THIRD EDITION

CORNERSTONES
OF FINANCIAL ACCOUNTING

Jay S. Rich
Illinois State University

Jefferson P. Jones
Auburn University

Maryanne M. Mowen
Oklahoma State University

Don R. Hansen
Oklahoma State University

SOUTH-WESTERN
CENGAGE Learning

Australia • Brazil • Japan • Korea • Mexico • Singapore • Spain • United Kingdom • United States

SOUTH-WESTERN
CENGAGE Learning

Cornerstones of Financial Accounting, 3e International Edition
Jay S. Rich, Jefferson P. Jones, Maryanne M. Mowen, Don R. Hansen

Senior Vice President, LRS/Acquisitions & Solutions Planning: Jack W. Calhoun

Editorial Director, Business & Economics: Erin Joyner

Editor-in-Chief: Rob Dewey

Executive Editor: Sharon Oblinger

Associate Developmental Editor: Julie Warwick

Editorial Assistant: A.J. Smiley

Brand Management Director: Jason Sakos

Sr. Brand Manager: Kristen Hurd

Market Development Manager: Lisa Lysne

Sr. Market Development Manager: Natalie Livingston

Marketing Coordinator: Eileen Corcoran

Sr. Content Project Manager: Tim Bailey

Media Editor: Lysa Kosins

Manufacturing Planner: Doug Wilke

Production Service: Cenveo Publishing Services

Sr. Art Director: Stacy Jenkins Shirley

Cover Designer: Patti Hudepohl

Internal Designer: Mike Stratton

Cover Images:

Black and white image: Getty Images/Rubberball

Color image: Shutterstock Images/hkeita

Library of Congress Control Number: 2012948958

International Edition with 10-K Report Appendix
ISBN-13: 978-1-285-06068-2
ISBN-10: 1-285-06068-7

International Edition
ISBN-13: 978-1-285-19757-9
ISBN-10: 1-285-19757-7

Asia
www.cengageasia.com
tel: (65) 6410 1200

Australia/New Zealand
www.cengage.com.au
tel: (61) 3 9685 4111

Brazil
www.cengage.com.br
tel: (55) 11 3665 9900

India
www.cengage.co.in
tel: (91) 11 4364 1111

Latin America
www.cengage.com.mx
tel: (52) 55 1500 6000

UK/Europe/Middle East/Africa
www.cengage.co.uk
tel: (44) 0 1264 332 424

Represented in Canada by Nelson Education, Ltd.
www.nelson.com
tel: (416) 752 9100/(800) 668 0671

Cengage Learning is a leading provider of customized learning solutions with office locations around the globe, including Singapore, the United Kingdom, Australia, Mexico, Brazil, and Japan. Locate your local office at: **www.cengage.com/global**

For product information and free companion resources:
www.cengage.com/international
Visit your local office: **www.cengage.com/global**
Visit our corporate website: **www.cengage.com**

Printed in Canada
3 4 5 6 7 16 15

BRIEF CONTENTS

APPENDIX 4: Financial Statement Information: Under Armour, Inc. and APPENDIX 5: Financial Statement Information: VF Corporation are found in print bundled with the book or online at www.cengagebrain.com.

NEW TO THIS EDITION

- **Increased Readability and Refined Design:** The new edition features better design for various features to improve readability including the Q&A, Cornerstones, capitalization of account titles, and better placement of exhibits.
- **New company financial statements** are included from recognizable companies like Under Armour, Inc., and VF Corporation, whose brands include The North Face, Timberland, and more. Each chapter includes an assignment that requires students to analyze and interpret actual financial data, better preparing them for their futures in the business world.
- **Additional Conceptual End-of-Chapter Material:** Additional Conceptual Connection questions are identified in the end-of-chapter content. These questions ask students to go beyond the calculations and articulate the conceptual context behind the work they've just completed and how that may impact a company's decision-making.
- **Addition of Brief Exercises** adds yet another layer of practice to reinforce the core concepts.

NEW TO CENGAGENOW

- **Author-Revised Feedback:** CengageNOW helps students get further outside the classroom and keeps them from getting stuck by providing them with meaningful, written feedback as they work. In this edition, that feedback has been fully revised by the author team to guide students and to be consistent with material presented in the text.
- **Post-Submission Feedback:** Also available in CengageNOW is the ability to show the full solution in addition to newly added source calculations to enhance the learning process. Now students can see where they may have gone wrong and correct their errors through further practice.
- **Animated Activities:** Animated Activities in CengageNOW are the perfect pre-lecture assignment to expose you to concepts before class! These illustrations visually guide students through selected core topics using a realistic company example to illustrate how the concepts relate to the everyday activities of a business. Animated Activities are assignable or available for self-study and review.
- **Blueprint Connections:** Blueprint Connections in CengageNOW are shorter extensions of the Blueprint Problems that build upon concepts covered and introduced within the Blueprint Problems. These scenario-based exercises help reinforce your knowledge of the concept and strengthen your analytical skills and are useful as in-class activities or as homework/review after lecture and before the exam.
- **Conceptual Conversion Questions:** End-of-chapter questions or requirements within larger questions that were previously short answer are now assignable and gradable within CengageNOW.

CHAPTER-BY-CHAPTER ENHANCEMENTS

Chapter 1: Accounting and the Financial Statements

- Updated chapter opener financial information and image for Apple Inc.
- Updated years throughout chapter
- Revised all financial information for exhibits
- Added 10 Brief Exercises
- Added one new Exercise
- Added Conceptual Connection/Illustrating Relationships features to selected exercises and problems
- Revised approximately 35% of end-of-chapter material
- Overall change (revisions plus new exercises) to approximately 45% of end-of-chapter material
- New design improves readability of the Q&A feature
- New companies for Comparative Analysis: Under Armour, Inc., vs. VF Corporation

Chapter 2: The Accounting Information System

- Updated chapter opener image for General Electric Company
- Updated years throughout chapter
- Revised all financial information for exhibits
- Replaced references to "matching principle" with the more inclusive term "expense recognition (or matching) principle"
- Added eight Brief Exercises
- Added Conceptual Connection feature to selected exercises
- Revised approximately 30% of end-of-chapter material
- Overall change (revisions plus new exercises) to approximately 43% of end-of-chapter material
- New design improves readability of the Q&A feature
- Revised Exhibit 2.1: Qualitative Characteristics of Useful Information
- New companies for Comparative Analysis: Under Armour, Inc., vs. VF Corporation

Chapter 3: Accrual Accounting

- Updated chapter opener financial information and image for FedEx
- Updated years throughout chapter
- Revised all financial information for exhibits
- Replaced references to "matching principle" with the more inclusive term "expense recognition (or matching) principle"
- Added reference to FASB/IASB project on revenue recognition
- Added 10 Brief Exercises
- Added three new Exercises
- Revised approximately 20% of end-of-chapter material
- Overall change (revisions plus new exercises) to approximately 44% of end-of-chapter material
- New design improves readability of the Q&A feature
- New companies for Comparative Analysis: Under Armour, Inc., vs. VF Corporation

Chapter 4: Internal Control and Cash

- Updated chapter opener image for Initech
- Updated years throughout chapter
- Revised all financial information for exhibits
- Added 14 Brief Exercises
- New design improves readability of the Q&A feature
- Revised 33% of end-of-chapter material
- New companies for Comparative Analysis: Under Armour, Inc., vs. VF Corporation

Chapter 5: Sales and Receivables

- Updated chapter opener financial information and image for Mitsubishi
- Updated years throughout chapter
- Revised all financial information for exhibits and examples including Wal-Mart and Nordstrom
- Added 20 Brief Exercises
- New design improves readability of the Q&A feature
- Revised 33% of end-of-chapter material
- Revised "Timing of Revenue Recognition" section due to FASB Exposure Draft
- New companies for Comparative Analysis: Under Armour, Inc., vs. VF Corporation

Chapter 6: Cost of Goods Sold and Inventory

- Updated chapter opener financial information and image for Wal-Mart Stores, Inc.
- Updated years throughout chapter
- Revised all financial information for exhibits and examples including Wal-Mart Stores, Inc., and Nordstrom
- Added 9 Brief Exercises
- Revised approximately 27% of end-of-chapter material
- Overall change (revisions plus new exercises) to approximately 38% of end-of-chapter material
- New design improves readability of the Q&A feature
- New companies for Comparative Analysis: Under Armour, Inc., vs. VF Corporation

Chapter 7: Operating Assets

- Updated chapter opener financial information for Verizon Communications, Inc.
- Updated years throughout chapter
- Revised all financial information for exhibits and financials including BP and AT&T

- Replaced references to "matching principle" with the more inclusive "expense recognition (or matching) principle"
- Added 11 Brief Exercises
- Revised 27% of end-of-chapter material
- Overall change (revisions plus new exercises) to approximately 42% of end-of-chapter material
- New design improves readability of the Q&A feature
- New companies for Comparative Analysis: Under Armour, Inc., vs. VF Corporation

Chapter 8: Current and Contingent Liabilities
- Updated chapter opener financial information for Ruth's Chris Steak House
- Updated years throughout chapter
- Revised all financial information for exhibits and examples including Live Nation Entertainment and Southwest Airlines Co.
- Added 25 Brief Exercises
- New design improves readability of the Q&A feature
- Revised 33% of end-of-chapter material
- New companies for Comparative Analysis: Under Armour, Inc., vs. VF Corporation

Chapter 9: Long-Term Liabilities
- Updated chapter opener financial information and image for American Airlines
- Updated years throughout chapter
- Revised all financial information for exhibits and examples including Whirlpool
- Added 25 Brief Exercises
- New design improves readability of the Q&A feature
- Revised 33% of end-of-chapter material
- New companies for Comparative Analysis: Under Armour, Inc., vs. VF Corporation

Chapter 10: Stockholders' Equity
- Updated chapter opener financial information and image for Google
- Updated years throughout chapter
- Revised all financial information for exhibits and examples including Procter & Gamble and Microsoft
- Added 17 Brief Exercises
- New design improves readability of the Q&A feature
- Revised 50% of end-of-chapter material
- New companies for Comparative Analysis: Under Armour, Inc., vs. VF Corporation

Chapter 11: The Statement of Cash Flows
- Updated chapter opener financial information and image for Deere & Company
- Updated years throughout chapter
- Revised all financial information for exhibits and examples including Brooke Sportswear Inc.
- Added 8 Brief Exercises
- Revised 34% of end-of-chapter material
- Overall change (revisions plus new exercises) to approximately 47% of end-of-chapter material
- New design improves readability of the Q&A feature
- New companies for Comparative Analysis: Under Armour, Inc., vs. VF Corporation

Chapter 12: Financial Statements Analysis
- Updated chapter opener financial information and image for Under Armour
- Updated years throughout chapter
- Revised all financial information for exhibits including VF Corporation
- Added 11 Brief Exercises
- New design improves readability of the Q&A feature
- Revised 20% of end-of-chapter material

Appendix 1: International Financial Reporting Standards
- Updated IFRS information
- Revised Exhibit A1.1 per IASB structure
- Added discussion of IASB Monitoring Board
- Revised Exhibit A1.2 per new adoptions of IFRS since last publication
- Revised Exhibits A1.4 and A1.5 per new IFRS survey information since last publication

Appendix 2: Investments
- Revised years throughout appendix
- Revised 33% of end-of-appendix material

Appendix 3: Time Value of Money
- Revised years throughout appendix
- Revised 33% of end-of-appendix material

Appendix 4: Financial Statement Information: Under Armour
- New financial information for 2011

Appendix 5: Financial Statement Information: VF Corporation
- New financial information for 2011

SUPERIOR SUPPLEMENTS

CengageNOW for *Cornerstones of Financial Accounting, 3e*

CengageNOW offers:

- **Auto-graded Homework** (static and algorithmic), Test Bank, Personalized Study Plan, Gradebook, and eBook are all in one resource.
- **Smart Entry** helps eliminate common data entry errors and prevents students from guessing their way through homework.
- **Learning Outcomes Reporting** and the ability to analyze student work from the gradebook. Each problem is tagged by topic, learning objective, level of difficulty, time estimates, Bloom's Taxonomy, AICPA, ACBSP, and other business program standards to allow greater guidance in developing assessments and evaluating student progress.
- **Assignments Options** are the most robust and flexible in the industry.
- **Enhanced Feedback** for additional pre- and post-submissions guidance.
- **Cornerstones Videos** further reinforce concepts and examples for visual learners.
- **Blueprint Problems and Connections** are scenario-based exercises that help reinforce knowledge of the concept and strengthen analytical skills and are best used as homework or review.
- **Animated Activities** are visual illustrations that guide students through selected core topics using a realistic company example to illustrate how concepts relate to everyday business activities.
- **Conceptual Conversion** to select problems and/or requirements that are short answer in the text are now converted to be assignable and gradeable in CNOW.

Solutions Manual

Author-written and carefully verified multiple times to ensure accuracy and consistency with the text, the Solutions Manual contains answers to all Discussion Questions, Multiple-Choice Exercises, Cornerstone Exercises, Brief Exercises, Exercises, Problem Set A, Problem Set B, and Cases that appear in the text. These solutions help you easily plan, assign, and efficiently grade assignments. All solutions are given in simplified Excel spreadsheets and also available in pdf format. The Solutions Manual is available electronically for instructors only on the IRCD and on the password-protected portion of the text's website at http://login.cengage.com.

Test Bank

Revised and verified to ensure accuracy, the Test Bank available in both Word® and ExamView® formats includes questions clearly identified by topic, learning objectives, level of difficulty, **Time Estimate**, **Bloom's Taxonomy**, AICPA, ACBSP, and other business program standards to allow greater guidance in developing assessments and evaluating student progress. The Test Bank is available electronically for instructors only on the IRCD and on the password-protected portion of the text's website at http://login.cengage.com. ExamView® testing software is only available on the IRCD.

PowerPoint® Lecture Slides

The PowerPoint® slides have been revised and "toned down" to allow for greater ease in preparing and presenting lectures to encourage lively classroom discussions. All Cornerstones within each chapter appear in the slides. The slides are available for instructors only on the IRCD and on the password-protected portion of the text's website at http://login.cengage.com. Student PowerPoint® slides are available at www.cengagebrain.com.

Spreadsheet Templates and Solutions

All spreadsheet problems and solutions, identified by a spreadsheet icon in the book, are available for instructors only on the IRCD and on the password-protected portion of the text's website at http://login.cengage.com. All spreadsheet template files are available for students at www.cengagebrain.com.

Instructor's Resource CD-ROM (ISBN-10: 1285055098 | ISBN-13: 9781285055091)

Place all of the key teaching resources you need at your fingertips with this all-in-one resource, which includes everything you need to plan, teach, grade, and assess student understanding and progress. This CD contains:

- Solutions Manual
- Test Bank in Microsoft® Word and ExamView®
- Microsoft PowerPoint® slides
- Instructor's Manual
- Spreadsheet Templates and Solutions

All resources on the IRCD are also available to instructors only on the password-protected portion of the text's website at http://login.cengage.com.

CengageBrain.com Free Study Tools for Students

This robust product website provides immediate access to a rich array of interactive learning resources for students that include flashcards, chapter-by-chapter online quizzes, final exam, crossword puzzles, PowerPoint® student slides, and the Cornerstones videos. Students should go to www.cengagebrain.com. At the CengageBrain.com homepage, search by the author, title, or ISBN of the book at the top of the page. CengageBrain.com will lead students to the product page to access the free study resources.

ACKNOWLEDGMENTS AND THANKS

We would like to thank the following reviewers whose valuable comments and feedback helped shape and refine this edition:

Dawn P. Addington, *Central New Mexico Community College*
Elizabeth Ammann, *Lindenwood University*
Sandra H. Bitenc, *University of Texas at Arlington*
Duane M. Brandon, *Auburn University*
Rada Brooks, *University of California at Berkeley*
Esther S. Bunn, *Stephen F. Austin State University*
Gayle Chaky, *Dutchess Community College*
Chiaho Chang, *Montclair State University*
Dr. Michel Charifzadeh, *Reutlingen University*
Linda Christiansen, *Indiana University Southeast*
Lawrence Chui, *University of St. Thomas*
Tony Cioffi, *Lorain County Community College*
Rita Kingery Cook, *University of Delaware*
Joseph R. D'Agostin, *Fairfield University*
Dori Danko, *Grand Valley State University*
John M. Davis, *Ashland Community & Technology College*
Peggy DeJong, *Kirkwood Community College*
Andrew DeJoseph, *Nassau Community College*
Michael P. Dole, *Marquette University*
Carleton M. Donchess, *Bridgewater State University*
Emily L. Drogt, *Grand Valley State University*
Peter Dryden, *University of Ballarat*
Richard J. Dumont, *Post University*
James M. Emig, *Villanova University*
Steven Ernest, *Baton Rouge Community College*
Alan Falcon, *Loyola Marymount University*
Dr. James Falter, *Marietta College*
Jack Fatica, *Terra Community College*
Annette Fisher, *Glendale Community College*
Anthony B. Flores, *Allan Hancock College*
Umit Gurun, *University of Texas at Dallas*
Penny Nunn Hahn, *Henderson Community College*
Rosemary Hall, *Bellevue College*
Dr. Helmi Hammami, *Qatar University*
Sheila Handy, *East Stroudsburg University*
Michael Harkness, *University of Michigan*
Dennis Heiner, *College of Southern Idaho*
Sueann Hely, *West Kentucky Community & Technical College*
Joshua Herbold, *University of Montana*
Joan Van Hise, *Fairfield University*
David R. Honodel, *University of Denver*
Carol Hughes, *Asheville Buncombe Technical College*
Nelson Ildefonso, *Coastline Community College*
Matthew I. Isaak, *University of Louisiana at Lafayette*
Sharon S. Jackson, *Samford University*
Marianne James, *California State University, Los Angeles*
Gene E. A. Johnson, *Clark College, Vancouver*
Linda Jones, *Neosho County Community College*
Daniel J. Kerch, *Pennsylvania Highlands Community College*
Shirly A. Kleiner, *Johnson County Community College*
Dr. Trevor M. Knox, *Muhlenberg College*
Susan Kowalske, *Salem State University*
A. J. Kreimer, *Temple University*
Barbara Kren, *Marquette University*
Steven J. LaFave, *Augsburg College*
David Laurel, *South Texas College*
Dr. Wayne Lewis, *Hudson Valley Community College*
Linda Lindsay, *University of Lethbridge*
Joseph LiPari, *Montclair State University*
Nancy P. Lynch, *West Virginia University*
Susan A. Lynn, *University of Baltimore*
Jennifer Malfitano, *Delaware County Community College*
Carol Mannino, *Milwaukee School of Engineering*
Herb Martin, *Hope College*
Carmen Martorana Jr., *Medaille College*
Josephine Mathias, *Mercer County Community College*
Jeanine Metzler, *Northampton Community College*
Lorie D. Milam, *University of Texas at San Antonio*
Shawn Miller, *Lone Star College*
Laurel Bond Mitchell, *University of Redlands*
Norma R. Montague, *Wake Forest University*
Charles T. Moores, *University of Nevada, Las Vegas*
Donata Muntean, *Charles Sturt University*
Lisa Murawa, *Mott Community College*
Debra Nelson, *Kalamazoo Valley Community College*
David W. O'Bryan, *Pittsburg State University*

Glenn E. Owen, *Allan Hancock College*
Glenn Pate, *Palm Beach State College*
Sy Pearlman, *California State University*
Richard Persaud, *Miami Dade College*
Judy Peterson, *Monmouth College*
Brandis Phillips, *North Carolina AT&T State University*
Janice Pitera, *Broome Community College*
Dr. Ronald Premuroso, *University of Montana*
Eric Press, *Temple University*
Kristen Quinn, *Northern Essex Community College*
Glenn Rechtschaffen, *University of Auckland*
Howard Rockness, *University of North Carolina at Wilmington*
Dr. Robert E. Rosacker, *University of Wisconsin, La Crosse*
Paul A. San Miguel, *Western Michigan University*
Angels H. Sandberg, *Shorter University*
Susan D. Sandblom, *Scottsdale Community College*
Gail Sanderson, *Lebanon Valley College*
Christine Schalow, *University of Wisconsin, Stevens Point*
Lee Schiffel, *Valparaiso University*
Joseph Schubert, *Delaware Technical Community College*
Randy Serrett, *University of Houston*
Amy Genson Sheneman, *Grand Valley State University*
Lynn R. Smith, *Utah Valley University*
Steven H. Smith, *Western Washington University*
Nancy Snow, *University of Toledo*
Barbara Squires, *Corning Community College*
Tim Stein, *Baker College of Muskegon*
Ronald Strittmater, *North Hennepin Community College*
Joel M. Strong, *St. Cloud State University*
Daniel Taylor, *University of Pennsylvania*
Steve Teeter, *Utah Valley University*
Dr. Thiruvadi, *Morgan State University*
Robert C. Urell, *Irvine Valley College*
Al Wallace, *Owensboro Community & Technical College*
Sharon Walters, *Morehead State University*
Larry Watkins, *Northern Arizona University*
Robert Wesoloskie, *Elizabethtown College*
Denise White, *Austin Community College*
Terry Willyard, *Baker College*
Wendy Wilson, *Southern Methodist University*
Candace Witherspoon, *University of Kentucky*
Glenn Van Wyhe, *Pacific Lutheran University*
Yan Xiong, *California State University Sacramento*

We would also like to thank the following instructors for their careful verification of the textbook and all end-of-chapter materials:

Eileen Byron, *CPA, PMP*
Timothy P. Dimond, *Northern Illinois University*
Nancy J. Emerson, *North Dakota State University*
Kurt Fredricks, *Valencia College*
Ms. Cathy Lumbattis, *Southern Illinois University Carbondale*
Christopher T. McKittrick, CPA, MBA, CFE, *North Carolina State University*
Jeanine M. Metzler, *Northampton Community College*
Tracy Newman, M.S. Ed
Linda S. Williams, *Tidewater Community College*

This book is dedicated to our students—past, present, and future—who are at the heart of our passion for teaching.

CONTENTS

APPENDIX 4: Financial Statement Information: Under Armour, Inc. and APPENDIX 5: Financial Statement Information: VF Corporation are found in print bundled with the book or online at www.cengagebrain.com.

ABOUT THE AUTHORS

Dr. Jay S. Rich is a Professor of Accounting at Illinois State University. He received his B.S., M.S., and Ph.D. from the University of Illinois. Prior to entering the Ph.D. program, he worked as an auditor at Price Waterhouse & Co. in Chicago and earned his CPA in 1985. He has published articles in *The Accounting Review*, *Auditing: A Journal of Practice & Theory*, *Accounting Horizons*, *Organizational Behavior and Human Decision Processes*, *Accounting Organizations and Society*, and others. He has also served on the editorial boards of *Auditing: A Journal of Practice & Theory* and *Current Issues in Auditing*. Dr. Rich has received both the Outstanding Dissertation Award and Notable Contribution to the Literature Award from the Audit Section of the American Accounting Association. His primary teaching interest is financial accounting, and he has taught numerous courses at the undergraduate, masters, and doctoral levels. His outside interests include his family, travel, reading, and watching sports, but he spends most of his free time driving his children to various activities. He also repeatedly develops plans to exercise and diet at some point in the future. By all accounts, he is a master at grilling meat, a mediocre skier, and a shameful golfer.

Dr. Jefferson P. Jones is the PricewaterhouseCoopers Associate Professor of Accounting in the School of Accountancy at Auburn University. He received his Bachelor's and Master of Accountancy degrees from Auburn University and his Ph.D. in accounting from Florida State University. While earning his CPA, he worked for Deloitte & Touche. Dr. Jones has received numerous teaching awards, including the Beta Alpha Psi Outstanding Teacher Award (six times), the Outstanding Master of Accountancy Professor Award (three times), the Auburn University College of Business McCartney Teaching Award, and the Auburn University School of Accountancy Teaching Award. In addition to an Intermediate Accounting text, his published articles appear in *Advances in Accounting*, *Review of Quantitative Finance and Accounting*, *Issues in Accounting Education*, *International Journal of Forecasting*, *The CPA Journal*, *Managerial Finance*, *Journal of Accounting and Finance Research*, and *The Journal of Corporate Accounting and Finance*. Dr. Jones has made numerous presentations around the country on research and pedagogical issues. He is a member of the American Accounting Association, the American Institute of Certified Public Accountants (AICPA), and the Alabama Society of CPAs (ASCPA). Dr. Jones is married, has two children, and enjoys traveling and playing golf.

Dr. Maryanne M. Mowen is Associate Professor Emerita of Accounting at Oklahoma State University. She currently teaches online classes in cost and management accounting for Oklahoma State University. She received her Ph.D. from Arizona State University. She brings an interdisciplinary perspective to teaching and writing in cost and management accounting, with degrees in history and economics. She has taught classes in ethics and the impact of the Sarbanes-Oxley Act on accountants. Her scholarly research is in the areas of management accounting, behavioral decision theory, and compliance with the Sarbanes-Oxley Act. She has published articles in journals such as *Decision Science, The Journal of Economics and Psychology,* and *The Journal of Management Accounting Research*. Dr. Mowen has served as a consultant to mid-sized and Fortune 100 companies and works with corporate controllers on management accounting issues. She is a member of the Northern New Mexico chapter of SCORE and serves as a mentor, assisting small and start-up businesses. Outside the classroom, she enjoys hiking, traveling, reading mysteries, and working crossword puzzles.

Dr. Don R. Hansen is Professor Emeritus of Accounting at Oklahoma State University. He received his Ph.D. from the University of Arizona in 1977. He has an undergraduate degree in mathematics from Brigham Young University. His research interests include activity-based costing and mathematical modeling. He has published articles in both accounting and engineering journals including *The Accounting Review*, *The Journal of Management Accounting Research*, *Accounting Horizons*, and *Accounting, Organizations, and Society*. He has served on the editorial board of *The Accounting Review*. His outside interests include family, church activities, reading, movies, and watching sports.

1

Accounting and the Financial Statements

© Pixelfabrik/Alamy

iStockphoto.com/dem10

After studying Chapter 1, you should be able to:

1. Explain the nature of accounting.
2. Identify the forms of business organizations and the types of business activities.
3. Describe the relationships shown by the fundamental accounting equation.
4. Prepare a classified balance sheet and understand the information it communicates.
5. Prepare an income statement and understand the information it communicates.
6. Prepare the retained earnings statement statement and understand the information it communicates.
7. Understand the information communicated by the statement of cash flows.
8. Describe the relationships among the financial statements.
9. Describe other information contained in the annual report and the importance of ethics in accounting.

EXPERIENCE FINANCIAL ACCOUNTING
with Apple

In 1976, Steve Jobs and Steve Wozniak, the founders of **Apple Inc.** began building personal computers in Jobs' parents' garage. By 1984, Apple had become a leader in the personal computing industry, and its Macintosh computer is regarded by many as a key contributor to the development of the desktop publishing market. Apple appeared invincible. However, the development of Microsoft's Windows operating system and several Apple product failures led many to predict the end of one of the computer industry's most prominent companies. How could a company with such a bright future experience failure? And, perhaps more remarkable, how could a company on the verge of extinction experience the kind of success that Apple has recently experienced? With the introduction of the iMac, the iPod, the iTunes Store, the iPhone, and the iPad, Apple's stock price increased from approximately $7 per share in June 1998 to more than $600 in March 2012.

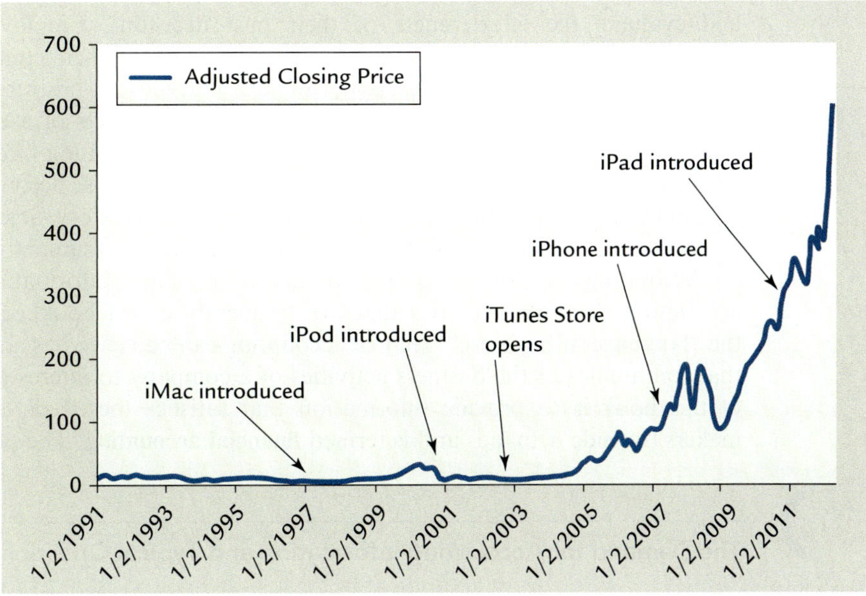

Source: Apple Inc. 2011 10-K.

What type of information can help someone predict the successes of a company like Apple? A good place to start is with the financial information contained in a company's annual report. This financial information is provided in the form of financial statements—a summary of the results of a company's operations. A study of a company's financial statements will help you determine how successful a company has been in the past as well as its prospects for the future. While this information is easily accessible and free of charge, your final judgment on a company's future prospects will be influenced by how well you understand the information contained in its financial statements.

OBJECTIVE 1

Explain the nature of accounting.

WHAT IS ACCOUNTING?

Our economy is comprised of many different businesses. Some companies, such as **Apple Inc.**, focus on providing goods, which for Apple take many forms including Macintosh computers, iPods, iPads, iPhones, and downloadable music. Other companies are primarily concerned with providing services. For example, **The Walt Disney Company** offers a variety of entertainment services from theme parks to motion pictures. While most entities, like Apple and Disney, exist in order to earn a profit, some are organized to achieve some other benefit to society (for example, school districts exist to meet the educational needs of a community). Regardless of their objective, all entities use accounting to plan future operations, make decisions, and evaluate performance.

Accounting is the process of identifying, measuring, recording, and communicating financial information about a company's business activities so decision-makers can make informed decisions. Accounting information is useful because it helps people answer questions and make better decisions.

The demand for accounting information comes from both inside and outside the business. Inside the business, managers use accounting information to help them plan and make decisions about the company. For example, managers can use accounting information to predict the consequences of their actions and to help decide which actions to take. They also use accounting information to control the operations of the company and evaluate the effectiveness of their past decisions. Employees use accounting information to help them judge the future prospects of their company, which should translate into future promotion opportunities. Outside the business, investors (owners) use accounting information to evaluate the future prospects of a company and decide where to invest their money. Creditors (lenders) use accounting information to evaluate whether to loan money to a company. Even governments use accounting information to determine taxes owed by companies, to implement regulatory objectives, and to make policy decisions. This demand for accounting information is summarized by Exhibit 1.1.

Accounting is more than the process of recording information and maintaining accounting records—activities that are frequently called bookkeeping. Accounting is the "language of business." That is, accounting can be viewed as an information system that communicates the business activities of a company to interested parties. The focus of this book is to provide information that satisfies the needs of external decision-makers (outside demand) and is termed **financial accounting**. The objectives of financial

EXHIBIT 1.1

The Demand for Accounting Information and Typical Questions

accounting involve providing decision-makers with information that assists them in assessing the amounts, timing, and uncertainties of a company's future cash flows. This information is provided through four basic financial statements: the balance sheet, the income statement, the retained earnings statement, and the statement of cash flows.

In this chapter, we will discuss the basic functioning of the accounting system within a business. We will address the following questions:

- What forms do businesses take?
- What are the basic business activities?
- How does the accounting system report these activities?
- How can decision-makers use the information provided by the accounting system?

Regardless of your major or future plans, knowledge of accounting and the ability to use accounting information will be critical to your success in business.

concept Q&A

How will accounting affect my life?

Answer:

Accounting will impact many aspects of your daily life. The business that sells you goods or services uses accounting to keep track of how much money it received as well as the cost of operating the business. Calculating the amount of tax that is owed to the government requires accounting. When you invest your money, you should use accounting to understand a company's business and its prospects for the future. Plans that you make for the future often involve accounting to determine how much money you will need.

BUSINESSES: FORMS AND ACTIVITIES

Accounting identifies, measures, records, and communicates financial information about an accounting entity. An accounting entity is a company that has an identity separate from that of its owners and managers and for which accounting records are kept.

OBJECTIVE 2

Identify the forms of business organizations and the types of business activities.

Forms of Business Organization

This text emphasizes accounting for entities which take one of three forms: sole proprietorship, partnership, or corporation.

Sole Proprietorship A **sole proprietorship** is a business owned by one person. Sole proprietorships, which account for more than 70% of all businesses, are usually small, local businesses such as restaurants, photography studios, retail stores, or website developers. This organizational form is popular because is it simple to set up and gives the owner control over the business. While a sole proprietorship is an accounting entity separate from its owner, the owner is personally responsible for the debt of the business. Sole proprietorships can be formed or dissolved at the wishes of the owner.

Partnership A **partnership** is a business owned jointly by two or more individuals. Small businesses and many professional practices of physicians, lawyers, and accountants are often organized as partnerships. Relative to sole proprietorships, partnerships provide increased access to financial resources as well as access to the individual skills of each of the partners. Similar to sole proprietorships, partnerships are accounting entities separate from the partners; however, the partners are jointly responsible for all the debt of the partnership.[1] Finally, the partnership is automatically dissolved when any partner leaves the partnership; of course, the remaining partners may form a new partnership and continue to operate.

Corporation A **corporation** is a business organized under the laws of a particular state. A corporation, such as Apple, is owned by one or more persons called *stockholders*, whose ownership interests are represented by shares of stock. A primary advantage of the corporate form is the ability to raise large amounts of money (capital) by issuing shares of stock. Unlike a sole proprietorship or a partnership, a corporation is an "artificial person" and the stockholders' legal responsibility for the debt of the business is limited to the amount they invested in the business. In addition, shares of stock can be

[1] Many professional partnerships—including the largest public accounting firms—have been reorganized as *limited liability partnerships* (LLPs), which protect the personal assets of the partners from being used to pay partnership debts.

easily transferred from one owner to another through capital markets without affecting the corporation that originally issued the stock. The ability to raise capital by selling new shares, the limited legal liability of owners, and the transferability of the shares give the corporation an advantage over other forms of business organization. However, the requirements to form a corporation are more complex compared to the other forms of business organization. In addition, owners of corporations generally pay more taxes than owners of sole proprietorships or partnerships for two reasons:

- First, the corporate income tax rate is greater than the individual income tax rate.
- Second, a corporation's income is taxed twice—at the corporate level as income is earned, and at the individual level as earnings are distributed to stockholders. This is known as double taxation.

Exhibit 1.2 illustrates the advantages and disadvantages of each form of organization. While the combined number of sole proprietorships and partnerships greatly exceeds that of corporations, the majority of business in the United States is conducted by corporations. Therefore, this book emphasizes the corporate form of organization.

EXHIBIT 1.2

Forms of Business Organization

Business Activities

Regardless of the form of a business, all businesses engage in activities that can be categorized as financing, investing, or operating activities. These activities are illustrated in Exhibit 1.3.

EXHIBIT 1.3

Business Activities

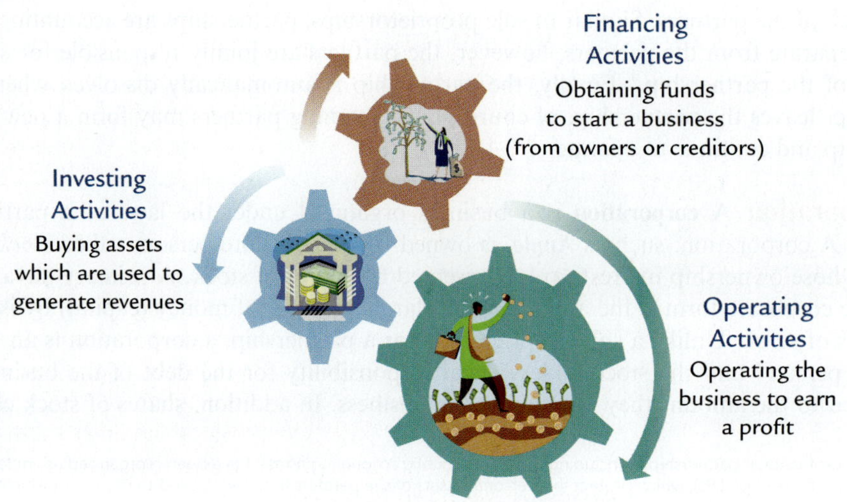

Financing Activities A company's financing activities include obtaining the funds necessary to begin and operate a business. These funds come from either issuing stock or borrowing money. Most companies use both types of financing to obtain funds.

When a corporation borrows money from another entity such as a bank, it must repay the amount borrowed. The person to whom the corporation owes money is called a **creditor**. This obligation to repay a creditor is termed a **liability** and can take many forms. A common way for a corporation to obtain cash is to borrow money with the promise to repay the amount borrowed plus interest at a future date. Such borrowings are commonly referred to as *notes payable*. A special form of note payable that is used by corporations to obtain large amounts of money is called a *bond payable*.

In addition to borrowing money from creditors, a corporation may issue shares of stock to investors in exchange for cash. The dollar amount paid to a corporation for these shares is termed *common stock* and represents the basic ownership interest in a corporation. As of September 24, 2011, Apple had issued 929,277,000 shares of common stock. The corporation is not obligated to repay the stockholder the amount invested; however, many corporations distribute a portion of their earnings to stockholders on a regular basis. These distributions are called *dividends*.

Creditors and stockholders have a claim on the **assets**, or economic resources, of a corporation. However, the claims on these resources differ. In the case of financial difficulty or distress, the claims of the creditors (liabilities) must be paid prior to the claims of the stockholders (called **stockholders' equity**). Stockholders' equity is considered a residual interest in the assets of a corporation that remain after deducting its liabilities.

Investing Activities Once a corporation has obtained funds through its financing activities, it buys assets that enable it to operate. For example, Apple has bought approximately $11.768 billion in land, buildings, machinery, and equipment that it uses in its operations. The corporation may also obtain intangible assets that lack physical substance, such as copyrights and patents. Apple reported $4,432 million of intangible assets that it uses in its operations. The purchase and sale of the assets that are used in operations (commonly referred to as property, plant, and equipment) are a corporation's investing activities.

Regardless of its form, assets are future economic benefits that a corporation controls. The assets purchased by a corporation vary depending on the type of business that the corporation engages in, and the composition of these assets is likely to vary across different companies and different industries. For example, in 2011, property, plant, and equipment made up approximately 6.7% of Apple's total assets. This is typical of many technology companies. In contrast, property, plant, and equipment made up 68.4% of the total assets of Southwest Airlines, a company that relies heavily on airplanes to produce revenue.

Operating Activities Once a corporation has acquired the assets that it needs, it can begin to operate. While different businesses have different purposes, they all want to generate revenue. **Revenue** is the increase in assets that results from the sale of products or services. For example, Apple reported revenue of $108.249 billion in 2011. In addition to revenue, assets such as *cash*, *accounts receivable* (the right to collect an amount due from customers), *supplies*, and *inventory* (products held for resale) often result from operating activities.

To earn revenue, a corporation will incur various costs or expenses. **Expenses** are the cost of assets used, or the liabilities created, in the operation of the business. Apple reported expenses of $64.431 billion related to the cost of iPods, iPhones, iPads, and other products sold in 2011.

The liabilities that arise from operating activities can be of different types. For example, if a corporation purchases goods on credit from a supplier, the obligation to repay the supplier is called an *account payable*. As of September 24, 2011, Apple reported $14.632 billion of accounts payable. Other examples of liabilities created by operating activities include *wages payable* (amounts owed to employees for work performed) and *income taxes payable* (taxes owed to the government).

The results of a company's operating activities can be determined by comparing revenues to expenses. If revenues are greater than expenses, a corporation has earned **net income**. If expenses are greater than revenues, a corporation has incurred a **net loss**.

YOU DECIDE Choice of Organizational Form

You are an entrepreneur who has decided to start a campus-area bookstore. In order to start your business, you have to choose among three organizational forms—sole proprietorship, partnership, or corporation. You have enough personal wealth to finance 40% of the business, but you must get the remaining 60% from other sources.

How does the choice of organizational form impact your control of the business and ability to obtain the needed funds?

The choice of organizational form can greatly impact many aspects of a business's operations. Each form has certain advantages and disadvantages that you should carefully consider.

- *Sole Proprietorship*: A sole proprietorship would give you the most control of your business. However, you would be forced to obtain the additional 60% of funds needed from a bank or other creditor. It often is difficult to get banks to support a new business.
- *Partnership*: If you choose to form a partnership, you would still have access to bank loans. In addition, you would also have the ability to obtain the additional funds from your partner or partners. In this situation, the partners would then have a 60% interest in the business, which may be an unacceptable loss of control.
- *Corporation*: If you choose to form a corporation, you could obtain the needed funds by issuing stock to investors. While a 60% interest may still be transferred to the stockholders, if the stock were widely dispersed among many investors, you might still retain effective control of the business with a 40% interest.

The choice of organizational form involves the consideration of many different factors.

OBJECTIVE 3

Describe the relationships shown by the fundamental accounting equation.

COMMUNICATION OF ACCOUNTING INFORMATION

The financing, investing, and operating activities of a company are recorded by accounting systems as detailed transactions. To effectively communicate a company's activities to decision-makers, these detailed transactions are summarized and reported in a set of standardized reports called **financial statements**. The role of financial statements is to provide information that helps investors, creditors, and others make judgments and predictions that serve as the basis for the various decisions they make. Financial statements help answer questions such as those shown in Exhibit 1.4.

EXHIBIT 1.4

Questions Answered by Financial Statements

How much better off is the company at the end of the year than it was at the beginning of the year?

What are the economic resources of the company and the claims against those resources?

From what sources did a company's cash come and for what did the company use cash during the year?

The Four Basic Financial Statements

Companies prepare four basic financial statements:

- The **balance sheet** reports the resources (assets) owned by a company and the claims against those resources (liabilities and stockholders' equity) at a specific point in time.

- The **income statement** reports how well a company has performed its operations (revenues, expenses, and income) over a period of time.
- The **retained earnings statement** reports how much of the company's income was retained in the business and how much was distributed to owners over a period of time.[2]
- The **statement of cash flows** reports the sources and uses of a company's cash over a period of time.

While financial statements can be prepared for any point or period of time (e.g., monthly, quarterly, or annually), most companies prepare financial statements at the end of each month, quarter, and year. Note that the balance sheet is a point-in-time description, whereas the other financial statements are period-of-time descriptions that explain the business activities between balance sheet dates as shown in Exhibit 1.5.

EXHIBIT 1.5

Financial Statement Time Periods

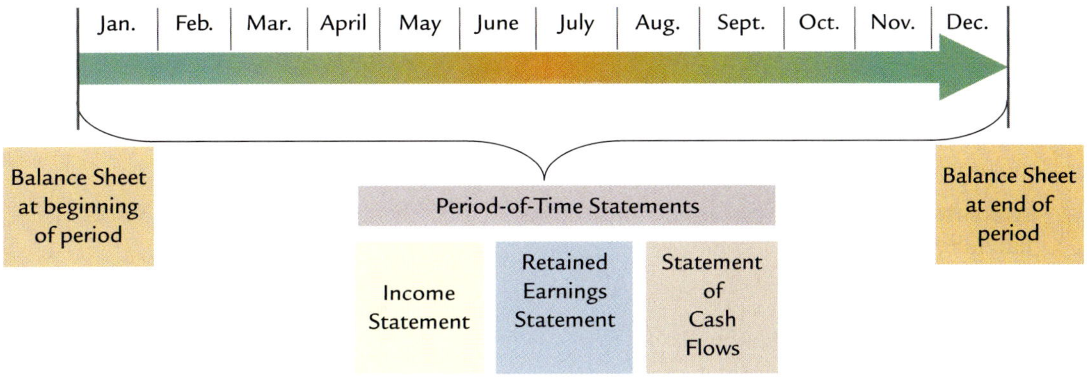

These four statements are prepared and issued at the end of an accounting period. While the accounting period can be a year, companies also issue statements monthly or quarterly to satisfy the users' needs for timely information. The financial statements are accompanied by supporting information and explanatory material called the notes to the financial statements.

In order to make it easier to use financial statements over time and across companies, a common set of rules and conventions have been developed to guide the preparation of financial statements. These rules and conventions, called **generally accepted accounting principles (GAAP)**, were developed by several different organizations over a number of years. In the United States, the **Securities and Exchange Commission (SEC)** has the power to set accounting rules for publicly traded companies. However, the SEC has delegated this authority to the **Financial Accounting Standards Board (FASB)**. While the FASB is the primary accounting standard setter in the United States, the FASB has been working closely with the **International Accounting Standards Board (IASB)** in its development of **international financial reporting standards (IFRS)**. While this text focuses on U.S. GAAP, the importance of IFRS cannot be ignored. Therefore, major differences between U.S. GAAP and IFRS are highlighted in margin notes throughout the text.

IFRS

IFRS describe an international set of generally accepted accounting standards used by over 120 countries in order to facilitate the conduct of business around the world.

While financial statements prepared under GAAP provide the kind of information users want and need, the financial statements do not interpret this information. The financial statement user must use his or her general knowledge of business and accounting to interpret the financial statements as a basis for decision-making.

[2] Information contained in the retained earnings statement is often included in a more comprehensive statement of changes in stockholders' equity, which describes changes in all components of stockholders' equity. This statement is presented in Chapter 10.

The Fundamental Accounting Equation

IFRS

The fundamental accounting equation is the same under IFRS and U.S. GAAP.

To understand financial statements, it is necessary that you understand how the accounting system records, classifies, and reports information about business activities. The **fundamental accounting equation** illustrates the foundation of the accounting system.

$$\text{Assets} = \text{Liabilities} + \text{Stockholders' Equity}$$

The fundamental accounting equation captures two basic features of any company. The left side of the accounting equation shows the assets, or economic resources of a company. The right side of the accounting equation indicates the claims on the company's assets. These claims may be the claims of creditors (liabilities) or they may be the claims of owners (stockholders' equity). The implication of the fundamental accounting equation is that what a company owns (its assets) must always be equal to what it owes (its liabilities and stockholders' equity). Cornerstone 1.1 illustrates this key relationship implied by the fundamental accounting equation.

CORNERSTONE 1.1

Using the Fundamental Accounting Equation

Why:

A company's resources (its assets) must always equal the claims on those resources (its liabilities and stockholders' equity).

Information:

On January 1, 2013, Gundrum Company reported assets of $125,000 and liabilities of $75,000. During 2013, assets increased by $44,000 and stockholders' equity increased by $15,000.

Required:

1. What is the amount reported for stockholders' equity on January 1, 2013?
2. What is the amount reported for liabilities on December 31, 2013?

Solution:

1. Stockholders' equity on January 1, 2013, is $50,000. This amount is calculated by rearranging the fundamental accounting equation as follows:

$$\begin{aligned}\text{Assets} &= \text{Liabilities} + \text{Stockholders' Equity}\\ \$125{,}000 &= \$75{,}000 + \text{Stockholders' Equity}\\ \text{Stockholders' Equity} &= \$125{,}000 - \$75{,}000 = \underline{\underline{\mathbf{\$50{,}000}}}\end{aligned}$$

2. At December 31, 2013, liabilities are $104,000. This amount is computed by adding the change to the appropriate balance sheet elements and then rearranging the fundamental accounting equation as follows:

$$\begin{aligned}\text{Assets} &= \text{Liabilities} + \text{Stockholders' Equity}\\ (\$125{,}000 + \$44{,}000) &= \text{Liabilities} + (\$50{,}000 + \$15{,}000)\\ \text{Liabilities} &= (\$125{,}000 + \$44{,}000) - (\$50{,}000 + \$15{,}000)\\ &= \$169{,}000 - \$65{,}000 = \underline{\underline{\mathbf{\$104{,}000}}}\end{aligned}$$

The fundamental accounting equation will be used to capture all of the economic activities recorded by an accounting system.

THE CLASSIFIED BALANCE SHEET

The purpose of the balance sheet is to report the financial position of a company (its assets, liabilities, and stockholders' equity) at a specific point in time. The relationship between the elements of the balance sheet is given by the fundamental accounting equation:

$$\text{Assets} = \text{Liabilities} + \text{Stockholders' Equity}$$

Note that the balance sheet gets its name because the economic resources of a company (assets) must always equal, or be in balance with, the claims against those resources (liabilities and stockholders' equity).

The balance sheet is organized, or classified, to help users identify the fundamental economic similarities and differences between the various items within the balance sheet. These classifications help users answer questions such as:

- how a company obtained its resources
- whether a company will be able to pay its obligations when they become due

While companies often use different classifications and different levels of detail on their balance sheets, some common classifications are shown in Exhibit 1.6.

OBJECTIVE 4

Prepare a classified balance sheet and understand the information it communicates.

IFRS

IFRS use the same balance sheet classifications, although terminology differences exist. For example, stockholders' equity may be called "capital and reserves."

EXHIBIT 1.6

Common Balance Sheet Classifications

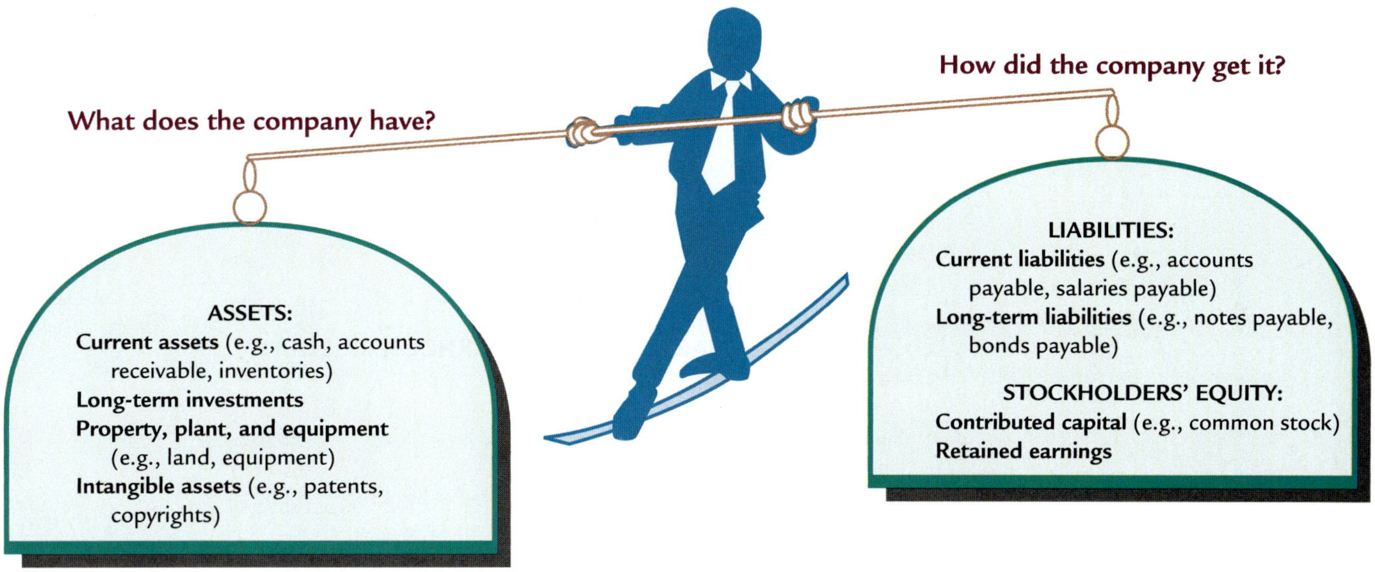

Let's examine the balance sheet classifications in more detail by looking at Apple's balance sheet shown in Exhibit 1.7 (p. 12).

With regard to the heading of the financial statement, several items are of interest:

- *Company name*: The company for which the accounting information is collected and reported is clearly defined.
- *Financial statement type*: The title of the financial statement follows the name of the company.
- *Date*: The specific date of the statement is listed. Apple operates on a fiscal year that ends in September. A **fiscal year** is an accounting period that runs for 1 year. While many companies adopt a fiscal year that corresponds to the calendar year, others adopt a fiscal year that more closely corresponds with their business cycle.

- *Amounts*: **Apple** reports its financial results rounded to the nearest million dollars. Large companies often round the amounts presented for a more clear presentation. For Apple, the reported cash amount of $9,815 is actually $9,815,000,000.

Current Assets

The basic classification of a company's assets is between current and noncurrent items. In a typical company, it is reasonable to designate 1 year as the dividing line between current and noncurrent items. However, if the operating cycle of a company is longer

EXHIBIT 1.7

Classified Balance Sheet of Apple Inc.

Apple Inc.
Balance Sheet
September 24, 2011
(in millions of dollars)

ASSETS		
Current assets:		
Cash	$ 9,815	
Short-term investments	16,137	
Accounts receivable, net	5,369	
Inventories	776	
Other current assets	12,891	
Total current assets		$ 44,988
Long-term investments		55,618
Property, plant, and equipment:		
Land and buildings	$ 2,059	
Machinery, equipment, and other	9,709	
Less: accumulated depreciation	(3,991)	
Total property, plant, and equipment		7,777
Intangible assets		4,432
Other assets		3,556
Total assets		$116,371
LIABILITIES AND STOCKHOLDERS' EQUITY		
Current liabilities:		
Accounts payable	$14,632	
Salaries payable	590	
Unearned revenue	4,091	
Other current liabilities	8,657	
Total current liabilities		$ 27,970
Long-term liabilities		11,786
Total liabilities		$ 39,756
Stockholders' equity:		
Contributed capital	$13,331	
Retained earnings	62,841	
Other equity*	443	
Total stockholders' equity		76,615
Total liabilities and stockholders' equity		$116,371

*The $443 million of other equity reported by Apple represents accumulated other comprehensive income. Accumulated other comprehensive income is discussed in Chapter 10.

Source: Apple Inc. 2011 10-K.

than 1 year, it may be necessary to extend this dividing line so that it corresponds to the length of the operating cycle. The **operating cycle** of a company is the average time that it takes a company to purchase goods, resell the goods, and collect the cash from customers. In other words, **current assets** consist of cash and other assets that are reasonably expected to be converted into cash within 1 year or one operating cycle, whichever is longer. Because most companies have operating cycles less than 1 year, we will use the 1-year dividing line to distinguish between current and noncurrent items. Common types of current assets are:

- Cash
- Short-term investments or marketable securities—investments in the debt and stock of other companies as well as government securities
- Accounts receivable—the right to collect an amount due from customers
- Inventories—goods or products held for resale to customers
- Other current assets—a "catch-all" category that includes items such as prepaid expenses (advance payments for rent, insurance, and other services) and supplies

Current assets are listed on the balance sheet in order of liquidity or nearness to cash. That is, the items are reported in the order in which the company expects to convert them into cash.

concept Q&A

Many classifications on the balance sheet are essentially subtotals. Is it really important to place accounts within the right category or is it enough to simply understand if they are assets, liabilities, or stockholders' equity?

Answer:

It is critical that you be able to identify accounts as assets, liabilities, or stockholders' equity accounts. However, the classifications are also important. Financial accounting is concerned with communicating useful information to decision-makers. These classifications provide decision-makers with information about the structure of assets, liabilities, and stockholders' equity that assists them in understanding a company's financial position.

Noncurrent Assets

Assets that are not classified as current are classified as long-term or noncurrent assets. These include long-term investments; property, plant, and equipment; intangible assets; and other noncurrent assets.

Long-Term Investments **Long-term investments** are similar to short-term investments, except that the company expects to hold the investment for longer than 1 year. This category also includes land or buildings that a company is not currently using in operations. Apple reported long-term investments of $55,618 million.

Property, Plant, and Equipment **Property, plant, and equipment** represents the tangible, long-lived, productive assets used by a company in its operations to produce revenue. This category includes land, buildings, machinery, manufacturing equipment, office equipment, and furniture. Apple reported property, plant, and equipment of $7,777 million, representing 6.7% ($7,777 million ÷ $116,371 million) of its total assets. Property, plant, and equipment is originally recorded at the cost to obtain the asset. Because property, plant, and equipment helps to produce revenue over a number of years, companies assign, or allocate, a portion of the asset's cost as an expense in each period in which the asset is used. This process is called *depreciation*. The *accumulated depreciation* shown on Apple's balance sheet represents the total amount of depreciation that the company has expensed over the life of its assets. Because accumulated depreciation is subtracted from the cost of an asset, it is called a *contra-asset*. The difference between the cost and the accumulated depreciation is the asset's *book value* (or *carrying value*).

Intangible Assets **Intangible assets** are similar to property, plant, and equipment in that they provide a benefit to a company over a number of years; however, these assets lack physical substance. Examples of intangible assets include patents, copyrights, trademarks, and goodwill.

Other Noncurrent Assets *Other noncurrent assets* is a catch-all category that includes items such as deferred charges (long-term prepaid expenses) and other long-term miscellaneous items.

IFRS

IFRS do not specify a particular order of the balance sheet classifications. International balance sheets often list noncurrent assets before current assets and stockholders' equity before non-current and current liabilities.

Current Liabilities

Current liabilities are closely related to current assets. **Current liabilities** consist of obligations that will be satisfied within 1 year or the operating cycle, whichever is longer. These liabilities can be satisfied through the payment of cash or by providing goods or services. **Current liabilities are typically listed in the order in which they will be paid** and include:

- Accounts payable—an obligation to repay a vendor or supplier for merchandise supplied to the company
- Salaries payable—an obligation to pay an employee for services performed
- Unearned revenue—an obligation to deliver goods or perform a service for which a company has already been paid
- Interest payable—an obligation to pay interest on money that a company has borrowed
- Income taxes payable—an obligation to pay taxes on a company's income

Long-Term Liabilities and Stockholders' Equity

Long-term liabilities are the obligations of the company that will require payment beyond 1 year or the operating cycle, whichever is longer. Common examples are:

- Notes payable—an obligation to repay cash borrowed at a future date
- Bonds payable—a form of an interest-bearing note payable issued by corporations in an effort to attract a large amount of investors

Stockholders' equity is the last major classification on a company's balance sheet. Stockholder's equity arises primarily from two sources:

- Contributed capital—the owners' contributions of cash and other assets to the company (includes the common stock of a company)
- Retained earnings—the accumulated net income of a company that has not been distributed to owners in the form of dividends

If a firm has been profitable for many years, and if its stockholders have been willing to forgo large dividends, retained earnings may be a large portion of equity. **Apple** reported approximately $62.841 billion of retained earnings, representing over 82% of its total stockholders' equity.

Together, a company's liabilities and equity make up the **capital** of a business. **Apple** has debt capital, capital raised from creditors, of $39.756 billion (total liabilities). Of this, $27.97 billion comes from current creditors, while $11.786 billion comes from long-term creditors. Apple's equity capital, which is the capital of the stockholders, is $76.6 billion (total stockholders' equity).

Using the fundamental accounting equation and the common classifications of balance sheet items, a company will prepare its balance sheet by following five steps:

Step 1. Prepare a heading that includes the name of the company, the title of the financial statement, and the time period covered.
Step 2. List the assets of the company in order of their liquidity or nearness to cash. Use appropriate classifications. Add the assets and double underline the total.
Step 3. List the liabilities of the company in order of their time to maturity. Use appropriate classifications.
Step 4. List the stockholders' equity balances with appropriate classifications.
Step 5. Add the liabilities and stockholders' equity and double underline the total.

In general, only the first items in a column as well as any subtotals or totals have dollar signs. Also when multiple items exist within a classification, these items are grouped together in a separate column (to the left of the main column) and their total is placed in the main column. Cornerstone 1.2 illustrates the steps in the preparation of a classified balance sheet.

Preparing a Classified Balance Sheet

CORNERSTONE 1.2

Why:

The balance sheet reports the financial position of a company (its assets, liabilities, and stockholders' equity) at a specific point in time.

Information:

Hightower Inc. reported the following account balances at December 31, 2013:

Inventories	$ 2,300	Accounts receivable	$ 4,200	Accounts payable	$ 3,750
Land	12,100	Cash	2,500	Common stock	14,450
Salaries payable	1,200	Equipment	21,000	Patents	2,500
Retained earnings	11,300	Accumulated depreciation	5,800	Notes payable, long-term	8,100

Required:

Prepare Hightower's balance sheet at December 31, 2013.

Solution:

Hightower Inc. Balance Sheet December 31, 2013			
ASSETS			Step 1
Current assets:			Step 2
Cash	$ 2,500		
Accounts receivable	4,200		
Inventories	2,300		
Total current assets		$ 9,000	
Property, plant, and equipment:			
Land	$12,100		
Equipment	21,000		
Less: accumulated depreciation	(5,800)		
Total property, plant, and equipment		27,300	
Intangible assets:			
Patents		2,500	
Total assets		$38,800	
LIABILITIES AND STOCKHOLDERS' EQUITY			
Current liabilities:			Step 3
Accounts payable	$ 3,750		
Salaries payable	1,200		
Total current liabilities		$ 4,950	
Long-term liabilities:			
Notes payable		8,100	
Total liabilities		$13,050	
Stockholders' equity:			Step 4
Common stock	$14,450		
Retained earnings	11,300		
Total stockholders' equity		25,750	
Total liabilities and stockholders' equity		$38,800	Step 5

Using Balance Sheet Information

The balance sheet conveys important information about the structure of assets, liabilities, and stockholders' equity, which is used to judge a company's financial health. For example, the relationship between current assets and current liabilities gives investors and creditors insights into a company's **liquidity**—the ability to pay obligations as they become due. Two useful measures of liquidity are *working capital* and the *current ratio*. Working capital and current ratios for a company are helpful when compared to other companies in the same industry. It is even more helpful to look at the trend of these measures over several years.

Working Capital **Working capital** is a measure of liquidity, computed as:

$$\text{Working Capital} = \text{Current Assets} - \text{Current Liabilities}$$

Because current liabilities will be settled with current assets, **Apple**'s working capital of \$17,018 million (\$44,988 million − \$27,970 million) signals that it has adequate funds with which to pay its current obligations. Because working capital is expressed in a dollar amount, the information it can convey is limited. For example, comparing Apple's working capital of \$17,018 million to **Dell**'s working capital of \$9,538 million would be misleading since Apple is almost \$69 billion larger (in terms of net assets).

Current Ratio The **current ratio** is an alternative measure of liquidity that allows comparisons to be made between different companies and is computed as:

$$\text{Current Ratio} = \frac{\text{Current Assets}}{\text{Current Liabilities}}$$

For example, **Apple**'s current ratio of 1.61 (\$44,988 million ÷ \$27,970 million) can be compared with its competitors (e.g., Dell's current ratio is 1.49).[3] Apple's current ratio tells us that for every dollar of current liabilities, Apple has \$1.61 of current assets. When compared to **Dell**, Apple is more liquid.

YOUDECIDE Assessing the Creditworthiness of a Prospective Customer

You are the regional credit manager for Nordic Equipment Company. Thin Inc., a newly organized health club, has offered to purchase \$50,000 worth of exercise equipment by paying the full amount plus 9% interest in 6 months. At your request, Thin provides the following figures from its balance sheet:

Current Assets		Current Liabilities	
Cash	\$10,000	Accounts payable	\$25,000
Accounts receivable	50,000	Notes payable	30,000
Supplies	4,000	Current portion of mortgage payable	18,000
Total	\$64,000	Total	\$73,000

[3] Information for Dell was obtained from Dell's fiscal year that ended on January 28, 2011.

Based on what you know about Thin's current assets and liabilities, do you allow the company to purchase the equipment on credit?

In making your decision, it is important to consider the relationship between a company's current assets and its current liabilities. Observe that Thin's current liabilities exceed current assets by $9,000 ($64,000 − $73,000) resulting in negative working capital. In addition, Thin's current ratio is 0.88 ($64,000 ÷ $73,000). By all indications, Thin is suffering from liquidity issues. Finally, there is no evidence presented that Thin's liquidity problem will improve. If Thin does fail to pay its liabilities, it is possible that the existing creditors could force Thin to sell its assets in order to pay off the debt. In such situations, it is possible that you will not receive the full amount promised. Unless Thin can demonstrate how it will pay its current short-term obligations, short-term credit should not be extended.

Allowing a company to purchase assets on credit requires evaluating the debtor's ability to repay the loan out of current assets.

THE INCOME STATEMENT

OBJECTIVE 5

Prepare an income statement and understand the information it communicates.

The income statement reports the results of a company's operations—the sale of goods and services and the associated cost of operating the company—for a given period. The long-term survival of a company depends on its ability to produce net income by earning revenues in excess of expenses. Income enables a company to pay for the capital it uses (dividends to stockholders and interest to creditors) and attract new capital necessary for continued existence and growth. Investors buy and sell stock and creditors loan money based on their beliefs about a company's future performance. The past income reported on a company's income statement provides investors with information about a company's ability to earn future income.

Elements of the Income Statement

The income statement consists of two major items: revenues and expenses. An income statement for Apple is presented in Exhibit 1.8.

EXHIBIT 1.8

Income Statement of Apple Inc.

Apple Inc.
Income Statement
For the fiscal year ended September 24, 2011
(in millions of dollars)

Revenues:		
Net sales	$108,249	
Interest and dividend income	519	$108,768
Expenses:		
Cost of goods sold	$ 64,431	
Selling, general, and administrative expenses	7,599	
Research and development	2,429	
Other expense	104	
Income taxes expense	8,283	82,846
Net income		$ 25,922

Source: Apple Inc. 2011 10-K.

Examining the heading of the income statement, notice that it follows the same general format as the balance sheet—it indicates the name of the company, the title of the financial statement, and the time period covered by the statement. However, the income statement differs from the balance sheet in that it covers a period of time instead of a specific date.

Revenues Revenues are the increase in assets that result from the sale of products or services. Revenues can arise from different sources and have different names depending on the source of the revenue. *Sales revenue* (or *service revenue* for companies that provide services) arises from the principal activity of the business. For **Apple**, its sales revenue comes from sales of hardware (such as iPods, Macintosh computers, iPhones, and iPads), software (operating systems), peripheral products and accessories, digital content (such as iTunes store sales), and service and support. Apple, like most other companies, generally recognizes sales revenue in the period that a sale occurs. Revenues also can be generated from activities other than the company's principal operations (nonoperating activities). For example, in addition to sales of its products, Apple also earns *interest income* and *dividend income* from investments.

Expenses Expenses are the cost of resources used to earn revenues during a period. Expenses have different names depending on their function. **Apple**'s income statement in Exhibit 1.8 reports five different expenses:

- *Cost of goods sold* (often called *cost of sales*)—the cost to the seller of all goods sold during the accounting period.[4]
- *Selling, general, and administrative expenses*—the expenses that a company incurs in selling goods, providing services, or managing the company that are not directly related to production. These expenses include advertising expenses; salaries paid to salespersons or managers; depreciation on administrative buildings; and expenses related to insurance, utilities, property taxes, and repairs.
- *Research and development expense*—the cost of developing new products.
- *Other expense*—a catch-all category used to capture other miscellaneous expenses incurred by the company.
- *Income taxes expense*—the income taxes paid on the company's pretax income.

Net Income Net income, or net earnings, is the difference between total revenues and expenses. **Apple** reported net income of $25,922 million ($108,768 million − $82,846 million). If total expenses are greater than total revenues, the company would report a net loss.

Preparing an Income Statement

The preparation of an income statement involves four steps:

Step 1. Prepare a heading that includes the name of the company, the title of the financial statement, and the time period covered.

Step 2. List the revenues of the company, starting with sales revenue (or service revenue) and then listing other revenue items. Add the revenues to get total revenue.

Step 3. List the expenses of the company, usually starting with cost of goods sold. Add the expenses to get total expenses.

Step 4. Subtract the expenses from the revenues to get net income (or net loss if expenses exceed revenues). Double-underline net income.

In general, only the first items in a column as well as any subtotals or totals have dollar signs. Also when multiple items exist within a classification, these items are grouped together in a separate column (to the left of the main column) and their total is placed in the main column. Cornerstone 1.3 shows how to prepare an income statement.

[4] We will discuss procedures for calculating cost of goods sold in Chapter 6.

Preparing an Income Statement

CORNERSTONE 1.3

Why:

The income statement reports the results of a company's operations (revenues minus expenses) for a given period of time.

Information:

Hightower Inc. reported the following account balances for the year ending December 31, 2013:

Cost of goods sold	$31,300	Interest expense	$ 540
Salaries expense	8,800	Sales revenue	50,600
Insurance expense	700	Depreciation expense	1,500
Interest income	1,200	Rent expense	2,100
Income taxes expense	2,000		

Required:

Prepare Hightower's income statement for the year ending December 31, 2013.

Solution:

Hightower Inc. Income Statement For the year ended December 31, 2013			Step 1
Revenues:			Step 2
Sales revenue	$50,600		
Interest income	1,200		
Total revenues		$51,800	
Expenses:			Step 3
Cost of goods sold	$31,300		
Salaries expense	8,800		
Rent expense	2,100		
Depreciation expense	1,500		
Insurance expense	700		
Interest expense	540		
Income taxes expense	2,000		
Total expenses		46,940	
Net income		$ 4,860	Step 4

Income Statement Formats

Companies prepare their income statements in one of two different formats: single-step income statements or multiple-step income statements.

Single-Step Income Statement The format that we illustrated in Cornerstone 1.3 is called a *single-step income statement*. In a single-step income statement, there are only two categories: total revenues and total expenses. Total expenses are subtracted from total revenues in a *single step* to arrive at net income. The advantage of a single-step income statement is its simplicity.

Multiple-Step Income Statement A second income statement format is the *multiple-step income statement*. The multiple-step income statement provides classifications of revenues and expenses that financial statement users find useful. A multiple-step income statement contains three important subtotals:

- **Gross margin (gross profit)**—the difference between net sales and cost of goods sold (or cost of sales)
- **Income from operations**—the difference between gross margin and operating expenses
- *Net income*—the difference between income from operations and any nonoperating revenues and expenses

A multiple-step income statement for **Apple** is shown in Exhibit 1.9.

EXHIBIT 1.9

Multiple-Step Income Statement for Apple Inc.

Apple Inc.
Income Statement
For the fiscal year ended September 24, 2011
(in millions of dollars)

Net sales	$108,249	
Cost of goods sold	64,431	
Gross margin		$43,818
Operating expenses:		
Research and development expense	$ 2,429	
Selling, general, and administrative expenses	7,599	
Total operating expenses		10,028
Income from operations		$33,790
Other income and expense:		
Interest income	$ 519	
Other expenses	(104)	415
Income before income taxes		$34,205
Income taxes expense		8,283
Net income		$25,922

Source: Apple Inc. 2011 10-K.

Gross Margin A company's *gross margin* or *gross profit* is calculated as:

$$\text{Gross Margin} = \text{Net Sales} - \text{Cost of Goods Sold}$$

Gross margin represents the initial profit made from selling a product, but it is *not* a measure of total profit because other operating expenses have not yet been subtracted. However, gross margin is closely watched by managers and other financial statement users. A change in a company's gross margin can give insights into a company's current pricing and purchasing policies, thereby providing insight into the company's future performance.

Income from Operations *Income from operations* is computed as:

$$\text{Income from Operations} = \text{Gross Margin} - \text{Operating Expenses}$$

Operating expenses are the expenses the business incurs in selling goods or providing services and managing the company. Operating expenses typically include research and development expenses, selling expenses, and general and administrative expenses. Income from operations indicates the level of profit produced by the principal activities of the company. **Apple** can increase its income from operations by either increasing its gross margin or decreasing its operating expenses.

Nonoperating Activities A multiple-step income statement reports nonoperating activities in a section which is frequently called *other income and expenses. Nonoperating activities* are revenues and expenses from activities other than the company's principal operations. They include gains and losses from the sale of equipment and other items that were not acquired for resale. For many companies, the most important nonoperating item is interest and investment revenue. Exhibit 1.10 lists some common nonoperating items.

EXHIBIT 1.10

Typical Nonoperating Items

Other Revenues and Gains

- Interest income on investments
- Dividend income from investments in stock of other companies
- Rent revenue
- Gains on disposal of property, plant, and equipment

Other Expenses and Losses

- Interest expense from loans
- Losses from disposal of property, plant, and equipment
- Losses from accidents or vandalism
- Losses from employee strikes
- Income taxes expense

Net Income Nonoperating items are subtracted from income from operations to obtain income before taxes. Income taxes expense is then subtracted to obtain net income. Regardless of the format used, notice that there is no difference in the amount of the revenue or expense items reported. That is, net income is the same under either the single-step or the multiple-step format. The only difference is how the revenues and expenses are classified.

Using Income Statement Information

A company's ability to generate current income is useful in predicting its ability to generate future income. When investors believe that future income will improve, they will buy stock. Similarly, creditors rely on their judgments of a company's future income to make loans. Investors' and creditors' estimates of the future profitability and growth of a company are aided by a careful examination of how a company has earned its revenue and managed its expenses.

Net Profit Margin A useful measure of a company's ability to generate profit is its **net profit margin** (sometimes called return on sales). Net profit margin shows the percentage of profit in each dollar of sales revenue (or service revenue) and is computed as:

$$\text{Net Profit Margin} = \frac{\text{Net Income}}{\text{Sales (or Service) Revenue}}$$

This ratio provides an indication of management's ability to control expenses. Future income depends on both maintaining (or increasing) market share while controlling expenses.

YOUDECIDE Assessing Future Profitability

You are looking to invest in one of two companies in the same industry—Growth Inc. or Stagnation Company. Your initial examination revealed that both companies reported the same amount of net income for 2014. Further analysis produced the following 5-year summary:

Growth Inc.

	2010	2011	2012	2013	2014
Sales revenues	$625,000	$750,000	$820,000	$920,000	$1,000,000
Net income	$ 30,000	$ 36,000	$ 40,000	$ 45,000	$ 50,000
Profit margin	4.8%	4.8%	4.9%	4.9%	5.0%

(Continued)

Stagnation Company

	2010	2011	2012	2013	2014
Sales revenue	$1,025,000	$975,000	$940,000	$1,020,000	$1,040,000
Net income	$ 51,000	$ 48,000	$ 46,000	$ 49,000	$ 50,000
Profit margin	5%	4.9%	4.9%	4.8%	4.8%

Which company is the better investment?

Investors seek those investments that will provide the largest return at the lowest risk. One factor associated with large returns is future profitability. Over the last 5 years, Growth's sales and net income have steadily increased while Stagnation's sales and net income have remained, on average, stable. Sales growth is an indicator of the possibility of increasing future income. Further, Growth's increasing profit margin (compared to a decreasing profit margin for Stagnation) indicates that Growth is doing a better job at controlling its expenses relative to Stagnation, enabling Growth to earn more profit on each dollar of sales. While the future never can be predicted with certainty, the data suggest that, if current trends continue, Growth will grow more rapidly than Stagnation. Therefore, an investment in Growth would probably yield the larger future return.

Accounting information can help you judge a company's potential for future profitability and growth.

OBJECTIVE 6

Prepare the retained earnings statement and understand the information it communicates.

RETAINED EARNINGS STATEMENT

The owners of a company contribute capital in one of two ways:

- directly, though purchases of common stock from the company
- indirectly, by the company retaining some or all of the net income earned each year rather than paying it out in dividends

As noted earlier, the income earned by the company but not paid out in the form of dividends is called retained earnings. The retained earnings statement summarizes and explains the changes in retained earnings during the accounting period.[5] The beginning balance in retained earnings is increased by net income earned during the year and decreased by any dividends that were declared. Exhibit 1.11 shows the retained earnings statement for **Apple**.

EXHIBIT 1.11

Retained Earnings Statement for Apple Inc.

Apple Inc.
Retained Earnings Statement
For the fiscal year ended September 24, 2011
(in millions of dollars)

Retained earnings, Sept. 25, 2010	$37,169
Add: Net income	25,922
	$63,091
Less: Dividends	0
Other*	(250)
Retained earnings, Sept. 24, 2011	$62,841

*The other item deducted in Apple's retained earnings statement is related to common stock issued under Apple's stock plans. This item is beyond the scope of this text.

Source: Apple Inc. 2011 10-K.

[5] Some companies may choose to report a statement of stockholders' equity, which explains the changes in all of the stockholders' equity accounts. This statement is discussed more fully in Chapter 10.

Notice the heading is similar to the heading for the income statement in that it covers a period of time (the fiscal year ended September 24, 2011). In addition, Apple declared no dividends for 2011 but chose to keep the net income earned within the company. Many growing companies, such as Apple, choose not to pay dividends in order to reinvest its earnings and support future growth.

The preparation of the retained earnings statement involves four steps:

Step 1. Prepare a heading that includes the name of the company, the title of the financial statement, and the time period covered.
Step 2. List the retained earnings balance at the beginning of the period obtained from the balance sheet.
Step 3. Add net income obtained from the income statement.
Step 4. Subtract any dividends declared during the period. Double-underline the total, which should equal retained earnings at the end of the period as reported on the balance sheet.

The preparation of a retained earnings statement is detailed in Cornerstone 1.4.

Preparing a Retained Earnings Statement

CORNERSTONE 1.4

Why:

The retained earnings statement summarizes and explains the changes in retained earnings during an accounting period.

Information:

Hightower Inc. reported the following account balances for the year ending December 31, 2013:

Net income	$4,860	Retained earnings, 1/1/2013	$ 9,440
Dividends	3,000	Retained earnings, 12/31/2013	11,300

Required:

Prepare Hightower's retained earnings statement for the year ending December 31, 2013.

Solution:

Hightower Inc. Retained Earnings Statement For the year ended December 31, 2013		Step 1
Retained earnings, January 1, 2013	$ 9,440	Step 2
Add: Net income	4,860	Step 3
Less: Dividends	(3,000)	Step 4
Retained earnings, December 31, 2013	**$11,300**	Step 4

Use of the Retained Earnings Statement

The retained earnings statement is used to monitor and evaluate a company's dividend payouts to its shareholders. For example, some older investors seek out companies with high dividend payouts so that they will receive cash during the year. Other investors are more interested in companies that are reinvesting a sufficient amount of earnings that will enable them to pursue profitable growth opportunities. Finally, creditors are interested in a company's dividend payouts. If a company pays out too much in dividends, the company may not have enough cash on hand to repay its debt when it becomes due.

YOUDECIDE Dividend Policy Decisions

You are the manager of a fast-growing software engineering firm. Over the last 5 years, your company has doubled the amount of its income every year. This tremendous growth has been financed through funds obtained from stockholders and cash generated from operations. The company has virtually no debt.

How would you respond to stockholders who have recently complained that the company's policy not to pay dividends is preventing them from sharing in the company's success?

Retained earnings can be an important source of financing for many companies. When companies feel that they have profitable growth opportunities, they should reinvest the earnings in the business instead of paying out the amount to stockholders as dividends. The reinvestment of these funds should result in higher stock prices (and increased wealth for the stockholders) as the company grows. If the company chose to pay a dividend, it would be forced to either abandon the growth opportunities or finance them through some other, more costly method (e.g., issuing debt).

When management feels that the company has growth opportunities that will increase the value of the company, the reinvestment of earnings is usually preferable.

OBJECTIVE 7

Understand the information communicated by the statement of cash flows.

STATEMENT OF CASH FLOWS

The last of the major financial statements, the statement of cash flows, describes the company's cash receipts (cash inflows) and cash payments (cash outflows) for a period of time. The statement of cash flows for Apple is shown in Exhibit 1.12.

EXHIBIT 1.12

Statement of Cash Flows

Apple Inc.
Statement of Cash Flows
For the fiscal year ended September 24, 2011
(in millions of dollars)

Net cash provided from operating activities	$ 37,529
Net cash used by investing activities	(40,419)
Net cash provided from financing activities	1,444
Net change in cash	$ (1,446)
Cash at the beginning of the year	11,261
Cash at the end of the year	$ 9,815

Source: Apple Inc. 2011 10-K.

Elements of the Statement of Cash Flows

Cash flows are classified into one of three categories:

- **Cash flows from operating activities**—any cash flows directly related to earning income. This category includes cash sales and collections of accounts receivable as well as cash payments for goods, services, salaries, and interest.

- **Cash flows from investing activities**—any cash flow related to the acquisition or sale of investments and long-term assets such as property, plant, and equipment.
- **Cash flows from financing activities**—any cash flow related to obtaining capital of the company. This category includes the issuance and repayment of debt, common stock transactions, and the payment of dividends.

The preparation of the statement of cash flows will be discussed in Chapter 11.

Use of the Statement of Cash Flows

Because cash is the lifeblood of any company and is critical to success, the statement of cash flows can be an important source of information as users attempt to answer how a company generated and used cash during a period. Such information is helpful as users assess the company's ability to generate cash in the future. Creditors can use the statement of cash flows to assess the creditworthiness of a company. A company with healthy cash flow—particularly if it comes from operating activities—is in a good position to repay debts as they come due and is usually a low-risk borrower. Stockholders are also interested in the adequacy of cash flows as an indicator of the company's ability to pay dividends and to expand its business. The statement of cash flows is covered in more detail in Chapter 11.

RELATIONSHIPS AMONG THE STATEMENTS

OBJECTIVE 8

Describe the relationships among the financial statements.

At this point, it is important to notice the natural relationships of the four basic financial statements and the natural progression from one financial statement to another. The accounting period begins with a balance sheet. During the year, the company earns net income from operating its business. Net income from the income statement increases retained earnings on the retained earnings statement. Ending retained earnings is then reported in the stockholders' equity section of the balance sheet at the end of the accounting period. Therefore, the income statement can be viewed as explaining, through the retained earnings statement, the change in the financial position during the year. Finally, the statement of cash flows explains the change in cash during the year. These relationships are shown in Exhibit 1.13 (p. 26).

OTHER ITEMS IN THE ANNUAL REPORT AND PROFESSIONAL ETHICS

OBJECTIVE 9

Describe other information contained in the annual report and the importance of ethics in accounting.

The financial statements discussed in the previous sections were reported to users in an *annual report.* For publicly traded companies that are required to file reports with the Securities and Exchange Commission, the annual report is contained within the company's 10-K filing. The annual report includes the financial statements of a company and other important information such as the notes to the financial statements, management's discussion and analysis of the condition of the company, and the auditor's report.

Notes to the Financial Statements

The **notes to the financial statements** (or **footnotes**) clarify and expand upon the information presented in the financial statements. The notes are an integral part of the financial statements and help to fulfill the accountant's responsibility for full disclosure of all relevant information. Without the information contained in the notes, the financial statements are incomplete and could not be adequately understood by users. The information contained in the notes can be either quantitative (numerical) or qualitative (nonnumerical).

EXHIBIT 1.13 Relationships Among the Financial Statements

Beginning of the Period → End of the Period

Hightower Inc.
Balance Sheet
Dec. 31, 2012

Assets:	
Cash	$ 2,030
Other assets	32,360
Total assets	$ 34,390
Liabilities:	
Total liabilities	$ 10,500
Stockholders' equity:	
Common stock	14,450
Retained earnings	9,440
Total liabilities & stockholders' equity	$ 34,390

Hightower Inc.
Income Statement
For the year ended Dec. 31, 2013

Revenues	$51,800
Expenses	46,940
Net income	$ 4,860

Hightower Inc.
Retained Earnings Statement
For the year ended Dec. 31, 2013

Retained earnings, 1/1	$ 9,440
Add: Net income	4,860
Less: Dividends	(3,000)
Retained earnings, 12/31	$11,300

Hightower Inc.
Statement of Cash Flows
For the year ended Dec. 31, 2013

Net cash provided from operating activities	$3,470
Net cash used by investing activities	(4,800)
Net cash provided from financing activities	1,800
Net change in cash	$ 470
Cash, 1/1/2013	2,030
Cash 12/31/2013	$2,500

Hightower Inc.
Balance Sheet
Dec. 31, 2013

Assets:	
Cash	$ 2,500
Other assets	36,300
Total assets	$38,800
Liabilities:	
Total liabilities	$13,050
Stockholders' equity:	
Common stock	14,450
Retained earnings	11,300
Total liabilities & stockholders' equity	$38,800

Generally, the first note contains a summary of significant accounting policies and rules used in the financial statements. For example, the following is an excerpt from Apple's notes to the financial statements concerning its accounting for revenues:

Revenue Recognition

The Company recognizes revenue when persuasive evidence of an arrangement exists, delivery has occurred, the sales price is fixed or determinable, and collection is probable. Product is considered delivered to the customer once it has been shipped and title and risk of loss have been transferred. For most of the Company's product sales, these criteria are met at the time the product is shipped.

Source: Apple Inc. 2011 10-K.

Other footnotes provide additional detail on line items presented in the financial statements. For example, while Apple only reports a single number on the balance sheet for property, plant, and equipment, the company provides a detailed breakdown of the components of property, plant, and equipment (land, building, machinery, equipment, and furniture) in the notes. Other notes provide disclosures about items not reported in the financial statements. For instance, Apple provides detailed explanations of its stock option activity over the last 3 years—an activity not directly reported on the financial statements yet of significant interest to users.

concept Q&A

Is there a single equation or financial statement that captures the business activities (operating, investing, and financing) in which all companies engage?

Answer:

The fundamental accounting equation captures the business activities of companies and encompasses all of the major financial statements. While certain statements provide more information on certain business activities (for example, the income statement provides information about a company's operating activities), information is also contained in other statements as well (for example, current assets and current liabilities provide insight into a company's operations). Therefore, all financial statements and the notes to the financial statements must be examined as an integrated whole.

Management's Discussion and Analysis

The annual report also includes a section entitled **Management's Discussion and Analysis**. In this section, management provides a discussion and explanation of various items reported in the financial statements. Additionally, management uses this opportunity to highlight favorable and unfavorable trends and significant risks facing the company. For example, in explaining the increase in sales from the previous years, Apple disclosed the following:

Net sales of iPhone and related products and services were $47.1 billion in 2011, representing an increase of $21.9 billion or 87% compared to 2010. iPhone year-over-year net sales growth reflected strong demand for iPhone 4 in all of the Company's operating segments. The expanded U.S. distribution of iPhone to the Verizon Wireless network, beginning in February 2011, continued expansion into new countries, and increased distribution with other new carriers and resellers also contributed to the year-over-year growth of iPhone.

Source: Apple Inc. 2011 10-K.

Report of Independent Accountants

An independent accountant (or auditor) is an accounting professional who conducts an examination of a company's financial statements. The objective of this examination is to gather evidence that will enable the auditor to form an opinion as to whether the financial statements fairly present the financial position and results of operations of the company. The auditor's opinion of the financial statements is presented in the form of an **audit report**. Exhibit 1.14 (p. 28) shows an excerpt from the audit report for Apple.

Because financial statement users cannot directly observe the company's accounting practices, companies hire auditors to give the users of the financial statements assurance or confidence that the financial statements are a fair presentation of the company's financial health. In performing an audit, it is impractical for an auditor to retrace every transaction of the company for the entire accounting period. Instead, the auditor performs procedures (e.g., sampling of transactions) that enable an opinion to be expressed on the financial statement as a whole.

EXHIBIT 1.14

Auditor's Report for Apple Inc.

Report of Independent Registered Public Accounting Firm (partial)

The Board of Directors and Shareholders of Apple Inc.:

We have audited the accompanying consolidated balance sheets of Apple Inc. as of September 24, 2011, and September 25, 2010, and the related consolidated statements of operations, shareholders' equity, and cash flows for each of the three years in the period ended September 24, 2011. These financial statements are the responsibility of the Company's management. Our responsibility is to express an opinion on these consolidated financial statements based on our audits.

We conducted our audits in accordance with the standards of the Public Company Accounting Oversight Board (United States). Those standards require that we plan and perform the audit to obtain reasonable assurance about whether the financial statements are free of material misstatement. An audit includes examining, on a test basis, evidence supporting the amounts and disclosures in the financial statements. An audit also includes assessing the accounting principles used and significant estimates made by management, as well as evaluating the overall financial statement presentation. We believe that our audits provide a reasonable basis for our opinion.

In our opinion, the financial statements referred to above present fairly, in all material respects, the consolidated financial position of Apple Inc. at September 24, 2011, and September 25, 2010, and the consolidated results of its operations and its cash flows for each of the three years in the period ended September 24, 2011, in conformity with U.S. generally accepted accounting principles.

We also have audited, in accordance with the standards of the Public Company Accounting Oversight Board (United States), Apple Inc.'s internal control over financial reporting as of September 24, 2011, based on criteria established in Internal Control—Integrated Framework issued by the Committee of Sponsoring Organizations of the Treadway Commission and our report dated October 26, 2011, expressed an unqualified opinion thereon.

/s/ Ernst & Young LLP
San Jose, California
October 26, 2011

Source: Apple Inc. 2011 10-K.

YOU DECIDE Career Analysis

As you consider various career options, keep in mind that virtually every organization must have an accounting system. Thus, accountants are employed in a wide range of businesses, including private companies, public accounting firms, governments, and banks. To help you evaluate whether an accounting career is right for you, consider the following question:

What skills and character traits are required for accountants?

Accountants must have well-developed analytical skills and must be effective communicators, both verbally and in writing. Most accounting assignments—whether in business, government, or public accounting—are team assignments in which team members must be able to communicate effectively and work quickly and cooperatively to a solution.

As a profession, accounting requires a high level of academic study and is subject to professional competence requirements. Most members of public accounting firms, and many management accountants and consultants, are (or are in the process of becoming) Certified Public Accountants (CPAs). Other valuable professional certifications are the Certified Management Accountant (CMA), the Certified Internal Auditor (CIA), and the Certified Fraud Examiner (CFE) designations. All of these designations are designed to ensure that the accountants who offer their services are properly qualified and maintain a high level of personal integrity and ethical behavior.

While the career opportunities for accountants are virtually boundless, even if you choose a different career path, the knowledge and experience that you can gain from accounting will prove invaluable in your career.

Accountants must possess strong analytical and communication skills, demonstrate professional competency, and behave ethically.

Professional Ethics

Confidence that standards of ethical behavior will be maintained—even when individuals have incentives to violate those standards—is essential to the conduct of any business activity. Owners of businesses must trust their managers, managers must trust each other and their employees, and the investing public must trust accountants to behave according to accepted ethical standards, which may or may not be reflected in formal written codes. The violation of ethical standards may bring clear and direct penalties but more often brings subtle and long-lasting negative consequences for individuals and companies.

For the economy to function effectively and efficiently, users must have faith that the information reported in financial statements is accurate and dependable. This can only be accomplished through ethical behavior of the accountants involved in the financial reporting process. The American Institute of Certified Public Accountants (AICPA), recognizing that its members have an obligation of self-discipline above and beyond the requirements of generally accepted accounting principles, has adopted a code of professional conduct which provides ethical guidelines for accountants in the performance of their duties. These ethical principles require accountants to serve the public interest with integrity. For example, auditors should fulfill their duties with objectivity, independence, and due professional care. In no situation should an auditor yield to pressure from management to report positively on financial statements that overstate the company's performance or prospects. Violation of these ethical standards can result in severe penalties, including revocation of an accountant's license to practice as a certified public accountant.

In recent years, there have been an increasing number of news reports about unethical behavior involving accounting practices. Acting ethically is not always easy. However, because of the important role of accounting in society, accountants are expected to maintain the highest level of ethical behavior. Throughout this book, you will be exposed to ethical dilemmas that we urge you to consider. As you analyze these cases, consider the guidelines in Exhibit 1.15.

EXHIBIT 1.15

Guidelines in Ethical Decision Making

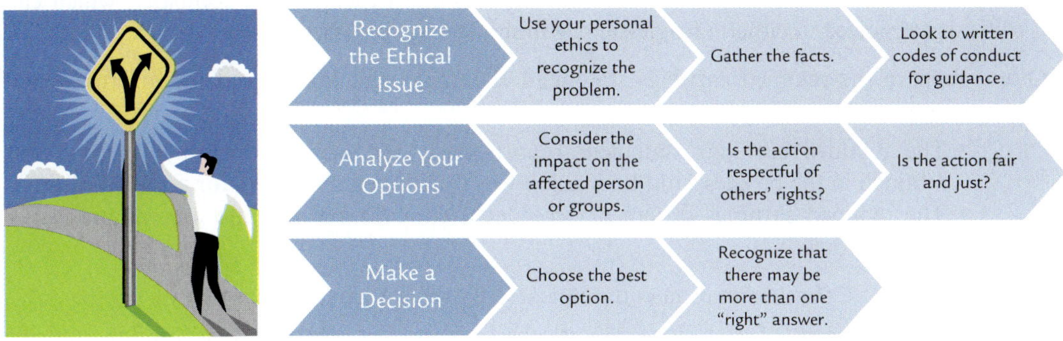

SUMMARY OF LEARNING OBJECTIVES

LO 1. Explain the nature of accounting.

- Accounting is the process of identifying, measuring, recording, and communicating financial information.
- This information is used both inside and outside of the business to make better decisions.

- Accounting is also called the language of business.
- Financial accounting focuses on the needs of external decision-makers.

LO 2. Identify the forms of business organizations and the types of business activities.

- The three forms of business organizations are the sole proprietorship (owned by one person), the partnership (jointly owned by two or more individuals), and the corporation (separate legal entity organized under the laws of a particular state).
- Regardless of the form of business, all businesses are involved in three activities. Financing activities include obtaining funds necessary to begin and operate a business. Investing activities involve buying the assets that enable a business to operate. Operating activities are the activities of a business that generate a profit.

LO 3. Describe the relationships shown by the fundamental accounting equation.

- The fundamental accounting equation captures all of the economic activities recorded by an accounting system.
- The left side of the accounting equation shows the assets, or economic resources of a company.
- The right side of the accounting equation shows the claims on the company's assets (liabilities or stockholders' equity).

LO 4. Prepare a classified balance sheet and understand the information it communicates.

- A balance sheet reports the resources (assets) owned by a company and the claims against those resources (liabilities and stockholders' equity) at a specific point in time.
- These elements are related by the fundamental accounting equation:
  Assets = Liabilities + Stockholders' Equity
- In order to help users identify the fundamental economic similarities and differences between the various items on the balance sheet, assets and liabilities are classified as either current or noncurrent (long-term). Stockholders' equity is classified as either contributed capital or retained earnings.

LO 5. Prepare an income statement and understand the information it communicates.

- The income statement reports how well a company has performed its operations over a period of time and provides information about the future profitability and growth of a company.
- The income statement includes the revenues and expenses of a company, which can be reported in either a single-step or multiple-step format.

LO 6. Prepare the retained earnings statement statement and understand the information it communicates.

- The retained earnings statement reports how much of a company's income was retained in the business and how much was distributed to owners for a period of time.
- The retained earnings statement provides users with insights into a company's dividend payouts.

LO 7. Understand the information communicated by the statement of cash flows.

- The statement of cash flows reports the sources of a company's cash inflow and the uses of a company's cash over time.
- The statement of cash flows can be used to assess the creditworthiness of a company.

LO 8. Describe the relationships among the financial statements.

- There is a natural relationship among the four basic financial statements so that financial statements are prepared in a particular order.
- Starting with the balance sheet at the beginning of the accounting period, financial statements are generally prepared in the following order: income statement, retained earnings statement, and balance sheet at the end of the accounting period.
- The statement of cash flows explains the change in cash on the balance sheets at the beginning and end of the accounting period.

LO 9. Describe other information contained in the annual report and the importance of ethics in accounting.

- The notes to the financial statements clarify and expand upon the information presented in the financial statements and are considered an integral part of a company's financial statements.
- Management's discussion and analysis provides a discussion and explanation of various items reported in the financial statements.
- The auditor's report gives the auditor's opinion as to whether the financial statements fairly present the financial condition and results of operations of the company.
- Standards of ethical behavior are essential to the conduct of any business activity. Violation of these standards often brings significant short- and long-term negative consequences for individuals and companies.
- The maintenance of a high ethical standard is necessary for users to have faith in the accuracy of the financial statements, which is a key factor in the effective and efficient functioning of the economy.

CORNERSTONES

CORNERSTONE 1.1	Using the fundamental accounting equation, page 10
CORNERSTONE 1.2	Preparing a classified balance sheet, page 15
CORNERSTONE 1.3	Preparing an income statement, page 19
CORNERSTONE 1.4	Preparing a retained earnings statement, page 23

KEY TERMS

Accounting, 4
Assets, 7
Audit report, 27
Balance sheet, 8
Capital, 14
Cash flows from financing activities, 25
Cash flows from investing activities, 25
Cash flows from operating activities, 24
Corporation, 5
Creditor, 7
Current assets, 13
Current liabilities, 14
Current ratio, 16
Expenses, 7
Financial accounting, 4
Financial Accounting Standards Board (FASB), 9
Financial statements, 8
Fiscal year, 11
Footnotes, 25
Fundamental accounting equation, 10
Generally accepted accounting principles (GAAP), 9
Gross margin (gross profit), 20
Income from operations, 20
Income statement, 9
Intangible assets, 13
International Accounting Standards Board (IASB), 9
International financial reporting standards (IFRS), 9
Liability, 7
Liquidity, 16
Long-term investments, 13
Long-term liabilities, 14
Management's Discussion and Analysis, 27
Net income, 8
Net loss, 8
Net profit margin, 21
Notes to the financial statements, 25
Operating cycle, 13
Partnership, 5
Property, plant, and equipment, 13
Retained earnings statement, 9
Revenue, 7
Securities and Exchange Commission (SEC), 9
Sole proprietorship, 5
Statement of cash flows, 9
Stockholders' equity, 7
Working capital, 16

REVIEW PROBLEM

Preparing Financial Statements

Concept:

A company's business activities are summarized and reported in its financial statements. The balance sheet reports the company's financial position (assets, liabilities, and stockholders' equity) at a specific point in time. The income statement reports the results of a company's operations (revenues minus expenses) for a given period of time. The retained earnings statement summarizes and explains the changes in retained earnings during the accounting period.

Information:

Enderle Company reported the following account balances at December 31, 2013:

Equipment	$19,800	Sales revenue	$82,500	Interest expense	$ 1,200
Retained earnings, 12/31/2013	15,450	Accumulated depreciation	5,450	Retained earnings, 1/1/2013	10,300
Copyright	1,200	Cash	2,900	Depreciation expense	3,500
Accounts payable	5,500	Salaries expense	18,100	Cost of goods sold	52,000
Interest income	2,300	Common stock	11,500	Inventory	5,600
Bonds payable	10,000	Land	15,000	Income taxes expense	3,000
Dividends	1,850	Accounts receivable	3,700	Interest payable	300

Required:

1. Prepare Enderle's single-step income statement for the year ending December 31, 2013.
2. Prepare Enderle's retained earnings statement for the year ending December 31, 2013.
3. Prepare Enderle's balance sheet at December 31, 2013.

Solution:

1.

Enderle Company
Income Statement
For the year ended December 31, 2013

Revenues:		
Sales revenue	$82,500	
Interest income	2,300	
Total revenues		$84,800
Expenses:		
Cost of goods sold	$52,000	
Salaries expense	18,100	
Depreciation expense	3,500	
Interest expense	1,200	
Income taxes expense	3,000	
Total expenses		77,800
Net income		$ 7,000

2.

Enderle Company
Retained Earnings Statement
For the year ended December 31, 2013

Retained earnings, January 1, 2013	$10,300
Add: Net income	7,000
Less: Dividends	(1,850)
Retained earnings, December 31, 2013	$15,450

3.

Enderle Company
Balance Sheet
December 31, 2013

ASSETS		
Current assets:		
Cash	$ 2,900	
Accounts receivable	3,700	
Inventory	5,600	
Total current assets		$12,200
Property, plant, and equipment:		
Land	$15,000	
Equipment	19,800	
Less: Accumulated depreciation	(5,450)	
Total property, plant, and equipment		29,350
Intangible assets:		
Copyright		1,200
Total assets		$42,750

LIABILITIES AND STOCKHOLDERS' EQUITY		
Current liabilities:		
Accounts payable	$ 5,500	
Interest payable	300	
Total current liabilities		$ 5,800
Long-term liabilities:		
Bonds payable		10,000
Total liabilities		$15,800
Stockholders' equity:		
Common stock	$11,500	
Retained earnings	15,450	
Total stockholders' equity		26,950
Total liabilities and stockholders' equity		$42,750

DISCUSSION QUESTIONS

1. Define *accounting*. How does accounting differ from *bookkeeping*?
2. Why is there a demand for accounting information? Name five groups that create demand for accounting information about businesses, and describe how each group uses accounting information.
3. What is an accounting entity?
4. Name and describe three different forms of business organization.
5. Name and describe the three main types of business activities.
6. Define the terms *assets*, *liabilities*, and *stockholders' equity*. How are the three terms related?
7. Define the terms *revenue* and *expense*. How are these terms related?
8. Name and briefly describe the purpose of the four financial statements.
9. What types of questions are answered by the financial statements?
10. What is point-in-time measurement? How does it differ from period-of-time measurement?
11. Write the fundamental accounting equation. Why is it significant?
12. What information is included in the heading of each of the four financial statements?
13. Define *current assets* and *current liabilities*. Why are current assets and current liabilities separated from noncurrent assets and long-term liabilities on the balance sheet?

14. Describe how items are ordered within the current assets and current liabilities sections on a balance sheet.
15. Name the two main components of stockholders' equity. Describe the main sources of change in each component.
16. What equation describes the income statement?
17. How does the multiple-step income statement differ from the single-step income statement?
18. Explain the items reported on a retained earnings statement.
19. Name and describe the three categories of the statement of cash flows.
20. How is the retained earnings statement related to the balance sheet? How is the income statement related to the retained earnings statement?
21. Describe the items (other than the financial statements) found in the annual report.
22. Give an example of unethical behavior by a public accountant and describe its consequences.

MULTIPLE-CHOICE QUESTIONS

1-1 Which of the following statements is *false* concerning forms of business organization?

a. A corporation has tax advantages over the other forms of business organization.
b. It is easier for a corporation to raise large sums of money than it is for a sole proprietorship or partnership.
c. A sole proprietorship is an easy type of business to form.
d. Owners of sole proprietorships and partnerships have personal liability for the debts of the business while owners of corporations have limited legal liability.

1-2 Which of the following statements regarding business activities is true?

a. Operating activities involve buying the long-term assets that enable a company to generate revenue.
b. Financing activities include obtaining the funds necessary to begin and operate a business.
c. Investing activities center around earning interest on a company's investments.
d. Companies spend a relatively small amount of time on operating activities.

1-3 At December 31, Pitt Inc. has assets of $12,900 and liabilities of $6,300. What is the stockholders' equity for Pitt at December 31?

a. $6,600
b. $6,300
c. $18,100
d. $19,200

1-4 Which of the following is *not* one of the four basic financial statements?

a. Balance sheet
b. Income statement
c. Statement of cash flows
d. Auditor's report

1-5 What type of questions do the financial statements help to answer?

a. Is the company better off at the end of the year than at the beginning of the year?
b. What resources does the company have?
c. For what did a company use its cash during the year?
d. All of the above.

1-6 Which of the following is *not* shown in the heading of a financial statement?

a. The title of the financial statement
b. The name of the company
c. The time period covered by the financial statement
d. The name of the auditor

Use the following information for Multiple-Choice Questions 1-7 and 1-8:
At December 31, Marker reported the following items: cash, $7,500; inventory, $3,900; accounts payable, $5,900; accounts receivable, $3,100; common stock, $6,000; property, plant, and equipment, $10,500; interest payable, $1,600; retained earnings, $11,500.

1-7 Refer to the information for Marker above. What is the total of Marker's current assets?

a. $12,100
b. $13,700
c. $14,500
d. $25,000

1-8 Refer to the information for Marker above. What is Marker's stockholders' equity?

a. $7,500
b. $17,500
c. $19,100
d. $25,000

1-9 Which of the following statements regarding the income statement is true?

a. The income statement provides information about the profitability and growth of a company.
b. The income statement shows the results of a company's operations at a specific point in time.
c. The income statement consists of assets, expenses, liabilities, and revenues.
d. Typical income statement accounts include sales revenue, unearned revenue, and cost of goods sold.

1-10 For the most recent year, Grant Company reported revenues of $182,300, cost of goods sold of $108,800, inventory of $8,500, salaries expense of $48,600, rent expense of $12,000, and cash of $12,300. What was Grant's net income?

a. $9,400
b. $12,900
c. $21,400
d. $24,900

1-11 Which of the following statements concerning retained earnings is true?

a. Retained earnings is the difference between revenues and expenses.
b. Retained earnings is increased by dividends and decreased by net income.
c. Retained earnings represents accumulation of the income that has not been distributed as dividends.
d. Retained earnings is reported as a liability on the balance sheet.

1-12 Which of the following sentences regarding the statement of cash flows is *false*?

a. The statement of cash flows describes the company's cash receipts and cash payments for a period of time.
b. The statement of cash flows reconciles the beginning and ending cash balances shown on the balance sheet.
c. The statement of cash flows reports cash flows in three categories: cash flows from business activities, cash flows from investing activities, and cash flows from financing activities.
d. The statement of cash flows may be used by creditors to assess the creditworthiness of a company.

1-13 Which of the following statements is true?

a. The auditor's opinion is typically included in the notes to the financial statements.
b. The notes to the financial statements are an integral part of the financial statements that clarify and expand on the information presented in the financial statements.
c. The management's discussion and analysis section does not convey any information that cannot be found in the financial statements themselves.
d. The annual report is required to be filed with the New York Stock Exchange.

CORNERSTONE EXERCISES

OBJECTIVE 3
CORNERSTONE 1.1

Cornerstone Exercise 1-14 Using the Accounting Equation

Listed below are three independent scenarios.

Scenario	Assets	Liabilities	Equity
1	$ (a)	$42,000	$56,000
2	115,000	(b)	77,000
3	54,000	18,500	(c)

Required:

Use the fundamental accounting equation to find the missing amounts.

OBJECTIVE 3
CORNERSTONE 1.1

Cornerstone Exercise 1-15 Using the Accounting Equation

At the beginning of the year, Morgan Company had total assets of $425,000 and total liabilities of $260,000.

Required:

Use the fundamental accounting equation to answer the following independent questions:

1. What is total stockholders' equity at the beginning of the year?
2. If, during the year, total assets increased by $73,000 and total liabilities increased by $32,000, what is the amount of total stockholders' equity at the end of the year?
3. If, during the year, total assets decreased by $52,000 and total stockholders' equity increased by $35,000, what is the amount of total liabilities at the end of the year?
4. If, during the year, total liabilities increased by $85,000 and total stockholders' equity decreased by $73,000, what is the amount of total assets at the end of the year?

OBJECTIVE 4 5 6 7
CORNERSTONE 1.2
CORNERSTONE 1.3
CORNERSTONE 1.4

Cornerstone Exercise 1-16 Financial Statements

Listed below are elements of the financial statements.

a. Liabilities
b. Net change in cash
c. Assets
d. Revenue
e. Cash flow from operating activities
f. Expenses
g. Stockholders' equity
h. Dividends

Required:

Match each financial statement item with its financial statement: balance sheet (B), income statement (I), retained earnings statement (RE), or statement of cash flows (CF).

OBJECTIVE 4
CORNERSTONE 1.2

Cornerstone Exercise 1-17 Balance Sheet

Listed below are items that may appear on a balance sheet.

Item	Classification
1. Accounts payable	a. Current assets
2. Machinery	b. Property, plant, and equipment
3. Inventory	c. Intangible assets
4. Common stock	d. Current liabilities
5. Notes payable (due in 5 years)	e. Long-term liabilities
6. Cash	f. Contributed capital
7. Copyright	g. Retained earnings
8. Net income less dividends	
9. Accumulated depreciation	
10. Accounts receivable	

Required:

Match each item with its appropriate classification on the balance sheet.

Cornerstone Exercise 1-18 Balance Sheet

OBJECTIVE 4
CORNERSTONE 1.2

An analysis of the transactions of Cavernous Homes Inc. yields the following totals at December 31, 2013: cash, $3,200; accounts receivable, $4,500; notes payable, $5,000; supplies, $8,100; common stock, $7,000; and retained earnings, $3,800.

Required:

Prepare a balance sheet for Cavernous Homes Inc. at December 31, 2013.

Cornerstone Exercise 1-19 Income Statement

OBJECTIVE 5
CORNERSTONE 1.3

An analysis of the transactions of Canary Cola Inc. for the year 2013 yields the following information: service revenue, $78,000; supplies expense, $33,200; rent expense, $20,500; and dividends, $7,000.

Required:

What is the amount of net income reported by Canary Cola for 2013?

Cornerstone Exercise 1-20 Retained Earnings Statement

OBJECTIVE 6
CORNERSTONE 1.4

Parker Company has a balance of $35,000 in retained earnings on January 1, 2013. During 2013, Parker reported revenues of $82,000 and expenses of $55,000. Parker also paid a dividend of $8,000.

Required:

What is the amount of retained earnings on December 31, 2013?

BRIEF EXERCISES

Brief Exercise 1-21 Users of Financial Information

OBJECTIVE 1

Listed below are several users of accounting information and decisions that user may make.

User of Accounting Information		Decision
1. Manager	a.	Determines whether the company paid the proper amount of taxes.
2. Employee	b.	Decides if a factory is profitable or should be closed.
3. Investor	c.	Determines if a company will be able to repay its obligations.
4. Creditor	d.	Decides if the reported net income will cause the stock price to rise or fall.
5. Government	e.	Estimates the amount of a possible bonus.

Required:

Indicate which user of accounting information is responsible for each of the decisions.

Brief Exercise 1-22 Forms of Business Organization

OBJECTIVE 2

Listed below are the forms of business organization and several related advantages or disadvantages.

Form of Business Organization		Advantage or Disadvantage
1. Sole proprietorship	a.	Most complex to organize
2. Partnership	b.	Owner(s) have personal responsibility for the debt of the organization
3. Corporation	c.	Access to the individual skills of each of the owners
	d.	Limited personal liability for the debt of the organization
	e.	Easier to raise large amounts of capital
	f.	The greatest percentage of businesses are organized in this manner
	g.	Owners generally pay higher taxes than owners of other forms of business organizations

(Continued)

Required:

Match each form of business organization with its respective advantage or disadvantage. (*Hint:* Some advantages or disadvantages may be related to more than one form of business organization.)

OBJECTIVE 2

Brief Exercise 1-23 Business Activities

Marni Restaurant Company engaged in the following transactions during March, its first month of operations.

a. Received $100,000 cash from the sale of stock.
b. Purchased $20,000 of inventory from J&J Wholesale Company.
c. Purchased $30,000 of kitchen equipment for its restaurants.
d. Obtained a $25,000 loan from First State Bank.
e. Sold $18,000 of food to customers.
f. Paid employee weekly salaries of $8,500.
g. Repaid $10,000 of principal relating to the loan in Item d.

Required:

For each of the above business activities, indicate whether it is an operating, investing, or financing activity.

OBJECTIVE 3

Brief Exercise 1-24 The Accounting Equation

Financial information for three independent cases is as follows:

a. The liabilities of Dent Company are $82,000, and its stockholders' equity is $120,000. What is the amount of Dent's total assets?
b. The total assets of Wayne Inc. are $55,000, and its stockholders' equity is $22,500. What is the amount of Wayne's total liabilities?
c. Gordon Company's total assets increased by $60,000 during the year, and its liabilities decreased by $35,000. Did Gordon's stockholders' equity increase or decrease? By how much?

Required:

Determine the missing amount for each case.

OBJECTIVE 4

Brief Exercise 1-25 Balance Sheet

Below are items that may appear on the balance sheet.

Item		Classification	
1.	Buildings	a.	Current assets
2.	Copyright	b.	Property, plant, and equipment
3.	Supplies	c.	Intangible assets
4.	Unearned service revenue	d.	Current liabilities
5.	Prepaid insurance	e.	Long-term liabilities
6.	Common stock	f.	Contributed capital
7.	Rent payable	g.	Retained earnings
8.	Accounts receivable		
9.	Allowance for doubtful accounts		
10.	Bonds payable		

Required:

Match each item with its appropriate classification.

Brief Exercise 1-26 Income Statement

OBJECTIVE 5

An analysis of the transactions of Rutherford Company for the year ended December 31, 2013, yields the following information: sales revenue, $65,000; insurance expense, $4,300; interest income, $3,900; cost of goods sold, $28,800; and loss on disposal of property, plant, and equipment, $1,200.

Required:

Prepare a single-step income statement.

Brief Exercise 1-27 Retained Earnings Statement

OBJECTIVE 6

Listed below are events that affect stockholders' equity.

a. Reported net income of $85,000.
b. Paid a cash dividend of $10,000.
c. Reported sales revenue of $120,000.
d. Issued common stock of $50,000.
e. Reported a net loss of $20,000.
f. Reported expenses of $35,000.

Required:

For each of the events, indicate whether it increases retained earnings (I), decreases retained earnings (D), or has no effect on retained earnings (NE).

Brief Exercise 1-28 Statement of Cash Flows

OBJECTIVE 7

Listed below are items that would appear on a statement of cash flows.

a. Cash received from customers
b. Cash paid for dividends
c. Cash received from a bank loan
d. Cash paid to suppliers
e. Cash paid to purchase equipment

Required:

Indicate in which part of the statement of cash flows each of the items would appear: operating activities (O), investing activities (I), or financing activities (F).

Brief Exercise 1-29 Relationships among the Financial Statements

OBJECTIVE 8

Listed below are three, independent scenarios.

Scenario	Balance Sheet: Retained Earnings	Income Statement: Net Income	Balance Sheet: Retained Earnings
1.	$30,000	$25,000	$ (a)
2.	(b)	30,000	94,000
3.	50,000	(c)	70,000

Required:

Compute the missing amount in each row. Assume no withdrawals or dividends.

OBJECTIVE 9

Brief Exercise 1-30 Annual Report Items

Listed below are several descriptions related to other items found in an annual report.

	Description		Location in the Annual Report
1.	An integral part of the financial statements that helps to fulfill the accountant's responsibility for full disclosure of all relevant information	a.	Notes to the financial statements
2.	An opinion as to whether the financial statements fairly present the financial position and result of operations of the company	b.	Management's discussion and analysis
3.	A discussion and explanation of various items reported in the financial statements	c.	Report of independent accountants
4.	Clarification or expansion upon the information presented in the financial statements		

Required:

Match each of the descriptions with the location in the annual report in which it may be found.

EXERCISES

OBJECTIVE 1

Exercise 1-31 Decisions Based on Accounting Information

Decision-makers use accounting information in a wide variety of decisions including the following:

1. Deciding whether or not to lend money to a business
2. Deciding whether or not an individual has paid enough in taxes
3. Deciding whether or not to place merchandise on sale in order to reduce inventory
4. Deciding whether or not to invest in a business
5. Deciding whether or not to demand additional benefits for employees

Required:

Match each decision with one of the following decision-makers who is primarily responsible for the decision: a government (G), an investor (I), a labor union (U), business managers (M), or a bank (B).

OBJECTIVE 2

Exercise 1-32 Forms of Business Organizations

Listed below are definitions, examples, or descriptions related to business entities.

1. Owned by one person
2. Can make and sell goods (manufacturing)
3. Owned by more than one person
4. Can sell goods (merchandising)
5. Can provide and sell services
6. Legally, a separate entity from the owner(s)
7. A law firm owned by some of the employees who are each liable for the financial obligations of the entity
8. The Coca-Cola Company

Required:

1. For each of the three types of business entities (sole proprietorship, partnership, and corporation), select as many of the definitions, examples, or descriptions as apply to that type of entity.
2. **CONCEPTUAL CONNECTION** Explain the advantages and disadvantages of each type of business entity.

Exercise 1-33 Business Activities

OBJECTIVE 2

Listed below are various activities that companies engage in during a period.

a. Purchase of equipment
b. Payment of a dividend
c. Purchase of supplies
d. Sale of equipment
e. Sale of goods or services
f. Borrow money from a bank
g. Contribution of cash by owners

Required:

For each of the activities listed above, classify the activity as operating (O), investing (I), or financing (F).

Exercise 1-34 Business Activities

OBJECTIVE 2

Bill and Steve recently formed a company that manufactures and sells high-end kitchen appliances. The following is a list of activities that occurred during the year.

a. Bill and Steve each contributed cash in exchange for common stock in the company.
b. Land and a building to be used as a factory to make the appliances were purchased for cash.
c. Machines used to make the appliances were purchased for cash.
d. Various materials used in the production of the appliances were purchased for cash.
e. Three employees were paid cash to operate the machines and make the appliances.
f. Running low on money, the company borrowed money from a local bank.
g. The money from the bank loan was used to buy advertising on local radio and television stations.
h. The company sold the appliances to local homeowners for cash.
i. Due to extremely high popularity of its products, Bill and Steve built another factory building on its land for cash.
j. The company paid a cash dividend to Bill and Steve.

Required:

Classify each of the business activities listed as either an operating activity (O), an investing activity (I), or a financing activity (F).

Exercise 1-35 Accounting Concepts

OBJECTIVE 4 5 6

A list of accounting concepts and related definitions is presented below.

Concept		Definition	
1.	Revenue	a.	Owner's claim on the resources of a company
2.	Expense	b.	The difference between revenues and expenses
3.	Net income (loss)	c.	Increase in assets from the sale of goods or services
4.	Dividend	d.	Economic resources of a company
5.	Asset	e.	Cost of assets consumed in the operation of a business
6.	Liability	f.	Creditors' claims on the resources of a company
7.	Stockholders' equity	g.	Distribution of earnings to stockholders

Required:

Match each of the concepts with its corresponding definition.

Exercise 1-36 The Fundamental Accounting Equation

OBJECTIVE 3

ILLUSTRATING RELATIONSHIPS

Financial information for three independent cases is given below.

	Assets	Liabilities	Equity
1.	$116,200	$ (a)	$55,400
2.	212,600	145,900	(b)
3.	(c)	22,500	48,300

(Continued)

Required:

Compute the missing numbers in each case.

OBJECTIVE 4

Exercise 1-37 Balance Sheet Structure

The following accounts exist in the ledger of Higgins Company: accounts payable, accounts receivable, accumulated depreciation, bonds payable, building, common stock, cash, equipment, income taxes payable, inventory, notes payable (due in 5 years), prepaid insurance, retained earnings, trademarks, and wages payable.

Required:

1. Organize the above items into a properly prepared classified balance sheet.
2. **CONCEPTUAL CONNECTION** Which information might be helpful to assess liquidity?

OBJECTIVE 4

Exercise 1-38 Identifying Current Assets and Liabilities

Dunn Sporting Goods sells athletic clothing and footwear to retail customers. Dunn's accountant indicates that the firm's operating cycle averages 6 months. At December 31, 2013, Dunn has the following assets and liabilities:

a. Prepaid rent in the amount of $8,500. Dunn's rent is $500 per month.
b. A $9,700 account payable due in 45 days.
c. Inventory in the amount of $46,230. Dunn expects to sell $38,000 of the inventory within 3 months. The remainder will be placed in storage until September 2014. The items placed in storage should be sold by November 2014.
d. An investment in marketable securities in the amount of $1,900. Dunn expects to sell $700 of the marketable securities in 6 months. The remainder are not expected to be sold until 2016.
e. Cash in the amount of $1,050.
f. An equipment loan in the amount of $60,000 due in March 2018. Interest of $4,500 is due in March 2014 ($3,750 of the interest relates to 2013, with the remainder relating to the first 3 months of 2014).
g. An account receivable from a local university in the amount of $2,850. The university has promised to pay the full amount in 3 months.
h. Store equipment at a cost of $9,200. Accumulated depreciation has been recorded on the store equipment in the amount of $1,250.

Required:

1. Prepare the current asset and current liability portions of Dunn's December 31, 2013, balance sheet.
2. Compute Dunn's working capital and current ratio at December 31, 2013.
3. **CONCEPTUAL CONNECTION** As in investor or creditor, what do these ratios tell you about Dunn's liquidity?

OBJECTIVE 4

Exercise 1-39 Current Assets and Current Liabilities

Hanson Construction has an operating cycle of 9 months. On December 31, 2013, Hanson has the following assets and liabilities:

a. A note receivable in the amount of $1,500 to be collected in 6 months
b. Cash totaling $1,380
c. Accounts payable totaling $2,100, all of which will be paid within 2 months
d. Accounts receivable totaling $12,000, including an account for $7,000 that will be paid in 2 months and an account for $5,000 that will be paid in 18 months
e. Construction supplies costing $6,200, all of which will be used in construction within the next 12 months
f. Construction equipment costing $60,000, on which depreciation of $22,400 has accumulated
g. A note payable to the bank in the amount of $6,800 is to be paid within the next year

Required:

1. Calculate the amounts of current assets and current liabilities reported on Hanson's balance sheet at December 31, 2013.
2. **CONCEPTUAL CONNECTION** Comment on Hanson's liquidity.

Exercise 1-40 Depreciation

OBJECTIVE 4 5

Swanson Products was organized as a new business on January 1, 2013. On that date, Swanson acquired equipment at a cost of $425,000, which is depreciated at a rate of $40,000 per year.

Required:

Describe how the equipment and its related depreciation will be reported on the balance sheet at December 31, 2013, and on the 2013 income statement.

Exercise 1-41 Stockholders' Equity

OBJECTIVE 4

On January 1, 2013, Mulcahy Manufacturing Inc., a newly formed corporation, issued 1,000 shares of common stock in exchange for $150,000 cash. No other shares were issued during 2013, and no shares were repurchased by the corporation. On November 1, 2013, the corporation's major stockholder sold 300 shares to another stockholder for $50,000. The corporation reported net income of $37,500 for 2013.

Required:

Prepare the stockholders' equity section of Mulcahy's balance sheet at December 31, 2013.

Exercise 1-42 Classified Balance Sheet

OBJECTIVE 4

College Spirit sells sportswear with logos of major universities. At the end of 2013, the following balance sheet account balances were available.

Accounts payable	$104,700	Income taxes payable	$ 11,400
Accounts receivable	6,700	Inventory	481,400
Accumulated depreciation	23,700	Long-term investment	110,900
Bonds payable	180,000	Note payable, short-term	50,000
Cash	13,300	Prepaid rent (current)	54,000
Common stock	300,000	Retained earnings, 12/31/2013	84,500
Furniture	88,000		

Required:

1. Prepare a classified balance sheet for College Spirit at December 31, 2013.
2. Compute College Spirit's working capital and current ratio at December 31, 2013.
3. **CONCEPTUAL CONNECTION** Comment on College Spirit's liquidity as of December 31, 2013.

Exercise 1-43 Classified Balance Sheet

OBJECTIVE 4

Jerrison Company operates a wholesale hardware business. The following balance sheet accounts and balances are available for Jerrison at December 31, 2013.

Accounts payable	$ 65,100	Equipment, data processing	$309,000
Accounts receivable	95,500	Income taxes payable	21,600
Accumulated depreciation		Interest payable	12,600
(on building)	216,800	Inventory	187,900
Accumulated depreciation		Investments (long-term)	32,700
(on data processing equipment)	172,400	Investments (short-term)	21,000
Accumulated depreciation	31,200	Land	41,000
(on trucks)		Notes payable (due June 1, 2014)	150,000
Bonds payable (due 2017)	200,000	Prepaid insurance (for 4 months)	5,700
Building (warehouse)	419,900	Retained earnings, 12/31/2013	?
Cash	11,400	Salaries payable	14,400
Common stock	150,000	Trucks	106,100

(Continued)

Required:

1. Prepare a classified balance sheet for Jerrison at December 31, 2013.
2. Compute Jerrison's working capital and current ratio at December 31, 2013.
3. **CONCEPTUAL CONNECTION** If Jerrison's management is concerned that a large portion of its inventory is obsolete and cannot be sold, how will Jerrison's liquidity be affected?

OBJECTIVE 4

Exercise 1-44 Balance Sheet Relationships

Balance sheet information for Milton Company is as follows:

	2013	2014
Current assets	$ (a)	$ 25,000
Long-term liabilities	(b)	34,900
Intangible assets	10,400	9,200
Long-term investments	19,200	(f)
Property, plant and equipment (net)	85,700	92,800
Current liabilities	14,500	12,300
Total assets	142,200	(g)
Retained earnings	56,900	67,000
Total liabilities	50,300	(h)
Contributed capital	(c)	(i)
Total stockholders' equity	(d)	(j)
Total liabilities and stockholders' equity	(e)	149,200

Required:

Compute the missing values (a)–(j). All the necessary information is provided. (*Hint:* It is not necessary to calculate your answers in alphabetical order.)

OBJECTIVE 5

Exercise 1-45 Income Statement Structure

The following accounts exist in the ledger of Butler Company: salaries expense, advertising expense, cost of goods sold, depreciation expense, interest expense, income taxes expense, sales revenue, and utilities expense.

Required:

1. Organize the above items into a properly prepared single-step income statement.
2. **CONCEPTUAL CONNECTION** What information would be helpful in assessing Butler's ability to generate future income?

OBJECTIVE 5

Exercise 1-46 Income Statement

ERS Inc. maintains and repairs office equipment. ERS had an average of 10,000 shares of common stock outstanding for the year. The following income statement account balances are available for ERS at the end of 2013.

Advertising expense	$24,200	Salaries expense (for administrative personnel)	$195,600
Depreciation expense (on service van)	16,250	Service revenue	933,800
Income taxes expense	15,150	Supplies expense	66,400
Insurance expense	11,900	Utilities expense	26,100
Interest expense	10,100	Wages expense (for service technicians)	448,300
Rent expense	58,400		

Required:

1. Prepare a single-step income statement for ERS for 2013.
2. **CONCEPTUAL CONNECTION** Compute net profit margin for ERS. If ERS is able to increase its service revenue by $100,000, what should be the effect on future income?

3. **CONCEPTUAL CONNECTION** Assume that ERS net profit margin was 8.5% for 2012. As an investor, what conclusions might you draw about ERS' future profitability?

Exercise 1-47 Multiple-Step Income Statement

OBJECTIVE 5

The following information is available for Bergin Pastry Shop.

Gross margin	$34,700
Income from operations	9,200
Income taxes expense (15% of income before taxes)	?
Interest expense	1,800
Net sales	85,300

Required:

Prepare a multiple-step income statement for Bergin.

Exercise 1-48 Income Statement

OBJECTIVE 5

The following information is available for Wright Auto Supply at December 31, 2013.

Cost of goods sold	$292,000	Rent expense	$ 21,000
Depreciation expense	31,250	Salaries (administrative)	33,800
Income taxes expense	32,520	Sales revenue	585,600
Interest expense	2,400	Wages expense (salespeople)	96,750

Required:

1. Prepare a single-step income statement for the year ended December 31, 2013.
2. Prepare a multiple-step income statement for the year ended December 31, 2013.
3. **CONCEPTUAL CONNECTION** Comment on the differences between the single-step and the multiple-step income statements.

Exercise 1-49 Retained Earnings Statement

OBJECTIVE 6

At the end of 2012, Sherwood Company had retained earnings of $18,240. During 2013, Sherwood had revenues of $837,400 and expenses of $792,100, and paid cash dividends in the amount of $38,650.

Required:

1. Determine the amount of Sherwood's retained earnings at December 31, 2013.
2. **CONCEPTUAL CONNECTION** Comment on Sherwood's dividend policy.

Exercise 1-50 Statement of Cash Flows

OBJECTIVE 7

Walters Inc. began operations on January 1, 2013. The following information relates to Walters' cash flows during 2013.

Cash received from owners	$201,500	Cash paid to purchase machine	$32,000
Cash paid for purchase of land and building	128,700	Cash paid to employees for salaries	46,400
Cash paid for advertising	34,200	Cash paid for dividends to stockholders	37,500
Cash received from customers	139,800	Cash paid for supplies	28,700

Required:

1. Calculate the cash provided/used for each cash flow category.
2. **CONCEPTUAL CONNECTION** Comment on Walters' creditworthiness.

OBJECTIVE 8

ILLUSTRATING RELATIONSHIPS

Exercise 1-51 Relationships Among the Financial Statements

Zachary Corporation's December 31, 2012 balance sheet included the following amounts:

Cash	$ 20,400
Retained earnings	105,600

Zachary's accountant provided the following data for 2013:

Revenues	$650,100	Cash inflow from operating activities	$ 892,250
Expenses	578,600	Cash outflow for investing activities	(990,300)
Dividends	30,000	Cash inflow from financing activities	108,400

Required:

Calculate the amount of cash and retained earnings at the end of 2013.

OBJECTIVE 8

ILLUSTRATING RELATIONSHIPS

Exercise 1-52 Relationships Among the Financial Statements

The following information for Kellman Inc. is available at the end of 2013.

Total assets on 12/31/2012	$82,400	Common stock on 12/31/2012	$50,000
Total assets on 12/31/2013	88,500	Common stock on 12/31/2013	50,000
Total liabilities on 12/31/2012	9,200	Net income for 2013	19,500
Total liabilities on 12/31/2013	11,300		

Required:

Calculate the amount of dividends reported on the retained earnings statement for 2013.

OBJECTIVE 8

ILLUSTRATING RELATIONSHIPS

Exercise 1-53 Relationships Among the Financial Statements

During 2013, Moore Corporation paid $20,000 of dividends. Moore's assets, liabilities, and common stock at the end of 2012 and 2013 were:

	12/31/2012	12/31/2013
Total assets	$152,200	$171,800
Total liabilities	56,600	63,750
Common stock	60,000	60,000

Required:

Using the information provided, compute Moore's net income for 2013.

OBJECTIVE 9

Exercise 1-54 Annual Report Items

DeSalle Company's annual report includes the following items: financial statements, notes to the financial statements, management's discussion and analysis, and a report of independent accountants.

Required:

For each of the following items, where would you most likely find the information in the annual report?

a. A description of the risks associated with operating the company in an international market
b. Detailed information on the outstanding debt of a company, including the interest rate being charged and the maturity date of the debt
c. A description of the accounting methods used by the company
d. The total resources and claims to the resources of a company
e. A discussion of the sales trends of the company's most profitable products
f. The amount of dividends paid to common stockholders
g. An opinion as to whether the financial statements are a fair presentation of the company's financial position and results of operations
h. The cost of operating a company over a period of time

Exercise 1-55 Professional Ethics

OBJECTIVE 9

Ethical behavior is essential to the conduct of business activity. Consider each of the following business behaviors:

a. A manager prepares financial statements that grossly overstate the performance of the business.
b. A CPA resigns from an audit engagement rather than allow a business client to violate an accounting standard.
c. An internal auditor decides against confronting an employee of the business with minor violations of business policy. The employee is a former college classmate of the auditor.
d. An accountant advises his client on ways to legally minimize tax payments to the government.
e. A manager legally reduces the price of a product to secure a larger share of the market.
f. Managers of several large companies secretly meet to plan price reductions designed to drive up-and-coming competitors out of the market.
g. An accountant keeps confidential details of her employer's legal operations that would be of interest to the public.
h. A recently dismissed accountant tells competitors details about her former employer's operations as she seeks a new job.

Required:

Identify each behavior as ethical (E) or unethical (U).

PROBLEM SET A

Problem 1-56A Applying the Fundamental Accounting Equation

OBJECTIVE 3

ILLUSTRATING RELATIONSHIPS

At the beginning of 2013, Huffer Corporation had total assets of $232,400, total liabilities of $94,200, common stock of $50,000, and retained earnings of $88,200. During 2013, Huffer had net income of $51,750, paid dividends of $10,000, and issued additional common stock for $15,000. Huffer's total assets at the end of 2013 were $285,500.

Required:

Calculate the amount of liabilities that Huffer must have at the end of 2013 in order for the balance sheet equation to balance.

Problem 1-57A Accounting Relationships

OBJECTIVE 4 5 6 8

ILLUSTRATING RELATIONSHIPS

Information for Beethoven Music Company is given below.

Total assets at the beginning of the year	$145,200	Equity at the beginning of the year	$ (b)
Total assets at the end of the year	(a)	Equity at the end of the year	104,100
Total liabilities at the beginning of the year	92,600	Dividends paid during the year	(c)
Total liabilities at the end of the year	126,900	Net income for the year	77,500
		Revenues	554,800
		Expenses	(d)

Required:

Use the relationships in the balance sheet, income statement, and retained earnings statement to determine the missing values.

Problem 1-58A Arrangement of the Income Statement

OBJECTIVE 5

Powers Wrecking Service demolishes old buildings and other structures and sells the salvaged materials. During 2013, Powers had $425,000 of revenue from demolition services and $137,000 of revenue from salvage sales. Powers also had $1,575 of interest income from investments. Powers incurred $243,200 of wages expense, $24,150 of depreciation expense, $48,575 of

(Continued)

supplies expense, $84,000 of rent expense, $17,300 of miscellaneous expense, and $43,900 of income taxes expense.

Required:

Prepare a single-step income statement for Powers for 2013.

OBJECTIVE 4 5 6 8

Problem 1-59A Income Statement and Balance Sheet Relationships

ILLUSTRATING RELATIONSHIPS

Each column presents financial information taken from one of four different companies, with one or more items of data missing.

	Company			
Financial Statement Item	**Floyd**	**Slater**	**Wooderson**	**O'Bannion**
Total revenue	$125	$ 715	$ (e)	$2,475
Total expense	92	(c)	54	(g)
Net income (net loss)	(a)	184	18	(600)
Total assets	905	1,988	(f)	8,140
Total liabilities	412	(d)	117	2,280
Total equity	(b)	823	80	(h)

Required:

Use your understanding of the relationships among financial statements and financial statement items to determine the missing values (a–h).

OBJECTIVE 4 5

Problem 1-60A Income Statement and Balance Sheet

The following information for Rogers Enterprises is available at December 31, 2013, and includes all of Rogers' financial statement amounts except retained earnings:

Accounts receivable	$72,920	Property, plant, and equipment	$ 90,000
Cash	13,240	Rent expense	135,000
Common stock (10,000 shares)	70,000	Retained earnings	?
Income taxes expense	12,800	Salaries expense	235,200
Income taxes payable	4,150	Salaries payable	14,800
Interest expense	16,000	Service revenue	463,500
Notes payable (due in 10 years)	25,000	Supplies	42,000
Prepaid rent (building)	31,500	Supplies expense	34,400

Required:

Prepare a single-step income statement and a classified balance sheet for the year ending December 31, 2013, for Rogers.

OBJECTIVE 6

Problem 1-61A Retained Earnings Statement

Dittman Expositions has the following data available:

Dividends, 2013	$ 10,250	Retained earnings, 12/31/2012	$ 20,900
Dividends, 2014	12,920	Revenues, 2013	407,500
Expenses, 2013	382,100	Revenues, 2014	451,600
Expenses, 2014	418,600		

Required:

Prepare retained earnings statements for 2013 and 2014.

OBJECTIVE 6

Problem 1-62A Retained Earnings Statements

ILLUSTRATING RELATIONSHIPS

The table below presents the retained earnings statements for Bass Corporation for 3 successive years. Certain numbers are missing.

	2012	2013	2014
Retained earnings, beginning	$21,500	$ (b)	$33,600
Add: Net income	9,200	10,100	(f)
	$30,700	$ (c)	$ (g)
Less: Dividends	(a)	(d)	(3,900)
Retained earnings, ending	$27,200	$ (e)	$41,200

Required:

Use your understanding of the relationship between successive retained earnings statements to calculate the missing values (a–g).

Problem 1-63A Income Statement, Retained Earnings Statement, and Balance Sheet

OBJECTIVE 4 5 6

The following information relates to Ashton Appliances for 2013.

Accounts payable	$ 16,800	Income taxes expense	$ 16,650
Accounts receivable	69,900	Income taxes payable	12,000
Accumulated depreciation (building)	104,800	Insurance expense	36,610
Accumulated depreciation (furniture)	27,600	Interest expense	15,500
		Inventory	59,850
Bonds payable (due in 7 years)	192,000	Other assets	92,800
Building	300,000	Rent expense (store equipment)	80,800
Cash	41,450	Retained earnings, 12/31/2012	54,000
Common stock	243,610	Salaries expense (administrative)	101,000
Cost of goods sold	511,350	Salaries payable	7,190
Depreciation expense (building)	11,050	Sales revenue	948,670
Depreciation expense (furniture)	12,000	Wages expense (store staff)	127,710
Furniture	130,000		

Required:

1. Prepare a single-step income statement for 2013, a retained earnings statement for 2013, and a properly classified balance sheet as of December 31, 2013.
2. **CONCEPTUAL CONNECTION** How would a multiple-step income statement be different from the single-step income statement you prepared for Ashton?

Problem 1-64A Stockholders' Equity Relationships

OBJECTIVE 8

ILLUSTRATING RELATIONSHIPS

Data from the financial statements of four different companies are presented in separate columns in the table below. Each column has one or more data items missing.

	Company			
Financial Statement Item	**Berko**	**Manning**	**Lucas**	**Corey**
Equity, 12/31/2012:				
Common stock	$50,000	$35,000	$ (i)	$15,000
Retained earnings	12,100	(e)	26,400	21,900
Total equity	$ (a)	$44,300	$66,400	$36,900
Net income (loss) for 2013	$ 7,000	$(1,800)	$ 6,000	$ (m)
Dividends during 2013	2,000	0	(j)	1,400
Equity, 12/31/2013:				
Common stock	50,000	35,000	55,000	15,000
Retained earnings	(b)	(f)	(k)	27,600
Total equity	$ (c)	$ (g)	$84,500	$ (n)
Total assets, 12/31/2013	92,500	(h)	99,200	(o)
Total liabilities, 12/31/2013	$ (d)	$14,800	$ (l)	$10,700

(Continued)

Required:

Use your understanding of the relationships among the financial statement items to determine the missing values (a–o).

OBJECTIVE 3 8 ILLUSTRATING RELATIONSHIPS

Problem 1-65A Relationships Among Financial Statements

Carson Corporation reported the following amounts for assets and liabilities at the beginning and end of a recent year.

	Beginning of Year	End of Year
Assets	$385,500	$420,250
Liabilities	152,800	156,600

Required:

Calculate Carson's net income or net loss for the year in each of the following independent situations:

1. Carson declared no dividends, and its common stock remained unchanged.
2. Carson declared no dividends and issued additional common stock for $40,000 cash.
3. Carson declared dividends totaling $15,000, and its common stock remained unchanged.
4. Carson declared dividends totaling $20,000 and issued additional common stock for $35,000.

PROBLEM SET B

OBJECTIVE 3 ILLUSTRATING RELATIONSHIPS

Problem 1-56B Applying the Fundamental Accounting Equation

At the beginning of 2013, KJ Corporation had total assets of $525,700, total liabilities of $290,800, common stock of $100,000, and retained earnings of $134,900. During 2013, KJ had net income of $205,500, paid dividends of $70,000, and issued additional common stock for $75,000. KJ's total assets at the end of 2013 were $710,100.

Required:

Calculate the amount of liabilities that KJ must have at the end of 2013 in order for the balance sheet equation to balance.

OBJECTIVE 4 5 6 8 ILLUSTRATING RELATIONSHIPS

Problem 1-57B The Fundamental Accounting Equation

Information for TTL Inc. is given below.

Total assets at the beginning of the year	$ (a)	Equity at the end of the year	$ (c)
Total assets at the end of the year	758,150	Dividends paid during the year	35,500
Total liabilities at the beginning of the year	368,200	Net income for the year	(d)
Total liabilities at the end of the year	(b)	Revenues	929,440
Equity at the beginning of the year	272,900	Expenses	835,320

Required:

Use the relationships in the balance sheet, income statement, and retained earnings statement to determine the missing values.

OBJECTIVE 5

Problem 1-58B Arrangement of the Income Statement

Parker Renovation Inc. renovates historical buildings for commercial use. During 2013, Parker had $763,400 of revenue from renovation services and $5,475 of interest income from miscellaneous investments. Parker incurred $222,900 of wages expense, $135,000 of depreciation expense, $65,850 of insurance expense, $109,300 of utilities expense, $31,000 of miscellaneous expense, and $61,400 of income taxes expense.

Required:

Prepare a single-step income statement for Parker for 2013.

Problem 1-59B Income Statement and Balance Sheet Relationships

OBJECTIVE 4 5 6 8

ILLUSTRATING RELATIONSHIPS

Each column presents financial information taken from one of four different companies, with one or more items of data missing.

	Company			
Financial Statement Item	**Crick**	**Pascal**	**Eiffel**	**Hilbert**
Total revenue	$925	$ 533	$ (e)	$1,125
Total expense	844	(c)	377	(g)
Net income (net loss)	(a)	289	126	(340)
Total assets	709	1,810	(f)	3,150
Total liabilities	332	(d)	454	2,267
Total equity	(b)	950	98	(h)

Required:

Use your understanding of the relationships among financial statements and financial statement items to find the missing values (a–h).

Problem 1-60B Income Statement and Balance Sheet

OBJECTIVE 4 5

Ross Airport Auto Service provides parking and minor repair service at the local airport while customers are away on business or pleasure trips. The following account balances (except for retained earnings) are available for Ross Airport Auto Service at December 31, 2013.

Accounts payable	$ 17,200	Interest payable	$ 4,800
Accounts receivable	39,200	Inventory (repair parts)	6,100
Accumulated depreciation (equipment)	42,300	Investments (long term)	35,000
Cash	7,700	Notes payable (due May 2, 2020)	160,000
Common stock (20,000 shares)	100,000	Prepaid rent (3 months)	27,300
Depreciation expense (equipment)	12,450	Rent expense	103,500
Dividends	6,300	Retained earnings, 12/31/2013	48,200
Equipment	270,800	Service revenue (parking)	232,600
Income taxes expense	2,700	Service revenue (repair)	198,500
Income taxes payable	1,100	Supplies expense (repair parts)	36,900
Interest expense	21,300	Wages expense	246,100
Interest income	4,100	Wages payable	12,500

Required:

Prepare a single-step income statement and a classified balance sheet for the year ended December 31, 2013.

Problem 1-61B Retained Earnings Statement

OBJECTIVE 6

Magical Experiences Vacation Company has the following data available:

Dividends, 2013	$ 14,000	Retained earnings, 12/31/2012	$ 55,300
Dividends, 2014	16,000	Revenues, 2013	221,900
Expenses, 2013	188,500	Revenues, 2014	325,400
Expenses, 2014	250,800		

Required:

Prepare retained earnings statements for 2013 and 2014.

OBJECTIVE 6

ILLUSTRATING RELATIONSHIPS

Problem 1-62B Retained Earnings Statements

The table below presents the retained earnings statements for Dillsboro Corporation for 3 successive years. Certain numbers are missing.

	2012	2013	2014
Retained earnings, beginning	$ (a)	$19,500	$26,700
Add: Net income	11,100	(c)	9,500
	$ 26,900	$ (d)	$ (f)
Less: Dividends	(7,400)	(5,200)	(g)
Retained earnings, ending	$ (b)	$ (e)	$34,100

Required:

Use your understanding of the relationship between successive retained earnings statements to calculate the missing values (a–g).

OBJECTIVE 4 5 6

Problem 1-63B Income Statement, Retained Earnings Statement, and Balance Sheet

McDonald Marina provides docking and cleaning services for pleasure boats at its marina in southern Florida. The following account balances are available:

Accounts payable	$ 26,400	Interest expense	$ 236,000
Accounts receivable	268,700	Interest payable	18,000
Accumulated depreciation (building)	64,500	Land	875,000
Accumulated depreciation (equipment)	950,400	Rent expense	14,600
Bonds payable (due 2018)	2,000,000	Rent payable	2,400
Building	197,300	Retained earnings, 12/31/2012	128,600
Cash	22,300	Service revenue (cleaning)	472,300
Common stock (40,000 shares)	600,000	Service revenue (docking)	1,460,000
Depreciation expense (building)	21,500	Supplies	9,800
Depreciation expense (equipment)	246,300	Supplies expense	89,100
Dividends	25,300	Utilities expense	239,400
Equipment	2,490,000	Wages expense	987,200
Income taxes expense	21,700	Wages payable	21,600

Required:

1. Prepare a single-step income statement, a retained earnings statement, and a classified balance sheet for the year ended December 31, 2013.
2. **CONCEPTUAL CONNECTION** How would a multiple-step income statement be different from the single-step income statement you prepared for McDonald Marina?

OBJECTIVE 8

ILLUSTRATING RELATIONSHIPS

Problem 1-64B Stockholders' Equity Relationships

Data from the financial statements of four different companies are presented in separate columns in the table below. Each column has one or more data items missing.

	Company			
Financial Statement Item	**Stackhouse**	**Compton**	**Bellefleur**	**Merlotte**
Equity, 12/31/2012:				
Common stock	$45,000	$39,000	$ 80,000	$25,000
Retained earnings	18,800	15,300	6,900	(k)
Total equity	$63,800	$ (d)	$ 86,900	$38,900
Net income (loss) for 2013	$ (a)	$ 7,100	$ 9,700	$ (4,500)
Dividends during 2013	2,100	800	(h)	0
Equity, 12/31/2013:				
Common stock	45,000	39,000	80,000	25,000
Retained earnings	21,700	(e)	(i)	(l)
Total equity	$ (b)	$ (f)	$ 95,300	$ (m)
Total assets, 12/31/2013	(c)	88,200	113,400	(n)
Total liabilities, 12/31/2013	$14,400	$ (g)	$ (j)	$15,700

Required:

Use your understanding of the relationships among the financial statement items to determine the missing values (a–n).

Problem 1-65B Relationships Among Financial Statements

OBJECTIVE 3 8

ILLUSTRATING RELATIONSHIPS

Leno Corporation reported the following amounts for assets and liabilities at the beginning and end of a recent year.

	Beginning of Year	End of Year
Assets	$256,500	$358,200
Liabilities	92,650	121,900

Required:

Calculate Leno's net income or net loss for the year in each of the following independent situations:

1. Leno declared no dividends, and its common stock remained unchanged.
2. Leno declared no dividends and issued additional common stock for $15,000 cash.
3. Leno declared dividends totaling $10,000, and its common stock remained unchanged.
4. Leno declared dividends totaling $12,000 and issued additional common stock for $20,000.

CASES

Case 1-66 Using Accounting Information

Jim Hadden is a freshman at Major State University. His earnings from a summer job, combined with a small scholarship and a fixed amount per term from his parents, are his only sources of income. He has a new MasterCard that was issued to him the week he began classes. It is spring term, and Jim finds that his credit card is "maxed out" and that he does not have enough money to carry him to the end of the term. Jim confesses that irresistible opportunities for spring term entertainment have caused him to overspend his resources.

Required:

Describe how accounting information could have helped Jim avoid this difficult situation.

Case 1-67 Analysis of Accounting Periodicals

The accounting profession is organized into three major groups: (a) accountants who work in nonbusiness entities, (b) accountants who work in business entities, and (c) accountants in public practice. The periodical literature of accounting includes monthly or quarterly journals that are written primarily for accountants within each of these groups.

Required:

1. Use your library and identify one journal published for each of the three professional groups. Identify the publisher of each journal and describe its primary audience.
2. Choose two of the three audiences you have just described. Briefly explain how members of one audience would benefit by reading a journal published primarily for members of the other audience.

Case 1-68 Career Planning

A successful career requires us to take advantage of opportunities that are difficult to foresee. Success is also aided by having a plan or strategy by which to choose among career alternatives as they arise.

Required:

1. How do you want to be employed in 5 years, and what must you do to get there?
2. How do you want to be employed in 10 years, and what must you do to get there?

Case 1-69 Financial Statement Analysis

Agency Rent-A-Car Inc. rents cars to customers whose vehicles are unavailable due to accident, theft, or repair ("Wheels while your car heals"). The company has a fleet of more than 40,000 cars located at 700 offices throughout the United States and Canada. Its balance sheets at January 31, 2013, and January 31, 2012, contain the following information (all dollar amounts are stated in thousands of dollars):

	1/31/2013	1/31/2012
Assets		
Cash	$ 5,210	$ 4,125
Accounts receivable	28,100	32,891
Supplies	7,152	7,853
Property and equipment	281,152	285,130
Other assets	15,250	9,563
	$336,864	$339,562
Liabilities and Stockholders' Equity		
Accounts payable	$ 19,655	$ 35,483
Other noncurrent liabilities	144,680	168,260
Stockholders' equity	172,529	135,819
	$336,864	$339,562

Required:

1. What is the dollar amount of current assets and current liabilities at January 31, 2013? At January 31, 2012? What does this information tell you about the company's liquidity?
2. Assume that stockholders were paid dividends of $21,000 during 2013 and that there were no other changes in stockholders' equity except for net income. How much net income did the business earn during the year?

Case 1-70 Financial Statement Analysis

Reproduced below are portions of the president's letter to stockholders and selected income statement and balance sheet data for the Wright Brothers Aviation Company. Wright Brothers is a national airline that provides both passenger service and package delivery service.

To Our Stockholders:

In 2013, the airline industry began to show some life. As fuel prices leveled and travelers showed an increased willingness to fly domestically, it was generally perceived that a gradual recovery was in place. The worldwide increase in the demand for air travel throughout the year translated into improved demand for the Company's services. In fact, revenues for both the passenger and package segments improved in every quarter of 2013. Most importantly, the Company started generating cash from operations in the last half of the year, and the passenger segments returned to generating profits in the third quarter....

With improved operating performance as the basis for negotiating a financial restructuring, the next critical step for the Company is to satisfactorily restructure its obligations in order to insure that the Company can operate effectively in the future. With that in mind, a strategic decision, albeit a difficult one, was made in February 2013—the Company filed for reorganization under Chapter 11 of the U.S. Bankruptcy Code....

	2013	2012	2011	2010	2009
Revenues:					
Passenger services	$ 141,343	$ 136,057	$354,246	$ 390,080	$ 337,871
Package services	35,199	60,968	145,940	203,675	202,615
Total revenues	176,542	197,025	500,186	593,755	540,486

	2013	2012	2011	2010	2009
Operating income	$ (54,584)	$ (92,613)	$(16,663)	$ 52,137	$ 39,527
Net income (loss)	(182,647)	(340,516)	(67,269)	(14,553)	(22,461)
Current assets	123,553	134,009	183,268	193,943	209,944
Total assets	542,523	678,846	952,623	1,040,903	1,133,498
Current liabilities	698,583	641,645	542,640	129,369	120,960
Long-term debt	116,572	119,481	144,297	576,446	655,383
Stockholders' equity	(272,632)	(82,280)	265,686	335,088	357,155

Required:

1. What trends do you detect in revenues, operating income, and net income for the period 2009–2013?
2. What happened to working capital over the 2009–2013 period? To what do you attribute this result?
3. The price of Wright Brothers stock declined steadily throughout the 2009–2013 period. Do you consider this decline to be a reasonable reaction to the financial results reported? Why or why not?

Case 1-71 Professional Ethics

Professional ethics guide public accountants in their work with financial statements.

Required:

Why is ethical behavior by public accountants important to society? Be sure to describe the incentives that public accountants have to behave *ethically* and *unethically*.

Case 1-72 Ethical Issues

Lola, the CEO of JB Inc., and Frank, the accountant for JB Inc., were recently having a meeting to discuss the upcoming release of the company's financial statements. Following is an excerpt of their conversation:

Lola: These financial statements don't show the hours of hard work that we've put in to restore this company to financial health. In fact, these results may actually prevent us from obtaining loans that are critical to our future.

Frank: Accounting does allow for judgment. Tell me your primary concerns, and let's see if we can work something out.

Lola: My first concern is that the company doesn't appear very liquid. As you can see, our current assets are only slightly more than current liabilities. The company has always paid its bills—even when cash was tight. It's not really fair that the financial statements don't reflect this.

Frank: Well, we could reclassify some of the long-term investments as current assets instead of noncurrent assets. Our expectation is that we will hold these investments for several years, but we could sell them at any time; therefore, it's fair to count these as current assets. We could also reclassify some of the accounts payable as noncurrent. Even though we expect to pay them within the next year, no one will ever look close enough to see what we've done. Together these two changes should make us appear more liquid and properly reflect the hard work we've done.

Lola: I agree. However, if we make these changes, our long-term assets will be smaller and our long-term debt will be larger. Many analysts may view this as a sign of financial trouble. Isn't there something we can do?

Frank: Our long-term assets are undervalued. Many were purchased years ago and recorded at historical cost. However, companies that bought similar assets are allowed to record them at an amount closer to their current market values. I've always thought this was misleading. If we increase the value of these long-term assets to their market value, this should provide the users of the financial statements with more relevant information and solve our problem, too.

Lola: Brilliant! Let's implement these actions quickly and get back to work.

(Continued)

Required:

Describe any ethical issues that have arisen as the result of Lola and Frank's conversation.

Case 1-73 Research and Analysis Using the Annual Report

Obtain **Apple Inc.**'s 2011 annual report either through the "Investor Relations" portion of their website (do a web search for Apple investor relations) or go to www.sec.gov and click "Search for Company Filings" under "Filings & Forms."

Required:

Answer the following questions:

1. On what date did Apple's fiscal year end? Was this date different from the previous year? If so, why?
2. How many years of balance sheet and income statement information does Apple present?
3. With regard to the balance sheet:
   a. What amounts did Apple report as total assets, liabilities, and stockholders' equity for 2011?
   b. Did the amounts reported as assets, liabilities, and stockholders' equity change over the last year? If so, by how much?
   c. What amounts were reported as current assets and current liabilities for the years presented?
   d. Provide an assessment of Apple's liquidity based on the information obtained in part b.
4. With regard to the income statement:
   a. What amounts did Apple report as revenues, expenses, and net income for 2011?
   b. Do you detect any trends with regard to revenues, expenses, or net income?
5. With regard to the statement of cash flows:
   a. What amounts did the company report for cash flow from operating activities, cash flow from investing activities, and cash flow from financing activities for 2011?
   b. How much cash did the company spend on purchasing PP&E in 2011?
6. With regard to management's discussion and analysis:
   a. What accounting policies and estimates does Apple consider critical? Where would these policies and estimates be described?
   b. Does management believe that the company performed well during the current year? On what do you base this assessment?
7. Are the financial statements audited? If so, by whom?

Case 1-74 Comparative Analysis: Under Armour, Inc., versus VF Corporation

Refer to the financial statements of **Under Armour, Inc.**, and **VF Corporation** that are supplied with this text.

Required:

Answer the following questions:

1. Describe each company's business and list some of the more common products or brands sold by each company.
2. a. What is the fiscal year-end of Under Armour? Of VF? Why would you expect these to be similar?
   b. Why does the date of VF's fiscal year end change each year?
3. With regard to the balance sheet:
   a. What amounts did each company report for total assets, liabilities, and stockholders' equity for the year ended December 31, 2011?
   b. What amounts were reported as current assets and current liabilities for the year ended December 31, 2011?
   c. Assess the liquidity of each company.
   d. Describe any other similarities and differences that you noticed between the two companies.

4. With regard to the income statement:
   a. What amounts did Under Armour report as revenues, expenses, and net income for the year ended December 31, 2011? What amounts did VF report as revenues, expenses, and net income for the fiscal year ended December 31, 2011?
   b. Compare any trends that you detect with regard to revenues, expenses, and net income.
5. What were the major sources and uses of cash for each company?
6. What is management's assessment of each company's past performance and future prospects? Where did you find this information?

Case 1-75 CONTINUING PROBLEM: FRONT ROW ENTERTAINMENT

Cam Mosley and Anna Newton met during their freshman year of college as they were standing in line to buy tickets to a concert. While waiting in line, the two shared various aspects of their lives. Cam, whose father was an executive at a major record label, was raised in New York. Some of his favorite memories were meeting popular musical artists—from the Rolling Stones to the Black Eyed Peas—as he accompanied his father on business trips. Anna, on the other hand, was born and raised in a small, rural town in southern Georgia. Her fondest childhood memories involved singing with her family, who often performed at county fairs and other small events. Even though they had different backgrounds, they felt an instant bond through their shared passion for music. Over the next couple of years, this friendship strengthened as they attended numerous concerts and other events together.

While on a road trip to see a new band during their senior year, Cam and Anna started discussing their future career plans. Both had an entrepreneurial spirit and were seeking a way to combine their majors in business with their passion for music. Cam had recently overheard his father discussing how many artists were unhappy with the current concert promoters. Anna had heard similar complaints from her cousin, whose band recently had their first top 25 hit. When Cam suggested that he and Anna form a concert promotion business, they both knew they had found the perfect careers.

Concert promoters sign artists, usually through the artists' agents, to contracts in which the promoter is responsible for organizing live concert tours. Typically, this includes booking the venue, pricing the tour, advertising the tour, and negotiating other services from local vendors. In general, the barriers to entry in the concert promotion industry are relatively low, with one of the more important items being forming a relationship with the various artists. Through their industry contacts (Cam's father, Anna's cousin), they felt that they could develop a client list relatively easily. A second major barrier would be to obtain the up-front cash necessary to promote the tour properly.

Since their friendship had started many years ago as they were trying to get front row seats, they decided to name their business Front Row Entertainment. With their first big decision made, it was time to get to work.

Required:

1. Discuss some of the typical business activities (financing, investing, and operating) that a business like Front Row Entertainment is likely to have. (*Hint*: You may want to perform an Internet search for concert promoters to obtain a better understanding of the industry.) Be sure to list some of the specific account names for assets, liabilities, stockholders' equity, revenues, and expenses that may arise from these activities.
2. Explain the advantages and disadvantages of the forms of business organization that Cam and Anna might choose for Front Row Entertainment. Which form would you recommend?
3. Cam and Anna will need to prepare financial statements to report company performance. What type of information does each financial statement provide? Be sure to describe the insights that each financial statement provides to users.

2

The Accounting Information System

© Pixelfabrik/Alamy

After studying Chapter 2, you should be able to:

1. Describe the qualitative characteristics, assumptions, and principles that underlie accounting.
2. Explain the relationships among economic events, transactions, and the expanded accounting equation.
3. Analyze the effect of business transactions on the accounting equation.
4. Discuss the role of accounts and how debits and credits are used in the double-entry accounting system.
5. Prepare journal entries for transactions.
6. Explain why transactions are posted to the general ledger.
7. Prepare a trial balance and explain its purpose.

© Viewfinders Stock Photography/Alamy

EXPERIENCE FINANCIAL ACCOUNTING

with General Electric

Tracing its roots back to Thomas Edison, the **General Electric Company (GE)** has become one of the largest and most diversified companies in the world, with customers in over 100 countries and about 300,000 employees worldwide. GE is comprised of five businesses:

- **NBC Universal**—one of the world's leading media and entertainment companies that provides network television services, produces television programs and movies, and operates theme parks.
- Technology Infrastructure—provides essential technologies in the aviation, transportation, enterprise solutions, and healthcare markets. Products include aircraft engines, power generation systems, energy technologies (such as solar and nuclear), water treatment facilities, and medical technologies such as x-rays, MRIs, and patient-monitoring systems.
- Energy Infrastructure—focuses on the development, implementation, and improvement of products and technologies that harness energy resources such as wind, oil, gas, and water.
- **GE Capital**—provides financial products and services to consumers and commercial businesses around the world. Products include business loans and leases, as well as home and personal loans, credit cards, and insurance.
- **GE Home & Business Solutions**—sells and services consumer products such as home appliances, telephones, and residential water systems as well as industrial products such as switchgear and circuit breakers.

With so many different activities throughout the world, GE faces a difficult task in measuring and reporting its many business activities.

Companies like GE rely on comprehensive accounting systems to capture, record, and report their various business activities.

Companies like GE rely on comprehensive accounting systems to capture, record, and report their various business activities. While the type of system depends on many factors such as the company's size and the volume of transactions it processes, most companies will use computerized accounting systems to efficiently provide information that is needed by the users of its financial statements. While GE invests heavily in its accounting system, it recognizes that no system is foolproof. Therefore, financial accounting systems should be based on several key principles, including rigorous oversight by management and dedication to a system of internal controls that are designed to ensure the accuracy and reliability of the accounting records. With such a major emphasis on its accounting system, users of GE's financial statements can feel confident that GE's business activities are recorded and reported properly. In short, it is GE's accounting system that brings "light" to GE's varied business activities.

OBJECTIVE 1

Describe the qualitative characteristics, assumptions, and principles that underlie accounting.

FUNDAMENTAL ACCOUNTING CONCEPTS

In the previous chapter, we described the typical business activities in which companies engage and how accounting systems report these activities through the financial statements. It's also important to understand the underlying concepts behind accounting systems. This chapter will discuss those concepts as well as the procedures that companies use to record information about business activities and how this information ultimately is transformed into financial statements. That is, you will see where the numbers on the financial statements actually come from. An understanding of these procedures is essential if you are to be an effective user of financial statements. As you review the financial statements, you are assessing a company's performance, cash flows, and financial position. To make those assessments, you need to be able to infer the actions of a company from what you see in the financial statements. That inference depends on your understanding of how companies transform the results of their activities into financial statements.

These transforming procedures are called the **accounting cycle**. The accounting cycle is a simple and orderly process, based on a series of steps and conventions. If the financial statements are to present fairly the effects of the company's activities, proper operation of the accounting cycle is essential. For example, if **General Electric** failed to properly apply accounting procedures, it is likely that many of its business activities would be improperly recorded (if they were even recorded at all) and its financial statements would be seriously misstated.

In this chapter, we will begin the discussion of the accounting cycle and how the completion of each step of the accounting cycle moves the accounting system toward its end product—the financial statements. We will address the following questions:

- What concepts and assumptions underlie accounting information?
- How do companies record business activities?
- What procedures are involved in transforming information about business activities into financial statements?
- How do business activities affect the financial statements?

The Conceptual Framework

IFRS

The conceptual framework is the result of a joint effort of the IASB and the FASB.

Generally accepted accounting principles rest on a conceptual framework of accounting. This framework flows logically from the fundamental objective of financial reporting: to provide information that is useful in making investment and credit decisions. The conceptual framework is designed to support the development of a consistent set of accounting standards and provide a consistent body of thought for financial reporting. An understanding of the conceptual framework should help you in understanding complex accounting standards by providing a logical structure to financial accounting; in other words, the concepts help to explain "why" accountants adopt certain practices. Exhibit 2.1 summarizes the characteristics of useful information as well as the underlying assumptions and principles that make up the conceptual framework and serve as the foundation of GAAP.

Qualitative Characteristics of Useful Information

Given the overall objective of providing useful information, the FASB has identified two fundamental characteristics that useful information should possess—relevance and faithful representation. The application of these criteria determines which economic events should be shown in the financial statements and how best to record these events.

- **Relevance:** Information is relevant if it is capable of making a difference in a business decision by helping users predict future events (*predictive value*) or providing feedback about prior expectations (*confirmatory value*). If the omission or misstatement of information could influence a decision, the information is said to be *material*. Therefore, materiality is also an aspect of relevance.

EXHIBIT 2.1

Qualitative Characteristics of Useful Information

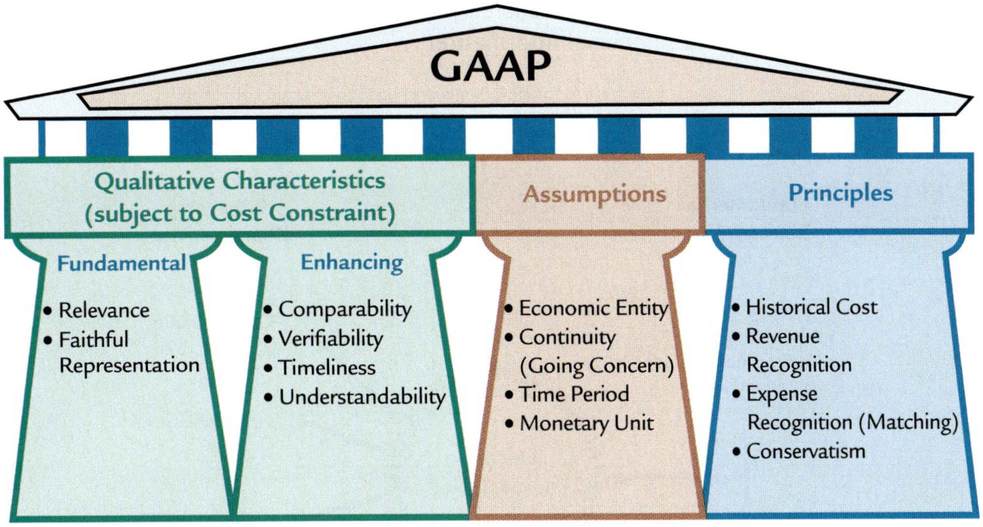

- **Faithful representation:** Accounting information should be a faithful representation of the real-world economic event that it is intending to portray. Faithfully represented information should be *complete* (includes all necessary information for the user to understand the economic event), *neutral* (unbiased), and *free from error* (as accurate as possible).

In applying these fundamental characteristics, the usual process is to identify the most relevant information and then determine if it can be faithfully represented. If so, the fundamental qualitative characteristics have been satisfied. If not, the process should be repeated with the next most relevant type of information.

In addition to the fundamental characteristics, four enhancing characteristics—comparability, verifiability, timeliness, and understandability—have been identified. These enhancing characteristics are considered complementary to the fundamental characteristics, and their presence should help determine the degree of the information's usefulness.

- **Comparability:** Comparable information allows external users to identify similarities and differences between two or more items. Information is useful when it can be compared with similar information about other companies or with similar information about the same company for a different time period. Included within comparability is consistency. **Consistency** can be achieved when a company applies the same accounting principles for the same items over time. Consistency can also be achieved when multiple companies use the same accounting principles in a single time period. Comparability should be viewed as the goal while consistency helps to achieve that goal.
- **Verifiability:** Information is verifiable when independent parties can agree on the measurement of the activity. When multiple independent observers can reach a general consensus, there is an implication that the information faithfully represents the economic event being measured.
- **Timeliness:** Information is timely if it is available to users before it loses its ability to influence decisions.
- **Understandability:** If users who have a reasonable knowledge of accounting and business can, with reasonable study effort, comprehend the meaning of the information, it is considered understandable.

Enhancing characteristics should be maximized to the extent possible.

These qualitative characteristics are bound by one pervasive constraint—the **cost constraint**. The cost constraint states that the benefit received from accounting information should be greater than the cost of providing that information. If the cost exceeds the benefit, the information is not considered useful. Exhibit 2.2 illustrates the qualitative characteristics of useful financial information.

EXHIBIT 2.2

Qualitative Characteristics of Accounting Information

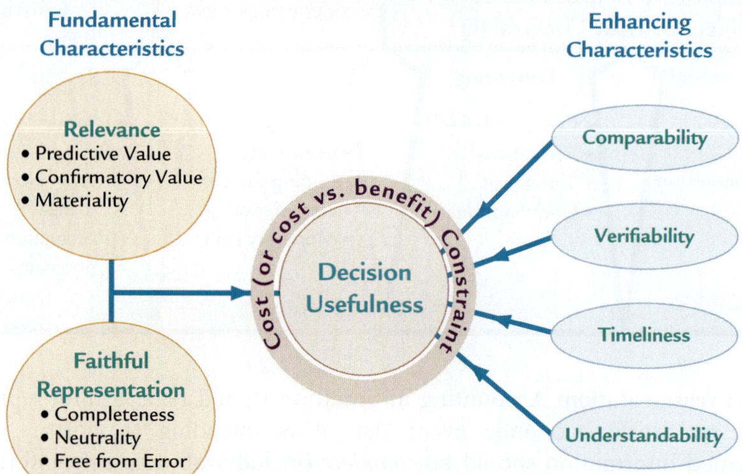

Trade-offs are often necessary in evaluating these criteria. For example, the most relevant information may not be able to be faithfully represented. Similarly, changing economic situations may require a change in the accounting principle used. Such a change may decrease the comparability of the information presented. In these situations, the accountant must exercise judgment in determining the accounting principles that would produce the most useful information for the decision-maker. In all situations, accountants should follow a **full disclosure** policy. That is, any information that would make a difference to financial statement users should be revealed.

Assumptions

The following four basic assumptions underlie accounting:

- **Economic entity assumption:** Under this assumption, each company is accounted for separately from its owners. Bill Gates' personal transactions, for instance, are not recorded in Microsoft's financial statements.
- **Continuity** (or **going-concern**) **assumption:** This assumption states that a company will continue to operate long enough to carry out its existing commitments. Without this assumption, many of our accounting procedures could not be followed. For example, if GE were expected to go bankrupt in the near future, its assets and liabilities would be reported on the balance sheet at an amount the company expects to receive if sold (minus any costs of disposal).
- **Time period assumption:** This assumption allows the life of a company to be divided into artificial time periods so net income can be measured for a specific period of time (e.g., monthly, quarterly, or annually). Without this assumption, a company's income could only be reported at the end of its life.
- **Monetary unit assumption:** This assumption requires that a company account for and report its financial results in monetary terms (such as U.S. dollar, euro, or Japanese yen). This assumption implies that certain nonmonetary items (such as brand loyalty or customer satisfaction) are not reported in a company's financial statements since they can't be measured in monetary terms.

Principles

Principles are general approaches that are used in the measurement and recording of business activities. The four basic principles of accounting are: the historical cost principle, the revenue recognition principle, the expense recognition (or matching) principle, and the conservatism principle.

- **Historical cost principle:** This principle requires that the activities of a company are initially measured at their cost—the exchange price at the time the activity occurs. For example, when GE buys equipment used in manufacturing its products, it initially records the equipment at the cost paid to acquire the equipment. Accountants use historical cost because it provides an objective and verifiable measure of the activity. However, the historical cost principle has been criticized because, after the date of acquisition, it does not reflect changes in market value. The FASB, aware of this criticism, has been developing standards that use market values to measure certain assets and liabilities (such as investments in marketable securities) after the date of acquisition.
- **Revenue recognition principle:** This principle is used to determine when revenue is recorded and reported. Under this principle, revenue is to be recognized or recorded in the period in which it is earned and the collection of cash is reasonably assured. Generally, this occurs when services are performed or goods are delivered to customers.[1]
- **Expense recognition (or matching) principle:** This principle requires that an expense be recorded and reported in the same period as the revenue that it helped generate. This may or may not be in the same period that cash is paid. Together, the application of the revenue and expense recognition principles determine a company's net income. These two principles will be discussed in more detail in Chapter 3.
- **Conservatism principle:** This principle states that accountants should take care to avoid overstating assets or income when they prepare financial statements. The idea behind this principle is that conservatism is a prudent reaction to uncertainty and offsets management's natural optimism about the company's future prospects. However, conservatism should not lead to biased financial information nor should it ever be used to justify the deliberate understatement of assets or income.

The application of these qualitative characteristics, assumptions, and principles is illustrated in Cornerstone 2.1.

concept Q&A

Companies assume they are going concerns. Wouldn't the valuation of a company's assets be more relevant if this assumption were relaxed and the net assets valued at their current selling costs?

Answer:

Current selling costs are only relevant if the company intends to sell the assets in the near term. However, many assets (such as machinery or buildings) are used over long periods of time, and in these situations, the use of current selling prices would be of little value to financial statement users. In addition, the cost of obtaining current values for these assets would greatly outweigh the benefits received.

Applying the Conceptual Framework

CORNERSTONE 2.1

Why:

The conceptual framework provides a logical structure and direction to financial accounting and reporting and supports the development of a consistent set of accounting standards.

Information:

Mario is faced with the following questions as he prepares the financial statements of DK Company:

1. Should the purchase of inventory be valued at what DK paid to acquire the inventory or at its estimated selling price?

(Continued)

[1] At the time of writing of this text, the FASB has proposed a change in the revenue recognition model. While this proposed change would alter the manner in which the revenue recognition principle is applied, the authors do not expect it to change the timing of revenue recognition for the revenue contracts covered in this text. For more detail on this proposed revenue recognition model, see this text's website.

CORNERSTONE **2.1**

(Continued)

2. Should information be provided that financial statement users might find helpful in predicting the DK's future income?
3. Faced with a choice between two equally acceptable estimates, should Mario choose the one that results in the higher or the lower amount for net income?
4. Although DK is profitable, should the financial statements be prepared under the assumption that DK will go bankrupt?
5. Should DK's inventory be reported in terms of the number of units on hand or the dollar value of those units?
6. Should equipment leased on a long-term basis be reported as an asset (the economic substance of the transaction) or should it be reported as a rental (the form of the transaction)?
7. Should DK recognize revenue from the sale of its products when the sale is made or when the cash is received?
8. Should DK record the purchase of a vacation home by one of its shareholders?
9. Should DK report income annually to its shareholders, or should it wait until all transactions are complete?
10. Should DK report salary expense in the period that the employees actually worked or when the employees are paid?

Required:

Which qualitative characteristic, assumption, or principle should Mario use in resolving the situation?

Solution:

1. *Historical cost:* The activities of a company (such as purchase of inventory) should be initially measured at the exchange price at the time the activity occurs.
2. *Relevance:* Material information that has predictive or confirmatory value should be provided.
3. *Conservatism:* When faced with a choice, accountants should avoid overstating assets or income.
4. *Continuity (going-concern):* In the absence of information to the contrary, it should be assumed that a company will continue to operate indefinitely.
5. *Monetary unit:* A company should account for and report its financial results in monetary terms.
6. *Faithful representation:* Information should portray the economic event that it is intending to portray completely, accurately, and without bias.
7. *Revenue recognition:* Revenue should be recognized when it is earned and the collection of cash is reasonably assured.
8. *Economic entity:* A company's transactions should be accounted for separately from its owners.
9. *Time period:* The life of a company can be divided into artificial time periods so that income can be measured and reported periodically to interested parties.
10. *Expense recognition (or matching):* Expenses should be recorded and reported in the same period as the revenue it helped generate.

Given this conceptual foundation, we will now turn our attention to the process of recording information about business activities in the accounting system.

MEASURING BUSINESS ACTIVITIES: THE ACCOUNTING CYCLE

OBJECTIVE 2

Explain the relationships among economic events, transactions, and the expanded accounting equation.

The sequence of procedures used by companies to transform the effects of business activities into financial statements is called the accounting cycle. The accounting cycle is shown in Exhibit 2.3.

EXHIBIT 2.3

The Accounting Cycle

The steps in the accounting cycle are performed each period and then repeated. Steps 1 through 4 are performed regularly each period as business activities occur. We will discuss these four steps in this chapter. Steps 5 through 7 are performed at the end of a period and are discussed in Chapter 3.

Economic Events

As we discussed in Chapter 1, a company engages in numerous activities that can be categorized as financing, investing, or operating activities. Each of these activities consists of different **events** that affect the company. Some of these events are *external* and result from exchanges between the company and another entity outside of the company. For example, when GE issues common stock to investors, purchases equipment used to make an aircraft engine, sells a home appliance to a local retail store, or pays its employees a salary, it is engaging in an exchange with another entity. Other events are *internal* and result from the company's own actions. When GE uses equipment to make its products, no other entity is involved; however, the event still has an impact on the company.

Accounting measures the effects of events that influence a company and incorporates these events into the accounting system which, ultimately, produces the financial statements. However, not every event that affects a company is recorded in the accounting records. In order for an event to be recorded, or recognized, in the accounting system, the items making up the event must impact a financial statement element (asset, liability, stockholders' equity, revenue, or expense) and should be a faithful representation of the event.

The first requirement usually is met when at least one party to a contract performs its responsibility according to the contract. For example, assume a buyer and seller agree upon the delivery of an asset and sign a contract. The signing of the contract usually is not recorded in the accounting system because neither party has performed its responsibility. Instead, recognition typically will occur once the buyer receives the asset or pays the seller, whichever comes first.

Even if the event impacts a financial statement element, a faithful representation of the event must be possible if it is to be recorded. A sudden increase in the price of oil or natural gas, for instance, may have an effect on GE's ability to sell its oil and natural gas compressors and turbines. However, the effects of this price increase cannot be faithfully represented, and the event will not be recognized in the financial statements. Providing a measurement that is complete, unbiased, and free from error is important in accounting to avoid misleading users of financial statements. A decision-maker would find it extremely difficult, if not impossible, to use financial statements that include amounts that failed to faithfully represent what has actually occurred. It is very important to pay attention to the recognition criteria as you consider an event for inclusion in the accounting system.

An accounting transaction results from an economic event that causes one of the elements of the financial statements (assets, liabilities, stockholders' equity, revenues, or expenses) to change and that can be faithfully represented. We will use the term **transaction** to refer to any event, external or internal, that is recognized in the financial statements. The process of identifying events to be recorded in the financial statements is illustrated in Exhibit 2.4.

EXHIBIT 2.4

Transaction Identification

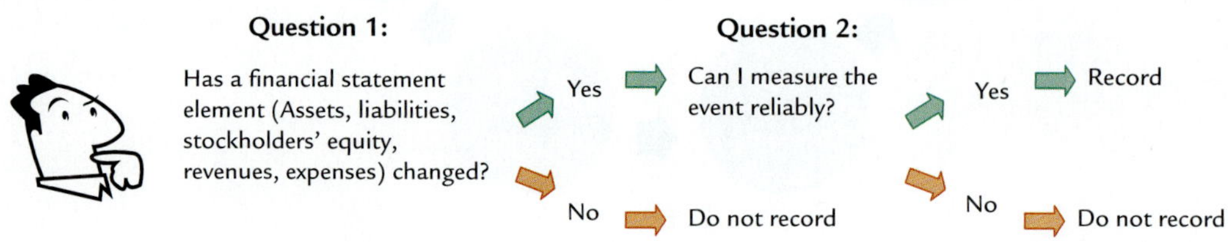

The Expanded Accounting Equation

Because accounting is concerned with the measurement of transactions and their effect on the financial statements, a starting point in the measurement and recording process is the fundamental accounting equation:

$$\text{Assets} = \text{Liabilities} + \text{Stockholders' Equity}$$

Recall from Chapter 1 that:

- The two sides of the accounting equation must always be equal or "in balance" as a company conducts its business. Accounting systems record these business activities in a way that maintains this equality. As a consequence, every transaction has a two-part, or double-entry, effect on the equation.
- The balance sheet and the income statement are related through retained earnings. Specifically net income (revenues minus expenses) increases retained earnings. Given this relationship, the fundamental accounting equation can be rewritten to show the elements that make up stockholders' equity.

With the expanded accounting equation shown in Exhibit 2.5, we are now ready to analyze how transactions affect a company's financial statements.

EXHIBIT 2.5

The Expanded Accounting Equation

Assets = Liabilities + Stockholders' Equity

Assets = Liabilities + Contributed Capital (e.g., Common Stock) + Retained Earnings

Assets = Liabilities + Contributed Capital + Beginning Retained Earnings + Revenues − Expenses − Dividends

YOUDECIDE Recognition of Economic Events

As you are analyzing the most recent financial statements of Big Oil (B&O) Company, you question if the company properly recorded an economic event. You know that B&O owns and operates several off-shore oil drilling platforms in the Gulf of Mexico. You also recall from news reports that a hurricane severely damaged two of the platforms, leading to a significant loss in revenue while the platforms were inactive. While you see evidence in the financial statements of the damage and repair to the platforms, you cannot find any evidence of the lost revenue in the financial statements.

Does the loss in revenue from the damaged oil platforms qualify for recognition in the financial statements?

To be recognized in the financial statements, the event must impact a financial statement element and be faithfully represented. While B&O may have been able to measure the loss in revenue, no financial statement element has been affected. While you may argue that this event affected revenue, revenue is an increase in assets resulting from the sale of products. Because the lost sales did not result in an inflow of assets, it is not considered revenue. In addition, expenses are defined as the cost of resources used to earn revenues. The lost revenue does not represent a use of resources and is therefore not an expense. Therefore, the lost revenue cannot be recognized in the financial statements.

Recognition of events in the financial statements requires analysis of whether the event impacted a financial statement element and can be faithfully represented.

STEP 1: ANALYZE TRANSACTIONS

OBJECTIVE 3

Analyze the effect of business transactions on the accounting equation.

Transaction analysis is the process of determining the economic effects of a transaction on the elements of the accounting equation. Transaction analysis usually begins with the gathering of *source documents* that describe business activities. Source documents can be internally or externally prepared and include items such as purchase orders, cash register tapes, and invoices that describe the transaction and monetary amounts involved. These documents are the beginning of a "trail" of evidence that a transaction was processed by the accounting system.

After gathering the source documents, accountants must analyze these business activities to determine which transactions meet the criteria for recognition in the accounting records. Once it is determined that a transaction should be recorded in the accounting system, the transaction must be analyzed to determine how it will affect the accounting equation. In performing transaction analysis, it is important to remember that the accounting equation must always remain in balance. Therefore, each transaction will have at least two effects on the accounting equation.

In summary, transaction analysis involves the following three steps:

Step 1. Write down the accounting equation. In this chapter, we often use an expanded version of the accounting equation because it provides more information in the analysis. However, the basic accounting equation could also be used.

Step 2. Identify the financial statement elements that are affected by the transaction.
Step 3. Determine whether the elements increased or decreased.

Cornerstone 2.2 illustrates the basic process of transaction analysis.

CORNERSTONE

2.2

Performing Transaction Analysis

Why:

The economic effect of a transaction will have a two-part, or dual, effect on the accounting equation that results in the equation remaining in balance.

Information:

Luigi Inc. purchases a $3,000 computer from WorstBuy Electronics on credit, with payment due in 60 days.

Required:

Determine the effect of the transaction on the elements on the accounting equation.

Solution:

A computer is an economic resource, or asset, that will be used by Luigi in its business. The purchase of the computer increased assets and also created an obligation, or liability, for Luigi. Therefore, the effect of the transaction on the accounting equation is as follows:

Assets	=	Liabilities	+	Stockholders' Equity		
				Contributed Capital	+	Retained Earnings
+$3,000		+$3,000				

Note that the transaction analysis in Cornerstone 2.2 conformed to the two underlying principles of transaction analysis:

- There was a dual effect on the accounting equation.
- The accounting equation remained in balance after the transaction.

All transactions can be analyzed using a similar process.

To provide a further illustration of the effect of transactions on the accounting equation, consider the case of HiTech Communications Inc. HiTech is a newly formed corporation that operates an advertising agency that specializes in promoting computer-related products in the Cincinnati area. We show the effects of 13 transactions on HiTech's financial position during its first month of operations, March 2013.

Transaction 1: Issuing Common Stock

On March 1, HiTech sold 1,000 shares of common stock to several investors for cash of $12,000. The effect of this transaction on the accounting equation is:

Assets	=	Liabilities	+	Stockholders' Equity		
				Contributed Capital	+	Retained Earnings
+$12,000				+$12,000		

The sale of stock increases assets, specifically cash, and also increases stockholders' equity (contributed capital or common stock). Notice that there is a dual effect, and although both assets and equity change, the equality of the equation is maintained. The issuance of stock would be considered a financing activity.

> **concept Q&A**
>
> Why must the accounting equation always remain in balance?
>
> **Answer:**
>
> The accounting equation captures the business activities of a company. The left side of the accounting equation describes the economic resources, or assets, that the company has acquired. The right side of the equation describes the claims on these assets—either from creditors (liabilities) or from stockholders (stockholders' equity). Because all resources belong to either the creditors or the stockholders, the equation must balance.

Transaction 2: Borrowing Cash

On March 2, HiTech raised additional funds by borrowing $3,000 from First Third Bank of Cincinnati. HiTech promised to pay the amount borrowed plus 8% interest to First Third Bank in 1 year. The financial effect of this transaction is:

Assets	=	Liabilities	+	Stockholders' Equity		
				Contributed Capital	+	Retained Earnings
+$3,000		+$3,000				

This borrowing has two effects: the asset cash is increased and a liability is created. HiTech has an obligation to repay the cash borrowed according to the terms of the borrowing. Such a liability is called a note payable. Because this transaction is concerned with obtaining funds to begin and operate a business, it is classified as a financing activity.

Transaction 3: Purchase of Equipment for Cash

On March 3, HiTech purchased office equipment (such as computer equipment) from MicroCenter Inc. for $4,500 in cash. The effect of this transaction on the accounting equation is:

Assets	=	Liabilities	+	Stockholders' Equity		
				Contributed Capital	+	Retained Earnings
+$4,500						
−$4,500						

There is a reduction in cash (an asset) as it is spent and a corresponding increase in another asset, equipment. The purchased equipment is an asset because HiTech will use it to generate future revenue. Notice that this transaction merely converts one asset (cash) into another (equipment). Total assets remain unchanged and the accounting equation remains in balance. Because Transaction 3 is concerned with buying long-term assets that enable HiTech to operate, it is considered an investing activity.

Transaction 4: Purchasing Insurance

On March 4, HiTech purchased a 6-month insurance policy for $1,200 cash. The effect of this transaction on the accounting equation is:

Assets	=	Liabilities	+	Stockholders' Equity		
				Contributed Capital	+	Retained Earnings
+$1,200						
−$1,200						

There is a reduction in cash (an asset) as it is spent and a corresponding increase in another asset, prepaid insurance. The purchased insurance is an asset because the insurance will benefit more than one accounting period. This type of asset is often referred to as a prepaid asset. Notice that, like Transaction 3, this transaction converts one asset (cash) into another (prepaid insurance). Total assets remain unchanged and the accounting equation remains in balance. Because Transaction 4 is concerned with the operations of the company, it is classified as an operating activity.

Transaction 5: Purchase of Supplies on Credit

On March 6, HiTech purchased office supplies from Hamilton Office Supply for $6,500. Hamilton Office Supply agreed to accept full payment in 30 days. As a result of this transaction, HiTech received an asset (supplies) but also incurred a liability to pay for these supplies in 30 days. The financial effect of this transaction is:

Assets	=	Liabilities	+	Stockholders' Equity		
				Contributed Capital	+	Retained Earnings
+$6,500		+$6,500				

A transaction where goods are purchased on credit is often referred to as a purchase "on account" and the liability that is created is referred to as an account payable. Because Transaction 5 is concerned with the operations of the company, it is classified as an operating activity.

Transaction 6: Sale of Services for Cash

On March 10, HiTech sold advertising services to Miami Valley Products in exchange for $8,800 in cash. Remember from Chapter 1 that revenue is defined as an increase in assets resulting from the sale of products or services. As an advertising company, the sale of advertising services is HiTech's primary revenue-producing activity. Therefore, this transaction results in an increase in assets (cash) and an increase in revenue.

Assets	=	Liabilities	+	Stockholders' Equity		
				Contributed Capital	+	Retained Earnings
+$8,800						+$8,800

As shown in the expanded accounting equation discussed earlier, *revenues increase retained earnings*. The dual effects (the increase in assets and the increase in retained earnings) maintain the balance of the accounting equation. Because Transaction 6 is concerned with the operations of the company, it is classified as an operating activity.

Transaction 7: Sale of Services for Credit

On March 15, HiTech sold advertising services to the *Cincinnati Enquirer* for $3,300. HiTech agreed to accept full payment in 30 days. When a company performs services for which they will be paid at a later date, this is often referred to as a sale "on account." Instead of receiving cash, HiTech received a promise to pay from the *Cincinnati Enquirer*. This right to collect amounts due from customers creates an asset called an account receivable. Similar to the cash sale in Transaction 6, the credit sale represents revenue for HiTech because assets (accounts receivable) were increased as a result of the sale of the advertising service. The financial effect of this transaction is:

Assets	=	Liabilities	+	Stockholders' Equity		
				Contributed Capital	+	Retained Earnings
+$3,300						+$3,300

Consistent with the revenue recognition principle, *revenue is recorded when earned* (for example, when the service is provided) and the collection of cash is reasonably assured, not when the cash is actually received. Because Transaction 7 is concerned with the operations of the company, it is classified as an operating activity.

Transaction 8: Receipt of Cash in Advance

On March 19, HiTech received $9,000 from the *OA News* for advertising services to be completed in the next 3 months. Similar to Transaction 6, HiTech received cash for services. However, due to the revenue recognition principle, HiTech cannot recognize revenue until it has performed the advertising service. Therefore, the receipt of cash creates a liability for HiTech for the work that is due in the future. The effect of this transaction on the accounting equation is:

Assets	=	Liabilities	+	Stockholders' Equity		
				Contributed Capital	+	Retained Earnings
+$9,000		+$9,000				

The liability that is created by the receipt of cash in advance of performing the revenue-generating activities is called an unearned revenue. Because Transaction 8 is concerned with the operations of the company, it is classified as an operating activity.

Transaction 9: Payment of a Liability

On March 23, HiTech pays $6,000 cash for the supplies previously purchased from Hamilton Office Supply on credit (Transaction 5). The payment results in a reduction of an asset (cash) and the settlement of HiTech's obligation (liability) to Hamilton Office Supply. The financial effect of this transaction is:

Assets	=	Liabilities	+	Stockholders' Equity		
				Contributed Capital	+	Retained Earnings
−$6,000		−$6,000				

As a result of this cash payment, the liability "Accounts Payable" is reduced to $500 ($6,500 − $6,000). This means that HiTech still owes Hamilton Office Supply $500. Notice that the payment of cash did not result in an expense. The expense related to supplies will be recorded as supplies are used. Because Transaction 9 is concerned with the operations of the company, it is classified as an operating activity.

Transaction 10: Collection of a Receivable

On March 25, HiTech collected $3,000 cash from the *Cincinnati Enquirer* for services sold earlier on credit (Transaction 7). The collection of cash increases assets. In addition, the accounts receivable (an asset) from the *Cincinnati Enquirer* is also reduced. The financial effect of this transaction is:

Assets	=	Liabilities	+	Stockholders' Equity		
				Contributed Capital	+	Retained Earnings
+$3,000						
−$3,000						

As a result of this cash payment, the *Cincinnati Enquirer* still owes HiTech $300. Notice that the cash collection did not result in the recognition of a revenue. The revenue was recognized as the service was performed (Transaction 7). Because Transaction 11 is concerned with the operations of the company, it is classified as an operating activity.

Transaction 11: Payment of Salaries

On March 26 (a Friday), HiTech paid weekly employee salaries of $1,800. Remember from Chapter 1 that an expense is the cost of an asset consumed in the operation of the business. Because an asset (cash) is consumed as part of HiTech's normal operations, salaries are an expense. As shown in the expanded accounting equation discussed earlier, *expenses decrease retained earnings*. The effect of this transaction on the accounting equation is:

Assets	=	Liabilities		Stockholders' Equity		
				Contributed Capital	+	Retained Earnings
−$1,800						−$1,800

Consistent with the expense recognition (or matching) principle, *expenses are recorded in the same period as the revenue that it helped generate*. Because Transaction 10 is concerned with the operations of the company, it is classified as an operating activity.

Transaction 12: Payment of Utilities

On March 30, HiTech paid its utility bill of $5,200 for March. Because an asset (cash) is consumed by HiTech as part of the operations of the business, the cost of utilities used during the month is an expense. The effect of this transaction on the accounting equation is:

Assets	=	Liabilities	+	Stockholders' Equity		
				Contributed Capital	+	Retained Earnings
−$5,200						−$5,200

Similar to the payment of salaries, utility expense is recorded as a decrease in retained earnings in the same period that it helped to generate revenue. Because Transaction 12 is concerned with the operations of the company, it is classified as an operating activity.

Transaction 13: Payment of a Dividend

On March 31, HiTech declared and paid a cash dividend of $500 to its stockholders. Dividends are not an expense. Dividends are a distribution of net income and are recorded as a direct reduction of retained earnings. The effect of this transaction on the accounting equation is:

Assets	=	Liabilities	+	Stockholders' Equity		
				Contributed Capital	+	Retained Earnings
−$500						−$500

The payment of a dividend is classified as a financing activity.

Overview of Transactions for HiTech Communications Inc.

Exhibit 2.6 summarizes HiTech's transactions in order to show their cumulative effect on the accounting equation. The transaction number is shown in the first column on the left. Revenue and expense items are identified on the right. Notice that this summary reinforces the two key principles discussed earlier:

- Each transaction has a dual effect on the elements of the accounting equation.
- The accounting equation always remains in balance—the total change in assets ($29,100) equals the change in liabilities plus stockholders' equity ($29,100).

Transaction analysis can be used to answer many important questions about a company and its activities. Using the information in Exhibit 2.6, we can answer the following questions:

- *What are the amounts of total assets, total liabilities, and total equity at the end of March?* At the end of March, HiTech has total assets of $29,100, total liabilities

EXHIBIT 2.6

Summary of Transactions for HiTech Communications Inc.

	Assets	=	Liabilities +	Stockholders' Equity: Contributed Capital +	Retained Earnings	
(1)	+ $12,000			+ $12,000		
(2)	+ $3,000		+ $3,000			
(3)	+ $4,500					
	- $4,500					
(4)	+ $1,200					
	- $1,200					
(5)	+ $6,500		+ $6,500			
(6)	+ $8,800				+ $8,800	Revenue
(7)	+ $3,300				+ $3,300	Revenue
(8)	+ $9,000		+ $9,000			
(9)	- $6,000		- $6,000			
(10)	+ $3,000					
	- $3,000					
(11)	- $1,800				- $1,800	Expense
(12)	- $5,200				- $5,200	Expense
(13)	- $500				- $500	Dividend
	$29,100		$12,500	$12,000	$4,600	
	$29,100	=		$29,100		

of $12,500, and total equity of $16,600 ($12,000 of contributed capital plus $4,600 of retained earnings). These amounts for assets, liabilities, and stockholders' equity at the end of March would be carried over as the beginning amounts for April.

- *What is net income for the month?* Net income is $5,100, which represents the excess of revenues of $12,100 ($8,800 + $3,300) over expenses of $7,000 ($5,200 + $1,800). Notice that dividends are not included in income; instead they are included on the retained earnings statement.
- *How much cash was received during the month? How much was spent? How much cash does HiTech have at the end of the month?* During March HiTech received a total of $35,800 in cash ($12,000 + $3,000 + $8,800 + $9,000 + $3,000) and spent a total of $19,200 ($4,500 + $1,200 + $6,000 + $1,800 + $5,200 + $500). At the end of the month, HiTech had cash on hand of $16,600 ($35,800 – $19,200).

The summary in Exhibit 2.6 can become quite cumbersome. For example, in order to determine the amount of cash that HiTech has at the end of the month, you may find it necessary to refer back to the actual transactions to determine which ones involved cash and which did not. In addition, what if an investor or creditor wanted to know not only net income but also the types of expenses that HiTech incurred? (For example, what was the dollar amount spent for salaries?) To answer these questions, more information is needed than the transaction summary provides. For a company like GE, a spreadsheet such as the preceding one would prove inadequate to convey its financial information to investors and creditors. A better way to record and track information that is consistent with the preceding model is necessary. The solution is double-entry accounting.

DOUBLE-ENTRY ACCOUNTING

OBJECTIVE 4

Discuss the role of accounts and how debits and credits are used in the double-entry accounting system.

Double-entry accounting describes the system used by companies to record the effects of transactions on the accounting equation. The effects of transactions are recorded in accounts. Under double-entry accounting, each transaction affects at least two accounts. In this section, we will explore accounts and the process by which transactions get reflected in specific accounts.

Accounts

To aid in the recording of transactions, an organizational system consisting of accounts has been developed. An **account** is a record of increases and decreases in each of the basic elements of the financial statements. Each financial statement element is composed of a variety of accounts. All changes in assets, liabilities, stockholders' equity, revenues, or expenses are then recorded in the appropriate account. The list of accounts used by the company is termed a **chart of accounts**.[2] A typical list of accounts is shown in Exhibit 2.7. These accounts were all discussed in Chapter 1.

EXHIBIT 2.7
Typical Accounts

Assets	Liabilities	Stockholders' Equity	Revenue	Expense
Cash	Accounts Payable	Common Stock	Sales Revenue	Cost of Goods Sold
Investments	Salaries Payable	Retained Earnings	Interest Income	Salaries Expense
Accounts Receivable	Unearned Sales Revenue		Rent Revenue	Rent Expense
Inventory	Interest Payable			Insurance Expense
Land	Income Taxes Payable			Depreciation Expense
Buildings	Notes Payable			Advertising Expense
Equipment	Bonds Payable			Utilities Expense
Patent				Repairs & Maintenance Expense
Copyright				Property Taxes Expense

Every company will have a different chart of accounts depending on the nature of its business activities. However, once a company selects which accounts will be used, all transactions must be recorded into these accounts. As the company engages in transactions, the transaction will either increase or decrease an account. The amount in an account at any time is called the *balance* of the account. For example, the purchase of equipment will increase the balance in the equipment account, whereas the disposal of equipment will decrease the balance of the equipment account. For financial reporting purposes, the balances of related accounts typically are combined and reported as a single amount. For example, **GE** reports a combined, or net, amount of property, plant, and equipment on its balance sheet. However, in its footnotes, GE discloses the amounts of individual accounts such as land, buildings, and machinery.

Although an account can be shown in a variety of ways, transactions are frequently analyzed using a **T-account**. The T-account gets its name because it resembles the capital letter T (see Exhibit 2.8). A T-account is a two-column record that consists of an account title and two sides divided by a vertical line—the left and the right side. The left side is referred to as the **debit** side and the right side is referred to as the **credit** side.

EXHIBIT 2.8
Form of a T-Account

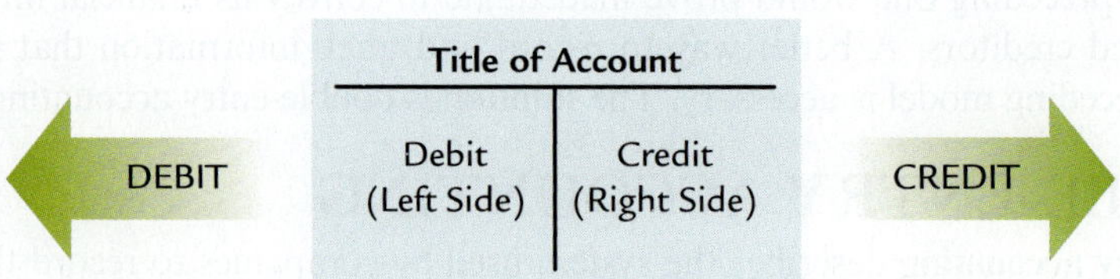

[2]This textbook uses a simplified and standardized chart of accounts that can be found on the inside cover of the book and on page 119. Account titles for real company financial statements may vary. Common alternate account titles are introduced, as appropriate, when accounts are introduced.

Note that the terms debit and credit simply refer to the left and the right side of an account. The left is always the debit side and the right is always the credit side. *Debit and credit do not represent increases or decreases.* (Increases or decreases to accounts are discussed in the next section.) Instead, debit and credit simply refer to *where* an entry is made in an account. The terms debit and credit will also be used to refer to the act of entering dollar amounts into an account. For example, entering an amount on the left side of an account will be called debiting the account. Entering an amount on the right side of an account is called crediting the account.

You may be tempted to associate the terms credit and debit with positive or negative events. For example, assume you returned an item that you purchased with a credit card to the local store and the store credited your card. This is generally viewed as a positive event since you now owe less money to the store. Or, if you receive a notice that your bank had debited your account to pay for service charges that you owe, this is viewed negatively because you now have less money in your account. Resist this temptation. In accounting, *debit means the left side of an account and credit means the right side of an account.*

concept Q&A

On a bank statement, a credit to a person's account means the account has increased. Similarly, a debit means the account has decreased. Why don't credit and debit always mean "add" and "subtract"?

Answer:

From the bank's perspective, a person's account is a liability since the bank must pay cash on demand. Because liabilities have normal credit balances, a credit will increase the account and a debit will decrease the account. However, from an individual's perspective, cash is an asset which has a normal debit balance. Therefore, debits increase cash and credits decrease cash. It is critical to always look at the normal balance of an account before determining if a transaction increases or decreases an account.

Debit and Credit Procedures

Using the accounting equation, we can incorporate debits and credits in order to determine how balance sheet accounts increase or decrease. There are three steps in determining increases or decreases to a balance sheet account:

Step 1. Draw a T-account and label each side of the T-account as either debit (left side) or credit (right side).

Step 2. Determine the normal balance of an account. All accounts have a **normal balance**. While individual transactions will increase and decrease an account, it would be unusual for an account to have a nonnormal balance.

Step 3. Increases or decreases to an account are based on the normal balance of the account.

This procedure is shown in Cornerstone 2.3.

Determining Increases or Decreases to a Balance Sheet Account

CORNERSTONE 2.3

Why:

Increases or decreases to an account are based on the normal balance of the account.

Information:

The balance sheet is comprised of three fundamental accounts—assets, liabilities, and stockholders' equity.

Required:

Determine how each of the three balance sheet accounts increases or decreases.

Solution:

- Because assets are located on the left side of the accounting equation, their normal balance is a debit. Therefore, debits will increase assets and credits will decrease assets.
- Because liabilities and stockholders' equity are on the right side of the accounting equation, their normal balance is a credit. Therefore, credits will increase liabilities and stockholders' equity while debits will decrease these accounts.

(Continued)

CORNERSTONE 2.3 *(Continued)*

This is illustrated in the following T-accounts:

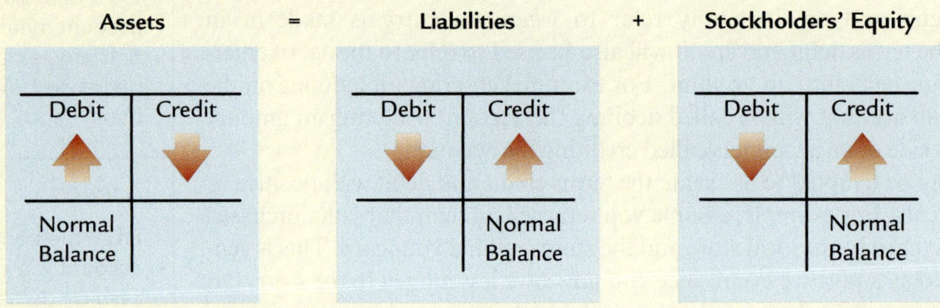

As we illustrated earlier in the chapter, every transaction will increase or decrease the elements of the accounting equation—assets, liabilities, and stockholders' equity. The direction of these increases and decreases must be such that the accounting equation stays in balance—the left side must equal the right side. In other words, *debits must equal credits*. This equality of debits and credits provides the foundation of double-entry accounting in which the two-sided effect of a transaction is recorded in the accounting system.

A similar procedure can be used to determine how increases and decreases are recorded for other financial statement elements. From the expanded accounting equation shown in Exhibit 2.5 (p. 67), we can see that stockholders' equity consists of both contributed capital (such as common stock) and retained earnings. As stockholders' equity accounts, both contributed capital and retained earnings have normal credit balances as shown in Exhibit 2.9. Because these accounts have normal credit balances, they are increased by credits and decreased by debits.

EXHIBIT 2.9

Normal Balances of Contributed Capital (e.g., Common Stock) and Retained Earnings

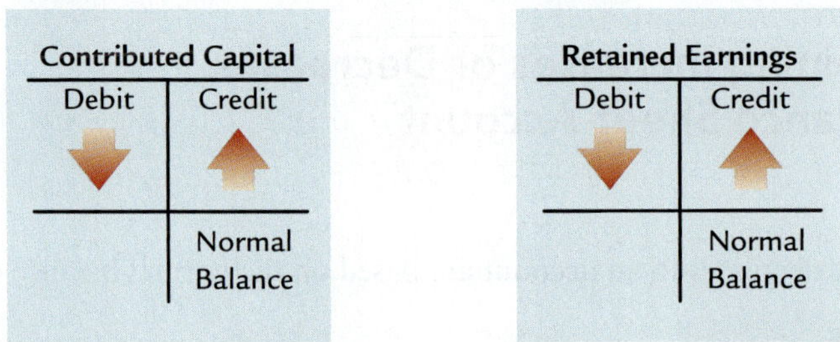

Retained earnings represent a company's accumulated net income (revenues minus expenses) minus any dividends. As we saw from the transaction analysis presented earlier in the chapter:

- Revenues increase retained earnings.
- Expenses decrease retained earnings.
- Dividends decrease retained earnings.

In order to determine increases or decreases in revenues, expenses, and dividends, we can use the following steps:

Step 1. Label each side of the t-account as either debit or credit.

Step 2. Determine the normal balance of an account.

Step 3. Increases or decreases to an account are based on the normal balance of the account.

Cornerstone 2.4 demonstrates how increases and decreases in these accounts are recorded.

Determining Increases or Decreases to Revenues, Expenses, and Dividends

CORNERSTONE 2.4

Why:

Increases or decreases to an account are based on the normal balance of the account.

Information:

Retained earnings is affected by three accounts—revenues, expenses, and dividends.

Required:

Determine how each of these three accounts increases or decreases.

Solution:

- Revenues increase stockholders' equity through retained earnings. Therefore, revenues have a normal credit balance. That means that credits will increase revenues and debits will decrease revenues.
- Expenses decrease stockholders' equity through retained earnings. Therefore, expenses have a normal debit balance. That means that debits will increase expenses and credits will decrease expenses.
- Dividends are defined as a distribution of retained earnings. Because dividends reduce retained earnings and stockholders' equity, dividends have a normal debit balance. That means that debits will increase dividends while credits will decrease dividends.

These procedures are summarized below.

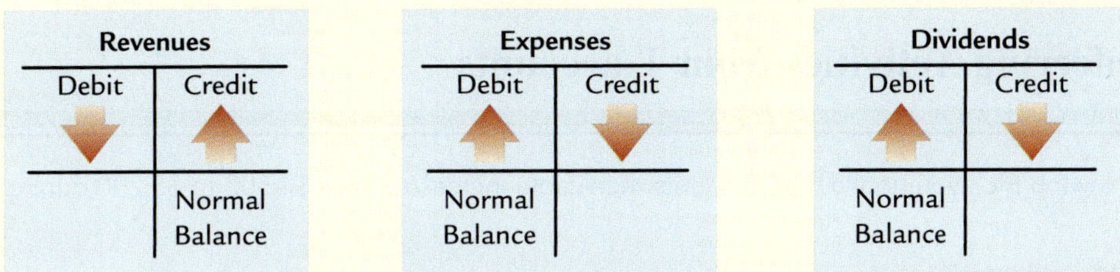

From Cornerstone 2.4, you should notice several items. First, revenues and expenses have opposite effects on retained earnings; therefore, revenues and expenses have opposite normal balances. Second, any change (increase or decrease) in revenue, expense, or dividends effects the balance of stockholders' equity. Specifically,

- an increase in revenue increases stockholders' equity
- a decrease in revenue decreases stockholders' equity
- an increase in expense or dividends decreases stockholders' equity
- a decrease in expense or dividends increases stockholders' equity

Finally, when revenues exceed expenses, a company has reported net income, which increases stockholders' equity. When revenues are less than expenses, a company has reported a net loss, which reduces stockholders' equity. These debit and credit procedures are summarized in Exhibit 2.10.

EXHIBIT 2.10

Summary of Debit and Credit Procedures

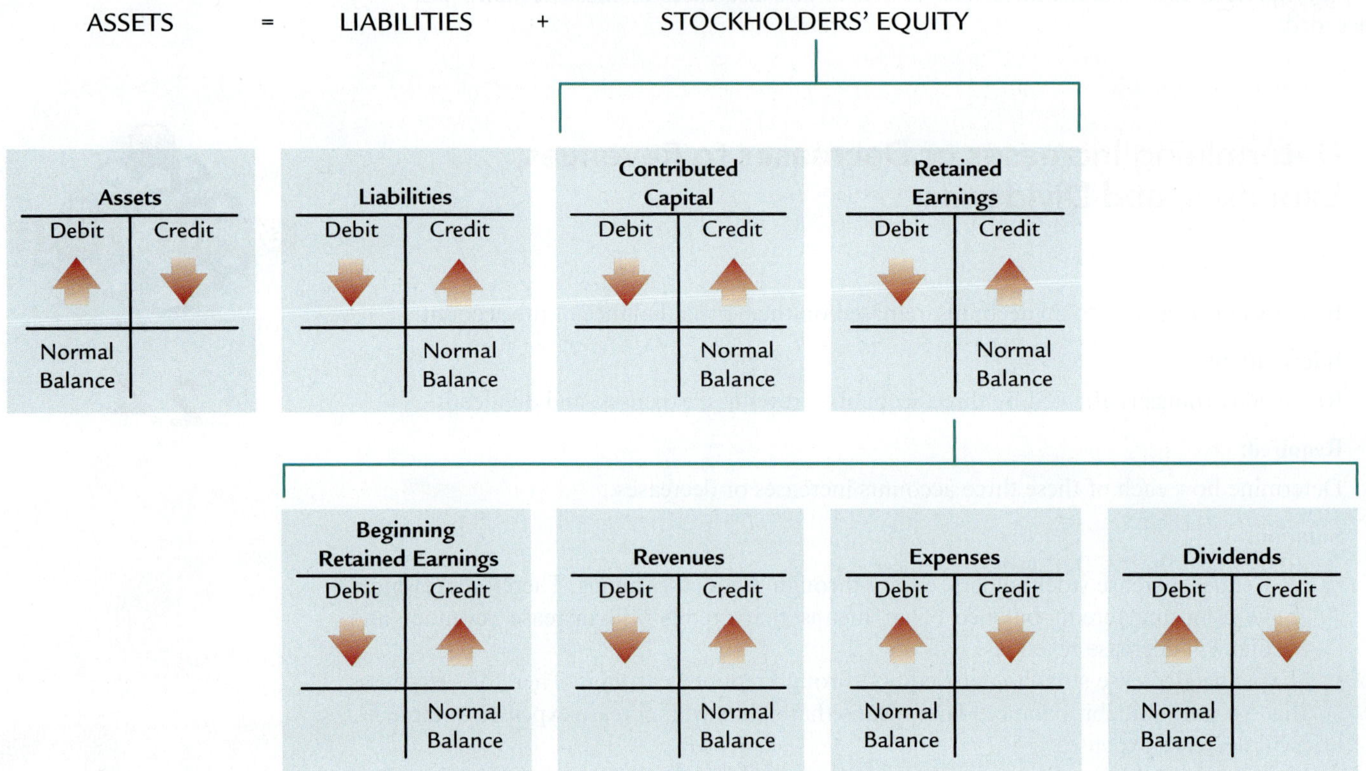

The important point from this analysis is that while debits are always on the left and credits are always on the right, the effect of a debit or credit on an account balance depends upon the normal balance of that account.

YOU DECIDE Inferring Activities from T-accounts

As you examine the accounting records of Newton Inc., you notice that accounts receivable increased from $4,500 to $5,200 during the year and that credit sales were $65,800.

What was the amount of accounts receivable collected?

The primary activities that affect accounts receivable are the sale goods and services on credit (increases in accounts receivable) and the collection of cash related to these credit sales (decreases in accounts receivable). To help visualize the account activity, prepare a T-account as follows:

Accounts Receivable			
Beginning balance	4,500		
Credit sales	65,800	?	Cash collections
Ending balance	5,200		

Because you know the beginning and ending balances of accounts receivable and the amount of credit sales, you can determine the cash collections as:

$$\text{Cash collections} = \$4{,}500 + \$65{,}800 - \$5{,}200 = \mathbf{\$65{,}100}$$

An understanding of how business activities affect individual accounts can yield valuable insights into the economic events that occurred during a period.

STEP 2: JOURNALIZE TRANSACTIONS

OBJECTIVE 5
Prepare journal entries for transactions.

While it would be possible to record transactions directly into accounts, most companies enter the effects of the transaction in a journal using the debit and credit procedures described in the previous section. A **journal** is a chronological record showing the debit and credit effects of transactions on a company. Each transaction is represented by a **journal entry** so that the entire effect of a transaction is contained in one place. The process of making a journal entry is often referred to as journalizing a transaction. Because a transaction first enters the accounting records through journal entries, the journal is often referred to as the book of original entry.

A journal entry consists of three parts: (1) the date of the transaction, (2) the accounts and amounts to be increased or decreased, and (3) a brief explanation of the transaction. Each journal entry shows the debit and credit effects of a transaction on specific accounts. In preparing a journal entry, the following steps should be followed: **Step 1.** Analyze the transaction using the procedures described in Cornerstone 2-2 (p. 68). **Step 2.** Determine which accounts are affected. **Step 3.** Prepare the journal entry using the debit and credit procedures in Cornerstones 2-3 (p. 75) and 2-4 (p. 77). This process is illustrated in Cornerstone 2.5.

Making a Journal Entry

CORNERSTONE 2.5

Why:

A journal entry records the effects of a transaction on accounts using debits and credits.

Information:

On January 1, Luigi Inc. purchases a $3,000 computer from WorstBuy Electronics on credit, with payment due in 60 days.

Required:

Prepare a journal entry to record this transaction.

Solution:

First, analyze the transaction using the procedures described in Cornerstone 2.2 (p. 68):

Assets	=	Liabilities	+	Stockholders' Equity		
				Contributed Capital	+	Retained Earnings
+$3,000		+$3,000				

The purchase of a computer has increased the asset account "Equipment," which is recorded with a debit. In addition, a liability, "Accounts Payable," was created and the increase in this account is recorded with a credit.

Date	Account and Explanation	Debit	Credit
Jan. 1	Equipment	3,000	
	Accounts Payable		3,000
	(Purchased office equipment on credit)		

From the journal entry in Cornerstone 2.5, notice several items:

- The date of the transaction is entered in the Date column.
- For each entry in the journal, the debit (the account and amount) is entered first and flush to the left. If there were more than one debit, it would be entered directly underneath the first debit on the next line. The credit (the account and the amount) is written below the debits and indented to the right. The purpose of this standard format is to make it possible for anyone using the journal to identify debits and credits quickly and correctly.
- *Total debits must equal total credits.*
- An explanation may appear beneath the credit.

In some instances, more than two accounts may be affected by an economic event. For example, assume that Luigi Inc. purchases a $3,000 computer from WorstBuy Electronics by paying $1,000 cash with the remainder due in 60 days. The purchase of this equipment increased the asset "Equipment," decreased the asset "Cash," and increased the liability "Accounts Payable" as shown in the analysis below:

Assets	=	Liabilities	+	Stockholders' Equity		
				Contributed Capital	+	Retained Earnings
+$3,000 −$1,000		+$2,000				

Luigi would make the following journal entry:

Date	Account and Explanation	Debit	Credit
Jan. 1	Equipment	3,000	
	Cash		1,000
	Accounts Payable		2,000
	(Purchased office equipment for cash and on credit)		

This type of entry is called a *compound journal entry* because more than two accounts were affected.

The use of a journal helps prevent the introduction of errors in the recording of business activities. Because all parts of the transaction appear together, it is easy to see whether equal debits and credits have been entered. If debits equal credits for *each* journal entry, then debits equal credits for *all* journal entries. At the end of the period, this fact leads to a useful check on the accuracy of journal entries. However, if the wrong amounts or the wrong accounts are used, debits can still equal credits, yet the journal entries will be incorrect. Additionally, each entry can be examined to see if the accounts that appear together are logically appropriate.

concept Q&A

If all journal entries have equal debits and credits, how can mistakes or errors occur?

Answer:

Mistakes or errors could still occur when entire transactions are not recorded, transactions are recorded for the wrong amounts or in the wrong accounts, or transactions are not recorded in the proper accounting period. While journal entries provide a safeguard against errors and mistakes, it will not prevent them all.

ETHICAL DECISIONS When an error is discovered in a journal entry, the accountant has an ethical responsibility to correct the error (subject to materiality), even if others would never be able to tell that the error had occurred. For example, if an accountant accidentally records a sale of merchandise by crediting Interest Revenue instead of Sales Revenue, total revenue would be unaffected. However, this error could significantly affect summary performance measures such as gross margin (sales minus cost of goods sold) that are important to many investors. When material errors are discovered, they should be corrected, even if this means embarrassment to the accountant. •

To provide a further illustration of recording transactions using journal entries, consider the case of HiTech Communications Inc. that was presented earlier in the chapter. For the remainder of the book, we will analyze each transaction and report its effects on the accounting equation in the margin next to the journal entry. Next, we identify the accounts that were affected by incorporating account titles into the transaction analysis model. Finally, we prepare the journal entry based on the analysis. You should always perform these steps as you prepare journal entries.

Transaction 1: Issuing Common Stock

On March 1, HiTech sold 1,000 shares of common stock to several investors for cash of $12,000.

Date	Account and Explanation	Debit	Credit
March 1	Cash	12,000	
	Common Stock		12,000
	(Issued common stock)		

Assets	= Liabilities +	Stockholders' Equity
+12,000		+12,000

Transaction 2: Borrowing Cash

On March 2, HiTech raised additional funds by borrowing $3,000 on a 1-year, 8% note payable to First Third Bank of Cincinnati.

Date	Account and Explanation	Debit	Credit
March 2	Cash	3,000	
	Notes Payable		3,000
	(Borrowed cash from bank)		

Assets	= Liabilities +	Stockholders' Equity
+3,000	+3,000	

Transaction 3: Purchase of Equipment for Cash

On March 3, HiTech purchased office equipment (computer equipment) from Micro-Center Inc. for $4,500 in cash.

Date	Account and Explanation	Debit	Credit
March 3	Equipment	4,500	
	Cash		4,500
	(Purchased equipment)		

Assets	= Liabilities +	Stockholders' Equity
+4,500 −4,500		

Transaction 4: Purchasing Insurance

On March 4, HiTech purchased a 6-month insurance policy for $1,200 in cash.

Date	Account and Explanation	Debit	Credit
March 4	Prepaid Insurance	1,200	
	Cash		1,200
	(Purchased insurance in advance)		

Assets	= Liabilities +	Stockholders' Equity
+1,200 −1,200		

Transaction 5: Purchase of Supplies on Credit

On March 6, HiTech purchased office supplies from Hamilton Office Supply for $6,500. Hamilton Office Supply agreed to accept full payment in 30 days.

Date	Account and Explanation	Debit	Credit
March 6	Supplies	6,500	
	Accounts Payable		6,500
	(Purchased supplies on account)		

Assets	= Liabilities +	Stockholders' Equity
+6,500	+6,500	

Transaction 6: Sale of Services for Cash

On March 10, HiTech sold advertising services to Miami Valley Products in exchange for $8,800 in cash.

Assets	=	Liabilities	+	Stockholders' Equity
+8,800				+8,800

Date	Account and Explanation	Debit	Credit
March 10	Cash	8,800	
	Service Revenue		8,800
	(Sold advertising services)		

Transaction 7: Sale of Services for Credit

On March 15, HiTech sold advertising services to the *Cincinnati Enquirer* for $3,300. HiTech agreed to accept full payment in 30 days.

Assets	=	Liabilities	+	Stockholders' Equity
+3,300				+3,300

Date	Account and Explanation	Debit	Credit
March 15	Accounts Receivable	3,300	
	Service Revenue		3,300
	(Sold advertising services)		

Transaction 8: Receipt of Cash in Advance

On March 19, HiTech received $9,000 in advance for advertising services to be completed in the next 3 months.

Assets	=	Liabilities	+	Stockholders' Equity
+9,000		+9,000		

Date	Account and Explanation	Debit	Credit
March 19	Cash	9,000	
	Unearned Service Revenue		9,000
	(Sold advertising services in advance)		

Transaction 9: Payment of a Liability

On March 23, HiTech pays $6,000 cash for the supplies previously purchased from Hamilton Office Supply (Transaction 5).

Assets	=	Liabilities	+	Stockholders' Equity
−6,000		−6,000		

Date	Account and Explanation	Debit	Credit
March 23	Accounts Payable	6,000	
	Cash		6,000
	(Paid accounts payable)		

Transaction 10: Collection of a Receivable

On March 25, HiTech collected $3,000 cash from the *Cincinnati Enquirer* for services sold earlier on credit (Transaction 7).

Assets	=	Liabilities	+	Stockholders' Equity
+3,000 −3,000				

Date	Account and Explanation	Debit	Credit
March 29	Cash	3,000	
	Accounts Receivable		3,000
	(Collected accounts receivable)		

Transaction 11: Payment of Salaries

On March 26, HiTech paid employees their weekly salaries of $1,800 cash.

Date	Account and Explanation	Debit	Credit
March 26	Salaries Expense	1,800	
	Cash		1,800
	(Paid employee salaries)		

Assets	=	Liabilities	+	Stockholders' Equity
−1,800				−1,800

Transaction 12: Payment of Utilities

On March 30, HiTech paid its utility bill of $5,200 for March.

Date	Account and Explanation	Debit	Credit
March 30	Utilities Expense	5,200	
	Cash		5,200
	(Paid for utilities used)		

Assets	=	Liabilities	+	Stockholders' Equity
−5,200				−5,200

Transaction 13: Payment of a Dividend

On March 31, HiTech declared and paid a cash dividend of $500 to its stockholders.

Date	Account and Explanation	Debit	Credit
March 31	Dividends	500	
	Cash		500
	(Declared and paid a cash dividend)		

Assets	=	Liabilities	+	Stockholders' Equity
−500				−500

YOUDECIDE Detecting Journal Entry Errors

You have been asked to inspect a delivery company's journal. Upon doing so, you find the following entry:

Date	Account and Explanation	Debit	Credit
June 29	Equipment, Delivery Truck	11,000	
	Prepaid Rent		11,000
	(Purchased delivery truck)		

Is this journal entry correct?

Because delivery trucks cannot be exchanged for prepaid rent, you conclude that an error was made in preparing this journal entry. Given the explanation contained in the journal entry, it's likely that the error was in the credit side of the entry. Instead of prepaid rent, the credit could be either to cash (if the purchase of the truck was for cash) or to note payable (if the purchase was on credit). Had the same data been entered directly into the accounts, this error would have been much more difficult to detect and correct.

The use of a journal helps prevent the introduction of errors in the recording of business activities.

STEP 3: POST TO THE LEDGER

OBJECTIVE 6

Explain why transactions are posted to the general ledger.

Because the journal lists each transaction in chronological order, it can be quite difficult to use the journal to determine the balance in any specific account. For example, refer to the journal entries shown earlier for HiTech Communications. What is the balance in cash at the end of the month? This relatively simple question is difficult to answer with the use of the journal.

To overcome this difficulty, companies will use a general ledger to keep track of the balances of specific accounts. A **general ledger** is simply a collection of all the individual

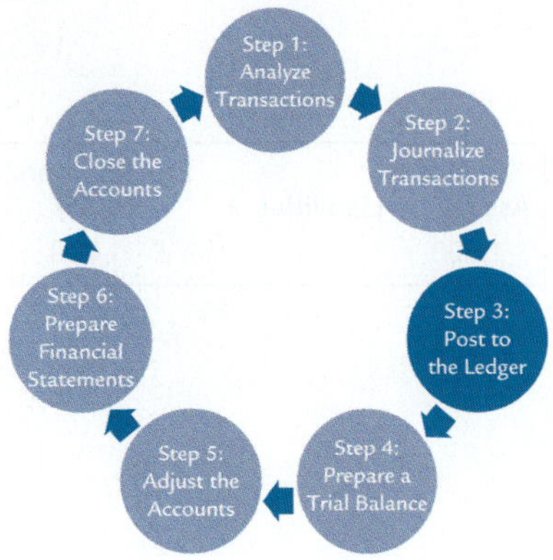

financial statement accounts that a company uses.[3] In a manual accounting system, a ledger could be as a simple as a notebook with a separate page for each account. Ledger accounts are often shown using the T-account format introduced earlier.

The process of transferring the information from the journalized transaction to the general ledger is called **posting**, and is illustrated in Exhibit 2.11. Posting is essentially copying the information from the journal into the ledger. Debits in the journal are posted as debits to the specific ledger account, and credits in the journal are posted as credits in the specific ledger account. To facilitate this process, most journals and ledgers have a column titled "Posting Reference." As the information is copied into the ledger, the number assigned to the account is placed in the "Posting Reference" column of the journal and the journal page number is placed in the "Posting Reference" column of the ledger.

EXHIBIT 2.11

The Posting Process for HiTech Communications Inc.

GENERAL JOURNAL

Page: 2

Date	Account and Explanation	Post. Ref.	Debit	Credit
Mar. 31	Dividends	3900	500	
	Cash	1000		500
	(Declared and paid cash dividend)			

GENERAL LEDGER

Account: CASH — Account Number: 1000

Date	Explanation	Post. Ref.	Debit	Credit	Balance
Mar. 1	Issued stock	1	12,000		12,000
2	Borrowed from bank	1	3,000		15,000
3	Purchased equipment	1		4,500	10,500
4	Purchased insurance	1		1,200	9,300
10	Sold advertising services	1	8,800		18,100
19	Sold advertising services in advance	1	9,000		27,100
23	Paid accounts payable	1		6,000	21,100
28	Paid salaries	1		1,800	19,300
29	Collected receivable	2	3,000		22,300
30	Paid utilities	2		5,200	17,100
31	Paid dividend	2		500	16,600

IFRS

Under IFRS, transactions are analyzed, journalized, and posted in the same manner as under U.S. GAAP.

This column provides a link between the ledger and journal that

- helps to prevent errors in the posting process
- allows you to trace the effects of a transaction through the accounting system

The general ledger accounts for HiTech are shown using T-accounts in Exhibit 2.12. The numbers in parentheses correspond to the transaction numbers.

[3]Most companies supplement the general ledger with subsidiary ledgers that record "subaccounts" that make up the larger general ledger account. For example, a single account such as Accounts Receivable may appear in the general ledger; however, the accounts receivable for individual customers are usually contained in a subsidiary ledger. The general ledger account will equal the total balance of all the accounts in the subsidiary ledger for that account.

EXHIBIT 2.12

General Ledger Accounts of HiTech Communications (T-account view)

Assets

Cash	
(T1) 12,000	4,500 (T3)
(T2) 3,000	1,200 (T4)
(T6) 8,800	6,000 (T9)
(T8) 9,000	1,800 (T11)
(T10) 3,000	5,200 (T12)
	500 (T13)
16,600	

Accounts Receivable	
(T7) 3,300	3,000 (T10)
300	

Supplies	
(T5) 6,500	
6,500	

Prepaid Insurance	
(T4) **1,200**	
1,200	

Equipment	
(T3) **4,500**	
4,500	

Liabilities

Accounts Payable	
(T9) 6,000	6,500 (T5)
	500

Unearned Service Revenue	
	9,000 (T8)
	9,000

Notes Payable	
	3,000 (T2)
	3,000

Stockholders' Equity

Common Stock	
	12,000 (T1)
	12,000

Service Revenue	
	8,800 (T6)
	3,300 (T7)
	12,100

Salaries Expense	
(T11) 1,800	
1,800	

Utilities Expense	
(T12) 5,200	
5,200	

Dividends	
(T13) 500	
500	

STEP 4: PREPARE A TRIAL BALANCE

OBJECTIVE 7

Prepare a trial balance and explain its purpose.

To aid in the preparation of financial statements, some companies will prepare a trial balance before they prepare financial statements. The **trial balance** is a list of all active accounts and each account's debit or credit balance. The accounts are listed in the order they appear in the ledger—assets first, followed by liabilities, stockholders' equity, revenues, and expenses. By organizing accounts in this manner, the trial balance serves as a useful tool in preparing the financial statements. The preparation of the trial balance for HiTech Communications is shown in Cornerstone 2.6.

CORNERSTONE

2.6

Preparing a Trial Balance

Why:

Refer to the general ledger for HiTech in Exhibit 2.12 (p. 85).

Required:

Prepare a trial balance for HiTech Communications Inc. at March 31, 2013.

Solution:

HiTech Communications Inc. Trial Balance March 31, 2013		
Account	**Debit**	**Credit**
Cash	$16,600	
Accounts Receivable	300	
Supplies	6,500	
Prepaid Insurance	1,200	
Equipment	4,500	
Accounts Payable		$ 500
Unearned Service Revenue		9,000
Notes Payable		3,000
Common Stock		12,000
Dividends	500	
Service Revenue		12,100
Salaries Expense	1,800	
Utilities Expense	5,200	
	$36,600	$36,600

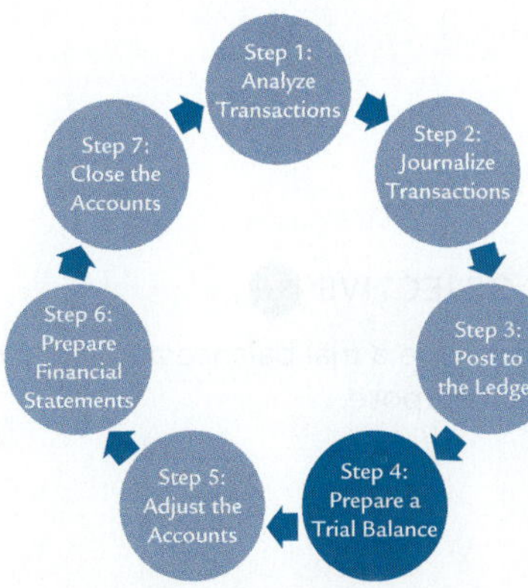

In addition, the trial balance is used to *prove the equality of debits and credits*. If debits did not equal credits, the accountant would quickly know that an error had been made. The error could have been in the journalizing of the transaction, the posting of the transaction, or in the computation of the balance in the ledger. However, a word of caution is necessary: a trial balance whose debits equal credits does *not* mean that all transactions were recorded correctly. A trial balance will not detect errors of analysis or amounts. Sometimes the wrong account is selected for a journal entry or an incorrect amount is recorded for a transaction. In other cases, a journal entry is omitted or entered twice. As long as both the debit and credit portions of the journal entry or posting reflect the incorrect information, the debit and credit totals in a trial balance will be equal.

SUMMARY OF LEARNING OBJECTIVES

LO 1. Describe the qualitative characteristics, assumptions, and principles that underlie accounting.

- The fundamental qualitative characteristics of accounting information are:
  - Relevance—refers to whether information is capable of making a difference in the decision-making process. Relevant information is material and helps to predict the future or provides feedback about prior expectations.
  - Faithful representation—refers to whether information faithfully represents the economic event that it is intending to portray. Faithfully presented information should be complete, neutral, and free from error.
- The enhancing qualitative characteristics are:
  - Comparability—allows external users to identify similarities and differences between two or more items. Comparability includes the characteristic of consistency.
  - Verifiability—results when independent parties can reach a consensus on the measurement of an activity.
  - Timeliness—available to users before the information loses its ability to influence decisions.
  - Understandability—able to be comprehended (with reasonable effort) by users who have a reasonable knowledge of accounting and business.
- The four assumptions are:
  - Economic entity—each company is accounted for separately from its owners
  - Continuity (going-concern)—assumption that a company will continue to operate long enough to carry out its commitments
  - Time-period—allows the life of a company to be divided into artificial time periods
  - Monetary unit—requires financial information to be reported in monetary terms
- The four principles are:
  - Historical cost—requires a business activity to be recorded at the exchange price at the time the activity occurs
  - Revenue recognition—requires revenue to be recognized when it is earned and cash collection is reasonably assured
  - Expense recognition (or matching) principle—requires that expenses be recognized in the same period as the revenue that it helped generate
  - Conservatism—requires care to be taken to avoid overstating assets or income

LO 2. Explain the relationships among economic events, transactions, and the expanded accounting equation.

- A company's business activities (operating, investing, and financing) consist of many different economic events that are both external to the company as well as internal to the company. Accounting attempts to measure the economic effect of these events. However, not all events are recognized, or recorded, in the accounting system.
- A transaction is an economic event that is recognized in the financial statements. An accounting transaction causes the elements of the accounting equation (assets, liabilities, contributed capital, retained earnings, revenues, expenses, or dividends) to change in a way that maintains the equality of their relationship.

LO 3. Analyze the effect of business transactions on the accounting equation.

- This is Step 1 of the accounting cycle.
- Transaction analysis is the process of determining the economic effects of a transaction on the elements of the accounting equation.

- Transaction analysis involves three steps:
  - Step 1: Write down the accounting equation (basic or expanded version).
  - Step 2: Identify the financial statement elements that are affected by the transaction.
  - Step 3: Determine whether the element increased or decreased.
- Each transaction will have a dual-effect on the accounting equation, and the accounting equation will remain in balance after the effects of the transaction are recorded.

LO 4. Discuss the role of accounts and how debits and credits are used in the double-entry accounting system.

- An account is a record of increases and decreases in each of the basic elements of the financial statements.
- Each financial statement element is made up of a number of different accounts.
- All transactions are recorded into accounts.
- The final account balance, after all changes are recorded, is used in the preparation of the financial statements.
- The left side of an account is referred to as a debit. The right side of an account is referred to as a credit.
- All accounts have a normal balance, which is a positive account balance. Assets, expenses, and dividends have a normal debit balance. Liabilities, stockholders' equity, and revenues have a normal credit balance.
- Increases or decreases to an account are based on the normal balance of an account. Normal debit balance accounts (assets, expenses, and dividends) are increased with debits and decreased with credits. Normal credit balance accounts (liabilities, equity, and stockholders' equity) are increased with credits and decreased with debits.

LO 5. Prepare journal entries for transactions.

- This is Step 2 of the accounting cycle.
- A journal entry represents the debit and credit effects of a transaction in the accounting records.
- A journal entry is prepared by following three steps:
  - Step 1: Analyzing the transaction.
  - Step 2: Determining which accounts are affected.
  - Step 3: Using the debit and credit procedures to record the effects of the transaction.
- A journal entry is recorded in chronological order and consists of the date of the transaction, the accounts affected, the amount of the transaction, and a brief explanation.

LO 6. Explain why transactions are posted to the general ledger.

- This is Step 3 of the accounting cycle.
- To overcome the difficulty of determining account balances listed chronologically in the journal, information in the journal is transferred to the general ledger in a process called posting.
- As result of posting, the general ledger accumulates the effects of transactions in individual financial statement accounts.

LO 7. Prepare a trial balance and explain its purpose.

- This is Step 4 of the accounting cycle.
- The trial balance is a list of all active accounts, in the order they appear in the ledger, and each account's debit or credit balance.
- The trial balance is used to prove the equality of debits and credits and helps to uncover errors in journalizing or posting transactions.
- The trial balance serves as a useful tool in preparing the financial statements.

- **CORNERSTONE 2.1** Applying the conceptual framework, page 63
- **CORNERSTONE 2.2** Performing transaction analysis, page 68
- **CORNERSTONE 2.3** Determining increases or decreases to a balance sheet account, page 75
- **CORNERSTONE 2.4** Determining increases or decreases to revenues, expenses, and dividends, page 77
- **CORNERSTONE 2.5** Making a journal entry, page 79
- **CORNERSTONE 2.6** Preparing a trial balance, page 86

KEY TERMS

Account, 74
Accounting cycle, 60
Chart of accounts, 74
Comparability, 61
Conservatism principle, 63
Consistency, 61
Continuity (or going-concern) assumption, 62
Cost constraint, 62
Credit, 74
Debit, 74
Double-entry accounting, 73
Economic entity assumption, 62
Events, 65
Expense recognition (or matching) principle, 63
Faithful representation, 61
Full disclosure, 62
General ledger, 83
Historical cost principle, 63
Journal, 79
Journal entry, 79
Monetary unit assumption, 62
Normal balance, 75
Posting, 84
Relevance, 60
Revenue recognition principle, 63
T-account, 74
Timeliness, 61
Time period assumption, 62
Transaction, 66
Transaction analysis, 67
Trial balance, 85
Understandability, 61
Verifiability, 61

REVIEW PROBLEM

I. The Accounting Cycle

Concept:
Economic events are recorded in the accounting system through a process of analyzing transactions, journalizing these transactions in a journal, and posting them to the ledger. These activities are the initial steps in the accounting cycle.

Information:
Boonville Delivery Service was recently formed to fill a need for speedy delivery of small packages. In December 2013, its first month of operations, the following transactions occurred.

a. On December 1, Boonville sells common stock to several investors for $32,000.
b. On December 2, Boonville borrows $20,000 on a 1-year note payable from Warrick National Bank, to be repaid with 8% interest on December 7, 2014.
c. On December 2, Boonville pays rent of $8,000 on its package sorting building for the month of December.
d. On December 6, Boonville purchases $7,000 worth of office furniture by paying $1,400 in cash and signing a 1-year, 12% note payable for the balance.

e. On December 20, Boonville completes a delivery contract for Tornado Corporation and bills its customer $15,000.
f. On December 24, Boonville makes a rush delivery for $5,300 cash.
g. On December 28, Tornado pays the $15,000 owed from Transaction e.
h. On December 28, Boonville signs an agreement with BigTime Computers to accept and deliver approximately 400 packages per business day during the next 12 months. Boonville expects to receive $400,000 of revenue for this contract, but the exact amount will depend on the number of packages delivered.
i. On December 29, Boonville receives a $1,500 bill from Mac's Catering for miscellaneous services performed at a Christmas party Boonville held for its clients. (No previous entry has been made for this activity.)
j. On December 31, Boonville pays $2,600 cash in salaries to its secretarial staff for work performed in December.
k. On December 31, Boonville declares and pays dividends of $5,000 on its common stock.

Required:

1. Analyze and journalize the Transactions a through k.
2. Post the transactions to the general ledger.
3. Prepare the December 31, 2013 trial balance for Boonville.

Solution:

1. **Analyzing and Journalizing Transactions**

Transaction a: *Issuing Common Stock.*

Assets	=	Liabilities	+	Stockholders' Equity		
				Contributed Capital	+	Retained Earnings
Cash +$32,000				Common Stock +$32,000		

Date	Account and Explanation	Debit	Credit
Dec. 1	Cash	32,000	
	Common Stock		32,000
	(Issued common stock)		

Transaction b: *Borrowing Cash*

Assets	=	Liabilities	+	Stockholders' Equity		
				Contributed Capital	+	Retained Earnings
Cash +$20,000		Notes Payable +$20,000				

Date	Account and Explanation	Debit	Credit
Dec. 2	Cash	20,000	
	Notes Payable		20,000
	(Borrowed cash from bank)		

Transaction c: *Paying Rent*

Assets	=	Liabilities	+	Stockholders' Equity		
				Contributed Capital	+	Retained Earnings
Cash −$8,000						Rent Expense −$8,000

Date	Account and Explanation	Debit	Credit
Dec. 2	Rent Expense	8,000	
	Cash		8,000
	(Paid rent for December)		

Transaction d: *Purchasing Asset with Cash and Credit*

Assets	=	Liabilities	+	Stockholders' Equity		
				Contributed Capital	+	Retained Earnings
Cash		Notes Payable				
−$1,400		+$5,600				
Furniture						
+$7,000						

Date	Account and Explanation	Debit	Credit
Dec. 6	Furniture	7,000	
	Cash		1,400
	Notes Payable		5,600
	(Purchased office furniture)		

Transaction e: *Performing Services for Credit*

Assets	=	Liabilities	+	Stockholders' Equity		
				Contributed Capital	+	Retained Earnings
Accounts Receivable						Service Revenue
+$15,000						+$15,000

Date	Account and Explanation	Debit	Credit
Dec. 20	Accounts Receivable	15,000	
	Service Revenue		15,000
	(Performed delivery services)		

Transaction f: *Performing Services for Cash*

Assets	=	Liabilities	+	Stockholders' Equity		
				Contributed Capital	+	Retained Earnings
Cash						Service Revenue
+$5,300						+$5,300

Date	Account and Explanation	Debit	Credit
Dec. 24	Cash	5,300	
	Service Revenue		5,300
	(Performed delivery services)		

Transaction g: *Collecting an Account Receivable*

Assets	=	Liabilities	+	Stockholders' Equity		
				Contributed Capital	+	Retained Earnings
Cash						
+$15,000						
Accounts Receivable						
−$15,000						

(Continued)

Date	Account and Explanation	Debit	Credit
Dec. 28	Cash	15,000	
	Accounts Receivable		15,000
	(Collected accounts receivable)		

Transaction h: *Signing of an Agreement to Provide Service*

This is an example of an important event that does not produce a journal entry at the time it occurs. There will be no recording of the transaction until one of the companies performs on its part of the contract (so, until Boonville provides the delivery service or BigTime Computers makes a payment to Boonville).

Transaction i: *Using Services*

Assets	=	Liabilities	+	Stockholders' Equity		
				Contributed Capital	+	Retained Earnings
		Accounts Payable				Miscellaneous Expense
		+$1,500				−$1,500

Date	Account and Explanation	Debit	Credit
Dec. 29	Miscellaneous Expense	1,500	
	Accounts Payable		1,500
	(Used catering service)		

Transaction j: *Payment of Salaries*

Assets	=	Liabilities	+	Stockholders' Equity		
				Contributed Capital	+	Retained Earnings
Cash						Salaries Expense
−$2,600						−$2,600

Date	Account and Explanation	Debit	Credit
Dec. 31	Salaries Expense	2,600	
	Cash		2,600
	(Paid secretarial staff salaries)		

Transaction k: *Declaring and Paying a Cash Dividend*

Assets	=	Liabilities	+	Stockholders' Equity		
				Contributed Capital	+	Retained Earnings
Cash						Dividends
−$5,000						−$5,000

Date	Account and Explanation	Debit	Credit
Dec. 31	Dividends	5,000	
	Cash		5,000
	(Declared and paid a cash dividend)		

2. **Posting of Transactions to the Ledger**

General Ledger of Boonville Delivery Service

Assets

Cash	
(a) 32,000	8,000 (c)
(b) 20,000	1,400 (d)
(f) 5,300	2,600 (j)
(g) 15,000	5,000 (k)
55,300	

Accounts Receivable	
(e) 15,000	15,000 (g)
0	

Furniture	
(d) 7,000	
7,000	

Liabilities

Accounts Payable	
	1,500 (i)
	1,500

Notes Payable	
	20,000 (b)
	5,600 (d)
	25,600

Stockholders' Equity

Common Stock	
	32,000 (a)
	32,000

Dividends	
(k) 5,000	
5,000	

Service Revenue	
	15,000 (e)
	5,300 (f)
	20,300

Salaries Expense	
(j) 2,600	
2,600	

Miscellaneous Expense	
(i) 1,500	
1,500	

Rent Expense	
(c) 8,000	
8,000	

3. **Preparing a Trial Balance**

Boonville Delivery Service
Trial Balance
December 31, 2013

Account	Debit	Credit
Cash	$55,300	
Accounts Receivable	0	
Furniture	7,000	
Accounts Payable		$ 1,500
Notes Payable		25,600
Common Stock		32,000
Dividends	5,000	
Service Revenue		20,300
Rent Expense	8,000	
Salaries Expense	2,600	
Miscellaneous Expense	1,500	
	$79,400	$79,400

DISCUSSION QUESTIONS

1. What is the conceptual framework of accounting?
2. Identify the characteristics of useful information.
3. Discuss the trade-offs that may be necessary between the qualitative characteristics.
4. Distinguish between comparability and consistency.
5. Describe the constraint on providing useful information.

6. Identify the four assumptions that underlie accounting.
7. Discuss the four principles that are used to measure and record business transactions.
8. How are the financial statements related to generally accepted accounting principles?
9. Of all the events that occur each day, how would you describe those that are recorded in a firm's accounting records?
10. In order for a transaction to be recorded in a business' accounting records, the effects of the transaction must be faithfully represented. What is faithful representation, and why is it important?
11. What is the basic process used in transaction analysis?
12. In analyzing a transaction, can a transaction only affect one side of the accounting equation? If so, give an example.
13. How do revenues and expenses affect the accounting equation?
14. What is a T-account? Describe the basic components of any account.
15. Do you agree with the statement that "debits mean increase and credits mean decrease"? If not, what do debit and credit mean?
16. The words *debit* and *credit* are used in two ways in accounting: "to debit an account" and "a debit balance." Explain both usages of the terms *debit and credit*.
17. All accounts have normal balances. What is the normal balance of each of these accounts?

    a. cash
    b. sales
    c. notes payable
    d. inventory
    e. retained earnings
    f. salary expense
    g. equipment
    h. unearned revenue

18. When a journal entry is made, what must be equal? Why?
19. Can accounting transactions be directly recorded in the general ledger? If so, why do most companies initially record transactions in the journal?
20. Why is the term *double-entry* an appropriate expression for describing an accounting system?
21. What are the initial steps in the accounting cycle and what happens in each step?
22. What kinds of errors will a trial balance detect? What kinds of errors will not be detectable by a trial balance?

MULTIPLE-CHOICE QUESTIONS

2-1 Which of the following is *not* a benefit derived from the conceptual framework?

a. Supports the objective of providing information useful for making business and economic decisions.
b. Provides a logical structure to aid in the understanding of complex accounting standards.
c. Provides specific guidance on how transactions should be recorded.
d. Supports the development of a consistent set of accounting standards.

2-2 Which of the following is *not* a characteristic of useful information?

a. Comparability
b. Relevance
c. Faithful representation
d. Conservatism

2-3 Information that provides feedback about prior expectations is:

	Relevant	Faithfully Represented
a.	Yes	Yes
b.	No	Yes
c.	Yes	No
d.	No	No

2-4 Relevant information possesses this quality:

	Freedom from Error	Predictive Value
a.	Yes	Yes
b.	No	Yes
c.	Yes	No
d.	No	No

2-5 Which of the following is *not* an assumption that underlies accounting?

a. Historical cost
b. Economic entity
c. Time-period
d. Continuity (going-concern)

2-6 Which principle requires that expenses be recorded and reported in the same period as the revenue that it helped generate?

a. Historical cost
b. Revenue recognition
c. Conservatism
d. Expense recognition or matching

2-7 Taylor Company recently purchased a piece of equipment for $2,000 which will be paid within 30 days after delivery. At what point would the event be recorded in Taylor's accounting system?

a. When Taylor signs the agreement with the seller
b. When Taylor receives an invoice (a bill) from the seller
c. When Taylor receives the asset from the seller
d. When Taylor pays $2,000 cash to the seller

2-8 The effects of purchasing inventory on credit are to:

a. increase assets and increase liabilities.
b. increase assets and increase stockholders' equity.
c. decrease assets and decrease stockholders' equity.
d. decrease assets and decrease liabilities.

2-9 The effects of paying salaries for the current period are to:

a. increase assets and increase stockholders' equity.
b. increase assets and increase liabilities.
c. decrease assets and decrease liabilities.
d. decrease assets and decrease stockholders' equity.

2-10 Which of the following statements is *false*?

a. The left side of a T-account is called the credit side.
b. All T-accounts have both a debit and a credit side.
c. Transactions are frequently analyzed using a T-account.
d. The amount in an account at any time is called the balance of the account.

2-11 Which of the following statements are true?

I. Debits represent decreases, and credits represent increases.
II. Debits must always equal credits.
III. Assets have normal debit balances while liabilities and stockholders' equity have normal credit balances.

a. I
b. I and II
c. II and III
d. All of these are true.

2-12 Debits will:

a. increase assets, expenses, and dividends.
b. decrease liabilities, revenues, and dividends.
c. increase assets, liabilities, revenues, expenses, and dividends.
d. decrease assets, liabilities, revenues, expenses, and dividends.

2-13 Which of the following statements are true?

I. A journal provides a chronological record of a transaction.
II. A journal entry contains the complete effect of a transaction.
III. The first step in preparing a journal entry involves analyzing the transaction.

a. I and II
b. II and III
c. I and III
d. All of these are true.

2-14 Posting:

a. involves transferring the information in journal entries to the general ledger.
b. is an optional step in the accounting cycle.
c. is performed after a trial balance is prepared.
d. involves transferring information to the trial balance.

2-15 A trial balance:

a. lists only revenue and expense accounts.
b. lists all accounts and their balances.
c. will help detect omitted journal entries.
d. detects all errors that could be made during the journalizing or posting steps of the accounting cycle.

CORNERSTONE EXERCISES

OBJECTIVE 1
CORNERSTONE 2.1

Cornerstone Exercise 2-16 Qualitative Characteristics

Three statements are given below.

a. When financial information is free from error or bias, the information is said to possess this characteristic.
b. Griffin Company uses the same depreciation method from period to period.
c. A trash can that is purchased for $10 is expensed even though it will be used for many years.

Required:

Give the qualitative characteristic or constraint that is most applicable to each of the statements.

OBJECTIVE 1
CORNERSTONE 2.1

Cornerstone Exercise 2-17 Qualitative Characteristics

Three statements are given below.

a. A financial item that may be useful to investors is not required to be reported because the cost of measuring and reporting this information is judged to be too great.
b. Timely information that is used to predict future events or provide feedback about prior events is said to possess this characteristic.
c. A quality of information that enables an analyst to evaluate the financial performance of two different companies in the same industry.

Required:

Give the qualitative characteristic or constraint that is most applicable to each of the statements.

OBJECTIVE 1
CORNERSTONE 2.1

Cornerstone Exercise 2-18 Accounting Assumptions

Four statements are given below.

a. Pewterschmidt Company values its inventory reported in the financial statements in terms of dollars instead of units.
b. Property, plant, and equipment is recorded at cost (minus any accumulated depreciation) instead of liquidation value.

c. The accounting records of a company are kept separate from its owners.
d. The accountant assigns revenues and expenses to specific years before preparing the financial statements.

Required:

Give the accounting assumption that is most applicable to each of the statements.

Cornerstone Exercise 2-19 Accounting Principles

OBJECTIVE 1
CORNERSTONE 2.1

Four statements are given below.

a. Quagmire Company recognizes revenue when the goods are delivered to a customer, even though cash will not be collected from the customer for 30 days.
b. Inventory, which was recently damaged by a flood, is reported at the lower of its cost or market value.
c. Land, located in a desirable location, is reported at the original acquisition price, even though its value has increased by over 100% since it was purchased.
d. The cost paid for a delivery truck is recorded as an asset and expensed over the next 5 years as it is used to help generate revenue.

Required:

Give the accounting principle that is most applicable to each of the statements.

Cornerstone Exercise 2-20 Transaction Analysis

OBJECTIVE 3
CORNERSTONE 2.2

Four transactions are listed below.

a. Sold goods to customers on credit.
b. Collected amounts due from customers.
c. Purchased supplies on account.
d. Used supplies in operations of the business.

Required:

Prepare three columns labeled assets, liabilities, and stockholders' equity. For each of the transactions, indicate whether the transaction increased (+), decreased (−), or had no effect (NE) on assets, liabilities, or stockholders' equity.

Cornerstone Exercise 2-21 Transaction Analysis

OBJECTIVE 3
CORNERSTONE 2.2

Morgan Inc. entered into the following transactions:

a. Issued common stock to investors in exchange for $30,000 cash.
b. Borrowed $10,000 cash from First State Bank.
c. Purchased $3,000 of supplies on credit.
d. Paid for the purchase in Transaction c.

Required:

Show the effect of each transaction using the following model.

Assets	=	Liabilities	+	Stockholders' Equity		
				Contributed Capital	+	Retained Earnings

Cornerstone Exercise 2-22 Transaction Analysis

OBJECTIVE 4
CORNERSTONE 2.2

The Mendholm Company entered into the following transactions:

a. Performed services on account, $21,500.
b. Collected $9,500 from client related to services performed in Item a.
c. Paid $500 dividend to stockholders.
d. Paid salaries of $4,000 for the current month.

(Continued)

Required:

Show the effect of each transaction using the following model:

Assets	=	Liabilities	+	Stockholders' Equity		
				Contributed Capital	+	Retained Earnings

OBJECTIVE 4
CORNERSTONE 2.3
CORNERSTONE 2.4

Cornerstone Exercise 2-23 Debit and Credit Procedures

Refer to the accounts listed below.

a. Accounts Payable
b. Accounts Receivable
c. Retained Earnings
d. Sales
e. Equipment
f. Common Stock
g. Salary Expense
h. Repair Expense

Required:

For each of the accounts, complete the following table by entering the normal balance of the account (debit or credit) and the word increase or decrease in the debit and credit columns.

Account	Normal Balance	Debit	Credit

OBJECTIVE 5
CORNERSTONE 2.5

Cornerstone Exercise 2-24 Journalize Transactions

Four transactions that occurred during June are listed below.

a. June 1: Issued common stock to several investors for $100,000.
b. June 8: Purchased equipment for $16,800 cash.
c. June 15: Made cash sales of $23,200 to customers.
d. June 29: Paid a $4,500 dividend to stockholders.

Required:

Prepare journal entries for the transactions.

OBJECTIVE 5
CORNERSTONE 2.5

Cornerstone Exercise 2-25 Journalize Transactions

Four transactions that occurred during May are listed below.

a. May 5: Borrowed cash of $40,000 from Middle State Bank.
b. May 10: Made cash sales of $28,500 to customers.
c. May 19: Paid salaries of $15,600 to employees for services performed.
d. May 22: Purchased and used $7,100 of supplies in operations of the business.

Required:

Prepare journal entries for the transactions.

OBJECTIVE 7
CORNERSTONE 2.6

Cornerstone Exercise 2-26 Preparing a Trial Balance

Listed below are the ledger accounts for Borges Inc. at December 31, 2013. All accounts have normal balances.

Service Revenue	$23,150	Dividends	$ 1,500
Cash	12,850	Salaries Expense	4,300
Accounts Payable	2,825	Equipment	12,725
Common Stock	15,000	Accounts Receivable	5,700
Rent Expense	2,400	Advertising Expense	1,500

Required:

Prepare a trial balance for Borges at December 31, 2013.

BRIEF EXERCISES

Brief Exercise 2-27 Qualitative Characteristics

OBJECTIVE 1

Six statements are given below:

a. The two fundamental qualitative characteristics that information should possess are __________ and __________.
b. __________ is the characteristic that allows external users to identify similarities and differences between two or more items.
c. __________ requires accounting information to be comprehensible to users who have a reasonable knowledge of business and economic activities and who are willing to study the information carefully.
d. When accounting information is complete, neutral, and free from error, it is said to be a _________ of the real world economic event that it is intending to portray.
e. When multiple, independent parties can agree on the measurement of an activity, the information is said to be __________.
f. The characteristic of __________ is illustrated by a financial analyst needing information within the next week in order to make an investment decision.

Required:

Complete each of the statements with the appropriate qualitative characteristic.

Brief Exercise 2-28 Assumptions and Principles

OBJECTIVE 1

Five common accounting practices are listed below:

a. A customer pays $20 to mail a package on December 30. The delivery company recognizes revenue when the package is delivered in January.
b. Jim Trotter owns C&S Heating Company. In preparing the financial statements, Trotter makes sure that the purchase of a new truck for personal use is not included in C&S's financial statements.
c. Moseley Inc. recorded land at its purchase price of $50,000. In future periods, the land is reflected in the financial statements at $50,000.
d. Mack Company purchases inventory in March. However, it does not expense that inventory until it is sold in April.
e. Mueller Inc. prepares quarterly and annual financial statements.

Required:

Identify the accounting principle or assumption that best describes each practice.

Brief Exercise 2-29 Events and Transactions

OBJECTIVE 2

Several events are listed below.

a. Paid $30,000 for land.
b. Purchased office supplies for cash.
c. Performed consulting services for a client with the amount to be collected in 30 days.
d. Signed a contract to perform consulting services over the next 6 months.

Required:

For each of the events, identify which ones qualify for recognition in the financial statements. If an event does not qualify for recognition, explain why.

Brief Exercise 2-30 Transaction Analysis

OBJECTIVE 3

Galle Inc. entered into the following transactions during January.

a. Borrowed $50,000 from First Street Bank by signing a note payable.
b. Purchased $25,000 of equipment for cash.

(Continued)

c. Paid $500 to landlord for rent for January.
d. Performed services for customers on account, $10,000.
e. Collected $3,000 from customers for services performed in Transaction d.
f. Paid salaries of $2,500 for the current month.

Required:

Show the effect of each transaction using the following model.

				Stockholders' Equity		
Assets	=	Liabilities	+	Contributed Capital	+	Retained Earnings

OBJECTIVE 4

Brief Exercise 2-31 Debit and Credit Procedures

Refer to the accounts listed below.

a. Accounts Receivable
b. Accounts Payable
c. Cash
d. Equipment
e. Notes Payable
f. Rent Expense
g. Salaries Expense
h. Service Revenue

Required:

For each of the accounts, indicate the normal balance of the account and the effect of a debit or a credit on the account.

OBJECTIVE 5

Brief Exercise 2-32 Journalize Transactions

Galle Inc. entered into the following transactions during January.

a. January 1: Borrowed $50,000 from First Street Bank by signing a note payable.
b. January 4: Purchased $25,000 of equipment for cash.
c. January 6: Paid $500 to landlord for rent for January.
d. January 15: Performed services for customers on account, $10,000.
e. January 25: Collected $3,000 from customers for services performed in Transaction d.
f. January 30: Paid salaries of $2,500 for the current month.

Required:

Prepare journal entries for the transactions.

OBJECTIVE 6

Brief Exercise 2-33 Posting Journal Entries

Listed below are selected T-accounts and their beginning balances for Galle Inc.

Cash	
12,000	

Accounts Receivable	
6,300	

Equipment	
5,000	

Notes Payable	
	0

Service Revenue	
	19,500

Salary Expense	
5,000	

Rent Expense	
1,000	

Required:

Post the journal entries from **Brief Exercise 2-32** to these accounts and compute the ending balance for each account.

Brief Exercise 2-34 Preparing a Trial Balance

OBJECTIVE 7

The following trial balance that was prepared by the bookkeeper of Mason Company does not balance.

Mason Company
Trial Balance
December 31, 2013

	Debit	Credit
Cash		$20,000
Accounts Payable	$ 3,000	
Insurance Expense	1,500	
Supplies	1,200	
Accounts Receivable		10,300
Salaries Payable	1,900	
Notes Payable		3,100
Common Stock		10,000
Dividends		2,000
Retained Earnings	8,000	
Service Revenue	19,200	
Unearned Service Revenue	2,100	
Prepaid Insurance		1,900
Salaries Expense	9,500	
Supplies Expense		900
	$46,400	$48,200

Required:

Prepare a correct trial balance. Assume all accounts have normal balances.

EXERCISES

Exercise 2-35 Qualitative Characteristics

OBJECTIVE 1

Listed below are the fundamental and enhancing qualitative characteristics that make accounting information useful.

- Relevance
- Faithful representation
- Comparability
- Verifiability
- Timeliness
- Understandability

Required:

1. Match the appropriate qualitative characteristic with the statements below (items can be used more than once).
   a. When information is provided before it loses its ability to influence decisions, it has this characteristic.
   b. When several accountants can agree on the measurement of an activity, the information possesses this characteristic.
   c. If users can comprehend the meaning of the information, the information is said to have this characteristic.
   d. If information confirms prior expectations, it possesses this characteristic.
   e. If information helps to predict future events, it possesses this characteristic.
   f. Freedom from bias is a component of this characteristic.
   g. When several companies in the same industry use the same accounting methods, this qualitative characteristic exists.
   h. Information that accurately portrays an economic event satisfies this characteristic.
2. **CONCEPTUAL CONNECTION** Explain the purpose of the conceptual framework.

OBJECTIVE 1

Exercise 2-36 Assumptions and Principles

Presented below are the four assumptions and four principles used in measuring and reporting accounting information.

Assumptions		Principles	
a.	Economic entity	e.	Historical cost
b.	Continuity (going-concern)	f.	Revenue recognition
c.	Time-period	g.	Expense recognition (matching)
d.	Monetary unit	h.	Conservatism

Required:

Identify the assumption or principle that best describes each situation below.

1. Requires that an activity be recorded at the exchange price at the time the activity occurred.
2. Allows a company to report financial activities separate from the activities of the owners.
3. Implies that items such as customer satisfaction cannot be reported in the financial statements.
4. Specifies that revenue should only be recognized when earned and the collection of cash is reasonably assured.
5. Justifies why some assets and liabilities are not reported at their value if sold.
6. Allows the life of a company to be divided into artificial time periods so accounting reports can be provided on a timely basis.
7. Is a prudent reaction to uncertainty.
8. Requires that expenses be recorded and reported in the same period as the revenue that it helped generate.

OBJECTIVE 2

Exercise 2-37 Events and Transactions

Several events are listed below.

a. Common stock is issued to investors.
b. An agreement is signed with a janitorial service to provide cleaning services over the next 12 months.
c. Inventory is purchased.
d. Inventory is sold to customers.
e. Two investors sell their common stock to another investor.
f. A 2-year insurance policy is purchased.

Required:

1. **CONCEPTUAL CONNECTION** For each of the events, identify which ones qualify for recognition in the financial statements.
2. **CONCEPTUAL CONNECTION** For events that do not qualify for recognition, explain your reasoning.

OBJECTIVE 2

Exercise 2-38 Events and Transactions

The following economic events related to K&B Grocery Store occurred during 2013:

a. On February 7, K&B received a bill from Indianapolis Power and Light indicating that it had used electric power during January 2013 at a cost of $220; the bill need not be paid until March 1, 2013.
b. On February 15, K&B placed an order for a new cash register with NCR, for which $800 would be paid after delivery.
c. On February 21, the cash register ordered on February 15 was delivered. Payment was not due until March.
d. On February 22, the K&B store manager purchased a new passenger car for $35,000 in cash. The car is entirely for personal use and was paid for from the manager's personal assets.

e. On February 24, K&B signed a 2-year extension of the lease on the store building occupied by the store. The new lease was effective on April 1, 2013, and required an increase in the monthly rental from $5,750 to $5,900.
f. On March 1, K&B paid $220 to Indianapolis Power and Light.
g. On March 5, K&B paid $5,750 to its landlord for March rent on the store building.

Required:

1. **CONCEPTUAL CONNECTION** Using the words "qualify" and "does not qualify," indicate whether each of the above events would qualify as a transaction and be recognized and recorded in the accounting system on the date indicated.
2. **CONCEPTUAL CONNECTION** For any events that did not qualify as a transaction to be recognized and recorded, explain why it does not qualify.

Exercise 2-39 Transaction Analysis

OBJECTIVE 3

The following events occurred for Parker Company.

a. Performed consulting services for a client in exchange for $3,200 cash.
b. Performed consulting services for a client on account, $1,700.
c. Paid $30,000 cash for land.
d. Purchased office supplies on account, $900.
e. Paid a $2,500 cash dividend to stockholders.
f. Paid $550 on account for supplies purchased in Transaction d.
g. Paid $800 cash for the current month's rent.
h. Collected $1,500 from client in Transaction b.
i. Stockholders invested $20,000 cash in the business.

Required:

1. Analyze the effect of each transaction on the accounting equation. For example, if salaries of $500 were paid, the answer would be "Decrease in stockholders' equity (expense) $500 and decrease in assets (cash) $500."
2. **CONCEPTUAL CONNECTION** For Event d, what accounting principle did you use to determine the amount to be recorded for supplies?

Exercise 2-40 Transaction Analysis

OBJECTIVE 3

Amanda Webb opened a home health care business under the name Home Care Inc. During its first month of operations, the business had the following transactions:

a. Issued common stock to Ms. Webb and other stockholders in exchange for $30,000 cash.
b. Paid $18,500 cash for a parcel of land on which the business will eventually build an office building.
c. Purchased supplies for $2,750 on credit.
d. Used the supplies purchased in Transaction c.
e. Paid rent for the month on office space and equipment, $800 cash.
f. Performed services for clients in exchange for $3,910 cash.
g. Paid salaries for the month, $1,100.
h. Paid $650 cash for advertising in the current month.
i. Paid $1,900 on account for supplies purchased in Transaction c.
j. Performed services for clients on credit in the amount of $1,050.
k. Paid a $600 dividend to stockholders.

Required:

Prepare an analysis of the effects of these transactions on the accounting equation of the business. Use the format below.

(Continued)

Assets	=	Liabilities	+	Stockholders' Equity		
				Contributed Capital	+	Retained Earnings

OBJECTIVE 3

Exercise 2-41 Transaction Analysis and Business Activities

The accountant for Compton Inc. has collected the following information:

a. Compton purchased a tract of land from Jacobsen Real Estate for $875,000 cash.
b. Compton issued 2,000 shares of its common stock to George Micros in exchange for $125,000 cash.
c. Compton purchased a John Deere tractor for $86,000 on credit.
d. Michael Rotunno paid Compton $10,400 cash for services performed. The services had been performed by Compton several months ago for a total price of $12,000 of which Rotunno had previously paid $1,600.
e. Compton paid its monthly payroll by issuing checks totaling $36,250.
f. Compton declared and paid its annual dividend of $5,000 cash.

Required:

1. Prepare an analysis of the effects of these transactions on the accounting equation of the business. Use the format below.

Assets	=	Liabilities	+	Stockholders' Equity		
				Contributed Capital	+	Retained Earnings

2. Indicate whether the transaction is a financing, investing, or operating activity.

OBJECTIVE 3

ILLUSTRATING RELATIONSHIPS

Exercise 2-42 Inferring Transactions from Balance Sheet Changes

Each of the following balance sheet changes is associated with a particular transaction:

a. Cash decreases by $22,000 and land increases by $22,000.
b. Cash decreases by $9,000 and retained earnings decreases by $9,000.
c. Cash increases by $100,000 and common stock increases by $100,000.
d. Cash increases by $15,000 and notes payable increases by $15,000.

Required:

CONCEPTUAL CONNECTION Describe each transaction listed above.

OBJECTIVE 3

Exercise 2-43 Transaction Analysis

Goal Systems, a business consulting firm, engaged in the following transactions:

a. Issued common stock for $75,000 cash.
b. Borrowed $35,000 from a bank.
c. Purchased equipment for $12,000 cash.
d. Prepaid rent on office space for 6 months in the amount of $7,800.
e. Performed consulting services in exchange for $6,300 cash.
f. Performed consulting services on credit in the amount of $18,750.
g. Incurred and paid wage expense of $9,500.
h. Collected $10,200 of the receivable arising from Transaction f.
i. Purchased supplies for $1,800 on credit.
j. Used $1,200 of the supplies purchased in Transaction i.
k. Paid for all of the supplies purchased in Transaction i.

Required:

For each transaction described above, indicate the effects on assets, liabilities, and stockholders' equity using the format below.

Assets	=	Liabilities	+	Stockholders' Equity		
				Contributed Capital	+	Retained Earnings

Exercise 2-44 Transaction Analysis

OBJECTIVE 3

During December, Cynthiana Refrigeration Service engaged in the following transactions:

a. On December 3, Cynthiana sold a 1-year service contract to Cub Foods for $12,000 cash.
b. On December 10, Cynthiana repaired equipment of the A&W Root Beer Drive-In. A&W paid $1,100 in cash for the service call.
c. On December 10, Cynthiana purchased a new Chevy truck for business use. The truck cost $36,500. Cynthiana paid $5,500 down and signed a 1-year note for the balance.
d. Cynthiana received a $3,200 order of repair parts from Carrier Corporation on December 19. Carrier is expected to bill Cynthiana for $3,200 in early January.
e. On December 23, Cynthiana purchased 20 turkeys from Cub Foods for $300 cash. Cynthiana gave the turkeys to its employees as a Christmas gift.

Required:

For each transaction described above, indicate the effects on assets, liabilities, and stockholders' equity using the format below.

Assets	=	Liabilities	+	Stockholders' Equity		
				Contributed Capital	+	Retained Earnings

Exercise 2-45 Inferring Transactions from Balance Sheet Changes

OBJECTIVE 3

ILLUSTRATING RELATIONSHIPS

Each of the balance sheet changes below is associated with a particular transaction:

a. Equipment increases by $5,000 and cash decreases by $5,000.
b. Cash increases by $4,100 and stockholders' equity increases by $4,100.
c. Supplies increases by $400 and accounts payable increases by $400.
d. Supplies decreases by $250 and stockholders' equity decreases by $250.

Required:

CONCEPTUAL CONNECTION Describe each transaction listed above.

Exercise 2-46 Normal Balances and Financial Statements

OBJECTIVE 4

The following accounts are available for Haubstadt Shoe Works:

Accounts Payable
Accounts Receivable
Accumulated Depreciation (Equipment)
Advertising Expense
Cash
Common Stock
Cost of Goods Sold
Depreciation Expense (Equipment)
Equipment
Interest Expense
Inventory
Notes Payable
Retained Earnings
Sales Revenue
Utilities Expense

Required:

Using a table like the one below, indicate whether each account normally has a debit or credit balance and indicate on which of the financial statements (income statement, retained earnings statement, or balance sheet) each account appears.

Account	Debit	Credit	Financial Statement

OBJECTIVE 4

Exercise 2-47 Debit and Credit Effects of Transactions

Lincoln Corporation was involved in the following transactions during the current year:

a. Lincoln borrowed cash from the local bank on a note payable.
b. Lincoln purchased operating assets on credit.
c. Lincoln paid dividends in cash.
d. Lincoln purchased supplies inventory on credit.
e. Lincoln used a portion of the supplies purchased in Transaction d.
f. Lincoln provided services in exchange for cash from the customer.
g. A customer received services from Lincoln on credit.
h. The owners invested cash in the business in exchange for common stock.
i. The payable from Transaction d was paid in full.
j. The receivable from Transaction g was collected in full.
k. Lincoln paid wages in cash.

Required:

Prepare a table like the one shown below and indicate the effect on assets, liabilities, and stockholders' equity. Be sure to enter debits and credits in the appropriate columns for each of the transactions. Transaction a is entered as an example:

Assets	=	Liabilities	+	Stockholders' Equity		
				Contributed Capital	+	Retained Earnings
a. Increase (Debit)		Increase (Credit)				

OBJECTIVE 4

Exercise 2-48 Debit and Credit Effect on Transactions

Jefferson Framers engaged in the following transactions:

a. Purchased land for $35,200 cash.
b. Purchased equipment for $16,400 in exchange for a 1-year, 8% note payable.
c. Purchased office supplies on credit for $1,500 from Office Depot.
d. Paid the $15,000 principal plus $600 interest on a note payable.
e. Paid an account payable in the amount of $3,150.
f. Provided $65,300 of services on credit.
g. Provided $15,400 of services for cash.
h. Collected $32,800 of accounts receivable.
i. Paid $10,300 of wages in cash.
j. Issued common stock for $40,000 cash.

Required:

Using a table like the one below, enter the necessary information for each transaction. Enter the debits before the credits. Transaction a is entered as an example.

Transaction	Account	Increase/Decrease	Debit/Credit	Amount
(a)	Land	Increase	Debit	$35,200
	Cash	Decrease	Credit	$35,200

OBJECTIVE 5

Exercise 2-49 Journalizing Transactions

Kauai Adventures rents and sells surfboards, snorkeling, and scuba equipment. During March, Kauai engaged in the following transactions:

March	2	Received $51,500 cash from customers for rental.
	3	Purchased on credit ten new surfboards (which Kauai classifies as inventory) for $180 each.
	6	Paid wages to employees in the amount of $9,200.
	9	Paid office rent for the month in the amount of $1,000.
	12	Purchased a new Ford truck for $40,800; paid $1,000 down in cash and secured a loan from Princeville Bank for the $39,800 balance.

March 13 Collected a $1,050 account receivable.
16 Paid an account payable in the amount of $950.
23 Borrowed $10,000 on a 6-month, 8% note payable.
27 Paid the monthly telephone bill of $185.
30 Paid a monthly advertising bill of $1,550.

Required:

Prepare a journal entry for each of these transactions.

Exercise 2-50 Journalizing Transactions

OBJECTIVE 5

Remington Communications has been providing cellular phone service for several years. During November and December 2013, the following transactions occurred:

Nov. 2 Remington received $2,400 for November phone service from Enrico Company.
6 Remington purchased $4,750 of supplies from Technology Associates on account.
10 Remington paid $5,250 to its hourly employees for their weekly wages.
15 Remington paid $4,750 to Technology Associates in full settlement of its account payable.
28 Remington paid $2,150 for utilities used during November.
30 Remington received a bill from Monticello Construction for $1,230 for repairs made to Remington's loading dock on November 15. Remington plans to pay the bill in early December.
Dec. 10 Remington paid $1,230 to Monticello Construction to settle the repair bill received on November 30.

Required:

1. Prepare a journal entry for each of these transactions.
2. **CONCEPTUAL CONNECTION** What accounting principle did you apply in recording the November 10 transaction?

Exercise 2-51 Transaction Analysis and Journal Entries

OBJECTIVE 5

Pasta House Inc. was organized in January 2013. During the year, the transactions below occurred:

a. On January 14, Pasta House sold Martin Halter, the firm's founder and sole owner, 10,000 shares of its common stock for $8 per share.
b. On the same day, Bank One loaned Pasta House $45,000 on a 10-year note payable.
c. On February 22, Pasta House purchased a building and the land on which it stands from Frank Jakubek for $34,000 cash and a 5-year, $56,000 note payable. The land and building had appraised values of $30,000 and $60,000, respectively.
d. On March 1, Pasta House signed an $15,000 contract with Cosby Renovations to remodel the inside of the building. Pasta House paid $4,000 down and agreed to pay the remainder when Cosby completed its work.
e. On May 3, Cosby completed its work and submitted a bill to Pasta House for the remaining $11,000.
f. On May 20, Pasta House paid $11,000 to Cosby Renovations.
g. On June 4, Pasta House purchased restaurant supplies from Glidden Supply for $650 cash.

Required:

Prepare a journal entry for each of these transactions.

Exercise 2-52 Accounting Cycle

OBJECTIVE 4 5 6 7

Rosenthal Decorating Inc. is a commercial painting and decorating contractor that began operations in January 2013. The following transactions occurred during the year:

a. On January 15, Rosenthal sold 500 shares of its common stock to William Hensley for $10,000.
b. On January 24, Rosenthal purchased $720 of painting supplies from Westwood Builders' Supply Company on account.
c. On February 20, Rosenthal paid $720 cash to Westwood Builders' Supply Company for the painting supplies purchased on January 24.

(Continued)

d. On April 25, Rosenthal billed Bultman Condominiums $12,500 for painting and decorating services performed in April.
e. On May 12, Rosenthal received $12,500 from Bultman Condominiums for the painting and decorating work billed in April.
f. On June 5, Rosenthal sent Arlington Builders a $9,500 bill for a painting job completed on that day.
g. On June 24, Rosenthal paid wages for work performed during the preceding week in the amount of $6,700.

Required:

1. Prepare a journal entry for each of the transactions.
2. Post the transactions to T-accounts.
3. Prepare a trial balance at June 30, 2013.

OBJECTIVE 7

Exercise 2-53 Preparing a Trial Balance Preparation

The following accounts and account balances are available for Badger Auto Parts at December 31, 2013:

Account	Balance	Account	Balance
Accounts Payable	$ 8,500	Income Taxes Payable	$ 3,600
Accounts Receivable	40,800	Interest Expense	6,650
Accumulated Depreciation (Furniture)	47,300	Interest Payable	1,800
Advertising Expense	29,200	Inventory	60,500
Cash	3,200	Notes Payable (Long-term)	50,000
Common Stock	100,000	Prepaid Rent	15,250
Cost of Goods Sold	184,300	Retained Earnings, 12/31/2012	15,900
Depreciation Expense (Furniture)	10,400	Sales Revenue	264,700
Furniture	128,000	Utilities Expense	9,700
Income Taxes Expense	3,800		

Required:

Prepare a trial balance. Assume that all accounts have normal balances.

OBJECTIVE 7

Exercise 2-54 Effect of Errors on a Trial Balance

The bookkeeper for Riley Inc. made the following errors:

a. A cash purchase of supplies of $348 was recorded as a debit to Supplies for $384 and a credit to Cash of $384.
b. A cash sale of $3,128 was recorded as a debit to Cash of $3,128 and a credit to Sales of $3,182.
c. A purchase of equipment was recorded once in the journal and posted twice to the ledger.
d. Cash paid for salaries of $5,270 was recorded as a debit to Salaries Expense of $5,270 and a credit to Accounts Payable of $5,270.
e. A credit sale of $7,600 was recorded as a credit to Sales Revenue of $7,600; however, the debit posting to Accounts Receivable was omitted.

Required:

Indicate whether or not the trial balance will balance after the error. If the trial balance will not balance, indicate the direction of the misstatement for any effected account (such as Cash will be overstated by $50).

PROBLEM SET A

OBJECTIVE 2 3

Problem 2-55A Events and Transactions

The accountant for Boatsman Products Inc. received the following information:

a. Boatsman sent its customers a new price list. Prices were increased an average of 3% on all items.

b. Boatsman accepted an offer of $150,000 for land that it had purchased 2 years ago for $130,000. Cash and the deed for the property are to be exchanged in 5 days.
c. Boatsman accepted $150,000 cash and gave the purchaser the deed for the property described in Item b.
d. Boatsman's president purchased 600 shares of the firm's common stock from another stockholder. The president paid $15 per share. The former stockholder had purchased the stock from Boatsman for $4 per share.
e. Boatsman leases its delivery trucks from a local dealer. The dealer also performs maintenance on the trucks for Boatsman. Boatsman received a $1,254 bill for maintenance from the dealer.

Required:

1. **CONCEPTUAL CONNECTION** Indicate whether or not each item qualifies as a transaction and should be recorded in the accounting system. Explain your reasoning.
2. **CONCEPTUAL CONNECTION** What accounting concept is illustrated by Item d?

Problem 2-56A Analyzing Transactions

OBJECTIVE 3 7

Luis Madero, after working for several years with a large public accounting firm, decided to open his own accounting service. The business is operated as a corporation under the name Madero Accounting Services. The following captions and amounts summarize Madero's balance sheet at July 31, 2013.

Assets					=	Liabilities			+	Equity		
Cash	+	Accounts Receivable	+	Supplies	=	Accounts Payable	+	Notes Payable	+	Common Stock	+	Retained Earnings
8,000		15,900		4,100		2,500		4,000		12,000		9,500

The following events occurred during August 2013.

a. Issued common stock to Ms. Garriz in exchange for $15,000 cash.
b. Paid $850 for first month's rent on office space.
c. Purchased supplies of $2,250 on credit.
d. Borrowed $8,000 from the bank.
e. Paid $1,080 on account for supplies purchased earlier on credit.
f. Paid secretary's salary for August of $2,150.
g. Performed accounting services for clients who paid cash upon completion of the service in the total amount of $4,700.
h. Used $3,180 of the supplies on hand.
i. Performed accounting services for clients on credit in the total amount of $1,920.
j. Purchased $500 in supplies for cash.
k. Collected $1,290 cash from clients for whom services were performed on credit.
l. Paid $1,000 dividend to stockholders.

Required:

1. Record the effects of the transactions listed above on the accounting equation. Use the format given in the problem, starting with the totals at July 31, 2013.
2. Prepare the trial balance at August 31, 2013.

Problem 2-57A Inferring Transactions from T-Accounts

OBJECTIVE 3 4 7

ILLUSTRATING RELATIONSHIPS

The following T-accounts summarize the operations of Chen Construction Company for July 2013.

(Continued)

Assets

Cash

Date	Debit	Credit	Date
7/1	200		
7/2	1,000	150	7/5
7/7	2,500	700	7/9
7/11	150	750	7/14

Accounts Receivable

Date	Debit	Credit	Date
7/1	1,400	150	7/11

Supplies

Date	Debit	Credit	Date
7/1	750		
7/4	250		

Land

Date	Debit	Credit	Date
7/1	3,000		
7/9	700		

Liabilities

Accounts Payable

Date	Debit	Credit	Date
		1,100	7/1
7/5	150	250	7/4

Stockholders' Equity

Common Stock

Date	Debit	Credit	Date
		4,000	7/1
		1,000	7/2

Retained Earnings

Date	Debit	Credit	Date
		250	7/1
7/14	750	2,500	7/7

Required:

1. **CONCEPTUAL CONNECTION** Assuming that only one transaction occurred on each day (beginning on July 2) and that no dividends were paid, describe the transactions that most likely took place.
2. Prepare a trial balance at July 31, 2013.

OBJECTIVE 4

Problem 2-58A Debit and Credit Procedures

A list of accounts for Montgomery Inc. appears below.

Accounts Payable
Accounts Receivable
Accumulated Depreciation
Cash
Common Stock
Depreciation Expense
Equipment
Income Taxes Expense
Interest Expense
Land
Notes Payable
Prepaid Rent
Retained Earnings
Salaries Expense
Service Revenue
Supplies

Required:

Complete the table below for these accounts. The information for the first account has been entered as an example.

Account	Type of Account	Normal Balance	Increase	Decrease
Accounts Payable	Liability	Credit	Credit	Debit

OBJECTIVE 5

Problem 2-59A Journalizing Transactions

Monroe Company rents and sells electronic equipment. During September 2013, Monroe engaged in the transactions described below.

Sept. 5	Purchased a Chevrolet truck for $38,900 cash.
8	Purchased inventory for $4,200 on account.
10	Purchased $1,250 of office supplies on credit.
11	Rented sound equipment to a traveling stage play for $13,600. The producer of the play paid for the service at the time it was provided.

Sept. 12	Rented sound equipment and lights to a local student organization for a school dance for $2,400. The student organization will pay for services within 30 days.
18	Paid employee wages of $4,750 that have been earned during September.
22	Collected the receivable from the September 12 transaction.
23	Borrowed $20,000 cash from a bank on a 3-year note payable.
28	Issued common stock to new stockholders for $35,000.
30	Paid a $3,250 cash dividend to stockholders.

Required:

Prepare a journal entry for each transaction.

Problem 2-60A Journalizing and Posting Transactions

OBJECTIVE 5 6

Cincinnati Painting Service Inc. specializes in painting houses. During June, its first month of operations, Cincinnati Painting engaged in the following transactions:

June 1	Issued common stock for $25,000.
3	Purchased painting supplies from River City Supply for $1,675 on credit.
8	Purchased a used truck from Hamilton Used Car Sales for $13,700, paying $1,500 down and agreeing to pay the balance in 6 months.
14	Paid $4,230 to hourly employees for work performed in June.
22	Billed various customers a total of $10,340 for June painting jobs.
26	Received $6,100 cash from James Eaton for a house painting job completed and previously billed.
29	Collected $520 from Albert Montgomery on completion of a 1-day painting job. This amount is not included in the June 22 bills.

Required:

1. Prepare a journal entry for each transaction.
2. Post the journal entries to the appropriate T-accounts.

Problem 2-61A The Accounting Cycle

OBJECTIVE 2 3 4 5 6 7

Karleen's Catering Service provides catered meals to individuals and businesses. Karleen's purchases its food ready to serve from Mel's Restaurant. In order to prepare a realistic trial balance, the events described below are aggregations of many individual events during 2013.

a. Common stock was issued for $22,000.
b. During the year, Karleen's paid office rent of $13,500.
c. Utilities expenses incurred and paid were $5,320.
d. Wages of $58,800 were earned by employees and paid during the year.
e. During the year, Karleen's provided catering services:

On credit	$128,200
For cash	18,650

f. Karleen's paid $59,110 for supplies purchased and used during the year.
g. Karleen's paid dividends in the amount of $3,500.
h. Karleen's collected accounts receivable in the amount of $109,400.

Required:

1. Analyze the events for their effect on the accounting equation.
2. Prepare journal entries. (*Note:* Ignore the date because these events are aggregations of individual events.)
3. Post the journal entries to the appropriate T-accounts.
4. Prepare a trial balance at December 31, 2013. Assume that all beginning account balances at January 1, 2013, are zero.

Problem 2-62A Comprehensive Problem

OBJECTIVE 2 3 4 5 6 7

Western Sound Studios records and masters audio tapes of popular artists in live concerts. The performers use the tapes to prepare "live" albums, CDs, and MP3s. The following account balances were available at the beginning of 2013:

(Continued)

Accounts Payable	$ 11,900
Accounts Receivable	384,000
Cash	16,300
Common Stock	165,000
Insurance Payable	1,000
Interest Payable	11,200
Notes Payable (Long-term)	100,000
Rent Payable (Building)	10,000
Retained Earnings, 12/31/2012	101,200

During 2013, the following transactions occurred (the events described below are aggregations of many individual events):

a. Taping services in the amount of $994,000 were billed.
b. The accounts receivable at the beginning of the year were collected.
c. In addition, cash for $983,000 of the services billed in Transaction a was collected.
d. The rent payable for the building was paid. In addition, $48,000 of building rental costs was paid in cash. There was no rent payable or prepaid rent at year-end.
e. The insurance payable on January 1 was paid. In addition, $4,000 of insurance costs was paid in cash. There was no insurance payable or prepaid insurance at year-end.
f. Utilities expense of $56,000 was incurred and paid in 2013.
g. Salaries expense for the year was $702,000. All $702,000 was paid in 2013.
h. The interest payable at January 1 was paid. During the year, an additional $11,000 of interest was paid. At year-end no interest was payable.
i. Income taxes for 2013 in the amount of $19,700 were incurred and paid.

Required:

1. Establish a T-account for the accounts listed above and enter the beginning balances. Use a chart of accounts to order the T-accounts.
2. Analyze each transaction. Journalize as appropriate. (*Note:* Ignore the date because these events are aggregations of individual events.)
3. Post your journal entries to the T-accounts. Add additional T-accounts when needed.
4. Use the ending balances in the T-accounts to prepare a trial balance.

PROBLEM SET B

OBJECTIVE 2 3

Problem 2-55B Events and Transactions

The following list contains events that occurred during January 2013 at the local Ford dealer, Malcom Motors:

a. California Central University (CCU) signed a contract to purchase a fleet of Ford Crown Victoria vehicles from Malcom Motors at a total price of $200,000, payable to Malcom in two equal amounts on August 1, 2013, and September 1, 2013. The cars will be delivered to CCU during August 2013.
b. The principal stockholder in Malcom Motors sold 10% of her stock in the company to John Lewis, the president of Malcom Motors, in exchange for $100,000 in cash.
c. Malcom Motors issued new stock to John Lewis in exchange for $50,000 in cash.
d. Malcom Motors owns the building it occupies; the company occupied the building during the entire month of January.
e. Malcom Motors owns land used for the storage of cars awaiting sale; the land was used by the company during the entire month of January.
f. Malcom Motors paid its lawyer $1,000 for services rendered in connection with the purchase agreement signed with California Central University.
g. Maintenance Management Company performed cleaning services for Malcom Motors during January under a contract that does not require payment for those services until March 1, 2013.

Required:

1. **CONCEPTUAL CONNECTION** Indicate whether each item qualifies as a transaction and should be recorded in the accounting system. Explain your reasoning.

2. **CONCEPTUAL CONNECTION** What concept is illustrated by Event b?

Problem 2-56B Analyzing Transactions

OBJECTIVE 3 7

Several years ago, Mary Emerson founded Emerson Consulting Inc., a consulting business specializing in financial planning for young professionals. The following captions and amounts summarize Emerson Consulting's balance sheet at December 31, 2012, the beginning of the current year:

Assets					=	Liabilities			+	Equity		
Cash	+	Accounts Receivable	+	Supplies	=	Accounts Payable	+	Notes Payable	+	Common Stock	+	Retained Earnings
3,000		6,600		4,800		500		1,000		10,000		2,900

During January 2013, the following transactions occurred:

a. Issued common stock to a new stockholder in exchange for $12,000 cash.
b. Performed advisory services for a client for $3,850 and received the full amount in cash.
c. Received $925 on account from a client for whom services had been performed on credit.
d. Purchased supplies for $1,140 on credit.
e. Paid $875 on accounts payable.
f. Performed advisory services for $2,980 on credit.
g. Paid cash of $1,350 for secretarial services during January.
h. Paid cash of $800 for January's office rent.
i. Paid utilities used in January 2013 in the amount of $1,340.
j. Paid a dividend of $500.

Required:

1. Record the effects of the transactions listed above on the accounting equation for the business. Use the format given in the problem, starting with the totals at December 31, 2012.
2. Prepare the trial balance at January 31, 2013.

Problem 2-57B Inferring Transactions from T-Accounts

OBJECTIVE 3 4 7

ILLUSTRATING RELATIONSHIPS

The following T-accounts summarize the operations of Brilliant Minds Inc., a tutoring service, for April 2013.

Assets

Cash

Date	Debit	Credit	Date
4/1	500	700	4/8
4/3	2,000	325	4/9
4/18	1,500	150	4/15
4/24	375		

Accounts Receivable

Date	Debit	Credit	Date
4/1	700	375	4/24

Supplies

Date	Debit	Credit	Date
4/1	900	140	4/11
4/15	150		

Equipment

Date	Debit	Credit	Date
4/1	1,200		
4/8	700		

Liabilities

Accounts Payable

Date	Debit	Credit	Date
4/9	325	625	4/1

Notes Payable

Date	Debit	Credit	Date
		2,000	4/3

Stockholders' Equity

Common Stock

Date	Debit	Credit	Date
		2,000	4/1

Retained Earnings

Date	Debit	Credit	Date
4/11	140	675	4/1
		1,500	4/18

(Continued)

Required:

1. **CONCEPTUAL CONNECTION** Assuming that only one transaction occurred on each day (beginning on April 3) and that no dividends were paid, describe the transaction that most likely took place.
2. Prepare a trial balance at April 30, 2013.

OBJECTIVE 3

Problem 2-58B Debit and Credit Procedures

A list of accounts for Montgomery Inc. appears below.

Accounts Payable
Accounts Receivable
Bonds Payable
Building
Cash
Common Stock
Copyright
Cost of Goods Sold
Depreciation Expense
Income Taxes Expense
Income Taxes Payable
Insurance Expense
Interest Expense
Inventory
Investments
Retained Earnings
Sales Revenue
Unearned Revenue
Utilities Expense

Required:

Complete the table below for these accounts. The information for the first account has been entered as an example.

Account	Type of Account	Normal Balance	Increase	Decrease
Accounts Payable	Liability	Credit	Credit	Debit

OBJECTIVE 5

Problem 2-59B Journalizing Transactions

Monilast Chemicals engaged in the following transactions during December 2013:

Dec.	2	Paid rent on office furniture, $1,200.
	3	Borrowed $25,000 on a 9-month, 8% note.
	7	Provided services on credit, $42,600.
	10	Purchased supplies on credit, $2,850.
	13	Collected accounts receivable, $20,150.
	19	Issued common stock, $50,000.
	22	Paid employee wages for December, $13,825.
	23	Paid accounts payable, $1,280.
	25	Provided services for cash, $13,500.
	30	Paid utility bills for December, $1,975.

Required:

Prepare a journal entry for each transaction.

OBJECTIVE 5 6

Problem 2-60B Journalizing and Posting Transactions

Findlay Testing Inc. provides water testing and maintenance services for owners of hot tubs and swimming pools. During September the following transactions occurred:

Sept.	1	Issued common stock for $20,000.
	2	Purchased chemical supplies for $1,880 cash.
	5	Paid office rent for October, November, and December; the rent is $800 per month.
	8	Purchased $1,290 of advertising for September on account.
	13	Billed the city of Bellefontaine $2,100 for testing the water in the city's outdoor pools during September.
	18	Received $8,250 from Alexander Blanchard upon completion of overhaul of his swimming pool water circulation system. Since the job was completed and collected for on the same day, no bill was sent to Blanchard.

Sept.	25	Received $835 from the city of Bellefontaine for water testing that was previously billed.
	30	Recorded and paid September salaries of $3,970.

Required:

1. Prepare a journal entry for each transaction.
2. Post the journal entries to the appropriate T-accounts.

Problem 2-61B The Accounting Cycle

OBJECTIVE 2 3 4 5 6 7

Sweetwater Temporary Clerical Help Service opened for business in June 2013. From the opening until the end of the year, Sweetwater engaged in the activities described below. So that a realistic trial balance can be prepared, the events described below are aggregations of many individual events.

a. Sold 10,000 shares of common stock for $4.50 per share.
b. Purchased office equipment from FurnitureMax Inc. for $18,710 cash.
c. Received $112,880 from clients for services provided.
d. Paid wages of $87,300.
e. Borrowed $20,000 from the Bank of America on a 3-year note payable.
f. Paid office rent of $10,200.
g. Purchased office supplies on credit for $2,120 from Office Supply Inc.
h. Paid $1,200 toward the payable established in Transaction g.
i. Paid utility charges incurred during the year of $3,250.

Required:

1. Analyze the events for their effect on the accounting equation.
2. Prepare journal entries. (*Note:* Ignore the date because these events are aggregations of individual events.)
3. Post the journal entries to T-accounts.
4. Prepare a trial balance at December 31, 2013.

Problem 2-62B Comprehensive Problem

OBJECTIVE 2 3 4 5 6 7

Mulberry Services sells electronic data processing services to firms too small to own their own computing equipment. Mulberry had the following accounts and account balances as of January 1, 2013:

Accounts Payable	$ 14,000
Accounts Receivable	130,000
Cash	6,000
Common Stock	114,000
Interest Payable	8,000
Notes Payable (Long-term)	80,000
Prepaid Rent (Short-term)	96,000
Retained Earnings, 12/31/2012	16,000

During 2013, the following transactions occurred (the events described below are aggregations of many individual events):

a. During 2013, Mulberry sold $690,000 of computing services, all on credit.
b. Mulberry collected $570,000 from the credit sales in Transaction a and an additional $129,000 from the accounts receivable outstanding at the beginning of the year.
c. Mulberry paid the interest payable of $8,000.
d. Wages of $379,000 were paid in cash.
e. Repairs and maintenance of $9,000 were incurred and paid.
f. The prepaid rent at the beginning of the year was used in 2013. In addition, $28,000 of computer rental costs were incurred and paid. There is no prepaid rent or rent payable at year-end.
g. Mulberry purchased computer paper for $13,000 cash in late December. None of the paper was used by year-end.
h. Advertising expense of $26,000 was incurred and paid.
i. Income tax of $10,300 was incurred and paid in 2013.
j. Interest of $5,000 was paid on the long-term loan.

(Continued)

Required:

1. Establish a ledger for the accounts listed above and enter the beginning balances. Use a chart of accounts to order the ledger accounts.
2. Analyze each transaction. Journalize as appropriate. (*Note:* Ignore the date because these events are aggregations of individual events.)
3. Post your journal entries to T-accounts. Add additional T-accounts when needed.
4. Use the ending balances in the T-accounts to prepare a trial balance.

CASES

Case 2-63 Analysis of the Accounting Cycle

Susan Eel wants to sell you her wholesale fish store. She shows you a balance sheet with total assets of $150,000 and total liabilities of $20,000. According to the income statement, last year's net income was $40,000.

When examining the accounting records, you notice that several accounts receivable in the $10,000 to $15,000 range are not supported by source documents. You also notice that there is no source documentation to support the $30,000 balance in the building account and the $10,000 balance in the equipment account. Susan tells you that she gave the building and refrigeration equipment to the business in exchange for stock. She also says that she has not had time to set up and monitor any paperwork for accounts receivable or accounts payable.

Required:

1. What requirements for transaction recognition appear to have been ignored when the accounts receivable, building, and equipment were recorded?
2. What would be the effect on the financial statements if the values appearing in the balance sheet for accounts receivable, building, and equipment were overstated? What would be the effect if the accounts payable were understated?
3. Assuming that you would like to purchase the company, what would you do to establish a reasonable purchase price?

Case 2-64 Analysis of the Effects of Current Asset and Current Liability Changes on Cash Flows

ILLUSTRATING RELATIONSHIPS

You have the following data for Cable Company's accounts receivable and accounts payable for 2013:

Accounts receivable, 1/1/2013	$ 6,325
2013 Sales on credit	93,680
Accounts receivable, 12/31/2013	7,950
Wages payable, 1/1/2013	4,960
2013 Wage expense	49,510
Wages payable, 12/31/2013	3,625

Required:

1. **CONCEPTUAL CONNECTION** How much cash did Cable collect from customers during 2013?
2. How would you classify cash collected from customers on the statement of cash flows?
3. How much cash did Cable pay for wages during 2013?
4. How would you classify the cash paid for wages on the statement of cash flows?

Case 2-65 Ethical Issues

Kathryn Goldsmith is the chief accountant for Clean Sweep, a national carpet-cleaning service with a December fiscal year-end. As Kathryn was preparing the 2013 financial statements for Clean Sweep, she noticed several odd transactions in the general ledger for December. For example, rent for January 2014, which was paid in December 2013, was recorded by debiting rent expense instead of prepaid rent. In another transaction, Kathryn noticed that the use of supplies was recorded with a debit to insurance expense instead of supplies expense. Upon further investigation, Kathryn discovered that the December ledger contained numerous such mistakes. Even with the mistakes, the trial balance still balanced.

Kathryn traced all of the mistakes back to a recently hired bookkeeper, Ben Goldsmith, Kathryn's son. Kathryn had hired Ben to help out in the accounting department over Christmas break so that he could earn some extra money for school. After discussing the situation with Ben, Kathryn determined that Ben's mistakes were all unintentional.

Required:

1. What ethical issues are involved?
2. What are Kathryn's alternatives? Which would be the most ethical alternative to choose?

Case 2-66 Research and Analysis Using the Annual Report

Obtain General Electric's 2011 annual report either through the "Investor Relations" portion of its website (do a web search for GE investor relations) or go to www.sec.gov and click "Search for Company Filings" under "Filings and Forms."

Required:

1. Determine the amounts in the accounting equation for the most recent year. Does it balance?
2. What is the normal balance for the following accounts?
   a. Current Receivables
   b. Short-Term Borrowings
   c. Sales of Services
   d. Property, Plant, and Equipment—Net
   e. Cost of Goods Sold
   f. Inventories
   g. Retained Earnings
3. Identify the additional account that is most likely involved when:
   a. Accounts Payable is decreased.
   b. Accounts Receivables is increased.
   c. Common Stock is increased.
   d. Wages Payable is increased.

Case 2-67 Comparative Analysis: Under Armour, Inc., versus VF Corporation

ILLUSTRATING RELATIONSHIPS

Refer to the financial statements of Under Armour, Inc., and VF Corporation that are supplied with this text.

Required:

1. Determine the amounts in the accounting equation for the year ending December 31, 2011, for each company. Does the accounting equation balance?
2. Set up a T-account for Under Armour's and VF's accounts receivable account and include the beginning and ending balances. Complete the T-account to reflect the sales and cash collections for the year for each company. Assume all sales are on account.
3. Prepare the journal entry to record the following two events for Under Armour and VF. For simplicity, assume the event was recorded in a single journal entry.
   a. What journal entry is necessary to record Under Armour's net sales for the year ending December 31, 2011? Assume that all sales were made on account.
   b. What journal entry is necessary to record Under Armour's cash collections from customers during the year ending December 31, 2011?

Case 2-68 Accounting for Partially Completed Events: a Prelude to Chapter 3

Ehrlich Smith, the owner of The Shoe Box, has asked you to help him understand the proper way to account for certain accounting items as he prepares his 2013 financial statements. Smith has provided the following information and observations:

(Continued)

a. A 3-year fire insurance policy was purchased on January 1, 2013, for $2,400. Smith believes that a part of the cost of the insurance policy should be allocated to each period that benefits from its coverage.

b. The store building was purchased for $80,000 in January 2005. Smith expected then (as he does now) that the building will be serviceable as a shoe store for 20 years from the date of purchase. In 2005, Smith estimated that he could sell the property for $6,000 at the end of its serviceable life. He feels that each period should bear some portion of the cost of this long-lived asset that is slowly being consumed.

c. The Shoe Box borrowed $20,000 on a 1-year, 8% note that is due on September 1 next year. Smith notes that $21,600 cash will be required to repay the note at maturity. The $1,600 difference is, he feels, a cost of using the loaned funds and should be spread over the periods that benefit from the use of the loan funds.

Required:

1. Explain what Smith is trying to accomplish with the three items. Are his objectives supported by the concepts that underlie accounting?
2. Describe how each of the three items should be reflected in the 2013 income statement and the December 31, 2013 balance sheet to accomplish Smith's objectives.

Case 2-69 CONTINUING PROBLEM: FRONT ROW ENTERTAINMENT

After much consideration, Cam and Anna decide to organize their company as a corporation. On January 1, 2013, Front Row Entertainment Inc. begins operations. Due to Cam's family connections in the entertainment industry, Cam assumes the major responsibility for signing artists to a promotion contract. Meanwhile, Anna assumes the financial accounting and reporting responsibilities. The following business activities occurred during January:

Jan. 1 Cam and Anna invest $8,000 each in the company in exchange for common stock.

1 The company obtains a $25,000 loan from a local bank. Front Row Entertainment agreed to pay annual interest of 9% each January 1, starting in 2014. It will repay the amount borrowed in 5 years.

1 The company paid $1,200 in legal fees associated with incorporation.

1 Office equipment was purchased with $7,000 in cash.

1 The company pays $800 to rent office space for January.

3 A 1-year insurance policy was purchased for $3,600.

3 Office supplies of $2,500 were purchased from Equipment Supply Services. Equipment Supply Services agreed to accept $1,000 in 15 days with the remainder due in 30 days.

5 The company signs Charm City, a local band with a growing cult following, to a four-city tour that starts on February 15.

8 Venues for all four Charm City concerts were reserved by paying $10,000 cash.

12 Advertising costs of $4,500 were paid to promote the concert tour.

18 Paid $1,000 to Equipment Supply Services for office supplies purchased on January 3.

25 To aid in the promotion of the upcoming tour, Front Row Entertainment arranged for Charm City to perform a 20-minute set at a local festival. Front Row Entertainment received $1,000 for Charm City's appearance. Of this total amount, $400 was received immediately with the remainder due in 15 days. The festival took place on January 25.

25 Paid Charm City $800 for performing at the festival. *Note:* Front Row Entertainment records the fees paid to the artist in an operating expense account called Artist Fee Expense.

28 Due to the success of the marketing efforts, Front Row Entertainment received $3,800 in advance ticket sales for the upcoming tour.

30 The company collected $200 of the amount due from the January 25 festival.

30 Paid salaries of $1,200 each to Cam and Anna for the month of January.

Required:

1. Analyze and journalize the January transactions.
2. Post the transactions to the general ledger.
3. Prepare a trial balance at January 31, 2013.

TYPICAL CHART OF ACCOUNTS

ASSETS

Accounts Receivable
Accumulated Depletion
Accumulated Depreciation
Allowance for Doubtful Accounts
Allowance to Adjust Available-for-Sale Securities to Market
Allowance to Adjust Trading Securities to Market
Buildings
Cash
Copyright
Equipment
Finished Goods Inventory
Franchise
Furniture
Goodwill
Interest Receivable
Inventory
Investments
Investments—Available-for-Sale Securities
Investments—Equity Method
Investments—Trading Securities
Land
Leasehold Improvements
Natural Resources
Notes Receivable
Other Assets
Patent
Petty Cash
Prepaid Advertising
Prepaid Insurance
Prepaid Rent
Prepaid Repairs & Maintenance
Prepaid Security Services
Raw Materials Inventory
Rent Receivable
Supplies
Tax Refund Receivable
Trademark
Trucks
Work-in-Process Inventory

LIABILITIES

Accounts Payable
Bonds Payable
Capital Lease Liability
Charitable Contributions
Commissions Payable
Discount on Bonds Payable
Discount on Notes Payable
Dividends Payable
Excise Taxes Payable
Income Taxes Payable
Interest Payable
Lawsuit Payable
Lease Liability
Leased Assets
Medicare Taxes Payable
Notes Payable
Premium on Bonds Payable
Premium on Notes Payable
Property Taxes Payable
Rent Payable
Repair & Maintenance Payable
Royalties Payable
Salaries Payable
Sales Taxes Payable
Social Security Taxes Payable
Unearned Rent Revenue
Unearned Sales Revenue
Unearned Service Revenue
Unemployment Taxes Payable
Union Dues Payable
Utilities Payable
Wages Payable
Warranty Liability

STOCKHOLDERS' EQUITY

Accumulated Other Comprehensive Income
Additional Paid-In Capital—Common Stock
Additional Paid-In Capital—Preferred Stock
Additional Paid-In Capital—Treasury Stock
Common Stock
Preferred Stock
Retained Earnings
Treasury Stock
Unrealized Gain (Loss) on Available-for-Sale Securities

EQUITY-RELATED ACCOUNTS

Dividends
Income Summary

REVENUES/GAINS

Dividend Income
Interest Income
Investment Income—Equity Method
Rent Revenue
Sales Discounts
Sales Returns and Allowances
Sales Revenue
Service Revenue

Gain on Disposal of Property, Plant, & Equipment
Gain on Sale of Intangibles
Gain on Sale of Investments
Gain on Settlement of Lawsuit
Unrealized Gain (Loss) on Trading Securities

EXPENSES/LOSSES

Advertising Expense
Amortization Expense
Artist Fee Expense
Bad Debt Expense
Bank Service Charge Expense
Cash Over and Short
Commissions Expense
Cost of Goods Sold
Delivery Expense
Depreciation Expense
Income Taxes Expense
Insurance Expense
Interest Expense
Legal Expense
Medicare Taxes Expense
Miscellaneous Expense
Organizational Costs
Other Expense
Postage Expense
Property Taxes Expense
Purchase Allowances
Purchase Discounts
Purchase Returns
Purchases
Rent Expense
Repairs & Maintenance Expense
Research and Development Expense
Royalties Expense
Salaries Expense
Security Services Expense
Service Charge Expense
Social Security Taxes Expense
Supplies Expense
Transportation-In
Unemployment Taxes Expense
Utilities Expense
Wages Expense
Warranty Expense

Loss from Impairment
Loss on Disposal of Property, Plant, & Equipment
Loss on Sale of Intangibles
Loss on Sale of Investments

Note:

The Chart of Accounts for this edition of *Cornerstones of Financial Accounting* has been simplified and standardized throughout all hypothetical in-chapter examples and end-of-chapter assignments in order to strengthen the pedagogical structure of the book. Account titles for real company financial statements will vary. Common alternate account titles are given in the textbook where the account is introduced, as appropriate, and real financial statement excerpts are included to help familiarize readers with alternate account titles.

When additional information is needed for an account title, it will be shown in parenthesis after the title [e.g., Accumulated Depreciation (Equipment), Excise Taxes Payable (State), Social Security Taxes Payable (Employer), etc.]

This Chart of Accounts is listed alphabetically by category for ease of reference. However, accounts in the textbook and in real financial statements are listed in order of liquidity.

3

Accrual Accounting

© Pixelfabrik/Alamy

© Leesniderp.../Dreamstime.com

After studying Chapter 3, you should be able to:

1. Explain the difference between cash-basis and accrual-basis accounting.
2. Explain how the time-period assumption, revenue recognition, and expense recognition (or matching) principles affect the determination of income.
3. Identify the kinds of transactions that may require adjustments at the end of an accounting period.
4. Prepare adjusting entries for accruals and deferrals.
5. Prepare financial statements from an adjusted trial balance.
6. Explain why and how companies prepare closing entries.
7. Understand the steps in the accounting cycle.
8. *(Appendix 3A)* Understand how to use a worksheet to prepare financial statements.

EXPERIENCE FINANCIAL ACCOUNTING

with FedEx®

FedEx began operations in 1973 with 14 jets that connected 25 U.S. cities. Some employees even used their own cars to deliver packages. As a pioneer of the hub and spoke model for overnight package delivery, FedEx is now the world's largest express transportation company with operations in over 220 countries. With more than 290,000 "team members," 688 aircraft, and 142,000 vehicles and trailers, FedEx has the ability to "absolutely, positively" get a package delivered overnight.

The end of the fiscal year, or accounting period, is a busy time as companies like FedEx make adjustments to the accounting information. Adjustments are necessary because a company's business activities often occur over several accounting periods. In its 2011 annual report, an excerpt of which is shown in Exhibit 3.1, FedEx's financial statements include many expenses that would not have been recognized without adjustments.

This sample of expenses, which doesn't include all the adjustments made, represents almost 14% of the total operating expenses that FedEx reported on its 2011 income statement. When FedEx recognized these expenses (except for depreciation and amortization), it also recorded a liability for them. These liabilities represented 65% of FedEx's current liabilities. The adjustment to recognize depreciation and amortization expense resulted in a decrease in assets of $1.973 million. Clearly, the failure to adjust for these expenses would significantly affect FedEx's financial statements.

EXHIBIT 3.1

Excerpt from FedEx's Financial Statements

FedEx Corporation
Consolidated Income Statement (partial)
For the Year Ended May 31, 2011

(in millions)	
Revenues	$ 39,304
Operating expenses	(36,926)
Other income (expense)	(113)
Income before income taxes	$ 2,265
Income taxes	(813)
Net income	$ 1,452

Sample of expenses resulting from adjustment (in millions):	
Salaries	$ 256
Employee benefits and compensated absences	1,012
Insurance	696
Taxes other than income taxes	357
Depreciation and amortization	1,973
Other	841
Total (14% of operating expenses)	$5,135

Source: FedEx 2011 10-K.

OBJECTIVE 1

Explain the difference between cash-basis and accrual-basis accounting.

COMPLETING THE ACCOUNTING CYCLE

In the previous chapter, we examined how companies use the double-entry accounting system to record business activities that occur during the accounting period. However, accountants also make numerous adjustments at the end of accounting periods for business activities that occur over several accounting periods—activities like performing services for customers, renting office space, and using equipment. As shown with **FedEx**, these adjustments can be significant.

Why are so many business activities recognized in the accounts through adjustments rather than through the normal journal entry process described in Chapter 2? The illustrations used in Chapter 2 excluded activities that were still underway at the end of the accounting period. However, the recognition of business activities in financial accounting uses the accrual basis of accounting. Accrual accounting requires that any incomplete activities be recognized in the financial statements. This often requires estimates and judgments about the timing of revenue and expense recognition. The result is that accountants must adjust the accounts to properly reflect these partially completed business activities.

In this chapter, we will review the concepts that form the basis for adjustments and then complete the accounting cycle that was introduced in Chapter 2 by exploring the preparation and effects of adjusting journal entries, preparing financial statements from the adjusted accounts, and closing the accounts in order to prepare for the next accounting period. We will address the following questions:

- What is the difference between the cash basis and the accrual basis of accounting?
- What is the purpose of adjusting entries?
- What types of transactions require adjustment, and how are the adjustments recorded in the accounting system?
- Which accounts are closed at the end of the period, and why is this necessary?

concept Q&A

Cash-basis accounting seems straightforward. Why complicate matters by introducing accrual accounting?

Answer:

The objective of financial reporting is to provide information that is useful in making business and economic decisions. Most of these decisions involve predicting a company's future cash flows. The use of accrual accounting through the application of the revenue recognition and expense recognition (or matching) principles links income recognition to the principal activity of the company, selling goods and services. Therefore, accrual accounting provides a better estimate of future cash flows than cash-basis accounting.

Accrual versus Cash Basis of Accounting

If you were asked what your net income (revenues minus expenses) for the month was, what would you do? Most likely, you would go online and look at your bank activity for the month. You would then list the total of the deposits as revenue and the total of the withdrawals as expenses. The difference would be your net income. This method of accounting is called **cash-basis accounting**. Under cash-basis accounting, revenue is recorded when cash is received, regardless of when it is actually earned. Similarly, an expense is recorded when cash is paid, regardless of when it is actually incurred. Therefore, cash-basis accounting does not link recognition of revenues and expenses to the actual business activity but rather the exchange of cash. In addition, by recording only the cash effect of transactions, cash-basis financial statements may not reflect all of the assets and liabilities of a company at a particular date. For this reason, most companies do not use cash-basis accounting.

Accrual-basis accounting (also called *accrual accounting*) is an alternative to cash-basis accounting that is required by generally accepted accounting principles. Under accrual accounting, transactions are recorded when they occur. Accrual accounting is superior to cash-basis because it links income measurement to selling, the principle activity of the company. That is, revenue is recognized as it is earned and expenses are recognized when they are incurred. In contrast to cash-basis accounting, accrual accounting is a more complex system that records both *cash and noncash* transactions.

OBJECTIVE 2

Explain how the time-period assumption, revenue recognition, and expense recognition (or matching) principles affect the determination of income.

KEY ELEMENTS OF ACCRUAL ACCOUNTING

As shown in Exhibit 3.2, an accrual accounting system rests on three elements of the conceptual framework that were introduced in Chapter 2—the time-period assumption, the revenue recognition principle, and the expense recognition (or matching) principle.

EXHIBIT 3.2

Key Elements of Accrual Accounting

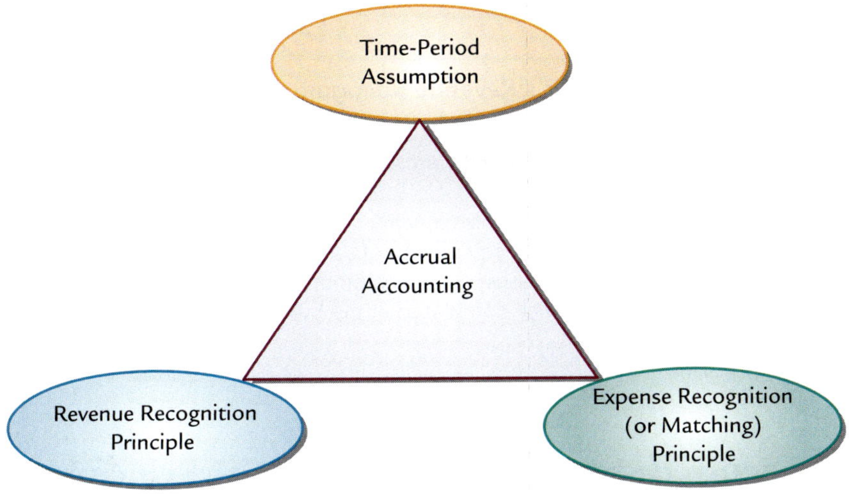

Time-Period Assumption

Investors, creditors, and other financial statement users demand timely information from companies. For that reason, companies report their financial results for specific periods of time—a month, a quarter, or a year. The **time-period assumption** allows companies to artificially divide their operations into time periods so they can satisfy users' demands for information.

Companies frequently engage in continuing activities that affect more than one time period. For example, FedEx often receives cash from a company to deliver products in one time period, although the actual delivery does not occur until a different time period. In addition, the aircraft and vehicles used by FedEx are purchased at a single point in time but are used over many years. To properly record the use of these aircraft and the providing of its service, accrual accounting requires that FedEx assign the revenue and expenses to the proper time period. This is quite often a difficult task and is guided by the revenue recognition and expense recognition (or matching) principles.

The Revenue Recognition Principle

IFRS

While revenue recognition concepts under IFRS are similar to U.S. GAAP, U.S. GAAP contains much more specific rules and guidance.

The **revenue recognition principle** determines when revenue is recorded and reported. Under this principle, revenue is recognized, or recorded, in the period in which both of the following conditions are met:

- The revenue has been earned.
- The collection of cash is reasonably assured.

These requirements are usually met when goods have been delivered to a customer or when services have been performed for a customer. At this point, the risks and rewards of ownership usually have been transferred from the seller to the buyer.[1] **Notice that revenue is recorded when these two conditions are met, regardless of when cash is received.**

To illustrate the revenue recognition principle, assume that on March 31, FedEx picks up a computer from Apple's distribution center and receives a cash payment of $30 to ship the computer to a customer. FedEx delivers the computer on April 2. Even though cash was received on March 31, FedEx will recognize the $30 of revenue on April 2, the date the computer is delivered to the customer. Notice that revenue is not recognized until it is earned by

[1] The Securities and Exchange Commission expanded upon this principle and stated that the revenue recognition criteria are normally met when (1) delivery has occurred or services have been rendered, (2) persuasive evidence of an arrangement exists, (3) the selling price is fixed or determinable, and (4) the collection of cash is reasonably assured. In addition, the FASB has proposed a comprehensive, contract-based revenue recognition model that would alter the manner in which the revenue recognition principle is applied. This model is described in more detail on this text's website.

FedEx (delivery of the computer) and that the receipt of cash prior to the delivery does not affect when revenue is recognized. Exhibit 3.3 shows an excerpt of FedEx's revenue recognition policy that is disclosed in the notes to its financial statements.

EXHIBIT 3.3

Annual Report Excerpt: FedEx's Revenue Recognition Policy

Note 1: Summary of Significant Accounting Policies (in part)

REVENUE RECOGNITION. We recognize revenue upon delivery of shipments for our transportation businesses and upon completion of services for our business services, logistics and trade services businesses. . . . For shipments in transit, revenue is recorded based on the percentage of service completed at the balance sheet date.

Source: FedEx 2011 10-K.

The Expense Recognition (or Matching) Principle

Companies incur expenses for a variety of reasons. Sometimes expenses are incurred when an asset is used. In other instances, expenses are incurred when a liability is created. For example, FedEx incurs fuel expense as fuel is used to deliver packages. FedEx also incurs salary expense when employees work but are not paid immediately. The key idea is that **an expense is recorded when it is incurred, regardless of when cash is paid.**

Expense recognition is the process of identifying an expense with a particular time period. Under accrual accounting, expenses are recognized following the **expense recognition (or matching) principle**, which requires that expenses be recorded and reported in the same period as the revenue that it helped to generate. Expenses for an accounting period should *include* only those costs used to earn revenue that was recognized in the accounting period. Expenses for an accounting period should *exclude* those costs used to earn revenue in an earlier period and those costs that will be used to earn revenue in a later period. Thus, the key to expense recognition is matching the expense with revenue.

ETHICAL DECISIONS The revenue recognition and expense recognition (or matching) principles can and have been abused in recent years. As companies strive to meet or exceed

EXHIBIT 3.4

Instances of Accounting Abuses

Company	Action
Regina Vacuum	Backdated sales invoices, improperly recorded revenue on consignment sales that had not been earned, and hid unpaid bills in a filing cabinet to reduce expenses. Chairman, CEO, and president Donald Sheelen pleaded guilty to fraud, fined $25,000, and sentenced to 1 year in a work release program in Florida.
Miniscribe	Improperly recognized revenue through a variety of means, including packaging and shipping bricks as finished products. Chief executive Q. T. Wiles fined $250 million.
Sunbeam	Used a variety of techniques to improperly recognize revenue (including bill and hold transactions and channel stuffing). CEO Al Dunlap fined $500,000 and barred from ever serving as an officer or director of a public company.
WorldCom	Improperly reduced operating expenses, which inflated income, by reversing (releasing) accrued liabilities and improperly classifying certain expenses as assets. Chief executive Bernard Ebbers was sentenced to 25 years in jail.
Bally Total Fitness	Recognized revenue on gym membership contracts before it was earned, and improperly delayed the recognition of expenses. In total, more than two dozen improprieties were discovered that caused stockholders' equity to be overstated by $1.8 billion. Bally's auditor paid $8.5 million to settle charges of improper auditing.

Wall Street expectations, management may be tempted to recognize revenue that has not yet been earned or to hide expenses that should be recognized. In recent years, the Securities and Exchange Commission (SEC) has conducted numerous investigations involving the abuse of both revenue and expense recognition. Some notable cases are listed in Exhibit 3.4.

While the actions summarized in Exhibit 3.4 were fraudulent and led to severe fines or jail time for many of the company executives, other innocent parties were also affected by these unethical actions. Stockholders, many of whom who had bought the stock at an inflated price, saw a significant drop in the stock's value after these actions were made public. In addition, innocent employees lost their jobs as the companies struggled to deal with the fraud that occurred. When faced with an ethical dilemma to manipulate the recognition of revenue or expenses, a good rule of thumb is to make the decision that best portrays the economic reality of your company. ●

Applying the Principles

In order to use the financial statements, it is important to understand how the revenue recognition and expense recognition (or matching) principles affect the amounts reported. Cornerstone 3.1 compares how the application of these principles results in accrual-basis income that differs from cash-basis income.

Applying the Revenue Recognition and Expense Recognition (or Matching) Principles

CORNERSTONE 3.1

Why:

Under accrual accounting, revenue is recognized when it is earned and the collection of cash is reasonably assured. Expenses are recognized in the same period as the revenue they helped generate.

Information:

The state of Georgia hired Conservation Inc., a consulting company specializing in the conservation of natural resources, to explore options for providing water resources to the Atlanta metropolitan area. In November 2013, Conservation incurred $60,000 of expenditures, on account, while investigating the water shortage facing the state. Conservation also delivered its recommendations and billed the state $100,000 for its work. In December 2013, Conservation paid the $60,000 of expenses. In January 2014, Conservation received the state's check for $100,000.

Required:

Calculate net income for November 2013, December 2013, and January 2014 using the following methods: (1) cash-basis accounting and (2) accrual-basis accounting.

Solution:

1. Cash-Basis Accounting:

November 2013		December 2013		January 2014	
Revenue	$0	Revenue	$ 0	Revenue	$100,000
Expense	0	Expense	60,000	Expense	0
Net income	$0	Net income	$(60,000)	Net income	$100,000

➡ Performed Service ➡ Paid Expenses ➡ Received Payment

(Continued)

CORNERSTONE 3.1 (Continued)

2. Accrual-Basis Accounting

November 2013		December 2013		January 2014	
Revenue	$100,000	Revenue	$0	Revenue	$0
Expense	60,000	Expense	0	Expense	0
Net income	$ 40,000	Net income	$0	Net income	$0
Performed Service		Paid Expenses		Received Payment	

Notice that, under accrual accounting, revenue is recognized when it is earned and expenses are matched with revenues. Even though Conservation did not receive the payment from the state of Georgia until January 2014, Conservation had performed services in November 2013 and appropriately recognized the revenue as the service was performed. The $60,000 of expenses were matched with revenues and also recognized in November 2013. If cash-basis accounting would have been used, $60,000 of expense would have been recognized in December 2013 (when the cash was paid) and $100,000 of revenue would have been recognized in January 2014 (when the cash was received). By following the revenue recognition and expense recognition (or matching) principles, net income was properly recognized in the period that the business activity occurred. In short, the difference between cash-basis and accrual-basis accounting is a matter of timing.

YOUDECIDE Recognizing a Security Service Contract

You are the chief financial officer of Secure Entry Inc., a security company, and it is your responsibility to develop the company's revenue and expense recognition policies. In April 2012, Secure Entry signed a 2-year contract with the Metropolis Stadium Authority (MSA) to provide security services at its stadium gates beginning in January 2013. Under the terms of the contract, MSA agrees to make 24 equal monthly payments to Secure Entry beginning in October 2012.

When should Secure Entry recognize revenue and expenses associated with the security contract?

To provide investors and creditors with the most useful information and be consistent with GAAP, you decide that Secure Entry should follow accrual accounting principles. Therefore, the contract is initially recognized in October 2012, when MSA makes the first payment. At that time, Secure Entry would record an increase in cash for the payment received and an equal increase in a liability (Unearned Revenue) to recognize that future services are owed. Secure Entry would not record the contract in its accounting system in April 2012 because the event does meet the recognition criteria discussed in Chapter 2.

Consistent with the revenue recognition principle, Secure Entry would recognize revenue each month, as services are performed, beginning in January 2013. Additionally, expenses related to the performance of security services should be matched against revenue from providing the security services and recognized monthly beginning in January 2013.

The proper recognition of revenue and expenses is critical in properly measuring and reporting income in the period that a business activity occurs.

OBJECTIVE 3

Identify the kinds of transactions that may require adjustments at the end of an accounting period.

ACCRUAL ACCOUNTING AND ADJUSTING ENTRIES

Which Transactions Require Adjustment?

Many business activities continue for a period of time—for example, the use of rented facilities or interest incurred on borrowed money. Because entries in the accounting system are made at particular points in time rather than continuously, adjustments are needed at the end of an accounting period to record partially complete activities.[2] **Adjusting entries** are journal entries made at the end of an accounting period to record the completed portion of partially completed transactions. Adjusting entries are necessary to apply the revenue recognition and expense recognition (or matching) principles and ensure that a company's financial statements include the proper amount for revenues, expenses, assets, liabilities, and stockholders' equity.

In Cornerstone 3.2, three representative transactions are described. The implications of the "length" of these transactions for recognition in the accounting system and for adjustment is discussed.

IFRS

The adjustment process under IFRS is the same as the adjustment process under U.S. GAAP.

Determining Which Transactions Require Adjustment

CORNERSTONE 3.2

Why:

Adjusting journal entries are required for continuous transactions that are partially complete at the end of an accounting period.

Information:

Computer Town sells computer equipment and provides computer repair service. Sales are typically made in cash or on account. Repairs are provided under service contracts, which customers purchase up front for a specified period of time (2, 3, or 5 years). Customers pay nothing when the computer is brought in for repair.

Required:

1. How should Computer Town account for cash and credit sales of equipment?
2. How should Computer Town account for repair services provided under service contracts?
3. How should Computer Town account for the use of office supplies?

Solution:

1. Cash sales should be recorded as they occur and the equipment is delivered, often at a cash register that tracks total sales for the day. When orders are received from customers who want to purchase equipment on credit, the sale should be recorded when the equipment is delivered to the customer. In both situations, the sale is complete at a single point in time (the delivery of the equipment) and no adjusting entry is needed.
2. Repair service contracts are continuous activities that require an adjustment at the end of the accounting period. Revenue is earned as time passes under the service contract and should be recorded in proportion to the period of time that has passed since the contract became effective. The unexpired portion of the service contract should be recorded as a liability (unearned revenue) until earned. Any expenses associated with the repair services should be recognized in the same period that service revenue is recognized (the expense recognition or matching principle).
3. The use of supplies can be viewed as a sequence of individual activities. However, the preparation of documents required to keep track of each activity individually would be too costly. Instead, the use of supplies can be treated as a continuous transaction and recognized through an adjusting entry. Any supplies used will be reported as an expense, and the unused portion of supplies will be reported as an asset.

[2] The distinction between business activities requiring adjustment and those that do not depends to some extent on our ability and willingness to keep track of activities. Some activities may occur so frequently or are so difficult to measure that no record of individual activities is maintained. In such cases, the sequence of individual activities becomes, for all intents and purposes, a continuous activity. For example, the use of office supplies is often treated as a continuous business activity because it is too costly to maintain a record of each time supplies are used.

Notice that in the second and third situations in Cornerstone 3.2, the preparation of adjusting entries is necessary to get the account balances properly stated and up to date. These end-of-period adjustments can have significant effects on a company's financial statements.

OBJECTIVE 4

Prepare adjusting entries for accruals and deferrals.

STEP 5: ADJUSTING THE ACCOUNTS

Adjustments are often necessary because timing differences exist between when a revenue or expense is recognized and cash is received or paid. These timing differences give rise to two categories of adjusting entries—accruals and deferrals. As shown in Exhibit 3.5, each category has two subcategories, resulting in four possible types of adjustments.

EXHIBIT 3.5

Types of Adjusting Entries

Accruals:

- **Accrued revenues:** Previously unrecorded revenues that have been earned but for which no cash has yet been received
- **Accrued expenses:** Previously unrecorded expenses that have been incurred but not yet paid in cash

Deferrals:

- **Deferred (unearned) revenues:** Liabilities arising from the receipt of cash for which revenue has not yet been earned
- **Deferred (prepaid) expenses:** Assets arising from the payment of cash which have not been used or consumed by the end of the period

The purpose of all adjustments is to make sure revenues and expenses get recorded in the proper time period. As the revenue and expense balances are adjusted, asset and liability balances will be adjusted also. Therefore, **all adjusting entries will affect at least one income statement account and one balance sheet account. Note that cash is never affected by adjustments.**

A 3-step procedure can be followed for making adjusting journal entries.

Step 1: Identify pairs of income statement and balance sheet accounts that require adjustment.

Step 2: Calculate the amount of the adjustment based on the amount of revenue that was earned or the amount of expense that was incurred during the accounting period.

Step 3: Record the adjusting journal entry.

This process is used for each of the four types of adjusting entries, as we will illustrate in the following sections.

concept Q&A

Why don't adjusting entries involve cash?

Answer:

Cash receipts and cash payments are recorded when they occur at a specific point in time. Adjusting entries are concerned with applying the revenue recognition and expense recognition (or matching) principles to continuous activities. Because revenue and expense recognition does not depend on cash receipt or cash payment, adjusting entries for continuous revenue and expense activities will not involve cash.

Accrued Revenues

Companies often engage in revenue-producing activities but are not paid until after the activities are complete. For example, FedEx has packages in transit at the end of an accounting period, meaning that FedEx has only partially completed its service. These transactions for which FedEx has earned revenue but not received the cash are called **accrued revenues**. Another example of an accrued revenue is interest earned, but not yet received, on a loan. While interest is earned as time passes, the company only receives the cash related to interest periodically (e.g., monthly, semiannually, or annually). Therefore, an adjustment is necessary to record the amount of interest earned but not yet received.

For accrued revenues, an adjustment is necessary to record the revenue and the associated increase in a company's assets, usually a receivable. Exhibit 3.6 demonstrates the process necessary to record accrued revenues. Note that *the accrual of revenue is necessary because the revenue was earned prior to the receipt of cash.*

EXHIBIT 3.6

Accrued Revenues

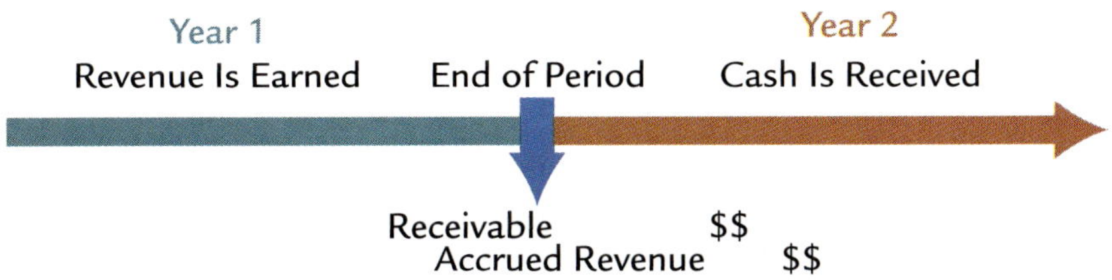

The adjusting entry required to record accrued revenues is shown in Cornerstone 3.3.

Recording Accrued Revenues

CORNERSTONE 3.3

Why:

Revenue is recognized when it is earned, regardless of when cash is received. The adjusting entry for an accrued revenue will result in an increase to a revenue account and an increase to an asset account.

Information:

Assume that Porter Properties Inc., a calendar-year company, rented office space, to be occupied immediately, to the Tiger Travel Agency on November 1, 2013, for $5,000 per month. Porter requires Tiger Travel to make a rental payment at the end of every 3 months. No payment was made on November 1.

Required:

1. Prepare the adjusting journal entry necessary for Porter on December 31, 2013.
2. Prepare the entry necessary on January 31, 2014, to record the receipt of cash.

Solution:

1. **Step 1: Identify the accounts that require adjustment.** Consistent with the revenue recognition principle, Rent Revenue needs to be increased because Porter has earned revenue from providing the office space. Because no payment was received, Porter would need to increase Rent Receivable to reflect their right to receive payment from Tiger Travel.

   Step 2: Calculate the amount of the adjustment. The amount of the adjustment would be calculated as:

   $5,000 per month × 2 months (office space occupied) = $10,000

   Step 3: Record the adjusting journal entry.

Date	Account and Explanation	Debit	Credit
Dec. 31, 2013	Rent Receivable	10,000	
	Rent Revenue		10,000
	(Record rent revenue earned in 2013 but not received)		

Assets	=	Liabilities	+	Stockholders' Equity
+10,000				+10,000

(Continued)

CORNERSTONE
3.3
(Continued)

Assets	= Liabilities +	Stockholders' Equity
+15,000		+5,000
−10,000		

2. The amount of cash received is calculated as:

$5,000 per month × 3 months (office space rented) = $15,000

Date	Account and Explanation	Debit	Credit
Jan. 31, 2014	Cash	15,000	
	Rent Revenue		5,000
	Rent Receivable		10,000
	(Record revenue earned in 2014 and the receipt of cash)		

The $5,000 of Rent Revenue represents the 1 month earned in 2014.

If the adjusting entry on December 31, 2013, was not made, assets, stockholders' equity, revenues, and income would be understated. The adjusting journal entry recognizes 2 months of revenue (November and December 2013) in the accounting period in which it was earned and updates the corresponding balance in Rent Receivable. The revenue has been earned because Porter has provided a service to Tiger Travel. Later, when cash is received, the remaining portion of the revenue that was earned in January 2014 is recognized and the receivable is reduced to reflect that it was paid. Consistent with the revenue recognition principle, revenue is recorded in the period that it is earned.

Accrued Expenses

Similar to the situation with accrued revenues, many companies incur expenses in the current accounting period but do not pay cash for these expenses until a later period. For example, Exhibit 3.1 showed that FedEx reported $256 million of salary expense related to services performed by FedEx employees but not paid as of the end of the year. This situation is quite common for operating costs such as payroll, taxes, utilities, rent, and interest. **Accrued expenses** are previously unrecorded expenses that have been incurred but not yet paid in cash.

For accrued expenses, an adjustment is necessary to record the expense and the associated increase in a company's liabilities, usually a payable. Exhibit 3.7 demonstrates the process necessary to record accrued expenses.

EXHIBIT 3.7

Accrued Expenses

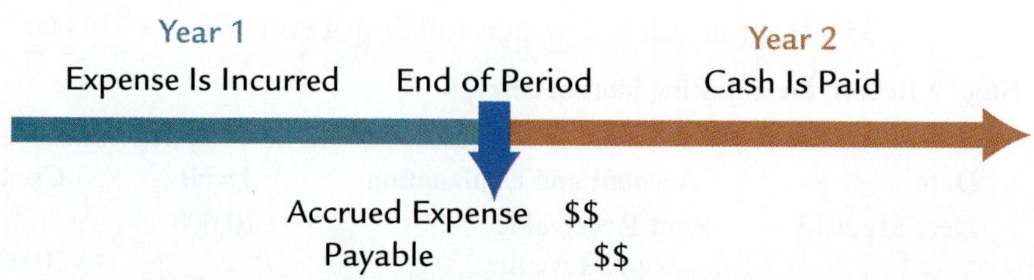

Note that *the accrual of the expense is necessary because the expense was incurred prior to the payment of cash.* The adjusting entry required to record accrued expenses is shown in Cornerstone 3.4.

Recording Accrued Expenses

CORNERSTONE 3.4

Why:

Expenses are recorded as they are incurred, regardless of when cash is paid. The adjusting entry for an accrued expense will result in an increase to an expense account and an increase to a liability account.

Information:

Assume that Porter Properties Inc., a calendar-year company, paid its clerical employees every 2 weeks. Employees work 5 days a week for a total of 10 work days every 2 weeks. Total wages for 10 days is $50,000. Also assume that December 31, 2013, is 4 days into a 10-day pay period.

Required:

1. Prepare the adjusting journal entry necessary for Porter on December 31, 2013.
2. Prepare the entry necessary on January 10, 2014, to record the payment of salaries.

Solution:

1. **Step 1: Identify the accounts that require adjustment.** Salaries Expense needs to be increased because Porter has incurred an expense related to its employees working for 4 days in December. This expense needs to be matched against December revenues (an application of the expense recognition principle). Because no payment to the employees was made, Porter would need to increase Salaries Payable to reflect its obligation to pay its employees.

   Step 2: Calculate the amount of the adjustment. The amount of the adjustment would be calculated as:

   $50,000 biweekly salaries × (4 days/10 days) worked in 2 weeks = $20,000

   Step 3: Record the adjusting entry.

Date	Account and Explanation	Debit	Credit
Dec. 31, 2013	Salaries Expense	20,000	
	Salaries Payable		20,000
	(Record expenses incurred not paid)		

Assets	= Liabilities +	Stockholders' Equity
	+20,000	−20,000

2. The amount of the salaries expense for the current year would be calculated as:

   $50,000 biweekly salaries × (6 days/10 days) worked in 2 weeks = $30,000

Date	Account and Explanation	Debit	Credit
Jan. 10, 2014	Salaries Expense	30,000	
	Salaries Payable	20,000	
	Cash		50,000
	(Record expense incurred in 2014 and the payment of cash)		

Assets	= Liabilities +	Stockholders' Equity
−50,000	−20,000	−30,000

If the adjusting journal entry on December 31, 2013, were not made, liabilities and expenses would be understated while income and stockholders' equity would be overstated. The adjusting journal entry recognizes the expense that was incurred during the accounting period and updates the balance in the corresponding liability. Later, when the cash is paid to the employees, the portion of the expense that was incurred in January 2014 is recognized and the previously created liability is reduced. Consistent with the expense recognition (or matching) principle, expenses are recorded in the period that they were incurred.

Deferred (Unearned) Revenues

Companies may collect payment for goods or services that it sells before it delivers those goods or services. For example, FedEx often collects cash for a package delivery prior to the actual performance of the delivery service. When the cash is collected, the revenue recognition is deferred, or delayed, until the service is performed. Transactions for which a company has received cash but has not yet earned the revenue are called **deferred (or unearned) revenues**. Other examples of deferred revenues include rent received in advance, magazine or newspaper subscriptions received in advance, and tickets (e.g., for airlines, sporting events, concerts) sold in advance. In all of these situations, the receipt of cash creates a liability for the company to deliver goods or perform services in the future. The unearned revenue account delays, or defers, the recognition of revenue by recording the revenue as a liability until it is earned.

As the goods are delivered or the service is performed, an adjustment is necessary to reduce the previously recorded liability and to recognize the portion of the revenue that has been earned. The portion of revenue that has not been earned remains in the liability account, unearned revenue, until it is earned. Therefore, revenue recognition is delayed, or deferred, until the revenue is earned. Exhibit 3.8 demonstrates the process necessary to record deferred revenues.

EXHIBIT 3.8

Deferred (Unearned) Revenues

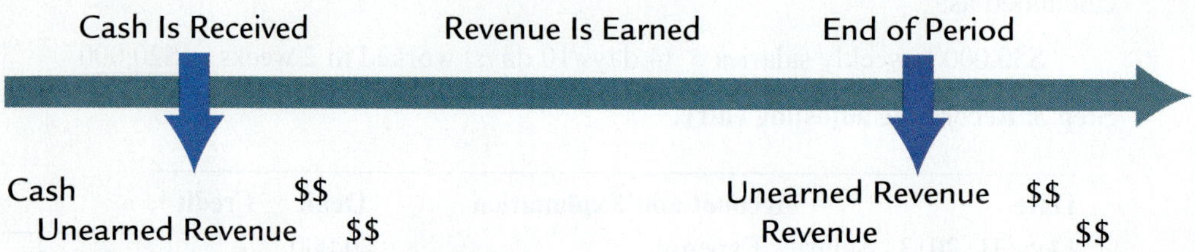

Note that *the deferral of revenue is necessary because the revenue was not earned at the time of cash receipt*. The adjusting entry recognizes the amount of revenue that has been earned from the time of cash receipt until the end of the accounting period. The adjusting entry required to adjust deferred revenues is shown in Cornerstone 3.5.

CORNERSTONE 3.5

Adjusting Deferred (Unearned) Revenues

Why:

Revenues are recognized when earned, regardless of when cash is received. The adjusting entry for deferred revenue will result in an increase to a revenue account and a decrease to a liability account.

(Continued)

Information:

Assume that Porter Properties Inc., a calendar-year company, rented office space to the Tiger Travel Agency on November 1, 2013, for $5,000 per month. Porter requires Tiger Travel to make a rental payment every 3 months. If Tiger Travel pays its entire 3-month rental in advance, Porter has agreed to reduce the monthly rental to $4,500. Tiger Travel agrees and pays Porter $13,500 for 3 months' rental in advance.

CORNERSTONE

3.5

(Continued)

Required:

1. Prepare the entry on November 1, 2013, to record the receipt of cash.
2. Prepare the adjusting journal entry necessary for Porter on December 31, 2013.

Solution:

1.

Date	Account and Explanation	Debit	Credit
Nov. 1, 2013	Cash	13,500	
	Unearned Rent Revenue		13,500
	(Record receipt of cash for 3 months' rent)		

Assets	=	Liabilities	+	Stockholders' Equity
+13,500		+13,500		

2. **Step 1: Identify the accounts that require adjustment.** Rent Revenue needs to be increased because Porter has earned revenue from providing the office space. Because a liability was previously recorded, Porter would need to decrease the liability, Unearned Rent Revenue, to reflect the decrease in their obligation to perform the service.

   Step 2: Calculate the amount of the adjustment. The amount of the adjustment would be calculated as:

   $4,500 per month × 2 months (office space rented) = $9,000

   Step 3: Record the adjusting entry.

Date	Account and Explanation	Debit	Credit
Dec. 31, 2013	Unearned Rent Revenue	9,000	
	Rent Revenue		9,000
	(Record rent revenue earned in 2013)		

Assets	=	Liabilities	+	Stockholders' Equity
		−9,000		+9,000

If the adjusting entry on December 31, 2013, was not made, liabilities (Unearned Rent Revenue) would be overstated while stockholders' equity, revenue, and net income would be understated. The adjusting journal entry recognizes 2 months of revenue (November and December 2013) in the accounting period in which it was earned and updates the corresponding balance in the liability, Unearned Rent Revenue. As a result of the adjusting entry, revenue is recorded in the period that it is earned.

Deferred (Prepaid) Expenses

Companies often acquire goods and services before they are used. These prepayments are recorded as assets called **deferred** (or **prepaid**) expenses. For example, **FedEx** reports prepaid expenses of $329 million on its December 31, 2011, balance sheet. Common prepaid expenses include items such as supplies, prepaid rent, prepaid advertising, and prepaid insurance. The purchases of buildings and equipment also are considered prepayments.

As the prepaid asset is used to generate revenue, an adjustment is necessary to reduce the previously recorded prepaid asset and recognize the related expense. The portion of the prepaid asset that has not been used represents the unexpired benefits and remains in the asset account until it is used. Therefore, expense recognition is delayed, or deferred, until the expense is incurred. Exhibit 3.9 demonstrates the process necessary to record deferred expenses.

EXHIBIT 3.9

Deferred (Prepaid) Expenses

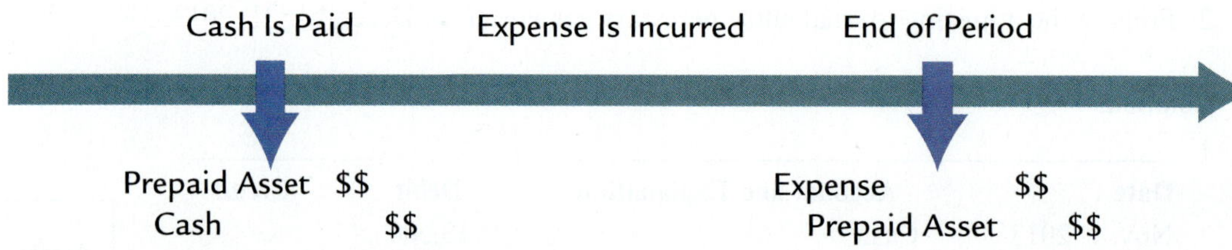

Note that *the deferral of the expense is necessary because the initial cash payment did not result in an expense*. Instead, an asset that provides future economic benefit was created. The adjusting entry recognizes the amount of expense that has been incurred from the time of the cash payment until the end of the accounting period. The adjusting entry required to adjust deferred expenses is shown in Cornerstone 3.6.

CORNERSTONE 3.6

Adjusting Deferred (Prepaid) Expenses

Why:

Expenses are recognized when incurred, regardless of when cash is paid. The adjusting entry for deferred expenses will result in an increase to an expense account and a decrease to an asset account.

Information:

Assume that Porter Properties Inc., a calendar-year company, had $4,581 of office supplies on hand at the beginning of November. On November 10, Porter purchased office supplies totaling $12,365. The amount of the purchase was added to the Supplies account. At the end of the year, the balance in Supplies was $16,946 ($4,581 + $12,365). A count of office supplies on hand indicated that $3,263 of supplies remained.

Required:

1. Prepare the entry on November 10, 2013, to record the purchase of supplies.
2. Prepare the adjusting journal entry necessary for Porter on December 31, 2013.

Solution:

1.

Assets	= Liabilities +	Stockholders' Equity
+12,365		
−12,365		

Date	Account and Explanation	Debit	Credit
Nov. 10, 2013	Supplies	12,365	
	Cash		12,365
	(Record purchase of office supplies)		

(Continued)

2. **Step 1: Identify the accounts that require adjustment.** Supplies Expense needs to be increased because Porter has used office supplies during November and December of 2013. The use of the supplies would also decrease the asset, Supplies.

   Step 2: Calculate the amount of the adjustment. The amount of the adjustment would be calculated as:

   $16,946 (supplies available to be used) – $3,263 (supplies on hand) = $13,683

   This amount represents the cost of supplies used during November and December 2013.

   Step 3: Record the adjusting entry.

Date	Account and Explanation	Debit	Credit
Dec. 31, 2013	Supplies Expense	13,683	
	Supplies		13,683
	(Record the use of office supplies during 2013)		

Assets	= Liabilities +	Stockholders' Equity
−13,683		−13,683

CORNERSTONE
3.6
(Continued)

If the adjusting entry on December 31, 2013, was not made, assets, stockholders' equity, and net income would be overstated and expenses would be understated. The adjusting journal entry recognizes the expense incurred during November and December 2013 and updates the corresponding balance in the asset, Supplies. As a result of the adjusting entry, the expense is recorded in the period that it is incurred.

Depreciation While most deferred (prepaid) expenses are accounted for in a manner similar to that illustrated in Cornerstone 3.6, the purchase of long-lived assets such as buildings and equipment presents a unique situation. Recall from Chapter 1 that these types of assets are classified as property, plant, and equipment on the balance sheet. Because property, plant, and equipment helps to produce revenue over a number of years (instead of just one period), the expense recognition (or matching) principle requires companies to systematically assign, or allocate, the asset's cost as an expense to each period in which the asset is used. This process is called **depreciation**. This concept and the methods used to compute depreciation expense are discussed in Chapter 7.

The depreciation process requires an adjustment to recognize the expense incurred during the period and reduce the long-lived asset. The unused portion of the asset is reported as property, plant, and equipment on the balance sheet. Therefore, the purchase of a long-lived asset is essentially a long-term prepayment for the service that the asset will provide.

Assume that Porter Properties purchased an office building on January 1, 2011, for $450,000. The depreciation expense on this building is $15,000 per year. Because depreciation is a continuous activity, Porter would need to make the following adjustment at the end of 2013.

Date	Account and Explanation	Debit	Credit
Dec. 31, 2013	Depreciation Expense	15,000	
	Accumulated Depreciation		15,000
	(Record depreciation for 2013)		

Assets	= Liabilities +	Stockholders' Equity
−15,000		−15,000

Depreciation expense represents the portion of the cost of the long-lived asset that is matched against the revenues that the asset helped to generate. In addition, the depreciation process reduces the asset. Accountants normally use a contra account to reduce the amount of a long-lived asset. **Contra accounts** are accounts that have a balance that is opposite of the balance in a related account. In this case, Accumulated Depreciation is a contra account to the building. Therefore, while the asset has a normal debit balance, the contra account has a normal credit balance. Contra accounts are deducted from the balance of the related asset account in the financial statements, and the resulting difference is known as the book value of the asset. Therefore, by increasing the contra account, the above journal entry reduces the book value of the asset. Exhibit 3.10 shows the financial statement presentation of the accumulated depreciation account.

EXHIBIT 3.10

Financial Statement Presentation of Accumulated Depreciation

Porter Properties Inc.
Balance Sheet
December 31, 2013

Assets:	
Current assets	$ 370,000
Property, plant, and equipment (net)	1,450,000
Other assets	80,000
Total assets	$ 1,900,000
Liabilities	$ 825,000
Equity	1,075,000
Total liabilities and equity	$ 1,900,000

Sample of accumulated depreciation presentation:

Building	$ 450,000
Less: Accumulated depreciation	(45,000)
Building (net)	$ 405,000

Notice that accumulated depreciation shows the total amount of depreciation taken in all years of the asset's life ($15,000 per year for 2011, 2012, and 2013). Therefore, the balance in the accumulated depreciation account will increase over the asset's life. The use of the contra account provides more information to users of the financial statements because it preserves both the original cost of the asset and the total cost that has expired to date.

Summary of Financial Statement Effects of Adjusting Entries

The effects of the adjustment process are summarized in Exhibit 3.11.

Adjusting entries are internal events that do not involve another company. The purpose of all adjustments is to make sure that revenues and expenses get recorded in the proper time period. As the revenue and expense balances are adjusted, asset and

EXHIBIT 3.11

Effects of Adjusting Entries on the Financial Statements

Type of Adjustment	Asset	Liability	Stockholders' Equity	Revenue	Expense
Accrued Revenue	↑		↑	↑	
Accrued Expense		↑	↓		↑
Deferred Revenue		↓	↑	↑	
Deferred Expense	↓		↓		↑

EXHIBIT 3.12

Trial Balance

HiTech Communications Inc.
Trial Balance
March 31, 2013

Account	Debit	Credit
Cash	$16,600	
Accounts Receivable	300	
Supplies	6,500	
Prepaid Insurance	1,200	
Equipment	4,500	
Accounts Payable		$ 500
Unearned Service Revenue		9,000
Notes Payable		3,000
Common Stock		12,000
Dividends	500	
Service Revenue		12,100
Salaries Expense	1,800	
Utilities Expense	5,200	
Totals	$36,600	$36,600

liability balances will be adjusted also. Therefore, *all adjusting entries will affect at least one income statement account and one balance sheet account.* Remember, *the cash account is never used in an adjusting entry.*

Comprehensive Example

To provide a comprehensive example of the adjusting process, consider the trial balance of HiTech Communications that was introduced in Chapter 2 (see Exhibit 3.12). Upon review of the trial balance, the accountant for HiTech noted that the following accounts needed to be adjusted.

Adjustment 1: Accrued Revenue HiTech's accountant noted that HiTech had performed $1,500 of advertising services for which it had not yet billed the customer. Because the services had not yet been billed, no entry was made in the accounting system. However, HiTech must record the revenue that was earned during the accounting period, even though the cash flow will not occur until a later date. The adjusting entry to record this accrued revenue is:

Date	Account and Explanation	Debit	Credit
Mar. 31	Accounts Receivable	1,500	
	Service Revenue		1,500
	(Recognize services earned)		

Assets	= Liabilities +	Stockholders' Equity
+1,500		+1,500

concept Q&A

What is the relationship between the cash receipt or payment and the recognition of accruals or deferrals?

Answer:

When the revenue is earned or the expense is incurred **before** the associated cash flow occurs, an accrual adjusting entry is necessary. When the revenue is earned or the expense is incurred **after** the associated cash flow occurs, a deferral adjusting entry is necessary.

Adjustment 2: Accrual of Interest The note payable for $3,000 that HiTech signed on March 2 required it to pay interest at an annual rate of 8%. The formula for computing interest is:

$$\text{Interest} = \text{Principal} \times \text{Interest Rate} \times \text{Time}$$

The principal amount of the loan is usually the face value of the note. The interest rate is stated as an annual rate, and the time period is the fraction of a year that the note is outstanding. For HiTech, interest expense for March 2011 is computed as:

$$\text{Interest} = \$3{,}000 \times 8\% \times 1/12 = \underline{\underline{\$20}}$$

Because interest expense has been incurred but the cash payment for interest will not occur until a later date, interest is an accrued expense that requires an increase to an expense account and an increase to a liability account. The adjusting entry to recognize accrued interest is:

Assets	= Liabilities +	Stockholders' Equity
	+20	−20

Date	Account and Explanation	Debit	Credit
Mar. 31	Interest Expense	20	
	Interest Payable		20
	(Recognize accrued interest)		

Adjustment 3: Accrual of Salaries HiTech paid its weekly salaries on March 26 and properly recorded an expense (Transaction 10 from Chapter 2). Salaries are $360 per day. HiTech will not pay salaries again until April 2. However, employees worked on March 29, March 30, and March 31. Because employees have worked but will not be paid until a later date, an adjustment is necessary to record the salaries incurred in March but not yet paid. Accrued salaries are $1,080 (3 days × $360 per day). The adjusting entry to recognize accrued salaries is:

Assets	= Liabilities +	Stockholders' Equity
	+1,080	−1,080

Date	Account and Explanation	Debit	Credit
Mar. 31	Salaries Expense	1,080	
	Salaries Payable		1,080
	(Recognize accrued salaries)		

Adjustment 4: Deferred (Unearned) Revenue HiTech's trial balance shows that a customer paid $9,000 in advance for services to be performed at a later date. This amount was originally recorded as a liability, Unearned Service Revenue. As HiTech performs services, the liability will be reduced and revenue will be recognized. Based on HiTech's analysis of work performed during March, it is determined that $3,300 of revenue has been earned. The adjusting entry to record this previously unearned revenue is:

Assets	= Liabilities +	Stockholders' Equity
	−3,300	+3,300

Date	Account and Explanation	Debit	Credit
Mar. 31	Unearned Service Revenue	3,300	
	Service Revenue		3,300
	(Recognize service revenue earned)		

Adjustment 5: Deferred (Prepaid) Expense—Supplies HiTech's trial balance shows a balance of $6,500 in the Supplies account. However, an inventory count at the close of business on March 31 determined that supplies on hand were $1,200. Because it was not efficient to record supplies expense during the period, HiTech must make an adjustment at the end of the period to record the supplies used during the period. It was determined that HiTech used $5,300 ($6,500 available to be used minus $1,200 not used) of supplies. The adjustment necessary to record the supplies used during March is:

Assets	= Liabilities +	Stockholders' Equity
−5,300		−5,300

Date	Account and Explanation	Debit	Credit
Mar. 31	Supplies Expense	5,300	
	Supplies		5,300
	(Recognize supplies used)		

Adjustment 6: Deferred (Prepaid) Expense—Insurance HiTech's trial balance shows a balance of $1,200 in the Prepaid Insurance account related to a 6-month insurance policy purchased at the beginning of March. Because time has passed since the purchase of the insurance policy, the asset, Prepaid Insurance, has partially expired and an expense needs to be recognized. The expired portion of the insurance is $200 ($1,200 × 1/6). The adjustment necessary to record insurance expense is:

Date	Account and Explanation	Debit	Credit
Mar. 31	Insurance Expense	200	
	Prepaid Insurance		200
	(Recognize insurance used)		

Assets	= Liabilities +	Stockholders' Equity
−200		−200

Adjustment 7: Depreciation HiTech's trial balance shows that $4,500 of equipment was purchased. Because this equipment is used to generate revenue, a portion of the cost of the equipment must be allocated to expense. HiTech computed depreciation expense as $125 per month. The adjustment necessary to record depreciation expense is:

Date	Account and Explanation	Debit	Credit
Mar. 31	Depreciation Expense	125	
	Accumulated Depreciation (Equipment)		125
	(Recognize depreciation on equipment)		

Assets	= Liabilities +	Stockholders' Equity
−125		−125

The ledger for HiTech Communications, after posting of the adjusting journal entries, is shown in Exhibit 3.13.

EXHIBIT 3.13

General Ledger of HiTech Communications

Assets

Cash	
16,600	
16,600	

Accounts Receivable	
300	
(A1) 1,500	
1,800	

Supplies	
6,500	5,300 (A5)
1,200	

Prepaid Insurance	
1,200	200 (A6)
1,000	

Equipment	
4,500	
4,500	

Accumulated Depreciation	
	125 (A7)
	125

Liabilities

Accounts Payable	
	500
	500

Notes Payable	
	3,000
	3,000

Interest Payable	
	20 (A2)
	20

Salaries Payable	
	1,080 (A3)
	1,080

Unearned Service Revenue	
(A4) 3,300	9,000
	5,700

Stockholders' Equity

Common Stock	
	12,000
	12,000

Service Revenue	
	12,100
	1,500 (A1)
	3,300 (A4)
	16,900

Salaries Expense	
1,800	
(A3) 1,080	
2,880	

Utility Expense	
5,200	
5,200	

Depreciation Expense	
(A7) 125	
125	

Interest Expense	
(A2) 20	
20	

Insurance Expense	
(A6) 200	
200	

Supplies Expense	
(A5) 5,300	
5,300	

Dividends	
500	
500	

Two major items should be apparent:

- Adjusting entries affect one balance sheet account and one income statement account. Without adjusting entries, the balances reported on both the balance sheet and the income statement would have been incorrect. If the adjustments were not recorded, HiTech would have understated revenue by $4,800 and understated expenses by $6,725.
- Adjusting entries do not affect cash.

YOUDECIDE Financial Statement Effects of Adjusting Entries

You are considering investing in Get Fit Inc., a chain of gymnasiums and wellness facilities. As you are analyzing the financial statements to determine if Get Fit is a good investment, three items catch your attention:

- Get Fit requires customers to pay the first 6 months' membership fees at the time the customer joins one of its facilities. These fees are recorded as revenue at the time of cash receipt since the amount is nonrefundable.
- Get Fit paid for and distributed flyers to advertise its recent membership drive. Because these flyers will circulate and attract customers for approximately a year, Get Fit recorded the expenditures as prepaid advertising that will be expensed over the next year.
- Get Fit provides healthy snacks to its customers by charging their membership account. Get Fit records revenue at the end of the month when it bills customers, although customers do not pay until the next month.

Do you feel that Get Fit is properly recording the above transactions? If not, what is the effect on the financial statements?

First, the membership fees are a continuous activity that Get Fit is incorrectly treating as a point-in-time activity. Because the revenue has not yet been earned, the membership fees should be initially recorded as unearned revenue. As the customers have use of the facility each month, an adjusting entry should be made to reduce unearned revenue and increase revenue. The fact that the fees are nonrefundable is irrelevant in deciding whether revenue should or should not be recognized. Second, because it is difficult to measure any future benefits associated with advertising costs, accountants take a conservative position and these costs should not be deferred; instead they should be expensed as incurred. Finally, Get Fit is appropriately recording an accrued revenue related to providing snacks. The fact that the customers do not pay until a later time period is not relevant in determining when the revenue is recorded.

If the above transactions had been properly recorded, Get Fit would have reported less revenue, higher expenses, and, therefore, lower net income. Financial statement users need to pay close attention to a company's policies with regard to revenue and expense recognition.

Adjusting entries can have a material impact on a company's reported revenues, expenses, and income.

OBJECTIVE 5

Prepare financial statements from an adjusted trial balance.

STEP 6: PREPARING THE FINANCIAL STATEMENTS

After a company has journalized and posted all of the adjusting entries, it updates the trial balance to reflect the adjustments that have been made. This trial balance is called an **adjusted trial balance**. Similar to the trial balance, the adjusted trial balance lists all of the active accounts and proves the equality of debits and credits. In addition, the adjusted trial balance is the primary source of information needed to prepare the financial statements. The adjusted trial balance for HiTech Communications is shown in Exhibit 3.14.

The financial statements can now be prepared using the balances obtained from the adjusted trial balance. As discussed in Chapter 1, the financial statements are interrelated. That is, there is a natural progression from one financial statement to another as the numbers in one financial statement flow into another financial statement. Because of this natural progression, financial statements are prepared in a particular order.

1. The income statement is prepared from the revenue and expense accounts.
2. Net income (obtained from the income statement) and dividends are used to prepare the retained earnings statement.
3. The balance sheet is prepared using the ending balance of retained earnings from the retained earnings statement.

EXHIBIT 3.14

Adjusted Trial Balance

HiTech Communications Inc.
Adjusted Trial Balance
March 31, 2013

Account		Debit	Credit
Cash	Balance Sheet Accounts	$16,600	
Accounts Receivable		1,800	
Supplies		1,200	
Prepaid Insurance		1,000	
Equipment		4,500	
Accumulated Depreciation (Equipment)			$ 125
Accounts Payable			500
Unearned Service Revenue			5,700
Interest Payable			20
Salaries Payable			1,080
Notes Payable			3,000
Common Stock			12,000
Dividends	Income Statement Accounts	500	
Service Revenue			16,900
Salaries Expense		2,880	
Utilities Expense		5,200	
Depreciation Expense		125	
Interest Expense		20	
Insurance Expense		200	
Supplies Expense		5,300	
Totals		$39,325	$39,325

YOUDECIDE Quality of Earnings

Investors and other users often assess the quality of a company's earnings when analyzing companies. The quality of earnings refers to how well a company's reported earnings reflect the company's true earnings. High quality earnings are generally viewed as permanent or persistent earnings that assist financial statement users in predicting future earnings and cash flows. Low quality earnings are temporary or transitory earnings from one-time transactions or events that do not aid in predicting future earnings or cash flows. While there is no consensus on how best to measure earnings quality, research suggests that investors recognize differences in earnings quality and these differences affect a company's stock price.

How do adjusting entries influence the quality of earnings?

Because adjusting entries always effect amounts reported on the income statement, the estimates and judgments involved in making accruals and deferrals can have a significant impact on a company's income. Companies that make relatively pessimistic estimates and judgments are said to follow conservative accounting practices and are generally viewed as having earnings that are of higher quality. In contrast, many companies use relatively optimistic estimates and judgments and employ aggressive accounting practices. These companies are normally viewed as having a lower quality of earnings.

More conservative adjusting entries usually lead to better predictors of future earnings or cash flows and are viewed as contributing to higher earnings quality.

The financial statements are prepared using the steps illustrated in Cornerstones 1.2, 1.3 and 1.4 (pages 15, 19, and 23). The financial statements of HiTech Communications and their interrelationship are shown in Exhibit 3.15.

EXHIBIT 3.15

Relationships Among the Financial Statements

HiTech Communications Inc.
Income Statement
For the month ended March 31, 2013

Service revenue		$16,900
Expenses:		
Supplies expense	$5,300	
Utilities expense	5,200	
Salaries expense	2,880	
Insurance expense	200	
Depreciation expense	125	
Interest expense	20	13,725
Net income		$ 3,175

HiTech Communications Inc.
Retained Earnings Statement
For the month ended March 31, 2013

Retained earnings, March 1, 2013	$ 0
Add: Net income	3,175
Less: Dividends	(500)
Retained earnings, March 31, 2013	$2,675

HiTech Communications Inc.
Balance Sheet
March 31, 2013

ASSETS

Current assets:		
Cash	$16,600	
Accounts receivable	1,800	
Supplies	1,200	
Prepaid insurance	1,000	
Total current assets		$20,600
Property, plant, and equipment:		
Equipment	$ 4,500	
Less: Accumulated depreciation	(125)	
Total property, plant, and equipment		4,375
Total assets		$24,975

LIABILITIES AND STOCKHOLDERS' EQUITY

Current liabilities:		
Accounts payable	$ 500	
Unearned service revenue	5,700	
Interest payable	20	
Salaries payable	1,080	
Total current liabilities		$ 7,300
Long-term liabilities:		
Notes payable		3,000
Total liabilities		$10,300
Stockholders' equity:		
Common stock	$12,000	
Retained earnings	2,675	
Total stockholders' equity		14,675
Total liabilities and stockholders' equity		$24,975

STEP 7: CLOSING THE ACCOUNTS

OBJECTIVE 6

Explain why and how companies prepare closing entries.

When we introduced the fundamental accounting equation in Chapter 1, we identified three kinds of balance sheet accounts: assets, liabilities, and stockholders' equity. These accounts are **permanent accounts** in that their balances are carried forward from the current accounting period to future accounting periods. We also identified three other accounts: revenues, expenses, and dividends. These accounts are used to collect the activities of only one period, so they are considered **temporary accounts**. The final step of the accounting cycle, closing the accounts, is done to:

- Transfer the effects of revenues, expenses, and dividends (the temporary accounts) to the permanent stockholders' equity account, Retained Earnings.
- Clear the revenue, expenses, and dividends (reduce their balances to zero) so they are ready to accumulate the business activities of the next accounting period. Without closing entries, the temporary accounts would accumulate the business activities of *all* accounting periods, not just the current time period.

The closing process is accomplished through a series of journal entries that are dated as of the last day of the accounting period. Often, another temporary account, called Income Summary, is used to aid the closing process. The use of the Income Summary account allows the company to easily identify the net income (or net loss) for the period. The closing process can be completed in a 4-step procedure:

Step 1: Close revenues to Income Summary.
Step 2: Close expenses to Income Summary. At this point, the balance in the Income Summary account should be equal to net income.
Step 3: Close Income Summary to Retained Earnings.
Step 4: Close Dividends to Retained Earnings.

The closing process is illustrated in Cornerstone 3.7.

concept Q&A

What would happen if we didn't make closing entries?

Answer:

The closing process transfers temporary account balances (revenues, expenses, and dividends) to retained earnings. If the accounts were not closed, these amounts would not get properly reflected in stockholders' equity and the accounting equation wouldn't balance. In addition, the temporary accounts would accumulate amounts from different accounting periods, making it extremely difficult to determine the effect of business activities for a specific accounting period.

Closing the Accounts

CORNERSTONE 3.7

Why:

The closing process is designed to transfer the balances in the temporary accounts to retained earnings and to prepare the temporary accounts for the next accounting period.

Information:

For 2013, Porter Properties' general ledger shows the following balances: Rent Revenue \$2,174,000; Salaries Expense \$1,300,000; Supplies Expense \$150,000; Interest Expense \$15,000; Insurance Expense \$20,000; Retained Earnings at the beginning of the year \$1,135,000; and Dividends \$5,000. All accounts have normal balances.

Required:

Prepare the closing entries for Porter at December 31, 2013.

(Continued)

CORNERSTONE **3.7** *(Continued)*

Solution:

Step 1: Close revenues to Income Summary.

Date	Account and Explanation	Debit	Credit
Dec. 31	Rent Revenue	2,174,000	
	Income Summary		2,174,000
	(Close revenue accounts)		

Step 2: Close expenses to Income Summary.

Date	Account and Explanation	Debit	Credit
Dec. 31	Income Summary	1,485,000	
	Salaries Expense		1,300,000
	Supplies Expense		150,000
	Interest Expense		15,000
	Insurance Expense		20,000
	(Close expense accounts)		

Step 3: Close Income Summary to Retained Earnings.

Date	Account and Explanation	Debit	Credit
Dec. 31	Income Summary	689,000	
	Retained Earnings		689,000
	(Close Income Summary)		

Step 4: Close Dividends to Retained Earnings.

Date	Account and Explanation	Debit	Credit
Dec. 31	Retained Earnings	5,000	
	Dividends		5,000
	(Close Dividends)		

Notice that revenues, which have a normal credit balance, are closed by debiting the revenue account. Similarly, expenses, which normally have a debit balance, are closed by crediting the expense accounts. Also, after the first two journal entries, the balance in the Income Summary account is $689,000 ($2,174,000 − $1,485,000), which is the amount of income for the period. This amount is then transferred to Retained Earnings. Finally, the Dividends account is not closed to Income Summary (because dividends are not part of income) but closed directly to Retained Earnings. The ending Retained Earnings account will have a balance of $1,819,000 ($1,135,000 + $689,000 − $5,000). The closing process for Porter is illustrated in Exhibit 3.16.

EXHIBIT 3.16

The Closing Process

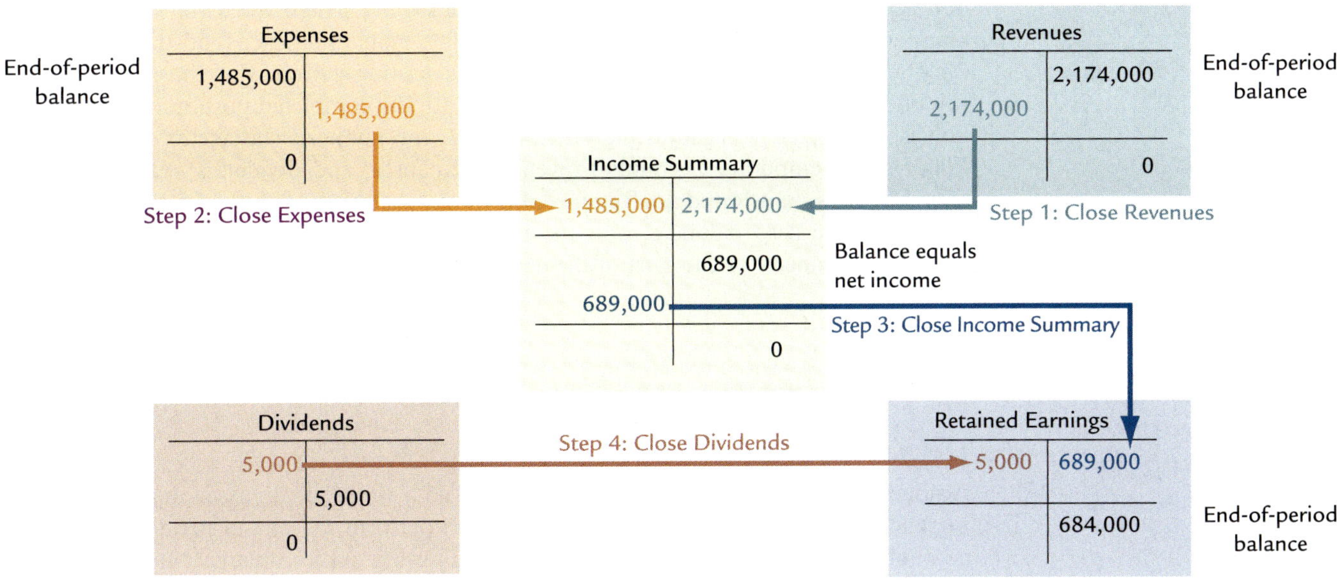

SUMMARY OF THE ACCOUNTING CYCLE

OBJECTIVE 7
Understand the steps in the accounting cycle.

In Chapter 2, we introduced the accounting cycle as a sequence of procedures that transforms business activities into financial statements. The accounting cycle is shown in Exhibit 3.17.

EXHIBIT 3.17

The Accounting Cycle

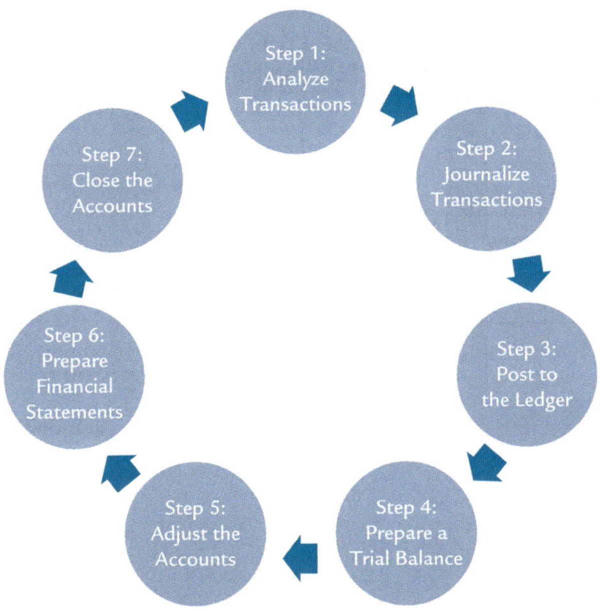

Notice that the accounting cycle begins with the analysis of transactions to determine which business activities are recognized in the accounting records and their effect on the fundamental accounting equation. Those activities that meet the recognition criteria are journalized and posted to the ledger. These three steps are repeated many times during an accounting period. The remaining steps of the accounting cycle are performed only at the end of the accounting period. For those transactions still underway at the end of the accounting period, the completed portion of the transaction is recognized with adjusting entries. Next, the financial statements are prepared. Finally, the temporary accounts—revenues, expenses, and dividends—are closed and their balances transferred to Retained Earnings. At this point, the income statement accounts have zero balances, and the balance sheet accounts all contain the correct beginning balances for the start of the next accounting period. The accounting cycle can begin again.

OBJECTIVE 8

Understand how to use a worksheet to prepare financial statements.

APPENDIX 3A: USING A WORKSHEET TO PREPARE FINANCIAL STATEMENTS

Accountants often use an informal schedule called a **worksheet** to assist them in organizing and preparing the information necessary to perform the end-of-period steps in the accounting cycle—namely the preparation of adjusting entries, financial statements, and closing entries. The worksheet is not a financial statement but simply an organizational tool that summarizes the information generated by the accounting system and enables the accountant to check the information for completeness and consistency. While worksheets can be completed manually, most worksheets today are created in computer spreadsheets.

A typical worksheet is shown in Exhibit 3.18. This exhibit uses the information for HiTech Communications that was presented in Chapter 2 and Chapter 3.

The completion of the worksheet requires the following six steps.

Step 1: Unadjusted Trial Balance

The worksheet starts with the unadjusted trial balance. The first column contains the listing of accounts used during the period in the same order as the accounts appear in the trial balance—the balance sheet accounts first followed by the income statement accounts. Note that a retained earnings account was added. Because this is the first month of operations, this account has a zero balance. The next two columns contain the unadjusted balances of these accounts and are totaled to ensure the equality of debits and credits.

Step 2: Adjusting Entry Columns

The next two columns contain the adjustments made to record the completed portion of business activities that remain underway at the end of the accounting period. Rather than take the time to make formal adjusting journal entries, the accountant typically enters the adjustments directly into the worksheet and then makes the formal journal entries after the worksheet has been completed. Two items should be noted:

- Adjustments often require the addition of accounts not included in the unadjusted trial balance. These additional accounts can be added, in no particular order, beneath the previous listing of accounts.
- Letters are typically used on a worksheet to identify the adjusting entries and to allow the accountant to easily match the debit and credit sides of each adjusting entry. The letters (a) through (g) correspond to the adjusting entries (1) through (7) shown earlier in the chapter.

The two columns are totaled to ensure the equality of debits and credits.

EXHIBIT 3.18

Worksheet

	A	B	C	D	E	F	G	H	I	J	K	L	M
1						HiTech Communications Inc.							
2						Work Sheet							
3						For the Month Ended March 31, 2012							
4		Unadjusted Trial Balance		Adjusting Entries		Adjusted Trial Balance		Income Statement		Retained Earnings Statement		Balance Sheet	
5	**Account Titles**	**Debit**	**Credit**	**Debit**	**Credit**	**Debit**	**Credit**	**Debit**	**Credit**	**Debit**	**Credit**	**Debit**	**Credit**
6	Cash	16,600				16,600						16,600	
7	Accounts Receivable	300		(a) 1,500		1,800						1,800	
8	Supplies	6,500			(e) 5,300	1,200						1,200	
9	Prepaid Insurance	1,200			(f) 200	1,000						1,000	
10	Equipment	4,500				4,500						4,500	
11	Accounts Payable		500				500						500
12	Unearned Revenue		9,000	(d) 3,300			5,700						5,700
13	Notes Payable		3,000				3,000						3,000
14	Common Stock		12,000				12,000						12,000
15	Retained Earnings, 3/1/2012		0				0				0		
16	Dividends	500				500				500			
17	Service Revenue		12,100		(a) 1,500		16,900		16,900				
18					(d) 3,300								
19	Salaries Expense	1,800		(c) 1,080		2,880		2,880					
20	Utility Expense	5,200				5,200		5,200					
21		36,600	36,600										
22													
23	Interest Expense			(b) 20		20		20					
24	Interest Payable				(b) 20		20						20
25	Salaries Payable				(c) 1,080		1,080						1,080
26	Supplies Expense			(e) 5,300		5,300		5,300					
27	Insurance Expense			(f) 200		200		200					
28	Depreciation Expense			(g) 125		125		125					
29	Accumulated Depreciation (Equipment)				(g) 125		125						125
30				11,525	11,525	39,325	39,325	13,725	16,900				
31	Net Income							(h) 3,175			(h) 3,175		
32								16,900	16,900	500	3,175		
33	Retained Earnings, 3/31/2012									(i) 2,675			(i) 2,675
34										3,175	3,175	25,100	25,100
35													

Step 3: Adjusted Trial Balance

The next two columns represent an adjusted trial balance. The adjustments entered in columns D and E are added to or subtracted from the unadjusted balances in columns B and C. The two columns are totaled to ensure the equality of debits and credits. The adjusted trial balance is the basis for preparing the financial statements.

Step 4: Income Statement

The income statement balances are transferred to the income statement columns of the worksheet and the columns are totaled. The difference between the two columns is the net income or loss of the period. In Exhibit 3.18, HiTech reports its net income of $3,175 in the debit column of the income statement and the credit column of the retained earnings statement. This entry is made (1) to balance the two income statement columns and (2) to transfer net income to retained earnings.

Step 5: Retained Earnings Statement

The amounts for beginning retained earnings and dividends are transferred from the adjusted trial balance columns (columns F and G) to the retained earnings statement columns (columns J and K). The columns are totaled and the difference is the amount of ending retained earnings. This amount is entered in the debit column of the retained earnings statement (to balance the two columns) and transferred to the credit column of the balance sheet as shown by letter (i).

Step 6: Balance Sheet

The final portion of the worksheet is completed by transferring all the balance sheet account balances from the adjusted trial balance columns (columns F and G) to the balance sheet columns (columns L and M).

At this point, the worksheet provides all the necessary information to prepare the financial statements. The completed financial statements are shown in Exhibit 3.15 (p. 142).

SUMMARY OF LEARNING OBJECTIVES

LO 1. Explain the difference between cash-basis and accrual-basis accounting.

- Cash-basis and accrual-basis accounting are two alternatives for recording business activities in the accounting records.
- Under cash-basis accounting, revenues and expenses are recorded when cash is received or paid, regardless of when the revenues are earned or the expenses are incurred.
- Accrual-basis accounting links income measurement to the selling activities of a company by recognizing revenues and expenses when they occur.

LO 2. Explain how the time-period assumption, revenue recognition, and expense recognition (or matching) principles affect the determination of income.

- The revenue recognition principle states that revenue is recognized or recorded in the period in which the revenue is earned and the collection of cash is reasonably assured (realized or realizable). These conditions are normally met when goods have been delivered or services have been performed.
- The expense recognition (or matching) principle requires that expenses be recognized in the same period as the revenue they helped generate.

- The application of these two principles results in income being measured as the business activity occurs, regardless of when cash is received or paid.

LO 3. Identify the kinds of transactions that may require adjustments at the end of an accounting period.

- Many business activities do not occur at a single point in time but continuously over time. Because entries in the accounting system are made at particular points in time, adjustments are needed at the end of an accounting period to record the completed portion of any partially completed activities.
- Adjusting entries apply the revenue recognition and expense recognition (or matching) principles to ensure that a company's financial statements reflect the proper amount for revenues, expenses, assets, liabilities, and stockholders' equity.
- Adjusting entries are categorized as either accruals (accrued revenues and accrued expenses) or deferrals (deferred revenues and deferred expenses).

LO 4. Prepare adjusting entries for accruals and deferrals.

- Accruals occur when revenues have been earned or expenses have been incurred but no cash has been received or paid.
- The adjusting entry for an accrued revenue will result in an increase to a revenue account and an increase to an asset account. The adjusting entry for an accrued expense account will result in an increase to an expense account and an increase to a liability account.
- Deferrals occur when cash has been received or paid prior to revenue being earned or the expense being incurred.
- The adjusting entry for a deferred (unearned) revenue will result in an increase to a revenue account and a decrease to a liability account. The adjusting entry for a deferred (prepaid) expense will result in an increase to an expense account and a decrease to an asset account.

LO 5. Prepare financial statements from an adjusted trial balance.

- An adjusted trial balance lists all of the active accounts and updates the trial balance to reflect the adjustments that have been made.
- The adjusted trial balance is the primary source of information needed to prepare the financial statements.
- Due to the interrelation between the financial statements, the income statement is prepared first, followed by the retained earnings statement, and finally, the balance sheet.

LO 6. Explain why and how companies prepare closing entries.

- Closing entries transfer the effects of revenues, expenses, and dividends to the stockholders' equity account, Retained Earnings, and clear the balances in revenues, expenses, and dividends (reduce their balances to zero) so that they are ready to accumulate the business activities of the next accounting period.
- To close the accounts, companies make a series of journal entries, dated as of the last day of the accounting period.

LO 7. Understand the steps in the accounting cycle.

- During the accounting period, transactions are analyzed to determine their effect on the accounting equation.
- Transactions that meet the recognition criteria are then journalized and posted to the general ledger.
- A trial balance is prepared to summarize the effects of these transactions.
- At the end of the accounting period, adjusting entries are prepared to recognize the completed portion of any partially completed business activities.

- The financial statements are prepared from the adjusted trial balance and the temporary accounts are closed.
- The accounting cycle repeats for the next accounting period.

LO 8. *(Appendix 3A)* Understand how to use a worksheet to prepare financial statements.

- A worksheet is an informal schedule that assists accountants in organizing and preparing the information necessary to perform the end-of-period steps in the accounting cycle.
- The worksheet begins with a trial balance and includes columns for adjusting entries, the adjusted trial balance, the income statement, the retained earnings statement, and the balance sheet.

CORNERSTONE 3.1 Applying the revenue recognition and expense recognition (or matching) principles, page 125

CORNERSTONE 3.2 Determining which transactions require adjustment, page 127

CORNERSTONE 3.3 Recording accrued revenues, page 129

CORNERSTONE 3.4 Recording accrued expenses, page 131

CORNERSTONE 3.5 Adjusting deferred (unearned) revenues, page 132

CORNERSTONE 3.6 Adjusting deferred (prepaid) expenses, page 134

CORNERSTONE 3.7 Closing the accounts, page 143

© Pixelfabrik/Alamy

KEY TERMS

Accrual-basis accounting, 122
Accrued expenses, 130
Accrued revenues, 128
Adjusted trial balance, 140
Adjusting entries, 127
Cash-basis accounting, 122
Contra accounts, 135
Deferred (or prepaid) expenses, 133
Deferred (or unearned) revenues, 132
Depreciation, 135
Expense recognition (or matching) principle, 124
Permanent accounts, 143
Revenue recognition principle, 123
Temporary accounts, 143
Time-period assumption, 123
Worksheet *(Appendix 3A)*, 146

REVIEW PROBLEM

The Adjustment Process

Concept:

Adjusting journal entries are required for continuous transactions that are partially complete at the end of an accounting period. This often requires estimates and judgments about the timing of revenue and expense recognition. Once the adjustments are made, financial statements can be prepared and the accounts are closed.

Information:

Kenny's Laundry has one laundry plant and uses five rented storefronts on the west side of Indianapolis as its retail locations. At the end of 2013, Kenny's had the following balances in its accounts before adjustment:

Account	Debit	Credit
Cash	4,800	
Accounts Receivable	26,000	
Supplies	128,000	
Land	124,400	
Building	249,000	
Accumulated Depreciation (Building)		36,000
Equipment	122,000	
Accumulated Depreciation (Equipment)		24,000
Other Assets	16,000	
Accounts Payable		8,000
Notes Payable (due 2019)		120,000
Unearned Service Revenue		12,000
Common Stock		240,000
Retained Earnings, 12/31/2012		69,000
Service Revenue		874,200
Rent Expense	168,000	
Wages Expense	431,000	
Insurance Expense	14,000	
Salaries Expense	92,000	
Interest Expense	8,000	

An examination identified the following items that require adjustment:

a. Kenny's launders shirts for the service staff of a local car dealer. At the end of 2013, the car dealer owes Kenny's $1,040 for laundry services that have been performed but will not be billed until early in 2014.
b. Kenny's supplies on hand at 12/31/2013 was $21,400.
c. Kenny's launders uniforms for a nearby McDonald's franchise. The franchisee pays Kenny's in advance for the laundry service once every 3 months. After examining the records, Kenny's accountant determines that the laundry has earned $8,400 of the $12,000 of unearned revenue.
d. Salaries in the amount of $1,500 are owed but unpaid and unrecorded.
e. Two months' interest at 8% on the note payable (due in 2019) is owed but unpaid and unrecorded.
f. Depreciation expense for the building is $12,000.
g. Depreciation expense for the equipment is $24,000.
h. Income taxes expense of $5,200 is owed but unpaid and unrecorded.

Required:

1. Determine and record the adjusting entries at 12/31/2013 for Kenny's Laundry.
2. Post the effects of the adjustments to the proper accounts, and determine the account balances.
3. Prepare an income statement, retained earnings statement, and a balance sheet for Kenny's using the adjusted account balances.
4. Close the necessary accounts.

Solution:

1. The adjustments for Kenny's are as follows:

a. The adjustment to record accrued revenue for services already provided is:

Assets	=	Liabilities	+	Stockholders' Equity
+1,040				+1,040

Date	Account and Explanation	Debit	Credit
Dec. 31	Accounts Receivable	1,040	
	Service Revenue		1,040
	(Recognize revenue for services performed but not billed)		

b. The before adjustment balance in supplies is $128,000. Supplies actually on hand are $21,400. Supplies expense (used) is $106,600 ($128,000 – $21,400):

Assets	=	Liabilities	+	Stockholders' Equity
–106,600				–106,600

Date	Account and Explanation	Debit	Credit
Dec. 31	Supplies Expense	106,600	
	Supplies		106,600
	(Recognize supplies used)		

c. The adjustment to record the amount of deferred (unearned) revenue earned in 2013 is:

Assets	=	Liabilities	+	Stockholders' Equity
		–8,400		+8,400

Date	Account and Explanation	Debit	Credit
Dec. 31	Unearned Service Revenue	8,400	
	Service Revenue		8,400
	(Recognize revenue earned)		

d. The entry to record the accrual of salaries is:

Assets	=	Liabilities	+	Stockholders' Equity
		+1,500		–1,500

Date	Account and Explanation	Debit	Credit
Dec. 31	Salaries Expense	1,500	
	Salaries Payable		1,500
	(Recognize salary expense incurred but not paid)		

e. Interest expense is $1,600 ($120,000 × 8% × 2/12). The entry to accrue interest expense is:

Assets	=	Liabilities	+	Stockholders' Equity
		+1,600		–1,600

Date	Account and Explanation	Debit	Credit
Dec. 31	Interest Expense	1,600	
	Interest Payable		1,600
	(Recognize interest expense incurred but not paid)		

f. The entry to record depreciation expense for the building is:

Assets	=	Liabilities	+	Stockholders' Equity
–12,000				–12,000

Date	Account and Explanation	Debit	Credit
Dec. 31	Depreciation Expense (Building)	12,000	
	Accumulated Depreciation (Building)		12,000
	(Record depreciation expense)		

g. The entry to record depreciation expense for the equipment is:

Assets	=	Liabilities	+	Stockholders' Equity
–24,000				–24,000

Date	Account and Explanation	Debit	Credit
Dec. 31	Depreciation Expense (Equipment)	24,000	
	Accumulated Depreciation (Equipment)		24,000
	(Record depreciation expense)		

h. The adjustment for income taxes expense is:

Assets	=	Liabilities	+	Stockholders' Equity
		+5,200		–5,200

Date	Account and Explanation	Debit	Credit
Dec. 31	Income Tax Expense	5,200	
	Income Taxes Payable		5,200
	(Record accrual of income taxes)		

2. The adjusted account balances for Kenny's Laundry are shown in Exhibit 3.19.

EXHIBIT 3.19

Kenny's Laundry Adjusted Account Balances

Assets

Cash

4,800	

Accounts Receivable

26,000	
(a) 1,040	
27,040	

Supplies

128,000	106,600 (b)
21,400	

Land

124,400	

Building

249,000	

Accumulated Depreciation (Building)

	36,000
	12,000 (f)
	48,000

Equipment

122,000	

Accumulated Depreciation (Equipment)

	24,000
	24,000 (g)
	48,000

Other Assets

16,000	

Liabilities

Accounts Payable

	8,000

Notes Payable (due 2019)

	120,000

Interest Payable

	1,600 (e)
	1,600

Salaries Payable

	1,500 (d)
	1,500

Income Taxes Payable

	5,200 (h)
	5,200

Unearned Service Revenue

(c) 8,400	12,000
	3,600

Stockholders' Equity

Common Stock

	240,000

Retained Earnings, 12/31/2012

	69,000

Service Revenue

	874,200
	1,040 (a)
	8,400 (c)
	883,640

Rent Expense

168,000	

Wages Expense

431,000	

Insurance Expense

14,000	

Salaries Expense

92,000	
(d) 1,500	
93,500	

Interest Expense

8,000	
(e) 1,600	
9,600	

Supplies Expense

(b) 106,600	
106,600	

Depreciation Expense (Building)

(f) 12,000	
12,000	

Depreciation Expense (Equipment)

(g) 24,000	
24,000	

Income Taxes Expense

(h) 5,200	
5,200	

3. The income statement, statement of changes in retained earnings, and balance sheet for Kenny's Laundry are prepared from the adjusted account balances and appear in Exhibit 3.20.

EXHIBIT 3.20

Financial Statements for Kenny's Laundry

Kenny's Laundry Income Statement For the year ended December 31, 2013		
Service revenue		$883,640
Less expenses:		
Wages expense	$431,000	
Rent expense	168,000	
Supplies expense	106,600	
Salaries expense	93,500	
Depreciation expense (equipment)	24,000	
Insurance expense	14,000	
Depreciation expense (building)	12,000	
Interest expense	9,600	
Income taxes expense	5,200	863,900
Net income		$ 19,740

Kenny's Laundry Retained Earnings Statement For the year ended December 31, 2013	
Retained earnings, 12/31/2012	$69,000
Add: Net income	19,740
Less: Dividends	0
Retained earnings, 12/31/2013	$88,740

Kenny's Laundry Balance Sheet December 31, 2013			
ASSETS			
Current assets:			
Cash		$ 4,800	
Accounts receivable		27,040	
Supplies		21,400	
Total current assets			$ 53,240
Property, plant, and equipment:			
Land		$124,400	
Building	$249,000		
Less: Accumulated depreciation	(48,000)	201,000	
Equipment	$122,000		
Less: Accumulated depreciation	(48,000)	74,000	
Total property, plant, and equipment			399,400
Other assets			16,000
Total assets			$468,640

LIABILITIES AND STOCKHOLDERS' EQUITY		
Current liabilities:		
Accounts payable	$ 8,000	
Salaries payable	1,500	
Interest payable	1,600	
Income taxes payable	5,200	
Unearned service revenue	3,600	
Total current liabilities		$ 19,900
Long-term liabilities:		
Notes payable (due 2019)		120,000
Total liabilities		$139,900
Stockholders' equity:		
Common stock	$240,000	
Retained earnings	88,740	
Total stockholders' equity		328,740
Total liabilities and stockholders' equity		$468,640

4. The entries to close the accounts are:

Date	Account and Explanation	Debit	Credit
Dec. 31	Service Revenue	883,640	
	Income Summary		883,640
	(Close revenues)		
31	Income Summary	863,900	
	Rent Expense		168,000
	Wages Expense		431,000
	Insurance Expense		14,000
	Salaries Expense		93,500
	Supplies Expense		106,600
	Depreciation Expense (Building)		12,000
	Depreciation Expense (Equipment)		24,000
	Interest Expense		9,600
	Income Tax Expense		5,200
	(Close expenses)		
31	Income Summary	19,740	
	Retained Earnings		19,740
	(Close Income Summary)		

DISCUSSION QUESTIONS

1. How does accrual-basis net income differ from cash-basis net income?
2. Explain when revenue may be recognized and give an example.
3. What happens during the accounting cycle?
4. Provide two examples of transactions that begin and end at a particular point in time and two examples of continuous transactions.
5. Why are adjusting entries needed?
6. What accounting concepts require that adjusting entries be employed?
7. Describe the recording of transactions that begin and end at a particular point in time and the recording of continuous transactions.
8. For each of the four categories of adjusting entries, describe the business activity that produces circumstances requiring adjustment.

9. What is the difference between an *accrual* and a *deferral*?
10. Which type of adjustment will (a) increase both assets and revenues, (b) increase revenues and decrease liabilities, (c) increase expenses and decrease assets, and (d) increase both expenses and liabilities?
11. How is the amount for an interest expense (or interest revenue) adjustment determined?
12. Describe the effect on the financial statements when an adjustment is prepared that records (a) unrecorded revenue and (b) unrecorded expense.
13. On the basis of what you have learned about adjustments, why do you think that adjusting entries are made on the last day of the accounting period rather than at several times during the accounting period?
14. What is the purpose of closing entries?
15. Describe the four steps in the closing process.
16. Identify each of the following categories of accounts as temporary or permanent: assets, liabilities, equity, revenues, expenses, dividends. How is the distinction between temporary and permanent accounts related to the closing process?
17. Why are only the balance sheet accounts permanent?
18. List the seven steps in the accounting cycle in the order in which they occur and explain what occurs at each step of the accounting cycle.
19. *(Appendix 3A)* What is the relationship between the accounting cycle and the worksheet?
20. *(Appendix 3A)* Describe the structure of the worksheet and the accounting information it contains.

MULTIPLE-CHOICE QUESTIONS

3-1 Which of the following statements is true?

a. Under cash-basis accounting, revenues are recorded when earned and expenses are recorded when incurred.
b. Accrual-basis accounting records both cash and noncash transactions when they occur.
c. Generally accepted accounting principles require companies to use cash-basis accounting.
d. The key elements of accrual-basis accounting are the revenue recognition principle, the expense recognition (or matching) principle, and the historical cost principle.

3-2 In December 2013, Swanstrom Inc. receives a cash payment of $3,500 for services performed in December 2013 and a cash payment of $4,500 for services to be performed in January 2014. Swanstrom also receives the December utility bill for $600 but does not pay this bill until 2014. For December 2013, under the accrual basis of accounting, Swanstrom would recognize:

a. $8,000 of revenue and $600 of expense.
b. $8,000 of revenue and $0 of expense.
c. $3,500 of revenue and $600 of expense.
d. $3,500 of revenue and $0 of expense.

3-3 Which transaction would require adjustment at December 31?

a. The sale of merchandise for cash on December 30.
b. Common stock was issued on November 30.
c. Salaries were paid to employees on December 31 for work performed in December.
d. A 1-year insurance policy (which took effect immediately) was purchased on December 1.

3-4 Which of the following statements is *false*?

a. Adjusting entries are necessary because timing differences exist between when a revenue or expense is recognized and cash is received or paid.
b. Adjusting entries always affect at least one revenue or expense account and one asset or liability account.
c. The cash account will always be affected by adjusting journal entries.
d. Adjusting entries can be classified as either accruals or deferrals.

3-5 Dallas Company loaned $10,000 to Ewing Company on December 1, 2013. Ewing will pay Dallas $720 of interest ($60 per month) on November 30, 2014. Dallas's adjusting entry at December 31, 2013, is:

a. Interest Expense	60		c. Interest Receivable	60	
Cash		60	Interest Revenue		60
b. Cash	60		d. No adjusting entry is required.		
Interest Revenue		60			

3-6 Ron's Diner received the following bills for December 2013 utilities:

- Electricity: $625 on December 29, 2013
- Telephone: $150 on January 5, 2014

Both bills were paid on January 10, 2014. On the December 31, 2013, balance sheet, Ron's Diner will report accrued expenses of:

a. $0
b. $150.
c. $625.
d. $775.

3-7 In September 2013, GolfWorld Magazine obtained $15,000 of subscriptions for 1 year of magazines and credited Unearned Sales Revenue. The magazines will begin to be delivered in October 2013. At December 31, 2013, GolfWorld should make the following adjustment:

a. Debit Sales Revenue by $3,750 and credit Unearned Sales Revenue by $3,750.
b. Debit Unearned Sales Revenue by $3,750 and credit Sales Revenue by $3,750.
c. Debit Sales Revenue by $11,250 and credit Unearned Sales Revenue by $11,250.
d. Debit Unearned Sales Revenue by $11,250 and credit Sales Revenue by $11,250.

3-8 Hurd Inc. prepays rent every 3 months on March 1, June 1, September 1, and December 1. Rent for the 3 months totals $3,600. On December 31, 2013, Hurd will report Prepaid Rent of:

a. $0
b. $1,200
c. $2,400
d. $3,600

3-9 Which of the following statements is *incorrect* regarding preparing financial statements?

a. The adjusted trial balance lists only the balance sheet accounts in a "debit" and "credit" format.
b. The adjusted trial balance is the primary source of information needed to prepare the financial statements.
c. The financial statements are prepared in the following order: (1) the income statement, (2) the retained earnings statement, and (3) the balance sheet.
d. The income statement and the balance sheet are related through the retained earnings account.

3-10 Reinhardt Company reported revenues of $122,000 and expenses of $83,000 on its 2013 income statement. In addition, Reinhardt paid $4,000 of dividends during 2013. On December 31, 2013, Reinhardt prepared closing entries. The net effect of the closing entries on retained earnings was a(n):

a. decrease of $4,000.
b. increase of $35,000.
c. increase of $39,000.
d. decrease of $87,000.

3-11 Which of the following is true regarding the accounting cycle?

a. The accounts are adjusted after preparing the financial statements.
b. Journal entries are made prior to the transaction being analyzed.
c. The temporary accounts are closed after the financial statements are prepared.
d. An adjusted trial balance is usually prepared after the accounts are closed.

CORNERSTONE EXERCISES

OBJECTIVE 1
CORNERSTONE 3.1

Cornerstone Exercise 3-12 Accrual- and Cash-Basis Revenue

McDonald Music sells used CDs for $4.00 each. During the month of April, McDonald sold 7,650 CDs for cash and 13,220 CDs on credit. McDonald's cash collections in April included $30,600 for the CDs sold for cash, $12,800 for CDs sold on credit during the previous month, and $29,850 for CDs sold on credit during April.

Required:

Calculate the amount of revenue recognized in April under (1) cash-basis accounting and (2) accrual-basis accounting.

OBJECTIVE 1
CORNERSTONE 3.1

Cornerstone Exercise 3-13 Accrual- and Cash-Basis Expenses

Speedy Delivery Company provides next-day delivery across the southeastern United States. During May, Speedy incurred $132,600 in fuel costs. Speedy paid $95,450 of the fuel cost in May, with the remainder paid in June. In addition, Speedy paid $15,000 in May to another fuel supplier in an effort to build up its supply of fuel.

Required:

Calculate the amount of expense recognized in May under (1) cash-basis accounting and (2) accrual-basis accounting.

OBJECTIVE 2
CORNERSTONE 3.1

Cornerstone Exercise 3-14 Revenue Recognition Principle

Heartstrings Gift Shoppe sells an assortment of gifts for any occasion. During October, Heartstrings started a Gift-of-the-Month program. Under the terms of this program, beginning in the month of the sale, Heartstrings would select and deliver a random gift each month, over the next 12 months, to the person the customer selects as a recipient. During October, Heartstrings sold 25 of these packages for a total of $11,280 in cash.

Required:

For the month of October, calculate the amount of revenue that Heartstrings will recognize.

OBJECTIVE 2
CORNERSTONE 3.1

Cornerstone Exercise 3-15 Expense Recognition (or Matching) Principle

The following information describes transactions for Morgenstern Advertising Company during July:

a. On July 5, Morgenstern purchased and received $24,300 of supplies on credit from Drexel Supply Inc. During July, Morgenstern paid $20,500 cash to Drexel and used $18,450 of the supplies.
b. Morgenstern paid $9,600 to salespeople for salaries earned during July. An additional $1,610 was owed to salespeople at July 31 for salaries earned during the month.
c. Paid $2,950 to the local utility company for electric service. Electric service in July was $2,300 of the $2,950 total bill.

Required:

Calculate the amount of expense recognized in July under (1) cash-basis accounting and (2) accrual-basis accounting.

OBJECTIVE 3
CORNERSTONE 3.2

Cornerstone Exercise 3-16 Identification of Adjusting Entries

Singleton Inc. uses the accrual basis of accounting and had the following transactions during the year.

a. Merchandise was sold to customers on credit.
b. Purchased equipment to be used in the operation of its business.
c. A 2-year insurance contract was purchased.

d. Received cash for services to be performed over the next year.
e. Paid weekly employee salaries.
f. Borrowed money from First Bank by signing a note payable due in 5 years.

Required:

Identify and explain why each transaction may or may not require adjustment.

Cornerstone Exercise 3-17 Accrued Revenue Adjusting Entries

OBJECTIVE 4
CORNERSTONE 3.3

Powers Rental Service had the following items that require adjustment at year end.

a. Earned $9,880 of revenue from the rental of equipment for which the customer had not yet paid.
b. Interest of $650 on a note receivable has been earned but not yet received.

Required:

1. Prepare the adjusting entries needed at December 31.
2. What is the effect on the financial statements if these adjusting entries are not made?

Cornerstone Exercise 3-18 Accrued Expense Adjusting Entries

OBJECTIVE 4
CORNERSTONE 3.4

Manning Manufacturing Inc. had the following items that require adjustment at year end.

a. Salaries of $5,320 that were earned in December are unrecorded and unpaid.
b. Used $1,970 of utilities in December, which are unrecorded and unpaid.
c. Interest of $925 on a note payable has not been recorded or paid.

Required:

1. Prepare the adjusting entries needed at December 31.
2. What is the effect on the financial statements if these adjusting entries are not made?

Cornerstone Exercise 3-19 Deferred Revenue Adjusting Entries

OBJECTIVE 4
CORNERSTONE 3.5

Olney Cleaning Company had the following items that require adjustment at year end.

a. For one cleaning contract, $14,520 cash was received in advance. The cash was credited to Unearned Service Revenue upon receipt. At year end, $1,210 of the service revenue was still unearned.
b. For another cleaning contract, $9,840 cash was received in advance and credited to Unearned Service Revenue upon receipt. At year end, $3,280 of the services had been provided.

Required:

1. Prepare the adjusting journal entries needed at December 31.
2. What is the effect on the financial statements if these adjusting entries are not made?
3. What is the balance in Unearned Service Revenue at December 31 related to the two cleaning contracts?

Cornerstone Exercise 3-20 Deferred Expense Adjusting Entries

OBJECTIVE 4
CORNERSTONE 3.6

Best Company had the following items that require adjustment at year end.

a. Cash for equipment rental in the amount of $3,800 was paid in advance. The $3,800 was debited to prepaid rent when paid. At year end, $2,950 of the prepaid rent had expired.
b. Cash for insurance in the amount of $8,200 was paid in advance. The $8,200 was debited to prepaid insurance when paid. At year end, $1,850 of the prepaid insurance was still unused.

Required:

1. Prepare the adjusting journal entries needed at December 31.
2. What is the effect on the financial statements if these adjusting entries are not made?
3. What is the balance in prepaid equipment rent and insurance expense at December 31?

OBJECTIVE 4
CORNERSTONE 3.6

Cornerstone Exercise 3-21 Adjustment for Supplies

Pain-Free Dental Group Inc. purchased dental supplies of $18,200 during the year. At the end of the year, a physical count of supplies showed $4,125 of supplies on hand.

Required:

1. Prepare the adjusting entry needed at the end of the year.
2. What is the amount of supplies reported on Pain-Free's balance sheet at the end of the year?

OBJECTIVE 4
CORNERSTONE 3.6

Cornerstone Exercise 3-22 Adjustment for Depreciation

LaGarde Company has a machine that it purchased for $125,000 on January 1. Annual depreciation on the machine is estimated to be $14,500.

Required:

1. Prepare the adjusting entry needed at the end of the year.
2. What is the book value of the machine reported on LaGarde's balance sheet at the end of the year?

OBJECTIVE 4
CORNERSTONE 3.3
CORNERSTONE 3.4
CORNERSTONE 3.5
CORNERSTONE 3.6

Cornerstone Exercise 3-23 Financial Statement Effects of Adjusting Entries

When adjusting entries were made at the end of the year, the accountant for Parker Company did not make the following adjustments.

a. $2,900 of wages had been earned by employees but were unpaid.
b. $3,750 of revenue had been earned but was uncollected and unrecorded.
c. $2,400 of revenue had been earned. The customer had prepaid for this service and the amount was originally recorded in the Unearned Sales Revenue account.
d. $1,200 of insurance coverage had expired. Insurance had been initially recorded in the Prepaid Insurance account.

Required:

Identify the effect on the financial statements of the adjusting entries that were omitted.

Use the following information for Cornerstone Exercises 3-24 through 3-27:
Sparrow Company had the following adjusted trial balance at December 31, 2013.

Sparrow Company
Adjusted Trial Balance
December 31, 2013

	Debit	Credit
Cash	$ 3,150	
Accounts Receivable	5,650	
Prepaid Insurance	4,480	
Equipment	42,000	
Accumulated Depreciation (Equipment)		$ 24,000
Accounts Payable		2,800
Salaries Payable		4,450
Unearned Service Revenue		3,875
Common Stock		8,000
Retained Earnings		2,255
Dividends	10,500	
Service Revenue		99,600
Salaries Expense	49,400	
Rent Expense	17,250	
Insurance Expense	2,200	
Depreciation Expense	4,950	
Income Taxes Expense	5,400	
Totals	$144,980	$144,980

Cornerstone Exercise 3-24 Preparing an Income Statement

OBJECTIVE 5
CORNERSTONE 1.3

Refer to the information for Sparrow Company on the previous page.

Required:

Prepare a single-step income statement for Sparrow for 2013.

Cornerstone Exercise 3-25 Preparing a Retained Earnings Statement

OBJECTIVE 5
CORNERSTONE 1.4

Refer to the information for Sparrow Company on the previous page.

Required:

Prepare a retained earnings statement for Sparrow for 2013.

Cornerstone Exercise 3-26 Preparing a Balance Sheet

OBJECTIVE 5
CORNERSTONE 1.2

Refer to the information for Sparrow Company on the previous page.

Required:

Prepare a classified balance sheet for Sparrow at December 31, 2013.

Cornerstone Exercise 3-27 Preparing and Analyzing Closing Entries

OBJECTIVE 6
CORNERSTONE 3.7

Refer to the information for Sparrow Company on the previous page.

Required:

1. Prepare the closing entries for Sparrow at December 31, 2013.
2. How does the closing process affect retained earnings?

BRIEF EXERCISES

Brief Exercise 3-28 Accrual- and Cash-Basis Accounting

OBJECTIVE 1

The following are several transactions for Halpin Advertising Company.

a. Purchased $1,000 of supplies.
b. Sold $5,000 of advertising services, on account, to customers.
c. Used $250 of supplies.
d. Collected $3,000 from customers in payment of their accounts.
e. Purchased equipment for $10,000 cash.
f. Recorded $500 depreciation on the equipment for the current period.

Required:

Identify the effect, if any, that each of the above transactions would have on net income under cash-basis accounting and accrual-basis accounting.

Brief Exercise 3-29 Revenue and Expense Recognition

OBJECTIVE 2

Lauhl Corporation provides janitorial services to several office buildings. During April, Lauhl engaged in the following transactions:

a. On April 1, Lauhl received $24,000 from Metro Corporation to provide cleaning services over the next 6 months.
b. On April 5, Lauhl purchased and received $8,500 of supplies on credit from Eagle Supply Company. During the month, Lauhl paid $5,000 to Eagle and used $1,300 of the supplies.
c. On April 20, Lauhl performed one-time cleaning services of $2,500 for Jones Company. Jones paid Lauhl the full amount on May 10.
d. On April 30, Lauhl paid employees wages of $3,400. An additional $850 was owed to employees for work performed in April.

Required:

Calculate the amount of net income that Lauhl should recognize in April under (1) cash-basis accounting and (2) accrual-basis accounting.

OBJECTIVE 3

Brief Exercise 3-30 Identification of Adjusting Entries

Examine the following accounts.

a. Prepaid Insurance
b. Inventory
c. Interest Payable
d. Unearned Service Revenue
e. Accumulated Depreciation

Required:

CONCEPTUAL CONNECTION Identify and explain why each account may or may not require adjustment.

OBJECTIVE 4

Brief Exercise 3-31 Adjusting Entries—Accruals

Nichols Company had the following items that required adjustment at December 31, 2013.

a. Electricity used during December was estimated to be $320. This amount will be paid in January.
b. Owed wages to employees of $3,250 that were earned in December but unrecorded and unpaid as of the end of the year.
c. Service revenue of $4,900 was earned in December but unbilled and unpaid as of year end.

Required:

1. Prepare the adjusting entries needed at December 31.
2. CONCEPTUAL CONNECTION What is the effect on the financial statements if these adjusting entries were not made?

OBJECTIVE 4

Brief Exercise 3-32 Adjusting Entries—Deferrals

Tyndal Company had the following items that required adjustment at December 31, 2013.

a. Purchased equipment for $40,000 on January 1, 2013. Tyndal estimates annual depreciation expense to be $3,100.
b. Paid $2,400 for a 2-year insurance policy on July 1, 2013. The amount was debited to Prepaid Insurance when paid.
c. Collected $1,200 rent for the period December 1, 2013 to March 30, 2014. The amount was credited to Unearned Service Revenue when received.

Required:

1. Prepare the adjusting entries needed at December 31.
2. CONCEPTUAL CONNECTION What is the effect on the financial statements if these adjusting entries were not made?

OBJECTIVE 5

Brief Exercise 3-33 Preparing an Income Statement

The adjusted trial balance of Pelton Company at December 31, 2013, includes the following accounts: Wages Expense, $22,400; Service Revenue, $38,400; Rent Expense, $3,200; Dividends, $4,000; Retained Earnings, $12,200; and Prepaid Rent, $1,000.

Required:

Prepare a single-step income statement for Pelton for 2013.

OBJECTIVE 5

Brief Exercise 3-34 Preparing a Retained Earnings Statement

Refer to the information presented in **Brief Exercise 3-33** for Pelton Company. The balance in Retained Earnings of $12,200 represents the balance as of January 1, 2013.

Required:

Prepare a retained earnings statement for Pelton for 2013.

Brief Exercise 3-35 Classifying Balance Sheet Items

OBJECTIVE 5

A classified balance sheet contains the following categories:

Current assets	Other assets
Long-term investments	Current liabilities
Property, plant, and equipment	Long-term liabilities
Intangible assets	Stockholders' equity

Required:

For each of the following accounts, list the correct balance sheet category where the item would typically appear.

a. Notes Payable (due in 5 years)
b. Accounts Receivable
c. Patent
d. Prepaid Rent
e. Accumulated Depreciation
f. Common Stock
g. Accounts Payable
h. Cash
i. Unearned Service Revenue
j. Equipment

Brief Exercise 3-36 Preparing and Analyzing Closing Entries

OBJECTIVE 6

At December 31, 2013, the ledger of Aulani Company includes the following accounts, all having normal balances: Sales Revenue, \$59,000; Cost of Goods Sold, \$31,000; Retained Earnings, \$20,000; Interest Expense, \$3,200; Dividends, \$5,000; Wages Expense \$8,000, and Interest Payable, \$2,100.

Required:

1. Prepare the closing entries for Aulani at December 31, 2013.
2. How does the closing process affect Aulani's retained earnings?

Brief Exercise 3-37 The Accounting Cycle

OBJECTIVE 7

Below are the steps of the accounting cycle.

Journalize transaction.	Analyze transaction.	Close the accounts.
Prepare financial statements.	Adjust the account.	Post to the ledger.
Prepare a trial balance.		

Required:

List these steps of the accounting cycle in their proper order.

EXERCISES

Exercise 3-38 Accrual- and Cash-Basis Expense Recognition

OBJECTIVE 1

The following information is taken from the accrual accounting records of Kroger Sales Company:

a. During January, Kroger paid \$9,150 for supplies to be used in sales to customers during the next 2 months (February and March). The supplies will be used evenly over the next 2 months.
b. Kroger pays its employees at the end of each month for salaries earned during that month. Salaries paid at the end of February and March amounted to \$4,925 and \$5,100, respectively.
c. Kroger placed an advertisement in the local newspaper during March at a cost of \$850. The ad promoted the pre-spring sale during the last week in March. Kroger did not pay for the newspaper ad until mid-April.

Required:

1. Under cash-basis accounting, how much expense should Kroger report for February and March?
2. Under accrual-basis accounting, how much expense should Kroger report for February and March?
3. **CONCEPTUAL CONNECTION** Which basis of accounting provides the most useful information for decision-makers? Why?

OBJECTIVE 2

Exercise 3-39 Revenue Recognition

Each of the following situations relates to the recognition of revenue:

a. A store sells a gift card in December which will be given as a Christmas present. The card is not redeemed until January.
b. A furniture store sells and delivers furniture to a customer in June with no payments and no interest for 6 months.
c. An airline sells an airline ticket and collects the fare in February for a flight in March to a spring break destination.
d. A theme park sells a season pass and collects the cash in January which allows entrance into the park for an entire year.
e. A package delivery service delivers a package in October but doesn't bill the customer and receive payment until November.

Required:

CONCEPTUAL CONNECTION For each situation, indicate when the company should recognize revenue on an accrual basis.

OBJECTIVE 2

Exercise 3-40 Revenue and Expense Recognition

Electronic Repair Company repaired a high-definition television for Sarah Merrifield in December 2013. Sarah paid $80 at the time of the repair and agreed to pay Electronic Repair $80 each month for 5 months beginning on January 15, 2014. Electronic Repair used $120 of supplies, which were purchased in November 2013, to repair the television. Assume that Electronic Repair uses accrual-basis accounting.

Required:

1. In what month or months should revenue from this service be recorded by Electronic Repair?
2. In what month or months should the expense related to the repair of the television be recorded by Electronic Repair?
3. **CONCEPTUAL CONNECTION** Describe the accounting principles used to answer the above questions.

OBJECTIVE 1 2

Exercise 3-41 Cash-Basis and Accrual-Basis Accounting

The records of Summers Building Company reveal the following information for 2013.

a. Cash receipts during 2013 (including $50,000 paid by stockholders in exchange for common stock) were $273,500.
b. Cash payments during 2013 (including $8,000 of dividends paid to stockholders) were $164,850.
c. Total selling price of services billed to customers during 2013 was $201,700.
d. Salaries earned by employees during 2013 were $114,250.
e. Cost of supplies used during 2013 in operation of the business was $47,325.

Required:

1. Calculate Summers Building's net income for 2013 on an accrual basis.
2. Calculate Summers Building's net income for 2013 on a cash basis.
3. **CONCEPTUAL CONNECTION** Explain how cash-basis accounting allows for the manipulation of income.

OBJECTIVE 2

Exercise 3-42 Revenue and Expense Recognition

Omega Transportation Inc., headquartered in Atlanta, Georgia, uses accrual-basis accounting and engaged in the following transactions:

- billed customers $3,580,000 for transportation services
- collected cash from customers in the amount of $2,479,000
- purchased fuel supplies for $1,655,000 cash
- used fuel supplies that cost $1,598,240
- employees earned salaries of $425,160
- paid employees $413,380 cash for salaries

Required:

Determine the amount of sales revenue and total expenses for Omega's income statement.

Exercise 3-43 Recognizing Expenses

OBJECTIVE 2

Treadway Dental Services gives each of its patients a toothbrush with the name and phone number of the dentist office and a logo imprinted on the brush. Treadway purchased 15,000 of the toothbrushes in October 2013 for $3,130. The toothbrushes were delivered in November and paid for in December 2013. Treadway began to give the patients the toothbrushes in February 2014. By the end of 2014, 4,500 of the toothbrushes remained in the supplies account.

Required:

1. How much expense should be recorded for the 15,000 toothbrushes in 2013 and 2014 to properly match expenses with revenues?
2. Describe how the 4,500 toothbrushes that remain in the supplies account will be handled in 2015.

Exercise 3-44 Revenue Expense and Recognition

OBJECTIVE 1 2

ILLUSTRATING RELATIONSHIPS

Carrico Advertising Inc. performs advertising services for several Fortune 500 companies. The following information describes Carrico's activities during 2013.

a. At the beginning of 2013, customers owed Carrico $45,800 for advertising services performed during 2012. During 2013, Carrico performed an additional $695,100 of advertising services on account. Carrico collected $708,700 cash from customers during 2013.
b. At the beginning of 2013, Carrico had $13,350 of supplies on hand for which it owed suppliers $8,150. During 2013, Carrico purchased an additional $14,600 of supplies on account. Carrico also paid $19,300 cash owed to suppliers for goods previously purchased on credit. Carrico had $2,230 of supplies on hand at the end of 2013.
c. Carrico's 2013 operating and interest expenses were $437,600 and $133,400, respectively.

Required:

1. Calculate Carrico's 2013 income before taxes.
2. Calculate the ending balance of accounts receivable, the supplies used, and the ending balance of accounts payable.
3. **CONCEPTUAL CONNECTION** Explain the underlying principles behind why the three accounts computed in Requirement 2 exist.

Exercise 3-45 Identification of Adjusting Entries

OBJECTIVE 3

Conklin Services prepares financial statements only once per year using an annual accounting period ending on December 31. Each of the following statements describes an entry made by Conklin on December 31 of a recent year.

a. On December 31, Conklin completed a service agreement for Pizza Planet and recorded the related revenue. The job started in August.
b. Conklin provides weekly service visits to the local C.J. Nickel department store to check and maintain various pieces of computer printing equipment. On December 31, Conklin recorded revenue for the visits completed during December. The cash will not be received until January.
c. Conklin's salaried employees are paid on the last day of every month. On December 31, Conklin recorded the payment of December salaries.
d. Conklin's hourly wage employees are paid every Friday. On December 31, Conklin recorded as payable the wages for the first three working days of the week in which the year ended.
e. On December 31, Conklin recorded the receipt of a shipment of office supplies from Office Supplies Inc. to be paid for in January.
f. On December 31, Conklin recorded the estimated use of supplies for the year. The supplies were purchased for cash earlier in the year.
g. Early in December, Conklin was paid in advance by Parker Enterprises for 2 months of weekly service visits. Conklin recorded the advance payment as a liability. On December 31, Conklin recorded revenue for the service visits to Parker Enterprises that were completed during December.
h. On December 31, Conklin recorded depreciation expense on office equipment for the year.

(Continued)

Required:

Indicate whether each entry is an *adjusting entry* or a *regular journal entry*, and, if it is an adjusting entry, identify it as one of the following types: (1) revenue recognized before collection of cash, (2) expense recognized before payment of cash, (3) revenue recognized after collection of cash, or (4) expense recognized after payment of cash.

OBJECTIVE 3

Exercise 3-46 Identification and Analysis of Adjusting Entries

Medina Motor Service is preparing adjusting entries for the year ended December 31, 2013. The following items describe Medina's continuous transactions during 2013:

a. Medina's salaried employees are paid on the last day of every month.
b. Medina's hourly employees are paid every other Friday for the preceding 2 weeks' work. The next payday falls on January 5, 2014.
c. In November 2013, Medina borrowed $600,000 from Bank One, giving a 9% note payable with interest due in January 2014. The note was properly recorded.
d. Medina rents a portion of its parking lot to the neighboring business under a long-term lease agreement that requires payment of rent 6 months in advance on April 1 and October 1 of each year. The October 1, 2013, payment was made and recorded as prepaid rent.
e. Medina's service department recognizes the entire revenue on every auto service job when the job is complete. At December 31, several service jobs are in process.
f. Medina recognizes depreciation on shop equipment annually at the end of each year.
g. Medina purchases all of its office supplies from Office Supplies Inc. All purchases are recorded in the supplies account. Supplies expense is calculated and recorded annually at the end of each year.

Required:

Indicate whether or not each item requires an adjusting entry at December 31, 2013. If an item requires an adjusting entry, indicate which accounts are increased by the adjustment and which are decreased.

OBJECTIVE 4

Exercise 3-47 Revenue Adjustments

Sentry Transport Inc. of Atlanta provides in-town parcel delivery services in addition to a full range of passenger services. Sentry engaged in the following activities during the current year:

a. Sentry received $5,000 cash in advance from Rich's Department Store for an estimated 250 deliveries during December 2013 and January and February of 2014. The entire amount was recorded as unearned revenue when received. During December 2013, 110 deliveries were made for Rich's.
b. Sentry operates several small buses that take commuters from suburban communities to the central downtown area of Atlanta. The commuters purchase, in advance, tickets for 50 one-way rides. Each 50-ride ticket costs $500. At the time of purchase, Sentry credits the cash received to unearned revenue. At year end, Sentry estimates that revenue from 10,160 one-way rides has been earned.
c. Sentry operates several buses that provide transportation for the clients of a social service agency in Atlanta. Sentry bills the agency quarterly at the end of January, April, July, and October for the service performed that quarter. The contract price is $7,500 per quarter. Sentry follows the practice of recognizing revenue from this contract in the period in which the service is performed.
d. On December 23, Delta Airlines chartered a bus to transport its marketing group to a meeting at a resort in southern Georgia. The meeting will be held during the last week in January 2014, and Delta agrees to pay for the entire trip on the day the bus departs. At year end, none of these arrangements have been recorded by Sentry.

Required:

1. Prepare adjusting entries at December 31 for these four activities.
2. **CONCEPTUAL CONNECTION** What would be the effect on revenue if the adjusting entries were not made?

Exercise 3-48 Expense Adjustments

OBJECTIVE 4

Faraday Electronic Service repairs stereos and DVD players. During 2013, Faraday engaged in the following activities:

a. On September 1, Faraday paid Wausau Insurance $4,860 for its liability insurance for the next 12 months. The full amount of the prepayment was debited to prepaid insurance.
b. At December 31, Faraday estimates that $1,520 of utility costs are unrecorded and unpaid.
c. Faraday rents its testing equipment from JVC. Equipment rent in the amount of $1,440 is unpaid and unrecorded at December 31.
d. In late October, Faraday agreed to become the sponsor for the sports segment of the evening news program on a local television station. The station billed Faraday $4,350 for 3 months' sponsorship—November 2013, December 2013, and January 2014—in advance. When these payments were made, Faraday debited prepaid advertising. At December 31, 2 months' advertising has been used and 1 month remains unused.

Required:

1. Prepare adjusting entries at December 31 for these four activities.
2. **CONCEPTUAL CONNECTION** What would be the effect on expenses if the adjusting entries were not made?

Exercise 3-49 Prepayments, Collections in Advance

OBJECTIVE 4

ILLUSTRATING RELATIONSHIPS

Greensboro Properties Inc. owns a building in which it leases office space to small businesses and professionals. During 2013, Greensboro Properties engaged in the following transactions:

a. On March 1, Greensboro Properties paid $10,500 in advance to Patterson Insurance Company for 1 year of insurance beginning March 1, 2013. The full amount of the prepayment was debited to prepaid insurance.
b. On May 1, Greensboro Properties received $30,000 for 1 year's rent from Angela Cottrell, a lawyer and new tenant. Greensboro Properties credited unearned rent revenue for the full amount collected from Cottrell.
c. On July 31, Greensboro Properties received $240,000 for 6 months' rent on an office building that is occupied by Newnan and Calhoun, a regional accounting firm. The rental period begins on August 1, 2013. The full amount received was credited to unearned rent revenue.
d. On November 1, Greensboro Properties paid $4,500 to Pinkerton Security for 3 months' security services beginning on that date. The entire amount was debited to prepaid security services.

Required:

1. Prepare the journal entry to record the receipt or payment of cash for each of the transactions.
2. Prepare the adjusting entries you would make at December 31, 2013, for each of these items.
3. **CONCEPTUAL CONNECTION** What would be the total effect on the income statement and balance sheet if these entries were not recorded?

Exercise 3-50 Prepayment of Expenses

OBJECTIVE 4

JDM Inc. made the following prepayments for expense items during 2013:

a. Prepaid building rent for 1 year on April 1 by paying $6,600. Prepaid rent was debited for the amount paid.
b. Prepaid 12 months' insurance on October 1 by paying $4,200. Prepaid insurance was debited.
c. Purchased $5,250 of office supplies on October 15, debiting supplies for the full amount. There were no office supplies on hand as of October 15. Office supplies costing $1,085 remain unused at December 31, 2013.
d. Paid $600 for a 12-month service contract for repairs and maintenance on a computer. The contract begins November 1. The full amount of the payment was debited to prepaid repairs and maintenance.

(Continued)

Required:

1. Prepare journal entries to record the payment of cash for each transaction.
2. Prepare adjusting entries for the prepayments at December 31, 2013.
3. **CONCEPTUAL CONNECTION** For all of the above items, assume that the accountant failed to make the adjusting entries. What would be the effect on net income?

OBJECTIVE 4

ILLUSTRATING RELATIONSHIPS

Exercise 3-51 Adjustment for Supplies

The downtown location of Chicago Clothiers purchases large quantities of supplies, including plastic garment bags and paper bags and boxes. At December 31, 2013, the following information is available concerning these supplies:

Supplies inventory, 1/1/2013	$ 4,150
Supplies inventory, 12/31/2013	5,220
Supplies purchased for cash during 2013	12,690

All purchases of supplies during the year are debited to the supplies inventory.

Required:

1. What is the expense reported on the income statement associated with the use of supplies during 2013?
2. What is the proper adjusting entry at December 31, 2013?
3. By how much would assets and income be overstated or understated if the adjusting entry were not recorded?

OBJECTIVE 4

Exercise 3-52 Adjusting Entries

Allentown Services Inc. is preparing adjusting entries for the year ending December 31, 2013. The following data are available:

a. Interest is owed at December 31, 2013, on a 6-month, 8% note. Allentown borrowed $120,000 from NBD on September 1, 2013.
b. Allentown provides daily building maintenance services to Mack Trucks for a quarterly fee of $2,700 payable on the fifteenth of the month following the end of each quarter. No entries have been made for the services provided to Mack Trucks during the quarter ended December 31, and the related bill will not be sent until January 15, 2014.
c. At the beginning of 2013, the cost of office supplies on hand was $1,220. During 2013, office supplies with a total cost of $6,480 were purchased from Office Depot and debited to office supplies inventory. On December 31, 2013, Allentown determined the cost of office supplies on hand to be $970.
d. On September 23, 2013, Allentown received a $7,650 payment from Bethlehem Steel for 9 months of maintenance services beginning on October 1, 2013. The entire amount was credited to unearned service revenue when received.

Required:

1. Prepare the appropriate adjusting entries at December 31, 2013.
2. **CONCEPTUAL CONNECTION** What would be the effect on the balance sheet and the income statement if the accountant failed to make the above adjusting entries?

OBJECTIVE 4

Exercise 3-53 Adjusting Entries

Reynolds Computer Service offers data processing services to retail clothing stores. The following data have been collected to aid in the preparation of adjusting entries for Reynolds Computer Service for 2013:

a. Computer equipment was purchased from IBM in 2010 at a cost of $540,000. Annual depreciation is $132,500.
b. A fire insurance policy for a 2-year period beginning September 1, 2013, was purchased from Good Hands Insurance Company for $12,240 cash. The entire amount of the

prepayment was debited to prepaid insurance. (Assume that the beginning balance of prepaid insurance was $0 and that there were no other debits or credits to that account during 2013.)

c. Reynolds has a contract to perform the payroll accounting for Dayton's Department Stores. At the end of 2013, $5,450 of services have been performed under this contract but are unbilled.

d. Reynolds rents 12 computer terminals for $65 per month per terminal from Extreme Terminals Inc. At December 31, 2013, Reynolds owes Extreme Terminals for half a month's rent on each terminal. The amount owed is unrecorded.

e. Perry's Tax Service prepays rent for time on Reynolds' computer. When payments are received from Perry's Tax Service, Reynolds credits unearned rent revenue. At December 31, 2013, Reynolds has earned $1,810 for computer time used by Perry's Tax Service during December 2013.

Required:

1. Prepare adjusting entries for each of the transactions.
2. **CONCEPTUAL CONNECTION** What would be the effect on the balance sheet and the income statement if the accountant failed to make the above adjusting entries?

Exercise 3-54 Recreating Adjusting Entries

OBJECTIVE 4

ILLUSTRATING RELATIONSHIPS

Selected balance sheet accounts for Gardner Company are presented below.

Prepaid Insurance (Dr.)	Prepaid Insurance (Cr.)	Wages Payable (Dr.)	Wages Payable (Cr.)	Unearned Sales Revenue (Dr.)	Unearned Sales Revenue (Cr.)	Interest Receivable (Dr.)	Interest Receivable (Cr.)
May 5 4,300			?		9,500 May 10	?	
	?			?			
1,250			5,400		2,250	825	

Required:

Analyze each account and recreate the journal entries that were made. For deferrals, be sure to include the original journal entry as well as the adjusting journal entry. Month end is May 31, 2013.

Exercise 3-55 Effect of Adjustments on the Financial Statements

OBJECTIVE 4

VanBrush Enterprises, a painting contractor, prepared the following adjusting entries at year end:

	Account	Debit	Credit
a.	Wages Expense	2,550	
	Wages Payable		2,550
b.	Accounts Receivable	8,110	
	Service Revenue		8,110
c.	Unearned Service Revenue	5,245	
	Service Revenue		5,245
d.	Rent Expense	3,820	
	Prepaid Rent		3,820

Required:

1. Show the effect of these adjustments on assets, liabilities, equity, revenues, expenses, and net income.
2. **CONCEPTUAL CONNECTION** If these adjustments were made with estimates that were considered conservative, how would this affect your interpretation of earnings quality?

Exercise 3-56 Preparing an Income Statement

OBJECTIVE 5

Oxmoor Corporation prepared the following adjusted trial balance.

(Continued)

Oxmoor Corporation
Adjusted Trial Balance
December 31, 2013

Account	Debit	Credit
Cash	$ 13,300	
Accounts Receivable	6,700	
Prepaid Rent	54,000	
Inventory	481,400	
Long-Term Investment	110,900	
Equipment	88,000	
Accumulated Depreciation		$ 23,700
Accounts Payable		111,700
Interest Payable		4,400
Note Payable (short-term)		50,000
Bonds Payable		180,000
Common Stock		300,000
Retained Earnings, 1/1/2013		45,635
Dividends	50,000	
Sales Revenue		583,900
Cost of Goods Sold	277,000	
Wages Expense	98,250	
Rent Expense	50,000	
Depreciation Expense	29,000	
Interest Expense	2,700	
Income Taxes Expense	38,085	
Totals	$1,299,335	$1,299,335

Required:

Prepare a single-step income statement for Oxmoor for the year ended December 31, 2013.

OBJECTIVE 5

Exercise 3-57 Preparing a Retained Earnings Statement

Refer to the unadjusted trial balance for Oxmoor Corporation in **Exercise 3-56**.

Required:

Prepare a retained earnings statement for Oxmoor for the year ended December 31, 2013.

OBJECTIVE 5

Exercise 3-58 Preparing a Balance Sheet

Refer to the unadjusted trial balance for Oxmoor Corporation in **Exercise 3-56**.

Required:

Prepare a classified balance sheet for Oxmoor at December 31, 2013.

OBJECTIVE 6

Exercise 3-59 Preparation of Closing Entries

Grand Rapids Consulting Inc. began 2013 with a retained earnings balance of $38,100 and has the following accounts and balances at year end:

Sales Revenue	$162,820	Supplies Expense	$ 4,348
Salaries Expense	91,660	Income Taxes Expense	13,800
Rent Expense	11,250	Dividends (declared and paid)	8,400
Utilities Expense	8,415		

Required:

1. Prepare the closing entries made by Grand Rapids Consulting at the end of 2013.
2. Prepare Grand Rapids Consulting's retained earnings statement for 2013.

Exercise 3-60 Preparation of Closing Entries

OBJECTIVE 6

James and Susan Morley recently converted a large turn-of-the-century house into a hotel and incorporated the business as Saginaw Enterprises. Their accountant is inexperienced and has made the following closing entries at the end of Saginaw's first year of operations:

Income Summary	210,000	
Service Revenue		177,000
Accumulated Depreciation		33,000
Depreciation Expense	33,000	
Income Taxes Expense	8,200	
Utilities Expense	12,700	
Wages Expense	66,000	
Supplies Expense	31,000	
Accounts Payable	4,500	
Income Summary		155,400
Income Summary	54,600	
Retained Earnings		54,600
Dividends	3,200	
Income Summary		3,200

Required:

1. Indicate what is wrong with the closing entries above.
2. Prepare the correct closing entries. Assume that all necessary accounts are presented above and that the amounts given are correct.
3. **CONCEPTUAL CONNECTION** Explain why closing entries are necessary.

Exercise 3-61 Preparation of a Worksheet *(Appendix 3A)*

OBJECTIVE 8

Unadjusted account balances at December 31, 2013, for Rapisarda Company are as follows:

Rapisarda Company
Unadjusted Trial Balance
December 31, 2013

Account	Debit	Credit
Cash	$ 2,000	
Accounts Receivable	33,000	
Prepaid Rent	26,000	
Equipment	211,000	
Accumulated Depreciation (Equipment)		$ 75,000
Other Assets	24,000	
Accounts Payable		12,000
Note Payable (due in 10 years)		40,000
Common Stock		100,000
Retained Earnings, 12/31/2012		11,000
Service Revenue		243,000
Rent Expense	84,000	
Wages Expense	97,000	
Interest Expense	4,000	
Totals	$481,000	$481,000

The following data are not yet recorded:

a. Depreciation on the equipment is $18,350.
b. Unrecorded wages owed at December 31, 2013: $4,680.
c. Prepaid rent at December 31, 2013: $9,240.
d. Income taxes expense: $5,463.

Required:

Prepare a completed worksheet for Rapisarda Company.

PROBLEM SET A

OBJECTIVE 1

Problem 3-62A Cash-Basis and Accrual-Basis Income

George Hathaway, an electrician, entered into an agreement with a real estate management company to perform all maintenance of basic electrical systems and air-conditioning equipment in the apartment buildings under the company's management. The agreement, which is subject to annual renewal, provides for the payment of a fixed fee of $6,600 on January 1 of each year plus amounts for parts and materials billed separately at the end of each month. Amounts billed at the end of 1 month are collected in the next month. During the first 3 months of 2013, George makes the following additional billings and cash collections:

	Billings for Parts and Materials	Cash Collected	Cash Paid for Parts and Materials	Cost of Parts and Materials Used
January	$280	$6,750*	$150	$160
February	0	250	185	170
March	320	0	290	300

* Includes $150 for parts and materials billed in December 2012.

Required:

1. Calculate the amount of cash-basis income reported for each of the first 3 months.
2. Calculate the amount of accrual-basis income reported for each of the first 3 months.
3. **CONCEPTUAL CONNECTION** Why do decision-makers prefer accrual-basis accounting?

OBJECTIVE 2

Problem 3-63A Revenue and Expense Recognition

Security Specialists performs security services for local businesses. During 2013, Security Specialists performed $1,425,700 of security services and collected $1,445,000 cash from customers. Security Specialist's employees earned salaries of $82,350 per month. During 2013, Security Services paid salaries of $980,200 cash for work performed. At the beginning of 2013, there were $2,875 of supplies on hand. Supplies of $65,800 were purchased during the year, and $9,225 of supplies were on hand at the end of the year. Other general and administrative expenses incurred during the year were $26,500.

Required:

1. Calculate revenue and expenses for 2013.
2. Prepare the 2013 income statement.
3. **CONCEPTUAL CONNECTION** Describe the accounting principles used to prepare the income statement.

OBJECTIVE 3 4

Problem 3-64A Identification and Preparation of Adjusting Entries

Kuepper's Day Care is a large daycare center in South Orange, New Jersey. The daycare center serves several nearby businesses as well as a number of individual families. The businesses pay $6,180 per child per year for daycare services for their employees' children. The businesses pay in advance on a quarterly basis. For individual families, daycare services are provided monthly and billed at the beginning of the next month. The following transactions describe Kuepper's activities during December 2013:

a. On December 1, Kuepper borrowed $50,000 by issuing a 5-year, $50,000, 9% note payable.
b. Daycare service in the amount of $13,390 was provided to individual families during December. These families will not be billed until January 2014.
c. At December 1, the balance in unearned service revenue was $26,780. At December 31, Kuepper determined that $10,300 of this revenue was still unearned.
d. On December 31, the daycare center collected $40,170 from businesses for services to be provided in 2014.
e. On December 31, the center recorded depreciation of $1,875 on a bus that it uses for field trips.

f. The daycare center had prepaid insurance at December 1 of $3,600. An examination of the insurance policies indicates that prepaid insurance at December 31 is $3,000.
g. Interest on the $50,000 note payable (see Transaction a) is unpaid and unrecorded at December 31.
h. Salaries of $35,480 are owed but unpaid on December 31.
i. Supplies of disposable diapers on December 1 are $4,200. At December 31, the cost of diapers in supplies is $750.

Required:

1. Identify whether each transaction is an adjusting entry or a regular journal entry. If the entry is an adjusting entry, identify it as an accrued revenue, accrued expense, deferred revenue, or deferred expense.
2. Prepare the entries necessary to record the transactions above and on the previous page.

Problem 3-65A Preparation of Adjusting Entries

OBJECTIVE 4

Bartow Photographic Services takes wedding and graduation photographs. At December 31, the end of Bartow's accounting period, the following information is available:

a. All wedding photographs are paid for in advance, and all cash collected for them is credited to Unearned Service Revenue. Except for a year end adjusting entry, no other entries are made for service revenue from wedding photographs. During the year, Bartow received $42,600 for wedding photographs. At year end, $37,400 of the $42,600 had been earned. The beginning-of-the-year balance of Unearned Service Revenue was zero.
b. During December, Bartow photographed 225 members of the next year's graduating class of Shaw High School. The school has asked Bartow to print one copy of a photograph of each student for the school files. Bartow delivers these photographs on December 28 and will bill the school $5.00 per student in January of next year. Revenue from photographs ordered by students will be recorded as the orders are received during the early months of next year.
c. Equipment used for developing and printing was rented for $22,500. The rental term was for 1 year beginning on August 1 and the entire year of rent was paid on August 1. The payment was debited to Prepaid Rent.
d. Depreciation on the firm's building for the current year is $9,400.
e. Wages of $4,170 are owed but unpaid and unrecorded at December 31.
f. Supplies at the beginning of the year were $2,400. During the year, supplies costing $19,600 were purchased from Kodak. When the purchases were made, their cost was debited to Supplies. At year end, a physical inventory indicated that supplies costing $4,100 were on hand.

Required:

1. Prepare the adjusting entries for each of these items.
2. **CONCEPTUAL CONNECTION** By how much would net income be overstated or understated if the accountant failed to make the adjusting entries?

Problem 3-66A Effects of Adjusting Entries on the Accounting Equation

OBJECTIVE 4

Four adjusting entries are shown below.

a.	Wages Expense	3,410	
	Wages Payable		3,410
b.	Accounts Receivable	8,350	
	Service Revenue		8,350
c.	Rent Expense	2,260	
	Prepaid Rent		2,260
d.	Unearned Service Revenue	5,150	
	Service Revenue		5,150

(Continued)

Required:

CONCEPTUAL CONNECTION Analyze the adjusting entries and identify their effects on the financial statement accounts. (*Note:* Ignore any income tax effects.) Use the following format for your answer:

Transaction	Assets	Liabilities	Common Stock	Retained Earnings	Revenues	Expenses

OBJECTIVE 4 5

Problem 3-67A Adjusting Entries and Financial Statements

You have the following unadjusted trial balance for Rogers Corporation at December 31, 2013:

Rogers Corporation
Unadjusted Trial Balance
December 31, 2013

Account	Debit	Credit
Cash	$ 3,100	
Accounts Receivable	15,900	
Supplies	4,200	
Prepaid Rent	9,500	
Equipment	625,000	
Accumulated Depreciation (Equipment)		$ 104,000
Other Assets	60,900	
Accounts Payable		9,400
Unearned Service Revenue		11,200
Note Payable (due 2016)		50,000
Common Stock		279,500
Retained Earnings, 12/31/2012		37,000
Service Revenue		598,000
Wages Expense	137,000	
Rent Expense	229,000	
Interest Expense	4,500	
Totals	$1,089,100	$1,089,100

At year end, you have the following data for adjustments:

a. An analysis indicates that prepaid rent on December 31 should be $2,300.
b. A physical inventory shows that $650 of office supplies is on hand.
c. Depreciation for 2013 is $35,250.
d. An analysis indicates that unearned service revenue should be $3,120.
e. Wages in the amount of $3,450 are owed but unpaid and unrecorded at year end.
f. Six months' interest at 8% on the note was paid on September 30. Interest for the period from October 1 to December 31 is unpaid and unrecorded.
g. Income taxes of $55,539 are owed but unrecorded and unpaid.

Required:

1. Prepare the adjusting entries.
2. Prepare an income statement, a retained earnings statement, and a balance sheet using adjusted account balances.
3. **CONCEPTUAL CONNECTION** Why would you not want to prepare financial statements until after the adjusting entries are made?

OBJECTIVE 4

Problem 3-68A Inferring Adjusting Entries from Account Balance Changes

ILLUSTRATING RELATIONSHIPS

The following schedule shows all the accounts of Fresno Travel Agency that received year end adjusting entries:

Account	Unadjusted Account Balance	Adjusted Account Balance
Prepaid Insurance	$ 23,270	$ 6,150
Prepaid Rent	3,600	2,100
Accumulated Depreciation	156,000	(a)
Wages Payable	0	6,750
Unearned Service Revenue	13,620	(b)
Service Revenue	71,600	78,980
Insurance Expense	0	(c)
Rent Expense	29,700	(d)
Depreciation Expense	0	12,500
Wages Expense	44,200	(e)

Required:

1. Calculate the missing amounts identified by the letters (a) through (e).
2. Prepare the five adjusting entries that must have been made to cause the account changes as indicated.

Problem 3-69A Preparation of Closing Entries and an Income Statement

OBJECTIVE 5 6

Round Grove Alarm Company provides security services to homes in northwestern Indiana. At year end 2013, after adjusting entries have been made, the following list of account balances is prepared:

Accounts Payable	$ 23,250	Prepaid Rent	$ 4,750
Accounts Receivable	36,800	Rent Expense	27,600
Accumulated Depreciation (Equipment)	124,000	Retained Earnings, 12/31/2012	29,400
Common Stock	150,000	Salaries Expense	148,250
Depreciation Expense (Equipment)	45,300	Salaries Payable	12,600
Dividends	6,000	Service Revenue	612,900
Equipment	409,500	Supplies	12,700
Income Taxes Expense	30,800	Supplies Expense	51,900
Income Taxes Payable	24,300	Utilities Expense	48,800
Interest Expense	4,800	Wages Expense	183,500
Notes Payable (due in 2016)	34,000	Wages Payable	7,950
Other Assets	7,700		

Required:

1. Prepare closing entries for Round Grove Alarm.
2. Prepare an income statement for Round Grove Alarm.

Problem 3-70A Comprehensive Problem: Reviewing the Accounting Cycle

OBJECTIVE 4 5 6 7

Tarkington Freight Service provides delivery of merchandise to retail grocery stores in the Northeast. At the beginning of 2013, the following account balances were available:

Cash	$ 92,100	Accumulated Depreciation (Equipment)	$ 580,000
Accounts Receivable	361,500	Land	304,975
Supplies	24,600	Accounts Payable	17,600
Prepaid Advertising	2,000	Wages Payable	30,200
Building (Warehouse)	2,190,000	Notes Payable (due in 2017)	1,000,000
Accumulated Depreciation (Warehouse)	280,000	Common Stock	1,400,000
Equipment	795,000	Retained Earnings, 12/31/2012	462,375

During 2013 the following transactions occurred:

a. Tarkington performed deliveries for customers, all on credit, for $2,256,700. Tarkington also made cash deliveries for $686,838.
b. There remains $286,172 of accounts receivable to be collected at December 31, 2013.

(Continued)

c. Tarkington purchased advertising of $138,100 during 2013 and debited the amount to prepaid advertising.
d. Supplies of $27,200 were purchased on credit and debited to the supplies account.
e. Accounts payable at the beginning of 2013 were paid early in 2013. There remains $5,600 of accounts payable unpaid at year end.
f. Wages payable at the beginning of 2013 were paid early in 2013. Wages were earned and paid during 2013 in the amount of $666,142.
g. During the year, Trish Hurd, a principal stockholder, purchased an automobile costing $42,000 for her personal use.
h. One-half year's interest at 6% annual rate was paid on the note payable on July 1, 2013.
i. Property taxes were paid on the land and buildings in the amount of $170,000.
j. Dividends were declared and paid in the amount of $25,000.

The following data are available for adjusting entries:

- Supplies in the amount of $13,685 remained unused at year end.
- Annual depreciation on the warehouse building is $70,000.
- Annual depreciation on the warehouse equipment is $145,000.
- Wages of $60,558 were unrecorded and unpaid at year end.
- Interest for 6 months at 6% per year on the note is unpaid and unrecorded at year end.
- Advertising of $14,874 remained unused at the end of 2013.
- Income taxes of $482,549 related to 2013 are unpaid at year end.

Required:

1. Post the 2013 beginning balances to T-accounts. Prepare journal entries for Transactions a through j and post the journal entries to T-accounts, adding any new T-accounts you need.
2. Prepare the adjustments and post the adjustments to the T-accounts, adding any new T-accounts you need.
3. Prepare an income statement.
4. Prepare a retained earnings statement.
5. Prepare a classified balance sheet
6. Prepare closing entries.
7. **CONCEPTUAL CONNECTION** Did you include Transaction g among Tarkington's 2013 journal entries? Why or why not?

OBJECTIVE 4 5 6 7 8

Problem 3-71A Preparing a Worksheet *(Appendix 3A)*

Marsteller Properties Inc. owns apartments that it rents to university students. At December 31, 2013, the following unadjusted account balances were available:

Cash	$ 4,600	Notes Payable (due in 2015)	$2,000,000
Rent Receivable	32,500	Common Stock	1,500,000
Supplies	4,700	Retained Earnings, 12/31/2012	39,200
Prepaid Insurance	60,000	Rent Revenue	660,000
Land	274,000	Repairs & Maintenance Expense	73,200
Buildings	4,560,000	Advertising Expense	58,700
Accumulated Depreciation		Wages Expense	84,300
(Buildings)	1,015,000	Utilities Expense	3,400
Other Assets	26,100	Interest Expense	90,000
Accounts Payable	57,300		

The following information is available for adjusting entries:

a. An analysis of apartment rental contracts indicates that $3,800 of apartment rent is unbilled and unrecorded at year end.
b. A physical count of supplies reveals that $1,400 of supplies are on hand at December 31, 2013.
c. Annual depreciation on the buildings is $204,250.
d. An examination of insurance policies indicates that $12,000 of the prepaid insurance applies to coverage for 2013.
e. Six months' interest at 9% is unrecorded and unpaid on the notes payable.

f. Wages in the amount of $6,100 are unpaid and unrecorded at December 31.
g. Utilities costs of $300 are unrecorded and unpaid at December 31.
h. Income taxes of $5,738 are unrecorded and unpaid at December 31.

Required:

1. Prepare a worksheet for Marsteller Properties.
2. Prepare an income statement, a retained earnings statement, and a classified balance sheet for Marsteller Properties.
3. Prepare the closing entries.

PROBLEM SET B

Problem 3-62B Cash-Basis and Accrual-Basis Income

OBJECTIVE 1

Martin Sharp operates a lawn mower repair business. He maintains an inventory of repair parts that are purchased from a wholesale supplier. Martin's records show the following information for the first 3 months of 2013.

	Cash Collected for Repair Work	Amounts Billed to Customers	Cash Payments to Supplier	Cost of Parts Used in Repairs
January	$3,200	$2,800	$1,165	$915
February	2,475	3,500	300	605
March	2,910	3,275	0	880

Required:

1. Ignoring expenses other than repair parts, calculate net income for each of the 3 months on a cash basis.
2. Ignoring expenses other than repair parts, calculate net income for each of the 3 months on an accrual basis.
3. **CONCEPTUAL CONNECTION** Why do decision-makers prefer accrual-basis accounting?

Problem 3-63B Revenue and Expense Recognition

OBJECTIVE 2

Aunt Bea's Catering Service provides catering service for special occasions. During 2013, Aunt Bea performed $228,500 of catering services and collected $218,200 of cash from customers. Salaries earned by Aunt Bea's employees during 2013 were $49,900. Aunt Bea paid employees $45,100 during 2013. Aunt Bea had $1,200 of supplies on hand at the beginning of the year and purchased an additional $12,640 of supplies during the year. Supplies on hand at the end of 2013 were $2,820. Other selling and administrative expenses incurred during 2013 were $10,800.

Required:

1. Calculate revenue and expenses for 2013.
2. Prepare the 2013 income statement.
3. **CONCEPTUAL CONNECTION** Describe the accounting principles used to prepare the income statement.

Problem 3-64B Identification and Preparation of Adjusting Entries

OBJECTIVE 3 4

Morgan Dance Inc. provides ballet, tap, and jazz dancing instruction to promising young dancers. Morgan began operations in January 2014 and is preparing its monthly financial statements. The following items describe Morgan's transactions in January 2014:

a. Morgan requires that dance instruction be paid in advance—either monthly or quarterly. On January 1, Morgan received $4,125 for dance instruction to be provided during 2014.
b. On January 31, Morgan noted that $825 of dance instruction revenue is still unearned.
c. On January 20, Morgan's hourly employees were paid $1,415 for work performed in January.

(Continued)

d. Morgan's insurance policy requires semiannual premium payments. Morgan paid the $3,000 insurance policy which covered the first half of 2014 in December 2013.
e. When there are no scheduled dance classes, Morgan rents its dance studio for birthday parties for $100 per two-hour party. Four birthday parties were held during January. Morgan will not bill the parents until February.
f. Morgan purchased $350 of office supplies on January 10.
g. On January 31, Morgan determined that office supplies of $85 were unused.
h. Morgan received a January utility bill for $770. The bill will not be paid until it is due in February.

Required:

1. Identify whether each transaction is an adjusting entry or a regular journal entry. If the entry is an adjusting entry, identify it as an accrued revenue, accrued expense, deferred revenue, or deferred expense.
2. Prepare the entries necessary to record the transactions above and on the previous page.

OBJECTIVE 4

Problem 3-65B Preparation of Adjusting Entries

West Beach Resort operates a resort complex that specializes in hosting small business and professional meetings. West Beach closes its fiscal year on January 31, a time when it has few meetings under way. At January 31, 2014, the following data are available:

a. A training meeting is under way for 16 individuals from Fashion Design. Fashion Design paid $4,500 in advance for each person attending the 10-day training session. The meeting began on January 28 and will end on February 6.
b. Twenty-one people from Northern Publishing are attending a sales meeting. The daily fee for each person attending the meeting is $280 (charged for each night a person stays at the resort). The meeting began on January 29, and guests will depart on February 2. Northern will be billed at the end of the meeting.
c. Depreciation on the golf carts used to transport the guests' luggage to and from their rooms is $11,250 for the year. West Beach records depreciation yearly.
d. At January 31, Friedrich Catering is owed $1,795 for food provided for guests through that date. This amount is unrecorded. West Beach classifies the cost of food as an "other expense" on the income statement.
e. An examination indicates that the cost of office supplies on hand at January 31 is $189. During the year, $850 of office supplies was purchased from Supply Depot. The cost of supplies purchased was debited to Office Supplies Inventory. No office supplies were on hand on January 31, 2013.

Required:

1. Prepare adjusting entries at January 31 for each of these items.
2. **CONCEPTUAL CONNECTION** By how much would net income be overstated or understated if the accountant failed to make the adjusting entries?

OBJECTIVE 4

Problem 3-66B Effects of Adjusting Entries on the Accounting Equation

Four adjusting entries are shown below.

	Account	Debit	Credit
a.	Interest Expense	1,875	
	Interest Payable		1,875
b.	Interest Receivable	1,150	
	Interest Revenue		1,150
c.	Insurance Expense	2,560	
	Prepaid Insurance		2,560
d.	Unearned Rent Revenue	4,680	
	Rent Revenue		4,680

Required:

CONCEPTUAL CONNECTION Analyze the adjusting entries and identify their effects on the financial statement accounts. (*Note:* Ignore any income tax effects.) Use the following format for your answer:

Transaction	Assets	Liabilities	Common Stock	Retained Earnings	Revenues	Expenses

Problem 3-67B Adjusting Entries and Financial Statements

OBJECTIVE 4 5

The unadjusted trial balance for Mitchell Pharmacy appears below.

Mitchell Pharmacy
Unadjusted Trial Balance
December 31, 2013

Account	Debit	Credit
Cash	$ 3,400	
Accounts Receivable	64,820	
Inventory	583,400	
Prepaid Insurance	11,200	
Building	230,000	
Accumulated Depreciation (Building)		$ 44,000
Land	31,200	
Other Assets	25,990	
Accounts Payable		47,810
Notes Payable (due 2015)		150,000
Common Stock		600,000
Retained Earnings, 12/31/2012		41,200
Service Revenue		950,420
Wages Expense	871,420	
Interest Expense	12,000	
Totals	$1,833,430	$1,833,430

The following information is available at year end for adjustments:

a. An analysis of insurance policies indicates that $2,180 of the prepaid insurance is coverage for 2014.
b. Depreciation expense for 2013 is $10,130.
c. Four months' interest at 10% is owed but unrecorded and unpaid on the note payable.
d. Wages of $4,950 are owed but unpaid and unrecorded at December 31.
e. Income taxes of $11,370 are owed but unrecorded and unpaid at December 31.

Required:

1. Prepare the adjusting entries.
2. Prepare an income statement, a retained earnings statement, and a balance sheet using adjusted account balances.
3. **CONCEPTUAL CONNECTION** Why would you not want to prepare financial statements until after the adjusting entries are made?

Problem 3-68B Inferring Adjusting Entries from Account Balance Changes

OBJECTIVE 4

ILLUSTRATING RELATIONSHIPS

The following schedule shows all the accounts of Eagle Imports that received year end adjusting entries:

Account	Unadjusted Account Balance	Adjusted Account Balance
Prepaid Insurance	$ 15,390	$ (a)
Accumulated Depreciation	92,500	103,000
Interest Payable	0	(b)
Wages Payable	0	(c)

(Continued)

Account	Unadjusted Account Balance	Adjusted Account Balance
Unearned Service Revenue	$ 12,250	$ 2,620
Service Revenue	122,500	(d)
Insurance Expense	1,500	12,746
Interest Expense	1,125	5,300
Depreciation Expense	0	(e)
Wages Expense	24,200	41,800

Required:

1. Calculate the missing amounts identified by the letters (a) through (e).
2. Prepare the five adjusting entries that must have been made to cause the account changes as indicated.

OBJECTIVE 5 6

Problem 3-69B Preparation of Closing Entries and an Income Statement

Port Austin Boat Repair Inc. has entered and posted its adjusting entries for 2013. The following are selected account balances after adjustment:

Sales Revenue	$692,500	Insurance Expense	$94,300
Interest Revenue	7,600	Wages Payable	11,700
Accounts Payable	8,330	Utilities Expense	12,300
Wages Expense	405,300	Interest Expense	9,500
Accounts Receivable, 12/31/2013	65,000	Depreciation Expense (Equipment)	20,000
Supplies Expense	68,350	Accumulated Depreciation (Equipment)	75,000
Supplies, 12/31/2013	179,000	Income Taxes Expense	12,300
Prepaid Rent	7,200	Income Taxes Payable	8,300
Rent Expense	28,800	Dividends	7,800
Unearned Sales Revenue	12,200		

Required:

1. Using the accounts and balances above, prepare the closing entries for 2013.
2. Prepare an income statement for Port Austin Boat Repair.

OBJECTIVE 4 5 6 7

Problem 3-70B Comprehensive Problem: Reviewing the Accounting Cycle

Wilburton Riding Stables provides stables, care for animals, and grounds for riding and showing horses. The account balances at the beginning of 2013 were:

Cash	$ 2,200	Accounts Payable	$ 23,700
Accounts Receivable	4,400	Income Taxes Payable	15,100
Supplies (Feed and Straw)	27,800	Interest Payable	2,700
Land	167,000	Wages Payable	14,200
Buildings	115,000	Notes Payable (due in 2017)	60,000
Accumulated Depreciation (Buildings)	36,000	Common Stock	150,000
Equipment	57,000	Retained Earnings	55,200
Accumulated Depreciation (Equipment)	16,500		

During 2013, the following transactions occurred:

a. Wilburton provided animal care services, all on credit, for $210,300. Wilburton rented stables to customers for $20,500 cash. Wilburton rented its grounds to individual riders, groups, and show organizations for $41,800 cash.
b. There remains $15,600 of accounts receivable to be collected at December 31, 2013.
c. Feed in the amount of $62,900 was purchased on credit and debited to the supplies account.
d. Straw was purchased for $7,400 cash and debited to the supplies account.
e. Wages payable at the beginning of 2013 were paid early in 2013. Wages were earned and paid during 2013 in the amount of $112,000.
f. The income taxes payable at the beginning of 2013 were paid early in 2013.
g. Payments of $73,000 were made to creditors for supplies previously purchased on credit.
h. One year's interest at 9% was paid on the note payable on July 1, 2013.

i. During 2013, Jon Wilburton, a principal stockholder, purchased a horse for his wife, Jennifer, to ride. The horse cost $7,000, and Wilburton used his personal credit to purchase it. The horse is stabled at the Wilburtons' home rather than at the riding stables.
j. Property taxes were paid on the land and buildings in the amount of $17,000.
k. Dividends were declared and paid in the amount of $7,200.

The following data are available for adjusting entries:

- Supplies (feed and straw) in the amount of $30,400 remained unused at year end.
- Annual depreciation on the buildings is $6,000.
- Annual depreciation on the equipment is $5,500.
- Wages of $4,000 were unrecorded and unpaid at year end.
- Interest for 6 months at 9% per year on the note is unpaid and unrecorded at year end.
- Income taxes of $16,500 were unpaid and unrecorded at year end.

Required:

1. Post the 2013 beginning balances to T-accounts. Prepare journal entries for Transactions a through k and post the journal entries to T-accounts, adding any new T-accounts you need.
2. Prepare the adjustments and post the adjustments to the T-accounts, adding any new T-accounts you need.
3. Prepare an income statement.
4. Prepare a retained earnings statement.
5. Prepare a classified balance sheet.
6. Prepare closing entries.
7. **CONCEPTUAL CONNECTION** Did you include Transaction i among Wilburton's 2013 journal entries? Why or why not?

Problem 3-71B Preparing a Worksheet *(Appendix 3A)*

OBJECTIVE 4 5 6 7 8

Flint Inc. operates a cable television system. At December 31, 2013, the following unadjusted account balances were available:

Cash	$ 2,000	Common Stock	$300,000
Accounts Receivable	89,000	Retained Earnings, 12/31/2012	14,700
Supplies	5,000	Dividends	28,000
Land	37,000	Service Revenue	985,000
Building	209,000	Royalties Expense	398,000
Accumulated Depreciation (Building)	40,000	Property Taxes Expense	10,500
Equipment	794,000	Wages Expense	196,000
Accumulated Depreciation (Equipment)	262,000	Utilities Expense	34,000
Other Assets	19,700	Miscellaneous Expense	44,000
Accounts Payable	29,500	Interest Expense	15,000
Notes Payable (due in 2017)	250,000		

The following data are available for adjusting entries:

a. At year end, $1,500 of office supplies remain unused.
b. Annual depreciation on the building is $20,000.
c. Annual depreciation on the equipment is $150,000.
d. The interest rate on the note is 8%. Four months' interest is unpaid and unrecorded at December 31, 2013.
e. At December 31, 2013, service revenue of $94,000 has been earned but is unbilled and unrecorded.
f. Utility bills of $2,800 are unpaid and unrecorded at December 31, 2013.
g. Income taxes of $49,633 were unpaid and unrecorded at year end.

Required:

1. Prepare a worksheet for Flint.
2. Prepare an income statement, a retained earnings statement, and a classified balance sheet for Flint.
3. Prepare the closing entries.

CASES

Case 3-72 Cash- or Accrual-Basis Accounting

Karen Ragsdale owns a business that rents parking spots to students at the local university. Karen's typical rental contract requires the student to pay the year's rent of $450 ($50 per month) on September 1. When Karen prepares financial statements at the end of December, her accountant requires that Karen spread the $450 over the 9 months that each parking spot is rented. Therefore, Karen can recognize only $200 of revenue (4 months) from each parking spot rental contract in the year the cash is collected and must defer (delay) recognition of the remaining $250 (5 months) to the next year. Karen argues that getting students to agree to rent the parking spot is the most difficult part of the activity so she ought to be able to recognize all $450 as revenue when the cash is received from a student.

Required:

Why do generally accepted accounting principles require the use of accrual accounting rather than cash-basis accounting for transactions like the one described here?

Case 3-73 Recognition of Service Contract Revenue

Zac Murphy is president of Blooming Colors Inc. which provides landscaping services in Tallahassee, Florida. On November 20, 2013, Mr. Murphy signed a service contract with Eastern State University. Under the contract, Blooming Colors will provide landscaping services for all of Eastern's buildings for a period of 2 years beginning on January 1, 2014, and Eastern will pay Blooming Colors on a monthly basis beginning on January 31, 2014. Although the same amount of landscaping services will be rendered in every month, the contract provides for higher monthly payments in the first year.

Initially, Mr. Murphy proposed that the revenue from the contract should be recognized when the contract is signed in 2013; however, his accountant, Sue Storm, convinced him that this would be inappropriate. Then Mr. Murphy proposed that the revenue should be recognized in an amount equal to the cash collected under the contract. Again, Ms. Storm argued against his proposal, indicating that generally accepted accounting principles (GAAP) required recognition of an equal amount of contract revenue each month.

Required:

1. Give a reason that might explain Mr. Murphy's desire to recognize contract revenue earlier rather than later.
2. Put yourself in the position of Sue Storm. How would you convince Mr. Murphy that his two proposals are unacceptable and that an equal amount of revenue should be recognized every month?
3. If Ms. Storm's proposal is adopted, how would the contract be reflected in the balance sheets at the end of 2013 and at the end of 2014?

Case 3-74 Revenue Recognition

Melaney Parks purchased HealthPlus Fitness in January 2013. Melaney wanted to increase the size of the business by selling 3-year memberships for $3,000, payable at the beginning of the membership period. The normal yearly membership fee is $1,500. Since few prospective members were expected to want to spend $3,000 at the beginning of the membership period, Melaney arranged for a local bank to provide a $3,000 installment loan to prospective members. By the end of 2013, 250 customers had purchased the 3-year memberships using the loan provided by the bank.

Melaney prepared her income statement for 2013 and included $750,000 ($3,000 × 250 members) as revenue because the club had collected the entire amount in cash. Melaney's accountant objected to the inclusion of the entire $750,000. The accountant argued that the $750,000 should be recognized as revenue as the club provides services for these members during the membership period. Melaney countered with a quotation from generally accepted accounting principles:

Profit is deemed to be realized when a sale in the ordinary course of business is effected, unless the circumstances are such that collection of the sale price is not reasonably assured.

Melaney notes that memberships have been sold and the collection of the selling price has occurred. Therefore, she argues that all $750,000 is revenue in 2013.

Required:

1. Write a short statement supporting either Melaney or the accountant in this dispute.
2. Would your answer change if the $3,000 fee were nonrefundable? Why or why not?

Case 3-75 Applying the Expense Recognition (or Matching) Principle

Newman Properties Inc. completed construction of a new shopping center in July 2013. During the first 6 months of 2013, Newman spent $550,000 for salaries, preparation of documents, travel, and other similar activities that was directly and incrementally associated with securing tenants (Nordstrom, Best Buy, and Office Depot) for the center. The center will open on August 1 with all its stores rented on 4-year leases. The rental revenue that Newman expects to receive from the current tenants is $8,500,000 per year for 4 years. The leases will be renegotiated at the end of the fourth year. The accountant for Newman wonders whether the $550,000 should be expensed in 2013 or whether it should be initially recorded as an asset and matched against revenues over the 4-year lease term.

Required:

Write a short statement indicating why you support expensing the $550,000 in the current period or spreading the expense over the 4-year lease term.

Case 3-76 Adjusting Entries for Refund Coupons

Cal-Lite Products Inc. manufactures a line of food products that appeals to persons interested in weight loss. To stimulate sales, Cal-Lite includes cash refund coupons in many of its products. Cal-Lite issues the purchaser a check when the coupon is returned to the company, which may be many months after the product is sold to stores and distributors. In addition, a significant number of coupons issued to customers are never returned.

Required:

1. Explain the conceptual basis for the determination of the expense in each year. Describe the information and calculations required to estimate the amount of expense for each year.
2. Describe the adjusting entry required at the end of each period of the program's existence.

Case 3-77 Adjusting Entries for Motion Picture Revenues

Link Pictures Inc. sells (licenses) the rights to exhibit motion pictures to theaters. Under the sales contract, the theater promises to pay a license fee equal to the larger of a guaranteed minimum or a percentage of the box office receipts. In addition, the contract requires the guaranteed minimum to be paid in advance. Consider the following contracts entered by Link during 2013:

a. Contract **A** authorizes a group of theaters in Buffalo, New York, to exhibit a film called Garage for 2 weeks ending January 7, 2014. Box office statistics indicate that first-week attendance has already generated licensing fees well in excess of the guaranteed minimum.
b. Contract **B** authorizes a chain of theaters in Miami, Florida, to exhibit a film called Blue Denim for a period of 2 weeks ending January 20, 2014. In most first-run cities, the film has attracted large crowds, and the percentage of box office receipts has far exceeded the minimum.
c. Contract **C** authorizes a chain of theaters in San Francisco to exhibit a film called Toast Points for a period of 2 weeks ending on December 12, 2013. The film is a "dog" and the theaters stopped showing it after the first few days. All prints of the film were returned by December 31, 2013.

The guaranteed minimum has been paid on all three contracts and recorded as unearned revenue. No other amounts have been received, and no revenue has been recorded for any of the contracts. Adjusting entries for 2013 are about to be made.

Required:

Describe the adjusting entry you would make at December 31, 2013, to record each contract.

Case 3-78 Effect of Adjusting Entries on Financial Statements (A Conceptual Approach)

Don Berthrong, the manager of the local Books-A-Million, is wondering how adjusting entries will affect his financial statements. Don's business has grown steadily for several years, and Don expects it to continue to grow for the next several years at a rate of 5 to 10% per year. Nearly all of Don's sales are for cash. Other than cost of goods sold, which is not affected by adjusting entries, most of Don's expenses are for items that require cash outflows (e.g., rent on the building, wages, utilities, and insurance).

Required:

1. Would Don's financial statement be affected significantly by adjusting entries?
2. Consider all businesses. What kinds of transactions would require adjustments that would have a significant effect on the financial statements? What kinds of businesses would be likely to require these kinds of adjustments?

Case 3-79 Interpreting Closing Entries

Barnes Building Systems made the following closing entries at the end of a recent year:

a.	Income Summary	129,750	
	Retained Earnings		129,750
b.	Retained Earnings	25,000	
	Dividends		25,000
c.	Sales Revenue	495,300	
	Income Summary		495,300
d.	Income Summary	104,100	
	Interest Expense		104,100

Required:

1. What was Barnes's net income?
2. By how much did Barnes's retained earnings change?
3. If the sales revenue identified in Entry c was Barnes's only revenue, what was the total amount of Barnes's expenses?

Case 3-80 Research and Analysis Using the Annual Report

Obtain **FedEx Corporation**'s 2011 annual report either through the "Investor Relations" portion of their website (do a web search for FedEx investor relations) or go to www.sec.gov and click "Search for Company Filings" under "Filings & Forms."

Required:

1. How does FedEx apply the revenue recognition principle?
2. With regard to the balance sheet and the income statement, what accounts may have required adjusting entries? Would these accounts require accruals or deferrals?
3. How much did FedEx owe its employees for services performed at the end of the 2011 fiscal year?
4. How much would FedEx credit to Income Summary for 2011? How much would be debited to Income Summary for 2011?
5. How much did FedEx report as income tax expense for 2011? How much did FedEx report as cash paid for taxes for 2011? Why are the amounts different and where does this difference get reported on FedEx's financial statements?

Case 3-81 Comparative Analysis: Under Armour, Inc., versus VF Corporation

Refer to the financial statements of **Under Armour, Inc.**, and **VF Corporation** that are supplied with this text.

Required:

1. Describe each company's revenue recognition policy. Is this policy consistent with the revenue recognition principle?

2. Which accounts on the balance sheet and income statement of each company may require adjusting entries? Would these accounts require accruals or deferrals?
3. How much would Under Armour credit and debit to Income Summary for the year ending December 31, 2011? How much would VF credit and debit to Income Summary for the fiscal year ending December, 2011?
4. Compare how much each company reported as income tax expense and as cash paid for taxes for the most recent year. Why are the amounts different, and where would this difference be reported on the financial statements?

Case 3-82 CONTINUING PROBLEM: FRONT ROW ENTERTAINMENT

Cam and Anna are very satisfied with their first month of operations. Their major effort centered on signing various artists to live performance contracts, and they had more success than they had anticipated. In addition to Charm City, they were able to use their contacts in the music industry to sign 12 other artists. With the tours starting in February, Cam and Anna were eager to hold their first big event. Over the next month, the following transactions occurred.

Feb.	1	Collected advance ticket sales of $28,400 relating to various concerts that were being promoted.
	1	Paid $800 to rent office space in February.
	2	Paid Equipment Supply Services $1,500, the balance remaining from the January 3 purchase of supplies.
	6	Paid $30,150 to secure venues for future concerts. (These payments are recorded as Prepaid Rent.)
	9	Received $325 related to the festival held on January 25.
	12	Purchased $475 of supplies on credit from Equipment Supply Services.
	15	Collected $3,400 of ticket sales for the first Charm City concert on the day of the concert.
	15	Paid Charm City $9,000 for performing the Feb. 15 concert. (*Remember:* Front Row records the fees paid to the artist in the Artist Fee Expense account.)
	20	Collected advance ticket sales of $10,125 relating to various concerts that were being promoted.
	21	Collected $5,100 of ticket sales for the second Charm City concert on the day of the concert.
	21	Paid Charm City $12,620 for performing the Feb. 21 concert.

At the end of February, Cam and Anna felt like their business was doing well; however, they decided that they needed to prepare financial statements to better understand the operations of the business. Anna gathered the following information relating to the adjusting entries that needed to be prepared at the end of February.

a. Two months of interest on the note payable is accrued. The interest rate is 9%.
b. A count of the supplies revealed that $1,825 of supplies remained on hand at the end of February.
c. Two months of the annual insurance has expired.
d. Depreciation related to the office equipment was $180 per month.
e. The rental of the venues for all four Charm City concerts was paid in advance on January 8. As of the end of February, Charm City has performed two of the four concerts in the contract.
f. An analysis of the unearned sales revenue account reveals that $8,175 of the balance relates to concerts that have not yet been performed.
g. Neither Cam nor Anna have received their salary of $1,200 each for February.
h. A utility bill of $435 relating to utility service on Front Row's office for January and February was received but not paid by the end of February.

Required:

1. Analyze and journalize the February transactions.
2. Set up T-accounts for each account, and post the transactions to the T-accounts. Be sure to use the balances computed in Chapter 2 as the beginning balances of the T-accounts.
3. Prepare a trial balance at February 28, 2013.
4. Prepare and post the adjusting entries needed at February 28, 2013.
5. By how much would net income be overstated or understated if the adjusting entries were not made?
6. Prepare an income statement and a retained earnings statement for the 2-month period ending February 28, 2013. Prepare a classified balance sheet as of February 28, 2013.
7. Prepare the necessary closing entries.

MAKING THE CONNECTION

INTEGRATIVE EXERCISE (CHAPTERS 1–3)

The Accounting Cycle

Begin with the following account balances for University Street Parking Garage (assume all accounts have normal balances) at December 31, 2013:

Accounts payable	$ 16,700
Accounts receivable	39,200
Accumulated depreciation (equipment)	36,800
Cash	6,700
Common stock (20,000 shares)	100,000
Depreciation expense (equipment)	12,300
Dividends	6,300
Equipment	269,500
Income taxes expense	2,700
Income taxes payable	1,100
Interest expense	16,500
Interest payable	0
Interest revenue	4,100
Inventory	4,900
Investments	35,000
Notes payable (due May 2, 2019)	160,000
Prepaid rent (4 months)	36,400
Rent expense	94,400
Retained earnings, 12/31/2012	43,000
Service revenue, parking	224,600
Service revenue, repair	208,100
Supplies expense	36,900
Wages expense	233,600
Wages payable	0

Required:

1. For the following transactions, provide the necessary adjusting entries and update the account balances to appropriately reflect these adjusting entries:
   a. The only lease held by University Street Parking required a rental payment of $9,100 per month. University Street Parking has prepaid rent through March 31, 2014.
   b. At December 31, 2013, University Street Parking owes employees wages of $12,500.
   c. University Street Parking should have total depreciation expense on equipment for 2013 of $14,300.
   d. The note payable of $160,000 has an interest rate of 6.75%. University Street Parking has paid interest through October 31, 2013.
2. Prepare a properly classified income statement for 2013, retained earnings statement for 2013, and a properly classified balance sheet as of December 31, 2013, using the post-adjustment account balances.

4 Internal Control and Cash

© Pixelfabrik/Alamy

After studying Chapter 4, you should be able to:

1. Discuss the role of internal controls in managing a business.
2. Discuss the five components of internal control.
3. Describe how businesses account for and report cash.
4. Describe how businesses control cash.
5. Describe the operating cycle and explain the principles of cash management.

EXPERIENCE FINANCIAL ACCOUNTING

with Initech

Peter Gibbons is a software engineer at Initech. He has an awful commute, an annoying boss, and a girlfriend he's pretty sure is cheating on him. Of course, Peter is the fictional star of the film *Office Space*. So, what do Peter and Initech have to do with accounting? In the movie, Initech is going through a downsizing and Peter finds out his best friends, Samir and (the unfortunately named) Michael Bolton, are about to be fired. To get back at Initech, the three friends decide to alter the company's software to take the fractions of a penny that are rounded off when calculating interest and deposit them into their personal account. They believe their scheme is undetectable because nobody will notice the gradual theft of these miniscule amounts. However, over time the sheer number of transactions will accumulate to a large sum.

"In this chapter, we discuss the policies and procedures companies put in place to prevent intentional and unintentional error, theft, and fraud. These policies and procedures are referred to as the internal control system."

The morning after altering Initech's software, Peter checks the account balance and finds it contains over $300,000. In a panic Peter calls his friends, and Michael Bolton concedes he made a "small" mistake. In the movie the three friends attempt to repay the money and are "saved" by a fire that burns Initech's offices. You may think that this could never happen, but such schemes are real and are known by various names such as "penny shaving" or "salami slicing."

In a somewhat related scheme, a hacker noticed that, when opening online brokering accounts (such as through **Google** checkout, **PayPal**, and many brokerage houses), it is common practice for the companies to send a confirming payment of a few cents to ensure you have access to the bank account or credit card. The hacker then wrote an automated program (known as a *bot*) to open almost 60,000 such accounts, collecting many thousands of these small payments into a few personal bank accounts. This isn't obviously illegal; however, he did run afoul of mail and bank fraud laws because he used false names, addresses, and Social Security numbers when opening the accounts.

In this chapter, we discuss the policies and procedures companies put in place to prevent intentional and unintentional error, theft, and fraud. These policies and procedures are referred to as the internal control system. For example, a commonly seen control that is designed to prevent use of bots to sign up or log in to web functions is a security check where the user must type in the distorted letters seen in a box (**Ticketmaster**, for example, does this to thwart scalpers).

OBJECTIVE 1

Discuss the role of internal controls in managing a business.

ROLE OF INTERNAL CONTROL

Except in very small businesses, top management delegates responsibility for engaging in business activities and recording their effects in the accounting system to other managers and employees. Management wants to make sure that these employees both:

- operate within the scope of their assigned responsibility
- act for the good of the business

To control employees' activities, management puts in place procedures that collectively are called the **internal control system**.

Internal control systems include all the policies and procedures established by top management and the board of directors to provide reasonable assurance that the company's objectives are being met in the following three areas (see the 3 columns in Exhibit 4.1):[1]

- Operations Objectives: effectiveness and efficiency of the entity's operations, including financial performance goals and safeguarding assets against loss.
- Reporting Objectives: reliability of reporting. They include internal and external financial and non-financial reporting.
- Compliance Objectives: compliance with applicable laws and regulations.

EXHIBIT 4.1

Relationship of Objectives, the Entity, and the Components of Internal Control

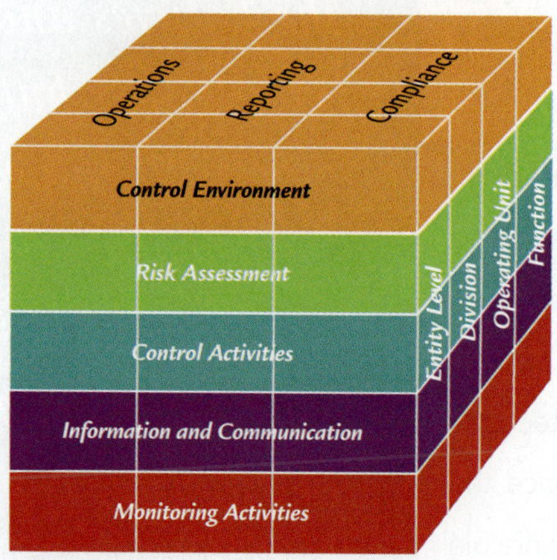

Source: COSO, *Internal Control—Integrated Framework*, 2011. Used with permission of COSO.

As such, internal control systems include many elements only indirectly related to our primary concern—the accounting system and financial statements. For example, policies and procedures concerning the extent and nature of research and development or advertising activities may have an important effect on the achievement of an entity's objectives but only indirectly affect its accounting system and financial statements.

IFRS

The documentation and assessment requirements of the Sarbanes-Oxley Act imposes a greater burden on U.S. companies relative to international companies.

Under the Sarbanes-Oxley Act of 2002, top management of publicly traded corporations have an increased responsibility for a system of internal controls that ensures the reliability of the financial statements. For example, the Act requires management to produce an internal control report. This report must acknowledge that management is responsible for establishing and maintaining an adequate internal control system and procedures for financial reporting and also that management assess the effectiveness of these controls. Further, the Act requires the principal executive and financial officers to certify that they are responsible for establishing and maintaining the system of internal control over financial reporting (see Exhibit 4.2). This certification was designed to prevent top management

[1] The Committee of Sponsoring Organizations of the Treadway Commission (COSO), *Internal Control-Integrated Framework*, 2011.

EXHIBIT 4.2

Section 302 Certification by Kevin Plank (CEO of Under Armour) Taken from SEC Filings (Exhibit 31.01 of 10-K) for the Year Ended December 31, 2011

I, Kevin A. Plank, certify that:

1. I have reviewed this annual report on Form 10-K of Under Armour, Inc.;

2. Based on my knowledge, this report does not contain any untrue statement of a material fact or omit to state a material fact necessary to make the statements made, in light of the circumstances under which such statements were made, not misleading with respect to the period covered by this report;

3. Based on my knowledge, the financial statements, and other financial information included in this report, fairly present in all material respects the financial condition, results of operations and cash flows of the registrant as of, and for, the periods presented in this report;

4. The registrant's other certifying officer and I are responsible for establishing and maintaining disclosure controls and procedures and internal control over financial reporting for the registrant and have:

a) designed such disclosure controls and procedures, or caused such disclosure controls and procedures to be designed under our supervision, to ensure that material information relating to the registrant, including its consolidated subsidiaries, is made known to us by others within those entities, particularly during the period in which this report is being prepared;

b) designed such internal control over financial reporting, or caused such internal control over financial reporting to be designed under our supervision, to provide reasonable assurance regarding the reliability of financial reporting and the preparation of financial statements for external purposes in accordance with generally accepted accounting principles;

c) evaluated the effectiveness of the registrant's disclosure controls and procedures and presented in this report our conclusions about the effectiveness of the disclosure controls and procedures, as of the end of the period covered by this report based on such evaluation; and

d) disclosed in this report any change in the registrant's internal control over financial reporting that occurred during the registrant's most recent fiscal quarter (the registrant's fourth fiscal quarter in the case of an annual report) that has materially affected, or is reasonably likely to materially affect, the registrant's internal control over financial reporting; and

5. The registrant's other certifying officer and I have disclosed, based on our most recent evaluation of internal control over financial reporting, to the registrant's auditors and the audit committee of the registrant's board of directors (or persons performing the equivalent functions):

a) all significant deficiencies and material weaknesses in the design or operation of internal control over financial reporting which are reasonably likely to adversely affect the registrant's ability to record, process, summarize and report financial information; and

b) any fraud, whether or not material, that involves management or other employees who have a significant role in the registrant's internal control over financial reporting.

Date: February 24, 2012

By:

Kevin A. Plank

President, Chief Executive Officer and Chairman of the Board of Directors

Source: Under Armour, Inc. 2011, Exhibit 31.01 10-K.

from denying knowledge or understanding of deceptive financial reporting as was tried in court by executives of **WorldCom**, among others.

In this chapter, we will examine the components of internal controls and demonstrate controls over cash, a company's most vulnerable asset. We will address the following questions:

- What are the five components of internal control?
- How are those controls applied to cash?
- How does the operating cycle affect cash?
- Why is cash management so important to a company?

OBJECTIVE 2

Discuss the five components of internal control.

COMPONENTS OF INTERNAL CONTROL

The Committee of Sponsoring Organizations of the Treadway Commission (COSO), identified five components of an internal control system: the control environment, risk assessment, control activities, information and communication, and monitoring activities (see the 5 rows of Exhibit 4.1). Each component is crucial to meeting the company's objectives. These components are relevant to every level of a company's organizational structure including the overall entity and its subsidiaries or divisions (if any). In addition, any individual operating units, functions, or other subset defined by the organization would be subject to such internal control components (see the 3rd dimension of Exhibit 4.1).

Control Environment and Ethical Behavior

The foundation of the internal control system is the **control environment**—the collection of environmental factors that influence the effectiveness of control procedures. The control environment includes the following:

- philosophy and operating style of management
- personnel policies and practices of the business
- overall integrity, attitude, awareness, and actions of everyone in the business concerning the importance of control (commonly called the *tone at the top*)

An important feature of the control environment is recognizing that an individual employee's goals may differ from the goals of other individuals and the goals of the business. For example, when managers receive a bonus based on certain accounting numbers, like sales, they have been known to ship a large quantity of merchandise to customers right before year-end—even if the merchandise was not ordered (done by such companies as **Bausch and Lomb**, **IBM**, etc.). Although much of the merchandise was returned in the following year, sales targets for the current year were met and bonuses were paid.

Resolving these conflicting incentives in an ethical manner that promotes organizational objectives is highly dependent on the tone at the top. For example, hiring and firing practices that put zero tolerance on unethical behavior are increasingly common. Additionally, the Sarbanes-Oxley Act requires publicly traded corporations to establish formal procedures to receive, retain, and address any information that may affect the company's accounting or auditing. To comply with this requirement, companies have created ethics hotlines that allow employees to anonymously report unethical behavior. While this was an important step in empowering subordinates to report unethical behavior by their superiors, hotlines only address procedures to receive the information. Companies must also have procedures in place to make sure such information is never destroyed and that it is communicated to those with the power to resolve any issues, such as the board of directors and upper management.

ETHICAL DECISIONS Donna Jones has just been hired as an accounting clerk. One of her jobs is to summarize invoices presented for payment by various creditors. Once prepared, the summary is first inspected by Carmen Adams, the assistant controller to whom Donna reports, and then presented to Dick Stewart, the controller, for approval. After signing and approving the summary, Dick passes along the summary to his secretary, Nancy, who prepares and mails the checks.

During Donna's second week on the job, Carmen tells her that City Consulting Services Inc. will make trouble for the company unless paid immediately. She says, "Dick is rarely at his desk, and he and Nancy never look at signatures anyway. It would cost us at least another day for Dick to review and sign the summary. Just put the unsigned summary in the approved pile on Dick's desk, and Nancy will have the check in the mail by the end of the day."

Donna suspects that Carmen will give her a low performance rating if she refuses to follow these instructions, and she wants to do well on her first job. Further, she is quite sure that Dick and Nancy will not notice the omitted control procedure. On the other hand, Donna knows that the controller's approval is an important control procedure. Consider two possible endings for this story:

1. *Donna goes along with Carmen.* Every month, Carmen tells Donna that City Consulting Services needs to be paid immediately. Donna places the unauthorized summary on Dick's unoccupied desk. All goes well until the internal auditor runs a routine check on the credit ratings of the entities with which the company does business and discovers that City Consulting is nothing more than a bank account established by Carmen. Carmen is charged with fraud, and Donna's role is exposed in the public trial that follows. Donna is not charged in the case, but she loses her job and has great difficulty finding another comparable position.
2. *Donna refuses to go along with Carmen.* Donna receives a negative review from Carmen and is asked to leave the company. During an exit interview, Donna tells Dick why she believes Carmen gave her a negative review. Dick asks the internal audit department to follow up on City Consulting Services, at which time it is discovered to be a bank account established by Carmen. Carmen is charged with fraud. Dick contacts Donna saying, "After investigating your comments regarding Carmen's request, we have uncovered her scheme to defraud the company and would like you to return to the company.

Like Donna, most people in business face difficult ethical dilemmas from time to time. The effectiveness of internal control systems depends on the ethical tone set by management and the ethical awareness of all company personnel. •

Risk Assessment

Risk assessment procedures (also called Enterprise Risk Management or ERM) are designed to identify, analyze, and manage **strategic risks** and **business process risks**.

Strategic Risks Strategic risks are possible threats to the organization's success in accomplishing its objectives and are *external* to the organization. These risks are often classified around industry forces such as competitors, customers, substitute products or services, suppliers, and threat of new competitors (these are known as Porter's Five Forces) or macro factors such as political, economic, social, and technological (also known as PEST factors).

Although entire courses are devoted to management of these strategic risks, the general idea is simple. For example, when **Amazon** was formed, **Barnes & Noble** was in the midst of high growth and was implementing cafes and music shops within supersized bookstores. Barnes & Noble was so deeply rooted in its "bricks-and-mortar" that it failed to respond to a technological factor: the Internet's transformation of the industry. By the time Barnesandnoble.com was launched, Amazon had secured the leading web presence for booksellers—a lead that Barnes & Noble has been unable to erode.

Business Process Risks Business processes are the *internal* processes of the company—specifically, how the company allocates its resources to meet its objectives. There are many business processes, but some of the more common ones are materials acquisition, production, logistics and distribution, branding and marketing, and human resources. The nature and relative importance of the business processes will vary from company to company based on their specific objectives. For example, **Dell** has adopted a low-cost provider objective. As such, it has concentrated on achieving operating efficiencies in order processing, production, and distribution. **Apple**, on the other hand, has adopted a product differentiation objective. This objective has led to an emphasis on product quality and continual research to develop better products with more features. As such, the risk assessment controls for these two companies will differ. Dell will be focused on monitoring inventory levels and production times, while Apple will focus on quality control and product development.

Control Activities

Control activities are the policies and procedures top management establishes to help insure that its objectives are met. The control activities most directly related to the accounting system and financial statements vary widely from one business to another, but generally can be identified with one of the following five categories.

Clearly Defined Authority and Responsibility The *authority* to perform important duties is delegated to specific individuals, and those individuals should be held *responsible* for the performance of those duties in the evaluation of their performance. Among the designated duties of an individual may be the authority to perform specified types of activities for the business or to authorize others to execute such transactions. The clear delegation of authority and responsibility motivates individuals to perform well because they know they are accountable for their actions. For example, at **Wal-Mart** and other retailers, cashiers enter a code into the cash register and maintain responsibility for cash entering and leaving the register. At the end of their shift, a supervisor counts the money. Should the register have too much or too little cash, the cashier would clearly be responsible for the error.

Segregation of Duties Accounting and administrative duties should be performed by different individuals so that no one person prepares all the documents and records for an activity. This **segregation of duties** (also called *separation of duties*) reduces the likelihood that records could be used to conceal *irregularities* (intentional misstatements, theft, or fraud) and increases the likelihood that irregularities will be discovered. Segregation of duties also reduces the likelihood that unintentional record-keeping errors will remain undiscovered.

Although segregation of duties cannot eliminate the possibility of fraud, it does require people to work together. For example, movie theaters like **AMC** and **Showcase** require one employee to collect the cash and another employee to collect the tickets to admit the customer into the theater. If one person was responsible for collecting cash and admitting customers, this person could pocket the cash and let the customer in without issuing a ticket. In this case, the number of tickets issued would match up with the cash collected because no ticket was issued and the cash was pocketed. Instead, movie theaters have one person collect the cash and issue the ticket and a second person admit customers with tickets. Cash can still be pocketed, but the segregation of duties will require both employees to engage in the fraudulent scheme (we call this *collusion*) or the cash collected will not match the tickets collected.

Perhaps the most important aspect of segregation of duties is separating the record-keeping responsibility from the physical control of the assets. For example, if a customer pays $1,000, the employee who collects the $1,000 could easily steal some or all of the money if he or she has access to the accounting records. In this case, the employee could record that the money was paid and hide the fact that the money was not in the company accounts or record that some or all of the money was not paid and that the debt was "bad."

Adequate Documents and Records Accounting records are the basis for the financial statements and other reports prepared for managers, owners, and others both inside and outside the business. Summary records and their underlying documentation must provide information about specific activities and help in the evaluation of individual performance. For example, prenumbered shipping documents provide a basis for monitoring shipments of goods to customers. When warehouse employees receive a shipping document, they ship the goods. If the shipping documents were not prenumbered, a shipping document could be sent to the warehouse and later destroyed. Without the missing number in the sequence to signal a missing document, nobody would realize that the document was missing.

Safeguards over Assets and Records Both assets and records must be secured against theft and destruction. **Safeguarding** requires physical protection of the assets through, for example, fireproof vaults, locked storage facilities, keycard access, and anti-theft tags on merchandise. An increasingly important part of safeguarding assets and records is access controls for computers. Safeguards must be provided for computer programs and data files, which are more fragile and susceptible to unauthorized access than manual record-keeping systems. For example, access controls often mandate use of both alpha and numeric characters and require password changes every few months.

Checks on Recorded Amounts Recorded amounts should be checked by an independent person to determine that amounts are correct and that they correspond to properly authorized activities. These procedures include clerical checks, reconciliations, comparisons of asset inspection reports with recorded amounts, computer-programmed controls, and management review of reports. For example, accounting records should be checked (or reconciled) to the bank statement and any discrepancies should be resolved immediately. Bank reconciliations are illustrated later in the chapter.

Such controls are effective at mitigating unintentional error, theft, and fraud. One of the elements typically cited in discussions of theft and fraud is opportunity. That is, persons committing theft or fraud believe they have the opportunity to "get away with it." Control activities are designed to prevent and detect theft and fraud by reducing employees' opportunity to conceal their actions. Yet, every year billions of dollars are lost to employee theft and fraud because effectively designed control activities are not followed.

Information and Communication

An internal control system will be unable to help a company achieve its objective unless adequate information is identified and gathered on a timely basis. Further, this information must be communicated to the appropriate employees in the organization. For example, consider a company like Mercedes that has a strategy of providing high-quality products. This company may gather information on the percentage of production that is rejected by quality control. If that percentage rises, it signals the possibility of problems in production (such as inferior material being used, poor training of new personnel, etc.). If such information is gathered and communicated, these problems can be addressed before the company's reputation for high quality is harmed. If, on the other hand, such information is not gathered and communicated, then management may not become aware of the problem until returns and complaints are made by dissatisfied customers. At this time, it may be too late to avoid damage to their reputation.

Monitoring

Monitoring is the process of tracking potential and actual problems in the internal control system. Monitoring is accomplished through normal supervising activities such as when a manager asks a subordinate how things are going. However, best practices for larger organizations suggest that an internal audit group help monitor the effectiveness of the internal control system. Monitoring the system of internal controls allows the organization to identify potential and actual weaknesses that could, if uncorrected, produce problems.

In fact, the Sarbanes-Oxley Act requires all publicly traded corporations to have an internal audit function that reports to the audit committee of the board of directors. The Act allows companies to outsource internal audit, but precludes the business that provides the (external) financial statement audit from performing internal audit services because it may impair the independence of the financial statement audit.

Relationship between Control Activities and the Accounting System

The **accounting system** consists of the methods and records used to identify, measure, record, and communicate financial information about a business. Although we distinguish between the accounting system and the internal control system, the two are really one integrated system designed to meet the needs of a particular business. It is difficult to generalize the relationship between internal control activities and accounting systems because it directly depends on the objectives of a particular business. Consequently, the relationship is best explored through an example.

Consider Hendrickson Theaters Inc. which operates 10 movie theaters in a single city. All the theaters are rented, as are the projection equipment and concession facilities. Hendrickson's administrative offices, furnishings, and office equipment are also rented. The following chart of accounts indicates the structure of Hendrickson's accounting system:

Chart of Accounts for Hendrickson Theaters Inc.

ASSETS	REVENUES
Cash	Admissions Revenue
Concessions Inventory	Concessions Revenue
Prepaid Rent	**EXPENSES**
LIABILITIES	Salaries Expense
Accounts Payable	Wages Expense
Salaries Payable	Cost of Concessions Sold
Wages Payable	Rent Expense (Movie)
EQUITY	Rent Expense (Theater)
Capital Stock	Rent (Equipment)
Retained Earnings	Rent (Office)
	Utilities Expense
	Advertising Expense
	Office Supplies Expense

Hendrickson's accountant makes journal entries daily for revenues, biweekly for wages, and monthly for the other expenses using general purpose accounting software. Because Hendrickson has a relatively small number of accounts, its accounting system is quite simple. The portion of Hendrickson's accounting system related to revenues and the associated control activities are described in Exhibit 4.3.

EXHIBIT 4.3

Relationship between the Accounting System and Control Procedures

Illustrations from the Internal Control Structure for Revenue and Cash for Hendrickson Theaters Inc.

Accounting System

Entries: Admissions and concessions revenues are recorded daily by increasing both cash and the appropriate revenue accounts.

Documentation: The cash register at each ticket booth and concession stand prepares a detailed list of cash transactions and a daily cash summary report. The daily summary reports from the 10 theaters are electronically transferred to the central office each night and are automatically summarized upon receipt. Each morning, the accountant generates a report and makes revenue entries in the computerized general ledger.

Reports: A variety of revenue analyses can be prepared on the computer system, including analyses by theater, movie, time of day, day of the week, and month.

Control Procedures

Authority and responsibility: Each theater manager is responsible for the control of cash in his or her theater, but the central office accountant makes all general ledger entries related to cash.

Segregation of duties: Maintenance of the general ledger is segregated from responsibility for local cash control. Ticket sellers and concession operators may assist in preparation of daily cash deposits, but the manager must check and sign deposit documents.

Documentation: Prenumbered admission tickets are dispensed by machine at each theater. The machine also prepares a report of the tickets issued each day, which is used by the theater manager to reconcile cash collected with the number of tickets sold.

Safeguards: The cash accumulates in each theater until the end of each day. When cash drawers reach a specified level, however, the cash register signals that a fixed amount of cash should be removed by the manager and placed in the theater's safe.

Checks: On an unannounced schedule, Hendrickson's accountant visits each theater and verifies cash receipts reported against the number of tickets issued. On these same visits, the accountant checks concession revenues against the amounts reported by inventorying concession supplies.

ACCOUNTING AND REPORTING CASH

OBJECTIVE 3

Describe how businesses account for and report cash.

Cash is not only currency and coins, but savings and checking accounts and negotiable instruments like checks and money orders. When cash is received, a cash account is increased by a debit; and when cash is paid out, a cash account is decreased by a credit. Receipt and payment of cash are frequently accomplished by a check sent through the mail, a process that may require several days, and additional time may pass between receipt of the check and its deposit in the bank by the payee. Despite the fact that there may be a time lag between the issuance of a check and the actual transfer of funds, the accounting system treats payment by check in exactly the same way that it treats the transfer of currency. The receipt of either a check or currency is recorded by a debit to cash. Conversely, either the issue of a check or the payment of currency is recorded by a credit to cash.

Cash is reported on both the balance sheet and the statement of cash flows. The balance sheet typically reports the amount of cash and equivalents available at the balance sheet date, as shown in Exhibit 4.4. The statement of cash flows shows the sources and uses of cash during the year. The statement of cash flows will be discussed in more detail in Chapter 11.

EXHIBIT 4.4

Balance Sheet Reporting of Cash for Under Armour, Inc.

Under Armour, Inc. and Subsidiaries
Consolidated Balance Sheets
(in thousands)

	Dec. 31, 2011	Dec. 31, 2010
ASSETS		
Current assets:		
Cash and Equivalents*	$175,384	$203,870

*The Company considers all highly liquid investments with an original maturity of three months or less at date of inception to be cash and cash equivalents.

Source: Under Armour, Inc. 2011 10-K.

As explained in the notes to **Under Armour**'s financial statements, **cash equivalents** include "all highly liquid investments with an original maturity of 3 months or less at date of inception." This is a standard definition and indicates that cash equivalents are both:

- easily convertible into known amounts of cash
- close enough to maturity that they are relatively insensitive to changes in interest rates

But why do companies bother to invest their cash in such short-term investments? The answer is that such investments earn a greater rate of return than cash sitting in a bank account. As shown in Exhibit 4.4, **Under Armour** had over $175,000,000 in cash and equivalents at December 31, 2011. If their investment strategy earns a mere 1% more than a bank account, they would earn an extra $1.75 million in interest for the year.

CASH CONTROLS

OBJECTIVE 4

Describe how businesses control cash.

Internal controls are designed to protect all assets. But the more liquid an asset (the more "liquid" an asset, the more easily it is converted into cash), the more likely it is to be stolen. In fact, an *Association of Certified Fraud Examiners'* fraud study suggested that 80% of all workplace frauds involved employee theft of company assets (i.e., embezzlement) and 90% of these thefts involved cash.[2] For example, casinos take in huge amounts of cash. At the **Mohegan Sun** casino in Connecticut, while counting cash, employees were required to wear jumpsuits with no pockets while supervisors observed them through one-way mirrors. That sounds good; however, one employee shoved an estimated $600,000 under the elastic wristband of his jumpsuit over the course of his employment. He would take the money out of his sleeve and put it in his pockets during bathroom breaks. On the day he was caught, he had $97,300 in $100 bills. Now the casino uses transparent jumpsuits for its cash counters.

Of course, casinos operate in a particularly difficult environment to control cash, but all companies must use internal control activities. As discussed, the following internal controls help businesses effectively control cash:

- The authority to collect, hold, and pay cash must be clearly assigned to specific individuals. Whenever feasible, cash-handling activities and cash record-keeping activities should be assigned to *different* individuals.
- Cash records should be examined often by an objective party as a basis for evaluating the performance of cash-handling activities.
- Controls should be supported by an appropriately designed record-keeping system.
- Cash should be safeguarded in vaults and banks.

Many of these controls are illustrated in the following YOU DECIDE.

YOU DECIDE Internal Control over Cash in a Student Organization

You are the treasurer of your sorority and have responsibility for collecting dues, depositing cash in the bank, writing all checks, maintaining accounting records, and preparing bank reconciliations and financial statements. After taking your financial accounting course, you realize that this is a clear violation of segregation of duties and mention this to your sorority president. She agrees, but says that segregation of duties is not nearly as important as simply finding someone willing to perform the treasurer's tasks.

What steps can you advise your student organization president to take to strengthen its internal control system?

You can advise the leader of your student organization to look into each of the following areas. A "no" answer to any question indicates a potential internal control weakness.

- *Is supporting documentation obtained from vendors whenever cash is paid or a liability is incurred?*
  The use of appropriate documentation assures the proper payment of bills and facilitates the appropriate accrual of liabilities on the year-end balance sheet.
- *Is every vendor invoice and all supporting documentation cancelled (e.g., by writing "Paid by check number 841 on November 29, 2013") at the time the check is written?*
  This action helps assure that duplicate payments are not made.
- *Does the organization's faculty advisor initial all checks written for amounts greater than some specified minimum (e.g., $500)?*
  This control reduces the possibility of unauthorized payments.
- *Are receipts of members' fees and dues deposited promptly (at least once a week)?*
  Prompt deposits help avoid misplacing receipts.
- *Does the organization have procedures to assist in the collection of membership dues?*
  Despite the mutual trust and friendship that are a part of most student organizations, uncollectible accounts can be a serious problem. The treasurer may need the assistance of formal procedures in collecting overdue accounts (e.g., placing sanctions on members who fail to pay).
- *Does the organization have an accounting policies and procedures manual?*
  Such a manual may be needed to prepare the year-end financial report in conformity with university and/or national governing body requirements.
- *Are complete minutes of all officers' meetings maintained?*
  The minutes should include (a) a listing of all changes in membership and officers, including the names of new members, (b) a schedule of dues that documents all financial obligations of members, (c) approval of payments, and (d) authorization of check signers. Including this information, along with descriptions of important decisions of the organization's governing body, documents all the important activities of the organization.

Businesses can effectively control cash with internal controls, which include guidelines for collecting, holding, and paying cash as well as keeping records and assigning individuals different responsibilities.

[2] The other 20% includes such things as fraudulent financial statements.

Although many of the cash controls with which you are most familiar (e.g., cash registers) might appear to be outside the accounting system, we will highlight three important areas where the accounting system interacts with the internal control system to strengthen cash controls:

- bank reconciliations
- cash over and short
- petty cash

Reconciliation of Accounting Records to Bank Statement

The use of a bank is one of the most important controls over cash. The bank duplicates the company's accounting by keeping their own accounting records of your account. Unfortunately, the bank's accounting records and company's accounting records often disagree because the transactions are not recorded at the same time (for example, a company writes a check on January 18 and credits cash immediately; however, the bank will not debit your account until the check is presented to the bank—typically many days later). Therefore, to ensure that the accounting records are consistent with the bank's accounting records, any differences must be "reconciled." This process is called the **bank reconciliation**.

Periodically—usually once a month—the bank returns all checks processed during the period, together with a detailed record of the activity of the account. The document is a *bank statement*, which shows the beginning and ending account balance and the individual deposits and withdrawals recorded by the bank during the period. Basically, the bank statement is a copy of the bank's accounting records showing each customer the increases and decreases in their balances (see Exhibit 4.5, p. 200). Remember, a checking account is a liability for the bank (the bank owes you the balance). Therefore, deposits and other events that increase your bank account balance are labeled "credits" on the bank statement (because they increase the bank's liability to you), and withdrawals and other events that decrease your bank account balance are labeled "debits" (because they decrease the bank's liability to you).

Reconciliation of these separately maintained records serves two purposes:

- It serves a control function by identifying errors and providing an inspection of detailed records that deters theft.
- It serves a transaction detection function by identifying transactions performed by the bank, so the business can make the necessary entries in its records.

> **concept Q&A**
>
> If a debit increases an asset and decreases a liability and a credit decreases an asset and increases a liability, why does the bank "credit" your account when you make a deposit and "debit" your account when you make a withdrawal?
>
> **Answer:**
>
> Because the "credit" and "debit" are from the bank's point of view. When you make a deposit, it actually increases the bank's liability to you—the bank now owes you more. When you make a withdrawal, it decreases the bank's liability to you.

In general, differences between the cash account balance (see Exhibit 4.6, p. 201) and the bank statement balance develop from three sources:

- transactions recorded by the business, but not recorded by the bank in time to appear on the current bank statement
- transactions recorded by the bank, but not yet recorded by the business
- errors in recording transactions on either set of records

Transactions Recorded by the Business, but Not Yet Recorded by the Bank

There are generally two types of transactions recorded by the business, but not recorded by the bank in time to appear on the current statement: outstanding checks and deposits in transit.

Outstanding Checks An **outstanding check** is a check issued and recorded by the business that has not been "cashed" by the recipient of the check. The business has (properly) recorded the check as lowering its cash balance and the bank has (properly) not recorded the check as lowering the business's account balance because it has not been

EXHIBIT 4.5 Bank Statement

T N B

THIRD NATIONAL BANK
123 W. Main Street
Batavia, OH 45103

Member FDIC

Account Statement

Statement Date:
August 31, 2013

OHIO ENTERPRISES INC.
519 MAIN STREET
BATAVIA, OH 45103

Account Number:
40056

Previous Balance	Checks and Debits	Deposits and Credits	Current Balance
$7,675.20	$10,685.26	$7,175.10	$4,165.04

Checks and Debits			Deposits and Credits		Daily Balance	
Date	No.	Amount	Date	Amount	Date	Amount
8/3/13	1883	182.00			8/3/13	7,493.20
8/4/13	1884	217.26	8/4/13	2,673.10	8/4/13	9,949.04
8/6/13	1885	1,075.00			8/6/13	8,874.04
8/7/13	1886	37.50	8/7/13	4,500.00	8/7/13	13,336.54
8/10/13	1887	826.00			8/10/13	12,510.54
8/11/13	1888	50.00			8/11/13	12,460.54
8/12/13	1889	2,670.00				
8/12/13	1890	67.90			8/12/13	9,722.64
8/13/13	1891	890.00			8/13/13	8,832.64
8/14/13	1892	27.50			8/14/13	8,805.14
8/17/13	1893	111.00			8/17/13	8,694.14
8/18/13	*DM*	380.00			8/18/13	8,314.14
8/19/13	1894	60.00				
8/19/13	1895	510.00			8/19/13	7,744.14
8/20/13	1896	30.00			8/20/13	7,714.14
8/21/13	1897	1,600.00			8/21/13	6,114.14
8/24/13	1898	78.00			8/24/13	6,036.14
8/25/13	*NSF*	200.00			8/25/13	5,836.14
8/26/13	1899	208.80			8/26/13	5,627.34
8/27/13	1900	1,250.00			8/27/13	4,377.34
8/28/13	1902	175.00			8/28/13	4,202.34
8/31/13	1903	25.30	8/31/13 *INT*	2.00		
8/31/13	*SC*	14.00			8/31/13	4,165.04

Symbols: **CM** Credit Memo **DM** Debit Memo **EC** Error Correction **INT** Interest Earned **NSF** Non-Sufficient Funds **SC** Service Charge

Reconcile your account immediately.

cashed. For example, when a check is written during December, but not cashed until January, the business's December 31 cash balance will be lower than its account balance on the December 31 bank statement.

Deposits in Transit A **deposit in transit** is an amount received and recorded by the business, but which has not been recorded by the bank in time to appear on the current bank statement. Deposits in transit cause the bank balance to be smaller than the business's cash account balance. Deposits in transit arise because many banks post any deposit received after 2:00 or 3:00 P.M. into their records on the next business day and because businesses often make deposits on weekends or holidays when the bank is not open for business, which could cause the deposit to appear on the next bank statement.

EXHIBIT 4.6

T-Account for Cash, Prior to Reconciliation

Ohio Enterprises Inc.

Cash

Date	Amount Deposited	Check Number	Check Amount	Check Number	Check Amount
Balance, 7/31/13	$6,200.94				
8/1	$2,673.10	1886	$ 37.50	1896	$ 30.00
8/5	4,500.00	1887	826.00	1897	1,600.00
8/31	300.00	1888	50.00	1898	87.00
Total deposits	$7,473.10	1889	2,670.00	1899	208.80
		1890	67.90	1900	1,250.00
		1891	890.00	1901	93.00
		1892	27.50	1902	175.00
		1893	111.00	1903	25.30
		1894	60.00	1904	72.50
		1895	510.00	1905	891.00
		Total disbursements			$9,682.50
Balance, 8/31/13	$3,991.54				

Transactions Recorded by the Bank, but Not Yet Recorded by the Business

Several types of transactions are recorded by the bank, but not yet recorded by the business, including service charges, non-sufficient funds checks, and debit and credit memos. After the reconciliation process, the business must make adjusting journal entries to record all the transactions that have been recorded by the bank but not yet recorded in the business's ledger cash account.

Service Charges **Service charges** are fees charged by the bank for checking account services. The amount of the fee is not known to the business (and therefore cannot be recorded) until the bank statement is received. Bank service charges unrecorded by the business at the end of a month cause the bank balance to be smaller than the business's cash account balance.

Non-Sufficient Funds Checks A **non-sufficient funds (NSF) check** is a check that has been returned to the depositor because funds in the issuer's account are not sufficient to pay the check (also called a *bounced check*). The amount of the check was added to the depositor's account when the check was deposited; however, since the check cannot be paid, the bank deducts the amount of the NSF check from the account. This deduction is recorded by the bank before it is recorded by the business. NSF checks cause the bank balance to be smaller than the cash account balance.

Debit and Credit Memos A debit memo might result, for example, if the bank makes a prearranged deduction from the business's account to pay a utility bill. Debit memos recorded by the bank but not yet recorded by the business cause the bank balance to be smaller than the cash account balance. A credit memo could result if the bank collected a note receivable for the business and deposited the funds in the business's account. Credit memos recorded by the bank but not recorded by the business cause the bank balance to be larger than the cash account balance.

Errors The previous differences between the accounting records and bank account balances are the result of time lags between the recording of a transaction by the business and its recording by the bank. Errors in recording transactions represent yet another source of difference between a business's cash account balance and the bank balance. Errors are inevitable in any accounting system and should be corrected as soon as discovered. In addition, an effort should be made to determine the cause of any error as a basis for corrective action. Obviously, an intentional error designed to hide misappropriation of funds calls for quite different corrective action than does an error resulting from human fatigue or machine failure.

Performing a Bank Reconciliation To begin the reconciliation, start with the "cash balance from the bank statement" and the "cash balance from company records." These two balances are then adjusted as necessary to produce identical "adjusted cash balances" by following these steps:

Step 1. Compare the deposits on the bank statement to the deposits debited to the cash account. Any deposits debited to the cash account but not on the bank statement are likely deposits in transit, so look at a deposit slip to ensure that these amounts were actually deposited. Deposits in transit should be added to the "cash balance from the bank statement."

Step 2. Compare the paid (often called *cancelled*) checks that are electronically returned with the bank statement to the amounts credited to the cash account and the list of outstanding checks from prior months. Any checks credited to the cash account but not on the bank statement are likely outstanding checks. These amounts should be subtracted from the "cash balance from the bank statement."

Step 3. Look for items on the bank statement that have not been debited or credited to the cash account. These include bank service charges, interest payments, NSF checks, automatic payments (debit memos), and bank collections on behalf of the company (credit memos). Bank debits should be subtracted from the "cash balance from company records," while bank credits should be added to the "cash balance from company records." Of course, all these amounts should be verified.

Step 4. If the "adjusted cash balances" are still not the same, search for errors. The most common error is a "transposition" error in which, for example, a check is written for $823, but recorded as $283 (the 8 and 2 are transposed). In this case, the accounting records will show a $283 credit to the cash account, but the bank will show a $823 debit to the company's account. All errors made by the company must be added or subtracted from the "cash balance from company records." All errors made by the bank must be added or subtracted from the "cash balance from the bank statement."

This process is illustrated in Cornerstone 4.1.

CORNERSTONE 4.1

Performing a Bank Reconciliation

Why:

Bank reconciliation is the process of comparing the accounting records and the bank statement, determining where discrepancies occur, and accounting for them.

Information:

Refer to the bank statement in Exhibit 4.5 (p. 200) and the cash account in Exhibit 4.6 (p. 201). Recognize that the beginning balance was reconciled at the end of last month (July). Assume that this was performed correctly and all outstanding checks (numbers 1883, 1884, and 1885) and deposits in transit from July cleared during August.

(Continued)

CORNERSTONE

4.1

(Continued)

Required:

1. Determine the adjustments needed by comparing the bank statement to the cash account.
2. Complete the bank reconciliation.

Solution:

1. Four items in the cash account do not appear on the bank statement: the August 31 deposit (in transit), and checks 1901, 1904, and 1905 (outstanding). There is also an error. The amount posted to the cash account for check 1898 does not equal the amount cleared on the bank statement. The cancelled check on record was written for $78.00, not $87.00, so the error is on the company's records.

2.

Cash balance from bank statement		$ 4,165.04
Add: Deposit in transit (8/31)		300.00
Less: Outstanding checks		
1901	$ (93.00)	
1904	(72.50)	
1905	(891.00)	(1,056.50)
Adjusted cash balance		**$ 3,408.54**

Cash balance from company records		$3,991.54
Add:		
Error in recording check 1898 (we recorded as $87, should be $78)	$ 9.00	
Interest	2.00	11.00
Less:		
Service charge	$ 14.00	
NSF check	200.00	
Electric bill (Debit Memo)	380.00	(594.00)
Adjusted cash balance		**$3,408.54**

Adjusted cash balances should equal.

If the person who writes the checks also performs the reconciliation, it is easier for him or her to cover up theft and fraud. Therefore, there are additional benefits when the bank reconciliation is performed by someone with no other responsibilities related to cash (the duties of reconciling cash and cash record keeping should be segregated).

Making Adjusting Entries as a Result of the Bank Reconciliation Once the bank reconciliation is completed, some adjustments to the accounting records may be necessary. No adjustments are necessary for outstanding checks or deposits in transit because the accounting records have correctly recorded these amounts. However, as shown in Cornerstone 4.2, adjustments are necessary for any company errors or items such as bank charges or interest that the company does not find out about until receiving the bank statement.

Making Adjusting Entries as a Result of the Bank Reconciliation

CORNERSTONE

4.2

(Continued)

Why:

Adjusting journal entries are required for all transactions correctly recorded by the bank that have not yet been included in the accounting records.

Information:

Refer to the bank reconciliation performed in Cornerstone 4.1. Assume that all checks from this account were written to satisfy accounts payable.

CORNERSTONE **4.2**

(Continued)

Required:

Prepare the necessary adjusting journal entries.

Solution:

Assets = Liabilities + Stockholders' Equity	Account and Explanation	Debit	Credit
Assets +9 = Liabilities +9 + Stockholders' Equity	Cash	9	
	Accounts Payable		9
	(Correct error in recording check 1898)		
Assets +2 = Liabilities + Stockholders' Equity +2	Cash	2	
	Interest Income		2
	(Record interest)		
Assets −14 = Liabilities + Stockholders' Equity −14	Bank Service Charge Expense	14	
	Cash		14
	(Record bank service charge)		
Assets +200 −200 = Liabilities + Stockholders' Equity	Accounts Receivable	200	
	Cash		200
	(Record NSF check)		
Assets −380 = Liabilities + Stockholders' Equity −380	Utilities Expense	380	
	Cash		380
	(Record debit memo for payment of electric bill)		

Cash Over and Short

Another important control activity requires that cash receipts be deposited in a bank daily. At the end of each day, the amount of cash received during the day is debited to the cash accounts to which it has been deposited. The amount deposited should equal the total of cash register tapes. If it does not (and differences will occasionally occur even when cash-handling procedures are carefully designed and executed), the discrepancy is recorded in an account called **cash over and short**, as illustrated in Cornerstone 4.3.

CORNERSTONE **4.3**

Recording Cash Over and Short

Why:

When the cash in the register does not reconcile with the register tapes, the discrepancy is recorded in cash over and short.

Information:

RSA has $20,671.12 prepared for deposit. However, the total of cash register tapes and other documents supporting the receipt of cash on that day is $20,685.14, including collections of accounts receivable of $6,760.50.

Required:

Prepare the necessary adjusting journal entry.

(Continued)

CORNERSTONE **4.3** *(Continued)*

Solution:

Account and Explanation	Debit	Credit
Cash	20,671.12	
Cash Over and Short	14.02	
Sales Revenue*		13,924.64
Accounts Receivable		6,760.50
(Record cash register collections)		

* $20,685.14 – $6,760.50

Assets	= Liabilities +	Stockholders' Equity
+20,671.12		−14.02
−6,760.50		+13,924.64

Observe that a cash *shortage* (as in Cornerstone 4.3) requires a debit to cash over and short, whereas a cash *overage* would require a credit.

One common source of cash over and short is errors in making change for cash sales. Significant amounts of cash over and short signal the need for a careful investigation of the causes and appropriate corrective action. Cash over and short is usually treated as an income statement account and is reported as a part of other expenses or other revenues.

Petty Cash

Cash controls are more effective when companies pay with a check for the following reasons:

- Only certain people have the authority to sign the check. Those authorized to sign do not keep the accounting records and only sign the check with the proper documentation supporting the payment (e.g., evidence that the goods being paid for were properly ordered and received).
- Supporting documents are marked paid to avoid duplicate payment.
- Checks are prenumbered, which makes it easy to identify any missing checks.

However, issuing checks to pay small amounts is usually more costly than paying cash.[3] Therefore, a company may establish a **petty cash** fund to pay for items such as stamps or a cake for an employee birthday party. The petty cash fund is overseen by a petty cash custodian, who both pays for small dollar amounts directly from the fund and reimburses employees who have receipts for items they've bought with their own money. At the end of the month, the custodian submits all receipts (and other supporting documentation) to the company. After company personnel (other than the petty cash custodian) determine that the documents are authentic and that each transaction is supported by appropriate documentation, the custodian is given an amount to replenish the petty cash fund. The company then records the amounts spent in the accounting records. Because the custodian replenishes petty cash at the end of the month, the accounting records are appropriately updated each month. This process is illustrated in Cornerstone 4.4 (p. 206).

Replenishment of petty cash may also occur during the month if the amount of petty cash available gets too low. However, to assure that all expenses are recorded in the appropriate accounting period, replenishment should occur at the end of the month or accounting period. As an additional control measure, a company should periodically verify its petty cash balances by counting the cash in the hands of custodians and comparing it to the custodian's petty cash record.

[3] Checks cost money to print, mail, and process. Some estimate the cost of processing a check to be over $1. Therefore, banks have developed ways for businesses to transfer money without the use of paper checks. For example, most employees do not see an actual paycheck; instead, money is automatically deposited into their bank account. These are called electronic fund transfers (EFT). Use of EFTs is quite common and has become commonplace at the individual level through the use of debit cards.

CORNERSTONE

4.4

Accounting for Petty Cash

Why:

Companies often establish a petty cash fund account to pay for small dollar amount items.

Information:

On January 1, Oregon Industries establishes a petty cash fund of $500. On January 31, the petty cash custodian presents the following records of the month's transactions, together with related documents, and requests reimbursement:

Jan. 12	Hansen's Grocery (coffee)	$ 30
15	U.S. Post Office (postage)	70
17	Northwest Messenger (package delivery)	25
19	Office Depot (office supplies)	175
25	Mr. Strand, Controller (food for lunch meeting)	63
	Total	$363

After approving the expenses, the company issues a check to the custodian for $363.00 to replenish the fund.

Required:

1. Prepare the journal entry to establish the petty cash fund on January 1.
2. Prepare the journal entry to record the replenishment of the fund on January 31.
3. Assuming the entry from Requirement 2 has been made, prepare the journal entry needed to increase the fund balance to $600.

Solution:

Assets	=	Liabilities	+	Stockholders' Equity
+500 −500				

Assets	=	Liabilities	+	Stockholders' Equity
−363				−175 −70 −25 −93

Assets	=	Liabilities	+	Stockholders' Equity
−100 +100				

Date	Account and Explanation	Debit	Credit
1. Jan. 1	Petty Cash	500.00	
	Cash		500.00
	(Establish petty cash fund)		
2. Jan. 31	Office Supplies	175.00	
	Postage Expense	70.00	
	Delivery Expense	25.00	
	Miscellaneous Expense	93.00	
	Cash*		363.00
	(Replenish petty cash fund and recognize expenses)		
3. Jan. 31	Petty Cash	100.00	
	Cash		100.00
	(Increase the fund balance to $600)		

* The expenditures of petty cash are not recorded in the accounting records until the fund is replenished. The replenishment does not alter the balance of the petty cash fund on Oregon's records; the balance remains $500.00.

We have spent considerable time discussing internal controls both in general and, over cash, in particular, for two reasons. First, internal controls are an integral part of the accounting system and business. Second, the accounting and reporting of cash is not that difficult. We will consider cash management strategies, but first we discuss the operating cycle because this affects the amount of cash needed.

OPERATING CYCLE

OBJECTIVE 5

Describe the operating cycle and explain the principles of cash management.

The **operating cycle** is the elapsed time between the purchase of goods for resale (or the purchase of materials to produce salable goods or services) and the collection of cash from customers (presumably a larger amount of cash than was invested in the goods sold). Although typically a year or less, the operating cycle can be as short as a few days for perishable goods, or as long as many years for the production and sale of products such as timber or wine (see Exhibit 4.7).

EXHIBIT 4.7

The Operating Cycle

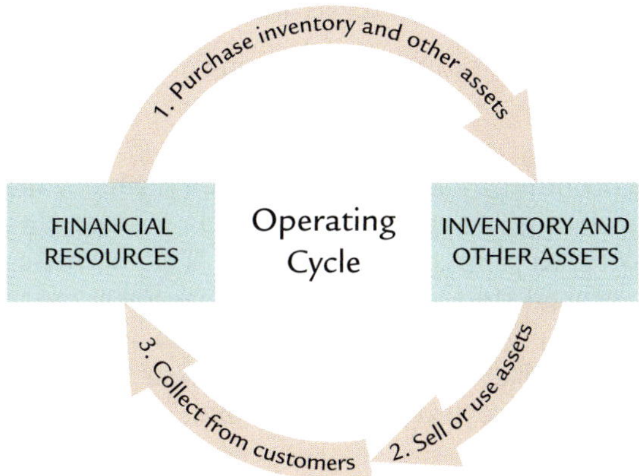

Consider the operating cycle for **H. H. Gregg**, a large appliance retailer that provides long-term financing for customers. Appliances remain in inventory for an average of 3 months before being sold. Most are sold on credit, and it takes an average of 12 months to collect the full amount of a sale. Thus, Gregg's operating cycle is 15 months, representing the average purchase-to-collection interval (3 months to sell plus 12 months to collect).

The length of the operating cycle influences the classification of assets and liabilities on balance sheets. In addition, the operating cycle plays an important role in the measurement of income. The length of the operating cycle also affects the amount of capital a business needs and the policies that govern its sales of goods and services, as the You Decide demonstrates.

YOU DECIDE Operating Cycle and Capital Requirements

You are the CFO of Tolland Gizmo. You sell, on credit, approximately 1,000 Gizmos per month at $10 per unit. In addition to the accounts receivable, you have an inventory of 200 Gizmos that were purchased at a cost of $6 per unit (a total inventory of $1,200) and $1,000 in cash. Currently, Tolland has 1 month's sales in accounts receivable and the following balance sheet:

ASSETS	
Cash	$ 1,000
Inventory	1,200
Accounts receivable	10,000
Total	$12,200
LIABILITIES AND STOCKHOLDERS' EQUITY	
Equity	$12,200
Total	$12,200

The sales force wants to lengthen the collection period of the accounts receivable to 3 months.

How would lengthening the collection period of the accounts receivable affect Tolland's financing requirements?

Tolland will now have interest expense. Presumably, the company would not allow its customers to take 3 months to pay unless compensated for doing so. Thus, Tolland will probably charge a higher price because of the extended payment terms.

Tolland's higher price to cover the interest expense it pays for a longer collection period will result in higher revenues.

IFRS

The management, control, and accounting for cash are the same under IFRS as under U.S. GAAP.

Cash Management

With an understanding of the operating cycle, we now turn our attention to cash management strategies. As discussed, the activities of the operating cycle transform cash into goods and services and then back, through sales, into cash. This sequence of activities includes a continual process of paying and receiving cash. A company can significantly increase its net income through its cash management policies. At a high level, cash management principles entail the following:

- delaying paying suppliers, so a company can earn as much interest on their cash as possible
- speeding up collection from customers in order to invest the cash sooner or reduce the need for additional financing
- earning the greatest return on any excess cash

We can follow these principles through the operating cycle.

Buying Inventory

The first stage of the operating cycle is buying inventory. Money that is tied up in inventory sitting on the shelves is not earning any return. As such, an important aspect of cash management is to keep inventory levels low. This decreases the need for cash. Companies have made great strides in inventory management over the last few decades. For example, **Dell** went from holding approximately 11 weeks of sales in inventory in 1991 to under one week in 2001, while car companies such as **Toyota** time the delivery of parts such as windows and seats down to the minute.

Paying for Inventory

The second stage of the operating cycle is paying for the inventory. As with all payments, a good cash management principle is to delay payments as long as possible while maintaining a good relationship with the payee. The longer a company keeps cash, the more interest it can collect. This may seem trivial, but consider a company like **Microsoft**. Its 2011 SEC filings reveal approximately $4.2 billion in accounts payable. If Microsoft can earn 5% on this money, it will earn over to $575,000 per day in interest. You may practice this in your own lives if you wait until April 15 to pay any income taxes owed or pay your tuition on the last possible day.

Selling Inventory

The third stage is selling the inventory, which often produces receivables. Good cash management suggests increasing the speed of receivable collections. This is an area that has become increasingly sophisticated over the last 20 years. In fact, many companies sell their receivables rather than wait for their customers to pay. Of course, they sell the receivables for less than they will receive (which represents interest and return for the buyer), but it also allows the company to receive the cash sooner and avoid hiring employees to service the receivables.

Short-Term Investments

Beyond delaying payments and speeding up collections, businesses try to keep their bank cash balances to a minimum because most bank accounts earn relatively small amounts of interest. Accordingly, short-term investments are purchased with temporary cash surpluses. The value and composition of short-term investment portfolios change continually in response to seasonal factors and other shifts in the business environment.

These investments will usually be liquidated (converted to cash through selling or maturity) before the business undertakes any significant short-term borrowing because the interest expense on short-term borrowings usually exceeds the return on short-term investments. Nonetheless, temporary shortages can result from the day-to-day ups and downs in the inflows and outflows of cash, as well as unforeseen needs for cash. A business with a good credit rating can borrow funds to resolve a temporary cash shortage. Such borrowings frequently are made under a line of credit, an agreement between the company and its bank in which the bank promises to lend the company funds up to a specified limit and at specified interest rates. The use of short-term investments as part of cash management is illustrated in the following You Decide.

YOUDECIDE Cash Management

You are the treasurer at Ohio Wire, a medium-size manufacturer of cable and wire used in building and bridge construction. Since most construction is seasonal, Ohio Wire tends to have far more cash inflows during the summer months. Further, during the winter their cash outflows are often greater than their inflows.

How do you manage the excess cash accumulated during the summer months knowing that cash will be needed during the winter?

Ohio Wire will use its excess cash to make short-term investments. These investments should be able to be easily liquidated by winter when the cash will be needed. Some examples of such investments could be certificates of deposit, Treasury Bills, and short-term equity holdings. Further, most companies will have lines of credit at a bank. These arrangements allow the company to borrow any amount up to some limit with a phone call.

Investing excess cash in short-term investments allows companies to have immediate access to cash to cover temporary short falls, while minimizing borrowing costs.

Effective cash management ultimately requires some understanding of future cash flows. For example, if the company is planning to expand or pay off a loan, it must make sure it has the necessary cash on hand. If a company receives most of its cash for the year around the holidays, it must effectively manage the excess until the time it is needed. These projections are made as part of the budgeting process and are an integral part of managerial accounting courses.

SUMMARY OF LEARNING OBJECTIVES

LO 1. Discuss the role of internal controls in managing a business.

- Internal control systems provide reasonable assurance that the company's objectives are being met in three areas:
  - effectiveness and efficiency of operations
  - reliability of financial reporting
  - compliance with applicable laws and regulations

LO 2. Discuss the five components of internal control.

- The internal control system includes:
  - the control environment
  - risk assessment
  - control activities
  - information and communication
  - monitoring
- Although we distinguish between the accounting system and the internal control system, the two are really one integrated system designed to meet the needs of a particular business.

LO 3. Describe how businesses account for and report cash.

- A cash account is debited when cash is received and credited when cash is paid out.
- Cash is reported on the balance sheet as the amount of cash and cash equivalents available on the balance sheet date.

- The statement of cash flows shows the sources and uses of cash during the accounting period.
- Cash equivalents are amounts that are easily convertible in to known amounts of cash and investments that are close to maturity.

LO 4. Describe how businesses control cash.

- Keeping control over cash is extremely difficult.
- It is important to:
  - safeguard cash
  - adequately segregate the custody of cash from the authorization of payments and the accounting records
- Cash accounts include:
  - Cash in Bank
  - Change Funds
  - Petty Cash
- Controls over these cash accounts include:
  - bank reconciliations
  - daily deposits and recording cash over and short amounts
  - accounting procedures for petty cash funds

LO 5. Describe the operating cycle and explain the principles of cash management.

- The operating cycle of the business starts when the business purchases inventory.
- When a business sells goods on credit, creating accounts receivable, cash is not replenished until the receivables are collected, which completes the operating cycle.
- Cash management is an important function at all companies because business is really a continuous cycle of paying and receiving cash.
- Although aspects of cash management have become extremely sophisticated, basic strategies are:
  - keeping inventory levels low
  - delaying payment of liabilities as long as possible
  - speeding up collection of receivables
  - investing idle cash to earn the greatest possible return while still being available when needed

CORNERSTONE 4.1 Performing a bank reconciliation, page 202

CORNERSTONE 4.2 Making adjusting entries as a result of the bank reconciliation, page 203

CORNERSTONE 4.3 Recording cash over and short, page 204

CORNERSTONE 4.4 Accounting for petty cash, page 206

© Pixelfabrik/Alamy

KEY TERMS

Accounting system, 195
Bank reconciliation, 199
Business process risks, 193
Cash equivalents, 197
Cash over and short, 204
Control activities, 194
Control environment, 192
Deposit in transit, 200
Internal control system, 190
Non-sufficient funds (NSF) check, 201

REVIEW PROBLEM

I. Bank Reconciliation

Fugazi Enterprises has the following information in its accounting records for their primary checking account:

Balance at April 30	$ 18,350
Checks written during May	114,700
Deposits during May	112,200

Fugazi's May bank statement contained the following information:

Balance per bank at April 30		$ 19,800
Credits during May:		
Deposits		109,600
Debits during May:		
Checks paid	$107,400	
Debit memo (May utilities)	8,000	
Bank service charge	80	115,480
Balance per bank at May 31		$ 13,920

The April bank reconciliation had deposits in transit of $850 and outstanding checks of $2,300. All these items cleared during May. These were the only reconciling items in April.

Required:

1. Prepare a bank reconciliation at May 31.
2. Prepare any adjusting entries necessary because of the bank reconciliation.

Solution:

1.

Cash balance from bank statement		$13,920
Add: Deposits in transit	$112,200 – ($109,600 – $850)*	3,450
Less: Outstanding checks	$114,700 – ($107,400 – $2,300)**	(9,600)
Adjusted cash balance		**$ 7,770**
Cash balance from company records	($18,350 + $112,200 – $114,700)	$15,850
Less:		
Debit memo (utilities)	$8,000	
Service charge	80	(8,080)
Adjusted cash balance		**$ 7,770**

*$112,200 was deposited during May, but the account was only credited for $109,600 during May. However, this $109,600 included $850 that was in transit at April 30, so only $108,750 ($109,600 – $850) of the May deposits were credited to the account.

**$114,700 in checks were written in May and $107,400 in checks cleared the bank during May. However, this $107,400 included $2,300 in checks that were outstanding from April, so only $105,100 ($107,400 – $2,300) in checks cleared that were written in May.

2.

Date	Account and Explanation	Debit	Credit
May 31	Utilities Expense	8,000	
	Bank Service Charge Expense	80	
	Cash		8,080

Assets	=	Liabilities	+	Stockholders' Equity
−8,080				−8,000
				−80

DISCUSSION QUESTIONS

1. What is the purpose of an internal control system?
2. Internal control systems include policies and procedures to do what?
3. Section 404 of the Sarbanes-Oxley Act increased top management's responsibility for what?
4. What are the five components of internal control?
5. What is meant by "tone at the top"? Why is it so important to an effective system of internal controls?
6. What are strategic risks?
7. What are business process risks?
8. What are the five categories of control activities?
9. How do these control activities help protect a company against error, theft, and fraud?
10. How do control activities relate to the accounting system?
11. Why does a company give particular attention to internal controls for cash?
12. Why is it important to segregate the duties for handling cash from the duties for keeping the accounting records for cash?
13. Describe two advantages of performing reconciliations of the cash account to the balances on the bank statements.
14. Describe the potential sources of difference between a cash account and its associated bank statement balance.
15. What kinds of bank reconciliation items require the firm to make adjusting entries?
16. Describe how cash over and short can be used for internal control purposes.
17. Why do most companies have petty cash funds?
18. What are cash equivalents?
19. Why do companies invest their cash in short-term investments?
20. What is the operating cycle?
21. Describe the basic cash management principles.
22. Why do companies hold short-term investments?

MULTIPLE-CHOICE EXERCISES

4-1 What is the primary role of internal controls in managing a business?

a. To prevent cash from being stolen
b. To ensure that the financial statements are presented in such a manner as to provide relevant and reliable information for financial statement users and the company's creditors
c. To constrain subordinates' activities in order to prevent employees from deviating from the scope of their responsibilities and encouraging them to act in the best interest of the business
d. To encourage theft and to ensure that segregation of duties does not take place

4-2 Which of the following is *not* one of the three areas for which internal control systems are intended to provide reasonable assurance?

a. Reliability of financial reporting
b. Compliance with applicable laws and regulations
c. Effectiveness and efficiency of operations
d. Certification that the financial statements are without error

4-3 Which of the following is *not* one of the five components of internal control?

a. Analysis of control procedures
b. Information and communication
c. Risk assessment
d. Control environment

4-4 Which of the following is *not* one of the five categories of control activities?

a. Checks on recorded amounts
b. Defalcation and financial reporting
c. Clearly defined authority and responsibility
d. Segregation of duties

4-5 The internal audit function is part of what element of the internal control system?

a. Control environment
b. Monitoring
c. Risk assessment
d. Control activities

4-6 Which of the following is *not* generally an internal control activity?

a. Establishing clear lines of authority to carry out specific tasks
b. Physically counting inventory in a perpetual inventory system
c. Reducing the cost of hiring seasonal employees
d. Limiting access to computerized accounting records

4-7 Allowing only certain employees to order goods and services for the company is an example of what internal control procedure?

a. Independent verifications
b. Proper authorizations
c. Safeguarding of assets and records
d. Segregation of duties

4-8 Deposits made by a company but not yet reflected in a bank statement are called

a. deposits in transit.
b. debit memoranda.
c. credit memoranda.
d. None of the above.

4-9 Which one of the following would *not* appear on a bank statement for a checking account?

a. Deposits
b. Interest earned
c. Service charges
d. Outstanding checks

4-10 Which one of the following is *not* a cash equivalent?

a. 180-day note issued by a local or state government
b. 90-day U.S. Treasury bill
c. 60-day corporate commercial paper
d. 30-day certificate of deposit

4-11 Business activity is best described as

a. lacking deviation.
b. predictable.
c. noncyclical.
d. cyclical.

4-12 The five primary activities of a business generally consist of

a. making a profit, issuing financial statements, repaying debts, issuing dividends to stockholders, and complying with laws and regulations.
b. receiving assets, selling assets, issuing financial statements, collecting cash, and making cash disbursements.
c. receiving assets, purchasing assets, selling goods or services, collecting cash from customers, and repaying owners and creditors.
d. receiving cash, disbursing cash, buying assets, issuing dividends, and paying off liabilities.

4-13 Effective cash management and control includes all of the following *except*

a. the use of a petty cash fund.
b. bank reconciliations.
c. purchase of stocks and bonds.
d. short-term investments of excess cash.

4-14 Cash management principles do *not* include

a. earning the greatest return possible on excess cash.
b. paying suppliers promptly.
c. speeding up collection from customers.
d. delaying payment of suppliers.

4-15 Which one of the following statements is true?

a. Sound internal control practice dictates that cash disbursements should be made by check, unless the disbursement is very small.
b. Petty cash can be substituted for a checking account to expedite the payment of all disbursements.
c. Good cash management practices dictate that a company should maintain as large a balance as possible in its cash account.
d. The person handling the cash should also prepare the bank reconciliation.

CORNERSTONE EXERCISES

OBJECTIVE 4
CORNERSTONE 4.1

Cornerstone Exercise 4-16 Bank Reconciliation

Firebird Corp. prepares monthly bank reconciliations of its checking account balance. The bank statement for February 2013 indicated the following:

Balance, February 28, 2013	$87,392
Service charge for February	100
Interest earned during February	875
NSF check from Valerie Corp. (deposited by Firebird)	630
Note ($12,000) and interest ($350) collected from a customer of Firebird's	12,350

An analysis of canceled checks and deposits and the records of Firebird Corp. revealed the following items:

Checking account balance per Firebird's books	$73,260
Outstanding checks as of February 28	6,440
Deposit in transit at February 28	4,785
Error in recording check 7853 issued by Firebird	18

The correct amount of check #7853 is $797. It was recorded as a cash disbursement of $779 by mistake. The check was issued to pay for merchandise purchases. The check appeared on the bank statement correctly.

Required:

1. Prepare a bank reconciliation schedule at February 28, 2013, in proper form.
2. What is the amount of cash that should be reported on the February 28, 2013 balance sheet?

OBJECTIVE 4
CORNERSTONE 4.1

Cornerstone Exercise 4-17 Bank Reconciliation

The accountant for Bellows Corp. was preparing a bank reconciliation as of April 30. The following items were identified:

Bellows' book balance	$28,750
Outstanding checks	900
Interest earned on checking account	75
Customer's NSF check returned by the bank	380

In addition, Bellows made an error in recording a customer's check; the amount was recorded in cash receipts as $370; the bank recorded the amount correctly as $730.

Required:

What amount will Bellows report as its adjusted cash balance at April 30, 2013?

Cornerstone Exercise 4-18 Adjusting Entry from Bank Reconciliation

OBJECTIVE 4
CORNERSTONE 4.2

A customer of Mutare paid for merchandise originally purchased on account with a check that has been erroneously entered into Mutare's cash account for $570 (it actually has been issued and paid for $750).

Required:

Record the appropriate journal entry to correct the error.

Cornerstone Exercise 4-19 Adjusting Entry from Bank Reconciliation

OBJECTIVE 4
CORNERSTONE 4.2

Pyramid Corporation is assessed a $40 fee as the result of a $126 NSF check received from a customer for services purchased on account. Neither the fee nor the NSF check has been accounted for on Pyramid's books.

Required:

Record the appropriate journal entry to update Pyramid's books.

Cornerstone Exercise 4-20 Bank Reconciliation

OBJECTIVE 4
CORNERSTONE 4.1
CORNERSTONE 4.2

Tiny Corp. prepares monthly bank reconciliations of its checking account balance. The bank statement indicated the following:

Balance, beginning of the month	$15,640
Service charge for October	65
Interest earned during October	80
NSF check from Green Corp. (deposited by Tiny) for goods purchased on account	615
Note ($2,500) and interest ($75) collected for Tiny from a customer	2,575

An analysis of canceled checks and deposits and the records of Tiny revealed the following items:

Checking account balance per Tiny's books	$12,951
Outstanding checks as of October 31	1,410
Deposit in transit at October 31	750
Error in recording a check issued by Tiny. (Correct amount of the check is $606, but was recorded as a cash disbursement of $660. The check was issued to pay for merchandise originally purchased on account).	54

Required:

1. Prepare a bank reconciliation at October 31, 2013, in proper form.
2. Record any necessary adjusting journal entries.
3. What is the amount of cash that should be reported on the October 31, 2013, balance sheet?

Cornerstone Exercise 4-21 Cash Over and Short

OBJECTIVE 4
CORNERSTONE 4.3

On a recent day, Pence Company obtained the following data from its cash registers:

	Cash Sales per Register Tape	Cash in Register after Removing Opening Change
Register 1	$12,675.12	$12,649.81
Register 2	11,429.57	11,432.16
Register 3	11,591.18	11,590.18

Pence deposits its cash receipts in its bank account daily.

Required:

Prepare a journal entry to record these cash sales.

OBJECTIVE 4
CORNERSTONE 4.3

Cornerstone Exercise 4-22 Cash Over and Short

Walker Department Store has one cash register. On a recent day, the cash register tape reported sales in the amount of $13,729.87. Actual cash in the register (after deducting and removing the opening change amount of $75) was $13,747.21, which was deposited in the firm's bank account.

Required:

Prepare a journal entry to record these cash collections.

OBJECTIVE 4
CORNERSTONE 4.4

Cornerstone Exercise 4-23 Petty Cash Fund

Murphy Inc. maintains a balance of $2,500 in its petty cash fund. On December 31, Murphy's petty cash account has a balance of $216. Murphy replenishes the petty cash account to bring it back up to $2,500. Murphy classifies all petty cash transactions as miscellaneous expense.

Required:

What entry is made to record the replenishment of the petty cash fund?

OBJECTIVE 4
CORNERSTONE 4.4

Cornerstone Exercise 4-24 Petty Cash with Change in Fund Balance

Basque Inc. maintains a petty cash fund with a balance of $800. On December 31, Basque's petty cash account has a balance of $60. Basque replenishes the petty cash account, as it does at the end of every month, but also decides to increase the fund balance to $1,000. Basque classifies all petty cash transactions as miscellaneous expense.

Required:

What entry is made to record this activity?

BRIEF EXERCISES

OBJECTIVE 1

Brief Exercise 4-25 Role of Internal Control

Internal controls play a crucial role in a business.

Required:

CONCEPTUAL CONNECTION Discuss why internal controls are important. What are the potential consequences of an internal control failure?

OBJECTIVE 2

Brief Exercise 4-26 Components of Internal Control

The Committee of Sponsoring Organizations of the Treadway Commission (COSO) discussed five components of internal control.

Required:

Define and discuss these five components of internal control.

OBJECTIVE 4

Brief Exercise 4-27 Bank Reconciliation

Hula Corp. utilizes J.P. Morgan Chase in its banking transactions. For the month of August, 2013, J.P. Morgan Chase presented Hula with its bank statement as follows:

Balance, August 31, 2013	$64,900
Service charge for August	100
Interest earned during August	875
NSF check from Jeffrey Corp. (deposited by Hula)	450
Note ($11,000) and interest ($425) collected for Hula from a customer	11,425

Upon receiving the bank statement, Hula's accountants analyzed its cash transactions for possible reconciling items between its cash balance per books and J.P. Morgan Chase's cash balance:

Checking account balance per Hula's books	$53,453
Outstanding checks as of August 31	3,700
Deposit in transit at August 31, 2013	3,940
Error in recording check 9288 issued by Hula	63

The correct amount of check 9288 is $770. It was recorded as a cash disbursement of $707 by mistake. The check was issued to pay for merchandise purchases. The check appeared on the bank statement correctly.

Required:

Prepare a bank reconciliation schedule at August 31, 2013, in proper form.

Brief Exercise 4-28 Adjusting Entry from Bank Reconciliation

OBJECTIVE 4

Engle, a furniture company, made an error in recording a check received from a customer. Last month, Engle's customer bought a table for $909. Upon receiving the check from the customer, Engel entered the check as an increase of cash of $990.

Required:

Record the appropriate journal entry to correct the error.

Brief Exercise 4-29 Adjusting Entry from Bank Reconciliation

OBJECTIVE 4

Samba Corporation operates in an industry with a high collectability issues. Recently, one of Samba's customers wrote a check for $235 for services performed. Samba's bank later informed Samba that its customer did not have cash available in his account to cover the $235 charge. As a result, Samba's bank assesses a $30 fee as the result of the NSF check received. Samba has not yet adjusted its books for the bank fee or the NSF check.

Required:

Record the appropriate journal entry to update Samba's books.

Brief Exercise 4-30 Bank Reconciliation

OBJECTIVE 4

Garrison Corporation was closing its books on May 31, 2014. Garrison's accountant prepared a bank reconciliation as of May 31, 2014, and has found the following possible reconciling items between its book balance and its cash balance per the bank:

Garrison's book balance	$80,760
Outstanding checks	660
Customer's NSF check returned by the bank	190
Interest earned on checking account	80

In the search for reconciling items, the accountant also discovered that Garrison made an error in recording a customer's check: the amount was recorded in cash receipts as $290; the bank recorded the amount correctly as $920.

Required:

What amount will Garrison report as its adjusted cash balance at May 31, 2014?

Brief Exercise 4-31 Bank Reconciliation

OBJECTIVE 4

Zing Corp. prepares monthly bank reconciliations as part of its cash controls. Zing's bank provided the following amount about Zing's cash balance at the bank for during the month of April 2014:

(Continued)

Balance, April 30, 2014	$74,350
Service charge for April	75
Note ($3,000) and interest ($90) collected for Zing from a customer	3,090
Interest earned during April	140
NSF check from Orange Corp. (deposited by Zing) for goods purchased on account	470

Zing then analyzed its cash balance on its own set of books, revealing the following details:

Checking account balance per Zing's books	$72,329
Deposit in transit at April 30	2,100
Outstanding checks as of April 30	1,400
Error in recording a check issued by Zing. (Correct amount of the check is $737, but was recorded as a cash disbursement of $773. The check was issued to pay for merchandise originally purchased on account.)	36

Required:

1. Prepare a bank reconciliation at April 30, 2014, in proper form.
2. Record any necessary adjusting journal entries.

OBJECTIVE 4

Brief Exercise 4-32 Cash Over and Short

At the end of each day, Spangle counts the cash in its cash registers. Spangle then compares the physical amount of cash to the amount of cash that the register tape indicates should be in the cash drawer. On a recent day, Spangle Company obtained the following data from its cash registers:

	Cash Sales per Register Tape	Cash in Register after Removing Opening Change
Register 1	$14,759.62	$14,757.98
Register 2	15,101.59	15,104.06
Register 3	14,802.18	14,798.87

Spangle deposits its cash receipts in its bank account daily.

Required:

Prepare a journal entry to record these cash sales.

OBJECTIVE 4

Brief Exercise 4-33 Cash Over and Short

Milner Department Store has one cash register on which it performs daily cash counts. Recently, the cash count indicated that there was $9,218.47 in the register after deducting and removing the opening change amount of $50. However, the cash register tape reported sales in the amount of $9,217.85. Milner deposited its cash collected in its bank account.

Required:

Prepare a journal entry to record these cash collections.

OBJECTIVE 4

Brief Exercise 4-34 Petty Cash Fund

Kingery Inc. maintains a balance of $3,000 in its petty cash fund for routine purchases such as supplies. During the year, Kingery's employees paid for various office supplies and food purchases for office birthdays. As a result, Kingery's petty cash account has a balance of $374 on December 31, 2013. At the end of each year, Kingery replenishes the petty cash in full. Kingery classifies all petty cash transactions as miscellaneous expense.

Required:

What entry is made to record the replenishment of the petty cash fund?

OBJECTIVE 4

Brief Exercise 4-35 Petty Cash with Change in Fund Balance

Canary Inc. maintains a petty cash fund with a balance of $1,800. During the month of September, Canary's employees made routine expenses using cash from the petty cash fund totaling $1,150. At the end of September, Canary replenishes the petty cash account, but it also decides to increase the fund balance to $2,000. Canary classifies all petty cash transactions as miscellaneous expense.

Required:

What entry is made to record this activity?

Brief Exercise 4-36 Cash Reporting

OBJECTIVE 3

Richter Industries has the following items:

Currency	$27,500
Customer checks that have not been deposited	850
U.S. government bonds that originally maturing in 3 months	11,000
U.S. government bonds that originally maturing in 12 months	14,000
Cash in saving and checking accounts	50,000
Certificates of deposits that originally maturing in 18 months	47,000

Required:

How much should Richter report as cash and equivalents on its balance sheet?

Brief Exercise 4-37 Operating Cycle

OBJECTIVE 5

Businesses must decide whether to issue credit to customers.

Required:

CONCEPTUAL CONNECTION Describe how selling to customers on credit affects the operating cycle.

Brief Exercise 4-38 Cash Management

OBJECTIVE 5

Effective cash management is very important to the operating performance of a business.

Required:

CONCEPTUAL CONNECTION Explain the principles of cash management. Why might it be advantageous to delay paying suppliers?

EXERCISES

Exercise 4-39 Internal Control System

OBJECTIVE 1 2

Required:

A list of terms and a list of definitions and examples are presented below. Make a list numbered 1 through 5 and match the letter of the most directly related definition or example with the number of each term.

Term	Definition or Example
1. Strategic risk	a. A member of upper management was fired for violating the company's code of conduct.
2. Control environment	b. The internal audit group is testing the operating effectiveness of various internal control activities.
3. Information and communication	c. Competitors begin offering extended warranty coverage on products.
4. Business process risk	d. Problems with our suppliers have resulted in lost sales because our stores were out of stock.
5. Monitoring	e. Reports documenting problems with production are forwarded to management.

OBJECTIVE 1 2

Exercise 4-40 Internal Control Terminology

Required:

A list of terms and a list of definitions and examples are presented below. Make a list numbered 1 through 7 and match the letter of the most directly related definition or example with the number of each term.

Term	Definition or Example
1. Accounting controls	a. Company policy prevents accountants from handling cash.
2. Adequate documents and records	b. Company policy requires receiving reports to be made for all deliveries by suppliers.
3. Checks on recorded amounts	c. Cash deposits are reconciled with cash register records at the end of every day.
4. Effective personnel policies	d. This includes the accounting system, all policies and procedures of the business, and the environment in which they operate.
5. Internal control structure	e. Every evening, a jewelry store removes all items of merchandise valued at over $100 from its display.
6. Safeguards over assets and records	f. These are policies and procedures that govern the identification, measurement, recording, and communication of economic information.
7. Segregation of duties	g. Every new employee is required to spend 2 days in training courses to learn company policies.

OBJECTIVE 2

Exercise 4-41 Classifying Internal Control Procedures

Required:

Match each of the control procedures listed below with the most closely related control procedures type. Your answer should pair each of the numbers 1 through 10 with the appropriate letter.

Control Procedure Types

a. Adequate documents and records
b. Checks on recorded amounts
c. Clearly defined authority and responsibility
d. Safeguards over assets and records
e. Segregation of duties

Control Procedures

1. Only the cashier assigned to the cash register is allowed to perform transactions.
2. Division managers are evaluated annually on the basis of their division's profitability.
3. Invoices received from outside suppliers are filed with purchase orders.
4. Employees with access to the accounting records are not permitted to open the mail because it contains many payments by check from customers.
5. The extent of access to the many segments of the company's computer system is tightly controlled by individual identification cards and passwords that change at regular intervals.
6. Each shipment to customers from inventory is recorded on a specially printed form bearing a sequential number; these forms are the basis for entries into the computer system, which makes entries to inventory records and produces periodic reports of sales and shipments.
7. At regular intervals, internal audit reviews a sample of expenditure transactions to determine that payment has been made to a bona fide supplier and that the related goods or services were received and appropriately used.
8. A construction company stores large steel girders in an open yard surrounded by a 5-foot fence and stores welding supplies in a controlled-access, tightly secured concrete building.
9. Cash registers display the price of each item purchased to the customer as it is recorded and produce a customer receipt that describes each item and gives its price.
10. The person in the controller's office who prepares and mails checks to suppliers cannot make entries in the general ledger system.

OBJECTIVE 2 3

Exercise 4-42 Internal Control of Cash

Hannah Thatcher, a longtime employee of a local shoe store, is responsible for maintaining the company's cash records and for opening the daily mail, through which the company receives about 25% of its daily cash receipts. Virtually all cash received by mail is in the form of checks made payable to the company. Thatcher is also responsible for preparing deposits of currency and checks for the bank at the end of each day.

Required:

1. **CONCEPTUAL CONNECTION** Explain briefly how Thatcher might be able to steal some of the company's cash receipts.
2. **CONCEPTUAL CONNECTION** What internal control procedures would you recommend to prevent this theft?

Exercise 4-43 Cash Over and Short

OBJECTIVE 4

Miller Enterprises deposits the cash received during each day at the end of the day. Miller deposited $48,287 on October 3 and $50,116 on October 4. Cash register records and other documents supporting the deposits are summarized as follows:

	10/3	10/4
Cash sales	$36,690	$40,310
Collections on account	10,875	9,813
Total receipts	$47,565	$50,123

Required:

1. Calculate the amount of cash over or cash short for each day.
2. Prepare the journal entry to record the receipt and deposit of cash on October 3.
3. Prepare the journal entry to record the receipt and deposit of cash on October 4.
4. **CONCEPTUAL CONNECTION** If you were the manager with responsibility over the cash registers, how would you use this information?

Exercise 4-44 Bank Reconciliation

OBJECTIVE 4

Johnson Corporation's bank statement for October reports an ending balance of $22,381, whereas Johnson's cash account shows a balance of $22,025 on October 31. The following additional information is available:

a. A $855 deposit made on October 31 was not recorded by the bank until November.
b. At the end of October, outstanding checks total $1,222.
c. The bank statement shows bank service charges of $125 not yet recorded by the company.
d. The company erroneously recorded as $973 a check that it had actually written for $379. It was correctly processed by the bank.
e. A $480 check from a customer, deposited by the company on October 29, was returned with the bank statement for lack of funds.

Required:

1. Prepare the October bank reconciliation for Johnson Corporation.
2. What amount will be reported as cash on the October 31 balance sheet?

Exercise 4-45 Bank Reconciliation (Partial)

OBJECTIVE 4

The cash account for Pitt Corporation contains the following information for June:

Cash balance, 5/31		$18,130
Cash received during June		42,650
		$60,780
Cash disbursements during June:		
Check 8255	$17,850	
Check 8256	22,375	
Check 8257	9,620	
Check 8258	2,735	52,580
Cash balance, 6/30		$ 8,200

(Continued)

The bank statement for April contains the following information:

Bank balance, 5/31		$34,525
Add: Deposits during June		42,650
		$77,175
Less: Checks paid during June:		
Check 8253	$ 1,720	
Check 8254	14,675	
Check 8255	17,850	
Check 8256	22,375	56,620
Bank balance, 6/30		$20,555

Required:

Assuming there were no deposits in transit at May 31 and that all outstanding checks at May 31 cleared during June, do the following:

1. Identify the outstanding checks at June 30.
2. Prepare the reconciliation of the bank and cash account balances at June 30.
3. Identify the outstanding checks at May 31.
4. Prepare the reconciliation of the bank and cash account balances at May 31.
5. **CONCEPTUAL CONNECTION** Why could you not perform the bank reconciliations without knowing that there were no deposits in transit on May 31 and that all outstanding checks at May 31 cleared during June?

OBJECTIVE 4

Exercise 4-46 Bank Reconciliation

Valentine Investigations has the following information for its cash account:

Balance, 1/31	$ 7,444
Deposits during February	106,780
Checks written during February	102,341

Valentine's bank statement for February contained the following information:

Balance per bank, 1/31		$ 8,910
Add: February deposits		104,950
		$ 113,860
Less:		
Checks paid in February	$(101,400)	
Bank service charge	(50)	
Debit memo (electric bill)	(800)	(102,250)
Balance per bank, 2/28		$ 11,610

A comparison of company records with the bank statement provided the following data:

	At 1/31	At 2/28
Deposits in transit	$2,750	$4,580
Outstanding checks	4,216	5,157

Required:

1. Prepare a bank reconciliation as of February 28.
2. Prepare adjusting entries for Valentine based on the information developed in the bank reconciliation.
3. What is the amount of cash that should be reported on the February 28 balance sheet?

OBJECTIVE 4

ILLUSTRATING RELATIONSHIPS

Exercise 4-47 Bank Reconciliation

Conway Company reported the following information:

Cash balance on balance sheet (12/31)	$22,066
Pre-reconciliation cash account balance (12/31)	23,916
Bank statement (12/31)	23,220

Bank service charges	$ 350
Bank debit memos (utility payments)	1,500
Deposits in transit (12/31)	9,160

Required:

1. Calculate the amount of outstanding checks as of December 31.
2. Prepare the adjusting entries that Conway must make at December 31.

Exercise 4-48 Adjusting Entries from a Bank Reconciliation

OBJECTIVE 4

Hawk Enterprises identified the following items on its January reconciliation that may require adjusting entries:

a. A deposit of $1,190 was recorded in Hawk's accounting records, but not on the January 31 bank statement.
b. A check for $3,371 was outstanding at January 31.
c. Included with the bank statement was a check for $560 written by Eagle Corporation. The bank had, in error, deducted this check from Hawk's account.
d. Bank service charges were $375.
e. An NSF check written by one of Hawk's customers in the amount of $1,150 was returned by the bank with Hawk's bank statement. This customer was paying for merchandise originally purchased on account.

Required:

For each of these five items, prepare an adjusting entry for Hawk's journal, if any is required.

Exercise 4-49 Recording Petty Cash Account Transactions

OBJECTIVE 4

During March, Anderson Company engaged in the following transactions involving its petty cash fund:

a. On March 1, Anderson Company established the petty cash fund by issuing a check for $1,500 to the fund custodian.
b. On March 4, the custodian paid $85 out of petty cash for freight charges on new equipment. This amount is properly classified as equipment.
c. On March 12, the custodian paid $140 out of petty cash for supplies. Anderson expenses supplies purchases as supplies expense.
d. On March 22, the custodian paid $25 out of petty cash for express mail services for reports sent to the Environmental Protection Agency. This is considered a miscellaneous expense.
e. On March 25, the custodian filed a claim for reimbursement of petty cash expenditures during the month totaling $250.
f. On March 31, Anderson issued a check for $250 to the custodian, replenishing the fund for expenditures during the month.

Required:

Prepare any journal entries required to record the petty cash account transactions that occurred during the month of March.

Exercise 4-50 Cash Reporting

OBJECTIVE 3

Brown Industries has the following items:

Currency	$15,500
Customer checks that have not been deposited	675
Cash in saving and checking accounts	35,000
Certificates of deposits that originally matured in 18 months	44,000
U.S. government bonds that originally matured in 2 months	8,000
U.S. government bonds that originally matured in 12 months	10,000

(Continued)

Required:

How much should Brown report as cash and equivalents on its balance sheet?

OBJECTIVE 3

Exercise 4-51 Components of Cash

The office manager for Stony Company had accumulated the following information at the end of a recent year:

Item	Amount
Accounts receivable	$22,470
Change for cash registers (currency and coin)	4,800
Amount on deposit in checking account (bank balance)	7,382
Amount on deposit in savings account (bank balance)	30,000
Balance in petty cash	500
Checks received from customers, but not yet deposited in bank	590
Checks sent by Stony to suppliers, but not yet presented at bank for payment	560
Deposits in transit	920
IOU from Richard Sandy, company president	10,000
Notes receivable	13,400
NSF check written by Liam Company	430
Prepaid postage	125

Required:

Calculate the total cash amount Stony will report on its balance sheet.

OBJECTIVE 5

Exercise 4-52 Operating Cycle

Business activity is often described as being cyclical in nature.

Required:

CONCEPTUAL CONNECTION Describe the cyclical nature of business activity.

OBJECTIVE 5

Exercise 4-53 Operating Cycle

A list of businesses is presented below:

Business	Operating-Cycle Description
1. Tree nursery	a. Very short—customers typically pay cash, and inventory is often held less than 1 day.
2. Fast food restaurant	b. A few months—merchandise is typically on hand for several weeks, and some customers may use credit.
3. Appliance store	c. More than 1 year—merchandise may be in inventory for several months, and most customers will pay for purchases after 1 or 2 years.
4. Electric utility	d. Several years—a number of years are required to prepare merchandise for sale. Customers probably pay cash for most items.
5. Clothing store	e. A few months—customers pay monthly. The current assets used to provide customer services are consumed within a few months.

Required:

1. Match each business with a description of the operating cycle for that business.
2. **CONCEPTUAL CONNECTION** How does a longer operating cycle (such as Description c or d) change a company's financing needs relative to a shorter operating cycle (such as Description a)?

Exercise 4-54 Operating Cycle and Current Receivables

OBJECTIVE 5

a. Dither and Sly are attorneys-at-law who specialize in federal income tax law. They complete their typical case in 6 months or less and collect from the typical client within 1 additional month.
b. Johnston's Market specializes in fresh meat and fish. All merchandise must be sold within one week of purchase. Almost all sales are for cash, and any receivables are generally paid by the end of the following month.
c. Mortondo's is a women's clothing store specializing in high-style merchandise. Merchandise spends an average of 7 months on the rack following purchase. Most sales are on credit, and the typical customer pays within 1 month of sale.
d. Trees Inc. grows Christmas trees and sells them to various Christmas tree lots. Most sales are for cash. It takes 6 years to grow a tree.

Required:

For each of the businesses described above, indicate the length of the operating cycle.

PROBLEM SET A

Problem 4-55A Role of Internal Control

OBJECTIVE 1 2

Internal control systems include policies and procedures designed to provide reasonable assurance that the corporation's objectives are being met in three areas: (a) effectiveness and efficiency of operations, (b) reliability of financial reporting, and (c) compliance with applicable laws and regulations. Like any other business, a grocery store uses internal control activities to meet their objectives in these three areas.

Required:

CONCEPTUAL CONNECTION Attempt to name a control for each area and describe how the control helps accomplish the store's objectives in these areas.

Problem 4-56A Internal Control Procedures for Cash Receipts

OBJECTIVE 2 3

Lee and Kim Cooper are planning to open and operate a clothing boutique in a newly developed subdivision. Lee and Kim are concerned that employees may try to pocket some of the cash collected from customers.

Required:

Identify some internal control procedures that could help ensure that all cash paid by customers is remitted to the business.

Problem 4-57A Internal Control for Cash

OBJECTIVE 2 3

After comparing cash register tapes with inventory records, the accountant for Benning Convenience Stores is concerned that someone at one of the stores is not recording some of that store's cash sales and is stealing the cash from the unreported sales.

Required:

1. **CONCEPTUAL CONNECTION** Explain why a comparison of sales and inventory records would reveal a situation in which cash sales are not being recorded and cash from those sales is being stolen.
2. **CONCEPTUAL CONNECTION** Describe how an employee might be able to steal cash from sales.
3. **CONCEPTUAL CONNECTION** What internal control procedures would you recommend to make the theft you described in Requirement 2 more difficult?

OBJECTIVE 4

Problem 4-58A Bank Reconciliation

Shortly after July 31, Morse Corporation received a bank statement containing the following information:

Date		Checks			Deposits	Balance
6/30	Beg. balance					$ 7,958
7/1					$ 1,200	9,158
7/2		$ 620	$ 550	$ 344	12,500	20,144
7/3		35	8,100			12,009
7/5		311	97	4,000	9,100	16,701
7/9		4,500	790	286		11,125
7/12		34	7,100			3,991
7/15		634	1,880		7,000	8,477
7/19		3,780	414			4,283
7/24		1,492	649			2,142
7/29		350	677*		4,620	5,735
7/31		575	18**			5,142

*NSF check
**Bank service charge

July cash transactions and balances on Morse's records are shown in the following T-account:

Cash

Balance, 6/30	$ 7,609				
Date	Amount Deposited	Check Number	Check Amount	Check Number	Check Amount
7/1	$12,500	176	$8,100	186	$ 1,880
7/5	9,100	177	97	187	634
7/15	7,000	178	4,000	188	3,780
7/29	4,620	179	311	189	649
7/30	2,050	180	7,100	190	1,492
Total deposits	$35,270	181	4,500	191	37
		182	790	192	350
		183	34	193	575
		184	286	194	227
		185	414	195	1,123
Balance, 7/31	$ 6,500		Total disbursements		$36,379

Required:

1. Prepare a bank reconciliation for July.
2. Prepare the adjusting entries made by Morse Corporation as a result of this reconciliation process.
3. What amount is reported as cash on the balance sheet at July 31?

OBJECTIVE 4

Problem 4-59A Bank Reconciliation

Raymond Corporation received the following bank statement for the month of October:

Date		Checks			Deposits	Balance
9/30	Beg. balance					$ 4,831.50
10/2		$1,204.50			$2,970.18	6,597.18
10/4		43.80	$ 321.70			6,231.68
10/8		905.36				5,326.32
10/10		100.20	60.00	$38.11		5,128.01
10/13					4,000.00	9,128.01
10/14		290.45*				8,837.56
10/17		516.11	309.24			8,012.21
10/19		106.39	431.15	21.72	2,850.63	10,303.58
10/21		3,108.42				7,195.16

Date	Checks		Deposits	Balance
10/23	63.89			$ 7,131.27
10/25	290.00**	111.90		6,729.37
10/27	88.90			6,640.47
10/31	20.00***	1,308.77		5,311.70

*NSF check
**Debit memo (Rent Expense)
***Service charge

The cash records of Raymond Corporation provide the following information:

Date	Item	Debit	Credit	Balance
10/1	Balance from 9/30			$ 6,553.38
10/2	Check #1908		$ 321.70	6,231.68
10/5	Check #1909		905.36	5,326.32
10/6	Check #1910		100.20	5,226.12
10/6	Check #1911		60.00	5,166.12
10/7	Check #1912		38.11	5,128.01
10/12	Deposit #411	$4,000.00		9,128.01
10/15	Check #1913		516.11	8,611.90
10/16	Check #1914		309.24	8,302.66
10/17	Check #1915		431.15	7,871.51
10/17	Check #1916		21.72	7,849.79
10/18	Deposit #412	2,850.63		10,700.42
10/18	Check #1917		106.39	10,594.03
10/20	Check #1918		63.89	10,530.14
10/20	Check #1919		3,108.42	7,421.72
10/23	Check #1920		111.90	7,309.82
10/25	Check #1921		88.90	7,220.92
10/29	Check #1922		1,803.77	5,417.15
10/30	Check #1923		284.77	5,132.38
10/31	Check #1924		628.32	4,504.06
10/31	Deposit #413	3,408.20		7,912.26

The items on the bank statement are correct. The debit memo is for the payment by the bank of Raymond's office furniture rent expense for October.

Required:

1. Prepare a bank reconciliation. (*Hint*: There is one transposition error in the cash account.)
2. Prepare adjusting entries based on the bank reconciliation.
3. What amount is reported for cash in bank in the balance sheet at October 31?

Problem 4-60A Bank Reconciliation

OBJECTIVE 4

The cash account of Dixon Products reveals the following information:

Cash			
Balance, 4/30	11,800	41,620	Checks written during May
Deposits during May	37,600		

The bank statement for May contains the following information:

Bank balance, 4/30		$ 11,750
Add: Deposits during May		37,250
		$ 49,000
Less: Checks paid during May	$(40,230)	
NSF check from Frolin Inc.	(190)	
Bank service charges	(40)	(40,460)
Bank balance, 5/31		$ 8,540

(Continued)

A comparison of detailed company records with the bank statement indicates the following information:

	At 4/30	At 5/31
Deposit in transit	$800	$1,150
Outstanding checks	750	2,140

The bank amounts are determined to be correct.

Required:

1. Prepare a bank reconciliation for May.
2. Prepare the adjusting entries made by Dixon as a result of the reconciliation process.
3. What amount is reported for cash on the balance sheet at May 31?

OBJECTIVE 4

Problem 4-61A Recording Petty Cash Transactions

Mallard Products had a balance of $350 in cash in its petty cash fund at the beginning of November. The following transactions took place in November:

a. On November 1, the custodian paid $72 out of petty cash for new pens with Mallard's newly designed logo prominently displayed. This is considered supplies expense.
b. On November 7, the custodian paid $120 out of petty cash for minor repairs to its equipment. This is a maintenance expense.
c. On November 9, the custodian paid $24 out of petty cash for transportation-in.
d. On November 15, the custodian paid $38 out of petty cash to have documents delivered to the accounting firm preparing the company's corporate tax return. This is considered an other expense.
e. On November 22, the custodian paid $86 out of petty cash to reimburse the Chief Financial Officer for costs he had incurred in traveling to the airport for an important international business conference. This is a travel expense.
f. On November 28, the custodian submitted receipts for the above expenditures and a check was drawn for the amount to replenish the fund.

Required:

Prepare any journal entries made by the corporation to record these transactions.

PROBLEM SET B

OBJECTIVE 1 2

Problem 4-55B Role of Internal Control

Internal control systems include policies and procedures designed to provide reasonable assurance that the corporation's objectives are being met in three areas: (a) effectiveness and efficiency of operations, (b) reliability of financial reporting, and (c) compliance with applicable laws and regulations. Like any other business, a bookstore uses internal control activities to meet its objectives in these three areas.

Required:

CONCEPTUAL CONNECTION Attempt to name a control for each area and describe how the control helps accomplish the store's objectives in these areas.

OBJECTIVE 2 3

Problem 4-56B Internal Control Procedures for Cash Receipts

Sean and Liz Kinsella are planning to open and operate a coffee shop on a university campus. Sean and Liz are concerned that part of the cash that customers pay for food might be kept by some of the store's employees.

Required:

CONCEPTUAL CONNECTION Identify some internal control procedures that could help ensure that all cash paid by customers is remitted to the business.

Problem 4-57B Internal Control for Cash

OBJECTIVE 2 3

After comparing cash register tapes with inventory records, the accountant for Good Times Music store is concerned that someone at one of the stores is not recording some of that store's cash sales and is stealing the cash from the unreported sales.

Required:

1. **CONCEPTUAL CONNECTION** Explain why a comparison of sales and inventory records would reveal a situation in which cash sales are not being recorded and cash from those sales is being stolen.
2. **CONCEPTUAL CONNECTION** Describe how an employee might be able to steal cash from sales.
3. **CONCEPTUAL CONNECTION** What internal control procedures would you recommend to make the theft you described in Requirement 2 more difficult?

Problem 4-58B Bank Reconciliation

OBJECTIVE 4

Shortly after July 31, Towanda Corporation received a bank statement containing the following information:

Date		Checks			Deposits	Balance
6/30	Beg. balance					$ 5,550
7/1					$ 300	5,850
7/2		$ 270	$ 150	$ 330	4,500	9,600
7/3		25	7,025			2,550
7/5		150	450	1,400	10,000	10,550
7/9		1,500	25	325		8,700
7/12		500	100			8,100
7/15		1,600	2,700		3,500	7,300
7/19		75	425			6,800
7/24		650	550			5,600
7/29			525*			5,075
7/31			25**			5,050

*NSF check (deposited in previous period, but withdrawn this period)
**Bank service charge

July cash transactions and balances on Towanda's records are shown in the following T-account:

Cash

Balance, 6/30	**$ 5,550**				
Date	Amount Deposited	Check Number	Check Amount	Check Number	Check Amount
7/1	$ 300	176	$ 270	186	$ 25
7/5	4,500	177	150	187	100
7/15	10,000	178	330	188	500
7/29	3,500	179	25	189	2,700
7/30	950	180	7,025	190	1,600
Total deposits	$19,250	181	150	191	75
		182	450	192	425
		183	1,400	193	550
		184	1,500	194	650
		185	325	195	275
Balance, 7/31	**$ 6,275**	Total disbursements			$18,525

Required:

1. Prepare a bank reconciliation for July.
2. Prepare the adjusting entries made by Towanda Corporation as a result of this reconciliation process.
3. What amount is reported as cash on the balance sheet at July 31?

OBJECTIVE 4

Problem 4-59B Bank Reconciliation

Donald Corporation received the bank statement shown below for the month of October:

Date		Checks			Deposits	Balance
9/30	Beg. balance					$ 5,205
10/2		$1,200			$2,950	6,955
10/4		50	$ 300			6,605
10/8		900				5,705
10/10		100	60	$35		5,510
10/13					4,000	9,510
10/14		300*				9,210
10/17		525	325			8,360
10/19		105	430	20	2,850	10,655
10/21		3,110				7,545
10/23		65				7,480
10/25		250**	110			7,120
10/27		90				7,030
10/31		25***	1,305			5,700

*NSF check
**Debit memo (Rent Expense)
***Service charge

The cash records of Donald Corporation provide the following information:

Date	Item	Debit	Credit	Balance
10/1	Balance from 9/30			$ 6,905
10/2	Check #1908		$ 300	6,605
10/5	Check #1909		900	5,705
10/6	Check #1910		100	5,605
10/6	Check #1911		60	5,545
10/7	Check #1912		35	5,510
10/12	Deposit #411	$4,000		9,510
10/15	Check #1913		525	8,985
10/16	Check #1914		325	8,660
10/17	Check #1915		430	8,230
10/17	Check #1916		20	8,210
10/18	Deposit #412	2,850		11,060
10/18	Check #1917		105	10,955
10/20	Check #1918		65	10,890
10/20	Check #1919		3,110	7,780
10/23	Check #1920		110	7,670
10/25	Check #1921		90	7,580
10/29	Check #1922		1,350	6,230
10/30	Check #1923		250	5,980
10/31	Check #1924		650	5,330
10/31	Deposit #413	3,300		8,630

The items on the bank statement are correct. The debit memo is for the payment by the bank of Donald's office furniture rent expense for October.

Required:

1. Prepare a bank reconciliation. (*Hint*: There is one transposition error in the cash account.)
2. Prepare adjusting entries based on the bank reconciliation.
3. What amount is reported for cash in bank on the balance sheet at October 31?

Problem 4-60B Bank Reconciliation

OBJECTIVE 4

The cash account of Mason Products reveals the following information:

Cash			
Balance, 4/30	10,100		
Deposits during May	39,600	40,000	Checks written during May

The bank statement for May contains the following information:

Bank balance, 4/30		$ 9,750
Add: Deposits during May		37,400
		$ 47,150
Less: Checks paid during May	$(38,500)	
NSF check from Higgins Inc.	(140)	
Bank service charges	(60)	(38,700)
Bank balance, 5/31		$ 8,450

A comparison of detailed company records with the bank statement indicates the following information:

	At 4/30	At 5/31
Deposit in transit	$900	$3,100
Outstanding checks	550	2,050

The bank amounts are determined to be correct.

Required:

1. Prepare a bank reconciliation for May.
2. Prepare the adjusting entries made by Mason Products as a result of the reconciliation process.
3. What amount is reported for cash on the balance sheet at May 31?

Problem 4-61B Recording Petty Cash Transactions

OBJECTIVE 4

Chicago Inc. had a balance of $1,200 in cash in its petty cash fund at the beginning of September. The following transactions took place in September:

a. On September 4, the custodian paid $75 out of petty cash for new stationery on which the company president's name appeared prominently. This is considered supplies expense.
b. On September 11, the custodian paid $350 out of petty cash for maintenance manuals for some equipment. This is a maintenance expense.
c. On September 15, the custodian paid $25 out of petty cash for transportation-in.
d. On September 23, the custodian paid $50 out of petty cash to have documents delivered to the lawyers who were defending the firm in a lawsuit. This is considered an other expense.
e. On September 27, the custodian paid $175 out of petty cash to reimburse the president for costs he had incurred when bad weather prevented the company jet from landing to pick him up after a meeting. This is a travel expense.
f. On September 30, the custodian submitted receipts for the above expenditures and a check was drawn for the amount to replenish the fund.

Required:

Prepare any journal entries made by the corporation to record these transactions.

CASES

Case 4-62 Ethics and Cash Controls

You have just been hired as a part-time clerk in a large department store. Each week you work three evenings and all day Saturday. Without the income provided by this job, you would be

(Continued)

unable to stay in college. Charles Riley, the manager in the clothing department to which you are assigned, has worked for the store for many years. Managers receive both a salary and a commission on their sales.

Late one afternoon, just as you begin work, Mr. Riley is ringing up a purchase. You observe that the purchase consists of two expensive suits, a coat, and several pairs of trousers and that the customer declines Mr. Riley's offer to have the store's tailor do the alterations. After the customer departs with his merchandise and as Mr. Riley is departing for the evening, you say, "See you tomorrow." Mr. Riley gives a brief, barely audible response and departs for the evening.

As you return to the sales counter, you glance at the paper tape displayed through a small opening in the cash register that records all sales on an item-by-item basis. You have just completed the store course in register operation, so you are quite familiar with the register and the tape it produces. To your surprise, you note that the last sale consisted of just a single pair of trousers.

Required:

1. What do you conclude about this transaction?
2. What are the possible consequences for the store, for Mr. Riley, and for you personally of reporting your observations to Mr. Riley's superiors?
3. What are the possible consequences for the store, for Mr. Riley, and for you personally of *not* reporting your observations to Mr. Riley's superiors?
4. What would your decision be?

Case 4-63 The Operating Cycle

There are two retail stores in Millersburgh. One is a full-service store that typically sells on credit to its customers; the other is a smaller discount store that usually sells for cash. Full-service stores typically charge higher prices than discount stores for identical items.

Required:

1. Does the operating cycle suggest some economic reason for a portion of this price difference? Explain your answer.
2. **CONCEPTUAL CONNECTION** Can you think of other reasons why a full-service store might charge more than a discount store for the same merchandise?

Case 4-64 Internal Controls for Cash Disbursements

Campus Supply Store purchases merchandise on credit from a large number of suppliers. During the past 5 years, Campus's annual sales have grown from $100,000 to $1,500,000. A recent article in the local newspaper disclosed that an employee of another firm had been arrested for embezzling funds from his employer by diverting payments for purchases to his own bank account. Because of that article, the accountant for Campus has decided to examine Campus's procedures for purchases and payables.

Currently three different employees are authorized to order merchandise for the store. These employees normally complete paperwork provided by the suppliers' sales representatives, keeping a copy for their records. When the ordered merchandise arrives, whomever the delivery person can locate signs for the package. Bills are sent to the store by suppliers and are paid by Campus's accountant when due.

Required:

1. Indicate which general principles of internal control are violated by Campus's procedures for purchases and payables.
2. **CONCEPTUAL CONNECTION** Recommend procedures that would incorporate the five general categories of internal control where possible.

Case 4-65 Internal Controls for Collection of Receivables

Carolyn Furniture Galleries sells traditional furniture from two stores in St. Louis. Carolyn's credit terms allow customers to pay for purchases over 3 months with no finance charges.

Carolyn's accountant has been responsible for approving customers for credit, recording cash received from customers in the accounting records, depositing cash collections in the bank, and following up on customers who are behind in their payments. Each month the accountant has prepared a report for Carolyn's president, indicating the cash collected, outstanding receivables, and uncollectible accounts.

Carolyn's president has been concerned about a significant increase in uncollectible accounts that began about 2 years ago, shortly after the current accountant was hired. Recently, a personal friend of Carolyn's president called. The caller had moved from St. Louis to Denver about 6 months ago. A month ago, the caller's new bank had refused a loan because a credit rating bureau in St. Louis had indicated that the caller had left bills unpaid at Carolyn Furniture. Carolyn's president knew that the caller had paid his account before leaving the community.

Carolyn's president called a detective agency and arranged for an investigation. Two weeks later, Carolyn's president was informed that the accountant had been spending much more money than his salary would warrant. Carolyn then called its auditor and arranged to have the accounting records for receivables and uncollectible accounts examined. This examination indicated that about $400,000 of cash had been stolen from the firm by the accountant. The accountant had identified customers who had moved and had recorded cash sales to continuing customers as credit sales in the accounts of the relocated customers. Carolyn's accountant had kept the cash received from the cash sales and had eventually written off the fictitious credit sales as uncollectible accounts. Without the accountant's knowledge, one of Carolyn's new employees had sent the names of the customers who had apparently defaulted on their accounts to the credit bureau.

Required:

CONCEPTUAL CONNECTION Identify the internal control weaknesses that permitted the accountant to steal the $400,000. Suggest internal control procedures that would make it difficult for someone else to repeat this theft.

Case 4-66 Cash Management

Hollis Corporation has the following budgeted schedule for expected cash receipts and cash disbursement.

Month	Expected Cash Receipts	Expected Cash Disbursements
July	$210,000	$200,000
August	280,000	210,000
September	230,000	190,000
October	160,000	180,000

Hollis begins July with a cash balance of $20,000, $15,000 of short-term debt, and no short-term investments. Hollis uses the following cash management policy:

a. End-of-month cash should equal $20,000 plus the excess of expected disbursements over receipts for the next month.
b. If receipts are expected to exceed disbursements in the next month, the current month ending cash balance should be $20,000.
c. Excess cash should be invested in short-term investments unless there is short-term debt, in which case excess cash should first be used to reduce the debt.
d. Cash deficiencies are met first by selling short-term investments and second by incurring short-term debt.

Required:

1. Calculate the expected buying and selling of short-term investments and the incurrence and repayment of short-term debt at the end of July, August, and September.
2. Discuss the general considerations that help accountants develop a cash management policy.

Case 4-67 Cash and Internal Controls

Identify a business with which you are familiar.

Required:

1. **CONCEPTUAL CONNECTION** Describe the ways in which it prevents theft of cash.
2. **CONCEPTUAL CONNECTION** Can you think of a way in which dishonest employees could circumvent the internal controls and steal cash?

Case 4-68 Researching and Analysis Using the Annual Report

Obtain **Microsoft**'s June 30, 2011, 10-K either through the "Investor Relations" portion of its website (do a search for Microsoft investor relations) or go to www.sec.gov and click "Search for Company Filings" under "Filings & Forms."

Required:

1. How much cash and equivalents and short-term investments did Microsoft hold as a percentage of total assets at the end of fiscal 2010 and 2011?
2. What is Microsoft's definition of a cash equivalent (see Note 1 under the "Financial Instruments" heading)? Does this appear consistent with other companies' definitions?
3. Look at Note 4 and specify how much of Microsoft's cash and equivalent balance is actually cash at the end of fiscal 2011. What is their largest (in dollar terms) cash equivalent?
4. Locate the certifications required by the CEO and CFO under Section 302 of the Sarbanes-Oxley Act. (*Hint*: It is in Exhibits 31-1 and 31-2 at the end of the 10-K.) Who signed these certifications?

Case 4-69 Comparative Analysis: Under Armour, Inc., versus VF Corporation

Refer to the financial statements of **Under Armour, Inc.**, and **VF Corporation** that are supplied with this text.

Required:

1. How much cash and equivalents and short-term investments (or current marketable securities) did VF and Under Armour hold as a percentage of total assets at the end of 2010 and 2011? (*Hint:* It may help to do a search for "equivalents" in a word or pdf version of the 10-K.)
2. **CONCEPTUAL CONNECTION** Speculate as to differences in cash management policies between the two companies.
3. **CONCEPTUAL CONNECTION** Describe the change in cash and equivalents and marketable securities as a percentage of total assets for Under Armour between 2010 and 2011.
4. Locate the Auditor's Opinion on the effectiveness of internal controls over financial reporting and describe the steps the auditors took to audit the effectiveness of Under Armour's and VF's internal controls over financial reporting.

Case 4-70 CONTINUING PROBLEM: FRONT ROW ENTERTAINMENT

Over the next 2 months, Front Row Entertainment continued to enjoy success in signing artists and promoting their events. However, the increased business has put considerable stress on keeping timely and up-to-date financial records. In particular, both Cam and Anna are concerned with the accounting and management of the company's cash.

The tour promotion industry is a cash-intensive industry, normally requiring large prepayments to secure venues and arrange advertising. When the number of artists under contract were small, Cam and Anna developed a simple system to manage the company's cash. Normally, any cash received was put in a file cabinet in the company's office. If the amount appeared to be getting large, a deposit was made. Similarly, if a large check needed to be written, either Cam or Anna would check the balance in the checkbook. If cash was not sufficient to cover the check, they'd get cash from the file cabinet and deposit the amount necessary to cover the check. However, with the increasing business, they would often forget to make deposits, causing several checks to be returned for non-sufficient funds. In addition, they were in the process of hiring additional office staff who would start work on May 1. They knew that leaving cash in a file cabinet would not be a good idea.

In order to obtain a better understanding of their cash position, Anna decides to perform a bank reconciliation—something she had failed to do since the company was started. According to the accounting records, the cash balance at April 30 was $7,495. Anna obtained the following information from Front Row's April bank statement and an analysis of canceled checks and deposits:

Balance per bank at April 30	$3,250
Deposits in transit at April 30	4,370
Outstanding checks as of April 30	1,160
Debit memo for April utilities	845
Bank service charge for April	50
Interest earned during April	450
NSF check from customer	590

Required:

1. **CONCEPTUAL CONNECTION** Discuss the purpose of an internal control system. How would the development of an internal control system benefit Front Row Entertainment? In your answer, be sure to highlight any problems that you noted with Front Row Entertainment's current system of accounting for cash.
2. Prepare a bank reconciliation for Front Row Entertainment for the period ending April 30, 2013.
3. Prepare any adjusting entries necessary because of the bank reconciliation.
4. **CONCEPTUAL CONNECTION** How did the failure to prepare a bank reconciliation affect the amounts reported on the previous financial statements?

5

Sales and Receivables

© Pixelfabrik/Alamy

After studying Chapter 5, you should be able to:

1. Explain the criteria for revenue recognition.
2. Measure net sales revenue.
3. Describe the principal types of receivables.
4. Measure and interpret bad debt expense and the allowance for doubtful accounts.
5. Describe the cash flow implications of accounts receivable.
6. Account for notes receivable from inception to maturity.
7. Describe internal control procedures for merchandise sales.
8. Analyze profitability and asset management using sales and receivables.

© Transtock Inc./Alamy

EXPERIENCE FINANCIAL ACCOUNTING
with Mitsubishi

Mitsubishi's U.S. sales increased from 191,000 cars in 1998 to 322,000 cars in 2001. This 68.5% sales growth made it the fastest growing auto brand in the U.S. Marketed toward Gen Y, Mitsubishi developed an "edgy" image with cross promotions including its leading role in Universal Film's *2 Fast 2 Furious.* Mitsubishi also offered a tempting "0-0-0" finance offer—0% down, 0% interest, and $0 monthly payments for 12 months.

Unfortunately, the economic downturn at the turn of the century hurt Mitsubishi's Gen Y target buyer particularly hard. Consequently, many buyers in the 0-0-0 financing program returned the car and never made a single payment (some reports put this never-paid number as high as 50 to 60% of the buyers in this program), leaving Mitsubishi with a year-old used car. This resulted in Mitsubishi taking a loss on bad debts of $454 million during the first half of 2003. Since Mitsubishi operates on a fiscal year of April 1–March 31, this loss was reported in fiscal year 2002.

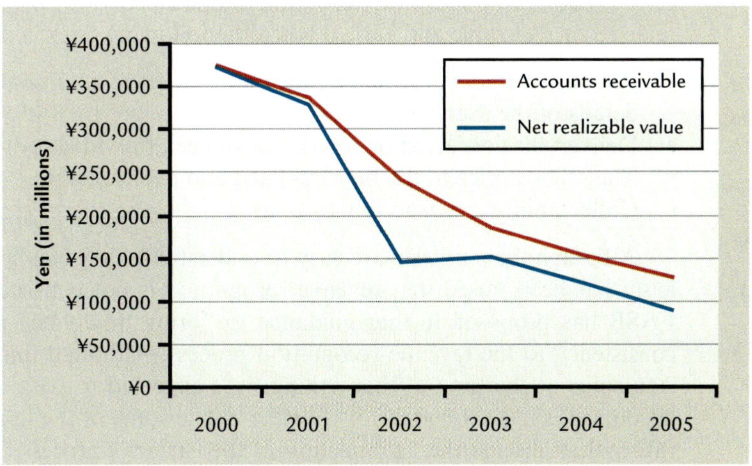

Courtesy of Mitsubishi Motors North America, Inc.

As you will learn in this chapter, net realizable value is the amount that a company expects to collect from its outstanding accounts receivable. Notice in the graph below, the drop in net realizable value in 2002, due to the loss on bad debts. A loss on bad debts is reported on the income statement, but as you can see here, the loss also impacts the balance sheet. This illustrates an important lesson. You must be careful to whom you give credit.

In this chapter, we discuss the reporting and analyzing of sales and any related receivables. First, we discuss the timing of revenue recognition. This is followed by accounting for three modifications to sales—sales discounts, sales returns, and sales allowances. We then shift our attention to receivables. When sales are made on credit, the seller recognizes a receivable. Because the collectability of these receivables is uncertain and the balances are often significant, as illustrated in the discussion of Mitsubishi, companies must attempt to appropriately value and manage these assets.

Turning our attention to sales, there are two primary questions in revenue recognition. First, in which period (for example, 2013 or 2014) should the revenue be recognized? Second, what amount of revenue should be recorded?

OBJECTIVE 1

Explain the criteria for revenue recognition.

TIMING OF REVENUE RECOGNITION

While cash-basis accounting recognizes revenue in the period payment is received (as on your tax return), accrual-basis accounting recognizes revenue when it is

1. **Realized** or **realizable** and
2. **Earned**.

The term "realized" means that noncash resources (such as inventory) have been exchanged for cash or near cash (accounts receivable). This happens, for example, when **Foot Locker** exchanges a pair of shoes (its inventory and a noncash resource) for cash or an account receivable. "Realizable" describes a situation where noncash resources (such as inventory) are readily convertible into known amounts of cash. For example, after a gold mine extracts the gold, the gold (a noncash resource) is readily convertible into cash because there is an active market for gold. Other examples of noncash resources readily convertible to cash include wheat, corn, and soybeans.

As for the second criterion, revenues are considered "earned" when the earnings process is substantially complete. For most retail sales, this occurs at the point of sale. That is, **Foot Locker** fulfills its obligation to you when it lets you walk out of the store with the pair of shoes you just bought. For a service organization, the earnings process is substantially complete when the service is performed. For example, if **Gold's Gym** collects $1,200 for a year-long membership, it should recognize $100 of revenue per month. Or, when **American Airlines** collects $450 in January for a flight to Mexico during spring break, it will recognize the revenue after the flight is provided.

Because sales transactions can be complicated and businesses frequently attempt to recognize revenue too soon, the Securities and Exchange Commission (SEC) has issued further guidance on revenue recognition. Specifically, the SEC maintains that revenue is realized or realizable and earned when the following criteria are met:[1]

- Persuasive evidence of an arrangement exists (e.g., a contract or other proof of the details of the exchange).
- Delivery has occurred or services have been provided.
- The seller's price to the buyer is fixed and determinable.
- Collectability is reasonably assured.

IFRS

The recognition of revenue under IFRS is similar to U.S. GAAP; however, IFRS provide less detailed guidance on when revenue should be recognized.

Although these criteria are easy to understand, they can be difficult to apply and criticism has been raised that revenue recognition is not consistently applied. As such, the FASB has proposed further guidance to "bring discipline" and, consequently, greater consistency to the revenue recognition process. Although this guidance is in the discussion stage at the time of this writing, it is expected to pass sometime during 2013 and become effective around 2015.[2] Further, while some of the terminology will change (e.g., rather than discuss the "completion of the earnings process," the new guidance focuses on "satisfaction of the performance obligation"), the timing of revenue recognition for the contracts covered in this text will remain unchanged. Specifically, the vast majority of sales contracts are relatively straightforward. As stated above, in these cases service companies (such as airlines, accountants, lawn care services, etc.) recognize revenue in the period they provide the services to the customer, and sellers of goods recognize revenue in the period when title passes to the customer. This book's website provides more current information on this transitional area.

ETHICAL DECISIONS Publicly traded corporations are under tremendous pressure to meet analyst targets for key financial-statement data, such as sales (and earnings per share). Many corporations, when faced with the reality of sales not meeting analysts' targets, resorted to a variety of practices to avoid such shortfalls. For example, **Bristol-Myers Squibb** was accused by the SEC of, among other things, "channel stuffing." In

[1] Staff Accounting Bulletin (SAB) 104.
[2] Early adoption will not be permitted for this standard.

channel stuffing, companies ship more goods to a customer than the customer ordered near the end of a period. However, because sales are recognized at the time of shipment, all these sales are recorded in the current period. Of course, this practice will result in lower sales in the subsequent period when the customer returns the unwanted goods. •

AMOUNT OF REVENUE RECOGNIZED

OBJECTIVE 2
Measure net sales revenue.

The appropriate amount of revenue to recognize is generally the cash received or the cash equivalent of the receivable. However, companies often induce customers to buy by modifying the terms of the sale. In this section, we discuss three changes to sales revenues: discounts, returns, and allowances.

Sales Discounts

To encourage prompt payment, businesses may offer a **sales discount**. This discount is a reduction of the normal selling price and is attractive to both the seller and the buyer. For the buyer, it is a reduction to the cost of the goods and services. For the seller, the cash is more quickly available and collection costs are reduced. For example, when cash is not available quickly, the seller may need to borrow money in order to pay its suppliers, employees, etc. The interest expense associated with borrowing money has a negative effect on net income.

Sales invoices use a standard notation to state discount and credit terms. For example, the invoice of a seller who expects payment in 30 days and offers a 2% discount if payment is made within 10 days would bear the notation 2/10, n/30 (which is read "2/10, net 30"). The notation n/30 indicates that the gross amount of the invoice (the full pre-discount amount) must be paid in 30 days. The notation 2/10 indicates that, if payment is made within the 10-day discount period, the amount owed is 2% less than the gross (pre-discount) amount of the invoice. Of course, if payment is made within the 20 days following the end of the discount period, then the amount owed is equal to the gross (pre-discount) amount of the invoice.

Most companies record the sale and the associated receivable at the gross (pre-discount) amount of the invoice. This is called the "gross method."[3] If payment is received after the discount period, the cash received equals the associated receivable so no adjustment is needed. But when a discount is taken, the amount of the discount is recorded in a contra-revenue account (i.e., it reduces Gross Sales Revenue to Net Sales Revenue) called *sales discounts,* which balances the entry. This method is illustrated in Cornerstone 5.1.

Recording Receivables Using the Gross Method

CORNERSTONE 5.1

Why:

Sales discounts offered to encourage prompt payment are recorded at the gross (pre-discount) amount of the invoice. If the discount is taken, a debit is made to Sales Discounts at the time of payment.

Information:

On May 5, 2013, GCD Advisors billed Richardson's Wholesale Hardware $15,000 for consulting services provided during April. GCD offered terms of 2/10, n/30.

(Continued)

[3] GAAP also allows the "net method" of accounting for receivables with sales discounts. This method is demonstrated in intermediate accounting courses.

CORNERSTONE

5.1

(Continued)

Required:

1. Prepare the journal entry to record the sale using the gross method.
2. Prepare the journal entry assuming the payment is received on May 15, 2013 (within the discount period).
3. Prepare the journal entry assuming the payment is received on May 25, 2013 (after the discount period).
4. How would sales revenues be disclosed on the income statement assuming the payment is made within 10 days?

Solution:

Assets	= Liabilities +	Stockholders' Equity
+15,000		+15,000

Assets	= Liabilities +	Stockholders' Equity
+14,700		−300
−15,000		

Assets	= Liabilities +	Stockholders' Equity
+15,000		
−15,000		

	Date	Account and Explanation	Debit	Credit
1.	May 5, 2013	Accounts Receivable	15,000	
		Sales Revenue		15,000
		(Record sale of merchandise)		
2.	May 15, 2013	Cash*	14,700	
		Sales Discounts**	300	
		Accounts Receivable		15,000
		(Record collection within the discount period)		
3.	May 25, 2013	Cash	15,000	
		Accounts Receivable		15,000
		(Record collection after the discount period)		

*$15,000 × 98%
**$15,000 × 2%

4. Partial income statement:

Sales revenue	$15,000
Less: Sales discounts	(300)
Net sales	$14,700

It is also important to monitor changes in how customers use sales discounts. For example, customers who stop taking sales discounts may be experiencing cash flow problems and therefore are potential credit risks. On the other hand, failure of a large number of customers to take discounts may indicate that an increase in the discount percentage is needed.

Finally, sales discounts must be distinguished from both trade and quantity discounts:

- A *trade discount* is a reduction in the selling price granted by the seller to a particular class of customers, for example, to customers who purchase goods for resale rather than for use.
- A *quantity discount* is a reduction in the selling price granted by the seller because selling costs per unit are less when larger quantities are ordered. This is why, for example, a 32-ounce soft drink does not cost double what a 16-ounce one costs at a restaurant.

For accounting purposes, the selling or invoice price is usually assumed to be the price after adjustment for the trade or quantity discounts; accordingly, trade and quantity discounts are not recorded separately in the accounting records.

Sales Returns and Allowances

Occasionally, a customer will return goods as unsatisfactory. In other cases, a customer may agree to keep goods with minor defects if the seller is willing to make an "allowance" by reducing the selling price. The accounting for sales returns and allowances, which is described in the paragraphs that follow, has the effect of reversing all or part of a previously recorded sale.

When goods or services arrive late, or in some other way are rendered less valuable, a customer may be induced to accept the goods/services if a price reduction, called a **sales allowance**, is offered by the seller. A contra-revenue account called *sales returns and allowances* (returns are discussed next) is used to record the price reduction. For example, on November 1, GCD Advisors completed a consulting project for Bolt Manufacturing for which the agreed upon price was $11,400. Because GCD had promised Bolt that the project would be completed by September 15, GCD offered and Bolt accepted, a $1,600 reduction as an allowance for the missed deadline. GCD made the following accounting entries to record these events:

Date	Account and Explanation	Debit	Credit
Nov. 1, 2013	Accounts Receivable	11,400	
	Sales Revenue		11,400
	(Record sale of services)		
Nov. 1, 2013	Sales Returns and Allowances	1,600	
	Accounts Receivable		1,600
	(Record allowance for missed deadline)		

Assets	= Liabilities +	Stockholders' Equity
+11,400		+11,400

Assets	= Liabilities +	Stockholders' Equity
−1,600		−1,600

If the bill has already been paid, the seller can either refund a portion of the purchase price and record a credit to cash or apply the allowance against future purchases by the customer by recording a credit to accounts receivable.

Merchandise or goods returned by the customer to the seller are **sales returns**. Companies also record these returned goods in *sales returns and allowances*. Sales returns will be discussed in Chapter 6 when we introduce inventory.

On the income statement, as indicated in Chapter 2, sales returns and allowances, like sales discounts, are subtracted from gross sales revenue to produce **net sales revenue**, as shown here:

Sales revenue	$752,000
Less: Sales returns and allowances	(1,600)
Net sales	$750,400

In other words, sales returns and allowances is a contra-revenue account. Presenting both gross sales revenue and sales returns and allowances, rather than net sales revenue alone, permits financial-statement users to respond to unusual behavior in either account. Careful users of financial statements look for unusual behavior in both sales revenue and sales returns and allowances in the income statement. Often, significant changes in these accounts help to explain other changes in income statement or balance sheet accounts, as illustrated in the You Decide feature below.

YOUDECIDE Sales Returns and Allowances

You are the Controller at Interplains Inc. Data for the past 4 years for sales revenue, sales returns and allowances, and net income are shown below.

	2010	2011	2012	2013
Sales revenue	$624,000	$653,000	$671,000	$887,000
Sales returns and allowances	6,100	6,400	6,300	14,800
Net income	30,000	29,000	31,500	12,200

(Continued)

What concerns are raised by the significant changes in sales revenue, sales returns and allowances, and net income in 2013?

Sales revenue, which had been relatively stable, increased by 32% in 2013. Often, significant growth in output is accompanied by quality assurance problems, as might be indicated by the 135% growth in sales returns and allowances. A check of production data might reveal the use of less highly trained workers or supervisors, or might indicate that the current workforce is being worked heavily on overtime.

Further, notice the significant decrease in net income despite the large increase in sales revenue. When this happens, you must attempt to discover why. For example, when a firm becomes significantly more or less profitable, the attitude of the employees toward their work can change, causing changes in the quality of output. Some key employees may leave a firm with declining profitability, thus causing quality difficulties.

Significant changes in sales revenue, sales returns and allowances, and net income can indicate important changes or trends in the workforce or workflow and should be analyzed so that management can take appropriate action.

OBJECTIVE 3

Describe the principal types of receivables.

IFRS

The recognition and valuation of receivables under IFRS is generally the same as U.S. GAAP.

TYPES OF RECEIVABLES

Now that we've addressed the timing of revenue recognition and measurement of net sales revenue, we will shift our attention to the accounting and analysis of the related receivables.

A receivable is money due from another business or individual. Receivables are typically categorized along three different dimensions:

- *Accounts Receivable or Notes Receivable:* A "note" is a legal document given by a borrower to a lender stating the timing of repayment and the amount (principal and/or interest) to be repaid. We discuss notes receivable later in the chapter. **Accounts receivable**, on the other hand, do not have a formal note. For example, while you likely signed a formal agreement to rent your apartment, you probably did not sign a formal agreement for your utilities.
- *Current or Noncurrent Receivables:* Although in practice both accounts and notes receivable are typically classified as current, accounts receivable are typically due in 30 to 60 days and do not have interest while notes receivable have interest and typically are due in anywhere from 3 to 12 months. Of course, if the due date is over 1 year, the note receivable typically will be classified as noncurrent.
- *Trade or Nontrade Receivables:* **Trade receivables** are due from customers purchasing inventory in the ordinary course of business while **nontrade receivables** arise from transactions not involving inventory (such as interest receivable or cash advances to employees).

OBJECTIVE 4

Measure and interpret bad debt expense and the allowance for doubtful accounts.

ACCOUNTING FOR BAD DEBTS

We discussed the recognition of accounts receivable in the sales section, but an equally important concept is ensuring that the proper amount for accounts receivable is shown on the balance sheet. GAAP requires accounts receivable to be shown at their "net realizable value," which is the amount of cash the company expects to collect. Unfortunately, the amount of cash collected will almost never equal the total amount recognized in accounts receivable because some customers will not pay (for example, a customer declares bankruptcy and ceases operations). When customers do not pay their accounts receivable, bad debts (also called uncollectible accounts) result. Although efforts are made to control bad debts, it is an expense of providing credit to customers. (The hope is that the increased business associated with providing credit will more than make up for the bad debts.)

As we saw in the previous section, when sales revenues are reduced to reflect sales returns and allowances, the reductions are accomplished through a contra-revenue account. Although it might seem logical to reduce sales revenues in the same way when customers default on accounts receivable arising from credit sales, this treatment is inappropriate. Reductions in sales revenue should be recorded only for transactions that result from actions of the seller, such as acceptance of returned merchandise (a sales return) or price reductions offered to purchasers (a sales allowance). Since defaults on credit sales arise from actions of the purchaser rather than the seller, bad debts cannot be recorded as revenue reductions. If bad debts are not treated as negative revenues, then they must be treated as expenses. And if they are expenses, the question then arises as to when the expense should be recorded.

There are two methods to record **bad debt expense**: the direct write-off method and the allowance method.

> **concept Q&A**
>
> Why is the direct write-off method not GAAP?
>
> **Answer:**
>
> The direct write-off method fails to "match" the bad debt expense to the sales revenue that it helped generate and does not show accounts receivable at net realizable value on the balance sheet.

Direct Write-Off Method

The direct write-off method waits until an account is deemed uncollectible before reducing accounts receivable and recording the bad debt expense. As you recall, the expense recognition (or matching) principle requires that expenses be matched with the related revenues in the period in which the revenues are recognized on the income statement. Since accounts are often determined to be uncollectible in accounting periods subsequent to the sale period, the direct write-off method is inconsistent with the matching concept and can only be used if bad debts are immaterial under GAAP.

Allowance Method

In the allowance method, bad debt expense is recorded in the period of sale, which allows it to be properly matched with revenues. The result is that bad debt expense is recognized before the actual default. Because defaults for the current period's sales have not actually occurred, the specific accounts receivable are not lowered; instead, an account is established to "store" the estimate until specific accounts are identified as uncollectible. This account is called **Allowance for Doubtful Accounts**.

For example, assume at the end of the first year of operations Hawthorne has an accounts receivable balance of $1,000,000. Although no customers have defaulted, Hawthorne estimates that $25,000 of that balance is uncollectible. At the end of the first year, Hawthorne would make the following adjusting entry:

Date	Account and Explanation	Debit	Credit
Dec. 31, 2014	Bad Debt Expense	25,000	
	Allowance for Doubtful Accounts		25,000
	(Record estimate of uncollectible accounts)		

Assets	=	Liabilities	+	Stockholders' Equity
−25,000				−25,000

This entry looks very similar to the entry that would be made under the direct write-off method. The major difference is the timing of the entry. The direct write-off method would make the entry in the period the customer defaults, while the allowance method makes the entry in the period of sale. Hawthorne's balance sheet would report accounts receivable as follows:

Accounts receivable	$1,000,000
Less: Allowance for doubtful accounts	(25,000)
Accounts receivable (net)	$ 975,000

However, it is important to recognize that Hawthorne's balance sheet would report the full $1,000,000 as accounts receivable under the direct write-off method at the end of the first year.

When a specific account is ultimately determined to be uncollectible under the allowance method, it is *written off* by a debit to the allowance account and a credit to accounts receivable. This write-off removes the defaulted balance from the accounts receivable balance and also removes it from the estimate "storage" account.

Under the allowance procedure, two methods commonly used to estimate bad debt expense are the *percentage of credit sales method* and the *aging method*.

Percentage of Credit Sales Method The simpler of the two methods for determining bad debt expense is the **percentage of credit sales method**. Using past experience and management's views of how the future may differ from the past (for example, if credit policies change), it is possible to estimate the percentage of the current period's credit sales that will eventually become uncollectible. This percentage is multiplied by the total credit sales for the period to calculate the estimated bad debt expense for the period:

$$\text{Total Credit Sales} \times \text{Percentage of Credit Sales Estimated to Default} = \text{Estimated Bad Debt Expense}$$

The adjusting entry is then prepared to recognize the bad debt expense as shown in Cornerstone 5.2.

CORNERSTONE 5.2

Estimating Bad Debt Expense Using the Percentage of Credit Sales Method

Why:

The percentage of credit sales method estimates the ending balance in bad debt expense based on past experience.

Information:

Crimson Company has credit sales of $620,000 during 2013 and estimates at the end of 2013 that 1.43% of these credit sales will eventually default. Also, during 2013, a customer defaults on a $524 balance related to goods purchased in 2012. Prior to the write-off and the adjusting entry, Crimson's accounts receivable and allowance for doubtful accounts balances were $304,000 and $134 (credit), respectively.

Required:

1. Estimate the bad debt expense for the period.
2. Prepare the journal entry to record the write-off of the defaulted $524 balance.
3. Prepare the adjusting entry to record the bad debt expense for 2013.
4. What is the net accounts receivable balance at the end of the year? How would this balance have changed if Crimson had not written off the $524 balance during 2013?

Solution:

1. $620,000 × 0.0143 = $8,866

2.

Date	Account and Explanation	Debit	Credit
Dec. 31, 2013	Allowance for Doubtful Accounts	524	
	Accounts Receivable		524
	(Record write-off of defaulted account)		

Assets	= Liabilities +	Stockholders' Equity
+524		
−524		

3. *Note*: The calculation in Solution 1 estimated the *ending* balance of bad debt expense. This amount is also the adjustment because the balance before the adjustment is zero. This is usually the case for income statement accounts because they were closed at the end of the prior year.

(Continued)

CORNERSTONE **5.2** *(Continued)*

Date	Account and Explanation	Debit	Credit
Dec. 31, 2013	Bad Debt Expense	8,866	
	Allowance for Doubtful Accounts		8,866
	(Record adjusting entry for bad debt expense estimate)		

Assets	= Liabilities +	Stockholders' Equity
−8,866		−8,866

Bad Debt Expense

Preadjustment balance, 12/31/13	0		
Adjustment	**8,866**		
Ending balance	8,866		

Allowance for Doubtful Accounts

		134	Beginning balance
Write-offs during 2013	524		
Preadjustment balance, 12/31/13	390		
		8,866	**Adjustment**
		8,476	Ending balance

4.

	Year End	Assuming No Write-Off
Accounts receivable	$303,476*	$304,000
Less: Allowance for doubtful accounts	(8,476)**	(9,000)***
Net accounts receivable	$295,000	$295,000

* $304,000 − $524 = $303,476
** $134 − $524 + $8,866 = $8,476 (see T-account in Solution 3.)
*** T-account from Solution 3 without the $524 debit for the write-off.

Note: Under the allowance method, the write-off of a specific account does not affect net accounts receivable.

Occasionally, accounts receivable that are written off are later partially or entirely collected. Suppose on February 5, 2014, Crimson receives $25 of the $524 that was written off at the end of the previous year (see Requirement 2 of Cornerstone 5.2). Crimson would make the following entries:

Date	Account and Explanation	Debit	Credit
Feb. 5, 2014	Accounts Receivable	25	
	Allowance for Doubtful Accounts		25
	(Reverse portion of write-off)		
	Cash	25	
	Accounts Receivable		25
	(Record collection of account receivable)		

Assets	= Liabilities +	Stockholders' Equity
+25		
−25		
+25		
−25		

Crimson's first entry reverses the appropriate portion of the write-off by restoring the accounts receivable and allowance for doubtful accounts balances. The second entry records the cash collection in the typical manner.

Aging Method Under the **aging method**, bad debt expense is estimated by determining the collectability of the accounts receivable rather than by taking a percentage of total credit sales. At the end of each accounting period, the individual accounts receivable are categorized by age. Then an estimate is made of the amount expected to default in each age category based on past experience and expectations about how the future may differ from the past. As you may expect, the overdue accounts are more likely to default than the currently due accounts, as shown in the example below.

Accounts Receivable Age	Amount	Proportion Expected to Default	Amount Expected to Default
Less than 15 days	$190,000	0.01	$1,900
16–30 days	40,000	0.04	1,600
31–60 days	10,000	0.10	1,000
Over 61 days	9,000	0.30	2,700
	$249,000		$7,200

The total amount expected to default on year end accounts receivable, $7,200 in the above example, is the amount that should be the ending balance in the allowance for doubtful accounts. Since the objective of the aging method is to estimate the ending balance in the allowance for doubtful accounts, any existing balance in the allowance account must be considered when determining the amount of the adjusting entry as shown in Cornerstone 5.3.

CORNERSTONE

5.3

Estimating the Allowance for Doubtful Accounts Using the Aging Method

Why:

An aging of the accounts receivable balance estimates the ending balance for the "allowance for doubtful accounts."

Information:

On January 1, 2013, Sullivan Inc. has the following balances for accounts receivable and allowance for doubtful accounts:

Accounts receivable	$224,000 (debit)
Allowance for doubtful accounts	6,700 (credit)

During 2013, Sullivan had $3,100,000 of credit sales, collected $3,015,000 of accounts receivable, and wrote off $60,000 of accounts receivable as uncollectible.

(Continued)

CORNERSTONE
5.3
(Continued)

Required:

1. What is Sullivan's preadjustment balance in accounts receivable on December 31, 2013?
2. What is Sullivan's preadjustment balance in allowance for doubtful accounts on December 31, 2013?
3. Assuming Sullivan's analysis of the accounts receivable balance indicates that $7,200 of the current accounts receivable balance is uncollectible, by what amount will the allowance for doubtful accounts need to be adjusted?
4. What will be the ending balance in bad debt expense?
5. Prepare the necessary adjusting entry for 2013.

Solution:

1.

Accounts Receivable			
Beginning balance	224,000		
Sales	3,100,000		
		3,015,000	Collections
		60,000	Write-offs
Preadjustment balance	249,000		

2.

Allowance for Doubtful Accounts			
		6,700	Beginning balance
Write-offs	60,000		
Preadjustment balance	53,300		

3.

Allowance for Doubtful Accounts			
Preadjustment balance	53,300		
		60,500*	**Adjusting entry**
		7,200**	Adjusted balance

* Necessary adjustment to end up with an ending balance of $7,200.
** Estimate of ending balance determined by analyzing the receivables aging. This information was given in Requirement 3.

4.

Bad Debt Expense		
Preadjustment balance	0	
Adjustment	**60,500**	
Ending balance	60,500	

5.

Date	Account and Explanation	Debit	Credit
Dec. 31, 2013	Bad Debt Expense	60,500	
	Allowance for Doubtful Accounts		60,500
	(Record adjusting entry for bad debt expense estimate)		

Assets	=	Liabilities	+	Stockholders' Equity
−60,500				−60,500

concept Q&A

What are the conceptual and practical differences between the percentage of credit sales and aging methods?

Answer:

The percentage of credit sales method estimates the amount to be shown as bad debt expense on the income statement. The aging method estimates the amount to be shown as the allowance for doubtful accounts on the balance sheet. The preadjustment balance in these accounts must be adjusted so that the ending balance equals the respective estimates. However, because bad debt expense is an income statement account that is closed to retained earnings at the end of every period, its preadjustment balance should be zero. As such, the adjustment is equal to the estimate of the ending balance. The allowance for doubtful accounts, on the other hand, is a balance sheet account and will typically have an existing balance.

Comparison of Percentage of Credit Sales Method and Aging Method The underlying difference between the percentage of credit sales method and the aging method is what is being estimated. The percentage of credit sales method is primarily concerned with appropriately estimating bad debt expense on the income statement. Because of the focus on the expense account, any existing balance in the allowance account is ignored when determining the amount of the adjusting entry. The aging method, on the other hand, is a balance sheet approach that analyzes the accounts receivable to estimate its net realizable value. This estimate provides the necessary ending allowance for doubtful accounts balance to report net accounts receivable at net realizable value.

Bad Debts from a Management Perspective

Although bad debts result from actions of the purchaser (nonpayment), the amount of bad debt expense is influenced by the credit policies of the seller, as the You Decide feature below illustrates.

YOU DECIDE Are Bad Debts Always Bad?

You are the owner/operator of Mt. Sterling Drug Company, a pharmaceutical wholesaler. In response to Mt. Sterling's "cash only" sales terms, competitors have attempted to lure business away by offering various incentives. Among these are credit terms whereby a customer typically has 30 to 60 days to pay for a purchase and receives a 1 to 2% discount for prompt payment (usually within 10 days of sale).

Which is worse, the potential bad debts that come with offering credit or the lost business from not offering credit?

There is no question that the inability to collect an account receivable is a serious problem. However, most wholesalers have come to accept bad debts as just another business expense. Certainly, no company would grant credit knowing that the specific customer will not pay for the goods purchased. Nonetheless, granting credit is a "necessary evil"—something that must be done to generate repeat business and maintain a competitive position.

An existing relationship with customers does not guarantee future business, especially if the customers can get a better deal elsewhere. Further, prudent screening of each customer's credit history should enable you to identify some of those who may have difficulty paying their accounts. Placing restrictions such as relatively low credit limits on these risky accounts or, in some cases, denying credit altogether should help keep bad debts to a minimum.

Suppose Mt. Sterling's gross margin is 30% of sales and that, as a result of the more liberal credit policy, sales increase by $100,000 and bad debts are limited to 3% of the new credit sales. Then Mt. Sterling's income from operations should increase by $27,000 (increased gross margin of $30,000 minus bad debt expense of $3,000), rather than decreasing.

When caution is used, most companies agree that the loss of business from not offering credit is more detrimental than the bad debt expenses incurred in doing so.

OBJECTIVE 5

Describe the cash flow implications of accounts receivable.

CASH MANAGEMENT PRINCIPLES RELATED TO ACCOUNTS RECEIVABLE

We now will focus on the cash management principles associated with accounts receivable.

Factoring Receivables

In Chapter 4, we mentioned that a principle of cash management is increasing the speed of cash collection for receivables. An increasingly common practice is to **factor**, or sell, receivables. When receivables are factored, the seller receives an immediate cash payment reduced by the factor's fees. The factor, the buyer of the receivables, acquires the right to collect the receivables and the risk of uncollectibility. In a typical factoring arrangement, the sellers of the receivables have no continuing responsibility for their collection.

Factoring arrangements vary widely, but typically the factor charges a fee ranging from 1% to 3%. This fee compensates the factor for the time value of money (i.e., interest), the risk of uncollectability, and the tasks of billing and collection. Large businesses and financial institutions frequently package factored receivables as financial instruments or securities and sell them to investors. This process is known as **securitization**. For example, **General Motors Acceptance Corporation (GMAC)** sells car loans to special financial institutions set up by investment banks. The financial institutions pay GMAC with funds raised from the sale of securities or notes, called certificates for automobile receivables (CARs). Banks use similar arrangements to package their credit card receivables into securities called certificates for amortizing revolving debts (CARDs).

Credit Cards

Bank **credit cards**, such as **Visa** and **MasterCard**, are really just a special form of factoring. The issuer of the credit card (i.e., the bank) pays the seller the amount of each sale minus a service charge (on the date of purchase) and then collects the full amount of the sale from the buyer (at some later date).[4] For example, if a retail customer uses a **Citibank** Visa Card to pay $100 for a haircut, the salon would make the following entry assuming Citibank charges a 1.55% service charge:

Account and Explanation	Debit	Credit
Cash	98.45	
Service Charge Expense	1.55	
Sales Revenue		100.00
(Record sales)		

Assets	= Liabilities +	Stockholders' Equity
+98.45		−1.55
		+100.00

Although a 1.55% service charge may seem expensive, credit card sales provide sellers with a number of advantages over supplying credit directly to customers, including the following:

- Sellers receive the money immediately.
- Sellers avoid bad debts because as long as the credit card verification procedures are followed, the credit card company absorbs the cost of customers who do not pay.
- Recordkeeping costs decrease because employees are not needed to manage these accounts.
- Sellers believe that by accepting credit cards their sales will increase. For example, how many of you have driven away from a gas station that does not accept credit cards or even one that merely does not allow you to pay at the pump?

Of course, many large retailers are willing to take on these costs to avoid the credit card service charge. For example, **Sears**, **Kohls**, **Target**, **Macy's**, and most other large retailers have internal credit cards. When these cards are used, the seller records it like any other accounts receivable and no service charge expense is incurred; however, they are accepting the risk of uncollectible accounts and the cost of servicing these accounts.

[4] The bank may also pay the full amount of the sale to the seller and then bill the service charge at the end of the period.

Nonbank credit cards, such as **American Express**, also result in a receivable for the seller because the issuer of the credit card (American Express) does not immediately pay the cash to the seller. American Express also charges a higher service charge to the seller. Consequently, sellers find American Express to be more costly than bank cards, such as **Visa** or **MasterCard**, which explains why many businesses do not accept American Express.

Debit Cards

A **debit card** authorizes a bank to make an immediate electronic withdrawal (debit) from the holder's bank account. The debit card is used like a credit card except that a bank electronically reduces (debits) the holder's bank account and increases (credits) the merchant's bank account for the amount of a sale made on a debit card.

Debit cards appear to be somewhat disadvantageous to the card holder as transactions cannot be rescinded by stopping payment. Further, a purchase using a debit card causes an immediate reduction in a bank account balance, while a check written at the same time will require at least 1 or 2 days to clear, allowing the depositor to benefit from the additional money in the account until the check is presented at the bank for payment. However, debit cards offer significant advantages to banks and merchants in reduced transaction-processing costs. Thus, banks and merchants have incentive to design debit cards that minimize or eliminate the disadvantages and costs to card users.

OBJECTIVE 6

Account for notes receivable from inception to maturity.

NOTES RECEIVABLE

Notes receivable are receivables that generally specify an interest rate and a maturity date at which any interest and principal must be repaid. Our discussion here is limited to simple notes that specify the repayment of interest and principal in a single payment on a given day (more complicated notes are described in Chapter 10).

The amount lent is the **principal**. The excess of the total amount of money collected over the amount lent is called **interest**. For example, as shown in Exhibit 5.1, if **Caterpillar** lends $500,000 to a customer and is repaid $580,000 at some later date, then $80,000 of interest was collected.

Interest can be considered compensation paid to the lender for giving up the use of resources for the period of a note (the time value of money). The interest rate specified

EXHIBIT 5.1

Principal and Interest in Loan Repayments

in the note is an annual rate. Therefore, when calculating interest, you must consider the duration of the note using the following formula:

$$\text{Interest} = \text{Principal} \times \text{Annual Interest Rate} \times \text{Fraction of 1 Year}$$

For example, in the example illustrated in Exhibit 5.1, what was the annual interest rate? The answer is that we have no way of knowing because the duration of the loan was not specified. If the duration of the loan was exactly 1 year, then the annual rate was 16%. If the duration was more (or less) than 1 year, however, then the annual rate is less (or more) than 16%.

Further, you will recall from Chapter 2 that the matching concept and the revenue recognition concept require that expenses and revenues be identified with specific accounting periods. If only 1 month of interest has been incurred by year end, an adjusting entry is required to recognize interest income and a corresponding interest receivable. Any remaining interest is recognized in subsequent periods.[5] The accounting for notes receivable is demonstrated in Cornerstone 5.4.

Accounting for Notes Receivable

CORNERSTONE 5.4

Why:

Notes receivable are recognized for the amount of cash loaned or goods/services sold. This is the principal amount of the note receivable. Any excess of the amount received over principal is recognized as interest income in the period the interest was earned.

Information:

Dover Electric Company purchased, on account, $50,000 of consulting services from Thomas Ltd. on November 1, 2013. The amount is due in full on January 1, 2014. Dover Electric is unable to pay the account by the due date and negotiates an extension with a 10% note in lieu of the unpaid account receivable.

Required:

1. Prepare Thomas's journal entries to record the sale on November 1, 2013, and the modification of payment terms on January 1, 2014.
2. How much interest will be paid if Dover Electric repays the note on (a) July 1, 2014, (b) December 31, 2014, or (c) March 31, 2015?
3. Prepare Thomas's adjusting entry to accrue interest on December 31, 2014, assuming the note is repaid on March 31, 2015.
4. Prepare Thomas's journal entries to record the cash received to pay off the note and interest on each of the three dates specified in Requirement 2.

(Continued)

[5] Interest is, in fact, often computed in terms of days rather than months. Suppose, for example, that the 3-month note runs for 92 days (two 31-day months and one 30-day month). The total interest on the 92-day note would be $302.47 [($10,000)(0.12)(92/365)], and the first 31-day month's interest would be $101.92 [($10,000)(0.12)(31/365)]. Observe that daily interest complicates the arithmetic associated with interest calculations but does not alter the basic form of the calculations. To simplify interest computations, we will use monthly interest throughout this chapter.

CORNERSTONE **5.4** *(Continued)*

Solution:

1.

Assets	= Liabilities +	Stockholders' Equity
+50,000		+50,000

Date	Account and Explanation	Debit	Credit
Nov. 1, 2013	Accounts Receivable	50,000	
	Sales Revenue		50,000
	(Record sale)		
Jan. 1, 2014	Notes Receivable	50,000	
	Accounts Receivable		50,000
	(Record issuance of note receivable)		

Assets	= Liabilities +	Stockholders' Equity
+50,000 −50,000		

2. Interest = Principal × Annual Interest Rate × Fraction of 1 Year

(a) July 1, 2014:
$= \$50,000 \times 10\% \times (6/12)$
$= \$2,500$

(b) Dec. 31, 2014:
$= \$50,000 \times 10\% \times (12/12)$
$= \$5,000$

(c) March 31, 2015:
$= \$50,000 \times 10\% \times (15/12)$
$= \$6,250$

3.

Assets	= Liabilities +	Stockholders' Equity
+5,000		+5,000

Date	Account and Explanation	Debit	Credit
Dec. 31, 2014	Interest Receivable	5,000	
	Interest Income		5,000
	(Record accrual of interest)		

4.

Assets	= Liabilities +	Stockholders' Equity
+52,500 −50,000		+2,500

Assets	= Liabilities +	Stockholders' Equity
+55,000 −50,000		+5,000

Assets	= Liabilities +	Stockholders' Equity
+56,250 −50,000 −5,000		+1,250

Date	Account and Explanation	Debit	Credit
July 1, 2014	Cash	52,500	
	Notes Receivable		50,000
	Interest Income		2,500
	(Record collection of note receivable)		
Dec. 31, 2014	Cash	55,000	
	Notes Receivable		50,000
	Interest Income		5,000
	(Record collection of note receivable)		
Mar. 31, 2015	Cash	56,250	
	Notes Receivable		50,000
	Interest Receivable		5,000
	Interest Income		1,250
	(Record collection of note receivable)		

OBJECTIVE 7

Describe internal control procedures for merchandise sales.

INTERNAL CONTROL FOR SALES

Since sales revenues have a significant effect on a company's net income, internal control procedures must be established to ensure that the amounts reported for these items are correct. For sales revenues, these controls normally involve the following documents and procedures:

- Accounting for a sale begins with the receipt of a purchase order or some similar document from a customer. The order document is necessary for the buyer to be obligated to accept and pay for the ordered goods.
- Shipping and billing documents are prepared based on the order document. Billing documents are usually called *invoices*.
- A sale and its associated receivable are recorded only when the order, shipping, and billing documents are all present.

As illustrated in Exhibit 5.2, sales revenue should be recorded only when these three control documents are completed. When any of these three internal controls is not present, it is possible for valid sales to be unrecorded and for invalid sales to be recorded.

For sales returns and allowances, internal control procedures must be established that identify the conditions and documentation required before a sales return or a sales allowance can be recorded. These controls protect the firm from unwarranted reductions in revenues and receivables.

EXHIBIT 5.2

Internal Controls for Recording Sales Revenue

PURCHASE ORDER No. R450
Richardson's Wholesale Hardware

Date: Sept. 1, 2013
To:
Bolt Manufacturing

QTY.	DESCRIPTION	PRICE	AMOUNT
30	Model No. SB100 snowblower	$500	$15,000

Ordered by: Jim Richardson
Jim Richardson

Purchase order number must appear on all shipments and invoice.

SHIPPING REPORT No. B275
Bolt Manufacturing

Date: Sept. 1, 2013
To:
Richardson's Wholesale Hardware

QTY.	DESCRIPTION
30	Model No. SB100 snowblower

Purchase order: R450

INVOICE No. B100
Bolt Manufacturing

Date: Sept. 1, 2013
Sold to:
Richardson's Wholesale Hardware
Purchase order: R450

QTY.	DESCRIPTION	PRICE	AMOUNT
30	Model No. SB100 snowblower	$500	$15,000
		SUBTOTAL	$15,000
		SALES TAX	0
		SHIPPING & HANDLING	0
		TOTAL DUE	$15,000

Date	Account and Explanation	Debit	Credit
Sept. 1	Accounts Receivable	15,000	
	Sales Revenue		15,000

ANALYZING SALES AND RECEIVABLES

OBJECTIVE 8
Analyze profitability and asset management using sales and receivables.

Analysts of the financial statements are extremely concerned with both sales and receivables.

Sales

Because sales revenue is such a key component of a company's success, analysts are interested in a large number of ratios that incorporate sales. Many of these ratios attempt to measure the return the company is earning on sales. These are called **profitability ratios**. For example, the ratio of income statement subtotals such as gross margin, operating income, and net income to sales are examined, but really any income statement subtotal deemed important can be of interest. The three most common ratios are gross profit margin, operating margin, and net profit margin:

$$\text{Gross Profit Margin} = \frac{\text{Gross Profit}}{\text{Net Sales}}$$

$$\text{Operating Margin} = \frac{\text{Operating Income}}{\text{Net Sales}}$$

$$\text{Net Profit Margin} = \frac{\text{Net Income}}{\text{Net Sales}}$$

Each of these ratios reveals information about a company's strategy and the competition it faces. For example, consider two large players in the retail industry—**Wal-Mart** and **Nordstrom**. Information available indicates that these two stores possess the following 5-year averages for these ratios:

	Wal-Mart	**Nordstrom**
Gross profit percentage	25.05%	38.62%
Operating margin percentage	5.87%	11.16%
Net profit margin percentage	3.61%	6.28%

Nordstrom's higher gross profit percentage suggests that Nordstrom is able to charge a premium on its merchandise. That is, Nordstrom follows a product differentiation strategy in which it tries to convince customers that its products are superior, distinctive, etc. **Wal-Mart**, on the other hand, is a low-cost provider who attempts to convince customers that it offers the lowest prices.

Analysts also like to look at the operating margin and net profit margin percentages to see how much is left from a sales dollar after paying for the product and all its operations. For these ratios, **Nordstrom** still retains a larger percentage of each sales dollar than **Wal-Mart**. How is it, then, that Wal-Mart makes so much money? It has a lot of sales dollars—its net sales revenue of $41 billion in 2011 is approximately 40 times greater than Nordstrom's $10.5 billion.

Receivables

Analysts are also concerned with asset management. Asset management refers to how efficiently a company is using the resources at its disposal. One of the most widely used asset management ratios is accounts receivable turnover:

$$\text{Accounts Receivable Turnover} = \frac{\text{Net Sales}}{\text{Average Net Accounts Receivable}}$$

This ratio provides a measure of how many times average trade receivables are collected during the period. In theory, net credit sales would be a much better numerator, but that figure is not normally disclosed. A higher number is better because it indicates that the company is more quickly collecting cash (through sales) from its inventory. As discussed in Chapter 4's section on cash management, this holds down borrowing costs and allows for a greater investment. Changes in this ratio over time are also very important. For example, a significant reduction in receivables turnover may indicate that management is extending credit to customers who are not paying.

Accounts receivable turnover for Wal-Mart and Nordstrom is:

	Wal-Mart	Nordstrom
Accounts receivable turnover	90.75	5.17

As expected, Wal-Mart is extremely efficient with its asset management because effective cash management is necessary for low cost providers. Of course, it is difficult to compare Nordstrom to Wal-Mart because they likely engage in different financing practices. For example, a greater proportion of Wal-Mart sales are made using cash or external credit cards (such as Visa), while Nordstrom has a larger proportion of sales using internal credit cards (a Nordstrom card). The internal credit cards result in lower accounts receivable turnover. Cornerstone 5.5 illustrates the calculation of these ratios for Wal-Mart.

Calculating the Gross Profit Margin, Operating Margin, Net Profit Margin, and Accounts Receivable Turnover Ratios

CORNERSTONE 5.5

Why:

The gross profit margin, operating margin, and net profit margin ratios provide measures of the return the company is earning on sales. The accounts receivable turnover ratio provides a measure of how many times average accounts receivable are collected during the period.

Information:

The following information (in millions) is available for Wal-Mart for its fiscal year ending January 31, 2012:

Net sales	\$443,854	Accounts receivable, 1/31/12	\$5,937
Gross profit	108,727	Accounts receivable, 1/31/11	5,089
Operating income	26,558		
Net income	15,699		

Required:

Compute the (1) gross profit margin, (2) operating margin, (3) net profit margin, and (4) accounts receivable turnover for Wal-Mart for fiscal 2011.

Solution:

1.
$$\text{Gross Profit Margin Ratio} = \frac{\text{Gross Profit}}{\text{Net Sales}} = \frac{\$108{,}727}{\$443{,}854} = 0.2450\text{, or } 24.50\%$$

2.
$$\text{Operating Margin Ratio} = \frac{\text{Operating Income}}{\text{Net Sales}} = \frac{\$26{,}558}{\$443{,}854} = 0.0598\text{, or } 5.98\%$$

3.
$$\text{Net Profit Margin Ratio} = \frac{\text{Net Income}}{\text{Net Sales}} = \frac{\$15{,}699}{\$443{,}854} = 0.0354\text{, or } 3.54\%$$

4.
$$\text{Accounts Receivable Turnover Ratio} = \frac{\text{Net Sales}}{\text{Average Net Accounts Receivable}} = \frac{\$443{,}854}{(\$5{,}089 + \$5{,}937) \div 2} = 80.51$$

SUMMARY OF LEARNING OBJECTIVES

LO 1. Explain the criteria for revenue recognition.

- Revenue is recognized when:
  - the earnings process is complete
  - collection has occurred or is reasonably certain to occur
- The earnings process is completed when delivery has occurred or services have been provided.

LO 2. Measure net sales revenue.

- The appropriate amount of revenue to recognize is generally the cash received or the cash equivalent of accounts receivable.
- Companies often induce customers to buy by offering:
  - sales discounts
  - sales returns
  - sales allowances
- Sales discounts are reductions of the normal selling price to encourage prompt payment.
- Sales returns occur when a customer returns goods as unsatisfactory.
- Sales allowances occur when a customer agrees to keep goods with minor defects if the seller reduces the selling price.
- These events are recorded in contra-revenue accounts that reduce gross sales to net sales.

LO 3. Describe the principal types of receivables.

- Receivables are classified along three different dimensions:
  - accounts and notes receivable
  - trade and nontrade receivables
  - current and noncurrent receivables

LO 4. Measure and interpret bad debt expense and the allowance for doubtful accounts.

- The primary issues in accounting for accounts receivable are when and how to measure bad debts (i.e., accounts that will not be paid).
- GAAP requires receivables to be shown at net realizable value on the balance sheet.
- The matching principle says that an expense should be recognized in the period in which it helps generate revenues.
- We must estimate and recognize bad debt expense in the period the sale is made—even though we do not know which accounts will be uncollectible.
- The estimate is made by using either:
  - the percentage of credit sales method
  - the aging method
- The percentage of credit sales method estimates the bad debt expense directly.
- The aging method estimates the ending balance needed in the allowance for doubtful accounts, and bad debt expense follows.

LO 5. Describe the cash flow implications of accounts receivable.

- Companies can increase the speed of cash collection on receivables by factoring, or selling, their receivables.
- The buyer of the receivables will charge a fee to compensate themselves for the time value of money, the risk of uncollectability, and the tasks of billing and collection.
- Receivables may be packaged as financial instruments or securities and sold to investors—called securitization.
- A special case of selling receivables is accepting credit cards like MasterCard and Visa.

LO 6. Account for notes receivable from inception to maturity.

- Notes receivable are recognized for the amount of cash borrowed or goods/services purchased.
- This initial amount is the principal amount of the note receivable.
- Any excess of amount repaid over principal is recognized as interest revenue in the period the interest was earned.

LO 7. Describe internal control procedures for merchandise sales.

- Since sales revenues have a significant effect on a company's net income, internal control procedures must be established to ensure that the amounts reported are correct.
- Typically sales are not recorded until a three-way match is performed between:
  - the customer purchase order (which indicates that the customer wants the goods)
  - the shipping document (which indicates that the goods have been shipped to the customer)
  - the invoice (which indicates that the customer has been billed)

LO 8. Analyze profitability and asset management using sales and receivables.

- Because sales revenue is such a key component of a company's success, analysts are interested in a large number of ratios that incorporate sales.
- Many of these ratios attempt to measure how much the company is making on sales. These are called profitability ratios.
  - Gross profit margin
  - Operating margin
  - Net profit margin
- Analysts are also concerned with asset management—how efficiently a company is using the resources at its disposal.
- One of the most widely used asset management ratios is accounts receivable turnover.

CORNERSTONE 5.1 Recording receivables using the gross method, page 239

CORNERSTONE 5.2 Estimating bad debt expense using the percentage of credit sales method, page 244

CORNERSTONE 5.3 Estimating the allowance for doubtful accounts using the aging method, page 246

CORNERSTONE 5.4 Accounting for notes receivable, page 251

CORNERSTONE 5.5 Calculating the gross profit margin, operating margin, net profit margin, and accounts receivable turnover ratios, page 255

KEY TERMS

Accounts receivable, 242
Aging method, 246
Allowance for Doubtful Accounts, 243
Bad debt expense, 243
Credit cards, 249
Debit card, 250
Earned, 238
Factor, 249
Interest, 250
Net sales revenue, 241
Nontrade receivables, 242
Notes receivable, 250
Percentage of credit sales method, 244
Principal, 250
Profitability ratios, 254
Realizable, 238
Realized, 238
Sales allowance, 241
Sales discount, 239
Sales returns, 241
Securitization, 249
Trade receivables, 242

REVIEW PROBLEM

I. Recording Sales and Receivables

Qwurk Productions performs graphic design services including designing and maintaining websites. The following activities occurred during 2013 and 2014:

11/1/13	Qwurk delivers a new logo to GCD Advisors and submits a bill for $2,000 with terms 2/10, n/30.
11/15/13	Qwurk delivers an overall web concept to Mutare, which Mutare approves. Qwurk submits a bill for $1,000 with terms 2/10, n/30.
11/20/13	Qwurk delivers paper and envelopes incorporating the new logo to GCD Advisors and submits a bill for $200.
11/22/13	Mutare pays for the 11/15 bill related to a new overall web concept.
11/25/13	GCD complains that the printing on much of the paper and envelopes is unacceptable. Qwurk offers to reduce the bill from $200 to $75. GCD accepts.
11/29/13	GCD pays for the 11/1 bill for a new logo and $75 for the 11/20 bill for paper and envelopes.
12/1/13	Qwurk installs a new website incorporating order fulfillment applications for Redbird Enterprises. Redbird signs a note to pay $20,000 plus 6% interest due on 7/1/14.
12/15/13	Qwurk writes off a $600 account receivable.
12/31/13	After performing an aging of its accounts receivable, Qwurk estimates that $2,000 of its accounts receivable will be uncollectible on a total balance of $600,000. The allowance for doubtful accounts has a credit balance of $300 prior to adjustment.
7/1/14	Redbird pays the note and interest in full.
12/31/14	For the year ended December 31, 2014, Qwurk has sales of $6,000,000; sales discounts of $15,000; sales returns and allowances of $20,000.

Required:

1. Provide the journal entry for November 1, 2013, assuming Qwurk uses the gross method of recording receivables.
2. Provide the journal entry for November 15, 2013, assuming Qwurk uses the gross method of recording receivables.
3. Provide the journal entry for November 20, 2013, assuming Qwurk uses the gross method of recording receivables.
4. Calculate how much Mutare paid and provide the journal entry for November 22, 2013.
5. Provide the journal entry for November 25, 2013.
6. Calculate how much GCD paid and provide the journal entry for November 29, 2013.
7. Provide the journal entry for December 1, 2013.
8. Provide the journal entry for December 15, 2013.
9. Provide the necessary adjusting entries for December 31, 2013, to accrue interest on the note and adjust the allowance account.
10. What is the net realizable value of Qwurk's accounts receivable at December 31, 2013?
11. Calculate how much interest Redbird paid and provide the journal entry for July 1, 2014.
12. Provide the income statement presentation of Qwurk's 2014 sales.

Solution:

	Date	Account and Explanation	Debit	Credit
	2013			
1.	Nov. 1	Accounts Receivable	2,000	
		Sales		2,000
		(Record sale)		
2.	Nov. 15	Accounts Receivable	1,000	
		Sales		1,000
		(Record sale)		

Assets	= Liabilities +	Stockholders' Equity
+2,000		+2,000

Assets	= Liabilities +	Stockholders' Equity
+1,000		+1,000

Date	Account and Explanation	Debit	Credit	Assets	= Liabilities +	Stockholders' Equity
2013						
3. Nov. 20	Accounts Receivable	200		+200		+200
	Sales		200			
	(Record sale)					
4. Nov. 22	Cash[a]	980		+980		−20
	Sales Discounts	20		−1,000		
	Accounts Receivable		1,000			
	(Record collection within the discount period)					
5. Nov. 25	Sales Returns and Allowances	125		−125		−125
	Accounts Receivable		125			
	(Record allowance for unacceptable merchandise)					
6. Nov. 29	Cash[b]	2,075		+2,075		
	Accounts Receivable		2,075	−2,075		
	(Record collection after discount period)					
7. Dec. 1	Notes Receivable	20,000		+20,000		+20,000
	Sales		20,000			
	(Record sale)					
8. Dec. 15	Allowance for Doubtful Accounts	600		+600		
	Accounts Receivable		600	−600		
	(Write off an accounts receivable)					
9. Dec. 31	Interest Receivable[c]	100		+100		+100
	Interest Income		100	−1,700		−1,700
	(Record 1 month's interest on Dec. 1 note receivable)					
	Bad Debt Expense	1,700				
	Allowance for Doubtful Accounts[d]		1,700			
	(Record adjusting entry for bad debt expense estimate)					

[a]	
Gross amount	$1,000
Less: Discount ($1,000 × 2%)	(20)
Total paid	$ 980

[b]	
Gross amount	$2,000
Less: Discount (not allowed; paid after 10 days)	0
Total paid	$2,000 + $75 = $2,075

[c] $20,000 × 6% × 1/12

[d] Qwurk's estimate warrants a $2,000 credit balance. Because the account already has a $300 credit balance, a $1,700 credit is needed.

10. December 31, 2013:		
	Accounts receivable accounts	$600,000
	Less: Allowance for doubtful accounts	(2,000)
	Net realizable value	$598,000

Net accounts receivable are shown at net realizable value.

11. July 1, 2014:

$$\text{Interest paid} = \$20{,}000 \times 6\% \times 7/12$$
$$= \$700$$

Interest paid to Qwurk is for the period December 1, 2013, through July 1, 2014. However, the interest income for December 2013 was already recognized in 2013 (see journal entry in 9). Interest income of $600 will be recognized in 2014.

Assets	= Liabilities +	Stockholders' Equity
+20,700		+600
−100		
−20,000		

Account and Explanation	Debit	Credit
Cash	20,700	
Interest Income		600
Interest Receivable (from 9)		100
Notes Receivable		20,000
(Record collection of note receivable)		

12.

Gross sales revenue	$6,000,000
Less: Sales discounts	(15,000)
Less: Sales returns and allowances	(20,000)
Net sales revenue	$5,965,000

DISCUSSION QUESTIONS

1. When is revenue recognized?
2. Explain the criteria for revenue recognition.
3. When is revenue generally considered earned?
4. What four criteria has the SEC issued as further guidance for revenue recognition?
5. How is net sales revenue calculated?
6. Why might users of financial statements prefer the separate disclosure of gross sales revenue and sales returns and allowances to the disclosure of a single net sales revenue amount?
7. Why are sales discounts offered?
8. What are sales returns?
9. What are sales allowances? How do sales allowances differ from sales discounts?
10. What are trade discounts and quantity discounts? From an accounting viewpoint, how does the effect of trade and quantity discounts on selling (or invoice) price differ from the effect of sales discounts?
11. What are the principal types of receivables?
12. Under the allowance method, why do we make an entry to record bad debt expense in the period of sale rather than in the period in which an account is determined to be uncollectible?
13. Why is the direct write-off method not GAAP?
14. What is the conceptual difference between the (1) percentage of credit sales and (2) aging methods of estimating bad debts?
15. What kind of account is *allowance for doubtful accounts*? What does it represent?
16. Why do companies issue credit when their past experience indicates that some customers will not pay?

17. How much interest will be due at maturity for each of the following interest-bearing notes?

	Principal	Months to Maturity	Annual Interest Rate
a.	$10,000	2	12%
b.	42,000	5	14
c.	18,000	4	13
d.	37,000	6	11

18. A business borrows $1,000, signing a note that requires repayment of the amount borrowed in two payments of $600 each, one at the end of each of the next two 6-month periods. Calculate the total interest on the note. What is the principal amount of the note?
19. A business borrows $1,000, signing a note that requires an interest rate of 12% per year and repayment of principal plus interest in a single payment at the end of 1 year. Calculate the total interest on the note. What is the amount of the single payment?
20. Describe what happens when receivables are factored.
21. Accepting major credit cards requires the seller to pay a service charge. What advantages does the seller obtain by accepting major credit cards?
22. Why is interest typically charged on notes receivable, but not on accounts receivable?
23. What documents must be present to trigger the recording of a sale (and associated receivable) in the accounting records?
24. Describe the documents that underlie the typical accounting system for sales. Give an example of a failure of internal control that might occur if these documents were not properly prepared.
25. How may analyzing sales and receivables provide information about a firm's profitability?
26. How may analyzing sales and receivables provide information about a firm's asset management?

MULTIPLE-CHOICE QUESTIONS

5-1 Which of the following is *not* one of the criteria for revenue recognition?

a. Delivery has occurred or services have been provided.
b. Persuasive evidence of an arrangement exists.
c. Collectability is certain.
d. The seller's price to the buyer is fixed and determinable.

5-2 Food To Go is a local catering service. Conceptually, when should Food To Go recognize revenue from its catering service?

a. At the date the meals are served
b. At the date the invoice is mailed to the customer
c. At the date the customer places the order
d. At the date the customer's payment is received

5-3 When is revenue from the sale of merchandise normally recognized?

a. When the customer takes possession of the merchandise, if sold for cash, or when payment is received, if sold on credit
b. When the customer pays for the merchandise
c. Either on the date the customer takes possession of the merchandise or the date on which the customer pays
d. When the customer takes possession of the merchandise

5-4 What does the phrase, "Revenue is recognized at the point of sale" mean?

a. Revenue is recorded in the accounting records when the cash is received from a customer and reported on the income statement when sold to the customer.
b. Revenue is recorded in the accounting records and reported on the income statement when goods are sold and delivered to the customer.
c. Revenue is recorded in the accounting records when the goods are sold to a customer and reported on the income statement when the cash payment is received from the customer.
d. Revenue is recorded in the accounting records and reported on the income statement when the cash is received from the customer.

5-5 On August 31, 2013, Montana Corporation signed a 4-year contract to provide services for Minefield Company at $30,000 per year. Minefield will pay for each year of services on the first day of each service year, starting with September 1, 2013. Using the accrual basis of accounting, when should Montana recognize revenue?

a. On the first day of each year when the cash is received
b. Equally throughout the year as services are provided
c. On the last day of each year after the services have been provided
d. Only at the end of the entire contract

5-6 Under the gross method, the seller records discounts taken by the buyer

a. at the time of sale.
b. at the end of the period in question.
c. never; discounts are irrelevant under the gross method.
d. in a contra-revenue account.

5-7 On April 20, McLean Company provides lawn care services to Tazwell Corporation for $3,000 with terms 1/10, n/30. On April 28, Tazwell pays for half of the services provided, and on May 19 it pays for the other half. What is the total amount of cash McLean received?

a. $3,000
b. $2,700
c. $2,985
d. $2,970

5-8 Which of the following statements concerning internal control procedures for merchandise sales is *not* correct?

a. A sale and its associated receivable are recorded only when the order, shipping, and billing documents are all present.
b. Shipping and billing documents are prepared based on the order document.
c. Accounting for a sale begins with the receipt of a purchase order or some similar document from a customer.
d. The order document is not necessary for the buyer to be obligated to accept and pay for the ordered goods.

5-9 All of the following are ways in which receivables are commonly distinguished *except*

a. collectible or uncollectible.
b. trade or nontrade receivable.
c. current or noncurrent.
d. accounts or notes receivable.

5-10 Which one of the following best describes the allowance for doubtful accounts?

a. Cash flow account
b. Income statement account
c. Contra-account
d. Liability account

5-11 If a company uses the direct write-off method of accounting for bad debts,

a. it will report accounts receivable on the balance sheet at their net realizable value.
b. it is applying the matching principle.
c. it will reduce the Accounts Receivable account at the end of the accounting period for estimated uncollectible accounts.
d. it will record bad debt expense only when an account is determined to be uncollectible.

5-12 Which of the following best describes the objective of estimating bad debt expense with the percentage of credit sales method?

a. To estimate the amount of bad debt expense based on an aging of accounts receivable
b. To determine the amount of uncollectible accounts during a given period
c. To estimate bad debt expense based on a percentage of credit sales made during the period
d. To facilitate the use of the direct write-off method

5-13 Which of the following best describes the concept of the aging method of receivables?

a. An accurate estimate of bad debt expense may be arrived at by multiplying historical bad debt rates by the amount of credit sales made during a period.
b. The precise amount of bad debt expense may be arrived at by multiplying historical bad debt rates by the amount of credit sales made during a period.
c. Estimating the appropriate balance for the allowance for doubtful accounts results in the appropriate value for net accounts receivable on the balance sheet.
d. Accounts receivable should be directly written off when the due date arrives and the customers have not paid the bill.

5-14 The aging method is closely related to the

a. income statement.
b. balance sheet.
c. statement of cash flows.
d. statement of retained earnings.

5-15 The percentage of credit sales approach is closely related to the

a. income statement.
b. balance sheet.
c. statement of retained earnings.
d. statement of cash flows.

5-16 The process by which firms package factored receivables as financial instruments or securities and sell them to investors is known as

a. credit extension.
b. bundling.
c. aging of accounts receivable.
d. securitization.

5-17 Which one of the following statements is true if a company's collection period for accounts receivable is unacceptably long?

a. Cash flows from operations may be higher than expected for the company's sales.
b. The company may offer trade discounts to lengthen the collection period.
c. The company should expand operations with its excess cash.
d. The company may need to borrow to acquire operating cash.

5-18 Zenephia Corp. accepted a 9-month note receivable from a customer on October 1, 2013. If Zenephia has an accounting period which ends on December 31, 2013, when would it most likely recognize interest income from the note?

a. December 31, 2013, and June 30, 2014
b. October 1, 2013
c. December 31, 2013, only
d. June 30, 2014, only

5-19 The "principal" of a note receivable refers to

a. the amount of interest due.
b. the amount of cash borrowed.
c. the present value of the note.
d. the financing company that is lending the money.

5-20 Net profit margin percentage is calculated by

a. dividing operating income by (net) sales.
b. subtracting operating income from (net) sales.
c. dividing net income by (net) sales.
d. subtracting net income from (net) sales.

CORNERSTONE EXERCISES

OBJECTIVE 1
CORNERSTONE 3.5

Cornerstone Exercise 5-21 Service Revenue

Kibitz Fitness received $30,000 from customers on August 1, 2013. These payments were advance payments of yearly membership dues.

Required:

At December 31, 2013, calculate what the balances in the Unearned Service Revenue and Service Revenue accounts will be.

OBJECTIVE 1
CORNERSTONE 3.5

Cornerstone Exercise 5-22 Service Revenue

Softball Magazine Company received advance payments of $75,000 from customers during 2013. At December 31, 2013, $20,000 of the advance payments still had not been earned.

Required:

After the adjustments are recorded and posted at December 31, 2013, calculate what the balances will be in the Unearned Magazine Revenue and Magazine Revenue accounts.

Use the following information for Cornerstone Exercises 5-23 and 5-24:
Bolton sold a customer service contract with a price of $37,000 to Sammy's Wholesale Company. Bolton offered terms of 1/10, n/30 and uses the gross method.

OBJECTIVE 2
CORNERSTONE 5.1

Cornerstone Exercise 5-23 Sales Discounts Taken

Refer to the information for Bolton above.

Required:

Prepare the journal entry to record the sale. Then prepare the journal entry assuming the payment is made within 10 days (within the discount period).

OBJECTIVE 2
CORNERSTONE 5.1

Cornerstone Exercise 5-24 Sales Discounts Not Taken

Refer to the information for Bolton above.

Required:

Prepare the journal entry assuming the payment is made after 10 days (after the discount period).

OBJECTIVE 2
CORNERSTONE 5.1

Cornerstone Exercise 5-25 Sales Discounts

Ramsden Inc. provided consulting services with a gross price of $25,000 and terms of 2/10, n/30.

Required:

1. Prepare the necessary journal entries to record the sale under the gross method.
2. Prepare the necessary journal entries to record collection of the receivable assuming the customer pays within 10 days.
3. Prepare the necessary journal entries to record collection of the receivable assuming the customer pays after 10 days.

OBJECTIVE 4
CORNERSTONE 5.2

Cornerstone Exercise 5-26 Percentage of Credit Sales

Clarissa Company has credit sales of $550,000 during 2013 and estimates at the end of 2013 that 2.5% of these credit sales will eventually default. Also, during 2013 a customer defaults on a $775 balance related to goods purchased in 2012. Prior to the write-off for the $775 default, Clarissa's accounts receivable and allowance for doubtful accounts balances were $402,000 and $129 (credit), respectively.

Required:

1. Prepare the journal entry to record the defaulted account.
2. Prepare the adjusting entry to record the bad debt expense for 2013.

Cornerstone Exercise 5-27 Write-Off of Uncollectible Accounts

OBJECTIVE 4
CORNERSTONE 5.2

The Rock has credit sales of $425,000 during 2013 and estimates at the end of 2013 that 1.5% of these credit sales will eventually default. Also, during 2013 a customer defaults on a $1,200 balance related to goods purchased in 2012.

Required:

1. Prepare the journal entry to record the defaulted balance.
2. Prepare the adjusting entry to record the bad debt expense for 2013.

Cornerstone Exercise 5-28 Aging Method

OBJECTIVE 4
CORNERSTONE 5.3

On January 1, 2013, Hungryman Inc. has the following balances for accounts receivable and allowance for doubtful accounts:

Accounts Receivable	$1,280,000
Allowance for Doubtful Accounts (a credit balance)	44,000

During 2013, Hungryman had $18,500,000 of credit sales, collected $17,945,000 of accounts receivable, and wrote off $60,000 of accounts receivable as uncollectible. At year end, Hungryman performs an aging of its accounts receivable balance and estimates that $52,000 will be uncollectible.

Required:

1. Calculate Hungryman's preadjustment balance in accounts receivable on December 31, 2013.
2. Calculate Hungryman's preadjustment balance in allowance for doubtful accounts on December 31, 2013.
3. Prepare the necessary adjusting entry for 2013.

Cornerstone Exercise 5-29 Aging Method

OBJECTIVE 4
CORNERSTONE 5.3

On January 1, 2013, Smith Inc. has the following balances for accounts receivable and allowance for doubtful accounts:

Accounts Receivable	$382,000
Allowance for Doubtful Accounts (a credit balance)	4,200

During 2013, Smith had $2,865,000 of credit sales, collected $2,905,000 of accounts receivable, and wrote off $3,850 of accounts receivable as uncollectible. At year end, Smith performs an aging of its accounts receivable balance and estimates that $3,800 will be uncollectible.

Required:

1. Calculate Smith's preadjustment balance in accounts receivable on December 31, 2013.
2. Calculate Smith's preadjustment balance in allowance for doubtful accounts on December 31, 2013.
3. Prepare the necessary adjusting entry for 2013.

Cornerstone Exercise 5-30 Percentage of Credit Sales Method

OBJECTIVE 4
CORNERSTONE 5.2

At December 31, 2013, Garner has a $15,000 credit balance in its allowance for doubtful accounts. Garner estimates that 3% of its 2013 credit sales will eventually default. During 2013, Garner had credit sales of $970,000.

(Continued)

Required:

Estimate the bad debt expense under the percentage of credit sales method.

OBJECTIVE 4
CORNERSTONE 5.3

Cornerstone Exercise 5-31 Accounts Receivable Balance

Beginning accounts receivable were $43,375. All sales were on account and totaled $187,600. Cash collected from customers totaled $182,450.

Required:

Calculate the ending accounts receivable balance.

OBJECTIVE 4
CORNERSTONE 5.3
ILLUSTRATING RELATIONSHIPS

Cornerstone Exercise 5-32 Accounts Receivable Balance

Beginning accounts receivable were $275,500, and ending accounts receivable were $302,300. Cash amounting to $2,965,000 was collected from customers' credit sales.

Required:

Calculate the amount of sales on account during the period.

OBJECTIVE 4
CORNERSTONE 5.3
ILLUSTRATING RELATIONSHIPS

Cornerstone Exercise 5-33 Accounts Receivable Balance

Beginning accounts receivable were $80,200, and ending accounts receivable were $83,700. All sales were on credit and totaled $562,900.

Required:

Determine how much cash was collected from customers.

OBJECTIVE 5

Cornerstone Exercise 5-34 Accounting for Credit Card Sales

Frank's Tattoos and Body Piercing operates near campus. At the end of a recent day, Frank's cash register included credit card documents for the following sales amounts:

MasterCard	$756
Visa	486

The merchant's charges are 1.8% for **MasterCard** and 2.1% for **Visa**. Frank's also had cash sales of $375 and $800 of sales on credit to a local business.

Required:

Prepare a journal entry to record these sales.

OBJECTIVE 6
CORNERSTONE 5.4

Cornerstone Exercise 5-35 Notes Receivable

Metzler Communications designs and programs a website for a local business. Metzler charges $46,000 for the project, and the local business signs an 8% note January 1, 2013.

Required:

1. Prepare the journal entry to record the sale on January 1, 2013.
2. Determine how much interest Metzler will receive if the note is repaid on October 1, 2013.
3. Prepare Metzler's journal entry to record the cash received to pay off the note and interest on October 1, 2013.

OBJECTIVE 6
CORNERSTONE 5.4

Cornerstone Exercise 5-36 Notes Receivable

Link Communications programs voicemail systems for businesses. For a recent project, they charged $135,000. The customer secured this amount by signing a note bearing 9% interest on February 1, 2013.

Required:

1. Prepare the journal entry to record the sale on February 1, 2013.
2. Determine how much interest Link will receive if the note is repaid on December 1, 2013.
3. Prepare Link's journal entry to record the cash received to pay off the note and interest on December 1, 2013.

Cornerstone Exercise 5-37 Ratio Analysis

OBJECTIVE 8
CORNERSTONE 5.5

The following information pertains to Cobb Corporation's financial results for the past year.

Net sales	$135,000
Cost of goods sold	48,000
Other expenses	37,000
Net income	50,000

Required:

Calculate Cobb's (1) gross profit margin ratio and (2) net profit margin ratio.

Cornerstone Exercise 5-38 Ratio Analysis

OBJECTIVE 8
CORNERSTONE 5.5

Diviney Corporation's net sales and average net trade accounts receivable were $8,750,000 and $630,000, respectively.

Required:

Calculate Diviney's accounts receivable turnover.

Cornerstone Exercise 5-39 Ratio Analysis

OBJECTIVE 8
CORNERSTONE 5.5

Bo Sports' net sales, average net trade accounts receivable, and net income were $5,700,000, $629,000, and $340,000, respectively.

Required:

Calculate Bo's (1) accounts receivable turnover and (2) net profit margin ratio.

BRIEF EXERCISES

Brief Exercise 5-40 Service Revenue

OBJECTIVE 1

H&R Wholesalers is a retailer providing low cost, bulk items to small companies. Companies must pay an annual membership fee of $100 to access H&R's warehouses. H&R received yearly membership fees from 320 companies on August 1, 2013.

Required:

At December 31, 2013, calculate the remaining amount of Unearned Revenue and the account balance of the Revenue account.

Brief Exercise 5-41 Service Revenue

OBJECTIVE 1

Melrose Milk Delivery provides weekly gourmet milk delivery to the residents of Nicetown. Melrose charges each customer $45 per week for its milk delivery, and it received advance payments for 2,000 weeks of milk delivery services in 2013. At December 31, 2013, two-thirds of the advance payments had been earned.

Required:

After the adjustments are recorded and posted at December 31, 2013, calculate what the balances will be in the Unearned Revenue and Revenue accounts?

OBJECTIVE 2

Brief Exercise 5-42 Sales Discounts Taken

Gordon's Grocers purchases bread from Buddy's Bread Company at $1.45 per loaf. Gordon's recently engaged in a customer service contract with Buddy's to purchase 20,000 loaves of Buddy's bread. Buddy offered credit to Gordon's at terms of 2/10, n/30.

Required:

Prepare the journal entry to record the sale using the gross method. Then, prepare the journal entry assuming the payment is made within 10 days (within the discount period).

OBJECTIVE 2

Brief Exercise 5-43 Sales Discounts Not Taken

Assume the same information as in **Brief Exercise 5-42**: Gordon's Grocers purchases bread from Buddy's Bread Company at $1.45 per loaf. Gordon's engaged in a customer service contract to purchase 20,000 loaves of Buddy's bread. Buddy offered credit at terms of 2/10, n/30 and uses the gross method.

Required:

Prepare the journal entry assuming the payment is made after 10 days (after the discount period).

OBJECTIVE 2

Brief Exercise 5-44 Sales Discounts

Harry Gardner provides tax services for small businesses. This year's tax season has proved especially lucrative for Harry; he earned $45,000 for providing his services. Harry uses terms of 1/10, n/30 in billing his customers.

Required:

1. Prepare the necessary journal entries to record the sale under the gross method.
2. Prepare the necessary journal entries to record collection of the receivable assuming the customer pays within 10 days.
3. Prepare the necessary journal entries to record collection of the receivable assuming the customer pays after 10 days.

OBJECTIVE 4

Brief Exercise 5-45 Percentage of Credit Sales

Roeker Company provides information systems consultation services to large companies in the Chicagoland area. Due to a dip in the economy, Roeker has increased the percentage of credit sales which it believes will be uncollectible from 3.0% to 3.2% for 2013. Roeker's consulting services provided revenues of $700,000 in 2013. During 2014, Roeker has write-offs of $750 related to goods purchased in 2013. Prior to the write-off for the $750 default, Roeker's accounts receivable and allowance for doubtful accounts balances were $480,000 and $232 (credit), respectively.

Required:

1. Prepare the journal entry to record the defaulted account.
2. Prepare the adjusting entry to record the bad debt expense for 2013.

OBJECTIVE 4

Brief Exercise 5-46 Write-Off of Uncollectible Accounts

King Enterprises had 27 customers utilizing its financial planning services in 2013. Each customer paid King $25,000 for receiving King's assistance. King estimates that 2% of its $675,000 credit sales in 2013 will be uncollectible. During 2014, King wrote off $2,700 related to services performed in 2013.

Required:

1. Prepare the journal entry to record the defaulted balance.
2. Prepare the adjusting entry to record the bad debt expense for 2013.

Brief Exercise 5-47 Aging Method

OBJECTIVE 4

Spotted Singer sells karaoke machines to businesses and consumers via the Internet. On January 1, 2013, Spotted Singer Inc. has an Accounts Receivable balance of $997,000 and a credit balance in its Allowance for Doubtful Accounts of $24,000. During 2013, Spotted Singer had $10,800,000 of credit sales, collected $1,725,000 of accounts receivable, and had customer defaults of $45,000. At year end, an aging analysis indicates that $28,000 of Spotted Singer's receivables will be uncollectible.

Required:

1. Calculate Spotted Singer's balance in accounts receivable on December 31, 2013, prior to the adjustment.
2. Calculate Spotted Singer's balance in allowance for doubtful accounts on December 31, 2013, prior to the adjustment.
3. Prepare the necessary adjusting entry for 2013.

Brief Exercise 5-48 Aging Method

OBJECTIVE 4

Ingrid Inc. has strict credit policies and only extends credit to customers with outstanding credit history. The company examined its accounts and determined that at January 1, 2013, it had balances in Accounts Receivable and Allowance for Doubtful Accounts of $478,000 and $7,900 (credit), respectively. During 2013, Ingrid extended credit for $3,075,000 of sales, collected $2,715,000 of accounts receivable, and had customer defaults of $4,280. Ingrid performed an aging analysis on its receivables at year end and determined that $6,800 of its receivables will be uncollectible.

Required:

1. Calculate Ingrid's balance in accounts receivable on December 31, 2013, prior to the adjustment.
2. Calculate Ingrid's balance in allowance for doubtful accounts on December 31, 2013, prior to the adjustment.
3. Prepare the necessary adjusting entry for 2013.

Brief Exercise 5-49 Percentage of Credit Sales Method

OBJECTIVE 4

Ruby Red manufactures, markets, and distributes citrus flavored soft drinks across the globe. Ruby Red hired a collection agency in 2012 to increase collection rates from customers. As a result, Ruby estimates that only 2% of its 2013 credit sales will be written off, compared to the 4% of 2012's credit sales that were estimated to be uncollectible. At December 31, 2013, Ruby Red has a $12,800 credit balance in its allowance for doubtful accounts and credit sales of $1,570,000.

Required:

Use the percentage of credit sales method to calculate the bad debt expense.

Brief Exercise 5-50 Collection of Amounts Previously Written Off

OBJECTIVE 4

Hannah purchased a laptop computer from Perry Corp. for $1,500. Hannah's receivable has been outstanding for over 180 days, and Perry determines that the total amount is uncollectible and writes off all of Hannah's debt. Hannah later receives a windfall and pays the amount of her balance to Perry Corp.

Required:

Make the appropriate journal entries (if any) to record the receipt of $450 by Perry Corp.

OBJECTIVE 5

Brief Exercise 5-51 Accounts Receivable Balance

Hart Inc. began the year with $315,700 of accounts receivable. During the year, Hart sold a considerable amount of merchandise on credit and collected $2,427,000 of its credit sales. At the end of the year, the accounts receivable balance is $16,800 lower than the beginning balance.

Required:

Calculate the amount of credit sales during the period.

OBJECTIVE 5

Brief Exercise 5-52 Accounts Receivable Balance

XYZ Corp sells widgets to consumers for $20 each. Its beginning accounts receivable balance was $24,975, and it sold 12,376 widgets throughout the year. The total cash collections for the year amounted to $217,750.

Required:

Calculate the ending accounts receivable balance.

OBJECTIVE 5

Brief Exercise 5-53 Accounts Receivable Balance

Ray's beginning and ending accounts receivables balances are $147,990 and $142,720, respectively. Ray's sold $3,745,060 of merchandise, of which 50% was on credit.

Required:

Determine the amount of cash collections for the period.

OBJECTIVE 5

Brief Exercise 5-54 Accounting for Credit Card Sales

Jarrod's Meat Shop doubles as a butcher shop and a sandwich shop that sells to both individuals and a nearby hospital system. On a particular day, Jarrod's had cash sales of $450, credit sales of $600, sales on MasterCard of $657, and sales on Visa of $923. The sales on credit cards incur merchant charges of 1.6% for MasterCard and 1.9% for Visa.

Required:

Prepare a journal entry to record these sales.

OBJECTIVE 6

Brief Exercise 5-55 Notes Receivable

Harrigan Enterprises utilizes Snoopy Systems to design and implement a cash management system. Due to Harrigan's cash management problems, it cannot currently pay for the system out of pocket. Snoopy chooses to extend a 6% note on January 1, 2013, for the $27,000 project cost.

Required:

1. Prepare Snoopy's journal entry to record the service performed on January 1, 2013.
2. Determine how much interest Snoopy will receive if the note is repaid on May 1, 2013.
3. Provide Snoopy's journal entry to record the cash received to pay off the note and interest on May 1, 2013.

OBJECTIVE 6

Brief Exercise 5-56 Notes Receivable

Kelsey's Kleening provides cleaning services for Clinton Inc., a business with four buildings. Kelsey's assigned different cleaning charges for each building based on the amount of square feet to be cleaned. The charges for the four buildings are $35,000, $27,000, $45,000, and $10,000. Clinton secured this amount by signing a note bearing 7% interest on March 1, 2013.

Required:

1. Prepare the journal entry to record the sale on March 1, 2013.
2. Determine how much interest Kelsey will receive if the note is repaid on December 1, 2013.
3. Prepare Kelsey's journal entry to record the cash received to pay off the note and interest on December 1, 2013.

Brief Exercise 5-57 Ratio Analysis

OBJECTIVE 8

Dobby's income statement lists net sales of $179,000 and a gross margin of $111,000. All other expenses not included in the gross margin totaled $46,500.

Required:

1. Calculate Dobby's gross profit ratio.
2. Calculate Dobby's net profit margin ratio.

Brief Exercise 5-58 Ratio Analysis

OBJECTIVE 8

Rose Corporation sells upscale lamps to boutiques across the country. The average net trade accounts receivable for Rose is $540,000. In addition, the company has average net sales of $6,950,000.

Required:

Calculate Rose's accounts receivable turnover.

Brief Exercise 5-59 Ratio Analysis

OBJECTIVE 8

Watts Inc. specializes in imported goods, focusing particularly on food products. For 2013, the company realized net sales of $9,700,000 and average net trade accounts receivable were $1,057,000. In 2012, Watts had realized a net loss for the year in the amount of $20,000; however, extraordinary efficiency efforts in 2013 increased net income by $445,000.

Required:

1. Calculate Watts' accounts receivable turnover.
2. Calculate Watts' net profit margin ratio.

EXERCISES

Exercise 5-60 Calculation of Revenue

OBJECTIVE 1

Wallace Motors buys and sells used cars. Wallace made the following sales during January and February:

a. Three cars were sold to Russell Taxi for a total of $75,000; the cars were delivered to Russell on January 18. Russell paid Wallace $20,000 on January 18 and the remaining $55,000 on February 12.
b. One car was sold to Hastings Classics for $28,000. The car was delivered to Hastings on January 25. Hastings paid Wallace on February 1.

Required:

Calculate the monthly revenue for Wallace for January and February.

Exercise 5-61 Revenue Recognition

OBJECTIVE 1

Volume Electronics sold a television to Sarah Merrifield on December 15, 2013. Sarah paid $100 at the time of the purchase and agreed to pay $100 each month for 5 months beginning January 15, 2014.

Required:

Determine in what month or months revenue from this sale should be recorded by Volume Electronics to ensure proper application of accrual accounting.

OBJECTIVE 1

ILLUSTRATING RELATIONSHIPS

Exercise 5-62 Calculation of Revenue from Cash Collection

Anderson Lawn Service provides mowing, weed control, and pest management services for a flat fee of $300 per lawn per month. During November, Anderson collected $9,900 in cash from customers, which included $1,200 for lawn care provided in October. At the end of November, Anderson had not collected from 6 customers who had promised to pay in December when they returned from vacation.

Required:

Calculate the amount of Anderson's revenue for November.

OBJECTIVE 2

Exercise 5-63 Effects of Sales Discounts

Citron Mechanical Systems makes all sales on credit, with terms 1/15, n/30. During 2013, the list price (prediscount) of services provided was $687,500. Customers paid $482,000 (list price) of these sales within the discount period and the remaining $205,500 (list price) after the discount period. Citron uses the gross method of recording sales.

Required:

1. Compute the amount of sales that Citron recorded for 2013.
2. Compute the amount of cash that Citron collected from these sales.
3. Prepare a summary journal entry to record these sales and a second summary entry to record the cash collected.

OBJECTIVE 2

Exercise 5-64 Sales Discount Recorded at Gross

Nevada Company provided services with a list price of $48,500 to Small Enterprises with terms 2/15, n/45. Nevada records sales at gross.

Required:

1. Prepare the entries to record this sale in Nevada's journal.
2. Prepare the entry for Nevada's journal to record receipt of cash in payment for the sale *within* the discount period.
3. Prepare the entry for Nevada's journal to record receipt of cash in payment for the sale *after* the discount period.
4. Assume that Nevada's customer does not have the available cash to pay Nevada within the discount period. How much interest should the customer be willing to pay for a loan to permit them to take advantage of the discount period (assuming no additional costs to the loan)?

OBJECTIVE 2

Exercise 5-65 Sales and Sales Returns and Allowances

Rubin Enterprises had the following sales-related transactions on a recent day:

a. List price of services provided on credit was $27,500; terms 2/10, n/30.
b. Collected $5,875 in cash for services to be provided in the future.
c. The customer complained about aspects of the services provided in Transaction a. To maintain a good relationship with this customer, Rubin granted an allowance of $1,500 off the list price. The customer had not yet paid for the services.
d. Rubin provided the services for the customer in Transaction b. Additionally, Rubin granted an allowance of $350 because the services were provided after the promised date. Because the customer had already paid, Rubin paid the $350 allowance in cash.

Required:

1. Prepare the necessary journal entry (or entries) for each of these transactions.
2. **CONCEPTUAL CONNECTION** What concerns would Rubin have assuming that the sales allowances for this period were significantly higher than in previous periods both in absolute turns and as a percentage of gross sales?

OBJECTIVE 4

Exercise 5-66 Average Uncollectible Account Losses and Bad Debt Expense

The accountant for Porile Company prepared the following data for sales and losses from uncollectible accounts:

Year	Credit Sales	Losses from Uncollectible Accounts*
2009	$ 883,000	$13,125
2010	952,000	14,840
2011	1,083,000	16,790
2012	1,189,000	16,850

* Losses from uncollectible accounts are the actual losses related to sales of that year (rather than write-offs of that year).

Required:

1. Calculate the average percentage of losses from uncollectible accounts for 2009 through 2012.
2. Assume that the credit sales for 2013 are $1,260,000 and that the weighted average percentage calculated in Requirement 1 is used as an estimate of losses from uncollectible accounts for 2013 credit sales. Determine the bad debt expense for 2013 using the percentage of credit sales method.
3. **CONCEPTUAL CONNECTION** Do you believe this estimate of bad debt expense is reasonable?
4. **CONCEPTUAL CONNECTION** How would you estimate 2013 bad debt expense if losses from uncollectible accounts for 2012 were $30,000? What other action would management consider?

OBJECTIVE 4

Exercise 5-67 Bad Debt Expense: Percentage of Credit Sales Method

Gilmore Electronics had the following data for a recent year:

Cash sales	$135,000
Credit sales	512,000
Accounts receivable determined to be uncollectible	9,650

The firm's estimated rate for bad debts is 2.2% of credit sales.

Required:

1. Prepare the journal entry to write off the uncollectible accounts.
2. Prepare the journal entry to record the estimate of bad debt expense.
3. If Gilmore had written off $3,000 of receivables as uncollectible during the year, how much would bad debt expense reported on the income statement have changed?
4. **CONCEPTUAL CONNECTION** If Gilmore's estimate of bad debts is correct (2.2% of credit sales) and the gross margin is 20%, by how much did Gilmore's income from operations increase assuming $150,000 of the sales would have been lost if credit sales were not offered?

OBJECTIVE 4

Exercise 5-68 Bad Debt Expense: Percentage of Credit Sales Method

Bradford Plumbing had the following data for a recent year:

Credit sales	$547,900
Allowance for doubtful accounts, 1/1 (a credit balance)	8,740
Accounts receivable, 1/1	42,340
Collections on account receivable	489,770
Accounts receivable written off	14,250

Bradford estimates that 2.7% of credit sales will eventually default.

(Continued)

Required:

1. Compute bad debt expense for the year (rounding to the nearest whole number).
2. Determine the ending balances in accounts receivable and allowance for doubtful accounts.

OBJECTIVE 4

Exercise 5-69 Bad Debt Expense: Aging Method

Glencoe Supply had the following accounts receivable aging schedule at the end of a recent year.

Accounts Receivable Age	Amount	Proportion Expected to Default	Allowance Required
Current	$310,500	0.005	$ 1,553
1–30 days past due	47,500	0.01	475
31–45 days past due	25,000	0.13	3,250
46–90 days past due	12,800	0.20	2,560
91–135 days past due	6,100	0.25	1,525
Over 135 days past due	4,200	0.60	2,520
			$11,883

The balance in Glencoe's allowance for doubtful accounts at the beginning of the year was $58,620 (credit). During the year, accounts in the total amount of $62,400 were written off.

Required:

1. Determine bad debt expense.
2. Prepare the journal entry to record bad debt expense.
3. If Glencoe had written off $90,000 of receivables as uncollectible during the year, how much would bad debt expense reported on the income statement have changed?

OBJECTIVE 4

Exercise 5-70 Aging Receivables and Bad Debt Expense

Perkinson Corporation sells paper products to a large number of retailers. Perkinson's accountant has prepared the following aging schedule for its accounts receivable at the end of the year.

Accounts Receivable Category	Amount	Proportion Expected to Default
Within discount period	$384,500	0.004
1–30 days past discount period	187,600	0.015
31–60 days past discount period	41,800	0.085
Over 60 days past discount period	21,400	0.200

Before adjusting entries are entered, the balance in the allowance for doubtful accounts is a *debit* of $480.

Required:

1. Calculate the desired postadjustment balance in Perkinson's allowance for doubtful accounts.
2. Determine bad debt expense for the year.

OBJECTIVE 4

ILLUSTRATING RELATIONSHIPS

Exercise 5-71 Allowance for Doubtful Accounts

At the beginning of the year, Kullerud Manufacturing had a credit balance in its allowance for doubtful accounts of $10,670, and at the end of the year it was a credit balance of $11,240. During the year, Kullerud made credit sales of $1,270,990, collected receivables in the amount of $1,240,830, and recorded bad debt expense of $42,550.

Required:

Compute the amount of receivables that Kullerud wrote off during the year.

Exercise 5-72 Collection of Amounts Previously Written Off

OBJECTIVE 4

Customer Rob Hufnagel owes Kellman Corp. $1,250. Kellman determines that the total amount is uncollectible and writes off all of Hufnagel's debt. Hufnagel later pays $350 to Kellman.

Required:

Make the appropriate journal entries (if any) to record the receipt of $350 by Kellman.

Exercise 5-73 Correcting an Erroneous Write-Off

OBJECTIVE 4

ILLUSTRATING RELATIONSHIPS

The new bookkeeper at Karlin Construction Company was asked to write off two accounts totaling $1,710 that had been determined to be uncollectible. Accordingly, he debited Accounts Receivable for $1,710 and credited Bad Debt Expense for the same amount.

Required:

1. Determine what was wrong with the bookkeeper's entry assuming Karlin uses the allowance method.
2. Give both the entry he should have made and the entry required to correct his error.

Exercise 5-74 Accounting for Notes Receivable

OBJECTIVE 6

On November 30, 2013, Tucker Products performed computer programming services for Thomas Inc. in exchange for a 5-month, $125,000, 9% note receivable. Thomas paid Tucker the full amount of interest and principal on April 30, 2014.

Required:

Prepare the necessary entries for Tucker to record the transactions described above.

Exercise 5-75 Recording Notes Receivable: Issuance, Payment, and Default

OBJECTIVE 6

Marydale Products permits its customers to defer payment by giving personal notes instead of cash. All the notes bear interest and require the customer to pay the entire note in a single payment 6 months after issuance. Consider the following transactions, which describe Marydale's experience with two such notes:

a. On October 31, 2013, Marydale accepts a 6-month, 9% note from Customer A in lieu of a $3,600 cash payment for services provided that day.
b. On February 28, 2014, Marydale accepts a 6-month, $2,400, 7% note from Customer B in lieu of a $2,400 cash payment for services provided on that day.
c. On April 30, 2014, Customer A pays the entire note plus interest in cash.
d. On August 31, 2014, Customer B pays the entire note plus interest in cash.

Required:

Prepare the necessary journal and adjusting entries required to record Transactions a through d in Marydale's records.

Exercise 5-76 Internal Control for Sales

OBJECTIVE 7

Arrow Products is a mail-order computer software sales outlet. Most of Arrow's customers call on its toll-free phone line and order software, paying with a credit card.

Required:

CONCEPTUAL CONNECTION Explain why the shipping and billing documents are important internal controls for Arrow.

OBJECTIVE 8

Exercise 5-77 Ratio Analysis

The following information was taken from Nash Inc.'s trial balances as of December 31, 2012, and December 31, 2013.

	12/31/2013	12/31/2012
Accounts receivable	$ 32,000	$ 39,000
Accounts payable	47,000	36,000
Sales	219,000	128,000
Sales returns	4,000	2,300
Retained earnings	47,000	16,000
Dividends	5,000	1,000
Net income	36,000	9,000

Required:

1. Calculate the net profit margin and accounts receivable turnover for 2013. (*Note:* Round answers to two decimal places.)
2. How much does Nash make on each sales dollar?
3. How many days does the average receivable take to be paid (assuming all sales are on account)?

OBJECTIVE 8

Exercise 5-78 Ratio Analysis

The following information was taken from Logsden Manufacturing's trial balances as of December 31, 2012, and December 31, 2013.

	12/31/2013	12/31/2012
Accounts receivable	$ 14,000	$ 18,000
Accounts payable	22,000	15,000
Cost of goods sold	144,000	127,000
Sales	279,000	239,000
Sales returns	12,000	10,000
Retained earnings	47,000	16,000
Dividends	3,000	2,000
Income from operations	25,000	16,000
Net income	19,000	18,000

Required:

1. Calculate the gross profit margin and operating margin percentage for 2013. (*Note:* Round answers to two decimal places.)
2. Assuming that all of the operating expenses are fixed (or, won't change as sales increase or decrease), what will be the operating margin percentage if sales increase by 25%?

PROBLEM SET A

OBJECTIVE 1

Problem 5-79A Revenue Recognition

Katie Vote owns a small business that rents computers to students at the local university for the 9-month school year. Katie's typical rental contract requires the student to pay the year's rent of $1,800 ($200 per month) in advance. When Katie prepares financial statements at the end of December, her accountant requires that Katie spread the $1,800 over the 9 months that a computer is rented. Therefore, Katie can recognize only $800 revenue (4 months) from each computer rental contract in the year the cash is collected and must defer recognition of the remaining $1,000 (5 months) to next year. Katie argues that getting students to agree to rent the computer is the most difficult part of the activity so she ought to be able to recognize all $1,800 as revenue when the cash is received from a student.

Required:

CONCEPTUAL CONNECTION Explain why generally accepted accounting principles require the use of accrual accounting rather than cash-basis accounting for transactions like the one described here.

Problem 5-80A Discount Policy and Gross Profit

OBJECTIVE 2

Compton Audio sells MP3 players. During 2013, Compton sold 1,750 units at an average of \$225 per unit. Each unit costs Compton \$150. At present, Compton offers no sales discounts. Compton's controller suggests that a generous sales discount policy would increase annual sales to 2,200 units and also improve cash flow. She proposes 5/10, n/30 and believes that 70% of the customers will take advantage of the discount.

Required:

1. If the controller is correct, determine how much the new sales discount policy would add to net sales and gross margin.
2. **CONCEPTUAL CONNECTION** Explain why the sales discount policy might improve cash flow.

Problem 5-81A Effects of Discounts on Sales and Purchases

OBJECTIVE 2

Helmkamp Products sells golf clubs and accessories to pro shops. Gross sales in 2013 were \$2,850,700 (Helmkamp's list price) on terms 2/15, n/45. Customers paid for \$2,000,000 (Helmkamp's list price) of the merchandise within the discount period and the remaining \$850,700 after the end of the discount period. Helmkamp records purchases and sales using the gross method to account for sales discounts.

Required:

1. Compute the amount of net sales.
2. Determine how much cash was collected from sales.

Problem 5-82A Sales Discounts

OBJECTIVE 2

Sims Company regularly provides services to Lauber Supply on terms 1/15, n/30 and records sales at gross. During a recent month, the two firms engaged in the following transactions:

a. Sims provided services with a list price of \$85,000.
b. Sims provided services with a list price of \$30,000.
c. Lauber paid for the purchase in Transaction a within the discount period.
d. Lauber paid for the purchase in Transaction b after the discount period.

Required:

1. Prepare the journal entries for Sims to record the sales in Transactions a and b (make separate entries).
2. Prepare the journal entry to record the receipt of Lauber's payment in Transaction c.
3. Prepare the journal entry to record the receipt of Lauber's payment in Transaction d.
4. **CONCEPTUAL CONNECTION** What implied annual interest rate is Lauber incurring by failing to take the sales discount and, instead, paying the gross amount after 30 days?

Problem 5-83A Internal Control for Sales

OBJECTIVE 7

Yancy's Hardware has three stores. Each store manager is paid a salary plus a bonus on the sales made by his or her store. On January 5, 2014, Bill Slick, manager of one of the stores, resigned. Bill's store had doubled its expected December 2013 sales, producing a bonus for Bill of \$6,000 in December alone. Charles Brook, an assistant manager at another store, was assigned as manager of Bill's store. Upon examination of the store's accounting records, Charles reports that the store's records indicated sales returns and allowances of \$96,000 in the first 4 days of January 2014, an amount equal to about half of December 2013 sales.

Required:

1. **CONCEPTUAL CONNECTION** Explain what the large amount of sales returns and allowances suggest that Bill might have done.
2. **CONCEPTUAL CONNECTION** Determine how Yancy could protect itself from a manager who behaved as Bill likely did.

OBJECTIVE 4

Problem 5-84A Bad Debt Expense: Percentage of Credit Sales Method

The Glass House, a glass and china store, sells nearly half its merchandise on credit. During the past 4 years, the following data were developed for credit sales and losses from uncollectible accounts:

Year of Sales	Credit Sales	Losses from Uncollectible Accounts*
2010	$197,000	$12,608
2011	202,000	13,299
2012	212,000	13,285
2013	273,000	22,274
Total	$884,000	$61,466

* Losses from uncollectible accounts are the actual losses related to sales of that year (rather than write-offs of that year).

Required:

1. Calculate the loss rate for each year from 2010 through 2013. (*Note:* Round answers to three decimal places.)
2. Determine whether there appears to be a significant change in the loss rate over time.
3. **CONCEPTUAL CONNECTION** If credit sales for 2014 are $400,000, determine what loss rate you would recommend to estimate bad debts. (*Note:* Round answers to three decimal places.)
4. Using the rate you recommend, record bad debt expense for 2014.
5. **CONCEPTUAL CONNECTION** Assume that the increase in The Glass House's sales in 2014 was largely due to granting credit to customers who would have been denied credit in previous years. How would this change your answer to Requirement 4? Describe a legitimate business reason why The Glass House would adopt more lenient credit terms.
6. **CONCEPTUAL CONNECTION** Using the data from 2010 through 2013, estimate the increase in income from operations in total for those 4 years assuming (a) the average gross margin is 25% and (b) 50% of the sales would have been lost if no credit was granted.

OBJECTIVE 4

Problem 5-85A Aging Method Bad Debt Expense

Cindy Bagnal, the manager of Cayce Printing Service, has provided the following aging schedule for Cayce's accounts receivable:

Accounts Receivable Category	Amount	Proportion Expected to Default
0–20 days	$ 86,550	0.01
21–40 days	19,400	0.06
41–60 days	10,250	0.12
Over 60 days	4,900	0.25
	$121,100	

Cindy indicates that the $121,100 of accounts receivable identified in the table does not include $4,600 of receivables that should be written off.

Required:

1. Journalize the $4,600 write-off.
2. Determine the desired postadjustment balance in allowance for doubtful accounts (round each aging category to the nearest dollar).
3. If the balance in allowance for doubtful accounts before the $4,600 write-off was a debit of $700, compute bad debt expense. Prepare the adjusting entry to record bad debt expense.

OBJECTIVE 4

Problem 5-86A Determining Bad Debt Expense Using the Aging Method

At the beginning of the year, Tennyson Auto Parts had an accounts receivable balance of $31,800 and a balance in the allowance for doubtful accounts of $2,980 (credit). During the year, Tennyson had credit sales of $624,300, collected accounts receivable in the amount of $602,700, wrote off

$18,600 of accounts receivable, and had the following data for accounts receivable at the end of the period:

Accounts Receivable Age	Amount	Proportion Expected to Default
Current	$20,400	0.01
1–15 days past due	5,300	0.02
16–45 days past due	3,100	0.08
46–90 days past due	3,600	0.15
Over 90 days past due	2,400	0.30
	$34,800	

Required:

1. Determine the desired postadjustment balance in allowance for doubtful accounts.
2. Determine the balance in allowance for doubtful accounts before the bad debt expense adjusting entry is posted.
3. Compute bad debt expense.
4. Prepare the adjusting entry to record bad debt expense.

Problem 5-87A Accounting for Notes Receivable

OBJECTIVE 6

Yarnell Electronics sells computer systems to small businesses. Yarnell engaged in the following activities involving notes receivable:

a. On September 1, 2013, Yarnell sold a $10,000 system to Ross Company. Ross gave Yarnell a 6-month, 7% note as payment.
b. On December 1, 2013, Yarnell sold a $6,000 system to Searfoss Inc. Searfoss gave Yarnell a 9-month, 9% note as payment.
c. On March 1, 2014, Ross paid the amount due on its note.
d. On September 1, 2014, Searfoss paid the amount due on its note.

Required:

Prepare the necessary journal and adjusting entries for Yarnell Electronics to record these transactions.

Problem 5-88A Ratio Analysis

OBJECTIVE 8

Selected information from Bigg Company's financial statements follows:

	Fiscal Year Ended December 31		
	2013	2012 (in thousands)	2011
Gross sales	$2,004,719	$1,937,021	$1,835,987
Less: Sales discounts	(4,811)	(4,649)	(4,406)
Less: Sales returns and allowances	(2,406)	(2,324)	(2,203)
Net sales	$1,997,502	$1,930,048	$1,829,378
Cost of goods sold	621,463	619,847	660,955
Gross profit	$1,376,039	$1,310,201	$1,168,423
Operating expenses	577,369	595,226	583,555
Operating income	$ 798,670	$ 714,975	$ 584,868
Other income (expenses)	15,973	(5,720)	(8,773)
Net income	$ 814,643	$ 709,255	$ 576,095

(Continued)

	At December 31		
	2013	2012 (in thousands)	2011
Accounts receivable	$201,290	$195,427	$182,642
Less: Allowance for doubtful accounts	(2,516)	(2,736)	(2,192)
Net accounts receivable	$198,774	$192,691	$180,450

Required:

1. Calculate the following ratios for 2012 and 2013: (a) gross profit margin, (b) operating margin, (c) net profit margin, and (d) accounts receivable turnover. (*Note:* Round answers to two decimal places.)
2. **CONCEPTUAL CONNECTION** For each of the first three ratios listed above, provide a plausible explanation for any differences that exist. (For example, why is the net profit margin higher or lower than it was the previous year?)
3. **CONCEPTUAL CONNECTION** Explain what each ratio attempts to measure. Make an assessment about Bigg Company based upon the ratios you have calculated. Are operations improving or worsening?

PROBLEM SET B

OBJECTIVE 1

Problem 5-79B Revenue Recognition

Mary Wade owns a small business that rents parking spaces to students at the local university. Mary's typical rental contract requires the student to pay the year's rent of $720 ($60 per month) in advance. When Mary prepares financial statements at the end of December, her accountant requires that Mary spread the $720 over the 12 months that a parking space is rented. Therefore, Mary can recognize only $240 revenue (4 months) from each contract in the year the cash is collected and must defer recognition of the remaining $480 (8 months) to next year. Mary argues that getting students to agree to rent the parking space is the most difficult part of the activity so she ought to be able to recognize all $720 as revenue when the cash is received from a student.

Required:

CONCEPTUAL CONNECTION Explain why generally accepted accounting principles require the use of accrual accounting rather than cash-basis accounting for transactions like the one described here.

OBJECTIVE 2

Problem 5-80B Discount Policy and Gross Profit

Parker Electronics sells cell phones. During 2013, Parker sold 1,500 units at an average of $500 per unit. Each unit cost Parker $350. At present, Parker offers no sales discounts. Parker's controller suggests that a generous sales discount policy would increase annual sales to 2,000 units and also improve cash flow. She proposes 3/15, n/20 and believes that 75% of the customers will take advantage of the discount.

Required:

1. If the controller is correct, determine how much the new sales discount policy would add to net sales and gross margin.
2. **CONCEPTUAL CONNECTION** Explain why the sales discount policy might improve cash flow.

OBJECTIVE 2

Problem 5-81B Effects of Discounts on Sales and Purchases

Smithson Products sells legal supplies to law firms. Gross sales in 2013 were $2,750,600 (Smithson's list price) on terms 3/10, n/30. Customers paid for $2,427,900 (Smithson's list price) of the merchandise within the discount period and the remaining $322,700 after the end of the discount period. Smithson records purchases and sales using the gross method to account for sales discounts.

Required:

1. Compute the amount of net sales.
2. Determine how much cash was collected from sales.

Problem 5-82B Sales Discounts

OBJECTIVE 2

Spartan Inc. regularly provides services to Grieder Supply on terms 3/10, n/40 and records sales at gross. During a recent month, the two firms engaged in the following transactions:

a. Spartan sold merchandise with a list price of $250,000.
b. Spartan sold merchandise with a list price of $75,000.
c. Grieder paid for the purchase in Transaction a within the discount period.
d. Grieder paid for the purchase in Transaction b after the discount period.

Required:

1. Provide the journal entries for Spartan to record the sales in Transactions a and b (make separate entries).
2. Provide the journal entry to record the receipt of Grieder's payment in Transaction c.
3. Provide the journal entry to record the receipt of Grieder's payment in Transaction d.
4. **CONCEPTUAL CONNECTION** What implied annual interest rate is Grieder incurring by failing to take the sales discount and, instead, paying the gross amount after 40 days?

Problem 5-83B Internal Control for Sales

OBJECTIVE 7

Johnson Tires has three stores. Each store manager is paid a salary plus a bonus on the sales made by his or her store. On January 5, 2014, Kevin Sampson, manager of one of the stores, resigned. Kevin's store had doubled its expected December 2013 sales, producing a bonus for Kevin of $7,000 in December alone. Jason Jones, an assistant manager at another store, was assigned as manager of Kevin's store. Upon examination of the store's accounting records, Jason reports that the store's records indicated sales returns and allowances of $124,000 in the first 4 days of January 2014, an amount equal to about half of December 2013 sales.

Required:

1. **CONCEPTUAL CONNECTION** Explain what the large amount of sales returns and allowances suggest that Kevin might have done.
2. **CONCEPTUAL CONNECTION** Determine how Johnson could protect itself from a manager who behaved as Kevin likely did.

Problem 5-84B Bad Debt Expense: Percentage of Credit Sales Method

OBJECTIVE 4

Kelly's Collectibles sells nearly half its merchandise on credit. During the past 4 years, the following data were developed for credit sales and losses from uncollectible accounts:

Year of Sales	Credit Sales	Losses from Uncollectible Accounts*
2010	$125,900	$10,007
2011	102,440	8,762
2012	131,120	9,849
2013	149,780	12,303
Total	$509,240	$40,921

*Losses from uncollectible accounts are the actual losses related to sales of that year (rather than write-offs of that year).

(Continued)

Required:

1. Calculate the loss rate for each year from 2010 through 2013. (*Note:* Round answers to three decimal places.)
2. Determine if there appears to be a significant change in the loss rate over time.
3. **CONCEPTUAL CONNECTION** If credit sales for 2014 are $182,000, explain what loss rate you would recommend to estimate bad debts. (*Note:* Round answers to three decimal places.)
4. Using the rate you recommend, record bad debt expense for 2014.
5. **CONCEPTUAL CONNECTION** Assume that the increase in Kelly's sales in 2014 was largely due to granting credit to customers who would have been denied credit in previous years. How would this change your answer to Requirement 4? Describe a legitimate business reason why Kelly's would adopt more lenient credit terms.
6. **CONCEPTUAL CONNECTION** Using the data from 2010 through 2013, estimate the increase in income from operations in total for those 4 years assuming (a) the average gross margin is 45% and (b) 20% of the sales would have been lost if no credit was granted (round to nearest dollar).

OBJECTIVE 4

Problem 5-85B Aging Method Bad Debt Expense

Carol Simon, the manager of Handy Plumbing has provided the following aging schedule for Handy's accounts receivable:

Accounts Receivable Category	Amount	Proportion Expected to Default
0–20 days	$ 92,600	0.03
21–40 days	12,700	0.09
41–60 days	17,800	0.14
Over 60 days	2,100	0.30
	$125,200	

Carol indicates that the $125,200 of accounts receivable identified in the table does not include $9,400 of receivables that should be written off.

Required:

1. Journalize the $9,400 write-off.
2. Determine the desired postadjustment balance in allowance for doubtful accounts.
3. If the balance in allowance for doubtful accounts before the $9,400 write-off was a debit of $550, compute bad debt expense. Prepare the adjusting entry to record bad debt expense.

OBJECTIVE 4

Problem 5-86B Determining Bad Debt Expense Using the Aging Method

At the beginning of the year, Lennon Electronics had an accounts receivable balance of $34,800 and a balance in the allowance for doubtful accounts of $3,640 (credit). During the year, Lennon had credit sales of $891,420, collected accounts receivable in the amount of $821,400, wrote off $28,990 of accounts receivable, and had the following data for accounts receivable at the end of the period:

Accounts Receivable Age	Amount	Proportion Expected to Default
Current	$42,350	0.01
1–15 days past due	11,200	0.04
16–45 days past due	9,600	0.09
46–90 days past due	7,200	0.17
Over 90 days past due	5,480	0.30
	$75,830	

Required:

1. Determine the desired postadjustment balance in allowance for doubtful accounts (round amounts to nearest dollar for each aging category).
2. Determine the balance in allowance for doubtful accounts before the bad debt expense adjusting entry is posted.

3. Compute bad debt expense.
4. Prepare the adjusting entry to record bad debt expense.

Problem 5-87B Accounting for Notes Receivable

OBJECTIVE 6

Sloan Systems sells voice mail systems to small businesses. Sloan engaged in the following activities involving notes receivable (round to nearest dollar):

a. On October 1, 2013, Sloan sold an $8,000 system to Majors Company. Majors gave Sloan a 7-month, 10% note as payment.
b. On November 1, 2013, Sloan sold a $6,000 system to Hadley Inc. Hadley gave Sloan a 10-month, 12% note as payment.
c. On May 1, 2014, Majors paid the amount due on its note.
d. On September 1, 2014, Hadley paid the amount due on its note.

Required:

Prepare the necessary journal and adjusting entries for Sloan Systems to record these transactions.

Problem 5-88B Ratio Analysis

OBJECTIVE 8

Selected information from Small Company's financial statements follows.

	Fiscal Year Ended December 31		
	2013	2012 (in thousands)	2011
Gross sales	$1,663,917	$1,697,195	$1,714,167
Less: Sales discounts	(2,995)	(3,055)	(3,086)
Less: Sales returns and allowances	(2,496)	(2,546)	(2,571)
Net sales	$1,658,426	$1,691,594	$1,708,510
Cost of goods sold	881,876	891,027	860,512
Gross profit	$ 776,550	$ 800,567	$ 847,998
Operating expenses	482,050	496,958	487,214
Operating income	$ 294,500	$ 303,609	$ 360,784
Other income (expenses)	3,534	(3,036)	(1,804)
Net income	$ 298,034	$ 300,573	$ 358,980

	At December 31		
	2013	2012 (in thousands)	2011
Accounts receivable	$376,062	$365,109	$341,223
Less: Allowance for doubtful accounts	(8,461)	(71,926)	(5,971)
Net accounts receivable	$367,601	$293,183	$335,252

Required:

1. Calculate the following ratios for 2012 and 2013: (a) gross profit margin, (b) operating margin, (c) net profit margin, and (d) accounts receivable turnover. (*Note:* Round answers to two decimal places.)
2. **CONCEPTUAL CONNECTION** For each of the first three ratios listed above provide a plausible explanation for any differences that exist. (For example, why is the net profit margin higher or lower than it was the previous year?)
3. **CONCEPTUAL CONNECTION** Explain what each ratio attempts to measure. Make an assessment about Small Company based upon the ratios you have calculated. Are operations improving or worsening?

CASES

Case 5-89 Ethics and Revenue Recognition

Alan Spalding is CEO of a large appliance wholesaler. Alan is under pressure from Wall Street Analysts to meet his aggressive sales revenue growth projections. Unfortunately, near the end of the year he realizes that sales must dramatically improve if his projections are going to be met. To accomplish this objective, he orders his sales force to contact their largest customers and offer them price discounts if they buy by the end of the year. Alan also offered to deliver the merchandise to a third-party warehouse with whom the customers could arrange delivery when the merchandise was needed.

Required:

1. Do you believe that revenue from these sales should be recognized in the current year? Why or why not?
2. What are the probable consequences of this behavior for the company in future periods?
3. What are the probable consequences of this behavior for investors analyzing the current year financial statements?

Case 5-90 Recognition of Service Contract Revenues

Jackson Dunlap is president of New Miami Maintenance Inc. which provides building maintenance services. On October 15, 2013, Jackson signed a service contract with Western College, and, Western made a down payment of $12,000. Under the contract, New Miami will provide maintenance services for all Western's buildings for a period of 2 years, beginning on January 1, 2014, and Western will pay New Miami $1,000 per month, beginning on January 31, 2014.

Initially, Jackson proposed that some portion of the revenue from the contract should be recognized in 2013; however, his accountant, Rita McGonigle, convinced him that this would be inappropriate. Then Jackson proposed that the revenue should be recognized in an amount equal to the cash collected under the contract in 2013. Again, Rita argued against his proposal, saying that generally accepted accounting principles required recognition of an equal amount of contract revenue each month.

Required:

1. Give a reason that might explain Jackson's desire to recognize contract revenue earlier rather than later.
2. Put yourself in Rita's position. How would you convince Jackson that his two proposals are unacceptable and that an equal amount of revenue should be recognized every month?
3. If Rita's proposal is adopted, how would the contract be reflected in the balance sheets at the end of 2013 and at the end of 2014?

Case 5-91 Revenue Recognition

Beth Rader purchased North Shore Health Club in June 2013. Beth wanted to increase the size of the business by selling 5-year memberships for $2,000, payable at the beginning of the membership period. The normal yearly membership fee is $500. Since few prospective members were expected to have $2,000, Beth arranged for a local bank to provide a $2,000 installment loan to prospective members. By the end of 2013, 250 customers had purchased the 5-year memberships using the loan provided by the bank.

Beth prepared her income statement for 2013 and included $500,000 as revenue because the club had collected the entire amount in cash. Beth's accountant objected to the inclusion of the entire $500,000. The accountant argued that the $500,000 should be recognized as revenue as the club provides services for these members during the membership period. Beth countered with a quotation from a part of "Generally Accepted Accounting Principles," *Accounting Research Bulletin 43, Chapter 1, Section A, No. 1:*

"Profit is deemed to be realized when a sale in the ordinary course of business is effected, unless the circumstances are such that collection of the sale price is not reasonably assured."

Beth notes that the memberships have been sold and that collection of the selling price has occurred. Therefore, she argues that all $500,000 is revenue in 2013.

Required:

Write a short statement supporting either Beth or the accountant in this dispute.

Case 5-92 Sales Discount Policies

Consider three businesses, all of which offer price reductions to their customers. The first is an independently owned gas station located at a busy intersection in Cincinnati, Ohio, that offers a 3% discount for cash purchases of gasoline. The second is a large home improvement store located near an interstate exit in suburban Cleveland that offers building contractors terms of 3/10, n/45. And third is a clothing manufacturer and catalog retailer located in Columbus. Several times during each year, a catalog is distributed in which men's dress shirts are heavily discounted if purchased in lots of four or more.

Required:

1. What are the main objectives of the discount policies in each of the three businesses?
2. How does accounting information assist each business in achieving its discount policy objectives?

Case 5-93 Financial Analysis of Receivables

A chain of retail stores located in Kansas and Nebraska has requested a loan from the bank at which you work. The balance sheet of the retail chain shows significant accounts receivable related to its in-house credit card. You have been assigned to evaluate these receivables.

Required:

1. What questions concerning the quality of these receivables can you answer by analyzing the retailer's financial statements?
2. What additional questions would you raise, and what information would you request from the retailer to answer these questions?

Case 5-94 Income Effects of Uncollectible Accounts

The credit manager and the accountant for Goldsmith Company are attempting to assess the effect on net income of writing off $100,000 of receivables. Goldsmith uses the aging method of determining bad debt expense and has the following aging schedule for its accounts receivable at December 31, 2013:

Accounts Receivable Category	Amount	Proportion Expected to Default
Current	$2,980,400	0.004
1–30 days past due	722,600	0.035
31–60 days past due	418,500	0.095
Over 60 days past due	322,800	0.250
	$4,444,300	

The receivables being considered for write-off are all over 60 days past due.

Required:

1. Assume that the tax rate is 30%. What will be the effect on net income if the $100,000 is written off?
2. What data would you examine to provide some assurance that a company was not holding uncollectible accounts in its accounts receivable rather than writing them off when they are determined to be uncollectible?

Case 5-95 Research and Analysis Using the Annual Report

Obtain **Whole Foods**'s Fiscal 2011 10-K (filed Nov. 23, 2011) through the "Investor Relations" portion of its website (do a web search for Whole Foods investor relations). Once at the Investor Relations section of the website, look for "SEC Filings." When you see the list of all the filings, either filter for the "Annual Filings" or search for "10-K." Another option is to go to www.sec.gov and click "Search for Company Filings" under "Filings & Forms."

Required:

1. Look at the "Accounts Receivable" heading to Note 2 (Summary of Significant Accounting Policies). Do you think Whole Foods uses the percentage of credit sales method or the aging method to estimate bad debt expense?
2. Looking at the same note, what was Whole Foods's allowance for doubtful accounts at fiscal year end 2010 and 2011?
3. Was a larger percentage of the gross accounts receivable considered uncollectible at fiscal year end 2010 or 2011?
4. Calculate Whole Foods's receivables turnover for fiscal 2010 and 2011 (Accounts Receivable, net, was $104,731 at the end of fiscal 2009). (*Note:* Round answers to two decimal places.) If the industry average for receivables turnover is 116.77, how do you evaluate their efficiency with receivables?
5. Calculate Whole Foods's gross profit margin, operating margin, and net profit margin for fiscal 2010 and 2011. (*Note:* Round answers to two decimal places.)
6. If the industry average for the gross profit ratio is 33.32%, what sort of strategy do you think Whole Foods is pursuing?
7. Evaluate the trend of Whole Foods's operating margin and net profit margin and relate the trend to the industry averages of 4.67% and 2.91%, respectively.

Case 5-96 Comparative Analysis: Under Armour, Inc., versus VF Corporation

Refer to the financial statements of **Under Armour, Inc.**, and **VF Corporation** that are supplied with this text.

Required:

1. Look at Under Armour's Note 2 (Summary of Significant Accounting Policies) under the heading Allowance for Doubtful Accounts. Based on this disclosure, describe the nature of Under Armour's receivables reported on the balance sheet. What is the balance in the allowance for doubtful accounts for 2010 and 2011?
2. Look at VF's Note C. What was VF's allowance for doubtful accounts as a percentage of total accounts receivable at the end of 2010 and 2011?
3. Using the balances reported on the balance sheets, what are Under Armour's and VF's receivables turnover for 2011? (*Note:* Round answer to two decimal places.)
4. Calculate Under Armour's and VF's gross profit margin for 2010 and 2011. (*Note:* Round answers to two decimal places.) What can you infer about the strategy pursued by these two companies based on these measures, assuming the industry average is around 32.7% ?
5. Calculate Under Armour's and VF's operating margin for 2010 and 2011. (*Note:* Round answers to two decimal places.) Comment on these measures assuming the industry average is around 7.7%.
6. Calculate Under Armour's and VF's net profit margin for 2010 and 2011. (*Note:* Round answers to two decimal places.) Comment on these measures assuming the industry average is 4.81%.

Case 5-97 CONTINUING PROBLEM: FRONT ROW ENTERTAINMENT

While Front Row Entertainment has had considerable success in signing artists and promoting concerts, Cam and Anna still had a few ideas to grow their business that they wanted to implement. One idea that they both agree on is to start an online fan "community" for each of their artists. By providing a more direct connection between the artists and their fans, each artist community would serve as an online fan club that should generate increased interest and attendance at the artists' concerts. In addition to marketing and promoting the artist, Front Row Entertainment could sell advertising space on these fan communities to companies interested in reaching the particular demographic that the artist attracts. Because the summer concert season is one of the busiest and most lucrative times of the year, Cam and Anna felt it was extremely important to get the fan communities in place prior to the beginning of the summer. Therefore, they engaged in the following selected transactions for the months of May and June:

May	1	Paid Web Design Inc. $8,500 to develop the fan websites. The fan websites were operational on May 10. Front Row charged this expenditure to other expense.
	10	Front Row Entertainment sold $550 worth of advertising to Little John's Restaurant with terms 2/10, n/30. The advertising will randomly appear on the artists' websites throughout the month of May.
	15	Front Row Entertainment sold $475 worth of advertising to Sherwood Media with terms 2/10, n/30. The advertising related to an in-store DVD promotion that Sherwood was holding later in the month.
	19	Front Row Entertainment received payment from Little John for the May 10 bill.
	20	Sherwood Media informed Front Row that an error had been made on its advertisement. Sherwood's promotion was supposed to run from May 20 to May 25; however, the advertisement stated that the promotion would run from May 15 to May 25. Because the error was Front Row's fault, Front Row agreed to reduce the amount owed by $150.
June	1	Front Row Entertainment sold $750 worth of advertising to Big House Entertainment Company with terms 2/10, n/30. The advertising will randomly appear on the artists' websites throughout the month of June.
	10	Sherwood paid Front Row the amount owed for the May 15 bill minus the allowance granted on May 20.
	20	Front Row learns that Big House Entertainment has filed for bankruptcy, and it writes off the $750 receivable.

Over the next few months, the fan communities continue to grow in popularity, with more and more companies purchasing advertising space. By the end of 2013, Front Row reports the following balances:

Accounts receivable	$17,900
Allowance for doubtful accounts	250 (debit)
Credit sales	45,000

Required:

1. Prepare journal entries for the May and June transactions.
2. Prepare the adjusting entry required at December 31, 2013, with regard to bad debt under each of the following independent assumptions.
   a. Assume that Front Row performed an aging of its accounts receivable. Front Row estimates that $895 of its accounts receivable will be uncollectible.
   b. Assume that Front Row uses the percentage of credit sales method and estimates that 2% of credit sales will be uncollectible.

6 Cost of Goods Sold and Inventory

After studying Chapter 6, you should be able to:

1. Describe the types of inventories held by merchandisers and manufacturers, and understand how inventory costs flow through a company.
2. Explain how to record purchases and sales of inventory using a perpetual inventory system.
3. Apply the four inventory costing methods to compute ending inventory and cost of goods sold under a perpetual inventory system.
4. Analyze the financial reporting and tax effects of the various inventory costing methods.
5. Apply the lower of cost or market rule to the valuation of inventory.
6. Evaluate inventory management using the gross profit and inventory turnover ratios.
7. Describe how errors in ending inventory affect income statements and balance sheets.
8. *(Appendix 6A)* Explain how to record purchases of inventory using a periodic inventory system.
9. *(Appendix 6B)* Compute ending inventory and cost of goods sold under a periodic inventory system.

EXPERIENCE FINANCIAL ACCOUNTING

with Wal-Mart

Wal-Mart Stores, Inc., based in Bentonville, Arkansas, is America's largest public corporation with almost $444 billion in sales for its 2012 fiscal year. Wal-Mart serves more than 200 million customers per week through 10,130 retail stores in 27 countries. Given the large volume of merchandise that is sold, Wal-Mart's profits depend heavily on the control and management of its inventory. After all, as shown in Exhibit 6.1, inventory makes 74% of Wal-Mart's current assets.

For many companies, inventory is at the heart of the operating cycle and must be carefully managed and controlled. If a company doesn't have enough inventory on its shelves to meet customers' demand, it will lose sales. On the other hand, too much inventory will increase carrying costs, such as storage and interest costs, as well as increase the risk of obsolescence. Wal-Mart has long been recognized as a world leader in its effective use of technology to manage and control its inventory and distribution.

As you will see in this chapter, even though inventory is an asset, it can have a major impact on net income. That is because all inventory accounting systems allocate the cost of inventory between ending inventory and cost of goods sold. Therefore, the valuation of inventory affects cost of goods sold, which in turn, affects net income. By managing and controlling its inventory, Wal-Mart has been able to tie up less of its money in inventory than its competitors, resulting in greater profits. This focus on inventory allows Wal-Mart shoppers to "Save Money. Live Better."

EXHIBIT 6.1

Composition of Wal-Mart's Current Assets

Wal-Mart Stores, Inc.
Consolidated Balance Sheets (partial)
January 31, 2012

(in millions)	2012
ASSETS:	
Current assets:	
Cash and cash equivalents	$ 6,550
Receivables	5,937
Inventories	40,714
Prepaid expenses and other	1,774
Total current assets	$54,975

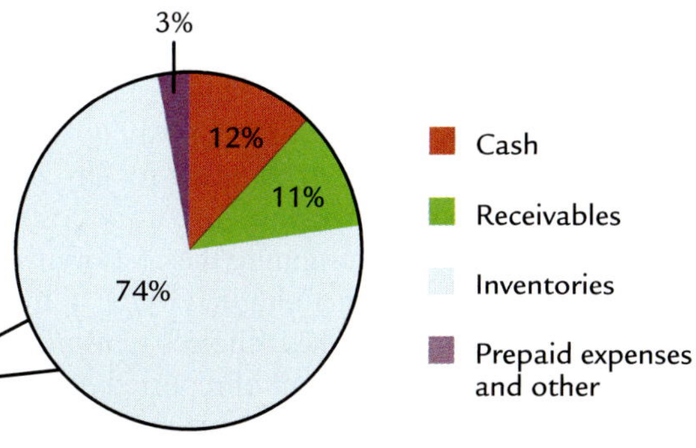

Source: Wal-Mart Stores, Inc. 2012 10K

OBJECTIVE 1

Describe the types of inventories held by merchandisers and manufacturers, and understand how inventory costs flow through a company.

NATURE OF INVENTORY AND COST OF GOODS SOLD

Inventory represents products held for resale and is classified as a current asset on the balance sheet. The inventories of large companies like General Electric, Procter and Gamble, and Wal-Mart are composed of thousands of different products or materials and millions of individual units that are stored in hundreds of different locations. For other companies, inventories are a much less significant portion of their total assets. Exhibit 6.2 shows the relative composition of inventory for Wal-Mart and Microsoft.

EXHIBIT 6.2

Relative Composition of Inventory for Different Companies

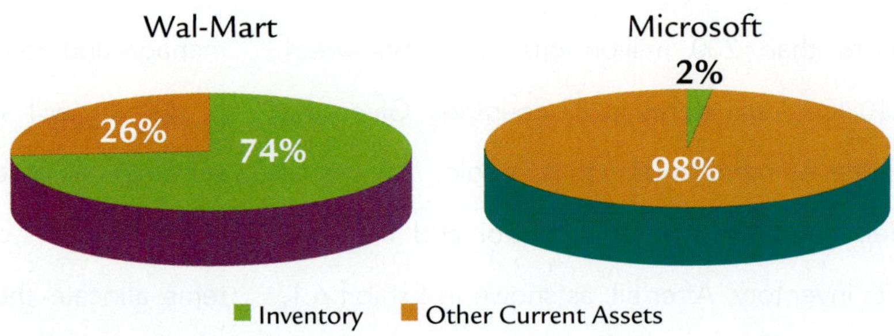

For companies like Wal-Mart, these vast and varied inventories are at the heart of company operations and must be carefully controlled and accounted for. For example, one of Wal-Mart's key performance measures is the comparison of inventory growth to sales growth. In the recessionary economy of 2009, Wal-Mart's sales grew by only 1%. In response, it was able to shrink its inventory by 4%—an indication that Wal-Mart was effectively managing and controlling its inventory in response to economic pressures.

When companies like Wal-Mart sell their inventory to customers, the cost of the inventory becomes an expense called cost of goods sold. **Cost of goods sold** (or **cost of sales**) represents the outflow of resources caused by the sale of inventory and is the most important expense on the income statement of companies that sell goods instead of services. **Gross margin** (also called **gross profit**), a key performance measure, is defined as sales revenue minus cost of goods sold. Thus, gross margin indicates the extent to which the resources generated by sales can be used to pay operating expenses (selling and administrative expenses) and provide for net income. For 2012, Wal-Mart reported a gross margin of $108,727,000,000, calculated as:

$$\text{Revenue} - \text{Cost of Goods Sold} = \text{Gross Margin}$$
$$\$443{,}854{,}000{,}000 - \$335{,}127{,}000{,}000 = \$108{,}727{,}000{,}000 \text{ (24.5\% of revenue)}$$

The cost of inventory has a direct effect on cost of goods sold and gross margin. To correctly interpret and analyze financial statements, one must understand inventory accounting. Accounting for inventories requires a matching of costs with revenues based on an appropriate inventory costing method. Management is allowed considerable latitude in determining the cost of inventory and may choose among several different costing methods. In addition, GAAP allows certain departures from historical cost accounting for inventory. These choices that managers make affect the balance sheet valuation of inventory, the amount of reported net income, and the income taxes payable from year to year.

In this chapter, we will examine the process of accounting for inventory and cost of goods sold. We will address the following questions:

- What are the different types of inventory?
- What costs should be included in inventory?

- Which inventory system (perpetual or periodic) should be employed?
- How are inventory transactions recorded?
- How is cost of goods sold computed?
- What are the financial effects of the four alternative inventory costing methods?
- How does application of the lower of cost or market rule affect inventory valuation?

An understanding of inventory accounting will help in the analysis of financial statements as well as in managing a business.

Types of Inventory and Flow of Costs

In previous chapters, we have generally discussed companies that sell services such as advertising agencies, delivery companies, repair companies, and accounting firms. For these companies, inventory plays a much smaller role. For example, in 2011, **Google** didn't even report an amount for inventory! Our focus in this chapter will be on companies that sell inventory. These companies are often referred to as either merchandisers or manufacturers.

Merchandisers are companies (either retailers or wholesalers) that purchase inventory in a finished condition and hold it for resale without further processing. **Retailers** such as **Wal-Mart**, **Sears**, and **Target** are merchandisers that sell directly to consumers, while **wholesalers** are merchandisers that sell to other retailers. For example, **McKesson** and **AmerisourceBergen** are wholesalers that supply pharmaceutical products to health-care providers; **United Natural Foods** is a wholesaler that distributes natural, organic, and specialty foods to various retailers. The inventory held by merchandisers is termed **merchandise inventory**. Merchandise inventory is an asset. When that asset is sold to a customer, it becomes an expense called cost of goods sold which appears on the income statement. Wal-Mart's inventory disclosure, shown earlier in Exhibit 6.1 (p. 289), is an example of a typical disclosure made by a merchandising company.

Manufacturers are companies that buy and transform raw materials into a finished product which is then sold. **Sony**, **Toyota**, and **Dell** are all manufacturing companies. Manufacturing companies classify inventory into three categories: raw materials, work-in-process, and finished goods.

- **Raw materials inventory** are the basic ingredients used to make a product. When these raw materials are purchased, the Raw Materials Inventory account is increased. As raw materials are used to manufacture a product, they become part of work-in-process inventory.
- **Work-in-process inventory** consists of the raw materials that are used in production as well as other production costs such as labor and utilities. These costs stay in this account until the product is complete. Once the production process is complete, these costs are moved to the Finished Goods Inventory account.
- **Finished goods inventory** represents the cost of the final product that is available for sale. When the finished goods inventory is sold to a customer, it becomes an expense called cost of goods sold, which appears on the income statement.

The inventory disclosure of **Dell**, shown in Exhibit 6.3 (p. 292), is an example of a typical disclosure made by a manufacturing company.

The relationship between the various inventory accounts and cost of goods sold is shown in Exhibit 6.4 (p. 292).

The concepts involved in accounting for inventories of manufacturers and merchandisers are similar. However, due to the additional complexities of accounting for manufacturing inventory, the remainder of this chapter will focus on merchandising companies.

EXHIBIT 6.3

Inventory Disclosure of Dell

February 3, 2012, and January 28, 2011

(in millions)	2012	2011
Current Assets		
Cash and cash equivalents	$13,852	$13,913
Accounts receivable, net	6,476	6,493
Inventories, net	1,404	1,301
Other current assets	7,716	7,314
Total current assets	$29,448	$29,021

Note 16: Supplemental Consolidated Financial Information

(in millions)	2012	2011
Raw materials	$ 753	$ 593
Work-in-process	239	232
Finished goods	412	476
Total inventories, net	$1,404	$1,301

Source: Dell, Inc. 2011 10K

Cost of Goods Sold Model

As shown in Exhibit 6.4, cost of goods sold is the cost to the seller of all goods sold during the accounting period. Recall that the *matching principle* requires that any costs used to generate revenue should be recognized in the same period that the revenue is recognized. Because revenue is recognized as goods are sold, cost of goods sold is an expense.

EXHIBIT 6.4

Flow of Inventory Costs

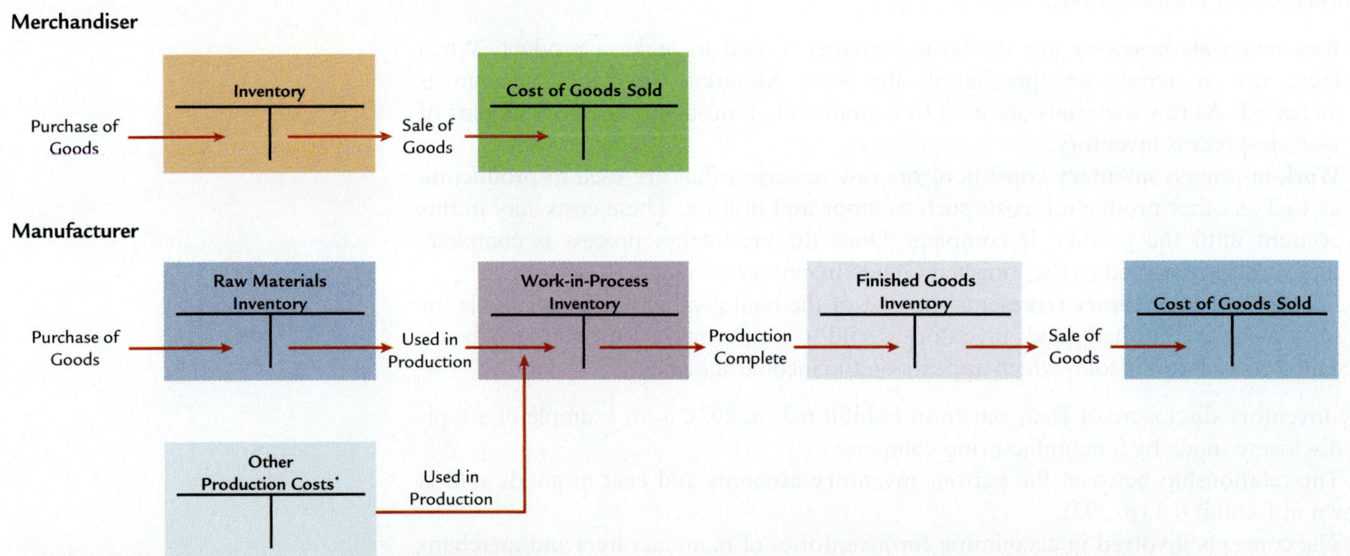

* Work-in-Process Inventory consists of raw materials used in production (also known as direct materials) as well as other production costs. These other production costs are called direct labor and factory overhead. The process by which these costs are converted to a final cost of a product is covered in managerial accounting.

The relationship between cost of goods sold and inventory is given by the cost of goods sold model:

	Beginning inventory
+	Purchases
=	Cost of goods available for sale
−	Ending inventory
=	Cost of goods sold

Except in the case of a new company, merchandisers and manufacturers will start the year with an amount of inventory on hand called *beginning inventory.* During the year, any *purchases* of inventory are added to the inventory account. The sum of beginning inventory and purchases represents the **cost of goods available for sale**. The portion of the cost of goods available for sale that remains unsold at the end of the year is the company's *ending inventory* (the ending inventory for one period becomes the beginning inventory of the next period). The portion of the cost of goods available for sale that is sold becomes *cost of goods sold.* The cost of goods sold model is illustrated in Exhibit 6.5.

EXHIBIT 6.5

Cost of Goods Sold Model

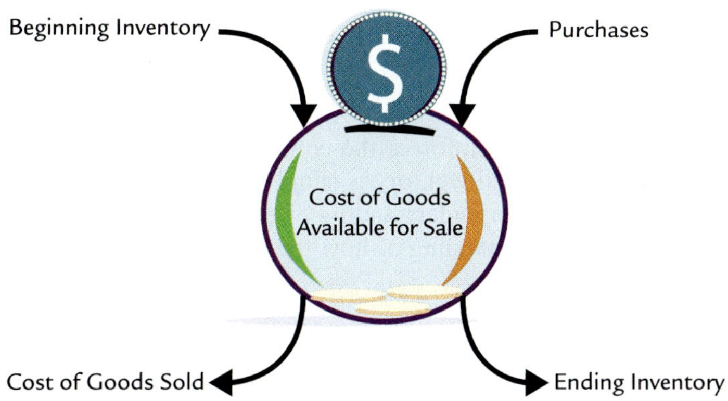

The determination of cost of goods sold requires an allocation of the cost of goods available for sale between ending inventory and cost of goods sold. An application of the cost of goods sold model is illustrated in Cornerstone 6.1.

Applying the Cost of Goods Sold Model

CORNERSTONE 6.1

Why:

The determination of cost of goods sold requires an allocation of the cost of goods available for sale between ending inventory and cost of goods sold.

Information:

Bargain Shops, a retail clothing store, had a beginning inventory of $26,000 on January 1, 2013. During 2013, the company purchased goods from a supplier costing $411,000. At the end of 2013, the cost of the unsold inventory was $38,000.

Required:

Compute cost of goods sold at December 31, 2013.

(Continued)

CORNERSTONE 6.1

(Continued)

Solution:

	Beginning inventory	$ 26,000
+	Purchases	411,000
=	Cost of goods available for sale	$437,000
−	Ending inventory	38,000
=	Cost of goods sold	$399,000

The general structure of the cost of goods sold model can be rearranged to solve for any missing amount if the other three amounts are known. For example, if Bargain Shops did not know the cost of ending inventory but knew the cost of goods sold was $399,000, the company could determine ending inventory by rearranging the model as follows:

	Beginning inventory	$ 26,000
+	Purchases	411,000
=	Cost of goods available for sale	$437,000
−	Cost of goods sold	399,000
=	Ending inventory	$ 38,000

concept Q&A

Because all inventories ultimately get expensed as cost of goods sold, why aren't all costs recorded as cost of goods sold when they are incurred?

Answer:

Costs related to inventories are initially recorded in an inventory account to help a company achieve a proper matching of expenses with revenues. By recording costs in an inventory account, a company can delay the recognition of the expense until the goods are sold. If all inventory related costs were expensed when incurred, users of financial statements would see a distorted picture of the company's profitability.

Cornerstone 6.1 reinforces the concept that the computation of cost of goods sold or ending inventory is simply an allocation of the cost of goods available for sale. An understanding of this cost of goods sold model should enhance your understanding of how the matching concept is applied to cost of goods sold.

Inventory Systems

Because inventory is at the heart of the operating cycle for most wholesalers and retailers, the inventory accounting systems that record purchases and sales and track the level of inventory are particularly important. These systems provide the information needed to determine cost of goods sold and analyze inventory. In addition, these systems signal the need to purchase additional inventory or the need to make special efforts to sell existing inventory. They also provide information necessary to safeguard the inventory from misappropriation or theft. In short, these systems provide the information that managers need to manage and control inventory.

Companies use one of two types of inventory accounting systems—a perpetual inventory system or a periodic inventory system.

Perpetual Inventory System In a **perpetual inventory system**, balances for inventory and cost of goods sold are continually (perpetually) updated with each sale or purchase of inventory. This type of system requires that detailed records be maintained on a transaction-by-transaction basis for each purchase and sale of inventory. For example, every time that **Wal-Mart** purchases inventory from a supplier, it records this purchase directly in its inventory records. Similarly, when Wal-Mart makes a sale to a customer, it will not only record the sale (as illustrated in Chapter 5) but will also update its inventory and cost of goods sold balances by decreasing inventory and increasing cost of goods sold. In other words, a perpetual inventory system records both the *revenue* and *cost* side of sales transactions.

With the volume of transactions that **Wal-Mart** has on a daily basis, this task may appear quite daunting. However, with the advent of "point of sale" cash register systems and optical bar code scanners, the implementation of perpetual inventory systems has become quite common. Some companies, such as Wal-Mart, are taking this idea a step further and using radio frequency identification (RFID) technology to track inventory. By attaching RFID tags to its inventory, Wal-Mart is able to more easily track inventory from its suppliers to the final customer, dramatically reducing inventory losses.

In a perpetual inventory system, the accounting system keeps an up-to-date record of both ending inventory and cost of goods sold at any point in time. However, a company that uses a perpetual system should still take a physical count of inventory at least once a year to confirm the balance in the inventory account. Any difference between the physical count of inventory and the inventory balance provided by the accounting system could be the result of errors, waste, breakage, or theft.

Periodic Inventory System A **periodic inventory system** does not require companies to keep detailed, up-to-date inventory records. Instead, a periodic system records the cost of purchases as they occur (in an account separate from the inventory account), takes a physical count of inventory at the end of the period, and applies the cost of goods sold model to determine the balances of ending inventory and cost of goods sold. Thus, a periodic system only produces balances for ending inventory and cost of goods sold at the end of each accounting period (periodically). If a company using the periodic system needs to know the balance of inventory or cost of goods sold during a period, it must do either of the following:

- perform a physical count of inventory
- estimate the amount of inventory using an acceptable estimation technique[1]

Comparison of Perpetual and Periodic Inventory Systems Perpetual and periodic systems offer distinct benefits and any choice between the two inventory systems must weigh each system's advantages against its operating costs. The principal advantage of a periodic system is that it is relatively inexpensive to operate. Because perpetual systems require entering and maintaining more data than periodic systems, the additional costs can be quite substantial for a company with thousands of different items in inventory. However, with technological advances, this advantage is rapidly disappearing. The perpetual system has the advantage of making the balances of inventory and cost of goods sold continuously available. This provides management with greater control over inventory than it would have under a periodic inventory system. Providing managers with more timely information can be a significant and extremely valuable advantage in a competitive business environment. For example, much of Wal-Mart's success has been attributed to its sophisticated inventory management and control system.

We will illustrate a perpetual inventory system in this chapter because of its growth and popularity in many different types of companies.

YOU DECIDE Just-in-Time Inventory Management

As the inventory manager for Goliath Inc., a large national merchandising company, it is your job to balance the costs of carrying inventory (e.g., finance costs, storage costs, etc.) against the costs of not meeting customer demand (e.g., the cost of lost sales). If Goliath can rely on its suppliers to deliver inventory on very short notice and in ready-to-use forms, then very low inventory levels can be maintained. This approach to inventory management is called **just in time (JIT)** and is consistent with both minimizing inventory carrying costs and "out-of-stock" costs.

[1] More information on the periodic inventory system is provided in Appendices 6A and 6B at the end of this chapter.

What information would you need to maintain a just-in-time inventory policy?

To synchronize the arrival of new inventory with the selling of the old inventory, you need detailed information about order-to-delivery times, receiving-to-ready-for-sale times, and inventory quantities. Delivery and make-ready times are used to control and minimize time lags between shipment of goods by suppliers and delivery to customers. In some retail stores, for example, merchandise arrives tagged, stacked, and ready for placement on the sales floor while in other retail stores several days may be required to get the merchandise ready for sale. Information on inventory quantities would also be useful as a signal to reorder a particular item of inventory. Perpetual inventory systems, which make inventory balances continuously available, can provide the needed information on inventory quantities.

Inventory management and control can lead to significant cost reductions and improved profitability.

OBJECTIVE 2

Explain how to record purchases and sales of inventory using a perpetual inventory system.

RECORDING INVENTORY TRANSACTIONS—PERPETUAL SYSTEM

The historical cost principle requires that the activities of a company are initially measured at their historical cost—the exchange price at the time the activity occurs. Applied to inventory, this principle implies that *inventory cost includes the purchase price of the merchandise plus any cost of bringing the goods to a salable condition and location.* Therefore, the cost of inventory will include the purchase price plus other "incidental" costs, such as freight charges to deliver the merchandise to the company's warehouse, insurance cost on the inventory while it is in transit, and various taxes. In general, a company should stop accumulating costs as a part of inventory once the inventory is ready for sale.[2]

Accounting for Purchases of Inventory

Let's first take a look at how a merchandising company would account for inventory purchases. In a perpetual inventory system, the inventory account is used to record the costs associated with acquiring merchandise.

Purchases **Purchases** refers to the cost of merchandise acquired for resale during the accounting period. The purchase of inventory is recorded by increasing the inventory account. All purchases should be supported by a source document, such as an *invoice,* that provides written evidence of the transaction as well as the relevant details of the purchase. A typical invoice is shown in Exhibit 6.6. Note the various details on the invoice, such as the names of the seller and the purchaser, the invoice date, the credit terms, the freight terms, a description of the goods purchased, and the total invoice amount.

Relying on the historical cost principle, the cost of purchases must include the effects of purchase discounts, purchase returns, and transportation charges.

Purchase Discounts As noted in Chapter 5, companies that sell goods on credit often offer their customers sales discounts to encourage prompt payment. From the viewpoint of the customer, such price reductions are called **purchase discounts**. The credit terms specify the amount and timing of payments. For example, credit terms of "2/10, n/30" mean that a 2% discount may be taken on the invoice price if payment is made within 10 days of the invoice date. This reduced payment period is known as the **discount period**. Otherwise, full payment is due within 30 days of the invoice date. If a purchase discount is taken, the purchaser reduces the inventory account for the amount of the discount taken, resulting in the inventory account reflecting the net cost of the purchase.

[2] For a manufacturing company, costs should be accumulated as raw materials inventory until the goods are ready for use in the manufacturing process.

EXHIBIT 6.6

Sample Invoice

Shoes Unlimited INVOICE

We Care About Your Feet

301 College Street
Irvine, California 92612
Phone 800-555-2389 Fax 949-555-2300

INVOICE #256
DATE: Sept. 1, 2013

TO:

J. Parker Jones, Purchasing Manager
Brandon Shoes
879 University Blvd.
Auburn, Alabama 36830

SALESPERSON	P.O. NUMBER	REQUISITIONER	SHIPPED VIA	F.O.B. POINT	TERMS
E. Higgins	4895721	J. Parker Jones	UPS	Shipping Point	2/10, n/30

QUANTITY	DESCRIPTION	UNIT PRICE	TOTAL
100	Model No. 754 Athletic Running Shoe	$100	$10,000
		SUBTOTAL	$10,000
		SHIPPING & HANDLING	150
		TOTAL DUE	$10,150

Generally, all available discounts should be taken. Failure to pay within the discount period is equivalent to paying interest for the use of money and can be quite expensive. For example, failure to take advantage of the 2% discount for credit terms of "2/10, n/30" is equivalent to an annual interest rate of 36.5%![3] Clearly, paying within the discount period is a good cash management policy.

Purchase Returns and Allowances Merchandise is inspected when received and may be tested in various ways before it becomes available for sale. The following issues may result in dissatisfaction with the merchandise:

- The wrong merchandise was delivered.
- The merchandise did not conform to specification.
- The merchandise was damaged or defective.
- The merchandise arrived too late at its destination.

[3] This implied interest rate is computed as [365 days ÷ (30 days – 10 days)] × 2%. Notice that this formula uses a 20-day interest period computed as the days until final payment is due (30 days) minus the days in the discount period (10 days). This period can be adjusted to fit the specific credit terms of the transaction.

If the purchaser is dissatisfied with the merchandise, it is frequently returned to the seller for credit or for a cash refund. The cost of merchandise returned to suppliers is called a **purchase return**. In some instances, the purchaser may choose to keep the merchandise if the seller is willing to grant a deduction (allowance) from the purchase price. This situation is called a **purchase allowance**. Increases in purchase returns and allowances may signal deteriorating supplier relationships; thus, purchase returns are monitored very closely by purchasing managers. Because inventory was increased when the purchase was initially made, a purchase return or allowance is recorded by decreasing inventory.

Transportation Costs Transportation, or freight, costs are expenditures made to move the inventory from the seller's location to the purchaser's location. The proper recording of transportation costs depends upon whether the buyer or the seller pays for the transportation. Effectively, this question is the same as asking at what point the ownership of the inventory transfers from the seller to the buyer. The point at which ownership, or title, of the inventory changes hands depends on the shipping terms of the contract. The shipping terms can be either F.O.B. (free on board) shipping point or F.O.B. destination as illustrated in Exhibit 6.7.

EXHIBIT 6.7

Shipping Terms

F.O.B. Shipping Point
- Ownership passes from the seller to the buyer when the goods are shipped.
- Buyer usually pays freight costs.
- Seller recognizes revenue at shipment.

F.O.B. Destination
- Ownership passes from the seller to the buyer when the goods are received.
- Seller usually pays freight costs.
- Seller recognizes revenue at delivery.

- ***F.O.B. shipping point***: If the shipping terms are **F.O.B. shipping point**, ownership of the inventory passes from the seller to the buyer at the shipping point. Under F.O.B. shipping point terms, the buyer normally pays the transportation costs, commonly termed **freight-in**. These costs are considered part of the total cost of purchases and the inventory account is increased. The seller would normally recognize revenue at the time of the shipment.
- ***F.O.B. destination:*** When the shipping terms are **F.O.B. destination**, ownership of the inventory passes when the goods are delivered to the buyer. Under F.O.B. destination shipping terms, the seller is usually responsible for paying the transportation costs, commonly termed **freight-out**. In this case, the transportation costs are not considered part of inventory; instead, the seller will expense these costs as a selling expense on the income statement. Revenue is not normally recognized until delivery of the goods has occurred.

Consigned Goods Sometimes goods owned by one party are held and offered for sale by another. This arrangement is called a **consignment**. In a consignment, the seller (or *consignee*) earns a fee when the consigned goods are sold, but the original owner (or *consignor*) retains ownership of the goods. Manufacturers often use consignments to encourage large retailers, such as **Wal-Mart** and **Target**, to offer their products for sale. Retailers find these arrangements attractive because it enables them to reduce their investment in inventory. In consignment arrangements, the goods are not included in the seller's inventory.

ETHICAL DECISIONS The proper determination of whether goods should or should not be considered part of the seller's inventory has created an ethical dilemma for some companies. With shipping terms of F.O.B. shipping point, managers may attempt to encourage customers to take delivery of more goods than are currently needed since such goods would generate revenue when the inventory is shipped. This practice, termed *channel stuffing,* effectively steals sales from the next period and distorts the results of the company's operations. The Securities and Exchange Commission (SEC) has closely examined transactions that were thought to be channel stuffing. For example, **Coca-Cola** recently paid $137.5 million due to channel stuffing allegations that allowed it to report artificially higher sales volumes to maintain a higher stock price. In addition, **Bristol-Myers Squibb** paid $150 million to settle allegations that included channel stuffing. •

Recording Purchase Transactions To summarize, the purchase price of inventory includes any cost of bringing the goods to a salable condition and location. Therefore, the inventory account is increased for the invoice price of a purchase as well as any transportation costs paid for by the buyer. Any purchase discounts, returns, or allowances reduce the inventory account. Cornerstone 6.2 illustrates the journal entries required to record purchases of merchandise inventory.

concept Q&A

The purchase transactions that affect inventory seem complicated. Why go to all that trouble and effort when the periodic inventory system could be used?

Answer:

A perpetual inventory system requires a number of entries that directly affect inventory. While this system is certainly more complex than a periodic inventory system, the numerous entries provide management with up-to-date information that allows them to better manage and control their inventory.

Recording Purchase Transactions in a Perpetual Inventory System

6.2

Why:

The cost of inventory includes the purchase price of the merchandise plus any cost of bringing the goods to a salable condition and location.

Information:

On September 1, Brandon Shoes purchased 50 pairs of hiking boots for $3,750 cash (or $75 a pair) and paid $150 of transportation costs. Also, on September 1, Brandon purchased 100 pairs of running shoes for $10,000; however, the seller paid the transportation costs of $300. The running shoes were purchased on credit with terms of 2/10, n/30. Brandon paid for one-half ($5,000) of the running shoes on September 10, within the discount period. After inspection, Brandon determined that running shoes costing $750 were defective and returned them on September 25. The remaining running shoes (cost of $4,250) were paid for on September 30.

Required:

Prepare the journal entries necessary to record the September transactions for Brandon Shoes.

(Continued)

CORNERSTONE **6.2** *(Continued)*

Solution:

Assets = Liabilities + Stockholders' Equity	Date		Account and Explanation	Debit	Credit
Assets +3,750 −3,750	Sept.	1	Inventory	3,750	
			Cash		3,750
			(Purchased inventory for cash)		
Assets +150 −150		1	Inventory	150	
			Cash		150
			(Recorded payment of freight costs)		
Assets +10,000; Liabilities +10,000		1	Inventory	10,000	
			Accounts Payable		10,000
			(Purchased inventory on credit)		
Assets −4,900 −100; Liabilities −5,000		10	Accounts Payable	5,000	
			Cash		4,900
			Inventory ($5,000 × 2%)		100
			(Recorded payment within the discount period)		
Assets −750; Liabilities −750		25	Accounts Payable	750	
			Inventory		750
			(Returned defective running shoes)		
Assets −4,250; Liabilities −4,250		30	Accounts Payable	4,250	
			Cash		4,250
			(Recorded payment outside the discount period)		

Note that the purchase of the hiking boots in Cornerstone 6.2 included the $150 of transportation costs (freight-in) because Brandon paid the freight. However, the purchase of the running shoes did not include freight costs because it was paid by the seller.

These journal entries illustrate that, under a perpetual inventory system, inventory is constantly updated with each purchase so that the net effect of purchases is reflected in the inventory account. The computation of net purchases for Brandon Shoes is summarized in Exhibit 6.8. Although the original invoice price was $13,750, the consideration of purchase discounts, returns, and transportation charges resulted in a much different value in the inventory account.

EXHIBIT 6.8

Calculation of Net Purchases

Invoice price of purchase	$13,750
Less: Purchase discounts	(100)
Purchase returns and allowances	(750)
Add: Transportation costs (freight-in)	150
Net cost of purchases	$13,050

Accounting for Sales of Inventory

In addition to purchase transactions, merchandising companies must also account for the inventory effects of sales and sales returns. Because a perpetual inventory system is being used, the Merchandise Inventory account is also affected.

IFRS

The purchase and sale of inventory is generally the same under IFRS as under U.S. GAAP.

Sales As discussed in Chapter 5, companies recognize sales revenue when it is earned and the collection of cash is reasonably assured. The recording of sales revenue involves two journal entries:

- In the first journal entry, sales revenue is recognized.
- The second journal entry recognizes, consistent with the matching principle, the cost of the goods that are sold. It also reduces the inventory account so that the perpetual inventory system will reflect an up-to-date balance for inventory.

Sales Returns and Allowances If a customer returns an item for some reason, the company will make an adjustment to sales as shown in Chapter 5. In addition, the company must make a second entry to decrease cost of goods sold and increase inventory to reflect the return of the merchandise.

Recording Inventory Effects of Sales Transactions The use of a perpetual inventory system requires that two journal entries be made for both sales and sales return transactions. These journal entries are illustrated in Cornerstone 6.3.

concept Q&A

Instead of making two entries to record a sale under a perpetual system, why not just make one entry for the net amount? Wouldn't gross margin be the same?

Answer:

A system could be developed that combines the two entries necessary to record a sale of inventory under a perpetual system; however, important information would be lost. If an entry were made to an account such as "Gross Margin" for the difference between sales revenue and cost of goods sold, no information would be provided on the gross amount of revenues or cost of goods sold. This loss of information would be inconsistent with the purpose of financial reporting.

Recording Sales Transactions in a Perpetual Inventory System

CORNERSTONE 6.3

Why:

The sale or return of inventory in a perpetual system requires two journal entries—one to record the revenue portion of the transaction and one to record the expense (and inventory) portion of the transaction.

Information:

On August 1, Brandon Shoes sold 100 pairs of football cleats to the local college football team for $12,000 cash (each pair of cleats was sold for $120 per pair). Brandon paid $10,000 (or $100 per pair) for the cleats from its supplier. On August 15, the local college football team returned 10 pairs of cleats for a cash refund of $1,200.

Required:

1. Prepare the journal entries to record the sale of the football cleats.
2. Prepare the journal entries to record the return of the football cleats.

(Continued)

CORNERSTONE 6.3 *(Continued)*

Solution:

Assets = Liabilities + Stockholders' Equity	Date		Account and Explanation	Debit	Credit
Assets +12,000 = Liabilities + Stockholders' Equity +12,000	1. Aug.	1	Cash	12,000	
			Sales Revenue		12,000
			(Recorded sale to customer)		
Assets −10,000 = Liabilities + Stockholders' Equity −10,000		1	Cost of Goods Sold	10,000	
			Inventory		10,000
			(Recorded cost of merchandise sold)		
Assets −1,200 = Liabilities + Stockholders' Equity −1,200	2.	15	Sales Returns and Allowances	1,200	
			Cash		1,200
			(Recorded return of merchandise)		
Assets +1,000 = Liabilities + Stockholders' Equity +1,000		15	Inventory	1,000	
			Cost of Goods Sold		1,000
			(Recorded cost of merchandise returned)		

In each of the transactions in Cornerstone 6.3, the external selling price of $120 was recorded as Sales Revenue. The cost of goods sold (or inventory) portion of the transaction was recorded at the cost to Brandon Shoes of $100. Therefore, for each pair of shoes sold, Brandon Shoes made a gross margin of $20 ($120 – $100). The total cost of goods sold recognized by Brandon Shoes is $9,000 ($10,000 – $1,000). *In dealing with sales to customers, it is important to remember to record revenues at the selling price and to record expenses (and inventory) at cost.*

YOU DECIDE Impact of Shipping Terms on Revenue Recognition

You are a CPA auditing the financial statements of Henderson Electronics, a computer retailer located in Duluth, Georgia. Henderson's policy is to record a sales transaction when the merchandise is shipped to customers (F.O.B. shipping point). During the audit, you notice that 50 computers were sold to the Itasca County School District near the end of the year. Further investigation reveals that these 50 computers are still in Henderson's warehouse. James Henderson, the owner, tells you that the school district wanted to purchase the computers with funds from the district's current fiscal year, but couldn't take delivery because the computer labs at the various schools were under renovation. Therefore, Henderson billed the district and recorded a credit sale in the current year.

Was this transaction accounted for properly?

Because the company has an F.O.B. shipping point policy and the inventory had not been delivered, the computers are not considered sold in the current year. Therefore, the recording of the credit sale should not have been made, and the inventory should be included in Henderson's ending inventory. This type of transaction is commonly referred to as a "bill and hold" sale. Although it may be perfectly legal, such transactions have come under scrutiny by the SEC as a means for companies to improperly inflate sales revenue and should be carefully scrutinized.

The proper determination of whether goods should or should not be included in inventory impacts both the balance sheet and the income statement.

COSTING INVENTORY

OBJECTIVE 3

Apply the four inventory costing methods to compute ending inventory and cost of goods sold under a perpetual inventory system.

A key feature of the cost of goods sold model illustrated in Cornerstone 6.1 (p. 293) is that the determination of cost of goods sold requires an allocation of the cost of goods available for sale between ending inventory and cost of goods sold. If the prices paid for goods are constant over time, this allocation is easy to compute—just multiply the cost per unit times the number of units on hand at year end (to determine the cost of ending inventory) or times the number of units sold (to determine the cost of goods sold). For example, if Speigel Company began operations by purchasing 1,000 units of a single product for $24 each, total goods available for sale would be $24,000, calculated as:

$$\text{Inventory Available for Sale} \times \text{Cost per Unit} = \text{Goods Available for Sale}$$
$$1{,}000 \text{ units} \times \$24 = \$24{,}000$$

If 800 units were sold during the period, the cost of the remaining 200-unit ending inventory is $4,800:

$$\text{Ending Inventory} \times \text{Cost per Unit} = \text{Cost of Ending Inventory}$$
$$\$24 \times 200 \text{ units} = \$4{,}800$$

Cost of goods sold is $19,200, calculated as:

$$\text{Units Sold} \times \text{Cost per Unit} = \text{Cost of Goods Sold}$$
$$800 \times \$24 = \$19{,}200$$

It makes no difference which of the 1,000 units remain in ending inventory because all units have the same cost ($24).

On the other hand, if the price paid for a good changes over time, the cost of goods available for sale may include units with different costs per unit. In such cases, the question arises: Which prices should be assigned to the units sold and which assigned to the units in ending inventory? For example, assume that Speigel Company purchased the same total of 1,000 units during a period at different prices:

Jan. 3	300 units purchased at $22 per unit	=	$ 6,600
Jan. 15	400 units purchased at $24 per unit	=	9,600
Jan. 24	300 units purchased at $26 per unit	=	7,800
	Cost of goods available for sale		$24,000

While the cost of goods available for sale is the same ($24,000), the cost of the 200-unit ending inventory depends on which goods remain in ending inventory. As illustrated by the cost of goods sold model discussed earlier, the cost assigned to ending inventory also affects the value of cost of goods sold.

	If ending inventory is made up of $22 per unit goods	**If ending inventory is made up of $26 per unit goods**
Ending inventory	$4,400	$5,200
	(200 units × $22/unit)	(200 units × $26/unit)
Cost of goods sold	$19,600	$18,800
	($24,000 – $4,400)	($24,000 – $5,200)

The determination of the value of ending inventory and cost of goods sold depends on management's choice of inventory system (perpetual or periodic) and method of allocating inventory costs.

Inventory Costing Methods

The inventory system (perpetual or periodic) determines *when* cost of goods sold is calculated—for every sales transaction or at the end of the period. An *inventory costing method* determines how costs are allocated to cost of goods sold and ending inventory. Although the assumption about how inventory costs flow could take many different forms, accountants typically use one of four inventory costing methods:

- specific identification
- first-in, first-out (FIFO)
- last-in, first-out (LIFO)
- average cost

Each of these four costing methods represents a different procedure for allocating the cost of goods available for sale between ending inventory and cost of goods sold. Only the specific identification method allocates the cost of purchases according to the *physical flow* of specific units through inventory. That is, specific identification is based on a *flow of goods* principle. In contrast, the other three methods—FIFO, LIFO, and average cost—are based on a *flow of cost* principle. When the FIFO, LIFO, or average cost methods are used, the physical flow of goods into inventory and out to the customers is generally unrelated to the flow of unit costs. We make this point here so that you will not be confused in thinking that a cost flow assumption describes the physical flow of goods in a company. *Generally accepted accounting principles do not require that the cost flow assumption be consistent with the physical flow of goods.*

Companies disclose their choice of inventory methods in a note to the financial statements. The 2012 annual report of **Wal-Mart** includes the following statement:

Notes to Consolidated Financial Statements

1. Summary of Significant Accounting Policies

Inventories.

The Company values inventories at the lower of cost or market as determined primarily by the retail method of accounting, using the last-in, first-out ("LIFO") method for substantially all of the Wal-Mart U.S. segment's merchandise inventories. The Sam's Club segment's merchandise is valued based on the weighted average cost using the LIFO method. Inventories for the Wal-Mart International operations are primarily valued by the retail method of accounting and are stated using the first-in, first-out ("FIFO") method. At January 31, 2012 and 2011, the Company's inventories valued at LIFO approximate those inventories as if they were valued at FIFO.

Source: Wal-Mart Stores, Inc. 2012 10K

Like many companies, **Wal-Mart** uses more than one method in determining the total cost of inventory. In general, LIFO and FIFO are the most widely used methods. Exhibit 6.9 shows the percentage of companies using each inventory costing method.

EXHIBIT 6.9

Use of Inventory Costing Methods

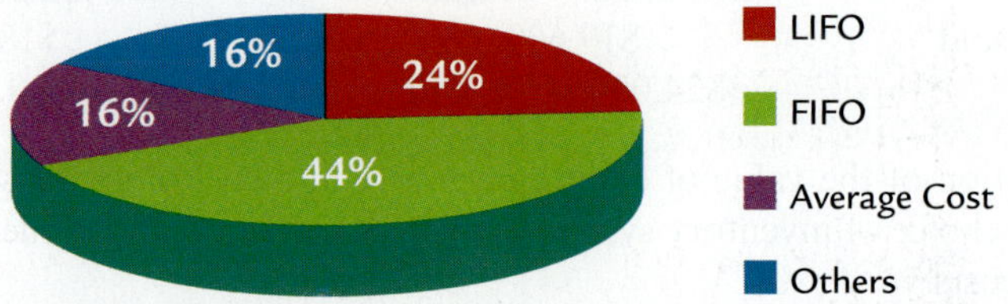

Source: AICPA, *Accounting Trends & Techniques*, 65th edition, 2011, par. 2.48, p. 174.

With the exception of specific identification, the inventory costing methods allocate cost of goods available for sale between ending inventory and cost of goods sold using the following process.

Step 1. Calculate the cost of goods available for sale *immediately prior* to any sale transaction.
Step 2. Apply the inventory costing method to determine ending inventory and cost of goods sold.
Step 3. Repeat Steps 1 and 2 for all inventory transactions during the period. The sum of the cost of goods sold computed in Step 2 is the cost of goods sold for the period. Ending inventory is the amount computed during the final application of Step 2 for the period.

To understand how inventory costing systems allocate costs (Step 2), it is useful to think of inventory as if it were a stack of separate layers, with each stack distinguished by the purchase price. Each time a purchase is made at a unit cost different from that of a previous purchase, a new layer of inventory cost is added to the stack. As inventory is sold, it is removed from the stack according to the cost flow assumption used. This process is illustrated in Exhibit 6.10 for the LIFO and FIFO methods.

EXHIBIT 6.10

Allocation of Inventory Costs

Specific Identification

The **specific identification method** determines the cost of ending inventory and the cost of goods sold based on the identification of the *actual* units sold and in inventory. This method does not require an assumption about the flow of costs but assigns cost based on the specific flow of inventory. It requires that detailed records of each purchase and sale be maintained so that a company knows exactly which items were sold and the cost of those items. Historically, this method was practical only for high-cost items with unique identifiers (e.g., serial numbers) that were sold in low numbers—for example, automobiles. With the introduction of bar coding, electronic scanners, and radio frequency identification, this method has become easier to implement, but its application is still relatively rare. The specific identification method is illustrated in Cornerstone 6.4.

Applying the Specific Identification Method

CORNERSTONE 6.4

Why:

Cost of goods sold and ending inventory are determined based on the identification of the actual units sold and in inventory.

Information:

Tampico Beachwear, a retail store specializing in beach apparel, has the following information related to purchases and sales of one of its more popular brand of shoes. (Each inventory layer is a different color.)

(Continued)

CORNERSTONE
6.4
(Continued)

Date		Description	Units Purchased at Cost	Units Sold at Retail
Oct.	1	Beg. inventory	300 units @ $16 = $ 4,800	
	3	Purchase 1	600 units @ $18 = $10,800	
	8	Sale 1		800 units @ $30
	15	Purchase 2	250 units @ $20 = $ 5,000	
	20	Purchase 3	150 units @ $22 = $ 3,300	
	25	Sale 2		300 units @ $30
			Goods available for sale: 1,300 units = $23,900	Sales: 1,100 units = $33,000

The following is a schedule of those units that were sold during the month and those that remain in ending inventory at the end of the month:

Description	Units Sold	Units in Ending Inventory
Beginning inventory	300	—
Purchase 1	550	50
Purchase 2	170	80
Purchase 3	80	70
Total	1,100	200

Required:

1. Compute the cost of ending inventory at October 31 under the specific identification method.
2. Compute the cost of goods sold at October 31 under the specific identification method.

Solution:

1. Ending inventory is:

50 units @ $18	$ 900
80 units @ $20	1,600
70 units @ $22	1,540
200 units	$4,040

2. Cost of goods sold is:

300 units @ $16	$ 4,800
550 units @ $18	9,900
170 units @ $20	3,400
80 units @ $22	1,760
1,100 units	$19,860

Three items in Cornerstone 6.4 are of interest.

- *Cost of Goods Available for Sale:* The sum of ending inventory ($4,040) and cost of goods sold ($19,860) equals cost of goods available for sale ($23,900). The specific identification method, like all inventory costing methods, allocates the cost of goods available for sale between ending inventory and cost of goods sold.

- *Cost of Goods Sold:* Because there are usually far fewer units in ending inventory than in cost of goods sold, it is often easier to compute the cost of ending inventory and then find the cost of goods sold by subtracting ending inventory from cost of goods available for sale ($23,900 – $4,040 = $19,860).
- *Financial Statement Effects:* The determination of inventory cost affects both the balance sheet and the income statement. The amount assigned to ending inventory will appear on the balance sheet. The amount assigned to cost of goods sold appears on the income statement and is used in the calculation of a company's gross margin.

First-In, First-Out (FIFO)

The **first-in, first-out (FIFO) method** is based on the assumption that costs move through inventory in an unbroken stream, with the costs entering and leaving the inventory in the same order. In other words, *the earliest purchases (the first in) are assumed to be the first sold (the first out), and the more recent purchases are in ending inventory.* Every time inventory is sold, the cost of the earliest (oldest) purchases that make up cost of goods available for sale is allocated to cost of goods sold, and the cost of the most recent purchases is allocated to ending inventory. In many instances, this cost flow assumption is an accurate representation of the physical flow of goods. **Hewlett-Packard** and restaurant companies such as **Ruby Tuesday** and **Yum Brands** all use FIFO. In addition, grocery stores such as **Publix** use FIFO for their perishable items. Cornerstone 6.5 illustrates the application of the FIFO method.

Applying the FIFO Inventory Costing Method

CORNERSTONE 6.5

Why:

The cost of the earliest purchases that make up cost of goods available for sale is allocated to cost of goods sold, and the cost of the most recent purchases is allocated to ending inventory.

Information:

Tampico Beachwear, a retail store specializing in beach apparel, has the following information related to purchases and sales of one of its more popular brand of shoes. (Each inventory layer is a different color.)

Date		Description	Units Purchased at Cost	Units Sold at Retail
Oct.	1	Beginning inventory	300 units @ $16 = $ 4,800	
	3	Purchase 1	600 units @ $18 = $10,800	
	8	Sale 1		800 units @ $30
	15	Purchase 2	250 units @ $20 = $ 5,000	
	20	Purchase 3	150 units @ $22 = $ 3,300	
	25	Sale 2		300 units @ $30
			Goods available for sale: 1,300 units = $23,900	Sales: 1,100 units = $33,000

Required:

Compute the cost of ending inventory and the cost of goods sold at October 31 using the FIFO method.

(Continued)

CORNERSTONE 6.5 (Continued)

Solution:

Step 1: Compute the cost of goods available for sale immediately prior to the first sale. This produces an inventory balance of $15,600 ($4,800 + $10,800). Notice that this inventory balance is made up of two layers—a $16 layer and an $18 layer.

Step 2: Apply FIFO to determine ending inventory and cost of goods sold. The cost of goods available for sale is allocated between inventory (the most recent purchases) and cost of goods sold (the earliest purchases).

Date	Description	Cost of Goods Sold		Inventory Balance	
Oct. 1	Beginning inventory			300 × $16	= $ 4,800
3	Purchase 1 (600 @ $18)			300 × $16 = $ 4,800 600 × $18 = $10,800	= $15,600
8	Sale 1 (800 @ $30)	300 × $16 = $4,800 500 × $18 = $9,000	= $13,800	100 × $18	= $ 1,800

Step 3: Repeat Steps 1 and 2 for the remaining inventory transactions during the period.

Date	Description	Cost of Goods Sold		Inventory Balance	
Oct. 8	Inventory on hand			100 × $18	= $ 1,800
15	Purchase 2 (250 @ $20)			100 × $18 = $1,800 250 × $20 = $5,000	= $ 6,800
20	Purchase 3 (150 @ $22)			100 × $18 = $1,800 250 × $20 = $5,000 150 × $22 = $3,300	= $10,100
25	Sale 2 (300 @ $30)	100 × $18 = $1,800 200 × $20 = $4,000	= $ 5,800	50 × $20 = $1,000 150 × $22 = $3,300	= $ 4,300
		Total	$ 19,600		

The application of FIFO in Cornerstone 6.5 resulted in the following:

- Ending inventory reported on the balance sheet is $4,300.
- Cost of goods sold reported on the income statement is $19,600 ($13,800 + $5,800).

Because the sum of ending inventory and cost of goods sold ($4,300 + $19,600) equals cost of goods available for sale ($23,900), Tampico could have also calculated cost of goods sold as the difference between cost of goods available for sale and ending inventory ($23,900 – $4,300).

Last-In, First-Out (LIFO)

IFRS
IFRS do not allow the use of LIFO.

The **last-in, first-out (LIFO) method** allocates the cost of goods available for sale between ending inventory and cost of goods sold based on the assumption that the most recent purchases (the last in) are the first to be sold (the first out). Under the LIFO method, *the most recent purchases (newest costs) are allocated to the cost of goods sold and the earliest purchases (oldest costs) are allocated to inventory.* Except for companies that stockpile inventory (e.g., piles of coal, stacks of hay, stacks of rock), this cost flow assumption rarely coincides with the actual physical flow of inventory. Companies such as **General Mills**, **Target**, and **Macy's** all use LIFO. Cornerstone 6.6 illustrates the application of the LIFO method.

Applying the LIFO Inventory Costing Method

CORNERSTONE 6.6

Why:

The cost of the most recent purchases that make up cost of goods available for sale is allocated to cost of goods sold, and the cost of the earliest purchases is allocated to ending inventory.

Information:

Tampico Beachwear, a retail store specializing in beach apparel, has the following information related to purchases and sales of one of its more popular brand of shoes. (Each inventory layer is a different color.)

Date		Description	Units Purchased at Cost	Units Sold at Retail
Oct.	1	Beginning inventory	300 units @ $16 = $ 4,800	
	3	Purchase 1	600 units @ $18 = $10,800	
	8	Sale 1		800 units @ $30
	15	Purchase 2	250 units @ $20 = $ 5,000	
	20	Purchase 3	150 units @ $22 = $ 3,300	
	25	Sale 2		300 units @ $30
			Goods available for sale: 1,300 units = $23,900	Sales: 1,100 units = $33,000

Required:

Compute the cost of ending inventory and the cost of goods sold at October 31 using the LIFO method.

Solution:

Step 1: Compute the cost of goods available for sale immediately *prior* to the first sale. This produces an inventory balance of $15,600 ($4,800 + $10,800). Notice that this inventory balance is made up of two layers—a $16 layer and an $18 layer.

Step 2: Apply LIFO to determine ending inventory and cost of goods sold. The cost of goods available for sale is allocated between inventory (the earliest purchases) and cost of goods sold (the most recent purchases).

Date		Description	Cost of Goods Sold		Inventory Balance	
Oct.	1	Beginning inventory			300 × $16	= $ 4,800
	3	Purchase 1 (600 @ $18)			300 × $16 = $ 4,800 600 × $18 = $10,800	= $15,600
	8	Sale 1 (800 @ $30)	600 × $18 = $10,800 200 × $16 = $ 3,200	= **$14,000**	100 × $16	= $ 1,600

Step 3: Repeat Steps 1 and 2 for the remaining inventory transactions during the period.

Date		Description	Cost of Goods Sold		Inventory Balance	
Oct.	8	Inventory on hand			100 × $16	= $1,600
	15	Purchase 2 (250 @ $20)			100×$16 = $1,600 250×$20 = $5,000	= $6,600
	20	Purchase 3 (150 @ $22)			100 × $16 = $1,600 250 × $20 = $5,000 150 × $22 = $3,300	= $9,900
	25	Sale 2 (300 @ $30)	150 × $22 = $3,300 150 × $20 = $3,000	= $ 6,300	100 × $16 = $1,600 100 × $20 = $2,000	= $3,600
			Total	= **$20,300**		

The application of LIFO in Cornerstone 6.6 resulted in the following:

- Ending inventory reported on the balance sheet is $3,600.
- Cost of goods sold reported on the income statement is $20,300, the sum of cost of goods sold during the period ($14,000 + $6,300).

Because the sum of ending inventory and cost of goods sold ($3,600 + $20,300) equals cost of goods available for sale ($23,900), Tampico could have also calculated cost of goods sold as the difference between cost of goods available for sale and ending inventory ($23,900 − $3,600).

Average Cost

The **average cost method** allocates the cost of goods available for sale between ending inventory and cost of goods sold based on a weighted average cost per unit. This weighted average cost per unit is calculated after each purchase of inventory as:

$$\text{Weighted Average Cost per Unit} = \frac{\text{Cost of Goods Available for Sale}}{\text{Units Available for Sale}}$$

Because a new average is computed after each purchase, this method is often called the moving-average method. This weighted average cost per unit is then used to calculate ending inventory and cost of goods sold as:

$$\text{Ending Inventory} = \text{Units on Hand} \times \text{Weighted Average Cost per Unit}$$
$$\text{Cost of Goods Sold} = \text{Units Sold} \times \text{Weighted Average Cost per Unit}$$

The average cost method is used by companies such as **Office Depot** and **OfficeMax**. Cornerstone 6.7 illustrates the application of the average cost method.

CORNERSTONE 6.7

Applying the Average Cost Inventory Costing Method

Why:

The cost of goods available for sale is allocated between ending inventory and cost of goods sold based on a weighted average cost of the goods available for sale.

Information:

Tampico Beachwear, a retail store specializing in beach apparel, has the following information related to purchases and sales of one of its more popular brand of shoes. (Each inventory layer is a different color.)

Date		Description	Units Purchased at Cost	Units Sold at Retail
Oct.	1	Beginning inventory	300 units @ $16 = $ 4,800	
	3	Purchase 1	600 units @ $18 = $10,800	
	8	Sale 1		800 units @ $30
	15	Purchase 2	250 units @ $20 = $ 5,000	
	20	Purchase 3	150 units @ $22 = $ 3,300	
	25	Sale 2		300 units @ $30
			Goods available for sale: 1,300 units = $23,900	Sales: 1,100 units = $33,000

(*Continued*)

CORNERSTONE
6.7
(Continued)

Required:

Compute the cost of ending inventory and the cost of goods sold at October 31 using the average cost method. (*Note:* Use four decimal places for per unit calculations and round all other numbers to the nearest dollar.)

Solution:

Step 1: Compute the cost of goods available for sale immediately *prior* to the first sale. This produces an inventory balance of $15,600 ($4,800 + $10,800) and inventory units of 900 (300 + 600).

Step 2: Apply the average cost method to determine ending inventory and cost of goods sold. The cost of goods available for sale is allocated between inventory and cost of goods sold using a weighted average cost per unit, calculated as:

$$\text{Weighted Average Cost per Unit} = \frac{\text{Cost of Goods Available for Sale}}{\text{Units Available for Sale}} = \frac{\$15{,}600}{900\text{ units}} = \$17.3333\text{ per unit}$$

Date	Description	Cost of Goods Sold	Inventory Balance	
Oct. 1	Beginning inventory		300 × $16	= $ 4,800 ($16/unit)
3	Purchase 1 (600 @ $18)		300 × $16 = $ 4,800 600 × $18 = $10,800	= $15,600 ($17.3333/unit)[a]
8	Sale 1 (800 @ $30)	800 × $17.3333 = $13,867	100 × $17.3333	= $ 1,733

[a] $15,600 ÷ 900 units = $17.3333/unit

Step 3: Repeat Steps 1 and 2 for the remaining inventory transactions during the period.

Date	Description	Cost of Goods Sold	Inventory Balance	
Oct. 8	Inventory on hand		100 × $17.3333	= $ 1,733 ($17.3333/unit)[a]
15	Purchase 2 (250 @ $20)		100 × $17.3333 = $1,733 250 × $20.00 = $5,000	= $ 6,733 ($19.2371/unit)[b]
20	Purchase 3 (150 @ $22)		350 × $19.2371 = $6,733 150 × $22.00 = $3,300	= $10,033 ($20.0660/unit)[c]
25	Sale 2 (300 @ $30)	300 × $20.0660 = $ 6,020	200 × $20.0660	= $ 4,013
		Total = $19,887		

[b] $6,733 ÷ 350 units = $19.2371/unit
[c] $10,033 ÷ 500 units = $20.0660/unit

The application of the average cost method in Cornerstone 6.7 results in the following:

- Ending inventory reported on the balance sheet is $4,013.
- Cost of goods sold reported on the income statement is $19,887, the sum of cost of goods sold during the period ($13,867 + $6,020).

Because the sum of ending inventory and cost of goods sold ($4,013 + $19,887) equals cost of goods available for sale ($23,900), Tampico could have also calculated cost of goods sold as the difference between cost of goods available for sale and ending inventory ($23,900 – $4,013).

The average cost method results in an allocation to ending inventory and cost of goods sold that is somewhere between the allocations produced by FIFO and LIFO.

OBJECTIVE 4

Analyze the financial reporting and tax effects of the various inventory costing methods.

ANALYSIS OF INVENTORY COSTING METHODS

Companies are free to choose among the four inventory costing methods, and the inventory accounting policy decisions that are made can have major effects on the financial statements. Proper management of these decisions, within the bounds of generally accepted accounting principles and good business ethics, can also affect the timing of income tax payments and the judgments of creditors, stockholders, and others. Therefore, it is important to understand the consequences of these accounting choices.

concept Q&A

Why doesn't the FASB simply mandate the most conceptually correct inventory costing method instead of giving companies a choice between alternative methods?

Answer:

All inventory costing methods provide an allocation of the total dollar amount of goods available for sale between ending inventory and cost of goods sold. No one cost method is conceptually superior to any other. For example, LIFO actually achieves a better matching of current costs with current revenues on the income statement; however, the resulting balance sheet valuation can be quite misleading about the current market value of inventory on the balance sheet. Companies make the choice between inventory methods for a variety of reasons unique to their own situation. Some companies will adopt LIFO for the tax benefits, while others will adopt FIFO because they want to report higher profits or simply because FIFO is less expensive to implement.

Illustrating Relationships: Financial Statement Effects of Alternative Costing Methods

Financial statement analysts frequently ask the hypothetical question, "How much would inventory and income have been if a different costing method had been used?" If the prices paid for purchased inventory are stable, all inventory costing methods will yield the same amounts for ending inventory and cost of goods sold. However, when purchase prices vary, the FIFO, LIFO and average cost methods will produce different amounts for ending inventory, cost of goods sold and, therefore, income. To properly analyze financial statements, it is necessary to understand the impact of changing prices on inventories and income.

To illustrate, consider the inventory data for Tampico Beachwear, which had revenues for the period of $33,000 (1,100 units sold × $30 per unit) and operating expenses of $4,000 (assumed amount). This information and the related FIFO, LIFO, and average cost inventory calculations in Cornerstones 6.5 through 6.7 produced the income statement amounts shown in Exhibit 6.11.

Notice that sales, purchases, and cost of goods available for sale are the same for each method. However the changing purchase prices of each inventory layer result in different amounts for cost of goods sold, gross margin, and net income.

When purchase prices are rising, as they are in our example (remember that shoes went from $16 to $18 to $20 to $22), the FIFO method produces the highest cost for ending inventory, the lowest cost of goods sold, and,

EXHIBIT 6.11

Financial Statement Effects of Alternative Inventory Costing Methods

Tampico Beachwear
Condensed Income Statements
For the month ending October 31

	FIFO		LIFO		Average Cost	
Sales		$33,000		$33,000		$33,000
Beginning inventory	$ 4,800		$ 4,800		$ 4,800	
Add: Purchases	19,100		19,100		19,100	
Cost of goods available for sale	$23,900		$23,900		$23,900	
Less: Ending inventory	(4,300)		(3,600)		(4,013)	
Cost of goods sold		19,600		20,300		19,887
Gross margin		$13,400		$12,700		$13,113
Operating expenses (given)		4,000		4,000		4,000
Income before taxes		$ 9,400		$ 8,700		$ 9,113
Income tax expense (30%)		2,820		2,610		2,734
Net income		$ 6,580		$ 6,090		$ 6,379

therefore, the highest gross margin (and net income) of the three methods. In contrast, the LIFO method produced the lowest cost for ending inventory, the highest cost of goods sold, and, therefore, the lowest gross margin (and net income) of the three methods. The average cost method produced amounts for inventory, cost of goods sold, and net income that fell between the FIFO and LIFO extremes. *When purchase prices are falling,* the situation is reversed. Exhibit 6.12 summarizes these relationships.

EXHIBIT 6.12

Financial Statement Effects of Alternative Inventory Costing Methods

↑ Rising Purchase Prices	↓ Falling Purchase Prices
FIFO produces:	FIFO produces:
• Highest ending inventory	• Lowest ending inventory
• Lowest cost of goods sold	• Highest cost of goods sold
• Highest income	• Lowest income
LIFO produces:	LIFO produces:
• Lowest ending inventory	• Highest ending inventory
• Highest cost of goods sold	• Lowest cost of goods sold
• Lowest income	• Highest income

During periods of rising prices, we expect LIFO companies to report lower amounts for inventory cost and higher amounts for cost of goods sold than comparable FIFO companies. And during periods of falling prices, we expect LIFO companies to report higher amounts of inventory cost and lower amounts for cost of goods sold than com parable FIFO companies. Due to these effects, it can be argued that:

- LIFO results in the more realistic amount for income because it matches the most current costs, which are closer to the current market value, against revenue.
- FIFO results in the more realistic amount for inventory because it reports the most current costs, which are closer to the current market value, on the balance sheet.

Income Tax Effects of Alternative Costing Methods

We have seen that in periods of rising prices, LIFO allocates the newest—and therefore highest—inventory purchase prices to cost of goods sold, resulting in a lower gross mar gin and lower net income. Therefore, in periods of rising prices, companies may choose LIFO because it produces the lowest current taxable income and the lowest current income tax payment. In Exhibit 6.11, LIFO produced income tax expense of $2,610 compared to income tax expense of $2,820 if FIFO had been used.

Of course, in the long run, all inventory costs will find their way to cost of goods sold and the income statement. Therefore, choosing LIFO to minimize current taxes does not avoid the payment of taxes; it merely postpones it, temporarily reducing the company's capital requirements for a period of time. The federal income tax code requires businesses that use LIFO for tax purposes to use LIFO for financial reporting purposes as well. This is known as the LIFO conformity rule.

ETHICAL DECISIONS When managers select an inventory costing method, it may not always be in the best interest of the company. For example, in a period of rising prices, the owners of the company may prefer that a company use LIFO in order to reduce the taxes that must be paid. However, many management bonus plans are based on net income, and the use of FIFO would result in larger bonuses. If managers let the choice of inventory costing method be guided solely by its effect on their compensation, the ethics of their behavior can certainly be questioned. •

Consistency in Application

Companies are free to choose whichever inventory costing method they prefer, regardless of whether the method matches the physical flow of goods. However, once a company adopts a particular costing method for an item, it must continue to use it consistently over time.[4] The consistent application of an accounting principle over time discourages changes in accounting methods from one period to another, even if acceptable alternative methods exist. This enhances the comparability and usefulness of accounting information. A change in accounting method may still be made; however, the effects of the change must be fully disclosed. The consistent application of accounting methods and the required disclosures of any accounting changes permit readers of financial statements to assume that accounting methods do not change over time unless specifically indicated.

YOUDECIDE Choosing Among Inventory Costing Methods

You are the owner and manager of Simply Fresh, a supermarket that specializes in selling fresh, organic food. You know that managing inventory is crucial to the company's success and that generally accepted accounting principles give you the freedom to choose between FIFO, LIFO, and average cost to report inventory and cost of goods sold.

What factors should you consider in selecting among the different inventory costing methods?

Three factors that should be considered are:

- *Actual physical flow of inventory*: Because most companies sell their oldest merchandise first, FIFO will give the closest approximation to the physical flow of inventory. However, GAAP does not require that the choice of inventory costing method be consistent with the physical flow of goods.
- *Financial statement effects*: During periods of rising prices, the use of FIFO will result in the highest cost for ending inventory, the lowest cost of goods sold, and the highest net income. These positive financial results may be desirable to satisfy stockholders who demand higher stock prices or meet lending agreements that are tied to financial performance. In addition, if management's bonus plan is tied to reported income, the use of FIFO may result in higher bonuses for management.
- *Tax benefits*: During periods of rising prices, the use of LIFO will result in lower income and possibly create significant tax savings for the company.

If financial statement users wish to make good decisions, it is important to understand the differences that result from management's choice of inventory method.

OBJECTIVE 5

Apply the lower of cost or market rule to the valuation of inventory.

LOWER OF COST OR MARKET RULE

The inventory accounting procedures described to this point have followed the historical cost principle—inventory is recorded in the firm's records at its historical purchase price (or cost). The price for which inventory items can be sold (their market value) may decline because the goods have become obsolete, have been damaged, or have otherwise diminished in value. For example, clothes that have gone out of style due to changing fashions or seasons have declined in value. Similarly, technology companies experience rapid obsolescence due to quickly changing technologies. In cases where the market value of inventory has dropped below its original cost, generally accepted accounting principles permit a departure from the historical cost concept.

IFRS

In applying the LCM rule, IFRS define market value as net realizable value (selling price minus cost of completion and disposal) instead of replacement cost.

This departure from the historical cost principle is called the **lower of cost or market (LCM) rule**. Under LCM, if the market value of a company's inventory is lower than its cost, the company reduces the amount recorded for inventory to its market value. To apply LCM, a company must first determine the cost of its inventory using one of the

[4] All items of inventory need not be accounted for by the same costing method. Many companies use LIFO for a portion of inventory and FIFO or average cost for another portion of their inventory.

inventory costing methods discussed earlier in the chapter (specific identification, FIFO, LIFO, or average cost). Next, the company will establish the market value of the inventory. Under LCM, market value is defined as current *replacement cost,* the current purchase price for identical goods.[5] Finally, the market value is compared with historical cost (usually on an item-by-item basis), and the lower of market value or historical cost is used as the cost for the inventory on the financial statements. Cornerstone 6.8 illustrates the application of the LCM rule.

Valuing Inventory at Lower of Cost or Market

CORNERSTONE 6.8

Why:

Inventory should be conservatively valued at the lower of its cost or market value.

Information:

MacKenzie Electronics prepared the following analysis of its inventory at December 31:

Product	Quantity	Historical Cost per Item	Replacement Cost (Market Value) per Item
42″ LED HDTV	12	$1,000	$1,100
60″ Plasma HDTV	7	1,300	1,000
DVD Recorders	20	120	100

Required:

1. Determine the lower of cost or market value for each item of inventory.
2. Prepare the journal entry needed on December 31 to value the inventory at LCM.

Solution:

1. The LCM amounts are shown in the last column of the analysis below.

Product	Cost	Market Value	Lower of Cost or Market
42″ LED HDTV	$12,000 (12 × $1,000)	$13,200 (12 × $1,100)	$12,000
60″ Plasma HDTV	9,100 (7 × $1,300)	7,000 (7 × $1,000)	7,000
DVD Recorders	2,400 (20 × $120)	2,000 (20 × $100)	2,000
	$23,500	$22,200	$21,000

2. To apply LCM, the inventory must be reduced by $2,500 ($23,500 – $21,000) as follows:

Date	Account and Explanation	Debit	Credit
Dec. 31	Cost of Goods Sold	2,500	
	Inventory		2,500
	(Reduced inventory to market value)		

Assets	=	Liabilities	+	Stockholders' Equity
−2,500				−2,500

[5] In determining the replacement cost (market value) of inventory, a company is subject to two constraints. First, the replacement cost cannot be more than the net realizable value (selling price minus costs to sell) of the inventory. Second, replacement cost cannot be less than the net realizable value minus a normal profit margin (markup). This concept is discussed more fully in intermediate accounting texts.

concept Q&A

If the Financial Accounting Standards Board (FASB) allows the value of inventory to be reduced to market value when the market value is less than cost, why can't the value of inventory be increased when the market value is greater than cost?

Answer:

For the same reason that the conservatism principle allows inventory to be written down to market value, it prevents inventory from being written up to market value. Given uncertainty as to the actual future selling price of the inventory, a prudent reaction would be to avoid being overly optimistic about the company's future prospects. Overly optimistic projections of the future usually have far more serious negative consequences for people relying on the financial statements than do understatements.

Note that, in Cornerstone 6.8, the market value of the LED HDTVs is greater than its historical cost; however, for the other two products, historical cost is greater than market value. Thus, only the plasma HDTVs and the DVD recorders are reduced to market; the LED HDTVs remain at historical cost. The journal entry reduces inventory to its market value, and the loss is recorded as an increase to cost of goods sold in the period that the market value of the item dropped.

The LCM rule is an application of the conservatism principle. The *conservatism principle* leads accountants to select the accounting methods or procedures that produce the lowest (most conservative) net income and net assets in the current period. Thus, accountants tend to recognize expenses and losses as early as possible and to recognize gains and revenues as late as possible. By conservatively valuing inventory, the LCM rule is designed to avoid overstating the current earnings and financial strength of a company by recognizing an expense in the period that there is a decline in market value of inventory rather than in the period that the inventory is sold.

YOU DECIDE An Ethical Dilemma Involving Overvalued Inventory

You are the controller for PC Location Inc., a retailer that operates six computer stores in the Chicago area. An analysis of year end inventory reveals a large number of obsolete laptop computers that require a $180,000 write-down to market value. When you inform the CEO of this issue, she reminds you that PC Location is currently negotiating with Second Chicago Bank to increase its long-term loan and the bank has asked to review PC Location's preliminary financial statements. The CEO asks you to delay recognizing the write-down until Second Chicago has seen the preliminary financial statements. "Let the auditors write down the inventory when they show up in February," she says. "That's what we pay them for."

What should you do in this situation?

If you agree to ignore the required lower of cost or market adjustment, the bank may decide to grant the loan on the basis of the misleading financial statements. But when they receive the audited financial statements several months later, an investigation will no doubt be launched, and you are likely to take the blame. The ethical course of action is for you to refuse to go along with the CEO. You should be prepared to support your adjustment and to argue the disastrous consequences of trying to mislead Second Chicago Bank. In addition, you should be prepared to present alternatives to proceeding with the new loan at this time. Of course, if you refuse to go along with the CEO, you may find yourself unemployed.

The application of judgment in accounting may lead to ethical dilemmas.

OBJECTIVE 6

Evaluate inventory management using the gross profit and inventory turnover ratios.

ANALYZING INVENTORY

Inventories are at the heart of many companies' operations and must be carefully con trolled and accounted for. Two measures of how successful a company is at managing and controlling its inventory are the gross profit ratio and the inventory turnover ratio.

Gross Profit Ratio The **gross profit ratio** is calculated as:

$$\text{Gross Profit Ratio} = \frac{\text{Gross Profit}}{\text{Net Sales}}$$

This ratio is carefully watched by managers, investors, and analysts as a key indicator of a company's ability to sell inventory at a profit. In short, the gross profit ratio tells us how many cents of every dollar are available to cover expenses other than cost of goods sold and to earn a profit. An increasing gross profit ratio could signal that a company is able to charge more for its products due to high demand or has effectively controlled the cost of its inventory. A decrease in this ratio could signal trouble. For example, a company may have reduced its selling price due to increased competition or it is paying more for its inventory.

Inventory Turnover Ratio The **inventory turnover ratio** is calculated as:

$$\text{Inventory Turnover Ratio} = \frac{\text{Cost of Goods Sold}}{\text{Average Inventory}}$$

This ratio describes how quickly inventory is purchased (or produced) and sold. Companies want to satisfy the conflicting goals of having enough inventory on hand to meet customer demand while minimizing the cost of holding inventory (e.g., storage costs, obsolescence, etc.). Inventory turnover provides an indicator of how much of the company's funds are tied up in inventory. High inventory turnover ratios indicate that a company is rapidly selling its inventory, thus reducing inventory costs. Low inventory turnover reflects that the company may be holding too much inventory, thereby incurring avoidable costs or signaling that demand for a company's products has fallen. Financial statement users can also compute the **average days to sell inventory** as:

$$\text{Average Days to Sell Inventory} = \frac{\text{365 days}}{\text{Inventory Turnover}}$$

Cornerstone 6.9 illustrates the analysis of these performance measures for Wal-Mart and Target.

Calculating the Gross Profit and Inventory Turnover Ratios

CORNERSTONE 6.9

Why:

The gross profit and inventory turnover ratios provide measures of how successful a company is at managing and controlling its inventory.

Information:

The following information is available for Wal-Mart and Target for the fiscal year ending in January 2012 (all amounts in millions):

Account	Wal-Mart	Target
Net sales	$443,854	$68,466
Cost of goods sold	335,127	47,860
Gross profit	108,727	20,606
Inventory, January 2011	36,437	7,596
Inventory, January 2012	40,714	7,918

(Continued)

CORNERSTONE 6.9 (Continued)

Required:

1. Compute the gross profit ratio for Wal-Mart and Target.
2. Compute the inventory turnover ratio and the average days to sell inventory for Wal-Mart and Target.

Solution:

1. $$\text{Gross Profit Ratio} = \frac{\text{Gross Profit}}{\text{Net Sales}}$$

Wal-Mart	**Target**
$\frac{\$108,727}{\$443,854} = 0.245, \text{ or } 24.5\%$	$\frac{\$20,606}{\$68,466} = 0.301, \text{ or } 30.1\%$

2. $$\text{Inventory Turnover Ratio} = \frac{\text{Cost of Goods Sold}}{\text{Average Inventory}}$$

Wal-Mart	**Target**
$\frac{\$335,127}{(\$36,437 + \$40,714) \div 2} = 8.688$	$\frac{\$47,860}{(\$7,596 + \$7,918) \div 2} = 6.170$

$$\text{Average Days to Sell Inventory} = \frac{365 \text{ days}}{\text{Inventory Turnover}}$$

Wal-Mart	**Target**
$\frac{365}{8.688} = 42.012 \text{ days}$	$\frac{365}{6.170} = 59.157 \text{ days}$

As you can see in Cornerstone 6.9, consistent with their position as low margin retailers, both Wal-Mart and Target have gross profit ratios below that of companies like Saks, which has a gross profit ratio of 40.8%. While Target generates a higher gross profit on each dollar of sales, Wal-Mart is able to more rapidly sell its inventory (approximately 17 days faster) than Target. This higher inventory turnover allows Wal-Mart to lower its cost of carrying inventory which leads to higher income.

LIFO Reserve Adjustments

Analysts and other users often wish to compare companies that use different inventory costing methods. To assist in these comparisons, companies that use LIFO are required to report the amount that inventory would increase (or decrease) if the company had used FIFO. This amount is referred to as the **LIFO reserve**. The LIFO inventory value can be found as follows:

$$\text{LIFO Inventory Value} = \text{Reported FIFO Inventory} - \text{LIFO Reserve}$$

In addition, the effect on income can be found by examining the difference in the LIFO reserve.

For example, General Mills' disclosure of its LIFO reserve for 2011 is shown in Exhibit 6.13.

This disclosure shows that inventories would have been $168.5 million higher under FIFO for the 2011 fiscal year. Analysts can adjust the inventory amount by substituting in the FIFO inventory values ($1,777.8 million and $1,486.3 million for fiscal years

EXHIBIT 6.13

LIFO Reserve Disclosure

General Mills Inc.
Notes to Consolidated Financial Statements
Note 17: Supplemental Information (in part)

(in millions)	May 29, 2011	May 30, 2010
Inventories, at FIFO	$1,777.8	$1,486.3
Excess of FIFO over LIFO	(168.5)	(142.3)
Inventories, at LIFO	$1,609.3	$1,344.0

Source: General Mills, Inc. 2011 10K

2011 and 2010, respectively) for the LIFO values reported on the balance sheet. In addition, income would have been higher under FIFO by $26.2 million ($168.5 million – $142.3 million)—the difference between the LIFO reserve for fiscal years 2011 and 2010.

YOUDECIDE LIFO Liquidations

You are the purchasing manager for Tomlinson Health Management, an aggressively managed new business that provides pharmacy services to retirement communities, nursing homes, and small hospitals in a three-state area. In order to secure tax benefits, Tomlinson uses LIFO for most of its inventories. Tomlinson's business has become increasingly competitive in recent years, and the current year's income has fallen significantly. Avery Tomlinson, the principal stockholder and CEO, has instructed you to hold year end inventories to the absolute minimum.

What could be Mr. Tomlinson's motivation to reduce inventories?

The LIFO inventory is composed of layers, each one representing a year's contribution to the inventory at the earliest purchase prices of that year. During a period of rising prices, the LIFO inventory will be made up of the relatively older costs trapped in the LIFO layers. If the quantity of inventory falls, some of these older costs, with relatively low unit prices, will be released to cost of goods sold. This produces a lower cost of goods sold, and higher income, than one computed at current FIFO prices.

Mr. Tomlinson may be engaging in the questionable practice of earnings management. Reducing inventories releases old, low-priced LIFO layers to the income statement, lowering cost of goods sold and raising net income. Of course, Tomlinson's act may also raise current income taxes and impair business operations due to insufficient quantities of inventory.

When analyzing inventory, it is important to understand how changing inventory levels affects the financial statements.

EFFECTS OF INVENTORY ERRORS

OBJECTIVE 7

Describe how errors in ending inventory affect income statements and balance sheets.

The cost of goods sold model, illustrated in Cornerstone 6.1 (p. 293), describes the relationship between inventory and cost of goods sold. This relationship implies that the measurement of inventory affects both the balance sheet and the income statement. Even with recent technological advances, it is easy to make errors in determining the cost of the hundreds of items in a typical ending inventory. Incorrect counts, mistakes in costing, or errors in identifying items are common. Because the ending inventory of one period is the beginning inventory of the next period, errors in the measurement of ending inventory affect two accounting periods.

To illustrate the effect of an error in valuing ending inventory on the financial statements, consider the information in Exhibit 6.14. The "Correct" column shows the financial statements for 2013 and 2014 as they would appear if no error were made. The "Erroneous" column shows the financial statements for the 2 years as they would appear if the firm understated its inventory at December 31, 2013, by $15,000. The "Error" column describes the effect of the error on each line of the statements.

The understatement of the 2013 ending inventory causes an overstatement of 2013 cost of goods sold. Thus, gross margin for 2013 is understated by $15,000. Ignoring income taxes, this error would then flow into both net income and retained earnings for 2013. However, the effect is not limited to 2013. Because the ending inventory for 2013 is the beginning inventory for 2014, the beginning inventory for 2014 is understated by $15,000. Assuming no other errors are made, this would lead to an understatement of cost of goods sold and an overstatement of gross margin (and net income) by $15,000. However, notice that when this flows into retained earnings, the understatement in 2013 is offset by the overstatement in 2014 so that retained earnings is correctly stated by the end of 2014. This illustrates the self correcting nature of inventory errors.

EXHIBIT 6.14

Effect of an Inventory Error

	(amounts in thousands)	Correct		Erroneous		Error*
2013 Financial Statements	**Income Statement** (partial)					
	Sales		$500		$500	
	Cost of goods sold:					
	Beginning inventory	$ 50		$ 50		
	Purchases	250		250		
	Cost of goods available for sale	$300		$300		
	Less: Ending inventory	(60)		(45)		−$15
	Cost of goods sold		240		255	+$15
	Gross margin		$260		$245	−$15
	Balance Sheet (partial)					
	Inventory		$ 60		$ 45	−$15
	Retained earnings		$100		$ 85	−$15
2014 Financial Statements	**Income Statement** (partial)					
	Sales		$600		$600	
	Cost of goods sold:					
	Beginning inventory	$ 60		$ 45		−$15
	Purchases	290		290		
	Cost of goods available for sale	$350		$335		−$15
	Less: Ending inventory	(50)		(50)		
	Cost of goods sold		300		285	−$15
	Gross margin		$300		$315	+$15
	Balance Sheet (partial)					
	Inventory		$ 50		$ 50	
	Retained earnings		180		180	

*A minus sign (−) indicates an understatement and a plus sign (+) indicates an overstatement.

Cornerstone 6.10 illustrates the analysis of inventory errors.

Analyzing Inventory Errors

CORNERSTONE 6.10

Why:

Errors in the measurement of ending inventory will affect both the current and subsequent period balance sheets as well as the current period income statement.

Information:

Dunn Corporation reported net income of $75,000 for 2013. Early in 2014, Dunn discovers that the December 31, 2013 ending inventory was overstated by $6,000.

Required:

Determine the financial statement effects of the inventory errors for 2013 and 2014.

Solution:

For 2013, assets (ending inventory) are overstated by $6,000. The overstatement of ending inventory causes an understatement of cost of goods sold (an expense) by $6,000. This error flows through to income and retained earnings (equity). Because the ending inventory for 2013 is the beginning inventory for 2014, the error has the opposite effects on income for 2014. Assuming no other errors are made, the inventory error self-corrects and the 2014 balance sheet is correctly stated. These effects are summarized below.

	Assets	Liabilities	Equity	Revenues	Expenses	Income
2013	$6,000 overstated	No effect	$6,000 overstated	No effect	$6,000 understated	$6,000 overstated
2014	No effect	No effect	No effect	No effect	$6,000 overstated	$6,000 understated

Even though inventory errors are self-correcting over two periods, it is still necessary to correct them in order to produce properly stated financial information. If the error is not corrected, both income statements and the 2013 balance sheet will be incorrect.

APPENDIX 6A: PERIODIC INVENTORY SYSTEM

OBJECTIVE 8

Explain how to record purchases of inventory using a periodic inventory system.

In a periodic inventory system, the inventory records are not kept continually, or perpetually, up to date. Instead, under a periodic inventory system, the inventory account is updated at the end of the period based on a physical count of the inventory on hand. The balance in the inventory account remains unchanged during the period. As purchase transactions occur, they are recorded in one of four temporary accounts:

- *Purchases:* The Purchases account accumulates the cost of the inventory acquired during the period.
- *Purchase Discounts:* The Purchase Discounts account accumulates the amount of discounts on purchases taken during the period.
- *Purchase Returns and Allowances:* The Purchase Returns and Allowances account accumulates the cost of any merchandise returned to the supplier or any reductions (allowances) in the purchase price granted by the seller.
- *Transportation-In:* The Transportation-In account accumulates the cost paid by the purchaser to transport inventory from suppliers.

The balances in these temporary accounts, along with the beginning and ending inventory balances obtained from the physical count of inventory, are used to compute cost of goods sold using the cost of goods sold model illustrated in Cornerstone 6.1 (p. 293).

Cornerstone 6.11 (p. 322) illustrates how to record purchase transactions in a periodic inventory system.

CORNERSTONE 6.11

Recording Purchase Transactions in a Periodic Inventory System

Why:

The cost of inventory includes the purchase price of the merchandise plus any cost of bringing the goods to a salable condition and location.

Information:

On September 1, Brandon Shoes purchased 50 pairs of hiking boots for $3,750 cash (or $75 a pair) and paid $150 of transportation costs. Also, on September 1, Brandon purchased 100 pairs of running shoes for $10,000; however, the seller paid the transportation costs of $300. The running shoes were purchased on credit with credit terms of 2/10, n/30. Brandon paid for one-half ($5,000) of the running shoes on September 10, within the discount period. After inspection, Brandon determined that running shoes costing $750 were defective and returned them on September 25. The remaining running shoes (cost of $4,250) were paid for on September 30.

Required:

Prepare the journal entries necessary to record the September transactions for Brandon Shoes.

Solution:

Assets = Liabilities + Stockholders' Equity	Date	Account and Explanation	Debit	Credit
Assets −3,750; Liabilities; Stockholders' Equity −3,750	Sept. 1	Purchases	3,750	
		Cash		3,750
		(Purchased inventory for cash)		
Assets −150; Liabilities; Stockholders' Equity −150	1	Transportation-In	150	
		Cash		150
		(Recorded payment of freight costs)		
Assets; Liabilities +10,000; Stockholders' Equity −10,000	1	Purchases	10,000	
		Accounts Payable		10,000
		(Purchased inventory on credit)		
Assets −4,900; Liabilities −5,000; Stockholders' Equity +100	10	Accounts Payable	5,000	
		Cash		4,900
		Purchase Discounts ($5,000 × 2%)		100
		(Recorded payment within the discount period)		
Assets; Liabilities −750; Stockholders' Equity +750	25	Accounts Payable (10 pairs × $75 per pair)	750	
		Purchase Returns and Allowances		750
		(Returned defective hiking boots)		
Assets −4,250; Liabilities −4,250; Stockholders' Equity	30	Accounts Payable	4,250	
		Cash		4,250
		(Recorded payment outside of the discount period)		

© Pixelfabrik/Alamy

Under either the periodic or the perpetual inventory system, the net cost of purchases (shown below) is the same.

Purchases	$13,750
Less: Purchase discounts	(100)
Purchase returns and allowances	(750)
Add: Transportation costs (freight-in)	150
Net cost of purchases	$13,050

Additionally, for sales transactions, there is no need to make a second journal entry to record the expense (and inventory) portion of a transaction. Instead, only the revenue portion is recorded as shown earlier in the text.

The differences between a periodic and perpetual inventory system are summarized in Exhibit 6.15.

EXHIBIT 6.15

Perpetual versus Periodic Inventory Systems

Activity	Perpetual System	Periodic System
Purchase	Inventory purchases are recorded in the *Inventory* account.	The costs of inventory purchases are recorded in the *Purchases account.*
Sale	When a sale is made, an entry is made to record the amount of sales revenue. *A second entry is made that increases the Cost of Goods Sold account and decreases the Inventory account.*	When a sale is made, an entry is made to record the amount of sales revenue only. *No entry is made to Cost of Goods Sold or Inventory.*
Costing ending inventory	At the end of the period, the *cost of ending* inventory is the balance in the Inventory account (which is verified by a physical count of inventory).	*The amount of ending inventory is determined at the end of the accounting by taking a physical count of inventory,* a procedure by which all items of inventory on a given date are identified and counted.
Determining cost of goods sold	Cost of goods sold for the period is the balance *in the Cost of Goods Sold account* at the end of the period.	Cost of Goods Sold is determined only at the end of the period by *applying the cost of goods sold model.*

APPENDIX 6B: INVENTORY COSTING METHODS AND THE PERIODIC INVENTORY SYSTEM

OBJECTIVE 9

Compute ending inventory and cost of goods sold under a periodic inventory system.

Regardless of whether a company uses a perpetual inventory system or a periodic inventory system, inventory costing methods are designed to allocate the cost of goods available for sale between ending inventory and cost of goods sold. Under a periodic inventory system, the inventory costing methods are applied *as if* all purchases during an accounting period take place prior to any sales of the period. While this is not a realistic assumption, it does simplify the computation of the ending inventory and cost of goods sold since only one allocation needs to be made, regardless of the number of purchases and sales. Given this assumption, the following steps can be applied to determine ending inventory and cost of goods sold:

Step 1. Calculate the cost of goods available for sale for the period.

Step 2. Apply the inventory costing method to determine ending inventory and cost of goods sold.

First-In, First-Out (FIFO)

Under the FIFO method, *the earliest purchases (the first in) are assumed to be the first sold (the first out) and the more recent purchases are in ending inventory.* Cornerstone 6.12 illustrates the application of the FIFO method. Notice that this is the same information used to illustrate the inventory costing methods applied to a perpetual inventory system (Cornerstones 6-5 through 6-7). However, the information on purchases is listed first and the sales can be combined because all purchases are assumed to occur prior to any sales.

CORNERSTONE

6.12

Applying the FIFO Inventory Costing Method in a Periodic Inventory System

Why:

The cost of the earliest purchases that make up cost of goods available for sale is allocated to cost of goods sold, and the cost of the most recent purchases is allocated to ending inventory.

Information:

Tampico Beachwear, a retail store specializing in beach apparel, has the following information related to purchases and sales of one of its more popular brand of shoes. (Each inventory layer is a different color.)

Date	Description	Units Purchased at Cost	Units Sold at Retail
Oct. 1	Beginning inventory	300 units @ $16 = $ 4,800	
3	Purchase 1	600 units @ $18 = $10,800	
8	Sale 1		800 units @ $30
15	Purchase 2	250 units @ $20 = $ 5,000	
20	Purchase 3	150 units @ $22 = $ 3,300	
25	Sale 2		300 units @ $30
		Goods available for sale: 1,300 units = $23,900	Sales: 1,100 units = $33,000

Ending inventory is made up of 200 units (1,300 units available for sale − 1,100 units sold).

Required:

Compute the cost of ending inventory and the cost of goods sold at October 31 using the FIFO method.

Solution:

Step 1: Compute the cost of goods available for sale for the period ($23,900).

Step 2: Apply FIFO to determine ending inventory and cost of goods sold. The cost of goods available for sale is allocated between inventory (the most recent purchases) and cost of goods sold (the earliest purchases) as follows:

Ending Inventory			Cost of Goods Sold		
150 units × $22	=	$3,300	300 units × $16	=	$ 4,800
50 units × $20	=	1,000	600 units × $18	=	10,800
200 units		$4,300	200 units × $20	=	4,000
			1,100 units		**$19,600**

Last-In, First-Out (LIFO)

Under the LIFO method, *the most recent purchases (newest costs) are allocated to the cost of goods sold and the earliest purchases (oldest costs) are allocated to ending inventory.* Cornerstone 6.13 illustrates the application of the LIFO method.

Applying the LIFO Inventory Costing Method in a Periodic Inventory System

CORNERSTONE 6.13

Why:

The cost of the most recent purchases that make up cost of goods available for sale is allocated to cost of goods sold, and the cost of the earliest purchases is allocated to ending inventory.

Information:

Tampico Beachwear, a retail store specializing in beach apparel, has the following information related to purchases and sales of one of its more popular brand of shoes. (Each inventory layer is a different color.)

Date	Description	Units Purchased at Cost	Units Sold at Retail
Oct. 1	Beginning inventory	300 units @ \$16 = \$ 4,800	
3	Purchase 1	600 units @ \$18 = \$10,800	
8	Sale 1		800 units @ \$30
15	Purchase 2	250 units @ \$20 = \$ 5,000	
20	Purchase 3	150 units @ \$22 = \$ 3,300	
25	Sale 2		300 units @ \$30
		Goods available for sale: 1,300 units = \$23,900	Sales: 1,100 units = \$33,000

Ending inventory is made up of 200 units (1,300 units available for sale – 1,100 units sold).

Required:

Compute the cost of ending inventory and the cost of goods sold at October 31 using the LIFO method.

Solution:

Step 1: Compute the cost of goods available for sale for the period (\$23,900).

Step 2: Apply LIFO to determine ending inventory and cost of goods sold. This cost of goods available for sale is allocated between inventory (the earliest purchases) and cost of goods sold (the most recent purchases) as follows:

Ending Inventory	Cost of Goods Sold		
200 units × \$16 = \$3,200	100 units × \$16	=	\$ 1,600
	150 units × \$22	=	3,300
	250 units × \$20	=	5,000
	600 units × \$18	=	10,800
	1,100 units		**\$20,700**

Average Cost Method

Under the average cost method, the weighted average cost per unit is multiplied by:

- the number of units in ending inventory to determine the cost of ending inventory
- the number of units sold to determine cost of goods sold

This method is commonly referred to as the weighted average method. In contrast to the perpetual inventory system, the weighted average cost per unit is not continually calculated. Rather it is calculated based on the total cost of goods available for sale and the total units available for sale. Cornerstone 6.14 illustrates the application of the average cost method.

CORNERSTONE

6.14

Applying the Average Cost Inventory Costing Method in a Periodic Inventory System

Why:

The cost of goods available for sale is allocated between ending inventory and cost of goods sold based on a weighted average cost of the goods available for sale.

Information:

Tampico Beachwear, a retail store specializing in beach apparel, has the following information related to purchases and sales of one of its more popular brand of shoes. (Each inventory layer is a different color.)

Date	Description	Units Purchased at Cost	Units Sold at Retail
Oct. 1	Beginning inventory	300 units @ $16 = $ 4,800	
3	Purchase 1	600 units @ $18 = $10,800	
8	Sale 1		800 units @ $30
15	Purchase 2	250 units @ $20 = $ 5,000	
20	Purchase 3	150 units @ $22 = $ 3,300	
25	Sale 2		300 units @ $30
		Goods available for sale: 1,300 units = $23,900	Sales: 1,100 units = $33,000

Ending inventory is made up of 200 units (1,300 units available for sale − 1,100 units sold).

Required:

Compute the cost of ending inventory and the cost of goods sold at October 31 using the average cost method.

(*Note:* Use four decimal places for per unit calculations and round all other numbers to the nearest dollar.)

Solution:

Step 1: Compute the cost of goods available for sale for the period ($23,900).

Step 2: Apply the average cost method to determine ending inventory and cost of goods sold. This method requires you to compute a weighted average cost of the goods available for sale:

$$\text{Weighted Average Cost per Unit} = \frac{\text{Cost of Goods Available for Sale}}{\text{Units Available for Sale}}$$

$$= \$23{,}900 \div 1{,}300 \text{ units} = \mathbf{\$18.3846 \text{ per unit}}$$

(*Continued*)

The cost of goods available for sale ($23,900) is allocated between inventory and cost of goods sold using the average cost of the inventory as follows:

Ending Inventory	Cost of Goods Sold
200 units × $18.3846 = $3,677	1,100 units × $18.3846 = **$20,223**

CORNERSTONE 6.14

(Continued)

Under all inventory costing methods, periodic inventory systems allocate the cost of purchased goods between cost of goods sold and ending inventory only at the end of the period. In contrast, the perpetual inventory system performs this allocation each time a sale is made. Because of this difference in the timing of cost allocations, the two systems usually yield different amounts for the cost of goods sold and ending inventory under both the LIFO and average cost assumptions. FIFO amounts, however, are always the same under both periodic and perpetual inventory systems.[6]

SUMMARY OF LEARNING OBJECTIVES

LO 1. Describe the types of inventories held by merchandisers and manufacturers, and understand how inventory costs flow through a company.

- Merchandising companies hold one type of inventory.
- Manufacturing companies have three types of inventory—raw materials, work-in-process, and finished goods.
- When goods are purchased, the cost of the purchase is recorded in inventory (for merchandisers) or raw materials inventory (for manufacturers). During the production process, manufacturers record the cost (raw materials, labor, and overhead) in work-in-process and then transfer the cost to finished goods inventory when the product is complete.
- Once the product is sold, the cost is transferred out of the inventory account (either Inventory or Finished Goods) and into Cost of Goods Sold to match it with Sales Revenue.
- The relationship between inventory and cost of goods sold is described by the cost of goods sold model.

LO 2. Explain how to record purchases and sales of inventory using a perpetual inventory system.

- In a perpetual inventory system, purchases of inventory are recorded by increasing the inventory account.
- If a purchase discount exists, inventory is reduced by the amount of the discount taken.
- When a purchased item is returned (purchase return) or a price reduction is granted by the seller (purchase allowance), the inventory item is reduced by the amount of the purchase return or allowance given.
- If transportation costs exist and the shipping terms are F.O.B shipping point, the transportation costs are considered part of the total cost of purchases, and the inventory account is increased.
- If transportation costs exist and the shipping terms are F.O.B. destination, the seller pays these costs and records them as a selling expense on the income statement.
- In a perpetual inventory system, sales require two entries that (1) record the sales reve-

[6] This occurs because FIFO always allocates the earliest items purchased to cost of goods sold, resulting in ending inventory being the latest items purchased. Under both the perpetual and periodic inventory systems, these are the same units of inventory at the same cost. Therefore, the timing of the cost allocation is irrelevant under FIFO.

nue and (2) recognize the expense (cost of goods sold) associated with the decrease in inventory.
- If an item is later returned, two entries must also be made: (1) increase Sales Returns and Allowances (a contra-revenue account) and (2) increase the inventory account and decrease Cost of Goods Sold.

LO 3. Apply the four inventory costing methods to compute ending inventory and cost of goods sold under a perpetual inventory system.

- The four inventory costing methods are specific identification; first-in, first-out (FIFO); last-in, first-out (LIFO); and average cost.
- The specific identification method determines the cost of ending inventory and the cost of goods sold based on the identification of the actual units sold and the units remaining in inventory.
- The other three inventory costing methods allocate cost of goods available for sale between ending inventory and cost of goods sold using the following process.

  Step 1. Calculate the cost of goods available for sale *immediately prior* to any sales transaction.
  Step 2. Apply the inventory costing method to determine ending inventory and cost of goods sold.
  Step 3. Repeat Steps 1 and 2 for all inventory transactions during the period. The sum of the cost of goods sold computed in Step 2 is the cost of goods sold for the period. Ending inventory is the amount computed during the final application of Step 2 for the period.

LO 4. Analyze the financial reporting and tax effects of the various inventory costing methods.

- If the prices paid for purchased inventory are stable, all inventory costing methods will yield the same amounts for ending inventory and cost of goods sold.
- When purchase prices vary, FIFO, LIFO and the average cost methods will produce different amounts for ending inventory, cost of goods sold, and, therefore, income.
- When prices are rising, the FIFO method produces the highest cost for ending inventory, the lowest cost of goods sold, and the highest gross margin (and net income).
- In contrast, the LIFO method produced the lowest cost for ending inventory, the highest cost of goods sold, and, therefore, the lowest gross margin (and net income) of the three methods. Because LIFO results in lower income, it results in the lowest income taxes.
- When purchase prices are *falling,* the situation is reversed.
- The average cost method produced amounts for inventory, cost of goods sold, and net income that fell between the FIFO and LIFO extremes.

LO 5. Apply the lower of cost or market rule to the valuation of inventory.

- If the market value of inventory has dropped below its original cost, generally accepted accounting principles permit a departure from the historical cost concept.
- A company is allowed to reduce the amount recorded for inventory to its market value, where market value is defined as the current replacement cost.
- This lower of cost or market rule is an application of the conservatism principle.

LO 6. Evaluate inventory management using the gross profit and inventory turnover ratios.

- Two useful measures of how successful a company is at managing and controlling its inventory are the gross profit ratio (Gross Profit ÷ Net Sales) and the inventory turnover ratio (Cost of Goods Sold ÷ Average Inventory).
- The gross profit ratio indicates how many cents of every dollar are available to cover expenses other than cost of goods sold and to earn a profit. The inventory turnover ratio describes how quickly inventory is purchased (or produced) and sold.

LO 7. Describe how errors in ending inventory affect income statements and balance sheets.

- Inventory errors can arise for a number of reasons, including incorrect counts of inventory, mistakes in costing, or errors in identifying items.
- Because the ending inventory of one period is the beginning inventory of the next period, an error in the measurement of ending inventory will affect the cost of goods sold and net income of two consecutive periods.
- Inventory errors are self-correcting; therefore, the assets and stockholders' equity of only the first period are misstated (assuming no other errors are made).

LO 8. *(Appendix 6A)* Explain how to record purchases of inventory using a periodic inventory system.

- In a periodic inventory system, purchases of inventory are recorded by increasing the Purchases account.
- If a purchase discount exists, the Purchases Discount account is increased by the amount of the discount taken.
- When a purchased item is returned (purchase return) or a price reduction is granted by the seller (purchase allowance), the Purchase Returns and Allowances account is increased by the amount of the purchase return or allowance given.
- If transportation costs exist and are paid by the purchaser, the transportation costs are considered part of the total cost of purchases and the Purchases account is increased.

LO 9. *(Appendix 6B)* Compute ending inventory and cost of goods sold under a periodic inventory system.

- Under a periodic inventory system, the inventory costing methods are applied as if all purchases during an accounting period take place prior to any sales of the period. Given this assumption, you will then apply the following steps:

  Step 1. Calculate the cost of goods available for sale for the period.
  Step 2. Apply the inventory costing method to determine ending inventory and cost of goods sold.

KEY TERMS

Average cost method, 310
Average days to sell inventory, 317
Consignment, 298
Cost of goods available for sale, 293
Cost of goods sold (cost of sales), 290
Discount period, 296
Finished goods inventory, 291
First-in, first-out (FIFO) method, 307
F.O.B. destination, 298
F.O.B. shipping point, 298
Freight-in, 298
Freight-out, 298
Gross margin (gross profit), 290
Gross profit ratio, 316
Inventory, 290
Inventory turnover ratio, 317
Just in time (JIT), 295
Last-in, first-out (LIFO) method, 308
LIFO reserve, 318
Lower of cost or market (LCM) rule, 314
Manufacturers, 291
Merchandise inventory, 291
Merchandisers, 291
Periodic inventory system, 295
Perpetual inventory system, 294
Purchase allowance, 298
Purchase discounts, 296
Purchase return, 298
Purchases, 296
Raw materials inventory, 291
Retailers, 291
Specific identification method, 305
Wholesalers, 291
Work-in-process inventory, 291

REVIEW PROBLEM

Accounting for Inventory

Why:

The cost of goods available for sale is allocated between ending inventory and cost of goods sold based on the inventory costing method chosen by management. Under a perpetual inventory system, the accounting records are continually (perpetually) updated for each sale or purchase of inventory.

Information:

Sagamore Supplies, an office supply wholesale store, uses a perpetual inventory system. Sagamore recorded the following activity for one of its inventory accounts:

Date	Activity	Number of Units	Cost per Unit
Oct. 1	Beginning inventory	2,500	$16
15	Purchase	5,100	$17
Nov. 3	Sale	5,900	
20	Purchase	4,800	$18
Dec. 10	Sale	5,300	

Additional information on the purchases and sales is:

- All purchases were cash purchases.
- All sales were cash sales, and all inventory items were sold for $25 per unit.

Required:

1. Compute the cost of ending inventory and the cost of goods sold using the following methods: (a) FIFO, (b) LIFO, and (c) average cost.
2. Assume that Sagamore uses the FIFO inventory costing method. Prepare the journal entries to record the purchases and sales of inventory.

Solution:

1.

a. Under FIFO, the cost of ending inventory is $21,600, and cost of goods sold is $191,500 ($97,800 + $93,700).

Date		Description	Cost of Goods Sold		Inventory Balance	
Oct.	1	Beginning inventory			2,500 × $16	= $ 40,000
	15	Purchase (5,100 @ $17)			2,500 × $16 = $40,000 5,100 × $17 = $86,700	= $126,700
Nov.	3	Sale (5,900 @ $25)	2,500 × $16 = $40,000 3,400 × $17 = $57,800	= **$97,800**	1,700 × $17	= $ 28,900

This is an interim calculation. Because the period is not over, these steps need to be repeated until the end of the accounting period.

Date		Description	Cost of Goods Sold		Inventory Balance	
Nov.	3	Inventory on hand			1,700 × $17	= $ 28,900
	20	Purchase (4,800 @ $18)			1,700 × $17 = $28,900 4,800 × $18 = $86,400	= $115,300
Dec.	10	Sale (5,300 @ $25)	1,700 × $17 = $28,900 3,600 × $18 = $64,800	= **$93,700**	1,200 × $18	= $ 21,600

b. Under LIFO, the cost of ending inventory is $19,200, and cost of goods sold is $193,900 ($99,500 + $94,400).

Date		Description	Cost of Goods Sold		Inventory Balance	
Oct.	1	Beginning inventory			2,500 × $16	= $ 40,000
	15	Purchase (5,100 @ $17)			2,500 × $16 = $40,000 5,100 × $17 = $86,700	= $126,700
Nov.	3	Sale (5,900 @ $25)	5,100 × $17 = $86,700 800 × $16 = $12,800	= **$99,500**	1,700 × $16	= $ 27,200

This is an interim calculation. Because the period is not over, these steps need to be repeated until the end of the accounting period.

Date		Description	Cost of Goods Sold		Inventory Balance	
Nov.	3	Inventory on hand			1,700 × $16	= $ 27,200
	20	Purchase (4,800 @ $18)			1,700 × $16 = $27,200 4,800 × $18 = $86,400	= $113,600
Dec.	10	Sale (5,300 @ $25)	4,800 × $18= $86,400 500 × $16= $ 8,000	= **$94,400**	1,200 × $16	= $ 19,200

(Continued)

c. Under average cost, the cost of ending inventory is \$21,183, and cost of goods sold is \$191,917 (\$98,359 + \$93,558).

Date		Description	Cost of Goods Sold	Inventory Balance	
Oct.	1	Beginning inventory		2,500 × \$16	= \$ 40,000 (\$16/unit)
	15	Purchase (5,100 @ \$17)		2,500 × \$16 = \$40,000 5,100 × \$17 = \$86,700	= \$126,700 (\$16.6711/unit)[a]
Nov.	3	Sale (5,900 @ \$25)	5,900 × \$16.6711 = **\$98,359**	1,700 × \$16.6711	= \$ 28,341

[a] \$126,700 ÷ 7,600 units = \$16.6711/unit

This is an interim calculation. Because the period is not over, these steps need to be repeated until the end of the accounting period.

Date		Description	Cost of Goods Sold	Inventory Balance	
Nov.	3	Inventory on hand		1,700 × \$16.6711	= \$ 28,341
	20	Purchase (4,800 @ \$18)		1,700 × \$16.6711 = \$28,341 4,800 × \$18 = \$86,400	= \$114,741 (\$17.6525/unit)[b]
Dec.	10	Sale 2 (5,300 @ \$25)	5,300 × \$17.6525 = **\$93,558**	1,200 × \$17.6525	= \$ 21,183

[b] \$114,741 ÷ 6,500 units = \$17.6525/unit

2.

Assets = Liabilities + Stockholders' Equity	Date	Account and Explanation	Debit	Credit
Assets +86,700 −86,700	Oct. 15	Inventory Cash *(Purchased inventory for cash)*	86,700	86,700
Assets +147,500; Stockholders' Equity +147,500	Nov. 3	Cash Sales Revenue *(Sold 5,900 units @ \$25 per unit)*	147,500	147,500
Assets −97,800; Stockholders' Equity −97,800	3	Cost of Goods Sold Inventory *(Recorded cost of sale of 5,900 units)*	97,800	97,800
Assets +86,400 −86,400	20	Inventory Cash *(Purchased inventory for cash)*	86,400	86,400
Assets +132,500; Stockholders' Equity +132,500	Dec. 10	Cash Sales Revenue *(Sold 5,300 units @ \$25 per unit)*	132,500	132,500
Assets −93,700; Stockholders' Equity −93,700	10	Cost of Goods Sold Inventory *(Recorded cost of sale of 5,300 units)*	93,700	93,700

DISCUSSION QUESTIONS

1. What are the differences between merchandisers and manufacturers?
2. Describe the types of inventories used by manufacturers and merchandisers.
3. Compare the flow of inventory costs between merchandisers and manufacturers.
4. What are the components of cost of goods available for sale and cost of goods sold?
5. How is cost of goods sold determined?
6. How do the perpetual and periodic inventory accounting systems differ from each other?
7. Why are perpetual inventory systems more expensive to operate than periodic inventory systems? What conditions justify the additional cost of a perpetual inventory system?
8. Why are adjustments made to the invoice price of goods when determining the cost of inventory?
9. Identify the accounting items for which adjustments are made to the invoice price of goods when determining the net cost of purchases.
10. Describe the difference between F.O.B. shipping point and F.O.B. destination.
11. Why do sales transactions under a perpetual inventory system require two journal entries?
12. Why do the four inventory costing methods produce different amounts for the cost of ending inventory and cost of goods sold?
13. The costs of which units of inventory (oldest or newest) are allocated to ending inventory or cost of goods sold using the FIFO, LIFO, and average cost methods?
14. If inventory prices are rising, which inventory costing method should produce the smallest payment for taxes?
15. How would reported income differ if LIFO rather than FIFO were used when purchase prices are rising? When purchase prices are falling?
16. How would the balance sheet accounts be affected if LIFO rather than FIFO were used when purchase prices are rising? When purchase prices are falling?
17. Why are inventories written down to the lower of cost or market?
18. What is the effect on the current period income statement and the balance sheet when inventories are written down using the lower of cost or market method? What is the effect on future period income statements and balance sheets?
19. What do the gross profit and inventory turnover ratios tell company management about inventory?
20. What is the LIFO reserve, and when is it used?
21. How does an error in the determination of ending inventory affect the financial statements of two periods?
22. *(Appendix 6A)* What accounts are used to record inventory purchase transactions under the periodic inventory system? Why aren't these accounts used in a perpetual inventory system?
23. *(Appendix 6B)* "For each inventory costing method, perpetual and periodic systems yield the same amounts for ending inventory and cost of goods sold." Do you agree or disagree with this statement? Explain.

MULTIPLE-CHOICE QUESTIONS

6-1 If beginning inventory is \$20,000, purchases are \$185,000, and ending inventory is \$30,000, what is cost of goods sold as determined by the cost of goods sold model?

a. \$135,000
b. \$175,000
c. \$195,000
d. \$235,000

6-2 Which of the following transactions would *not* result in an entry to the inventory account in the buyer's accounting records under a perpetual inventory system?

a. Purchase of merchandise on credit
b. Return of merchandise to the supplier
c. Payment of a credit purchase of merchandise within the discount period
d. Payment of freight by the seller for goods received from a supplier

6-3 Briggs Company purchased $15,000 of inventory on credit with credit terms of 2/10, n/30. Briggs paid for the purchase within the discount period. How much did Briggs pay for the inventory?

a. $14,700 c. $15,000
b. $14,850 d. $15,300

6-4 Which of the following transactions would *not* result in an adjustment to the inventory account under a perpetual inventory system?

a. Sale of merchandise for cash
b. Sale of merchandise on credit
c. Receipt of payment from a customer within the discount period
d. Return of merchandise by a customer

6-5 U-Save Automotive Group purchased 10 vehicles during the current month. Two trucks were purchased for $20,000 each, two SUVs were purchased for $31,000 each, and six hybrid cars were purchased for $27,000 each. A review of the sales invoices revealed that five of the hybrid cars were sold and both trucks were sold. What is the cost of U-Save's ending inventory if it uses the specific identification method?

a. $89,000 c. $135,000
b. $129,000 d. $175,000

Use the following information for Multiple-Choice Questions 6-6 through 6-8:
Morgan Inc. has the following units and costs for the month of April:

	Units Purchased at Cost	Units Sold at Retail
Beginning inventory, April 1	1,200 units at $25	
Purchase 1, April 9	1,500 units at $28	
Sale 1, April 12		2,400 units at $45
Purchase 2, April 22	1,000 units at $30	

6-6 Refer to the information for Morgan Inc. above. If Morgan uses a perpetual inventory system, what is the cost of ending inventory under FIFO at April 30?

a. $32,500 c. $63,600
b. $38,400 d. $69,500

6-7 Refer to the information for Morgan Inc. above. If Morgan uses a perpetual inventory system, what is the cost of goods sold under LIFO at April 30?

a. $37,500 c. $63,600
b. $38,400 d. $64,500

6-8 Refer to the information for Morgan Inc. above. If Morgan uses a perpetual inventory system, what is the cost of ending inventory under average cost at April 30? (*Note:* Use four decimal places for per-unit calculations and round to the nearest dollar.)

a. $35,838 c. $64,000
b. $38,000 d. $66,162

6-9 When purchase prices are rising, which of the following statements is true?

a. LIFO produces a higher cost of goods sold than FIFO.
b. LIFO produces a higher cost for ending inventory than FIFO.
c. FIFO produces a lower amount for net income than LIFO.
d. Average cost produces a higher net income than FIFO or LIFO.

6-10 Which method results in a more realistic amount for income because it matches the most current costs against revenue?

a. FIFO
b. Average cost
c. Specific identification
d. LIFO

6-11 Which of the following statements regarding the lower of cost or market (LCM) rule is true?

a. The LCM rule is an application of the historical cost principle.
b. When the replacement cost of inventory drops below the historical cost of inventory, an adjustment is made to decrease inventory to its market value and decrease income.
c. If a company uses the LCM rule, there is no need to use a cost flow assumption such as FIFO, LIFO, or average cost.
d. When the market value of inventory is above the historical cost of inventory, an adjustment is made to increase inventory to its market value and increase income.

6-12 Which of the following statements is true with regard to the gross profit ratio?

1. An increase in cost of goods sold would increase the gross profit rate (assuming sales remain constant).
2. An increase in the gross profit rate may indicate that a company is efficiently managing its inventory.
3. An increase in selling expenses would lower the gross profit rate.

a. 1
b. 2
c. 1 and 2
d. 2 and 3

6-13 An increasing inventory turnover ratio indicates that a company:

a. has reduced the time it takes to purchase and sell inventory.
b. is having trouble selling its inventory.
c. may be holding too much inventory.
d. has sold inventory at a higher profit.

6-14 Ignoring taxes, if a company understates its ending inventory by $10,000 in the current year:

a. assets for the current year will be overstated by $10,000.
b. net income for the subsequent year will be overstated by $10,000.
c. cost of goods sold for the current year will be understated by $10,000.
d. retained earnings for the current year will be unaffected.

6-15 *(Appendix 6A)* Which of the following statements is true for a company that uses a periodic inventory system?

a. The purchase of inventory requires a debit to Inventory.
b. The return of defective inventory requires a debit to Purchase Returns and Allowances.
c. The payment of a purchase within the discount period requires a credit to Purchase Discounts.
d. Any amounts paid for freight are debited to Inventory.

Use the following information for Multiple-Choice Questions 6-16 through 6-18:
Morgan Inc. has the following units and costs for the month of April:

	Units Purchased at Cost	Units Sold at Retail
Beginning inventory, April 1	1,200 units at $25	
Purchase 1, April 9	1,500 units at $28	
Sale 1, April 12		2,400 units at $45
Purchase 2, April 22	1,000 units at $30	

6-16 *(Appendix 6B)* Refer to the information for Morgan Inc. above. If Morgan uses a periodic inventory system, what is the cost of goods sold under FIFO at April 30?

a. $32,800
b. $38,400
c. $63,600
d. $69,200

6-17 *(Appendix 6B)* Refer to the information for Morgan Inc. above. If Morgan uses a periodic inventory system, what is the cost of ending inventory under LIFO at April 30?

a. $32,800
b. $38,400
c. $63,600
d. $69,200

6-18 *(Appendix 6B)* Refer to the information for Morgan Inc. above. If Morgan uses a periodic inventory system, what is the cost of ending inventory under average cost at April 30? (*Note:* Use four decimal places for per-unit calculations and round all other numbers to the nearest dollar.)

a. $34,667
b. $35,838
c. $66,162
d. $67,333

CORNERSTONE EXERCISES

OBJECTIVE 1
CORNERSTONE 6.1

Cornerstone Exercise 6-19 Applying the Cost of Goods Sold Model

Hempstead Company has the following data for 2013:

Item	Units	Cost
Inventory, 12/31/2012	940	$10,340
Purchases	4,510	49,610
Inventory, 12/31/2013	770	8,470

Required:

1. How many units were sold?
2. Using the cost of goods sold model, determine the cost of goods sold.

Use the following information for Cornerstone Exercises 6-20 and 6-21:
Mathis Company and Reece Company use the perpetual inventory system. The following transactions occurred during the month of April:

a. On April 1, Mathis purchased merchandise on account from Reece with credit terms of 2/10, n/30. The selling price of the merchandise was $3,100, and the cost of the merchandise sold was $2,225.
b. On April 1, Mathis paid freight charges of $250 cash to have the goods delivered to its warehouse.
c. On April 8, Mathis returned $800 of the merchandise which had originally cost Reece $500.
d. On April 10, Mathis paid Reece the balance due.

Cornerstone Exercise 6-20 Recording Purchase Transactions

OBJECTIVE 2
CORNERSTONE 6.2

Refer to the information for Mathis and Reece companies on the previous page.

Required:

1. Prepare the journal entry to record the April 1 purchase of merchandise and payment of freight by Mathis.
2. Prepare the journal entry to record the April 8 return of merchandise.
3. Prepare the journal entry to record the April 10 payment to Reece.

Cornerstone Exercise 6-21 Recording Sales Transactions

OBJECTIVE 2
CORNERSTONE 6.3

Refer to the information for Mathis and Reece companies on the previous page.

Required:

Prepare the journal entries to record these transactions on Reece's books.

Use the following information for Cornerstone Exercises 6-22 through 6-25:
Filimonov Inc. has the following information related to purchases and sales of one of its inventory items:

Date	Description	Units Purchased at Cost	Units Sold at Retail
June 1	Beginning inventory	200 units @ \$10 = \$2,000	
9	Purchase 1	300 units @ \$12 = \$3,600	
14	Sale 1		400 units @ \$25
22	Purchase 2	250 units @ \$14 = \$3,500	
29	Sale 2		225 units @ \$25

Cornerstone Exercise 6-22 Inventory Costing: FIFO

OBJECTIVE 3
CORNERSTONE 6.5

Refer to the information for Filimonov Inc. and assume that the company uses a perpetual inventory system.

Required:

Calculate the cost of goods sold and the cost of ending inventory using the FIFO inventory costing method.

Cornerstone Exercise 6-23 Inventory Costing: LIFO

OBJECTIVE 3
CORNERSTONE 6.6

Refer to the information for Filimonov Inc. and assume that the company uses a perpetual inventory system.

Required:

Calculate the cost of goods sold and the cost of ending inventory using the LIFO inventory costing method.

Cornerstone Exercise 6-24 Inventory Costing: Average Cost

OBJECTIVE 3
CORNERSTONE 6.7

Refer to the information for Filimonov Inc. and assume that the company uses a perpetual inventory system.

Required:

Calculate the cost of goods sold and the cost of ending inventory using the average cost method. (*Note:* Use four decimal places for per-unit calculations and round all other numbers to the nearest dollar.)

OBJECTIVE 4
CORNERSTONE 6.5, 6.6, 6.7

Cornerstone Exercise 6-25 Effects of Inventory Costing Methods

Refer to your answers for Filimonov Inc. in **Cornerstone Exercises 6-22** through **6-24.**

Required:

1. In a period of rising prices, which inventory costing method produces the highest amount for ending inventory?
2. In a period of rising prices, which inventory costing method produces the highest net income?
3. In a period of rising prices, which inventory costing method produces the lowest payment for income taxes?
4. In a period of rising prices, which inventory method generally produces the most realistic amount for cost of goods sold? For inventory? Would your answer change if inventory prices were decreasing during the period?

OBJECTIVE 5
CORNERSTONE 6.8

Cornerstone Exercise 6-26 Lower of Cost or Market

The accountant for Murphy Company prepared the following analysis of its inventory at year end:

Item	Units	Cost per Unit	Market Value
RSK-89013	600	$38	$47
LKW-91247	420	47	40
QEC-57429	510	26	32

Required:

1. Compute the carrying value of the ending inventory using the lower of cost or market method applied on an item-by-item basis.
2. Prepare the journal entry required to value the inventory at lower of cost or market.

OBJECTIVE 6
CORNERSTONE 6.9

Cornerstone Exercise 6-27 Inventory Analysis

Singleton Inc. reported the following information for the current year:

Net sales	$650,000	Inventory, 1/1	$21,250
Cost of goods sold	495,000	Inventory, 12/31	24,850
Gross profit	$155,000		

Required:

Compute Singleton's (a) gross profit ratio, (b) inventory turnover ratio, and (c) average days to sell inventory. (*Note:* Round all answers to two decimal places.)

OBJECTIVE 7
CORNERSTONE 6.10

Cornerstone Exercise 6-28 Inventory Errors

McLelland Inc. reported net income of $175,000 for 2013 and $210,000 for 2014. Early in 2014, McLelland discovers that the December 31, 2013 ending inventory was overstated by $20,000. For simplicity, ignore taxes.

Required:

1. What is the correct net income for 2013? For 2014?
2. Assuming the error was not corrected, what is the effect on the balance sheet at December 31, 2013? At December 31, 2014?

OBJECTIVE 8
CORNERSTONE 6.11

Cornerstone Exercise 6-29 *(Appendix 6A)* Recording Purchase Transactions

Refer to the information for Mathis Company (p. 336) and assume that Mathis uses a periodic inventory system.

Required:

1. Prepare the journal entry to record the April 1 purchase of merchandise and payment of freight by Mathis.
2. Prepare the journal entry to record the April 8 return of merchandise.
3. Prepare the journal entry to record the April 10 payment to Reece.

Cornerstone Exercise 6-30 *(Appendix 6B)* Inventory Costing Methods: Periodic FIFO

OBJECTIVE 9
CORNERSTONE 6.12

Refer to the information for Filimonov Inc. (p. 337) and assume that the company uses a periodic inventory system.

Required:

Calculate the cost of goods sold and the cost of ending inventory using the FIFO inventory costing method.

Cornerstone Exercise 6-31 *(Appendix 6B)* Inventory Costing Methods: Periodic LIFO

OBJECTIVE 9
CORNERSTONE 6.13

Refer to the information for Filimonov Inc. (p. 337) and assume that the company uses a periodic inventory system.

Required:

Calculate the cost of goods sold and the cost of ending inventory using the LIFO inventory costing method.

Cornerstone Exercise 6-32 *(Appendix 6B)* Inventory Costing Methods: Periodic Average Cost

OBJECTIVE 9
CORNERSTONE 6.14

Refer to the information for Filimonov Inc. (p. 337) and assume that the company uses a periodic inventory system.

Required:

Calculate the cost of goods sold and the cost of ending inventory using the average cost method. (*Note:* Use four decimal places for per-unit calculations and round all other numbers to the nearest dollar.)

BRIEF EXERCISES

Brief Exercise 6-33 Applying the Cost of Goods Sold Model

OBJECTIVE 1

Milton Company reported inventory of $60,000 at the beginning of 2013. During the year, it purchased inventory of $625,000 and sold inventory for $950,000. A count of inventory at the end of the year determined that the cost of inventory on hand was $50,000.

Required:

1. What was Milton's cost of goods sold for 2013?
2. What is Milton's gross margin for the year?

Brief Exercise 6-34 Recording Purchase and Sales Transactions

OBJECTIVE 2

Raymond Company and Geeslin Company both use a perpetual inventory system. The following transactions occurred during the month of January:

Jan. 1	Raymond purchased $5,000 of merchandise on account from Geeslin with credit terms of 2/10, n/30. The cost of the merchandise was $3,750.
8	Raymond returned $500 of the merchandise to Geeslin. The cost of the merchandise returned was $375.
10	Raymond paid invoices totaling $3,000 to Geeslin for the merchandise purchased on January 1.
30	Raymond paid Geeslin the balance due.

(Continued)

Required:

Prepare the journal entries to record these transactions on the books of Raymond and Geeslin.

Use the following information for Brief Exercises 6-35 and 6-36.

Tyler Company has the following information related to purchases and sales of one of its inventory items.

Date	Description	Units Purchased at Cost	Units Sold at Retail
Sept. 1	Beginning inventory	20 units @ $5	
10	Purchase	30 units @ $8	
20	Sales		40 units @ $15
25	Purchase	25 units at $10	

OBJECTIVE 3

Brief Exercise 6-35 Inventory Costing Methods

Refer to the information for Tyler Company above and assume the company uses a perpetual inventory system.

Required:

Calculate ending inventory and cost of goods sold using the FIFO, LIFO, and average cost methods.

OBJECTIVE 4

Brief Exercise 6-36 Effects of Inventory Costing Methods

Refer to the information for Tyler Company above.

Required:

1. Which inventory costing method produces the highest amount for net income?
2. Which inventory costing method produces the lowest amount for taxes?
3. Which inventory costing method produces the highest amount for ending inventory?
4. How would your answers to Requirements 1–3 change if inventory prices declined during the period?

OBJECTIVE 5

Brief Exercise 6-37 Lower of Cost or Market

Garcia Company's inventory at the end of the year was recorded in its accounting records at $17,800. Due to technological changes in the market, Garcia would be able to replace its inventory for $16,500.

Required:

1. Using the lower of cost or market method, what amount should Garcia report for inventory on its balance sheet at the end of the year?
2. Prepare the journal entry required to value the inventory at the lower of cost or market.

OBJECTIVE 6

Brief Exercise 6-38 Inventory Analysis

Callahan Company reported the following information for the current year:

Net sales revenue	$280,000
Cost of goods sold	120,000
Beginning inventory	5,000
Ending inventory	10,000

Required:

1. Compute Callahan's (a) gross profit ratio, (b) inventory turnover ratio, and (c) average days to sell inventory. (Round all answers to two decimal places.)
2. Explain the meaning of each number.

Brief Exercise 6-39 Inventory Errors OBJECTIVE 7

Haywood Inc. reported the following information for 2013:

Beginning inventory	$ 25,000
Ending inventory	50,000
Sales revenue	1,000,000
Cost of goods sold	620,000

A physical count of inventory at the end of the year showed that ending inventory was actually $65,000.

Required:

1. What is the correct cost of goods sold and gross profit for 2013?
2. Assuming the error was not corrected, what is the effect on the balance sheet at December 31, 2013? At December 31, 2014?

Brief Exercise 6-40 *(Appendix 6A)* Recording Purchase and Sales Transactions OBJECTIVE 8

Refer to the information for Raymond Company in **Brief Exercise 6-34** and assume that the company uses the periodic inventory system.

Required:

Prepare the journal entries to record these transactions on the books of Raymond Company.

Brief Exercise 6-41 *(Appendix 6B)* Inventory Costing Methods: Periodic Inventory Systems. OBJECTIVE 9

Refer to the information for Tyler Company in **Brief Exercise 6-35** and assume that the company uses the periodic inventory system.

Required:

Calculate the cost of goods sold and the cost of ending inventory using the FIFO, LIFO, and average cost methods. (*Note:* Use four decimal places for per-unit calculations and round all other numbers to the nearest whole dollar.)

EXERCISES

Exercise 6-42 Applying the Cost of Goods Sold Model OBJECTIVE 1

Wilson Company sells a single product. At the beginning of the year, Wilson had 150 units in stock at a cost of $8 each. During the year, Wilson purchased 825 more units at a cost of $8 each and sold 240 units at $13 each, 210 units at $15 each, and 335 units at $14 each.

Required:

1. Using the cost of goods sold model, what is the amount of ending inventory and cost of goods sold?
2. What is Wilson's gross margin for the year?

Exercise 6-43 Applying the Cost of Goods Sold Model OBJECTIVE 1

ILLUSTRATING RELATIONSHIPS

The following amounts were obtained from the accounting records of Steed Company:

	2011	2012	2013
Beginning inventory	$ 9,600	(b)	(d)
Net purchases	(a)	$55,300	$51,100
Ending inventory	11,200	(c)	13,750
Cost of goods sold	44,500	49,800	(e)

Required:

Compute the missing amounts.

OBJECTIVE 2

Exercise 6-44 Perpetual and Periodic Inventory Systems

Below is a list of inventory systems options.

a. Perpetual inventory system
b. Periodic inventory system
c. Both perpetual and periodic inventory systems

Required:

Match each option with one of the following:

1. Only revenue is recorded as sales are made during the period; the cost of goods sold is recorded at the end of the period.
2. Cost of goods sold is determined as each sale is made.
3. Inventory purchases are recorded in an inventory account.
4. Inventory purchases are recorded in a purchases account.
5. Cost of goods sold is determined only at the end of the period by subtracting the cost of ending inventory from the cost of goods available for sale.
6. Both revenue and cost of goods sold are recorded during the period as sales are made.
7. The inventory is verified by a physical count.

OBJECTIVE 2

Exercise 6-45 Recording Purchases

Compass Inc. purchased 1,250 bags of insulation, on account, from Glassco Inc. The bags of insulation cost $5.50 each. Compass paid Turner Trucking $320 to have the bags of insulation shipped to its warehouse. Compass returned 50 bags that were defective and paid for the remainder. Assume that Compass uses the perpetual inventory system and that Glassco did not offer a purchase discount.

Required:

1. Prepare a journal entry to record the purchase of the bags of insulation.
2. Prepare the entry to record the payment for shipping.
3. Prepare the entry for the return of the defective bags.
4. Prepare the entry to record the payment for the bags kept by Compass.
5. What is the total cost of this purchase?

OBJECTIVE 2

Exercise 6-46 Recording Purchases

Dawson Enterprises uses the perpetual system to record inventory transactions. In a recent month, Dawson engaged in the following transactions:

a. On April 1, Dawson purchased merchandise on credit for $25,150 with terms 2/10, n/30.
b. On April 2, Dawson purchased merchandise on credit for $28,200 with terms 3/15, n/25.
c. On April 9, Dawson paid for the purchase made on April 1.
d. On April 25, Dawson paid for the merchandise purchased on April 2.

Required:

Prepare journal entries for these four transactions.

OBJECTIVE 2

Exercise 6-47 Recording Purchases and Shipping Terms

On May 12, Digital Distributors received three shipments of merchandise. The first was shipped F.O.B. shipping point, had a total invoice price of $142,500, and was delivered by a trucking company that charged an additional $8,300 for transportation charges from Digital. The second was shipped F.O.B. shipping point and had a total invoice price of $87,250, including transportation charges of $5,700 that were prepaid by the seller. The third shipment was shipped F.O.B. destination and had an invoice price of $21,650, excluding transportation charges of $1,125 paid by the seller. Digital uses a perpetual inventory system. Digital has not paid any of the invoices.

Required:

Prepare journal entries to record these purchases.

Exercise 6-48 Recording Sales and Shipping Terms

OBJECTIVE 2

Stanley Company shipped the following merchandise during the last week of December 2013. All sales were on credit.

Sales Price	Shipping Terms	Date Goods Shipped	Date Goods Received
$5,460	F.O.B. shipping point	December 27	January 3
$3,800	F.O.B. destination	December 29	January 5
$4,250	F.O.B. destination	December 29	December 31

Required:

1. Compute the total amount of sales revenue recognized by Stanley in December 2013.
2. **CONCEPTUAL CONNECTION** If Stanley included all of the above shipments as revenue, what would be the effect on Stanley's assets, liabilities, stockholders' equity, revenues, expenses, and net income for 2013?

Exercise 6-49 Recording Purchases and Sales

OBJECTIVE 2

Printer Supply Company sells computer printers and printer supplies. One of its products is a toner cartridge for laser printers. At the beginning of 2013, there were 225 cartridges on hand that cost $62 each. During 2013, Printer Supply purchased 1,475 cartridges at $62 each. After inspection, Printer Supply determined that 15 cartridges were defective and returned them to the supplier. Printer Supply also sold 830 cartridges at $95 each and sold an additional 710 cartridges at $102 each after a midyear selling price increase. Customers returned 20 of the cartridges that were purchased at $102 to Printer Supply for miscellaneous reasons. Assume that Printer Supply uses a perpetual inventory system.

Required:

1. Prepare summary journal entries to record the purchases, sales, and return of inventory. Assume that all purchases and sales are on credit but no discounts were offered.
2. What is the cost of ending inventory, cost of goods sold, and gross profit for 2013?

Exercise 6-50 Inventory Costing Methods

OBJECTIVE 3 4

Crandall Distributors uses a perpetual inventory system and has the following data available for inventory, purchases, and sales for a recent year:

Activity	Units	Purchase Price (per unit)	Sale Price (per unit)
Beginning inventory	110	$7.10	
Purchase 1, Jan. 18	575	7.20	
Sale 1	380		$12.00
Sale 2	225		12.00
Purchase 2, Mar. 10	680	7.50	
Sale 3	270		12.00
Sale 4	290		12.50
Purchase 3, Sept. 30	230	7.70	
Sale 5	240		12.50

Required:

1. Compute the cost of ending inventory and the cost of goods sold using the specific identification method. Assume the ending inventory is made up of 40 units from beginning inventory, 30 units from Purchase 1, 80 units from Purchase 2, and 40 units from Purchase 3.
2. Compute the cost of ending inventory and cost of goods sold using the FIFO inventory costing method.
3. Compute the cost of ending inventory and cost of goods sold using the LIFO inventory costing method.
4. Compute the cost of ending inventory and cost of goods sold using the average cost inventory costing method. (*Note:* Use four decimal places for per-unit calculations and round all other numbers to the nearest dollar.)

(Continued)

5. **CONCEPTUAL CONNECTION** Compare the ending inventory and cost of goods sold computed under all four methods. What can you conclude about the effects of the inventory costing methods on the balance sheet and the income statement?

OBJECTIVE 3 4 6

Exercise 6-51 Inventory Costing Methods

On June 1, Welding Products Company had a beginning inventory of 210 cases of welding rods that had been purchased for $88 per case. Welding Products purchased 1,150 cases at a cost of $95 per case on June 3. On June 19, the company purchased another 950 cases at a cost of $112 per case. Sales data for the welding rods are:

Date	Cases Sold
June 9	990
June 29	975

Welding Products uses a perpetual inventory system, and the sales price of the welding rods was $130 per case.

Required:

1. Compute the cost of ending inventory and cost of goods sold using the FIFO method.
2. Compute the cost of ending inventory and cost of goods sold using the LIFO method.
3. Compute the cost of ending inventory and cost of goods sold using the average cost method. (*Note:* Use four decimal places for per-unit calculations and round all other numbers to the nearest dollar.)
4. **CONCEPTUAL CONNECTION** Assume that operating expenses are $21,600 and Welding Products has a 30% tax rate. How much will the cash paid for income taxes differ among the three inventory methods?
5. **CONCEPTUAL CONNECTION** Compute Welding Products' gross profit ratio (rounded to two decimal places) and inventory turnover ratio (rounded to three decimal places) under each of the three inventory costing methods. How would the choice of inventory costing method affect these ratios?

OBJECTIVE 4

Exercise 6-52 Financial Statement Effects of FIFO and LIFO

The chart below lists financial statement items that may be affected by the use of either the FIFO or LIFO inventory costing methods.

	FIFO	LIFO
Ending inventory		
Cost of goods sold		
Gross margin		
Income before taxes		
Payments for income taxes		
Net income		

Required:

CONCEPTUAL CONNECTION Assuming that prices are rising, complete the chart by indicating whether the specified item is (a) higher or (b) lower under FIFO and LIFO.

OBJECTIVE 4

Exercise 6-53 Effects of Inventory Costing Methods

Jefferson Enterprises has the following income statement data available for 2013:

Sales revenue	$828,600
Operating expenses	370,400
Interest expense	42,100
Income tax rate	34%

Jefferson uses a perpetual inventory accounting system and the average cost method. Jefferson is considering adopting the FIFO or LIFO method for costing inventory. Jefferson's accountant prepared the following data:

	If Average Cost Used	If FIFO Used	If LIFO Used
Ending inventory	$ 65,950	$ 78,500	$ 40,100
Cost of goods sold	399,050	386,500	424,900

Required:

1. Compute income before taxes, income taxes expense, and net income for each of the three inventory costing methods. (Round to the nearest dollar.)
2. **CONCEPTUAL CONNECTION** Why are the cost of goods sold and ending inventory amounts different for each of the three methods? What do these amounts tell us about the purchase price of inventory during the year?
3. **CONCEPTUAL CONNECTION** Which method produces the most realistic amount for net income? For inventory? Explain your answer.

Exercise 6-54 Inventory Costing Methods

OBJECTIVE 3 4

Neyman Inc. has the following data for purchases and sales of inventory:

Date	Units	Cost per Unit
Beginning inventory	22	$400
Purchase 1, Feb. 24	130	370
Sale 1	145	
Purchase 2, July 2	180	330
Purchase 3, Oct. 31	90	250
Sale 2	265	

All sales were made at a sales price of $450 per unit. Assume that Neyman uses a perpetual inventory system.

Required:

1. Compute the cost of goods sold and the cost of ending inventory using the FIFO, LIFO, and average cost methods. (*Note:* Use four decimal places for per-unit calculations and round all other numbers to the nearest dollar.)
2. **CONCEPTUAL CONNECTION** Why is the cost of goods sold lower with LIFO than with FIFO?

Exercise 6-55 Effects of FIFO and LIFO

OBJECTIVE 3 4

Sheepskin Company sells to colleges and universities a special paper that is used for diplomas. Sheepskin typically makes one purchase of the special paper each year on January 1. Assume that Sheepskin uses a perpetual inventory system. You have the following data for the 3 years ending in 2013:

2011	
Beginning inventory	0 pages
Purchases	10,000 pages at $1.60 per page
Sales	8,500 pages
2012	
Beginning inventory	1,500 pages
Purchases	16,200 pages at $2.00 per page
Sales	15,000 pages
2013	
Beginning inventory	2,700 pages
Purchases	18,000 pages at $2.50 per page
Sales	20,100 pages

(Continued)

Required:

1. What would the ending inventory and cost of goods sold be for each year if FIFO is used?
2. What would the ending inventory and cost of goods sold be for each year if LIFO is used?
3. **CONCEPTUAL CONNECTION** For each year, explain the cause of the differences in cost of goods sold under FIFO and LIFO.

OBJECTIVE 5

Exercise 6-56 Lower of Cost or Market

Meredith's Appliance Store has the following data for the items in its inventory at the end of the accounting period:

Item	Number of Units	Historical Cost per Unit	Market Value per Unit
Window air conditioner	25	$180	$105
Dishwasher	22	225	210
Refrigerator	35	420	425
Microwave	15	220	175
Washer (clothing)	28	180	220
Dryer (clothing)	18	210	225

Required:

1. Compute the carrying value of Meredith's ending inventory using the lower of cost or market rule applied on an item-by-item basis.
2. Prepare the journal entry required to value the inventory at lower of cost or market.
3. **CONCEPTUAL CONNECTION** What is the conceptual justification for valuing inventory at the lower of cost or market?

OBJECTIVE 5

Exercise 6-57 Lower of Cost or Market

Shaw Systems sells a limited line of specially made products, using television advertising campaigns in large cities. At year end, Shaw has the following data for its inventory:

Item	Number of Units	Historical Cost per Unit	Market Value per Unit
Phone	625	$ 24	$ 20
Stereo	180	177	190
Electric shaver	215	30	28
MP3 alarm clock	450	26	25
Handheld game system	570	40	42

Required:

1. Compute the carrying value of the ending inventory using the lower of cost or market rule applied on an item-by-item basis.
2. Prepare the journal entry required to value the inventory at lower of cost or market.
3. **CONCEPTUAL CONNECTION** What is the impact of applying the lower of cost or market rule on the financial statements of the current period? What is the impact on the financial statements of a subsequent period in which the inventory is sold?

OBJECTIVE 6

Exercise 6-58 Analyzing Inventory

The recent financial statements of McLelland Clothing Inc. include the following data:

Sales	$754,690
Cost of goods sold:	
Computed under FIFO	528,600
Computed under LIFO	555,000
Average inventory:	
Computed under FIFO	72,200
Computed under LIFO	45,800

Required:

1. Calculate McLelland's gross profit ratio (rounded to two decimal places), inventory turnover ratio (rounded to three decimal places), and the average days to sell inventory (assume a 365-day year and round to two decimal places) using the FIFO inventory costing method. Be sure to explain what each ratio means.
2. Calculate McLelland's gross profit ratio (rounded to two decimal places), inventory turnover ratio (rounded to three decimal places), and the average days to sell inventory (assume a 365-day year and round to two decimal places) using the LIFO inventory costing method. Be sure to explain what each ratio means.
3. **CONCEPTUAL CONNECTION** Which ratios—the ones computed using FIFO or LIFO inventory values—provide the better indicator of how successful McLelland was at managing and controlling its inventory?

Exercise 6-59 Effects of an Error in Ending Inventory

OBJECTIVE 7

Waymire Company prepared the partial income statements presented below for 2013 and 2012.

	2013		2012	
Sales revenue		$ 538,200		$ 483,700
Cost of goods sold:				
Beginning inventory	$ 39,300		$ 32,100	
Purchases	343,200		292,700	
Cost of goods available for sale	$382,500		$324,800	
Ending inventory	(46,800)	335,700	(39,300)	285,500
Gross margin		$ 202,500		$ 198,200
Operating expenses		(167,200)		(151,600)
Income before taxes		$ 35,300		$ 46,600

During 2014, Waymire's accountant discovered that ending inventory for 2012 had been understated by $6,500.

Required:

1. Prepare corrected income statements for 2013 and 2012.
2. Prepare a schedule showing each financial statement item affected by the error and the amount of the error for that item (ignore the effect of income taxes). Indicate whether each error is an overstatement (+) or an understatement (−).

Exercise 6-60 *(Appendix 6A)* Recording Purchases

OBJECTIVE 8

Compass Inc. purchased 1,250 bags of insulation, on account, from Glassco Inc. The bags of insulation cost $5.50 each. Compass paid Turner Trucking $320 to have the bags of insulation shipped to its warehouse. Compass returned 50 bags that were defective and paid for the remainder. Assume that Compass uses the periodic inventory system.

Required:

1. Prepare a journal entry to record the purchase of the bags of insulation.
2. Prepare the entry to record the payment for shipping.
3. Prepare the entry for the return of the defective bags.
4. Prepare the entry to record the payment for the bags kept by Compass.
5. What is the total cost of this purchase?
6. **CONCEPTUAL CONNECTION** If you have previously worked **Exercise 6-45**, compare your answers. What are the differences? Be sure to explain why the differences occurred.

Exercise 6-61 *(Appendices 6A and 6B)* Recording Purchases and Sales

OBJECTIVE 8 9

Printer Supply Company sells computer printers and printer supplies. One of its products is a toner cartridge for laser printers. At the beginning of 2013, there were 225 cartridges on hand at

(Continued)

a cost of $62 each. During 2013, Printer Supply purchased 1,475 cartridges at $62 each, sold 830 cartridges at $95 each, and sold an additional 710 cartridges at $102 each after a midyear selling price increase. Printer Supply returned 15 defective cartridges to the supplier. In addition, customers returned 20 cartridges that were purchased at $102 to Printer Supply for various reasons. Assume that Printer Supply uses a periodic inventory system.

Required:

1. Prepare journal entries to record the purchases, sales, and return of inventory. Assume that all purchases and sales are on credit but no discounts were offered.
2. What is the cost of ending inventory, cost of goods sold, and gross profit for 2013?
3. **CONCEPTUAL CONNECTION** If you have previously worked **Exercise 6-49**, compare your answers. What are the differences? Be sure to explain why the differences occurred.

OBJECTIVE 9

Exercise 6-62 *(Appendix 6B)* Inventory Costing Methods: Periodic Inventory System

Jackson Company had 400 units in beginning inventory at a cost of $20 each. Jackson's 2013 purchases were:

Date	Purchases
Feb. 21	5,200 units at $24 each
July 15	4,800 units at $28 each
Sept. 30	8,500 units at $30 each

Jackson uses a periodic inventory system and sold 18,500 units at $50 each during 2013.

Required:

1. Calculate the cost of ending inventory and the cost of goods sold using the FIFO, LIFO and average cost methods. (*Note:* Use four decimal places for per-unit calculations and round all other numbers to the nearest dollar.)
2. Prepare income statements through gross margin using each of the costing methods in Requirement 1.
3. **CONCEPTUAL CONNECTION** What is the effect of each inventory costing method on income?

OBJECTIVE 9

Exercise 6-63 *(Appendix 6B)* Inventory Costing Methods: Periodic Inventory System

The inventory accounting records for Lee Enterprises contained the following data:

Beginning inventory	1,400 units at $12 each
Purchase 1, Feb. 26	2,400 units at $16 each
Sale 1, March 9	2,300 units at $27 each
Purchase 2, June 14	2,200 units at $20 each
Sale 2, Sept. 22	1,900 units at $29 each

Required:

1. Calculate the cost of ending inventory and the cost of goods sold using the FIFO, LIFO, and average cost methods. (*Note:* Use four decimal places for per-unit calculations and round all other numbers to the nearest dollar.)
2. **CONCEPTUAL CONNECTION** Compare the ending inventory and cost of goods sold computed under all three methods. What can you conclude about the effects of the inventory costing methods on the balance sheet and the income statement?

Exercise 6-64 *(Appendix 6B)* Inventory Costing Methods: Periodic System

OBJECTIVE 9

Harrington Company had the following data for inventory during a recent year:

	Units		Cost per Unit	Total Cost	
Beginning inventory		500	$ 9.00		$ 4,500
Purchase 1, Jan. 28	1,600		9.40	$15,040	
Purchase 2, May 2	1,200		10.20	12,240	
Purchase 3, Aug. 13	1,400		10.80	15,120	
Purchase 4, Nov. 9	1,100		11.30	12,430	
Total purchases		5,300			54,830
Goods available for sale		5,800			$59,330
Less: Sales		(5,240)			
Ending inventory		560			

Assume that Harrington uses a periodic inventory accounting system.

Required:

1. Using the FIFO, LIFO, and average cost methods, compute the ending inventory and cost of goods sold. (*Note:* Use four decimal places for per-unit calculations and round all other numbers to the nearest dollar.)
2. **CONCEPTUAL CONNECTION** Which method will produce the most realistic amount for income? For inventory?
3. **CONCEPTUAL CONNECTION** Which method will produce the lowest amount paid for taxes?

PROBLEM SET A

Problem 6-65A Applying the Cost of Goods Sold Model

OBJECTIVE 9

ILLUSTRATING RELATIONSHIPS

The following amounts were obtained from the accounting records of Rabren Supply Company:

	2012		2013	
Net sales		$359,620		$423,150
Cost of goods sold:				
Beginning inventory	$36,800		(d)	
Purchases	(a)		301,600	
Goods available for sale	(b)		(e)	
Ending inventory	42,780		(f)	
Cost of goods sold		(c)		289,700
Gross margin		$116,450		(g)

Required:

Compute the missing amounts.

Problem 6-66A Recording Sale and Purchase Transactions

OBJECTIVE 2

Alpharack Company sells a line of tennis equipment to retailers. Alpharack uses the perpetual inventory system and engaged in the following transactions during April 2013, its first month of operations:

a. On April 2, Alpharack purchased, on credit, 360 Wilbur T-100 tennis rackets with credit terms of 2/10, n/30. The rackets were purchased at a cost of $30 each. Alpharack paid Barker Trucking $195 to transport the tennis rackets from the manufacturer to Alpharack's warehouse, shipping terms were F.O.B. shipping point, and the items were shipped on April 2.

b. On April 3, Alpharack purchased, for cash, 115 packs of tennis balls for $10 per pack.

(Continued)

c. On April 4, Alpharack purchased tennis clothing, on credit, from Designer Tennis Wear. The cost of the clothing was $8,250. Credit terms were 2/10, n/25.
d. On April 10, Alpharack paid for the purchase of the tennis rackets in Transaction a.
e. On April 15, Alpharack determined that $325 of the tennis clothing was defective. Alpharack returned the defective merchandise to Designer Tennis Wear.
f. On April 20, Alpharack sold 118 tennis rackets at $90 each, 92 packs of tennis balls at $12 per pack, and $5,380 of tennis clothing. All sales were for cash. The cost of the merchandise sold was $7,580.
g. On April 23, customers returned $860 of the merchandise purchased on April 20. The cost of the merchandise returned was $450.
h. On April 25, Alpharack sold another 55 tennis rackets, on credit, for $90 each and 15 packs of tennis balls at $12 per pack, for cash. The cost of the merchandise sold was $1,800.
i. On April 29, Alpharack paid Designer Tennis Wear for the clothing purchased on April 4 minus the return on April 15.
j. On April 30, Alpharack purchased 20 tennis bags, on credit, from Bag Designs for $320. The bags were shipped F.O.B. destination and arrived at Alpharack on May 3.

Required:

1. Prepare the journal entries to record the sale and purchase transactions for Alpharack during April 2013.
2. Assuming operating expenses of $8,500 and income taxes of $1,180, prepare Alpharack's income statement for April 2013.

OBJECTIVE 2 3 4

Problem 6-67A Inventory Costing Methods

Anderson's Department Store has the following data for inventory, purchases, and sales of merchandise for December:

Activity	Units	Purchase Price (per unit)	Sale Price (per unit)
Beginning inventory	10	$8.00	
Purchase 1, Dec. 2	22	8.80	
Purchase 2, Dec. 5	26	9.05	
Sale 1, Dec. 7	19		$20.00
Sale 2, Dec. 10	25		20.00
Purchase 3, Dec. 12	12	9.80	
Sale 3, Dec. 14	20		20.00

Anderson's uses a perpetual inventory system. All purchases and sales were for cash.

Required:

1. Compute cost of goods sold and the cost of ending inventory using FIFO.
2. Compute cost of goods sold and the cost of ending inventory using LIFO.
3. Compute cost of goods sold and the cost of ending inventory using the average cost method. (*Note:* Use four decimal places for per-unit calculations.)
4. Prepare the journal entries to record these transactions assuming Anderson chooses to use the FIFO method.
5. **CONCEPTUAL CONNECTION** Which method would result in the lowest amount paid for taxes?

OBJECTIVE 3 4 6

Problem 6-68A Inventory Costing Methods

Gavin Products uses a perpetual inventory system. For 2012 and 2013, Gavin has the following data:

Activity	Units	Purchase Price (per unit)	Sale Price (per unit)
2012			
Beginning inventory	200	$ 9	
Purchase 1, Feb. 15	300	11	
Sale 1, Mar. 10	320		$25
Purchase 2, Sept. 15	500	12	
Sale 2, Nov. 3	550		25
Purchase 3, Dec. 20	150	13	
2013			
Sale 3, Apr. 4	200		25
Purchase 4, June 25	200	14	
Sale 4, Dec. 18	150		25

Required:

1. For each year, compute cost of goods sold, the cost of ending inventory, and gross margin using FIFO.
2. For each year, compute cost of goods sold, the cost of ending inventory, and gross margin using LIFO.
3. For each year, compute cost of goods sold, the cost of ending inventory, and gross margin using the average cost method. (*Note:* Use four decimal places for per-unit calculations and round all other numbers to the nearest dollar.)
4. **CONCEPTUAL CONNECTION** Which method would result in the lowest amount paid for taxes?
5. **CONCEPTUAL CONNECTION** Which method produces the most realistic amount for income? For inventory? Explain your answer.
6. **CONCEPTUAL CONNECTION** Compute Gavin's gross profit ratio and inventory turnover ratio under each of the three inventory costing methods. (*Note:* Round answers to two decimal places.) How would the choice of inventory costing method affect these ratios?

Problem 6-69A Lower of Cost or Market

OBJECTIVE 5

Sue Stone, the president of Tippecanoe Home Products, has prepared the following information for the company's television inventory at the end of 2013:

Model	Quantity	Cost per Unit	Market Value per Unit
T-260	15	$250	$445
S-256	28	325	300
R-193	20	210	230
Z-376	15	285	250

Required:

1. Determine the carrying amount of the inventory using lower of cost or market applied on an item-by-item basis.
2. Prepare the journal entry required to value the inventory at lower of cost or market.
3. **CONCEPTUAL CONNECTION** What is the impact of applying the lower of cost or market rule on the financial statements of the current period? What is the impact on the financial statements of a subsequent period in which the inventory is sold?

Problem 6-70A Inventory Costing and LCM

OBJECTIVE 3 5

Ortman Enterprises sells a chemical used in various manufacturing processes. On January 1, 2013, Ortman had 5,000,000 gallons on hand, for which it had paid $0.50 per gallon. During 2013, Ortman made the following purchases:

(Continued)

Date	Gallons	Cost per Gallon	Total Cost
Feb. 20	10,000,000	$0.52	$ 5,200,000
May 15	25,000,000	0.56	14,000,000
Sept. 12	32,000,000	0.60	19,200,000

During 2013, Ortman sold 65,000,000 gallons at $0.75 per gallon (35,000,000 gallons were sold on June 29 and 30,000,000 gallons were sold on Nov. 22), leaving an ending inventory of 7,000,000 gallons. Assume that Ortman uses a perpetual inventory system. Ortman uses the lower of cost or market for its inventories, as required by generally accepted accounting principles.

Required:

1. Assume that the market value of the chemical is $0.76 per gallon on December 31, 2013. Compute the cost of ending inventory using the FIFO, LIFO, and average cost methods, and then apply LCM. (*Note:* Use four decimal places for per-unit calculations and round all other numbers to the nearest dollar.)
2. Assume that the market value of the chemical is $0.58 per gallon on December 31, 2013. Compute the cost of ending inventory using the FIFO, LIFO, and average cost methods, and then apply LCM. (*Note:* Use four decimal places for per-unit calculations and round all other numbers to the nearest dollar.)

OBJECTIVE 7

Problem 6-71A Effects of an Inventory Error

The income statements for Graul Corporation for the 3 years ending in 2013 appear below.

	2013	2012	2011
Sales revenue	$ 4,643,200	$ 4,287,500	$ 3,647,900
Cost of goods sold	(2,475,100)	(2,181,600)	(2,006,100)
Gross margin	$ 2,168,100	$ 2,105,900	$ 1,641,800
Operating expense	(1,548,600)	(1,428,400)	(1,152,800)
Income from operations	$ 619,500	$ 677,500	$ 489,000
Other expenses	(137,300)	(123,600)	(112,900)
Income before taxes	$ 482,200	$ 553,900	$ 376,100
Income tax expense (34%)	(163,948)	(188,326)	(127,874)
Net income	$ 318,252	$ 365,574	$ 248,226

During 2013, Graul discovered that the 2011 ending inventory had been misstated due to the following two transactions being recorded incorrectly.

a. A purchase return of inventory costing $42,000 was recorded twice.
b. A credit purchase of inventory made on December 20 for $28,500 was not recorded. The goods were shipped F.O.B. shipping point and were shipped on December 22, 2011.

Required:

1. Was ending inventory for 2011 overstated or understated? By how much?
2. Prepare correct income statements for all 3 years.
3. **CONCEPTUAL CONNECTION** Did the error in 2011 affect cumulative net income for the 3-year period? Explain your response.
4. **CONCEPTUAL CONNECTION** Why was the 2013 net income unaffected?

OBJECTIVE 8 9

Problem 6-72A *(Appendices 6A and 6B)* Inventory Costing Methods

Spiegel Department Store has the following data for inventory, purchases, and sales of merchandise for December:

Activity	Units	Purchase Price (per unit)	Sale Price (per unit)
Beginning inventory	10	$8.00	
Purchase 1, Dec. 2	22	8.80	
Purchase 2, Dec. 5	26	9.05	
Sale 1, Dec. 7	19		$20.00
Sale 2, Dec. 10	25		20.00
Purchase 3, Dec. 12	12	9.80	
Sale 3, Dec. 14	20		20.00

Spiegel uses a periodic inventory system. All purchases and sales are for cash.

Required:

1. Compute cost of goods sold and the cost of ending inventory using FIFO.
2. Compute cost of goods sold and the cost of ending inventory using LIFO.
3. Compute cost of goods sold and the cost of ending inventory using the average cost method. (*Note:* Use four decimal places for per-unit calculations.)
4. Prepare the journal entries to record these transactions assuming Spiegel chooses to use the FIFO method.
5. **CONCEPTUAL CONNECTION** Which method would result in the lowest amount paid for taxes?
6. **CONCEPTUAL CONNECTION** Refer to **Problem 6-67A** and compare your results. What are the differences? Be sure to explain why the differences occurred.

Problem 6-73A *(Appendix 6B)* Inventory Costing Methods

OBJECTIVE 9

Jet Black Products uses a periodic inventory system. For 2012 and 2013, Jet Black has the following data:

Activity	Units	Purchase Price (per unit)	Sale Price (per unit)
2012			
Beginning inventory	200	$ 9.00	
Purchase 1, Feb. 15	300	11.00	
Sale 1, Mar. 10	320		$25.00
Purchase 2, Sept. 15	500	12.00	
Sale 2, Nov. 3	550		25.00
Purchase 3, Dec. 20	150	13.00	
2013			
Sale 3, Apr. 4	200		25.00
Purchase 4, June 25	200	14.00	
Sale 4, Dec. 18	150		25.00

All purchases and sales are for cash.

Required:

1. Compute cost of goods sold, the cost of ending inventory, and gross margin for each year using FIFO.
2. Compute cost of goods sold, the cost of ending inventory, and gross margin for each year using LIFO.
3. Compute cost of goods sold, the cost of ending inventory, and gross margin for each year using the average cost method. (*Note:* Use four decimal places for per unit calculations and round all other numbers to the nearest dollar.)
4. **CONCEPTUAL CONNECTION** Which method would result in the lowest amount paid for taxes?

(Continued)

5. **CONCEPTUAL CONNECTION** Which method produces the most realistic amount for income? For inventory? Explain your answer.
6. **CONCEPTUAL CONNECTION** What is the effect of purchases made later in the year on the gross margin when LIFO is employed? When FIFO is employed? Be sure to explain why any differences occur.
7. **CONCEPTUAL CONNECTION** If you worked **Problem 6-68A**, compare your answers. What are the differences? Be sure to explain why any differences occurred.

PROBLEM SET B

OBJECTIVE 1

ILLUSTRATING RELATIONSHIPS

Problem 6-65B Applying the Cost of Goods Sold Model

The following amounts were obtained from the accounting records of Wachter Sports Products Inc.:

	2012		2013	
Net sales		(a)		$154,810
Cost of goods sold:				
Beginning inventory	(b)		(d)	
Purchases	104,250		(e)	
Goods available for sale	(c)		$127,500	
Ending inventory	6,940		(f)	
Cost of goods sold		104,730		(g)
Gross margin		$ 28,600		$ 38,980

Required:

Compute the missing amounts.

OBJECTIVE 2

Problem 6-66B Recording Sale and Purchase Transactions

Jordan Footwear sells athletic shoes and uses the perpetual inventory system. During June, Jordan engaged in the following transactions its first month of operations:

a. On June 1, Jordan purchased, on credit, 100 pairs of basketball shoes and 210 pairs of running shoes with credit terms of 2/10, n/30. The basketball shoes were purchased at a cost of $85 per pair, and the running shoes were purchased at a cost of $60 per pair. Jordan paid Mole Trucking $310 cash to transport the shoes from the manufacturer to Jordan's warehouse, shipping terms were F.O.B. shipping point, and the items were shipped on June 1 and arrived on June 4.
b. On June 2, Jordan purchased 88 pairs of cross-training shoes for cash. The shoes cost Jordan $65 per pair.
c. On June 6, Jordan purchased 125 pairs of tennis shoes on credit. Credit terms were 2/10, n/25. The shoes were purchased at a cost of $45 per pair.
d. On June 10, Jordan paid for the purchase of the basketball shoes and the running shoes in Transaction a.
e. On June 12, Jordan determined that $585 of the tennis shoes were defective. Jordan returned the defective merchandise to the manufacturer.
f. On June 18, Jordan sold 50 pairs of basketball shoes at $116 per pair, 92 pairs of running shoes for $85 per pair, 21 pairs of cross-training shoes for $100 per pair, and 48 pairs of tennis shoes for $68 per pair. All sales were for cash. The cost of the merchandise sold was $13,295.
g. On June 21, customers returned 10 pairs of the basketball shoes purchased on June 18. The cost of the merchandise returned was $850.
h. On June 23, Jordan sold another 20 pairs of basketball shoes, on credit, for $116 per pair and 15 pairs of cross-training shoes for $100 cash per pair. The cost of the merchandise sold was $2,675.

i. On June 30, Jordan paid for the June 6 purchase of tennis shoes minus the return on June 12.
j. On June 30, Jordan purchased 60 pairs of basketball shoes, on credit, for $85 each. The shoes were shipped F.O.B. destination and arrived at Jordan on July 3.

Required:

1. Prepare the journal entries to record the sale and purchase transactions for Jordan during June 2013.
2. Assuming operating expenses of $5,300 and income taxes of $365, prepare Jordan's income statement for June 2013.

Problem 6-67B Inventory Costing Methods

OBJECTIVE 2 3 4

Ein Company began operations in February 2013. Ein's accounting records provide the following data for the remainder of 2013 for one of the items the company sells:

Activity	Units	Purchase Price (per unit)	Sale Price (per unit)
Beginning inventory	9	$58	
Purchase 1, Feb. 15	6	72	
Purchase 2, Mar. 22	8	80	
Sale 1, Apr. 9	10		$150
Purchase 3, May 29	9	86	
Sale 2, July 10	15		150
Purchase 4, Sept. 10	8	96	
Sale 3, Oct. 15	12		150

Ein uses a perpetual inventory system. All purchases and sales were for cash.

Required:

1. Compute cost of goods sold and the cost of ending inventory using FIFO.
2. Compute cost of goods sold and the cost of ending inventory using LIFO.
3. Compute cost of goods sold and the cost of ending inventory using the average cost method. (*Note:* Use four decimal places for per-unit calculations and round all other numbers to the nearest penny.)
4. Prepare the journal entries to record these transactions assuming Ein chooses to use the FIFO method.
5. **CONCEPTUAL CONNECTION** Which method would result in the lowest amount paid for taxes?

Problem 6-68B Inventory Costing Methods

OBJECTIVE 3 4 6

Terpsichore Company uses a perpetual inventory system. For 2012 and 2013, Terpsichore has the following data:

Activity	Units	Purchase Price (per unit)	Sale Price (per unit)
2012			
Beginning inventory	100	$45	
Purchase 1, Feb. 25	700	52	
Sale 1, Apr. 15	600		$90
Purchase 2, Aug. 30	500	56	
Sale 2, Nov. 13	600		90
Purchase 3, Dec. 20	400	58	
2013			
Sale 3, Mar. 8	400		90
Purchase 4, June 28	900	62	
Sale 4, Dec. 18	200		90

(Continued)

Required:

1. For each year, compute cost of goods sold, the cost of ending inventory, and gross margin using FIFO.
2. For each year, compute cost of goods sold, the cost of ending inventory, and gross margin using LIFO.
3. For each year, compute cost of goods sold, the cost of ending inventory, and gross margin using the average cost method. (*Note:* Use four decimal places for per-unit calculations and round all other numbers to the nearest dollar.)
4. **CONCEPTUAL CONNECTION** Which method would result in the lowest amount paid for taxes?
5. **CONCEPTUAL CONNECTION** Which method produces the most realistic amount for income? For inventory? Explain your answer.
6. **CONCEPTUAL CONNECTION** Compute Terpsichore's gross profit ratio and inventory turnover ratio under each of the three inventory costing methods. (*Note:* Round answers to two decimal places.) How would the choice of inventory costing method affect these ratios?

OBJECTIVE 5

Problem 6-69B Lower of Cost or Market

Kevin Spears, the accountant of Tyler Electronics Inc. has prepared the following information for the company's inventory at the end of 2013:

Model	Quantity	Cost per Unit	Market Value per Unit
RSQ535	30	$100	$120
JKY942	52	140	125
LLM112	84	85	80
KZG428	63	105	128

Required:

1. Determine the carrying amount of the inventory using lower of cost or market applied on an item-by-item basis.
2. Prepare the journal entry required to value the inventory at lower of cost or market.
3. **CONCEPTUAL CONNECTION** What is the impact of applying the lower of cost or market rule on the financial statements of the current period? What is the impact on the financial statements of a subsequent period in which the inventory is sold?

OBJECTIVE 3 5

Problem 6-70B Inventory Costing and LCM

J&J Enterprises sells paper cups to fast-food franchises. On January 1, 2013, J&J had 5,000 cups on hand, for which it had paid $0.10 per cup. During 2013, J&J made the following purchases and sales:

Date	Units	Cost per Unit	Total Cost
Feb. 20	100,000	$0.12	$12,000
May 15	57,000	0.14	7,980
Sept. 12	85,000	0.15	12,750

During 2013, J&J sold 240,000 cups at $0.35 per cup (80,000 cups were sold on April 2 and 160,000 cups were sold on October 20), leaving an ending inventory of 7,000 cups. Assume that J&J uses a perpetual inventory system. J&J uses the lower of cost or market for its inventories, as required by generally accepted accounting principles.

Required:

1. Assume that the market value of the cups is $0.38 per cup on December 31, 2013. Compute the cost of ending inventory using the FIFO, LIFO, and average cost methods, and then apply LCM. (*Note:* Use four decimal places for per-unit calculations and round all other numbers to the nearest dollar.)

2. Assume that the market value of the cups is $0.12 per cup on December 31, 2013. Compute the cost of ending inventory using the FIFO, LIFO, and average cost methods, and then apply LCM. (*Note:* Use four decimal places for per-unit calculations and round all other numbers to the nearest dollar.)

Problem 6-71B Effects of an Inventory Error

OBJECTIVE 7

The income statements for Picard Company for the 3 years ending in 2013 appear below.

	2013	2012	2011
Sales revenue	$1,168,500	$ 998,400	$ 975,300
Cost of goods sold	(785,800)	(675,450)	(659,800)
Gross margin	$ 382,700	$ 322,950	$ 315,500
Operating expense	(162,500)	(142,800)	(155,300)
Income from operations	$ 220,200	$ 180,150	$ 160,200
Other expenses	(73,500)	(58,150)	(54,500)
Income before taxes	$ 146,700	$ 122,000	$ 105,700
Income tax expense (34%)	(49,878)	(41,480)	(35,938)
Net income	$ 96,822	$ 80,520	$ 69,762

During 2013, Picard discovered that the 2011 ending inventory had been misstated due to the following two transactions being recorded incorrectly:

a. Inventory costing $37,000 that was returned to the manufacturer (a purchase return) was not recorded. The items were included in ending inventory.
b. A credit purchase of inventory made on August 30, 2011, for $12,800 was recorded twice. The goods were shipped F.O.B. shipping point and were shipped on September 5, 2011.

Required:

1. Was ending inventory for 2011 overstated or understated? By how much?
2. Prepare correct income statements for all 3 years.
3. **CONCEPTUAL CONNECTION** Did the error in 2011 affect cumulative net income for the 3-year period? Explain your response.
4. **CONCEPTUAL CONNECTION** Why was the 2013 net income unaffected?

Problem 6-72B *(Appendices 6A and 6B)* Inventory Costing Methods

OBJECTIVE 8 9

Edwards Company began operations in February 2013. Edwards accounting records provide the following data for the remainder of 2013 for one of the items the company sells:

Activity	Units	Purchase Price (per unit)	Sale Price (per unit)
Beginning inventory	9	$58	
Purchase 1, Feb. 15	6	72	
Purchase 2, Mar. 22	8	80	
Sale 1, Apr. 9	10		$150
Purchase 3, May 29	9	86	
Sale 2, July 10	15		150
Purchase 4, Sept. 10	8	96	
Sale 3, Oct. 15	12		150

Edwards uses a periodic inventory system. All purchases and sales were for cash.

Required:

1. Compute cost of goods sold and the cost of ending inventory using FIFO.
2. Compute cost of goods sold and the cost of ending inventory using LIFO.
3. Compute cost of goods sold and the cost of ending inventory using the average cost method. (*Note:* Use four decimal places for per-unit calculations and round all other numbers to the nearest dollar.)

(Continued)

4. Prepare the journal entries to record these transactions assuming Edwards chooses to use the FIFO method.
5. **CONCEPTUAL CONNECTION** Which method would result in the lowest amount paid for taxes?
6. **CONCEPTUAL CONNECTION** Refer to **Problem 6-67B** and compare your results. What are the differences? Be sure to explain why the differences occurred.

OBJECTIVE 9

Problem 6-73B *(Appendix 6B)* Inventory Costing Methods

Grencia Company uses a periodic inventory system. For 2012 and 2013, Grencia has the following data (assume all purchases and sales are for cash):

Activity	Units	Purchase Price (per unit)	Sale Price (per unit)
2012			
Beginning inventory	100	$45	
Purchase 1, Feb. 25	700	52	
Sale 1, Apr. 15	600		$90
Purchase 2, Aug. 30	500	56	
Sale 2, Nov. 13	600		90
Purchase 3, Dec. 20	400	58	
2013			
Sale 3, Mar. 8	400		90
Purchase 4, June 28	900	62	
Sale 4, Dec. 18	200		90

Required:

1. Compute cost of goods sold, the cost of ending inventory, and gross margin for each year using FIFO.
2. Compute cost of goods sold, the cost of ending inventory, and gross margin for each year using LIFO.
3. Compute cost of goods sold, the cost of ending inventory, and gross margin for each year using the average cost method. (*Note:* Use four decimal places for per-unit calculations and round all other numbers to the nearest dollar.)
4. **CONCEPTUAL CONNECTION** Which method would result in the lowest amount paid for taxes?
5. **CONCEPTUAL CONNECTION** Which method produces the most realistic amount for income? For inventory? Explain your answer.
6. **CONCEPTUAL CONNECTION** What is the effect of purchases made later in the year on the gross margin when LIFO is employed? When FIFO is employed? Be sure to explain why any differences occur.
7. **CONCEPTUAL CONNECTION** If you worked **Problem 6-68B**, compare your answers. What are the differences? Be sure to explain why any differences occurred.

CASES

Case 6-74 Inventory Valuation and Ethics

Mary Cravens is an accountant for City Appliance Corporation. One of Mary's responsibilities is developing the ending inventory amount for the calculation of cost of goods sold each month. At the end of September, Mary noticed that the ending inventory for a new brand of televisions was much larger than she had expected. In fact, there had been hardly any change since the end of the previous month when the shipments of televisions arrived. Mary knew that the firm's advertising had featured the new brand's products, so she had expected that a substantial portion of the televisions would have been sold.

Because of these concerns, Mary went to the warehouse to make sure the numbers were correct. While at the warehouse, Mary noticed that 30 of the televisions in question were on the loading dock for delivery to customers, and another, larger group of 200 sets were in an area set aside for sales returns. Mary asked Barry Tompkins, the returns supervisor, why so many of the televisions had been returned. Barry said that the manufacturer had used a cheap circuit board that failed on many of the sets after they had been in service for a week or two. Mary then asked how the defective televisions had been treated when the inventory was taken at the end of September. Barry said that the warehouse staff had been told to include in the ending inventory any item in the warehouse that was not marked for shipment to customers. Therefore, all returned merchandise was considered part of ending inventory.

Mary asked Barry what would be done with the defective sets. Barry said that they would probably have to be sold to a liquidator for a few cents on the dollar. Mary knew from her examination of the inventory data that all the returned sets had been included in the September inventory at their original cost.

Mary returned to the office and prepared a revised estimate of ending inventory using the information Barry Tompkins had given her to revalue the ending inventory of the television sets. She submitted the revision along with an explanatory note to her boss, Susan Grant. A few days later, Susan stopped by Mary's office to report on a conversation with the chief financial officer, Herb Cobb. Herb told Susan that the original ending inventory amount would not be revised. Herb said that the television sets in question had been purchased by his brother and adequate documentation existed to support the sale.

Required:

1. What would happen to cost of goods sold, gross margin, income from operations, and net income if the cost of the returned inventory had been reduced to its liquidation price as Mary had proposed?
2. What should Mary do now?

Case 6-75 Inventory Costing When Inventory Quantities Are Small

A number of companies have adopted a just-in-time procedure for acquiring inventory. These companies have arrangements with their suppliers that require the supplier to deliver inventory just as the company needs the goods. As a result, just-in-time companies keep very little inventory on hand.

Required:

1. Should the inventory costing method (FIFO or LIFO) have a material effect on cost of goods sold when a company adopts the just-in-time procedure and reduces inventory significantly?
2. Once a company has switched to the just-in-time procedure and has little inventory, should the inventory costing method (LIFO or FIFO) affect cost of goods sold?

Case 6-76 Inventory Purchase Price Volatility

In 2013, Steel Technologies Inc. changed from the LIFO to the FIFO method for its inventory costing. Steel Technologies' annual report indicated that this change had been instituted because the price at which the firm purchased steel was highly volatile.

Required:

Explain how FIFO cost of goods sold and ending inventory would be different from LIFO when prices are volatile.

Case 6-77 The Effect of Reductions in Inventory Quantities

Hill Motor Company, one of the country's largest automobile manufacturers, disclosed the following information about its inventory in the notes to its financial statements:

(Continued)

Inventories are stated generally at cost, which is not in excess of market value. The cost of inventory is determined by the last-in, first-out (LIFO) method. If the first-in, first-out (FIFO) method of inventory valuation had been used, inventory would have been about $2,519 million higher at December 31, 2013, and $2,668 million higher at December 31, 2012. As a result of decreases in inventory, certain inventory quantities carried at lower LIFO costs prevailing in prior years, as compared with costs of current purchases, were liquidated in 2013 and 2012. These inventory adjustments improved pretax operating results by approximately $134 million in 2013 and $294 million in 2012.

Required:

1. Explain why the reduction in inventory quantities increased Hill Motor Company's net income.
2. **CONCEPTUAL CONNECTION** If Hill Motor Company had used the FIFO inventory costing method, would the reduction in ending inventory quantities have increased net income?

Case 6-78 Errors in Ending Inventory

From time to time, business news will report that the management of a company has misstated its profits by knowingly establishing an incorrect amount for its ending inventory.

Required:

1. Explain how a misstatement of ending inventory can affect profit.
2. Why would a manager intent on misstating profits choose ending inventory to achieve the desired effect?

Case 6-79 Ethics and Inventory

An electronics store has a large number of computers that use outdated technology in its inventory. These computers are reported at their cost. Shortly after the December 31 year end, the store manager insists that the computers can be sold for well over their cost. But the store's accountant has been told by the sales staff that it will be difficult to sell these computers for more than half of their inventory cost.

Required:

1. Why is the store manager reluctant to admit that these computers have little sales value?
2. What are the consequences for the business of failing to recognize the decline in value?
3. What are the consequences for the accountant of participating in a misrepresentation of the inventory's value?

Case 6-80 Research and Analysis Using the Annual Report

Obtain **Wal-Mart**'s 2012 annual report either through the "Investor Relations" portion of its website (do a web search for Wal-Mart investor relations) or go to www.sec.gov and click "Search for company filings" under "Filings and Forms (EDGAR)."

Required:

1. What amount did Wal-Mart report for inventories in its consolidated balance sheets at January 31, 2012? At January 31, 2011?
2. What inventory valuation method does Wal-Mart use to determine the cost of its inventories? (*Hint:* You may need to refer to the notes to the consolidated financial statements.)
3. What amount did Wal-Mart report for cost of goods sold for 2012, 2011, and 2010?
4. Compute the gross profit (rounded to one decimal place) and inventory turnover (rounded to two decimal places) ratios for 2012. What do these ratios tell you?
5. Does Wal-Mart use the lower of cost or market method to account for its inventory? Does it appear that Wal-Mart will write down its inventory to market value?

6. What would be the effect on the financial statements if Wal-Mart were to overstate its inventory by 1%?

Case 6-81 Comparative Analysis: Under Armour, Inc., vs. VF Corporation

Refer to the financial statements of **Under Armour, Inc.**, and **VF Corporation** that are supplied with this text.

Required:

1. What amounts do Under Armour and VF report for inventories in their consolidated balance sheets at December 2011 and December 2010?
2. Do Under Armour and VF use the same method to value their inventories?
3. What amount does Under Armour report for cost of goods sold for the years ending December 2011, 2010 and 2009? What amount does VF report for cost of goods sold for the years ending December 2011, 2010, and 2009?
4. Compute the gross profit and inventory turnover ratios for fiscal year ending December 2011. (*Note:* Round answers to two decimal places.) What do these ratios tell you about the success of each company in managing and controlling their inventory?
5. Do Under Armour and VF use the lower of cost or market method to account for their inventories? By what amount have they written inventories down in the fiscal year ending December 2011?

Case 6-82 CONTINUING PROBLEM: FRONT ROW ENTERTAINMENT

In addition to developing online fan communities, Cam and Anna believe that they could increase Front Row Entertainment's revenue by selling live-performance DVDs at the concert. Front Row records the following activity between May and August 2013 for one of its artists:

Date	Activity	Number of Units	Cost per Unit
May 10	Purchase inventory	240	$8.25
25	Sale	180	
June 5	Purchase inventory	300	8.75
12	Sale	150	
July 5	Sale	135	
Aug. 8	Purchase inventory	190	9.25
20	Sale	110	

Front Row sells all of its DVDs for $15 each and uses a perpetual inventory system.

Required:

1. Compute ending inventory and cost of goods sold using the FIFO, LIFO, and average cost methods. (*Note:* Use four decimal places for per-unit calculations and round all other numbers to the nearest penny.)
2. Discuss the advantages and disadvantages of each method.
3. Assume that Front Row decides to use FIFO. Prepare the journal entries necessary to record the above transactions. Assume all purchases and sales were for cash.

7

Operating Assets

© Pixelfabrik/Alamy

After studying Chapter 7, you should be able to:

1. Define, classify, and describe the accounting for operating assets.
2. Explain how the historical cost principle applies to recording the cost of a fixed asset.
3. Understand the concept of depreciation.
4. Compute depreciation expense using various depreciation methods.
5. Distinguish between capital and revenue expenditures.
6. Understand and account for revisions in depreciation.
7. Describe the process of recording the disposal of a fixed asset.
8. Evaluate the use of fixed assets.
9. Understand the measurement and reporting of intangible assets.
10. Understand the measurement and reporting of natural resources.
11. *(Appendix 7A)* Describe the process of recording an impairment of a fixed asset.

Adrian Weinbrecht/Cultura/Jupiterimages

EXPERIENCE FINANCIAL ACCOUNTING

with Verizon

With revenues exceeding $110 billion, **Verizon Communications, Inc.**, is one of the world's leading providers of telecommunications services. Verizon boasts 32.8 million voice and broadband connections as well as 92.2 million subscribers to its wireless voice and data communication services. With users demanding enhanced data-carrying capabilities, higher transmission speeds, and increased multimedia capabilities, Verizon has chosen to use its network to differentiate itself from its competitors. As a result, Verizon has spent over $110 billion between 2006 and 2010 to maintain, upgrade, and expand its technology infrastructure. This amount includes an average of $6 billion per year on its wireless network alone. The results of these investments have led Verizon to claim that it operates the most reliable wireless network in the country, which has resulted in impressive growth in the number of subscribers to its wireless services. For a company like Verizon, effective management of its long-term operating assets (e.g., its wireless network) is essential for the generation of revenue and profit.

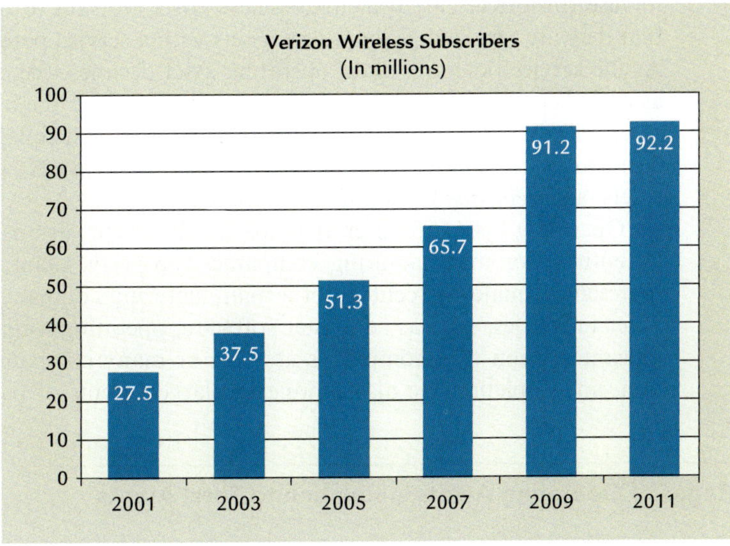

Source: Verizon Wireless 2011 10-K.

Verizon's strategy for success rests on two key premises which relate to its network. First, the network must provide reliable access to every location that its customers need to access. For a simple call home or in crises, customers must be able to count on Verizon's network to function effectively. Second, Verizon is committed to investing in new technology in order to maintain a high level of customer satisfaction and remain competitive. Without continual investment, Verizon knows it will lose customers. Consistent with these goals, Verizon spent $16.2 billion in 2011 related to the build-up, expansion, and upgrade of its network. These expenditures represent an asset on Verizon's balance sheet that it hopes will provide a future benefit in terms of growth in market share and profitability. By closely analyzing a company's expenditures on productive assets, you will be able to better assess the company's long-term productivity, profitability, and ability to generate cash flow.

OBJECTIVE 1

Define, classify, and describe the accounting for operating assets.

UNDERSTANDING OPERATING ASSETS

In this chapter, we will examine the measurement and reporting issues related to **operating assets**, which are the long-lived assets that are used by the company in the normal course of operations. Unlike inventory, operating assets are not sold to customers. Instead, operating assets are used by a company in the normal course of operations to generate revenue. They are usually held by a company until they are no longer of service to the company. In other words, operating assets are held until their *service potential* has been exhausted. The typical operating asset is used for a period of 4 to 10 years, although some are held for only 2 or 3 years and others for as long as 30 or 40 years. Operating assets are divided into three categories:

- *Property, plant, and equipment (PP&E)*, often called *fixed assets* or *plant assets*, are tangible operating assets that can be seen and touched. They include, among other things, land, buildings, machines, and automobiles.
- *Intangible assets*, which generally result from legal and contractual rights, do not have physical substance. They include patents, copyrights, trademarks, licenses, and goodwill.
- *Natural resources* are naturally occurring materials that have economic value. They include timberlands and deposits such as coal, oil, and gravel.

IFRS

The determination of the cost of operating assets and the accounting for depreciation under IFRS are similar to U.S. GAAP.

Operating assets represent future economic benefits, or service potential, that will be used in the normal course of operations. At acquisition, an operating asset is recorded at its cost, including the cost of acquiring the asset and the cost of preparing the asset for use (historical cost principle). These costs are said to be *capitalized*, which means that they are reported as long-term assets with a service potential of greater than 1 year. As the service potential of an operating asset declines, the cost of the asset is allocated as an expense among the accounting periods in which the asset is used and benefits are received (the expense recognition, or matching, principle). This allocation is called *depreciation* for property, plant, and equipment assets, *amortization* for intangible assets, and *depletion* for natural resources.

Operating assets are often the most costly of the various types of assets acquired by an entity. For manufacturing companies, property, plant, and equipment frequently represents a major percentage of a manufacturing company's total assets. However, in other industries, such as computer software, operating assets may be a relatively insignificant portion of a company's assets. For many companies, depreciation, amortization, and depletion are also among the largest items of periodic expense. Exhibit 7.1

EXHIBIT 7.1

Percentages of Operating Assets in Relation to Total Assets

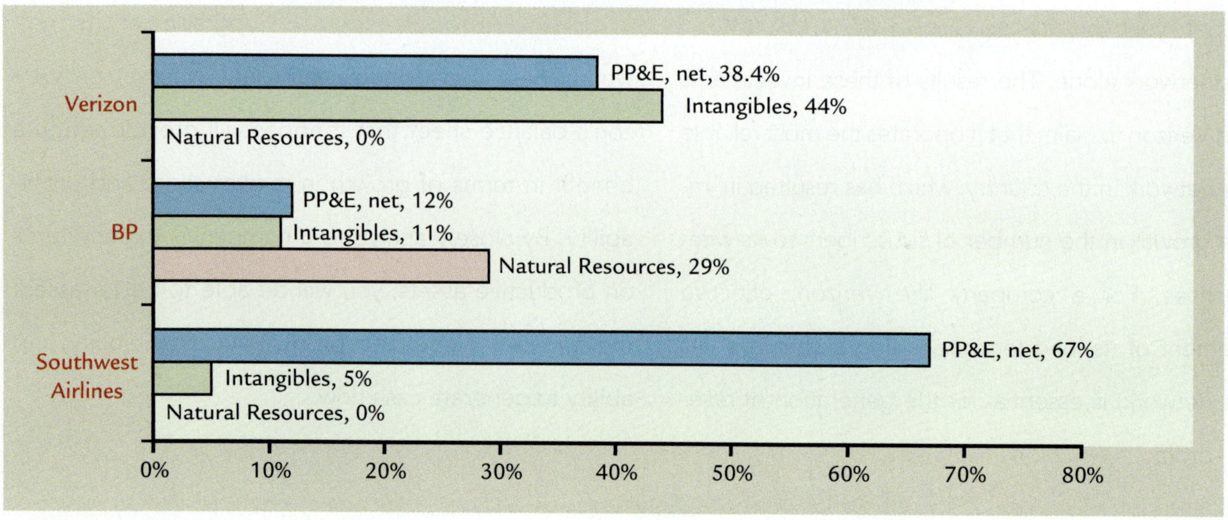

Source: Information obtained from the 2011 10-K reports of each company.

shows the percentages of operating assets in relation to total assets for various companies.

For Verizon, operating assets (property, plant, and equipment plus intangible assets) comprise approximately 83% of its total assets. Fixed assets include the expenditures required to build, upgrade, and expand its wireless network. In addition, Verizon has significant investments in intangible operating assets, primarily licenses that provide Verizon with the exclusive right to use certain radio frequencies to provide wireless services. In contrast, companies such as BP (one of the largest oil companies in the world) have relatively more natural resources (oil and natural gas properties), while Southwest Airlines' operating assets are made up primarily of its airplanes. Information about a company's operating assets gives financial statement users insights into a company's ability to satisfy customer demands (productive capacity) and the effectiveness of management in using the company's assets to generate revenue. While the relative mix of operating assets may vary among companies, it is clear that the management of operating assets is critical to a company's long-term success.

In this chapter, we will discuss the measurement and reporting issues related to the initial acquisition, use, and disposition of operating assets. We will address the following questions:

- What is included in the cost of an operating asset?
- How should an operating asset's cost be allocated to expense?
- How should expenditures after acquisition be treated?
- How is the retirement of an operating asset recorded?

ACQUISITION OF PROPERTY, PLANT, AND EQUIPMENT

OBJECTIVE 2

Explain how the historical cost principle applies to recording the cost of a fixed asset.

Property, plant, and equipment are the tangible operating assets used in the normal operations of a company. These assets are tangible in the sense that they have a visible, physical presence in the company. Property, plant, and equipment includes:

- Land: the site of a manufacturing facility or office building used in operations[1]
- Land Improvements: structural additions or improvements to land (such as driveways, parking lots, fences, landscaping, lighting)
- Buildings: structures used in operations (factory, office, warehouse)
- Equipment: assets used in operations (machinery, furniture, automobiles)

It is important to note that land has an unlimited life and service potential and is not subject to depreciation. However, land improvements, buildings, and equipment have limited lives and limited service potential. Therefore, the cost of these assets is recorded in separate accounts and depreciated over the periods in which they are used to generate revenue.

Measuring the Cost of a Fixed Asset

The cost of a fixed asset is any expenditure necessary to acquire the asset and to prepare the asset for use. For example, the cost of a machine would be its purchase price (minus any discount offered) plus sales taxes, freight, installation costs, and the cost of labor and materials for trial runs that check its performance. Expenditures that are included as part of the cost of the asset are said to be *capitalized*. Exhibit 7.2 (p. 366) shows expenditures that are typically included as part of the cost of various types of property, plant, and equipment.

Expenditures that are *not* included as part of the cost of the asset are expensed immediately. Generally, recurring costs that benefit a period of time, not the asset's life,

[1] Land purchased for future use or as an investment is not considered part of property, plant, and equipment.

EXHIBIT 7.2

Typical Costs of Acquiring Property, Plant, and Equipment

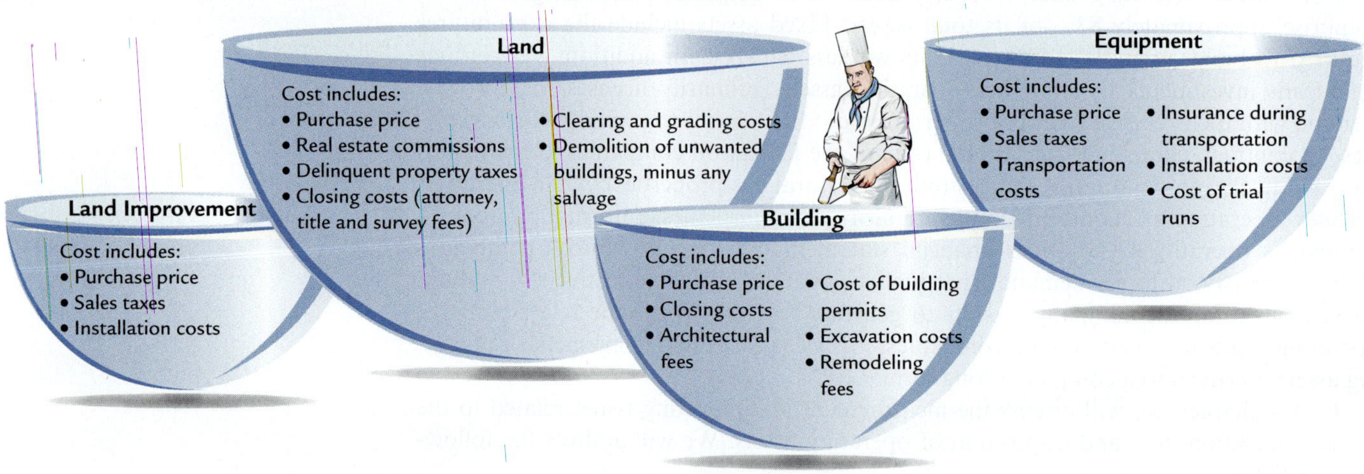

concept Q&A

If a company did not record all of the costs necessary to acquire an asset and prepare it for use, what would be the effect on the financial statements?

Answer:

If costs were not recorded as an asset, these costs would be immediately expensed, which would lower income in the current period. By recording these costs as assets, the company delays the recognition of expense until the service potential of the asset is used.

are expensed instead of capitalized. Careful judgment should be exercised in determining which costs should be capitalized and which costs should be expensed.

ETHICAL DECISION The distinction between whether an expenditure should be capitalized or expensed can have dramatic consequences for a company's financial statements. WorldCom's handling of this issue triggered one of the largest financial restatements in U.S. history. When WorldCom used the telecommunications lines of another company, it paid a fee which should have been expensed in the current period. By improperly capitalizing \$3.8 billion of these costs, WorldCom was able to increase its income and its operating cash flow, thereby concealing large losses. •

Recording the Cost of a Fixed Asset

The historical cost principle requires that a company record its fixed assets at the exchange price at the time the asset is purchased. When cash is paid in exchange for an asset, the amount of cash given, plus any other expenditure necessary to prepare the asset for use, becomes part of the historical cost of the acquired asset. In addition to cash purchases, companies often purchase fixed assets by issuing debt. In this situation, the asset is valued at the fair value of the liability on the date the asset is acquired. Interest paid on the debt is generally viewed as resulting from a financing decision rather than from the decision to acquire the asset. Therefore, interest on borrowed funds normally is not added to the purchase price of an asset.[2]

When noncash consideration, such as land or other noncash assets, is given in exchange for an asset, the purchase price of the acquired asset is the fair value of the asset given up or the fair value of the asset received, whichever is more clearly determinable. The fair value of an asset is the estimated amount of cash that would be required to acquire the asset. This cash equivalent cost can be inferred from information about similar assets in comparable transactions.

Cornerstone 7.1 illustrates the accounting procedures for the measurement and recording of the cost of a fixed asset. It shows that all costs necessary to acquire the machine and prepare it for use—freight (\$2,900) and installation costs (\$5,300 + \$800 + \$1,500)—are

[2] For assets that require a long period of preparation for use, such as ships, large plants, or buildings, GAAP does permit the addition of interest to the cost of the asset. This topic is addressed in Intermediate Accounting.

Measuring and Recording the Cost of a Fixed Asset

CORNERSTONE 7.1

Why:

The cost of a fixed asset is any expenditure necessary to acquire the asset and to prepare it for use.

Information:

On June 29, Drew Company acquired a new automatic milling machine from Dayton Inc. Drew paid $20,000 in cash and signed a 1-year, 10% note for $80,000. Following the purchase, Drew incurred freight charges, on account, of $2,900 to ship the machine from Dayton's factory to Drew's plant. After the machine arrived, Drew paid J. B. Contractors $5,300 for installation. Drew also used $800 of supplies and $1,500 of labor on trial runs.

Required:

1. Determine the cost of the machine.
2. Prepare the journal entry necessary to record the purchase of the machine.

Solution:

1. $20,000 + $80,000 + $2,900 + $5,300 + $800 + $1,500 = $110,500
2.

Date	Account and Explanation	Debit	Credit
June 29	Equipment	110,500	
	Cash ($20,000 + $5,300)		25,300
	Notes Payable		80,000
	Accounts Payable (for freight charges)		2,900
	Supplies		800
	Wages Payable		1,500
	(Record purchase of equipment)		

Assets	= Liabilities +	Stockholders' Equity
+110,500	+80,000	
−25,300	+2,900	
−800	+1,500	

included in the machine's historical cost. Interest on the note payable, however, is excluded from the machine's cost and is added to interest expense as it accrues. Finally, note that the cost is capitalized (recorded as an asset), and there is no effect on the income statement.

Had Drew given 1,600 shares of its own stock, which was selling for $50 per share, instead of the 10% note, the acquisition would have been recorded as:

Date	Account and Explanation	Debit	Credit
June 29	Equipment	110,500	
	Cash ($20,000 + $5,300)		25,300
	Common Stock		80,000
	Accounts Payable		2,900
	Supplies		800
	Wages Payable		1,500
	(Record purchase of equipment)		

Assets	= Liabilities +	Stockholders' Equity
+110,500	+2,900	+80,000
−25,300	+1,500	
−800		

Because the fair value of the stock ($50 × 1,600 = $80,000) equals the amount of the note, the cost of the asset is the same in both entries.

YOU DECIDE The Purchase Decision

You are the controller of Stanley Inc., a struggling manufacturing company that is experiencing cash flow problems. You are reviewing two proposals that would enable the company to obtain a piece of equipment that is critical to its operations. The first proposal would allow the company to purchase the equipment by signing a long-term note payable. The second proposal involves having the company rent the equipment.

What factors should you consider in making the decision of whether to purchase or rent the equipment?

Given the company's financial situation, renting (or leasing) the equipment may provide several advantages.

- Renting often requires little or no down payment, allowing a company with cash flow problems access to fixed assets that it would otherwise not be able to afford while freeing up cash for more immediate needs.
- Renting may allow the company to keep assets and, more importantly, liabilities off of the balance sheet, which increases the perceived borrowing ability of the company. For example, the purchase of the equipment would increase both fixed assets (property, plant, and equipment) and liabilities at the time of the purchase. In contrast, the rental of the equipment would require no entry at the time the agreement is signed. Therefore, the purchase of the asset on credit would cause an immediate increase in the company's debt to equity ratio.
- Renting the equipment may protect the renter against obsolescence since the rented asset can be exchanged for a newer model at the end of the rental agreement.
- Rental agreements may provide the renter with an increased tax benefit.

However, renting also has disadvantages, such as interest rates that may be higher than normal long-term borrowing rates. In short, the decision to purchase or rent is a strategic decision that must be carefully considered.

Managers are often confronted with the decision to purchase or rent fixed assets. In fact, renting assets through leasing arrangements has become one of the more frequently used strategies for acquiring fixed assets.[3]

OBJECTIVE 3

Understand the concept of depreciation.

DEPRECIATION

We observed earlier that the cost of a fixed asset represents the cost of future benefits or service potential to a company. With the exception of land, this service potential declines over the life of each asset as the asset is used in the operations of the company. **Depreciation** is the process of allocating, in a systematic and rational manner, the cost of a tangible fixed asset (other than land) to expense over the asset's useful life. The matching principle provides the conceptual basis for measuring and recognizing depreciation and requires that the cost of a fixed asset be allocated as an expense among the accounting periods in which the asset is used and revenues are generated by its use.

The amount of depreciation expense is recorded each period by making the following adjusting journal entry:

Depreciation Expense	xxx	
Accumulated Depreciation		xxx

The amount of depreciation recorded each period, or **depreciation expense**, is reported on the income statement. **Accumulated depreciation**, which represents the total amount of depreciation expense that has been recorded for an asset since the asset was acquired, is reported on the balance sheet as a contra-asset. That is, accumulated depreciation is deducted from the cost of the asset to get the asset's **book value** (or **carrying value**). Exhibit 7.3 shows the disclosures relating to property, plant, and equipment and depreciation made by Verizon in its 2011 annual report.

Before continuing, it is critical to understand the following points:

- Depreciation is a *cost allocation process*. It is *not* an attempt to measure the fair value of the asset or obtain some other measure of the asset's value. In fact, the book value (cost minus accumulated depreciation) of an asset that is reported on a company's balance sheet is often quite different from the market value of the asset.

[3] Lease arrangements and their effects are discussed more fully in Chapter 9.

EXHIBIT 7.3

Excerpt from Verizon's 2011 Annual Report

Notes to Consolidated Financial Statements

NOTE 4 Plant, Property, and Equipment:

Land	$ 862
Buildings and equipment	21,969
Central office and other network equipment	107,322
Cable, poles, and conduit	67,190
Leasehold improvements	5,030
Work in progress	3,417
Furniture, vehicles, and other	9,836
	$215,626
Less: Accumulated depreciation	127,192
Property, plant, and equipment, net	$ 88,434

Source: Verizon Wireless 2011 10-K.

- Depreciation is *not* an attempt to accumulate cash for the replacement of an asset. Depreciation is a cost allocation process that does not involve cash.

Information Required for Measuring Depreciation

The following information is necessary in order to measure depreciation:

- cost of the fixed asset
- useful life (or expected life) of the fixed asset
- residual value (salvage value) of the fixed asset

Cost As discussed earlier in the chapter, the **cost** of a fixed asset is any expenditure necessary to acquire the asset and to prepare the asset for use. In addition to cost, we also need to examine two other items—useful life and estimates of residual value—to measure depreciation. Exhibit 7.4 shows the relationship among the factors used to compute depreciation expense.

EXHIBIT 7.4

Components of Depreciation Expense

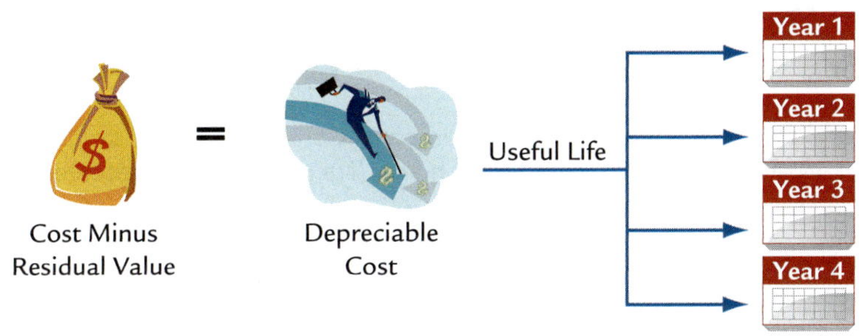

Useful Life The **useful life** of an asset is the period of time over which the company anticipates deriving benefit from the use of the asset.[4] The useful life of any fixed asset

[4] The useful life can be estimated in *service units* as well as in *units of time*. For example, an airline may choose to measure the useful life of its aircraft in hours of use rather than years.

reflects both the physical capacities of the asset and the company's plans for its use. Many companies plan to dispose of assets before their entire service potential is exhausted. For example, major automobile rental companies typically use an automobile for only a part of its entire economic life before disposing of it. The useful life also is influenced by technological change. Many assets lose their service potential through obsolescence long before the assets are physically inoperable. As shown in Exhibit 7.5, Verizon uses an estimated useful life of 3 to 50 years for its fixed assets.

EXHIBIT 7.5

Excerpt from Verizon's 2011 Annual Report

Notes to Consolidated Financial Statements

NOTE 4 Property, Plant, and Equipment

	Lives (Years)
Land	—
Buildings and equipment	*15–45*
Central office and other network equipment	*3–15*
Cable, poles, and conduit	*11–50*
Leasehold improvements	*5–20*
Work in progress	—
Furniture, vehicles, and other	*3–12*

Source: Verizon Wireless 2011 10-K.

Residual Value The **residual value** (also called **salvage value**) is the amount of cash or trade-in consideration that the company expects to receive when an asset is retired from service. Accordingly, the residual value reflects the company's plans for the asset and its expectations about the value of the asset once its expected life with the company is over. A truck used for 3 years may have a substantial residual value, whereas the same truck used for 12 years may have minimal residual value. Residual value is based on projections of some of the same future events that are used to estimate an asset's useful life. Since depreciation expense depends on estimates of both useful life and residual value, depreciation expense itself is an estimate.

The cost of the asset minus its residual value gives an asset's **depreciable cost**. The depreciable cost of the asset is the amount that will be depreciated (expensed) over the asset's useful life.

YOUDECIDE Impact of Depreciation Estimates

You are a loan officer of the Prairie State Bank. The president of a ready-mix concrete company, Concrete Transit Company, has applied for a 5-year, $150,000 loan to finance his company's expansion. You have examined Concrete Transit's financial statements for the past 3 years and found the following:

	2013	2012	2011
Depreciation expense (calculated using the straight-line method)	$ 15,000	$ 15,000	$ 15,000
Income before taxes	$ 15,000	$ 17,000	$ 21,000
Depreciable assets (cost)	$470,000	$470,000	$470,000

Based on other customers in the same business that use the same depreciation method as Concrete Transit, you expected depreciation expense to be approximately 15% of the cost of the depreciable assets.

Should you make the loan?

Since Concrete Transit has similar assets and is using a similar depreciation method to its competitors, the most obvious reason for reporting a lower percentage of depreciation expense is that Concrete Transit is using different estimates of residual value and/or useful life than its competitors. As you will see in the next section, if higher estimates of residual value or useful life are used, depreciation expense will be lower and income will be higher. If you adjust Concrete Transit's depreciation expense to 15% of the cost of its depreciable assets, depreciation expense will increase from $15,000 to $70,500 ($470,000 × 0.15) for each year. This would cause a decrease in income before taxes of $55,500 each year. These adjusted amounts suggest that Concrete Transit has been increasingly unprofitable. Given the difficulties it would likely have in making the required loan payments, the loan should not be made.

While most companies establish policies for depreciable assets that specify the estimation of useful lives and residual values, the measurement of depreciation expense (and income) ultimately relies on judgment.

DEPRECIATION METHODS

OBJECTIVE 4

Compute depreciation expense using various depreciation methods.

The service potential of a fixed asset is assumed to decline with each period of use, but the pattern of decline is not the same for all assets. Some assets decline at a constant rate each year while others decline sharply in the early years of use and then more gradually as time goes on. For other assets, the pattern of decline depends on how much the asset is used each period. *Depreciation methods* are the standardized calculations required to determine periodic depreciation expense. The most common depreciation methods are:

- straight-line
- declining balance
- units-of-production

For any of these depreciation methods, the total amount of depreciation expense that has been recorded (accumulated depreciation) over the life of the asset will never exceed the depreciable cost (cost minus residual value) of the asset.

Exhibit 7.6 shows the methods most commonly used by 500 of the largest U.S. companies.

concept Q&A

Why does the FASB allow companies to use different depreciation methods instead of requiring the use of a single depreciation method that would improve comparability?

Answer:

The depreciation method chosen by a company should capture the declining service potential of a fixed asset. Because assets are used differently, alternative methods are allowed so that the use of the asset can be better matched with the revenue it helped generate.

Straight-Line Method

As its name implies, the **straight-line depreciation method** allocates an equal amount of an asset's cost to depreciation expense for each year of the asset's useful life. It is appropriate to apply this method to those assets for which

EXHIBIT 7.6

The Relative Use of Depreciation Methods

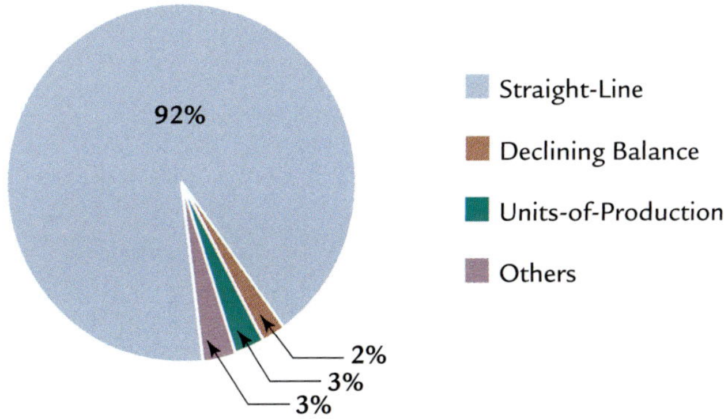

Source: AICPA, *Accounting Trends & Techniques*, 65th Edition, 2011, par. 3.80, p. 394.

an equal amount of service potential is considered to be used each period. The straight-line method is the most widely used method because it is simple to apply and is based on a pattern of declining service potential that is reasonable for many fixed assets.

The computation of straight-line depreciation expense is based on an asset's depreciable cost, which is the excess of the asset's cost over its residual value. Straight-line depreciation expense for each period is calculated by dividing the depreciable cost of an asset by the asset's useful life:

$$\text{Straight-Line Depreciation} = \frac{(\text{Cost} - \text{Residual Value})}{\text{Expected Useful Life}}$$

Alternatively, some companies will calculate an annual rate at which the asset should be depreciated. The fraction, (1 ÷ Useful Life), is called the *straight-line rate*. Using the straight-line rate, a company would compute depreciation expense by multiplying the straight-line rate by the asset's depreciable cost. Cornerstone 7.2 illustrates the computation of depreciation expense using the straight-line method.

CORNERSTONE 7.2

Computing Depreciation Expense Using the Straight-Line Method

Why:

As the service potential of a fixed asset declines, the cost of the asset is allocated as an expense among the accounting periods in which the asset is used and benefits are received (the matching principle).

Information:

On January 1, 2013, Morgan Inc. acquired a machine for $50,000. Morgan expects the machine to be worth $5,000 at the end of its 5-year useful life. Morgan uses the straight-line method of depreciation.

Required:

1. Compute the straight-line rate of depreciation for the machine.
2. Compute the annual amount of depreciation expense.
3. Prepare a depreciation schedule that shows the amount of depreciation expense for each year of the machine's life.
4. Prepare the journal entry required to record depreciation expense in 2013.

Solution:

1. $\text{Straight-Line Rate} = \frac{1}{\text{Useful Life}} = \frac{1}{5 \text{ years}} = \underline{\underline{20\%}}$

2. $\text{Straight-Line Depreciation Expense} = \frac{\$50{,}000 - \$5{,}000}{5 \text{ years}}$

   $= \underline{\underline{\$9{,}000}} \text{ per year}$

   Note: Depreciation expense may also be found by multiplying the straight-line rate (20%) by the asset's depreciable cost ($45,000).

(*Continued*)

CORNERSTONE 7.2

(Continued)

3.

End of Year	Depreciation Expense	Accumulated Depreciation	Book Value
			$50,000
2013	$ 9,000	$ 9,000	41,000
2014	9,000	18,000	32,000
2015	9,000	27,000	23,000
2016	9,000	36,000	14,000
2017	9,000	45,000	5,000
	$45,000		

4.

Date	Account and Explanation	Debit	Credit
Dec. 31, 2013	Depreciation Expense	9,000	
	Accumulated Depreciation		9,000
	(Record straight-line depreciation expense)		

Assets	= Liabilities +	Stockholders' Equity
−9,000		−9,000

Cornerstone 7.2 illustrates three important points:

- The straight-line depreciation method results in the recording of the same amount of depreciation expense ($9,000) each year, as shown in Exhibit 7.7.
- The contra-asset account, accumulated depreciation, increases at a constant rate of $9,000 per year until it equals the depreciable cost ($45,000).
- The book value of the machine (cost minus accumulated depreciation) decreases by $9,000 per year until it equals the residual value ($5,000) at the end of the asset's useful life.

EXHIBIT 7.7

Straight-Line Pattern of Depreciation

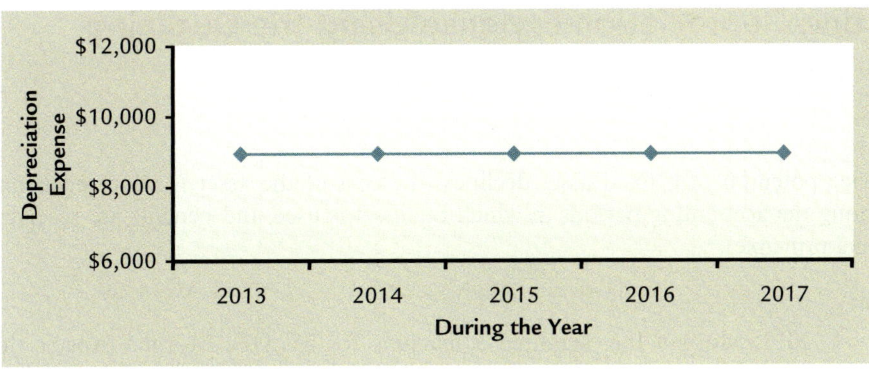

Declining Balance Method

The **declining balance depreciation method** is an accelerated depreciation method that produces a declining amount of depreciation expense each period by multiplying the declining book value of an asset by a constant depreciation rate. It is called an accelerated method because it results in a larger amount of depreciation expense in the early years of an asset's life relative to the straight-line method. However, because the total amount of depreciation expense (the depreciable cost) must be the same under any depreciation method, accelerated methods result in a smaller amount of depreciation expense in the later years of an asset's life. The declining balance method is appropriate for assets that are subject to a rapid decline in service potential due to factors such as rapid obsolescence.

The declining balance depreciation rate is some multiple (m) of the straight-line rate:

$$\text{Declining Balance Rate} = (m) \times \text{Straight-Line Rate}$$

The multiple (m) is often 2, in which case the declining balance method is called the *double-declining-balance method*.[5]

Depreciation expense for each period of an asset's useful life equals the declining balance rate times the asset's book value (cost minus accumulated depreciation) at the beginning of the period as shown by the following equation:

$$\text{Declining Balance Depreciation Expense} = \text{Declining Balance Rate} \times \text{Book Value}$$

The calculation of declining balance depreciation expense differs from the calculation of straight-line depreciation expense in two important ways:

- The straight-line method applies a depreciation rate to the *depreciable cost* of the asset. However, the declining balance method multiplies a depreciation rate by the *book value* of the asset. Because the book value declines as depreciation expense is recorded, this produces a declining pattern of depreciation expense over time.
- The straight-line method records an equal amount of depreciation expense *each period* of the asset's life. However, it is likely that the computation of depreciation expense under the declining balance method would cause the asset's book value to fall below its residual value. Because an asset's book value cannot be depreciated below its residual value, a lower amount of depreciation expense (relative to what is calculated under the declining balance method) must be recorded in the last year of the asset's life so that depreciation stops once the residual value is reached.

Cornerstone 7.3 illustrates the computation of depreciation expense using the declining balance method.

CORNERSTONE 7.3

Computing Depreciation Expense Using the Declining Balance Method

Why:

As the service potential of a fixed asset declines, the cost of the asset is allocated as an expense among the accounting periods in which the asset is used and benefits are received (the matching principle).

Information:

On January 1, 2013, Morgan Inc. acquired a machine for $50,000. Morgan expects the machine to be worth $5,000 at the end of its 5-year useful life. Morgan uses the double-declining-balance method of depreciation.

Required:

1. Compute the double-declining-balance rate of depreciation for the machine.

(Continued)

[5] In this text, a multiple of 2 is used for the declining balance method unless otherwise noted.

CORNERSTONE 7.3

(Continued)

2. Prepare a depreciation schedule that shows the amount of depreciation expense for each year of the machine's life.
3. Prepare the journal entry required to record depreciation expense in 2013.

Solution:

1. $\frac{1}{\text{Useful Life}} \times 2 = \frac{1}{5} \times 2 = \frac{2}{5}$ or 40%

2.

End of Year	Depreciation Expense (Rate × Book Value)	Accumulated Depreciation	Book Value
			$50,000
2013	40% × $50,000 = $20,000	$20,000	30,000
2014	40% × $30,000 = 12,000	32,000	18,000
2015	40% × $18,000 = 7,200	39,200	10,800
2016	40% × $10,800 = 4,320	43,520	6,480
2017	1,480*	45,000	5,000
	$45,000		

* The computed amount of $2,592 (40% × $6,480) would cause book value to be lower than residual value. Therefore, depreciation expense of $1,480 is taken in 2017 so that the book value equals the residual value.

3.

Date	Account and Explanation	Debit	Credit
Dec. 31, 2013	Depreciation Expense	20,000	
	Accumulated Depreciation		20,000
	(Record declining balance depreciation expense)		

Assets	= Liabilities +	Stockholders' Equity
−20,000		−20,000

Relative to the straight-line method, the double-declining-balance method results in the recognition of higher depreciation expense in the early years of the asset's life and lower depreciation expense in the later years of the asset's life, as shown in Exhibit 7.8.

EXHIBIT 7.8

Declining Balance Pattern of Depreciation

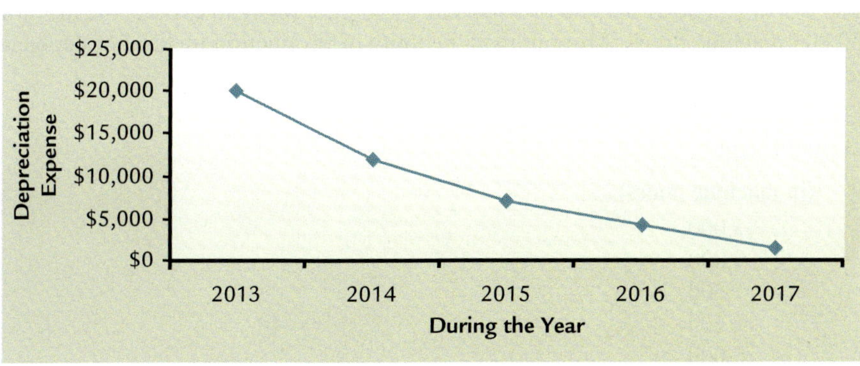

This pattern of expense is consistent with an asset whose service potential is used more rapidly (and its contribution to revenue is greater) in the early years of the asset's life. For this reason, the declining balance method is often used by companies in industries that experience rapid obsolescence.

Units-of-Production Method

The two previous depreciation methods resulted in a pattern of expense that was related to the passage of time. However, when the decline in an asset's service potential is proportional to the usage of the asset and asset usage can be measured, depreciation expense can be computed using the **units-of-production depreciation method**. Usage is typically gauged by a measure of productive capacity (such as units produced, hours worked, or miles driven). An automobile is an example of an asset having service potential that usually declines with use, where usage is measured by the number of miles traveled.

To compute depreciation expense under the units-of-production method, the depreciation cost per unit is determined as shown in the equation:

$$\text{Depreciation Cost per Unit} = \frac{(\text{Cost} - \text{Residual Value})}{\text{Expected Usage of the Asset}}$$

Next, the depreciation cost per unit is multiplied by the actual usage of the asset:

$$\begin{array}{c}\text{Units-of-Production}\\ \text{Depreciation Expense}\end{array} = \text{Depreciation Cost per Unit} \times \text{Actual Usage of the Asset}$$

An example of depreciation expense computed by the units-of-production method is shown in Cornerstone 7.4. Depending on the use of the asset during the year, the units-of-production depreciation method can result in a pattern of depreciation expense that may appear accelerated, straight-line, decelerated, or erratic.

CORNERSTONE

7.4

Computing Depreciation Expense Using the Units-of-Production Method

Why:

As the service potential of a fixed asset declines (as measured by usage), the cost of the asset is allocated as an expense among the accounting periods in which the asset is used and benefits are received (the matching principle).

Information:

On January 1, 2013, Morgan Inc. acquired a machine for $50,000. Morgan expects the machine to be worth $5,000 at the end of its 5-year useful life. Morgan expects the machine to run for 30,000 machine hours. Morgan uses the units-of-production method of depreciation. The actual machine hours are:

Year	Actual Usage (in machine hours)
2013	3,000
2014	9,000
2015	7,500
2016	4,500
2017	6,000

(Continued)

CORNERSTONE
7.4
(Continued)

Required:

1. Compute the depreciation cost per machine hour.
2. Prepare a depreciation schedule that shows the amount of depreciation expense for each year of the machine's life.
3. Prepare the journal entry required to record depreciation expense in 2013.

Solution:

1. $\frac{\text{Depreciable Cost}}{\text{Estimated Usage}} = \frac{(\$50{,}000 - \$5{,}000)}{30{,}000 \text{ machine hours}} = \underline{\underline{\$1.50}}$

2.

End of Year	Cost per Machine Hour	×	Actual Usage	=	Depreciation Expense	Accumulated Depreciation	Book Value
							$50,000
2013	$1.50		3,000		$ 4,500	$ 4,500	45,500
2014	1.50		9,000		13,500	18,000	32,000
2015	1.50		7,500		11,250	29,250	20,750
2016	1.50		4,500		6,750	36,000	14,000
2017	1.50		6,000		9,000	45,000	5,000
					$45,000		

3.

Date	Account and Explanation	Debit	Credit
Dec. 31, 2013	Depreciation Expense	4,500	
	Accumulated Depreciation		4,500
	(Record units-of-production depreciation expense)		

Assets	=	Liabilities	+	Stockholders' Equity
−4,500				−4,500

Note that when production varies widely and irregularly from period to period, the units-of-production method will result in an erratic pattern of depreciation expense, as shown in Exhibit 7.9.

Relative to the prior year, Morgan reported an increase (over the previous year) in depreciation expense in 2014 and 2017; depreciation expense decreased in all other

EXHIBIT 7.9

Units-of-Production Pattern of Depreciation

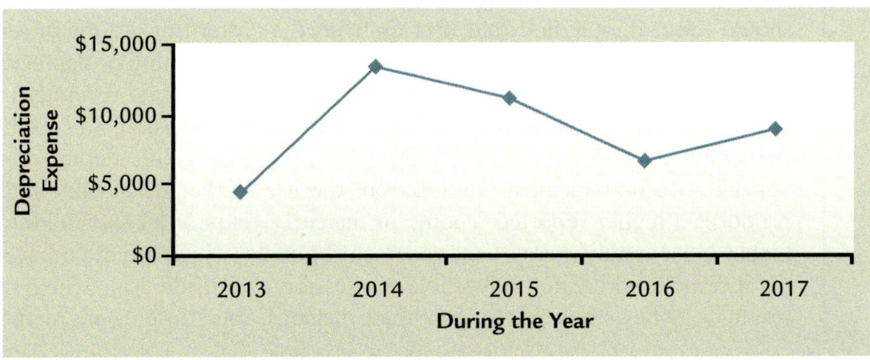

years. Thus, the units-of-production method does not produce a predictable pattern of depreciation expense. While this method does an excellent job of matching depreciation expense to usage of the asset, it is difficult to apply because it requires estimation of expected usage (which is a more difficult task than simply estimating useful life in years) and is used less widely than the other two depreciation methods.

Choosing Between Depreciation Methods

The three depreciation methods can be summarized as follows:

- The straight-line depreciation method produces a constant amount of depreciation expense in each period of the asset's life and is consistent with a constant rate of decline in service potential.
- The declining balance depreciation method accelerates the assignment of an asset's cost to depreciation expense by allocating a larger amount of cost to the early years of an asset's life. This is consistent with a decreasing rate of decline in service potential and a decreasing amount for depreciation expense.
- The units-of-production depreciation method is based on a measure of the asset's use in each period, and the periodic depreciation expense rises and falls with the asset's use. In this sense, the units-of-production depreciation method is based not on a standardized pattern of declining service potential but on a pattern tailored to the individual asset and its use.

IFRS

IFRS allow for companies to increase the value of their property, plant, and equipment up to fair value. This is not permitted under U.S. GAAP.

Exhibit 7.10 compares the depreciation expense recorded by Morgan Inc. under each of the depreciation methods discussed. Note that the total amount of depreciation

EXHIBIT 7.10

Depreciation Patterns over Time

Year	Straight-Line	Double-Declining-Balance	Units-of-Production
2013	$ 9,000	$20,000	$ 4,500
2014	9,000	12,000	13,500
2015	9,000	7,200	11,250
2016	9,000	4,320	6,750
2017	9,000	1,480	9,000
Total	$45,000	$45,000	$45,000

expense ($45,000) recognized by Morgan Inc. was the same under all three methods. This resulted in the asset having a book value of $5,000 at the end of 2017. At this point, book value is equal to residual value. While the total depreciation expense for each method was the same, the yearly amounts of depreciation expense recognized were different.

Because each method is acceptable under GAAP, what factors does management use in selecting a depreciation method? Ideally, management should select the method that best matches the pattern of decline in service potential of the asset. This would result in the best matching of depreciation expense to the period in which the asset helped to generate revenue. However, in reality, other factors also help motivate this decision. For example, the simplicity and ease of application of the straight-line method is very appealing to management. In addition, the use of the straight-line method produces a higher reported income in the early years of an asset's life. This higher income may increase management bonuses (which are often based on net income) and create a favorable impression to outside users which could result in higher stock prices. For these reasons, the straight-line method is

concept Q&A

If all depreciation methods result in the same amount being recorded as an expense over the life of the fixed asset, why would a financial statement user be concerned with the depreciation method chosen?

Answer:

The choice of depreciation method affects the amount recognized as an expense during each year of the fixed asset's life. Therefore, the company's reported income each year would be different based on the depreciation method chosen.

the most popular depreciation method. However, once a depreciation method is chosen, that method should be consistently applied over time to enhance the comparability of the financial information.

ETHICAL DECISION The use of estimates in depreciation calculations presents an ethical issue for accountants. If an estimate is biased upward or downward, it can have significant financial statement impacts. For example, accountants may face pressures to increase the useful life of an asset beyond what is reasonable. This upwardly biased estimate of useful life decreases the amount of depreciation expense recorded and increases the company's net income. Accountants must resist these pressures and provide an unbiased estimate that faithfully portrays the service potential of the asset. •

Depreciation for Partial Years

Fixed assets are purchased (or disposed of) at various times throughout the year. If the fixed asset is purchased (or disposed of) at the beginning or end of an accounting period, a full year of depreciation is recorded. If, however, the asset is purchased (or disposed of) during the accounting period, the matching principle requires that depreciation be recorded only for the portion of the year that the asset was used to generate revenue.

To illustrate, consider an asset purchased on April 1, 2013, for \$100,000, which is being depreciated using the straight-line method over 5 years with no residual value. For a full year (12 months), depreciation expense would be \$20,000, calculated as:[6]

$$\frac{(\text{Cost} - \text{Residual Value})}{\text{Expected Useful Life}} = \frac{(\$100{,}000 - \$0)}{5 \text{ years}}$$

However, this asset was purchased in April, so it was only depreciated for the partial year (9 months) of 2013. Depreciation expense for the partial year would be \$15,000, calculated as:

$$\$20{,}000 \times (9/12)$$

A full year of depreciation expense, \$20,000, would be recorded for the next 4 years. Because a full year of depreciation was not taken in 2013, a partial year of depreciation (3 months) of \$5,000 would need to be recorded in 2018 to fully depreciate the asset, calculated as:

$$\$20{,}000 \times (3/12)$$

At this point, the asset would be fully depreciated.[7]

Depreciation and Income Taxes

A company can choose between the three depreciation methods discussed earlier as it prepares its financial statements, but the depreciation method used in preparing its tax return does not need to be the same. The Internal Revenue Code specifies which depreciation method a company should use to prepare tax returns. Tax depreciation rules are designed to stimulate investment in operating assets and, therefore, are not guided by the matching principle. Tax depreciation rules provide for the rapid (accelerated) expensing of depreciable assets, which lowers taxes. By bringing forward the bulk of depreciation expense, tax depreciation rules enable companies to save cash by delaying the payment of taxes. Most companies use the Modified Accelerated Cost Recovery System (MACRS) to compute depreciation expense for their tax returns, which is similar to the declining balance method. MACRS is not acceptable for financial reporting purposes.

[6] Although acquisitions may occur *during* a month, for purposes of simplifying depreciation calculations, many companies follow the policy of substituting the date of the nearer first of the month for the actual transaction date. Thus, acquisitions on March 25 or April 9 would be treated as acquisitions on April 1 for purposes of calculating depreciation expense.

[7] For the sake of simplicity, most examples, exercises, and problems in this book assume that asset purchases (and disposals) occur at the beginning of the accounting period.

YOU DECIDE Impact of Depreciation Method on Income

You are a financial analyst trying to assess the earnings performance and profitability of two companies, Cobine Inc. and Stabler Inc., which both began operations within the last year. Both companies report the same amount of income and are comparable in most every respect. However, one item catches your attention. While both companies report the same amount of property, plant, and equipment, Cobine reports a much smaller amount for depreciation expense. In the notes to the financial statements, Cobine indicates that it uses the straight-line depreciation method while Stabler uses the double-declining-balance depreciation method.

How does the difference in depreciation methods affect your assessment of the two companies?

When companies use different depreciation methods, significant variations may result in income although no real economic differences exist. As shown in Exhibit 7.10 (p. 378), all depreciation methods result in the same amount being expensed over the life of the asset; however, the amount expensed each year will differ.

Because its assets are relatively new, Cobine's use of the straight-line depreciation method will result in less expense and higher income compared to Stabler, which uses the double-declining-balance method. However, if the company's fixed assets were relatively older, the situation will be reversed—the use of the accelerated depreciation method will result in lower expense and higher income relative to the straight-line method. In both cases, the differences in expense and income are merely the result of an accounting choice and reflect no real underlying economic differences between the two firms.

Financial statement users must be able to "see through" the financial statement effects of accounting choices and base their decision on the underlying economics of the business.

OBJECTIVE 5

Distinguish between capital and revenue expenditures.

EXPENDITURES AFTER ACQUISITION

In addition to expenditures made when property, plant, and equipment is purchased, companies incur costs over the life of the asset that range from ordinary repairs and maintenance to major overhauls, additions, and improvements. Companies must decide whether these expenditures should be capitalized (added to an asset account) or expensed (reported in total on the income statement).

Revenue Expenditures

Expenditures that do not increase the future economic benefits of the asset are called **revenue expenditures** and are expensed in the same period the expenditure is made. Verizon's policy with regard to revenue expenditures, as disclosed in the notes to the financial statements, is shown below.

> *We charge the cost of maintenance and repairs, including the cost of replacing minor items not constituting substantial betterments, principally to Cost of Services and Sales as these costs are incurred.*
>
> *Source:* Verizon Wireless 2011 10-K.

These expenditures maintain the level of benefits provided by the asset, relate only to the current period, occur frequently, and typically involve relatively small dollar amounts. An example of a revenue expenditure is the ordinary repair and maintenance of an asset.

Capital Expenditures

Expenditures that extend the life of the asset, expand the productive capacity, increase efficiency, or improve the quality of the product, are called **capital expenditures**. Because these expenditures provide benefits to the company in both current and future periods, capital expenditures are added to an asset account and are subject to depreciation. These expenditures typically involve relatively large dollar amounts. Examples of capital expenditures include extraordinary or major repairs, additions, remodeling of buildings, and improvements (sometimes called betterments). For example, Verizon reported capital expenditures of approximately $16.2 billion related to the build-out, upgrade, and expansion of both its wired and wireless network capacity and the introduction of new technology.

Exhibit 7.11 summarizes different expenditures and how they would be accounted for.

EXHIBIT 7.11

Types of Expenditures

Type of Expenditure	Description	Examples	Accounting Treatment
Ordinary Repairs and Maintenance	Expenditures that keep an asset in normal operating condition	• Oil change for a truck • Painting of a building • Replacement of a minor part • Normal cleaning costs	*Expense* in the current period
Extraordinary or Major Repairs	Expenditures that extend the asset's useful life	• Overhaul or rebuilding of an engine • Fixing structural damage to a building	*Capitalize and depreciate* over the asset's remaining useful life
Additions	Adding a new or major component to an existing asset	• Adding a new wing to a building • Installing a pollution-control device on a machine	*Capitalize and depreciate* over the shorter of the remaining life of the asset or the addition
Improvements (or Betterments)	The replacement of a component of an asset with a better one that increases efficiency or productivity	• Replacing an old air conditioning unit with a more efficient one • Replacing a manual machine control with computer-controlled controls	*Capitalize and depreciate* over the improved asset's remaining useful life

Because it is often difficult to distinguish capital and revenue expenditures, managers must exercise professional judgment in deciding to capitalize or expense these costs. Many companies develop simple policies to aid them in making this decision. For example, a company may decide to expense all costs under $1,000.

REVISION OF DEPRECIATION

OBJECTIVE 6

Understand and account for revisions in depreciation.

Depreciation expense is based on estimates of useful life and residual value. As new or additional information becomes available, a company will often find it necessary to revise its estimates of useful life, residual value, or both. The change of these estimates will result in a recalculation of depreciation expense. In addition, when a capital expenditure is made, it is also necessary for a company to recalculate its depreciation expense. In such situations, the company does not change previously recorded amounts related to depreciation. Instead, any revision of depreciation expense is accounted for in current and future periods.

To revise depreciation expense, the following steps are performed:

Step 1. Obtain the book value of the asset at the date of the revision of depreciation.
Step 2. Compute depreciation expense using the revised amounts for book value, useful life, and/or residual value.

Cornerstone 7.5 illustrates the accounting for a revision in depreciation.

Revising Depreciation Expense

CORNERSTONE 7.5

Why:

A revision in depreciation is accounted for in current and future periods.

Information:

On January 1, 2005, Parker Publishing Company bought a printing press for $300,000. Parker estimated that the printing press would have a residual value of $50,000 and a useful

(Continued)

CORNERSTONE 7.5

(Continued)

life of 10 years. Parker uses the straight-line depreciation method and the book value of the asset on December 31, 2012, was $100,000. On January 1, 2013, Parker paid $90,000 to add a digital typesetting component to the printing press. After the addition, the printing press is expected to have a remaining useful life of 6 years and a residual value of $10,000.

Required:

1. What is the book value of the printing press on January 1, 2013?
2. What amount should Parker record for depreciation expense for 2013?

Solution:

1. Because the digital typesetting component is a capital expenditure, the cost of the addition is added to the book value of the asset, resulting in a revised book value of $190,000 ($90,000 + $100,000).
2. Using the revised book value, the revised estimate of residual value, and the revised estimate of useful life, Parker would recognize depreciation expense in 2013 of $30,000, calculated as:

$$\text{Depreciation Expense} = \frac{\$190{,}000 - \$10{,}000}{6 \text{ years}} = \underline{\underline{\$30{,}000}} \text{ per year}$$

Note that only the current and future years are affected by this revision. Parker does *not* need to adjust the prior years' financial statements based on this new information. However, if the change in estimate is a material amount, it should be disclosed in the notes to the financial statements.

Impairments

Because depreciation is a cost allocation process and does not attempt to measure the fair value of the asset, the book value of an asset and the fair value of an asset may be quite different. When the fair value of the asset falls significantly below the book value of the asset, the asset may be impaired. An *impairment* is a permanent decline in the future benefit or service potential of an asset. The impairment may be due to numerous factors, including too little depreciation expense being recorded in previous years or obsolescence of the asset. Consistent with the principle of conservatism, if a fixed asset is impaired, a company should reduce the asset's book value to its fair value in the year the impairment occurs. The accounting for impairments is discussed more fully in Appendix 7A.

OBJECTIVE 7

Describe the process of recording the disposal of a fixed asset.

DISPOSAL OF FIXED ASSETS

Although companies usually dispose of fixed assets voluntarily, disposition may also be forced.

- **Voluntary disposal** occurs when the company determines that the asset is no longer useful. The disposal may occur at the end of the asset's useful life or at some other time. For example, obsolescence due to unforeseen technological developments may lead to an earlier than expected disposition of the asset.
- **Involuntary disposal** occurs when assets are lost or destroyed through theft, acts of nature, or by accident.

In either case, disposals rarely occur on the first or last day of an accounting period. Therefore, the disposal of property, plant, and equipment usually requires two journal entries:

1. An entry to record depreciation expense up to the date of disposal.
2. An entry to:

- Remove the asset's book value (the cost of the asset **and** the related accumulated depreciation).
- Record a gain or loss on disposal of the asset, which is computed as the difference between the proceeds from the sale and the book value of the asset.

Gains and losses on the disposal of property, plant, and equipment are normally reported as "other revenues or gains" or "other expenses and losses," respectively, and appear immediately after income from operations on a multiple-step income statement.

Verizon's policy for recording disposals, as shown in the notes to its 2011 financial statements, is shown below.

> *When the depreciable assets . . . are retired or otherwise disposed of, the related cost and accumulated depreciation are deducted from the plant accounts, and any gains or losses on disposition are recognized in income.*
>
> *Source:* Verizon Wireless 2011 10-K.

Cornerstone 7.6 illustrates the accounting for the disposal of property, plant, and equipment.

Recording the Disposition of Property, Plant, and Equipment

CORNERSTONE 7.6

Why:

When a company disposes of an asset, the book value at the date of disposition is removed and any related gain or loss is recognized.

Information:

Dickerson Corporation sold a machine on July 1, 2013, for $22,000. The machine had originally cost $100,000. Accumulated depreciation on January 1, 2013, was $80,000. Depreciation expense for the first 6 months of 2013 was $5,000.

Required:

1. Prepare the journal entry to record depreciation expense up to the date of disposal.
2. Compute the gain or loss on disposal of the machine.
3. Prepare the journal entry to record the disposal of the machine.

Solution:

1.

Date	Account and Explanation	Debit	Credit
July 1, 2013	Depreciation Expense	5,000	
	Accumulated Depreciation		5,000
	(Record depreciation expense)		

Assets	=	Liabilities	+	Stockholders' Equity
−5,000				−5,000

2.

Proceeds from sale		$22,000
Less: Book value of asset sold:		
Cost	$100,000	
Accumulated depreciation ($80,000 + $5,000)	(85,000)	15,000
Gain on disposal		$ 7,000

(Continued)

CORNERSTONE **7.6** *(Continued)*

Assets	= Liabilities +	Stockholders' Equity
+22,000		+7,000
+85,000		
−100,000		

3.

Date	Account and Explanation	Debit	Credit
July 1, 2013	Cash	22,000	
	Accumulated Depreciation	85,000	
	Equipment		100,000
	Gain on Disposal of Property, Plant, and Equipment		7,000
	(Record disposal of machine)		

Note that Dickerson recorded depreciation expense up to the date of disposal. Once this journal entry is made, the book value is updated to reflect the increased accumulated depreciation. This revised book value is then used to compute the Gain on Disposal of Property, Plant, and Equipment which appears in the "other revenues and gains" section of the income statement.

If Dickerson had received $12,000 for the asset, the following computation would be made:

Proceeds from sale		$12,000
Less: Book value of asset sold:		
Cost	$100,000	
Accumulated depreciation ($80,000 + $5,000)	(85,000)	15,000
Loss on disposal of property, plant, and equipment		$ (3,000)

Because the proceeds from the sale were less than the book value, Dickerson would record a loss as follows:

Assets	= Liabilities +	Stockholders' Equity
+12,000		−3,000
+85,000		
−100,000		

Date	Account and Explanation	Debit	Credit
July 1, 2013	Cash	12,000	
	Accumulated Depreciation	85,000	
	Loss on Disposal of Property, Plant, and Equipment	3,000	
	Equipment		100,000
	(Record disposal of machine)		

Dickerson would report the loss in the "other expenses and losses" section of the income statement.

YOU DECIDE Future Asset Replacement

You are considering a major investment in one of two long-haul trucking companies. Both companies are about the same size, travel competitive routes, and have similar net incomes. However, the balance sheets reveal a significant difference in the accumulated depreciation for the trucks as shown at right.

	Halpin Company	Long Company
Trucks	$ 600,000	$ 550,000
Less: Accumulated depreciation	(138,000)	(477,000)
Book value	$ 462,000	$ 73,000

What conclusions can you make regarding the future cash outflows each company will have to make for future asset replacements?

Assuming that the assets' estimates of useful life are consistent with their economic lives, the closer that accumulated depreciation is to historical cost, the older the assets and the more likely that they will have to be replaced. Long Company's assets are closer to being fully depreciated than those of Halpin Company. Therefore, Long is more likely to make cash outflows for the replacement of its assets. Although more information would be needed about Long in order to know the precise impact of the impending replacement, the comparison of the two accumulated depreciation amounts does provide you with valuable insights. While the recording of depreciation expense does not alter cash flow, accumulated depreciation signals the approaching future replacement of fixed assets, which usually requires cash.

A comparison of accumulated depreciation to historical cost can provide financial statement users with an approximation of the remaining life of the assets.

ANALYZING FIXED ASSETS

OBJECTIVE 8

Evaluate the use of fixed assets.

Because fixed assets are a major productive asset of most companies, it is useful to understand if the company is using these assets efficiently. In other words, how well is the company using its fixed assets to generate revenue? One measure of how efficiently a company is using its fixed assets is the **fixed asset turnover ratio**. It is calculated as:

$$\text{Fixed Asset Turnover Ratio} = \frac{\text{Net Sales}}{\text{Average Net Fixed Assets}}$$

The more efficiently a company uses its fixed assets, the higher the ratio will be.

In addition to the fixed asset turnover ratio, investors are also concerned with the condition of a company's fixed assets. Because older assets tend to be less efficient than newer assets, the age of a company's fixed assets can provide useful insights into the company's efficiency. The age of a company's fixed assets also can provide an indication of a company's capital replacement policy and assist managers in estimating future capital expenditures. A rough estimate of the **average age of fixed assets** can be computed as:

$$\text{Average Age of Fixed Assets} = \frac{\text{Accumulated Depreciation}}{\text{Depreciation Expense}}$$

Cornerstone 7.7 illustrates the calculation of the fixed asset turnover ratio and the average age of fixed assets.

Analyzing Fixed Asset Ratios

CORNERSTONE 7.7

Why:

The analysis of fixed assets can provide useful information as to how efficiently the assets have been used as well as the condition of the assets.

Information:

The following information was obtained from the financial statements of Verizon and AT&T (all amounts in millions):

(Continued)

CORNERSTONE
7.7
(Continued)

Account	Verizon	AT&T
Property, plant, and equipment, net, 12/31/10	$ 87,711	$103,196
Property, plant, and equipment, net, 12/31/11	88,434	107,087
Accumulated depreciation, 12/31/11	127,192	153,192
Net sales	110,875	126,723
Depreciation expense	14,991	16,368

Required:

1. Compute the fixed asset turnover ratio for Verizon and AT&T.
2. Compute the average age of Verizon's and AT&T's fixed assets as of 12/31/2011.

Solution:

1. $\text{Fixed Asset Turnover Ratio} = \dfrac{\text{Net Sales}}{\text{Average Net Fixed Assets}}$

Verizon

$$\frac{\$110{,}875}{\left[\dfrac{(\$87{,}711 + \$88{,}434)}{2}\right]} = \underline{\underline{1.26}} \text{ times}$$

AT&T

$$\frac{\$126{,}723}{\left[\dfrac{(\$103{,}196 + \$107{,}087)}{2}\right]} = \underline{\underline{1.21}} \text{ times}$$

2. $\text{Average Age of Fixed Assets} = \dfrac{\text{Accumulated Depreciation}}{\text{Depreciation Expense}}$

Verizon

$$\frac{\$127{,}192}{\$14{,}991} = \underline{\underline{8.48}} \text{ years}$$

AT&T

$$\frac{\$153{,}192}{\$16{,}368} = \underline{\underline{9.36}} \text{ years}$$

In Cornerstone 7.7, the fixed asset ratio tells us that for each dollar invested in fixed assets, Verizon generated sales of $1.26 while AT&T generated sales of $1.21. In comparison with the industry average of 1.24, it appears that both AT&T and Verizon are efficiently using their fixed assets to generate sales. In addition, Verizon's assets are, on average, 8.48 years old, while AT&T's assets are approximately 9.36 years old. Because Verizon's primary fixed asset is network equipment, which is depreciated between 3 and 15 years (see Exhibit 7.3 and Exhibit 7.5), this signals that Verizon will most likely be making significant capital expenditures over the next several years to replace its network equipment.

In addition to comparing a company's fixed asset turnover ratio with that of prior years and its competitors, it is necessary to gain an understanding of a company's operations to appropriately assess how efficiently a company is using its fixed assets. For example, Verizon's fixed asset turnover may be lower than some of its competitors because it is currently spending large amounts to expand its network in anticipation of future sales. These expansion activities (which are capitalized in the current period) could depress Verizon's fixed asset turnover ratio.

INTANGIBLE ASSETS

OBJECTIVE 9
Understand the measurement and reporting of intangible assets.

Intangible operating assets, like tangible assets, represent future economic benefit to the company, but unlike tangible assets, they lack physical substance. Patents, copyrights, trademarks, leaseholds, organization costs, franchises, and goodwill are all examples of intangible assets. The economic benefits associated with most intangible assets are in the form of legal rights and privileges conferred on the owner of the asset. The economic value of a patent, for example, is the legal right to restrict, control, or charge for the use of the idea or process covered by the patent.

Because intangible assets lack physical substance, it is often easy to overlook their importance to the overall value of a company. Recent research suggests that between 60% and 80% of a company's market value may be tied to intangible assets. For many companies, intangible assets may be the most important asset it has. A pharmaceutical company such as GlaxoSmithKline could easily argue that the true value of the company lies with its intellectual capital and patents, not its tangible property, plant, and equipment. However, due to unique issues with intangibles (such as the highly uncertain nature of future benefits and the possibility of wide fluctuations in value), the value of many intangible assets is not adequately captured by current accounting standards. For example, GlaxoSmithKline's intangible assets only make up approximately 29% of its total assets. As the value of intangible assets continues to be a key driver of company value, the measurement and evaluation of intangibles will certainly be a crucial issue.

concept Q&A

If intangible assets represent a major amount of many companies' value, wouldn't any estimate of the intangible asset's value be better than not recording the asset at all?

Answer:

While intangible assets are certainly relevant to financial statement users, information must be reliably measured to be recorded in the financial statements. For many intangibles, the inability to measure the intangible asset reliably results in the inability to record the intangible asset. This trade-off between the relevance and reliability of information is often a matter of judgment.

Accounting for Intangible Assets

Intangible assets are recorded at cost, consistent with the historical cost principle. Similar to fixed assets, the cost of an intangible asset is any expenditure necessary to acquire the asset and to prepare the asset for use. For intangible assets purchased from outside the company, the primary element of the cost is the purchase price. Costs such as registration, filing, and legal fees are considered necessary costs and are capitalized as part of the intangible asset.

For internally developed intangible assets, the cost of developing the asset is expensed as incurred and normally recorded as **research and development (R&D) expense**. While expenditures for R&D may lead to intangible assets such as patents and copyrights, R&D is not an intangible asset. While many disagree with this position, current accounting standards require that all R&D be recorded as an expense. Exhibit 7.12 provides a listing of some typical intangible assets.

IFRS
Under IFRS, research costs are expensed while development costs are capitalized if it is probable that future benefits will be received.

Companies also incur significant costs such as legal fees, stock issue costs, accounting fees, and promotional fees when they are formed. It can be argued that these **organizational costs** are an intangible asset that provides a benefit to a company indefinitely. However, current accounting standards treat organizational costs as an expense in the period the cost is incurred.

Once an intangible asset is recorded, companies must determine if the asset has a finite life or an indefinite life. The cost of an intangible asset with a *finite life*, like the cost of a tangible asset, is allocated to accounting periods over the life of the asset to reflect the decline in service potential. This process is referred to as **amortization**. Most companies will amortize the cost of an intangible asset on a straight-line basis over the shorter of the economic or legal life of the asset. For example, a patent has a legal life of 20 years from the date it is granted. However, the economic advantage offered by a patent often expires before the end of its legal life as a result of other technological developments. Therefore, the shorter economic life should be used to amortize the cost of the patent.

If an intangible asset is determined to have an *indefinite life*, it is *not* amortized but is reviewed at least annually for impairment. Cornerstone 7.8 illustrates the accounting for the acquisition and amortization of intangible assets.

EXHIBIT 7.12

Common Types of Intangible Assets

Intangible Asset	Description	Cost Includes	Amortization
Patent	Right to manufacture, sell, or use a product. The legal life is 20 years from the date of grant.	Purchase price, registration fees, legal costs	Shorter of the economic life or legal life
Copyright	Right to publish, sell, or control a literary or artistic work. The legal life is life of author plus 70 years.	Purchase price, registration fees, legal costs	Shorter of the economic life or legal life
Trademark	Right to the exclusive use of a distinctive name, phrase, or symbol (for example, the iPod name or the Nike "swoosh"). The legal life is 10 years but it can be renewed indefinitely.	Purchase price, registration fees, legal costs	Not amortized since it has an indefinite life; reviewed at least annually for impairment
Franchise	Exclusive right to conduct a certain type of business in some particular geographic area. Life of the franchise depends on specific terms of the franchise contract.	Initial cost paid to acquire the franchise	Shorter of the economic life or legal life
Goodwill	Unidentifiable intangible asset that arises from factors such as customer satisfaction, quality products, skilled employees, and business location. Goodwill is only recognized in business combinations.	The excess of the purchase price over the fair value of the identifiable net assets acquired in a business combination	Not amortized since it has an indefinite life; reviewed at least annually for impairment

CORNERSTONE 7.8

Accounting for Intangible Assets

Why:

Intangible assets are recorded at the cost necessary to acquire the asset and to prepare the asset for use. The cost of the asset is allocated as an expense among the accounting periods in which the asset is used and benefits are received (the matching principle).

Information:

On January 1, 2013, King Company acquired a patent from Queen Inc. for $40,000. The patent was originally granted on January 1, 2007 and has 14 years of its legal life remaining. However, due to technological advancements, King estimates the patent will only provide benefits for 10 years. In addition, King purchased a trademark from Queen for $60,000.

Required:

1. Prepare any journal entries necessary to record the acquisition of the patent and the trademark.
2. Compute the amortization expense for the patent and the trademark.
3. Prepare any adjusting journal entries necessary to record the amortization expense for 2013.

(Continued)

Solution: CORNERSTONE **7.8** *(Continued)*

1.

Date	Account and Explanation	Debit	Credit
Jan. 1, 2013	Patent	40,000	
	Trademark	60,000	
	Cash		100,000
	(To purchase patent and trademark)		

Assets	= Liabilities +	Stockholders' Equity
+40,000		
+60,000		
−100,000		

2. $$\frac{\text{Cost} - \text{Residual Value}}{\text{Useful Life}} = \frac{\$40,000 - \$0}{10 \text{ years}} = \underline{\underline{\$4,000}}$$

Note: Because the trademark has an indefinite life, no amortization is necessary.

3.

Date	Account and Explanation	Debit	Credit
Dec. 31, 2013	Amortization Expense	4,000	
	Patent		4,000
	(To record amortization of patent)		

Assets	= Liabilities +	Stockholders' Equity
−4,000		−4,000

In Cornerstone 7.8, several items are of note:

- Most intangible assets do not have a residual value. Therefore, the cost that is being amortized is usually the entire cost of the intangible asset.
- King amortized the patent over the shorter of its remaining legal life (14 years) or its economic life (10 years). This is consistent with recognizing amortization expense over the period that the intangible asset is expected to provide benefits.
- King recorded the amortization expense by directly crediting the intangible asset, Patent. After the amortization expense is recorded, the book value of the patent is $36,000 ($40,000 − $4,000).
- Amortization expense is reported as operating expense on the income statement.

YOUDECIDE Measuring and Estimating the Dimensions of a Patent

You are the controller for Marietta Corporation, a research intensive company engaged in the design and sale of ceramic products. For the past year, half of Marietta's research staff has been engaged in designing a process for coating iron and steel with a ceramic material for use in high-temperature areas of automobile engines. The company has secured a patent for its process and is about to begin marketing equipment that uses the patented process. The assistant controller has argued that half of the year's cost of research activities should be assigned to the patent, including the salaries paid to researchers. Additionally, while Marietta expects the patented equipment to be a viable product for only 5 years, the assistant controller recommends that the patent should be amortized over its legal life of 20 years.

What is the impact of the assistant controller's recommendation, and how should you account for the patent?

If these costs were capitalized as part of the patent as the assistant controller recommended, current period assets and income would be overstated. In future periods, the higher recorded value of the intangible asset would result in an increase in amortization expense. While many analysts agree with the assistant controller that some research and development expenditures create an intangible asset, current accounting standards require that all research activities should be expensed when incurred.

If the patent were amortized over its legal life, the cost of the patent would be spread over 20 years, resulting in lower yearly amounts of amortization expense and higher income. However, accounting standards require that intangible assets be amortized over the shorter of their legal lives or their economic lives. Therefore, a relatively higher amortization expense should be recognized over the 5-year useful life of the patent.

Current accounting standards should be followed to avoid misstating the financial statements.

OBJECTIVE 10

Understand the measurement and reporting of natural resources.

NATURAL RESOURCES

Natural resources, such as coal deposits, oil reserves, and mineral deposits, make up an important part of the operating assets for many companies. For example, **BP** has oil and gas properties of over $83 billion, representing approximately 29% of its total assets. Like intangible assets, natural resources present difficult estimation and measurement problems. However, natural resources differ from other operating assets in two important ways:

- Unlike fixed assets, natural resources are physically consumed as they are used by a company.
- Natural resources can generally be replaced or restored only by an act of nature. (Timberlands are renewed by replanting and growth, but coal deposits and most mineral deposits are not subject to renewal.)

The accounting for natural resources is quite similar to the accounting for intangible assets and fixed assets. At acquisition, all the costs necessary to ready the natural resource for separation from the earth are capitalized. At the time a company acquires the property on which a natural resource is located (or the property rights to the natural resource itself), only a small portion of the costs necessary to ready the asset for removal are likely to have been incurred. Costs such as sinking a shaft to an underground coal deposit, drilling a well to an oil reserve, or removing the earth over a mineral deposit can be several times greater than the cost of acquiring the property.

As a natural resource is removed from the earth, the cost of the natural resource is allocated to each unit of natural resource removed. This process of allocating the cost of the natural resource to each period in which the resource is used is called **depletion**. Depletion is computed by using a procedure similar to that for the units-of-production method of depreciation. First, a depletion rate is computed as:

$$\text{Depletion Rate} = \frac{\text{Cost} - \text{Residual Value}}{\text{Recoverable Units}}$$

Second, depletion is calculated by multiplying the depletion rate by the number of units of the natural resource recovered during the period:

$$\text{Depletion} = \text{Depletion Rate} \times \text{Units Recovered}$$

As the natural resource is extracted, the natural resource is reduced and the amount of depletion computed is added to inventory. As the inventory is sold, the company will recognize an expense (cost of goods sold) related to the natural resource. Cornerstone 7.9 illustrates how to account for depletion of a natural resource.

CORNERSTONE 7.9

Accounting for Depletion of a Natural Resource

Why:

All costs necessary to acquire the natural resource and prepare it for use are capitalized as part of the natural resource. The depletion of the natural resource is added to inventory as the resource is depleted.

Information:

In 2012, the Miller Mining Company purchased a 4,000-acre tract of land in southern Indiana for $12,000,000, on which it developed an underground coal mine. Miller spent $26,000,000 to sink shafts to the coal seams and otherwise prepare the mine for operation.

(Continued)

CORNERSTONE
7.9
(Continued)

Miller estimates that there are 10,000,000 tons of recoverable coal and that the mine will be fully depleted 8 years after mining begins in early 2013. The land has a residual value of $500,000. During 2013, 800,000 tons of coal were mined.

Required:

1. Compute the cost of the natural resource.
2. Compute the depletion rate.
3. How much depletion is taken in 2013?
4. Prepare the journal entry necessary to record depletion and the related cost of goods sold.

Solution:

1. The cost of the natural resource includes all costs necessary to get the mine ready for use:

Cost	$12,000,000
Development/preparation costs	26,000,000
Cost	$38,000,000

2. Depletion Rate $= \frac{(\$38{,}000{,}000 - \$500{,}000)}{10{,}000{,}000 \text{ tons}} = \underline{\underline{\$3.75}}$ per ton

3. Depletion $= \$3.75 \times 800{,}000 = \underline{\underline{\$3{,}000{,}000}}$

4.

Date	Account and Explanation	Debit	Credit
Dec. 31, 2013	Inventory	3,000,000	
	Accumulated Depletion		3,000,000
	(Record depletion of coal mine)		

Assets	= Liabilities +	Stockholders' Equity
+3,000,000		
−3,000,000		

Assuming all of the coal is sold in 2013, the following entry should also be made:

Date	Account and Explanation	Debit	Credit
Dec. 31, 2013	Cost of Goods Sold	3,000,000	
	Inventory		3,000,000
	(Record cost of goods sold)		

Assets	= Liabilities +	Stockholders' Equity
−3,000,000		−3,000,000

In Cornerstone 7.9, the following items are of particular importance:

- Miller records depletion initially increasing an inventory account. As the coal is sold, inventory will be reduced and cost of goods sold will be recognized. Thus, the expense related to depletion will be matched with the revenue that is generated from the sale of the natural resource.
- Depletion increases the accumulated depletion account.[8] At December 31, 2013, Miller could present the coal mine among its assets in the balance sheet as shown in Exhibit 7.13.

[8] An alternative practice allowed by GAAP is to credit depletion directly to the asset account.

EXHIBIT 7.13

Disclosure of Natural Resource by Miller Mining Company

Property, plant, and equipment:	
Land	$ 2,200,000
Equipment and machinery	19,800,000
Coal mine (cost of $38,000,000 minus accumulated depletion of $3,000,000)	35,000,000
Total property, plant, and equipment	$57,000,000

Companies will often incur costs for tangible fixed assets in connection with the use of a natural resource (such as buildings, equipment, roads to access the resource). Because the useful life of these assets is often limited by the life of the natural resource, these tangible assets should be depreciated using the units-of-production method on the same basis as the natural resource. However, if the assets have a life shorter than the expected life of the natural resource or will be used for the extraction of other natural resources, the assets should be depreciated over their own useful lives.

OBJECTIVE 11

Describe the process of recording an impairment of a fixed asset.

APPENDIX 7A: IMPAIRMENT OF PROPERTY, PLANT, AND EQUIPMENT

An **impairment** is a permanent decline in the future benefit or service potential of an asset. The impairment may be due to numerous factors, including too little depreciation expense being recorded in previous years or obsolescence of the asset. A company is required to review an asset for impairment if events or circumstances lead the company to believe that an asset may be impaired. Consistent with the principle of conservatism, if a fixed asset is impaired, a company should reduce the asset's book value to its fair value in the year the impairment occurs.

IFRS

The impairment model under IFRS is a single-step process that measures the impairment as the difference between the book value and the higher of the fair value or value in use.

The impairment test consists of two steps:

Step 1. Existence: An impairment exists if the future cash flows expected to be generated by the asset are less than the asset's book value.

Step 2. Measurement: If an impairment exists, the impairment loss is measured as the difference between the book value and the fair value of the asset.

Cornerstone 7.10 illustrates the accounting for an impairment.

CORNERSTONE

7.10

Recording an Impairment of Property, Plant, and Equipment

Why:

If there is a permanent decline in the service potential of an operating asset, the asset's book value should be reduced to reflect this reduction in service potential.

Information:

Tabor Company acquired a machine on January 1, 2006, for $150,000. On January 3, 2013, when the machine has a book value of $60,000, Tabor believes that recent technological innovations may have led to an impairment in the value of the machine. Tabor estimates the machine will generate future cash flows of $50,000 and its current fair value is $42,000.

(Continued)

CORNERSTONE
7.10
(Continued)

Required:

1. Determine if the machine is impaired as of January 2013.
2. If the machine is impaired, compute the loss from impairment.
3. Prepare the journal entry to record the impairment.

Solution:

1. The machine is impaired because the estimated future cash flows expected to be generated by the machine ($50,000) are less than the book value of the machine ($60,000).
2. Fair Value – Book Value = Loss from Impairment

   $42,000 – $60,000 = ($18,000)

3.

Date	Account and Explanation	Debit	Credit
Jan. 3, 2013	Loss from Impairment	18,000	
	Equipment		18,000
	(Record impairment of asset)		

Assets	=	Liabilities	+	Stockholders' Equity
−18,000				−18,000

SUMMARY OF LEARNING OBJECTIVES

LO 1. Define, classify, and describe the accounting for operating assets.

- Operating assets are the long-lived assets used by the company in the normal course of operations to generate revenue.
- Operating assets consist of three categories: property, plant, and equipment; intangible assets; and natural resources.
- Generally, operating assets are recorded at cost.
- As the service potential of the asset is used, the asset's cost is allocated as an expense (called depreciation, amortization, or depletion).

LO 2. Explain how the historical cost principle applies to recording the cost of a fixed asset.

- The cost of a fixed asset is any expenditure necessary to acquire the asset and to prepare the asset for use.
- This amount is generally the cash paid.
- If noncash consideration is involved, cost is the fair value of the asset received or the fair value of the asset given up, whichever is more clearly determinable.

LO 3. Understand the concept of depreciation.

- Depreciation is the process of allocating the cost of a tangible fixed asset to expense over the asset's useful life.
- Depreciation is not an attempt to measure fair value.
- Instead, depreciation is designed to capture the declining service potential of a fixed asset.
- Three factors are necessary to compute depreciation expense: cost, useful life, and residual value.

LO 4. Compute depreciation expense using various depreciation methods.

- The straight-line method allocates an equal amount of the asset's cost to each year of the asset's useful life by dividing the asset's depreciable cost (cost minus residual value) by the asset's useful life.

- The declining balance method is an accelerated method of depreciation that produces a declining amount of depreciation expense each period by multiplying the declining book value of an asset by a constant depreciation rate (computed as a multiple of the straight-line rate of depreciation).
- The units-of-production method recognizes depreciation expense based on the actual usage of the asset.

LO 5. Distinguish between capital and revenue expenditures.

- Revenue expenditures are expenditures that do not increase the future benefit of an asset and are expensed as incurred.
- Capital expenditures extend the life of the asset, expand productive capacity, increase efficiency, or improve the quality of the product. Capital expenditures are added to the asset account and are subject to depreciation.

LO 6. Understand and account for revisions in depreciation.

- When new or additional information becomes available, a company will revise its calculation of depreciation expense.
- A revision in depreciation will be recorded in current and future periods.

LO 7. Describe the process of recording the disposal of a fixed asset.

- When a fixed asset is disposed of (either voluntarily or involuntarily), a gain or loss is recognized.
- The gain or loss is the difference between the proceeds from the sale and the book value of the asset.
- The gain or loss is reported on the income statement as "other revenues or gains" or "other expenses and losses," respectively.

LO 8. Evaluate the use of fixed assets.

- The efficiency with which a company uses its fixed assets can be analyzed by using the fixed asset turnover ratio (net sales divided by average net fixed assets).
- The condition of a company's assets and insights into the company's capital replacement policy can be examined by computing the average age of fixed assets (accumulated depreciation divided by depreciation expense).

LO 9. Understand the measurement and reporting of intangible assets.

- Intangible assets are recorded at cost, which is any expenditure necessary to acquire the asset and prepare it for use.
- If the intangible asset has a finite life, it is amortized over the shorter of the economic or legal life of the asset.
- If the intangible asset has an indefinite life, it is not amortized but is reviewed at least annually for impairment.

LO 10. Understand the measurement and reporting of natural resources.

- The cost of natural resources is any cost necessary to acquire and prepare the resource for separation from the earth.
- As the natural resource is removed, the cost is allocated to each unit of the natural resource that is removed and recorded in an inventory account. This process is called depletion.
- Depletion is calculated using a procedure similar to the units-of-production depreciation method.

LO 11. *(Appendix 7A)* Describe the process of recording an impairment of a fixed asset.

- Impairment exists when the future cash flows expected to be generated by an asset are less than the book value of the asset.
- An impairment loss, the difference between the book value and fair value of the asset, is recognized and the asset is reduced.

CORNERSTONES

KEY TERMS

Accumulated depreciation, 368
Amortization, 387
Average age of fixed assets, 385
Book value, 368
Capital expenditures, 380
Carrying value, 368
Cost, 369
Declining balance depreciation method, 373
Depletion, 390
Depreciable cost, 370
Depreciation, 368
Depreciation expense, 368
Fixed asset turnover ratio, 385
Impairment, 392
Intangible operating assets, 387
Involuntary disposal, 382
Natural resources, 390
Operating assets, 364
Organizational costs, 387
Property, plant, and equipment, 365
Research and development (R&D) expense, 387
Residual value, 370
Revenue expenditures, 380
Salvage value, 370
Straight-line depreciation method, 371
Units-of-production depreciation method, 376
Useful life, 369
Voluntary disposal, 382

REVIEW PROBLEM

Accounting for Operating Assets

Concept:

At acquisition, operating assets are capitalized at their historical cost. As the service potential of an operating asset declines, the cost of the asset is allocated as an expense among the accounting periods in which the asset is used and benefits are received.

Information:

The Carroll Company manufactures a line of cranes, shovels, and hoists, all of which are electronically controlled. During 2013, the following transactions occurred:

a. On January 2, Carroll purchased a building by signing a note payable for $702,900. The building is expected to have a useful life of 30 years and a residual value of $3,900.
b. On January 3, Carroll purchased a delivery truck for $34,650 cash. The delivery truck is expected to have a useful life of 5 years and a $5,000 residual value.
c. Immediately after the acquisition, Carroll spent $5,350 on a new engine for the truck. After installing the engine, Carroll estimated that this expenditure increased the useful life of the truck to 8 years. The residual value is still expected to be $5,000.
d. In order to assure a coal supply for its heating plant, Carroll acquired a small operating coal mine for $1,980,000. Carroll estimated that the recoverable coal reserves at acquisition were 495,000 tons. Carroll's mine produced 40,000 tons of coal during 2013.
e. Carroll purchased a patent on January 3 for $100,000. The patent has 12 years remaining on its legal life, but Carroll estimated its economic life to be 8 years. Carroll uses the straight-line amortization method.

Required:

1. Record the acquisition of the building and the delivery truck.
2. Prepare a depreciation schedule and record a full year's depreciation expense for 2013 on the building (use the straight-line depreciation method) and on the truck (use the double-declining-balance depreciation method).
3. Compute and record 2013 depletion for the coal mine.
4. Compute and record the amortization expense on the patent for 2013 on a straight-line basis.
5. Assume Carroll had sales of $8,800,000, fixed assets with an average net book value of $3,200,000, depreciation expense of $375,000, and accumulated depreciation of $2,062,500. Compute the fixed asset turnover ratio and the average age of the fixed assets. Comment on what the ratios mean.

Solution:

1. The cost of the building is $702,900 and is recorded as:

Assets	= Liabilities +	Stockholders' Equity
+702,900	+702,900	

Date	Account and Explanation	Debit	Credit
Jan. 2, 2013	Buildings	702,900	
	Notes Payable		702,900
	(Purchased building by issuing note payable)		

The cost of the truck is $40,000 ($34,650 acquisition price + $5,350 from the overhaul of the engine). The purchase of the truck is recorded as:

Assets	= Liabilities +	Stockholders' Equity
−40,000		
+40,000		

Date	Account and Explanation	Debit	Credit
Jan. 3, 2013	Truck	40,000	
	Cash		40,000
	(Purchase of truck for cash)		

2. Depreciation on the items of property, plant, and equipment:

STRAIGHT-LINE DEPRECIATION ON THE BUILDING

$$\text{Straight-Line Depreciation Expense} = \frac{\text{Cost} - \text{Residual Value}}{\text{Expected Life}}$$

$$= \frac{\$702{,}900 - \$3{,}900}{30 \text{ years}} = \underline{\underline{\$23{,}300}} \text{ per year}$$

Assets	= Liabilities +	Stockholders' Equity
−23,300		−23,300

Date	Account and Explanation	Debit	Credit
Dec. 31, 2013	Depreciation Expense	23,300	
	Accumulated Depreciation		23,300
	(To record depreciation on building)		

DOUBLE-DECLINING-BALANCE DEPRECIATION FOR THE TRUCK

Declining Balance Depreciation Expense = Declining Balance Rate × Book Value

Declining Balance Rate = (1/Useful Life) × 2 = (1/8) × 2 = 2/8, or 25%

Cost = $34,650 (from Transaction b) + $5,350 overhaul (from Transaction c)
= $40,000

End of Year	Depreciation Expense	Accumulated Depreciation	Book Value
			$40,000
2013	25% × $40,000 = $10,000	$10,000	30,000
2014	25% × 30,000 = 7,500	17,500	22,500
2015	25% × 22,500 = 5,625	23,125	16,875
2016	25% × 16,875 = 4,219	27,344	12,656
2017	25% × 12,656 = 3,164	30,508	9,492
2018	25% × 9,492 = 2,373	32,881	7,119
2019	25% × 7,119 = 1,780	34,661	5,339
2020	339*	35,000	5,000
	$35,000		

* The amount needed to achieve a $5,000 book value.

Date	Account and Explanation	Debit	Credit
Dec. 31, 2013	Depreciation Expense	10,000	
	Accumulated Depreciation		10,000
	(To record depreciation on truck)		

Assets	= Liabilities +	Stockholders' Equity
−10,000		−10,000

3. Depletion on the coal mine:

$$\text{Depletion Rate} = \frac{\text{Cost} - \text{Residual Value}}{\text{Recoverable Units}}$$

$$= \frac{\$1{,}980{,}000}{495{,}000} = \$4.00 \text{ per ton}$$

$$\text{Depletion} = \text{Depletion Rate} \times \text{Units Recovered}$$

$$= \$4.00 \times 40{,}000 = \underline{\underline{\$160{,}000}}$$

Date	Account and Explanation	Debit	Credit
Dec. 31, 2013	Inventory	160,000	
	Accumulated Depletion		160,000
	(To record depletion)		

Assets	= Liabilities +	Stockholders' Equity
+160,000		
−160,000		

4. Amortization of the patent:

$$\text{Straight-Line Amortization Expense} = \frac{\text{Cost} - \text{Residual Value}}{\text{Expected Life}}$$

$$= \frac{\$100{,}000 - \$0}{8 \text{ years}}$$

$$= \underline{\underline{\$12{,}500}} \text{ per year}$$

Date	Account and Explanation	Debit	Credit
Dec. 31, 2013	Amortization Expense	12,500	
	Patent		12,500
	(To record amortization of patent)		

Assets	= Liabilities +	Stockholders' Equity
−12,500		−12,500

5. The fixed asset turnover ratio is computed as its net sales divided by the average of its fixed assets. Carroll Company's fixed asset turnover ratio is 2.75 ($8,800,000/$3,200,000). This ratio describes how efficiently Carroll is using its fixed assets to generate revenue. The average age of fixed assets is computed as accumulated depreciation divided by depreciation expense. Carroll's fixed assets are approximately 5½ years old ($2,062,500/$375,000). For every dollar of fixed assets, Carroll is generating $2.75 of sales.

DISCUSSION QUESTIONS

1. How do operating assets differ from nonoperating assets? What benefits do operating assets provide to the company?
2. What are the classifications of operating assets? How do they differ from one another?
3. How does the cost concept affect accounting for operating assets? Under this concept, what is included in the cost of a fixed asset?
4. How is the cost of a fixed asset measured in a cash transaction? In a noncash transaction?
5. What is the effect on the financial statements if a company incorrectly records an expense as an asset?
6. How does the matching principle affect accounting for operating assets?
7. What factors must be known or estimated in order to compute depreciation expense?
8. How do the accelerated and straight-line depreciation methods differ?
9. What objective should guide the selection of a depreciation method for financial reporting purposes?
10. What objective should be of primary importance in the selection of a depreciation method for income tax reporting?
11. What accounting concepts should be considered when evaluating the accounting for expenditures that are made for fixed assets after acquisition? Be sure to distinguish between revenue and capital expenditures.
12. What is the proper accounting for depreciation when new or additional information becomes available that causes a company to change its estimates of useful life or residual value?
13. How is the sale of equipment at an amount greater than its book value recorded? How would your answer change if the equipment is sold at an amount less than its book value?
14. What information does the fixed asset turnover ratio and the average age of fixed assets provide users of financial statements?
15. Describe the benefits that intangible assets provide to a company.
16. What factors should be considered when selecting the amortization period for an intangible asset?
17. What basis underlies the computation of depletion?
18. *(Appendix 7A)* What is an impairment of a fixed asset?

MULTIPLE-CHOICE QUESTIONS

7-1 Anniston Company purchased equipment and incurred the following costs:

Purchase price	$68,500
Cost of trial runs	400
Installation costs	325
Sales tax	3,425

What is the cost of the equipment?

a. $68,500
b. $71,925
c. $72,250
d. $72,650

7-2 The cost principle requires that companies record fixed assets at:

a. fair value.
b. book value.
c. historical cost.
d. market value.

7-3 When depreciation is recorded each period, what account is debited?

a. Depreciation Expense
b. Cash
c. Accumulated Depreciation
d. The fixed asset account involved

Use the following information for Multiple-Choice Questions 7-4 through 7-6:
Cox Inc. acquired a machine for $800,000 on January 1, 2013. The machine has a salvage value of $20,000 and a 5-year useful life. Cox expects the machine to run for 15,000 machine hours. The machine was actually used for 4,200 hours in 2013 and 3,450 hours in 2014.

7-4 Refer to the information for Cox Inc. above. What would be the balance in the accumulated depreciation account at December 31, 2014, if the straight-line method were used?

a. $156,000
b. $160,000
c. $312,000
d. $328,000

7-5 Refer to the information for Cox Inc. above. What amount would Cox record as depreciation expense at December 31, 2014, if the double-declining-balance method were used?

a. $187,200
b. $192,000
c. $195,200
d. $312,000

7-6 Refer to the information for Cox Inc. above. What amount would Cox record as depreciation expense for 2013 if the units-of-production method were used (*Note:* Round your answer to the nearest dollar)?

a. $179,400
b. $184,000
c. $218,400
d. $224,000

7-7 Which of the following statements is true regarding depreciation methods?

a. The use of a declining balance method of depreciation will produce lower depreciation charges in the early years of an asset's life compared to the straight-line depreciation method.
b. Over the life of an asset, a declining balance depreciation method will recognize more depreciation expense relative to the straight-line method.
c. The use of a declining balance method instead of the straight-line method will produce higher book values for an asset in the early years of the asset's life.
d. The use of a higher estimated life and a higher residual value will lower the annual amount of depreciation expense recognized on the income statement.

7-8 Normal repair and maintenance of an asset is an example of what?

a. Revenue expenditure
b. Capital expenditure
c. An expenditure that will be depreciated
d. An expenditure that should be avoided

7-9 Chapman Inc. purchased a piece of equipment in 2012. Chapman depreciated the equipment on a straight-line basis over a useful life of 10 years and used a residual value of $12,000. Chapman's depreciation expense for 2013 was $11,000. What was the original cost of the building? ILLUSTRATING RELATIONSHIPS

a. $98,000
b. $110,000
c. $122,000
d. $134,000

7-10 Bradley Company purchased a machine for $34,000 on January 1, 2011. It depreciates the machine using the straight-line method over a useful life of 8 years and a $2,000 residual value. On January 1, 2013, Bradley revised its estimate of residual value to $1,000 and shortened the machine's useful life to 4 more years. Depreciation expense for 2013 is:

a. $4,000.
b. $5,750.
c. $6,000.
d. $6,250.

7-11 Jerabek Inc. decided to sell one of its fixed assets that had a cost of $55,000 and accumulated depreciation of $35,000 on July 1, 2013. On that date, Jerabek sold the fixed asset for $15,000. What was the resulting gain or loss from the sale of the asset?

a. $5,000 loss
b. $5,000 gain
c. $15,000 loss
d. $15,000 gain

7-12 Which of the following statements is true?

a. The fixed asset turnover ratio assists managers in determining the estimated future capital expenditures that are needed.
b. The average age of the fixed assets is computed by dividing accumulated depreciation by depreciation expense.
c. If net sales increases, the fixed asset turnover ratio will decrease.
d. A relatively low fixed asset turnover ratio signals that a company is efficiently using its assets.

7-13 Which of the following is *not* an intangible asset?

a. Patent
b. Trademark
c. Research and development
d. Goodwill

7-14 Heston Company acquired a patent on January 1, 2013, for $75,000. The patent has a remaining legal life of 15 years, but Heston expects to receive benefits from the patent for only 5 years. What amount of amortization expense does Heston record in 2013 related to the patent?

a. $5,000
b. $7,500
c. $15,000
d. $0—patents are not amortized.

7-15 Howton Paper Company purchased $1,400,000 of timberland in 2012 for its paper operations. Howton estimates that there are 10,000 acres of timberland, and it cut 2,000 acres in 2013. The land is expected to have a residual value of $200,000 once all the timber is cut. Which of the following is true with regard to depletion?

a. Depletion will cause Howton's timber inventory to increase.
b. Howton will record depletion expense of $280,000 in 2013.
c. Howton's depletion rate is $140 per acre of timber.
d. Howton should deplete the timber at a rate of 20% (2,000 acres ÷ 10,000 acres) per year.

7-16 *(Appendix 7A)* Murnane Company purchased a machine on February 1, 2009, for $100,000. In January 2013, when the book value of the machine is $70,000, Murnane believes the machine is impaired due to recent technological advances. Murnane expects the machine to generate future cash flow of $10,000 and has estimated the fair value of the machine to be $55,000. What is the loss from impairment?

a. $5,000
b. $15,000
c. $30,000
d. $45,000

CORNERSTONE EXERCISES

OBJECTIVE 2
CORNERSTONE 7.1

Cornerstone Exercise 7-17 Cost of a Fixed Asset

Borges Inc. recently purchased land to use for the construction of its new manufacturing facility and incurred the following costs: purchase price, $125,000; real estate commissions, $9,500; delinquent property taxes, $1,800; closing costs, $3,500; clearing and grading of the land, $12,800.

Required:

Determine the cost of the land.

Cornerstone Exercise 7-18 Acquisition Cost

OBJECTIVE 2
CORNERSTONE 7.1

Cox Company recently purchased a machine by paying $8,500 cash and signing a 6-month, 10% note for $10,000. In addition to the purchase price, Cox incurred the following costs related to the machine: freight charges, $800; interest charges, $500; special foundation for machine, $400; installation costs, $1,100.

Required:

Determine the cost of the machine.

> *Use the following information for Cornerstone Exercises 7-19 through 7-21:*
> Irons Delivery Inc. purchased a new delivery truck for $45,000 on January 1, 2013. The truck is expected to have a $3,000 residual value at the end of its 5-year useful life.

Cornerstone Exercise 7-19 Straight-Line Depreciation

OBJECTIVE 3 4
CORNERSTONE 7.2

Refer to the information for Irons Delivery Inc. above. Irons uses the straight-line method of depreciation.

Required:

Prepare the journal entry to record depreciation expense for 2013 and 2014.

Cornerstone Exercise 7-20 Declining Balance Depreciation

OBJECTIVE 3 4
CORNERSTONE 7.3

Refer to the information for Irons Delivery Inc. above. Irons uses the double-declining-balance method of depreciation.

Required:

Prepare the journal entry to record depreciation expense for 2013 and 2014.

Cornerstone Exercise 7-21 Units-of-Production Depreciation

OBJECTIVE 3 4
CORNERSTONE 7.4

Refer to the information for Irons Delivery Inc. above. Irons uses the units-of-production method of depreciation. Irons expects the truck to run for 160,000 miles. The actual miles driven in 2013 and 2014 were 40,000 and 36,000, respectively.

Required:

Prepare the journal entry to record depreciation expense for 2013 and 2014.

Cornerstone Exercise 7-22 Revision of Depreciation

OBJECTIVE 6
CORNERSTONE 7.5

On January 1, 2011, Slade Inc. purchased a machine for $90,000. Slade depreciated the machine with the straight-line depreciation method over a useful life of 10 years, using a residual value of $4,000. At the beginning of 2013, a major overhaul, costing $35,000, was made. After the overhaul, the machine's residual value is estimated to be $2,500, and the machine is expected to have a remaining useful life of 12 years.

Required:

Determine the depreciation expense for 2013.

Cornerstone Exercise 7-23 Disposal of an Operating Asset

OBJECTIVE 7
CORNERSTONE 7.6

On August 30, Williams Manufacturing Company decided to sell one of its fabricating machines that was 15 years old for $6,000. The machine, which originally cost $105,000, had accumulated depreciation of $102,500.

Required:

Prepare the journal entry to record the disposal of the machine.

OBJECTIVE 8
CORNERSTONE 7.7

Cornerstone Exercise 7-24 Analyze Fixed Assets

At December 31, 2013, Clark Corporation reported beginning net fixed assets of $94,150, ending net fixed assets of $103,626, accumulated depreciation of $49,133, net sales of $212,722, and depreciation expense of $12,315.

Required:

Compute Clark Corporation's fixed asset turnover ratio and the average age of its fixed assets. (*Note:* Round answers to two decimal places.)

OBJECTIVE 9
CORNERSTONE 7.8

Cornerstone Exercise 7-25 Cost of Intangible Assets

Advanced Technological Devices Inc. acquired a patent for $91,500. It spent an additional $31,250 successfully defending the patent in legal proceedings.

Required:

Determine the cost of the patent.

OBJECTIVE 9
CORNERSTONE 7.8

Cornerstone Exercise 7-26 Amortization of Intangible Assets

MicroSystems Inc. acquired a patent for $180,000. MicroSystems amortizes the patent on a straight-line basis over its remaining economic life of 12 years.

Required:

Prepare the journal entry to record the amortization expense related to the patent.

OBJECTIVE 10
CORNERSTONE 7.9

Cornerstone Exercise 7-27 Depletion of Natural Resources

Brandon Oil Company recently purchased oil and natural gas reserves in a remote part of Alaska for $1,850,000. Brandon spent $10,000,000 preparing the oil for extraction from the ground. Brandon estimates that 108,000,000 barrels of oil will be extracted from the ground. The land has a residual value of $20,000. During 2013, 15,000,000 barrels are extracted from the ground.

Required:

Calculate the amount of depletion taken in 2013. (*Note*: Use two decimal points for calculations.)

OBJECTIVE 11
CORNERSTONE 7.10

Cornerstone Exercise 7-28 *(Appendix 7A)* Impairment

Brown Industries had two machines that it believes may be impaired. Information on the machines is shown below.

	Book Value	Estimated Future Cash Flows	Fair Value
Machine 1	$42,000	$50,000	$40,000
Machine 2	50,000	40,000	32,000

Required:

For each machine, determine if the machine is impaired. If so, calculate the amount of the impairment loss.

BRIEF EXERCISES

OBJECTIVE 1

Brief Exercise 7-29 Understanding Operating Assets

Descriptions of operating assets are listed below.

a. Naturally occurring materials that have economic value
b. Tangible assets that can be seen and touched

c. Do not have physical substance
d. Depreciated over the accounting periods in which the asset is used and benefits are received
e. Generally result from legal and contractual rights

Required:

Identify the category of operating asset associated with each description as property, plant, and equipment; intangible assets; or natural resources.

Brief Exercise 7-30 Acquisition Cost

OBJECTIVE 2

Desert State University installed a HD video board with an invoice price of $5,000,000 in its football stadium. Desert State paid an additional $100,000 of delivery and installation costs relating to this board. Because this is one of the largest boards in the world, Desert State also installed ten 5-ton air conditioning units at a total cost of $120,000 to keep the board cool in the desert heat.

Required:

Determine the cost of the video board.

Brief Exercise 7-31 Depreciation Concepts

OBJECTIVE 3

Listed below are concepts and terminology related to depreciation.

Concepts	Terminology
1. The period of time over which the company anticipates deriving benefit from the use of the asset	a. Depreciation
2. The cost of the asset minus its accumulated depreciation	b. Accumulated depreciation
3. The total amount of depreciation expense that has been recorded for an asset since the asset was acquired	c. Book value
4. The amount of cash or trade-in consideration that the company expects to receive when an asset is retired from service	d. Useful life
5. A process of cost allocation, not an attempt to measure the fair value of an asset	e. Residual value

Required:

Match each concept with the related terminology.

Brief Exercise 7-32 Depreciation Methods

OBJECTIVE 4

On January 1, 2013, Loeffler Company acquired a machine at a cost of $200,000. Loeffler estimates that it will use the machine for 4 years or 8,000 machine hours. It estimates that after 4 years the machine can be sold for $20,000. Loeffler uses the machine for 2,100 and 1,800 machine hours in 2013 and 2014, respectively.

Required:

Compute depreciation expense for 2013 and 2014 using the (1) straight-line, (2) double-declining-balance, and (3) units-of-production methods of depreciation.

Brief Exercise 7-33 Expenditures After Acquisition

OBJECTIVE 5

Listed below are several transactions:

a. Paid $80 cash to replace a minor part of an air conditioning system.
b. Paid $40,000 to fix structural damage to a building.
c. Paid $8,000 for monthly salaries.
d. Paid $12,000 to replace a manual cutting machine with a computer-controlled machine.
e. Paid $1,000 related to the annual painting of a building.

Required:

Classify each transaction as either a revenue expenditure, a capital expenditure, or neither.

OBJECTIVE 6

Brief Exercise 7-34 Revision of Depreciation

On January 1, 2013, the Kelley Company ledger showed a building with a cost of $250,000 and related accumulated depreciation of $96,000. The depreciation resulted from using straight-line depreciation with a useful life of 20 years and no residual value. On this date, Kelley determined that the building had a remaining useful life of 16 years and a residual value of $14,000.

Required:

Determine the depreciation expense for 2013.

OBJECTIVE 7

Brief Exercise 7-35 Disposal of an Operating Asset

Jolie Company owns equipment with a cost of $85,500 and accumulated depreciation of 76,200.

Required:

Prepare the journal entry to record the disposal of the equipment on April 9 assuming:

1. Jolie sold the equipment for $11,200 cash.
2. Jolie sold the equipment for $7,900 cash.

OBJECTIVE 8

Brief Exercise 7-36 Analyzing Fixed Assets

Pitt reported the following information for 2012 and 2013:

	2012	2013
Property, plant, and equipment, cost	$550,000	$ 550,000
Accumulated depreciation	170,000	220,000
Net sales		4,600,000
Depreciation expense		50,000

Required:

Compute Pitt's fixed asset turnover ratio and the average age of its fixed assets. (*Note*: Round all answers to two decimal places.)

OBJECTIVE 9

Brief Exercise 7-37 Cost and Amortization of Intangible Assets

On January 2, 2013, Frazier Company purchased a restaurant franchise for $85,000. The terms of the franchise agreement allowed Frazier to have exclusive rights to operate a restaurant under the "Simply Fried" brand name for the next 10 years.

Required:

Prepare any journal entries related to the franchise that Frazier should make during 2013.

OBJECTIVE 10

Brief Exercise 7-38 Natural Resources and Depletion

Luper Company acquired a tract of land which contained iron deposits for $2,500,000. Luper spent $120,000 to access the iron ore. Luper estimates that 2,000,000 tons of ore will be extracted. The estimated value of the land after the ore is extracted is $100,000. During the current year, Luper extracts 150,000 tons of iron ore.

Required:

Compute the cost of the natural resource and the amount of depletion taken during the year.

OBJECTIVE 11

Brief Exercise 7-39 (*Appendix 7A*) Impairment

Listed below is information related to three assets reported in the financial statements of Grant Company:

Asset	Book Value	Estimated Future Cash Flows	Fair Value
a. Building	$180,000	$200,000	$190,000
b. Equipment	50,000	45,000	40,000
c. Furniture	15,000	16,000	13,000

Required:

For each scenario, indicate whether the asset has been impaired and, if so, the amount of the impairment loss that should be recorded.

EXERCISES

Exercise 7-40 Balance Sheet Presentation

OBJECTIVE 1

Listed below are items that may appear on a classified balance sheet.

1. Land
2. Amounts due from customers
3. Office building
4. Truck
5. Goods held for resale
6. Amounts owed to suppliers
7. Patent
8. Timberland
9. Land held as investment
10. Goodwill

Required:

Indicate whether each item is included as an operating asset on a classified balance sheet. If the item is an operating asset, indicate whether the item is property, plant, and equipment; an intangible asset; or a natural resource as well as the cost allocation process used (depreciation, amortization, or depletion). If the item is not an operating asset, indicate the proper balance sheet classification.

Exercise 7-41 Balance Sheet Classification

OBJECTIVE 1

Micro-Technologies Inc., a computer manufacturer, has the following items on its balance sheet—office furniture delivery truck, patent, computer assembly machine, building, memory chips.

Required:

Indicate the proper balance sheet classification of each item and the cost allocation process used (depreciation, amortization, depletion).

Exercise 7-42 Acquisition Cost

OBJECTIVE 2

Items that may relate to property, plant, and equipment follow:

1. Purchase price of a machine
2. Delinquent property taxes at the time of purchase
3. Interest on debt used to purchase equipment
4. Sales taxes paid on purchase of equipment
5. Costs to install a machine
6. Ordinary repairs to equipment
7. Cost to remodel a building
8. Architectural fees paid for design of a building
9. Cost of training employees to run equipment
10. Transportation costs to have furniture delivered

Required:

CONCEPTUAL CONNECTION Determine whether each item is included as part of the cost of property, plant, and equipment. For any item excluded from the cost of property, plant, and equipment, explain why the item was excluded.

Exercise 7-43 Cost of a Fixed Asset

OBJECTIVE 2

Laurel Cleaners purchased an automatic dry cleaning machine for $165,000 from TGF Corporation on April 1, 2013. Laurel paid $25,000 in cash and signed a 5-year, 10% note for $140,000. Laurel will pay interest on the note each year on March 31, beginning in 2014. Transportation charges of $4,250 for the machine were paid by Laurel. Laurel also paid $1,500 for the living expenses of the TGF installation crew. Solvent, necessary to operate the machine, was acquired for $1,000. Of this amount, $800 of the solvent was used to test and adjust the machine.

(Continued)

Required:

1. Compute the cost of the new dry cleaning machine.
2. **CONCEPTUAL CONNECTION** Explain why you excluded any expenditures from the cost of the dry cleaning machine.

OBJECTIVE 2

Exercise 7-44 Cost of a Fixed Asset

Colson Photography Service purchased a new digital imaging machine on April 15 for $11,200. During installation Colson incurred and paid in cash the following costs:

Rental of drill	$ 150
Electrical contractor	1,300
Plumbing contractor	785

Colson also paid $160 to replace a bracket on the digital imager that was damaged when one of Colson's employees dropped a box on it while it was being installed.

Required:

1. Determine the cost of the digital imaging machine.
2. **CONCEPTUAL CONNECTION** Explain why you included or excluded the $160 bracket replacement cost.

OBJECTIVE 2

Exercise 7-45 Cost of Fixed Assets

Mooney Sounds, a local stereo retailer, needed a new store because it had outgrown the leased space it had used for several years. Mooney acquired and remodeled a former grocery store. As a part of the acquisition, Mooney incurred the following costs:

Cost of grocery store	$277,400	Wire and electrical supplies	$ 4,290
Cost of land (on which the grocery store is located)	83,580	New doors	6,400
New roof for building	74,000	New windows	3,850
Lumber used for remodeling	23,200	Wages paid to workers for remodeling	12,500
Paint	515	Additional inventory purchased for grand opening sale	45,300

Required:

1. Determine the cost of the land and the building.
2. **CONCEPTUAL CONNECTION** If management misclassified a portion of the building's cost as part of the cost of the land, what would be the effect on the financial statements?

OBJECTIVE 2 4

Exercise 7-46 Cost and Depreciation

On January 1, 2013, Quick Stop, a convenience store, purchased a new soft-drink cooler. Quick Stop paid $15,380 cash for the cooler. Quick Stop also paid $750 to have the cooler shipped to its location. After the new cooler arrived, Quick Stop paid $222 to have the old cooler dismantled and removed. Quick Stop also paid $1,020 to a contractor to have new wiring and drains installed for the new cooler. Quick Stop estimated that the cooler would have a useful life of 8 years and a residual value of $500. Quick Stop uses the straight-line method of depreciation.

Required:

1. Prepare any necessary journal entries to record the cost of the cooler.
2. Prepare the adjusting entry to record 2013 depreciation expense on the new cooler.
3. What is the book value of the cooler at the end of 2013?
4. **CONCEPTUAL CONNECTION** If Quick Stop had used a useful life of 12 years and a residual value of $800, how would this effect depreciation expense for 2013 and the book value of the cooler at the end of 2013?

Exercise 7-47 Characteristics of Depreciation Methods

OBJECTIVE 3

Below is a common list of depreciation methods and characteristics related to depreciation.

Depreciation Methods

a. Straight-line depreciation method
b. Declining balance depreciation method
c. Units-of-production depreciation method when actual units produced increases over the life of the asset

Characteristics

1. Results in depreciation expense that decreases over the life of the asset.
2. Results in depreciation expense that increases over the life of the asset.
3. Allocates the same amount of cost to each period of a depreciable asset's life.
4. Calculated by multiplying a *constant* depreciation rate by depreciable cost.
5. Calculated by applying a *constant* depreciation rate to the asset's book value at the beginning of the period.
6. Results in lowest income taxes in early years of the asset's life.
7. Consistent with the matching principle.

Required:

Match one or more of the depreciation methods with each characteristic.

Exercise 7-48 Depreciation Methods

OBJECTIVE 3 4

Berkshire Corporation purchased a copying machine for $8,700 on January 1, 2013. The machine's residual value was $425 and its expected life was 5 years or 2,000,000 copies. Actual usage was 480,000 copies the first year and 400,000 the second year.

Required:

1. Compute depreciation expense for 2013 and 2014 using the (a) straight-line method, (b) double-declining-balance method, and (c) units-of-production method.
2. For each depreciation method, what is the book value of the machine at the end 2013? At the end of the 2014?
3. **CONCEPTUAL CONNECTION** Assume that Berkshire uses the double-declining-balance method of depreciation. What is the effect on assets and income relative to if Berkshire had used the straight-line method of depreciation instead of the double-declining-balance method of depreciation?

Exercise 7-49 Depreciation Methods

OBJECTIVE 3 4

Clearcopy, a printing company, acquired a new press on January 1, 2013. The press cost $173,400 and had an expected life of 8 years or 4,500,000 pages and an expected residual value of $15,000. Clearcopy printed 675,000 pages in 2013.

Required:

1. Compute 2013 depreciation expense using the (a) straight-line method, (b) double-declining-balance method, and (c) units-of-production method.
2. What is the book value of the machine at the end of 2013 under each method?

Exercise 7-50 Depreciation Methods

OBJECTIVE 3 4

Quick-as-Lightning, a delivery service, purchased a new delivery truck for $45,000 on January 1, 2013. The truck is expected to have a useful life of 10 years or 150,000 miles and an expected residual value of $3,000. The truck was driven 15,000 miles in 2013 and 13,000 miles in 2014.

(*Continued*)

Required:

1. Compute depreciation expense for 2013 and 2014 using the (a) straight-line method, (b) double-declining-balance method, and (c) units-of-production method.
2. For each method, what is the book value of the machine at the end 2013? At the end of 2014?
3. **CONCEPTUAL CONNECTION** If Quick-as-Lightning used an 8-year useful life or 100,000 miles and a residual value of $1,000, what would be the effect on (a) depreciation expense and (b) book value under each of the depreciation methods?

OBJECTIVE 3 4

ILLUSTRATING RELATIONSHIPS

Exercise 7-51 Inferring Original Cost

Barton Construction Company purchased a piece of heavy equipment on January 1, 2011, which it is depreciating using the straight-line method. The equipment's useful life is 5 years and its residual value is $5,000. Barton recorded depreciation expense of $44,000 in 2012.

Required:

Determine the original cost of the equipment.

OBJECTIVE 3 4

Exercise 7-52 Choice Among Depreciation Methods

Walnut Ridge Production Inc. purchased a new computerized video editing machine at a cost of $450,000. The system has a residual value of $64,000 and an expected life of 5 years.

Required:

1. Compute depreciation expense, accumulated depreciation, and book value for the first 3 years of the machine's life using the (a) straight-line method and (b) double-declining-balance method.
2. Which method would produce the largest income in the first, second, and third years of the asset's life?
3. **CONCEPTUAL CONNECTION** Why might the controller of Walnut Ridge Production be interested in the effect of choosing a depreciation method? Evaluate the legitimacy of these interests.

OBJECTIVE 3 4

Exercise 7-53 Revision of Depreciation

On January 1, 2011, Blizzards-R-Us purchased a snow-blowing machine for $125,000. The machine was expected to have a residual value of $12,000 at the end of its 5-year useful life. On January 1, 2013, Blizzards-R-Us concluded that the machine would have a remaining useful life of 6 years with a residual value of $3,600.

Required:

1. Determine the revised annual depreciation expense for 2013 using the straight-line method.
2. **CONCEPTUAL CONNECTION** How does the revision in depreciation affect the Blizzards-R-Us financial statements?

OBJECTIVE 5

Exercise 7-54 Capital versus Revenue Expenditure

Warrick Water Company, a privately owned business, supplies water to several communities. Warrick has just performed an extensive overhaul on one of its water pumps. The overhaul is expected to extend the life of the pump by 10 years. The residual value of the pump is unchanged. You have been asked to determine which of the following costs should be capitalized as a part of this overhaul. Those costs not capitalized should be expensed.

Element of Cost	Classification and Explanation
New pump motor	
Repacking of bearings (performed monthly)	
New impeller (rotating component of a pump)	
Painting of pump housing (performed annually)	
Replacement of pump foundation	

Element of Cost	Classification and Explanation
New wiring (needed every 5 years)	
Installation labor, motor	
Installation labor, impeller	
Installation labor, wiring	
Paint labor (performed annually)	
Placement of fence around pump*	

* A requirement of the Occupational Safety and Health Administration that will add to maintenance costs over the remaining life of the pump.

Required:

CONCEPTUAL CONNECTION Classify each cost as part of the overhaul or as an expense. Be sure to explain your reasoning for each classification.

Exercise 7-55 Expenditures After Acquisition

OBJECTIVE 5

The following expenditures were incurred during the year:

a. Paid $4,000 for an overhaul of an automobile engine.
b. Paid $20,000 to add capacity to a cellular phone company's wireless network.
c. Paid $200 for routine maintenance of a manufacturing machine.
d. Paid $10,000 to remodel an office building.
e. Paid $300 for ordinary repairs

Required:

1. Classify the expenditures as either capital or revenue expenditures.
2. **CONCEPTUAL CONNECTION** If management improperly classified these expenditures, what would be the impact on the financial statements?

Exercise 7-56 Expenditures After Acquisition

OBJECTIVE 5

Roanoke Manufacturing placed a robotic arm on a large assembly machine on January 1, 2013. At the time, the assembly machine, which was acquired on January 1, 2006, was expected to last another 3 years. The following information is available concerning the assembly machine.

Cost, assembly machine	$750,000
Accumulated depreciation, 1/1/2013	480,000

The robotic arm cost $225,000 and was expected to extend the useful life of the machine by 3 years. Therefore, the useful life of the assembly machine, after the arm replacement, is 6 years. The assembly machine is expected to have a residual value of $120,000 at the end of its useful life.

Required:

1. Prepare the journal entry necessary to record the addition of the robotic arm.
2. Compute 2013 depreciation expense for the machine using the straight-line method, and prepare the necessary journal entry.
3. What is the book value of the machine at the end of 2013?
4. **CONCEPTUAL CONNECTION** What would have been the effect on the financial statements if Roanoke had expensed the addition of the robotic arm?

Exercise 7-57 Expenditures After Acquisition and Depreciation

OBJECTIVE 5

Eastern National Bank installed a wireless encryption device in January 2009. The device cost $120,000. At the time the device was installed, Eastern estimated that it would have an expected life of 8 years and a residual value of $10,000. By 2012, the bank's business had expanded and modifications to the device were necessary. At the beginning of 2013, Eastern spent $35,000 on modifications for the device. Eastern estimates that the new expected life of the device (from

(Continued)

January 2013) is 6 years and the new residual value is $4,000. Eastern uses the straight-line method of depreciation. Had Eastern not modified the device, it estimates that processing delays would have caused the bank to lose at least $50,000 of business per year.

Required:

1. Compute the accumulated depreciation for the device at the time the modifications were made (4 years after acquisition).
2. What is the book value of the device before and after the modification?
3. What will be annual straight-line depreciation expense for the device after the modification?
4. **CONCEPTUAL CONNECTION** The bank's president notes, "Since the after-modification, depreciation expense exceeds the before-modification depreciation expense. This modification was a poor idea." Comment on the president's assertion.

OBJECTIVE 7

Exercise 7-58 Disposal of Fixed Asset

Perfect Auto Rentals sold one of its cars on January 1, 2013. Perfect had acquired the car on January 1, 2011, for $23,400. At acquisition Perfect assumed that the car would have an estimated life of 3 years and a residual value of $3,000. Assume that Perfect has recorded straight-line depreciation expense for 2011 and 2012.

Required:

1. Prepare the journal entry to record the sale of the car assuming the car sold for (a) $9,800 cash, (b) $7,500 cash, and (c) $11,500 cash.
2. How should the gain or loss on the disposition (if any) be reported on the income statement?

OBJECTIVE 7

Exercise 7-59 Disposal of Fixed Asset

Pacifica Manufacturing retired a computerized metal stamping machine on December 31, 2013. Pacifica sold the machine to another company and did not replace it. The following data are available for the machine:

Cost (installed), 1/1/2008	$880,000
Residual value estimated on 1/1/2008	60,000
Estimated life as of 1/1/2008	10 years

The machine was sold for $225,000 cash. Pacifica uses the straight-line method of depreciation.

Required:

1. Prepare the journal entry to record depreciation expense for 2013.
2. Compute accumulated depreciation at December 31, 2013.
3. Prepare the journal entry to record the sale of the machine.
4. **CONCEPTUAL CONNECTION** Explain how the disposal of the fixed asset would affect the 2013 financial statements. Ignore income taxes.

OBJECTIVE 3 4 5 7

ILLUSTRATING RELATIONSHIPS

Exercise 7-60 Depreciation and Disposal of Fixed Assets

Stanley Company reported the following information regarding its equipment:

Account	Amount
Equipment, Jan. 1, 2013	$745,120
Equipment, Dec. 31, 2013	831,410
Accumulated depreciation, Jan. 1, 2013	224,350
Accumulated depreciation, Dec. 31, 2013	257,690
Capital expenditures	148,735
Accumulated depreciation on equipment sold	50,320
Cash received for equipment sold	14,150

Required:

1. What journal entry did Stanley make to record depreciation expense for 2013?
2. What journal entry did Stanley make to record the disposal of the equipment?

Exercise 7-61 Analyze Fixed Assets

OBJECTIVE 8

Tabor Industries is a technology company that operates in a highly competitive environment. In 2010, management had significantly curtailed its capital expenditures due to cash flow problems. Tabor reported the following information for 2013:

- Net fixed assets (beginning of year), $489,000
- Net fixed assets (end of year), $505,000
- Net sales, $1,025,000
- Accumulated depreciation (end of year), $543,000
- Depreciation expense, $126,000

An analyst reviewing Tabor's financial history noted that Tabor had previously reported fixed asset turnover ratios and average age of its assets as follows:

	2008	2009	2010	2011	2012
Fixed asset turnover	2.48	2.45	2.74	2.57	2.33
Average age of assets (years)	1.81	1.79	1.94	2.81	3.74

During this time frame, the industry average fixed asset turnover ratio is 2.46 and the industry average age of assets is 1.79 years.

Required:

1. Compute Tabor's fixed asset turnover ratio for 2013.
2. Compute the average age of Tabor's fixed assets for 2013.
3. **CONCEPTUAL CONNECTION** Comment on Tabor's fixed asset turnover ratios and the average age of the fixed assets.

Exercise 7-62 Acquisition and Amortization of Intangible Assets

OBJECTIVE 9

TLM Technologies had these transactions related to intangible assets during 2013.

Jan. 2	Purchased a patent from Luna Industries for $175,000. The remaining legal life of the patent is 15 years, and TLM expects the patent to be useful for 8 years.
Jan. 5	Paid legal fees in a successful legal defense of the patent of $90,000.
June 29	Registered a trademark with the federal government. Registration costs were $4,000. TLM expects to use the trademark indefinitely.
Sept. 2	Paid research and development costs of $478,200.

Required:

1. Prepare the journal entries necessary to record the transactions.
2. Prepare the entries necessary to record amortization expense for the intangible assets.
3. What is the balance of the intangible assets at the end of 2013?

Exercise 7-63 Balance Sheet Presentation

OBJECTIVE 1 3 4 8 9

The following information relates to the assets of Westfield Semiconductors as of December 31, 2013. Westfield uses the straight-line method for depreciation and amortization.

Asset	Acquisition Cost	Expected Life	Residual Value	Time Used
Land	$104,300	Infinite	$100,000	10 years
Building	430,000	25 years	30,000	10 years
Machine	285,000	5 years	10,000	2 years
Patent	80,000	10 years	0	3 years
Truck	21,000	100,000 miles	3,000	44,000 miles

(*Continued*)

Required:

Use the information above to prepare the property, plant, and equipment and intangible assets portions of a classified balance sheet for Westfield.

OBJECTIVE 9

Exercise 7-64 Amortization of Intangibles

On January 1, 2013, Boulder Investments Inc. acquired a franchise to operate a Burger Doodle restaurant. Boulder paid $225,000 for a 10-year franchise and incurred organization costs of $15,000.

Required:

1. Prepare the journal entry to record the cash payment for the franchise fee and the organization costs.
2. Prepare the journal entry to record the annual amortization expense at the end of the first year.

OBJECTIVE 10

Exercise 7-65 Depletion Rate

Oxford Quarries purchased 45 acres of land for $185,000. The land contained stone that Oxford will remove from the ground, finish, and then sell as facing material for buildings. Oxford spent $435,000 preparing the quarry for operation. Oxford estimates that the quarry contains 55,000 tons of usable stone and that it will require 6 years to remove all the usable stone once quarrying begins. Upon completion of quarrying, Oxford estimates that the land will have a residual value of $11,150. During 2013, Oxford extracted 8,500 tons of stone.

Required:

1. Compute the depletion rate per ton.
2. Prepare the journal entry to record the extraction of the stone.

OBJECTIVE 10

Exercise 7-66 Depletion of Timber

Bedford Ridge Development purchased a 5,000-acre tract of forested land in southern Georgia. The tract contained about 1,650,000 pine trees that, when mature, can be used for utility poles. Bedford paid $800 per acre for the timberland. The land has a residual value of $107 per acre when all the trees are harvested. During 2013, Bedford harvested 180,000 trees.

Required:

1. Compute the depletion per tree.
2. Prepare the journal entry to record the harvesting of the trees for 2013.

OBJECTIVE 11

Exercise 7-67 *(Appendix 7A)* Impairment

On January 1, 2006, the Key West Company acquired a pie-making machine for $75,000. The machine was expected to have a useful life of 10 years with no residual value. Key West uses the straight-line depreciation method. On January 1, 2013, due to technological changes in the bakery industry, Key West believed that the asset might be impaired. Key West estimates the machine will generate net cash flows of $12,000 and has a current fair value of $10,000.

Required:

1. What is the book value of the machine on January 1, 2013?
2. Compute the loss related to the impairment.
3. Prepare the journal entry necessary to record the impairment of the machine.

PROBLEM SET A

Problem 7-68A Financial Statement Presentation of Operating Assets

OBJECTIVE 1

Olympic Acquisitions Inc. prepared the following post-closing trial balance at December 31, 2013:

	Debit	Credit
Cash	$ 5,400	
Accounts Receivable	16,200	
Supplies	25,800	
Land	42,350	
Buildings	155,900	
Equipment	278,650	
Truck	31,100	
Franchise	49,600	
Goodwill	313,500	
Natural Resources	94,600	
Accounts Payable		$ 4,250
Accumulated Depreciation (Buildings)		112,000
Accumulated Depreciation (Equipment)		153,000
Accumulated Depreciation (Truck)		16,300
Wages Payable		6,850
Interest Payable		7,125
Income Taxes Payable		12,125
Notes Payable (due in 8 years)		185,550
Common Stock		304,500
Retained Earnings		211,400
Totals	$1,013,100	$1,013,100

Required:

Prepare a classified balance sheet for Olympic at December 31, 2013. (*Note*: Olympic reports the three categories of operating assets in separate subsections of assets.)

Problem 7-69A Cost of a Fixed Asset

OBJECTIVE 2

Mist City Car Wash purchased a new brushless car-washing machine for one of its bays. The machine cost $41,700. Mist City borrowed the purchase price from its bank on a 1-year, 8% note payable. Mist City paid $975 to have the machine transported to its place of business and an additional $200 in shipping insurance. Mist City incurred the following costs as a part of the installation:

Plumbing	$2,150
Electrical	1,125
Water (for testing the machine)	20
Soap (for testing the machine)	10

During the testing process, one of the motors became defective when soap and water entered the motor because its cover had not been installed properly by Mist City's employees. The motor was replaced at a cost of $640.

Required:

1. Compute the cost of the car-washing machine.
2. **CONCEPTUAL CONNECTION** Explain why any costs were excluded from the cost of the machine.

Problem 7-70A Depreciation Methods

OBJECTIVE 3 4

Hansen Supermarkets purchased a radio frequency identification (RFID) system for one of its stores at a cost of $190,000. Hansen determined that the system had an expected life of 8 years (or 50,000,000 items scanned) and an expected residual value of $12,000.

(*Continued*)

Required:

1. Determine the amount of depreciation expense for the first and second years of the system's life using the (a) straight-line and (b) double-declining-balance depreciation methods.
2. If the number of items scanned the first and second years were 6,100,000 and 5,600,000, respectively, compute the amount of depreciation expense for the first and second years of the system's life using the units-of-production depreciation method.
3. Compute the book values for all three depreciation methods as of the end of the first and second years of the system's life.
4. **CONCEPTUAL CONNECTION** What factors might management consider when selecting among depreciation methods?

OBJECTIVE 3 4

Problem 7-71A Depreciation Schedules

Wendt Corporation acquired a new depreciable asset for $94,000. The asset has a 4-year expected life and a residual value of zero.

Required:

1. Prepare a depreciation schedule for all 4 years of the asset's expected life using the straight-line depreciation method.
2. Prepare a depreciation schedule for all 4 years of the asset's expected life using the double-declining-balance depreciation method.
3. **CONCEPTUAL CONNECTION** What questions should be asked about this asset to decide which depreciation method to use?

OBJECTIVE 3 4 5

Problem 7-72A Expenditures After Acquisition

Pasta, a restaurant specializing in fresh pasta, installed a pasta cooker in early 2011 at a cost of $12,400. The cooker had an expected life of 5 years and a residual value of $900 when installed. As the restaurant's business increased, it became apparent that renovations would be necessary so the cooker's output could be increased. In January 2014, Pasta spent $8,200 to install new heating equipment and $4,100 to add pressure-cooking capability. After these renovations, Pasta estimated that the remaining useful life of the cooker was 10 years and that the residual value was now $1,500.

Required:

1. Compute 1 year's straight-line depreciation expense on the cooker before the renovations.
2. Assume that 3 full years of straight-line depreciation expense had been recorded on the cooker before the renovations were made. Compute the book value of the cooker immediately after the renovations were made.
3. Compute 1 year's straight-line depreciation expense on the renovated cooker.

OBJECTIVE 5

Problem 7-73A Repair Decision

Clermont Transit operates a summer ferry service to islands in the Ohio River. Farmers use the ferry to move farming equipment to and from the islands. Clermont's ferry is in need of repair. A new engine and steering assembly must be installed, or the Coast Guard will not permit the ferry to be used. Because of competition, Clermont will not be able to raise its rates for ferry service if these repairs are made. Costs of providing the ferry service will not be decreased if the repairs are made.

Required:

1. Identify the factors that Clermont should consider when evaluating whether or not to make the repairs.
2. **CONCEPTUAL CONNECTION** Since the revenue rate cannot be increased and costs will not be decreased if the repairs are made, can the cost of the repairs be capitalized? Why or why not?

Problem 7-74A Disposition of Fixed Assets

OBJECTIVE 7

In order to provide capital for new hotel construction in other locations, Wilton Hotel Corporation has decided to sell its hotel in Pierre, South Dakota. Wilton auctions the hotel and its contents on October 1, 2013, with the following results:

Land	$600,000
Building	225,000
Furniture	120,000

Wilton's accounting records reveal the following information about the assets sold:

Asset	Acquisition Cost	Accumulated Depreciation
Land	$ 55,000	
Building	350,000	$155,000
Furniture	285,500	133,000

Required:

1. Prepare a separate journal entry to record the disposition of each of these assets.
2. **CONCEPTUAL CONNECTION** Explain how the disposals of the fixed assets above would affect the current period financial statements.

Problem 7-75A Natural Resource and Intangible Accounting

OBJECTIVE 9 10

McLeansboro Oil Company acquired a small oil company with only three assets during a recent year. The assets were acquired for $1,350,000 cash.

Asset	Fair Value	Expected Life
Oil	$1,125,000	55,000 barrels
Land	78,000	Indefinite
Equipment	62,000	550,000 barrels

Required:

1. Prepare the entry to record this acquisition in McLeansboro's journal. (*Hint*: Record the cost in excess of fair value as goodwill.)
2. If McLeansboro pumps and sells 11,000 barrels of oil in 1 year, compute the amount of depletion.
3. Prepare journal entries to record depletion for the 11,000 barrels of oil pumped and sold.
4. **CONCEPTUAL CONNECTION** Is the goodwill amortized? Explain your reasoning.
5. **CONCEPTUAL CONNECTION** Why are the land and the equipment capitalized separately from the oil well?

Problem 7-76A Accounting for Intangible Assets

OBJECTIVE 9

On January 1, 2007, Technocraft Inc. acquired a patent that was used for manufacturing semiconductor-based electronic circuitry. The patent was originally recorded in Technocraft's ledger at its cost of $1,780,000. Technocraft has been amortizing the patent using the straight-line method over an expected economic life of 10 years. Residual value was assumed to be zero. Technocraft sued another company for infringing on its patent. On January 1, 2014, Technocraft spent $50,000 on this suit and won a judgment to recover the $50,000 plus damages of $200,000. The sued company paid the $250,000.

Required:

1. Compute and record amortization expense on the patent for 2013 (prior to the lawsuit).
2. Prepare the necessary journal entry on January 1, 2014, to record the expenditure of $50,000 to defend the patent.
3. Prepare the journal entry to record the award of $250,000 on January 1, 2014.
4. Indicate the entry you would have made had Technocraft lost the suit. (*Note:* Assume that the patent would be valueless if Technocraft had lost the suit.)
5. **CONCEPTUAL CONNECTION** What are the financial statement effects of capitalizing or expensing the cost of defending the patent?

PROBLEM SET B

OBJECTIVE 1

Problem 7-68B Financial Statement Presentation of Operating Assets

Athens Inc. prepared the following post-closing trial balance at December 31, 2013:

	Debit	Credit
Cash	$ 3,325	
Accounts Receivable	27,975	
Prepaid Insurance	8,350	
Land	21,150	
Buildings	305,520	
Equipment	126,310	
Patent	9,970	
Goodwill	42,400	
Natural Resources	134,800	
Accounts Payable		$ 7,775
Accumulated Depreciation (Buildings)		101,950
Accumulated Depreciation (Equipment)		47,875
Unearned Revenue		9,825
Interest Payable		3,625
Income Taxes Payable		17,150
Notes Payable (due in 10 years)		170,000
Common Stock		125,000
Retained Earnings		196,600
Totals	$679,800	$679,800

Required:

Prepare a classified balance sheet for Athens at December 31, 2013. (*Note*: Athens reports the three categories of operating assets in separate subsections of assets.)

OBJECTIVE 2

Problem 7-69B Cost of a Fixed Asset

Metropolis Country Club purchased a new tractor to be used for golf course maintenance. The tractor cost $64,200. Metropolis borrowed the purchase price from its bank on a 1-year, 7% note payable. Metropolis incurred the following costs:

Shipping costs	$925
Shipping insurance	180
Calibration of cutting height	75

Required:

1. Compute the cost of the tractor.
2. **CONCEPTUAL CONNECTION** Explain why any costs were excluded from the cost of the tractor.

OBJECTIVE 3 4

Problem 7-70B Depreciation Methods

Graphic Design Inc. purchased a state-of-the-art laser engraving machine for $65,200. Graphic Design determined that the system had an expected life of 10 years (or 1,500,000 items engraved) and an expected residual value of $8,200.

Required:

1. Determine the amount of depreciation expense for the first and second years of the machine's life using the (a) straight-line and (b) double-declining-balance depreciation methods.
2. If the number of items engraved the first and second years was 120,000 and 135,000, respectively, compute the amount of depreciation expense for the first and second years of the machine's life using the units-of-production depreciation method.

3. Compute the book values for all three depreciation methods as of the end of the first and second years of the system's life.
4. **CONCEPTUAL CONNECTION** What factors might management consider when selecting among depreciation methods?

Problem 7-71B Depreciation Schedules

OBJECTIVE 3 4

Dunn Corporation acquired a new depreciable asset for $135,000. The asset has a 5-year expected life and a residual value of zero.

Required:

1. Prepare a depreciation schedule for all 5 years of the asset's expected life using the straight-line depreciation method.
2. Prepare a depreciation schedule for all 5 years of the asset's expected life using the double-declining-balance depreciation method.
3. **CONCEPTUAL CONNECTION** What questions should be asked about this asset to decide which depreciation method to use?

Problem 7-72B Expenditures After Acquisition

OBJECTIVE 3 4 5

Murray's Fish Market, a store that specializes in providing fresh fish to the Nashville, Tennessee, area, installed a new refrigeration unit in January 2012 at a cost of $27,500. The refrigeration unit has an expected life of 8 years and a residual value of $500 when installed. As the fish market's business increased, it became apparent that renovations were necessary so that the capacity of the refrigeration unit could be increased. In January 2014, Murray's spent $18,785 to install an additional refrigerated display unit (that was connected to the original unit) and replace the refrigeration coils. After this addition and renovation, Murray's Fish Market estimated that the remaining useful life of the original refrigeration unit was 12 years and that the residual value was now $1,000.

Required:

1. Compute 1 year's straight-line depreciation expense on the refrigeration unit before the addition and renovations.
2. Assume that 2 full years of straight-line depreciation expense were recorded on the refrigeration unit before the addition and renovations were made. Compute the book value of the refrigeration unit immediately after the renovations were made.
3. Compute 1 year's straight-line depreciation expense on the renovated refrigeration unit. Round your answer to the nearest dollar.

Problem 7-73B Remodeling Decision

OBJECTIVE 5

Ferinni Company operates a travel agency out of a historic building in Smalltown. Ferinni's CEO believes that the building needs to be remodeled in order to reach a wider customer base. The CEO proposes building a new entry that would be adjacent to Main Street in order to attract more foot traffic. The current entry faces a parking deck at the rear of the building and is easily overlooked by customers. The new entry will require the rearrangement of several offices inside the building. Because of competition from Internet travel sites, Ferinni will not be able to raise rates for its travel service after the remodeling is made.

Required:

1. Identify the factors that Ferinni should consider when evaluating whether to remodel the building.
2. **CONCEPTUAL CONNECTION** Since the revenue rate cannot be increased, can the cost of the remodeling be capitalized? Why or why not?

OBJECTIVE 7

Problem 7-74B Disposition of Operating Assets

Salva Pest Control disposed of four assets recently. Salva's accounting records provided the following information about the assets at the time of their disposal:

Asset	Cost	Accumulated Depreciation
Pump	$ 6,200	$ 4,800
Truck	18,600	17,500
Furniture	4,200	3,850
Chemical testing apparatus	6,800	4,000

The truck was sold for $2,450 cash, and the chemical testing apparatus was donated to the local high school. Because the pump was contaminated with pesticides, $500 in cash was paid to a chemical disposal company to decontaminate the pump and dispose of it safely. The furniture was taken to the local landfill.

Required:

1. Prepare a separate journal entry to record the disposition of each of these assets.
2. **CONCEPTUAL CONNECTION** Explain how the disposals of the fixed assets would affect the current period financial statements.

OBJECTIVE 9 10

Problem 7-75B Natural Resource and Intangible Accounting

In 2013, the Mudcat Gas Company purchased a small natural gas company with two assets—land and natural gas reserves—for $158,000,000. The fair value of the land was $1,500,000 and the fair value of the natural gas reserves was $155,250,000. At that time, estimated recoverable gas was 105,000,000 cubic feet.

Required:

1. Prepare the entry to record this acquisition in Mudcat's journal. (*Hint*: Record any cost in excess of fair value as goodwill.)
2. If Mudcat recovers and sells 2,500,000 cubic feet in 1 year, compute the depletion. Round your answer to the nearest dollar.
3. Prepare journal entries to record depletion for the 2,500,000 cubic feet of natural gas recovered and sold.
4. **CONCEPTUAL CONNECTION** Is the goodwill amortized? Explain your reasoning.
5. **CONCEPTUAL CONNECTION** Why is the land capitalized separately from the natural gas reserves?

OBJECTIVE 9

Problem 7-76B Accounting for Intangible Assets

Blackford and Medford Publishing Company own the copyrights on many top authors. On January 5, 2014, Blackford and Medford acquired the copyright on the literary works of Susan Monroe, an underground novelist in the 1960s, for $825,000 cash. Due to a recent resurgence of interest in the 1960s, the copyright has an estimated economic life of 5 years. The residual value is estimated to be zero.

Required:

1. Prepare a journal entry to record the acquisition of the copyright.
2. Compute and record the 2014 amortization expense for the copyright.

CASES

Case 7-77 Ethics, Internal Controls, and the Capitalization Decision

James Sage, an assistant controller in a large company, has a friend and former classmate, Henry Cactus, who sells computers. Sage agrees to help Cactus get part of the business that has been going to a large national computer manufacturer for many years. Sage knows that the controller would not approve a shift away from the national supplier but believes that he can authorize a number of small orders for equipment that will escape the controller's notice. Company policy requires that all capital expenditures be approved by a management committee; however, expenditures under $2,000 are considered expenses and are subject to much less scrutiny. The assistant controller orders four computers to be used in a distant branch office. In order to keep the size of the order down, he makes four separate orders over a period of several months.

Required:

1. What are the probable consequences of this behavior for the company? For the assistant controller?
2. Describe internal control procedures that would be effective in discouraging and detecting this kind of behavior.

Case 7-78 Management's Depreciation Decision

Great Basin Enterprises, a large holding company, acquired North Spruce Manufacturing, a medium-sized manufacturing business, from its founder who wishes to retire. Despite great potential for development, North Spruce's income has been dropping in recent years. Great Basin has installed a new management group (including a new controller, Christie Carmichael) at North Spruce and has given the group 6 years to expand and revitalize the operations. Management compensation includes a bonus based on net income generated by the North Spruce operations. If North Spruce does not show considerable improvement by the end of the sixth year, Great Basin will consider selling it. The new management immediately makes significant investments in new equipment but finds that new revenues develop slowly. Most of the new equipment will be replaced in 8 to 10 years. To defer income taxes to the maximum extent, Ms. Carmichael uses accelerated depreciation methods and the minimum allowable "expected lives" for the new equipment, which average 5 years. In preparing financial statements, Ms. Carmichael uses the straight-line depreciation method and expected lives that average 12 years for the new equipment.

Required:

1. Why did the controller compute depreciation expense on the financial statements as she did?
2. What are the possible consequences of the controller's decision on the amount of depreciation expense shown on the financial statements if this decision goes unchallenged?

Case 7-79 Effect of Estimates of Life and Residual Value on Depreciation Expense

Hattiesburg Manufacturing purchased a new computer-integrated system to manufacture a group of fabricated metal and plastic products. The equipment was purchased from Bessemer Systems at a cost of $550,000. As a basis for determining annual depreciation expense, Hattiesburg's controller requests estimates of the expected life and residual value for the new equipment. The engineering and production departments submit the following divergent estimates:

	Engineering Department Estimates	Production Department Estimates
Expected life	10 years	8 years
Residual value	$90,000	0

Before considering depreciation expense for the new equipment, Hattiesburg Manufacturing has net income in the amount of $250,000. Hattiesburg uses the straight-line method of depreciation.

Required:

1. Compute a full year's depreciation expense for the new equipment, using each of the two sets of estimates.
2. Ignoring income taxes, what will be the effect on net income of including a full year's depreciation expense based on the engineering estimates? Based on the production estimates?

(*Continued*)

3. If a business has a significant investment in depreciable assets, the expected life and residual value estimates can materially affect depreciation expense and therefore net income. What might motivate management to use the highest or lowest estimates? How would cash outflows for income taxes be affected by the estimates?

Case 7-80 Research and Analysis Using the Annual Report

Obtain **Verizon Communications, Inc.**'s 2011 annual report either through the "Investor Relations" portion of its website (do a web search for Verizon Communications investor relations) or go to www.sec.gov and click "Search for Company Filings" under "Filings & Forms."

Required:

1. What method of depreciation does Verizon use? What are the typical useful lives of Verizon's operating assets?
2. What is the cost of Verizon's property, plant, and equipment on December 31, 2011? List the major components of Verizon's property, plant, and equipment.
3. What amount of accumulated depreciation is associated with property, plant, and equipment as of December 31, 2011?
4. Refer to the statement of cash flows:
   a. What is the amount of depreciation and amortization expense reported for each of the last 3 years?
   b. How much did Verizon spend on the acquisition of operating assets (capital expenditures) in each of the last 3 years?
   c. How much property, plant, and equipment was disposed of in 2011? (*Hint:* Also refer to the balance sheet.)
   d. Is the change in depreciation and amortization expense consistent with the pattern of capital expenditures observed? Why or why not?
5. What is the change in accumulated depreciation for the most recent year? Is this change explained by the depreciation and amortization expense reported? If not, what other items might cause accumulated depreciation to change?
6. Describe Verizon's capital expenditure plans for the future. (*Hint*: Refer to the Management Discussion and Analysis section.)
7. Explain Verizon's accounting policy with regard to intangible assets. (*Hint*: Refer to Note 1.)
8. List the types of intangible assets that Verizon possesses. What is Verizon's largest intangible asset?

Case 7-81 Comparative Analysis: Under Armour, Inc., versus VF Corporation

Refer to the financial statements of **Under Armour, Inc.**, and **VF Corporation** that are supplied with this text.

Required:

1. With regard to depreciation methods:
   a. What depreciation method does Under Armour use? What depreciation method does VF use?
   b. What are the typical useful lives of each company's operating assets?
   c. What effect will the useful lives have on the company's financial statements?
2. Refer to the statement of cash flows:
   a. What is the amount of depreciation and amortization expense that each company reported for the 3 years presented?
   b. How much did each company spend on the acquisition of operating assets (capital expenditures) in each of the last 3 years?
   c. Is the change in depreciation and amortization expense consistent with the pattern of capital expenditures observed? Why or why not?
3. Compute the fixed asset turnover and the average age of fixed assets for each company for 2011. What conclusions can you draw from these ratios?

Case 7-82 CONTINUING PROBLEM: FRONT ROW ENTERTAINMENT

After a successful first year, Cam and Anna decide to expand Front Row Entertainment's operations by becoming a venue operator as well as a tour promoter. A venue operator contracts with promoters to rent the venue (which can range from amphitheaters to indoor arenas to nightclubs) for specific events on specific dates. In addition to receiving revenue from renting the venue, venue operators also provide services such as concessions, parking, security, and ushering services. By vertically integrating their business, Cam and Anna can reduce the expense that they pay to rent venues. In addition, they will generate additional revenue by providing services to other tour promoters.

After a little investigation, Cam and Anna locate a small venue operator that owns The Chicago Music House, a small indoor arena with a rich history in the music industry. The current owner has experienced severe health issues and has let the arena fall into a state of disrepair. However, he would like the arena to be preserved and its musical legacy to continue. After a short negotiation, on January 1, 2014, Front Row purchases the venue by paying $10,000 in cash and signing a 15-year 10% note for $380,000. In addition, Front Row purchases the right to use the "Chicago Music House" name for $25,000 cash.

During the month of January 2014, Front Row incurred the following expenditures as they renovated the arena and prepared it for the first major event scheduled for February.

Jan. 5	Paid $21,530 to repair damage to the roof of the arena.
10	Paid $45,720 to remodel the stage area.
21	Purchased concessions equipment (e.g., popcorn poppers, soda machines) for $12,350.

Renovations were completed on January 28, and the first concert was held in the arena on February 1. The arena is expected to have a useful life of 30 years and a residual value of $35,000. The concessions equipment will have a useful life of 5 years and a residual value of $250.

Required:

1. Prepare the journal entries to record the acquisition of the arena, the concessions equipment, and the trademark.
2. Prepare the journal entries to record the expenditures made in January.
3. Compute and record the depreciation for 2014 (11 months) on the arena (use the straight-line method) and on the concessions equipment (use the double-declining-balance method). Round all answers to the nearest dollar.
4. Would amortization expense be recorded for the trademark? Why or why not?

© Pixelfabrik/Alamy

MAKING THE CONNECTION

INTEGRATIVE EXERCISE (CHAPTERS 4–7)

Integrating Asset Accounting

Obtain **Apple**'s fiscal 2011 10-K (filed October 26, 2011) either through the "Investor Relations" portion of its website (do a web search for "Apple Investor Relations") or go to www.sec.gov and click "Search for Company Filings" under "Filings & Forms."

Required:

Using Apple's 10-K, answer the following questions:

1. Looking at Note 1 (*Summary of Significant Accounting Policies*), how does Apple define cash equivalents?
2. Looking at the "Report of Independent Registered Public Accounting Firm" supplying an opinion on Apple's internal controls over financial reporting (p. 77 of the 10-K), what was the auditor's opinion regarding the effectiveness of Apple's internal control over financial reporting? What criteria were used to evaluate the effectiveness of these controls?
3. What was Apple's accounts receivable turnover (rounded to two decimal places) in 2010 and 2011? (Accounts receivable were $3,361,000,000 at the end of 2009.) Assuming the industry average for 2011 was 8.32, describe Apple's relative efficiency with its accounts receivable.
4. What was Apple's inventory turnover (rounded to two decimal places) in 2010 and 2011? (Inventories were $455,000,000 at the end of 2009.) Assuming the industry average for 2011 was 17.83, describe Apple's relative efficiency with its inventory.
5. Describe the trend in Apple's accounts receivable and inventory turnover.
6. How many days' sales does Apple have in receivables and inventory for 2010 and 2011? (When added together, this is its operating cycle.) (*Note:* Round all answers to two decimal places.)
7. **CONCEPTUAL CONNECTION** Assuming 10% interest, how much interest expense did Apple save by improving its accounts receivable and inventory turnovers (remember, the numbers are in millions)?
8. What were Apple's gross profit, operating margin, and net profit ratios in 2011? (*Note:* Round answers to two decimal places.) Assuming industry averages for 2011 were 17.41%, 6.93%, and 5.19%, respectively, describe Apple's profitability.
9. Looking at Note 1 (*Summary of Significant Accounting Policies*), what method of depreciation does Apple use? What is the range of useful life for internally used software? Do you think this useful life is appropriate?

8

© Pixelfabrik/Alamy

Current and Contingent Liabilities

© Jamie Richards/Alamy

After studying Chapter 8, you should be able to:

1. Explain liability recognition and measurement criteria.
2. Identify and record the kinds of activities that produce current liabilities.
3. Describe contingent liabilities and the alternatives for their recognition and measurement.
4. Measure warranty liabilities and warranty expense.
5. Analyze liquidity ratios using information contained in the current liabilities section.

EXPERIENCE FINANCIAL ACCOUNTING

with Ruth's Chris Steak House

Ruth's Chris Steak House was founded in 1965 when Ruth Fertel mortgaged her home for $33,000 to purchase the "Chris Steak House," a 60-seat restaurant located near the New Orleans Fair Grounds racetrack. Today this brand is considered one of the top restaurants in the world with revenues of over $300 million. Interestingly, in fiscal 2011 approximately $50.0 million worth of gift cards were sold. Gift cards have become a popular holiday gift among business professionals. According to the National Retail Federation, gift cards are the most requested holiday item with $27.8 billion spent on holiday gift cards in 2011. Further, restaurants are the second most popular category after department stores.

> *"Gift cards have become a popular holiday gift among business professionals. According to the National Retail Federation, gift cards are the most requested holiday item with $23.6 billion spent on holiday gift cards in 2009. Further, restaurants are the second most popular catagory."*

As you will learn in this chapter, Ruth's Chris has a liability (unearned revenues) related to the sale of gift cards until the meal is provided. That is, gift-card revenue should not be recognized until the services (in this case, a meal) are provided. Gift card revenue should not be recognized until the card is redeemed (for goods or services), and, therefore, Ruth's Chris would not expect to see the revenue benefit from this transaction immediately. Generally this would occur within 18 months after the gift card was purchased.

CURRENT AND CONTINGENT LIABILITIES

Chapters 4, 5, 6, and 7 explained accounting and reporting for assets. Now we will move to the other side of the balance sheet and discuss liabilities and equity, which are the sources of cash and other financial resources used to acquire assets. We begin by examining liabilities.

Finding potential creditors, arranging attractive credit terms, structuring borrowings with lenders, and arranging to have enough cash coming in to pay the liabilities as they come due are several of the most important managerial functions. The result of liability management and the accounting recognition, measurement, and reporting issues for those activities appears in the liabilities portion of the balance sheet. The information provided by **Live Nation Entertainment** in its 2011 balance sheet is typical:

Live Nation Entertainment
Consolidated Balance Sheets (Partial)
(in thousands)
December 31, 2011

LIABILITIES AND STOCKHOLDER'S EQUITY	2011
Current liabilities:	
Accounts payable, client accounts	$ 473.956
Accounts payable	87,627
Accrued expenses	579,566
Deferred revenue	273,536
Current portion of long-term debt	52,632
Other current liabilities	25,236
Total current liabilities	$1,492,553
Long-term debt, net	1,663,056
Long-term deferred income taxes	186,298
Other long-term liabilities	120,693

Source: Live Nation 2011 10-K

Naturally, existing and potential creditors also find this information useful when they want to know about the obligations management has assumed.

In this chapter and the next we discuss the three kinds of business obligations: current liabilities, contingent liabilities, and long-term debt. Current liabilities are those obligations that are (1) expected to be retired with existing current assets or creation of new current liabilities and (2) due within 1 year or one operating cycle, whichever is longer. All other liabilities are considered long-term. Contingent liabilities can be either current or long-term, but they are "iffy" in two ways. They may or may not turn into actual obligations and, for those contingencies that do become obligations, the timing and amount of the required payment is uncertain. In this chapter we focus on current and contingent liabilities and address the following questions:

- When are liabilities recognized?
- How are liabilities measured?
- What kinds of activities produce current liabilities and how are they recorded in the accounting records?
- What are contingent liabilities and how are they recorded in the accounting records?
- How do you measure and record warranty liabilities?

OBJECTIVE 1

Explain liability recognition and measurement criteria.

RECOGNITION AND MEASUREMENT OF LIABILITIES

Liabilities are probable future sacrifices of economic benefits. These commitments, which arise from activities that have already occurred, require the business to transfer assets or provide services to another entity sometime in the future. For example, an account payable arises from a transaction in which the business receives goods or services in return for a cash payment at some future time.

Within this general definition, liabilities have a wide variety of characteristics, as shown in Exhibit 8.1:

EXHIBIT 8.1

Characteristics of Liabilities

Payment of cash:
Although liabilities frequently require the payment of cash, some may require the transfer of assets other than cash, or the performance of services.

Certainty:
Although the exact amount and timing of future payments are usually known, for some liabilities they may not be.

Legal enforceability:
Although many liabilities are legally enforceable claims, some may represent merely *probable* claims.

Payment recipient:
Although liabilities usually identify the entity to be paid, the definition does not exclude payment to as yet unidentified recipients.

Thus, the future outflow associated with a liability may or may not involve the payment of cash, may or may not be known with certainty, may or may not be legally enforceable, and may or may not be payable to a known recipient.

Recognition of Liabilities

Most liabilities are recognized when goods or services are received or money is borrowed. When a liability depends on a future event (i.e., a **contingent liability**), such as the outcome of a lawsuit, recognition depends on how likely the occurrence of the event is and whether a good estimate of the payment amount can be made. If the future payment is judged to be less than likely to occur or the payment is not estimable, the obligation should not be recognized. Such obligations may require disclosure in footnotes to the financial statements, as explained later in this chapter.

Measurement of Liabilities

We all know that when you owe money you typically pay interest. That is, if you borrow \$100 at 10% interest, then when you pay it back 1 year later you must repay \$110:

$$\begin{aligned}\text{Total Payment} &= \text{Principal} + (\text{Principal} \times \text{Interest Rate} \times \text{Period})\\ &= \$100 + (\$100 \times 10\% \times 12/12)\end{aligned}$$

Sometimes companies will appear to give you a 0% interest loan. For example, furniture and electronics retailers frequently advertise "no interest, no money down for 12 months" or similar terms. Of course, we know this really means that the "interest" is included in the sales price because no business is going to truly provide 0% interest.

In theory, the amount of the liability reported on the balance sheet should not include any interest that has not yet occurred. For example, on a balance sheet prepared 6 months after borrowing the \$100 at 10% interest described above, you should report a liability of \$105:

$$\$100 + (\$100 \times 10\% \times 6/12)$$

However, many liabilities are more like your credit card or utilities bill. For example, you might owe your power company \$150 for the use of electricity during September. You likely do not receive this bill until sometime during October, and you do not have to pay it until near the end of November. Further, there appears to be no interest because you owe $150 whether you pay the bill when you receive it in October or wait until the November due date.

Despite the apparent lack of interest, theoretically interest exists. Consequently, in theory we should calculate the interest on such liabilities. For example, if we made a balance sheet at the end of September, then a liability for the power company should be calculated to exclude the theoretical interest included in the $150 payment at the end of November (i.e., 2 months' interest at the market rate). Fortunately, we ignore the interest for most current liabilities because the amount of interest is relatively small. So most current liabilities are simply recorded and reported at the total amount owed, as we will see in the next section.

OBJECTIVE 2

Identify and record the kinds of activities that produce current liabilities.

CURRENT LIABILITIES

Current liabilities are obligations that require the firm to pay cash or another current asset, create a new current liability, or provide goods or services within the longer of 1 year or one operating cycle. Since most firms have operating cycles shorter than 1 year, the 1-year rule usually applies.

Some firms combine their current liabilities into a very short list, while others provide considerable detail. Exhibit 8.2 compares the current liabilities sections of the

EXHIBIT 8.2

Current Liability Sections from Two Balance Sheets

Southwest Airlines Co.
Consolidated Balance Sheets
(in millions)

LIABILITIES AND SHAREHOLDER'S EQUITY

	December 31, 2011	December 31, 2010
Current liabilities:		
Accounts payable	$1,057	$ 739
Accrued liabilities	996	863
Air traffic liability	1,836	1,198
Current maturities of long-term debt	644	505
Total current liabilities	$4,533	$3,305

Source: Southwest Airlines Co. 2011 10-K

United Continental Holdings, Inc.
Consolidated Balance Sheets
(in millions)

	December 31	
	2011	2010
LIABILITIES AND SHAREHOLDERS' EQUITY		
Current liabilities:		
Advance ticket sales	$ 3,114	$ 2,998
Frequent flyer deferred revenue	2,405	2,582
Accounts payable	1,998	1,805
Accrued salaries and benefits	1,509	1,470
Current maturities of long-term debt	1,186	2,411
Current maturities of capital leases	125	252
Other	1,057	1,127
	$11,394	$12,645

Source: United Continental Holdings, Inc. 2011 10-K

balance sheets for two airlines—**Southwest** and **UAL (United Airlines)**. Although it's reasonable to assume that both airlines have similar types of current liabilities, Southwest combines theirs into a relatively short list while UAL provides more detail. Further, UAL orders its individual current liabilities from largest to smallest (with "other" at the end), while Southwest appears to order its current liabilities in alphabetical order, or perhaps the order in which the liabilities will be paid (order of liquidity).

IFRS

IFRS commonly reports current liabilities in reverse order relative to U.S. GAAP—from least liquid to most liquid.

In the sections that follow, we will briefly describe how various types of current liabilities arise and the principles that underlie their recognition, measurement, and reporting.

Accounts Payable

An **account payable** arises when a business purchases goods or services on credit. It is really just the flip side of an account receivable—when you have a payable, the business you owe has a receivable. Credit terms generally require that the purchaser pay the amount due within 30 to 60 days and seldom require the payment of interest. Accounts payable do not require a formal agreement or contract. For example, your account with the power company usually does not require you to sign a formal contract.

You may recall from Chapter 5 that accounts receivable have some valuation issues related to estimating bad debts. Accounts payable, on the other hand, have no such issues. They are measured and reported at the total amount required to satisfy the account, which is the cost of the goods or services acquired. For example, if Game Time Sporting Goods buys and receives running shoes on May 15, 2013, for which it pays its supplier $2,000 on June 15, 2013, it would need to make the following journal entries:

Date	Account and Explanation	Debit	Credit
May 15	Inventory	2,000	
	Accounts Payable		2,000
	(Record purchase of inventory)		
June 15	Accounts Payable	2,000	
	Cash		2,000
	(Record payment to supplier)		

Assets	=	Liabilities	+	Stockholders' Equity
+2,000		+2,000		

Assets	=	Liabilities	+	Stockholders' Equity
−2,000		−2,000		

Accrued Liabilities

Unlike accounts payable, which are recognized when goods or services change hands, **accrued liabilities** are recognized by adjusting entries. They usually represent the completed portion of activities that are in process at the end of the period. For example, Green's Landscaping pays wages of $10,000 (or $1,000 per work day) to its employees every other Friday. The standard entry is:

Date	Account and Explanation	Debit	Credit
Dec. 20	Wages Expense	10,000	
	Cash		10,000
	(Record payment of wages)		

Assets	=	Liabilities	+	Stockholders' Equity
−10,000				−10,000

What happens, however, when December 31 falls on the Tuesday before the Friday payday? In this case, the expense for the 7 days that have already been worked (5 days from last week and Monday and Tuesday of this week) must be matched to the proper period. Additionally, because the work has been performed but the employees have not yet been paid, Green's Landscaping has a liability to its employees. As such, on December 31 Green's would make the following adjusting entry:

Assets	=	Liabilities	+	Stockholders' Equity
		+7,000		−7,000

Date	Account and Explanation	Debit	Credit
Dec. 31	Wages Expense	7,000	
	Wages Payable		7,000
	(Record accrual of wages expense)		

Further, when Green's pays $10,000 to its employees on January 3, pay for 3 days is an expense of the current year (Wednesday, January 1 through Friday, January 3) and 7 days' pay retires the Wages Payable from December 31:

Assets	=	Liabilities	+	Stockholders' Equity
−10,000		−7,000		−3,000

Date	Account and Explanation	Debit	Credit
Jan. 3	Wages Expense	3,000	
	Wages Payable	7,000	
	Cash		10,000
	(Record payment of wages)		

This sort of process is used for a wide variety of activities that are completed over time. For example, taxes are paid on April 15 based on the previous year's net income. As such, on December 31 an adjusting entry will match the appropriate income taxes expense to the current year and set up a liability (income taxes payable) that will be paid off by April 15. The same logic applies to other similar situations, such as property taxes and interest expense.

Notes Payable

A **note payable** typically arises when a business borrows money or purchases goods or services from a company that requires a formal agreement or contract (like when you sign a contract to lease an apartment or buy a car). This formal agreement or contract is what distinguishes the note payable from an account payable. The agreement typically states the timing of repayment and the amount (principal and/or interest) to be repaid. Notes payable typically mature in anywhere from 3 to 12 months, but it can be longer (if it does not mature for over 12 months, it will be classified as a long-term liability). These longer maturities explain why creditors are more likely to impose interest on notes payable than with accounts payable.

Notes Payable from Borrowing from a Bank Notes payable normally specify the amount to be repaid indirectly, by stating the amount borrowed (the principal) and an interest rate. These notes are called *interest-bearing notes* because they explicitly state an **interest rate**. The maturity amount of an interest-bearing note is not stated explicitly but is determined from the interest rate, the principal amount, and the maturity date.

When a business borrows using a short-term, interest-bearing note, the transaction is recorded at the amount borrowed. This is illustrated in Cornerstone 8.1.

8.1

Recording Notes Payable and Accrued Interest

Why:

Notes payable are recognized when a business transfers assets (or provides services) to another entity at some point in the future for activities that have already occurred. Interest must be matched to the period in which it helped generate revenues.

Information:

Korsgard Auto Parts borrowed $100,000 from a bank on October 1, 2013, at 10% interest. The interest and principal are due on October 1, 2014.

(Continued)

CORNERSTONE **8.1**

(Continued)

Required:

1. Prepare the required journal entry on October 1, 2013.
2. Prepare the adjusting journal entry on December 31, 2013.
3. Prepare the journal entry (or entries) on October 1, 2014.

Solution:

Date	Account and Explanation	Debit	Credit
1. Oct. 1, 2013	Cash	100,000	
	Notes Payable		100,000
	(Record issuance of note payable)		
2. Dec. 31, 2013	Interest Expense	2,500*	
	Interest Payable		2,500
	(Record accrual of interest expense)		
3. Oct. 1, 2014	Notes Payable	100,000	
	Interest Expense	7,500**	
	Interest Payable	2,500	
	Cash		110,000
	(Record payment of note and interest)		

* $100,000 × 10% × 3/12
** $100,000 × 10% × 9/12

Assets	= Liabilities +	Stockholders' Equity
+100,000	+100,000	

Assets	= Liabilities +	Stockholders' Equity
	+2,500	−2,500

Assets	= Liabilities +	Stockholders' Equity
−110,000	−2,500 −100,000	−7,500

Exhibit 8.3 illustrates the financial statement effects of the transactions recorded in Cornerstone 8.1. Notice that the interest payment of $10,000 is recorded as interest expense of $2,500 in 2013 and $7,500 in 2014.

EXHIBIT 8.3

Effect of Borrowing Money on the Annual Income Statement and Balance Sheet

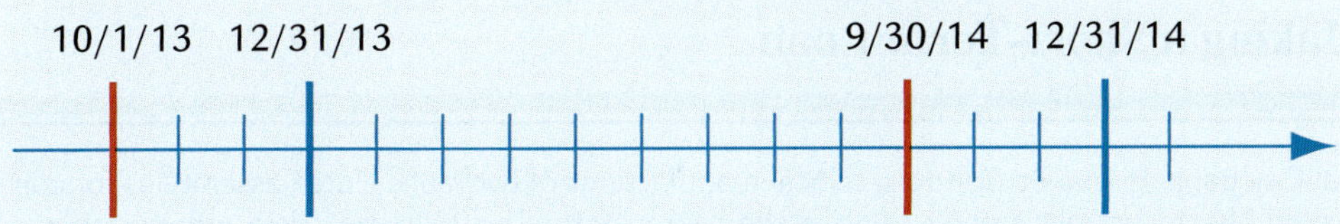

	2013	2014
Annual income statement:		
Interest expense	$ 2,500	$ 7,500
Annual balance sheet:		
Notes payable	$100,000	$ 0
Interest payable	2,500	0
Transactions:		
Cash borrowed	$100,000	
Principal payment		$100,000
Interest payment		10,000

Notes Payable from a Payment Extension In addition to short-term borrowings, notes payable are often created when a borrower is unable to pay an account payable in a timely manner. In this case, the borrower is typically granted a payment extension, but the creditor requires that a formal note be signed to impose interest. As discussed, a current liability can be retired through creation of a new current liability. Rolling an account payable into a short-term note payable would be an example of this.

Assume that on March 8, 2013, Gibson Shipping orders $25,000 of packing materials from Ironman Enterprises on account. This amount is due on May 15, 2013. Gibson would need to make the following journal entry:

Assets	= Liabilities +	Stockholders' Equity
+25,000	+25,000	

Date	Account and Explanation	Debit	Credit
Mar. 8	Supplies	25,000	
	Accounts Payable		25,000
	(Record purchase of packing materials)		

On May 15, Gibson cannot make the $25,000 payment and asks Ironman for a payment extension. If Ironman grants the extension on the condition that Gibson sign a note that specifies 7% interest beginning on May 15, 2013, with a due date of November 15, 2013, Gibson would make the following journal entry:

Assets	= Liabilities +	Stockholders' Equity
	+25,000 −25,000	

Date	Account and Explanation	Debit	Credit
May 15	Accounts Payable	25,000	
	Notes Payable		25,000
	(Record issuance of note payable)		

Finally, on November 15, 2013, when Gibson pays the amount in full, the journal entry would be as follows:

Assets	= Liabilities +	Stockholders' Equity
−25,875	−25,000	−875

Date	Account and Explanation	Debit	Credit
Nov. 15	Notes Payable	25,000	
	Interest Expense	875*	
	Cash		25,875
	(Record payment of note and interest)		

* $25,000 × 7% × 6/12

YOUDECIDE Making a Short-Term Loan

You are a commercial loan officer at National City Bank. Hydraulic Controls, a local manufacturer of hydraulic clutch assemblies for compact foreign and domestic automobiles, would like to borrow money using a short-term note. The following data are available on Hydraulic's current liabilities, current assets, sales revenue, and net income (loss) for the past 3 years:

Item	2013	2012	2011
Accounts payable	$ 174,000	$ 146,000	$ 104,000
Short-term notes payable	332,000	291,000	291,000
Income taxes payable	0	43,000	50,000
Total current liabilities	$ 506,000	$ 480,000	$ 445,000
Total current assets	485,000	546,000	611,000
Sales revenue	5,047,000	5,293,000	5,538,000
Net income (loss)	(10,000)	89,000	130,000

Hydraulic Controls asks its bank to increase its short-term notes payable by $100,000.

Should you approve a short-term note payable for Hydraulic?

To determine whether to extend additional credit to Hydraulic, you should consider the following:

- *How will the short-term notes be repaid?* The short-term notes would be repaid from current assets. But decline in the amount of current assets relative to current liabilities suggests that even the present amount of current liabilities may not be payable with the resources currently available.
- *What might be causing the recent increases in current liabilities and decreases in current assets?* Because profitability is declining, the firm may not be able to borrow from outside sources or secure cash from operations. Therefore, it may be drawing down current assets and increasing current liabilities to provide capital.

The decline in profitability, the trend in the ratio of current assets to current liabilities, and the present excess of current liabilities over current assets suggest that it would be unwise to extend additional credit at this time.

Current Portion of Long-Term Debt

The current portion of long-term debt is the amount of long-term debt principal that is due within the next year. At the end of each accounting period, the long-term debt that is due during the next year is reclassified as a current liability (see Exhibit 8.2, p. 428). Since the reclassification of most long-term debt as current does not usually change the accounts or amounts involved, journal entries are not required. In some cases, long-term debt that is due within the next year will be paid with the proceeds of a new long-term debt issue. Remember that current liabilities must be retired with existing current assets or creation of new current liabilities—a new long-term debt issue is creation of a new *long-term*, not current, liability. When such refinancing is expected, the maturing obligation is not transferred to current liabilities but is left as a long-term debt.[1]

Other Payables

So far we have discussed accounts payable, accrued liabilities, and notes payable. However, businesses will have other current liabilities that do not fall into these categories. There are many situations that can give rise to these other payables, and we will discuss some of the most common.

Sales Tax At the time of a sale, most retail businesses collect **sales taxes**, usage taxes, or excise taxes for various state, local, and federal taxing authorities. These taxes, although collected as part of the total selling price, are not additions to revenue. Instead, they are money collected from the customer for the governmental unit levying the tax. These tax collections are liabilities until they are paid to the taxing authority. For example, businesses typically must remit sales tax collected to the state every quarter. Cornerstone 8.2 illustrates the accounting for sales tax.

Recording Liabilities at the Point of Sale

CORNERSTONE 8.2

Why:

The law often requires companies to collect taxes from customers and remit them to a taxing authority. Upon collection, these represent liabilities until they are paid.

Information:

During the first quarter of 2014, McLean County Tire sold, on credit, 3,000 truck tires at $75 each plus State of Illinois sales tax of 7% and City of Bloomington municipal taxes of 1%. These taxes are paid to the appropriate taxing authority each quarter.

(Continued)

[1] We discuss long-term liabilities in more detail in Chapter 9.

CORNERSTONE 8.2 *(Continued)*

Required:

Prepare the journal entry to record (1) first quarter sales and (2) payment of taxes to the appropriate taxing authority.

Solution:

Assets	= Liabilities +	Stockholders' Equity
+243,000	+15,750 +2,250	+225,000

	Date	Account and Explanation	Debit	Credit
1.	Mar. 31	Accounts Receivable	243,000	
		Sales Revenue		225,000*
		Sales Taxes Payable (State)		15,750**
		Sales Taxes Payable (City)		2,250***
		(Record sale of truck tires)		

* 3,000 tires × $75
** 3,000 tires × $75 × 7%
*** 3,000 tires × $75 × 1%

Assets	= Liabilities +	Stockholders' Equity
−18,000	−15,750 −2,250	

	Date	Account and Explanation	Debit	Credit
2.	Apr. 10	Sales Taxes Payable (State)	15,750	
		Sales Taxes Payable (City)	2,250	
		Cash		18,000
		(Record payment of first quarter sales taxes)		

Note: The receivable is larger than the sales revenue because of the amount of taxes McLean collects for the state and municipal governments—liabilities to McLean until the governmental units are paid.

Withholding and Payroll Taxes Businesses are required to withhold taxes from employees' earnings and to pay taxes based on wages and salaries paid to employees. These **withholding** and **payroll taxes** are liabilities until they are paid to the taxing authority. Note that there are really two sources for these taxes: employees and employers.

Employees Employees must pay certain taxes that are "withheld" from their paycheck. This is the difference between gross pay and net pay. The business does not have any rights to this money; instead, as with sales tax, they must pay these amounts to the proper authority. The standard withholdings are federal, state, and possibly city or county income taxes, as well as Social Security and Medicare. Employees may also have amounts withheld for such things as retirement accounts (e.g., 401-K), parking, and health insurance, among other things, but these are not taxes.

Employers The business itself must pay certain taxes based on employee payrolls. These amounts are not withheld from employee pay; they are additional amounts that must be paid over and above gross pay. For example, employers match employee contributions to Social Security and Medicare (together these are called FICA). That is, if you have $400 withheld from your paycheck for Social Security, your employer pays the federal government $800 related to your employment. Employers also pay federal and state unemployment taxes (these are used to fund unemployment benefits) based on their history of firing employees (because fired employees are eligible to collect unemployment benefits). Finally, employers do have other costs—typically called fringe benefits—associated with employees, but these are not taxes. Examples of fringe benefits include employer contributions to retirement accounts and health insurance. Exhibit 8.4 shows the obligations most U.S. businesses pay in taxes or withhold from employee earnings. Cornerstone 8.3 illustrates the accounting for these obligations.

EXHIBIT 8.4

Employer Payroll Taxes and Withheld Earnings

Private industry employers (which excludes state and local government employers) break down as follows as of December 7, 2011:

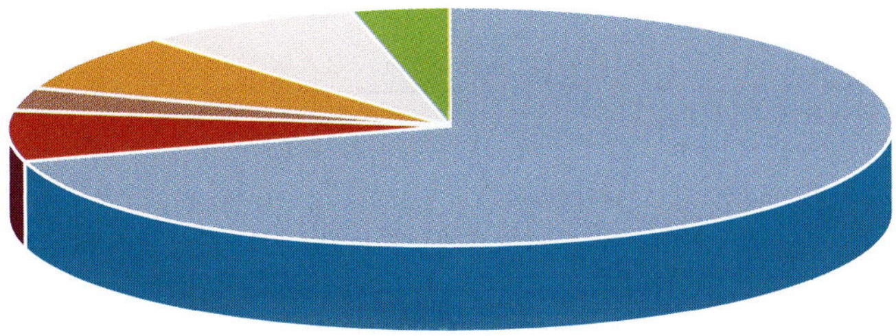

- Wages & Salaries, $19.91 (70.5%)
- Legally Required (FICA, etc.), $2.34 (8.3%)
- Insurance Benefits, $2.28 (8.1%)
- Paid Leave, $1.90 (6.7%)
- Retirement & Savings, $1.02 (3.6%)
- Supplemental Pay, $0.80 (2.8%)

Total Compensation per hour, $28.24* (100.0%)

*Difference from addition of individual expenditures due to rounding.

Source: Bureau of Labor Statistics; news release USDL-11-1718.

Recording Payroll Taxes

CORNERSTONE 8.3

Why:

Employers not only withhold taxes from employees' gross pay, but also pay amounts over and above gross pay.

Information:

Assume that McLean County Tire's hourly employees earned $48,500 in the pay period ending March 31. Income taxes withheld are $10,185. Additionally, a 3% state unemployment tax and an 0.8% federal unemployment tax are withheld.

Required:

1. Prepare the journal entry related to the gross pay earned by employees (assume no employees have reached their annual Social Security limit of $110,100 for 2012).
2. Prepare the journal entry related to the payroll taxes on top of gross pay.

Solution:

	Date	Account and Explanation	Debit	Credit
1.	Mar. 31	Wages Expense	48,500.00	
		Income Taxes Payable		10,185.00
		Social Security Taxes Payable (Employee)[g]		2,037.00[a]
		Medicare Taxes Payable (Employee)		703.25[b]
		Cash		35,574.75
		(Record wages and liabilities)		
2.	31	Unemployment Taxes Expense (Federal)	388.00	
		Unemployment Taxes Expense (State)	1,455.00	
		Social Security Taxes Expense	3,007.00	
		Medicare Taxes Expense	703.25	

Assets	=	Liabilities	+	Stockholders' Equity
−35,574.75		+10,185.00		−48,500.00
		+2,037.00		
		+703.25		

Assets	=	Liabilities	+	Stockholders' Equity
		+388.00		−388.00
		+1,455.00		−1,455.00
		+3,007.00		−3,007.00
		+703.25		−703.25

(Continued)

CORNERSTONE 8.3 (*Continued*)

Unemployment Taxes Payable (Federal)		388.00[c]
Unemployment Taxes Payable (State)		1,455.00[d]
Social Security Taxes Payable (Employer)		3,007.00[e]
Medicare Taxes Payable (Employer)		703.25[f]
(Record employer payroll taxes)		

[a] $48,500 × 4.2%
[b] $48,500 × 1.45%
[c] $48,500 × 0.8%
[d] $48,500 × 3%
[e] $48,500 × 6.2%
[f] $48,500 × 1.45%
[g] Employee limits were reduced to 4.2% by the Tax Relief, Unemployment Insurance Reauthorization, and Job Creation Act of 2010. At the time of this writing, Congress continues to discuss extending this tax relief. However, should Congress choose to let the deadline expire, employee contributions will return to 6.2%.

Note: The $48,500.00 payroll is (1) smaller than the total expense of $54,053.25 (i.e., the sum of expenses from both journal entries) and (2) larger than the $35,574.75 cash paid (i.e., net pay) to employees. In other words, the actual cost of an employee is more than his or her gross pay.

YOU DECIDE Full-Time Employee or Consultant?

You are the HR manager of Berndt Chocolates. The marketing department wants to hire a full-time employee at an annual salary of approximately $52,000. They argue that this will save the company money because Berndt will no longer have to pay an outside marketing consultant approximately $60,000 per year to do the same job.

What factors should you consider in deciding whether to hire the full-time employee?

Businesses often make the decision of whether to hire a full-time employee or pay a consultant. Of course, of primary concern is which person will perform the function better, but there are other factors to consider. Hiring a consultant can provide several advantages. First, a full-time employee will incur costs in addition to salary. For example, assuming federal and state unemployment tax rates totaling 3.5% for a full-time employee earning $52,000, Berndt's payroll taxes will increase as follows:

Employer Payroll Taxes	Cost
OASDI (Social Security at 6.2%)	$3,224
Medicare (at 1.45%)	754
Federal and state unemployment (at 3.5%)	245
Total employer payroll taxes	$4,223

Further, most companies have fringe benefits such as medical insurance, life insurance, retirement contributions, and bonuses. Assuming these fringe benefits are 30% of the employee's annual salary, this employee would cost $71,823 [$52,000 + $4,223 + ($52,000 × 30%)] per year. Second, it is much easier and less costly to decrease or eliminate consultants than full-time employees.

Aside from qualifications, the costs of federal and state taxes and benefits should be considered when deciding whether to hire full-time employees.

Unearned Revenues **Unearned revenue** is the liability created when customers pay for goods or services in advance. In such instances, the amount of the prepayment is a liability for the seller. This liability is discharged either by providing the goods or services purchased (at which time revenue is recognized) or by refunding the amount of the prepayment.[2] Cornerstone 8.4 illustrates the accounting for unearned revenues.

[2] If the goods or services are not provided, the seller may also be liable for legal damages. The amount of such damages would be recorded as an expense.

Recording Unearned Revenues

CORNERSTONE 8.4

Why:

When customers pay for goods or services in advance, the business recognizes a liability. The revenue is recognized at the time the goods or services are provided.

Information:

Ron's Cajun Connection sells $100,000 of gift cards in December 2013. These gift cards may be redeemed at any time; however, they expire on December 31, 2014. During 2014, $98,875 of gift cards are redeemed.

Required:

1. Prepare the journal entry related to the sale of gift cards.
2. Prepare the journal entry related to redemption of the gift cards.
3. Prepare the journal entry related to the expiration of the remaining gift cards.

Solution:

	Date	Account and Explanation	Debit	Credit
1.	Dec. 2013	Cash	100,000	
		Unearned Sales Revenue		100,000
		(Record sale of gift cards)		
2.*	Dec. 31, 2014	Unearned Sales Revenue	98,875	
		Sales Revenue		98,875
		(Record redemption of gift cards)		
3.**	Dec. 31, 2014	Unearned Sales Revenue	1,125	
		Sales Revenue		1,125
		(Record expiration of gift cards)		

Assets	=	Liabilities	+	Stockholders' Equity
+100,000		+100,000		

Assets	=	Liabilities	+	Stockholders' Equity
		−98,875		+98,875

Assets	=	Liabilities	+	Stockholders' Equity
		−1,125		+1,125

*These entries are made individually as each gift card is redeemed.

**When gift cards expire, the sales revenue is recognized because the business does not need to provide any additional goods or services.

A similar *long-term* liability, called *customer deposits,* is recorded when customers make advance payments or security deposits that are not expected to be earned or returned soon enough to qualify as current liabilities.

Cornerstone 8-4 demonstrates that revenue will not be recognized until it is realized (or realizable) and earned. Here, revenue is realized because the cash has been collected, so the first criterion is met; however, it is not earned until the goods or services are provided. Recall the chapter opener discussion of **Ruth's Chris Steak House** and how they sold approximately $50.0 million in gift cards during 2011. This is how Ruth's Chris accounts for these gift cards.

concept Q&A

Why is a liability recognized when a customer prepays for a good or service (i.e., an unearned revenue)?

Answer:

Liabilities are probable future sacrifices of economic benefits which arise from activities that have already occurred. Because the business here will provide the goods or services purchased by the customer at a future point, the prepayment is a liability.

OBJECTIVE 3

Describe contingent liabilities and the alternatives for their recognition and measurement.

CONTINGENT LIABILITIES

Measurement of the liabilities described so far was not affected by uncertainties about the amount, timing, or recipient of future asset outflows. However, such uncertainties exist. In financial accounting, a contingency is an ". . . existing condition, situation, or set of circumstances involving uncertainty" as to possible gain or loss.

A contingent liability is not recognized in the accounts unless both of the following are true:

- the event on which it is contingent is probable
- a reasonable estimate of the loss can be made

IFRS

IFRS refers to contingencies as "provisions." In addition, IFRS defines probable as "more likely than not" while U.S. GAAP defines probable as "likely." Therefore, more events will be recognized as provisions under IFRS.

If the contingent event is likely to occur, reliable measurement of the liability is usually possible, so recognition is appropriate. For example, contingent liabilities arising from product warranties and pensions are recognized because previous experience allows for reliable measurements to be made. On the other hand, if occurrence of the contingent event is not probable or reliable measurement of the obligation is impossible, the potential obligation is not recorded as a liability. Instead, as shown in Exhibit 8.5, it may be disclosed in footnotes to the financial statements.

EXHIBIT 8.5

Recognition of Contingent Liabilities

	A Reasonable Estimate Can Be Made	No Reasonable Estimate Can Be Made
Probable	Make a journal entry to record the liability.	No journal entry is made: disclose information in footnote to the financial statements.
Reasonably Possible	No journal entry is made: disclose information in footnote to the financial statements.	No journal entry is made: disclose information in footnote to the financial statements.
Remote	Neither record as a liability nor disclose in a footnote to the financial statements.	Neither record as a liability nor disclose in a footnote to the financial statements.

Lawsuits filed against a business are a classic example of contingent liabilities. Most large companies are party to multiple lawsuits at any point in time. Estimating when a loss is probable and determining a reasonable estimate requires information from the attorneys, but businesses rarely record a contingent liability prior to the jury deciding against them. We've probably all heard of such lawsuits as when Stella Liebeck sued **McDonald's** in 1992. Liebeck spilled coffee while removing the lid to add sugar, burning her legs. She suffered third degree burns over 6% of her body. McDonald's could have settled the case for $20,000, but they refused. Liebeck ultimately was awarded $200,000 in compensatory damages and $2.7 million in punitive damages.[3]

The accounting question becomes: When is a liability (and corresponding expense) recorded? Proper matching suggests that the expense would be recorded at the time Liebeck spilled the coffee. However, at this time, the loss was contingent. Since the liability and expense were not recorded until it was deemed probable that **McDonald's** would lose the lawsuit and a reasonable estimate could be made, McDonald's did not record a liability for this amount until they lost the lawsuit.

Of course, the likelihood that a contingent event will occur may change over time. A contingent liability that should not be recorded or disclosed at one time may need to be recorded or disclosed later because the facts and circumstances change. This frequently happens to contingent liabilities arising from litigation.

[3] Liebek's compensatory damages were reduced to $160,000 because she was found to be 20% at fault.

ETHICAL DECISIONS The contingent liability rules create an interesting ethical dilemma in lawsuits. Consider the fictional case of a a class action lawsuit being filed against Giant Pharmaceuticals by patients who used one of Giant's best selling drugs. Company attorneys believe it is probable that Giant will settle the lawsuit for approximately \$3 billion. However, if Giant were to recognize a \$3 billion liability and expense, the plaintiff attorneys would likely refuse to settle for less. After all, what would you think if you were on the jury and the defendants' attorney showed you Giant's financial statements, explained the contingency rule, and said, "See, even Giant thinks it's probable that they will lose this lawsuit and pay damages of \$3 billion." As you might expect, companies are extremely reluctant to record expenses and liabilities related to lawsuits for this reason or to even disclose that a loss is probable. Is this ethical? It probably isn't ethical, but it is an area that all parties seem to allow. As such, users of the financial statements cannot place too much reliance on the lack of expenses and liabilities related to lawsuits. •

concept Q&A

Accounts receivable have a contingent loss related to bad debts. A group of customers owes money (the accounts receivable); however, there is uncertainty about whether the customers will pay. How do we account for this contingency and why do we account for it in this way?

Answer:

As discussed in Chapter 5, companies typically use an estimate of uncollectible receivables to recognize "bad debt expense" and reduce the accounts receivable valuation through a credit to the "allowance for doubtful accounts." This is done because it is probable that amounts will be uncollectible and this amount is reasonably estimated (generally based on past experience). So, although bad debt expense does not produce a liability (instead, it reduces an asset), the accounting for this contingency is consistent with contingent liabilities.

WARRANTIES

When goods are sold, the customer is often provided with a warranty against certain defects. A **warranty** usually guarantees the repair or replacement of defective goods during a period (ranging from a few days to several years) following the sale.

OBJECTIVE 4

Measure warranty liabilities and warranty expense.

The use of parts and labor to satisfy warranty claims may occur in the accounting period in which the sale is made, but it is also likely to occur in some subsequent accounting period. The matching concept requires that all expenses required to produce sales revenue for a given period be recorded in that period. Since warranty costs are sales-related, they must be recorded in the sales period. And since all warranty costs probably have not been incurred by the end of the sales period, they must be estimated. Businesses are likely able to make reasonable estimates of their warranty costs based on past experience.

The recognition of warranty expense and (estimated) warranty liability is normally recorded by an adjustment at the end of the accounting period. As warranty claims are paid to customers or related expenditures are made, the liability is reduced. Cornerstone 8.5 illustrates the accounting for warranties.

Recording Warranty Liabilities

CORNERSTONE 8.5

Why:

Future warranty expenses must be recognized, or matched, in the period of sale.

Information:

Nolan Electronics offers a 12-month warranty on all its computers. Nolan estimates that one computer of each 2,000 sold will require warranty service and that the average warranty claim will cost Nolan \$155.

Required:

1. Prepare the journal entry to recognize warranty expense and associated liability, assuming Nolan sells 3,000,000 computers during 2013, for which no warranty work has yet been performed.

(Continued)

CORNERSTONE 8.5 (Continued)

2. Prepare the journal entry for warranty repairs, assuming that in January 2014, Nolan sends $10,400 cash and parts costing $8,300 to its dealers for warranty repairs.

Solution:

1. $$(3{,}000{,}000 \text{ computers sold}) \times \left(\frac{1 \text{ failure}}{2{,}000 \text{ sold}}\right) \times \left(\frac{\$155}{1 \text{ failure}}\right) = \$232{,}500$$

Assets	= Liabilities +	Stockholders' Equity
	+232,500	−232,500

Date	Account and Explanation	Debit	Credit
Dec. 31, 2013	Warranty Expense	232,500	
	Warranty Liability		232,500
	(Record warranty expense for 2013)		

2.

Assets	= Liabilities +	Stockholders' Equity
−10,400	−18,700	
−8,300		

Date	Account and Explanation	Debit	Credit
Jan. 2014	Warranty Liability	18,700	
	Cash		10,400
	Parts Inventory		8,300
	(Record payment for warranty repairs for January 2014)		

Note: The income statement effect of warranties (activity in the equity column) occurs when goods are sold. Payments or other asset outflows associated with the satisfaction of warranty claims do not affect the income statement.

concept Q&A

Why are warranties expensed at the point of sale when a company often does not incur warranty costs until later periods?

Answer:

Remember, the matching principle says that expenses will be recognized in the periods in which they helped generate revenues. The presence of the warranty "helped" sell the item. Additionally, warranties are contingencies—if the product fails, then the company will experience a loss. When loss contingencies are probable and a reasonable estimate can be made, a journal entry is made to record the expense and recognize a liability.

Actual warranty claims are unlikely to exactly equal the business's estimate. Any small overestimate or underestimate is usually combined with the next warranty estimate. However, large overestimates or underestimates must be recognized in the accounts and reported on the income statement as other income or other expenses as soon as they become apparent.

OBJECTIVE 5

Analyze liquidity ratios using information contained in the current liabilities section.

ANALYZING CURRENT LIABILITIES

Both investors and creditors are interested in a company's liquidity—that is, its ability to meet its short-term obligations. Failure to pay current liabilities can lead to suppliers refusing to sell to the company and employees leaving. As such, even companies with good business models can be forced into bankruptcy by their inability to pay current liabilities.

The following ratios are often used to analyze a company's ability to meet its current obligations:

$$\text{Current Ratio} = \frac{\text{Current Assets}}{\text{Current Liabilities}}$$

$$\text{Quick Ratio} = \frac{(\text{Cash} + \text{Marketable Securities} + \text{Accounts Receivable})}{\text{Current Liabilities}}$$

$$\text{Cash Ratio} = \frac{(\text{Cash} + \text{Marketable Securities})}{\text{Current Liabilities}}$$

$$\text{Operating Cash Flow Ratio} = \frac{\text{Cash Flows from Operating Activities}}{\text{Current Liabilities}}$$

The first three ratios compare all or parts of current assets to current liabilities. The logic is that current liabilities need to be paid over approximately the same time frame that current assets are turned into cash. "Acceptable" current ratios vary from industry to industry, but the thought is that current assets must exceed current liabilities (which implies a current ratio > 1) to be able to meet current obligations. In fact, the general rule of thumb appears to be that a current ratio greater than 2 is appropriate.

However, the second and third ratios recognize that some current assets are harder to liquidate. Both the quick and cash ratio exclude inventories because including inventories assumes that sales will be made. The quick ratio assumes that accounts receivable are liquid. This is true when customers have low credit risk and pay in relatively short amounts of time. Of course, such an assumption is not true for all industries. Consequently, the use of the cash ratio may be more appropriate in these cases.

Operating cash flow, on the other hand, looks at the ability of cash generated from operating activities to meet current obligations. As with the current ratio, the operating cash flow ratio assumes that sales will continue into the future. Cornerstone 8.6 illustrates the analysis of current liabilities.

Calculating Liquidity Ratios

CORNERSTONE 8.6

Why:

Information contained in current liabilities provides investors and creditors with an idea of a company's ability to meet its current obligations.

Information:

Consider the following information from **Standard Pacific**, a large builder of single-family homes, as of December 31, 2011 (in thousands):

Current liabilities	$203,719	Receivables	$ 11,525
Cash & equivalents	406,785	Inventories	1,537,079
Marketable securities	0	Cash flows from operating activities	(322,613)

Required:

Calculate the following: (1) current ratio, (2) quick ratio, (3) cash ratio, and (4) operating cash flow ratio.

Solution:

1. Current ratio: $\dfrac{\$406{,}785 + \$0 + \$11{,}525 + \$1{,}537{,}079}{\$203{,}719} = 9.60$

2. Quick ratio: $\dfrac{\$406{,}785 + \$0 + \$11{,}525}{\$203{,}719} = 2.05$

3. Cash ratio: $\dfrac{\$406{,}785 + \$0}{\$203{,}719} = 2.00$

4. Operating cash flow ratio: $\dfrac{-\$322{,}613}{\$203{,}719} = -1.58$

Note: Most of the information to calculate these ratios can also be found on the balance sheet (except for cash flows from operating activities, which is on the statement of cash flows).

In isolation, the current ratio in Cornerstone 8.6 appears very strong. For most industries, a current ratio greater than seven is rare. However, a vast majority of the current assets is inventory (unsold homes). In strong real estate markets, new homes can sell quite fast, but when a real estate slump hits, such homes can remain unsold for long periods of time. During the 2007 real estate market slump, for example, home builders experienced much slower sales (**Standard Pacific**'s sales were down approximately 30%). A few home builders even resorted to selling homes at a loss to generate needed cash.

The quick ratio and cash ratio in Cornerstone 8.6 show that **Standard Pacific** can meet its current obligations with its cash reserves alone, which means Standard Pacific has little short-term solvency risk. However, the highly negative cash flows from operations are primarily due to growing inventory in 2011. Although this growing inventory could be interpreted as expanding operations, it could also signal slowing sales.

SUMMARY OF LEARNING OBJECTIVES

LO 1. Explain liability recognition and measurement criteria.

- Most liabilities are recognized in exchange for goods and services or the borrowing of money.
- In theory, the amount reported on the balance sheet should not include interest that has not yet accrued.
- For nearly all current liabilities, unaccrued interest is deemed immaterial, so most current liabilities are simply recorded and reported at the total amount due.

LO 2. Identify and record the kinds of activities that produce current liabilities.

- Current liabilities are obligations to outsiders that require the firm to pay cash or another current asset or provide goods or services within the longer of 1 year or one operating cycle.
- Current liabilities are the result of many common transactions such as:
  - purchasing goods or services on credit (i.e., accounts payable)
  - the completed portion of activities that are in process at the end of the period such as wages or interest (i.e., accrued liabilities)
  - sales tax collected from customers
  - payroll taxes such as income taxes withheld from employees and Social Security
  - notes payable
  - goods or services paid for in advance by customers (i.e., unearned revenues)
  - the portion of long-term debt due within the year

LO 3. Describe contingent liabilities and the alternatives for their recognition and measurement.

- A contingent liability is an obligation whose amount, timing, or recipient depends on future events.
- A contingent liability is not recognized in the accounts unless the event on which it is contingent is probable (likely to occur) and a reasonable estimate of the liability can be made.
- If occurrence of the contingent event is not probable or reliable measurement of the obligation is impossible, the potential obligation is not recorded as a liability, but may be disclosed in the footnotes.

LO 4. Measure warranty liabilities and warranty expense.

- Since warranties help generate sales, the estimated future cost of servicing the warranty must be recorded in the sales period (this is an example of the matching principle).
- Matching the costs servicing the warranty to the sales period is done by expensing the estimate of the future cost of servicing the warranty and creating a liability.
- As warranty claims are paid to customers or related expenditures are made, the estimated liability is reduced.

LO 5. Analyze liquidity ratios using information contained in the current liabilities section.

- Both investors and creditors are interested in a company's liquidity—that is, its ability to meet its short-term obligations.
- Failure to pay current liabilities can lead to suppliers refusing to sell needed inventory and employees leaving.
- Even companies with good business models can be forced into bankruptcy by their inability to pay current liabilities.
- Common ratios used to analyze a company's ability to meet its current obligations are:
  - current ratio
  - quick ratio
  - cash ratio
  - operating cash flow ratio

CORNERSTONE 8.1	Recording notes payable and accrued interest, page 430
CORNERSTONE 8.2	Recording liabilities at the point of sale, page 433
CORNERSTONE 8.3	Recording payroll taxes, page 435
CORNERSTONE 8.4	Recording unearned revenues, page 437
CORNERSTONE 8.5	Recording warranty liabilities, page 439
CORNERSTONE 8.6	Calculating liquidity ratios, page 441

KEY TERMS

Account payable, 429
Accrued liabilities, 429
Contingent liability, 427
Current liabilities, 428
Interest rate, 430
Liabilities, 426
Note payable, 430
Payroll taxes, 434
Sales taxes, 433
Unearned revenue, 436
Warranty, 439
Withholding taxes, 434

REVIEW PROBLEM

Recording Current Liabilities and Calculating the Current Ratio

ABC Co. has the following balances in its accounts as of the beginning of the day on December 31 (this is not all of the accounts):

Account	Debit	Credit
Accounts payable		$ 100,000
Accounts receivable	$150,000	
Cash	75,000	
Interest payable		0
Inventory	270,000	
Long-term notes payable		1,000,000
Other current assets	60,000	
Other current liabilities		45,000
Sales taxes payable		10,000
Short-term notes payable		0
Unearned revenues		30,000

(Continued)

The following additional information is *not* reflected in these balances:

a. On December 1, ABC bought equipment for $200,000 with a short-term note payable bearing 12% interest. ABC has not made any journal entries related to this transaction.
b. On December 31, ABC accepted delivery of $30,000 of inventory. ABC has not yet paid its suppliers.
c. Customers prepaid $10,600 related to services ABC will perform next year. This price included 6% state sales tax.
d. Gross salaries and wages in the amount of $20,000 are paid. Assume all employees are below the Social Security maximum, 5.4% state unemployment taxes and 0.8% federal unemployment taxes are paid on $3,225.81 of wages, and $2,500 federal income taxes are withheld from employees. Assume both employees and employers pay 6.2% to Social Security.

Required:

1. Prepare the necessary journal entries for Items a–d.
2. Determine the current ratio before accounting for the additional information.
3. Determine the current ratio after accounting for the additional information.
4. Explain why ABC's current ratio deteriorated so badly.

Solution:

1. The necessary journal entries for each item are as follows:

Assets	=	Liabilities +	Stockholders' Equity
+200,000		+200,000	

Assets	=	Liabilities +	Stockholders' Equity
+30,000		+30,000	

Assets	=	Liabilities +	Stockholders' Equity
		+2,000	−2,000

Assets	=	Liabilities +	Stockholders' Equity
+10,600		+10,000	
		+600	

Assets	=	Liabilities +	Stockholders' Equity
−15,970		+1,240	−20,000
		+290	
		+2,500	

Assets	=	Liabilities +	Stockholders' Equity
		+174.19	−174.19
		+25.81	−25.81
		+1,240.00	−1,240.00
		+290.00	−290.00

	Date	Account and Explanation	Debit	Credit
a.	Dec. 1	Equipment	200,000	
		Short-term Notes Payable		200,000
		(Record issue of note for equipment purchase)		
b.	31	Inventory	30,000	
		Accounts Payable		30,000
		(Record purchase of inventory)		
		ABC must also accrue interest on December 31.		
	31	Interest Expense[a]	2,000	
		Interest Payable		2,000
		(Record interest accrued on short-term note)		
c.	31	Cash	10,600	
		Unearned Revenue		10,000
		Sales Taxes Payable (State)		600
		(Record unearned revenue and state sales taxes)		
d.	31	Wages Expense	20,000	
		Social Security Taxes Payable (Employee)[b]		1,240
		Medicare Taxes Payable (Employee)[c]		290
		Income Taxes Payable (Federal)		2,500
		Cash		15,970
		(Record wages expense and related liabilities)		
	31	Social Security Taxes Expense	1,240.00	
		Medicare Taxes Expense	290.00	
		Unemployment Taxes Expense (State)[d]	174.19	
		Unemployment Taxes Expense (Federal)[e]	25.81	
		Social Security Taxes Payable (Employer)		1,240.00
		Medicare Taxes Payable (Employer)		290.00
		Unemployment Taxes Payable (State)[d]		174.19
		Unemployment Taxes Payable (Federal)[e]		25.81
		(Record employer payroll taxes)		

[a] $200,000 × 12% × 1/12
[b] $20,000 × 6.2%
[c] $20,000 × 1.45%
[d] $3,225.81 × 5.4%
[e] $3,225.81 × 0.8%

2. Before accounting for the additional information:

Current assets:	
Cash	$ 75,000
Accounts receivable	150,000
Inventory	270,000
Other current assets	60,000
Total current assets	$555,000
Current liabilities:	
Accounts payable	$100,000
Interest payable	0
Sales taxes payable	10,000
Short-term notes payable	0
Unearned revenues	30,000
Other current liabilities	45,000
Total current liabilities	$185,000

Current Ratio = $555,000/$185,000 = 3.0

3. After accounting for the additional information:

		Debit	Credit	
Current assets:				
Cash	$ 75,000	$10,600 (c)	$ 15,970 (d)	$ 69,630
Accounts receivable	150,000			150,000
Inventory	270,000	30,000 (b)		300,000
Other current assets	60,000			60,000
Total current assets				$579,630
Current liabilities:				
Accounts payable	100,000		30,000 (b)	$130,000
Interest payable	0		2,000 (b)	2,000
Sales taxes payable	10,000		600 (c)	10,600
Short-term notes payable	0		200,000 (a)	200,000
Unearned revenues	30,000		10,000 (c)	40,000
Other current liabilities	45,000		5,760 (d)*	50,760
Total current liabilities				$433,360

* $1,240 + $290 + $2,500 + $1,240 + $290 + $174.19 + $25.81 = $5,760

Current Ratio = $579,630/$433,360 = 1.34

4. The primary cause of the deterioration of ABC's current ratio is the addition of the short-term note payable related to the equipment. This transaction almost doubled the current liabilities, but current assets were unaffected by the addition of equipment. Another way to think about this is that ABC financed long-term operational assets with short-term financing.

DISCUSSION QUESTIONS

1. What are liabilities?
2. How is the amount of a liability measured?
3. When are most liabilities recognized?
4. What are current liabilities? Provide some common examples.
5. Describe at least two ways in which current liabilities are frequently ordered on the balance sheet.
6. What is the difference between an account payable and a note payable?

7. What sort of transaction typically creates an account payable?
8. What do we mean by accrued liabilities? Provide some common examples.
9. What type of transaction typically creates a note payable?
10. Why is interest ignored when valuing accounts payable?
11. How is interest computed on an interest-bearing short-term note?
12. When would debt that must be repaid within the next year be classified as long-term instead of current?
13. Provide examples of payroll taxes that are paid by the employee through reduction of their gross pay. Provide some examples of payroll taxes that are paid by the employer.
14. Why do unearned revenues and customers' deposits qualify as liabilities?
15. What are contingent liabilities? Provide an example.
16. When is a contingency recognized as a liability?
17. Why is the liability for warranties recognized when products are sold rather than when the warranty services are performed?
18. Describe the circumstances under which the current, quick, and cash ratios, respectively, are more appropriate measures of short-term liquidity than the other ratios.
19. Describe the differences between the current, quick, and cash ratios. Which one is the most conservative measure of short-term liquidity?
20. How does the rationale for the operating cash flow ratio differ from the rationale for the current, quick, and cash ratios?

MULTIPLE-CHOICE QUESTIONS

8-1 Liabilities are recognized in exchange for

a. borrowing money.
b. services.
c. goods.
d. all of these.

8-2 When reporting liabilities on a balance sheet, in theory, what measurement should be used?

a. Present value of the present outflow
b. Present value of the future outflow
c. Future value of the present outflow
d. Future value of the future outflow

Use the following information for Multiple-Choice Questions 8-3 and 8-4:
Kinsella Seed borrowed $200,000 on October 1, 2013, at 10% interest. The interest and principal are due on October 1, 2014.

8-3 Refer to the information for Kinsella Seed above. What journal entry should be recorded on December 31, 2013?

a. Debit Interest Expense 5,000; credit Interest Payable 5,000.
b. Debit Interest Payable 5,000; credit Interest Expense 5,000.
c. Debit Interest Receivable 20,000; credit Interest Expense 20,000.
d. No entry is necessary.

8-4 Refer to the information for Kinsella Seed above. What journal entry should be made with respect to the interest payment on October 1, 2014?

a. Debit Interest Expense 15,000; debit Interest Payable 5,000; credit Cash 20,000.
b. Debit Interest Expense 15,000; credit Cash 15,000.
c. Debit Cash 20,000; credit Interest Expense 15,000; credit Interest Payable 5,000.
d. Debit Interest Expense 20,000; credit Cash 20,000.

8-5 Which of the following is *not* a current liability?

a. Accounts payable
b. Unearned revenue
c. Sales taxes payable
d. Bonds payable due in 5 years

8-6 Which of the following is *not* an example of an accrued liability?

a. Accounts payable
b. Interest payable
c. Wages payable
d. Property taxes payable

8-7 Kramerica Inc. sold 350 oil drums to Thompson Manufacturing for $75 each. In addition to the $75 sale price per drum, there is a $1 per drum federal excise tax and a 7% state sales tax. What journal entry should be made to record this sale?

a. Debit Accounts Receivable 28,438; credit Sales Revenue 28,438.
b. Debit Accounts Receivable 26,250; credit Sales Revenue 26,250.
c. Debit Accounts Receivable 26,250; debit Taxes Expense 2,188; credit Excise Taxes Payable (Federal) 350; credit Sales Taxes Payable (State) 1,838; credit Sales Revenue 26,250.
d. Debit Accounts Receivable 28,438; credit Excise Taxes Payable (Federal) 350; credit Sales Taxes Payable (State) 1,838; credit Sales Revenue 26,250.

8-8 All of the following represent taxes commonly collected by businesses from customers *except*

a. City sales taxes
b. Federal excise taxes
c. Unemployment taxes
d. State sales taxes

8-9 Payroll taxes typically include all of the following *except*

a. Social Security taxes
b. Federal excise taxes
c. Medicare taxes
d. Federal unemployment taxes

8-10 When a credit is made to the income taxes payable account related to taxes withheld from an employee, the corresponding debit is made to

a. Wages Expense
b. Taxes Expense
c. Taxes Payable
d. Cash

8-11 When should a contingent liability be recognized?

a. When a reasonable estimation can be made
b. When the contingent liability is probable
c. neither a nor b
d. a and b

8-12 Which of the following is true?

a. No journal entries or footnotes are necessary if the probability of a contingent liability is remote.
b. A contingent liability should always be recorded in the footnotes to the financial statements.
c. A contingent liability should always be recorded within the financial statements.
d. A company can choose to record a contingent liability either within its financial statements or in the footnotes to the financial statements.

8-13 ABC Advisors is being sued by a former customer. ABC's lawyers say that it is possible, but not probable, that the company will lose the lawsuit and the trial should last approximately 18 more months. Should ABC lose, they will most likely have to pay approximately $750,000. How should this lawsuit be reported in the financial statements?

a. Current liability of $750,000 and Expense of $750,000
b. Long-term liability of $750,000 and Expense of $750,000
c. No disclosure is required.
d. No effect on the balance sheet or income statement, but described in the footnotes.

8-14 Warranty expense is

a. recorded as it is incurred.
b. recorded in the period of sale.
c. capitalized as a warranty asset.
d. none of these.

8-15 To record warranties, the adjusting journal entry would be

a. a debit to Warranty Liability and a credit to Warranty Expense.
b. a debit to Warranty Expense and a credit to Warranty Liability.
c. a debit to Warranty Expense and a debit to Cash.
d. a debit to Warranty Liability and a credit to Cash.

8-16 How is the current ratio calculated?

a. Current Assets/Current Liabilities
b. Cash Flows from Operating Activities/Current Liabilities
c. (Cash + Marketable Securities)/Current Liabilities
d. (Cash + Marketable Securities + Accounts Receivable)/Current Liabilities

8-17 How is the cash ratio calculated?

a. Current Assets/Current Liabilities
b. Cash Flows from Operating Activities/Current Liabilities
c. (Cash + Marketable Securities)/Current Liabilities
d. (Cash + Marketable Securities + Accounts Receivable)/Current Liabilities

8-18 Which of the following transactions would cause the current ratio to increase (assuming the current ratio is currently greater than 1)?

a. Purchased inventory on credit.
b. Purchased property, plant, and equipment for cash.
c. Received money from a customer related to an accounts receivable.
d. Paid off a payable.

CORNERSTONE EXERCISES

OBJECTIVE 2
CORNERSTONE 8.1

Cornerstone Exercise 8-19 Issuing Notes Payable

On June 30, Carmean Inc. borrows $250,000 from 1st National Bank with an 8-month, 7% note.

Required:

What journal entry is made on June 30?

OBJECTIVE 2
CORNERSTONE 8.1

Cornerstone Exercise 8-20 Notes Payable

Rogers Machinery Company borrowed $330,000 on February 1, with a 6-month, 10%, interest-bearing note.

Required:

1. Record the borrowing transaction.
2. Record the repayment transaction.

OBJECTIVE 2
CORNERSTONE 8.1

Cornerstone Exercise 8-21 Accrued Interest

On August 1, Wilshire Company borrowed $150,000 from People's National Bank on a 1-year, 8% note.

Required:

What adjusting entry should Wilshire make at December 31?

OBJECTIVE 2
CORNERSTONE 8.1

Cornerstone Exercise 8-22 Accrued Interest

On March 1, the Garner Corporation borrowed $75,000 from the First Bank of Midlothian on a 1-year, 5% note.

Required:

If the company keeps its records on a calendar year, what adjusting entry should Garner make on December 31?

Cornerstone Exercise 8-23 Accrued Wages

OBJECTIVE 2
CORNERSTONE 8.4

Skiles Company's weekly payroll amounts to $15,000, and payday is every Friday. Employees work 5 days per week, Monday through Friday. The appropriate journal entry was recorded at the end of the accounting period, Tuesday, December 31, 2013.

Required:

What journal entry is made on Friday, January 3, 2013?

Cornerstone Exercise 8-24 Sales and Excise Tax

OBJECTIVE 2
CORNERSTONE 8.2

Garner's Antique Hot Rods recently sold a 1957 Chevy for $75,000 on account. The state sales tax is 6%, and there is a $500-per-car federal excise tax.

Required:

Prepare the journal entry to record the sale.

Cornerstone Exercise 8-25 Sales Tax

OBJECTIVE 2
CORNERSTONE 8.2

Cobb Baseball Bats sold 45 bats for $50 each, plus an additional state sales tax of 6%. The customer paid cash.

Required:

Prepare the journal entry to record the sale.

Cornerstone Exercise 8-26 Payroll Taxes

OBJECTIVE 2
CORNERSTONE 8.3

Hernandez Builders has a gross payroll for January amounting to $500,000. The following amounts have been withheld:

Income taxes	$63,000
Social Security	31,000
Medicare	7,250
Charitable contributions	1% of gross pay
Union dues	2% of gross pay

Also, the federal unemployment tax rate is 6.2% and applies to all but $50,000 of the gross payroll.

Required:

1. What is the amount of net pay recorded by Hernandez?
2. Prepare the journal entries to record the payroll.

Cornerstone Exercise 8-27 Payroll Taxes

OBJECTIVE 2
CORNERSTONE 8.3

Kinsella Inc. has a gross payroll of $13,500 for the pay period. The entire payroll is subject to Social Security and Medicare taxes. Kinsella must also withhold $1,750 in income taxes from the employees and pay state unemployment taxes of $60. Assume employees pay 6.2% to Social Security.

Required:

Prepare the necessary journal entries for Kinsella to record both the gross pay earned by employees and the employer portion of these payroll taxes (round to nearest dollar).

Cornerstone Exercise 8-28 Payroll Taxes

OBJECTIVE 2
CORNERSTONE 8.3

During October, Seger Insurance employees earned $100,000 in wages. Social Security applied to $86,000 of these wages (assume employees pay 6.2% of Social Security), while Medicare applies to all $100,000. State and federal unemployment taxes of $1,300 and $650 are owed, respectively.

(Continued)

Required:

Prepare the necessary journal entry for Seger to record the employer portion of these payroll taxes.

OBJECTIVE 2
CORNERSTONE 8.4

Cornerstone Exercise 8-29 Unearned Sales Revenue

Brand Landscaping offers a promotion where a customer's lawn will be mowed 20 times if the customer pays $700 in advance.

Required:

Prepare the journal entry to record (1) the customers' prepayment of $700 and (2) Brand's mowing of the lawn one time.

OBJECTIVE 2
CORNERSTONE 8.4

Cornerstone Exercise 8-30 Unearned Rent Revenue

EWO Property Management leases commercial properties. A new client signs a 3-year lease and agrees to pay the first 2 months in advance. The monthly rent is $85,000.

Required:

Prepare the journal entry to record (1) the customers' prepayment of 2 months' rent and (2) the necessary adjusting entry after 1 month has passed.

OBJECTIVE 4
CORNERSTONE 8.5

Cornerstone Exercise 8-31 Warranties

In 2013, BMJ Plumbing Company sold 250 water heaters for $1,050 each. The water heaters carry a 5-year warranty for repairs. BMJ Plumbing estimates that repair costs will average 2% of the total selling price.

Required:

1. How much is recorded in the warranty liability account as a result of selling the water heaters during 2013, assuming no warranty service has yet been performed?
2. Prepare the necessary adjusting entry at December 31, 2013.

OBJECTIVE 4
CORNERSTONE 8.5

Cornerstone Exercise 8-32 Warranties

In 2013, Waldo Balloons sold 50 hot air balloons at $25,000 each. The balloons carry a 5-year warranty for defects. Waldo estimates that repair costs will average 3% of the total selling price. The estimated warranty liability at the beginning of the year was $40,000. Claims of $15,000 were actually incurred during the year to honor their warranties.

Required:

What was the balance in the warranty liability at the end of the year?

OBJECTIVE 5
CORNERSTONE 8.6

Cornerstone Exercise 8-33 Liquidity Ratios

NWA's financial statements contain the following information:

Cash	$300,000	Accounts payable	$ 500,000
Accounts receivable	650,000	Accrued expenses	150,000
Inventory	800,000	Long-term debt	1,000,000
Marketable securities	100,000		

Note: Round answers to two decimal places.

Required:

1. What is its current ratio?
2. What is its quick ratio?
3. What is its cash ratio?
4. Discuss NWA's liquidity using these ratios.

Cornerstone Exercise 8-34 Liquidity Ratios

OBJECTIVE 5
CORNERSTONE 8.6

GER's financial statements contain the following information:

Cash	$3,125,000	Accounts payable	$ 3,500,000
Accounts receivable	3,150,000	Accrued expenses	1,800,000
Inventory	4,200,000	Long-term debt	10,000,000
Marketable securities	1,850,000		

Note: Round answers to two decimal places.

Required:

1. What is the current ratio?
2. What is the quick ratio?
3. What is the cash ratio?
4. Discuss GER's liquidity using these ratios.

BRIEF EXERCISES

Brief Exercise 8-35 Accounts Payable

OBJECTIVE 2

On May 18, Stanton Electronics purchased, on credit, 1,000 TV sets for $400 each. Stanton plans to resell these TVs in its store. Stanton paid the supplier on June 30.

Required:

Prepare the necessary journal entry (or entries) on May 18 and June 30.

Brief Exercise 8-36 Accounts and Notes Payable

OBJECTIVE 2

On February 15, Barbour Industries buys $800,000 of inventory on credit. On March 31, Barbour approaches its supplier because it cannot pay the $800,000. The supplier agrees to roll the amount into a note due on September 30 with 10% interest.

Required:

Prepare the necessary journal entries from February 15 through payment on September 30.

Brief Exercise 8-37 Issuing Notes Payable

OBJECTIVE 2

On September 30, Bello International borrows $320,000 from Chase Bank with a 9-month, 8% note.

Required:

What journal entry is made at Bello's year-end, December 31?

Brief Exercise 8-38 Notes Payable

OBJECTIVE 2

Renchen Company, which manufactures steel tubing and casing for automobile production, borrowed $500,000 on January 1 to finance the purchase of a new piece of machinery with new heating technology. The terms of Renchen's note dictate that it is a 4-month, 9%, interest-bearing note.

Required:

1. Record the borrowing transaction.
2. Record the repayment transaction.

Brief Exercise 8-39 Accrued Interest

OBJECTIVE 2

On July 1, Brimley Company issued a note with First National Bank with terms of 2 years and 10% interest to finance its inventory purchase of 1,000 plasma televisions with a list price of $2,750 each.

(Continued)

Required:

What adjusting entry should Brimley make at December 31?

OBJECTIVE 2

Brief Exercise 8-40 Accrued Interest

On May 1, the Garnett Corporation wanted to purchase a $200,000 piece of equipment, but Garnett was only able to furnish $75,000 of its own cash to purchase the equipment. Garnett borrowed the remainder of the $200,000 from the People's National Bank on a 3-year, 4% note.

Required:

If the company keeps its records on a calendar year, what adjusting entry should Garnett make on December 31?

OBJECTIVE 2

Brief Exercise 8-41 Accrued Property Taxes

Annual property taxes covering the preceding 12 months are always paid on July 1. Lou Inc. is always assessed $11,000 property taxes.

Required:

Given this information, determine the adjusting journal entry that Lou must make on December 31.

OBJECTIVE 2

Brief Exercise 8-42 Accrued Income Taxes

Nolan Inc. had taxable income of $400,000 in 2013. Its effective tax rate is 35%. Nolan pays its 2013 income taxes on April 15, 2014.

Required:

1. Given this information, determine the adjusting journal entry that Nolan must make on December 31, 2013.
2. Prepare the journal entry to record the tax payment.

OBJECTIVE 2

Brief Exercise 8-43 Accrued Wages

Natalie's Bakery pays its 20 hourly employees every Friday. Each of Natalie's employees earns a wage of $10 per hour and works 35 hours per week, spread evenly from Monday through Sunday. During the current year December 31 falls on a Tuesday.

Required:

Given this information, determine the adjusting journal entry that Natalie's Bakery must make on December 31.

OBJECTIVE 2

Brief Exercise 8-44 Accrued Wages

A company employs a part-time staff of 50 employees, each earning $10 per hour and working 30 hours per week. Employees work 5 days per week, Monday through Friday, and are paid weekly on Fridays. The appropriate journal entry was recorded at the end of the accounting period, Tuesday, April 30, 2013.

Required:

What journal entries are made on Tuesday, April 30, and Friday, May 3, 2013?

OBJECTIVE 2

Brief Exercise 8-45 Accrued Wages

Employees earn $2,500 per day, work 5 days per week, Monday through Friday, and get paid every Friday. The previous payday was Friday, March 22, and the accounting period ends on Monday, March 31.

Required:

What is the ending balance in the wages payable account on March 31?

Brief Exercise 8-46 Accrued Wages and Payment of Payroll

OBJECTIVE 2

Hansen Legal offices are open Monday through Friday, and Hansen pays employees salaries of $35,000 every other Friday. During the current year December 31 falls on a Wednesday, and the next payday is January 7.

Required:

Given this information, determine the adjusting journal entry that Hansen must make on December 31 as well as the journal entry to record the payment of the payroll on January 7.

Brief Exercise 8-47 Sales and Excise Tax

OBJECTIVE 2

Betty's Antique Shop, a shop specializing in antiques from the 19th century, recently sold a chair from the Civil War era for $60,000 on account. The state sales tax is 5%, and there is a $400-per-antique federal excise tax.

Required:

Provide the journal entry to record the sale.

Brief Exercise 8-48 Sales Tax

OBJECTIVE 2

Farrah's Furniture sold 35 couches to Angel's Inc. for $850 each plus an additional state sales tax of 7%. Angel's Inc. purchased on credit.

Required:

Provide the journal entry to record the sale (round to nearest penny).

Brief Exercise 8-49 Payroll Taxes

OBJECTIVE 2

Sid's Grocery Store has 100 employees who earn a wage of $18.75 per hour. Each of Sid's employees has worked a total of 160 hours over the month of July. At the time of recording July's monthly payroll, the following amounts have been withheld:

Federal income tax	$30,000
State income tax	8,000
Social Security	22,000
Medicare	4,750
Charitable contributions	1% of gross pay
Union dues	1% of gross pay

Also, the unemployment tax rate is 2% and applies to all but $30,000 of the gross payroll.

Required:

1. What is the amount of net pay recorded by Sid's?
2. Make the journal entries to record the payroll.

Brief Exercise 8-50 Payroll Taxes

OBJECTIVE 2

Champaign Inc., a company that provides educational consulting services to large universities across the nation, has a gross payroll of $25,000 for the pay period. The entire payroll is subject to Social Security and Medicare taxes. Champaign must also withhold $2,400 in federal income tax from the employees and pay state unemployment tax of $75. Assume employees pay 6.2% of Social Security.

Required:

Provide the necessary journal entries for Champaign to record these payroll taxes (round to nearest penny).

Brief Exercise 8-51 Payroll Taxes

OBJECTIVE 2

It's the Tooth Dental works to provide high quality pediatric dental services in a fun-loving environment for children. During December, It's the Tooth Dental employees earned $90,000 in

(*Continued*)

wages. Social Security applied to $86,000 of these wages, while Medicare applies to all $90,000. Federal and state income taxes withheld were $1,100 and $500, respectively. Assume employees pay 6.2% of Social Security.

Required:

Provide the necessary journal entries for It's the Tooth Dental to record this activity.

OBJECTIVE 2

Brief Exercise 8-52 Unearned Sales Revenue

Curtis's Carpet Cleaning normally charges $90 to clean one room of carpeting. During the holiday season, Curtis offers a promotion to clean the customer's carpet 10 times at a discounted rate if the customer pays $600 in advance.

Required:

Make the journal entry to record the following transactions.

1. A customer's prepayment of $600
2. Curtis's cleaning of the carpet one time

OBJECTIVE 2

Brief Exercise 8-53 Unearned Rent Revenue

Mannion Property Management leases commercial properties and expects its clients to pay rent on a monthly basis. A new client signs a 4-year lease with a yearly rent of $420,000 and agrees to pay the first 6 months in advance.

Required:

Make the journal entry to record the following transactions.

1. The customer's prepayment of 6 months' rent
2. The necessary adjusting entry after 1 month has passed

OBJECTIVE 3

Brief Exercise 8-54 Contingent Liabilities

Many companies provide warranties with their products. Such warranties typically guarantee the repair or replacement of defective goods for some specified period of time following the sale.

Required:

CONCEPTUAL CONNECTION Why do most warranties require companies to make a journal entry to record a liability for future warranty costs?

OBJECTIVE 3

Brief Exercise 8-55 Contingent Liabilities

SLC Electronics is the plaintiff in a class action lawsuit. Their attorney has written a letter that it is now extremely likely that SLC will lose the lawsuit and be forced to pay $3,000,000 in damages.

Required:

Prepare the necessary journal entry. If no entry is required state "none." Any recognition will be to Other Expense and Lawsuit Payable.

OBJECTIVE 4

Brief Exercise 8-56 Warranties

In 2013, Lee Electronics, a franchise of electronics stores located in small towns throughout the United States, sold 450 32-inch televisions for $575 each. The televisions carry an attached 3-year warranty for repairs. Lee Electronics estimates that repair costs will average 2% of the total selling price.

Required:

1. How much is recorded in the Warranty Liability account as a result of selling the televisions during 2013, assuming no warranty service has yet been performed?
2. Provide the necessary adjusting entry at December 31, 2013.

Brief Exercise 8-57 Warranties

OBJECTIVE 4

Wally's Party Warehouse provides wholesale party equipment and materials to Party Shops. In 2013, Wally's Party sold 30 bounce houses at $30,000 each. The bounce houses carry a 3-year warranty for defects. Wally estimates that repair costs will average 2% of the total selling price. The estimated warranty liability at the beginning of the year was $26,000. Claims of $19,000 were actually incurred during the year to honor warranties.

Required:

What was the balance in the Estimated Warranty Liability account at the end of the year?

Brief Exercise 8-58 Liquidity Ratios

OBJECTIVE 5

JRL's financial statements contain the following information:

Cash	$400,000	Accounts payable	$575,000
Accounts receivable	800,000	Accrued expenses	180,000
Inventory	950,000	Long-term debt	900,000
Marketable securities	115,000		

Required:

1. What is its current ratio?
2. What is its quick ratio?
3. What is its cash ratio?
4. Discuss JRL's liquidity using these ratios.

Brief Exercise 8-59 Liquidity Ratios

OBJECTIVE 5

SJM's financial statements contain the following information:

Cash	$2,725,000	Accounts payable	$3,275,000
Accounts receivable	3,050,000	Accrued expenses	1,700,000
Inventory	3,950,000	Long-term debt	9,100,000
Marketable securities	1,725,000		

Required:

1. What is the current ratio?
2. What is the quick ratio?
3. What is the cash ratio?
4. Discuss SJM's liquidity using these ratios.

EXERCISES

Exercise 8-60 Accrued Wages

OBJECTIVE 2

Rising Stars Gymnastics pays its hourly employees every Saturday. The weekly payroll for hourly employees is $5,000, and the employees' hours are spread evenly from Monday through Saturday. During the current year December 31 falls on a Wednesday.

Required:

Given this information, determine the adjusting journal entry that Rising Stars must make on December 31.

Exercise 8-61 Recording Various Liabilities

OBJECTIVE 2

Glenview Hardware had the following transactions that produced liabilities during 2014:

a. Purchased merchandise on credit for $30,000. (*Note:* Assume a periodic inventory system.)
b. Year-end wages of $10,000 were incurred, but not paid. Related income taxes of $1,200, Social Security of $620 (employee portion), and Medicare taxes of $145 were withheld.

(*Continued*)

c. Year-end estimated income taxes payable, but unpaid, for the year were $42,850.
d. Sold merchandise on account for $1,262, including state sales taxes of $48. (*Note:* Assume a periodic inventory system.)
e. Employer's share of Social Security and Medicare taxes for the period were $620 and $145, respectively.
f. Borrowed cash under a 90-day, 9%, $25,000 note.

Required:

Prepare the entry to record each of these transactions (treat each transaction independently).

OBJECTIVE 2

Exercise 8-62 Recording Various Liabilities

Plymouth Electronics had the following transactions that produced liabilities during 2014:

a. Purchased merchandise on credit for $80,000. (*Note:* Assume a periodic inventory system.)
b. Year-end wages of $40,000 were incurred, but not paid. Related income taxes of $13,000 and Medicare taxes of $580 were withheld. Employee wages are all above the Social Security maximum, so only Medicare was paid.
c. Year-end estimated income taxes payable, but unpaid, for the year were $113,615.
d. Sold merchandise on account for $3,636, including state sales taxes of $180. (*Note:* Assume a periodic inventory system.)
e. Employer's share of Medicare taxes for the period was $580. The taxes will be paid at a later date.
f. Borrowed cash under a 180-day, 8%, $155,000 note.

Required:

Prepare the entry to record each of these transactions (treat each transaction independently).

OBJECTIVE 1 2 4

Exercise 8-63 Reporting Liabilities

Morton Electronics had the following obligations:

a. A legally enforceable claim against the business to be paid in 3 months.
b. A guarantee given by a seller to a purchaser to repair or replace defective goods during the first 6 months following a sale.
c. An amount payable to Bank One in 10 years.
d. An amount to be paid next year to Citibank on a long-term note payable.

Required:

CONCEPTUAL CONNECTION Describe how each of these items should be reported in the balance sheet.

OBJECTIVE 2

Exercise 8-64 Accounts Payable

Sleek Ride, a company providing limo services, has a December 31 year-end date. For Sleek Ride, the following transactions occurred during the first 10 days of June:

a. Purchased, on credit, space for classified advertisements in the *New York Times* for $1,950. The advertising was run the day the space was purchased.
b. Purchased office supplies from Office Max on credit in the amount of $475.
c. One of Sleek Ride's sales staff signed a $20,000 contract to provide exclusive limo services for a large company for the remainder of the month. The salesperson's commission is 10% of service revenue. The commission will be paid July 10. (*Note:* Concern yourself only with the commission.)
d. Received electric bill for May. The bill is $4,200 and is due June 15.
e. Received a bill for $970 from Harry's Auto. Harry's repaired 10 limos for Sleek Ride in late May. Payment is due June 18.

Required:

Prepare journal entries for the above transactions.

Exercise 8-65 Accrued Liabilities

OBJECTIVE 2

Charger Inc. had the following items that require adjusting entries at the end of the year.

a. Charger pays its employees $5,000 every Friday for a 5-day work week. This year December 31 falls on a Wednesday.
b. Charger earned income of $800,000 for the year for tax purposes. Its effective tax rate is 35%. These taxes must be paid by April 15 of next year.
c. Charger borrowed $280,000 with a note payable dated August 1. This note specifies 6%. The interest and principal are due on March 31 of the following year.
d. Charger's president earns a bonus equal to 10% of income in excess of $650,000. Income for the year was $800,000. This bonus is paid in May of the following year and any expense is charged to wages expense.

Required:

Prepare the adjusting journal entries to record these transactions at the end of the current year.

Exercise 8-66 Accrued Liabilities

OBJECTIVE 2

Thornwood Tile had the following items that require adjusting entries at the end of the year.

a. Thornwood pays payroll of $180,000 every other Friday for a 2-week period. This year the last payday is Friday, December 26. (*Note:* The work week is Monday through Friday.)
b. Thornwood purchased $350,000 of tile on June 1 with a note payable requiring 12% interest. The interest and principal on this note are due within 1 year. As of December 31, Thornwood had not made any principal or interest payments.
c. Thornwood's earned income is $900,000 for the year for tax purposes. Its effective tax rate is 30%. These taxes must be paid by April 15 of next year.

Required:

Prepare the adjusting journal entries to record these transactions at the end of the current year.

Exercise 8-67 Sales Tax

OBJECTIVE 2

Far and Wide Broadband provides Internet connection services to customers living in remote areas. During February 2014, it billed a customer a total of $295,000 before taxes. Weston also must pay the following taxes on these charges:

a. State of Kansas sales tax of 6%
b. Federal excise tax of 0.2%
c. State of Kansas use tax of 0.4%

Required:

Assuming Far and Wide collects these taxes from the customer, what journal entry would Far and Wide make when the customers pay their bills?

Exercise 8-68 Payroll Accounting and Discussion of Labor Costs

OBJECTIVE 2

Blitzen Marketing Research paid its weekly and monthly payroll on January 31. The following information is available about the payroll:

Item	Amount
Monthly salaries	$237,480
Hourly wages	585,000
FICA:	
Social Security (both employee and employer)	6.20%
Medicare (both employee and employer)	1.45%
Withholding for income taxes	$108,500
Federal unemployment taxes	1,200
State unemployment taxes	4,000

(Continued)

Blitzen will pay both the employer's taxes and the taxes withheld on April 15.

Required:

1. Prepare the journal entries to record the payroll payment and the incurrence of the associated expenses and liabilities. (*Note:* Round to nearest penny.)
2. What is the employees' gross pay? What amount does Blitzen pay in excess of gross pay as a result of taxes? (*Note:* Provide both an absolute dollar amount and as a percentage of gross pay, rounding to two decimal places.)
3. How much is the employees' net pay as a percentage of total payroll related expenses? (*Note:* Round answer to two decimal places.)
4. **CONCEPTUAL CONNECTION** If another employee can be hired for $60,000 per year, what would be the total cost of this employee to Blitzen?

OBJECTIVE 2

Exercise 8-69 Unearned Revenue

Jennifer's Landscaping Services signed a $400-per-month contract on November 1, 2013, to provide plant watering services for Lola Inc.'s office buildings. Jennifer's received 4 months' service fees in advance on signing the contract.

Required:

1. Prepare Jennifer's journal entry to record the cash receipt for the first 4 months.
2. Prepare Jennifer's adjusting entry at December 31, 2013.
3. **CONCEPTUAL CONNECTION** How would the advance payment [account(s) and amount(s)] be reported in Jennifer's December 31, 2013, balance sheet? How would the advance payment [account(s) and amount(s)] be reported in Lola's December 31, 2013, balance sheet?

OBJECTIVE 3

Exercise 8-70 Recognition and Reporting of Contingent Liabilities

A list of alternative accounting treatments is followed by a list of potential contingent liabilities.

Alternative Accounting Treatments

a. Estimate the amount of liability and record.
b. Do not record as a liability but disclose in a footnote to the financial statements.
c. Neither record as a liability nor disclose in a footnote to the financial statements.

Potential Contingent Liabilities

1. Income taxes related to revenue included in net income this year but taxable in a future year
2. Potential costs in future periods associated with performing warranty services on products sold this period
3. Estimated cost of future services under a product warranty related to past sales
4. Estimated cost of future services under a product warranty related to future sales
5. Estimated cost of pension benefits related to past employee services that has yet to be funded
6. Potential loss on environmental cleanup suit against company; a court judgment against the company is considered less than probable but more than remotely likely
7. Potential loss under class-action suit by a group of customers; during the current year, the likelihood of a judgment against the company has increased from remote to possible but less than probable
8. Potential loss under an affirmative action suit by a former employee; the likelihood of a judgment against the company is considered to be remote
9. Potential loss from a downturn in future economic activity
10. Loss from out-of-court settlement of lawsuit that is likely to occur toward the end of next year

Required:

Match the appropriate alternative accounting treatment with each of the potential contingent liabilities listed above. Your answer should list the numbers 1 through 10 and, next to each number, the letter of the appropriate accounting treatment.

Exercise 8-71 Warranties

OBJECTIVE 4

Ed's Athletics sells bicycles and other sports and athletic equipment. Sales and expected warranty claims for the year are as follows:

Item	Unit Sales	Expected Warranty Claims for Warranty Period	Cost per Claim
Mountain bikes	300	3 claims per 100 sold	$30
Racing bikes	120	1 claims per 20 sold	75
Snowboards	650	2 claim per 100 sold	20

Required:

1. Prepare the entry to record warranty expense for Ed's for the year.
2. CONCEPTUAL CONNECTION Why does Ed's have to record a liability for future warranty claims?

Exercise 8-72 Ratio Analysis

OBJECTIVE 5

ILLUSTRATING RELATIONSHIPS

Intel Corporation provided the following information on its balance sheet and statement of cash flows:

Current liabilities	$8,514,000,000	Inventories	$ 4,314,000,000
Cash and equivalents	6,598,000,000	Other current assets	2,146,000,000
Marketable securities	3,404,000,000	Cash flows from operating activities	10,620,000,000
Receivables	2,709,000,000		

Required:

1. Calculate the (a) current ratio, (b) quick ratio, (c) cash ratio, and (d) operating cash flow ratio. (*Note:* Round answers to two decimal places.)
2. CONCEPTUAL CONNECTION Interpret these results.
3. CONCEPTUAL CONNECTION Assume that Intel, as a requirement of one of its loans, must maintain a current ratio of at least 2.30. Given the large amount of cash, how could Intel accomplish this on December 31 (be specific as to dollar amounts)?

PROBLEM SET A

Problem 8-73A Payable Transactions

OBJECTIVE 2

Richmond Company engaged in the following transactions during 2013:

a. Purchased $160,000 of supplies from ABC Supplies on February 16. Amount due in full on March 31.
b. Paid for 25% of the purchased merchandise (Transaction a) on February 26.
c. On March 31 negotiated a payment extension with ABC for the remainder of the balance from the February 16 purchase by signing a 1-year, 10% note.
d. Borrowed $300,000 on a 10-month, 8% interest-bearing note on April 30.
e. Purchased $78,000 of merchandise on June 4. Amount due in full on June 30.
f. Paid for the purchased merchandise (Transaction e) on June 24.
g. Received from Haywood Inc. on August 19, a $22,000 deposit against a total selling price of $220,000 for services to be performed for Haywood.
h. Paid quarterly installments of Social Security and Medicare and individual income tax withholdings, as shown below, on October 15. The Social Security and Medicare were previously recorded as expenses during the quarter and the amounts paid represent both the employee and employer shares (50% each):

Social Security taxes	$185,000
Medicare taxes	43,266
Income taxes withheld	319,000

i. On December 15, Richmond completed the services ordered by Haywood on August 19. Haywood's remaining balance of $198,000 is due on January 31.

(*Continued*)

Required:

1. Prepare journal entries for these transactions.
2. Prepare any adjusting entries necessary at December 31, 2013.

OBJECTIVE 2

Problem 8-74A Payroll Accounting

Jet Enterprises has the following data available for its April 30, 2013, payroll:

Wages earned	$485,000*
Income taxes withheld	92,300

* All subject to Social Security and Medicare matching and withholding of 6.2% and 1.45%, respectively.

Federal unemployment taxes of 0.70% and state unemployment taxes of 0.90% are payable on $405,700 of the wages earned.

Required:

1. Compute the amounts of taxes payable and the amount of wages that will be paid to employees. Then prepare the journal entries to record the wages earned and the payroll taxes. (*Note:* Round to the nearest penny.)
2. **CONCEPTUAL CONNECTION** Jet would like to hire a new employee at a salary of $65,000. Assuming payroll taxes are as described above (with unemployment taxes paid on the first $9,000) and fringe benefits (e.g., health insurance, retirement, etc.) are 25% of gross pay, what will be the total cost of this employee for Jet?

OBJECTIVE 2

Problem 8-75A Note Payable and Accrued Interest

Fairborne Company borrowed $600,000 on an 8%, interest-bearing note on October 1, 2013. Fairborne ends its fiscal year on December 31. The note was paid with interest on May 1, 2014.

Required:

1. Prepare the entry for this note on October 1, 2013.
2. Prepare the adjusting entry for this note on December 31, 2013.
3. Indicate how the note and the accrued interest would appear in the balance sheet at December 31, 2013.
4. Prepare the entry to record the repayment of the note on May 1, 2014.

OBJECTIVE 2

Problem 8-76A Interest-Bearing Note Replacing an Unpaid Account Payable

Conti Products owed $80,000 on account for inventory purchased on December 1, 2014. Conti uses a perpetual inventory system and has a fiscal year that ends on December 31. Conti was unable to pay the amount owed by the March 1, 2015, due date because of financial difficulties. On March 1, 2015, Conti signed a 4-month, $80,000, 6% interest-bearing note. This note was repaid with interest on July 1, 2015.

Required:

1. Prepare the entry recorded on December 1, 2014.
2. Prepare the adjusting entry recorded on December 31, 2014.
3. Prepare the entry recorded on March 1, 2015.
4. Prepare the entry recorded on July 1, 2015.

OBJECTIVE 2

Problem 8-77A Excise Taxes

Reagan Gas provides gas utilities to a wide area of eastern Illinois. During May 2013 it billed 36,000 of its residential customers located in the town of Moline a total of $3,295,000 for electricity (this is considered revenue). In addition Reagan is required to collect the following taxes:

a. State excise tax: A tax of $5.00 per customer plus 3% of billing used to fund the Illinois Energy Commission
b. Federal excise tax: A tax of $0.45 per customer plus 0.2% of billing used to fund the Federal Energy Commission

Required:

1. Determine how much Reagan will bill these customers in total for the month of May 2013.
2. Prepare the entry to record the billing of these amounts.
3. Prepare the entry to record the collection of these amounts.
4. Prepare the entry to record the payment of the state excise taxes to the appropriate governmental unit.

Problem 8-78A Unearned Revenue and Customer Deposits

OBJECTIVE 2

On November 20, 2013, Green Bay Electronics agreed to manufacture and supply 750 electronic control units used by Wausau Heating Systems in large commercial and industrial installments. On that date, Wausau deposited $250 per unit upon signing the 3-year purchase agreement, which set the selling price of each control unit at $1,000. Green Bay's inventory cost is $225 per unit. No units were delivered during 2013. The first 200 units will be delivered in 2014, 300 units will be delivered during 2015, and the remaining units will be delivered during 2016. Assume Green Bay uses a perpetual inventory system, and Wausau pays in cash upon delivery of units for amounts not covered by the deposit.

Required:

1. **CONCEPTUAL CONNECTION** Prepare the entry by Green Bay to record receipt of the deposit during 2013. How would the deposit be reported in the financial statements at the end of 2013?
2. **CONCEPTUAL CONNECTION** Prepare the entry by Green Bay to record the delivery of 200 units during 2014. How would the deposit be reported in the financial statements at the end of 2014?
3. Prepare the entry by Green Bay to record the delivery of 300 units during 2015.

Problem 8-79A Warranties

OBJECTIVE 4

Lincoln Repairs and Detailing has recently opened its doors to provide quality auto repair services. To encourage business, Lincoln offers a 9-month warranty on all repairs. The following data are available for 2013:

Transmissions repaired, 2013	1,980
Expected frequency of warranty claims	0.05 per repair
Actual warranty claims, 2013	$26,200
Estimated warranty liability, 1/1/13	$28,000
Estimated cost of each warranty claim	$ 220

Assume that warranty claims are paid in cash.

Required:

1. Compute the warranty expense for 2013.
2. Prepare the entry to record the payment of the 2013 warranty claims.
3. **CONCEPTUAL CONNECTION** What is the December 31, 2013, balance in the estimated warranty liability account? Why has the balance in the warranty liability account changed from January 1, 2013?

OBJECTIVE 5

Problem 8-80A Ratio Analysis

Consider the following information taken from GER's financial statements:

	September 30 (in thousands)	
	2014	2013
Current assets:		
Cash and cash equivalents	$ 1,274	$ 6,450
Receivables	30,071	16,548
Inventories	31,796	14,072
Other current assets	4,818	2,620
Total current assets	$67,959	$39,690
Current liabilities:		
Current portion of long-term debt	$ 97	$ 3,530
Accounts payable	23,124	11,228
Accrued compensation costs	5,606	1,929
Accrued expenses	9,108	5,054
Other current liabilities	874	777
Total current liabilities	$38,809	$22,518

Also, GER's operating cash flows were $12,829 and $14,874 in 2014 and 2013, respectively.
Note: Round all answers to two decimal places.

Required:

1. Calculate the current ratios for 2014 and 2013.
2. Calculate the quick ratios for 2014 and 2013.
3. Calculate the cash ratios for 2014 and 2013.
4. Calculate the operating cash flow ratios for 2014 and 2013.
5. **CONCEPTUAL CONNECTION** Provide some reasons why GER's liquidity may be considered to be improving and some reasons why it may be worsening.

PROBLEM SET B

OBJECTIVE 2

Problem 8-73B Payable Transactions

Daniels Company engaged in the following transactions during 2014:

a. Purchased $25,000 of merchandise from XYZ Supplies on January 26. Amount due in full on February 28.
b. Paid for 40% of the purchased merchandise (Transaction a) on February 26.
c. On February 28, negotiate a payment extension with XYZ for the remainder of the balance from the January 26 purchase by signing a 1-year, 8% note.
d. Borrowed $300,000 on an 8-month, 9% interest-bearing note on July 31.
e. Purchased $150,000 of merchandise on August 2. Amount due in full on September 30.
f. Paid for the purchased merchandise (Transaction e) on September 28.
g. Received from Martel Inc. on October 4, a $40,000 deposit against a total selling price of $400,000 for services to be performed for Martel.
h. Paid quarterly installments of Social Security, Medicare, and individual income tax withholdings, as shown below, on October 10. The Social Security and Medicare were previously recorded as expenses during the quarter and the amounts paid represent both the employee and employer shares (50% each).

Social Security taxes	$280,000
Medicare taxes	65,484
Income taxes withheld	730,000

i. On December 15, Daniels completed the services ordered by Martel on October 4. Martel's remaining balance of $360,000 is due on January 31.

Required:

1. Prepare journal entries for these transactions.
2. Prepare any adjusting entries necessary at December 31, 2014.

Problem 8-74B Payroll Accounting

OBJECTIVE 2

McLaughlin Manufacturing has the following data available for its March 31, 2013, payroll:

Wages earned	$1,250,000*
Income taxes withheld	180,600

* All subject to Social Security and Medicare matching and withholding at 6.2% and 1.45%, respectively.

Federal unemployment taxes of 0.50% and state unemployment taxes of 0.80% are payable on the first $1,000,000.

Required:

1. Compute the taxes payable and wages that will be paid to employees. Then prepare the journal entries to record the wages earned and the payroll taxes. (*Note:* Round to the nearest penny.)
2. **CONCEPTUAL CONNECTION** McLaughlin Manufacturing would like to hire a new employee at a salary of $80,000. Assuming payroll taxes are as described above (with unemployment taxes paid on the first $7,000) and fringe benefits (e.g., health insurance, retirement, etc.) are 28% of gross pay, what will be the total cost of this employee for McLaughlin?

Problem 8-75B Note Payable and Accrued Interest

OBJECTIVE 2

Ellsworth Enterprises borrowed $425,000 on an 8%, interest-bearing note on September 30, 2014. Ellsworth ends its fiscal year on December 31. The note was paid with interest on March 31, 2015.

Required:

1. Prepare the entry for this note on September 30, 2014.
2. Prepare the adjusting entry for this note on December 31, 2014.
3. Indicate how the note and the accrued interest would appear on the balance sheet at December 31, 2014.
4. Prepare the entry to record the repayment of the note on March 31, 2015.

Problem 8-76B Interest-Bearing Note Replacing an Unpaid Account Payable

OBJECTIVE 2

Monte Cristo Products, which uses a perpetual inventory system, owed $770,000 on account for inventory purchased on November 1, 2014. The company's fiscal year ends on December 31. Monte Cristo was unable to pay the amount owed by the February 1 due date because of financial difficulties. On February 1, 2015, it signed a $770,000, 12% interest-bearing note. This note was repaid with interest on September 1, 2015.

Required:

1. Prepare the entry recorded on November 1, 2014.
2. Prepare the adjusting entry recorded on December 31, 2014.
3. Prepare the entry recorded on February 1, 2015.
4. Prepare the entry recorded on September 1, 2015.

Problem 8-77B Excise Taxes

OBJECTIVE 2

Yossarian Power Corporation provides electricity to a wide area of eastern Maine. During March 2014, it billed 3,000 of its residential customers located in the town of Maryville a total of $393,000 for electricity. In addition Yossarian Power is required to collect the following taxes:

(*Continued*)

a. State excise tax: A tax of $3.50 per customer plus 2% of billing used to fund the Maine Energy Commission
b. Federal excise tax: A tax of $0.50 per customer plus 0.15% of billing used to fund the Federal Energy Commission

Required:

1. Determine how much Yossarian Power will bill these 3,000 customers in total for the month of March 2014.
2. Prepare the entry to record the billing of these amounts.
3. Prepare the entry to record the collection of these amounts.
4. Prepare the entry to record the payment of the state excise taxes to the appropriate governmental unit.

OBJECTIVE 2

Problem 8-78B Unearned Revenue and Customer Deposits

On December 10, 2013, Kool-Air Solutions agreed to manufacture and supply 800 refrigerators used by Vandelay Industries. Vandelay deposited $150 per unit upon signing the 3-year purchase agreement, which set the selling price of each refrigerator at $950. Kool-Air's inventory cost is $425 per unit. No units were delivered during 2013. During 2014, 175 units will be delivered; during 2015, 325 units will be delivered; and during 2016, the remaining units will be delivered. Assume Kool-Air uses a perpetual inventory system and Vandelay pays in cash upon delivery of units for amounts not covered by the deposit.

Required:

1. **CONCEPTUAL CONNECTION** Prepare the entry by Kool-Air to record receipt of the deposit during 2013. How would the deposit be reported in the financial statements at the end of 2013?
2. **CONCEPTUAL CONNECTION** Prepare the entry by Kool-Air to record the delivery of 175 units during 2014. How would the deposit be reported in the financial statements at the end of 2014?
3. Prepare the entry by Kool-Air to record the delivery of 325 units during 2015.

OBJECTIVE 4

Problem 8-79B Warranties

Montague Auto Repair specializes in the repair of foreign car transmissions. To encourage business, Montague offers a 6-month warranty on all repairs. The following data are available for 2013:

Transmissions repaired, 2013	4,500
Expected frequency of warranty claims	0.09 per repair
Actual warranty claims, 2013	$110,000
Estimated warranty liability, 1/1/13	$ 25,000
Estimated cost of each warranty claim	$ 250

Assume that warranty claims are paid in cash.

Required:

1. Compute the warranty expense for 2013.
2. Prepare the entry to record the payment of the 2013 warranty claims.
3. **CONCEPTUAL CONNECTION** What is the December 31, 2013, balance in the warranty liability account? Why has the balance in the warranty liability account changed from January 1, 2013?

OBJECTIVE 5

Problem 8-80B Ratio Analysis

Consider the following information taken from Chicago Water Slide's (CWS's) financial statements:

4. Compare Under Armour's and VF's short-term liquidity based on the values and trends of the current ratios.
5. Calculate Under Armour's and VF's quick ratios and cash ratios for 2010 and 2011. (*Note:* Round answers to two decimal places.)
6. Compare the values and trends of these ratios when evaluating Under Armour's and VF's short-term liquidity.
7. Calculate Under Armour's and VF's operating cash flows ratios for 2010 and 2011. (*Note:* Round answers to two decimal places.)
8. Compare Under Armour's and VF's short-term liquidity based on the values and trends of the operating cash flows ratio.

Case 8-85 CONTINUING PROBLEM: FRONT ROW ENTERTAINMENT

Front Row has the following selected balances at the February 28, 2014:

Account	Debit	Credit
Cash	$12,480	
Accounts receivable	3,900	
Inventory	20,380	
Other current assets	31,000	
Accounts payable		$ 8,640
Interest payable		375
Sales taxes payable		1,200
Unearned sales revenue		26,100
Other current liabilities		8,300

The following information is *not* reflected in these balances:

a. On February 28, 2014, Front Row accepted delivery of $5,325 of live-performance DVDs from the supplier. Front Row has not yet paid the supplier.
b. On February 1, Front Row purchased $8,000 of equipment for its Chicago Music House venue by issuing a 1-year note payable bearing 10% interest. Front Row has not made any journal entries related to this transaction and should accrue for this at month's end. (*Note:* Round any calculations to the nearest dollar.)
c. Front Row collected $3,745 of advance ticket sales related to an upcoming concert. This price included 7% state sales tax.
d. Amanda Wilson was paid $2,000 in wages to update and monitor the online fan communities. Federal and state unemployment taxes are $16 and $108, respectively. All of Amanda's wages are subject to Social Security (assume employees pay 6.2% of Social Security and 1.45% of Medicare). In addition, $375 of income taxes were withheld. (*Note:* Round any calculations to the nearest dollar.)

In addition, several individuals were injured during a concert in February when they pushed past security and rushed the stage. A personal injury lawsuit was filed against Front Row in the amount of $250,000. After investigating the incident and consultation with legal counsel, it was determined that the likelihood of a judgment against Front Row is remote.

Required:

1. Prepare the necessary journal entries for Transactions a through d. (*Note:* Round all calculations to the nearest dollar.)
2. Determine the current ratio before and after the additional information (round to 2 decimal places).
3. How should this contingent event be recorded?

9

Long-Term Liabilities

© Pixelfabrik/Alamy

After studying Chapter 9, you should be able to:

1. Describe debt securities and the markets in which they are issued.
2. Account for the issuance of long-term debt.
3. Use the straight-line method to account for premium/discount amortization.
4. Use the effective interest rate method to account for premium/discount amortization.
5. Determine the after-tax cost of financing with debt and explain financial leverage.
6. Compare and contrast operating and capital leases.
7. Analyze a company's long-term solvency using information related to long-term liabilities.
8. *(Appendix 9A)* Calculate the market price of long-term debt using present value techniques.

razihusin/Shutterstock.com

EXPERIENCE FINANCIAL ACCOUNTING

with American Airlines

AMR Corporation is the parent company of **American Airlines**, **AMR Eagle**, and **AmericanConnection** airlines. These airlines serve more than 250 cities in approximately 50 countries and average about 3,400 flights per day with approximately 900 airplanes. In 2011, AMR had revenues of just under $24 billion and total assets of $23.8 billion. However, AMR also has long-term debt and pension obligations (including current portions) of $17.4 billion.

Industries that use property, plant, and equipment to generate revenues (such as airlines and hotels) typically have higher debt than industries that use intangible assets (such as pharmaceuticals and software).

Companies use long-term debt, along with issuing stock (see Chapter 10), as a way to finance and expand their operations. One measure used to evaluate the mix of debt and equity financing is the long-term debt to equity ratio. A ratio above 1.0 indicates that liabilities are greater than stockholders' equity. According to **Reuters Finance**, the long-term debt to equity ratio for the airline industry is 1.32. Compare this with the pharmaceutical industry that has an average long-term debt to equity ratio of 0.12. Why do airlines have so much more debt than pharmaceutical companies?

Industries that use property, plant, and equipment (PP&E) to generate revenues (such as airlines and hotels) typically have higher debt than industries that use intangible assets (such as pharmaceuticals and software). There are a number of reasons for this, but one is that PP&E is readily transferable to creditors in the event of financial distress, so creditors are more receptive to lending at lower rates.

There is a long history of finance research investigating the optimal mix of debt and equity financing because there are advantages and disadvantages for both. Factors affecting the optimal mix are difficult to quantify.

Relatively large amounts of long-term debt are not necessarily bad. Although more long-term debt means more interest expense, interest expense has the advantage of being tax deductible, unlike dividends paid to stockholders. Another advantage is that creditors do not share in the profits of the company, while stockholders do. Thus, if the borrowed money creates a return that is greater than the interest expense on the debt, the stockholders benefit. This is the concept of leverage. We will discuss this concept more in Chapter 12.

Long-term debt generally refers to obligations that extend beyond 1 year. Bonds, long-term notes, debentures, and capital leases belong in this category of liabilities. Exhibit 9.1 shows Whirlpool's long-term debt obligations.[1]

EXHIBIT 9.1

Excerpt from Whirlpool's 2011 10-K (Note 5)

NOTE 5
FINANCING ARRANGEMENTS

	December 31	
	2011	**2010**
	Millions of dollars	
Senior note—6.125%, maturing 2011	$ —	$ 300
Senior note—8.0%, maturing 2012	350	350
Medium-term note—5.5%, maturing 2013	500	500
Maytag medium-term note—6.5%, maturing 2014	101	101
Senior note—8.6%, maturing 2014	500	500
Maytag medium-term note—5.0%, maturing 2015	195	193
Senior note—6.5%, maturing 2016	249	249
Debentures—7.75%, maturing 2016	244	244
Senior note—4.85%, maturing 2021	300	—
Other (various maturing through 2019)	51	70
	2,490	2,507
Less current maturities	361	312
Total long-term debt, net of current maturities	$2,129	$2,195

Source: Whirlpool Corporation, 2011 10-K

On the balance sheet, long-term debt is typically reported as a single number. The more detailed list, like this one for Whirlpool, is usually included in the notes to the financial statements.

Notice that Whirlpool subtracted current maturities (just before the bottom line) from the rest of its long-term debt. The difference ($2,129 for 2011) is the amount included as long-term debt on the balance sheet. As we noted in Chapter 8, long-term debt that is due to mature over the next year is reported as a current liability. For simplification, we will disregard the reclassification of long-term debt as current liabilities throughout this chapter.

OBJECTIVE 1

Describe debt securities and the markets in which they are issued.

BONDS PAYABLE AND NOTES PAYABLE

When a company borrows money from a bank, it typically signs a formal agreement or contract called a "note." Frequently, notes are also issued in exchange for a noncash asset such as equipment. Collectively, we refer to these notes as **notes payable**. Larger corporations typically elect to issue bonds instead of notes. A **bond** is a type of note that requires the issuing entity to pay the face value of the bond to the holder when it

[1] We use the term *debt* instead of *liabilities* in this chapter because this is the term used in real financial statements.

matures and usually to pay interest periodically at a specified rate.[2] A bond issue essentially breaks down a large debt (large corporations frequently borrow hundreds of millions of dollars) into smaller chunks (usually $1,000) because the total amount borrowed is too large for a single lender. For example, rather than try to find a single bank willing (and able) to lend $800,000,000 at a reasonable interest rate, corporations typically find it easier and more economical to issue 800,000 bonds with a $1,000 face value. However, the concept behind the way we account for notes and bonds is identical (the only difference is the account title—either "Bonds Payable" or "Notes Payable"), and analysts typically do not distinguish between the two. As such, the terms have come to be used somewhat interchangeably.

All such contracts require the borrower to repay the **face value** (also called **par value** or **principal**). Typically the face value is repaid at **maturity**, which is a specified date in the future. However, some contracts require the principal to be repaid in, for example, monthly installments. These contracts typically require equal payments to be made each period. A portion of each payment is interest and a portion is principal. Car, student, and home loans are examples of installment loans.

Most debt contracts also require that the borrower make regular interest payments. Historically, interest payments were made when a bondholder detached a coupon from the debt contract and mailed it to the company on the interest payment date. These obligations are called *coupon notes*, *coupon debentures*, or *coupon bonds*, and the required interest payments are *coupon payments*. The terminology for coupons is still used today, but now the payments are automatically sent to the registered bondholder.

The amount of each interest payment can be calculated from the face amount, the interest rate, and the number of payments per year, all stated in the debt contract. (The **interest rate** identified in the contract goes by various names, including **stated rate**, **coupon rate**, and **contract rate**.) Recall the formula for calculating interest:

$$\text{Face Value} \times \text{Interest Rate} \times \text{Time (in years)}$$

To illustrate, consider a contract with a face amount of $1,000, a stated interest rate of 8%, and semiannual interest payments. For this $1,000 note, the amount of each semiannual interest payment is $40:

$$\$1{,}000 \times 8\% \times 6/12 = \$40$$

Types of Bonds

In practice, bonds also differ along a number of other dimensions, as illustrated in Exhibit 9.2 (p. 472).

Secured Bonds A **secured** bond has some collateral pledged against the corporation's ability to pay. For example, **mortgage bonds** are secured by real estate. In this case, should the borrower fail to make the payments required by the bond, the lender can take possession of (repossess) the real estate that secures the bond. The real estate provides "security" for the lender in case the debt is not paid. Bonds are also frequently secured by the stocks or bonds of other corporations and, in theory, can be secured by anything of value.

Unsecured Bonds Most bonds, however, are **unsecured**. These are typically called **debenture bonds**. In this case, there is no collateral; instead, the lender is relying on the general credit of the corporation. What this really means is, should the borrower go bankrupt, any secured bondholders will get their collateral before the unsecured bondholders receive a single penny. That is, unsecured bondholders are the last lenders to be paid in bankruptcy (only the stockholders follow).

[2] Interest is generally paid semiannually. We use both semiannual and annual interest payments in the text to better illustrate interest amortization.

EXHIBIT 9.2

Long-Term Debt Terms

Notes/Bonds	Debt instruments that require borrowers to pay the lender the face value and usually to make periodic interest payments.
Face Value/Par Value/Principal	Amount of money the borrower agrees to repay at maturity.
Maturity Date	Date on which the borrower agrees to pay the creditor the face (or par) value.
Stated/Coupon/Contract Rate	Rate of interest paid on the face (or par) value. The borrower pays the interest to the creditor each period until maturity.
Market/Yield Rate	Market rate of interest demanded by creditors. This is a function of economic factors and the creditworthiness of the borrower. It may differ from the stated rate.
Secured Bonds	Secured debt provides collateral (such as real estate or another asset) for the lender. If the borrower fails to make the payments required by the debt, the lender can take steps to "repossess" the collateral.
Unsecured/Debenture Bonds	Debt that does not have collateral is unsecured. Unsecured bonds typically are called debenture bonds.
Junk Bonds	Unsecured bonds that are relatively risky and, therefore, pay a high rate of interest to compensate the lender for the added risk.
Callable Bonds	Bonds that give the borrower the option to pay off the debt prior to maturity. Borrowers typically exercise this option when the interest being paid on the debt is substantially greater than the current market rate of interest.
Convertible Bonds	Bonds that give the lender the option to convert the bond into other securities—typically shares of common stock. Lenders will typically exercise this option when the value of the shares of common stock is more attractive than the interest and principal payments supplied by the debt instrument.

You may have heard of the term **junk bonds**. These are unsecured bonds where the risk of the borrower failing to make the interest and/or principal payments is relatively high. Why would anyone lend money under such circumstances? Because they receive a high enough rate of interest to compensate them for the risk.

Callable Bonds **Callable bonds** give the borrower the right to pay off (or call) the bonds prior to their due date. The borrower typically "calls" debt when the interest rate being paid is much higher than the current market conditions. This is similar to homeowners "refinancing" to obtain a lower interest rate on their home mortgage.

Convertible Bonds **Convertible bonds** allow the bondholder to convert the bond into another security—typically common stock. Convertible bonds will specify the conversion ratio. For example, each $1,000 bond may be convertible into 20 shares of common stock. In this case, bondholders will convert when the value of the 20 shares becomes more attractive than the interest payments and repayment of the $1,000 principal.

Selling New Debt Securities

Borrowing, through the use of notes or bonds, is attractive to businesses as a source of money because the relative cost of issuing debt (the interest payments) is often lower than the cost of issuing equity (giving up ownership shares). Businesses may sell bonds directly to institutions such as insurance companies or pension funds. However, bonds are frequently sold to the public through an underwriter. Underwriters generate a profit either by offering a price that is slightly less than the expected market price (thereby producing a profit on resale) or by charging the borrower a fee.

Underwriters examine the provisions of the instrument (secured or unsecured, callable or not callable, convertible or not convertible), the credit standing of the borrowing business, and the current conditions in the credit markets and the economy as a whole to determine the **market rate** of interest (or **yield**) for the bond. The yield may differ from the stated rate because the underwriter disagrees with the borrower as to the correct yield or because of changes in the economy or creditworthiness of the borrower between the setting of the stated rate and the date of issue.

As shown in Exhibit 9.3, there are three possible relationships between the stated interest rate and yield: (1) they can be equal, (2) the yield can be less than the stated rate, or (3) the yield can be greater than the stated rate. If the yield is equal to the stated rate, the bonds sell for the face value, or par. If the yield is less than the stated rate, the bonds represent particularly good investments because the interest payments are higher than market. In this case, the demand for such bonds will bid the selling price up above face value. When this happens, bonds are said to sell at a **premium**. On the other hand, if the yield is greater than the stated rate of interest, the below market interest payments will drive the selling price below the face value, in which case, the bond would sell at a **discount**.

concept Q&A

Why is the market value of bonds not always equal to their face value?

Answer:

If, for example, the stated rate of interest is higher than the market rate of interest, the bonds represent particularly good investments. As such, the demand for such bonds will bid the price up above face value. On the other hand, if the stated rate of interest is lower than the market rate of interest, the lack of demand for such bonds will bid the market price below face value.

EXHIBIT 9.3

The Relationships between Stated Interest Rate and Yield

Bonds Sold at	Yield Compared to Stated Rate	Interest over the Life of the Bonds
Premium (above Par)	Yield < Stated Rate	Interest Expense < Interest Paid
Par	Yield = Stated Rate	Interest Expense = Interest Paid
Discount (below Par)	Yield > Stated Rate	Interest Expense > Interest Paid

YOUDECIDE Fixed versus Variable-Rate Debt

You are the CFO of Carmean Corp. Carmean has decided to borrow $100,000,000 to finance expansion plans. One option is to issue 20-year bonds with a fixed rate of 8%. Carmean's investment bankers believe these will sell for par. Another option is to issue 20-year bonds with a variable rate of 1-year LIBOR (London Interbank Offered Rate) plus 5.4%. For the first year, this will result in a 6.5% rate, but the rate will be adjusted annually.

What types of things should you consider in making the decision about which borrowing option is best for Carmean?

Borrowers must trade off the potential benefit of lower rates with the risk of the rate increasing in the future. In fact, risk is what the difference in rates is all about. With a fixed rate, the lender bears all the risk of changing rates. Specifically, if fixed rates increase dramatically, the lender is stuck with a below market return. Admittedly, if rates were to drop, the lender has an above market return, but this uncertainty is the definition of risk. With a variable rate, on the other hand, the borrower bears the risk (and rewards) of changing rates. The shift of risk from the lender to the borrower is why the lender is willing to accept a lower rate initially.

Borrowers must consider terms of the contract, such as how frequently the rate is adjusted, the length of the loan, limits on how much the rate can increase each year, or how high the rate can go, etc. Additionally, the borrower must consider its ability to handle increased interest payments should the rate adjust up.

In this case, Carmean should only opt for the lower variable rate if the company can absorb the higher interest payments should the rate adjust up.

OBJECTIVE 2

Account for the issuance of long-term debt.

ACCOUNTING FOR LONG-TERM DEBT

The accounting for notes and bonds is conceptually identical, so keep in mind that, in the bond and note examples that follow, everything would stay the same if we substituted the word note for bond and vice versa.

There are three basic cash flows for which the issuing corporation must account:

- issuance: the cash received when the bonds are issued (the issue or selling price)
- interest: the interest payments
- repayment: the repayment of the principal (or face value)

IFRS

The accounting for notes payable and bonds payable is generally the same under IFRS as it is for U.S. GAAP.

Assume that a corporation issues bonds with a total face value of $500,000, with a stated rate of 6.5% payable annually, and the principal is due in 5 years. Exhibit 9.4 depicts all three cash flows.

EXHIBIT 9.4

Cash Flows for a Bond

Face value:	$500,000	**Stated rate:**	6.5%
Due:	5 years	**Interest payments:**	$500,000 × 6.5% × (12/12)

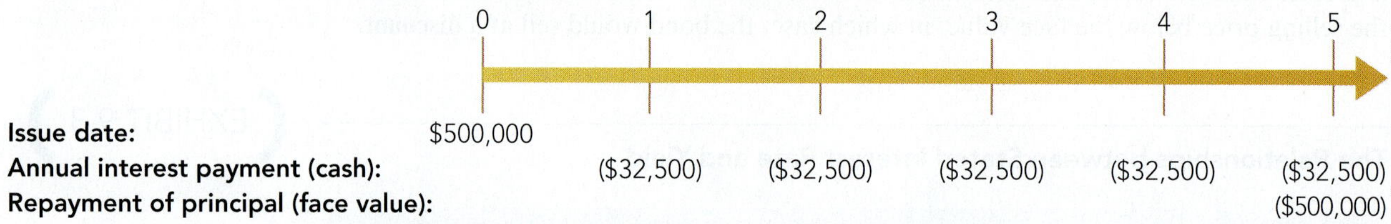

Recording Issuance

The market price for debt is typically quoted as a percentage of face value. For example, if $100,000 face value bonds are issued at 103, their selling price is 103% of face value, or $103,000. Any amount paid above the face value is called a *premium*. In this case, a $3,000 premium was paid. If the bond is issued below face value, this difference is called a *discount*. For example, if these $100,000 face value bonds were issued at 96, there would be a $4,000 discount.

At the time of issue, the borrower records the face value of the bonds in a bond payable account and records any premium or discount in a separate account called Premium on Bonds Payable or Discount on Bonds Payable. The premium and discount accounts are called "valuation" accounts because they affect the value at which the liability is shown on the balance sheet. That is, as shown in Exhibit 9.5, both the premium and discount accounts are netted with bonds payable on the balance sheet, so on the date of issue the book value of the bonds payable is equal to the market value.

EXHIBIT 9.5

Balance Sheet Presentation

Long-term liabilities:				Long-term liabilities:		
Bonds payable	$100,000		**OR**	Bonds payable	$100,000	
Add: Premium on bonds payable	3,000			Less: Discount on bonds payable	(4,000)	
		$103,000				$96,000

Cornerstone 9.1 illustrates recording the issuance of bonds.

Recording the Issuance of Bonds

CORNERSTONE 9.1

Why:

When bonds are issued, any premium or discount is recorded in a separate valuation account.

Information:

On December 31, 2013, Vampatella Co. issued $100,000 face value of bonds, with a stated rate of 8%, due in 5 years with interest payable annually on December 31.

Required:

Prepare the journal entries assuming the bonds sell (1) for par, (2) for 103, and (3) for 96.

Solution:

Date	Account and Explanation	Debit	Credit
1. Dec. 31, 2013	Cash	100,000	
	Bonds Payable		100,000
	(Record issuance of bonds at par)		
2. Dec. 31, 2013	Cash (100,000 × 103%)	103,000	
	Bonds Payable		100,000
	Premium on Bonds Payable		3,000
	(Record issuance of bonds at premium)		
3. Dec. 31, 2013	Cash (100,000 × 96%)	96,000	
	Discount on Bonds Payable	4,000	
	Bonds Payable		100,000
	(Record issuance of bonds at discount)		

Assets	= Liabilities +	Stockholders' Equity
+100,000	+100,000	

Assets	= Liabilities +	Stockholders' Equity
+103,000	+100,000 +3,000	

Assets	= Liabilities +	Stockholders' Equity
+96,000	+100,000 −4,000	

RECOGNIZING INTEREST EXPENSE AND REPAYMENT OF PRINCIPAL

OBJECTIVE 3

Use the straight-line method to account for premium/discount amortization.

Recognizing repayment of the principal at maturity is trivial. Recall that the principal amount repaid is equal to the face value of the note. This is also the amount that was originally credited to the note or bond payable. As such, you merely need to debit the note or bond payable and credit the cash.

Recognizing the interest expense, on the other hand, is a bit more challenging because, conceptually, any premium received or discount granted by the borrower should be offset against future interest payments. In our examples above, when the bonds were issued at par (face value) the amount of cash received when issued was equal to the amount to be repaid at maturity. When the bonds were issued at a premium, the amount of cash received when issued was $103,000 ($3,000 greater than the face value), but only the face value ($100,000) is repaid at maturity. The $3,000 difference represents an effective reduction of the amount of interest paid to the borrower. In contrast, when the bonds were issued at a discount, the amount of cash received was $96,000 ($4,000 less than the face value), but the entire face value ($100,000) must be repaid at maturity. The additional $4,000 effectively represents additional interest.

> **concept Q&A**
>
> Why are premiums and discounts on bonds payable amortized to Interest Expense?
>
> **Answer:**
>
> Discounts occur when the stated rate of interest is below the market rate of interest. In this case, lenders lend less than the face value to the borrower but are repaid the entire face value at maturity. This difference between the amount lent and the amount repaid conceptually represents an additional interest payment to compensate the lender for accepting a below market interest rate. Similarly, premiums occur when the stated rate of interest is above the market rate of interest. In this case, lenders lend more than the face value to the borrower but are only repaid the face value at maturity. This difference represents a prepayment of interest by the lender to compensate the borrower for providing above market interest payments.

When an obligation extends over several interest periods, the amount of interest associated with each period also must be determined. **Interest amortization** is the process used to determine the amount of interest to be recorded in each of the periods the liability is outstanding.[3]

This allocation has two parts:

- actual interest payment made to the lender during the period
- amortizing any premium or discount on the bond

Interest Amortization Methods

Although the interest payment made to the lender during the period is always a component of the period's interest expense, there are two methods for amortizing any premium or discount:

- The **effective interest rate method** is based on compound interest calculations. Interest expense for the period is always the yield (the effective interest rate) times the carrying (or book) value of the bonds at the beginning of the period.
- The **straight-line method**, on the other hand, represents a simple approximation of effective interest amortization. Equal amounts of premium or discount are amortized to interest expense each period.

Although the effective interest rate method is GAAP, the straight-line method may be used if it produces approximately the same numerical results as the effective interest rate method. Frequently, the two methods do, in fact, produce quite similar results.

THE STRAIGHT-LINE METHOD

We will now discuss how interest expense is allocated to the various accounting periods using the straight-line method for:

- debt with regular interest payments sold at their face or par value
- debt with regular interest payments sold for more (a premium) or less (a discount) than the face or par value

Debt with Regular Interest Payments Sold at Par

When debt is sold at par, there is no premium or discount to amortize. In this case, the interest expense reported on the income statement is equal to the interest payment(s) made to the creditor during the period. This situation typically happens when a business borrows from a single creditor. In this case, the two parties can easily agree on a stated rate that equals the appropriate yield. Cornerstone 9.2 illustrates how interest expense is recorded in this case.

CORNERSTONE 9.2

Recording Interest Expense for Bonds Sold at Par

Why:

When bonds are issued at par, there is no discount or premium to amortize, so the only component of interest expense is the interest paid to the lender for the period.

Information:

On December 31, 2013, Vampatella Co. issued $100,000 of 8% bonds at par. These bonds are due in 5 years with interest payable annually on December 31.

(Continued)

[3] The same interest amortization procedures used by borrowers to account for liabilities are also used by lenders to account for the corresponding assets.

Required:

1. Calculate the interest payment made on December 31 of each year.
2. Prepare the journal entries necessary to recognize (a) the interest expense on December 31, 2014–2018, and (b) the repayment of the loan principal on December 31, 2018.

CORNERSTONE **9.2**

(Continued)

Solution:

1. The interest payment on December 31 of each year will be:

$$\$100{,}000 \times 8\% = \$8{,}000$$

2.

	Date	Account and Explanation	Debit	Credit
a.	Dec. 31, 2014–2018	Interest Expense	8,000	
		Cash		8,000
		(Record interest expense)		
b.	Dec. 31, 2018	Bonds Payable	100,000	
		Cash		100,000
		(Record repayment of bond principal)		

Assets	= Liabilities +	Stockholders' Equity
−8,000		−8,000

Assets	= Liabilities +	Stockholders' Equity
−100,000	−100,000	

Note, from Cornerstone 9.2, that the interest expense recorded is equal to the cash paid to the lender when the bond is issued at par.

Debt with Regular Interest Payments Sold at a Premium or Discount

As mentioned previously, the sale of a bond at a discount or premium affects the borrower's interest expense. This is because total interest expense is the difference between the payments to the lenders and the amount received by the borrowing business. Let us compare a $1,000,000, 10%, 5-year bond contract with semiannual interest payments that are sold at a $10,000 discount (99% of par) with the same issue sold at a $20,000 premium (102% of par).

	Bond Sold at a Discount	Bond Sold at a Premium
Face amount payment at maturity	$1,000,000	$ 1,000,000
Interest payments (10 at $50,000 each)	500,000	500,000
Total payments to lenders	$1,500,000	$ 1,500,000
Less: Proceeds at issue	(990,000)	(1,020,000)
Total interest expense over life of bond	$ 510,000	$ 480,000

For the discounted bond, total interest expense ($510,000) exceeds interest payments ($500,000) by $10,000. For the bond issued at a premium, total interest expense ($480,000) is $20,000 less than the cash interest payments ($500,000).

This total interest expense is spread over the life of the bond. For the 10%, $1,000,000 bond sold at 99, interest expense would be $51,000 per 6-month interest period:

$$\frac{\$510{,}000}{10} = \$51{,}000 \text{ per 6-month interest period}$$

Another way of calculating this would be as:

Interest paid	$50,000
Amortization of discount (10,000/10 periods)	1,000
Total interest expense per period	$51,000

In fact, amortization tables like those in Cornerstones 9.3 and 9.4 (p. 480) are used to help calculate these amounts. Although such tables aren't really necessary when using the straight-line method for amortizing bond discount or premium, they are extremely helpful when the effective interest rate method is used, as is shown later in the chapter.

Cornerstone 9.3 shows how to record interest expense when the bond is issued at a discount.

CORNERSTONE

9.3

Recording Interest Expense for Bonds Sold at a Discount Using the Straight-Line Method

Why:

When interest-bearing bonds are issued at a discount, the interest expense for the period is the amount of interest payment for the period *plus* the discount amortization for the period. Under the straight-line method, an equal amount of discount is amortized each period.

Information:

On December 31, 2013, Franzen Inc. issues 5-year, $100,000,000, 8% bonds at 99 ($99,000,000). The discount at the time of the sale is $1,000,000. Interest is paid semiannually on June 30 and December 31.

Required:

1. Prepare the journal entry to record the issuance of the bonds on December 31, 2013.
2. Calculate the amount of discount that will be amortized each semiannual period.
3. Calculate the amount of interest expense for each semiannual period.
4. Complete an amortization table for each of the 10 semiannual periods.
5. Prepare the journal entries necessary to (a) recognize the interest expense on June 30 and December 31, 2014–2018, and (b) record the repayment of the loan principal on December 31, 2018.

Solution:

1.

Date	Account and Explanation	Debit	Credit
Dec. 31, 2013	Cash	99,000,000	
	Discount on Bonds Payable	1,000,000	
	Bonds Payable		100,000,000
	(Record issuance of bonds at a discount)		

Assets	=	Liabilities	+	Stockholders' Equity
+99,000,000		−1,000,000		
		+100,000,000		

2. $$\text{Discount Amortization} = \frac{\text{Total Discount}}{\text{Number of Interest Periods}} = \frac{\$1{,}000{,}000}{10 \text{ periods}} = \underline{\underline{\$100{,}000}} \text{ per period}$$

3. $$\begin{aligned} \text{Interest Expense} &= \text{Interest Payment} + \text{Discount Amortization} \\ &= (\$100{,}000{,}000 \times 8\% \times 6/12) + \$100{,}000 \\ &= \$4{,}000{,}000 + \$100{,}000 \\ &= \underline{\underline{\$4{,}100{,}000}} \end{aligned}$$

(Continued)

CORNERSTONE **9.3** *(Continued)*

4.

Semiannual Period	Cash Payment (Credit)	Interest Expense (Debit)	Discount on Bonds Payable (Credit)	Discount on Bonds Payable Balance	Carrying Value
At issue				$1,000,000	$ 99,000,000
1	$4,000,000	$4,100,000	$100,000	900,000	99,100,000
2	4,000,000	4,100,000	100,000	800,000	99,200,000
3	4,000,000	4,100,000	100,000	700,000	99,300,000
4	4,000,000	4,100,000	100,000	600,000	99,400,000
5	4,000,000	4,100,000	100,000	500,000	99,500,000
6	4,000,000	4,100,000	100,000	400,000	99,600,000
7	4,000,000	4,100,000	100,000	300,000	99,700,000
8	4,000,000	4,100,000	100,000	200,000	99,800,000
9	4,000,000	4,100,000	100,000	100,000	99,900,000
10	4,000,000	4,100,000	100,000	0	100,000,000

Note: The discount on bonds payable is amortized to $0 at maturity.

5.

	Date	Account and Explanation	Debit	Credit
a.	June 30/Dec. 31	Interest Expense	4,100,000	
		Cash		4,000,000
		Discount on Bonds Payable		100,000
		(Record interest payment on bonds)		
b.	Dec. 31, 2018	Bonds Payable	100,000,000	
		Cash		100,000,000
		(Record repayment of bond principal)		

Assets	=	Liabilities	+	Stockholders' Equity
−4,000,000		+100,000		−4,100,000

Assets	=	Liabilities	+	Stockholders' Equity
−100,000,000		−100,000,000		

EXHIBIT 9.6

Carrying Value over the Life of a Bond Issued at a Discount

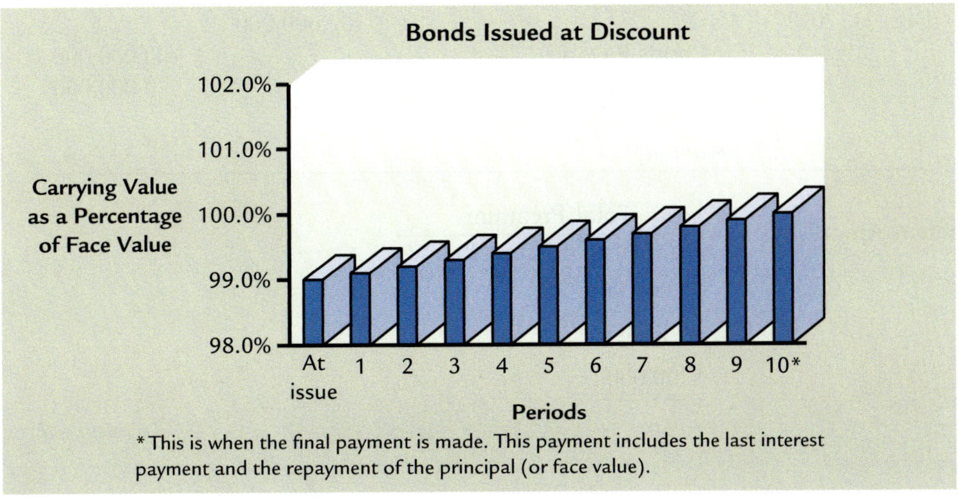

* This is when the final payment is made. This payment includes the last interest payment and the repayment of the principal (or face value).

Exhibit 9.6 (p. 479) illustrates how the carrying value of the bond shown in Cornerstone 9.3 moves closer to face value. In fact, the carrying value will be the face value at maturity because the discount balance will be $0 (i.e., it will be completely amortized). Notice that the beginning carrying value is 99% of the face value. This indicates that although the 8% stated rate is below market yield, it is only slightly below—8.25%.

Cornerstone 9.4 shows how things change when the bond is issued at a premium.

Exhibit 9.7 illustrates how the carrying value of the bond shown in Cornerstone 9.4 declines over time due to the premium amortization. Notice that the beginning carrying value is 102% of the face value. This indicates that the 8% stated rate is slightly above market yield—7.51%. Notice that in this case, the carrying value is the face value of the bond plus the premium because both the bond payable and the premium have credit balances. Further, as the premium is amortized, the premium balance declines and the carrying value moves closer to face value.

CORNERSTONE 9.4

Recording Interest Expense for Bonds Sold at a Premium Using the Straight-Line Method

Why:

When interest-bearing bonds are issued at a premium, the interest expense for the period is the amount of interest payment for the period *minus* the premium amortization for the period. Under the straight-line method, an equal amount of premium is amortized each period.

Information:

On December 31, 2013, Ames Inc. issues 5-year, $100,000,000, 8% bonds at 102 ($102,000,000). The premium at the time of the sale is $2,000,000. Interest is paid semiannually on June 30 and December 31.

Required:

1. Prepare the journal entry to record the issuance of the bonds on December 31, 2013.
2. Calculate the amount of premium that will be amortized each semiannual period.
3. Calculate the amount of interest expense for each semiannual period.
4. Complete an amortization table for the 10 semiannual periods.
5. Prepare the journal entry necessary to (a) recognize the interest expense on June 30 and December 31, 2014–2018, and (b) record the repayment of the loan principal on December 31, 2018.

Solution:

1.

Date	Account and Explanation	Debit	Credit
Dec. 31, 2013	Cash	102,000,000	
	Bonds Payable		100,000,000
	Premium on Bonds Payable		2,000,000
	(Record issuance of bonds at a premium)		

Assets	=	Liabilities	+	Stockholders' Equity
+102,000,000		+2,000,000		
		+100,000,000		

2. $$\text{Premium Amortization} = \frac{\text{Total Premium}}{\text{Number of Interest Periods}} = \frac{\$2{,}000{,}000}{10 \text{ periods}} = \underline{\underline{\$200{,}000}}$$

(Continued)

CORNERSTONE **9.4** *(Continued)*

3. Interest Expense = Interest Payment – Premium Amortization
= (\$100,000,000 × 8% × 6/12) – \$200,000
= \$4,000,000 – \$200,000
= \$3,800,000

4.

Semiannual Period	Cash Payment (Credit)	Interest Expense (Debit)	Premium on Bonds Payable (Debit)	Premium on Bonds Payable Balance	Carrying Value
At issue				\$2,000,000	\$102,000,000
1	\$4,000,000	\$3,800,000	\$200,000	1,800,000	101,800,000
2	4,000,000	3,800,000	200,000	1,600,000	101,600,000
3	4,000,000	3,800,000	200,000	1,400,000	101,400,000
4	4,000,000	3,800,000	200,000	1,200,000	101,200,000
5	4,000,000	3,800,000	200,000	1,000,000	101,000,000
6	4,000,000	3,800,000	200,000	800,000	100,800,000
7	4,000,000	3,800,000	200,000	600,000	100,600,000
8	4,000,000	3,800,000	200,000	400,000	100,400,000
9	4,000,000	3,800,000	200,000	200,000	100,200,000
10	4,000,000	3,800,000	200,000	0	100,000,000

Note: The premium on bonds payable is amortized to \$0 at maturity.

5.

Date	Account and Explanation	Debit	Credit
a. June 30/ Dec. 31	Interest Expense	3,800,000	
	Premium on Bonds Payable	200,000	
	Cash		4,000,000
	(Record interest payment on bonds)		
b. Dec. 31, 2018	Bonds Payable	100,000,000	
	Cash		100,000,000
	(Record repayment of principal)		

Assets	=	Liabilities	+	Stockholders' Equity
–4,000,000		–200,000		–3,800,000

Assets	=	Liabilities	+	Stockholders' Equity
–100,000,000		–100,000,000		

EXHIBIT 9.7

Carrying Value over the Life of a Bond Issued at a Premium

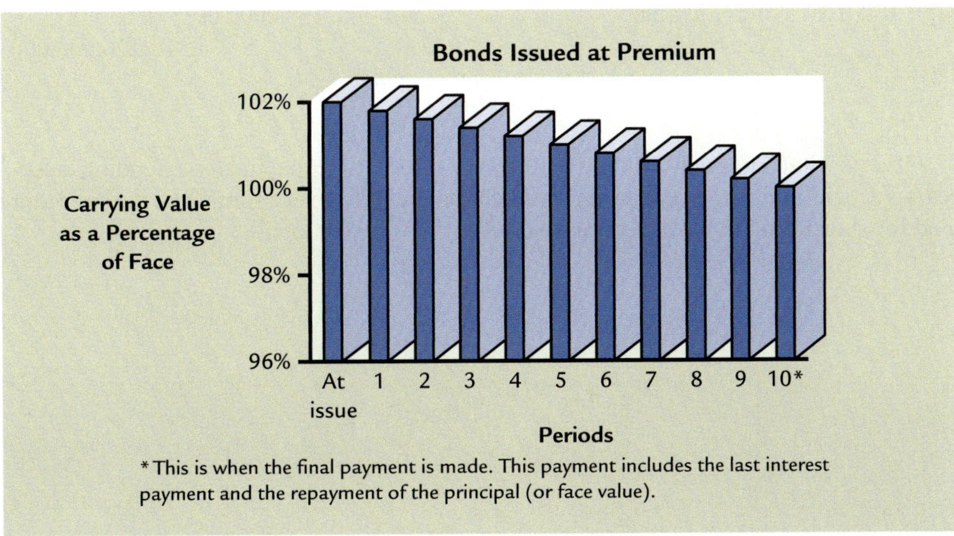

Accruing Interest

In the previous discussion, interest payments were made on the last day of the period—December 31. This is frequently not the case in the real world. Assume that on September 1, 2013, Nadel Communications borrows $120,000,000 on a 3-year, 7% note. The note requires annual interest payments (each equal to 7% of $120,000,000) and repayment of the principal plus the final year's interest at the end of the third year. This borrowing would be recognized in Nadel's accounts as:

Assets	=	Liabilities	+	Stockholders' Equity
+120,000,000		+120,000,000		

Date	Account and Explanation	Debit	Credit
Sept. 1, 2013	Cash	120,000,000	
	Notes Payable		120,000,000
	(Record issuance of note)		

Since no interest payment is made at Nadel's year end (December 31), interest must be accrued for the period. Interest expense for the 4-month period from September through December is $2,800,000 ($120,000,000 × 0.07 × 4/12). That means interest expense for the 8-month period from January through August is $5,600,000 ($120,000,000 × 0.07 × 8/12). Nadel would recognize interest expense and the payment of interest on this note during 2013 through 2016 as:

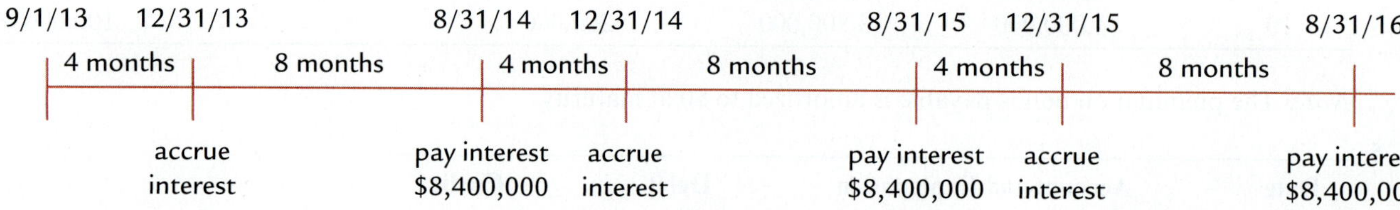

Assets	=	Liabilities	+	Stockholders' Equity
		+2,800,000		−2,800,000

Date	Account and Explanation	Debit	Credit
Dec. 31	Interest Expense	2,800,000	
	Interest Payable		2,800,000
	(Record interest expense and interest payable on 12/31/13, 12/31/14, and 12/31/15)		

Assets	=	Liabilities	+	Stockholders' Equity
−8,400,000		−2,800,000		−5,600,000

Date	Account and Explanation	Debit	Credit
Sept. 1	Interest Expense	5,600,000	
	Interest Payable	2,800,000	
	Cash		8,400,000
	[Record interest expense (8 months) and payment of 12 months' interest on 9/1/14, 9/1/15, and 9/1/16]		

Assets	=	Liabilities	+	Stockholders' Equity
−120,000,000		−120,000,000		

Date	Account and Explanation	Debit	Credit
Sept. 1, 2016	Notes Payable	120,000,000	
	Cash		120,000,000
	(Record repayment of principal on note)		

Observe that although Nadel's note involves multiple payments extending over 3 years, recognition of the borrowing and its repayment are very similar to the procedure used for short-term, interest-bearing notes illustrated in Chapter 8.

YOU DECIDE Financial Statement Effects of Refinancing

You are the CFO of Global Industries. Eight years ago, Global issued $100,000,000 of bonds that yielded 11%. Global's borrowing costs are currently 9%. If Global were to refinance the debt, interest payments would drop by $2,000,000 per year.

Should Global refinance? How would the refinancing affect net income?

Unlike debt at a bank (such as a car loan or home mortgage), bonds are not paid off by merely repaying the principal; instead, bonds must be repurchased in the market at their fair market value. To illustrate, assume these bonds were issued at par. This means that their fair value was $100,000,000 on the date of issue. However, the fair value is $100,000,000 only when the market rate of interest is 11% (such as at issue) and on the maturity date (because no interest payments remain). If market rates fall below the 11% yield, the fair value of the debt will increase because the lenders will demand a premium to sell the above-market interest payments of 11%. Accordingly, to refinance, Global must pay more than $100,000,000. This premium, coupled with the additional costs of refinancing, will more than offset the decrease in interest payments.

As for the effect on net income, because the carrying value of the existing debt is its amortized cost, not its fair market value, refinancing typically results in a gain or loss on refinancing being recognized. In this case, Global will pay more than the $100,000,000 carrying value of the bonds. The amount of this premium will be a loss on Global's income statement, thus lowering net income.

In this case, Global should only consider the cash flow implications. Specifically, Global should refinance if the present value of the interest saved exceeds the costs of refinancing. In reality, however, management also considers the financial-statement effects of the transaction, although any loss on refinancing does not affect the cash flows.

THE EFFECTIVE INTEREST RATE METHOD: RECOGNIZING INTEREST EXPENSE AND REPAYMENT OF PRINCIPAL

OBJECTIVE 4

Use the effective interest rate method to account for premium/discount amortization.

The straight-line and effective interest rate methods are identical when a bond is issued at par because there are no premiums or discounts to amortize. Further, even when premiums or discounts exist, the *total* interest expense over the life of the bonds is identical. However, the interest expense allocated to the individual accounting periods differs because premiums and discounts are amortized in different manners.

Under the effective interest rate method, the amortization of premiums and discounts results in the interest expense for each accounting period being equal to a constant percentage of the bond book value (also called *carrying value*). That is, the interest expense changes every period, but the effective interest rate on the bond book value is constant. The straight-line method, on the other hand, has a constant interest expense each period, but the effective interest rate on the bond book value changes every period.

To use the effective interest method, you must distinguish between interest payments, which are calculated as:

$$\text{Face Value} \times \text{Stated Rate} \times \text{Time (in years)}$$

and effective interest expense, which is calculated as:

$$\text{Carrying Value} \times \text{Yield Rate} \times \text{Time (in years)}$$

concept Q&A

Is the total amount of interest expense over the life of the bond higher when we use straight-line amortization or the effective interest rate method?

Answer:

Neither—the total amount of interest expense is identical under both methods. What changes is the interest expense allocated to each period (see Exhibit 9.8).

This difference is so important it bears emphasis. Interest payments are calculated with face value and the stated rate of interest. These payments are the same each period. Interest expense, under the effective rate method, is calculated by using the Carrying Value (Face Value − Discount Balance or Face Value + Premium Balance) and the yield, or market rate, of interest.

Cornerstone 9.5 illustrates how discounts are amortized under the effective interest rate method.

CORNERSTONE 9.5

Recording Interest Expense for Bonds Sold at a Discount Using the Effective Interest Rate Method

Why:

When interest-bearing bonds are issued at a discount, the interest expense for the period is the amount of interest payment for the period *plus* the discount amortization for the period. Under the effective interest rate method, a constant (or effective) rate of interest on the bond book (or carrying) value is allocated to the period.

Information:

On December 31, 2013, Brannigan Co. issued $1,000,000 of 8% bonds, due in 5 years with interest payable annually on December 31. The market rate of interest is 9%. Assume the bond was issued at $961,103. This was calculated using time value of money concepts [see Cornerstone 9.8 (p. 493) in Appendix 9A for the calculation].

Required:

1. Complete an amortization table for each of the five annual periods.
2. Prepare the journal entry necessary to (a) recognize the interest expense on December 31, 2014 and 2015, and (b) record the repayment of the loan principal on December 31, 2018.

Solution:

1.

Annual Period	Cash Payment[a] (Credit)	Interest Expense[b] (Debit)	Discount on Bonds Payable[c] (Credit)	Discount on Bonds Payable Balance	Carrying Value[d]
At issue				$38,897	$ 961,103
Dec. 31, 2014	$80,000	$86,499	$6,499	32,398	967,602
Dec. 31, 2015	80,000	87,084	7,084	25,314	974,686
Dec. 31, 2016	80,000	87,722	7,722	17,592	982,408
Dec. 31, 2017	80,000	88,417	8,417	9,175	990,825
Dec. 31, 2018	80,000	89,175	9,175	0	1,000,000

[a] Cash Payment = Face Value × 8% × 12/12 = $80,000
[b] Interest Expense = Carrying Value × 9% × 12/12
[c] Change in Discount Balance = Interest Expense − Cash Payment
[d] New Carrying Value = Previous Carrying Value + Change in Discount on Bonds Payable Balance

(Continued)

CORNERSTONE

9.5

(Continued)

2.

	Date	Account and Explanation	Debit	Credit
a.	Dec. 31, 2014	Interest Expense	86,499	
		Cash		80,000
		Discount on Bonds Payable		6,499
		(Record interest expense)		
	Dec. 31, 2015	Interest Expense	87,084	
		Cash		80,000
		Discount on Bonds Payable		7,084
		(Record interest expense)		
b.	Dec. 31, 2018	Bonds Payable	1,000,000	
		Cash		1,000,000
		(Record repayment of principal)		

Assets	= Liabilities +	Stockholders' Equity
−80,000	+6,499	−86,499

Assets	= Liabilities +	Stockholders' Equity
−80,000	+7,084	−87,084

Assets	= Liabilities +	Stockholders' Equity
−1,000,000	−1,000,000	

As in the straight-line method, recording interest expense for bonds issued at a premium is the mirror image of bonds issued at a discount. Cornerstone 9.6 illustrates how premiums are amortized under the effective interest rate method.

Recording Interest Expense for Bonds Sold at a Premium Using the Effective Interest Rate Method

CORNERSTONE

9.6

Why:

When interest-bearing bonds are issued at a premium, the interest expense for the period is the amount of interest payment for the period *minus* the premium amortization for the period. Under the effective interest rate method, a constant (or effective) rate of interest on the bond book (or carrying) value is allocated to the period.

Information:

On December 31, 2013, Cutler Co. issued \$1,000,000 of 8% bonds, due in 5 years with interest payable annually on December 31. The market rate of interest is 7%. Assume the bond was issued at \$1,041,002 [see Cornerstone 9.8 (p. 493) in Appendix 9A for the calculation].

Required:

1. Complete an amortization table for each of the five periods.
2. Prepare the journal entry necessary to (a) recognize the interest expense on December 31, 2014 and 2015, and (b) record the repayment of the loan principal on December 31, 2018.

(Continued)

CORNERSTONE **9.6**

(Continued)

Solution:

1.

Annual Period	Cash Payment[a] (Credit)	Interest Expense[b] (Debit)	Premium on Bonds Payable[c] (Debit)	Premium on Bonds Payable Balance	Carrying Value[d]
At issue				$41,002	$1,041,002
Dec. 31, 2014	$80,000	$72,870	$7,130	33,872	1,033,872
Dec. 31, 2015	80,000	72,371	7,629	26,243	1,026,243
Dec. 31, 2016	80,000	71,837	8,163	18,080	1,018,080
Dec. 31, 2017	80,000	71,266	8,734	9,346	1,009,346
Dec. 31, 2018	80,000	70,654	9,346	0	1,000,000

[a] Cash Payment = Face Value × 8% × 12/12 = $80,000
[b] Interest Expense = Carrying Value × 7% × 12/12
[c] Change in Premium Balance = Cash Payment − Interest Expense
[d] New Carrying Value = Previous Carrying Value − Change in Premium on Bonds Payable Balance

2.

	Date	Account and Explanation	Debit	Credit
a.	Dec. 31, 2014	Interest Expense	72,870	
		Premium on Bonds Payable	7,130	
		Cash		80,000
		(Record interest expense)		
	Dec. 31, 2015	Interest Expense	72,371	
		Premium on Bonds Payable	7,629	
		Cash		80,000
		(Record interest expense)		
b.	Dec. 31, 2018	Bonds Payable	1,000,000	
		Cash		1,000,000
		(Record repayment of principal)		

Assets	=	Liabilities	+	Stockholders' Equity
−80,000		−7,130		−72,870

Assets	=	Liabilities	+	Stockholders' Equity
−80,000		−7,629		−72,371

Assets	=	Liabilities	+	Stockholders' Equity
−1,000,000		−1,000,000		

Note that the interest expense using the straight-line method is the same each period. In contrast, the interest expense using the effective interest method results in a different amount each period. This is because the interest expense is based on a constant *rate*. This rate is applied to the remaining carrying value of the bonds each period. Exhibit 9.8, on the facing page, illustrates how the carrying value of the bonds are different between the straight-line and effective interest methods for both a premium and a discount.

concept Q&A

Why is the effective interest rate method GAAP?

Answer:

The effective interest rate method does a better job allocating, or matching, the time value of money to the proper period. Under the effective interest rate method, the interest expense is equal to market rate of interest (or yield) at issue on the bond book value. This makes sense because market forces will ensure that the creditor receives the market rate of return on the investment.

Installment Debt

Instead of paying off the principal at maturity, some debt requires a portion of the principal to be paid off each period (usually monthly), along with some interest. Classic installment debt payments are home mortgages or car payments. Installment debt payments are the same each period, but the portion that is considered interest changes because the outstanding principal balance is changing. To illustrate, consider buying a car for $20,000, at 6% annual interest, and 48 monthly payments. In this case, each monthly payment would be $469.70. After 48 payments you would have paid a total of

EXHIBIT 9.8

Long-Term Debt Carrying Value Using Straight-Line and Effective Interest Methods to Amortize Premium and Discount

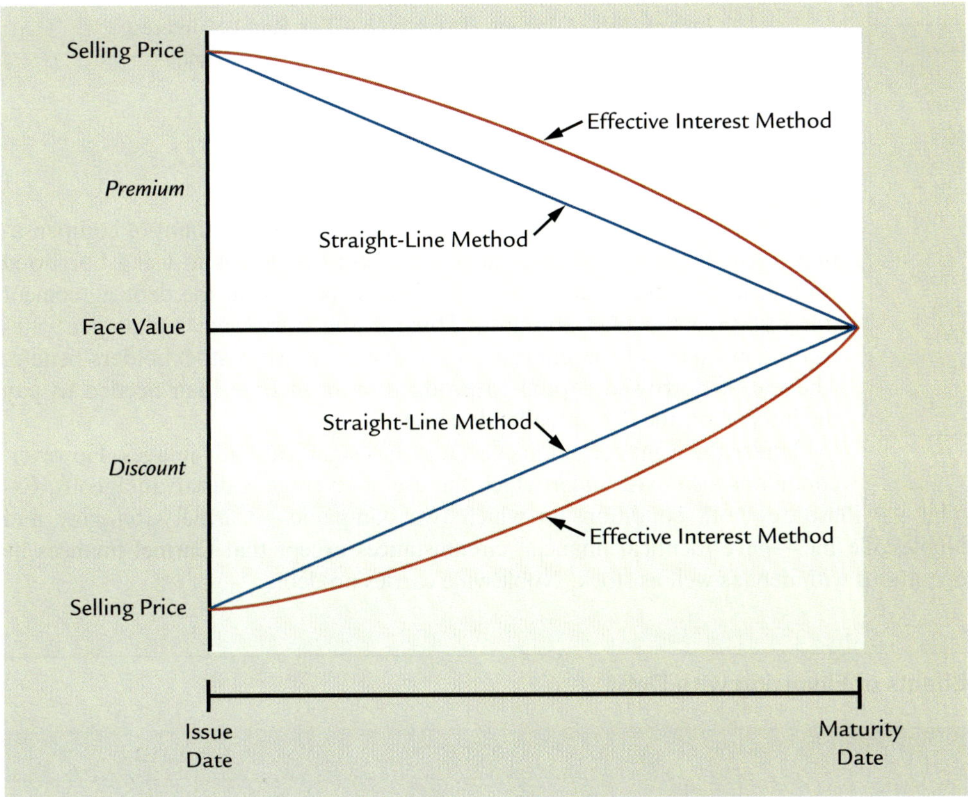

$22,545.60 ($469.70 × 48). This means you would have paid $2,545.60 of interest and $20,000 of principal. However, the initial monthly payments would have a relatively high portion allocated to interest because your outstanding loan balance is relatively high. Your last few payments, on the other hand, would have a relatively low portion allocated to interest because your outstanding loan balance is relatively low.

PROS AND CONS OF DEBT FINANCING

OBJECTIVE 5

Determine the after-tax cost of financing with debt and explain financial leverage.

A business must weigh both the negative and positive aspects of debt financing in deciding whether or not to take the risk. This extremely complex decision is treated more fully in finance courses, but some general points follow.[4]

Tax Deductible Interest Expense

A significant advantage of financing with debt rather than stock is the fact that the interest expense on debt is deductible for income tax purposes. Consider the case of Carmel Company, which issued $1,000,000 of 8% bonds that resulted in interest expense of $80,000 per year. The net cash outflow for Carmel's bonds is significantly less than $80,000, however, because of the effect of interest deductibility.

Since interest expense is deductible, taxable income is $80,000 less than it is without the bond issue. At a rate of 30% ($80,000 × 30%), income taxes were reduced by

[4] The following discussion explains the accounting concepts and procedures for debt used by borrowers. Although the concepts and procedures used by investors in debt securities are based on the same measurements and calculations, the reporting conventions are somewhat different. The most fundamental difference is that investors record debt acquired as assets rather than liabilities and record the interest as revenue rather than expense.

$24,000, yielding a net cash outflow for the bonds of $56,000 ($80,000 – $24,000). In other words, the cost of financing with bonds (or any other form of debt with tax-deductible interest payments) is the interest *net of income taxes*, which is determined using the following formula:

Interest Net of Income Taxes = (1 – Tax Rate) × Interest
= (1 – 0.30) × $80,000
= $56,000

Leverage

Another potential advantage of debt is that it fixes the amount of compensation to the lender. No matter how successful the firm is in using borrowed capital, its creditors receive only the return specified in the debt agreement (interest plus the face amount). Thus, if the borrowed capital generates income in excess of the interest on the debt, the firm's stockholders benefit. The use of borrowed capital to produce more income than needed to pay the interest on the debt is called **leverage**.

Under the right conditions, leverage has significant advantages. However, conditions also exist under which the use of leverage is disadvantageous. Exhibit 9.9 illustrates both conditions in which two companies—Carmel Company and Noblesville Inc.—have identical financial circumstances except that Carmel finances its operations with debt as well as stock; Noblesville carries no debt.

concept Q&A

How do credit cards calculate interest?

Answer:

Although terms vary from card to card, they all charge some percentage of our average balance for the period. If your card charges 1.5% of the average balance for the month and you have a $5,000 average balance, then interest charge would be $75. Interest of 1.5% may not sound that bad, but remember that this is per month. That equates to 18% per year (1.5% × 12 months). If all you do is pay the interest, you are not lowering your outstanding balance at all.

EXHIBIT 9.9

Effects of Financing with Debt

	2012		2013	
	Carmel Company	**Noblesville Inc.**	**Carmel Company**	**Noblesville Inc.**
Balance sheet:*				
Assets	$3,000,000	$3,000,000	$3,000,000	$3,000,000
Bonds payable	$1,000,000	—	$1,000,000	—
Stockholders' equity	$2,000,000	$3,000,000	$2,000,000	$3,000,000
Number of common stock shares	100,000	150,000	100,000	150,000
Income statement:				
Income from operations	$ 600,000	$ 600,000	$ 200,000	$ 200,000
Interest expense (8%)	80,000	—	80,000	—
Income before taxes	$ 520,000	$ 600,000	$ 120,000	$ 200,000
Income taxes expense (30%)	156,000	180,000	36,000	60,000
Net income	$ 364,000	$ 420,000	$ 84,000	$ 140,000
Earnings per share	$ 3.64	$ 2.80	$ 0.84	$ 0.93

*Annual averages (assume that current liabilities are negligible).

In 2012, favorable economic conditions allow Carmel to make the most of its leverage. Carmel's stockholders earn $3.64 per share, which includes an amount attributable to earnings in excess of the cost of borrowing. In contrast, Noblesville's stockholders earn only $2.80 per share in 2012. However, income from operations falls sharply in 2013. As a result, Carmel's stockholders earn only $0.84 per share compared with $0.93 per share for Noblesville's stockholders. Just as stockholders receive earnings in excess of the interest on debt, so they must bear the burden when the interest on debt exceeds earnings.

Inflation

A third advantage of financing with debt is that in periods of inflation, debt permits the borrower to repay the lender in dollars that have declined in purchasing power. For instance, based on changes in the consumer price index (CPI), $1,000,000 borrowed in 1992 and repaid in 2012 provided the lender with approximately 59% of the purchasing power of the amount loaned in 1992.

Payment Schedule

The primary negative attribute of debt is the inflexibility of the payment schedule. Debt requires specified payments to creditors on specified dates. If a payment is not made as scheduled, the borrower can be forced into bankruptcy. This attribute of debt makes it a more risky source of capital than equity. The larger the proportion of debt an entity uses to finance its capital needs, the greater the risk of default. As risk increases (because of a higher proportion of debt), the cost of the debt increases. At a certain point, the risk becomes so great that additional debt cannot be issued at any cost. For firms whose operational and competitive circumstances produce substantial fluctuations in earnings, even low levels of debt may be considered too risky.

Occasionally, a business finds that it is unable to make the interest or principal payments required by its long-term debt. If there is reason to expect that the firm will eventually be able to secure enough cash to make part of or all the required payments, creditors may permit a restructuring of the cash payment schedule. The amount at which the firm's liabilities are measured may or may not be changed by such a restructuring. In such cases, creditors must analyze the situation to ensure that they are better off than they would be if they forced a bankruptcy.

LEASES

OBJECTIVE 6

Compare and contrast operating and capital leases.

Many companies choose to **lease**, instead of purchase, some of their assets. For example, AMR (the parent of American Airlines) reports that of their approximately 900 airplanes, 239 are under operating leases and 60 are under capital leases.

Operating Leases

In an **operating lease**, the **lessor** (the legal owner of the asset) retains substantially all of the risks and obligations of ownership, while the **lessee** uses the asset during the term of the lease. Automobiles, apartments, retail space, and office space are usually rented with operating leases. All discussions of rental arrangements considered earlier in this book have been operating leases.

Under an operating lease, the leased asset does not appear in the records of the lessee because the legal owner of the asset retains the risks and obligations of ownership. Rent paid in advance of the use of the asset is reported as prepaid rent, and rent expense is recognized in the period in which the leased asset is used. However, because many financial statement users view leases as liabilities, the sum of all payments required by noncancelable operating leases for the next 5 years must be disclosed in a footnote to the lessee's financial statements. Exhibit 9.10 (p. 490) is taken from AMR's 2011 10-K.

To further illustrate, although AMR reports the present value of the net minimum lease payments ($679 million) of its capital leases as a liability, no liability is recorded for the $10.6 billion in future operating lease obligations. For this reason, many companies will intentionally structure the lease to qualify as an operating lease.

IFRS

IFRS refers to a capital lease as a financial lease.

Capital Leases

A **capital lease**, on the other hand, is a noncancelable agreement that is in substance a purchase of the leased asset. If a lease has any of the following characteristics, it is essentially a purchase, and is therefore considered a capital lease:

- A transfer of the leased asset to the lessee occurs at the end of the lease at no cost or at a "bargain price."
- The term for the lease is at least 75% of the economic life of the leased asset.
- The present value of the lease payments is at least 90% of the fair value of the leased asset.

EXHIBIT 9.10

Excerpts from AMR's 2011 10-K

Note 6
Leases
Minimum future rental payments under capital and operating lease obligations as of December 31, 2011, are as follows *(in millions)*:

Year Ending December 31	Capital leases	Operating leases
2012	$ 167	$ 1,176
2013	149	1,091
2014	129	942
2015	118	779
2016	78	685
2017 and thereafter	477	5,940
	$1,118	$10,613
Less amount representing interest	439	
Present value of net minimum lease payments	$ 679	

Source: AMR Corporation, 2011 10-K

Although the lessor remains the legal owner of the leased asset, a capital lease transfers virtually all the benefits of ownership to the lessee. Therefore, a capital lease is appropriately shown among the lessee's assets and liabilities. At the beginning of such a lease, a capital lease liability is recorded at the present value of the future lease payments. At this time, an asset is recorded in the same amount. Over the life of the lease the asset is depreciated, using an appropriate depreciation method. The lease liability is reduced and interest expense recorded as lease payments are made.

OBJECTIVE 7

Analyze a company's long-term solvency using information related to long-term liabilities.

RATIO ANALYSIS

Although long-term creditors are concerned with a company's short-term liquidity, they are primarily concerned with its long-term solvency. As such, long-term creditors focus on ratios that incorporate (1) long-term debt and (2) interest expense/payments.

The following ratios are often used to analyze a company's debt load:

$$\text{Debt to Equity} = \frac{\text{Total Liabilities}}{\text{Total Equity}}$$

$$\text{Debt to Total Assets} = \frac{\text{Total Liabilities}}{\text{Total Assets}}$$

$$\text{Long-Term Debt to Equity} = \frac{\text{Long-Term Debt}}{\text{Total Equity}}$$

The long-term debt to equity ratio is designed to look at the mix of debt and equity financing. For example, if the ratio is 1.00, then 50% of the company's financing comes from stockholders while the other 50% comes from creditors. However, over the last few decades borrowing arrangements have become much more varied. Historically, when companies borrowed, they locked themselves into long-term debt contracts. Now many companies use short-term borrowing, such as revolving credit, as part of their financing plan. This has the advantage of allowing companies to more frequently adjust their levels of borrowing based on current conditions. The downside is that short-term credit exposes them to greater risk of interest rate changes. For example, when interest rates increase, short-term borrowers may be forced to refinance at these higher rates while long-term borrowers will be locked in at the lower rates. Of course, short-term borrowers can, and do, hedge these interest rate risks, but that is a topic for advanced accounting and finance courses.

Because it is increasingly common to use short-term debt financing, the debt to equity and debt to total asset ratios contain all debt. Although the denominators for these two ratios differ, they both give a sense of the extent to which a company is financed with debt. You can see this more clearly by remembering that Total Assets = Total Liabilities + Total Equity. Both ratios therefore measure the relative size of Total Liabilities in the accounting equation.

Other ratios focus a company's ability to make interest payments. These ratios are often called coverage ratios because they provide information on the company's ability to meet or cover its interest payments. The most common ratios focus either on accrual basis interest expense or the cash basis interest payment and are typically measured pretax because interest expense is tax deductible.

> **concept Q&A**
>
> Is it always better to have lower debt to equity, debt to total assets, and long-term debt to equity ratios?
>
> **Answer:**
>
> No. Debt provides opportunities for leverage. Think about it in this way—if you're guaranteed a return greater than your interest payments, it would not make sense to avoid borrowing. Of course, the reality is that while no returns are guaranteed, interest payments are unavoidable.

$$\text{Times Interest Earned (Accrual Basis)} = \frac{\text{Operating Income}}{\text{Interest Expense}}$$

$$\text{Times Interest Earned (Cash Basis)} = \frac{(\text{Cash Flows from Operations} + \text{Taxes Paid} + \text{Interest Paid})}{\text{Interest Payments}}$$

See Cornerstone 9.7 for an example of calculating these ratios and using them to analyze the long-term debt of a company.

Calculating and Analyzing Long-Term Debt Ratios

CORNERSTONE 9.7

Why:

Investors and creditors are interested in a company's ability to meet its long-term obligations. Analysis of information about long-term liabilities and interest expense and payments provides such information.

Information:

Consider the following information from the 2011 10-Ks for United Continental Holdings (hereafter, UAL) and Southwest Airlines (in millions).

UAL			
Long-term debt	$12,735	Interest expense	$ 949
Total liabilities	36,182	Operating income	1,822
Total assets	37,988	Interest payments	855
Total equity	1,806	Cash flows from operations	2,408
		Income tax expense	5
		Income tax payments	10

(Continued)

CORNERSTONE 9.7 (*Continued*)

Southwest Airlines			
Long-term debt	$ 3,751	Interest expense	$ 194
Total liabilities	11,191	Operating income	693
Total assets	18,068	Interest payments	185
Total equity	6,877	Cash flows from operations	1,385
		Income tax expense	145
		Income tax payments	13

Required:

1. Calculate the following ratios for both companies: (a) debt to equity, (b) debt to total assets, (c) long-term debt to equity, (d) times interest earned (accrual basis), and (e) times interest earned (cash basis).
2. Interpret these results.

Solution:

1.

	UAL	Southwest Airlines
a. debt to equity	$36,182 ÷ $1,806 = 20.03	$11,191 ÷ $6,877 = 1.63
b. debt to total assets	$36,182 ÷ $37,988 = 0.95	$11,191 ÷ $18,068 = 0.62
c. long-term debt to equity	$12,735 ÷ $1,806 = 7.05	$3,751 ÷ $6,877 = 0.55
d. times interest earned (accrual basis)	$1,822 ÷ $949 = 1.92	$693 ÷ $194 = 3.57
e. times interest earned (cash basis)	($2,408 + $10 + $855) ÷ $855 = 3.83	($1,385 + $13 + $185) ÷ $185 = 8.56

2. Southwest's solvency risk is clearly far lower than UAL's. Although UAL has a relatively high debt load, its operations are covering its interest payments. Southwest, on the other hand, has a relatively low debt load and can more easily make its interest payments.

   Not surprisingly, UAL is well below industry averages on most ratios while Southwest is an industry leader. These ratios are also reflected in their credit ratings. UAL has typically fluctuated between B and B– while Southwest has historically ranged between A or A– (although it is currently BBB).

ETHICAL DECISIONS When evaluating a company's solvency, a major concern is whether all debt was properly recorded. Companies have long engaged in transactions designed to hide debt. Such transactions are typically called *off-balance-sheet financing*. Interestingly, many such transactions are legal and considered to be ethical by most. For example, as discussed previously, many companies structure their lease agreements to avoid meeting the criteria for capital leases that require recording an asset and liability related to the future lease obligation. Because these leases are then treated as operating leases, no asset or liability is recorded on the books.

Because many financial-statement users view operating leases as unavoidable obligations, FASB requires disclosure of operating lease obligations for each of the subsequent 5 years and in total. This disclosure allows users to adjust ratios. For example, in the footnotes of its 2011 10-K, **United Continental Holdings** (the parent company of United and Continental Airlines) reports future minimum lease payments of $19.816 billion related to its operating leases. If we capitalize these amounts, UAL's long-term debt to equity ratio goes from 7.05 (see solution to Cornerstone 9.7) to 18.02 [($12,735 + $19,816) ÷ $1,806].

Many companies also create other legal entities (called "special purpose entities" or SPEs) to "hide" debt. As with leases, such transactions are legal when certain rules are met involving outside investors. **Enron**, however, created some SPEs in which the documentation appeared to meet the outside investor rules to keep the debt off Enron's balance sheet. In hindsight, however, either unwritten side-agreements or complicated aspects of some of the contracts indicate that the debt should have been included on Enron's balance sheet. Keeping this debt off the balance sheet was important for Enron in maintaining its credit rating, but these unwritten side-agreements and complicated aspects of the contracts were necessary to attract the outside investors. While virtually nobody considers structuring their leases to allow treatment as an operating lease to be unethical, the side-agreements and subterfuge used by Enron was not only unethical, but in many cases criminal. •

APPENDIX 9A: PRICING LONG-TERM DEBT

OBJECTIVE 8

Calculate the market price of long-term debt using present value techniques.

Debt agreements create contractually defined cash flows for the lender. Specifically, lenders typically receive:

- periodic interest payments
- repayment of the loan principal at some future date (loan maturity)

To receive these cash flows, the lender must decide how much to lend. When you borrow from a bank or car dealer, this single lender will set the interest rate to reflect the desired market, or yield, rate. However, there are notable exceptions. For example, if you buy a car for $25,000 at 0.9% interest, does that mean the car dealer's yield is 0.9%? No, it really means that they would have been happy to sell you the car for something below $25,000, such as $24,250. In this case, the "extra" principal you repay ($25,000 – $24,250 = $750) represents interest.

Of course, similar situations happen to businesses, but by far the most common situation has to do with bonds because the stated rate of interest (e.g., 8%) on the bond does not provide the desired yield. As discussed, if the yield is above the stated rate, the bond will sell at a discount (e.g., 98), and if the yield is below the stated rate, it will sell at a premium (e.g., 103). But how are these prices determined?

Bonds are priced at the present value of the two future cash flows—the periodic interest payments provide an annuity, while the repayment of the principal is a lump sum. This calculation is shown in Cornerstone 9.8.

Determining the Market Value of a Bond

CORNERSTONE 9.8

Why:

Bonds are issued at the present value of future cash flows. The interest payments and repayment of the bond principal (or face value) are the future cash flows. These amounts must be discounted at the market rate of interest (or yield).

Information:

On December 31, 2013, Chu Co. issued $1,000,000 of 8% bonds, due in 5 years with interest payable annually on December 31.

Required:

1. Draw the cash flow diagram.
2. What is the market value of these bonds if sold to yield (a) 8%, (b) 9%, and (c) 7%?

(Continued)

CORNERSTONE

9.8

(Continued)

Solution:

1. PV = ?

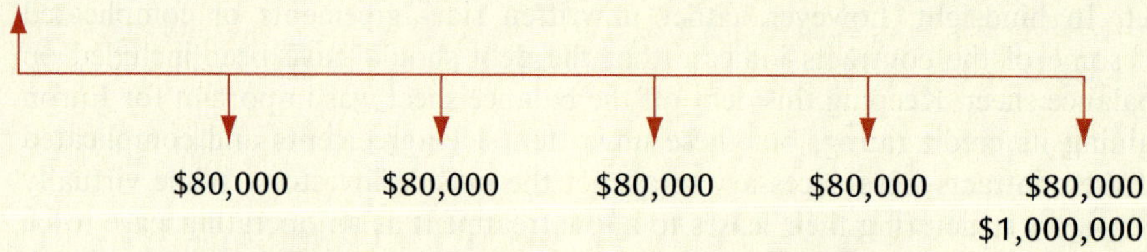

2. a. PV of interest payments = Interest Payment × PV of an annuity, 5 periods, 8%
= $80,000 × 3.992710* = $319,417

PV of principal payments = Principal Payment × PV of a single sum, 5 periods, 8%
= $1,000,000 × 0.680583* = $680,583

Market price of bonds = $319,417 + $680,583 = $1,000,000

*Although present and future value tables provided at the end of Appendix 3 (Exhibits A3.7, A3.8, A3.9, and A3.10) only show five decimal places, we have used factors to six decimal places in these calculations (and those that follow). Use of six decimal places allows the market price of the bond when issued at par to be calculated with no rounding error.

b. PV of interest payments = Interest Payment × PV of an annuity, 5 periods, 9%
= $80,000 × 3.889651 = $311,172

PV of principal payments = Principal Payment × PV of a single sum, 5 periods, 9%
= $1,000,000 × 0.649931 = $649,931

Market price of bonds = $311,172 + $649,931 = $961,103

c. PV of interest payments = Interest Payment × PV of an annuity, 5 periods, 7%
= $80,000 × 4.100197 = $328,016

PV of principal payments = Principal Payment × PV of a single sum, 5 periods, 7%
= $1,000,000 × 0.712986 = $712,986

Market price of bonds = $328,016 + $712,986 = $1,041,002

SUMMARY OF LEARNING OBJECTIVES

LO 1. Describe debt securities and the markets in which they are issued.

- Debt securities are issued in exchange for borrowed cash.
- In return for the borrowed cash, the borrower typically makes periodic interest payments and repays the face, or par, value at maturity.
- These securities may be placed directly with a creditor such as a bank or pension fund or they may be more widely distributed with the help of an underwriter.

LO 2. Account for the issuance of long-term debt.

- The issue price of long-term debt is typically quoted as a percentage of face value.
- At the time of issuance the borrower records the face value of the debt in bonds payable (or notes payable).

- Any amount of cash received over the face value is credited to a premium.
- Any amount of cash received under the face value is debited to a discount.

• The bonds payable (or notes payable) is netted with the premium or discount when reported on the balance sheet.

LO 3. Use the straight-line method to account for premium/discount amortization.

- In the straight-line method, equal amounts of premium or discount are amortized to interest expense each period.
- This results in a constant interest expense each period.
- Although GAAP requires use of the effective interest rate method, the straight-line method may be used if the results are not materially different from the effective interest rate method.

LO 4. Use the effective interest rate method to account for premium/discount amortization.

- GAAP requires the effective interest rate method to be used to amortize any premium or discount, unless the straight-line method is not materially different.
- Under this method, premiums and discounts are amortized in a manner that results in the interest expense for each accounting period being equal to a constant percentage of the bond book, or carrying, value.
- That is, the interest expense changes every period, but the effective interest rate on the bond book value is constant.
- This constant percentage is called the "yield" and represents the market rate of interest at the date of issue.

LO 5. Determine the after-tax cost of financing with debt and explain financial leverage.

- Since interest expense is deductible for tax purposes, the presence of interest expense lowers the taxes owed.
- The formula for the after-tax effect of interest expense is (1 − Tax Rate) × Interest Expense.

LO 6. Compare and contrast operating and capital leases.

- A capital lease is a noncancelable agreement that is, in substance, a purchase of the leased asset.
- If a lease includes one of the following requirements, it is considered a capital lease:
  - A transfer of the leased asset to the lessee occurs at the end of the lease at no cost or at a "bargain price."
  - The term for the lease is at least 75% of the economic life of the leased asset.
  - The present value of the lease payments is at least 90% of the fair value of the leased asset.
- If a lease qualifies as a capital lease, an asset and a liability must be recorded.
- If the lease does not meet requirements to be treated as a capital lease, then it is treated as an operating lease.
- Under an operating lease, the leased asset does not appear in the records of the lessee because the legal owner of the asset retains the risks and obligations of ownership.

LO 7. Analyze a company's long-term solvency using information related to long-term liabilities.

- Although long-term creditors are concerned with a company's short-term liquidity, they are primarily concerned with its long-term solvency.
- Long-term creditors focus on ratios that incorporate:
  - Long-term debt
  - interest expense/payments

LO 8. *(Appendix 9A)* Calculate the market price of long-term debt using present value techniques.

- Bonds are issued at the present value of future cash flows.
- The interest payments and repayment of the bond principal (or face value) are the future cash flows.
- These amounts must be discounted at the market rate of interest (or yield).

CORNERSTONES

CORNERSTONE 9.1 Recording the issuance of bonds, page 475
CORNERSTONE 9.2 Recording interest expense for bonds sold at par, page 476
CORNERSTONE 9.3 Recording interest expense for bonds sold at a discount using the straight-line method, page 478
CORNERSTONE 9.4 Recording interest expense for bonds sold at a premium using the straight-line method, page 480
CORNERSTONE 9.5 Recording interest expense for bonds sold at a discount using the effective interest rate method, page 484
CORNERSTONE 9.6 Recording interest expense for bonds sold at a premium using the effective interest rate method, page 485
CORNERSTONE 9.7 Calculating and analyzing long-term debt ratios, page 491
CORNERSTONE 9.8 *(Appendix 9A)* Determining the market value of a bond, page 493

KEY TERMS

Bond, 470
Callable bonds, 472
Capital lease, 489
Contract rate, 471
Convertible bonds, 472
Coupon rate, 471
Debenture bonds, 471
Discount, 473
Effective interest rate method, 476
Face value, 471
Interest amortization, 476
Interest rate, 471
Junk bonds, 472
Lease, 489
Lessee, 489
Lessor, 489
Leverage, 488
Long-term debt, 470
Market rate, 473
Maturity, 471
Mortgage bonds, 471
Notes payable, 470
Operating lease, 489
Par value, 471
Premium, 473
Principal, 471
Secured bond, 471
Stated rate, 471
Straight-line method, 476
Unsecured bond, 471
Yield, 473

REVIEW PROBLEMS

I. Straight-Line Method

To finance a new hydroelectric plant, Midwest Electric issues $100,000,000 of 9%, 15-year bonds on December 31, 2013. The bonds pay interest semiannually on June 30 and December 31. Assume the market rate of interest on December 31, 2013, was above 9%.

Required:

1. Will the bonds be issued at par, a premium, or a discount? Why?
2. Describe the cash payments made by Midwest Electric.
3. Prepare the journal entry to record the bond issue assuming the bonds were issued at 91.
4. What is the amount of discount amortization per 6-month interest period assuming the bonds were issued at 91?
5. Complete an amortization table through June 30, 2016.
6. Prepare the journal entries for December 31, 2015, and June 30, 2016.

7. How will the bonds be shown on the December 31, 2015 balance sheet?
8. Prepare the journal entry to record the repayment of principal at maturity.

Solution:

1. The bonds will be issued at a discount (below par) because the stated rate is below the market rate. Thus, Midwest Electric will have to lower the price below face value to compensate creditors for accepting a below market interest payment.
2. The interest payments are made semiannually, so the interest payments are:

$$\$100{,}000{,}000 \times 9\% \times 6/12 = \underline{\underline{\$4{,}500{,}000}}$$

There are 30 interest payments over the 15-year life of the bonds, so total interest payments are:

$$\$4{,}500{,}000 \times 30 = \underline{\underline{\$135{,}000{,}000}}$$

At maturity, the face value of $100,000,000 is also repaid. Thus, total payments (interest plus principal) of $235,000,000 are made.

3.

Date	Account and Explanation	Debit	Credit
Dec. 31, 2013	Cash	91,000,000	
	Discount on Bonds Payable	9,000,000	
	Bonds Payable		100,000,000
	(Record issuance of bonds)		

Assets	=	Liabilities	+	Stockholders' Equity
+91,000,000		−9,000,000 +100,000,000		

4.

$$\text{Discount Amortization} = \frac{\text{Total Discount}}{\text{Number of Interest Periods}} = \frac{\$9{,}000{,}000}{30 \text{ periods}} = \underline{\underline{\$300{,}000}}$$

5.

Semiannual Period	Cash Payment (Credit)	Interest Expense (Debit)	Discount on Bonds Payable (Credit)	Discount on Bonds Payable Balance	Carrying Value
At issue				$9,000,000	$91,000,000
06/30/14	$4,500,000	$4,800,000	$300,000	8,700,000	91,300,000
12/31/14	4,500,000	4,800,000	300,000	8,400,000	91,600,000
06/30/15	4,500,000	4,800,000	300,000	8,100,000	91,900,000
12/31/15	4,500,000	4,800,000	300,000	7,800,000	92,200,000
06/30/16	4,500,000	4,800,000	300,000	7,500,000	92,500,000

6.

Account and Explanation	12/31/15 Debit	12/31/15 Credit	6/30/16 Debit	6/30/16 Credit
Interest Expense	4,800,000		4,800,000	
Cash		4,500,000		4,500,000
Discount on Bonds Payable		300,000		300,00
(Record interest payment on bonds)				

12/31/15

Assets	=	Liabilities	+	Stockholders' Equity
−4,500,000		+300,000		−4,800,000

6/30/16

Assets	=	Liabilities	+	Stockholders' Equity
−4,500,000		+300,000		−4,800,000

7. Long-term liabilities:

Bonds payable	$100,000,000	
Less: Discount on bonds payable	(7,800,000)	92,200,000

8.

Date	Account and Explanation	Debit	Credit
Dec. 31, 2028	Bonds Payable	100,000,000	
	Cash		100,000,000
	(Record repayment of bonds)		

Assets	=	Liabilities	+	Stockholders' Equity
−100,000,000		−100,000,000		

II. Effective Interest Method

To finance a new hydroelectric plant, Midwest Electric issues $100,000,000 of 9%, 15-year bonds on December 31, 2013. The bonds pay interest semiannually on June 30 and December 31. Assume the market rate of interest on January 1, 2014, was 10%.

Required:

1. Will the bonds be issued at par, a premium, or a discount? Why?
2. Describe the cash flows.
3. Using present value techniques, verify the bond issue price of $92,314,025. (*Note*: This requires the use of Appendix 9A and Appendix 3.)
4. Prepare the journal entry to record the bond issue.
5. Complete an amortization table through June 30, 2016 (round to the nearest dollar).
6. Prepare the journal entries for December 31, 2015, and June 30, 2016.
7. How will the bonds be shown on the December 31, 2015 balance sheet?
8. Prepare the journal entry to record the repayment of principal at maturity.

Solution:

1. The bonds will be issued at a discount (below par) because the stated rate is below the market rate. Thus, Midwest Electric will have to lower the price below face value to compensate creditors for accepting a below market interest payment.
2. The interest payments are made semiannually, so the interest payments are:

$$\$100,000,000 \times 9\% \times 6/12 = \underline{\underline{\$4,500,000}}$$

There are 30 interest payments over the 15-year life of the bonds, so total interest payments are:

$$\$4,500,000 \times 30 = \underline{\underline{\$135,000,000}}$$

At maturity the face value of $100,000,000 is also repaid. Thus, total payments (interest plus principal) of $235,000,000 are made.

3. The issue price is the present value of the cash flows:

PV of Interest Payments = Interest Payment × PV of an annuity, 30 semiannual periods, 5%
= $4,500,000 ×15.37245 = $69,176,025

PV of Principal Payments = Principal Payment × PV of a single sum, 30 semiannual periods, 5%
= $100,000,000 × 0.23138 = $23,138,000

Market price of bonds = $69,176,025 + $23,138,000 = $92,314,025

4.

Date	Account and Explanation	Debit	Credit
Dec. 31, 2013	Cash	92,314,025	
	Discount on Bonds Payable	7,685,975	
	Bonds Payable		100,000,000
	(Record issuance of bonds)		

Assets	=	Liabilities	+	Stockholders' Equity
+92,314,025		−7,685,975 + 100,000,000		

5.

Annual Period	Cash Payment (Credit)	Interest Expense (Debit)	Discount on Bonds Payable (Credit)	Discount on Bonds Payable Balance	Carrying Value
At issue				$7,685,975	$92,314,025
06/30/14	$4,500,000	$4,615,701	$115,701	7,570,274	92,429,726
12/31/14	4,500,000	4,621,486	121,486	7,448,788	92,551,212
06/30/15	4,500,000	4,627,561	127,561	7,321,227	92,678,773
12/31/15	4,500,000	4,633,939	133,939	7,187,288	92,812,712
06/30/16	4,500,000	4,640,636	140,636	7,046,652	92,953,348

6.

Account and Explanation	12/31/15 Debit	12/31/15 Credit	6/30/16 Debit	6/30/16 Credit
Interest Expense	4,633,939		4,640,636	
Cash		4,500,000		4,500,000
Discount on Bonds Payable		133,939		140,636
(Record interest payment on bonds)				

12/31/15

Assets	=	Liabilities	+	Stockholders' Equity
−4,500,000		+133,939		−4,633,939

6/30/16

Assets	=	Liabilities	+	Stockholders' Equity
−4,500,000		+140,636		−4,640,636

7.

Long-term liabilities:		
Bonds payable	$100,000,000	
Less: Discount on bonds payable	(7,187,288)	92,812,712

8.

Date	Account and Explanation	Debit	Credit
Dec. 31, 2028	Bonds Payable	100,000,000	
	Cash		100,000,000
	(Record repayment of bonds)		

Assets	=	Liabilities	+	Stockholders' Equity
−100,000,000		−100,000,000		

DISCUSSION QUESTIONS

1. What is long-term debt?
2. What is the difference between a bond and a note? How do the accounting treatments differ?
3. What does the face (or par) value of a bond represent?
4. What is the maturity date of a bond?
5. What is the stated or coupon rate of a bond?
6. How does a bond's stated rate differ from its yield rate? Which one is used to calculate the interest payment?
7. How does a secured bond differ from an unsecured bond?
8. What does it mean if a bond is "callable"?
9. What does it mean if a bond is "convertible"?
10. What is a junk bond?
11. How is total interest for long-term debt calculated?
12. Describe the process that businesses follow to sell new issues of long-term debt.
13. Describe how the relationship between the stated rate and yield rate affect the price at which bonds are sold.
14. How are premiums and discounts presented on the balance sheet?
15. How do premiums and discounts on long-term debt securities affect interest expense?
16. What is the difference between the straight-line and effective interest rate methods of amortizing premiums and discounts?
17. How can there be interest expense each period for noninterest-bearing bonds if there are no interest payments?
18. Under the effective interest rate method, describe the difference in calculating the (a) interest payment and (b) interest expense for the period.
19. How does a firm "leverage" its capital structure? When is leverage advantageous? When is it disadvantageous? Who receives the advantage or bears the disadvantage of leverage?
20. Name and describe two kinds of leases.
21. Which type of lease requires that a long-term debt and an asset be recorded at the inception of the lease?
22. *(Appendix 9A)* Describe how the bond issue price is calculated.

MULTIPLE-CHOICE QUESTIONS

9-1 Which of the following statements regarding bonds payable is true?

a. Generally, bonds are issued in denominations of $100.
b. When an issuing company's bonds are traded in the "secondary" market, the company will receive part of the proceeds when the bonds are sold from the first purchaser to the second purchaser.
c. The entire principal amount of most bonds mature on a single date.
d. A debenture bond is backed by specific assets of the issuing company.

9-2 Bonds are sold at a premium if the

a. market rate of interest was more than the stated rate at the time of issue.
b. market rate of interest was less than the stated rate at the time of issue.
c. company will have to pay a premium to retire the bonds.
d. issuing company has a better reputation than other companies in the same business.

9-3 If bonds are issued at 101.25, this means that

a. a $1,000 bond sold for $1,012.50.
b. a $1,000 bond sold for $101.25.
c. the bonds sold at a discount.
d. the bond rate of interest is 10.125% of the market rate of interest.

9-4 What best describes the discount on bonds payable account?

a. A liability
b. An asset
c. A contra liability
d. An expense

9-5 The premium on bonds payable account is shown on the balance sheet as

a. a contra asset.
b. a reduction of an expense.
c. an addition to a long-term liability.
d. a subtraction from a long-term liability.

9-6 When bonds are issued by a company, the accounting entry typically shows an

a. increase in liabilities and a decrease in stockholders' equity.
b. increase in assets and an increase in stockholders' equity.
c. increase in liabilities and an increase in stockholders' equity.
d. increase in assets and an increase in liabilities.

9-7 Bower Company sold $100,000 of 20-year bonds for $95,000. The stated rate on the bonds was 7%, and interest is paid annually on December 31. What entry would be made on December 31 when the interest is paid? (Numbers are omitted.)

a. Interest Expense
   Cash
b. Interest Expense
   Bonds Payable
   Cash
c. Interest Expense
   Discount on Bonds Payable
   Cash
d. Interest Expense
   Discount on Bonds Payable
   Cash

9-8 Bonds in the amount of $100,000 with a life of 10 years were issued by the Roundy Company. If the stated rate is 6% and interest is paid semiannually, what would be the total amount of interest paid over the life of the bonds?

a. $120,000
b. $60,000
c. $30,000
d. $6,000

9-9 Sean Corp. issued a $40,000, 10-year bond, with a stated rate of 8%, paid semiannually. How much cash will the bond investors receive at the end of the first interest period?

a. $800
b. $1,600
c. $3,200
d. $4,000

9-10 When bonds are issued at a discount, the interest expense for the period is the amount of interest payment for the period

a. plus the premium amortization for the period.
b. minus the premium amortization for the period.
c. plus the discount amortization for the period.
d. minus the discount amortization for the period.

9-11 When bonds are issued at a premium, the interest expense for the period is the amount of interest payment for the period

a. minus the premium amortization for the period.
b. plus the premium amortization for the period.
c. plus the discount amortization for the period.
d. minus the discount amortization for the period.

9-12 Installment bonds differ from typical bonds in what way?

a. Essentially they are the same.
b. The entire principal balance is paid off at maturity for installment bonds.
c. Installment bonds do not have a stated rate.
d. A portion of each installment bond payment pays down the principal balance.

9-13 In 2013, Drew Company issued $200,000 of bonds for $189,640. If the stated rate of interest was 6% and the yield was 6.73%, how would Drew calculate the interest expense for the first year on the bonds using the effective interest method?

a. $189,640 × 8%
b. $189,640 × 6.73%
c. $200,000 × 8%
d. $200,000 × 6.73%

9-14 The result of using the effective interest method of amortization of the discount on bonds is that

a. the cash interest payment is greater than the interest expense.
b. the amount of interest expense decreases each period.
c. the interest expense for each amortization period is constant.
d. a constant interest rate is charged against the debt carrying value.

9-15 Serenity Company issued $100,000 of 6%, 10-year bonds when the market rate of interest was 5%. The proceeds from this bond issue were $107,732. Using the effective interest method of amortization, which of the following statements is true? Assume interest is paid annually.

a. Amortization of the premium for the first interest period will be $1,464.
b. Amortization of the premium for the first interest period will be $613.
c. Interest payments to bondholders each period will be $5,000.
d. Interest payments to bondholders each period will be $6,464.

9-16 Bonds are a popular source of financing because

a. a company having cash flow problems can postpone payment of interest to bondholders.
b. financial analysts tend to downgrade a company that has raised large amounts of cash by frequent issues of stock.
c. bond interest expense is deductible for tax purposes, while dividends paid on stock are not.
d. the bondholders can always convert their bonds into stock if they choose.

9-17 Which of the following statements regarding leases is *false*?

a. If a lease is classified as a capital lease, the lessee records a lease liability on its balance sheet.
b. If a lease is classified as an operating lease, the lessee records a lease liability on its balance sheet.
c. Accounting recognizes two types of leases—operating and capital leases.
d. Lease agreements are a popular form of financing the purchase of assets because leases do not require a large initial outlay of cash.

9-18 Which of the following lease conditions would result in a capital lease to the lessee?

a. The lessee will return the property to the lessor at the end of the lease term.
b. The lease term is 70% of the property's economic life.
c. The fair market value of the property at the inception of the lease is $18,000; the present value of the minimum lease payments is $15,977.
d. The lessee can purchase the property for $1 at the end of the lease term.

9-19 On January 2, 2013, Sylvester Metals Co. leased a mining machine from EDH Leasing Corp. The lease qualifies as an operating lease. The annual payments are $4,000 paid at the end of each year, and the life of the lease is 10 years. What entry would Sylvester make when the machine is delivered by EDH?

a. Prepaid Rent	40,000	
Lease Liability		40,000
b. Leased Assets	40,000	
Lease Liability		40,000
c. Prepaid Rent	4,000	
Lease Liability		4,000

d. No entry is necessary.

9-20 WVA Mining Company has leased a machine from Franklin Machinery Company. The annual payments are $6,000, and the life of the lease is 8 years. It is estimated that the useful life of the machine is 9 years. How would WVA record the acquisition of the machine?

a. The machine would be recorded as an asset with a cost of $54,000.
b. The machine would be recorded as an asset, at the present value of $6,000 for 8 years.
c. The machine would be recorded as an asset, at the present value of $6,000 for 9 years.
d. The company would not record the machine as an asset but would record rent expense of $6,000 per year.

9-21 Willow Corporation's balance sheet showed the following amounts: current liabilities, $5,000; bonds payable, $1,500; lease obligations, $2,300. Total stockholders' equity was $6,000. The debt to equity ratio is

a. 1.47.
b. 1.42.
c. 0.83.
d. 0.63.

9-22 Kinsella Corporation's balance sheet showed the following amounts: current liabilities, $75,000; total liabilities, $100,000; total assets, $200,000. What is the long-term debt to equity ratio?

a. 0.75
b. 0.375
c. 0.25
d. 0.125

9-23 McLaughlin Corporation's balance sheet showed the following amounts: current liabilities, $75,000; total liabilities, $100,000; total assets, $200,000. What is the debt to total assets ratio?

a. 2
b. 1
c. 0.875
d. 0.50

9-24 *(Appendix 9A)* The bond issue price is determined by calculating the

a. present value of the stream of interest payments and the present value of the maturity amount.
b. future value of the stream of interest payments and the future value of the maturity amount.
c. future value of the stream of interest payments and the present value of the maturity amount.
d. present value of the stream of interest payments and the future value of the maturity amount.

CORNERSTONE EXERCISES

Cornerstone Exercise 9-25 Reporting Long-Term Debt on the Balance Sheet

OBJECTIVE 2
CORNERSTONE 9.1

Dennis Corp. has the following bonds:

a. $2,000,000 in bonds that have $10,000 of unamortized discount associated with them.
b. $500,000 in bonds that have $25,000 of unamortized premium associated with them.

Required:

Prepare the balance sheet presentation for these two bonds.

Cornerstone Exercise 9-26 Issuance of Long-Term Debt

OBJECTIVE 2
CORNERSTONE 9.1

Anne Corp. issued $600,000, 5% bonds.

Required:

Prepare the necessary journal entries to record the issuance of these bonds assuming the bonds were issued (a) at par, (b) at 102, and (c) at 92.

Cornerstone Exercise 9-27 Issuance of Long-Term Debt

OBJECTIVE 2
CORNERSTONE 9.1

EWO Enterprises issues $4,500,000 of bonds payable.

Required:

Prepare the necessary journal entries to record the issuance of the bonds assuming the bonds were issued (a) at par, (b) at 104.5, and (c) at 99.

Cornerstone Exercise 9-28 Issuance of Long-Term Debt

OBJECTIVE 2
CORNERSTONE 9.1

M. Nickles Company issued $1,500,000 of bonds for $1,487,200. Interest is paid semiannually.

Required:

1. Prepare the necessary journal entry to record the issuance of the bonds.
2. Is the yield greater or less than the stated rate? How do you know?

Cornerstone Exercise 9-29 Debt Issued at Par

OBJECTIVE 3
CORNERSTONE 9.2

On December 31, 2012, Brock & Co. issued $600,000 of bonds payable at par. The bonds have a 9% stated rate, pay interest on March 31, June 30, September 30, and December 31, and mature on December 31, 2013.

Required:

Prepare the journal entries to record the interest payment on June 30, 2013.

> *Use the following information for Cornerstone Exercises 9-30 and 9-31:*
> On December 31, 2013, Drew Company issued $350,000, 5-year bonds for $320,000. The stated rate of interest was 7% and interest is paid annually on December 31.

Cornerstone Exercise 9-30 Debt Issued at a Discount (Straight Line)

OBJECTIVE 3
CORNERSTONE 9.3

Refer to the information for Drew Company above.

Required:

Prepare the necessary journal entry on December 31, 2015, assuming the straight-line method is followed.

Cornerstone Exercise 9-31 Debt Issued at a Discount (Straight Line)

OBJECTIVE 3
CORNERSTONE 9.3

Refer to the information for Drew Company above.

(Continued)

Required:

Prepare the amortization table for Drew Company's bonds. (*Note:* Round to the nearest dollar.)

> *Use the following information for Cornerstone Exercises 9-32 and 9-33:*
> On December 31, 2013, Ironman Steel issued $1,300,000, 8-year bonds for $1,340,000. The stated rate of interest was 7% and interest is paid annually on December 31.

OBJECTIVE 3
CORNERSTONE 9.4

Cornerstone Exercise 9-32 Debt Issued at a Premium (Straight Line)

Refer to the information for Ironman Steel above.

Required:

Prepare the necessary journal entry on December 31, 2017, assuming the straight-line method is followed.

OBJECTIVE 3
CORNERSTONE 9.4

Cornerstone Exercise 9-33 Debt Issued at a Premium (Straight Line)

Refer to the information for Ironman Steel above.

Required:

Prepare the amortization table for Ironman Steel's bonds. (*Note:* Round to the nearest dollar.)

> *Use the following information for Cornerstone Exercises 9-34 and 9-35:*
> Sicily Corporation issued $300,000 in 5% bonds (payable on December 31, 2023) on December 31, 2013, for $257,363. Interest is paid on June 30 and December 31. The market rate of interest is 7%.

OBJECTIVE 4
CORNERSTONE 9.5

Cornerstone Exercise 9-34 Bonds Issued at a Discount (Effective Interest)

Refer to the information for Sicily Corporation above.

Required:

Prepare the amortization table through December 31, 2015, using the effective interest rate method. (*Note:* Round to the nearest dollar. Rounding differences may occur in spreadsheet software.)

OBJECTIVE 4
CORNERSTONE 9.5

Cornerstone Exercise 9-35 Bonds Issued at a Discount (Effective Interest)

Refer to the information for Sicily Corporation above.

Required:

Prepare the journal entries for December 31, 2014 and 2015.

> *Use the following information for Cornerstone Exercises 9-36 and 9-37:*
> Crafty Corporation issued $475,000 of 5%, 7-year bonds on December 31, 2013, for $448,484. Interest is paid annually on December 31. The market rate of interest is 6%.

OBJECTIVE 4
CORNERSTONE 9.5

Cornerstone Exercise 9-36 Bonds Issued at a Discount (Effective Interest)

Refer to the information for Crafty Corporation above.

Required:

Prepare the amortization table using the effective interest rate method. (*Note:* Round to the nearest dollar. Rounding differences may occur in spreadsheet software.)

OBJECTIVE 4
CORNERSTONE 9.5

Cornerstone Exercise 9-37 Issued at a Discount (Effective Interest)

Refer to the information for Crafty Corporation above.

Required:

Prepare the journal entry for December 31, 2014 and 2015.

Use the following information for Cornerstone Exercises 9-38 and 9-39:
Cookie Dough Corporation issued $850,000 in 9%, 10-year bonds (payable on December 31, 2024) on December 31, 2014, for $907,759. Interest is paid on June 30 and December 31. The market rate of interest is 8%.

Cornerstone Exercise 9-38 Bonds Issued at a Premium (Effective Interest)

OBJECTIVE 4
CORNERSTONE 9.6

Refer to the information for Cookie Dough Corporation above.

Required:

Prepare the amortization table through December 31, 2017, using the effective interest rate method. (*Note:* Round to the nearest dollar. Rounding differences may occur in spreadsheet software.)

Cornerstone Exercise 9-39 Bonds Issued at a Premium (Effective Interest)

OBJECTIVE 4
CORNERSTONE 9.6

Refer to the information for Cookie Dough Corporation above.

Required:

Prepare the journal entries for December 31, 2016 and 2017.

Use the following information for Cornerstone Exercises 9-40 and 9-41:
Charger Battery issued $200,000 of 11%, 7-year bonds on December 31, 2013, for $220,132. Interest is paid annually on December 31. The market rate of interest is 9%.

Cornerstone Exercise 9-40 Bonds Issued at a Premium (Effective Interest)

OBJECTIVE 4
CORNERSTONE 9.6

Refer to the information for Charger Battery above.

Required:

Prepare the amortization table using the effective interest rate method. (*Note:* Round to the nearest dollar. Rounding differences may occur in spreadsheet software.)

Cornerstone Exercise 9-41 Bonds Issued at a Premium (Effective Interest)

OBJECTIVE 4
CORNERSTONE 9.6

Refer to the information for Charger Battery above.

Required:

Prepare the journal entries for December 31, 2015 and 2016.

Cornerstone Exercise 9-42 Ratio Analysis

OBJECTIVE 7
CORNERSTONE 9.7

Watterson Corporation's balance sheet showed the following amounts: current liabilities, $70,000; bonds payable, $150,000; and lease obligations, $20,000. Total stockholders' equity was $90,000.

Required:

Calculate the debt to equity ratio. (*Note:* Round answer to three decimal places.)

Cornerstone Exercise 9-43 Ratio Analysis

OBJECTIVE 7
CORNERSTONE 9.7

Blue Corporation has $2,000,000 in total liabilities and $3,500,000 in total assets.

Required:

Calculate Blue's debt to equity ratio. (*Note:* Round answer to three decimal places.)

OBJECTIVE 7
CORNERSTONE 9.7

Cornerstone Exercise 9-44 Ratio Analysis

Red Corporation had $1,750,000 in total liabilities and $3,000,000 in total assets as of December 31, 2014. Of Red's total liabilities, $600,000 is long-term.

Required:

Calculate Red's debt to assets ratio and its long-term debt to equity ratio. (*Note:* Round answers to four decimal places.)

OBJECTIVE 8
CORNERSTONE 9.8

Cornerstone Exercise 9-45 *(Appendix 9A)* Bond Issue Price

On December 31, 2013, Garner Hot Rods issued $2,000,000 of 6%, 10-year bonds. Interest is payable semiannually on June 30 and December 31.

Required:

What is the issue price if the bonds are sold to yield 8%? (*Note:* Round to the nearest dollar.)

OBJECTIVE 8
CORNERSTONE 9.8

Cornerstone Exercise 9-46 *(Appendix 9A)* Bond Issue Price

On December 31, 2014, Callahan Auto issued $900,000 of 9%, 10-year bonds. Interest is payable semiannually on June 30 and December 31.

Required:

What is the issue price if the bonds are sold to yield 8%? (*Note:* Round to the nearest dollar.)

BRIEF EXERCISES

OBJECTIVE 2

Brief Exercise 9-47 Reporting Long-Term Debt on the Balance Sheet

Scott Corp. provides contracted home staging services to real estate agencies and their clients. Scott issued the following bonds in the current year:

a. 1,500 bonds with $1,000 face value which the market has valued at $45,000 below its face value
b. 2,700 bonds with $1,000 face value which the market has valued at $85,000 above its face value

Required:

Prepare the balance sheet presentation for these two bonds.

OBJECTIVE 2

Brief Exercise 9-48 Issuance of Long-Term Debt

Natalie Corp. provides medical supplies to hospitals located in Western Washington and Oregon. This year, Natalie Corp. issued 8,000 bonds with a $1,000 face value. The nominal rate for each bond is 7%.

Required:

Prepare the necessary journal entries to record the issuance of these bonds assuming the bonds were issued (a) at par, (b) at 103, and (c) at 96.

OBJECTIVE 2

Brief Exercise 9-49 Issuance of Long-Term Debt

APL Enterprises required an infusion of cash in order to purchase a large piece of equipment. To finance its equipment purchase, APL issued $3,600,000 of 8% bonds payable.

Required:

Prepare the necessary journal entries to record the issuance of the bonds assuming the bonds were issued (a) at par, (b) at 102, and (c) at 97.

Brief Exercise 9-50 Issuance of Long-Term Debt OBJECTIVE 2

H. Simpson Company is an entertainment company located in Springfield, IL. H. Simpson recently issued $200,000 of bonds to finance large expenditures for an upcoming television production. H. Simpson received cash of $194,620 upon the issuance of the bonds and plans to pay interest semiannually.

Required:

1. Prepare the necessary journal entry to record the issuance of the bonds.
2. Is the stated rate greater or less than the yield? How do you know?

Brief Exercise 9-51 Debt Issued at Par OBJECTIVE 3

On December 31, 2013, Desmond & Co. issued 5,000 bonds with a $1,000 par value at 100. The bonds have an 8% stated rate, pay interest on June 30 and December 31, and mature on December 31, 2014.

Required:

Prepare the journal entries to record the interest payment on June 30, 2014.

Brief Exercise 9-52 Debt Issued at a Discount (Straight Line) OBJECTIVE 3

On December 31, 2013, Mayor Company issued 40,000 5-year bonds with a $1,000 par value each. The market values the bonds at $30,000 less than the face value of the bonds. The stated rate of interest is 6%, and interest is paid annually on December 31.

Required:

Prepare the necessary journal entry on December 31, 2014, assuming the straight-line method is followed.

Brief Exercise 9-53 Debt Issued at a Discount (Straight Line) OBJECTIVE 3

Use the information from **Brief Exercise 9-52**.

Required:

Prepare the amortization table for Mayor Company's bonds.

Brief Exercise 9-54 Debt Issued at a Premium (Straight Line) OBJECTIVE 3

On December 31, 2013, Solomon Crafts issued 60,000 8-year bonds with $1,000 face value. External markets value the bonds at $630,000 more than face value. The stated rate of interest on Solomon's bonds is 5%, and interest is paid annually on December 31.

Required:

Prepare the necessary journal entry on December 31, 2015, assuming the straight-line method is followed.

Brief Exercise 9-55 Debt Issued at a Premium (Straight Line) OBJECTIVE 3

Use the information from **Brief Exercise 9-54**.

Required:

Prepare the amortization table for Solomon's bonds.

Use the following information for Brief Exercises 9-56 and 9-57:
Roman Corporation decided to issue long-term debt in order to pay off its short-term obligations. On December 31, 2014, Roman issued $900,000 in 7% bonds (payable on December 31, 2024) at 87. Interest is paid on June 30 and December 31. The market rate of interest is 9%.

OBJECTIVE 4

Brief Exercise 9-56 Bonds Issued at a Discount (Effective Interest)

Refer to the information for Roman Corporation on the previous page.

Required:

Prepare the amortization table through December 31, 2016, using the effective interest rate method.

OBJECTIVE 4

Brief Exercise 9-57 Bonds Issued at a Discount (Effective Interest)

Refer to the information for Roman Corporation on the previous page.

Required:

Prepare the journal entries for December 31, 2015 and 2016.

Use the following information for Brief Exercises 9-58 and 9-59:
Crafty Corporation received $472,088 of cash upon issuance of 500 $1,000 par value bonds. Each bond has a stated rate of 5% and will mature on December 31, 2020, 7 years after the issuance of the bonds. Interest is paid annually on December 31. The market rate of interest is 6%.

OBJECTIVE 4

Brief Exercise 9-58 Bonds Issued at a Discount (Effective Interest)

Refer to the information for Crafty Corporation above.

Required:

Prepare the amortization table using the effective interest rate method.

OBJECTIVE 4

Brief Exercise 9-59 Bonds Issued at a Discount (Effective Interest)

Refer to the information for Crafty Corporation above.

Required:

Prepare the journal entry for December 31, 2016 and 2017.

Use the following information for Brief Exercises 9-60 and 9-61:
Haley Industries issued $120,000 of 11%, 7-year bonds on December 31, 2013, with a $5,842 premium. Interest is paid annually on December 31. The market rate of interest is 10%.

OBJECTIVE 4

Brief Exercise 9-60 Bonds Issued at a Premium (Effective Interest)

Refer to the information above for Haley Industries.

Required:

Prepare the amortization table using the effective interest rate method.

OBJECTIVE 4

Brief Exercise 9-61 Bonds Issued at a Premium (Effective Interest)

Refer to the information above for Haley Industries.

Required:

Record the journal entries for December 31, 2015 and 2016.

OBJECTIVE 5

Brief Exercise 9-62 Cost of Debt Financing

Topple Corporation leases skyscrapers in cities throughout the world to large corporations. Topple's cost of debt financing is 9%, its cost of equity is 12%, and its tax rate is 35%.

Required:

Calculate the after-tax interest rate to two-tenths of 1%.

Brief Exercise 9-63 Cost of Debt Financing

OBJECTIVE 5

Crackle Company instituted an aggressive plan to lower its cost of financing over the next decade. Currently Crackle's cost of debt financing is 8%, its cost of equity financing is 14%, and its tax rate is 35%. Crackle currently has $2,500,000 of debt.

Required:

1. Calculate the after-tax cost amount of interest expense.
2. How does the tax effect of interest expense affect financial leverage?

Brief Exercise 9-64 Leases

OBJECTIVE 6

Overland Airlines leased an aircraft from JRL Aircraft Company. Overland believes it may have been able to purchase an aircraft at a cost lower than the cost of leasing the aircraft; however, Overland does not want the obligation of including an aircraft as an asset in its financial statements. The annual payments of the lease are $1,250,000, and the life of the lease is 15 years. It is estimated that the useful life of the aircraft is 18 years. The present value of the future lease payments is $9,235,730.

Required:

CONCEPTUAL CONNECTION Would Overland Aircraft record the lease as an operating or capital lease? Why?

Brief Exercise 9-65 Ratio Analysis

OBJECTIVE 7

Whitten Corporation's balance sheet shows the following amounts: current assets, $200,000; current liabilities, $80,000; bonds payable, $155,000; and lease obligations, $25,000. Total stockholders' equity is $120,000.

Required:

Calculate the debt to equity ratio. (*Note:* Round to two decimal places.)

Brief Exercise 9-66 Ratio Analysis

OBJECTIVE 7

Valiant Corporation has $1,800,000 in total liabilities, $800,000 of which are current. Valiant has $400,000 of cash and cash equivalents, $300,000 of other current assets, and $2,000,000 in property, plant, and equipment.

Required:

Calculate Valiant's debt to equity ratio.

Brief Exercise 9-67 Ratio Analysis

OBJECTIVE 7

Trevor Corporation had $2,900,000 in total liabilities and $4,300,000 in total assets as of December 31, 2013. Trevor calculates that 40% of assets are designated as current, while $500,000 of Trevor's total liabilities are long-term.

Required:

Calculate Trevor's debt to assets ratio and its long-term debt to equity ratio. (*Note:* Round to two decimal places.)

Brief Exercise 9-68 *(Appendix 9A)* Bond Issue Price

OBJECTIVE 8

On December 31, 2013, Ruby Inc. issued 3,000 $1,000 par value bonds with a stated rate of 6% and a 10-year maturity. Interest is payable semiannually on June 30 and December 31.

(Continued)

Required:

What is the issue price if the bonds are sold to yield 8%? (*Note:* Round to nearest dollar.)

OBJECTIVE 8

Brief Exercise 9-69 *(Appendix 9A)* Bond Issue Price

On December 31, 2013, Nelson Construction issued 3,500 of $1,000 par value bonds with a stated rate of 8%, maturing in 10 years. Interest is payable semiannually on June 30 and December 31.

Required:

What is the issue price if the bonds are sold to yield 6%? (*Note:* Round to nearest dollar.)

EXERCISES

OBJECTIVE 1 2

Exercise 9-70 Issuing at Par, a Premium, or a Discount

Dash Enterprises is planning to issue 1,500 bonds, each having a face amount of $1,000.

Required:

1. Prepare the journal entry to record the sale of the bonds at par.
2. Prepare the journal entry to record the sale of the bonds at a premium of $19,000.
3. Prepare the journal entry to record the sale of the bonds at a discount of $32,000.
4. **CONCEPTUAL CONNECTION** Assuming the stated rate is identical for the previous three scenarios, in which scenario is the market rate of interest (yield) highest? How do you know?

OBJECTIVE 1 2

Exercise 9-71 Bond Premium and Discount

Markway Inc. is contemplating selling bonds. The issue is to be composed of 750 bonds, each with a face amount of $1,000.

Required:

1. Calculate how much Markway is able to borrow if each bond is sold at a premium of $30.
2. Calculate how much Markway is able to borrow if each bond is sold at a discount of $10.
3. Calculate how much Markway is able to borrow if each bond is sold at 92% of par.
4. Calculate how much Markway is able to borrow if each bond is sold at 103% of par.
5. Assume that the bonds are sold for $975 each. Prepare the entry to recognize the sale of the 750 bonds.
6. Assume that the bonds are sold for $1,015 each. Prepare the entry to recognize the sale of the 750 bonds.

OBJECTIVE 2 3

Exercise 9-72 Bonds with Annual Interest Payments

Kiwi Corporation issued at par $350,000, 9% bonds on December 31, 2013. Interest is paid annually on December 31. The principal and the final interest payment are due on December 31, 2015.

Required:

1. Prepare the entry to recognize the issuance of the bonds.
2. Prepare the journal entry for December 31, 2014.
3. Prepare the journal entry to record repayment of the principal on December 31, 2015.
4. **CONCEPTUAL CONNECTION** How would the interest expense for 2014 change if the bonds had been issued at a premium?

Exercise 9-73 Issuance and Interest Amortization for Zero Coupon Note (Straight Line)

OBJECTIVE 2 3

Kerwin Company borrowed $10,000 on a 2-year, zero coupon note. The note was issued on December 31, 2013. The face amount of the note, $12,544, is to be paid at maturity on December 31, 2015.

Required:

1. Assuming straight line amortization, calculate the interest expense for 2013 and 2014.
2. Prepare the entries to recognize the borrowing, the first year's interest expense, and the second year's interest expense plus redemption of the note at maturity.

Exercise 9-74 Interest Payments and Interest Expense for Bonds (Straight Line)

OBJECTIVE 2 3

Swiss Inc. sold 15-year bonds with a total face amount of $2,000,000 and a stated rate of 6%. The bonds sold for $2,090,000 on December 31, 2013, and pay interest semiannually on June 30 and December 31.

Required:

1. Prepare the entry to recognize the sale of the bonds.
2. Determine the amount of the semiannual interest payment required by the bonds.
3. Prepare the journal entry made by Swiss at June 30, 2014, to recognize the interest expense and an interest payment.
4. Determine the amount of interest expense for 2014.
5. **CONCEPTUAL CONNECTION** If Swiss issued bonds with a variable interest rate, would you expect the market rate of interest (i.e., yield) to increase, decrease, or stay the same? Why?
6. **CONCEPTUAL CONNECTION** What should Swiss consider in deciding whether to use a fixed or variable rate?

Exercise 9-75 Interest Payments and Interest Expense for Bonds (Straight Line)

OBJECTIVE 2 3

On December 31, 2013, Harrington Corporation sold $425,000 of 15-year, 11% bonds. The bonds sold for $395,000 and pay interest semiannually on June 30 and December 31.

Required:

1. Prepare the journal entry to record the sale of the bonds.
2. Calculate the amount of the semiannual interest payment.
3. Prepare the entry at June 30, 2014, to recognize the payment of interest and interest expense.
4. Calculate the annual interest expense for 2014.

Exercise 9-76 Interest Payments and Interest Expense for Bonds (Straight Line)

OBJECTIVE 3

On December 31, 2013, Perry Manufacturing issued bonds with a total face amount of $3,000,000 and a stated rate of 9%.

Required:

1. Calculate the interest expense for 2014 if the bonds were sold at par.
2. Calculate the interest expense for 2014 if the bonds were sold at a premium and the straight-line premium amortization for 2014 is $12,000.
3. Calculate the interest expense for 2014 if the bonds were sold at a discount and the straight-line discount amortization for 2014 is $33,000.

Exercise 9-77 Completing a Debt Amortization Table (Straight Line)

OBJECTIVE 3

ILLUSTRATING RELATIONSHIPS

Cagney Company sold $200,000 of bonds on December 31, 2013. A portion of the amortization table follows.

(Continued)

Period	Cash Payment (Credit)	Interest Expense (Debit)	Discount on Bonds Payable (Credit)	Discount on Bonds Payable Balance	Carrying Value
At issue				$8,000	$192,000
06/30/14	$12,000	$12,800	$800	7,200	192,800
12/31/14	12,000	12,800	800	6,400	193,600
06/30/15	?	?	?	?	?

Required:

1. Determine the stated interest rate on these bonds.
2. Calculate the interest expense and the discount amortization for the interest period ending June 30, 2015.
3. Calculate the liability balance shown on a balance sheet after the interest payment is recorded on June 30, 2015.

OBJECTIVE 3

Exercise 9-78 Using a Premium Amortization Table (Straight Line)

For Dingle Corporation, the following amortization table was prepared when $400,000 of 5-year, 7% bonds were sold on December 31, 2013, for $420,000.

Period	Cash Payment (Credit)	Interest Expense (Debit)	Premium on Bonds Payable (Debit)	Premium on Bonds Payable Balance	Carrying Value
At issue				$20,000	$420,000
06/30/14	$14,000	$12,000	$2,000	18,000	418,000
12/31/14	14,000	12,000	2,000	16,000	416,000
06/30/15	14,000	12,000	2,000	14,000	414,000
12/31/15	14,000	12,000	2,000	12,000	412,000
06/30/16	14,000	12,000	2,000	10,000	410,000
12/31/16	14,000	12,000	2,000	8,000	408,000
06/30/17	14,000	12,000	2,000	6,000	406,000
12/31/17	14,000	12,000	2,000	4,000	404,000
06/30/18	14,000	12,000	2,000	2,000	402,000
12/31/18	14,000	12,000	2,000	0	400,000

Required:

1. Prepare the entry to recognize the issuance of the bonds on December 31, 2013.
2. Prepare the entry to recognize the first interest payment on June 30, 2014.
3. Determine what interest expense for this bond issue Dingle will report in its 2015 income statement.
4. Indicate how these bonds will appear in Dingle's December 31, 2017 balance sheet.

OBJECTIVE 3

Exercise 9-79 Using a Discount Amortization Table (Straight Line)

Panamint Candy Company prepared the following amortization table for $300,000 of 5-year, 9% bonds issued and sold by Panamint on December 31, 2014, for $285,000:

Period	Cash Payment (Credit)	Interest Expense (Debit)	Discount on Bonds Payable (Credit)	Discount on Bonds Payable Balance	Carrying Value
				$15,000	$285,000
06/30/15	$13,500	$15,000	$1,500	13,500	286,500
12/31/15	13,500	15,000	1,500	12,000	288,000
06/30/16	13,500	15,000	1,500	10,500	289,500
12/31/16	13,500	15,000	1,500	9,000	291,000
06/30/17	13,500	15,000	1,500	7,500	292,500
12/31/17	13,500	15,000	1,500	6,000	294,000
06/30/18	13,500	15,000	1,500	4,500	295,500
12/31/18	13,500	15,000	1,500	3,000	297,000
06/30/19	13,500	15,000	1,500	1,500	298,500
12/31/19	13,500	15,000	1,500	0	300,000

Required:

1. Prepare the entry to recognize the sale of the bonds on December 31, 2014.
2. Prepare the entry to recognize the first interest payment on June 30, 2015.
3. Determine the interest expense for these bonds that Panamint will report on its 2017 income statement.
4. Indicate how these bonds will appear in Panamint's December 31, 2018 balance sheet.

Exercise 9-80 Completing an Amortization Table (Straight Line)

OBJECTIVE 3

Richter Corporation sold $1,000,000 face value of bonds at 104 on December 31, 2013. These bonds have a 7% stated rate and mature in 4 years. Interest is payable on June 30 and December 31 of each year.

Required:

1. Prepare a bond amortization table assuming straight-line amortization.
2. Prepare the journal entry for December 31, 2015.
3. Indicate how these bonds will appear in Richter's balance sheet at December 31, 2015.

Exercise 9-81 Zero Coupon Bond

OBJECTIVE 3

Johnson Company sold for $90,000 a $102,400, 2-year zero coupon bond on December 31, 2013. The bond matures on December 31, 2015.

Required:

1. Prepare the entry to record the issuance of the bond.
2. Prepare the adjusting entry to recognize 2014 interest expense.
3. Prepare the entry to recognize the 2015 interest expense and the repayment of the bond on December 31, 2015.

Exercise 9-82 Zero Coupon Note

OBJECTIVE 3

Dodge City Products borrowed $100,000 cash by issuing a 36-month, $120,880 zero coupon note on December 31, 2014. The note matures on December 31, 2017.

Required:

1. Prepare the entry to recognize the issuance of the note.
2. Prepare the adjustments to recognize 2015 and 2016 interest.
3. Prepare the entry to recognize 2017 interest and repayment of the note at maturity.

Exercise 9-83 Note Interest Payment and Interest Expense (Effective Interest)

OBJECTIVE 4

Jones Manufacturing sold $900,000 of 15-year, 7% notes for $822,186. The notes were sold December 31, 2013, and pay interest semiannually on June 30 and December 31. The effective interest rate was 8%. Assume Jones uses the effective interest rate method.

Required:

1. Prepare the entry to record the sale of the notes.
2. Determine the amount of the semiannual interest payments for the notes.
3. Prepare the amortization table through 2015. (*Note:* Round to the nearest dollar.)
4. Prepare the entry for Jones' journal at June 30, 2014, to record the payment of 6 months' interest and the related interest expense.
5. Determine interest expense for 2015.

Exercise 9-84 Bond Interest Payments and Interest Expense (Effective Interest)

OBJECTIVE 4

On December 31, 2012, Hawthorne Corporation issued for $155,989, 5-year bonds with a face amount of $150,000 and a stated (or coupon) rate of 9%. The bonds pay interest annually and have an effective interest rate of 8%. Assume Hawthorne uses the effective interest rate method.

(*Continued*)

Required:

1. Prepare the entry to record the sale of the bonds.
2. Calculate the amount of the interest payments for the bonds.
3. Prepare the amortization table through 2014. (*Note:* Round to the nearest dollar.)
4. Prepare the journal entry for December 31, 2013, to record the payment of interest and the related interest expense.
5. Calculate the annual interest expense for 2013 and 2014.

OBJECTIVE 4

ILLUSTRATING RELATIONSHIPS

Exercise 9-85 Completing a Bond Amortization Table (Effective Interest Rate Method)

Cagney Company sold $200,000 of bonds on June 30, 2012. A portion of the amortization table appears below.

Period	Cash Payment (Credit)	Interest Expense (Debit)	Discount on Bonds Payable (Credit)	Discount on Bonds Payable Balance	Carrying Value
12/31/13	$9,000	$9,277	$277	$2,340	$197,660
06/30/14	9,000	9,290	290	2,050	197,950
12/31/14	?	?	?	?	?

Required:

1. Indicate the stated interest rate on these bonds.
2. Calculate the effective annual interest rate on these bonds. (*Note:* Round to the nearest 0.1%.)
3. Determine the interest expense and discount amortization for the interest period ending December 31, 2014. (*Note:* Round to the nearest dollar.)
4. Determine the liability balance after the interest payment is recorded on December 31, 2014.

OBJECTIVE 4

ILLUSTRATING RELATIONSHIPS

Exercise 9-86 Completing a Bond Amortization Table (Effective Interest Rate Method)

MacBride Enterprises sold $200,000 of bonds on December 31, 2013. A portion of the amortization table appears below.

Period	Cash Payment (Credit)	Interest Expense (Debit)	Premium on Bonds Payable (Debit)	Premium on Bonds Payable Balance	Carrying Value
At issue				$6,457	$206,457
06/30/14	$9,000	$8,465	$535	5,922	205,922
12/31/14	9,000	8,443	557	5,365	205,365
06/30/15	9,000	8,420	580	4,785	204,785
12/31/15	?	?	?	?	?

Required:

1. Indicate the stated annual interest rate on these bonds.
2. Calculate the effective annual interest rate on these bonds. (*Note:* Round to the nearest 0.1%.)
3. Determine the interest expense and premium amortization for the interest period ending December 31, 2015. (*Note:* Round to the nearest dollar.)
4. Determine when the bonds will mature.

Use the following information for Exercises 9-87 and 9-88:
Dandy Candy bought a delivery vehicle for $45,000 by issuing an 8% installment note on December 31, 2014. Dandy will make 12 monthly payments of $3,914.50 at the end of each month.

OBJECTIVE 4

ILLUSTRATING RELATIONSHIPS

Exercise 9-87 Installment Notes

Refer to the information for Dandy Candy above.

Required:

Prepare the amortization table using the effective interest rate method. (*Note:* Round to the nearest penny.)

Exercise 9-88 Installment Notes

OBJECTIVE 4

Refer to the information for Dandy Candy on the previous page.

Required:

Prepare the journal entries for the end of March and the end of April.

Exercise 9-89 Installment Notes

OBJECTIVE 4

ABC bank loans $250,000 to Yossarian to purchase a new home. Yossarian will repay the note in equal monthly payments over a period of 30 years. The interest rate is 12%.

Required:

If the monthly payment is $2,571.53, how much of the first payment is interest expense and how much is principal repayment? (*Note:* Round to the nearest cent.)

Exercise 9-90 Noninterest-Bearing Bonds (Straight Line)

OBJECTIVE 3

Dean Plumbing issues $1,000,000 face value, noninterest-bearing bonds on December 31, 2014. The bonds are issued at 65 and mature on December 31, 2018.

Required:

Assuming the straight-line amortization method is followed, prepare the journal entry on December 31, 2017.

Exercise 9-91 Cost of Debt Financing

OBJECTIVE 5

Stinson Corporation's cost of debt financing is 6%. Its tax rate is 30%.

Required:

Calculate the after-tax interest rate. (*Note:* Round answer to one decimal place.)

Exercise 9-92 Cost of Debt Financing

OBJECTIVE 5

Diamond Company's cost of debt financing is 10%. Its tax rate is 35%. Diamond has $3,000,000 of debt.

Required:

1. Calculate the after-tax cost amount of interest expense.
2. **CONCEPTUAL CONNECTION** How does the tax effect of interest expense affect financial leverage?

Exercise 9-93 Leases

OBJECTIVE 6

Meyer Bus Services has leased a tour bus from Ground Bus Company. The annual payments are $200,000, and the life of the lease is 12 years. It is estimated that the useful life of the tour bus is 14 years. The present value of the future lease payments is $1,988,200.

Required:

CONCEPTUAL CONNECTION Would Meyer record the lease as an operating or capital lease? Why?

Exercise 9-94 Ratio Analysis

OBJECTIVE 7

Rising Stars Academy provided the following information on its 2013 balance sheet and statement of cash flows:

Long-term debt	$ 4,400	Interest expense	$ 398
Total liabilities	8,972	Net income	559
Total assets	38,775	Interest payments	432
Total equity	29,803	Cash flows from operations	1,015
Operating income	1,223	Income tax expenses	266
		Income taxes paid	150

(*Continued*)

Required:

1. Calculate the following ratios for Rising Stars: (a) debt to equity, (b) debt to total assets, (c) long-term debt to equity, (d) times interest earned (accrual basis), and (e) times interest earned (cash basis). (*Note:* Round answers to three decimal places.)
2. **CONCEPTUAL CONNECTION** Interpret these results.

OBJECTIVE 8

Exercise 9-95 *(Appendix 9A)* Calculating Bond Issue Price

On December 31, 2013, University Theatres issued $500,000 face value of bonds. The stated rate is 8%, and interest is paid semiannually on June 30 and December 31. The bonds mature in 15 years.

Required:

Calculate the price at which the bonds are issued assuming the market rate of interest is (a) 6% and (b) 10%.

PROBLEM SET A

OBJECTIVE 2

Problem 9-96A Reporting Long-Term Debt

Fridley Manufacturing's accounting records reveal the following account balances after adjusting entries are made on December 31, 2014:

Accounts payable	$ 62,500	Interest payable	$ 38,700
Bonds payable (9.4%, due in 2021)	800,000	Installment note payable (8%, equal installments due 2015 to 2018)	120,000
Lease liability*	41,500	Notes payable (7.8%, due in 2019)	400,000
Bonds payable (8.7%, due in 2017)	50,000	Premium on notes payable (7.8%, due in 2019)	6,100
Deferred tax liability*	133,400	Note payable, 4% $50,000 face amount, due in 2020 (net of discount)	31,900
Discount on bonds payable (9.4%, due in 2021)	12,600		
Income taxes payable	26,900		

* Long-term liability

Required:

Prepare the current liabilities and long-term debt portions of Fridley's balance sheet at December 31, 2014. Provide a separate line item for each issue (do not combine separate bonds or notes payable), but some items may need to be split into more than one item.

OBJECTIVE 2 3

Problem 9-97A Entries for and Financial Statement Presentation of a Note

Augustine Corporation borrowed $150,000 from the J.P Morgan Chase Bank on June 1, 2013, on a 3-year, 6.4% note. Interest is paid annually on June 1.

Required:

1. Record the borrowing transaction in Augustine's journal.
2. Prepare the adjusting entries made at December 31, 2013 and 2014.
3. Prepare the necessary journal entry to recognize the first interest payment on June 1, 2014.
4. Indicate how the note and associated interest would be presented in Augustine's December 31, 2014 balance sheet.
5. Prepare the necessary journal entries to record the repayment of the note and the last year's interest payment on June 1, 2016.

OBJECTIVE 2 3

Problem 9-98A Preparing a Bond Amortization Table (Straight Line)

On December 31, 2014, Distel Company borrowed $102,700 by issuing 3-year, 9% bonds with a face amount of $100,000. Interest is paid annually on December 31.

Required:

Prepare an amortization table using the following column headings:

Period	Cash Payment (Credit)	Interest Expense (Debit)	Premium on Bonds Payable (Debit)	Premium on Bonds Payable Balance	Carrying Value

Problem 9-99A Note Computations and Entries (Straight Line)

OBJECTIVE 3

On December 31, 2013, Sisek Company borrowed $800,000 with a 10-year, 9.75% note, interest payable semiannually on June 30 and December 31. Cash in the amount of $792,800 was received when the note WAS issued.

Required:

1. Prepare the necessary journal entry at December 31, 2013.
2. Prepare the necessary journal entry at June 30, 2014.
3. Prepare the necessary journal entry at December 31, 2014.
4. Determine the carrying amount of these notes at the end of the fifth year (December 31, 2018).

Problem 9-100A Preparing a Bond Amortization Table (Straight Line)

OBJECTIVE 3

Edmonton-Alston Corporation issued 5-year, 9.5% bonds with a total face value of $700,000 on December 31, 2013, for $726,000. The bonds pay interest on June 30 and December 31 of each year.

Required:

1. Prepare an amortization table.
2. Prepare the entries to recognize the interest payments made on June 30, 2014, and December 31, 2014.

Problem 9-101A Preparing a Bond Amortization Table (Straight Line)

OBJECTIVE 3

Sonoma Company, issued 5-year, 8.6% bonds with a total face value of $750,000 on December 31, 2013, for $711,450. The bonds pay interest on June 30 and December 31 of each year.

Required:

1. Prepare an amortization table.
2. Prepare the entries to recognize the bond issuance and the interest payments made on June 30, 2014, and December 31, 2014.

Problem 9-102A Preparing and Using an Amortization Table (Straight Line)

OBJECTIVE 3

Girves Development Corporation has agreed to construct a plant in a new industrial park. To finance the construction, the county government issued $5,000,000 of 10-year, 4.75% revenue bonds for $5,125,000 on December 31, 2013. Girves will pay the interest and principal on the bonds. When the bonds are repaid, Girves will receive title to the plant. In the interim, Girves will pay property taxes as if it owned the plant. This financing arrangement is attractive to Girves, as state and local government bonds are exempt from federal income taxation and thus carry a lower interest rate. The bonds are attractive to investors, as both Girves and the county are issuers. The bonds pay interest semiannually on June 30 and December 31.

Required:

1. Prepare an amortization table through December 31, 2015, for these revenue bonds assuming straight-line amortization.
2. **CONCEPTUAL CONNECTION** Discuss whether or not Girves should record the plant as an asset after it is constructed.
3. **CONCEPTUAL CONNECTION** Discuss whether or not Girves should record the liability for these revenue bonds.

Problem 9-103A Noninterest-Bearing Note (Straight Line)

OBJECTIVE 3

On December 31, 2013, Athena Corporation borrowed $110,000 cash on a $155,000, 24-month 0% note. Athena uses the straight-line method of amortization.

(Continued)

Required:

1. Record the borrowing in Athena's journal.
2. Prepare the adjusting entry for December 31, 2014.
3. Prepare the entries to recognize the 2015 interest expense and repayment of the note on December 31, 2015.

OBJECTIVE 3

Problem 9-104A Preparing an Amortization Table for Noninterest-Bearing Bonds (Straight Line)

On December 31, 2014, Georgetown Distributors borrowed $2,180,000 by issuing 4-year, zero coupon bonds. The face value of the bonds is $3,000,000. Georgetown uses the straight-line method to amortize any premium or discount.

Required:

Prepare an amortization table for these bonds, using the following column headings:

Period	Cash Payment (Credit)	Interest Expense (Debit)	Discount on Bonds Payable (Credit)	Discount on Bonds Payable Balance	Carrying Value

OBJECTIVE 6

Problem 9-105A Capital and Operating Leases

Sheldon Products has decided to lease its new office building. The following information is available for the lease:

Lease:	
Payments	$80,000 per year*
Length of lease	10 years
Economic life of building	12 years
Appropriate interest rate	5.2%
Cost of building if purchased	$620,000

* The first payment is due at the end of the first year of the lease.

Required:

1. Determine whether this is a capital lease or an operating lease.
2. Regardless of your answer to the preceding question, assume that this is a capital lease and that the present value of the lease payments is $611,783. Record the liability and corresponding asset for this acquisition. (*Note:* Round to the nearest dollar.)
3. Record the interest expense on the capital lease at the end of the first year. Also assume no residual value and a 10-year lease for the building. Record the first year's straight-line depreciation of the cost of the leased asset. (*Note:* Round to the nearest dollar.)

PROBLEM SET B

OBJECTIVE 2

Problem 9-96B Reporting Long-Term Debt

Craig Corporation's accounting records reveal the following account balances after adjusting entries are made on December 31, 2013:

Accounts payable	$ 73,000	Interest payable	$ 33,400
Bonds payable (9.4%, due in 2018)	900,000	Installment note payable (9%, equal installments due 2014 to 2024)	110,000
Lease liability*	30,000	Notes payable (7.8%, due in 2022)	350,000
Bonds payable (8.3%, due in 2017)	60,000	Premium on notes payable (7.8%, due in 2022)	5,000
Deferred tax liability*	127,600	3% note payable, $50,000 face amount, due in 2024	29,800
Discount on bonds payable (9.4%, due in 2018)	11,900		
Income taxes payable	28,100		

*Long-term liability

Required:

Prepare the current liabilities and long-term debt portions of Craig's balance sheet at December 31, 2013. Provide a separate line item for each issue (do not combine separate bonds or notes payable), but some items may need to be split into more than one item.

Problem 9-97B Entries for and Financial Statement Presentation of a Note

OBJECTIVE 2 3

Griddley Company borrowed $200,000 from the East Salvador Bank on February 1, 2013, on a 3-year, 8.6% note. Interest is paid annually on February 1.

Required:

1. Record the borrowing transaction in Griddley's journal.
2. Prepare the adjusting entries made at December 31, 2013 and 2014. (*Note:* Round to the nearest dollar.)
3. Prepare the necessary journal entry to recognize the first interest payment on February 1, 2014. (*Note:* Round to the nearest dollar.)
4. Indicate how the note and associated interest would be presented in Griddley's December 31, 2014 balance sheet.
5. Prepare the necessary journal entries to record the repayment of the note and the last year's interest payment on February 1, 2016. (*Note:* Round to the nearest dollar.)

Problem 9-98B Preparing a Bond Amortization Table (Straight Line)

OBJECTIVE 2 3

On December 31, 2013, Peacock Products borrowed $447,000 by issuing 3-year, 8% bonds with a face amount of $400,000. Interest is payable annually on December 31.

Required:

Prepare an amortization table using the following column headings. (*Note:* Round to the nearest dollar.)

Period	Cash Payment (Credit)	Interest Expense (Debit)	Premium on Bonds Payable (Debit)	Premium on Bonds Payable Balance	Carrying Value

Problem 9-99B Note Computations and Entries (Straight Line)

OBJECTIVE 3

On December 31, 2013, Benton Corporation borrowed $1,000,000 with 10-year, 8.75% notes, interest payable semiannually on June 30 and December 31. Cash in the amount of $985,500 was received when the note was issued.

Required:

1. Prepare the necessary journal entry at December 31, 2013.
2. Prepare the necessary journal entry at June 30, 2014.
3. Prepare the necessary journal entry at December 31, 2014.
4. Determine the carrying amount of these notes at the end of the fifth year (December 31, 2018).

Problem 9-100B Preparing a Bond Amortization Table (Straight Line)

OBJECTIVE 3

Dalton Company issued 5-year, 7.5% bonds with a total face value of $900,000 on December 31, 2013, for $950,000. The bonds pay interest on June 30 and December 31 of each year.

Required:

1. Prepare an amortization table
2. Prepare the entries to recognize the interest payments made on June 30, 2014, and December 31, 2014.

Problem 9-101B Preparing a Bond Amortization Table (Straight Line)

OBJECTIVE 3

Pennington Corporation issued 5-year, 8.6% bonds with a total face value of $700,000 on December 31, 2014, for $680,000. The bonds pay interest on June 30 and December 31 of each year.

(*Continued*)

Required:

1. Prepare an amortization table.
2. Prepare the entries to recognize the bond issuance and the interest payments made on June 30, 2015, and December 31, 2015.

OBJECTIVE 3

Problem 9-102B Preparing a Bond Amortization Table (Straight Line)

Cook Construction has agreed to construct a factory in a new industrial park. To finance the construction, the county government issued $6,500,000 of 10-year, 4.75% revenue bonds for $6,950,000 on December 31, 2013. Cook will pay the interest and principal on the bonds. When the bonds are repaid, Cook will receive title to the factory. In the interim, Cook will pay property taxes as if it owned the factory. This financing arrangement is attractive to Cook, as state and local government bonds are exempt from federal income taxation and thus carry a lower interest rate. The bonds are attractive to investors, as both Cook and the county are issuers. The bonds pay interest semiannually on June 30 and December 31.

Required:

1. Prepare an amortization table through December 31, 2015, for these revenue bonds assuming straight-line amortization.
2. **CONCEPTUAL CONNECTION** Discuss whether or not Cook should record the factory as an asset after it is constructed.
3. **CONCEPTUAL CONNECTION** Discuss whether or not Cook should record the liability for these revenue bonds.

OBJECTIVE 3

Problem 9-103B Noninterest-Bearing Note (Straight Line)

On December 31, 2013, Sorenson Financing Corporation borrowed $90,000 cash on a $110,300, 24-month zero coupon note. Sorenson uses the straight-line method of amortization.

Required:

1. Record the borrowing in Sorenson's journal.
2. Prepare the adjusting entry for December 31, 2014.
3. Prepare the entries to recognize the 2015 interest expense and repayment of the note on December 31, 2015.

OBJECTIVE 3

Problem 9-104B Preparing an Amortization Table for Noninterest-Bearing Bonds (Straight Line)

On December 31, 2013, Birch Inc. borrowed $2,500,000 by issuing 3-year, zero coupon bonds. The face value of the bonds is $2,680,000. Birch uses the straight-line method to amortize any premium or discount.

Required:

Prepare an amortization table for these bonds using the following column headings:

Period	Cash Payment (Credit)	Interest Expense (Debit)	Discount on Bonds Payable (Credit)	Discount on Bonds Payable Balance	Carrying Value

OBJECTIVE 6

Problem 9-105B Capital and Operating Leases

Kleinfelder Company has decided to lease its new office building. The following information is available for the lease:

Lease:	
Payments	$75,000 per year*
Length of lease	15 years
Economic life of building	16 years
Appropriate interest rate	7.3%
Cost of building if purchased	$750,000

*The first payment is due at the end of the first year of the lease.

Required:

1. Determine whether this is a capital lease or an operating lease.
2. Regardless of your answer to the preceding question, assume that this is a capital lease and that the present value of the lease payments is $740,000. Record the liability and corresponding asset for this acquisition.
3. Record the interest expense on the capital lease at the end of the first year. Also assume no residual value and a 15-year lease for the building. Record the first year's straight-line depreciation of the cost of the leased asset. (*Note:* Round to the nearest dollar.)

CASES

Case 9-106 **Long-Term Debt and Ethics**

You are the CFO of Diversified Industries. Diversified has suffered through 4 or 5 tough years. This has deteriorated its financial condition to the point that Diversified is in danger of violating two loan covenants related to its largest loan, which is not due for 12 more years. The loan contract states that if Diversified violates any of these covenants, the loan principal becomes immediately due and payable. Diversified would be unable to make this payment, and any additional loans taken to repay this loan would likely be at higher rates, forcing Diversified into bankruptcy. An investment banker suggests forming another entity (called "special purpose entities" or SPE) and transferring some debt to this SPE. Structuring the SPE very carefully will have the effect of moving enough debt off Diversified's balance sheet to keep the company in compliance with all its loan covenants. The investment banker assures you that accounting rules permit such accounting treatment.

Required:

How do you react to the investment banker?

Case 9-107 **Debt Covenants and Financial Reporting Standards**

Debtholders receive note contracts, one for each note, that describe the payments promised by the issuer of the debt. In addition, the issuing corporation frequently enters a supplementary agreement, called a *note indenture*, with a trustee who represents the debtholders. The provisions or covenants of the indenture may place restrictions on the issuer for the benefit of the debtholders. For example, an indenture may require that the issuer's debt to equity ratio never rise above a specified level or that periodic payments be made to the trustee who administers a "sinking fund" to provide for the retirement of debt.

Consider Roswell Manufacturing's debt indenture, which requires that Roswell's debt to equity ratio never exceed 2:1. If Roswell violates this requirement, the debt indenture specifies very costly penalties, and if the violation continues, the entire debt issue must be retired at a disadvantageous price and refinanced. In recent years, Roswell's ratio has averaged about 1.5:1 ($15 million in total liabilities and $10 million in total stockholders' equity). However, Roswell has an opportunity to purchase one of its major competitors, Ashland Products. The acquisition will require $4.5 million in additional liabilities, but it will double Roswell's net income. Roswell does not believe that a stock issue is feasible in the current environment. The Financial Accounting Standards Board issued a new standard concerning accounting for post employment benefits, which is strongly supported by the Securities and Exchange Commission. Implementation of the new standard will add about $2 million to Roswell's long-term liabilities. Roswell's CEO, Martha Cooper, has written a strong letter of objection to the FASB. The FASB received similar letters from over 300 companies.

Required:

1. Write a paragraph presenting an analysis of the impact of the new standard on Roswell Manufacturing.
2. If you were a member of the FASB and met Martha Cooper at a professional meeting, how would you respond to her objection?

Case 9-108 Evaluating Leverage

Gearing Manufacturing Inc. is planning a $1,000,000 expansion of its production facilities. The expansion could be financed by the sale of $1,250,000 in 8% notes or by the sale of $1,250,000 in common stock, which would raise the number of shares outstanding from 50,000 to 75,000. Gearing pays income taxes at a rate of 30%.

Required:

1. Suppose that income from operations is expected to be $550,000 per year for the duration of the proposed debt issue. Should Gearing finance with notes or stock? Explain your answer.
2. Suppose that income from operations is expected to be $275,000 per year for the duration of the proposed debt issue. Should Gearing finance with notes or stock? Explain your answer.
3. Suppose that income from operations varies from year to year but is expected to be above $300,000, 40% of the time and below $300,000, 60% of the time. Should Gearing finance with notes or stock? Explain your answer.
4. As an investor, how would you use accounting information to evaluate the risk of excessive use of leverage? What additional information would be useful? Explain.

Case 9-109 Leverage

Cook Corporation issued financial statements at December 31, 2013, that include the following information:

Balance sheet at December 31, 2013:

Assets	$8,000,000
Liabilities	$1,200,000
Stockholders' equity (300,000 shares)	$6,800,000

Income statement for 2013:

Income from operations	$1,200,000
Less: Interest expense	(100,000)
Income before taxes	$1,100,000
Less: Income taxes expense (0.30)	(330,000)
Net income	$ 770,000

The levels of assets, liabilities, stockholders' equity, and operating income have been stable in recent years; however, Cook Corporation is planning a $1,800,000 expansion program that will increase income from operations by $350,000 to $1,550,000. Cook is planning to sell 8.5% notes at par to finance the expansion.

Required:

1. What earnings per share does Cook report before the expansion?
2. What earnings per share will Cook report if the proposed expansion is undertaken? Would this use of leverage be advantageous to Cook's stockholders? Explain.
3. Suppose income from operations will increase by only $150,000. Would this use of leverage be advantageous to Cook's stockholders? Explain.
4. Suppose that income from operations will increase by $200,000 and that Cook could also raise the required $1,800,000 by issuing an additional 100,000 shares of common stock (assume the additional shares were outstanding for the entire year). Which means of financing would stockholders prefer? Explain.

Case 9-110 Research and Analysis Using the Annual 10-K

Obtain **Marriott**'s 2011 10-K through the "Investor Relations" portion of Marriott's website. (do a web search for Marriott investor relations). Once at the Investor Relations part of the website look for "SEC Filings." When you see the list of all the filings, either filter for the "Annual Filings" or search for "10-K" when you find the list of all SEC Filings.

Another option is to or go to www.sec.gov and click "Search for Company Filings" under "Filings & Forms."

Required:

1. What are Marriott's total liabilities for 2011?
2. How much of these liabilities are classified as long-term debt (not noncurrent liabilities, but classified as long-term debt)?
3. Look at Marriott's long-term debt footnote and answer the following questions:
   a. When does the debt with the highest stated rate mature?
   b. How much of the debt is maturing in each of the next 5 years (2012–2016)? How much is maturing in more than 5 years (2015 and beyond)?
   c. How much debt was repurchased on the open market during 2009? What was the gain or loss recognized on this debt repurchase?
4. Calculate and discuss Marriott's debt to equity and times interest earned (accrual basis) ratios.

Case 9-111 Comparative Analysis: Under Armour, Inc., versus VF Corporation

Refer to the financial statements of **Under Armour, Inc.**, and **VF Corporation** that are supplied with this text.

Required:

1. Look at Under Armour's and VF's footnotes. Describe their largest borrowing arrangements and balances at the end of 2011.
2. Calculate Under Armour's and VF's interest earned (accrual) for 2010 and 2011. For Under Armour, the income tax expense can be found on the income statement, while the interest expense can be found in the last paragraph of Note 7. The interest payments and income tax payments can be found on the statement of cash flows. For VF, the interest and income tax expenses are on the income statement, while information about the payments is in Note V.
3. Calculate Under Armour's and VF's long-term debt to equity ratios for 2010 and 2011. (*Note:* Round answers to two decimal places.)
4. Calculate Under Armour's and VF's debt to equity ratios for 2010 and 2011. (*Note:* Round answers to two decimal places.)
5. Calculate Under Armour's and VF's long-term debt to total assets ratios for 2010 and 2011. (*Note:* Round answers to two decimal places.)
6. Calculate Under Armour's and VF's debt to total assets ratios for 2010 and 2011. (*Note:* Round answers to two decimal places.)
7. Comment on Under Armour's and VF's debt management.

Case 9-112 CONTINUING PROBLEM: FRONT ROW ENTERTAINMENT

In June 2014, Front Row Entertainment had the opportunity to expand its venue operations by purchasing five different venues. To finance this purchase, Front Row issued $1,500,000 of 6%, 5-year bonds on July 1, 2014. The bonds were issued for $1,378,300 and pay interest semiannually on June 30 and December 31.

Required:

1. Prepare the journal entry to record the bond issue at July 1, 2014.
2. Assume that Front Row uses the straight-line method of amortization.
   a. Prepare an amortization table through December 31, 2015. (*Note:* Round to the nearest dollar.)
   b. Prepare the journal entry required at December 31, 2014.
   c. How will the bonds be shown on the December 31, 2014 balance sheet?
3. Assume that Front Row uses the effective interest method of amortization and the annual market rate of interest was 8%.
   a. Prepare an amortization table through December 31, 2015. (*Note:* Round to the nearest dollar.)
   b. Prepare the journal entry required at December 31, 2014.
   c. How will the bonds be shown on the December 31, 2014 balance sheet?

10

Stockholders' Equity

© Pixelfabrik/Alamy

After studying Chapter 10, you should be able to:

1. Distinguish between common and preferred stock and describe their use in raising capital.
2. Record capital stock.
3. Account for the distribution of assets to stockholders.
4. Describe the accounting issues related to retained earnings and accumulated other comprehensive income.
5. Analyze stockholder payout and profitability ratios using information contained in the stockholders' equity section.

iStockphoto.com/Cliff Wassmann

EXPERIENCE FINANCIAL ACCOUNTING

with Google

In 1998, Sergey Brin and Larry Page, two Ph.D. students at Stanford University, founded **Google**. The incredible growth of Google is evidenced in the fact that, by 2011, Google had revenues of almost $40 billion and net income of over $9.7 billion. These figures are drastically larger than in 2004, when Google first sold its stock to the public. Since 2004, Google's revenue is up almost 1,100%, while its net income is up over 2,340%.

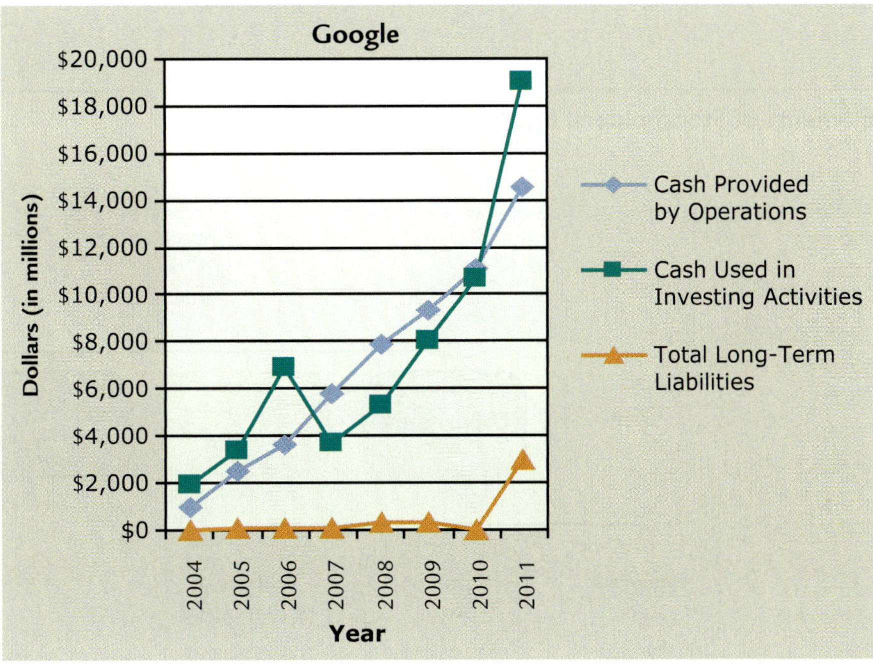

Source: Google, Inc. 2011 10-K

One way that stockholders earn a return on their investment is by receiving dividends; yet, despite their profitability, Google has never paid a dividend to stockholders. Instead Google chooses to invest in growth opportunities.

You may be aware of some of these growth opportunities, like Google's purchases of **YouTube**, **DoubleClick**, and **AdMob**, as well as its roll out of features such as Google+ and Google Chrome. However, Google's investments do not stop there. In fact, Google's 2011 statement of cash flows shows that Google spent more than $19 billion on investing activities. Since past investment is responsible for Google's large growth in revenues and net income, the hope is that the 2011 investments will fuel profitable growth in the coming years. Review the graph above, and notice Google's investing activities over the last 8 years with very little increase in long-term debt. It is apparent that the investing dollars came from operations.

IFRS

IFRS typically refers to stockholders' equity as *capital and reserves.*

Stockholders' equity, which also is called **equity**, represents the owners' claims against the assets of a corporation after all liabilities have been deducted. The stockholders' equity section of the balance sheet clearly identifies various elements of equity according to their source. The most common sources are (see Exhibit 10.1):

- capital stock—split between (1) preferred and common stock and (2) the associated additional paid-in capital
- retained earnings or deficit
- accumulated other comprehensive income
- treasury stock

In this chapter, we describe how common and preferred stock are used to raise capital for the corporation, discuss how corporations account for the various elements of stockholders' equity, and analyze stockholder payout and stockholder profitability using information contained in stockholders' equity.

EXHIBIT 10.1

Elements of Stockholders' Equity

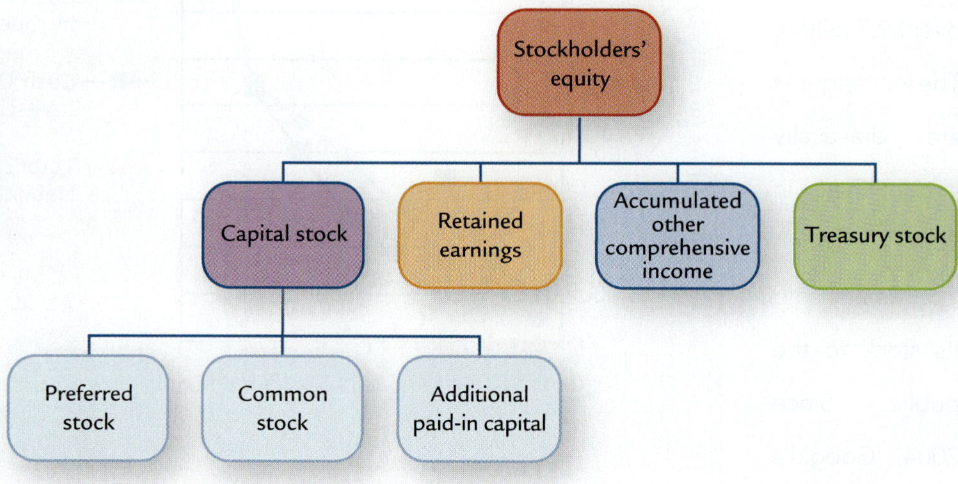

OBJECTIVE 1

Distinguish between common and preferred stock and describe their use in raising capital.

RAISING CAPITAL WITHIN A CORPORATION

Recall from Chapter 1 that most large businesses are organized as corporations because incorporation increases the company's ability to raise cash (or capital) by easing the transfer of ownership and limiting the liability of owners. Ownership of a corporation is divided into a large number of equal parts or *shares.* Shares are owned in varying numbers by the owners of the corporation called **stockholders** or **shareholders**.

Authorization to Issue Stock

Corporations are authorized, or *chartered,* in accordance with the provisions of state laws that govern the structure and operation of corporations. These laws differ from state to state, and a corporation can charter in any state. For instance, although Google is headquartered in Mountain View, California, it is chartered in Delaware, as are many corporations due to Delaware's favorable laws.

Although the provisions of incorporation laws vary from state to state, all states require persons who wish to form a corporation to apply to a prescribed state official for the issuance of a charter. The **corporate charter**, which is sometimes called the

articles of incorporation, is a document that authorizes the creation of the corporation, setting forth its name and purpose and the names of the incorporators.

The typical corporate charter contains provisions that describe how stock may be issued by the corporation. First, it authorizes the corporation to issue stock in a limited number of classes. It also sets an upper limit on the number of shares that the corporation may issue in each class. And finally, it sets a lower limit on the amount for which each share must be sold.

Shares of stock are sold, or issued, when a corporation is formed. Additional shares may be issued later. The maximum number of shares the business may issue in each class of stock is referred to as the number of **authorized shares**. This must be distinguished from the number of **issued shares**, which is the number of shares actually sold to stockholders. A corporation rarely issues all of its authorized shares.

Corporations can buy back their own stock for reasons explained later in this chapter. Thus, the number of shares issued is further distinguished from the number of **outstanding shares**, which is the number of issued shares actually in the hands of stockholders. When firms reacquire their own stock, the reacquired shares are not considered to be outstanding. Exhibit 10.2 illustrates how the share quantities are determined.

EXHIBIT 10.2

Determination of Share Quantities

	500,000 shares are authorized	200,000 of the authorized shares are sold to the public	10,000 of the issued shares are bought back by the corporation	50,000 of the authorized shares (previously unissued) are sold to the public
Authorized	500,000	500,000	500,000	500,000
Issued	0	200,000	200,000	250,000
Outstanding	0	200,000	190,000	240,000

These three share quantities—the number of shares authorized, issued, and outstanding—are reported for each class of stock on the balance sheet or in its accompanying notes.

Common Stock

All classes of stock are designated as either common stock or preferred stock. These come with different financial benefits and provide different rights regarding the governance of the corporation. The primary rights for owners of **common stock** are:

- voting in the election of the board of directors. You will recall that the board controls the operating and financial policies of the company.
- sharing in the profits and dividends of the company. We will talk more about this below.
- keeping the same percentage of ownership if new stock is issued (preemptive right).
- sharing in the assets in liquidation in proportion to their holdings. This is referred to as the "residual claim" because common stockholders are only paid after all creditors and preferred stockholders are paid in full (which is very rare in liquidation).

When you hear of someone who "made money by investing in stock," it is almost invariably through an investment in common stock. This is because, although the "residual claim" means common stockholders are only paid after the creditors and preferred stockholders are paid in full, it also means that common stockholders get *everything* that is left over after the creditors and preferred stockholders are paid in full. As such, the common stockholders receive the bulk of the financial gain from a profitable company through stock appreciation and dividends:

- *Stock appreciation*: The value of the stock increases above the price initially paid (of course, it is also possible that the stock's value decreases if the company is unprofitable—this is a risk of owning stock).
- *Dividends*: **Dividends** are payments to a company's stockholders from earnings. These payments are usually in the form of cash, but noncash assets and stock can also be given as dividends. Payment of dividends to common stockholders, however, depends on a company's alternatives. The company may elect to pay down debt or, if the company has growth opportunities, they may elect to keep (or retain) earnings to fund these investment options rather than pay dividends. In fact, many companies do not pay dividends to common stockholders.

Preferred Stock

Preferred stock generally pays a regular dividend. In this regard, preferred stock is similar to debt, with the preferred stock dividend equating to interest payments. Additionally, the value of preferred stock, like the value of debt, is most closely tied to interest rate levels and the company's overall creditworthiness; the value of common stock, on the other hand, is most closely tied to the performance of the company. In this respect, preferred stock is a less risky investment than common stock. Preferred stockholders also receive priority over common stockholders in the payment of dividends and the distribution of assets in the event of liquidation.

Comparison of Common and Preferred Stock

Some differences between preferred stock and common stock favor the preferred stockholder; other differences favor the common stockholder. Most differences between preferred and common stock are designated in the company's corporate charter and take one or more of the following forms:

- *Dividend preferences:* Preferred stock frequently requires that the issuing corporation pay dividends to preferred stockholders before paying dividends to common stockholders. Additionally, preferred dividends may be *cumulative and participating,* as explained on p. 540.
- *Conversion privileges:* Preferred stock may be convertible into common shares if the preferred stockholder elects to do so and certain conditions are satisfied. For example, each share of preferred stock might be convertible into, for example, 10 shares of common stock after a certain date.
- *Liquidation preferences:* If and when a corporation is dissolved, liquidating distributions are made to stockholders. Corporate charters frequently require the claims of preferred stockholders to be satisfied before those of common stockholders. Additionally, the charter may specify a liquidating amount for preferred shares.
- *Call provisions (redeemable):* The corporate charter may authorize or even require the corporation to repurchase (or redeem) any preferred shares that are sold. In such cases, the charter usually fixes the *call price* (the amount to be paid to the preferred stockholders) and specifies a date on or after which the shares may or must be repurchased. Note that this feature is similar to the repaying of the principal on a loan at the maturity date—particularly when the charter requires redemption at a specific date.
- *Denial of voting rights:* Most preferred stock does not confer voting rights, which means that preferred stockholders, unlike common stockholders, cannot vote at stockholders' meetings.

The first three characteristics of preferred stock are advantageous for preferred stockholders. The last two characteristics usually work in the interest of common stockholders.

Because of the relative advantages of different forms of stock, corporations are typically authorized by their charters to issue several classes of preferred stock and several classes of common stock, each with a different set of terms and provisions. The 2011 edition of *Accounting Trends & Techniques* (an American Institute of Certified Public Accountants publication that surveys accounting practices followed in 600 sampled financial statements) indicates that only 28 of the 600 companies (a little under 6%) had outstanding preferred stock, but all corporations have outstanding common stock.[1] This excerpt from Procter & Gamble's 10-K illustrates how the different classes of stock are shown:

Classes of Stock for Procter & Gamble (amounts in millions)

	2011	2010
Convertible Class A preferred stock, stated value \$1 per share (600 shares authorized)	\$1,234	\$1,277
Nonvoting Class B preferred stock, stated value \$1 per share (200 shares authorized)	—	—
Common stock, stated value \$1 per share (10,000 shares authorized; issued: 2011—4,007.9, 2010—4,007.6)	4,008	4,008

Source: Procter & Gamble, Inc. 2011 10-K

YOU DECIDE Issuing Debt or Preferred Stock

You are the CFO of Canova Manufacturing. Your company needs to raise capital to pursue an expansion project, but the company does not want to sell additional common stock.

What factors should you consider in deciding whether to issue debt or preferred stock?

In making your decision, it would be helpful to consider the following differences between debt and preferred stock.

Advantage of debt:

- Interest payments are tax deductible, while preferred dividends are not.

Advantages of preferred stock:

- Preferred stock is historically classified as equity, rather than debt, on the balance sheet. If Canova prefers to, or must, show lower debt totals, preferred stock is advantageous. For example, provisions of existing debt contracts may not allow Canova to issue additional debt.
- Preferred stock is less risky than debt because, unlike interest payments, missing a preferred dividend payment does not trigger bankruptcy. If Canova fears cash flow problems, this will be important.
- Companies with a history of operating losses typically do not pay income taxes. If Canova has these so-called net operating loss carryforwards, then debt no longer has the tax advantage.
- Preferred stock is generally sold to other corporations because these corporations do not pay taxes on the full amount of the dividends (i.e., there is a big tax break relative to receiving interest payments).

Although preferred stock and debt have many similarities, they have some important differences.

ACCOUNTING FOR ISSUANCE OF COMMON AND PREFERRED STOCK

OBJECTIVE 2
Record capital stock.

In examples in previous chapters, we recorded the contributions of stockholders in exchange for stock in a single account. In practice, however, cash or other assets (capital) contributed by stockholders is usually divided between two accounts, on the basis of the par value of the stock. **Par value** is an arbitrary monetary amount printed on each share of stock that establishes a minimum price for the stock when issued, but does not

IFRS
The accounting for stockholders' equity is generally the same under IFRS as under U.S. GAAP.

[1] *Accounting Trends and Techniques for 2011, 65th edition,* Table 5-5, p. 490.

determine its market value.[2] When a corporation receives more than par value for newly issued stock, as it usually does (stock rarely sells for exactly its par value), the par value and the excess over par are recorded in separate accounts. The par value multiplied by the number of shares sold is recorded in an account that describes the type of stock—for example, common stock or preferred stock. The amount received in excess of the par value is recorded in an account called **Additional Paid-In Capital**. These accounts are the first accounts shown in the stockholders' equity section of the balance sheet and taken together are known as **capital stock**. Cornerstone 10.1 illustrates the accounting procedures for recording the sale of stock.

CORNERSTONE

10.1

Recording the Sale of Common and Preferred Stock

Why:

When companies sell common or preferred stock to raise capital, the resulting ownership claims are recorded in the capital stock section of stockholders' equity.

Information:

Spectator Corporation is authorized to issue 1,000 shares of preferred stock with a 9% dividend rate and a par value of $20 per share and 50,000 shares of common stock with a par value of $2 per share. On January 2, 2013, Spectator issues 200 shares of preferred stock at $22 per share and 20,000 shares of common stock at $2.50 per share.

Required:

1. How much cash did Spectator raise through its stock issuance?
2. Prepare the journal entries necessary to record the sale of common and preferred stock separately.
3. Prepare the stockholders' equity section of Spectator's balance sheet. (*Note:* Assume Spectator has yet to engage in any operations.)

Solution:

1.

Preferred stock ($22 × 200 shares)	$ 4,400
Common stock ($2.50 × 20,000 shares)	50,000
Total proceeds	**$54,400**

2.

Date	Account and Explanation	Debit	Credit
Jan. 2	Cash	4,400	
	Preferred Stock[a]		4,000
	Additional Paid-In Capital—Preferred Stock[b]		400
	(Record sale of preferred stock at $22 per share)		

Assets	=	Liabilities	+	Stockholders' Equity
+4,400				+4,000
				+400

[a]200 shares × $20 par = $4,000

[b]200 shares × ($22 − $20) = $400

(Continued)

[2] The precise meaning of par value is established by securities laws that vary somewhat from state to state.

CORNERSTONE **10.1** *(Continued)*

Date	Account and Explanation	Debit	Credit
Jan. 2	Cash	50,000	
	Common Stock[c]		40,000
	Additional Paid-In Capital—Common Stock[d]		10,000
	(Record sale of common stock at $2.50 per share)		

Assets	=	Liabilities	+	Stockholders' Equity
+50,000				+40,000
				+10,000

[c] 20,000 shares × $2 par = $40,000
[d] 20,000 shares × ($2.50 − $2.00) = $10,000

3.

Stockholders' equity:		
Preferred stock, 9%, $20 par, 1,000 shares authorized, 200 shares issued and outstanding	$ 4,000	
Common stock, $2 par, 50,000 shares authorized, 20,000 shares issued and outstanding	40,000	
Additional paid-in capital:		
Preferred stock	400	
Common stock	10,000	
Total capital stock		$54,400
Retained earnings*		0
Total stockholders' equity		$54,400

*Note that retained earnings displays a zero balance because Spectator is a newly formed corporation.

Stated Capital and No-Par Stock

The stock issued by Spectator Corporation carried a par value that represents the stated capital of the corporation. **Stated capital (legal capital)** is the amount of capital that, under law, cannot be returned to the corporation's owners unless the corporation is liquidated. Even when state law permits the issuance of **no-par stock** (stock without a par value), it frequently requires that no-par stock have a stated (legal) value, set by the corporation, in order to establish the corporation's stated or legal capital. Further, this is a relatively infrequent occurrence.[3]

Stated value, like par value, is recorded separately in the *Common* (or *Preferred*) *Stock* account, while any excess paid over its stated value is recorded in *Additional Paid-In Capital—Common* (or *Preferred*) *Stock.*[4]

Warrants

A **stock warrant** is the right granted by a corporation to purchase a specified number of shares of its common stock at a stated price and within a stated time period. Corporations issue stock warrants in the following two situations:

concept Q&A

How do we account for stock issued in exchange for noncash assets or services (such as legal services in connection with incorporation)?

Answer:

The amount recorded should be the fair market value of the stock or the fair market value of the asset/service, whichever is more clearly determinable. In the case of a newly organized corporation, the fair market value of the asset/service is usually more clearly determinable. But in the case of established corporations with widely traded stock, the fair market value of the stock is more clearly determinable than the fair market value of the asset/service.

[3] *Accounting Trends & Techniques* for 2011 indicated that 53 of the 502 stock issues outstanding for the companies surveyed (approximately 10%) had "no par value" common stock (Table 5-4, p. 489).
[4] In some states, stated value functions exactly as does the par value of stock to identify the legal capital portion of total capital stock. However, in other states, legal capital is defined as the entire capital stock amount associated with the no-par stock. In these states, the entire capital stock amount is recorded in a single Common or Preferred Stock account.

- First, they may issue warrants along with bonds or preferred stock as an "equity kicker" to make the bonds or preferred stock more attractive. Such warrants often have a duration of 5 or more years.
- Second, they may issue warrants to existing stockholders who have a legal right to purchase a specified share of a new stock issue, in order to maintain their relative level of ownership in the corporation. Such warrants usually have a duration of less than 6 months.

Options

Corporations also grant employees and executives the right to buy stock at a set price as compensation for their services. These "rights" are called *stock options.* **Stock options** are frequently given to employees and executives as compensation for their services. For example, the employer may give an executive the right to purchase in 2 years 5,000 shares of the company's stock at $50 per share, today's market price. If in 2 years the market price of the stock is higher than $50 (for example, $62), the executive can purchase the 5,000 shares for $50 each and receive effective compensation of $60,000 [($62 − $50) × 5,000 shares]. Of course, if the price is lower than $50, the executive will not exercise the option.

The number of U.S. employees holding stock options increased dramatically through the 1990s and 2000s. The National Center for Employee Ownership estimated that in 1992 approximately 1 million employees held stock options, but by 2006 this number had soared to 10.6 million.

ETHICAL DECISIONS The compensation expense recorded by a company when they grant stock options depends on many factors including the price at which employees can buy the stock (called the **exercise** or **strike price**) and the market value of the stock on the date of grant. As discussed, the strike price of the options and the market value of the stock are generally the same on the date of grant. However, during 2006, many companies came under investigation for "back dating" stock options. That is, companies waited to announce the granting of options and then picked the date in the past when the stock price was lowest. This maximized the value of each individual option to the employee.

This practice has been curtailed by the Sarbanes-Oxley Act, but in and of itself, this is not illegal. However, if on December 20 a company backdates options to May 1 (the lowest stock price of the year), the value of each option will be greater on December 20 than on May 1. As such, the company should calculate compensation expense using the market value of the stock on December 20. We will never know exactly how widespread the practice of backdating was, but approximately 80 firms were initially the subject of an SEC probe and research estimates that 29.2% of firms backdated grants to top executives between 1996 and 2005. •

Corporations elect to grant stock options for two primary reasons:

- First, stock options allow cash-poor companies to compete for top talent in the employee market. For example, market salary for a manager of systems quality and assurance may be $200,000 per year—well beyond the means of many start-up companies. However, such a person may agree to work for $100,000 per year and a significant number of stock options.
- Second, stock options are believed to better align the incentives of the employee with those of the owners. This concept is easy to understand with a bit of exaggeration. Employees would like to be paid millions of dollars a year to do nothing, while owners would like the employees to work hundreds of hours a week for free. Stock options help align these incentives because now an employee's personal wealth is tied to the success of the company's stock price—just like the owners. Knowledge of these uses of equity is important, but discussion of the complications of accounting for stock warrants and options is left for more advanced accounting courses.

YOU DECIDE Going Public

You are CEO of Georgian Inc., a successful manufacturer of electronic components for computer hardware. Georgian wishes to double its scale of operations in order to meet both existing and expected demand for its products. Georgian is a *privately held corporation*. High interest rates preclude Georgian from borrowing the necessary expansion capital, and its current owners are unable to invest significantly more capital at this time.

What effect will going public have on corporate control and expenses?

Raising enough capital to double the scale of operations will likely require giving away a substantial ownership interest. If the new owners are sufficiently well-organized and cohesive, they could elect a majority of directors and control the company. On the other hand, if the new shares were purchased by a large number of investors with no organized interest in controlling Georgian, then effective control would remain in the hands of the original owners. Of course, the risk of losing control at some future time would still exist. Going public will also substantially increase the costs of financial reporting and corporate governance to comply with requirements of the Sarbanes-Oxley Act of 2002.

Going public will most likely require giving up control of the company and will also increase expenses in order to comply with financial reporting standards.

ACCOUNTING FOR DISTRIBUTIONS TO STOCKHOLDERS

OBJECTIVE 3

Account for the distribution of assets to stockholders.

As discussed, owners invest in corporations through the purchase of stock. Corporations can distribute cash to stockholders in the following ways:

- The corporation can repurchase the shares from owners.
- The corporation can issue dividends.

Historically, dividends were the most common method of distributing cash. Over recent years, however, repurchasing shares has become a more frequent method of cash distribution because it has tax advantages for stockholders relative to dividends.[5] First, dividends are paid to *all* stockholders, thus creating tax consequences for everyone. Stock repurchases, on the other hand, only trigger tax consequences for those stockholders who elect to sell their stock back to the company. Thus, if a stockholder does not want to incur tax consequences in the current year, he or she can elect not to sell the shares back to the company. Second, dividends have usually been taxed at higher rates than gains from selling stock.[6] Dividends do have the advantage of allowing stockholders to receive assets from the corporation without reducing their ownership share.

Stock Repurchases (Treasury Stock)

When a corporation purchases its own previously issued stock, the stock that it buys is called **treasury stock**. Corporations purchase treasury stock for many reasons:

- to buy out the ownership of one or more stockholders
- to reduce the size of corporate operations
- to reduce the number of outstanding shares of stock in an attempt to increase earnings per share and market value per share
- to acquire shares to be transferred to employees under stock bonus, stock option, or stock purchase plans
- to satisfy the terms of a business combination in which the corporation must give a quantity of shares of its stock as part of the acquisition of another business
- to reduce vulnerability to an unfriendly takeover

[5] In fact, one study shows that the number of stock repurchases increased from 87 and $1.4 billion in 1988 to 1,570 and $222 billion in 1998 (Grullon, G. and D. Ikenberry. 2000. "What do we know about stock repurchases?" *Journal of Applied Corporate Finance*. Spring: 31–51).

[6] Dividends were taxed at the same rates as gains from selling stocks from 2003 through 2010 as a result of the *Jobs and Growth Tax Relief Reconciliation Act of 2003*. However, this favorable tax treatment for dividends is scheduled to expire at the end of 2012, unless Congress continues to extend the cuts.

> **concept Q&A**
>
> If a corporation buys the stock of another corporation and later sells that stock for a different price, a gain or loss is recorded on the income statement. However, when a corporation buys its own stock and later sells it for a different price, the income statement is not affected. Why is this?
>
> **Answer:**
>
> Transactions with a corporation's owners cannot be included on the income statement.

The stock may be purchased on the open market, by a general offer to the stockholders (called a *tender offer*), or by direct negotiation with a major stockholder. If the objective of acquiring treasury stock is to reduce the size of corporate operations, the treasury shares may be retired after purchase. More frequently, however, repurchased stock is held in the corporation's treasury until circumstances favor its resale, or until it is needed to meet obligations of the corporation that must be satisfied with shares of its stock. Transactions in treasury stock, even very large ones, usually do not require stockholder approval.

The 2011 edition of *Accounting Trends & Techniques* indicates that 323 of the 500 companies surveyed hold treasury shares.[7] Interestingly, a few companies hold a relatively large portion of their issued shares in treasury. For example, at the end of 2011 **Coca-Cola Company** held approximately 35.7% of its shares in treasury at a repurchase cost of $31.3 billion.

Purchase At first thought, one might consider recording the acquisition of treasury stock as an exchange of cash for an investment in stock (an exchange of one asset for another). However, that approach fails to recognize that the treasury stock is already represented by amounts in the corporation's equity accounts. Although the shares would represent an asset to another entity if it acquired them, they cannot represent an asset to the entity that issued them. Thus, the purchase of treasury stock is a reduction of equity rather than the acquisition of an investment. Instead of requiring a debit to an investment account, the reacquisition of treasury stock requires a debit to a contra-equity account, Treasury Stock. This interpretation is consistent with the provisions of most state incorporation laws, which prohibit the payment of dividends on treasury stock.[8]

Resale If the treasury shares are reissued at some point in the future, the original cost of the shares is removed from the Treasury Stock account. Any excess of proceeds over the cost of the shares is not considered a gain because a corporation cannot generate income by buying and selling its own stock (income is reserved for transactions with nonowners); instead, a credit is made to a special paid-in capital account—*Additional Paid-In Capital—Treasury Stock*. If the treasury shares are sold for less than their cost, a debit is first made to "Additional Paid-In Capital—Treasury Stock." If the credit balance in Additional Paid-In Capital—Treasury Stock is not large enough to absorb the shortfall, then the unabsorbed debit reduces Retained Earnings. Cornerstone 10.2 illustrates how to account for treasury stock.

CORNERSTONE 10.2

Accounting for Treasury Stock

Why:

When purchasing its own previously issued stock, a corporation records a reduction to stockholders' equity by debiting treasury stock.

Information:

On July 1, 2013, Spectator Corporation repurchases 1,000 shares of its outstanding common stock for $15 per share. On September 15, 2013, Spectator sells 500 shares of treasury stock for $18 per share, and on December 1, 2013, Spectator sells 400 shares of treasury stock for $11 per share.

(Continued)

[7] *Accounting Trends and Techniques for 2011, 65th edition,* Table 5-8, p. 512.

[8] The method of accounting for treasury stock demonstrated here is called the *cost method*. This method is used by approximately 95% of the companies engaging in treasury stock transactions. An alternative method, called the *par value method*, is demonstrated in Intermediate Accounting courses.

CORNERSTONE 10.2

(*Continued*)

Required:

Prepare the journal entries to record (1) the purchase of treasury stock, (2) the sale of treasury stock on September 15, 2013, and (3) the sale of treasury stock on December 1, 2013.

Solution:

	Date	Account and Explanation	Debit	Credit
1.	July 1, 2013	Treasury Stock[a]	15,000	
		Cash		15,000
		(Record purchase of treasury shares)		
2.	Sept. 15, 2013	Cash[b]	9,000	
		Treasury Stock[c]		7,500
		Additional Paid-In Capital—Treasury Stock[d]		1,500
		(Record reissue of treasury shares)		
3.	Dec. 1, 2013	Cash[e]	4,400	
		Additional Paid-In Capital—Treasury Stock[f]	1,500	
		Retained Earnings[g]	100	
		Treasury Stock[h]		6,000
		(Record reissue of treasury shares)		

Assets	=	Liabilities	+	Stockholders' Equity
−15,000				−15,000

Assets	=	Liabilities	+	Stockholders' Equity
+9,000				+7,500 +1,500

Assets	=	Liabilities	+	Stockholders' Equity
+4,400				−1,500 −100 +6,000

[a] 1,000 shares × \$15 = \$15,000
[b] 500 shares × \$18 = \$9,000
[c] 500 shares × \$15 = \$7,500
[d] 500 shares × (\$18 − \$15) = \$1,500
[e] 400 shares × \$11 = \$4,400
[f] Additional Paid-In Capital—Treasury Stock can be debited in a journal entry, but the result of the journal entry cannot be a debit *balance* to the account. Thus, there is a limit of \$1,500 due to the credit in Requirement 2.
[g] Retained Earnings is debited if there is any remaining debit needed after Additional Paid-In Capital—Treasury Stock is zeroed out.
[h] 400 shares × \$15 = \$6,000

Transfers among Stockholders We have been considering the effects on the equity accounts when a corporation buys or sells its own stock. However, treasury stock transactions constitute a special case. In general, the purchase or sale of stock after it is first issued does *not* alter the equity accounts of the issuing corporation, unless that corporation is itself the purchaser or seller. Although the issuing corporation's accounts do not change when shares are sold by one stockholder to another, the corporation's stockholder list must be updated. Large corporations usually retain an independent *stock transfer agent* to maintain their stockholder lists, which include the quantity and serial numbers of the shares held. Stock transfer agents also arrange for the transfer of certificates among stockholders and the issuance of new certificates to stockholders.[9]

Retirement of Treasury Shares Occasionally, treasury shares are permanently retired. That is, these particular shares will no longer be traded. In such cases, the Common Stock account is debited for the par value of the stock and the Additional Paid-In Capital account is reduced for any excess of the purchase price of the treasury shares over par. If Spectator had retired the 1,000 shares it repurchased for \$15/share in

[9] Although the transfer of shares among stockholders does not affect the accounts of the issuing corporation, such transactions obviously require entries into the accounts of the buyers and sellers of the shares.

Cornerstone 10-2, it would have made the following entry assuming the par value of the stock was $2:

Assets	=	Liabilities	+	Stockholders' Equity
−15,000				−2,000 −13,000

Date	Account and Explanation	Debit	Credit
July 1, 2013	Common Stock*	2,000	
	Additional Paid-In Capital—Common Stock	13,000	
	Cash		15,000
	(Record purchase and retirement of shares)		

*1,000 shares × $2 = $2,000

Dividends

A dividend is an amount paid periodically by a corporation to a stockholder as a return on invested capital. Dividends represent distributions of accumulated net income. They are usually paid in cash but may also be paid in the form of noncash assets or even additional shares of a corporation's own stock. All dividends, whatever their form, reduce retained earnings (see Exhibit 10.3).

EXHIBIT 10.3

Dividends

Dividends reduce Retained Earnings.

Cash dividends distribute cash to stockholders.

Stock dividends distribute additional shares to stockholders.

Stock splits transfer additional shares to stockholders without changing equity.

Cash Dividends

Cash dividends are by far the most common form of dividend. The payment of a cash dividend is preceded by an official announcement or declaration by the board of directors of the company's intention to pay a dividend. The dividend declaration specifies the:

- **declaration date**—the date on which a corporation announces its intention to pay a dividend on common or preferred stock
- dollar amount of the dividend—usually stated as the number of dollars per share
- **date of record**—the date on which a stockholder must own one or more shares of stock in order to receive the dividend
- **payment date**—the date on which the dividend will actually be paid

Since the stock of most corporations is continually changing hands, it is necessary to set a date on which the ownership of shares is established as a basis for the payment of dividends. If a share of stock is sold between the date of record and the dividend payment date, the former owner of the share, rather than the new owner, receives the dividend. On the other hand, if a share of stock is sold between the declaration date and the date of record, the new owner, rather than the former owner, receives the dividend. The accounting for cash dividends is illustrated in Cornerstone 10.3.

concept Q&A

Why are dividends not an expense on the income statement?

Answer:

Transactions with owners are not included on the income statement.

Recording Cash Dividends

CORNERSTONE 10.3

Why:

Dividends are generally paid out of retained earnings.

Information:

The Kingsmill Corporation has issued 3,000 shares of common stock, all of the same class; 2,800 shares are outstanding and 200 shares are held as treasury stock. On November 15, 2013, Kingsmill's board of directors declares a cash dividend of $2.00 per share payable on December 15, 2013, to stockholders of record on December 1, 2013.

Required:

Prepare the journal entries at (1) the date of declaration, (2) the date of record, and (3) the payment.

Solution:

1. Dividends are not paid on treasury stock. Further, a liability is incurred on the date of declaration because the corporation has the legal obligation to pay after declaring the dividend.

Date	Account and Explanation	Debit	Credit
Nov. 15, 2013	Retained Earnings (or Dividends*)	5,600	
	Dividends Payable		5,600
	(Record liability for dividends)		

Assets	= Liabilities +	Stockholders' Equity
	+5,600	−5,600

*Dividends is closed to Retained Earnings at the end of the period (2,800 shares × $2 = $5,600)

2. No journal entry is needed because the date of record is the date at which ownership is recorded to determine who will receive the dividend.

3.

Date	Account and Explanation	Debit	Credit
Dec. 15, 2013	Dividends Payable	5,600	
	Cash		5,600
	(Record payment of dividends)		

Assets	= Liabilities +	Stockholders' Equity
−5,600	−5,600	

Dividend Policy The corporation's record of dividends and retained earnings provides useful information to:

- boards of directors and managers who must formulate a dividend policy
- stockholders and potential investors who wish to evaluate past dividend policies and assess prospects for future dividends

Historical records and long-term future projections of earnings and dividends are of particular interest to stockholders because the dividend policies of most large corporations are characterized by long-term stability. In other words, they are designed to produce a smooth pattern of dividends over time. For this reason, directors approach increases in the per-share dividend very cautiously and avoid decreases at all costs.

Liquidating Dividends When retained earnings has been reduced to zero, any additional dividends must come from capital stock. Such dividends are called **liquidating dividends** and must be charged first against additional paid-in capital, then the Common (or

Preferred) Stock accounts. The payment of liquidating dividends usually accompanies the dissolution of the corporation and is regulated by various laws designed to protect the interests of creditors and other holders of nonresidual equity. Thus, the presence of significant liabilities will usually prevent, or at least require close monitoring of, liquidating dividends. Since these dividends are a return of paid-in capital, they are not taxed as income to the recipients.

Stock Dividends A cash dividend transfers cash from the corporation to its stockholders. In contrast, a **stock dividend** transfers shares of stock from the corporation to its stockholders—additional shares of the corporation's own stock. For each share outstanding, a fixed number of new shares is issued, and an amount of retained earnings is transferred to contributed capital accounts in a process known as *capitalization of retained earnings.* While a cash dividend reduces both total assets and total equity, a stock dividend alters neither total assets nor total equity. A stock dividend merely notifies investors that the equity section of the balance sheet has been rearranged.

The amount of retained earnings capitalized for each new share depends on the size of the stock dividend.

- *Small stock dividends* increase the number of outstanding shares by less than 25%; they are capitalized using the stock's market value just before the dividend.
- *Large stock dividends* increase the number of outstanding shares by 25% or more and are capitalized at par.

This is illustrated in Cornerstone 10.4.

CORNERSTONE 10.4

Recording Small and Large Stock Dividends

Why:

Small stock dividends are capitalized using the stock's market value, while large stock dividends are capitalized at the stock's par value.

Information:

On May 18, 2013, Arlington Corporation has 6,000,000 shares of $10 par common stock outstanding. This stock is currently trading at $12 per share.

Required:

1. Determine how many new shares are issued and prepare the necessary journal entry assuming Arlington declares and pays a 5% stock dividend.
2. Determine how many new shares are issued and prepare the necessary journal entry assuming Arlington declares and pays a 30% stock dividend.

Solution:

1. 6,000,000 × 0.05 = 300,000 shares

Assets	= Liabilities +	Stockholders' Equity
		−3,600,000 +3,000,000 +600,000

Account and Explanation	Debit	Credit
Retained Earnings*	3,600,000	
Common Stock**		3,000,000
Additional Paid-In Capital—Common Stock		600,000
(Record small stock dividend)		

*300,000 shares × $12 = $3,600,000
**300,000 shares × $10 = $3,000,000

(Continued)

CORNERSTONE **10.4** *(Continued)*

2. 6,000,000 × 0.30 = 1,800,000 shares

Account and Explanation	Debit	Credit
Retained Earnings***	18,000,000	
Common Stock***		18,000,000
(Record large stock dividend)		

Assets	= Liabilities +	Stockholders' Equity
		−18,000,000 +18,000,000

***1,800,000 shares × $10 = $18,000,000

Note that the stock dividend merely transfers dollars from Retained Earnings to the Capital Stock accounts.

Although a stock dividend increases the *number* of shares held by each stockholder, it does not alter the *proportion* of shares held. For example, if an investor held 100,000 out of 2,000,000 outstanding shares before a 10% stock dividend, that investor would hold 110,000 out of 2,200,000 outstanding shares after the dividend. Thus the investor would hold 5% of the outstanding shares both before and after the stock dividend and would have a 5% claim on earnings and stockholders' equity both before and after:

$$\frac{100{,}000}{2{,}000{,}000} = \frac{110{,}000}{2{,}200{,}000} = \underline{\underline{0.05}}$$

Further, despite the popular belief to the contrary among stockholders and even some financial managers, research shows that neither stock dividends nor stock splits, which we will consider next, enhance the total market value of a corporation's outstanding common stock. Stock dividends should be distinguished from dividend plans that allow stockholders to choose between receiving a cash dividend and a share of stock with equivalent current value. Such plans may enhance a stockholder's proportionate ownership and also avoid brokerage fees.

Stock Splits A stock split, like a stock dividend, increases the number of outstanding shares without altering the proportionate ownership of a corporation. Unlike a stock dividend, however, a stock split involves a *decrease* in the per-share par value (or stated value), with no capitalization of retained earnings. In other words, a **stock split** is a stock issue that increases the number of outstanding shares of a corporation without changing the balances of its equity accounts.

Consider a corporation that has 10,000 common shares outstanding with a par value of $30 per share. In a two-for-one stock split, stockholders will exchange each of their 10,000 original shares for two new shares; the number of shares will rise from 10,000 to 20,000; and the par value of each share will be reduced to $15 per share. The total par value of all stock will remain $300,000:

$$\$30 \times 10{,}000 \text{ shares} = \$15 \times 20{,}000 \text{ shares} = \underline{\underline{\$300{,}000}}$$

The split has the effect of distributing the par value over a larger number of shares.

Stock splits are used to reduce the per-share price of a stock. If nothing else changes, a two-for-one split should cut the market price of a stock in half. A corporation may wish to reduce the per-share price to encourage trading of its stock. The assumption is that a higher per-share price is an obstacle to purchases and sales of stock, particularly for small investors.

No entry is required to record a stock split because no account balances change. The changes in the par value and the number of outstanding shares are merely noted in the corporation's records.

To illustrate how companies use stock splits, look at the Microsoft data in Exhibit 10.4 (p. 540). Note that Microsoft stock has split nine times in its history. That means if

EXHIBIT 10.4

Microsoft's Stock Price History

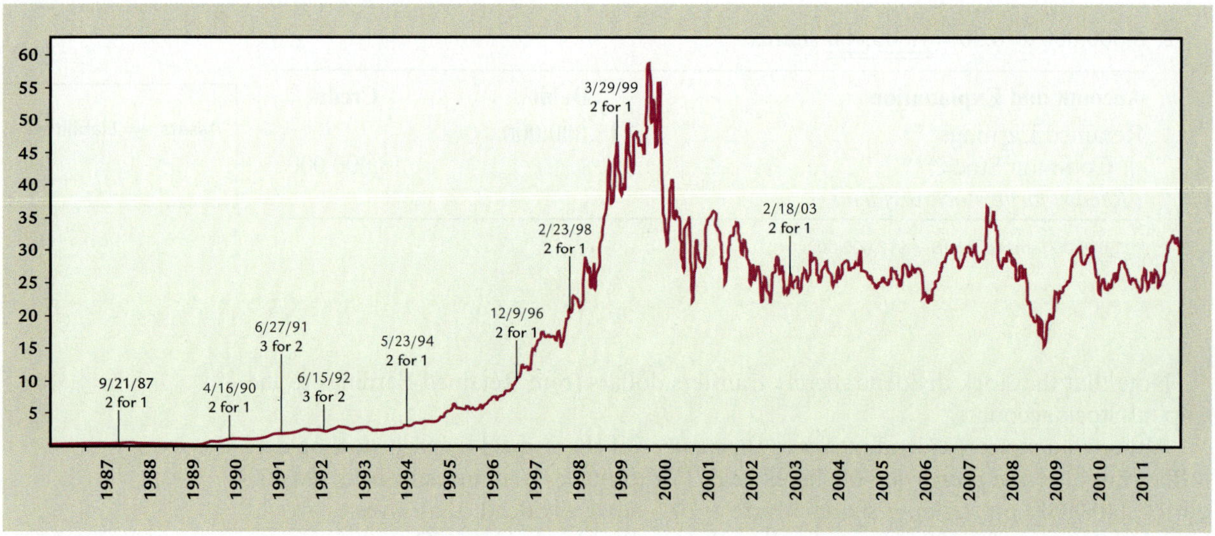

Source: Microsoft, Inc. 2011 10-K

you had owned 1,000 shares of Microsoft stock prior to September 21, 1987, and you never bought nor sold a single share, you would now have 288,000 shares:

$$1{,}000 \text{ shares} \times 2 \times 2 \times \frac{3}{2} \times \frac{3}{2} \times 2 \times 2 \times 2 \times 2 \times 2$$

These shares would have been worth approximately $9,300,000 in April 2012. Further, if we assume that splits have no effect on price, the price of a share of Microsoft stock during April 2012 (which was trading slightly above $32 per share), would have been approximately $9,300 per share if there had been no stock splits.

Not many individual investors can pay $9,300 per share, but two notable companies—**Berkshire Hathaway** (Warren Buffet's company) and **Google**—do not issue stock splits. As a consequence, during April 2012, a share of Google stock was selling for approximately $645 per share (down from over $700 in late 2007), while Berkshire Hathaway Class A common was selling for approximately $122,000 per share (down from over $150,000 in late 2007). In fact, check to see what Berkshire Hathaway is selling for today by going to **Google Finance** or **Yahoo! Finance** and typing in "Berkshire Hathaway."

Preferred Dividend Preferences While dividends on common stock are set by the corporation's board of directors, dividends on preferred stock are usually established as one of the terms of the issue. Most preferred stock issues fix their dividend rate as a percentage of the par value. For example, an 8% preferred share with a $100 par value has an annual dividend of $8 ($100 par × 8%). Of course, both preferred and common dividends are subject to various restrictions imposed by statute, corporate charter, terms of preferred stock issues, and contracts with bondholders and others.

Although preferred stockholders have no voting rights, they are "preferred" in the sense that corporations are required to pay dividends to them before paying dividends to common stockholders. Such dividend preferences can take three forms:

- current dividend preference
- cumulative dividend preference
- participating dividend preference

Most preferred stock issues grant a current dividend preference, and some also grant one or both of the other preferences, thereby further enhancing the likelihood of dividend payments.

Current Dividend Preference Preferred stock always has a **current dividend preference**, which provides that current dividends must be paid to preferred stockholders before any dividends are paid to common stockholders. However, the current dividend preference does not guarantee payment of preferred dividends. In lean years, both common and preferred stockholders may fail to receive dividends.

The following illustration demonstrates the impact of the current dividend preference. During the period 2012 through 2015, Cook Corporation maintained the following capital structure:

Preferred stock, 8%, $10 par, 5,000 shares authorized, 4,000 shares issued and outstanding	$ 40,000
Common stock, $5 par, 50,000 shares authorized, 30,000 shares issued and outstanding	150,000
Additional paid-in capital—common stock	60,000
Total capital stock	$250,000

Cook's board of directors determined the total dollar amount available for preferred and common dividends in each year from 2012 through 2015 as shown in the second column of the following schedule:

Year	Amount Available for Dividends	Dividends to Preferred	Dividends to Common
2012	$12,200	$3,200*	$9,000**
2013	7,000	3,200	3,800
2014	2,000	2,000	0
2015	0	0	0

*0.08 × $40,000 = $3,200
**$12,200 − $3,200 = $9,000

This schedule shows that the common dividend is any positive amount remaining after the full preferred dividend has been paid. If the total amount available for dividends is less than the full preferred dividend, the entire amount is paid to preferred stockholders.

Cumulative Dividend Preference Most preferred stock is cumulative. The **cumulative dividend preference** requires the eventual payment of all preferred dividends—both **dividends in arrears** and current dividends—before any dividends are paid to common stockholders. (Preferred stock dividends remaining unpaid for 1 or more years are considered to be in arrears.) In other words, no dividends can be paid to common stockholders until all prior and current preferred dividends have been paid. The cumulative dividend preference thus includes the current dividend preference. This is illustrated in Cornerstone 10.5.

Calculating Cumulative Preferred Dividends

CORNERSTONE 10.5

Why:

The cumulative feature of preferred stock requires corporations to pay all current and unpaid prior-period dividends to preferred stockholders before paying any dividends to common stockholders.

Information:

Jefferson Manufacturing has a single class of common stock and a single class of cumulative preferred stock. The cumulative preferred stock requires the corporation to pay an annual dividend of $6,500 to preferred stockholders. On January 1, 2013, Jefferson's preferred dividends were 1 year in arrears, which means that Jefferson declared neither preferred nor common dividends in 2012. From 2013 to 2015, Jefferson's board of directors determined they would be able to pay $9,000, $12,000, and $15,000, respectively.

Required:

Show how these anticipated payments will be split between preferred and common stockholders.

(*Continued*)

CORNERSTONE **10.5**

(Continued)

Solution:

Year	Amount Available for Dividends	Dividends to Preferred	Dividends to Common
2013	$ 9,000	$ 9,000*	$ 0
2014	12,000	10,500**	1,500**
2015	15,000	6,500	8,500

*The $9,000 dividend paid to preferred stockholders in 2013 removes the $6,500 in arrears from 2012, but leaves dividends in arrears at January 1, 2014, of $4,000—the excess of preferred dividends for 2012 and 2013 over the amount paid in 2013 [(2 × $6,500) − $9,000 = $4,000].

**The $10,500 dividend to preferred stockholders in 2014 pays the current preferred dividend ($6,500), removes the $4,000 in arrears, and leaves $1,500 to be paid to common stockholders ($12,000 − $6,500 − $4,000 = $1,500).

Dividends do not become a liability of a corporation until they have been declared by the board of directors. If preferred dividends in arrears have not been declared, they are not recorded as liabilities but are disclosed in a footnote to the financial statements.

Participating Dividend Preference For some classes of preferred stock, dividends are not restricted to a fixed rate. Preferred stock that pays dividends in excess of its stated dividend rate is called *participating preferred stock.* Preferred stock that cannot pay dividends in excess of the current dividend preference plus cumulative dividends in arrears, if any, is called *nonparticipating preferred stock.*

The **participating dividend preference** provides that stockholders of participating preferred shares receive, in addition to the stated dividend, a share of amounts available for distribution as dividends to other classes of stock. Participating preferred stock may be either fully participating or partially participating:

- Fully participating preferred stock receives a share of *all* amounts available for dividends. Common stock is allocated a dividend at the same rate on par as the current dividend preference, and any remainder is divided between preferred and common stockholders—usually in proportion to the total par value of the two classes of stock.
- Partially participating preferred stock also receives a share of all amounts available for dividends, but the share is limited to a specified percentage of preferred par value.

YOUDECIDE Stock Repurchase or Dividend

You are the controller at Cohen Industries. The Board of Directors has decided to distribute $5,000,000 in excess cash to common stockholders.

In what ways can this distribution be accomplished? What factors should be considered when determining the best way?

You could either declare and pay a cash dividend or enter a stock repurchase plan. The primary difference between the two methods relates to tax consequences. First, the tax rate for dividends is higher than the rate on gains from selling stock. Second, while all common stockholders participate in dividends and, thus, incur tax consequence, only those stockholders who choose to sell their stock back to Cohen will experience tax consequences. Additionally, you should consider the future of any such distributions to stockholders. Generally, companies do not like to lower dividends. Finally, you should consider the price of the stock. Stock repurchases are most attractive when you believe your stock to be undervalued.

Therefore, if this distribution is a one-time event, a stock repurchase would be the way to go; however, if excess cash is anticipated in future periods, instituting a cash dividend would make sense.

OBJECTIVE 4

Describe the accounting issues related to retained earnings and accumulated other comprehensive income.

ACCOUNTING FOR RETAINED EARNINGS AND ACCUMULATED OTHER COMPREHENSIVE INCOME

Retained earnings (or **deficit**) is the accumulated earnings (or losses) over the entire life of the corporation that have not been paid out in dividends. Generally, ending retained earnings is calculated with a simple formula:

Beginning Retained Earnings
+ Net Income
− Dividends
= Ending Retained Earnings

Restrictions on Retained Earnings

Under most corporate charters, the balance of a corporation's retained earnings represents an upper limit on the entity's ability to pay dividends. (Dividends cannot reduce retained earnings below zero.) A corporation's capacity to pay dividends may be further restricted by agreements with lenders, by the corporation's board of directors, and by various provisions of state law, as follows:

- An agreement between the corporation and bondholders may require that retained earnings never fall below a specified level so long as the bonds are outstanding.
- The firm's board of directors may set aside a portion of retained earnings and declare it unavailable for the payment of dividends. Such an action may be used to communicate to stockholders changes in dividend policy made necessary by expansion programs or other decisions of the board.
- State law may require that dividends not reduce retained earnings below the cost of treasury stock.

Restrictions of this sort are usually disclosed in footnotes to the financial statements to signify that the restricted amount is unavailable for dividends. In rare cases, a separate "reserve" account is established for the restricted portion of retained earnings. The reserve account is called either *Restricted Earnings* or *Appropriation of Retained Earnings*. The account title frequently indicates, quite specifically, the nature of the restriction or the appropriation, as, for example, "Restricted Retained Earnings under Agreements with Bondholders" or "Appropriation of Retained Earnings for Plant Expansion." When reserve accounts are used, retained earnings is reported on two or more lines in the equity section of the balance sheet (see Exhibit 10.5 on p. 544). One line is devoted to each restriction, and to "Unrestricted retained earnings" or "Unappropriated retained earnings."

Error Corrections and Prior Period Adjustments Errors in recording transactions can distort the financial statements. If errors are discovered and corrected before the closing process, then no great harm is done. However, if errors go undetected, then flawed financial statements are issued. No matter when they are discovered, errors should be corrected.

If an error resulted in a misstatement of net income, then correction may require a direct adjustment to retained earnings, called a **prior period adjustment**. To illustrate, suppose that Byrnes Corporation uses a computer program to calculate depreciation expense. In 2012, a programming error caused the 2012 depreciation expense to be understated by $16,000. The error was not discovered until August 2013; consequently, 2012 net income after income taxes (which are paid at a rate of 25%) was

EXHIBIT 10.5 Information from Deere & Co. 2011 10-K

Deere & Co. 2011 10-K

The following was included in Note 18 of **Deere & Co.**'s 2011 10-K:

The credit agreements also require the equipment operations to maintain a ratio of total debt to total capital (total debt and stockholders' equity excluding accumulated other comprehensive income (loss)) of 65 percent or less at the end of each fiscal quarter. Under this provision, the company's excess equity capacity and retained earnings balance free of restriction at October 31, 2011, was $8,503 million.

Although Deere & Co. did not choose to show this restriction in the stockholders' equity portion of their balance sheet, if they had it would have appeared as follows:

STOCKHOLDERS' EQUITY (Partial)

		2011
Common stock, $1 par value (authorized — 1,200,000,000 shares; issued – 536,431,204 shares in 2011, at paid-in amount)		3,251.7
Common stock in treasury, 130,361,345 shares in 2011, at cost		(7,292.8)
Retained earnings:		
Restricted for credit agreement	6,016.4	
Unrestricted	8,503.0	14,519.4

Source: Deer & Company, 2011 10-K

overstated by $12,000 [$16,000 × (1 – 0.25)]. The error correction would be recorded in 2013 as follows:

Assets	=	Liabilities	+	Stockholders' Equity
+4,000				−12,000
−16,000				

Date	Account and Explanation	Debit	Credit
Aug. 31, 2013	Retained Earnings	12,000	
	Tax Refund Receivable	4,000	
	Accumulated Depreciation		16,000
	(Record prior period adjustment)		

Byrnes' retained earnings statement for 2013 incorporates the $12,000 prior period adjustment as follows:

Byrnes Corporation
Retained Earnings Statement
For the year ended December 31, 2013

Retained earnings, January 1, 2013		$157,000
Less: Prior period adjustment:		
Correction of error in calculation of 2012 depreciation expense (net of tax)		(12,000)
Retained earnings as adjusted, January 1, 2013		$145,000
Add: Net income for 2013		65,000
Less: Dividends declared in 2013:		
Cash dividend, preferred stock	$ (4,000)	
Stock dividend, common stock	(20,000)	(24,000)
Retained earnings, December 31, 2013		$186,000

Notice that the adjustment is deducted from the beginning balance of retained earnings to produce an *adjusted* beginning balance.

Financial accounting standards define prior period adjustments in a way that specifically excludes adjustments arising from estimation errors and changes from one accounting principle to another. These changes are corrected by adjusting the related income accounts for the period in which they are discovered.

concept Q&A

Assume that a standard condition in a loan contract (called a *loan covenant*) requires a borrower to maintain retained earnings of $3,000,000 on a $500,000 loan. The borrower does not like this covenant and asks why it has to be there. What would you say?

Answer:

Loan covenants such as these are there to protect the lender from the borrower removing money from the company, then declaring bankruptcy, and never repaying the loan. For example, in the absence of this covenant, an unscrupulous borrower could borrow $500,000 from the bank then pay out all this cash to stockholders as dividends leaving little (or at least far less) collateral within the company.

Accounting for Accumulated Other Comprehensive Income

Financial accounting theory suggests that income represents the changes in the assets and liabilities of the company as a result of transactions with nonowners. However, over time the FASB has allowed the gains and losses from certain nonowner transactions to bypass the income statement and go directly to stockholders' equity. These instances are rare, and the transactions that produce them are somewhat complicated, but one example is unrealized gains and losses on investments classified as available-for-sale securities. To illustrate, if a company buys a share of stock for $10 and at the end of the year that share is worth $12, the company has a $2 unrealized gain (a gain or loss is realized when the share is actually sold). It seems logical that this gain would appear on the income statement, but FASB has ruled that these gains and losses, when the investment is available-for-sale, are excluded from net income to reduce volatility due to fluctuations in fair value. At the same time, companies are required to include these gains and losses, along with net income in a measure called *comprehensive income*.

The FASB permits comprehensive income to be reported in one of two methods. The first method is a single statement approach in which both net income and comprehensive income are shown on the same statement. In this method, comprehensive income items will be added to or subtracted from net income to obtain total comprehensive income. The second method is a two-statement approach where total net income is shown on the first statement. That statement is followed by a statement of comprehensive income, which shows the components of comprehensive income and total comprehensive income. You can see an example of the two-statement approach in **VF**'s financial statements on pp. 35–36 of Appendix 5. You may also note that **Under Armour** does not use either method. This is because a third method of disclosing comprehensive income, within the statement of stockholders' equity, was permitted for fiscal years beginning before December 15, 2011. So, in its 2012 financial statements Under Armour is required to use either the one- or two-statement approach.

Regardless of which option is used to disclose comprehensive income for the period, **accumulated other comprehensive income** is shown in the stockholders' equity section of the balance sheet. Accumulated other comprehensive income is the total of comprehensive income for all periods. By disclosing this information, companies communicate the changes in assets and liabilities resulting from all transactions with nonowners.

Although it is not a required statement, a majority of corporations traded on U.S. stock exchanges also provide a statement of stockholders' equity. This latter statement reconciles the beginning and ending balances for each of the elements of stockholders' equity changes.

EQUITY ANALYSIS

OBJECTIVE 5

Analyze stockholder payout and profitability ratios using information contained in the stockholders' equity section.

Stockholders want to understand the following:

- how the value of their shares of stock will change
- how the company will distribute any excess cash to stockholders

We all know that investors buy stock to increase their personal wealth. But how do stockholders use the financial statements to better understand these two dimensions?

Stockholder Profitability Ratios

A primary driver of an increase in stock price is profitability. Profitability refers to the return that the company earns (in other words, its net income). However, the magnitude of the net income also matters because it shows how much had be to invested to earn the return. That is, would you rather earn \$10 on a \$100 investment or \$20 on a \$500 investment? Although the latter return is twice as large as the former, it also took an investment that was five times bigger. Assuming equal risk, etc., most investors would prefer to invest \$100 to earn \$10 because they then could use the extra \$400 to invest somewhere else.

The two most common ratios used to evaluate stockholder profitability are return on common equity and earnings per share (EPS).

Return on Common Equity

Return on common equity shows the growth in equity from operating activities. It is calculated as:

$$\text{Return on Common Equity} = \frac{\text{Net Income} - \text{Preferred Dividends}}{\text{Average Common Stockholders' Equity}}$$

Common stockholders' equity is calculated by taking total stockholders' equity and subtracting preferred stock.

Earnings per Share (EPS)

Earnings per share (EPS) measures the net income earned by each share of common stock. It is calculated as:

$$\text{EPS} = \frac{\text{Net Income} - \text{Preferred Dividends}}{\text{Average Common Shares Outstanding}}$$

Cornerstone 10.6 illustrates how to calculate stockholder profitability.

10.6

Calculating Stockholder Profitability Ratios

Why:

Analysis of information contained in the financial statements allows stockholders to assess profitability.

Information:

Consider the following information from VF's financial statements (all numbers in thousands other than per-share amounts).

Common stock price (12/31/11)	\$126.99/share	Avg. common shares outstanding	109,287
Common dividends	\$285,722	Dividends per common share	\$2.61/share
Preferred dividends	\$0	Net income (available to common shareholders)	\$888,089
2011 Preferred stock	\$0	2010 Preferred stock	\$0
2011 Total stockholders' equity	\$4,525,991	2010 Total stockholders' equity	\$3,861,319
Purchases of treasury stock	\$7,420		

Required:

Calculate the following stockholder profitability ratios: (1) return on common equity and (2) EPS.

(Continued)

Solution:

CORNERSTONE 10.6 *(Continued)*

1. $$\text{Return on Common Equity} = \frac{\text{Net Income} - \text{Preferred Dividends}}{\text{Average Common Stockholders' Equity Outstanding}}$$
$$= \frac{(\$888{,}089 - 0)}{[(\$4{,}525{,}991 - \$0) + (\$3{,}861{,}319 - \$0)] \div 2} = 21.18\%$$

2. $$\text{EPS} = \frac{\text{Net Income} - \text{Preferred Dividends}}{\text{Average Common Shares Outstanding}} = \frac{(\$888{,}089 - \$0)}{109{,}287} = \$8.13$$

Stockholder Payout

Stockholders not only experience an increase in wealth through an increasing stock price, but may also receive cash, or a payout, from the company. The most common stockholder payout ratios relate to dividends. Dividend yield considers the ratio of dividends paid to stock price. This ratio is conceptually similar to an interest rate for debt:

$$\text{Dividend Yield} = \frac{\text{Dividends per Common Share}}{\text{Common Stock Price}}$$

Another common dividend ratio calculates the proportion of dividends to earnings:

$$\text{Dividend Payout} = \frac{\text{Common Dividends}}{\text{Net Income}}$$

However, as discussed earlier, payouts to stockholders can also take the form of stock repurchases. As such, the stock repurchase payout ratio is:

$$\text{Stock Repurchase Payout} = \frac{\text{Common Stock Repurchases}}{\text{Net Income}}$$

By using these two ratios, stockholders can easily calculate the total payout:

$$\text{Total Payout} = \text{Dividend Payout} + \text{Stock Repurchase Payout}$$

Or, it can be calculated directly as:

$$\text{Total Payout} = \frac{\text{Common Dividends} + \text{Common Stock Repurchases}}{\text{Net Income (or Comprehensive Income)}}$$

Cornerstone 10.7 illustrates how to calculate payout ratios.

Calculating Stockholder Payout Ratios

CORNERSTONE 10.7 *(Continued)*

Why:

Analysis of information contained in the financial statements allows stockholders to assess payout.

Information:

Consider the following information from VF's financial statements (all numbers in thousands other than per-share amounts).

CORNERSTONE **10.7** *(Continued)*

Common stock price (12/31/11)	\$126.99/share	Avg. common shares outstanding	109,287
Common dividends	\$285,722	Dividends per common share	\$2.61/share
Preferred dividends	\$0	Net income (available to common shareholders)	\$888,089
2011 Preferred stock	\$0	2010 Preferred stock	\$0
2011 Total stockholders' equity	\$4,525,991	2010 Total stockholders' equity	\$3,861,319
Purchases of treasury stock	\$7,420		

Required:

Calculate the following stockholder payout ratios: (1) dividend yield, (2) dividend payout, (3) stock repurchase payout, and (4) total payout.

Solution:

1. $\text{Dividend Yield} = \dfrac{\text{Dividends per Common Share}}{\text{Common Stock Price}} = \dfrac{\$2.61}{\$126.99} = 2.06\%$
2. $\text{Dividend Payout} = \dfrac{\text{Common Dividends}}{\text{Net Income}} = \dfrac{\$285{,}722}{\$888{,}089} = 32.17\%$
3. $\text{Stock Repurchase Payout} = \dfrac{\text{Common Stock Repurchases}}{\text{Net Income}} = \dfrac{\$7{,}420}{\$888{,}089} = 0.84\%$
4. Total Payout = Dividend Payout + Stock Repurchase Payout = 32.17% + 0.84% = 33.01%

Note: This can also be calculated directly as (Dividends + Stock Repurchases) ÷ Net Income.

Interpreting Ratios

What do these stockholder profitability and payout ratios mean? The results of these ratios are usually used in two ways:

- *Compared over time to evaluate trends*: For example, in 2011 **VF**'s EPS was \$8.13. This might be great news if EPS in 2010 were \$2.15 or bad news if it were \$10.25. In fact, EPS for 2009 and 2010 were \$4.18 and \$5.25, respectively, so EPS is up more than 94% in 2 years. This is great news, but perhaps not completely surprising as the economy was at its worst in 2009.
- *Compared to results for other companies in the industry*: For example, the 2011 return on common equity for **Columbia Sportswear** was 13.91% and for **Perry Ellis** it was 1.90%. This makes VF's return on common equity of 21.18% look great. You can also look at industry averages. **Reuters** reports an industry average of 2.19%, so VF is well ahead of the industry averages.

YOU DECIDE Providing Shares for Employee Stock Options

You are the CFO of DTR Technology, a small, publicly traded software firm. Your stock price has increased by 120% over the last 2 years and is now at \$22 per share. Of course, this is great news. However, one side effect is that DTR employees own approximately 750,000 stock options with an average exercise price of \$5 per share.

What factors must be considered in handling the anticipated exercise of these options?

DTR could issue previously unissued shares and take in the exercise price, or \$3,750,000 in total (750,000 × \$5). Although this seems reasonable, very few companies follow this course of action. Instead, most companies engage in a stock repurchase plan. For example, **Microsoft** repurchased 318 million shares of stock in 2009, at least partly because there were 327 million employee stock options outstanding (and the number is that low because Microsoft has not issued employee stock options other than in mergers since 2004). This is despite the fact that Microsoft stock closed fiscal year 2009 at \$23.77, while the average exercise price of the options was \$9.50. In other words, if Microsoft plans to buy back shares of stock for \$23.77 per share while only receiving \$9.50 per option exercised, they will lose \$14.27 per share (or over

$46.5 billion if all options were excised). The reason most companies choose this latter option is because simply issuing previously unissued shares will increase the number of shares outstanding, which will, in turn, decrease (or dilute) earnings per share.

For DTR, repurchasing shares on the open market to cover its 750,000 in options would cost $12,750,000 [750,000 options × ($22 − $5)], but would prevent earnings per share from being diluted.

SUMMARY OF LEARNING OBJECTIVES

LO 1. Distinguish between common and preferred stock and describe their use in raising capital.

- Corporations sell both common stock and preferred stock to raise capital.
- Preferred stock generally guarantees a regular dividend and receives priority over common stock in the payment of dividends and distribution of assets in liquidation.
- Common stock has voting rights and receives all benefits not assigned to the preferred stockholders or creditors.
- Selling different classes of stock (with different features) attracts stockholders with diverse risk preferences and tax situations.

LO 2. Record capital stock.

- Both preferred and common stock are generally recorded at par or stated value.
- Any extra consideration received is recorded as "additional paid-in capital."

LO 3. Account for the distribution of assets to stockholders.

- Assets are distributed to stockholders by either:
  - repurchasing their shares of stock
  - paying dividends
- Generally the cost of stock repurchases is recorded as a reduction in stockholders' equity (a debit to treasury stock).
- Typically the corporation pays dividends with cash.
- Stock dividends and stock splits do not represent a payout to stockholders. These transactions have no effect on total stockholders' equity.
- Preferred stock generally has dividend preferences such as being cumulative or participating.

LO 4. Describe the accounting issues related to retained earnings and accumulated other comprehensive income.

- Retained earnings represents the earnings that the corporation elects not to pay out in dividends.
- Ending retained earnings is calculated by adding net income and subtracting dividends to beginning retained earnings.
- Retained earnings can be restricted, which communicates to stockholders that this portion of retained earnings is not eligible for dividend payout.
- Certain nonowner transactions are not included on the income statement. These transactions are included in the Accumulated Other Comprehensive Income account in the stockholders' equity section of the balance sheet.

LO 5. Analyze stockholder payout and profitability ratios using information contained in the stockholders' equity section.

- Stockholders are primarily interested in two things:
  - creation of value
  - distribution of value
- Analysis of the stockholders' equity section of the balance sheet in conjunction with the statement of stockholders' equity allows stockholders to separate these concepts.

CORNERSTONE 10.1 Recording the sale of common and preferred stock, page 530
CORNERSTONE 10.2 Accounting for treasury stock, page 534
CORNERSTONE 10.3 Recording cash dividends, page 537
CORNERSTONE 10.4 Recording small and large stock dividends, page 538
CORNERSTONE 10.5 Calculating cumulative preferred dividends, page 541
CORNERSTONE 10.6 Calculating stockholder profitability ratios, page 546
CORNERSTONE 10.7 Calculating stockholder payout ratios, page 547

KEY TERMS

Accumulated other comprehensive income, 545
Additional Paid-In Capital, 530
Articles of incorporation, 527
Authorized shares, 527
Capital stock, 530
Common stock, 527
Corporate charter, 526
Cumulative dividend preference, 541
Current dividend preference, 540
Date of record, 536
Declaration date, 536
Dividends, 528
Dividends in arrears, 541
Earnings per share (EPS), 546
Equity, 526
Exercise (or strike) price, 532
Issued shares, 527
Liquidating dividends, 537
No-par stock, 531
Outstanding shares, 527
Par value, 529
Participating dividend preference, 542
Payment date, 536
Preferred stock, 528
Prior period adjustment, 543
Retained deficit, 543
Retained earnings, 543
Return on common equity, 546
Shareholders, 526
Stated capital (legal capital), 531
Stock dividend, 538
Stock options, 532
Stock split, 539
Stock warrant, 531
Stockholders, 526
Stockholders' equity, 526
Treasury stock, 533

REVIEW PROBLEM

Stockholders' Equity

Grace Industries, a privately held corporation, has decided to go public. The current ownership group has 10,000,000 common shares (purchased at an average price of $0.50 per share) and the articles of incorporation authorize 50,000,000, $0.10 par, common shares and 1,000,000, 10%, $30 par, cumulative, preferred shares. On January 1, 2012, the public offering issues 8,000,000 common shares at $14 per share and 100,000 preferred shares at $33 per share.

On October 3, 2013, Grace Industries repurchases 750,000 common shares at $12 per share. After the repurchase, Grace's board of directors decides to declare dividends totaling $4,050,000 (no dividends were declared or paid in 2012). This dividend will be declared on November 15, 2013, to all stockholders of record on December 8, 2013. This dividend will be paid on December 23, 2013. On December 28, 2013, 100,000 of the treasury shares are reissued for $15 per share.

At December 31, 2013, Grace Industries has $12,000,000 of retained earnings and accumulated other comprehensive income of ($250,000).

Required:

1. Prepare the journal entry to record the January 1, 2012 issuance of the common and preferred stock.
2. Prepare the journal entry to record the October 3, 2013 stock repurchase.
3. Determine how much of the dividend will go to preferred stockholders.
4. Calculate what the dividends per common share will be.
5. Prepare the journal entry for the dividend declaration on November 15, 2013.
6. Prepare the journal entry on the date of record (December 8, 2013).
7. Prepare the journal entry on the dividend payment date (December 23, 2013).
8. Prepare the journal entry for the reissuance of treasury shares on December 28, 2013.
9. Prepare the stockholders' equity section of the balance sheet at December 31, 2013.

Solution:

1.

Date	Account and Explanation	Debit	Credit
Jan. 1, 2012	Cash[a]	3,300,000	
	Preferred Stock[b]		3,000,000
	Additional Paid-In Capital—Preferred Stock[c]		300,000
	(Record issuance of preferred stock)		
	Cash[d]	112,000,000	
	Common Stock[e]		800,000
	Additional Paid-In Capital—Common Stock[f]		111,200,000
	(Record issuance of common stock)		

Assets	= Liabilities +	Stockholders' Equity
+3,300,000		+3,000,000
+112,000,000		+300,000
		+800,000
		+111,200,000

[a] 100,000 shares × $33 = $3,300,000
[b] 100,000 shares × $30 par = $3,000,000
[c] 100,000 shares × ($33 – $30) = $300,000
[d] 8,000,000 shares × $14 = $112,000,000
[e] 8,000,000 shares × $0.10 par = $800,000
[f] 8,000,000 shares × ($14 – $0.10) = $111,200,000

2.

Date	Account and Explanation	Debit	Credit
Oct. 3, 2013	Treasury Stock*	9,000,000	
	Cash		9,000,000
	(Record repurchase of common stock)		

Assets	= Liabilities +	Stockholders' Equity
−9,000,000		−9,000,000

*750,000 shares × $12 = $9,000,000

3. The preferred stock is cumulative, so the preferred stockholders must be paid their annual dividend for 2013 (the current year) and for 2012 (dividends in arrears).

Preferred Dividends* $600,000

*100,000 shares × ($30 par × 10% × 2 years) = $600,000

4. The common stockholders receive any dividend remaining after the preferred dividend has been paid (because the preferred is not participating). Because common dividends are only paid to outstanding stock, the treasury shares must be subtracted from the issued shares. Remember that the ownership group owned 10,000,000 shares then issued 8,000,000 shares in the initial public offering.

$$\text{Common Dividends} = \frac{\$4{,}050{,}000 - \$600{,}000}{18{,}000{,}000 \text{ issued shares} - 750{,}000 \text{ treasury shares}} = \underline{\underline{\$0.20}} \text{ per share}$$

5.

Date	Account and Explanation	Debit	Credit
Nov. 15, 2013	Dividends*	4,050,000	
	Cash Dividends Payable		4,050,000
	(Record declaration of cash dividends)		

Assets	= Liabilities +	Stockholders' Equity
	+4,050,000	−4,050,000

*Dividends is closed to Retained Earnings.

6. No entry is necessary on the date of record.

7.

Assets	=	Liabilities	+	Stockholders' Equity
−4,050,000		−4,050,000		

Date	Account and Explanation	Debit	Credit
Dec. 23, 2013	Cash Dividends Payable	4,050,000	
	Cash		4,050,000
	(Record payment of cash dividends)		

8.

Assets	=	Liabilities	+	Stockholders' Equity
+1,500,000				+1,200,000
				+300,000

Date	Account and Explanation	Debit	Credit
Dec. 28, 2013	Cash*	1,500,000	
	Treasury Stock**		1,200,000
	Additional Paid-In Capital—Treasury Stock		300,000
	(Record reissuance of treasury shares)		

*100,000 shares × $15 = $1,500,000
**100,000 shares × $12 = $1,200,000

9. Stockholders' equity:

Preferred stock, 10%, $30 par, cumulative, 1,000,000 shares authorized, 100,000 shares issued and outstanding	$ 3,000,000[a]
Common stock, $0.10 par, 50,000,000 shares authorized, 18,000,000 shares issued, and 17,350,000 outstanding	1,800,000[b]
Additional paid-in capital:	
Preferred stock	300,000[c]
Common stock	115,200,000[d]
Treasury stock	300,000[e]
Total capital stock	$120,600,000
Retained earnings	12,000,000[f]
Less:	
Accumulated other comprehensive income	(250,000)[f]
Treasury stock (650,000 shares at cost)	(7,800,000)[g]
Total stockholders' equity	$124,550,000

[a] 100,000 shares issued at $30 par (see journal entry from 1).
[b] 18,000,000 shares issued at $0.10 par.
[c] 100,000 shares issued at $3 more than par ($33 selling price minus $30 par). See journal entry from 1.
[d] 10,000,000 shares issued to original ownership group at an average price of $0.50 per share ($0.40 per share in excess of par) plus 8,000,000 shares issued in IPO at $14 ($13.90 per share in excess of par).
[e] 100,000 treasury shares issued at $15 per share, which is $3 per share in excess of $12 cost (see journal entry from 8).
[f] Given in information.
[g] 750,000 shares repurchased at $12 per share minus 100,000 shares reissued.

DISCUSSION QUESTIONS

1. What does stockholders' equity represent?
2. What does a share of stock represent?
3. Why do corporations issue stock?
4. What is the difference between a privately and publicly held corporation?
5. What are authorized shares?
6. Why would the number of shares issued be different from the number of shares outstanding?
7. What are the benefits that common stockholders may receive?
8. How do common stock and preferred stock differ?
9. Discuss the similarities between preferred stock and debt.
10. Why do corporations utilize different forms of equity?
11. Describe how cumulative preferred stock differs from noncumulative preferred stock.

12. How is a preferred stock dividend calculated?
13. What balance sheet accounts are affected by the issuance of stock?
14. What is the difference between par value and stated value?
15. Why might a corporation grant stock options to employees in lieu of a higher salary?
16. What is a stock warrant? How are they used by corporations?
17. Describe two ways corporations make payouts to stockholders.
18. What is treasury stock?
19. Give four reasons why a company might purchase treasury stock.
20. How would the purchase of treasury stock affect the stockholders' equity section of a corporation's balance sheet?
21. A corporation repurchases 10,000 shares of its common stock at $7 per share and later resells it for $11 per share. What is the affect on the income statement of this resell?
22. What entries are made (if any) at the declaration date, date of record, and date of payment for cash dividends?
23. Compare and contrast cash dividends and liquidating dividends.
24. Describe the effect of a cash versus a stock dividend on a company's stockholders' equity.
25. What is a stock dividend? How does it differ from a stock split?
26. What is the effect of a stock split on stockholders' equity account balances?
27. Explain each of the following preferred stock dividend preferences: (1) current dividend preference, (2) cumulative dividend preference, and (3) participating dividend preference.
28. Are dividends in arrears reported among the liabilities of the dividend-paying firm? If not, how are they reported, and why?
29. What are retained earnings?
30. How may a corporation's retained earnings be restricted?
31. When are prior period adjustments used?
32. Distinguish between retained earnings and accumulated other comprehensive income.
33. Describe the statement of changes in stockholders' equity.
34. How are dividend payout and profitability ratios useful to investors?

MULTIPLE-CHOICE QUESTIONS

10-1 Which of the following is *not* a component of stockholders' equity?

a. retained earnings
b. net income
c. loss on sale of equipment
d. dividends payable

10-2 Which of the following statements is true?

a. The outstanding number of shares is the maximum number of shares that can be issued by a corporation.
b. The shares that are in the hands of the stockholders are said to be outstanding.
c. It is very unlikely that corporations will have more than one class of stock outstanding.
d. Preferred stock is stock that has been retired.

10-3 Authorized stock represents the:

a. number of shares that are currently held by stockholders.
b. number of shares that have been sold.
c. number of shares that have been repurchased by the corporation.
d. maximum number of shares that can be issued.

10-4 McKean Corporation authorized 500,000 shares of common stock in its articles of incorporation. On May 1, 2013, 100,000 shares were sold to the company's founders. However, on October 15, 2013, McKean repurchased 20,000 shares to settle a dispute among the founders. At this date, how many shares were issued and outstanding, respectively?

a. 80,000 and 100,000
b. 100,000 and 80,000
c. 100,000 and 100,000
d. 500,000 and 100,000

10-5 Harvey Corporation shows the following in the stockholders' equity section of its balance sheet: The par value of its common stock is $0.25 and the total balance in the Common Stock account is $50,000. Also noted is that 15,000 shares are currently designated as treasury stock. The number of shares *outstanding* is:

a. 185,000.
b. 196,250.
c. 200,000.
d. 215,000.

10-6 Ames Corporation repurchases 10,000 shares of its common stock for $12 per share. The shares were originally issued at an average price of $10 per share. Later it resells 6,000 of the shares for $15 per share and the remaining 4,000 shares for $17 per share. How much gain or loss should Ames report on its income statement as a result of these transactions?

a. $38,000 gain
b. $20,000 loss and $38,000 gain
c. $0
d. $20,000 loss

10-7 With regard to preferred stock,

a. its stockholders may have the right to participate, along with common stockholders, if an extra dividend is declared.
b. its issuance provides no flexibility to the issuing company because its terms always require mandatory dividend payments.
c. no dividends are expected by the stockholders.
d. there is a legal requirement for a corporation to declare a dividend on preferred stock.

10-8 DAE Parts Shop began business on January 1, 2013. The corporate charter authorized issuance of 20,000 shares of $5 par value common stock and 5,000 shares of $10 par value, 5% cumulative preferred stock. DAE issued 12,000 shares of common stock at $25 per share on January 2, 2013. What effect does the entry to record the issuance of stock have on total stockholders' equity?

a. increase of $340,000
b. increase of $300,000
c. increase of $150,000
d. increase of $120,000

10-9 Thornwood Partners began business on January 1, 2013. The corporate charter authorized issuance of 75,000 shares of $1 par value common stock and 8,000 shares of $3 par value, 10% cumulative preferred stock. On July 1, Thornwood issued 20,000 shares of common stock in exchange for 2 years' rent on a retail location. The cash rental price is $3,000 per month, and the rental period begins on July 1. What is the correct entry to record the July 1 transaction?

a. Debit to Cash, $72,000; credit to Prepaid Rent, $57,600
b. Debit to Prepaid Rent, $72,000; credit to Common Stock, $72,000
c. Debit to Prepaid Rent, $72,000; credit to Common Stock, $20,000; credit to Additional Paid-In Capital—Common Stock, $52,000
d. Debit to Prepaid Rent, $72,000; credit to Common Stock, $60,000; credit to Additional Paid-In Capital—Common Stock, $12,000

10-10 A company would repurchase its own stock for all of the following reasons *except*:

a. it wishes to prevent unwanted takeover attempts.
b. it wishes to increase the earnings per share.
c. it believes the stock is overvalued.
d. it needs the stock for employee bonuses.

10-11 When a company purchases treasury stock, which of the following statements is true?

a. Dividends continue to be paid on the treasury stock.
b. It is no longer considered to be issued.
c. The cost of the treasury stock reduces stockholders' equity.
d. Treasury stock is considered to be an asset because cash is paid for the stock.

10-12 If a company purchases treasury stock for $6,000 and then reissues it for $5,000, the difference of $1,000 is:

a. a decrease in stockholders' equity.
b. a gain in stockholders' equity.
c. treated as a loss on the sale.
d. treated as a gain on the sale.

10-13 When a company retires its own common stock, the company must:

a. record a gain or loss depending on the difference between original selling price and repurchase cost.
b. decrease the Common Stock account balances by the original issue price.
c. get the approval of the state to do so.
d. issue a different class of stock to the former stockholders.

10-14 Which of the following should be considered when a company decides to declare a cash dividend on common stock?

a. the retained earnings balance only
b. the cash available and the retained earnings balance
c. the amount of authorized shares of common stock
d. the book value of the company's stock

10-15 When a company declares a cash dividend, which of the following is true?

a. Assets are decreased.
b. Assets are increased.
c. Stockholders' equity is increased.
d. Liabilities are increased.

10-16 What is the effect of a stock dividend on stockholders' equity?

a. Stockholders' equity is decreased.
b. Retained earnings is increased.
c. Additional paid-in capital is decreased.
d. Total stockholders' equity stays the same.

10-17 As a result of a stock split,

a. stockholders' equity is increased.
b. the stockholders have a higher proportionate ownership of the company.
c. the par value of the stock is changed in the reverse proportion as the stock split.
d. the market price of the outstanding stock is increasing because a split is evidence of a profitable company.

10-18 The balance of the $2.50 par value Common Stock account for Patriot Company was $240,000,000 before its recent 2-for-1 stock split. The market price of the stock was $50 per share before the stock split. What occurred as a result of the stock split?

a. The balance in the common stock account was increase to $480,000.
b. The balance in the retained earnings account decreased.
c. The market price of the stock dropped to approximately $25 per share.
d. The market price of the stock was not affected.

10-19 When a company declares a 3-for-1 stock split, the number of outstanding shares:

a. is reduced by one-third.
b. is reduced by one-third and the number of issued shares is tripled.
c. stays the same, but the number of issued shares triples.
d. triples.

10-20 Shea Company has 100,000 shares of 6%, $50 par value, cumulative preferred stock. In 2012, no dividends were declared on preferred stock. In 2013, Shea had a profitable year and decided to pay dividends to stockholders of both preferred and common stock. If they have $750,000 available for dividends in 2013, how much could it pay to the common stockholders?

a. $750,000
b. $450,000
c. $150,000
d. $0

10-21 RVR Enterprises shows net income of $100,000 for 2013 and retained earnings of $500,000 on its December 31, 2013 balance sheet. During the year, RVR declared and paid $60,000 in dividends. What was RVR's retained earnings balance at December 31, 2012?

a. $400,000
b. $440,000
c. $460,000
d. $540,000

10-22 Comprehensive income:

a. includes transactions that affect stockholders' equity with the exception of those transactions that involve owners.
b. is considered an appropriation of retained earnings.
c. includes all transactions that are under management's control.
d. is the result of all events and transactions reported on the income statement.

10-23 FASB's concept of comprehensive income:

a. excludes the payment of dividends.
b. has a primary drawback because it allows management to manipulate the income figure to a certain extent.
c. requires that all transactions must be shown on the income statement.
d. allows items that are not necessarily under management's control, such as natural disasters, to be shown as an adjustment of retained earnings.

10-24 Garner Corporation issued $50,000 in common stock dividends. Its net income for the year was $250,000. What is Garner's dividend payout ratio?

a. 5
b. 2.5
c. 0.5
d. 0.2

CORNERSTONE EXERCISES

OBJECTIVE 2
CORNERSTONE 10.1

Cornerstone Exercise 10-25 Recording the Sale of Common and Preferred Stock

Donahue Corporation is authorized by its charter from the State of Illinois to issue 2,000 shares of 7% preferred stock with a par value of $30 per share and 125,000 shares of common stock with a par value of $0.01 per share. On January 1, 2013, Donahue issues 1,300 shares of preferred stock at $35 per share and 84,000 shares of common stock at $12.50 per share.

Required:

Prepare the journal entry to record the issuance of the stock.

OBJECTIVE 2
CORNERSTONE 10.1

Cornerstone Exercise 10-26 Recording the Sale of Common Stock

Plymouth Company issues 150,000 shares of common stock (par value $3) for $19 per share on June 30, 2013.

Required:

Prepare the journal entry to record this transaction.

Cornerstone Exercise 10-27 Calculating the Number of Shares Issued

OBJECTIVE 2
CORNERSTONE 10.1

Castalia Inc. issued shares of its $0.80 par value common stock on September 4, 2013, for $8 per share. The Additional Paid-In Capital—Common Stock account was credited for $612,000 in the journal entry to record this transaction.

Required:

How many shares were issued on September 4, 2013?

Cornerstone Exercise 10-28 Accounting for Treasury Stock

OBJECTIVE 3
CORNERSTONE 10.2

On January 20, 2013, Spring Hope Corporation repurchases 2,600 shares of its outstanding common stock for $9 per share. On April 3, 2013, Spring Hope sells 700 shares of treasury stock for $13 per share. On October 29, 2013, Spring Hope sells the remaining 1,900 shares of its treasury stock for $6 per share.

Required:

Prepare the journal entries to record these transactions.

Cornerstone Exercise 10-29 Accounting for Treasury Stock

OBJECTIVE 3
CORNERSTONE 10.2

On January 3, 2013, Tommyboy Corporation repurchases 250,000 shares of its outstanding common stock for $18 per share. On May 1, 2013, Tommyboy sells 80,500 shares of treasury stock for $12 per share. On October 1, 2013, Tommyboy sells 40,000 shares of its treasury stock for $31 per share.

Required:

1. Prepare the journal entries to record these transactions.
2. How will these transactions affect Tommyboy's 2013 income statement?

Use the following information for Cornerstone Exercises 10-30 and 10-31:
Kellman Company purchases 110,000 shares of treasury stock for $8 per share on September 4, 2014.

Cornerstone Exercise 10-30 Treasury Stock

OBJECTIVE 3
CORNERSTONE 10.2

Refer to the information for Kellman Company above.

Required:

1. How will this transaction affect stockholders' equity?
2. How will this transaction affect net income?

Cornerstone Exercise 10-31 Treasury Stock

OBJECTIVE 3
CORNERSTONE 10.2

Refer to the information for Kellman Company above.

Required:

What is the appropriate journal entry to record the transaction?

Cornerstone Exercise 10-32 Cash Dividends

OBJECTIVE 3
CORNERSTONE 10.3

King Tut Corporation issued 19,000 shares of common stock, all of the same class; 12,000 shares are outstanding and 7,000 shares are held as treasury stock. On December 1, 2013, King Tut's board of directors declares a cash dividend of $0.50 per share payable on December 15, 2013, to stockholders of record on December 10, 2013.

Required:

Prepare the appropriate journal entries for the date of declaration, date of record, and date of payment.

OBJECTIVE 3
CORNERSTONE 10.3

Cornerstone Exercise 10-33 Declaration of Cash Dividend

Wilson Corporation declares a cash dividend of $80,000 on December 31, 2013.

Required:

What is the appropriate journal entry to record this declaration?

OBJECTIVE 3
CORNERSTONE 10.4

Cornerstone Exercise 10-34 Stock Dividend

Bower Corporation reported the following information: common stock, $2 par; 120,000 shares authorized; 65,000 shares issued and outstanding.

Required:

1. What is the appropriate journal entry to record a 5% stock dividend if the market price of the common stock is $45 per share when the dividend is declared?
2. What is the appropriate journal entry to record a 35% stock dividend if the market price of the common stock is $45 per share when the dividend is declared?
3. How do these transactions affect Bower's total stockholders' equity?

OBJECTIVE 3
CORNERSTONE 10.5

Cornerstone Exercise 10-35 Preferred and Common Stock Dividends

Barstow Corporation has a single class of common stock and a single class of cumulative preferred stock. The cumulative preferred stock requires the corporation to pay an annual dividend of $8,000 to preferred stockholders. On January 1, 2013, Barstow's preferred dividends were 1 year in arrears, which means that Barstow declared neither preferred nor common dividends in 2012. During the 3 years (2013–2015), Barstow's board of directors determined they would be able to pay $9,500, $17,000, and $20,000, respectively.

Required:

Show how these anticipated payments will be split between preferred and common stockholders.

OBJECTIVE 3
CORNERSTONE 10.5

Cornerstone Exercise 10-36 Preferred Stock Dividends

Seashell Corporation has 25,000 shares outstanding of 8%, $10 par value, cumulative preferred stock. In 2011 and 2012, no dividends were declared on preferred stock. In 2013, Seashell had a profitable year and decided to pay dividends to stockholders of both preferred and common stock.

Required:

If Seashell has $200,000 available for dividends in 2013, how much could it pay to the common stockholders?

OBJECTIVE 5
CORNERSTONE 10.6

Cornerstone Exercise 10-37 Stockholder Profitability Ratios

The following information pertains to Montague Corporation:

Net income	$1,800,000
Average common equity	$22,350,000
Preferred dividends	$375,000
Average common shares outstanding	805,000

Required:

Calculate the return on common equity and the earnings per share. (*Note:* Round answers to two decimal places.)

OBJECTIVE 5
CORNERSTONE 10.7

Cornerstone Exercise 10-38 Stockholder Payout Ratios

The following information pertains to Milo Mindbender Corporation:

Net income	$123,000
Dividends per common share	$2.00
Common shares	12,000
Purchases of treasury stock	$85,000
Common share price	$20

Required:

Calculate the dividend yield, dividend payout, and total payout. (*Note*: Round answers to two decimal places.)

BRIEF EXERCISES

Brief Exercise 10-39 Common Stock versus Preferred Stock

OBJECTIVE 1

Corporations issue two general types of stock—common and preferred.

Required:

Describe the major differences between common and preferred stock.

Brief Exercise 10-40 Recording the Sale of Common and Preferred Stock

OBJECTIVE 2

At the end of its first year of operations, Mulligan Corporation has outstanding shares of 96,000 common stock and 1,900 preferred stock. The State of Ohio authorized Mulligan to issue 3,000 shares of 6% preferred stock with a par value of $40 per share and 110,000 shares of common stock with a par value of $0.01 per share. Any common stock sold during the year had a selling price of $47 per share. Mulligan's preferred stock was issued at $17.50.

Required:

Prepare the journal entry to record any issuance of stock during the year.

Brief Exercise 10-41 Recording the Sale of Common Stock

OBJECTIVE 2

Green Company, a food coloring manufacturer that provides its products to large processed-food corporations, issues 450,000 shares of common stock (par value $0.10) for $22 per share on September 30, 2013.

Required:

Prepare the necessary journal entry to record this transaction.

Brief Exercise 10-42 Calculating the Number of Shares Issued

OBJECTIVE 2

Castanet Inc. issued shares of its $1.50 par value common stock on November 9, 2013, for $13 per share. In recording the issuance of the stock, Castanet credited the Additional Paid-In Capital—Common Stock account for $416,300.

Required:

How many shares were issued on November 9, 2013?

Brief Exercise 10-43 Accounting for Treasury Stock

OBJECTIVE 3

On August 19, 2013, Portland Corporation repurchases 1,400 shares of its outstanding common stock for $9 per share. On October 31, 2013, Portland sells 600 shares of treasury stock for $13 per share. Any additional sales of treasury stock during the year were sold for $4 per share. On December 31, 2013, Portland had no remaining treasury stock.

Required:

Prepare the necessary journal entries to record any transactions associated with treasury stock.

Brief Exercise 10-44 Accounting for Treasury Stock

OBJECTIVE 3

Paris Corporation provides travel planning services for large corporations across the world. On January 23, 2013, Paris Corporation repurchases 275,000 shares of its outstanding common stock for $12 per share. On May 19, 2013, Paris sells 100,500 shares of treasury stock for $8 per share. On November 1, 2013, Paris sells 60,000 shares of its treasury stock for $27 per share.

(*Continued*)

Required:

1. Prepare the necessary journal entries to record these transactions.
2. **CONCEPTUAL CONNECTION** How will these transactions affect Paris's 2013 income statement?

Use the following information for Brief Exercises 10-45 and 10-46:
Heitman Company purchases 170,000 shares of treasury stock for $11 per share.

OBJECTIVE 3

Brief Exercise 10-45 Treasury Stock

Refer to the information for Heitman Company above.

Required:

1. How will this transaction affect stockholders' equity?
2. How will this transaction affect net income?

OBJECTIVE 3

Brief Exercise 10-46 Treasury Stock

Refer to the information for Heitman Company above.

Required:

What is the appropriate journal entry to record the transaction?

OBJECTIVE 3

Brief Exercise 10-47 Cash Dividends

Cyprus Corporation issued 12,000 shares of common stock. At the beginning of the year, Cyprus held 5,000 shares of treasury stock, but it reissued 1,000 of those shares in October. On December 1, 2013, Cyprus's board of directors declares a cash dividend of $0.95 per share payable on December 20, 2013, to stockholders of record on December 15, 2013.

Required:

Prepare the appropriate journal entries for the date of declaration, date of record, and date of payment.

OBJECTIVE 3

Brief Exercise 10-48 Declaration of Cash Dividend

Travis Corporation expected to pay its stockholders a dividend in January 2014. The cash dividend of $75,000 was declared on December 31, 2013.

Required:

What is the appropriate journal entry to record this declaration?

OBJECTIVE 3

Brief Exercise 10-49 Stock Dividend

Augusta Corporation reported the following information: 35,000 shares of $3 par value common stock authorized, 30,000 shares common stock issued, 10,000 shares treasury stock.

Required:

1. What is the appropriate journal entry to record a 5% stock dividend if the market price of the common stock is $40 per share when the dividend is declared?
2. What is the appropriate journal entry to record a 20% stock dividend if the market price of the common stock is $40 per share when the dividend is declared?
3. **CONCEPTUAL CONNECTION** How do these transactions affect Augusta's total stockholders' equity?

OBJECTIVE 3

Brief Exercise 10-50 Preferred and Common Stock Dividends

Brookshed Corporation has a single class of common stock and a single class of cumulative preferred stock. The cumulative preferred stock requires the corporation to pay an annual dividend of $11,000 to preferred stockholders. On January 1, 2013, Brookshed's preferred dividends were 1 year in arrears, which means that Brookshed declared neither preferred nor common dividends in 2012. During the 3 years (2013–2015), Brookshed's board of directors determined they would be able to pay $17,000, $18,000, and $21,000, respectively.

Required:

Show how these anticipated payments will be split between preferred and common stockholders.

Brief Exercise 10-51 Preferred Stock Dividends

OBJECTIVE 3

Eugene Corporation issued 25,000 shares outstanding of 6%, $5 par value, cumulative preferred stock. Eugene purchased 5,000 shares of its preferred stock to remain in its treasury. In 2011 and 2012, no dividends were declared on preferred stock. In 2013, Seashell had a profitable year and decided to pay dividends to stockholders of both preferred and common stock.

Required:

If Eugene has $75,000 available for dividends in 2013, how much could it pay to the common stockholders?

Use the following information for Brief Exercises 10-52 and 10-53:
Titanic Corporation's net income for the year ended December 31, 2013, is $380,000. On June 30, 2013, a $0.75 per-share cash dividend was declared for all common stockholders. Common stock in the amount of 38,000 shares was outstanding at the time. The market price of Titanic's stock at year end (12/31/13) is $18 per share. Titanic had a $1,100,000 credit balance in retained earnings at December 31, 2012.

Brief Exercise 10-52 Retained Earnings

OBJECTIVE 4

Refer to the information for Titanic Corporation above.

Required:

Calculate the ending balance (12/31/13) of retained earnings.

Brief Exercise 10-53 Retained Earnings

OBJECTIVE 4

Refer to the information for Titanic Corporation above. Assume that on July 31, 2013, Titanic discovered that 2012 depreciation was overstated by $75,000.

Required:

Prepare Titanic's retained earnings statement for the year ended December 31, 2013, assuming the 2012 tax rate was 30%.

Brief Exercise 10-54 Stockholder Payout Ratios

OBJECTIVE 5

Super Duper Corporation had a string of successful years. Super Duper's executives wish to examine how its stockholders have been compensated for their contributed capital. The following information pertains to Super Duper Corporation:

Net income	$104,000
Dividends per common share	$1.50
Common shares	16,000
Purchases of treasury stock	$65,000
Common stock price	$25

Required:

Calculate the dividend yield, dividend payout, and total payout.

OBJECTIVE 5

Brief Exercise 10-55 Stockholder Profitability Ratios

The following information pertains to Capital Corporation:

Net income	$1,005,000
Average common equity	$16,500,000
Preferred stock, $10 par, 230,000 issued, 10% cumulative	$2,300,000
Average common shares outstanding	525,000

Required:

Calculate the return on common equity and the earnings per share.

EXERCISES

OBJECTIVE 1

Exercise 10-56 Accounting for Shares

Kress Products' corporate charter authorized the firm to sell 800,000 shares of $10 par common stock. At the beginning of 2013, Kress sold 318,000 shares and reacquired 4,500 of those shares. The reacquired shares were held as treasury stock. During 2013, Kress sold an additional 24,350 shares and purchased 8,200 more treasury shares.

Required:

Determine the number of issued and outstanding shares at December 31, 2013.

OBJECTIVE 1

Exercise 10-57 Outstanding Stock

Lars Corporation shows the following information in the stockholders' equity section of its balance sheet: The par value of common stock is $5, and the total balance in the Common Stock account is $225,000. There are 13,000 shares of treasury stock.

Required:

What is the number of shares outstanding?

Use the following information for Exercises 10-58 and 10-59:
Stahl Company was incorporated as a new business on January 1, 2013. The company is authorized to issue 600,000 shares of $2 par value common stock and 80,000 shares of 6%, $20 par value, cumulative preferred stock. On January 1, 2013, the company issued 75,000 shares of common stock for $15 per share and 5,000 shares of preferred stock for $25 per share. Net income for the year ended December 31, 2013, was $500,000.

OBJECTIVE 1

Exercise 10-58 Capital Stock

Refer to the information for Stahl Company above.

Required:

What is the amount of Stahl's total contributed capital at December 31, 2013?

OBJECTIVE 1

Exercise 10-59 Preparation of Stockholders' Equity Section

Refer to the information for Stahl Company above.

Required:

Prepare the stockholders' equity section of the balance sheet for Stahl Company.

OBJECTIVE 2

Exercise 10-60 Issuing Common Stock

Carmean Products Inc. sold 32,350 shares of common stock to stockholders at the time of its incorporation. Carmean received $42 per share for the stock.

Required:

1. Assume that the stock has a $22 par value per share. Prepare the journal entry to record the sale and issue of the stock.
2. Assume that the stock has a $8 stated value per share. Prepare the journal entry to record the sale and issue of the stock.
3. Assume that the stock has no par value and no stated value. Prepare the journal entry to record the sale and issue of the stock.
4. **CONCEPTUAL CONNECTION** How do the different par values affect total contributed capital and total stockholders' equity?

Exercise 10-61 Issuing and Repurchasing Stock

OBJECTIVE 2

Mohawk Company had the following transactions related to its common and preferred stock:

March 22	Sold 180,000 shares of $1 par common stock for $33 per share.
	Sold 1,500 shares of $5 par preferred stock at $11 per share.
November 9	Repurchased 25,000 shares of the common stock at $35 per share.

Required:

Prepare the journal entries for these transactions.

Exercise 10-62 Prepare the Stockholders' Equity Section

OBJECTIVE 2

Renee Corporation has the following stockholders' equity information:

	$5 Par Common	$10 Par Preferred
Additional paid-in capital	$2,250,000	$50,000
Shares:		
Authorized	750,000	40,000
Issued	300,000	8,000
Outstanding	250,000	8,000

Retained earnings is $1,837,000, and the cost of treasury shares is $1,200,000.

Required:

Prepare the stockholders' equity portion of Renee's balance sheet.

Exercise 10-63 Prepare the Stockholders' Equity Section

OBJECTIVE 2

Wildcat Drilling has the following accounts on its trial balance.

	Debit	Credit
Retained Earnings		600,000
Cash	825,000	
Additional Paid-In Capital—Common		3,100,000
Additional Paid-In Capital—Preferred		400,000
Accounts Payable		345,000
Accounts Receivable	410,000	
Common Stock, $1 par		600,000
Preferred Stock, $10 par		340,000
Inventory	1,300,000	
Treasury Stock—Common (30,000 shares)	382,000	
Accumulated Other Comprehensive Income		70,000

Required:

Prepare the stockholders' equity portion of Wildcat's balance sheet.

OBJECTIVE 2

ILLUSTRATING RELATIONSHIPS

Exercise 10-64 Interpret the Stockholders' Equity Section

Medici Inc. has the following stockholders' equity section of the balance sheet:

Medici Inc.
Balance Sheet (Partial)

Stockholders' equity:		
Preferred stock, 100,000 shares authorized; 30,000 issued and outstanding		$ 300,000
Common stock, 1,000,000 shares authorized; 600,000 issued; 550,000 outstanding		1,200,000
Additional paid-in capital:		
Preferred stock	$ 90,000	
Common stock	4,800,000	4,890,000
Total capital stock		$6,390,000
Retained earnings		450,000
Accumulated other comprehensive income		22,000
Less: Treasury stock, at cost		(800,000)
Total stockholders' equity		$6,062,000

Required:

1. How many shares of preferred stock are authorized?
2. How many shares of common stock are outstanding?
3. What was the average selling price for the common stock when issued?
4. What was the average repurchase price for the treasury shares?
5. If the annual dividends on the preferred stock are $0.80 per share, what is the dividend rate on the preferred stock?

OBJECTIVE 3

Exercise 10-65 Treasury Stock Transactions

Garrett Inc. had no treasury stock at the beginning of the year. During February, Garrett purchased 12,600 shares of treasury stock at $23 per share. In May, Garrett sold 4,500 of the treasury shares for $25 per share. In November, Garrett sold the remaining treasury shares for $18 per share.

Required:

Prepare journal entries for the February, May, and November treasury stock transactions.

OBJECTIVE 3

Exercise 10-66 Cash Dividends on Common Stock

Berkwild Company is authorized to issue 2,000,000 shares of common stock. At the beginning of 2013, Berkwild had 248,000 issued and outstanding shares. On July 2, 2013, Berkwild repurchased 4,610 shares of its common stock at $28 per share. On March 1 and September 1, Berkwild declared a cash dividend of $1.10 per share. The dividends were paid on April 1 and October 1.

Required:

1. Prepare the journal entries to record the declaration of the two cash dividends.
2. Prepare the journal entries to record the payment of the two dividends.
3. **CONCEPTUAL CONNECTION** Explain why the amounts of the two dividends are different.

OBJECTIVE 3

ILLUSTRATING RELATIONSHIPS

Exercise 10-67 Cash Dividends on Common and Preferred Stock

Lemon Inc. has the following information regarding its preferred and common stock:

Preferred stock, $30 par, 12% cumulative; 300,000 shares authorized; 150,000 shares issued and outstanding

Common stock, $2 par; 2,500,000 shares authorized; 1,200,000 shares issued; 1,000,000 outstanding

As of December 31, 2013, Lemon was 3 years in arrears on its dividends. During 2014, Lemon declared and paid dividends. As a result, the common stockholders received dividends of $0.45 per share.

Required:

1. What was the total amount of dividends declared and paid?
2. What journal entry was made at the date of declaration?

Exercise 10-68 Distribution to Stockholders

OBJECTIVE 3

Owners invest in corporations through the purchase of stock.

Required:

CONCEPTUAL CONNECTION Describe two ways that corporations distribute assets to stockholders (without liquidating the company). Discuss their relative advantages and disadvantages.

Exercise 10-69 Stock Dividends

OBJECTIVE 3

Crystal Corporation has the following information regarding its common stock: $10 par, with 500,000 shares authorized, 213,000 shares issued, and 183,700 shares outstanding.

On August 22, 2013, Crystal declared and paid a 15% stock dividend when the market price of the common stock was $30 per share.

Required:

1. Prepare the journal entries to record declaration and payment of this stock dividend.
2. Prepare the journal entries to record declaration and payment assuming it was a 30% stock dividend.

Exercise 10-70 Stock Dividend

OBJECTIVE 3

ILLUSTRATING RELATIONSHIPS

The balance sheet of Cohen Enterprises includes the following stockholders' equity section:

Common stock, $1 par, 330,000 shares authorized, 150,000 shares issued and outstanding	$150,000
Additional paid-in capital—common stock	341,800
Total capital stock	$491,800
Retained earnings	173,000
Total equity	$664,800

Required:

1. On April 15, 2013, when its stock was selling for $18 per share, Cohen Enterprises issued a small stock dividend. After making the journal entry to recognize the stock dividend, Cohen's total capital stock increased by $270,000. In percentage terms, what was the size of the stock dividend?
2. Ignoring the small stock dividend discussed in Requirement 1, assume that on June 1, 2013, when its stock was selling for $22 per share, Cohen issued a large stock dividend. After making the journal entry to recognize the stock dividend, Cohen's retained earnings decreased by $75,000. In percentage terms, what was the size of the stock dividend?

Exercise 10-71 Stock Split

OBJECTIVE 3

Birch Enterprises reported the following information: common stock, $3 par; 750,000 shares authorized; 400,000 shares issued and outstanding.

Required:

What is the typical effect of a 4-for-1 stock split on the information Birch Enterprises reports above? If the market value of the common stock is $600 per share when the stock split is declared, what would you expect the approximate market value per share to be immediately after the split?

OBJECTIVE 3

ILLUSTRATING RELATIONSHIPS

Exercise 10-72 Stock Dividends and Stock Splits

The balance sheet of Castle Corporation includes the following stockholders' equity section:

Common stock, $2 par, 80,000 shares authorized, 60,000 shares issued and outstanding	$120,000
Additional paid-in capital—common stock	371,800
Total capital stock	$491,800
Retained earnings	173,000
Total equity	$664,800

Required:

1. Assume that Castle issued 60,000 shares for cash at the inception of the corporation and that no new shares have been issued since. Determine how much cash was received for the shares issued at inception.
2. Assume that Castle issued 30,000 shares for cash at the inception of the corporation and subsequently declared a 2-for-1 stock split. Determine how much cash was received for the shares issued at inception.
3. Assume that Castle issued 57,000 shares for cash at the inception of the corporation and that the remaining 3,000 shares were issued as the result of stock dividends when the stock was selling for $53 per share. Determine how much cash was received for the shares issued at inception.

OBJECTIVE 3

Exercise 10-73 Preferred Dividends

Eastern Inc.'s equity includes 8%, $25 par preferred stock. There are 100,000 shares authorized and 45,000 shares outstanding. Assume that Eastern declares and pays preferred dividends quarterly.

Required:

1. Prepare the journal entry to record declaration of one quarterly dividend.
2. Prepare the journal entry to record payment of the one quarterly dividend.

OBJECTIVE 3

Exercise 10-74 Cumulative Preferred Dividends

Capital stock of Barr Company includes:

Common stock, $5 par, 650,000 shares outstanding	$3,250,000
Preferred stock, 15% cumulative, $60 par, 10,000 shares outstanding	600,000

As of December 31, 2012, 2 years' dividends are in arrears on the preferred stock. During 2013, Barr plans to pay dividends that total $360,000.

Required:

1. Determine the amount of dividends that will be paid to Barr's common and preferred stockholders in 2013.
2. If Barr paid $280,000 of dividends, determine how much each group of stockholders would receive.

OBJECTIVE 4

Exercise 10-75 Retained Earnings

Tigress Manufacturing had beginning retained earnings of $650,000. During the year, Tigress paid cash dividends of $70,000 to preferred stockholders and $55,000 to common stockholders. Net income for the year was $340,000.

Required:

1. Reproduce the Retained Earnings T-account for the year starting with the beginning balance.
2. Determine what Tigress's ending retained earnings is assuming that during the year it discovers that net income was overstated by $13,000 in prior years due to an error. The error was corrected and the current year's net income is correct.

Exercise 10-76 Retained Earnings

OBJECTIVE 4

ILLUSTRATING RELATIONSHIPS

The December 31, 2014 comparative balance sheet of Smith Industries includes the following stockholders' equity section:

	2014	2013
Common stock, $2 par, 80,000 shares authorized, 60,000 shares issued and outstanding	$120,000	$120,000
Additional paid-in capital—common stock	371,800	371,800
Total capital stock	$491,800	$491,800
Retained earnings	173,000	116,000
Total equity	$664,800	$607,800

Required:

During 2014 Smith paid dividends of $0.50 per share. What was Smith's net income for 2014?

Exercise 10-77 Restrictions on Retained Earnings

OBJECTIVE 2 5

At December 31, 2012, Longfellow Clothing had $226,700 of retained earnings, all unrestricted. During 2013, Longfellow earned net income of $92,000 and declared and paid cash dividends on common stock of $21,800. During 2013, Longfellow sold a bond issue with a covenant that required Longfellow to transfer from retained earnings to restricted retained earnings an amount equal to the principal of the bond issue, $50,000. At December 31, 2013, Longfellow has 30,000 shares of $5 par common stock issued and outstanding. Additional paid-in capital—common stock is $236,500.

Required:

Prepare the stockholders' equity portion of Longfellow's December 31, 2013 balance sheet.

Exercise 10-78 Ratio Analysis

OBJECTIVE 5

Consider the following information.

Stock price	$55/share	Avg. common shares outstanding	850,000
Common dividends	$765,000	Dividends per common share	$0.90/share
Preferred dividends	$238,800	Net income	$15,485,000
2013 preferred stock	$6,162,000	2012 preferred stock	$5,299,000
2013 total stockholders' equity	$28,435,000	2012 total stockholders' equity	$25,483,000
Purchases of treasury stock	$120,000		

Required:

1. Calculate the stockholder payout ratios. (*Note:* Round answers to two decimal places.)
2. Calculate the stockholder profitability ratios. (*Note:* Round answers to two decimal places.)

Exercise 10-79 Ratio Analysis

OBJECTIVE 2

ILLUSTRATING RELATIONSHIPS

MJO Inc. has the following stockholders' equity section of the balance sheet:

MJO Inc.
Balance Sheet (Partial)

Stockholders' equity:		
Preferred stock, 100,000 shares authorized; 30,000 issued and outstanding		$ 300,000
Common stock, 1,000,000 shares authorized; 600,000 issued; 550,000 outstanding		1,200,000
Additional paid-in capital:		
Preferred stock	$ 90,000	
Common stock	4,800,000	4,890,000
Total capital stock		$6,390,000
Retained earnings		450,000
Accumulated other comprehensive income		22,000
Less: Treasury stock, at cost		(800,000)
Total stockholders' equity		$6,062,000

(*Continued*)

On the balance sheet date, MJO's stock was selling for $25 per share.

Required:

1. Assuming MJO's dividend yield is 1%, what are the dividends per common share?
2. Assuming MJO's dividend yield is 1% and its dividend payout is 20%, what is MJO's net income?

OBJECTIVE 1 2 3 4

Exercise 10-80 Stockholders' Equity Terminology

A list of terms and a list of definitions or examples are presented below. Make a list of the numbers 1 through 12 and match the letter of the most directly related definition or example with each number.

Terms

1. stock warrant
2. date of record
3. par value
4. stock split
5. treasury stock
6. stock dividend
7. preferred stock
8. outstanding shares
9. authorized shares
10. declaration date
11. comprehensive income
12. retained earnings

Definitions and Examples

a. Capitalizes retained earnings.
b. Shares issued minus treasury shares.
c. Emerson Electric will pay a dividend to all persons holding shares of its common stock on December 15, 2013, even if they just bought the shares and sell them a few days later.
d. The accumulated earnings over the entire life of the corporation that have not been paid out in dividends.
e. Common Stock account balance divided by the number of shares issued.
f. The state of Louisiana set an upper limit of 1,000,000 on the number of shares that Gump's Catch Inc. can issue.
g. Shares that never earn dividends.
h. Any changes to stockholders' equity from transactions with nonowners.
i. A right to purchase stock at a specified future time and specified price.
j. A stock issue that requires no journal entry.
k. Shares that may earn guaranteed dividends.
l. On October 15, 2013, General Electric announced its intention to pay a dividend on common stock.

PROBLEM SET A

OBJECTIVE 1

Problem 10-81A Presentation of Stockholders' Equity

Green Line Corporation was organized in January 2013. During 2013, Green Line engaged in the following stockholders' equity activities:

a. Secured approval for a corporate charter that authorizes Green Line to sell 1,500,000, $2 par common shares and 200,000, $25 par preferred shares.
b. Sold 120,000 of the common shares for $9 per share.
c. Sold 65,000 of the preferred shares for $32 per share.
d. Repurchased 15,000 shares of the common stock at a cost of $11 per share.
e. Earned net income of $460,000.
f. Paid dividends of $52,000.

Required:

Prepare the stockholders' equity portion of Green Line's balance sheet as of December 31, 2013.

Problem 10-82A Issuing Common and Preferred Stock

OBJECTIVE 2

Klaus Herrmann, a biochemistry professor, organized Bioproducts Inc. early this year. The firm will manufacture antibiotics using gene splicing technology. Bioproducts' charter authorizes the firm to issue 10,000 shares of 7%, \$70 par preferred stock and 150,000 shares of \$5 par common stock. During the year, the firm engaged in the transactions listed below.

a. Issued 50,000 common shares to Klaus Herrmann in exchange for \$550,000 cash.
b. Sold 8,000 common shares to a potential customer for \$12 per share.
c. Issued 4,000 shares of preferred stock to a venture capital firm for \$85 per share.
d. Gave 100 shares of common stock to Margaret Robb, a local attorney, in exchange for Margaret's work in arranging for the firm's incorporation. Margaret usually charges \$1,200 for comparable work.

Required:

Prepare a journal entry for each of these transactions.

Problem 10-83A Treasury Stock Transactions

OBJECTIVE 3

Hansen Inc. engaged in the following transactions during the current year:

a. Repurchased 13,000 shares of its own \$1 par common stock for \$14 per share on January 14.
b. Sold 2,000 treasury shares to employees for \$6 per share on January 31.
c. Repurchased 3,000 more shares of the \$1 par common stock for \$16 per share on July 24.
d. Sold the remaining 11,000 shares from the January 14 purchase and 1,200 of the shares from the July 24 purchase to employees for \$6.50 per share on August 1.

Required:

1. Prepare journal entries for each of these transactions.
2. **CONCEPTUAL CONNECTION** Determine what the effect on total stockholders' equity is for each of the four transactions.

Problem 10-84A Statement of Stockholders' Equity

OBJECTIVE 1 2

At the end of 2013, Haley Corporation had the following equity accounts and balances:

Common stock, \$10 par	\$800,000
Additional paid-in capital—common stock	200,000
Retained earnings	279,000

During 2014, Haley engaged in the following transactions involving its equity accounts:

a. Sold 5,000 shares of common stock for \$19 per share.
b. Sold 1,200 shares of 12%, \$50 par preferred stock at \$75 per share.
c. Declared and paid cash dividends of \$22,000.
d. Repurchased 1,000 shares of treasury stock (common) for \$24 per share.
e. Sold 300 of the treasury shares for \$26 per share.

Required:

1. Prepare the journal entries for Transactions a through e.
2. Assume that 2014 net income was \$123,700. Prepare a statement of stockholders' equity at December 31, 2014.

Problem 10-85A Common Dividends

OBJECTIVE 3

Fusion Payroll Service began 2013 with 1,200,000 authorized and 375,000 issued and outstanding \$5 par common shares. During 2013, Fusion entered into the following transactions:

a. Declared a \$0.30 per-share cash dividend on March 10.
b. Paid the \$0.30 per-share dividend on April 10.
c. Repurchased 8,000 common shares at a cost of \$18 each on May 2.
d. Sold 1,500 unissued common shares for \$23 per share on June 9.

(*Continued*)

e. Declared a \$0.45 per-share cash dividend on August 10.
f. Paid the \$0.45 per-share dividend on September 10.
g. Declared and paid a 5% stock dividend on October 15 when the market price of the common stock was \$25 per share.
h. Declared a \$0.50 per-share cash dividend on November 10.
i. Paid the \$0.50 per-share dividend on December 10.

Required:

1. Prepare journal entries for each of these transactions. (*Note:* Round to the nearest dollar.)
2. Determine the total dollar amount of dividends (cash and stock) for the year.
3. **CONCEPTUAL CONNECTION** Determine the effect on total assets and total stockholders' equity of these dividend transactions.

OBJECTIVE 3

Problem 10-86A Stock Dividends and Stock Splits

Lance Products' balance sheet includes total assets of \$587,000 and the following equity account balances at December 31, 2013:

Common stock, \$2 par, 80,000 shares issued and outstanding	\$160,000
Additional paid-in capital—common stock	24,000
Total capital stock	\$184,000
Retained earnings	217,000
Total stockholders' equity	\$401,000

Lance's common stock is selling for \$12 per share on December 31, 2013.

Required:

1. How much would Lance Products have reported for total assets and retained earnings on December 31, 2013, if the firm had declared and paid a \$15,000 cash dividend on December 31, 2013? Prepare the journal entry for this cash dividend.
2. How much would Lance have reported for total assets and retained earnings on December 31, 2013, if the firm had issued a 15% stock dividend on December 31, 2013? Prepare the journal entry for this stock dividend.
3. **CONCEPTUAL CONNECTION** How much would Lance have reported for total assets and retained earnings on December 31, 2013, if the firm had effected a 2-for-1 stock split on December 31, 2013? Is a journal entry needed to record the stock split? Why or why not?

OBJECTIVE 3

Problem 10-87A Preferred Dividends

Stevens Industries had the following preferred stock outstanding at the end of a recent year:

\$5 par, 9%	12,000 shares
\$10 par, 9%, cumulative	6,000 shares
\$25 par, 10%, cumulative, convertible	9,000 shares
\$50 par, 12%, nonparticipating	10,000 shares

Required:

1. Determine the amount of annual dividends on each issue of preferred stock and the total annual dividend on all four issues.
2. Calculate what the amount of dividends in arrears would be if the dividends were omitted for 1 year.

Problem 10-88A Ratio Analysis

OBJECTIVE 5

Consider the following information taken from the stockholders' equity section:

	(dollar amounts in thousands)	
	2014	2013
Preferred stock	$ 1,000	$ 1,000
Common stock, 334,328,193 and 330,961,869 shares issued in 2014 and 2013, respectively	3,343	3,310
Additional paid-in capital—common stock	766,382	596,239
Retained earnings	5,460,629	4,630,390
Accumulated other comprehensive (loss) income	(206,662)	58,653
Treasury stock (76,275,837 and 56,960,213 shares in 2014 and 2013, respectively) at cost	(3,267,955)	(2,205,987)
Total stockholders' equity	$ 2,756,737	$ 3,083,605

Additional Information (all numbers in thousands other than per-share information):	2014
Weighted average common shares outstanding	184,000
Price per share at year end	$105.45
Net income	$1,358,950
Preferred dividends	$100,000
Common dividends	$213,440
Common dividends per share	$1.16
Stock repurchases	$834,975

Required:

1. Calculate the following for 2014. (*Note:* Round answers to two decimal places.)

Stockholder Payout	Stockholder Profitability
Dividend yield	Return on common equity
Dividend payout	EPS
Total payout	
Stock repurchase payout	

2. **CONCEPTUAL CONNECTION** Assume 2013 ratios were:

Stockholder Payout	Stockholder Profitability
Dividend yield: 0.85%	Return on common equity: 34.26%
Dividend payout: 9.80%	EPS: $3.51
Total payout: 70.00%	
Stock repurchase payout: 60.20%	

and the current year industry averages are:

Stockholder Payout	Stockholder Profitability
Dividend yield: 0.76%	Return on common equity: 23.81%
Dividend payout: 12.35%	EPS: $1.23
Total payout: 48.37%	
Stock repurchase payout: 36.02%	

How do you interpret the company's payout and profitability performance?

PROBLEM SET B

Problem 10-81B Presentation of Stockholders' Equity

OBJECTIVE 1

Steven's Restorations was organized in January 2013. During 2013, Steven's engaged in the following stockholders' equity activities:

(*Continued*)

a. Secured approval for a corporate charter that authorizes Steven's to sell 1,000,000, $10 par common shares and 75,000, $100 par preferred shares.
b. Sold 480,000 of the common shares for $15 per share.
c. Sold 25,000 of the preferred shares for $105 per share.
d. Repurchased 2,000 shares of the common stock at a cost of $18 per share.
e. Earned net income of $107,000.
f. Paid dividends of $13,000.

Required:

Prepare the stockholders' equity portion of Steven's balance sheet as of December 31, 2013.

OBJECTIVE 2

Problem 10-82B Issuing Common and Preferred Stock

Mallard Furniture recently became an incorporated furniture manufacturer after years of being run as a successful family business. Mallard's charter authorizes the firm to issue 10,000 shares of 8%, $25 par preferred stock and 50,000 shares of $2 par common stock. During the year, the company engaged in the following transactions:

a. Issued 25,000 common shares to Mallard's founding family in exchange for $140,000 cash.
b. Sold 5,000 common shares to a potential customer for $13 per share.
c. Issued 2,000 shares of preferred stock to a venture capital firm for $45 per share.
d. Gave 50 shares of common stock to Kelsey Kennedy, a local attorney, in exchange for Kelsey's help on a legal matter. Kelsey usually charges $1,500 for comparable work and this amount should be classified as a legal expense.

Required:

Prepare a journal entry for each of these transactions.

OBJECTIVE 3

Problem 10-83B Treasury Stock Transactions

Bentonite Adhesives Inc. engaged in the following transactions during the current year:

a. Repurchased 8,000 shares of its own $5 par common stock for $13 per share on January 14.
b. Sold 2,600 of the treasury shares to employees for $8 per share on January 31.
c. Repurchased 2,000 more shares of the $5 par common stock for $17 each on July 24.
d. Sold the remaining 5,400 shares from the January 14 purchase and 800 of the shares from the July 24 purchase to employees for $9 per share on August 1.

Required:

1. Prepare journal entries for each of these transactions.
2. **CONCEPTUAL CONNECTION** Determine the effect on total stockholders' equity for each of the four transactions.

OBJECTIVE 1 2

Problem 10-84B Statement of Stockholders' Equity

At the end of 2013, Stanley Utilities Inc. had the following equity accounts and balances:

Common stock, $1 par	$4,500,000
Additional paid-in capital—common stock	1,375,000
Retained earnings	188,000

During 2014, Stanley Utilities engaged in the following transactions involving its equity accounts:

a. Sold 3,300 shares of common stock for $15 per share.
b. Sold 1,000 shares of 12%, $100 par preferred stock at $105 per share.
c. Declared and paid cash dividends of $8,000.
d. Repurchased 1,000 shares of treasury stock (common) for $38 per share.
e. Sold 400 of the treasury shares for $42 per share.

Required:

1. Prepare the journal entries for Transactions a through e.
2. Assume that 2014 net income was $87,000. Prepare a statement of stockholders' equity at December 31, 2014.

Problem 10-85B Common Dividends

OBJECTIVE 3

Thompson Payroll Service began in 2013 with 1,500,000 authorized and 820,000 issued and outstanding $8 par common shares. During 2013, Thompson entered into the following transactions:

a. Declared a $0.20 per-share cash dividend on March 24.
b. Paid the $0.20 per-share dividend on April 6.
c. Repurchased 13,000 common shares for the treasury at a cost of $12 each on May 9.
d. Sold 2,500 unissued common shares for $15 per share on June 19.
e. Declared a $0.40 per-share cash dividend on August 1.
f. Paid the $0.40 per-share dividend on September 14.
g. Declared and paid a 10% stock dividend on October 25 when the market price of the common stock was $15 per share.
h. Declared a $0.45 per-share cash dividend on November 20.
i. Paid the $0.45 per-share dividend on December 20.

Required:

1. Prepare journal entries for each of these transactions. (*Note:* Round to the nearest dollar.)
2. What is the total dollar amount of dividends (cash and stock) for the year?
3. **CONCEPTUAL CONNECTION** Determine the effect on total assets and total stockholders' equity of these dividend transactions.

Problem 10-86B Stock Dividends and Stock Splits

OBJECTIVE 3

Heller Company's balance sheet includes total assets of $3,872,000 and the following equity account balances at December 31, 2013:

Common stock, $5 par, 10,000 shares issued and outstanding	$ 95,000
Additional paid-in capital—common stock	162,000
Total capital stock	$257,000
Retained earnings	411,000
Total stockholders' equity	$668,000

Heller's common stock is selling for $23 per share on December 31, 2013.

Required:

1. Determine how much Heller's Products would have reported for total assets and retained earnings on December 31, 2013, if the firm had declared and paid a $22,000 cash dividend on December 31, 2013. Prepare the journal entry for this cash dividend.
2. Determine how much Heller would have reported for total assets and retained earnings on December 31, 2013, if the firm had issued a 12% stock dividend on December 31, 2013. Prepare the journal entry for this stock dividend.
3. **CONCEPTUAL CONNECTION** How much would Heller have reported for total assets and retained earnings on December 31, 2013, if the firm had effected a 2-for-1 stock split on December 31, 2013? Is a journal entry needed to record the stock split? Why or why not?

Problem 10-87B Preferred Dividends

OBJECTIVE 3

Steel Corporation had the following preferred stock outstanding at the end of a recent year:

$20 par, 9%	30,000 shares
$25 par, 10%, cumulative	15,000 shares
$100 par, 6%, cumulative, convertible	20,000 shares
$100 par, 8%, nonparticipating	8,000 shares

(*Continued*)

Required:

1. Determine the amount of annual dividends on each issue of preferred stock and the total annual dividend on all four issues.
2. Calculate what the amount of dividends in arrears would be if the dividends were omitted for 1 year.

OBJECTIVE 5

Problem 10-88B Ratio Analysis

Consider the following information taken from the stockholders' equity section:

	(dollar amounts in thousands)	
	2014	**2013**
Preferred stock	$ 1,000	$ 2,000
Common stock, 230,000,000 and 176,000,000 shares issued in 2014 and 2013, respectively	2,300	1,760
Additional paid-in capital—common stock	567,000	432,000
Retained earnings	4,604,600	3,700,000
Accumulated other comprehensive (loss) income	(454,600)	147,000
Treasury stock (37,000,000 and 19,000,000 shares in 2014 and 2013, respectively) at cost	(1,750,000)	(975,000)
Total stockholders' equity	$ 2,970,300	$3,307,760

Additional Information (all numbers in thousands other than per-share information):	2014
Weighted average common shares outstanding	200,000
Price per share at year end	$58.30
Net income	$1,584,000
Preferred dividends	$50,000
Common dividends	$300,000
Common dividends per share	$1.50
Stock repurchases	$850,000

Required:

1. Calculate the following. (*Note:* Round answers to two decimal places.)

Stockholder Payout	Stockholder Profitability
Dividend yield	Return on common equity
Dividend payout	EPS
Total payout	
Stock repurchase payout	

2. **CONCEPTUAL CONNECTION** Assume last year's ratios were:

Stockholder Payout	Stockholder Profitability
Dividend yield: 2.31%	Return on common equity: 37.41%
Dividend payout: 13.65%	EPS: $6.12
Total payout: 78.59%	
Stock repurchase payout: 64.94%	

and the current year industry averages are:

Stockholder Payout	Stockholder Profitability
Dividend yield: 2.50%	Return on common equity: 44.44%
Dividend payout: 15.10%	EPS: $6.48
Total payout: 55.10%	
Stock repurchase payout: 40.00%	

How do you interpret the company's payout and profitability performance?

CASES

Case 10-89 Ethics and Equity

Roger and Gordon are middle managers at a large, publicly traded corporation. Roger tells Gordon that the company is about to sign an exclusive product distribution agreement with a small, publicly traded manufacturer. This contract will quadruple the manufacturer's revenue. Roger mentions to Gordon that the manufacturer's stock price will likely go "through the roof." Gordon says, "Maybe we should buy some stock."

Required:

1. Are Roger and Gordon being smart, being unethical but not breaking the law, or breaking the law?
2. How does the SEC monitor such activity?

Case 10-90 Stock Transactions and Ethics

Marilyn Cox is the office manager for DTR Inc. DTR constructs, owns, and manages apartment complexes. Marilyn has been involved in negotiations between DTR and prospective lenders as DTR attempts to raise $425 million to use to build apartments in a growing area of Tulsa. Based on her experience with past negotiations, Marilyn knows that lenders are concerned about DTR's debt to equity ratio. When the negotiations began, DTR had debt of $80 million and equity of $50 million. Marilyn believes that DTR's debt to equity ratio of 1.6 is probably the minimum that lenders will accept.

Marilyn is also aware that DTR issued $10 million of common stock to a long-time friend of the corporation's president in exchange for some land just before the negotiations with lenders began. The president's friend constructs and sells single family homes. The land is in an area zoned only for single family housing and would be an attractive site for single family homes. Thus, the land is worth at least $10 million. However, DTR does not intend to build any single family homes.

Required:

1. What would have been DTR's debt to equity ratio if the $10 million of stock had not been issued for the land?
2. If Marilyn believes that the $10 million stock issue was undertaken only to improve DTR's debt to equity ratio and that it will be reversed whenever the president's friend wants the land back or when DTR's debt to equity position improves, what should she do?

Case 10-91 Common and Preferred Stock

Expansion Company now has $2,500,000 of equity (100,000 common shares). Current income is $400,000 and Expansion Company needs $500,000 of additional capital. The firm's bankers insist that this capital be acquired by selling either common or preferred stock. If Expansion sells common stock, the ownership share of the current stockholders will be diluted because 20,000 more shares will be sold. If preferred stock is sold, the dividend rate will be 15% of the $500,000. Furthermore, the preferred stock will have to be cumulative, participating, and convertible into 20,000 shares of common stock.

Required:

Indicate whether Expansion should sell additional common or preferred stock, and explain the reasons for your choice.

Case 10-92 Leverage

Enrietto Aquatic Products' offer to acquire Fiberglass Products for $2,000,000 cash has been accepted. Enrietto has $1,000,000 of liquid assets that can be converted into cash and plans to either sell common stock or issue bonds to raise the remaining $1,000,000. Before this acquisition, Enrietto's condensed balance sheet and condensed income statement were as follows:

(*Continued*)

Enrietto Aquatic Products
Preacquisition Condensed Balance Sheet

Assets		Liabilities and Equity	
Assets	$20,000,000	Liabilities	$ 8,000,000
		Common stock, $10 par	6,000,000
		Retained earnings	6,000,000
		Total liabilities & stockholders' equity	$20,000,000

Enrietto Aquatic Products
Preacquisition Condensed Income Statement

Income from operations	$ 6,000,000
Less: Interest expense	(1,000,000)
Income before taxes	$ 5,000,000
Less: Income taxes expense (0.34)	(1,700,000)
Net income	$ 3,300,000

Enrietto's policy is to pay 60% of net income to stockholders as dividends. Enrietto expects to be able to raise the $1,000,000 it needs for the acquisition by selling 50,000 shares of common stock at $20 each or by issuing $1,000,000 of 20-year, 12% bonds. Enrietto expects income from operations to grow by $700,000 after Fiberglass Products has been acquired. (Interest expense will increase if debt is used to finance the acquisition.)

Required:

1. Determine the return on equity (net income/total equity) before the acquisition and for both financing alternatives (round percentages to two decimal places).
2. If Enrietto sells additional stock, what will be the cash outflow for dividends?
3. If Enrietto sells bonds, what will be the net cash outflows for new interest and for all dividends? (Remember that interest is tax-deductible.)
4. Assume that Enrietto sells stock and that none of the preacquisition stockholders buy any of the 50,000 new shares. What total amount of dividends will the preacquisition stockholders receive after the acquisition? How does this amount compare with the dividends they receive before the acquisition?
5. Which alternative is better for Enrietto's preacquisition stockholders?

Case 10-93 Research and Analysis Using the Annual Report

Obtain **Priceline.com**'s 2011 10-K (remember, the 2011 10-K is filed with the SEC in early 2012) either through the "Investor Relations" portion of its website (do a web search for Priceline investor relations), or go to www.sec.gov and click "Search for Company Filings" under "Filings & Forms."

Required:

1. How many shares of common stock are authorized, issued, and outstanding at December 31, 2011?
2. What is Priceline.com's dividend policy? Why didn't Priceline.com pay dividends to common stockholders in any of the 3 years shown?
3. What is the common stockholders' equity at December 31, 2011 (in thousands)?
4. How many shares of treasury stock were held at the end of 2011? What did they cost?
5. Calculate the dividend and stock repurchase payouts. (*Note:* Round answers to two decimal places and use "Net income attributable to VF Corporation" instead of net income in the ratio calculations.)
6. Taking the weighted average number of basic common shares outstanding from the EPS information at the bottom of the income statement, calculate the stockholder profitability ratios. (Use "Net income attributable to VF Corporation" instead of net income in the ratio calculations.)

Case 10-94 Comparative Analysis: Under Armour, Inc., versus VF Corporation

Refer to the financial statements of **Under Armour, Inc.**, and **VF Corporation** that are supplied with this text.

Common Stock Price:

	Dec. 31, 2011	Dec. 31, 2010
Under Armour	$ 71.79	$54.84
VF	126.99	86.18

Note: Round all answers to two decimal places. Numbers, other than per-share amounts, are in thousands.

Required:

1. What percentage of the total common shares issued have Under Armour and VF repurchased and retained as treasury shares at December 31, 2011?
2. Calculate Under Armour's and VF's dividend yield and dividend payout for the years ended January 31, 2011 and 2010. Use "Net income attributable to VF Corporation" instead of net income in the ratio calculations.
3. Calculate Under Armour's and VF's total payout and stock repurchase payout for 2010 and 2011. Use "Net income attributable to VF Corporation" instead of net income in the ratio calculations.
4. Compare Under Armour's and VF's stockholder payouts based on the values and trends identified in these stockholder payout ratios.
5. Calculate Under Armour's and VF's return on common equity and earnings per share for 2010 and 2011. Common stockholders' equity for 2009 was $399,997 and $3,813,285 for Under Armour and VF, respectively. Use "Net income attributable to VF Corporation" instead of net income in the ratio calculations.
6. Compare the values and trends of these stockholder profitability ratios for Under Armour and VF.

Case 10-95 CONTINUING PROBLEM: FRONT ROW ENTERTAINMENT

After purchasing the five venues in June 2014, Front Row needed additional cash to renovate and operate these venues. While the company had successfully borrowed money before (from bank loans as well as from the issuance of bonds), it could not find a lender willing to invest in the business due to the large amount of debt that the company currently has on its balance sheet.

With debt financing out of the question, Front Row considers its other options. The name of an old college friend, Steve Trotter, immediately comes to Cam and Anna's mind. Steve has previous work experience in the retail industry and expressed a desire to manage Front Row's current merchandising operations (the sale of DVDs). His vision was to expand the operations to include apparel (t-shirts, hats, etc.) and other items (such as bobble-head dolls of the artists). In addition, several other family members have expressed an interest in investing in the company.

Front Row was authorized to issue 25,000 shares of its $1 par common stock. On January 1, 2013, it issued Cam and Anna 8,000 shares each for $1 per share. Front Row was also authorized to issue 20,000 shares of 8%, $50 par preferred stock. The following transactions occurred during the remainder of 2014.

June 15	Issued 2,000 shares of $1 par common stock to Steve for $20 per share.
July 1	Issued 3,000 shares of $50 preferred stock to family members for $75 per share.
10	Repurchased 700 common shares at $16 per share.
Aug. 5	The board of directors declared a $25,000 dividend to all stockholders of record on August 31, 2014. The dividend will be paid on September 15, 2014.
Sept. 15	The $25,000 dividend was paid.
Dec. 15	300 of the treasury shares were reissued at $22 per share.

Front Row had $53,250 of retained earnings to be included in the December 31, 2014 balance sheet.

Required:

1. Prepare the journal entries to record the above transactions.
2. Prepare the stockholders' equity section of the balance sheet at December 31, 2014.

© Pixelfabrik/Alamy

MAKING THE CONNECTION

INTEGRATIVE EXERCISE (CHAPTERS 8–10)

Integrating Accounting for Liabilities and Equity

Obtain **Apple**'s 2011 10-K (filed October 26, 2011) either through the "Investor Relations" portion of its website (do a web search for "Apple Investor Relations") or go to www.sec.gov and click "Search for Company Filings" under "Filings & Forms."

Required:

Using Apple's 10-K, answer the following questions (*Hint*: It may be easier to use the Word or PDF file and use the search feature within the program):

1. Calculate Apple's current, quick, and cash ratios for 2010 and 2011. The industry averages for these ratios for 2011 were 1.45, 1.12, and 0.62, respectively. Comment on Apple's short-term liquidity.

2. Calculate Apple's debt to equity, long-term debt to equity, and times interest earned (accrual basis) for 2010 and 2011. The industry averages for these ratios for 2011 were 44.40%, 17.24%, and 3.41, respectively. You will need to read the "Other Income and Expense" section of the Management, Discussion & Analysis section to find the amount of interest expense. Comment on Apple's mix of debt and equity and long-term solvency.

3. Calculate Apple's return on equity for 2010 and 2011 (stockholders' equity for 2009 was $31,640,000,000). The industry average for 2011 was 13.44%. Comment on Apple's profitability.

4. Apple did not pay any dividends or repurchase any stock during 2010 or 2011. Why might Apple elect not to make any payouts to stockholders?

11 The Statement of Cash Flows

© Pixelfabrik/Alamy

After studying Chapter 11, you should be able to:

1. Explain the purpose of a statement of cash flows.
2. Identify and classify business activities that produce cash inflows and outflows.
3. Understand the relationship between changes in cash and the changes in the balance sheet accounts.
4. Prepare the cash flows from operating activities section of a statement of cash flows using the indirect method.
5. Prepare the cash flows from investing activities section of a statement of cash flows.
6. Prepare the cash flows from financing activities section of a statement of cash flows.
7. Analyze information contained in the statement of cash flows.
8. *(Appendix 11A)* Prepare the cash flows from operating activities section of a statement of cash flows using the direct method.
9. *(Appendix 11B)* Use a spreadsheet to prepare the statement of cash flows.

Rick Dalton/Agstockusa/age fotostock

EXPERIENCE FINANCIAL ACCOUNTING
with Deere & Company

Founded in 1837, **Deere & Company** (collectively known as John Deere) is an American success story. From humble beginnings as a blacksmith shop in Illinois, John Deere has grown into one of the world's largest corporations. Not only is John Deere the world's leading manufacturer of farm and forestry equipment, it also sells a broad line of lawn tractors and other outdoor consumer products. In addition, John Deere is one of the world's largest equipment finance companies with a managed portfolio of almost $28 billion.

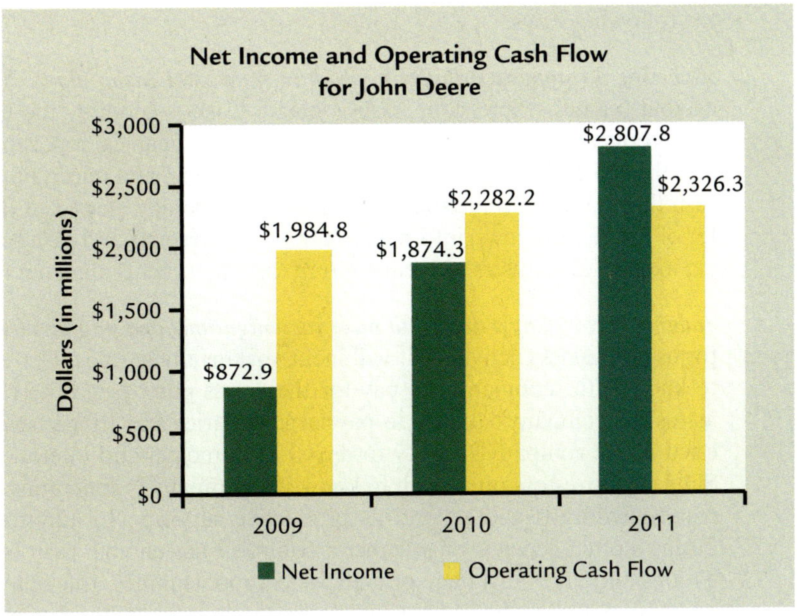

Source: Deere & Company 2011 10K.

In addition to the income statement, balance sheet, and retained earnings statement, companies are also required to provide a statement of cash flows. The statement of cash flows measures a company's inflows (sources) and outflows (uses) of cash during a period of time. While net income provides important information, the recognition of revenues and expenses can occur at different times than the related cash inflow or outflow. Therefore, a company's net income does not always equal the amount of cash that it received and spent. In addition to providing important information that aids in understanding how a company generates and uses cash, the statement of cash flows also allows users to identify differences between net income and cash flow.

Cash is the lifeblood of any business. A healthy cash flow is required if a company is to meet its current operating obligations, replace its worn machinery and equipment, pursue profitable new opportunities, or provide dividends to its stockholders. With operating cash flow of more than $2.3 billion, John Deere appears to have no problem in generating cash flow. From this perspective, it is easy to see why some think the color of money is John Deere green!

OBJECTIVE 1

Explain the purpose of a statement of cash flows.

ROLE OF THE STATEMENT OF CASH FLOWS

In addition to being interested in the information in the accrual-basis financial statements, most financial statement users also want to know how a company obtained and used its cash. The purpose of the **statement of cash flows** is to provide relevant information about a company's cash receipts (inflows of cash) and cash payments (outflows of cash) during an accounting period.

The statement of cash flows is one of the primary financial statements. Because the other financial statements—the income statement, balance sheet, and statement of retained earnings—provide only limited information about a company's cash flows, the statement of cash flows can be viewed as a complement to these other financial statements. That is, while the income statement provides information about the company's performance on an accrual basis, it does not tell how much cash was generated or used as a result of the company's operations. Similarly, the balance sheet provides information on the changes in net assets, but it doesn't provide information on how much cash was used or received in relation to these changes. The statement of cash flows fills this void by explaining the sources from which a company has acquired cash (inflows of cash) and the uses to which the business has applied cash (outflows of cash).

The information in a statement of cash flows helps investors, creditors, and others in the following ways.

Assessing a company's ability to produce future net cash inflows You may have heard the age-old business expression "cash is king." Cash is certainly the life-blood of a company and is critical to a company's success. One goal of financial reporting is to provide information that is helpful in predicting the amounts, timing, and uncertainty of a company's future cash flows. While accrual-basis net income is generally viewed to be the best single predictor of future cash flows, information about cash receipts and cash payments can, along with net income, allow users to predict future cash flows better than net income alone.

Judging a company's ability to meet its obligations and pay dividends As a company performs its business activities, it will incur various obligations. For example, suppliers want to know if the company can pay for the goods purchased on credit. Employees want to assess the company's ability to pay larger salaries and fringe benefits. Lenders are interested in the company's ability to repay the principal and interest on amounts borrowed. Similarly, investors often wish to know if a company is generating enough cash to be able to pay dividends and expand its productive capacity. In addition, success or failure in business often depends on whether a company has enough cash to meet unexpected obligations and take advantage of unexpected opportunities. Information about cash receipts and cash payments helps financial statement users make these important judgments.

Estimating the company's needs for external financing As companies operate, various expenditures can be financed through either internally generated funds or by external financing (debt or equity). Knowing the amount of cash that a company generates internally helps financial statement users assess whether a company will have to borrow additional funds from creditors or seek additional cash from investors.

Understanding the reasons for the differences between net income and related cash receipts and cash payments As you have already noticed, the amount of a company's net income and the amount of cash generated from operations are often different amounts due to the application of accrual accounting concepts. Because of the judgments and estimates involved in accrual accounting, many financial statement users question the usefulness of reported income. However, when provided with cash flow information, these users can gain insights into the quality and reliability of the reported income amounts.

Evaluating the balance sheet effects of both cash and noncash investing and financing transactions Not all changes in cash are directly related to a company's operations (such as manufacturing a product or selling a good or service). Instead, a company may make investments in productive assets as it expands its operations or upgrades its facilities. In addition, a company may seek sources of cash by issuing debt or equity. These activities can be just as crucial to a company's long-term success as its current operations.

In summary, information about a company's cash receipts and cash payments, along with information contained in the balance sheet and the income statement, is critical to understanding and analyzing a company's operations.

In this chapter, we will explain how a statement of cash flows is prepared from the information contained in the balance sheet and the income statement. We will explore the measurement, presentation, and analysis of cash flow information and address the following questions:

- What are the principal sources and uses of cash?
- How is the statement of cash flows prepared and reported to external users?
- How is the statement of cash flows used by investors, creditors, and others?

concept Q&A

If we already have the balance sheet and income statement, why is a statement of cash flows so important?

Answer:

The statement of cash flows provides information about a company's sources and uses of cash. Knowing how companies obtain and use cash provides users with a good idea of a company's financial strength and its long-term viability. The decision to invest in a company is much safer if a potential investor—be it a bank or stockholder—knows how much cash is being produced and where it is coming from.

CASH FLOW CLASSIFICATIONS

OBJECTIVE 2

Identify and classify business activities that produce cash inflows and outflows.

Because our focus is on cash flows, it is important to have a clear understanding of what is included in the term *cash*. For purposes of the statement of cash flows, cash includes both funds on hand (coins and currency) and cash equivalents. Recall from Chapter 4 that cash equivalents are short-term, highly liquid investments that are readily convertible to cash and have original maturities of 3 months or less. Examples of cash equivalents include money market funds and investments in U.S. government securities (for example, treasury bills). Because of their high liquidity or nearness to cash, cash equivalents are treated as cash in the statement of cash flows.

During an accounting period, a company engages in the three fundamental business activities discussed in Chapter 1—operating activities, investing activities, and financing activities. Each of these activities can contribute to (a cash inflow) or reduce (a cash outflow) a company's cash balance. Therefore, the statement of cash flows reconciles the beginning and ending balances of cash by describing the effects of business activities on a company's cash balance. This relationship is shown in Exhibit 11.1.

EXHIBIT 11.1

How the Statement of Cash Flows Links the Two Balance Sheets

Balance Sheet 12/31/2013	
Assets	
Cash	$1,800
Other	6,300
Total	$8,100
Liabilities and Equity	
Liabilities	$4,200
Equity	3,900
Total	$8,100

Statement of Cash Flows For the year ended 12/31/2014	
Operating activities	$ 3,400
Investing activities	(5,100)
Financing activities	2,300
Net change in cash	$ 600
Beginning cash	1,800
Ending cash	$ 2,400

Balance Sheet 12/31/2014	
Assets	
Cash	$2,400
Other	7,100
Total	$9,500
Liabilities and Equity	
Liabilities	$4,400
Equity	5,100
Total	$9,500

Cash Flows from Operating Activities

Cash flows from operating activities (or operating cash flows) are the cash inflows and outflows that relate to acquiring (purchasing or manufacturing), selling, and delivering goods or services. Cash inflows from operating activities include:

- cash sales to customers
- collection of accounts receivable arising from credit sales
- cash dividends received
- interest received on investments in equity and debt securities

Cash outflows from operating activities include payments:

IFRS

IFRS allow companies to report taxes paid as an investing or financing transaction if it can be indentified with an investing or financing activity.

- to suppliers for goods and services
- to employees for wages and salaries
- to governments for taxes
- to lenders for interest on debt

Operating cash flows correspond to the *types* of items that determine net income (revenues and expenses). However, the *amounts* are different because the income statement is accrual-based while the statement of cash flows is cash-based. Therefore, to isolate the current period operating cash flow, companies must adjust the current period income statement items for any related noncash items, which can be determined by examining the changes in the related current assets and current liabilities.

John Deere reported operating cash flow of $2,326.3 million compared to net income of $2,807.8 million (see Exhibit 11.5, p. 591). While various reasons exist for this difference, two major factors include adjustments for noncash items (such as depreciation and amortization) and accrual accounting adjustments of current assets and liabilities. The adjustments needed to reconcile net income with operating cash flow are discussed later in the chapter.

Cash Flows from Investing Activities

Cash flows from investing activities (or investing cash flows) are the cash inflows and outflows that relate to acquiring and disposing of operating assets and investments in other companies (current and long-term), lending money, and collecting loans. Cash inflows from investing activities include cash received from the:

- sale of property, plant, and equipment
- collection of the principal amount of a loan (a note receivable)
- sale of investments in other companies

Cash outflows from investing activities include payments made to:

- acquire property, plant, and equipment
- purchase debt or equity securities of other companies as an investment
- loan money to others (notes receivable)

In general, investing cash flows relate to increases or decreases of long-term assets and investments.

John Deere reported a $2,620.7 million cash outflow related to investing activities. Its major investing activities were related to the purchase and collection of receivables related to its equipment financing business and purchases of property and equipment.

Cash Flows from Financing Activities

Cash flows from financing activities (or financing cash flows) relate to obtaining resources from creditors and owners, providing owners a return on their investment, and repaying creditors. Cash inflows from financing activities include cash received from the:

IFRS

IFRS allow companies to report the payment of dividends as either an operating or a financing activity.

- issuance of stock
- issuance of debt (bonds or notes payable)

Cash outflows from financing activities include cash payments to:

- repay the principal amount borrowed (bonds or notes payable)
- repurchase a company's own stock (treasury stock)
- pay dividends

In general, financing cash flows involve cash receipts and payments that affect long-term liabilities and stockholders' equity.

John Deere reported a cash inflow of $139.6 million related to financing activities. Its major source of funds was from the issuance of long-term debt. It also paid dividends of $593.1 million to its stockholders.

Noncash Investing and Financing Activities

Occasionally, investing and financing activities take place without affecting cash. For example, a company may choose to acquire an operating asset (such as a building) by issuing long-term debt. Alternatively, a company may acquire one asset by exchanging it for another. These types of activities are referred to as **noncash investing and financing activities**. Because these activities do not involve cash, they are not reported on the statement of cash flows. However, these transactions still provide useful information about a company's overall investing and financing activities. Any significant noncash investing and financing activities are required to be reported in a supplementary schedule that is shown either at the bottom of the statement of cash flows or in the notes to the financial statements. This requirement to disclose any significant noncash investing and financing activities is consistent with the full-disclosure principle—any information that would make a difference to financial statement users should be made known.

Exhibit 11.2 summarizes the classification of business activities as either operating, investing, or financing activities. Two particular activities—interest and dividends—are often misclassified by students. Interest (received or paid) and cash dividends received are classified as operating activities because they go into the determination of income. Cash dividends paid, on the other hand, are not an expense but are a reduction of retained earnings. Therefore, cash dividends paid are classified as a financing activity.

IFRS

IFRS allow companies to report dividends and interest paid as either an operating or a financing activity. Additionally, IFRS allow companies to report dividends and interest received as either an operating or an investing activity.

EXHIBIT 11.2

Classification of Cash Flows

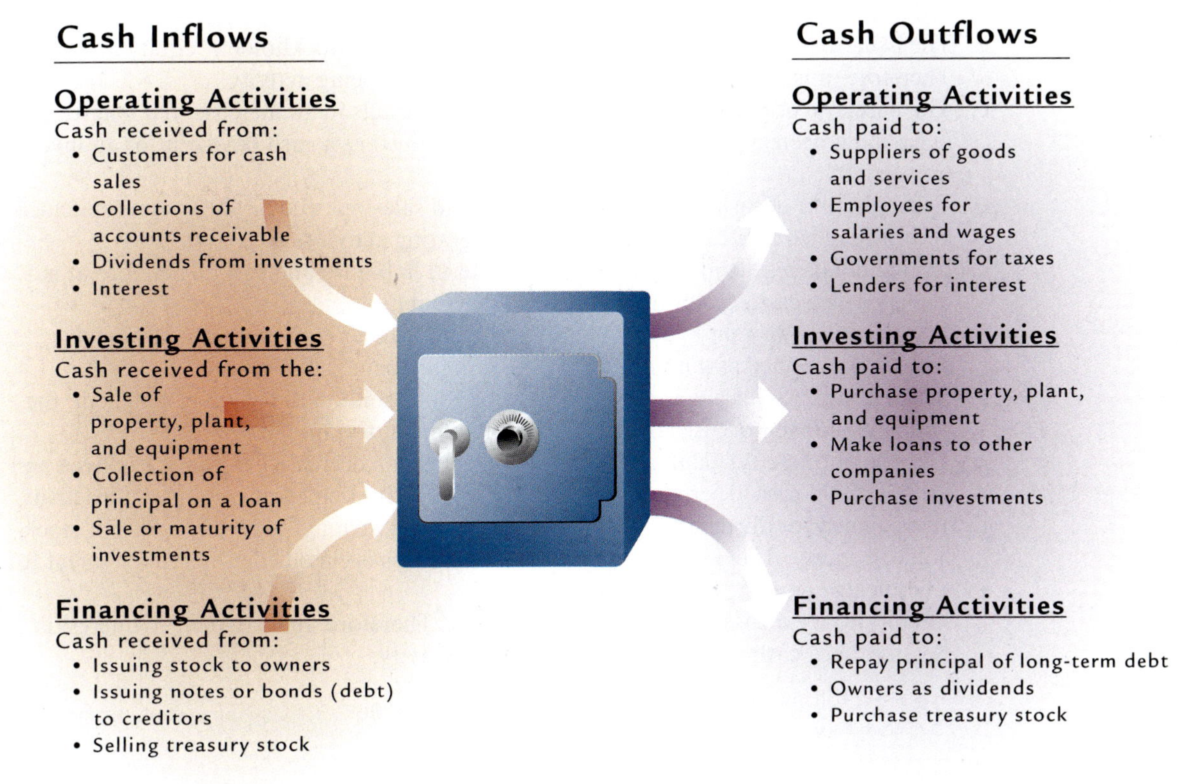

Cornerstone 11.1 shows how business activities can be classified as either operating, investing, financing, or noncash activities.

CORNERSTONE 11.1

Classifying Business Activities

Why:

Cash flows from operating activities correspond to the cash effects of items that determine net income. Cash flows from investing activities relate to increases or decreases in long-term assets and investments. Cash flows from financing activities involve cash receipts and payments that affect long-term liabilities and stockholders' equity.

Information:

Moore Inc. engaged in the following activities during the current year:

a. Payment of wages to employees
b. Issuance of common stock
c. Purchase of property, plant, and equipment
d. Collection of cash from customers
e. Issuance of bonds
f. Retirement of debt by issuing stock
g. Purchase of inventory
h. Sale of property, plant, and equipment
i. Payment of dividends
j. Payment of interest

Required:

Classify each of the above activities as an operating, investing, or financing activity and indicate whether the activity involved a cash receipt or cash payment. If the transaction does not involve cash, classify it as a noncash investing and financing activity.

Solution:

a. Because wages are an expense on the income statement, the payment of wages is classified as a cash payment for an operating activity.
b. The issuance of common stock results in an increase of stockholders' equity and cash. Therefore, it is classified as a cash receipt from a financing activity.
c. The purchase of property, plant, and equipment results in an increase to a long-term asset and a decrease of cash. Therefore, it is classified as a cash payment for an investing activity.
d. The collection of cash from customers relates to sales revenue on the income statement and is classified as a cash receipt from an operating activity.
e. Issuing bonds results in an increase to long-term liabilities and cash. Therefore, it is classified as a cash receipt from a financing activity.
f. The retirement of debt by issuing stock is a financing activity that does not involve cash. It is classified as a noncash investing and financing activity.
g. Because inventory is a component of cost of goods sold on the income statement, the purchase of inventory is classified as a cash payment for an operating activity.
h. The sale of property, plant, and equipment results in a decrease in a long-term asset and an increase in cash. Therefore, it is classified as a cash receipt from an investing activity.
i. The payment of dividends is a reduction in retained earnings, which is a part of stockholders' equity. Therefore, the payment of dividends is classified as a cash payment for a financing activity.
j. Interest is an expense on the income statement. Therefore, the payment of interest is classified as a cash payment for an operating activity.

Format of the Statement of Cash Flows

Once a company has properly classified its cash inflows and outflows as operating, investing, or financing activities, it reports each of these three categories as shown in Exhibit 11.3. Note that the three cash flow categories are summed to obtain the net increase or decrease in cash. This change in cash reconciles the beginning and ending balances of cash as noted in Exhibit 11.1 (p. 583).

EXHIBIT 11.3

Format of the Statement of Cash Flows

Brooke Sportswear Inc. Statement of Cash Flows For the year ended December 31, 2013		
Cash flows from operating activities		
Cash inflows	$ xxx	
Cash outflows	(xxx)	
Net cash provided (used) by operating activities		$xxx
Cash flows from investing activities		
Cash inflows	$ xxx	
Cash outflows	(xxx)	
Net cash provided (used) by investing activities		xxx
Cash flows from financing activities		
Cash inflows	$ xxx	
Cash outflows	(xxx)	
Net cash provided (used) by financing activities		xxx
Net increase (decrease) in cash and cash equivalents		$xxx
Cash and cash equivalents at beginning of year		xxx
Cash and cash equivalents at end of year		$xxx
Schedule or note disclosure of noncash investing and financing activities		

YOUDECIDE Statement of Cash Flow Classifications

You are preparing the statement of cash flows for Sienna Corporation and consult the CFO about how to properly classify the cash paid for interest. The CFO states that the company chose to finance its recent expansion activities with large amounts of debt. Because the interest payments resulted from this financing decision, he believes that the cash paid for interest should be classified as a financing activity. In addition, the CFO points out that you shouldn't waste any more time on this since it's simply a classification issue. No matter where the interest payment is reported, the total change in cash will be the same and no one will care.

How should you classify the cash paid for interest?

The CFO certainly makes a good argument to classify interest payments as a financing cash flow. Similar to dividend payments (which are paid for the use of equity capital), interest is paid for the use of debt capital. However, the FASB states that operating cash flows should reflect the cash effects of transactions that enter into the determination of income. Because interest is an expense, it should be classified as an operating activity. While this is a classification issue, the CFO's assertion that the proper classification makes no difference is incorrect. The various classifications on a statement of cash flows provide insights into how a company generated and used its cash.

The proper classification of items in the statement of cash flows is critical for financial statement users.

OBJECTIVE 3

Understand the relationship between changes in cash and the changes in the balance sheet accounts.

ANALYZING THE ACCOUNTS FOR CASH FLOW DATA

Unlike the balance sheet and the income statement, the statement of cash flows cannot be prepared by simply using information obtained from an adjusted trial balance prepared using the accrual basis of accounting. Instead, each item on the balance sheet and the income statement must be analyzed to *explain* why cash changed by the amount that it did. In other words, the accrual-basis numbers in the balance sheet and the income statement must be adjusted to a cash basis. Notice that our concern is not with determining the change in cash but the *reasons why* cash changed.

The recording of any business activity creates two types of financial measures—*balances* and *changes*. Balances measure the dollar amount of an account at a given time. Changes measure the increases or decreases in account balances over a period of time. For example, consider the following T-account:

Accounts Receivable			
Balance, 1/1/2013	11,000		
2013 credit sales	90,000	92,000	Cash collections for 2013
Balance, 12/31/2013	9,000		

concept Q&A

Why do we analyze changes in the balance sheet accounts to determine the inflows and outflows of cash? Wouldn't it be easier to simply look at the Cash account in the general ledger?

Answer:

It is correct that the Cash account in the general ledger will contain all cash inflows and cash outflows and a statement of cash flows could be prepared by analyzing this account. However, this would require individuals to identify, understand, and classify every single cash receipt or cash payment. With the large volume of cash transactions, this would be an extremely time-consuming and inefficient task. It is much easier to determine cash flows by analyzing the changes in the balance sheet accounts.

This T-account shows two balances and two changes. The beginning and ending balances ($11,000 and $9,000) measure accounts receivable at January 1, 2013 and December 31, 2013, respectively. The credit sales ($90,000) and cash collections ($92,000) are changes that measure the effects of selling goods and collecting cash. Like accounts receivable, every balance sheet account can be described in terms of balances and changes.

To understand a company's cash flows, the relationships between the *changes* in balance sheet accounts and the company's cash flows need to be analyzed. We will begin our analysis with the fundamental accounting equation:

$$\text{Assets} = \text{Liabilities} + \text{Stockholders' Equity}$$

Next, we will restate this equation in terms of changes (Δ):

$$\Delta\ \text{Assets} = \Delta\ \text{Liabilities} + \Delta\ \text{Stockholders' Equity}$$

Separating assets into cash and noncash accounts:

$$\Delta\ \text{Cash} + \Delta\ \text{Noncash Assets} = \Delta\ \text{Liabilities} + \Delta\ \text{Stockholders' Equity}$$

Finally, moving the changes in noncash assets to the right side:

$$\Delta\ \text{Cash} = \Delta\ \text{Liabilities} + \Delta\ \text{Stockholders' Equity} - \Delta\ \text{Noncash Assets}$$

Where:

Increases in Cash = Increases in Liabilities + Increases in Stockholders' Equity + Decreases in Noncash Assets

Decreases in Cash = Decreases in Liabilities + Decreases in Stockholders' Equity + Increases in Noncash Assets

This analysis reveals that **all cash receipts or cash payments are associated with changes in other balance sheet accounts.** Cornerstone 11.2 illustrates how to classify specific balance sheet accounts as increases in cash or decreases in cash.

Classifying Changes in Balance Sheet Accounts

CORNERSTONE

11.2

Why:

Increases in cash result from increases in liabilities, increases in stockholders' equity, and decreases in noncash assets. Decreases in cash result from decreases in liabilities, decreases in stockholders' equity, and increases in noncash assets.

Information:

The following changes in the balance sheet accounts have been observed for the current period:

Account	1/1/2013	12/31/2013	Change
a. Accounts receivable	$ 25,000	$ 18,000	$ (7,000)
b. Bonds payable	400,000	300,000	(100,000)
c. Equipment	145,000	175,000	30,000
d. Inventory	15,000	18,000	3,000
e. Common stock	150,000	175,000	25,000
f. Retained earnings	75,000	95,000	20,000
g. Accounts payable	12,000	10,000	(2,000)
h. Unearned revenue	17,000	19,000	2,000

Required:

Classify each change as either an increase in cash or a decrease in cash.

Solution:

a. Increase in cash
b. Decrease in cash
c. Decrease in cash
d. Decrease in cash
e. Increase in cash
f. Increase in cash
g. Decrease in cash
h. Increase in cash

Exhibit 11.4 integrates the analysis of the relationships between the *changes* in balance sheet accounts and the company's cash flows with the cash flow classifications discussed in the previous section. Examining Exhibit 11.4, several items are of interest:

- Cash flows from operating activities generally involve income statement items (which are reflected in retained earnings) and changes in current assets or liabilities.
- Investing activities are related to changes in long-term assets.
- Financing activities are related to changes in long-term liabilities and stockholders' equity.
- Retained earnings affects both cash flows from operating activities (for example, revenues, expenses, net income, or a net loss) and cash flows from financing activities (for example, payment of dividends).
- Each item on the balance sheet and the income statement must be analyzed to explain the change in cash.

EXHIBIT 11.4

Cash Flow Classifications and Changes in Balance Sheet Accounts

Classification	Cash Effect	Balance Sheet Items Affected	Example
Operating	Inflow (+)	Decreases in current assets	Collecting an account receivable
		Increases in current liabilities	Receipt of revenue in advance
		Increases in retained earnings	Making a cash sale
	Outflow (−)	Increases in current assets	Purchasing inventory
		Decreases in current liabilities	Paying an account payable
		Decreases in retained earnings	Paying interest
Investing	Inflow (+)	Decreases in long-term assets	Selling equipment
	Outflow (−)	Increases in long-term assets	Buying equipment
Financing	Inflow (+)	Increases in long-term liabilities	Issuing long-term debt
		Increases in stockholders' equity	Issuing stock
	Outflow (−)	Decreases in long-term liabilities	Retiring long-term debt
		Decreases in stockholders' equity	Paying dividends

PREPARING A STATEMENT OF CASH FLOWS

After the accounts have been analyzed to identify cash inflows and outflows, a statement of cash flows can be prepared. To prepare a statement of cash flows, you need:

- *Comparative balance sheets:* Used to determine the changes in assets, liabilities, and stockholders' equity during a period
- *A current income statement:* Used to determine cash flows from operating activities
- *Additional information about selected accounts:* Used to determine the reason why cash was received or paid

Using this information, there are five basic steps in preparing the statement of cash flows.

Step 1. Compute the net cash flow from operating activities. This involves adjusting the amounts on the income statement for noncash changes reflected in the balance sheet. Two methods, the indirect or direct method (explained in the next section), may be used to determine this amount.

Step 2. Compute the net cash flow from investing activities. Information from the balance sheet as well as any additional information provided will need to be analyzed to identify the cash inflows and outflows associated with long-term assets.

Step 3. Compute the net cash flow from financing activities. Information from the balance sheet as well as any additional information provided will need to be analyzed to identify the cash inflows and outflows associated with long-term liabilities and stockholders' equity.

Step 4. Combine the net cash flows from operating, investing, and financing activities to obtain the net increase (decrease) in cash for the period.

Step 5. Compute the change in cash for the period and compare this with the change in cash from Step 4. The change in cash, computed from the beginning balance of cash and the ending balance of cash as shown on the balance sheet, should reconcile with the net cash flow computed in Step 4.

The statement of cash flows for John Deere is shown in Exhibit 11.5.

OBJECTIVE 4

Prepare the cash flows from operating activities section of a statement of cash flows using the indirect method.

PREPARING CASH FLOWS FROM OPERATING ACTIVITIES

The cash flows from operating activities section of the statement of cash flows may be prepared using either of two methods: the direct method or the indirect method. Both

EXHIBIT 11.5

Statement of Cash Flows for John Deere

Deere and Company
Statement of Consolidated Cash Flows*
For the Year Ended October 31, 2011
(in millions of dollars)

Cash Flows from Operating Activities		
Net income	$ 2,807.8	
Adjustments to reconcile net income to net cash provided by operating activities:		
Bad debt expense	13.5	
Depreciation and amortization	914.9	
Other noncash items	(87.9)	
Changes in assets and liabilities:		
Increase in receivables related to sales	(808.9)	
Increase in inventories	(1,730.5)	
Increase in accounts payable and accrued expenses	1,287.0	
Net increase (decrease) in accrued income taxes payable/receivable	1.2	
Net increase (decrease) in retirement benefits	495.3	
Other	(566.1)	
Net cash provided by operating activities		$ 2,326.3
Cash Flows from Investing Activities		
Collections of notes receivable	$ 12,151.4	
Proceeds from sales of businesses, net of cash sold	911.1	
Proceeds from maturities and sales of marketable securities	32.4	
Proceeds from sales of equipment on operating leases	683.4	
Cost of receivables acquired	(13,956.8)	
Purchases of marketable securities	(586.9)	
Purchases of property, plant, and equipment	(1,056.6)	
Cost of equipment on operating leases acquired	(624.2)	
Acquisitions of businesses, net of cash acquired	(60.8)	
Other	(113.7)	
Net cash used for investing activities		(2,620.7)
Cash Flows from Financing Activities		
Decrease in short-term borrowings	$ (226.1)	
Proceeds from long-term borrowings	5,655.0	
Payments of long-term borrowings	(3,220.8)	
Proceeds from issuance of common stock	170.0	
Repurchases of common stock	(1,667.0)	
Dividends paid	(593.1)	
Other	21.6	
Net cash provided by financing activities		139.6
Effect of exchange rate changes on cash and cash equivalents		11.4
Net increase (decrease) in cash and cash equivalents		$ (143.4)
Cash and cash equivalents at beginning of year		3,790.6
Cash and cash equivalents at end of year		$ 3,647.2

*The statement of cash flows information was taken from the 10-K report of Deere and Company and has been summarized and reformatted by the authors.

Source: Deere & Company 2011 10-K.

methods arrive at an identical amount—the net cash provided (used) by operating activities. The two methods differ only in how this amount is computed.

The Direct Method

In the **direct method**, cash inflows and cash outflows are listed for each type of operating activity that a company performs. These cash flows are generally computed by adjusting *each item* on the income statement by the changes in the related current asset or liability accounts. Typical cash flow categories reported are cash collected from customers, cash paid to suppliers, cash paid to employees, cash paid for interest, and cash paid for taxes. The cash outflows are subtracted from the cash inflows to determine the net cash flow from operating activities. If the direct method is used, companies must also provide a supplementary schedule that shows the reconciliation of net income with operating cash flow. While the FASB prefers the use of the direct method because it is more consistent with the purpose of the statement of cash flows, it is not widely used.

The Indirect Method

The indirect method does not report individual cash inflows and outflows. Instead, it focuses on the *differences* between net income and operating cash flow. The **indirect method** begins with net income and then adjusts it for noncash items to produce net cash flow from operating activities. These adjustments to net income are necessary for two reasons:

- to eliminate income statement items that do not affect cash (such as depreciation and gains/losses on sales of assets)
- to adjust accrual-basis revenues and expenses to cash receipts and cash payments

The changes in the related current asset and current liability accounts contain the information necessary to make the adjustments to revenue and expense accounts.

Generally, companies prefer the indirect method because it is easier and less costly to prepare. In fact, approximately 98% of U.S. companies use the indirect method, as shown in Exhibit 11.6.

EXHIBIT 11.6

Use of the Indirect and Direct Methods

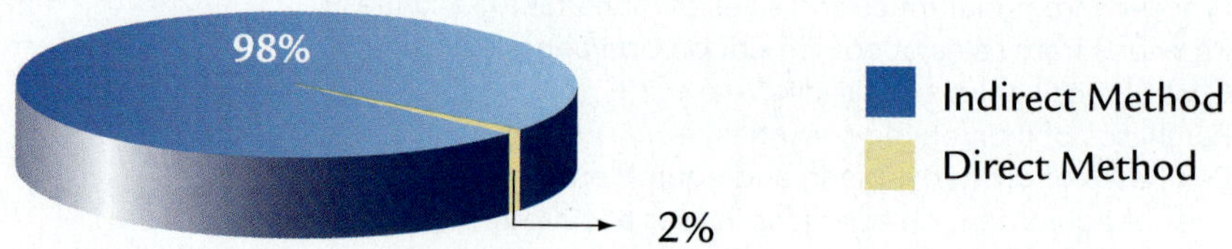

Source: Accounting Trends and Techniques, 2011.

ETHICAL DECISIONS By highlighting the differences between operating cash flows and net income, financial statement users may be able to more easily see attempts at earnings management. If managers try to manage earnings by manipulating the accrual accounting process (for example, increase revenues or decrease expenses on the income statement to increase income), these actions will often have no cash flow effect but will instead reveal themselves through changes in the accrual-basis accounts. When there are growing differences between operating cash flow and net income, the indirect method highlights the changes in the accrual accounts and allows users to judge the cause of these differences. •

Applying the Indirect Method

We will illustrate the preparation of cash flows from operating activities for Brooke Sportswear using the more popular indirect method. The direct method is illustrated in Appendix 11A. However, remember two important points:

- Cash flow from operating activities is the same under either method.
- The indirect and direct methods only apply to the operating activities section of the statement of cash flows. The investing and financing sections will be prepared the same way regardless of which method is used to prepare the operating activities section.

The income statement and comparative balance sheets for Brooke Sportswear are shown in Exhibit 11.7.

EXHIBIT 11.7

Financial Statements for Brooke Sportswear

Brooke Sportswear
Balance Sheets
December 31, 2013 and 2012

	2013	2012
ASSETS		
Current assets:		
Cash	$ 15,000	$ 13,000
Accounts receivable	53,000	46,000
Prepaid insurance	1,000	2,000
Inventory	63,000	51,000
Total current assets	$ 132,000	$ 112,000
Long-term investments	53,000	41,000
Property, plant, and equipment:		
Land	325,000	325,000
Equipment	243,000	210,000
Accumulated depreciation	(178,000)	(150,000)
Total assets	$ 575,000	$ 538,000
LIABILITIES AND EQUITY		
Current liabilities:		
Accounts payable	$ 13,000	$ 17,000
Wages payable	3,500	2,000
Interest payable	1,500	1,000
Income taxes payable	3,000	6,000
Total current liabilities	$ 21,000	$ 26,000
Long-term liabilities:		
Notes payable	109,000	115,000
Total liabilities	$130,000	$141,000
Equity:		
Common stock	$165,000	$151,000
Retained earnings	280,000	246,000
Total equity	$445,000	$397,000
Total liabilities and equity	$575,000	$538,000

Brooke Sportswear
Income Statement
For the year ended December 31, 2013

Sales revenue	$ 472,000
Less: Cost of goods sold	(232,000)
Gross margin	$ 240,000
Less operating expenses:	
Wages expense	(142,000)
Insurance expense	(15,000)
Depreciation expense	(40,000)
Income from operations	$ 43,000
Other income and expenses:	
Loss on disposal of property, plant, and equipment	(6,000)
Gain on sale of investments	15,000
Interest expense	(5,000)
Income before taxes	$ 47,000
Less: Income taxes expense	(8,000)
Net income	$ 39,000

Additional Information:

1. Equipment with a cost of $20,000 and accumulated depreciation of $12,000 was sold for $2,000 cash. Equipment was purchased for $53,000 cash.
2. Long-term investments with a cost of $16,000 were sold for $31,000 cash. Additional investments were purchased for $28,000 cash.
3. Notes payable in the amount of $35,000 were repaid, and new notes payable in the amount of $29,000 were issued for cash.
4. Common stock was issued for $14,000 cash.
5. Cash dividends of $5,000 were paid (obtained from the retained earnings statement).

Because income statements are prepared on an accrual basis, the revenues and expenses recognized on the income statement are not necessarily the same as the cash receipts and cash payments for a period. For example, revenues may include credit sales for which the company has not collected cash and exclude collections of cash from credit sales made in a previous period. Similarly, expenses may have been incurred for which no cash has been paid, or cash may have been paid related to expenses incurred in a previous period. Therefore, net income must be adjusted for these timing differences between the recognition of net income and the receipt or payment of cash.

Under the indirect method, four types of adjustments must be made to net income to adjust it to net cash flow from operating activities:

1. Add to net income any noncash expenses and subtract from net income any noncash revenues.
2. Add to net income any losses and subtract from net income any gains.

concept Q&A

Why are there differences between net income and net cash flow from operating activities?

Answer:

Net income is prepared under the accrual basis of accounting which records business activities when they occur instead of when cash is received or paid. Therefore, all of the adjustments that are made to net income reflect timing differences between the reporting of revenues and expenses and the related inflow or outflow of cash.

3. Add to net income any decreases in current assets or increases in current liabilities that are related to operating activities.
4. Subtract from net income any increases in current assets and decreases in current liabilities that are related to operating activities.

These adjustments and the computation of net cash flow from operating activities are illustrated in Cornerstone 11.3.

The adjustments made in Cornerstone 11.3 are explained below.

Adjustment of Noncash Revenues and Expenses The income statement often includes various noncash items such as depreciation expense, amortization expense, and bad debt expense.

- Noncash expenses reduce net income but do not reduce cash. Therefore, under the indirect method, **noncash expenses are added back to net income.**
- Noncash revenues increase income but do not increase cash. Therefore, under the indirect method, **noncash revenues are subtracted from net income.**

CORNERSTONE 11.3

Calculating Net Cash Flow from Operating Activities: Indirect Method

Why:

The calculation of net cash flow from operating activities requires adjustments to net income for noncash items, gains and losses, and changes in current assets and current liabilities.

Information:

Refer to the income statement and the current assets and current liabilities sections of Brooke Sportswear's balance sheets found in Exhibit 11.7 (p. 593).

Required:

Compute the net cash flow from operating activities using the indirect method.

Solution:

Net income		$39,000
Adjustments to reconcile net income to net cash flow from operating activities:*		
Depreciation expense	$ 40,000	
Loss on disposal of equipment	6,000	
Gain on sale of long-term investments	(15,000)	
Increase in accounts receivable	(7,000)	
Decrease in prepaid insurance	1,000	
Increase in inventory	(12,000)	
Decrease in accounts payable	(4,000)	
Increase in wages payable	1,500	
Increase in interest payable	500	
Decrease in income taxes payable	(3,000)	8,000
Net cash provided by operating activities		$47,000

* The explanation of these adjustments is given in the text of this section.

Adjustment of Gains and Losses The sale of a long-term asset or the extinguishment of a long-term liability often produces either a gain or loss that is reported on the income statement. However, the gain or loss does not affect cash flow and should, therefore, not be included as an operating activity. Furthermore, the gain or loss does not reveal the total amount of cash received or paid. Instead, it only gives the amount received or paid in excess of the book value of the asset or liability. The correct procedure is to eliminate the gain or loss from net income and record the full amount of the cash flow as either an investing activity or a financing activity.

- Because gains increase net income, under the indirect method, **gains are subtracted from net income.**
- Because losses decrease net income, under the indirect method, **losses are added back to net income.**

Adjustments for Changes in Current Assets and Current Liabilities As discussed earlier in the chapter, all cash receipts or cash payments are associated with changes in one or more balance sheet accounts. Generally, current assets and liabilities are related to the operating activities of a company, and changes in these accounts cause a difference between net income and cash flows from operating activities. Based on the earlier analysis of the balance sheet accounts, two general rules emerge:

- **Increases in current assets and decreases in current liabilities are subtracted from net income.**
- **Decreases in current assets and increases in current liabilities are added to net income.**

The adjustments to net income required to calculate cash flow from operating activities are summarized in Exhibit 11.8.

EXHIBIT 11.8

Adjustments Required to Calculate Cash Flow from Operating Activities

+ Add to Net Income	− Subtract from Net Income
• Noncash expenses	• Noncash revenues
• Losses	• Gains
• Decreases in current assets	• Increases in current assets
• Increases in current liabilities	• Decreases in current liabilities

The explanations of these adjustments for Brook Sportswear are shown below.

Accounts Receivable The Accounts Receivable account increases when credit sales are recorded and decreases when cash is collected from customers.

Accounts Receivable			
Balance, 1/1/2013	46,000		
Credit sales	XXX	XXX	Cash collections
Balance, 12/31/2013	53,000		

The increase of accounts receivable implies that credit sales were $7,000 greater than the cash collected from customers. This is consistent with the results of our earlier analysis indicating that increases in noncash assets are related to decreases in cash. Because cash collections were less than the sales reported on in the income statement, the company would need to subtract the increase in accounts receivable from net income when computing net cash flow from operating activities. (A decrease in accounts receivable would be added to net income when computing net cash flow from operating activities.)

Prepaid Insurance The Prepaid Insurance account increases when cash prepayments are made and decreases when expenses are incurred.

Prepaid Insurance

Balance, 1/1/2013	2,000		
Cash prepayments	xxx	xxx	Expense incurred
Balance, 12/31/2013	1,000		

The decrease in prepaid insurance indicates that expenses incurred and recorded on the income statement were $1,000 higher than the cash payments. Because more expenses were incurred than were paid in cash, the company actually has more cash available at the end of the period than at the beginning of the period (because less cash was paid). This is consistent with the results of our earlier analysis indicating that decreases in noncash assets are related to increases in cash. The decrease in the Prepaid Insurance account needs to be added to net income when computing net cash flow from operating activities. (Increases in prepaid insurance would be subtracted from net income.)

Inventory The Inventory account increases when inventory is purchased and decreases as inventory is sold.

Inventory

Balance, 1/1/2013	51,000		
Purchases	xxx	xxx	Cost of goods sold
Balance, 12/31/2013	63,000		

The increase in inventory implies that purchases of inventory exceeded the cost of the inventory sold reported on the income statement by $12,000. Therefore, the company made "extra" cash purchases that were not included in cost of goods sold. To adjust net income to net cash flow from operating activities, the increase in the Inventory account, which represents the extra cash purchases, needs to be subtracted from net income. (Decreases in inventory would be added to net income.)

Accounts Payable The Accounts Payable account increases when credit purchases are made and decreases when cash payments are made to suppliers.

Accounts Payable

		17,000	Balance, 1/1/2013
Cash payments	xxx	xxx	Credit purchases
		13,000	Balance, 12/31/2013

The decrease in accounts payable indicates that the cash payments to suppliers exceeded the credit purchases of inventory by $4,000. Because the purchase of inventory is part of cost of goods sold, this implies that more cash was paid than was reflected in expenses. This is consistent with the results of our earlier analysis indicating that decreases in liabilities are related to decreases in cash. Therefore, the decrease in accounts payable needs to be subtracted from net income when computing the net cash flow from operating activities. (Increases of accounts payable are added to net income.)

Wages Payable The Wages Payable account increases when wages are accrued (incurred but not yet paid) and decreases when wages are paid.

Wages Payable

		2,000	Balance, 1/1/2013
Cash payments	xxx	xxx	Wages expense
		3,500	Balance, 12/31/2013

The increase in wages payable indicates that wages expense recorded on the income statement was greater than the cash paid for wages by $1,500. Because less cash was paid than expensed, the company actually has more cash available. This is consistent with the results of our earlier analysis indicating that increases in liabilities are related to increases in cash. Therefore, the increase in wages payable is added to net income when computing the net cash flow from operating activities. (Decreases in wages payable are subtracted from net income.)

Interest Payable Interest payable increases when interest expense is recorded and decreases when interest is paid.

Interest Payable			
		1,000	Balance, 1/1/2013
Cash payments	XXX	XXX	Interest expense
		1,500	Balance, 12/31/2013

The increase in interest payable implies that interest expense recorded on the income statement was $500 greater than the cash paid for interest. This is consistent with the results of our earlier analysis indicating that increases in liabilities are related to increases in cash. Therefore, the increase in interest payable is added to net income when computing the net cash flow from operating activities. (Decreases in interest payable are subtracted from net income.)

Income Taxes Payable The Income Taxes Payable account increases when income tax expense is incurred and decreases when income taxes are paid.

Income Taxes Payable			
		6,000	Balance, 1/1/2013
Cash payments	XXX	XXX	Income tax expense
		3,000	Balance, 12/31/2013

The decrease in income taxes payable implies that the cash payments for income taxes were $3,000 greater than the income tax expense reported on the income statement. This is consistent with the results of our earlier analysis indicating that decreases in liabilities are related to decreases in cash. Therefore, less cash is available at the end of the period and the decrease in income taxes payable is subtracted from net income when computing the net cash flow from operating activities. (Increases in income taxes payable are added to net income.)

YOUDECIDE Operating Cash Flow and the Quality of Earnings

You are analyzing the financial statements of Slater Inc., a retail company that operates primarily in the southeastern United States. While Slater has reported increasing net income, you notice that its operating cash flow has been declining. Further investigation reveals increasing accounts receivable and inventory balances.

What inferences can you make about the quality of Slater's earnings?

Many analysts will compare net income to operating cash flow as a means of assessing the quality of a company's earnings. All other things equal, the higher a company's operating cash flow relative to its net income, the greater the quality of the company's earnings. In Slater's situation, increasing income with declining operating cash flow is a warning sign that requires closer scrutiny. The increasing accounts receivable balances could simply signal rapidly growing operations. However, it may also signal that a company is attempting to boost sales by allowing customers to take longer to pay or lending to riskier customers. Similarly, increasing inventory balances may be due to seasonal factors (for example, the normal inventory growth during a "slow" quarter) or could signal that the company was not able to sell its merchandise as it had planned. When differences between net income and operating cash flow are noted, it is critical to fully understand their implications for the company's prospects.

Understanding the differences between net income and operating cash flow can provide useful insights into the quality of a company's earnings.

OBJECTIVE 5

Prepare the cash flows from investing activities section of a statement of cash flows.

PREPARING CASH FLOWS FROM INVESTING ACTIVITIES

The second major section of the statement of cash flows reports the net cash flow from investing activities. Information for preparing the investing activities portion of the statement of cash flows is obtained from the investment and long-term asset accounts. Because all of these accounts are assets, increases that were financed by cash would be treated as outflows of cash. Decreases in the assets that produced cash receipts would be treated as inflows of cash.

Although the beginning and ending balance sheets are useful sources for identifying changes in these accounts, you must refer to any additional data provided to determine the actual amount of investing cash inflows and outflows. For example, a company might purchase land at a cost of $200,000 and, during the same accounting period, sell land that had a cost of $145,000. If only the beginning and ending amounts for land are examined, one would erroneously conclude that there had been a single cash outflow of $55,000 for land, instead of two separate cash flows—a cash outflow for the purchase of land and a cash inflow related to the sale of land.

Analyzing Investing Activities

To analyze investing activities, follow the three basic steps outlined in Exhibit 11.9.

EXHIBIT 11.9

Analyzing Investing Activities

Step 1.
Recreate the journal entries to describe the activities that took place during the period.

Step 2.
Record the cash flows as inflows or outflows of cash in the investing activities section of the statement of cash flows.

Step 3.
Analyze the account using all available information to make sure the account activity has been completely explained.

To illustrate the analysis of the relevant accounts and the recreation of the journal entries, consider the information in Brooke Sportswear's financial statements in Exhibit 11.7 (p. 593).

Land Notice that no change occurred in the Land account, nor was any additional information given concerning this account. Therefore, you may conclude that there was no cash flow associated with land for the year.

Property, Plant, and Equipment To get a full picture of the Equipment account you must examine both the equipment and the related Accumulated Depreciation account. (For any operating asset that depreciates, you will need to analyze the two related accounts together.) Using the information from the financial statements and the additional information in Exhibit 11.7 (p. 593), you can recreate the activity in these accounts by making the following journal entries:

Repayment of Principal	Notes Payable	35,000	
	Cash		35,000

Assets	= Liabilities +	Stockholders' Equity
−35,000		−35,000

Issuance of Note	Cash	29,000	
	Notes Payable		29,000

Assets	= Liabilities +	Stockholders' Equity
+29,000		+29,000

Notice that there are two cash flows related to financing activities:

- a $35,000 cash outflow associated with the repayment of principal
- a $29,000 cash inflow associated with issuing the note

The payment of interest is considered an operating activity and is not relevant to this analysis. The analysis performed above is used to reconcile the change in the Notes Payable account as shown in the following T-account:

Notes Payable

		115,000	Balance, 1/1/2013
Repaid principal	35,000	29,000	Issued note
		109,000	Balance, 12/31/2013

Common Stock Using information in Exhibit 11.7 (p. 593), you can recreate activity in the common stock account by making the following journal entry:

Issuance of Stock	Cash	14,000	
	Common Stock		14,000

Assets	= Liabilities +	Stockholders' Equity
+14,000		+14,000

One cash inflow ($14,000) has caused the change in common stock. The credit entry to the Common Stock account is used to reconcile the change in the Common Stock account, as shown in the following T-account:

Common Stock

		151,000	Balance, 1/1/2013
Retired stock	0	14,000	Issued stock
		165,000	Balance, 12/31/2013

Retained Earnings Using information in Exhibit 11.7 (p. 593), you can recreate the activity in the Retained Earnings account by making the following journal entry:

Payment of Dividends	Dividends	5,000	
	Cash		5,000

Assets	= Liabilities +	Stockholders' Equity
−5,000		−5,000

The only cash flow, the payment of dividends, is a financing activity. The following T-account summarizes the activity in the Retained Earnings account:

Retained Earnings

		246,000	Balance, 1/1/2013
Dividends	5,000	39,000	Net income
		280,000	Balance, 12/31/2013

Note that retained earnings is increased by net income and decreased by the payment of dividends.[1] Net income does not affect cash flow from financing activities but is considered an operating activity.

Cornerstone 11.5 (p. 602) shows how to compute the financing activities section of the statement of cash flows for Brooke Sportswear.

[1] Dividends declared but not paid also reduce retained earnings but are classified as a noncash activity.

CORNERSTONE

11.5

Reporting Net Cash Flow from Financing Activities

Why:

The cash flow effects of changes in long-term liabilities and equity are reported as financing cash flows.

Information:

Refer to the income statement, long-term assets, liabilities, and equity sections of Brooke Sportswear's balance sheet, and Items 3–5 of additional information in Exhibit 11.7 (p. 593).

Required:

Compute the net cash flow from financing activities.

Solution:

Cash flows from financing activities:	
Cash paid to retire principal on notes payable	$(35,000)
Cash received from issuing notes payable	29,000
Cash received from issuance of common stock	14,000
Cash paid for dividends	(5,000)
Net cash provided by financing activities	$ 3,000

Combining Cornerstones 11-3 through 11-5, a complete statement of cash flows is presented in Exhibit 11.10. This exhibit presents cash flows from operating activities using the indirect method. Notice that the statement of cash flows explains the change in cash shown on the balance sheet of Brooke Sportswear in Exhibit 11.7 (p. 593).

YOUDECIDE Understanding Patterns in the Statement of Cash Flows

During a recent conference call with analysts, the CEO of Waggoner Inc. said that the company expects future sales growth as it expands into several new geographical markets. To corroborate the CEO's statements, you examine the statement of cash flows and find that the company reported negative operating cash flows, positive investing cash flows, and positive financing cash flows.

Does the statement of cash flows support the CEO's statements?

It does not appear that the CEO's statements are supported by the company's cash flows. An expanding company should exhibit negative investing cash flows as it invests in the long-term assets necessary for expansion. The positive investing cash flows shown by Waggoner indicate that it is a net seller of its fixed assets—not a purchaser. In addition, one would like to see any expansion supported by positive operating cash flows. Instead of being an expanding company, the pattern of cash flows exhibited by Waggoner suggests a company that is experiencing problems in generating operating cash flows. Further, it appears the company may be selling its fixed assets and obtaining capital through borrowing or stockholder contributions in order to cover the operating cash flow shortfall.

Careful analysis of the patterns and interrelationships of a company's cash flows can provide users with insights into a company's operations.

EXHIBIT 11.10

Statement of Cash Flows for Brooke Sportswear

Brooke Sportswear
Statement of Cash Flows
For the year ended December 31, 2013

Cash flows from operating activities		
Net income	$ 39,000	
Adjustments to reconcile net income to net cash flow from operating activities:		
Depreciation expense	40,000	
Loss on disposal of equipment	6,000	
Gain on sale of long-term investments	(15,000)	
Increase in accounts receivable	(7,000)	
Decrease in prepaid insurance	1,000	
Increase in inventory	(12,000)	
Decrease in accounts payable	(4,000)	
Increase in wages payable	1,500	
Increase in interest payable	500	
Decrease in income taxes payable	(3,000)	
Net cash provided by operating activities		$ 47,000
Cash flows from investing activities		
Cash received from sale of equipment	$ 2,000	
Purchase of equipment	(53,000)	
Cash received from sale of investments	31,000	
Purchase of investments	(28,000)	
Net cash used for investing activities		(48,000)
Cash flows from financing activities		
Cash paid to retire principal on notes payable	$(35,000)	
Cash received from issuing notes payable	29,000	
Cash received from issuance of common stock	14,000	
Cash paid for dividends	(5,000)	
Net cash provided by financing activities		3,000
Net increase (decrease) in cash		$ 2,000
Cash and cash equivalents, 1/1/2013		13,000
Cash and cash equivalents, 12/31/2013		$ 15,000

USING THE STATEMENT OF CASH FLOWS

OBJECTIVE 7

Analyze information contained in the statement of cash flows.

Effective analysis of the statement of cash flows requires:

- an examination of the statement of cash flows itself
- a comparison of the information on the current statement of cash flows with earlier statements
- a comparison of the information in the current statement of cash flows with information from other companies' statements of cash flow

Examining the Statement of Cash Flows

One of the most important insights that can be gained by inspecting the current period's statement of cash flows is an estimate of how long it will take to recover the cash outflow associated with long-term uses of cash (such as purchase of property, plant, and equipment or payment of dividends). Investments in property, plant, and equipment are likely to require several profitable years before the investment is completely recovered through the sale of goods or services. Therefore, prudent managers will seek long-term sources of cash, such as long-term debt or equity, which will not need to be repaid before the original investment has been recovered through profitable operations.

The sources most frequently used to provide long-term cash inflows are operations, the sale of long-term debt, and the sale of stock. Of these three, operations is generally considered the least risky, or the most controllable. The sale of debt or equity requires that investors or creditors make sizable commitments to the company. Although cash inflows from operations also require that an outsider (the customer) make a commitment, the size and timing of a customer's cash commitments are more flexible. Thus, it is more likely that the company can produce cash inflows from customers on a regular basis. For this reason, most companies attempt to secure a sizable portion of their total cash inflows from operations. Generally, analysts view cash flows from operations as the most important section of the statement of cash flows because, in the long-run, this will be the company's source of cash used to provide a return to investors and creditors.

Because the cost of selling large debt or equity issues in the public capital markets is high, most large companies sell debt or equity in relatively large amounts. They also make smaller long-term or short-term borrowings directly from banks, insurance companies, and other financial intermediaries. Many businesses arrange a "pre-approved" line of credit that can be used, up to some limit, for borrowing whenever cash is needed. Sales of small amounts of stock to employees through stock option and stock bonus plans also help increase cash inflows.

Comparing the Statement of Cash Flows from Several Periods

An analysis of the statement of cash flows also requires a comparison of the company's current statement of cash flows with earlier statements of cash flow. Typically, several consecutive years should be analyzed in order to determine trends in cash inflows and cash outflows. The following questions may be helpful in beginning the analysis of a series of cash flow statements:

- What proportions of cash have come from operating, financing, and investing activities?
- Are there discernible trends in these proportions?
- What proportions of long-term uses of cash are financed by long-term sources of cash?
- How has the company financed any permanent increases in current assets?
- Has the company begun any investment programs that are likely to require significant cash outflows in the future?
- What are the probable sources for the cash inflows the company will need in the near future?
- Are these sources likely to be both able and willing to provide the cash that is needed?
- If the company is unable to secure all the cash it needs, could cash outflows be restricted to the available supply of cash without seriously affecting operations?

Financial statement users will rely on summary cash flow measures to help them make these assessments. Two such measures are a company's free cash flow and its cash flow adequacy ratio.

Free Cash Flow A company's **free cash flow** represents the cash flow that a company is able to generate after considering the maintenance or expansion of its assets (capital expenditures) and the payment of dividends. Free cash flow is computed as:

$$\text{Free Cash Flow} = \text{Net Cash Flow from Operating Activities} - \text{Capital Expenditures} - \text{Cash Dividends}$$

Having positive free cash flow allows a company to pursue profit-generating opportunities. However, negative free cash flow is not necessarily a bad thing. For example, a company making large investments in productive assets (large capital expenditures) may show negative free cash flow. If these investments provide a high rate of return, this strategy will be good for the company in the long run.

Cash Flow Adequacy Ratio A second useful measure is the **cash flow adequacy ratio**. The cash flow adequacy ratio provides a measure of the company's ability to meet its maturing debt obligations with its operating cash flow. This ratio is calculated as:

$$\text{Cash Flow Adequacy} = \frac{\text{Free Cash Flow}}{\text{Average Amount of Debt Maturing over the Next 5 Years}}$$

The cash flow adequacy ratio is also an indicator of the company's credit quality. Generally, a higher cash flow adequacy ratio signals that a company is a better credit risk than a company that must seek outside sources of capital to repay its obligations.

Cornerstone 11.6 illustrates the computation and analysis of these ratios for John Deere and Caterpillar.

Analyzing Free Cash Flow and Cash Flow Adequacy

CORNERSTONE 11.6

Why:

Cash flow measures can be used to help assess a company's ability to expand its operations, meet its obligations, obtain financing, and pay dividends.

Information:

The following information was obtained from the 2011 10-K reports of John Deere and Caterpillar.

(amounts in millions)	John Deere	Caterpillar
Operating cash flows	$2,326.3	$7,010
Capital expenditures	1,056.6	2,515
Cash dividends	593.1	1,159
Average maturities of long-term debt over the next 5 years	3,343.8	4,260.8

Required:

Compute John Deere's and Caterpillar's free cash flow and cash flow adequacy ratios.

Solution:

Free Cash Flow = Net Cash from Operating Activities − Capital Expenditures − Cash Dividends

John Deere	Caterpillar
$2,326.3 − $1,056.6 − $593.1 = **$676.6**	$7,010 − $2,515 − $1,159 = **$3,336**

$$\text{Cash Flow Adequacy} = \frac{\text{Free Cash Flow}}{\text{Average Amount of Debt Maturing over the Next 5 Years}}$$

John Deere	Caterpillar
$\frac{\$676.6}{\$3,343.8} = \mathbf{20.2\%}$	$\frac{\$3,336}{\$4,260.8} = \mathbf{78.3\%}$

Source: Deere & Company and Caterpillar 2011 10-Ks.

As you can see in Cornerstone 11.6, with over $3.3 billion in free cash flow, **Caterpillar** certainly has the financial flexibility to take advantage of profit-generating opportunities and internally finance its expansion needs. **John Deere**, with approximately $676.6 million of free cash flow also appears to have a significant amount of free cash flow. However, both companies have a cash flow adequacy ratio of less than one. This implies that both companies may have to seek outside sources of capital in order to repay their maturing debt obligations.

Comparing the Statement of Cash Flows to Similar Companies

Finally, the analysis of the statement of cash flows requires comparing information from similar companies. Such comparisons provide good reference points because similar companies generally secure cash from similar sources and are likely to spend cash for similar activities. Comparative analysis can reveal significant deviations in the:

- amounts of cash inflows
- sources of those inflows
- types of activities to which cash is applied

When significant differences are found among similar companies, an explanation should be sought in the other financial statements, in the notes accompanying the statements, or from management.

OBJECTIVE 8

(Appendix 11A) Prepare the cash flows from operating activities section of a statement of cash flows using the direct method.

APPENDIX 11A: THE DIRECT METHOD

In the direct method of computing net cash flow from operating activities, inflows and outflows of cash are listed for each type of operating activity that a company performs. This involves adjusting *each item* on the income statement by the changes in the related current asset or liability accounts. Typical operating cash flows and the adjustments necessary to compute them are given below. All numbers are taken from the financial statements for Brooke Sportswear given in Exhibit 11.7 (p. 593).

Cash Collected from Customers

Sales revenue includes both cash sales and credit sales. When all sales are for cash, the cash collected from customers equals sales. However, when credit sales are made, the amount of cash that was collected during a period must be determined by analyzing the Sales and Accounts Receivable accounts. The Accounts Receivable account increases when credit sales are recorded and decreases when cash is collected from customers.

Accounts Receivable			
Balance, 1/1/2013	46,000		
Credit sales	XXX	XXX	Cash collections
Balance, 12/31/2013	53,000		

The increase of accounts receivable implies that credit sales were $7,000 greater than the cash collected from customers. This is consistent with increases in noncash assets reflecting decreases in cash. Because cash collections were less than reported sales ($472,000), Brooke Sportswear would subtract the increase in accounts receivable from sales when computing cash collected from customers. A general formula to compute cash collections from customers is:

$$\text{Cash Collected from Customers} = \text{Sales}\begin{cases} + \text{ Decrease in Accounts Receivable} \\ - \text{ Increase in Accounts Receivable} \end{cases}$$

Other Cash Collections

If other revenues exist (such as interest or rent), similar adjustments are made to determine the cash collections. For example, interest revenue is adjusted for any change in interest receivable as follows:

$$\text{Cash Collected for Interest} = \text{Interest Revenue}\begin{cases} + \text{ Decrease in Interest Receivable} \\ - \text{ Increase in Interest Receivable} \end{cases}$$

Cash Paid to Suppliers

A company pays its suppliers for inventory which it later sells to customers, as represented by cost of goods sold. These purchases of inventory from suppliers may be either cash purchases or credit purchases, reflected as accounts payable. To compute cash paid to suppliers, it is necessary to analyze two accounts—Inventory and Accounts Payable—and make two adjustments.

Inventory			
Balance, 1/1/2013	51,000		
Purchases	XXX	XXX	Cost of goods sold
Balance, 12/31/2013	63,000		

Accounts Payable			
		17,000	Balance, 1/1/2013
Cash payments	XXX	XXX	Credit purchases
		13,000	Balance, 12/31/2013

The increase in inventory implies that purchases of inventory exceeded the cost of goods sold by $12,000. (A decrease in inventory would imply that purchases of inventory were less than cost of goods sold.) Therefore, cost of goods sold needs to be increased to reflect the "extra" cash purchases that were not included as an expense. A general formula to capture this relationship is:

$$\text{Cost of Purchases} = \text{Cost of Goods Sold}\begin{cases} + \text{ Increases in Inventory} \\ - \text{ Decreases in Inventory} \end{cases}$$

Next, the cost of purchases must be adjusted by the change in accounts payable to compute the cash paid to suppliers. The decrease in accounts payable implies that the cash payments to suppliers exceeded the purchases of inventory by $4,000. (An increase in accounts payable would imply that cash payments were less than the cost of purchases.) Therefore, Brooke Sportswear would add the increase in accounts payable to the cost of purchases to compute the cash paid to suppliers. A general formula that captures this relationship is:

$$\text{Cash Paid to Suppliers} = \text{Cost of Purchases}\begin{cases} + \text{ Decreases in Accounts Payable} \\ - \text{ Increases in Accounts Payable} \end{cases}$$

Combining this adjustment with the first adjustment, the cash paid to suppliers is computed as:

$$\text{Cash Paid to Suppliers} = \begin{cases} + \text{ Increases in Inventory} \\ - \text{ Decreases in Inventory} \end{cases}\begin{cases} + \text{ Decreases in Accounts Payable} \\ - \text{ Increases in Accounts Payable} \end{cases}$$

Cash Paid for Operating Expenses

Recall that operating expenses are the expenses the business incurs in selling goods or providing services and managing the company. These are usually divided into selling and administrative expenses and include items such as advertising expense, salaries and wages, insurance expense, utilities expense, property tax expense, and depreciation. These expenses are recognized when goods and services are used, not when cash is paid. Therefore, the expense amounts reported on the income statement will probably not equal the amount of cash actually paid during the period. Some expenses are paid before they are actually recognized (such as prepaid insurance); other expenses are paid for after they are recognized, creating a payable account at the time of the cash payment (such as salaries payable).

To determine the amount of cash payments for operating expenses, it is necessary to analyze the changes in the balance sheet accounts that are related to operating expenses—prepaid expenses and accrued liabilities. A prepaid expense increases when cash prepayments are made and decreases when expenses are incurred. An accrued liability increases when expenses are accrued (incurred but not yet paid) and decreases when cash payments are made. Brooke Sportswear has two balances that need to be analyzed—prepaid insurance and wages payable.

Prepaid Insurance

Balance, 1/1/2013	2,000		
Cash prepayments	XXX	XXX	Expense incurred
Balance, 12/31/2013	1,000		

Wages Payable

		2,000	Balance, 1/1/2013
Cash payments	XXX	XXX	Wages expense
		3,500	Balance, 12/31/2013

The decrease in prepaid insurance indicates that expenses recorded on the income statement were $1,000 higher than the cash payments. Because more expenses were incurred than were paid in cash, the company actually has more cash available at the end of the period than at the beginning of the period. (An increase in prepaid expenses means that cash payments were higher than the expenses recognized on the income statement and a company would have less cash available at the end of the period.) Therefore, Brooke Sportswear should add the increase in prepaid insurance ($1,000) to insurance expense ($15,000) to compute the cash paid for insurance.

The increase in wages payable indicates that wages expense recorded on the income statement was greater than the cash paid for wages by $1,500. Because less cash was paid than expensed, the company actually has more cash available. (A decrease in wages payable would imply that cash payments were greater than the expense recorded on the income statement.) Therefore, Brooke Sportswear should subtract the increase in wages payable ($1,500) from wages expense to compute cash paid for wages.

Combining these two adjustments, a general formula to compute cash paid for operating expenses is:

Cash Paid for Operating Expenses	=	Operating Expenses	+ Increases in Prepaid Expenses − Decreases in Prepaid Expenses
			+ Decrease in Accrued Liabilities − Increase in Accrued Liabilities

Cash Paid for Interest and Income Taxes

Computing cash paid for interest and income taxes is similar to that for operating expenses. Interest payable increases when interest expense is recorded and decreases when interest is paid.

Interest Payable

		1,000	Balance, 1/1/2013
Cash payments	XXX	XXX	Interest expense
		1,500	Balance, 12/31/2013

The increase in interest payable implies that interest expense recorded on the income statement was $500 greater than the cash paid for interest. (A decrease in interest expense indicates that the cash paid for interest is greater than the interest expense recorded on the income statement.) Therefore, Brooke Sportswear would subtract the $500 increase in interest payable from interest expense ($5,000) to compute the cash paid for interest. A general formula to capture this relationship is:

$$\text{Cash Paid for Interest} = \text{Interest Expense}\begin{cases} + \text{ Decreases in Interest Payable} \\ - \text{ Increases in Interest Payable} \end{cases}$$

The Income Taxes Payable account increases when income tax expense is incurred and decreases when income taxes are paid.

Income Taxes Payable			
		6,000	Balance, 1/1/2013
Cash payments	XXX	XXX	Income tax expense
		3,000	Balance, 12/31/2013

The decrease in income taxes payable implies that the cash payments for income taxes were $3,000 greater than the income tax expense reported on the income statement. (An increase in income taxes payable implies that income tax expense reported on the income statement is greater than the cash paid for income taxes.) Therefore, Brooke Sportswear would add the increase in income taxes payable ($3,000) to income taxes expense ($8,000) to compute cash paid for income taxes. A general formula to capture this relationship is:

$$\begin{matrix}\text{Cash Paid for} \\ \text{Income Taxes}\end{matrix} = \text{Income Tax Expense}\begin{cases} + \text{ Decrease in Income Taxes Payable} \\ - \text{ Increase in Income Taxes Payable} \end{cases}$$

Other Items

Noncash Revenues and Expenses The income statement often includes various noncash items such as depreciation expense, amortization expense, and bad debt expense. Noncash items do not affect cash flow. Therefore, under the direct method, **noncash items are not reported on the statement of cash flows**. Sometimes, depreciation expense (or some other noncash expense) is included as part of operating expenses. In this case, depreciation expense must be subtracted from operating expenses to compute the cash paid for operating expenses.

Gains and Losses The sale of a long-term asset or the extinguishment of a long-term liability often produces either a gain or loss that is reported on the income statement. However, the gain or loss does not affect cash flow and should not be included as an operating activity. Furthermore, the gain or loss does not reveal the total amount of cash received or paid. Instead, it only gives the amount received or paid in excess of the book value of the asset or liability. Therefore, **gains and losses are not reported on the statement of cash flows under the direct method.**

Applying the Direct Method

Cornerstone 11.7 (p. 610) illustrates and summarizes the computation of the net cash flow from operating activities using the direct method. Because each item on the income statement is adjusted under the direct method, it is common to begin the analysis with the first item on the income statement (sales) and proceed down the income statement in the order that the accounts are listed.

It is important to note that both the indirect and direct methods arrive at the identical amount for the net cash provided (used) by operating activities. Therefore, the net cash provided by operating activities of $47,000 computed on the next page is the same as the net cash flow from operating activities computed under the indirect method shown in

CORNERSTONE

11.7

Calculating Net Cash Flows from Operating Activities: Direct Method

Why:

To compute net cash flow from operating activities under the direct method, each item on the income statement must be adjusted for changes in the related asset and liability accounts.

Information:

Refer to the financial statements for Brooke Sportswear in Exhibit 11.7 (p. 593).

Required:

Compute the net cash flow from operating activities using the direct method.

Solution:

Cash flows from operating activities		
Cash collected from customers[a]		$ 465,000
Cash paid:		
To suppliers of merchandise[b]	$(248,000)	
For wages[c]	(140,500)	
For insurance[d]	(14,000)	
For interest[e]	(4,500)	
For income taxes[f]	(11,000)	(418,000)
Net cash provided by operating activities		$ 47,000

[a] $472,000 sales − $7,000 change in accounts receivable = $465,000
[b] $232,000 cost of goods sold + $12,000 change in inventory + $4,000 change in accounts payable = $248,000
[c] $142,000 wages expense − $1,500 change in wages payable = $140,500
[d] $15,000 insurance expense − $1,000 change in prepaid insurance = $14,000
[e] $5,000 interest expense − $500 change in interest payable = $4,500
[f] $8,000 income taxes expense + $3,000 change in income taxes payable = $11,000

Cornerstone 11.3 (p. 594). The two methods differ only in how this amount is computed and the presentation of the details on the statement of cash flows. In addition, if the direct method is used, companies must also provide a supplementary schedule that shows the reconciliation of net income with net cash flow from operating activities. This supplementary schedule is, in effect, the presentation shown under the indirect method in Cornerstone 11.3.

OBJECTIVE 9

(Appendix 11B) Use a spreadsheet to prepare the statement of cash flows.

APPENDIX 11B: USING A SPREADSHEET TO PREPARE THE STATEMENT OF CASH FLOWS

The use of a spreadsheet provides a means of systematically analyzing changes in the balance sheet amounts, along with the information from the income statement and any additional information, to produce a statement of cash flows. This approach produces spreadsheet entries (made only on the spreadsheet and not in the general ledger) that simultaneously reconstruct and explain the changes in the balance sheet account balances and identify the cash inflows and outflows. The spreadsheet is based on the same underlying principles as discussed in the chapter. Its primary advantage is that it provides a systematic approach to analyze the data, which is helpful in complex situations.

To construct the spreadsheet, follow these steps:

Step 1. Construct five columns. The first column will contain the balance sheet account titles. Immediately beneath the balance sheet accounts, set up the three sections of the statement of cash flows. The second column will contain the beginning balances of the balance sheet accounts (enter the amounts at this time). The third and fourth column will contain the debit and credit adjustments, respectively. The fifth column will contain the ending balances of the balance sheet accounts (enter the amounts at this time).

Step 2. Analyze each change in the balance sheet accounts in terms of debits and credits. Enter the effects in the adjustments column. Note that each entry will adjust both the balance sheet account being considered and either a statement of cash flows section of the spreadsheet or another balance sheet account (other than cash). Note that all inflows of cash are recorded as debits and all outflows of cash are recorded as credits.

Step 3. Prepare the statement of cash flows from the information contained in the statement of cash flows section of the spreadsheet.

Exhibit 11.11 (p. 612) illustrates how to use a spreadsheet to prepare the statement of cash flows for Brooke Sportswear. The required adjustments, labeled as (a) - (r) in Exhibit 11.11 are explained below. Refer to the information given earlier in the chapter regarding the logic behind the analysis of these changes.

Net Income

a. Net income is listed as a cash inflow in the operating activities section. Because net income flows into retained earnings during the closing process, a credit to retained earnings reflects the effect of the closing entry.

Adjusting for Noncash Items

b. For Brooke Sportswear, the only noncash item was depreciation expense, which is added back to net income in the operating activities section and is reflected as a credit to accumulated depreciation.

Adjusting for Gains and/or Losses Due to Investing and Financing Activities

c. The actual proceeds from the sale of equipment are shown as a cash inflow in the investing activities section. The loss on the disposal of equipment is added back to net income in the operating activities section. In addition, both equipment and accumulated depreciation should be adjusted to reflect the sale.

d. The cash paid to purchase equipment is shown as a cash outflow in the investing activities section. At this point, note that the beginning and ending balances of the Equipment and Accumulated Depreciation accounts are reconciled.

e. The actual proceeds from the sale of the investment are shown as a cash inflow in the investing activities section. The gain on the sale of the investment is subtracted from net income in the operating activities section. In addition, the Investments account should be adjusted to reflect the sale.

f. The cash paid to purchase the investment is shown as a cash outflow in the investing activities section. At this point, note that the beginning and ending balances of the Investments account are reconciled.

Adjusting for Changes in Current Assets and Current Liabilities

g. The increase in accounts receivable is subtracted from net income and reconciles the change in the Accounts Receivable account.

EXHIBIT 11.11

Spreadsheet to Prepare Statement of Cash Flows

	A	B	C	D	E	F	G
1	**Brooke Sportswear**						
2	**Spreadsheet to Prepare the Statement of Cash Flows**						
3	**For the year ended December 31, 2013**						
4							
5		**Beginning**		**Adjustments**			**Ending**
6		**Balance**		**Debit**	**Credit**		**Balance**
7	**Balance Sheet Accounts**						
8	Cash	13,000	(r)	2,000			15,000
9	Accounts Receivable	46,000	(g)	7,000			53,000
10	Prepaid Insurance	2,000			1,000	(h)	1,000
11	Inventory	51,000	(i)	12,000			63,000
12	Land	325,000					325,000
13	Equipment	210,000	(d)	53,000	20,000	(c)	243,000
14	Accumulated Depreciation	150,000	(c)	12,000	40,000	(b)	178,000
15	Investments	41,000	(f)	28,000	16,000	(e)	53,000
16							
17	Accounts Payable	17,000	(j)	4,000			13,000
18	Wages Payable	2,000			1,500	(k)	3,500
19	Interest Payable	1,000			500	(l)	1,500
20	Income Taxes Payable	6,000	(m)	3,000			3,000
21	Notes Payable	115,000	(n)	35,000	29,000	(o)	109,000
22	Common Stock	151,000			14,000	(p)	165,000
23	Retained Earnings	246,000	(q)	5,000	39,000	(a)	280,000
24							
25	**Statement of Cash Flows**						
26	Cash flow from operating activities						
27	Net income		(a)	39,000			
28	Adjustments to reconcile net						
29	income to net cash flow from						
30	operating activities						
31	Depreciation expense		(b)	40,000			
32	Loss on disposal of equipment		(c)	6,000			
33	Gain on sale of investments				15,000	(e)	
34	Increase in accounts receivable				7,000	(g)	
35	Decrease in prepaid insurance		(h)	1,000			
36	Increase in inventory				12,000	(i)	
37	Decrease in accounts payable				4,000	(j)	
38	Increase in wages payable		(k)	1,500			
39	Increase in interest payable		(l)	500			
40	Decrease in income taxes payable				3,000	(m)	
41							
42	Cash flows from investing activities						
43	Sale of equipment		(c)	2,000			
44	Purchase equipment				53,000	(d)	
45	Sale of investments		(e)	31,000			
46	Purchase of investment				28,000	(f)	
47							
48	Cash flows from financing activities						
49	Repaid note payable				35,000	(n)	
50	Issued note payable		(o)	29,000			
51	Issued common stock		(p)	14,000			
52	Paid dividend				5,000	(q)	
53							
54	Net change in cash				2,000	(r)	
55							
56				325,000	325,000		

h. The decrease in prepaid insurance is added to net income and reconciles the change in the Prepaid Insurance account.
i. The increase in inventory is subtracted from net income and reconciles the change in the Inventory account.
j. The decrease in accounts payable is subtracted from net income and reconciles the change in the Accounts Payable account.
k. The increase in wages payable is added to net income and reconciles the change in the Wages Payable account.
l. The increase in interest payable is added to net income and reconciles the change in the Interest Payable account.
m. The decrease in income taxes payable is subtracted from net income and reconciles the change in the Income Taxes Payable account.

Adjusting for Cash Inflows and Outflows Associated with Financing Activities

n. The repayment of the notes payable is a cash outflow from a financing activity and adjusts the Notes Payable account.
o. The issuance of a notes payable is a cash inflow from a financing activity and reconciles the change in the Notes Payable account.
p. The issuance of common stock is a cash inflow from a financing activity and reconciles the change in the Common Stock account.
q. The payment of dividends is a cash outflow from a financing activity and, together with the first entry, Item a, reconciles the change in retained earnings. The final entry reconciles the cash balance.
r. The summation of the three sections of the statement of cash flows equals the change in cash for the period. This amount can be checked by summing the net cash flows from operating, investing, and financing activities computed in the previous steps.

Completing the Statement of Cash Flows

The statement of cash flows can now be prepared from the information developed in the statement of cash flows portion of the spreadsheet. The statement of cash flows for Brooke Sportswear is shown in Exhibit 11.10 (p. 603).

SUMMARY OF LEARNING OBJECTIVES

LO 1. Explain the purpose of a statement of cash flows.

- The statement of cash flows is one of the primary financial statements whose purpose is to provide information about a company's cash receipts (inflows of cash) and cash payments (outflows of cash) during an accounting period.
- The statement of cash flows is complementary to the information contained in the income statement and the balance sheet and is critical to understanding and analyzing a company's operations.

LO 2. Identify and classify business activities that produce cash inflows and outflows.

- The statement of cash flows is divided into three main sections based on the fundamental business activities that a company engages in during a period:
  - cash flows from operating activities, which encompass the cash inflows and outflows that relate to the determination of net income
  - cash flows from investing activities, which are related to acquisitions and disposals of long-term assets and investments
  - cash flows from financing activities, which are related to the external financing of the company (debt or stockholders' equity)
- Some business activities take place without affecting cash and are referred to as noncash investing and financing activities.

LO 3. Understand the relationship between changes in cash and the changes in the balance sheet accounts.

- Because of timing issues between the recognition of revenues and expenses and the inflows and outflows of cash, information about a company's cash flows can be obtained by examining the changes in the balance sheet account balances over a period.
- Increases in cash result from increases in liabilities, increases in stockholders' equity, and decreases in noncash assets.
- Decreases in cash result from decreases in liabilities, decreases in stockholders' equity, and increases in noncash assets.

LO 4. Prepare the cash flows from operating activities section of a statement of cash flows using the indirect method.

- The indirect method for reporting cash flows from operating activities begins with net income and adjusts it for noncash items to produce net cash flow from operating activities.
- The adjustments to net income are necessary to eliminate income statement items that do not affect cash and to adjust accrual-basis revenues and expenses to cash receipts and cash payments.
- Four types of adjustments are necessary:
  - add to net income any noncash expenses and subtract from net income any noncash revenues
  - add to net income any losses and subtract from net income any gains
  - add to net income any decreases in current assets or increases in current liabilities that are related to operating activities
  - subtract from net income any increases in current assets and decreases in current liabilities that are related to operating activities

LO 5. Prepare the cash flows from investing activities section of a statement of cash flows.

- The cash flows from the investing activities section reports the net cash flow related to buying and selling property, plant, and equipment or other operating assets, purchasing and selling investments in other companies, and lending and collecting the principal amount of loans from borrowers.
- The preparation of the investing activities section of a statement of cash flows involves a careful analysis of the information in the financial statements as well as a recreation of the journal entries that describe the activities that took place during a period.

LO 6. Prepare the cash flows from financing activities section of a statement of cash flows.

- The cash flows from financing activities section reports the net cash flow related to the borrowing and repayment of the principal amount of long-term debt, sale of common or preferred stock, payment of dividends, and purchase and sale of treasury stock.
- The preparation of the financing activities section of a statement of cash flows involves a careful analysis of the information in the financial statements as well as a recreation of the journal entries that describe the activities that took place during a period.

LO 7. Analyze information contained in the statement of cash flows.

- Effective analysis of the statement of cash flows requires an examination of the statement of cash flows itself, a comparison of the information on the current statement of cash flows with earlier statements, and a comparison of the information in the current statement of cash flows with information from other companies' statements of cash flow.
- Financial statement users may also rely on summary cash flow measures such as free cash flow (the cash flow that a company is able to generate after considering the maintenance or expansion of its assets) and the cash flow adequacy ratio (a measure of a company's ability to meet its debt obligations with its operating cash flow).

LO 8. *(Appendix 11A)* Prepare the cash flows from operating activities section of a statement of cash flows using the direct method.

- The direct method for reporting cash flows from operating activities lists cash inflows and cash outflows for each type of operating activity that a company performs.
- Cash flows from operating activities are generally computed by adjusting each item on the income statement by the changes in the related current asset or current liability accounts.
- Typical cash flow categories reported under the direct method include cash collected from customers, cash paid to suppliers, cash paid to employees, cash paid for interest, and cash paid for taxes.

LO 9. *(Appendix 11B)* Use a spreadsheet to prepare the statement of cash flows.

- A spreadsheet provides a means of systematically analyzing changes in the balance sheet amounts, along with the information from the income statement and any additional information, to produce a statement of cash flows.

CORNERSTONE 11.1 Classifying business activities, page 586

CORNERSTONE 11.2 Classifying changes in balance sheet accounts, page 589

CORNERSTONE 11.3 Calculating net cash flow from operating activities: indirect method, page 594

CORNERSTONE 11.4 Reporting net cash flow from investing activities, page 600

CORNERSTONE 11.5 Reporting net cash flow from financing activities, page 602

CORNERSTONE 11.6 Analyzing free cash flow and cash flow adequacy, page 605

CORNERSTONE 11.7 Calculating net cash flows from operating activities: direct method, page 610

KEY TERMS

Cash flow adequacy ratio, 605
Cash flows from financing activities, 584
Cash flows from investing activities, 584
Cash flows from operating activities, 583
Direct method, 591
Free cash flow, 604
Indirect method, 592
Noncash investing and financing activities, 585
Statement of cash flows, 582

REVIEW PROBLEM

The Statement of Cash Flows

Why:

The statement of cash flows measures a company's inflows (sources) and outflows (uses) of cash during a period of time. These cash inflows and cash outflows are classified as operating, investing, and financing activities.

Information:

The income statement and comparative balance sheet for Solar System Company are shown on the next page.

(Continued)

Solar System Company
Balance Sheets
December 31, 2013 and 2012

	2013	2012
ASSETS		
Current assets:		
Cash	$ 56,000	$ 47,000
Accounts receivable	123,000	107,000
Prepaid expenses	10,000	9,000
Inventory	52,000	46,000
Total current assets	$ 241,000	$ 209,000
Property, plant, and equipment:		
Equipment	270,000	262,000
Accumulated depreciation	(118,000)	(109,000)
Total assets	$ 393,000	$ 362,000
LIABILITIES AND EQUITY		
Current liabilities:		
Accounts payable	$ 18,000	$ 11,000
Salaries payable	5,000	9,000
Income taxes payable	7,000	5,000
Total current liabilities	$ 30,000	$ 25,000
Long-term liabilities:		
Notes payable	120,000	130,000
Total liabilities	$150,000	$155,000
Equity:		
Common stock	$213,000	$200,000
Retained earnings	30,000	7,000
Total equity	$243,000	$207,000
Total liabilities and equity	$393,000	$362,000

Solar System Company
Income Statement
For the year ended December 31, 2013

Sales revenue	$1,339,000
Less: Cost of goods sold	(908,000)
Gross margin	$ 431,000
Less operating expenses:	
Salaries expense	(230,000)
Depreciation	(24,000)
Other operating expenses	(116,000)
Income from operations	$ 61,000
Other income and expenses:	
Gain on disposal of equipment	3,000
Interest expense	(14,000)
Income before taxes	$ 50,000
Less: Income taxes expense	(12,000)
Net income	$ 38,000

Additional Information:

1. Equipment with a cost of $24,000 and accumulated depreciation of $15,000 was sold for $12,000 cash. Equipment was purchased for $32,000 cash.
2. Notes payable in the amount of $10,000 were repaid.
3. Common stock was issued for $13,000 cash during 2013.
4. Cash dividends of $15,000 were paid during 2013.

Required:

Prepare a statement of cash flows for Solar System Company using the indirect method.

Solution:

Solar System Company
Statement of Cash Flows
For the year ended December 31, 2013

Cash flows from operating activities		
Net income	$ 38,000	
Adjustments to reconcile net income to net cash flow from operating activities:		
Depreciation expense	24,000	
Gain on disposal of equipment	(3,000)	
Increase in accounts receivable	(16,000)	
Increase in prepaid expenses	(1,000)	
Increase in inventory	(6,000)	
Increase in accounts payable	7,000	
Decrease in salaries payable	(4,000)	
Increase in income taxes payable	2,000	
Net cash provided by operating activities		$ 41,000

(Continued)

Solar System Company
Statement of Cash Flows—(Continued)
For the year ended December 31, 2013

Cash flows from investing activities		
Cash received from sale of equipment	$ 12,000	
Purchase of equipment	(32,000)	
Net cash used by investing activities		$(20,000)
Cash flows from financing activities		
Cash paid to retire notes payable	$(10,000)	
Cash received from issuance of common stock	13,000	
Cash paid for dividends	(15,000)	
Net cash used by financing activities		(12,000)
Net increase (decrease) in cash		$ 9,000
Cash and cash equivalents, 1/1/2013		47,000
Cash and cash equivalents, 12/31/2013		$ 56,000

DISCUSSION QUESTIONS

1. What is a statement of cash flows?
2. How do investors, creditors, and others typically use the information in the statement of cash flows?
3. How is a statement of cash flows different from an income statement?
4. What are cash equivalents? How are cash equivalents reported on the statement of cash flows?
5. What are the three categories into which inflows and outflows of cash are divided? Be sure to describe what is included in each of these three categories.
6. Why are companies required to report noncash investing and financing activities? How are these activities reported?
7. Why are direct exchanges of long-term debt for items of property, plant, and equipment included in supplementary information for the statement of cash flows even though the exchanges do not affect cash?
8. Describe the relationship between changes in cash and changes in noncash assets, liabilities, and stockholders' equity.
9. What are two ways to report a company's net cash flow from operating activities? Briefly describe each method.
10. Why are depreciation, depletion, and amortization added to net income when the indirect method is used to report net cash flows from operating activities?
11. Where do the components of the changes in retained earnings appear in the statement of cash flows? Assume the indirect method is used to prepare the statement of cash flows.
12. How is the sale of equipment at a loss reported on the statement of cash flows? Assume the indirect method is used to prepare the statement of cash flows.
13. What does an increase in inventory imply? How would this increase in inventory be reported under the indirect method?
14. What does an increase in accounts payable imply? How would this increase in accounts payable be reported under the indirect method?
15. Does the fact that the cash flow from operating activities is normally positive imply that cash and cash equivalents usually increase each year?
16. What are the most common sources of cash inflows from financing and investing activities?
17. What are the most common cash outflows related to investing and financing activities?
18. What balance sheet account changes might you expect to find for a company that must rely on sources other than operations to fund its cash outflows?

19. From what source(s) should most companies secure the majority of cash inflows? Why?
20. Why should companies attempt to secure cash for investment in property, plant, and equipment from long-term or permanent sources?
21. *(Appendix 11A)* When using the direct method, which items usually constitute the largest components of cash inflows from operating activities?
22. *(Appendix 11A)* Describe how to compute each of the cash inflows and cash outflows from operating activities under the direct method.
23. *(Appendix 11A)* Why is depreciation expense not generally reported on the statement of cash flows when using the direct method?
24. *(Appendix 11B)* Why do companies often use a spreadsheet to prepare the statement of cash flows?

MULTIPLE-CHOICE QUESTIONS

11-1 Which of the following is *not* a use of the statement of cash flows?

a. Aids in the prediction of future cash flow.
b. Provides a measure of the future obligations of the company.
c. Helps estimate the amount of funds that will be needed from creditors or stockholders.
d. Provides insights into the quality and reliability of reported income.

11-2 Which of the following would be classified as a cash outflow from an operating activity?

a. Purchase of an investment
b. Payment of dividends
c. Purchase of equipment
d. Payment of goods purchased from suppliers

11-3 Which of the following is an example of a cash inflow from an operating activity?

a. Collection of cash relating to a note receivable
b. Sale of property, plant, and equipment
c. Collection of an account receivable from a credit sale
d. None of these

11-4 Which of the following is an example of a cash outflow from a financing activity?

a. Payment of cash dividends to stockholders
b. Payment of interest on a note payable
c. Payment of wages to employees
d. Issuance of common stock for cash

11-5 Which of the following is true?

a. An increase in cash may result from an increase in liabilities.
b. An increase in cash may result from a decrease in stockholders' equity.
c. An increase in cash may result from an increase in noncash assets.
d. A decrease in cash may result from an increase in liabilities.

11-6 Which of the following statements is true?

a. Net cash flow from operating activities must be determined using the indirect method.
b. The indirect method adjusts sales for changes in noncash items to produce net cash flow from operating activities.
c. Many companies prefer the indirect method because it is easier and less costly to prepare.
d. The FASB prefers the indirect method.

11-7 Mullinix Inc. reported the following information: net income, \$55,000; decrease in accounts receivable, \$12,000; decrease in accounts payable, \$6,500; and depreciation expense, \$10,000. What amount did Mullinix report as cash flow from operating activities on its statement of cash flows?

a. \$50,500
b. \$59,500
c. \$70,500
d. \$83,500

11-8 Which item is added to net income when computing cash flows from operating activities?

a. Gain on the disposal of property, plant, and equipment
b. Increase in wages payable
c. Increase in inventory
d. Increase in prepaid rent

Use the following information for Multiple-Choice Questions 11-9 and 11-10:
Cornett Company reported the following information: cash received from the issuance of common stock, $150,000; cash received from the sale of equipment, $14,800; cash paid to purchase an investment, $20,000; cash paid to retire a note payable, $50,000; and cash collected from sales to customers, $225,000.

11-9 Refer to the information for Cornett Company above. What amount should Cornett report on its statement of cash flows as net cash flows provided by investing activities?

a. $(5,200)
b. $55,200
c. $144,800
d. None of these

11-10 Refer to the information for Cornett Company above. What amount should Cornett report on its statement of cash flows as net cash flows from financing activities?

a. $65,200
b. $94,800
c. $100,000
d. None of these

11-11 Chasse Building Supply Inc. reported net cash provided by operating activities of $243,000, capital expenditures of $112,900, cash dividends of $35,800, and average maturities of long-term debt over the next 5 years of $122,300. What is Chasse's free cash flow and cash flow adequacy ratio?

a. $94,300 and 0.77, respectively
b. $94,300 and 0.82, respectively
c. $130,100 and 1.06, respectively
d. $165,900 and 1.36, respectively

11-12 Smoltz Company reported the following information for the current year: cost of goods sold, $252,500; increase in inventory, $21,700; and increase in accounts payable, $12,200. What is the amount of cash paid to suppliers that Smoltz would report on its statement of cash flows under the direct method?

a. $218,600
b. $243,000
c. $262,000
d. $286,400

11-13 Romo Inc. reported the following information for the current year: operating expenses, $325,000; increase in prepaid expenses, $6,200; and decrease in accrued liabilities, $8,800. What is the amount of cash paid for operating expenses that Romo would report on its statement of cash flows under the direct method?

a. $310,000
b. $322,400
c. $327,600
d. $340,000

CORNERSTONE EXERCISES

Cornerstone Exercise 11-14 Classification of Cash Flows

OBJECTIVE 2
CORNERSTONE 11.1

Stanfield Inc. reported the following items in its statement of cash flows presented using the indirect method.

a. Decrease in inventory
b. Paid a cash dividend to stockholders
c. Purchased equipment for cash
d. Issued long-term debt
e. Depreciation expense
f. Sold a building for cash

Required:

Indicate whether each item should be classified as a cash flow from operating activities, a cash flow from investing activities, or a cash flow from financing activities.

OBJECTIVE 2
CORNERSTONE 11.1

Cornerstone Exercise 11-15 Classification of Cash Flows

Patel Company reported the following items in its statement of cash flows presented using the indirect method.

a. Issuance of common stock
b. Cash paid for interest
c. Sold equipment for cash
d. Receipt of cash dividend on investment
e. Repayment of principal on long-term debt
f. Loss on disposal of equipment.

Required:

Indicate whether each item should be classified as a cash flow from operating activities, a cash flow from investing activities, or a cash flow from financing activities.

Use the following information for Cornerstone Exercises 11-16 and 11-17:
A review of the balance sheet of Peterson Inc. revealed the following changes in the account balances:

a. Increase in long-term investment
b. Increase in accounts receivable
c. Increase in common stock
d. Increase in long-term debt
e. Decrease in accounts payable
f. Decrease in supplies inventory
g. Increase in prepaid insurance
h. Decrease in retained earnings

OBJECTIVE 2
CORNERSTONE 11.1

Cornerstone Exercise 11-16 Classification of Cash Flows

Refer to the information for Peterson Inc. above.

Required:

Classify each change in the balance sheet account as a cash flow from operating activities, a cash flow from investing activities, a cash flow from financing activities, or a noncash investing and financing activity.

OBJECTIVE 3
CORNERSTONE 11.2

Cornerstone Exercise 11-17 Analyzing Changes in Balance Sheet Accounts

Refer to the information for Peterson Inc. above.

Required:

Indicate whether each of the changes above produces a cash increase, a cash decrease, or is a noncash activity.

OBJECTIVE 4
CORNERSTONE 11.3

Cornerstone Exercise 11-18 Determining Net Cash Flow from Operating Activities

An analysis of the balance sheet and income statement of Sanchez Company revealed the following: net income, \$12,750; depreciation expense, \$32,600; decrease in accounts receivable, \$21,500; increase in inventory, \$18,300; increase in accounts payable, \$19,800; and decrease in interest payable of \$1,200.

Required:

Compute the net cash flows from operating activities using the indirect method.

OBJECTIVE 4
CORNERSTONE 11.3

Cornerstone Exercise 11-19 Determining Net Cash Flow from Operating Activities

Brandon Inc. reported the following items in its balance sheet and income statement: net income, \$105,600; gain on disposal of equipment, \$10,800; increase in accounts receivable, \$6,200; decrease in accounts payable, \$14,900; and increase in common stock, \$50,000.

Required:

Compute the net cash flows from operating activities using the indirect method.

Cornerstone Exercise 11-20 Determining Net Cash Flow from Investing Activities

OBJECTIVE 5
CORNERSTONE 11.4

Davis Inc. reported the following information:

	12/31/2013	12/31/2012
Equipment	$ 220,000	$155,000
Accumulated depreciation	(135,000)	115,200
Investment (long-term)	20,200	12,000

In addition, Davis sold equipment costing $22,900 with accumulated depreciation of $18,150 for $3,500 cash, producing a $1,250 loss. Davis reported net income for 2013 of $122,350.

Required:

Compute net cash flow from investing activities.

Cornerstone Exercise 11-21 Determining Net Cash Flow from Financing Activities

OBJECTIVE 6
CORNERSTONE 11.5

Hebert Company reported the following information for 2013:

Repaid long-term debt	$75,000
Paid interest on note payable	1,570
Issued common stock	30,000
Paid dividends	18,000

Required:

Compute net cash flow from financing activities.

Cornerstone Exercise 11-22 Analyzing the Statement of Cash Flows

OBJECTIVE 7
CORNERSTONE 11.6

Rollins Inc. is considering expanding its operations into different regions of the country; however, this expansion will require significant cash flow as well as additional financing. Rollins reported the following information for 2013: cash provided by operating activities, $387,200; cash provided by investing activities, $108,700; average debt maturing over the next 5 years, $345,500; capital expenditures, $261,430; cash dividends, $40,000.

Required:

Compute free cash flow and the cash flow adequacy ratio. (*Note:* Round ratio to two decimal places.) Comment on Rollins' ability to expand its operations.

Cornerstone Exercise 11-23 *(Appendix 11A)* Cash Receipts from Customers

OBJECTIVE 8
CORNERSTONE 11.7

Singleton Inc. had accounts receivable of $22,150 at January 1, 2013, and $26,850 at December 31, 2013. Net income for 2013 was $125,300 and sales revenue was $1,240,000.

Required:

Compute the amount of cash collected from customers using the direct method.

Cornerstone Exercise 11-24 *(Appendix 11A)* Cash Payments to Suppliers

OBJECTIVE 8
CORNERSTONE 11.7

Blackmon Company reported net income of $805,000 and cost of goods sold of $1,525,000 on its 2013 income statement. In addition, Blackmon reported an increase in inventory of $65,410, a decrease in prepaid insurance of $12,800, and a decrease in accounts payable of $43,190.

Required:

Compute the amount of cash payments to suppliers using the direct method.

Cornerstone Exercise 11-25 *(Appendix 11A)* Cash Payments for Operating Expenses

OBJECTIVE 8
CORNERSTONE 11.7

Luna Inc. reported operating expenses of $174,500, excluding depreciation expense of $36,200 for 2013. During 2013, Luna reported a decrease in prepaid expenses of $8,500 and a decrease in accrued liabilities of $18,200.

(Continued)

Required:

Compute the amount of cash payments for operating expenses using the direct method.

BRIEF EXERCISES

OBJECTIVE 1

Brief Exercise 11-26 Uses of the Statement of Cash Flows

Listed below are the three major financial statements and some of the ways in which they are used by investors, creditors and others.

Use	Financial Statement
a. Aids in understanding the differences between net income and cash flow.	1. Balance Sheet
b. Helps to assess a company's ability to produce future cash flows.	2. Income Statement
c. Assists in judging a company's ability to meets its obligations.	3. Statement of Cash Flows
d. Helps in estimating the need for external financing.	

Required:

Match each financial statement with its use. (Each use may be related to more than one financial statement, and financial statements may be used more than one time.)

OBJECTIVE 2

Brief Exercise 11-27 Classification of Cash Flows

Foster Company reported the following items in its statement of cash flows presented using the indirect method.

a. Interest paid on long-term note payable
b. Proceeds from sale of building
c. Increase in accounts payable
d. Increase in retained earnings
e. Cash dividend paid to stockholders
f. Taxes paid to the federal government

Required:

Indicate whether each item should be classified as a cash flow from operating activities, a cash flow from investing activities, or a cash flow from financing activities.

OBJECTIVE 2 3

Brief Exercise 11-28 Analyzing Balance Sheet Accounts

A review of the balance sheet of Dixon Company revealed the following changes in the account balances:

a. Increase in retained earnings
b. Increase in equipment
c. Increase in interest receivable
d. Decrease in bonds payable
e. Increase in unearned rent revenue
f. Decrease in prepaid insurance
g. Decrease in long-term investment
h. Increase in accounts payable

Required:

1. Classify each change in the balance sheet account as a cash flow from operating activities, a cash flow from investing activities, a cash flow from financing activities, or a noncash investing and financing activity.
2. Indicate whether each of the changes in the balance sheet accounts produces an increase in cash, produces a decrease in cash, or is a noncash activity.

OBJECTIVE 4

Brief Exercise 11-29 Determining Net Cash Flow from Operating Activities

Presented below are selected balance sheet information and the income statement for Burch Company.

Selected Balance Sheet Information		
	Dec. 31, 2013	Dec. 31, 2012
Cash	$20,000	$17,500
Accounts receivable	10,500	8,000
Inventory	18,000	21,000
Accounts payable	15,000	10,000
Income taxes payable	1,000	2,500

Burch Company Income Statement For the year ended December 31, 2013	
Sales	$ 250,000
Cost of goods sold	(160,000)
Depreciation expense	(15,000)
Other expenses	(35,000)
Income tax expense	(12,000)
Net income	$ 28,000

Required:

Compute the net cash flows from operating activities using the indirect method.

Brief Exercise 11-30 Determining Net Cash Flow from Investing Activities

OBJECTIVE 5

Orlando Inc. reported the following information:

	12/31/2013	12/31/2012
Furniture	$46,000	$32,000
Accumulated depreciation	15,900	12,500
Investment (long-term)	38,000	50,000

In addition, Orlando sold furniture costing $8,000 with accumulated depreciation of $5,000 for $3,500. Orlando also reported a $3,000 gain on the sale of long-term investments.

Required:

Compute net cash flow from investing activities.

Brief Exercise 11-31 Determining Net Cash Flow from Financing Activities

OBJECTIVE 6

Madison Company reported the following information:

	12/31/2013	12/31/2012
Notes payable	$ 95,000	$75,000
Common stock	120,000	80,000
Retained earnings	20,000	36,000

Madison reported net income of $26,000 for the year ended December 31, 2013. In addition, Madison repaid $35,000 of the notes payable during 2013.

Required:

Compute net cash flow from financing activities.

Brief Exercise 11-32 Analyzing the Statement of Cash Flows

OBJECTIVE 7

Manning Company reported the following information for 2013: cash provided by operating activities, $425,000; cash used by investing activities, $200,000; average debt maturing over the next 5 years, $80,000; capital expenditures, $275,000; cash dividends, $60,000.

Required:

Compute free cash flow and the cash flow adequacy ratio. (*Note:* Round ratios to two decimal places.) Comment on each ratio.

OBJECTIVE 8

Brief Exercise 11-33 *(Appendix 11A)* Determining Net Cash Flow from Operating Activities—Direct Method

Presented below are selected balance sheet information and the income statement for Burch Company.

Selected Balance Sheet Information

	Dec. 31, 2013	Dec. 31, 2012
Cash	$20,000	$17,500
Accounts receivable	10,500	8,000
Inventory	18,000	21,000
Accounts payable	15,000	10,000
Income taxes payable	1,000	2,500

Burch Company
Income Statement
For the year ended December 31, 2013

Sales	$ 250,000
Cost of goods sold	(160,000)
Depreciation expense	(15,000)
Other expenses	(35,000)
Income tax expense	(12,000)
Net income	$ 28,000

Required:

Compute the net cash flows from operating activities using the direct method.

EXERCISES

OBJECTIVE 2

Exercise 11-34 Classification of Cash Flows

A review of the financial records for Rogers Inc. uncovered the following items:

a. Collected accounts receivable
b. Paid cash to purchase equipment
c. Received cash from the issuance of bonds
d. Paid interest on long-term debt
e. Sold equipment at book value
f. Depreciation on equipment
g. Issued common stock for land
h. Paid rent on building for the current period
i. Paid cash to settle an account payable
j. Declared and paid dividends to stockholders
k. Received cash dividend on investment
l. Repaid the principal amount of long-term debt
m. Amortization of a copyright
n. Sold a long-term investment at a gain

Rogers uses the indirect method to prepare the operating activities of its statement of cash flows.

Required:

Indicate whether each item should be classified as a cash flow from operating activities, cash flow from investing activities, cash flow from financing activities, or noncash investing and financing activity.

OBJECTIVE 2

Exercise 11-35 Classification of Cash Flows

The following are several items that might be disclosed on a company's statement of cash flows presented using the indirect method.

a. Net income
b. Depreciation expense
c. Issuance of common stock
d. Loss on disposal of equipment
e. Purchase of a building
f. Decrease in accounts payable
g. Converted bonds into common stock
h. Sale of long-term investment
i. Payment of interest
j. Increase in inventory

Required:

1. Indicate whether each item should be classified as a cash flow from operating activities, cash flow from investing activities, cash flow from financing activities, or noncash investing and financing activity.
2. **CONCEPTUAL CONNECTION** Why is the proper classification of cash flows important?

Exercise 11-36 Analyzing Changes in Balance Sheet Accounts

OBJECTIVE 3

A review of the balance sheet of Mathews Company revealed the following changes in the account balances:

a. Increase in accounts receivable
b. Increase in retained earnings
c. Decrease in salaries payable
d. Increase in common stock
e. Decrease in inventory
f. Increase in accounts payable
g. Decrease in long-term debt
h. Increase in property, plant, and equipment

Required:

1. For each of the above items, indicate whether it produces a cash inflow or a cash outflow.
2. Classify each change as a cash flow from operating activities (indirect method), cash flow from investing activities, or cash flow from financing activities.

Exercise 11-37 Analyzing the Accounts

OBJECTIVE 3

Casey Company uses a perpetual inventory system and engaged in the following transactions:

a. Made credit sales of $825,000. The cost of the merchandise sold was $560,000.
b. Collected accounts receivable in the amount of $752,600.
c. Purchased goods on credit in the amount of $574,300.
d. Paid accounts payable in the amount of $536,200.

Required:

Prepare the journal entries necessary to record the transactions. Indicate whether each transaction increased cash, decreased cash, or had no effect on cash.

Exercise 11-38 Analyzing the Accounts

OBJECTIVE 3

The controller for Summit Sales Inc. provides the following information on transactions that occurred during the year:

a. Purchased supplies on credit, $18,600
b. Paid $14,800 cash toward the purchase in Transaction a
c. Provided services to customers on credit, $46,925
d. Collected $39,650 cash from accounts receivable
e. Recorded depreciation expense, $8,175
f. Employee salaries accrued, $15,650
g. Paid $15,650 cash to employees for salaries earned
h. Accrued interest expense on long-term debt, $1,950
i. Paid a total of $25,000 on long-term debt, which includes $1,950 interest from Transaction h
j. Paid $2,220 cash for 1 year's insurance coverage in advance
k. Recognized insurance expense, $1,340, that was paid in a previous period
l. Sold equipment with a book value of $7,500 for $7,500 cash
m. Declared cash dividend, $12,000
n. Paid cash dividend declared in Transaction m
o. Purchased new equipment for $28,300 cash.
p. Issued common stock for $60,000 cash
q. Used $10,700 of supplies to produce revenues

Summit Sales uses the indirect method to prepare its statement of cash flows.

Required:

1. Construct a table similar to the one shown at the top of the next page. Analyze each transaction and indicate its effect on the fundamental accounting equation. If the transaction increases a financial statement element, write the amount of the increase preceded by a plus sign (+) in the appropriate column. If the transaction decreases a financial statement element, write the amount of the decrease preceded by a minus sign (−) in the appropriate column.
2. Indicate whether each transaction results in a cash inflow or a cash outflow in the "Effect on Cash Flows" column. If the transaction has no effect on cash flow, then indicate this by placing "none" in the "Effect on Cash Flows" column.

(Continued)

3. For each transaction that affected cash flows, indicate whether the cash flow would be classified as a cash flow from operating activities, cash flow from investing activities, or cash flow from financing activities. If there is no effect on cash flows, indicate this as a noncash activity.

Effect on Accounting Equation

	Assets		Liabilities and Equity			
Transaction	Current	Noncurrent	Current Liabilities	Noncurrent Liabilities	Equity	Effect on Cash Flows

OBJECTIVE 4

Exercise 11-39 Reporting Net Cash Flow from Operating Activities

The following information is available for Cornelius Inc.:

Selected Income Statement Information	Amount
Net income	$52,000
Depreciation expense	11,300

Selected Balance Sheet Information	Beginning Balance	Ending Balance
Accounts receivable	$11,500	$17,650
Inventory	33,800	27,825
Accounts payable	15,900	24,600

Required:

1. Compute the net cash flows from operating activities using the indirect method.
2. **CONCEPTUAL CONNECTION** Explain why Cornelius was able to report net cash flow from operating activities that was higher than net income.
3. **CONCEPTUAL CONNECTION** What could the difference between net income and cash flow from operating activities signal to financial statement users?

OBJECTIVE 4

Exercise 11-40 Reporting Net Cash Flow from Operating Activities

The following information is available for Bernard Corporation for 2013:

Net income	$185,200	Decrease in income taxes payable	$ 3,870
Decrease in accounts receivable	8,300	Increase in notes payable (due 2017)	50,000
Increase in inventory	19,900	Depreciation expense	52,700
Decrease in prepaid rent	4,410	Loss on disposal of equipment	6,450
Increase in salaries payable	7,100		

Required:

1. Compute the net cash flows from operating activities using the indirect method.
2. **CONCEPTUAL CONNECTION** What are the causes of the major differences between net income and net cash flow from operating activities?

OBJECTIVE 5

ILLUSTRATING RELATIONSHIPS

Exercise 11-41 Determining Cash Flows from Investing Activities

Burns Company's 2013 and 2012 balance sheets presented the following data for equipment:

	12/31/2013	12/31/2012
Equipment	$325,000	$262,000
Accumulated depreciation	133,900	108,000
Book value	$191,100	$154,000

During 2013, equipment costing $41,000 with accumulated depreciation of $36,700 was sold for cash, producing a $3,200 gain.

Required:

1. Calculate the amount of depreciation expense for 2013.
2. Calculate the amount of cash spent for equipment during 2013.
3. Calculate the amount that should be included as a cash inflow from the disposal of equipment.

Exercise 11-42 Determining Cash Flows from Investing Activities

OBJECTIVE 5

ILLUSTRATING RELATIONSHIPS

Airco owns several aircraft and its balance sheet indicated the following amounts for its aircraft accounts at the end of 2013 and 2012:

	12/31/2013	12/31/2012
Equipment, aircraft	$32,700,000	$22,250,000
Accumulated depreciation	13,900,000	13,125,000
Book value	$18,800,000	$ 9,125,000

Required:

1. Assume that Airco did not sell any aircraft during 2013. Determine the amount of depreciation expense for 2013 and the cash spent for aircraft purchases in 2013.
2. If Airco sold for cash aircraft that cost $4,100,000 with accumulated depreciation of $3,825,000 producing a gain of $193,000, determine (a) the amount of depreciation expense, (b) the cash paid for aircraft purchases in 2013, and (c) the cash inflow from the disposal of aircraft.

Exercise 11-43 Determining Cash Flows from Financing Activities

OBJECTIVE 6

ILLUSTRATING RELATIONSHIPS

Solomon Construction Company reported the following amount on its balance sheet at the end of 2013 and 2012 for notes payable:

	12/31/2013	12/31/2012
Notes payable	$200,000	$120,000

Required:

1. If Solomon did not repay any notes payable during 2013, determine how much cash Solomon received from the issuance of notes payable.
2. If Solomon repaid $40,000 of notes payable during 2013, determine what amounts Solomon would report in the financing activities section of the statement of cash flows.

Exercise 11-44 Determining Cash Flows from Financing Activities

OBJECTIVE 6

ILLUSTRATING RELATIONSHIPS

Nichols Inc. reported the following amounts on its balance sheet at the end of 2013 and 2012 for equity:

	12/31/2013	12/31/2012
Common stock	$210,000	$135,000
Retained earnings	495,300	412,800

Required:

Assume that Nichols did not retire any stock during 2013, it reported $105,610 of net income for 2013, and any dividends declared were paid in cash. Determine the amounts Nichols would report in the financing section of the statement of cash flows.

Exercise 11-45 Partial Statement of Cash Flows

OBJECTIVE 4 5 6

Service Company had net income during the current year of $65,800. The following information was obtained from Service's balance sheet:

Accounts receivable	$26,540 increase
Inventory	32,180 increase
Accounts payable	9,300 decrease
Interest payable	2,120 increase
Accumulated depreciation (Building)	14,590 increase
Accumulated depreciation (Equipment)	32,350 increase

(Continued)

Additional Information:

1. Equipment with accumulated depreciation of $18,000 was sold during the year.
2. Cash dividends of $29,625 were paid during the year.

Required:

1. Prepare the net cash flows from operating activities using the indirect method.
2. **CONCEPTUAL CONNECTION** How would the cash proceeds from the sale of equipment be reported on the statement of cash flows?
3. **CONCEPTUAL CONNECTION** How would the cash dividends be reported on the statement of cash flows?
4. **CONCEPTUAL CONNECTION** What could the difference between net income and cash flow from operating activities signal to financial statement users?

OBJECTIVE 7

Exercise 11-46 Analyzing the Statement of Cash Flows

Information for Ditka Inc. and McMahon Company is given below:

	Ditka Inc.	McMahon Company
Cash provided by operating activities	$2,475,000	$1,639,000
Capital expenditures	1,157,000	748,000
Dividends	285,000	189,000
Average debt maturity over next 5 years	985,000	1,212,000

Required:

1. Compute Ditka's and McMahon's free cash flow and cash flow adequacy ratio. (*Note:* Round ratio to two decimal places.)
2. **CONCEPTUAL CONNECTION** What information do these cash-based performance measures provide with regard to the two companies?

OBJECTIVE 4 5 6 7

Exercise 11-47 Preparing the Statement of Cash Flows

The comparative balance sheets for Beckwith Products Company are presented below.

	2013	2012
Assets:		
Cash	$ 36,950	$ 25,000
Accounts receivable	75,100	78,000
Inventory	45,300	36,000
Property, plant, and equipment	256,400	153,000
Accumulated depreciation	38,650	20,000
Total assets	$375,100	$272,000
Liabilities and Equity:		
Accounts payable	$ 13,100	$ 11,000
Interest payable	11,500	8,000
Wages payable	8,100	9,000
Notes payable	105,000	90,000
Common stock	100,000	50,000
Retained earnings	137,400	104,000
Total liabilities and equity	$375,100	$272,000

Additional Information:

1. Net income for 2013 was $58,400.
2. Cash dividends of $25,000 were declared and paid during 2013.
3. During 2013, Beckwith issued $50,000 of notes payable and repaid $35,000 principal relating to notes payable.

4. Common stock was issued for $50,000 cash.
5. Depreciation expense was $18,650, and there were no disposals of equipment.

Required:

1. Prepare a statement of cash flows (indirect method) for Beckwith Products for 2013.
2. Compute the following cash-based performance measures: (a) free cash flow and (b) cash flow adequacy. (*Note:* Assume that the average amount of debt maturing over the next 5 years is $85,000. Round ratio to two decimal places.)
3. **CONCEPTUAL CONNECTION** What can you conclude by examining the patterns in Beckwith's cash flows?

Exercise 11-48 *(Appendix 11A)* Preparing Net Cash Flows from Operating Activities—Direct Method

OBJECTIVE 8

Colassard Industries has the following data available for preparation of its statement of cash flows:

Sales revenue	$385,800	Inventory, increase	$ 8,710
Cost of goods sold	203,100	Prepaid insurance, increase	1,550
Wages expense	62,400	Accounts payable, increase	3,680
Insurance expense	13,780	Notes payable, increase	40,000
Interest expense	15,150	Interest payable, increase	1,240
Income taxes expense	27,400	Wages payable, decrease	6,700
Accounts receivable, decrease	15,600		

Required:

Prepare the cash flows from operating activities section of the statement of cash flows using the direct method.

Exercise 11-49 *(Appendix 11A)* Preparing a Statement of Cash Flows—Direct Method

OBJECTIVE 8

The controller of Newstrom Software Inc. provides the following information as the basis for a statement of cash flows:

Cash collected from customers	$785,400	Income taxes paid	$ 58,300
Cash paid for interest	22,100	Payment of dividends	35,000
Cash paid to employees and other suppliers of goods and services	221,750	Principal payments on mortgage payable	60,000
Cash paid to suppliers of merchandise	395,540	Principal payments on long-term debt	22,000
Cash received from the issuance of long-term debt	40,000	Proceeds from the issuance of common stock	85,000
Cash received from disposal of equipment	42,500	Purchase of equipment	120,000
Cash received from sale of long-term investments	71,400	Purchase of long-term investments	75,800

Required:

1. Calculate the net cash provided (used) by operating activities.
2. Calculate the net cash provided (used) by investing activities.
3. Calculate the net cash provided (used) by financing activities.

OBJECTIVE 8

Exercise 11-50 *(Appendix 11A)* Preparing a Statement of Cash Flows—Direct Method

Financial statements for Rowe Publishing Company are presented below.

Rowe Publishing Company
Balance Sheets
December 31, 2013 and 2012

	2013		2012	
ASSETS				
Current assets:				
Cash		$ 85,000		$ 66,000
Accounts receivable		240,000		231,000
Inventory		190,000		170,000
Total current assets		$515,000		$467,000
Property, plant, and equipment:				
Building	$ 400,000		$ 400,000	
Equipment	155,000		130,000	
	$ 555,000		$ 530,000	
Accumulated depreciation	(375,000)		(350,000)	
Net property, plant, and equipment		180,000		180,000
Total assets		$695,000		$647,000
LIABILITIES AND EQUITY				
Current liabilities:				
Accounts payable	$133,000		$121,000	
Salaries payable	15,000		11,000	
Income taxes payable	10,000		17,000	
Total current liabilities		$158,000		$149,000
Long-term liabilities:				
Notes payable	$115,000		$150,000	
Bonds payable	50,000		0	
Total long-term liabilities		165,000		150,000
Total liabilities		$323,000		$299,000
Equity:				
Common stock	$300,000		$300,000	
Retained earnings	72,000		48,000	
Total equity		372,000		348,000
Total liabilities and equity		$695,000		$647,000

Rowe Publishing Company
Income Statement
For the year ended December 31, 2013

Sales		$1,051,000
Less: Cost of goods sold		(578,000)
Gross margin		$ 473,000
Less operating expenses:		
Salaries	$(351,000)	
Depreciation	(25,000)	(376,000)
Income from operations		$ 97,000
Less: Interest expense		(16,000)
Income before taxes		$ 81,000
Less: Income taxes expense		(22,000)
Net income		$ 59,000

Additional Information:

1. No buildings or equipment were sold during 2013. Equipment was purchased for $25,000 cash.
2. Notes payable in the amount of $35,000 were repaid during 2013.
3. Bonds payable of $50,000 were issued for cash during 2013.
4. Rowe Publishing declared and paid dividends of $35,000 during 2013.

Required:

Prepare a statement of cash flows for 2013, using the direct method to determine net cash flow from operating activities.

Exercise 11-51 *(Appendix 11B)* Using a Spreadsheet to Prepare a Statement of Cash Flows

OBJECTIVE 9

Comparative balance sheets for Cincinnati Health Club are presented below.

Cincinnati Health Club
Balance Sheets
December 31, 2013 and 2012

	2013		2012	
ASSETS				
Current assets:				
Cash		$ 5,300		$ 9,200
Accounts receivable		10,500		8,900
Inventory		19,800		18,600
Total current assets		$ 35,600		$ 36,700
Property, plant, and equipment:				
Building	$ 490,000		$ 490,000	
Equipment	280,000		270,000	
	$ 770,000		$ 760,000	
Accumulated depreciation	(148,000)		(120,000)	
Net property, plant, and equipment		622,000		640,000
Total assets		$657,600		$676,700
LIABILITIES AND EQUITY				
Current liabilities:				
Accounts payable	$ 55,300		$ 36,100	
Salaries payable	9,500		11,700	
Income taxes payable	1,100		9,900	
Total current liabilities		$ 65,900		$ 57,700
Long-term liabilities:				
Bonds payable		350,000		400,000
Total liabilities		$415,900		$457,700
Equity:				
Common stock	$180,000		$150,000	
Retained earnings	61,700		69,000	
Total equity		241,700		219,000
Total liabilities and equity		$657,600		$676,700

Additional Information:

1. Cincinnati Health Club reported net income of $2,700 for 2013.
2. No buildings or equipment were sold during 2013. Equipment was purchased for $10,000 cash.
3. Depreciation expense for 2013 was $28,000.
4. Bonds payable of $50,000 were issued for cash during 2013.
5. Common stock of $30,000 was issued during 2013.
6. Cash dividends of $10,000 were declared and paid during 2013.

Required:

Using a spreadsheet, prepare a statement of cash flows for 2013. Assume Cincinnati Health Club uses the indirect method.

PROBLEM SET A

Problem 11-52A Classifying and Analyzing Business Activities

OBJECTIVE 2 3

CTT Inc. reported the following business activities during 2013:

a. Purchased property, plant, and equipment for cash
b. Purchased merchandise inventory for cash
c. Recorded depreciation on property, plant, and equipment
d. Issued common stock for cash

(Continued)

e. Purchased merchandise inventory on credit
f. Collected cash sales from customers
g. Paid cash dividends
h. Purchased a 2-year insurance policy for cash
i. Paid salaries of employees
j. Borrowed cash by issuing a note payable
k. Sold property, plant, and equipment for cash
l. Paid cash for principal amount of mortgage
m. Paid interest on mortgage

Required:

1. Indicate whether each activity should be classified as a cash flow from operating activities, cash flow from investing activities, cash flow from financing activities, or noncash investing and financing activity. Assume that CTT uses the indirect method.
2. For each activity that is reported on the statement of cash flows, indicate whether it produces a cash inflow, cash outflow, or no cash effect.

OBJECTIVE 4

Problem 11-53A Reporting Net Cash Flow from Operating Activities

The income statement for Granville Manufacturing Company is presented below.

Granville Manufacturing Company
Income Statement
For the year ended December 31, 2013

Sales		$4,199,830
Cost of goods sold		2,787,210
Gross margin		$1,412,620
Operating expenses:		
Salaries expense	$831,800	
Depreciation expense	246,100	
Administrative expense	131,000	
Bad debt expense	51,700	
Other expenses	43,900	1,304,500
Net income		$ 108,120

The following balance sheet changes occurred during the year:

- Accounts receivable increased by $182,400.
- Inventory increased by $98,725.
- Prepaid expenses decreased by $64,100.
- Accounts payable increased by $43,850.
- Salaries payable increased by $54,900.

Required:

1. Prepare the net cash flows from operating activities using the indirect method.
2. **CONCEPTUAL CONNECTION** What are the causes of the major differences between net income and net cash flow from operating activities?

OBJECTIVE 2 3 4

Problem 11-54A Classification of Cash Flows

Rolling Meadows Country Club Inc. is a privately owned corporation that operates a golf club. Rolling Meadows reported the following inflows and outflows of cash during 2013:

Net income	$125,800	Cash received from sale of used golf carts	$12,700
Decrease in accounts receivable	7,175	Depreciation expense (buildings)	35,100
Increase in pro shop inventory	23,300	Depreciation expense (golf carts)	21,250
Increase in prepaid insurance	12,600	Proceeds from issuance of note payable	60,000
Increase in accounts payable	13,210	Payment on mortgage payable	42,000
Decrease in wages payable	7,400	Cash received from issuance of common stock	41,375
Increase in income taxes payable	2,125	Payment of cash dividends	40,000
Cash paid for new golf carts	85,000		

Rolling Meadows had cash on hand at 1/1/2013 of $8,500.

Required:

1. Prepare a properly formatted statement of cash flows using the indirect method.
2. **CONCEPTUAL CONNECTION** What can you conclude by examining the patterns in Rolling Meadow's cash flows?

Problem 11-55A Preparing a Statement of Cash Flows

OBJECTIVE 4 5 6

Erie Company reported the following comparative balance sheets:

	2013	2012
Assets:		
Cash	$ 33,200	$ 12,750
Accounts receivable	53,000	44,800
Inventory	29,500	27,500
Prepaid rent	2,200	6,200
Investments (long-term)	17,600	31,800
Property, plant, and equipment	162,000	149,450
Accumulated depreciation	(61,600)	(56,200)
Total assets	$235,900	$216,300
Liabilities and Equity:		
Accounts payable	$ 16,900	$ 19,500
Interest payable	3,500	4,800
Wages payable	9,600	7,100
Income taxes payable	5,500	3,600
Notes payable	28,000	53,000
Common stock	100,000	68,500
Retained earnings	72,400	59,800
Total liabilities and equity	$235,900	$216,300

Additional Information:

1. Net income for 2013 was $20,500.
2. Cash dividends of $7,900 were declared and paid during 2013.
3. Long-term investments with a cost of $28,600 were sold for cash at a gain of $4,100. Additional long-term investments were purchased for $14,400 cash.
4. Equipment with a cost of $14,800 and accumulated depreciation of $13,500 was sold for $3,800 cash. New equipment was purchased for $27,350 cash.
5. Depreciation expense was $18,900.
6. A principal payment of $25,000 was made on long-term notes.
7. Common stock was sold for $31,500 cash.

Required:

Prepare a statement of cash flows for Erie using the indirect method to compute net cash flow from operating activities.

Problem 11-56A Preparing a Statement of Cash Flows

OBJECTIVE 4 5 6

Monon Cable Television Company reported the following financial statements for 2013:

(Continued)

Monon Cable Television Company
Balance Sheets
December 31, 2013 and 2012

	2013		2012	
ASSETS				
Current assets:				
Cash		$ 2,000		$ 8,000
Accounts receivable		11,300		6,000
Supplies		1,200		1,700
Total current assets		$ 14,500		$ 15,700
Property, plant, and equipment:				
Equipment (antenna)	$ 60,000		$ 35,000	
Buildings	210,000		190,000	
Trucks	81,000		75,000	
	$ 351,000		$ 300,000	
Accumulated depreciation	(125,000)		(131,000)	
Net property, plant, and equipment		226,000		169,000
Total assets		$240,500		$184,700
LIABILITIES AND EQUITY				
Current liabilities:				
Accounts payable	$ 6,500		$ 8,000	
Rent payable	4,900		13,600	
Royalties payable	3,300		3,100	
Total current liabilities		$ 14,700		$ 24,700
Long-term liabilities:				
Notes payable (long-term)		40,000		0
Total liabilities		$ 54,700		$ 24,700
Equity:				
Common stock	$100,000		$100,000	
Retained earnings	85,800		60,000	
Total equity		185,800		160,000
Total liabilities and equity		$240,500		$184,700

Monon Cable Television Company
Income Statement
For the year ended December 31, 2013

Sales		$519,000
Less operating expenses:		
Royalties expense	$240,000	
Salaries expense	26,000	
Utilities expense	83,000	
Supplies expense	13,000	
Rent expense	79,000	
Depreciation expense	28,000	469,000
Income from operations		$ 50,000
Other income (expenses):		
Gain on disposal of property, plant, and equipment	$ 800	
Interest expense	(1,800)	(1,000)
Income before taxes		$ 49,000
Less: Income taxes expense		(9,000)
Net income		$ 40,000

Additional Information:

1. Equipment (an old antenna) with a cost of $35,000 and accumulated depreciation of $34,000 was taken down and sold as scrap for $1,800 cash during 2013. A new antenna was purchased for cash at an installed cost of $60,000.
2. A building was purchased for $20,000 cash.
3. Trucks were purchased for $6,000 cash.
4. Depreciation expense for 2013 was $28,000.
5. A long-term note payable was issued for $40,000 cash.
6. Dividends of $14,200 were paid during 2013.

Required:

1. Prepare a statement of cash flows using the indirect method to compute net cash flow from operating activities.
2. **CONCEPTUAL CONNECTION** Explain what has been responsible for the decrease in cash.

OBJECTIVE 8

Problem 11-57A *(Appendix 11A)* Preparing Net Cash Flows from Operating Activities—Direct Method

Yogurt Plus, a restaurant, collected the following information on inflows and outflows for 2013:

Inflows		**Outflows**	
Sales (all for cash)	$334,500	Cash payments made for merchandise sold	$176,450
Cash received from sale of common stock	72,000	Cash payments for operating expenses	115,210
Proceeds from issuance of long-term notes payable	50,000	Cash payments for interest	24,600
Proceeds from sale of used restaurant furniture	11,300	Cash payments for income taxes	9,475
Proceeds from issuance of short-term note payable	15,000	Purchase of restaurant furniture for cash	108,800
Notes payable issued in exchange for kitchen equipment	30,000	Principal payment on mortgage	35,000
		Payment of dividends	10,000
		Cost of kitchen equipment acquired in exchange for note payable	30,000

Yogurt Plus had a cash balance of $21,800 at 1/1/2013.

Required:

1. Prepare a statement of cash flows using the direct method to determine net cash flow from operating activities.
2. **CONCEPTUAL CONNECTION** What can you conclude by examining the patterns in Yogurt Plus's cash flows?

Problem 11-58A *(Appendix 11A)* Preparing Net Cash Flows from Operating Activities—Direct Method

OBJECTIVE 8

Refer to the information for Granville Manufacturing Company in **Problem 11-53A**.

Required:

Prepare the cash flows from operating activities section of the statement of cash flows using the direct method.

Problem 11-59A *(Appendix 11B)* Using a Spreadsheet to Prepare a Statement of Cash Flows

OBJECTIVE 9

Jane Bahr, a controller of Endicott & Thurston, prepared the following balance sheets at the end of 2013 and 2012:

Endicott & Thurston Associates
Balance Sheets
December 31, 2013 and 2012

	2013		2012	
ASSETS				
Current assets:				
Cash		$ 2,000		$ 17,000
Accounts receivable		78,000		219,000
Prepaid rent		29,000		104,000
Total current assets		$109,000		$340,000
Long-term investments		51,000		40,000
Property, plant, and equipment:				
Equipment, computing	$ 488,000		$ 362,000	
Furniture	400,000		365,000	
	$ 888,000		$ 727,000	
Accumulated depreciation	(366,000)		(554,000)	
Net property, plant, and equipment		522,000		173,000
Total assets		$682,000		$553,000
LIABILITIES AND EQUITY				
Current liabilities:				
Accounts payable	$ 56,000		$ 58,000	
Salaries payable	89,000		105,000	
Total current liabilities		$145,000		$163,000
Long-term liabilities:				
Notes payable		80,000		105,000
Bonds payable		140,000		0
Total liabilities		$365,000		$268,000
Equity:				
Common stock	$225,000		$225,000	
Retained earnings	92,000		60,000	
Total equity		317,000		285,000
Total liabilities and equity		$682,000		$553,000

Additional Information:

1. Computing equipment with a cost of $250,000 and accumulated depreciation of $230,000 was sold for $5,000. New computing equipment was purchased for $376,000.
2. New office furniture was purchased at a cost of $35,000.
3. Depreciation expense for 2013 was $42,000.
4. Investments costing $20,000 were sold for cash at a loss of $2,000. Additional investments were purchased for $31,000 cash.
5. A $25,000 principal payment on the long-term note was made during 2013.
6. A portion of the cash needed to purchase computing equipment was secured by issuing bonds payable for $140,000 cash.
7. Net income was $70,000 and dividends were $38,000.

(Continued)

Required:

1. Using a spreadsheet, prepare a statement of cash flows for 2013. Assume Endicott & Thurston use the indirect method.
2. **CONCEPTUAL CONNECTION** Discuss whether Endicott & Thurston appear to have matched the timing of inflows and outflows of cash.

PROBLEM SET B

OBJECTIVE 2 3

Problem 11-52B Classifying and Analyzing Business Activities

Cowell Company had the following business activities during 2013:

a. Paid cash dividend to stockholders
b. Paid cash for inventory
c. Purchased equipment for cash
d. Paid interest on long-term debt
e. Acquired land in exchange for common stock
f. Issued common stock for cash
g. Paid salaries to employees
h. Received cash from the sale of merchandise
i. Recorded amortization related to an intangible asset
j. Issued bonds payable in exchange for cash
k. Sold equipment for cash
l. Purchased inventory on account

Cowell Company uses the indirect method to prepare its statement of cash flows.

Required:

1. Indicate whether each activity should be classified as a cash flow from operating activities, cash flow from investing activities, cash flow from financing activities, or noncash investing and financing activity.
2. For each activity that is reported on the statement of cash flows, indicate whether each activity produces a cash inflow, cash outflow, or no cash effect.

OBJECTIVE 4

Problem 11-53B Reporting Net Cash Flow from Operating Activities

The income statement for Dunn Products Inc. is presented below.

Dunn Products Inc. Income Statement For the year ended December 31, 2013		
Sales		$3,584,600
Cost of goods sold		2,557,500
Gross margin		$1,027,100
Other expenses:		
Salaries expense	$455,100	
Administrative expense	247,000	
Depreciation expense	214,500	
Bad debt expense	37,000	
Income taxes expense	28,200	981,800
Net income		$ 45,300

The following balance sheet changes occurred during the year:

- Accounts receivable decreased by $85,150.
- Inventory decreased by $138,620.
- Prepaid expenses increased by $112,400.
- Accounts payable decreased by $67,225.
- Salaries payable increased by $18,300.

Required:

1. Prepare the net cash flows from operating activities using the indirect method.
2. **CONCEPTUAL CONNECTION** What are the causes of the major differences between net income and net cash flow from operating activities?

Problem 11-54B Classification of Cash Flows

OBJECTIVE 2 3 4

Fannin Company is a manufacturer of premium athletic equipment. Fannin reported the following inflows and outflows of cash during 2013.

Net income	$594,600	Cash received from sale of investment	$ 22,850
Increase in accounts receivable	23,400	Cash paid for property, plant, and equipment	101,325
Decrease in inventory	61,250	Depreciation expense	93,410
Decrease in prepaid insurance	47,600	Proceeds from issuance of note payable	50,000
Decrease in accounts payable	31,550	Payment on bonds payable	200,000
Decrease in income taxes payable	7,600	Cash received from issuance of common stock	20,000
Increase in wages payable	18,200	Payment of cash dividends	30,000

Fannin had cash on hand at 1/1/2013 of $118,250.

Required:

1. Prepare a properly formatted statement of cash flows using the indirect method.
2. **CONCEPTUAL CONNECTION** What can you conclude by examining the patterns in Fannin's cash flows?

Problem 11-55B Preparing a Statement of Cash Flows

OBJECTIVE 4 5 6

Volusia Company reported the following comparative balance sheets for 2013:

Volusia Company
Balance Sheet
December 31, 2012 and 2013

	2013	2012
ASSETS		
Cash	$ 28,100	$ 16,300
Accounts receivable	26,500	32,725
Inventory	24,100	28,200
Prepaid rent	3,900	1,800
Investments, long-term	37,200	25,500
Property, plant, and equipment	115,000	102,975
Accumulated depreciation	(47,100)	(38,600)
Total assets	$187,700	$168,900
LIABILITIES AND EQUITY		
Accounts payable	$ 24,900	$ 21,200
Interest payable	4,700	3,300
Wages payable	4,600	6,900
Income taxes payable	3,500	5,200
Notes payable	35,000	30,000
Common stock	72,900	65,000
Retained earnings	42,100	37,300
Total liabilities and equity	$187,700	$168,900

Additional Information:

1. Net income for 2013 was $18,300.
2. Cash dividends of $13,500 were declared and paid during 2013.
3. Long-term investments with a cost of $21,200 were sold for cash at a loss of $1,500. Additional long-term investments were purchased for $32,900 cash.
4. Equipment with a cost of $25,000 and accumulated depreciation of $16,300 was sold for $4,500 cash. New equipment was purchased for $37,025 cash.
5. Depreciation expense was $24,800.
6. A principal payment of $15,000 was made on long-term notes. Volusia issued notes payable for $20,000 cash.
7. Common stock was sold for $7,900 cash.

Required:

Prepare a statement of cash flows for Volusia using the indirect method to compute net cash flow from operating activities.

OBJECTIVE 4 5 6

Problem 11-56B Preparing a Statement of Cash Flows

SDPS Inc. provides airport transportation services in southern California. An income statement for 2013 and balance sheets for 2013 and 2012 appear below.

SDPS Inc.
Balance Sheets
December 31, 2013 and 2012

	2013		2012	
ASSETS				
Current assets:				
Cash		$ 40,000		$ 82,000
Accounts receivable		126,000		109,000
Supplies, fuel		11,000		25,000
Total current assets		$177,000		$216,000
Property, plant, and equipment:				
Equipment, vehicles	$ 524,000		$ 409,000	
Accumulated depreciation	(174,000)		(136,000)	
Net property, plant, and equipment		350,000		273,000
Total assets		$527,000		$489,000
LIABILITIES AND EQUITY				
Current liabilities:				
Accounts payable	$103,000		$ 58,000	
Wages payable	22,000		29,000	
Repair and maintenance payable	41,000		34,000	
Rent payable	92,000		51,000	
Total current liabilities		$258,000		$172,000
Long-term liabilities:				
Notes payable		100,000		125,000
Total liabilities		$358,000		$297,000
Equity:				
Common stock	$150,000		$150,000	
Retained earnings	19,000		42,000	
Total equity		169,000		192,000
Total liabilities and equity		$527,000		$489,000

SDPS Inc.
Income Statement
For the year ended December 31, 2013

Sales		$937,000
Less operating expenses:		
Wages expense	$278,000	
Rent expense	229,000	
Supplies expense	83,000	
Maintenance expense	138,000	
Depreciation expense	215,000	943,000
Income (loss) from operations		$ (6,000)
Other income (expenses):		
Loss on disposal of property, plant, and equipment	$ (3,000)	
Interest expense	(14,000)	(17,000)
Net loss		$ (23,000)

Additional Information:

1. Vehicles with a cost of $310,000 and accumulated depreciation of $177,000 were sold for $130,000 cash. New vehicles were purchased for $425,000 cash.
2. A $25,000 principal payment on the long-term note was made during 2013.
3. No dividends were paid during 2013.

Required:

1. Prepare a statement of cash flows using the indirect method to compute net cash flow from operating activities.
2. **CONCEPTUAL CONNECTION** Explain what has been responsible for the decrease in cash.
3. **CONCEPTUAL CONNECTION** Determine how SDPS financed its increase in net property, plant, and equipment during a period in which it had a substantial net loss.

Problem 11-57B *(Appendix 11A)* Preparing Net Cash Flows from Operating Activities—Direct Method

OBJECTIVE 8

Befuddled Corporation collected the following information on inflows and outflows for 2013:

Inflows		**Outflows**	
Cash collections from sales	$956,500	Cash payments for cost of goods sold	$534,900
Proceeds from disposal of equipment	11,250	Cash payments for operating expenses	193,200
Proceeds received from issuance of notes payable	30,000	Cash payments for interest	36,400
		Cash payments for income taxes	21,300
		Cash payments for purchases of equipment	217,150
		Repayment of short-term notes payable	20,000
		Payment of cash dividends	38,000

Befuddled had a cash balance of $89,200 on 1/1/2013.

Required:

1. Prepare a statement of cash flows using the direct method to determine net cash flow from operating activities.
2. CONCEPTUAL CONNECTION What can you conclude by examining the patterns in Befuddled's cash flows?

Problem 11-58B *(Appendix 11A)* Preparing Net Cash Flows from Operating Activities—Direct Method

OBJECTIVE 8

Refer to the information for Dunn Products Inc. in **Problem 11-53B**.

Required:

Prepare the cash flows from operating activities section of the statement of cash flows using the direct method.

OBJECTIVE 9

Problem 11-59B *(Appendix 11B)* Using a Spreadsheet to Prepare a Statement of Cash Flows

Fleet Limousine Service Inc. began operations in late March 2013. At the end of 2013, the following balance sheet was prepared for Fleet.

Fleet Limousine Service Inc.
Balance Sheets
December 31, 2013

ASSETS		
Current assets:		
Cash	$ 7,200	
Accounts receivable	15,900	
Supplies	3,100	
Total current assets		$ 26,200
Long-term investments		15,000
Property, plant, and equipment:		
Land	$ 11,000	
Building	175,000	
Equipment	233,400	
	$419,400	
Accumulated depreciation	(35,500)	
Net property, plant, and equipment		383,900
Total assets		$425,100
LIABILITIES AND EQUITY		
Current liabilities:		
Accounts payable	$ 12,700	
Unearned service revenue	21,800	
Salaries payable	4,600	
Rent payable	8,200	
Total current liabilities		$ 47,300
Long-term liabilities:		
Notes payable		95,000
Total liabilities		$142,300
Equity:		
Common stock	$300,000	
Retained earnings	(17,200)	
Total equity		282,800
Total liabilities and equity		$425,100

Additional Information:

1. During 2013, land was purchased for $11,000, a building was purchased for $175,000, and equipment was purchased for $233,400.
2. Depreciation expense for 2013 was $35,500.
3. The long-term note was issued for $100,000, and a principal payment of $5,000 was made during 2013.
4. Common stock was issued for $300,000 cash during 2013.
5. During 2013, there was a net loss of $17,200, and no dividends were paid.

Required:

1. Using a spreadsheet, prepare a statement of cash flows for 2013. Assume Fleet Limousine uses the indirect method.
2. **CONCEPTUAL CONNECTION** Discuss whether Fleet Limousine appears to have matched the timing of inflows and outflows of cash.

CASES

Case 11-60 The Statement of Cash Flows and Credit Analysis

June's Camera Shop sells cameras and photographic supplies of all types to retail customers. June's also repairs cameras and provides color prints. To compete with other camera departments, June's offers fast, efficient, and effective repairs and photographic processing. For fiscal 2013 and 2012, June's accountant prepared the following statements of cash flows:

June's Camera Shop
Statements of Cash Flows
For the years ended January 31, 2013 and 2012

	2013		2012	
Cash flows from operating activities				
Net income		$ 87,000		$ 63,000
Adjustments to reconcile net income to net cash provided by operating activities:				
Depreciation expense	$ 41,000		$ 37,000	
Increase in accounts receivable	(17,000)		(12,000)	
Increase in inventory	(19,000)		(11,000)	
Increase in accounts payable	15,000		14,000	
Increase in wages payable	11,000		5,000	
Increase in income taxes payable	6,000		3,000	
Total adjustments		37,000		36,000
Net cash provided by operating activities		$124,000		$ 99,000
Cash flows from investing activities				
Purchase of long-term investments	$(15,000)		$(10,000)	
Purchase of equipment	(45,000)		(40,000)	
Net cash used by investing activities		(60,000)		(50,000)
Cash flows from financing activities				
Principal payments on mortgage	$(15,000)		$(15,000)	
Payment of dividends	(12,000)		(10,000)	
Net cash used by financing activities		(27,000)		(25,000)
Net increase in cash and cash equivalents		$ 37,000		$ 24,000
Cash and cash equivalents at beginning of year		158,000		134,000
Cash and cash equivalents at end of year		$195,000		$158,000

Required:

1. Does June's Camera Shop appear to have grown (in terms of property, plant, and equipment) during the past 2 years?
2. June's president, June Smith, would like to open a second store. Smith believes that $225,000 is needed to equip the facility properly. The business has $100,000 of cash and liquid investments to apply toward the $225,000 required. Do the data in the 2013 and 2012 statements of cash flow suggest whether or not June's Camera Shop is likely to be able to secure a loan for the remaining $125,000 needed for the expansion?
3. How long should it take June's Camera Shop to pay back the $125,000?

Case 11-61 Profitability Declines and the Statement of Cash Flows

The Bookbarn Inc. is a retail seller of new books in a moderate-sized city. Although initially very successful, The Bookbarn's sales volume has declined since the opening of two competing bookstores 2 years ago. The accountant for The Bookbarn prepared the following statement of cash flows at the end of the current year:

The Bookbarn Inc.
Statement of Cash Flows
For the year ended December 31, 2013

Cash flows from operating activities		
Net income		$ 26,500
Adjustments to reconcile net income to net cash provided by operating activities:		
Depreciation expense	$ 38,500	
Loss on disposal of property, plant, and equipment	2,100	
Increase in accounts receivable	(1,200)	
Increase in inventory	(3,800)	
Increase in accounts payable	6,700	
Decrease in wages payable	(1,200)	
Total adjustments		41,100
Net cash provided by operating activities		$ 67,600
Cash flows from investing activities		
Purchase of equipment	$(12,000)	
Proceeds from disposal of equipment	2,300	
Net cash used by investing activities		(9,700)
Cash flows from financing activities		
Payment of dividends	$ (4,000)	
Repayment of mortgage	(10,000)	
Net cash used by financing activities		(14,000)
Net increase in cash		$ 43,900

Your analysis suggests that The Bookbarn's net income will continue to decline by $8,000 per year to $18,500 as sales continue to fall. Thereafter, you expect sales to stabilize.

Required:

1. What will happen to the amount of cash provided by operations as net income decreases?
2. Assume that equipment is nearly fully depreciated but that it will be fully serviceable for several years. What will happen to cash flows from operations as depreciation declines?
3. Do the operations of businesses experiencing declining sales volumes always consume cash? Explain your answer.
4. Can current assets and current liabilities buffer operating cash flows against the impact of declines in sales volume in the short run? In the long run? Explain your answer.

Case 11-62 Preparing a Prospective Statement of Cash Flows

Jane and Harvey Wentland have decided to open a retail athletic supply store, Fitness Outfitters Inc. They will stock clothing, shoes, and supplies used in running, swimming, bicycling, weight lifting, and other exercise and athletic activities. During their first year of operations, 2013, they expect the following results. (Subsequent years are expected to be more successful.)

Sales revenue	$ 629,000
Less: Cost of goods sold	(291,000)
Gross margin	$ 338,000
Less: Operating expenses	(355,000)
Net loss	$ (17,000)

By the end of 2013, Fitness Outfitters needs to have a cash balance of $5,000 and is expected to have the following partial balance sheet:

ASSETS		
Inventory		$ 53,000
Equipment	$97,000	
Accumulated depreciation, equipment	15,000	82,000
LIABILITIES AND EQUITY		
Accounts payable		$ 37,000
Common stock		100,000
Retained earnings		(17,000)

Assume that all sales will be for cash and that equipment will be acquired for cash.

Required:

1. Prepare as much of the statement of cash flows for 2013 as you can. Use the direct method to determine cash flows from operations.
2. In the statement that you prepared for Requirement 1, by how much does the prospective cash balance exceed or fall short of the desired cash balance? If a shortfall occurs, where would you suggest that Jane and Harvey seek additional cash?
3. Does the preparation of a prospective statement of cash flows seem worthwhile for an ongoing business? Why?

Case 11-63 Income, Cash Flow, and Future Losses

On January 1, 2011, Cermack National Bank loaned $5,000,000 under a 2-year, zero coupon note to a real estate developer. The bank recognized interest revenue on this note of approximately $400,000 per year. Due to an economic downturn, the developer was unable to pay the $5,800,000 maturity amount on December 31, 2012. The bank convinced the developer to pay $800,000 on December 31, 2012, and agreed to extend $5,000,000 credit to the developer despite the gloomy economic outlook for the next several years. Thus, on December 31, 2012, the bank issued a new 2-year, zero coupon note to the developer to mature on December 31, 2014, for $6,000,000. The bank recognized interest revenue on this note of approximately $500,000 per year.

The bank's external auditor insisted that the riskiness of the new loan be recognized by increasing the allowance for uncollectible notes by $1,500,000 on December 31, 2012, and $2,000,000 on December 31, 2013. On December 31, 2014, the bank received $1,200,000 from the developer and learned that the developer was in bankruptcy and that no additional amounts would be recovered.

Required:

1. Prepare a schedule showing annual cash flows for the two notes in each of the 4 years.
2. Prepare a schedule showing the effect of the notes on net income in each of the 4 years.
3. Which figure, net income or net cash flow, does the better job of telling the bank's stockholders about the effect of these notes on the bank? Explain by reference to the schedules prepared in Requirements 1 and 2.
4. A commonly used method for predicting future cash flows is to predict future income and adjust it for anticipated differences between net income and net cash flow. Does the Cermack National Bank case shed any light on the justification for using net income in this way rather than simply predicting future cash flows by reference to past cash flows?

Case 11-64 Researching Accounting Standards: Dissenting Views and the Statement of Cash Flows

The preparation of cash flow statements is required by generally accepted accounting principles. This accounting standard was initially adopted by a four-to-three vote of the FASB. Several members of the Board took exception to various aspects of the statement including (1) the classification of interest and dividends received and interest paid as cash flows from operations and (2) the use of the indirect method.

(Continued)

Required:

Obtain the *Statement of Financial Accounting Standards No. 95 (FAS 95)* from the FASB website. Go to www.fasb.org, highlight the "Standards" tab, select "Pre-Codification Standards," select "Statement of Financial Accounting Standards No. 95," and click on the "As Issued" link.

1. How did dissenting members of the FASB prefer that interest and dividends received and interest paid be classified? (See the section following paragraph 34 of the full text of *Statement No. 95*.) How did the FASB justify classifying these items as cash flows from operations? (See paragraph 90 of *Statement No. 95*.)
2. Why did dissenting members of the FASB take exception to the indirect method? (See the section following paragraph 34 of the full text of *Statement No. 95*.) How did the FASB justify permitting use of the indirect method? (See paragraphs 108, 109, and 119 of *Statement No. 95*.)

Case 11-65 Research and Analysis Using the Annual Report

Obtain **John Deere**'s 2011 annual report either through the "Investor Relations" portion of their website (do a web search for John Deere investor relations) or go to www.sec.gov and click "Search for Company Filings" under "Filings & Forms."

Required:

1. What method of computing net cash flow from operating activities did John Deere use?
2. What was the amount of net cash provided by operating activities for the 2 most current years? What were the most significant adjustments that caused a difference between net income and net cash provided by operating activities?
3. What amount did the company pay for interest during the most current year? For taxes during the most current year? (*Hint*: You may need to refer to the notes to the financial statements.)
4. Why was the provision for depreciation and amortization added to net income to compute the net cash provided by operating activities?
5. Refer to John Deere's investing and financing activities. What were some of John Deere's significant uses of cash? What were some of John Deere's significant sources of cash?
6. What was the amount of cash dividends paid by John Deere for the most current year?
7. Are the time commitments of inflows and outflows well matched by John Deere?
8. Are debt and equity likely to be available as inflows of cash in the near future?

Case 11-66 Comparative Analysis: Under Armour, Inc., versus VF Corporation

Refer to the financial statements of **Under Armour, Inc.**, and **VF Corporation** that are supplied with this text.

Required:

1. What method of computing net cash flow from operating activities did Under Armour use? What method of computing net cash flow from operating activities did VF use? Would you expect these to be the same? Why or why not?
2. Find net cash provided by operating activities for each company:
   a. What was the amount of cash provided by operating activities for the year ending December 31, 2011 for Under Armour? What was the amount of cash provided by operating activities for the year ending December 2011 for VF?
   b. What was the most significant adjustment that caused a difference between net income and net cash provided by operating activities?
   c. Comparing net income to net cash provided by operating activities, can you draw any conclusions as to the quality of each company's earnings?
3. Refer to each company's investing and financing activities. What were some of the more significant uses of cash? What were some of the more significant sources of cash?
4. Does each company match the time commitments of inflows and outflows of cash well?
5. Are debt and equity likely to be available as inflows of cash in the near future?

Case 11-67 CONTINUING PROBLEM: FRONT ROW ENTERTAINMENT

The income statement and comparative balance sheet for Front Row Entertainment are shown below:

Front Row Entertainment Inc.
Balance Sheets
December 31, 2014 and 2013

	2014	2013
ASSETS		
Current assets:		
Cash	$ 30,322	$ 9,005
Accounts receivable, net	98,250	17,000
Prepaid expenses	133,400	57,200
Supplies	2,200	3,700
Inventory	61,380	2,850
Total current assets	$ 325,552	$89,755
Property, plant, and equipment:		
Building	1,857,250	0
Equipment	27,350	7,000
Accumulated depreciation	(53,835)	(2,160)
Trademark	25,000	—
Total assets	$2,181,317	$94,595
LIABILITIES AND EQUITY		
Current liabilities:		
Accounts payable	$ 2,450	$12,240
Salaries payable	2,500	3,690
Interest payable	40,917	2,250
Unearned sales revenue	1,780	28,650
Income taxes payable	550	2,180
Notes payable (short-term)	8,000	0
Total current liabilities	$ 56,197	$49,010
Long-term liabilities:		
Notes payable	$ 405,000	$25,000
Bonds payable, net	1,500,000	0
Less: Discount on bond payable	(109,530)	
Total long-term liabilities	$1,795,470	$25,000
Equity:		
Preferred stock	$ 150,000	$ 0
Common stock	18,000	16,000
Paid-in capital in excess of par:		
Preferred stock	75,000	0
Common stock	38,000	0
Treasury stock	1,800	0
Retained earnings	53,250	4,585
Less: Treasury stock	(6,400)	0
Total equity	$ 329,650	$20,585
Total liabilities and equity	$2,181,317	$94,595

Front Row Entertainment Inc.
Income Statement
For the year ended December 31, 2014

Revenues:	
Sales revenue	$3,142,800
Service revenue	636,000
Total revenues	$3,778,800
Expenses:	
Artist fee expense	$2,134,260
Rent expense	952,663
Cost of goods sold	74,800
Salaries and wages expense	345,100
Depreciation expense	51,675
Interest expense	98,087
Income taxes expense	22,000
Other expenses	26,550
Total expenses	$3,705,135
Net income	$ 73,665

Additional Information:

1. Bonds payable of $1,500,000 were issued for $1,378,300 on July 1, 2014. During 2014, $12,170 of the discount on the bonds payable was amortized.
2. In January 2014, a $380,000 long-term note payable was issued in exchange for a building. No buildings were sold during the year.
3. On February 29, an $8,000 short-term note payable was issued in exchange for equipment. No equipment was sold during the year.
4. Cash dividends of $25,000 were declared and paid during 2014.
5. Common stock was issued for $40,000 cash during 2014.
6. Preferred stock was issued for $225,000 cash during 2014.
7. Treasury stock was purchased for $11,200 during 2014. Front Row reissued $4,800 of treasury stock in December 2014 for $6,600.

Required:

1. Prepare a statement of cash flows using the indirect method.
2. What conclusions can you draw about Front Row from the observed pattern of cash flows?

12

Financial Statement Analysis

© Pixelfabrik/Alamy

After studying Chapter 12, you should be able to:

1. Explain how creditors, investors, and others use financial statements in their decisions.
2. Become familiar with the most important SEC filings.
3. Understand the difference between cross sectional and time series analysis.
4. Analyze financial statements using horizontal and vertical analysis.
5. Calculate and use financial statement ratios to evaluate a company.

Ronald Martinez/Getty Images for Under Armour

EXPERIENCE FINANCIAL ACCOUNTING

with Under Armour

The **Under Armour** brand was founded by Kevin Plank in 1996. Kevin was 23 years old and had just completed his career on the University of Maryland football team. Although he loved football, Kevin hated the wetness and weight of sweat-drenched T-shirts. He noticed, however, that compression shorts, which were designed to keep muscles relaxed, managed to stay dry and comfortable.

During his senior year in 1995, Kevin visited a fabric store and found a synthetic fabric that was similar in feel to the tight-fitting, stretchy, compression shorts. Kevin had some sample shirts made and had his teammates try them out. His teammates loved them.

Using cash advances from credit cards and his own savings, Kevin gathered $40,000 and launched Under Armour out of his grandmother's house. He began to market the gear out of the trunk of his car to college sports teams around the country. Georgia Tech and Arizona State were Under Armour's first customers. By the end of the company's first year, Kevin had sold approximately 500 shirts, which produced sales of about $17,000.

In 1997, cold weather, turf protection, and all-season apparel lines were added to the original HeatGear line, and by the end of that year over 7,500 products had been sold. Then in 1998, Under Armour became the official supplier for NFL Europe. In addition, Under Armour apparel was worn in the Oliver Stone movie *Any Given Sunday* and in *The Replacements*, starring Gene Hackman and Keanu Reeves. By the end of 1999, Under Armour outfitted 8 Major League Baseball teams, over 20 NFL teams, 4 NHL teams, and dozens of NCAA teams. In that year, it sold over 250,000 items and sales topped $1 million.

"Under Armour apparel was worn in the Oliver Stone movie Any Given Sunday *and in* The Replacements, *starring Gene Hackman and Keanu Reeves. By the end of 1999, Under Armour outfitted 8 Major League Baseball teams, over 20 NFL teams, 4 NHL teams, and dozens of NCAA teams."*

The new millenium saw Under Armour's sales take off. The year 2001 produced sales of approximately $25 million, and sales were over $100 million by 2003. With a stable of athlete endorsements, Under Armour became a must-have piece of equipment for recreational and youth athletes. Undoubtedly most of us have seen Under Armour being worn around our campuses and towns. Yet, how do we know whether Under Armour would be a good company in which to invest? In reading this chapter, you will learn about a number of tools used by investors and creditors to analyze the financial status of Under Armour and other companies.

Throughout this book, you have learned how to use debits and credits to record many of the most common transactions in which companies engage. You have also studied how these debits and credits are summarized in the financial statements and how this information is useful to those interested in the company. In this chapter, we review, extend, and summarize the role of financial statements in business decision-making. The types of decisions facing customers, suppliers, employees, creditors, and investors are discussed. However, we concentrate primarily on investment and credit decisions and the techniques used for comparison to other companies or previous years.

Reading this chapter will help you answer the following questions:

- What decision-making groups use financial statements and what questions are they able to answer by analyzing the financial statements?
- What information can be found in SEC filings?
- Where can various information be found in the Form 10-K?
- How are financial statements analyzed?

OBJECTIVE 1

Explain how creditors, investors, and others use financial statements in their decisions.

USE OF FINANCIAL STATEMENTS IN DECISIONS

As we discussed in Chapter 1, the role of financial statements is to provide information that will help creditors, investors, and others make judgments which serve as the foundation for various decisions. While customers, suppliers, employees, creditors, and investors all use financial statement data to make decisions, as shown in Exhibit 12.1, each group uses the accounting information to answer different questions.

Customer Decisions

Customers want to buy from companies that will:

- continue to produce goods or provide services in the future
- provide repair or warranty service if required

The financial statements contain data describing the profitability and efficiency of a company's operations which customers can use to estimate the likelihood that a supplier will be able to deliver goods or services now and in the future.

EXHIBIT 12.1

Users of Financial Statements and Typical Questions

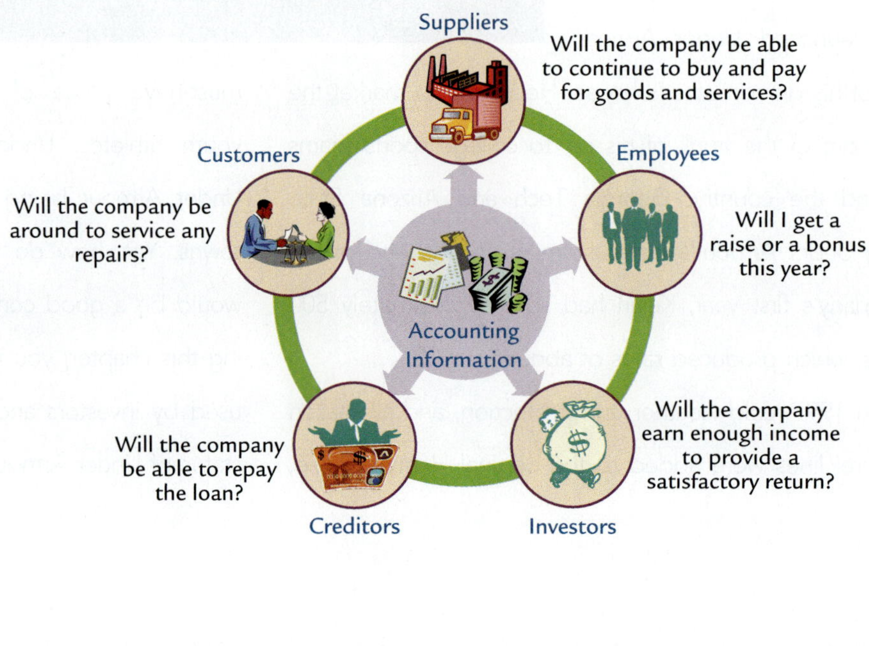

Supplier Decisions

A company that is considering selling goods or providing services to another company wants to know whether its customer will be able to:

- pay for the purchase as agreed
- continue to purchase and pay for goods and services

Suppliers can use balance sheet data to estimate the likelihood that a customer will be able to pay for current purchases. They can use income statement data to analyze whether a customer will be able to continue purchasing and paying for goods or services in the future.

Employment Decisions

When you select an employer, you want to be sure that the company will provide:

- competitive salary and benefits
- experiences that will prepare you to assume increased responsibility
- a secure position for the foreseeable future

Income statement data can help a prospective employee assess the likelihood that a company will provide the growth and profits necessary to support a successful career. For example, examining a company's return on assets and sales growth can help prospective employees determine a company's profitability and growth.

In related decisions, unions representing employees use the financial statements. For example, when the employer's income statement suggests the employer is performing very well, the union will seek greater wages and benefits. Conversely, when the income statement suggests the employer is performing poorly (such as in the airline industry), unions may accept lower wages and benefits to help the employer stay in operation.

Credit Decisions

An individual or an organization that is considering making a loan needs to know whether the borrower will be able to repay the loan and its interest. For short-term loans (those of 1 year or less), the principal and interest will be repaid from current assets—cash on hand and cash that can be secured by selling inventory and collecting accounts receivable. A short-term lender, then, is most interested in the composition and amounts of a borrowing company's current assets and current liabilities. The excess of the current assets over current liabilities, an amount called *working capital*, is particularly important.

For a long-term loan, the principal and interest will be repaid from cash provided by profits earned over the period of the loan. A long-term lender, then, is most interested in estimating:

- future profits of the enterprise
- amounts of other claims against those profits, such as dividends to stockholders, payments to other lenders, and future investments by the firm

Information from three different statements is useful in making credit decisions:

- An analysis of the balance sheet can provide information about the borrower's current liquidity.
- Profitability data developed from current and previous income statements are often helpful in forecasting future profitability.
- Sources and uses of cash presented in the statement of cash flows are helpful in forecasting the amount and timing of future claims against profits.

Investment Decisions

Investors who buy stock in a corporation expect to earn returns on their investment from:

- dividends
- increases in the value of the stock (capital gains)

Both dividends and increases in the value of the stock depend on the future profitability of the company. The larger the profits, the more resources the company has available for payment of dividends and for investment in new assets to use in creating additional profits.

Although detailed analysis of the corporation is where you find the best information for predicting (or forecasting) future profits, this cannot be done in a vacuum. You must also understand economic and industry factors. For example, if you ignore how economic factors such as rising interest rates affect home construction (it slows it down), then forecasts of corporations whose performances are tied to this industry, such as Lowe's or Home Depot, may be overly optimistic. As such, most analysts take a top-down approach when trying to predict future profits. This approach starts with gathering economic and industry data. In fact, professional analysts typically specialize in certain industries so that their knowledge of how the economy and industry interact will be applicable to all the corporations they analyze (or "follow"). Yet, at some point, you must begin to analyze the corporation itself.

OBJECTIVE 2

Become familiar with the most important SEC filings.

SEC FILINGS

Publicly traded corporations must file a variety of financial information, including audited financial statements, with the Securities and Exchange Commission (SEC) on an ongoing basis. For example, annual reports on **Form 10-K**, quarterly reports on **Form 10-Q**, and current reports for numerous specified events on **Form 8-K**, as well as many other disclosure requirements must be submitted to the SEC in a timely manner. These filings are the most important and complete source of financial information about the corporation and are the major source of information about the business for most investors (and creditors). A summary of the most important SEC filings is provided in Exhibit 12.2. A complete list of mandatory filings with more detailed descriptions is provided at www.sec.gov/about/forms/secforms.htm.

EXHIBIT 12.2

The Most Important SEC Filings

Filing	Description*
Form 10-K	The annual report on Form 10-K provides a comprehensive overview of the corporation's business and financial condition and includes *audited* financial statements. Although similarly named, the annual report on Form 10-K is distinct from the "annual report to shareholders," which a corporation must send to its stockholders when it holds an annual meeting to elect directors. For larger filers, the 10-K must be filed within 60 days of their fiscal year end.
Form 10-Q	The Form 10-Q includes *unaudited* financial statements and provides a continuing view of the corporation's financial position during the year. The report must be filed for each of the first three fiscal quarters of the corporation's fiscal year. For larger filers, this must be done within 40 days of the end of the quarter.
Form 8-K	In addition to filing Forms 10-K and 10-Q, public corporations must report material corporate events on a more current basis. Form 8-K is the "current report" companies must file with the SEC to announce major events that are important to investors and creditors.
Form DEF 14A (Proxy Statement)	The Proxy Statement notifies stockholders of issues that will be voted on at the annual stockholders' meeting. For example, stockholders commonly vote on the audit firm, executive compensation issues, and representation on the Board of Directors.
Forms 3, 4, and 5	Corporate officers, directors, and 10+ percent stockholders are collectively known as "insiders." Form 3 must be filed upon becoming an officer, director, or 10+ percent stockholders. Insiders must file Form 4 within 2 business days of buying or selling the corporation's stock. Form 5 is a special annual filing.
Forms S-1 and S-2 (Registration Statements) **Rule 424 (Prospectus)**	Corporations must file these forms to "register" their securities with the SEC prior to offering them to investors. Each form contains information for potential investors related to the sale of stock by the corporation. When the corporation sells stock to the public for the first time, it is called an "Initial Public Offering" or IPO. Subsequent offerings are referred to as Secondary Offerings.

*Descriptions taken from the SEC website.

Format and Content of Form 10-K

The most useful filing is Form 10-K, which is filed after each fiscal year end. We provide excerpts from **Under Armour**'s and **VF Corporation**'s 10-Ks at the end of the book in Appendices 4 and 5, respectively. The 10-K includes audited financial statements, but there is also a wealth of additional information. As seen in Appendices 4 and 5, 10-Ks are quite long (frequently well over 100 pages; remember these are just excerpts); however, all 10-Ks must follow a format mandated by the SEC. If you familiarize yourself with the mandated format, you will be able to find information of interest more efficiently.

Item 1 outlines the history of the company, discusses recent developments, and provides an overview of its industry and competitors. There is a detailed discussion of such things as major products, major suppliers and sources of raw materials, key customers, seasonalities, government regulations, and risk factors. A thorough read of this section is a good way to better understand the business and determine whether the company has a good strategy for creating profits.

Typically there is little important information in Items 2, 3, and 4. However, you should scan these items for anything of interest. **Item 2** describes the property holdings of the company; **Item 3** discusses lawsuits in which the company is involved; **Item 4** discusses anything brought to a stockholder vote in the fourth quarter (the 10-Qs handle this matter for the first three quarters). Item 3 is likely the most important of these items, as you will want to be aware of any serious litigation facing the company. However, most companies are parties to multiple lawsuits at any point in time, and a vast majority of these lawsuits will not materially affect the company.

Item 5 provides a summary of recent stock price and dividend activity, while **Item 6** summarizes financial data for the last 5 years. There is not much detail to these sections, but they do provide a nice overview. Further, Item 6 often provides information about key performance indicators, such as sales per square foot in the retail industry or revenues per passenger mile in the airline industry, which are not included in the financial statements.

Item 7 is Management's Discussion and Analysis, more frequently referred to as **MD&A**. This is one of the key parts of the 10-K. In this section, management discusses its views of the financial condition and performance of the company. Management is required to disclose trends, events, or known uncertainties that would materially affect the company. Included in this section are many statements about what will likely happen in the future. Although there is obviously uncertainty about whether these future events will happen, this information is designed to provide investors with information management believes necessary to understand the company and predict, or forecast, future performance. Item 7A is where the effect of market risk factors, such as fluctuating interest rates or currency exchange rates, on the company's financial performance is discussed. It is important to read the MD&A.

Item 8 contains the corporation's balance sheets for the last 2 years and income statements and statements of cash flows for the last 3 years. These three financial statements are the primary sources of information for analysts. Specifically, as discussed in other chapters and later in this chapter, financial statement ratio analysis provides analysts with a wealth of information to evaluate such things as the corporation's profitability, asset and debt management, and short-term liquidity. One part of Item 8 that should not be ignored is the footnotes provided as a supplement to the financial statements. This is where you will find information about the corporation's accounting policies (such as, does the company use LIFO or FIFO?) as well as disclosures providing additional detail about various accounts listed on the financial statements.

Finally, Item 8 also includes the auditor's opinions on (1) the effectiveness of the corporation's system of internal controls over financial reporting and (2) the fairness of presentation of the financial statements and accompanying footnotes. Although these opinions are typically "unqualified," indicating no major problems, you should definitely look at these opinions to ensure this is true. Auditing financial statements is one of the primary services provided by CPAs and is the focus of multiple courses for accounting majors.

Item 9 is reserved for changes in or disagreements with the auditors. This item also rarely indicates a problem, but you should look at it just in case. Item 9A is a recent addition to 10-Ks in response to requirements made by the passage of the Sarbanes-Oxley Act. Here management acknowledges its responsibility for establishing and maintaining a system of internal controls over financial reporting, its testing of this system's effectiveness, and its opinion of its effectiveness. It is this system of internal controls on which the auditors provide an opinion, although as discussed in the previous paragraph, the opinion is frequently included in Item 8.

Items 10 through 14 provide information that is usually provided in the proxy statement (see Form DEF 14A in Exhibit 12.2, p. 650) because stockholders typically vote on whether to retain directors and auditors (or principal accountants). Of course, the names of the parties are disclosed, as are their business experience or any family relationships with other directors or officers. Finally, **Item 15** is a listing of the financial statements (discussed as part of Item 8) and other required filings.

OBJECTIVE 3

Understand the difference between cross sectional and time series analysis.

ANALYZING FINANCIAL STATEMENTS WITH CROSS SECTIONAL AND TIME SERIES ANALYSIS

As with many things in life, context is important in financial statement analysis. For example, how well do you believe a corporation with \$3.3 billion in net sales is performing? Your answer should be that it depends. That is, if net sales for the previous 2 years were \$4.5 billion and \$3.9 billion, respectively, you would say the trend is negative. However, if net sales for the previous 2 years were \$2.0 billion and \$2.8 billion, respectively, then you would conclude the trend is positive. Or, to make the judgement, you could see how this corporation's sales growth stacks up against a major competitor's.

The context with which we placed our hypothetical corporation's net sales and sales growth demonstrates the two general comparisons we make when analyzing financial statements—cross sectional analysis and time series (or trend) analysis.

Cross Sectional Analysis

Cross sectional analysis compares one corporation to another corporation and to industry averages. Although this method is useful, it is often difficult to find a good comparison corporation, and even corporations classified in the same industry frequently have different aspects to their operations. For example, the Apparel and Accessories industry in which **Under Armour** and **VF** are placed also includes **Coach, Inc.** Nonetheless, it is useful to highlight similarities, differences, strengths, and weaknesses of the corporation as compared to the competition and the industry as a whole. For example, for 2011:

- Under Armour's gross profit margin percentage was 48.4%.
- VF's gross profit margin percentage was 45.78%.
- The Apparel and Accessories industry had gross profit margin percentages of 32.52%.

Along this dimension, both Under Armour and VF outperformed the industry. We will discuss more comparisons between Under Armour, VF, and the Apparel and Accessories industry later in the chapter.

Time Series Analysis

Time series (or trend) analysis compares a single corporation across time. For example, if you look at **Under Armour**'s income statement in Appendix 4, you see that its net sales were:

- \$0.856 billion in 2009
- \$1.064 billion in 2010
- \$1.473 billion in 2011

This shows a positive trend.

Year-to-year comparisons of important accounts and account groups help to identify the causes of changes in a company's income or financial position. Knowing the causes of these changes is helpful in forecasting a company's future profitability and financial position. In fact, the SEC requires comparative financial statements (2 years for the balance sheet and 3 years for both the income statement and statement of cash flows) in the 10-K, which facilitates trend analysis.

Cross Sectional and Time Series Analysis Illustrated

Cross sectional and time series analysis are demonstrated in Cornerstone 12.1.

Interpreting Cross Sectional and Time Series (or Trend) Analysis

CORNERSTONE 12.1

Why:

When analyzing a corporation's financial statements, cross sectional analysis compares the corporation's financial statements to a competitor or industry averages, and time series analysis compares specific line items of the financial statements over multiple years.

Information:

Information from **Under Armour**'s and **VF**'s financial statements follows.

	Under Armour (in thousands)		
	2011	**2010**	**2009**
Net sales	$1,472,684	$1,063,927	$856,411
Cost of goods sold	759,848	533,420	446,286
Gross profit	$ 712,836	$ 530,507	$410,125

	VF (in thousands)		
	2011	**2010**	**2009**
Net sales	$9,459,232	$7,702,589	$7,220,286
Cost of goods sold	5,128,602	4,105,201	4,025,122
Gross profit	$4,330,630	$3,597,388	$3,195,164

Required:

1. Using time series analysis, comment on the trend of Under Armour's cost of goods sold and gross profit.
2. What is the primary weakness of using raw financial statement numbers in cross sectional and time series analysis? What can you do about it?
3. Using cross sectional analysis, compare VF's gross profit to that of Under Armour's.

Solution (all $ are in thousands):

1. Under Armour's cost of goods sold increased by $87,134 ($533,420 – $446,286) from 2009 to 2010 and by $226,428 between 2010 and 2011. In isolation this may seem bad, but the primary reason for this increase is that sales were also increasing. In fact, Under Armour has a positive trend in gross profit, which increased by $120,382 between 2009 and 2010 and by $182,329 between 2010 and 2011.

Source: Under Armour 2011 10-K and VF Corporation 2011 10-K.

(Continued)

CORNERSTONE 12.1 (*Continued*)

2. The primary weakness is that raw financial statement numbers can be difficult to compare. For example, Under Armour's net sales increased by over $600 million from 2009 to 2011, while its gross profit only increased by about $300 million. However, if you look at the percentage change, both net sales and gross profit increased by about 70%. Further, when comparing two competitors—like Under Armour and VF—making comparisons with raw financial statement numbers is difficult because they are often vastly different in size. Using percentage changes from year to year or between two financial statement line items helps overcome the differences in the relative sizes of items of interest.

3. When we look at the percentage change in gross margin from year to year we discover the following:

Growth in Gross Profit:	2010 to 2011*	2009 to 2010**
Under Armour	34.37%	29.35%
VF	20.38%	12.59%

* (2011 Gross Profit − 2010 Gross Profit) ÷ 2010 Gross Profit
** (2010 Gross Profit − 2009 Gross Profit) ÷ 2009 Gross Profit

This analysis suggests that, while both companies increased their growth profit, Under Armour is growing faster.

Source: Under Armour 2011 10-K and VF Corporation 2011 10-K.

OBJECTIVE 4
Analyze financial statements using horizontal and vertical analysis.

ANALYZING THE FINANCIAL STATEMENTS WITH HORIZONTAL AND VERTICAL ANALYSIS

The comparative financial statements included in the 10-K report the results in dollar amounts. This makes it easy to detect large changes between years in accounts or groups of accounts. These changes may indicate that the corporation is changing or that the conditions under which the corporation operates are changing. However, while comparative financial statements show changes in the amounts of financial statement items, analysts often prefer to restate the financial statements in percentages using common size statements. **Common size statements** express each financial statement line item in percentage terms, which highlights differences. Typically, this conversion from dollar amounts to percentages is done with horizontal or vertical analysis.

Horizontal Analysis

In **horizontal analysis**, each financial statement line item is expressed as a percent of the base year (typically the first year shown). Cornerstone 12.2 shows how to prepare a common size income statement for horizontal analysis.

CORNERSTONE 12.2

Preparing Common Size Statements for Horizontal Analysis

Why:

Horizontal analysis expresses each financial statement line item as a percent of the base year.

Information:

Under Armour's income statement from its 2011 10-K follows.

(Continued)

CORNERSTONE
12.2

(Continued)

Under Armour, Inc. and Subsidiaries
Consolidated Statements of Income

	Year Ended December 31,		
	2011	2010 (in thousands)	2009
Net revenues	$1,472,684	$1,063,927	$856,411
Cost of goods sold	759,848	533,420	446,286
Gross profit	712,836	530,507	410,125
Selling, general and administrative expenses	550,069	418,152	324,852
Income from operations	162,767	112,355	85,273
Interest expense, net	3,841	2,258	2,344
Other expense, net	2,064	1,178	511
Income before income taxes	156,862	108,919	82,418
Provision for income taxes	59,943	40,442	35,633
Net income	$ 96,919	$ 68,477	$ 46,785

Required:

Prepare a common size income statement to be used for horizontal analysis for Under Armour using 2009 as the base year.

Solution:

Under Armour, Inc. and Subsidiaries
Consolidated Statements of Income

	Year Ended December 31,		
	2011	2010 (in thousands)	2009
Net revenues	171.96%	124.23%	100.00%
Cost of goods sold	170.26%	119.52%	100.00%
Gross profit	173.81%	129.35%	100.00%
Selling, general and administrative expenses	169.33%	128.72%	100.00%
Income from operations	190.88%	131.76%	100.00%
Interest expense, net	163.87%	96.33%	100.00%
Other expense, net	403.91%	230.53%	100.00%
Income before income taxes	190.32%	132.15%	100.00%
Provision for income taxes	168.22%	113.50%	100.00%
Net income	207.16%	146.37%	100.00%

Source: Under Armour 2011 10-K and VF Corporation 2011 10-K.

Horizontal analysis is good for highlighting the growth (or shrinkage) in financial statement line items from year to year and is particularly useful for trend analysis. For example, looking at Under Armour's common size income statement in Cornerstone 12.2, we see that cost of goods sold has grown slightly slower than sales when comparing 2011 to 2009. This has resulted in the gross profit growth exceeding sales growth.

Vertical Analysis

Vertical analysis, on the other hand, expresses each financial statement line item as a percent of the largest amount on the statement. On the income statement, this is net sales and on the balance sheet it is total assets. Vertical analysis helps distinguish between changes in account balances that result from growth and changes that are likely to have arisen from other causes. Cornerstone 12.3 shows how to prepare a common size income statement and balance sheet for vertical analysis.

CORNERSTONE 12.3

Preparing Common Size Statements for Vertical Analysis

Why:

Vertical analysis expresses each financial statement line item as a percent of the largest amount on the statement.

Information:

Under Armour's income statements and balance sheets (from the 2011 and 2010 10-Ks) follow.

Under Armour, Inc. and Subsidiaries
Consolidated Statements of Income

	Year Ended December 31,		
	2011	**2010**	**2009**
		(in thousands)	
Net revenues	$1,472,684	$1,063,927	$856,411
Cost of goods sold	759,848	533,420	446,286
Gross profit	712,836	530,507	410,125
Selling, general and administrative expenses	550,069	418,152	324,852
Income from operations	162,767	112,355	85,273
Interest expense, net	3,841	2,258	2,344
Other expense, net	2,064	1,178	511
Income before income taxes	156,862	108,919	82,418
Provision for income taxes	59,943	40,442	35,633
Net income	$ 96,919	$ 68,477	$ 46,785

Under Armour, Inc. and Subsidiaries
Consolidated Balance Sheets

	December 31,		
	2011	**2010**	**2009**
		(in thousands)	
ASSETS			
Current assets			
Cash and equivalents	$175,384	$203,870	$187,297
Accounts receivable (gross)	138,143	106,934	84,556
Allowance for doubtful accounts	4,100	4,900	5,200
Accounts receivable (net)	134,043	102,034	79,356
Inventories	324,409	215,355	148,488
Prepaid expenses and other current assets	39,643	19,326	19,989
Deferred income taxes	16,184	15,265	12,870
Total current assets	689,663	555,850	448,000

Source: Under Armour 2011 10-K and VF Corporation 2011 10-K.

(Continued)

CORNERSTONE 12.3

(Continued)

	December 31,		
	2011	2010 (in thousands)	2009
Property, plant and equipment	159,135	76,127	72,926
Intangible assets, net	5,535	3,914	5,681
Deferred income taxes	15,885	21,275	13,908
Other long term assets	48,992	18,212	5,073
Total assets	$919,210	$675,378	$545,588
LIABILITIES AND STOCKHOLDERS' EQUITY			
Current liabilities			
Accounts payable	$100,527	$ 84,679	$ 68,710
Accrued expenses	69,285	55,138	40,885
Current maturities of long term debt	6,882	6,865	9,178
Current maturities of capital lease obligations	–	–	97
Other current liabilities	6,913	2,465	1,292
Total current liabilities	183,607	149,147	120,162
Long term debt, net of current maturities	70,842	9,077	10,948
Other long term liabilities	28,329	20,188	14,481
Total liabilities	282,778	178,412	145,591
Stockholders' equity'			
Class A common stock	13	13	13
Class B convertible common stock	4	4	4
Additional paid-in capital	268,223	224,887	197,342
Retained earnings	366,164	270,021	202,188
Unearned compensation	–	–	(14)
Accumulated other comprehensive income	2,028	2,041	464
Total stockholders' equity	636,432	496,966	399,997
Total liabilities and stockholders' equity	$919,210	$675,378	$545,588

Required:

Prepare common size income statements and balance sheets to be used in vertical analysis for Under Armour.

Solution:

Under Armour, Inc. and Subsidiaries
Consolidated Statements of Income

	Year Ended December		
	2011	2010 (in thousands)	2009
Net revenues	100.00%	100.00%	100.00%
Cost of goods sold	51.60%	50.14%	52.11%
Gross profit	48.40%	49.86%	47.89%
Selling, general and administrative expenses	37.35%	39.30%	37.93%
Income from operations	11.05%	10.56%	9.96%
Interest expense, net	0.26%	0.21%	0.27%
Other expense, net	0.14%	0.11%	0.06%
Income before income taxes	10.65%	10.24%	9.62%
Provision for income taxes	4.07%	3.80%	4.16%
Net income	6.58%	6.44%	5.46%

Source: Under Armour 2011 10-K and VF Corporation 2011 10-K.

(Continued)

CORNERSTONE 12.3

(Continued)

Under Armour, Inc. and Subsidiaries
Consolidated Balance Sheets

	December 31		
	2011	**2010**	**2009**
		(in thousands)	
ASSETS			
Current assets			
Cash and equivalents	19.08%	30.19%	34.33%
Accounts receivable (gross)	15.03%	15.83%	15.50%
Allowance for doubtful accounts	0.45%	0.73%	0.95%
Accounts receivable (net)	14.58%	15.11%	14.55%
Inventories	35.29%	31.89%	27.22%
Prepaid expenses and other current assets	4.31%	2.86%	3.66%
Deferred income taxes	1.76%	2.26%	2.36%
Total current assets	75.03%	82.30%	82.11%
Property, plant and equipment	17.31%	11.27%	13.37%
Intangible assets, net	0.60%	0.58%	1.04%
Deferred income taxes	1.73%	3.15%	2.55%
Other long term assets	5.33%	2.70%	0.93%
Total assets	100.00%	100.00%	100.00%
LIABILITIES AND STOCKHOLDERS' EQUITY			
Current liabilities			
Accounts payable	10.94%	12.54%	12.59%
Accrued expenses	7.54%	8.16%	7.49%
Current maturities of long term debt	0.75%	1.02%	1.68%
Current maturities of capital lease obligations	0.00%	0.00%	0.02%
Other current liabilities	0.75%	0.36%	0.24%
Total current liabilities	19.97%	22.08%	22.02%
Long term debt, net of current maturities	7.71%	1.34%	2.01%
Other long term liabilities	3.08%	2.99%	2.65%
Total liabilities	30.76%	26.42%	26.69%
Stockholders' equity			
Class A common stock	0.00%	0.00%	0.00%
Class B convertible common stock	0.00%	0.00%	0.00%
Additional paid-in capital	29.18%	33.30%	36.17%
Retained earnings	39.83%	39.98%	37.06%
Unearned compensation	0.00%	0.00%	0.00%
Accumulated other comprehensive income	0.22%	0.30%	0.09%
Total stockholders' equity	69.24%	73.58%	73.31%
Total liabilities and stockholders' equity	100.00%	100.00%	100.00%

Source: Under Armour 2011 10-K and VF Corporation 2011 10-K.

Identifying non-growth changes and their causes can help forecast a company's future profitability or its future financial position. For example, in Cornerstone 12.3, Under Armour's cost of sales decreased from approximately 52.11% of net sales in 2009 to 51.60% in 2011. This may not seem like much of a change, and it's not, but if cost of sales had remained at 52.11% of net sales, then gross profit would be over $7.5 million lower. Determining whether this improved cost of sales percentage is sustainable may have a large effect on forecasting the future. Further, vertical analysis of the balance sheet reveals that Under Armour has made a significant investment in property, plant, and equipment. The question is what is the nature of this investment? If the investment represents new production capacity, it could translate into future sales. However, if the investment is a new "palace" for corporate headquarters, our forecasted growth would not be as great.

Of course, you can, and should, get much more depth with such analysis. A careful horizontal and vertical analysis serves as a starting point for an inquiry into the causes of these changes, with the objective being forecasting the corporation's future financial statements.

ANALYZING THE FINANCIAL STATEMENTS WITH RATIO ANALYSIS

OBJECTIVE 5

Calculate and use financial statement ratios to evaluate a company.

Ratio analysis is an examination of financial statements conducted by preparing and evaluating a series of ratios. **Ratios** (or **financial ratios**), like other financial analysis data, normally provide meaningful information only when compared with ratios from previous periods for the same firm (i.e., time series, or trend, analysis) or similar firms (i.e., cross sectional analysis). Ratios help by removing most of the effects of size differences. When dollar amounts are used, size differences between firms may make a meaningful comparison impossible. However, properly constructed financial ratios permit the comparison of firms regardless of size.

We discuss six categories of ratio analysis:

- *Short-term liquidity ratios* are particularly helpful to short-term creditors, but all investors and creditors have an interest in these ratios.
- *Debt management ratios* and *profitability ratios* provide information for long-term creditors and stockholders.
- *Asset efficiency (or operating) ratios* help management operate the firm and indicate to outsiders the efficiency with which certain of the company's activities are performed.
- *Stockholder ratios* are of interest to a corporation's stockholders.
- *Dupont analysis* decomposes return on equity into margin, turnover, and leverage.

All these ratios are shown and defined in Exhibit 12.4 at the conclusion of this section (pp. 680–681). We will use data from Under Armour's financial statements in Appendix 4 to illustrate each of these types of financial statement ratios. Also note that in the following discussion all dollar amount are in thousands, except per share data, to match up with the financial statements.

Short-Term Liquidity Ratios

Analysts want to know the likelihood that a company will be able to pay its current obligations as they come due. Failure to pay current liabilities can lead to suppliers refusing to sell needed inventory and employees leaving. As such, even companies with good business models can be forced into bankruptcy by their inability to pay current liabilities.

The cash necessary to pay current liabilities will come from existing cash or from receivables and inventory, which should turn into cash approximately at the same time the current liabilities become due. Property, plant, and equipment and other long-lived assets are much more difficult to turn into cash in time to meet current obligations without harming future operations. Accordingly, the **short-term liquidity ratios** compare some combination of current assets or operations to current liabilities.

Current Ratio Since a company must meet its current obligations primarily by using its current assets, the current ratio is especially useful to short-term creditors. The **current ratio** is expressed as follows:

$$\text{Current Ratio} = \frac{\text{Current Assets}}{\text{Current Liabilities}}$$

Using information from Under Armour's 2011 balance sheet, the current ratio for Under Armour is calculated as:

	2011	2010
Total current assets	$689,663	$555,850
Total current liabilities	$183,607	$149,147
Current ratio	**3.76**	**3.73**

Source: Under Armour 2011 10-K.

Under Armour's current assets increased at approximately the same rate as its current liabilities. As such, Under Armour's current ratio is essentially the same.

There are no absolute standards for ratios, so a company's ratios are typically compared to the industry averages and/or competitors. The average for the Apparel and Accessories industry is 1.49. By these standards, Under Armour's current ratio was relatively strong in both years.

Quick Ratio Some analysts believe that the current ratio overstates short-term liquidity. They argue that prepaid expenses (expenses for which payments are made before consumption) often cannot be converted into cash. Further, inventories must be sold and receivables collected from those sales before cash is obtained to pay maturing current liabilities. Both the sale of inventory and collection of receivables can require a lengthy period. Conservative analysts argue that only those current assets that can be turned into cash almost immediately should be used to measure short-term liquidity.

A more conservative measure of short-term liquidity is based on *quick assets* (usually cash, receivables, and short-term investments) and current liabilities. The **quick ratio** (or *acid test ratio*) is expressed as follows:

$$\text{Quick Ratio} = \frac{\text{Cash} + \text{Short-Term Investments} + \text{Receivables}}{\text{Current Liabilities}}$$

Looking at the detail of Under Armour's current assets, the quick ratio is calculated as follows:

	2011	2010
Current assets:		
Cash and equivalents	$175,384	$203,870
Marketable securities	0	0
Receivables, net	134,043	102,034
Inventories	324,409	215,355
Prepaid expenses and other current assets	39,643	19,326
Deferred income taxes	16,184	15,265
Total current assets	$689,663	$555,850
Quick assets	$309,427	$305,904
Total current liabilities	$183,607	$149,147
Quick ratio	**1.69**	**2.05**

Source: Under Armour 2011 10-K.

Generally, a quick ratio above 1.0 is considered adequate because there are enough liquid assets available to meet current obligations. Using this guideline, we see that Under Armour had little difficulty meeting its current obligations in 2010 or 2011. Further, Under Armour's quick ratio is well above the industry average of 1.07.

Cash Ratio An even more conservative short-term liquidity ratio is the cash ratio. Specifically, while the current and quick ratios assume that receivables will be collected, the cash ratio does not make this assumption. This ratio may be more appropriate for industries in which collectability is uncertain or for corporations with high credit risk receivables. The **cash ratio** is expressed as:

$$\text{Cash Ratio} = \frac{\text{Cash} + \text{Short-Term Investments}}{\text{Current Liabilities}}$$

Although Under Armour does not have high credit risk receivables, the cash ratio is calculated as:

	2011	2010
Current assets:		
Cash and equivalents	$175,384	$203,870
Marketable securities	0	0
Receivables, net	134,043	102,034
Inventories	324,409	215,255
Prepaid expenses and other current assets	39,643	19,326
Deferred income taxes	16,184	15,265
Total current assets	$689,663	$555,850
Liquid assets	$175,384	$203,870
Total current liabilities	$183,607	$149,147
Cash ratio	**0.96**	**1.37**

Source: Under Armour 2011 10-K.

If you questioned the collectability of Under Armour's receivables, the cash ratio indicates that Under Armour had more than enough cash and marketable securities to pay off its current liabilities in 2010, but not quite enough in 2011. Note that the cash ratio of below 1.0 in 2011 only indicates liquidity issues if you do not believe in the collectibility of Under Armour's receivables.

Operating Cash Flow Ratio The operating cash flow ratio takes a slightly different approach. This ratio looks at the ability of operations to generate cash, which recognizes the more general concept that current obligations will be paid through operations (after all, selling inventory and collecting receivables is a big part of operations). The **operating cash flow ratio** is expressed as:

$$\text{Operating Cash Flow Ratio} = \frac{\text{Cash Flows from Operating Activities}}{\text{Current Liabilities}}$$

Looking at Under Armour's statement of cash flows and balance sheet, the operating cash flow ratio is calculated as follows:

	2011	2010
Cash flows from operating activities	$15,218	$50,114
Total current liabilities	$183,607	$149,147
Operating cash flow ratio	**0.08**	**0.34**

Source: Under Armour 2011 10-K.

In 2010 and 2011, Under Armour operations did not generate enough cash to meet the current obligations due at the end of the year. Obviously, this is not ideal. However, closer examination of the statement of cash flows and balance sheet suggests that the primary reason cash flows from operating activities are low is due to a build up in receivables, inventories, and prepaid expenses. Growth in these areas is consistent with growth in operations. Of course, the real key is whether Under Armour be able to sell this growing inventory and collect associated receivables.

Overview of Short-Term Liquidity Ratios Most of the short-term liquidity ratios declined in 2011, which indicates Under Armour's short-term liquidity worsened. However, because Under Armour's ratios are so much better than industry averages, this doesn't yet warrant real concern. Nonetheless, for creditors, generally this is not good news. Creditors typically prefer all these measures of short-term liquidity be as high as possible. However, because investments in current assets (especially cash, receivables, and inventory) earn very small returns compared with the returns on investments in noncurrent assets, management must minimize the proportion of capital invested in current assets if it is to maximize profit. Using the income statement and balance sheet shown in Exhibit 12.3, Cornerstone 12.4 illustrates how to calculate and interpret short-term liquidity ratios for VF Corporation.

EXHIBIT 12.3

VF Corporation Income Statement and Balance Sheet

VF Corporation
Consolidated Statements of Income*

	Year Ended December		
	2011	2010 (in thousands)	2009
Net Sales	$9,365,477	$7,624,599	$7,143,074
Royalty Income	93,755	77,990	77,212
Total Revenues	9,459,232	7,702,589	7,220,286
Costs and Operating Expenses			
Cost of goods sold	5,128,602	4,105,201	4,025,122
Marketing, administrative and general expenses	3,085,839	2,574,790	2,336,394
Impairment of goodwilll and intangible assets	–	201,738	121,953
Total Costs and Operating Expenses	8,214,441	6,881,729	6,483,469
Operating Income	1,244,791	820,860	736,817
Other Income (Expense)			
Interest income	4,778	2,336	2,230
Interest expense	(77,578)	(77,738)	(85,902)
Miscellaneous, net	(7,248)	4,754	1,528
Total Other Income (Expense)	(80,048)	(70,648)	(82,144)
Income Before Income Taxes	1,164,743	750,212	654,673
Income Taxes	274,350	176,700	196,215
Net Income before Noncontrolling Interests	890,393	573,512	458,458
Net (Income) Loss Attributable to Noncontrolling Interests	(2304)	(2150)	2813
Net Income	$ 888,089	$ 571,362	$ 461,271

*The income statement information was taken from the 10-K report of VF Corporation and has been summarized and reformatted by the authors.

Source: VF Corporation 2011 10-K.

EXHIBIT 12.3

VF Corporation Income Statement and Balance Sheet (*Continued*)

VF Corporation
Consolidated Balance Sheets

	December 2011	2010 (in thousands)	2009
ASSETS			
Current Assets			
Cash and equivalents	$ 341,228	$ 792,239	$ 731,549
Accounts receivable (gross)	1,174,256	817,682	836,520
Allowance for doubtful accounts	54,010	44,599	60,380
Accounts receivable (net)	1,120,246	773,083	776,140
Inventories	1,453,645	1,070,694	958,639
Deferred income taxes	106,717	68,220	64,959
Other current assets	166,108	121,824	101,275
Total current assets	3,187,944	2,826,060	2,632,562
Property, Plant and Equipment	737,451	602,908	614,178
Intangible Assets	2,958,463	1,490,925	1,535,121
Goodwill	2,023,460	1,166,638	1,367,680
Other Assets	405,808	371,025	324,322
Total assets	$9,313,126	$6,457,556	$6,473,863
LIABILITIES AND STOCKHOLDERS' EQUITY			
Current Liabilities			
Short-term borrowings	$ 281,686	$ 36,576	$ 45,453
Current portion of long-term debt	2,744	2,737	203,179
Accounts payable	637,116	510,998	373,186
Accrued liabilities	744,486	559,164	473,971
Total current liabilities	1,666,032	1,109,475	1,095,789
Long-term Debt	1,831,781	935,882	938,494
Other Liabilities	1,290,138	550,880	626,295
Commitments and Contingencies	–	–	–
Stockholders' Equity			
Preferred stock	–	–	–
Common stock	110,557	107,938	110,285
Additional paid-in capital	2,316,107	2,081,367	1,864,499
Accumulated other comprehensive income (loss)	(421,477)	(268,594)	(209,742)
Retained earnings	2,520,804	1,940,508	2,050,109
Total equity attributable to VF Corp.	4,525,991	3,861,219	3,815,151
Noncontrolling interests	(816)	100	(1,866)
Total stockholders' equity	4,525,175	3,861,319	3,813,285
Total liabilities and stockholders' equity	$9,313,126	$6,457,556	$6,473,863

Source: VF Corporation 2011 10-K.

From Cornerstone 12.4, you can see that VF's current ratio is safely above the industry average of 1.49. However, its quick and cash ratios are below the 1.0 threshold considered adequate. The questions, in this case, are how confident are you in the collectibility of the receivable and is there an adequate allowance for doubtful accounts. Further, the operating cash flow ratio may require some investigation to determine whether operations are generating sufficient cash to meet current obligations.

CORNERSTONE

12.4

Calculating and Interpreting Short-Term Liquidity Ratios

Why:

Short-term liquidity ratios assess the corporation's ability to meet its current obligations.

Information:

Refer to the information in VF's income statement and balance sheet in Exhibit 12.3 (pp. 662–663). VF's cash flows from operations were (in thousands) $1,001,282 and $1,081,371 in 2010 and 2011, respectively.

Required:

Calculate the following short-term liquidity ratios for VF for 2010 and 2011: (1) current ratio, (2) quick ratio, (3) cash ratio, and (4) operating cash flow ratio (operating cash flows are provided in the Information section).

Solution:

	2011 (in thousands)	2010 (in thousands)
1. Current Ratio $= \dfrac{\text{Current Assets}}{\text{Current Liabilities}}$	$\dfrac{\$3{,}187{,}944}{\$1{,}666{,}032} = \underline{\underline{1.91}}$	$\dfrac{\$2{,}826{,}060}{\$1{,}109{,}475} = \underline{\underline{2.55}}$
2. Quick Ratio $= \dfrac{\text{Cash + Short-Term Investments + Receivables}}{\text{Current Liabilities}}$	$\dfrac{(\$341{,}228 + \$0 + \$1{,}120{,}246)}{\$1{,}666{,}032} = \underline{\underline{0.88}}$	$\dfrac{(\$792{,}239 + \$0 + \$773{,}083)}{\$1{,}109{,}475} = \underline{\underline{1.41}}$
3. Cash Ratio $= \dfrac{\text{Cash + Short-Term Investments}}{\text{Current Liabilities}}$	$\dfrac{(\$341{,}228 + \$0)}{\$1{,}666{,}032} = \underline{\underline{0.20}}$	$\dfrac{(\$792{,}239 + \$0)}{\$1{,}109{,}475} = \underline{\underline{0.71}}$
4. Operating Cash Flow Ratio $= \dfrac{\text{Cash Flows from Operating Activities}}{\text{Current Liabilities}}$	$\dfrac{\$1{,}081{,}371^{*}}{\$1{,}666{,}032} = \underline{\underline{0.65}}$	$\dfrac{\$1{,}001{,}282^{*}}{\$1{,}109{,}475} = \underline{\underline{0.90}}$

*Taken from the statement of cash flows. The numbers were provided in the Information section of this Cornerstone.

Source: VF Corporation 2011 10-K.

Compared to Under Armour's short term liquidity ratios shown previously in the text, VF's short-term liquidity ratios are generally weaker, albeit adequate. This suggests that VF's risk of short-term insolvency is higher, although neither corporation is in much danger.

Debt Management Ratios

Debt management ratios provide information on two aspects of debt. First, they provide information on the relative mix of debt and equity financing (often referred to as its capital structure). The primary advantages of debt over equity are:

- Interest payments are tax-deductible.
- Creditors do not share in profits.

Debt, however, is riskier than equity, because, unless the interest and principal payments are made when due, the firm may fall into bankruptcy. In most corporations, management attempts to achieve an appropriate balance between the cost advantage of debt and its extra risk.

Second, debt management ratios also try to show the corporation's ability to meet or cover its debt obligations through operations because interest and principal payments must be made as scheduled or a company can be declared bankrupt. The times interest earned ratio is an example of the latter type of measurement.

Times Interest Earned Ratio Some liabilities, like accounts payable, have flexible payment schedules that can be modified when necessary. Other liabilities—primarily short-term and long-term debt—have specific payment schedules that must be met. The cash used to make these payments must come from operations. Analysts use the times interest earned ratio to gauge a firm's ability to repay its debt from recurring operations. This ratio can focus either on accrual-basis interest expense or the cash-basis interest payments and are typically measured pretax because interest expense is tax deductible. The **times interest earned ratio** is expressed as:

$$\text{Times Interest Earned } (\textit{Accrual Basis}) = \frac{\text{Operating Income}}{\text{Interest Expense}}$$

$$\text{Times Interest Earned } (\textit{Cash Basis}) = \frac{\text{Cash Flows from Operations} + \text{Income Tax Payments} + \text{Interest Payments}}{\text{Interest Payments}}$$

The times interest earned ratios for Under Armour are calculated as:

	2011	2010
Cash flows from operating activities	$ 15,218*	$ 50,114*
Operating income	162,767	112,355
Interest payments	2,305*	992*
Interest expense	3,900**	2,300**
Income tax payments	56,940*	38,773*
Times interest earned (cash)	**32.30**	**90.60**
Times interest earned (accrual)	**41.74**	**48.85**

* Taken from the statement of cash flows.
** Taken from the last paragraph of Note 7.
Source: Under Armour 2011 10-K.

Note that interest expense is often included in the financial statement footnotes because many corporations, including Under Armour, net interest income with interest expense on the face of the income statement. Under Armour appears to have an easy time covering its interest expense/payments.

While times interest earned ratio provides information on the company's ability to meet, or cover, its debt obligations, other debt management ratios assess the relative mix of debt and equity financing. We will consider four different ways of measuring the proportion of debt within a corporation's capital structure.

Long-Term Debt to Equity Ratio Despite its apparent misnomer, we prefer to define long-term debt as the sum of long-term debt and the debt-like obligations in current liabilities (notes or short-term loans). It is called the long-term debt to equity ratio because historically when corporations borrowed money, they locked themselves into long-term debt contracts. The long-term debt to equity ratio provides information on the proportion of capital provided by creditors and by stockholders. Of course, this type of debt also includes any current portion (i.e., long-term debt principal that must be repaid within the next 12 months). Additionally, it can include more flexible borrowing arrangements, such as lines of credit, that may be classified as current liabilities. The **long-term debt to equity ratio** is expressed as:

$$\text{Long-Term Debt to Equity Ratio} = \frac{\text{Long-Term Debt (including current portion)}}{\text{Total Equity}}$$

Under Armour has a long-term debt to equity ratio of 0.12 and 0.03 in 2011 and 2010, respectively, based on long-term debt of $77,724 in 2011 and $15,942 in 2010 (including $6,882 in 2011 and $6,865 in 2010 of current portion of long-term debt). This represents a substantial increase in long-term debt which helped fund the substantial increase in property, plant, and equipment and inventory. It also is above the industry average of 0.09, so some monitoring of debt is warranted.

Debt to Equity Ratio Debt is also occasionally defined as all liabilities. This is a more inclusive view of debt recognizing that if corporations did not have current liabilities such as accounts payable, they would have to take out other borrowings or sell stock to finance its assets. The **debt to equity ratio** is expressed as:

$$\text{Debt to Equity Ratio} = \frac{\text{Total Liabilities}}{\text{Total Equity}}$$

Under Armour's debt to equity ratio was 0.44 in 2011 and 0.36 in 2010.

Long-Term Debt or Debt to Total Assets The proportion of total capital provided by creditors is also shown by the **long-term debt to total assets ratio** and the **debt to total assets ratio**. These measures are more useful when equity is small or subject to substantial changes. These ratios are expressed as:

$$\text{Long-Term Debt to Total Assets Ratio} = \frac{\text{Long-Term Debt (including current portion)}}{\text{Total Assets}}$$

$$\text{Debt to Total Assets Ratio} = \frac{\text{Total Liabilities}}{\text{Total Assets}}$$

Overview of Debt Management Ratios Cornerstone 12.5 demonstrates how to calculate and interpret debt management ratios.

CORNERSTONE 12.5

Calculating and Interpreting Debt Management Ratios

Why:

Debt management ratios provide information on the company's ability to meet its debt obligations through operations.

Information:

Refer to the information in VF's income statement and balance sheet in Exhibit 12.3 (pp. 662–663). Additional financial statement information follows (all $ amount are in thousands).

	2011 (in thousands)	2010 (in thousands)
Cash flows from operations*	$1,081,371	$1,001,282
Interest payments**	66,775	81,083
Income tax payments**	205,333	262,802

* Taken from the statement of cash flows.
** Taken from Note V of the financial statements.

Required:

Calculate the following debt management ratios for VF for 2010 and 2011: (1) times interest earned ratio (both cash and accrual), (2) long-term debt to equity ratio, (3) debt to equity ratio, (4) long-term debt to total assets ratio, and (5) debt to total assets ratio.

Source: VF Corporation 2011 10-K.

(Continued)

CORNERSTONE **12.5** *(Continued)*

Solution:

		2011 (in thousands)	**2010 (in thousands)**
1. Times Interest Earned (*Accrual Basis*)	$= \dfrac{\text{Operating Income}}{\text{Interest Expense}}$	$\dfrac{\$1,244,791}{\$77,578} = \underline{\underline{16.05}}$	$\dfrac{\$820,860}{\$77,738} = \underline{\underline{10.56}}$
Times Interest Earned (*Cash Basis*)	$= \dfrac{\text{Cash Flows from Operations + Income Tax Payments + Interest Payments}}{\text{Interest Payments*}}$	$\dfrac{\$1,081,371+\$205,333+\$66,775}{\$66,775} = \underline{\underline{20.27}}$	$\dfrac{\$1,001,282+\$262,802+\$81,083}{\$81,083} = \underline{\underline{16.59}}$
2. Long-Term Debt to Equity	$= \dfrac{\text{Long-Term Debt (including current portion)}}{\text{Total Equity}}$	$\dfrac{\$1,831,781 + \$2,744}{\$4,525,175} = \underline{\underline{0.41}}$	$\dfrac{\$935,882 + \$2,737}{\$3,861,319} = \underline{\underline{0.24}}$
3. Debt to Equity	$= \dfrac{\text{Total Liabilities}}{\text{Total Equity}}$	$\dfrac{\$1,666,032+\$1,831,781+\$1,290,138}{\$4,525,175} = \underline{\underline{1.06}}$	$\dfrac{\$1,109,475+935,882+\$550,880}{\$3,861,319} = \underline{\underline{0.67}}$
4. Long-Term Debt to Total Assets	$= \dfrac{\text{Long-Term Debt (including current portion)}}{\text{Total Assets}}$	$\dfrac{\$1,831,781 + \$2,744}{\$9,313,126} = \underline{\underline{0.20}}$	$\dfrac{\$935,882 + \$2,737}{\$6,457,556} = \underline{\underline{0.15}}$
5. Debt to Total Assets	$= \dfrac{\text{Total Liabilities}}{\text{Total Assets}}$	$\dfrac{\$1,666,032 + 1,831,781 + \$1,290,138}{\$9,313,126} = \underline{\underline{0.51}}$	$\dfrac{\$1,109,475 + 935,882 + \$550,880}{\$6,457,556} = \underline{\underline{0.40}}$

*Taken from Note 6

Source: VF Corporation 2011 10-K.

From the times interest earned ratios in Cornerstone 12.5, you can see that VF Corporation produced sufficient operating income and cash flows from operations to easily meet its interest expense in both years.

The long-term debt to equity, debt to equity, long-term debt to total assets, and debt to total asset ratios suggest a company financed approximately half by debt and half by equity. The trend, however, indicates that VF has taken on additional debt in the last year. It may be wise to consider more years to get a better picture of the trend and investigate reasons for the increasing debt burden.

YOUDECIDE Credit Analysis

You are a loan officer at First National Bank. Your assistant has prepared the following financial statement and debt management ratio information to help you evaluate Carmody Manufacturing's loan application:

	2013	**2012**	**2011**	**Industry (2011–2013)**
Sales	171.2%	131.9%	100%	183.2%
Gross margin	168.7%	129.4%	100%	184.6%
Operating expenses	180.3%	134.7%	100%	160.5%
Operating income	160.5%	124.3%	100%	202.4%
Net income	162.2%	125.7%	100%	201.7%

(Continued)

You also have the following data for the year ended December 31, 2013:

For the Years 2009–2013	Carmody Manufacturing	Industry
Average current ratio	2.06	1.55
Average debt to equity ratio	19.47	80.14
Average long-term debt to equity ratio	17.23	49.83
Average times interest earned (accrual)	9.55	3.87

Carmody has asked First National for a long-term loan that will double its long-term debt.

Should you approve the loan for Carmody?

The data you have is somewhat mixed. The debt management ratios are outstanding for the industry. Even after doubling the amount of long-term debt, it is apparent that Carmody will remain better than the industry averages for the debt to equity, long-term debt to equity, and times interest earned ratios. The operating results, however, are not as encouraging. Carmody's growth is somewhat below industry averages. Further, the growth in operating expenses signals a problem—especially when you consider that many operating expenses are fixed (such as salaries).

Although you probably want to follow up with Carmody regarding its projected results of operations, given its low debt burden, First National should probably grant the loan.

Asset Efficiency Ratios

Asset efficiency ratios (or **operating ratios**) are measures of how efficiently a company uses its assets. The principal asset efficiency ratios are measures of **turnover**, that is, the average length of time required for assets to be consumed or replaced. The faster an asset is turned over, the more efficiently it is being used. These ratios provide managers and other users of a corporation's financial statements with easily interpreted measures of the time required to turn receivables into cash, inventory into cost of goods sold, or total assets into sales.

But managers are not the only people interested in asset efficiency ratios. Since well-managed efficiently operated companies are usually among the most profitable, and since profits are the sources of cash from which long-term creditors receive their interest and principal payments, creditors seek information about the corporation's profit prospects from asset efficiency ratios. And stockholders find that larger profits are usually followed by increased dividends and higher stock prices, so they, too, are concerned with indicators of efficiency.

Accounts Receivable Turnover Ratio

The length of time required to collect the receivable from a credit sale is the time required to turn over accounts receivable. The accounts receivable turnover ratio indicates how many times accounts receivable is turned over each year. The more times accounts receivable turns over each year, the more efficient are the firm's credit-granting and credit-collection activities. The **accounts receivable turnover ratio** is expressed as:

$$\text{Accounts Receivable Turnover Ratio} = \frac{\text{Net Credit Sales or Net Sales}}{\text{Average Accounts Receivable}}$$

In the equation above, "net credit sales" means credit sales minus sales returns and allowances. While some firms make all their sales on credit, many also make a substantial proportion of their sales for cash (or on credit cards, which are essentially cash sales). It is unusual for a company making cash and credit sales to report the proportion that is credit sales. For that reason, the accounts receivable turnover ratio is often computed using whatever number the firm reports for sales. In addition, to find the average balance for any financial statement account, like average accounts receivable, divide the sum of the beginning and ending balances by two.

Using net sales, Under Armour's receivables turnover ratios were 11.73 and 12.48 for 2010 and 2011, respectively. This is far better than the 2011 industry average of 7.96, so Under Armour is very efficient at collecting cash from its sales.

Careful analysts examine quarterly or monthly financial statements, when available, to determine whether the amount of receivables recorded in the annual statements is representative of the receivables carried during the year. For example, businesses in the apparel industry, like Under Armour, often have much larger receivables after the Christmas selling season than during other parts of the year.

Inventory Turnover Ratio Inventory turnover is the length of time required to sell inventory to customers. The more efficient a firm, the more times inventory will be turned over. The **inventory turnover ratio** indicates the number of times inventory is sold during the year and is expressed as:

$$\text{Inventory Turnover Ratio} = \frac{\text{Cost of Goods Sold}}{\text{Average Inventory}}$$

Average inventory is beginning inventory plus ending inventory divided by 2.

Under Armour's inventory turnover ratios were 2.93 and 2.82 for 2010 and 2011, respectively. This means that Under Armour turns over its inventory a little under three times per year or about once every 4 months. Remember that inventory sitting in the warehouse or on the shelf is not earning a return. The weakening inventory turnover deserves some attention, although it's not a drastic decrease. For example, does the slower moving inventory indicate weakening sales? Further, the industry average is 2.28, so Under Armour is relatively efficient with its inventory.

Now that we have examined both receivables and inventory turnover, let us combine these measurements to approximate the length of the operating cycle (the length of time required for an investment in inventory to produce cash). Under Armour's 2011 operating cycle can be estimated by adding the number of days needed to turn over both receivables and inventory. The inventory turns over in approximately 129 days (365 days ÷ 2.82 inventory turnover ratio) and the receivables turn over in approximately 29 days (365 days ÷ 12.48 receivables turnover ratio), which gives an operating cycle of approximately 158 days.

The longer the operating cycle, the larger the investment necessary in receivables and inventory. When assets are larger, more liabilities and equity are required to finance them. Large amounts of capital negatively affect net income and cash flows for dividends. Therefore, firms attempt to maintain as short an operating cycle as possible. Under Armour's operating cycle is between 5 and 6 months.

Asset Turnover Ratio Another measure of the efficiency of a corporation's operations is the **asset turnover ratio**. This ratio measures the efficiency with which a corporation's assets are used to produce sales revenues. The more sales dollars produced by each dollar invested in assets, the more efficiently a firm is considered to be operating. The asset turnover ratio is expressed as:

$$\text{Asset Turnover Ratio} = \frac{\text{Net Sales}}{\text{Average Total Assets}}$$

Average total assets equals beginning total assets plus ending total assets divided by 2.

Under Armour's asset turnover ratios were 1.74 and 1.85 in 2010 and 2011, respectively, which means about every 197 days (365 ÷ 1.85) in 2011. The asset turnover average for the industry is 0.71, so Under Armour is far above the industry average.

Care must be exercised when evaluating the asset turnover ratio. Some industries (such as electric utilities and capital intensive manufacturers) require a substantially larger investment in assets to produce a sales dollar than do other industries (such as fast-food restaurants or footwear and catalog merchants). And obviously, a company's total assets turn over much more slowly than its inventories and receivables.

Overview of Asset Efficiency Ratios Cornerstone 12.6 illustrates how to calculate and interpret asset efficiency ratios.

CORNERSTONE

12.6

Calculating and Interpreting Asset Efficiency Ratios

Why:

Asset efficiency ratios are measures of how efficiently a corporation uses its assets.

Information:

Refer to the information in VF's income statements and balance sheet in Exhibit 12.3 (pp. 662–663).

Required:

Calculate the following asset efficiency ratios for VF for 2010 and 2011: (1) accounts receivable turnover ratio, (2) inventory turnover ratio, and (3) asset turnover ratio.

Solution:

Ratio	Formula	2011 (in thousands)	2010 (in thousands)
1. Accounts Receivable Turnover Ratio	= Net Sales / Average Accounts Receivable*	$9,365,477 / [($1,120,246 + $773,083) ÷ 2] = 9.89	$7,624,599 / [($773,083 + $776,140) ÷ 2] = 9.84
2. Inventory Turnover Ratio	= Cost of Goods Sold / Average Inventories	$5,128,602 / [($1,453,645 + $1,070,694) ÷ 2] = 4.06	$4,105,201 / [($1,070,694 + $958,639) ÷ 2] = 4.05
3. Asset Turnover Ratio	= Net Sales / Average Total Assets	$9,365,477 / [($9,313,126 + $6,457,556) ÷ 2] = 1.19	$7,624,599 / [($6,457,556 + $6,473,863) ÷ 2] = 1.18

*Note: Average Balance = (Beginning Balance + Ending Balance) / 2

Source: VF Corporation 2011 10-K.

While Under Armour has a significantly stronger receivables turnover than VF, VF's inventory turnover is much stronger than Under Armour's. Further, VF's operating cycle of approximately 126 days is considerable shorter than Under Armour's of about 158 days. Interestingly, despite this operating cycle advantage, Under Armour possesses an asset turnover advantage.

It is important to note that turnover ratios must be interpreted carefully. A company's ability to increase its receivables turnover is limited by competitive considerations. If competitors allow customers a lengthy period before payment is expected, then the firm must offer similar credit terms or lose customers. In periods of high interest rates, the cost of carrying customers' receivables should not be underestimated. For example, a firm with credit sales of $10,000 per day that collects in 30 rather than 90 days would save $72,000 per year at a 12% annual interest rate (60 days × $10,000 × 12%).

However, a corporation's ability to increase its inventory turnover is also affected by its strategy and what the competition is doing. For example, if its strategy is to offer a wide selection or if its competitors stock large quantities of inventory, a corporation will be forced to keep more inventory on hand. This, of course, leads to lower inventory turnover.

Asset efficiency ratios measure the efficiency of a corporation's operations—a factor ultimately related to the corporation's profits. Let us now examine some direct measures of a corporation's profitability.

Profitability Ratios

Profitability ratios measure two aspects of a corporation's profits:

- elements of operations that contribute to profit
- the relationship of profit to total investment and investment by stockholders

The first group of profitability ratios, which includes gross profit (or gross margin) percentage, operating margin percentage, and net profit margin percentage, expresses income statement elements as percentages of net sales. The second group of profitability ratios, which includes return on assets and return on equity, divides measures of income by measures of investment.

Gross Profit (or Gross Margin) Percentage **Gross profit percentage** is a measurement of the proportion of each sales dollar that is available to pay other expenses and provide profit for owners. It indicates the effectiveness of pricing, marketing, purchasing, and production decisions. Gross profit percentage is expressed as:

$$\text{Gross Profit Percentage} = \frac{\text{Gross Profit}}{\text{Net Sales}}$$

Under Armour's gross profit percentage was 49.86% in 2010 and 48.40% in 2011. This means that for every dollar in sales the merchandise cost approximately 51 cents, which results in approximately 49 cents in gross profit. This is far above the industry average of 32.85%.

Operating Margin Percentage The operating margin percentage measures the profitability of a company's operations in relation to its sales. All operating revenues and expenses are included in income from operations, but expenses, revenues, gains, and losses that are unrelated to operations are excluded. For example, a retailer would exclude interest revenues produced by its credit activities from income from operations. The **operating margin percentage** is expressed as:

$$\text{Operating Margin Percentage} = \frac{\text{Income from Operations}}{\text{Net Sales}}$$

Under Armour's operating margin percentage was 10.56% in 2010 and 11.05% in 2011. The difference between the gross profit and operating margin percentage of approximately 37% in 2011 (48.40% gross margin percentage – 11.05% operating margin percentage) means that approximately 37 cents of every dollar of sales were spent on operating expenses in 2011. Although an operating margin of 11.05% may not sound very good, it is well above the industry average of 7.72% for the year.

Net Profit Margin Percentage The net profit margin percentage measures the proportion of each sales dollar that is profit. The **net profit margin percentage** is expressed as:

$$\text{Net Profit Margin Percentage} = \frac{\text{Net Income}}{\text{Net Sales}}$$

Under Armour's net profit margin percentage was 6.44% in 2010 and 6.58% in 2011. The 2011 figure is far above the industry average of 4.82%.

In evaluating the gross profit, operating margin, and net profit margin percentage, it is important to recognize that there is substantial variation in profit margins from industry to industry. For example, retail grocery stores, such as Kroger and Safeway, earn a relatively small amount of gross profit, operating margin, and net income per sales dollar. Pharmaceutical manufacturers, such as Pfizer and Eli Lilly, on the other hand, earn much more per sales dollar. Since the magnitude of these percentages is affected by many factors, changes from period to period must be investigated to determine the cause.

Return on Assets The return on assets ratio measures the profit earned by a corporation through use of all its capital, or the total of the investment by both creditors and owners. The **return on assets ratio** is expressed as:

$$\text{Return on Assets} = \frac{\text{Net Income} + [\text{Interest Expense} \times (1 - \text{Tax Rate})]}{\text{Average Total Assets}}$$

Profit, or return, is determined by adding interest expense net of tax to net income. Interest expense net of tax is expressed as:

$$\text{Interest Net of Tax} = \text{Interest Expense} \times (1 - \text{Tax Rate})$$

Interest expense is added to net income because it is a return to creditors for their capital contributions. Because the actual capital contribution made by creditors is included in the denominator (average total assets), the numerator must be computed on a comparable basis.

Under Armour's return on assets was 11.45% in 2010 and 12.46% in 2011. As with the percentages discussed above, appropriate values for this ratio vary from industry to industry because of differences in risk. Over a several-year period, the average return on assets for an electric utility ought to be smaller than the average return on assets for a company that makes and sells home appliances. Companies in the home appliance industry, such as Whirlpool Corporation, have a much larger variability of net income because their operations are more sensitive to economic conditions. The average for the Apparel and Accessories industry is 4.93%, so Under Armour is well above the mean in 2011 for this ratio.

Return on Equity The return on equity ratio measures the profit earned by a firm through the use of capital supplied by stockholders. Return on equity is similar to return on assets, except that the payments to creditors are removed from the numerator and the creditors' capital contributions are removed from the denominator. The **return on equity ratio** is expressed as:

$$\text{Return on Equity} = \frac{\text{Net Income}}{\text{Average Equity}}$$

One of the primary objectives of the management of a firm is to maximize returns for its stockholders. Although the link between a corporation's net income and increases in dividends and share price return is not perfect, the return on equity ratio is still an effective measure of management's performance for the stockholders. As is the case with return on assets, firms often differ in return on equity because of differences in risk. For example, the average several-year return on equity for a grocery store should be lower than the average return on equity for a retail department store because of the lower sensitivity to economic conditions.

The return on equity for Under Armour was 15.27% and 17.10% in 2010 and 2011, respectively, which is also significantly greater than the industry average of 8.35% in 2011.

Overview of Profitability Ratios Cornerstone 12.7 demonstrates how to calculate and interpret profitability ratios.

Calculating and Interpreting Profitability Ratios

CORNERSTONE 12.7

Why:

Profitability ratios measure elements of operations that contribute to profit and the relationship of profit to total investment and investment by stockholders.

Information:

Refer to the information in VF's income statement and balance sheet in Exhibit 12.3 (pp. 662–663).

Required:

Calculate the following profitability ratios for VF for 2010 and 2011: (1) gross profit percentage, (2) operating margin percentage, (3) net profit margin percentage, (4) return on assets, and (5) return on equity.

Solution:

2011 (in thousands) | **2010 (in thousands)**

1. Gross Profit Percentage $= \dfrac{\text{Gross Profit}}{\text{Net Sales}}$

2011: $\dfrac{\$9{,}365{,}477 - \$5{,}128{,}602}{\$9{,}365{,}477} = \underline{\underline{45.24\%}}$

2010: $\dfrac{\$7{,}624{,}599 - \$4{,}105{,}201}{\$7{,}624{,}599} = \underline{\underline{46.16\%}}$

2. Operating Margin Percentage $= \dfrac{\text{Income from Operations}}{\text{Net Sales}}$

2011: $\dfrac{\$1{,}244{,}791}{\$9{,}365{,}477} = \underline{\underline{13.29\%}}$

2010: $\dfrac{\$820{,}860}{\$7{,}624{,}599} = \underline{\underline{10.77\%}}$

3. Net Profit Margin Percentage $= \dfrac{\text{Net Income}}{\text{Net Sales}}$

2011: $\dfrac{\$888{,}089}{\$9{,}365{,}477} = \underline{\underline{9.48\%}}$

2010: $\dfrac{\$571{,}362}{\$7{,}624{,}599} = \underline{\underline{7.49\%}}$

4. Return on Assets $= \dfrac{\text{Net Income} + [\text{Interest Expense} \times (1 - \text{Tax Rate*})]}{\text{Average Total Assets**}}$

2011

$\dfrac{\$888{,}089 + [77{,}578 \times (1 - 23.55\%)]}{[(\$9{,}313{,}126 + \$6{,}457{,}556) \div 2]} = \underline{\underline{12.01\%}}$

2010

$\dfrac{\$571{,}362 + [77{,}738 \times (1 - 23.55\%)]}{[(\$6{,}457{,}556 + \$6{,}473{,}863) \div 2]} = \underline{\underline{9.76\%}}$

**Note:* $\left(\text{Tax Rate} = \dfrac{\text{Income Taxes}}{\text{Income before Taxes}}\right)$

***Note:* Average Total Assets $= \dfrac{\text{Beginning Total Assets} + \text{Ending Total Assets}}{2}$

5. Return on Equity $= \dfrac{\text{Net Income}}{\text{Average Equity*}}$

2011

$\dfrac{\$888{,}089}{[(\$4{,}525{,}175 + \$3{,}861{,}319) \div 2]} = \underline{\underline{21.18\%}}$

2010

$\dfrac{\$571{,}362}{[(\$3{,}861{,}319 + \$3{,}813{,}285) \div 2]} = \underline{\underline{14.89\%}}$

**Note:* Average Equity $= \dfrac{\text{Beginning Equity} + \text{Ending Equity}}{2}$

Source: VF Corporation 2011 10-K.

As you can see in Cornerstone 12.7, although **Under Armour** has a slightly better gross profit percentage, **VF** is slightly better for all other profitability ratios in 2011. We will discuss how VF likely creates this advantage more fully in the Dupont Analysis section.

Stockholder Ratios

Stockholders are primarily interested in two things:

- the creation of value
- the distribution of value

Stockholder ratios such as earnings per share and return on common equity provide information about the creation of value for stockholders. As discussed in Chapter 10, value is distributed to stockholders in one of two ways. Either the corporation issues dividends or repurchases stock. The remainder of the stockholder ratios—dividend yield, dividend payout, stock repurchase payout, and total payout—address this distribution of value.

Earnings per Share (EPS) Earnings per share ratio (EPS) measures the income available for common stockholders on a per-share basis and is examined by nearly all statement users. **Earnings per share ratio (EPS)** is expressed as:

$$\text{Earnings per Share Ratio} = \frac{\text{Net Income} - \text{Preferred Dividends}}{\text{Average Number of Common Shares Outstanding}}$$

For the average number of common shares outstanding, remember that treasury shares are not considered to be outstanding. Preferred dividends are subtracted from net income because those payments are a return to holders of shares other than common stock. In fact, the numerator, net income minus preferred dividends, is often called *income available for common shareholders.*

Although this formula allows you to calculate EPS on your own, corporations are also required to disclose EPS on the income statement. For example, **Under Armour**'s EPS was $1.35 in 2010 and $1.88 in 2011.

Return on Common Equity The return on common equity ratio is arguably the most important ratio for investors. It's similar to the return on equity discussed in the profitability ratio section, but it uses the return on *common* equity rather than equity. Common equity is expressed as:

$$\text{Common Equity} = \text{Total Equity} - \text{Preferred Stock}$$

The **return on common equity ratio** is expressed as:

$$\text{Return on Common Equity} = \frac{\text{Net Income}}{\text{Average Common Equity}}$$

When there is no preferred stock, as is the case for **Under Armour**, return on common equity will equal traditional return on equity (ROE) because common equity will equal total equity.

Dividend Yield Ratio The dividend yield ratio measures the rate at which dividends provide a return to stockholders by comparing dividends with the market price of a share of stock. This ratio is conceptually similar to an interest rate on debt where the dividend is like the interest payment and the cost of the share of stock is the principal. The **dividend yield ratio** is expressed as:

$$\text{Dividend Yield Ratio} = \frac{\text{Dividends per Common Share}}{\text{Closing Market Price per Share for the Year}}$$

For 2011, Under Armour did not pay dividends, and the closing market value of its common shares was $71.79. This gives a dividend yield ratio of 0%, which is below the industry average of 1.14%.

Dividend yield is affected by both the corporation's dividend policy and the behavior of its stock price. Because stock prices often change by substantial amounts over short periods, the dividend yield ratio is not stable. In fact, when a stock is traded regularly, the market price is likely to change many times each day. For this reason, some analysts compute dividend yield based on the average stock price for a given period. Others use the highest and the lowest prices for a period and present the dividend yield as a range. For ease, we calculate dividend yield using the closing market price for the year.

Dividend Payout Ratio The dividend payout ratio measures the proportion of a corporation's profits that are returned to the stockholders immediately as dividends. The **dividend payout ratio** is expressed as:

$$\text{Dividend Payout Ratio} = \frac{\text{Common Dividends}}{\text{Net Income}}$$

You could also calculate dividend payout using per share amounts (Dividends per Share ÷ EPS). You can find the dividends paid in the retained earnings column of the statement of stockholders' equity.

As stated above, Under Armour did not pay dividends in 2011, which also means its dividend payout ratio is 0%.

The dividend payout ratio varies from corporation to corporation, even within a given industry. Many corporations attempt to pay some stable proportion of earnings as dividends, while others never pay a dividend. Corporations are reluctant to reduce dividends unless absolutely necessary. The result of these two tendencies is that dividends per share are usually increased only when management is confident that higher earnings per share can be sustained. An increase in the dividend payout ratio is usually a signal that management expects future net income to be larger and sustainable.

Stock Repurchase Payout Ratio The **stock repurchase payout ratio** is expressed as:

$$\text{Stock Repurchase Payout Ratio} = \frac{\text{Common Stock Repurchases}}{\text{Net Income}}$$

You can find stock repurchases by looking at the Treasury Stock column of the statement of stockholders' equity.

Under Armour did not repurchase any stock during 2010 or 2011. Failing to pay dividends and repurchase stock is not unusual for companies in a high-growth phase, because they are using their cash to expand operations.

Total Payout Ratio The **total payout ratio** is expressed as:

$$\text{Total Payout Ratio} = \frac{\text{Common Dividends} + \text{Common Stock Repurchases}}{\text{Net Income}}$$

This ratio can also be calculated indirectly as:

$$\text{Total Payout Ratio} = \text{Dividend Payout Ratio} + \text{Stock Repurchase Payout Ratio}$$

Of course, the total payout ratio for Under Armour is also 0%.

Overview of Stockholder Ratios Cornerstone 12.8 demonstrates how to calculate and interpret the stockholder ratios.

CORNERSTONE

12.8

Calculating and Interpreting Stockholder Ratios

Why:

Stockholder ratios measure the creation of value and the distribution of value to stockholders.

Information:

Refer to the information for VF's income statement and balance sheet in Exhibit 12.3 (pp. 662–663). All following dollar amount are in thousands, except for per share amounts. VF's average common shares for 2011 and 2010 were 109,287 and 108,764, respectively. They paid dividends of $285,722 ($2.61 per share) and $264,281 ($2.43 per share) for 2011 and 2010, respectively. VF repurchased $7,420 of common shares in 2011 and $411,838 of common shares in 2010. (Average common shares are typically disclosed on the income statement. Information regarding dividends and stock repurchases can be found in the statement of stockholders' equity and/or the statement of cash flows.) The price of VF's stock was $126.99 and $86.18 at the end of 2011 and 2010, respectively.

Required:

Calculate the following stockholder ratios for VF for 2010 and 2011: (1) earnings per share, (2) return on common equity, (3) dividend yield, (4) dividend payout, (5) total payout, and (6) share repurchase payout.

Solution:

1. $$\text{EPS} = \frac{\text{Net Income} - \text{Preferred Dividends}}{\text{Average Number of Common Shares Outstanding}}$$

$$\textbf{2011: } \frac{\$888{,}089 - \$0}{109{,}287} = \underline{\underline{\$8.13}} \qquad \textbf{2010: } \frac{\$571{,}362 - \$0}{108{,}764} = \underline{\underline{\$5.25}}$$

2. $$\text{Return on Common Equity} = \frac{\text{Net Income}}{\text{Average Common Equity*}}$$

$$\textbf{2011: } \frac{\$888{,}089}{[(\$4{,}525{,}175 - \$0 - \$0) + (\$3{,}861{,}319 - \$0 - \$0) \div 2]} = \underline{21.18\%}$$

$$\textbf{2010: } \frac{\$571{,}362}{[(\$3{,}861{,}319 - \$0 - \$0) + (\$3{,}813{,}285 - \$0 - \$0) \div 2]} = \underline{14.89\%}$$

*Common Equity = Total Equity − Preferred Stock – Additional Paid-In Capital–Preferred Stock

3. $$\text{Dividend Yield Ratio} = \frac{\text{Dividends per Common Share**}}{\text{Closing Market Price per Share for the Year}}$$

$$\textbf{2011: } \frac{\$2.61}{\$126.99} = \underline{\underline{2.06\%}} \qquad \textbf{2010: } \frac{\$2.43}{\$86.18} = \underline{\underline{2.82\%}}$$

**Dividends per share are taken from the Selected Financial Data. Amounts are given in the Information section of this Cornerstone.

4. $$\text{Dividend Payout Ratio} = \frac{\text{Common Dividends}}{\text{Net Income}}$$

$$\textbf{2011: } \frac{\$285{,}722}{\$888{,}089} = \underline{\underline{32.17\%}} \qquad \textbf{2010: } \frac{\$264{,}281}{\$571{,}362} = \underline{\underline{46.25\%}}$$

5. $$\text{Stock Repurchase Payout Ratio} = \frac{\text{Common Stock Repurchases}}{\text{Net Income}}$$

$$\textbf{2011: } \frac{\$7{,}420}{\$888{,}089} = \underline{\underline{0.84\%}} \qquad \textbf{2010: } \frac{\$411{,}838}{\$571{,}362} = \underline{\underline{72.08\%}}$$

6. $$\text{Total Payout Ratio} = \frac{\text{Common Dividends} + \text{Common Stock Repurchases}}{\text{Net Income}}$$

$$\textbf{2011: } \frac{\$285{,}722 + \$7{,}420}{\$888{,}089} = \underline{\underline{33.01\%}} \qquad \textbf{2010: } \frac{\$264{,}281 + \$411{,}838}{\$571{,}362} = \underline{\underline{118.33\%}}$$

Source: VF Corporation 2011 10-K.

As you can see in Cornerstone 12.8, VF's 2010 and 2011 EPS of $5.25 and $8.13, respectively, are much higher than Under Armour's EPS of $1.35 and $1.88 in 2010 and 2011, respectively.

As for stockholder payout, the firms pursued quite different strategies. Under Armour did not pay dividends or make stock repurchases. VF, on the other hand, paid dividends of $2.43 per share and $2.61 per share in 2010 and 2011, respectively. This represents over 32% of VF's net income in 2011 and over 46% of VF's net income in 2010. Additionally, VF spent 72.08% of net income on stock repurchases in 2010 and 0.84% in 2011. To summarize, Under Armour is not paying out anything to its stockholders. This is most likely because it is a relatively new company and is reinvesting any cash into growing the business. VF, on the other hand, paid out over 118% of its 2010 net income and over 33% of its 2011 net income to stockholders in the form of dividends and stock repurchases.

Dupont Analysis

Return on common equity (or return on equity, hereafter abbreviated as ROE) is the most important measure of profitability for investors. It represents the amount of income generated per dollar of book value of equity or common equity. In that way, it is conceptually similar to an interest rate. Recall that ROE is calculated as:

$$\text{ROE} = \frac{\text{Net Income}}{\text{Average Equity}}$$

Dupont analysis recognizes that ROE can be broken down into three important aspects of return—net profit margin, asset turnover, and leverage.

$$\text{ROE} = \frac{\text{Net Income}}{\text{Sales}} \times \frac{\text{Sales}}{\text{Average Total Assets}} \times \frac{\text{Average Total Assets}}{\text{Average Equity}}$$

$$= \text{Net Profit Margin} \times \text{Asset Turnover} \times \text{Total Leverage}$$

The logic of this breakdown is compelling. First, profitability requires that the corporation is able to earn an adequate gross profit margin. That is, Under Armour and VF must be able to sell their products for more than it costs to buy them. Net profit margin carries this idea down the income statement from gross profit to net income. As we learned earlier in the chapter, the net profit margin represents how many cents of profit there are on every sales dollar.

Second, how efficient is the corporation with its net assets? The desire for asset efficiency is obvious. Everyone knows that you would rather earn $1,000,000 on an investment of $5,000,000 than an investment of $50,000,000. Before discussing leverage, we will focus a little more closely on net profit margin and asset turnover, which taken together, give us return on assets (Net Income÷Average Total Assets), albeit ignoring the after-tax effect of interest expense in the numerator (see p. 672). To illustrate, consider Under Armour and VF for 2010. Their net profit margins and asset turnovers were:

	Net Profit Margin	Asset Turnover	Return on Assets
Under Armour	6.44%	1.74	11.21%*
VF	7.42%	1.19	8.83%*

* This differs from the return on assets shown on p. 672 for Under Armour and in Part 4 of Cornerstone 12.7 for VF because a Dupont analysis does not add back the after-tax effect of interest expense to net income (see discussion on p. 672).

Although Under Armour and VF had similar net profit margins in 2010, their return on assets are quite different because Under Armour has a much higher asset turnover. This highlights different strategies for achieving profitability. Under Armour is more efficient with its assets. This is consistent with a corporation that is seeking to compete on price because to keep costs down you must be efficient with net assets. Companies with higher margins, on the other hand, are product differentiators. A successful product differentiator can earn higher margins on its products because customers view the products as sufficiently different from the competition's to warrant paying higher prices. Although not specifically part of the Dupont analysis, both Under Armour and VF are likely considered product differentiators as is evidenced by gross profit margin percentages that are well above industry averages.

Most product differentiators experience lower asset turnover. You can probably think of these distinctions within and between industries. For example, **Wal-Mart** is a low-cost leader. Wal-Mart has very low margins but makes up for it by being extremely efficient with assets. **Nordstrom**, on the other hand, has much higher margins, but this is offset by lower turnover. Grocery stores, such as **Trader Joe's** and **Albertson's**, have low margins and high turnover; auto dealers and jewelry stores, such as **Toyota** and **Tiffany & Co.**, have high margins and low turnover. Further, the trade-off between margins and turnover is evident in a number of decisions. For example, if a store puts an item on sale, it sacrifices margins and hopes to make up for it with higher turnover.

Notice that 2010 ROE of 15.27% for **Under Armour** and 14.89% for **VF** is higher than their respective returns on assets. Return on *equity* can be made larger than return on *assets* by leveraging these assets through the use of debt. The idea of leverage is simple. For example, if you can borrow at 8% and earn 10% (assuming the same tax rates on the interest and return), then you win. If you could guarantee these two figures after taxes, you should borrow all you can because you are netting 2% on every dollar. That is, if you borrow $1,000,000, you will make $20,000 (a $100,000 return minus $80,000 in interest). If you can borrow $1,000,000,000, then you will make $20,000,000.

This effect is captured by the total leverage component of the Dupont analysis. Recall that a company can obtain money to finance its business by either selling stock or borrowing. If it chooses to sell stock, then stockholders are entitled to their share of the returns. If it borrows the money, on the other hand, the creditors do not share in the returns. So why don't all corporations use debt instead of equity? There are two reasons:

- They may not be able to find a low enough interest rate.
- While interest is guaranteed, returns are not. That is, while the returns may seem better than the interest right now, in a few years it may not be so. For evidence of this, consider stories of people who borrowed money at 15% on credit cards to invest in the stock market in the late 1990s.

Cornerstone 12.9 illustrates how to perform and interpret a Dupont analysis.

CORNERSTONE

12.9

Performing and Interpreting a Dupont Analysis

Why:

A Dupont analysis decomposes a corporation's ROE into net profit margin, asset turnover, and total leverage.

Information:

Refer to the information for **VF**'s income statement and balance sheet in Exhibit 12.3 (pp. 662–663) in addition to the following information for **Under Armour** (all dollar amounts are in thousands):

Net income	$ 96,919	Ending total assets	$919,210
Sales	1,472,684	Beginning stockholders' equity	496,966
Beginning total assets	675,378	Ending stockholders' equity	636,432

Source: VF Corporation 2011 10-K and Under Armour 2011 10-K.

(Continued)

Required:

Perform a Dupont analysis for both corporations for 2011.

CORNERSTONE

12.9

(*Continued*)

Solution:

VF

$$\text{Dupont Analysis: ROE} = \left(\frac{\text{Net Income}}{\text{Sales}}\right) \times \left(\frac{\text{Sales}}{\text{Average Total Assets}}\right) \times \left(\frac{\text{Average Total Assets}}{\text{Average Equity}}\right)$$

$$= \left(\frac{\$888{,}089}{\$9{,}365{,}477}\right) \times \left[\frac{\$9{,}365{,}477}{(\$6{,}457{,}556 + \$9{,}313{,}126) \div 2}\right] \times \left[\frac{(\$6{,}457{,}556 + \$9{,}313{,}126) \div 2}{(\$3{,}861{,}319 + \$4{,}525{,}175) \div 2}\right]$$

$$= 9.48\% \times 1.19 \times 1.88$$

$$= \underline{\underline{21.21^{*}\%}}$$

*Does not equal ROE of 21.18% shown in Cornerstone 12.7 because of rounding in the individual components.

Under Armour

$$= \left(\frac{\$96{,}919}{\$1{,}472{,}684}\right) \times \left[\frac{\$1{,}472{,}684}{(\$675{,}378 + \$919{,}210) \div 2}\right] \times \left[\frac{(\$675{,}378 + \$919{,}210) \div 2}{(\$496{,}966 + \$636{,}432) \div 2}\right]$$

$$= 6.58\% \times 1.85 \times 1.41$$

$$= \underline{\underline{17.16\%}}$$

Source: VF Corporation 2011 10-K and Under Armour 2011 10-K.

The Dupont analysis in Cornerstone 12.9 shows that although Under Armour and VF have similar return on assets in 2011, they get there in slightly different ways. VF has superior margins, while Under Armour has superior turnover. Further, despite their similar return on assets, VF's ROE is much better than Under Armour's. This is because VF is more highly levered, which means VF has a higher proportion of debt financing. This higher proportion of debt financing "leverages" VF's return on assets to produce an even higher ROE. Remember that while higher leverage is positive for stockholders in good times, it can be catastrophic in bad times.

Summary of Financial Ratios

Exhibit 12.4 (pp. 680–681) summarizes the financial ratios presented in this chapter. More advanced accounting texts may present additional ratios; however, those introduced here are among the most widely used.

Data for Ratio Comparisons

As we pointed out earlier in the chapter, developing information from financial ratios requires that comparisons be made among the ratios of:

- the same corporation over time
- similar corporations over time
- similar corporations at the present time

Analysts rely on several sources to fulfill their need for a broad range of data for individual corporations as well as for industries and the economy.

We believe the best source of information about a corporation starts with the investor relations section of its website. This part of the website should contain links to the corporation's 10-K (and other SEC filings), analyst conference calls, and press releases. You can also gain information through the financial press (*The Wall Street Journal,* etc.) and investor discussion boards, although the latter must be evaluated with a critical eye.

EXHIBIT 12.4

Summary of Financial Ratios

Short-Term Liquidity Ratios

1. $\text{Current Ratio} = \dfrac{\text{Current Assets}}{\text{Current Liabilities}}$

2. $\text{Quick Ratio} = \dfrac{\text{Cash} + \text{Short-Term Investments} + \text{Receivables}}{\text{Current Liabilities}}$

3. $\text{Cash Ratio} = \dfrac{\text{Cash} + \text{Short-Term Investments}}{\text{Current Liabilities}}$

4. $\text{Operating Cash Flow Ratio} = \dfrac{\text{Cash Flows from Operating Activities}}{\text{Current Liabilities}}$

Debt Management Ratios

5a. $\text{Times Interest Earned } (\textit{Accrual Basis}) = \dfrac{\text{Operating Income}}{\text{Interest Expense}}$

5b. $\text{Times Interest Earned } (\textit{Cash Basis}) = \dfrac{\text{Cash Flows from Operations} + \text{Income Tax Payments} + \text{Interest Payments}}{\text{Interest Payments}}$

6. $\text{Long-Term Debt to Equity Ratio} = \dfrac{\text{Long-Term Debt (including current portion)}}{\text{Total Equity}}$

7. $\text{Debt to Equity Ratio} = \dfrac{\text{Total Liabilities}}{\text{Total Equity}}$

8. $\text{Long-Term Debt to Total Assets Ratio} = \dfrac{\text{Long-Term Debt (including current portion)}}{\text{Total Assets}}$

9. $\text{Debt to Total Assets Ratio} = \dfrac{\text{Total Liabilities}}{\text{Total Assets}}$

Asset Efficiency Ratios

10. $\text{Accounts Receivable Turnover Ratio} = \dfrac{\text{Net Credit Sales or Net Sales}}{\text{Average Accounts Receivable}}$

11. $\text{Inventory Turnover Ratio} = \dfrac{\text{Cost of Goods Sold}}{\text{Average Inventory}}$

12. $\text{Asset Turnover Ratio} = \dfrac{\text{Net Sales}}{\text{Average Total Assets}}$

Profitability Ratios

13. $\text{Gross Profit Percentage} = \dfrac{\text{Gross Profit}}{\text{Net Sales}}$

14. $\text{Operating Margin Percentage} = \dfrac{\text{Income from Operations}}{\text{Net Sales}}$

15. $\text{Net Profit Margin Percentage} = \dfrac{\text{Net Income}}{\text{Net Sales}}$

16. $\text{Return on Assets} = \dfrac{\text{Net Income} + [\text{Interest Expense} \times (1 - \text{Tax Rate})]}{\text{Average Total Assets}}$

17. $\text{Return on Equity} = \dfrac{\text{Net Income}}{\text{Average Equity}}$

EXHIBIT 12.4

Summary of Financial Ratios (*Continued*)

Stockholder Ratios

18. Earnings per Share (EPS) Ratio $= \frac{\text{Net Income} - \text{Preferred Dividends}}{\text{Average Number of Common Shares Outstanding}}$

19. Return on Common Equity $= \frac{\text{Net Income}}{\text{Average Common Equity}}$

20. Dividend Yield Ratio $= \frac{\text{Dividends per Common Share}}{\text{Closing Market Price per Share for the Year}}$

21. Dividend Payout Ratio $= \frac{\text{Common Dividends}}{\text{Net Income}}$

22. Stock Repurchase Payout Ratio $= \frac{\text{Common Stock Repurchases}}{\text{Net Income}}$

23. Total Payout Ratio $= \frac{\text{Common Dividends} + \text{Common Stock Repurchases}}{\text{Net Income}}$

Dupont Analysis

24. Return on Equity $= \frac{\text{Net Income}}{\text{Sales}} \times \frac{\text{Sales}}{\text{Average Total Assets}} \times \frac{\text{Average Total Assets}}{\text{Average Equity}}$

$= \text{Net Profit Margin} \times \text{Asset Turnover} \times \text{Total Leverage}$

Information on the industry can be obtained from industry guides such as Standard & Poor's and IBISWorld. These are often available through your university library website or in hard copy at the library. Also helpful are websites like Google Finance, Yahoo! Finance, BizStats, and MSN.

SUMMARY OF LEARNING OBJECTIVES

LO 1. Explain how creditors, investors, and others use financial statements in their decisions.

- The role of financial statements is to provide information for:
  - creditors
  - investors
  - customers
  - suppliers
  - employees

This information will help these groups form judgments, which will serve as the foundation for various decisions.

LO 2. Become familiar with the most important SEC filings.

- Publicly traded corporations must file a variety of financial information, including audited annual financial statements, with the Securities and Exchange Commission (SEC) on an ongoing basis. For example:
  - annual reports on Form 10-K
  - quarterly reports on Form 10-Q
  - current reports for numerous specified events on Form 8-K

- The annual report on Form 10-K provides a comprehensive overview of the corporation's business and financial condition and includes *audited* financial statements.
- Although similarly named, the annual report on Form 10-K is distinct from the "annual report to shareholders," which a corporation must send to its stockholders when it holds an annual meeting to elect directors.
- For larger filers, the 10-K must be filed within 60 days of the corporation's fiscal year end.

LO 3. Understand the difference between cross sectional and time series analysis.

- Cross sectional analysis entails comparing a corporation's financial statements to its primary competitors and industry averages.
- Time series (or trend) analysis involves comparisons of the current year to previous years.
- Differences may exist in the size of two corporations or even in the same corporation from year to year (perhaps due to the acquisition of another corporation). Analysts address this problem by restating the financial statements in percentage terms.

LO 4. Analyze financial statements using horizontal and vertical analysis.

- In horizontal analysis, each financial statement line item is expressed as a percent of the base year (typically the least recent year shown).
- In vertical analysis, each financial statement line item is expressed as a percent of the largest statement amount—net sales on the income statement and total assets on the balance sheet.

LO 5. Calculate and use financial statement ratios to evaluate a company.

- Ratios help remove the effects of size differences (as measured in dollars).
- Six categories of ratios are discussed:
  - short-term liquidity
  - debt management
  - profitability
  - asset efficiency (or operating)
  - stockholder
  - Dupont
- More advanced accounting and finance texts may present additional ratios; however, those introduced here are among the most widely used.

CORNERSTONE 12.1 Interpreting cross sectional and time series (or trend) analysis, page 653

CORNERSTONE 12.2 Preparing common size statements for horizontal analysis, page 654

CORNERSTONE 12.3 Preparing common size statements for vertical analysis, page 656

CORNERSTONE 12.4 Calculating and interpreting short-term liquidity ratios, page 664

CORNERSTONE 12.5 Calculating and interpreting debt management ratios, page 666

CORNERSTONE 12.6 Calculating and interpreting asset efficiency ratios, page 670

CORNERSTONE 12.7 Calculating and interpreting profitability ratios, page 673

CORNERSTONE 12.8 Calculating and interpreting stockholder ratios, page 676

CORNERSTONE 12.9 Performing and interpreting a Dupont analysis, page 678

KEY TERMS

REVIEW PROBLEM

Ratio Analysis

Following are consolidated balance sheets and income statements for Kellman Company:

Kellman Company and Subsidiaries
Consolidated Balance Sheets
(in thousands)

	December 31,		
	2012	2011	2010
ASSETS			
Current assets:			
Cash and cash equivalents	$ 40,588	$ 70,655	$ 62,977
Accounts receivable, net	93,515	71,867	53,132
Inventories	166,082	81,031	53,607
Income taxes receivable	614	4,310	0
Other current assets	11,028	8,944	5,252
Deferred income taxes	10,418	8,145	6,822
Total current assets	**$322,245**	**$244,952**	**$181,790**
Property and equipment, net	52,332	29,923	20,865
Intangible assets, net	6,470	7,875	0
Deferred income taxes	8,173	5,180	0
Other noncurrent assets	1,393	1,438	1,032
Total assets	**$390,613**	**$289,368**	**$203,687**

(Continued)

LIABILITIES AND STOCKHOLDERS' EQUITY			
Current liabilities:			
Accounts payable	$ 55,012	$ 42,718	$ 31,699
Accrued expenses	36,111	25,403	11,449
Income taxes payable	0	0	716
Current maturities of long-term debt	4,111	2,648	1,967
Current maturities of capital lease obligations	465	794	1,841
Total current liabilities	**$ 95,699**	**$ 71,563**	**$ 47,672**
Long-term debt, net of current maturities	9,298	1,893	2,868
Capital lease obligations, net of current maturities	458	922	1,715
Deferred income taxes	0	0	330
Other long-term liabilities	4,673	602	272
Total liabilities	**$110,128**	**$ 74,980**	**$ 52,857**
Stockholders' equity:			
Class A common stock	$ 12	$ 12	$ 10
Class B common stock	4	4	5
Additional paid-in capital—common stock	162,362	148,562	124,803
Retained earnings	117,782	66,376	28,067
Unearned compensation	(182)	(463)	(1,889)
Notes receivable from stockholders	0	0	(163)
Accumulated other comprehensive income	507	(103)	(3)
Total stockholders' equity	**$280,485**	**$214,388**	**$150,830**
Total liabilities and stockholders' equity	**$390,613**	**$289,368**	**$203,687**

Kellman Company and Subsidiaries
Consolidated Income Statements
(in thousands)

	December 31,		
	2012	**2011**	**2010**
Net sales	$ 606,561	$ 430,689	$ 281,053
Cost of goods sold	301,517	215,089	145,203
Gross profit	**$305,044**	**$215,600**	**$135,850**
Operating expenses			
Selling, general and administrative expenses	218,779	158,682	100,040
Income from operations	**$ 86,265**	**$ 56,918**	**$ 35,810**
Interest income	1,549	2,231	273
Interest expense	(800)	(774)	(3,188)
Other income, net	2,029	712	79
Income before income taxes	**$ 89,043**	**$ 59,087**	**$ 32,974**
Income tax expense	36,485	20,108	13,255
Net income	**$ 52,558**	**$ 38,979**	**$ 19,719**
Cumulative preferred dividends on preferred stock	0	0	5,307
Net income available to common stockholders	**$ 52,558**	**$ 38,979**	**$ 14,412**

Additionally, you will need the following information:

Weighted average common shares outstanding	48,021	46,983	37,199
Cash flows from operating activities	$(14,628)	$10,701	$15,795
Dividends per share	$0	$0	$0
Dividends	$0	$0	$0
Stock repurchases	$0	$0	$0
Market price per share at year end	$43.67	$50.45	$38.31

Required:

1. Calculate the short-term liquidity ratios for Kellman Company for 2011 and 2012.
2. Calculate the debt management ratios for Kellman Company for 2011 and 2012.
3. Calculate the asset efficiency ratios for Kellman Company for 2011 and 2012.
4. Calculate the profitability ratios for Kellman Company for 2011 and 2012.
5. Calculate the stockholder ratios for Kellman Company for 2011 and 2012.
6. Perform a Dupont analysis for Kellman Company for 2011 and 2012.

Solution:

1. Short-term liquidity ratios:

$$\text{Current Ratio} = \frac{\text{Current Assets}}{\text{Current Liabilities}}$$

	2012	2011
Current assets	$322,245	$244,952
Current liabilities	95,699	71,563
Current ratio	**3.37**	**3.42**

$$\text{Quick Ratio} = \frac{\text{Cash} + \text{Short-Term Investments} + \text{Receivables}}{\text{Current Liabilities}}$$

	2012	2011
Cash	$40,588	$70,655
Short-term investments	0	0
Accounts receivable	93,515	71,867
Current liabilities	95,699	71,563
Quick ratio	**1.40**	**1.99**

$$\text{Cash Ratio} = \frac{\text{Cash} + \text{Short-Term Investments}}{\text{Current Liabilities}}$$

	2012	2011
Cash	$40,588	$70,655
Short-term investments	0	0
Current liabilities	95,699	71,563
Cash ratio	**0.42**	**0.99**

$$\text{Operating Cash Flow Ratio} = \frac{\text{Cash Flows from Operating Activities}}{\text{Current Liabilities}}$$

	2012	2011
Cash flows from operating activities	$(14,628)*	$10,701*
Current liabilities	95,699	71,563
Operating cash flow ratio	**(0.15)**	**0.15**

*Provided in the Information section.

2. Debt management ratios:

$$\text{Times Interest Earned} = \frac{\text{Operating Income}}{\text{Interest Expense}}$$

	2012	2011
Operating income	$86,265	$56,918
Interest expense	800	774
Times interest earned (accrual)	**107.83**	**73.54**

(Continued)

$$\text{Long-Term Debt to Equity Ratio} = \frac{\text{Long-Term Debt (including current portion)}}{\text{Total Equity}}$$

	2012	2011
Long-term debt	$ 9,298	$ 1,893
Current portion of long-term debt	4,111	2,648
Total equity	280,485	214,388
Long-term debt to equity	**0.05**	**0.02**

$$\text{Debt to Equity Ratio} = \frac{\text{Total Liabilities}}{\text{Total Equity}}$$

	2012	2011
Total liabilities	$110,128	$ 74,980
Total equity	280,485	214,388
Debt to equity	**0.39**	**0.35**

$$\text{Long-Term Debt to Total Assets Ratio} = \frac{\text{Long-Term Debt (including current portion)}}{\text{Total Assets}}$$

	2012	2011
Long-term debt	$ 9,298	$ 1,893
Current portion of long-term debt	4,111	2,648
Total assets	390,613	289,368
Long-term debt to total assets	**0.03**	**0.02**

$$\text{Debt to Total Assets Ratio} = \frac{\text{Total Liabilities}}{\text{Total Assets}}$$

	2012	2011
Total liabilities	$110,128	$ 74,980
Total assets	390,613	289,368
Debt to total assets	**0.28**	**0.26**

3. Asset efficiency ratios:

$$\text{Accounts Receivable Turnover Ratio} = \frac{\text{Net Sales}}{\text{Average Accounts Receivable*}}$$

$$^{*}\text{Average Balance} = \frac{(\text{Beginning Balance} + \text{Ending Balance})}{2}$$

	2012	2011	2010
Net sales	$606,561	$430,689	$281,053
Receivables	93,515	71,867	53,132
Accounts receivable turnover ratio	**7.34**	**6.89**	

$$\text{Inventory Turnover Ratio} = \frac{\text{Cost of Goods Sold}}{\text{Average Inventories}}$$

	2012	2011	2010
Cost of goods sold	$301,517	$215,089	$145,203
Inventories	166,082	81,031	53,607
Inventory turnover ratio	**2.44**	**3.20**	

$$\text{Asset Turnover Ratio} = \frac{\text{Net Sales}}{\text{Average Total Assets}}$$

	2012	2011	2010
Net sales	$606,561	$430,689	$281,053
Total assets	390,613	289,368	203,687
Asset turnover ratio	**1.78**	**1.75**	

4. Profitability ratios:

$$\text{Gross Profit Percentage} = \frac{\text{Gross Profit}}{\text{Net Sales}}$$

	2012	2011
Net sales	$606,561	$430,689
Gross profit	305,044	215,600
Gross profit percentage	**50.29%**	**50.06%**

$$\text{Operating Margin Percentage} = \frac{\text{Income from Operations}}{\text{Net Sales}}$$

	2012	2011
Net sales	$606,561	$430,689
Income from operations	86,265	56,918
Operating margin percentage	**14.22%**	**13.22%**

$$\text{Net Profit Margin Percentage} = \frac{\text{Net Income}}{\text{Net Sales}}$$

	2012	2011
Net sales	$606,561	$430,689
Net income	52,558	38,979
Net profit margin percentage	**8.67%**	**9.05%**

$$\text{Return on Assets} = \frac{\text{Net Income} + [\text{Interest Expense} \times (1 - \text{Tax Rate})]}{\text{Average Total Assets*}}$$

$$\text{*Average Balance} = \frac{(\text{Beginning Balance} + \text{Ending Balance})}{2}$$

	2012	2011	2010
Total assets	$390,613	$289,368	$203,687
Income taxes expense	36,485	20,108	
Net income	52,558	38,979	
Interest expense	800	774	
Income before taxes	89,043	59,087	
Tax rate*	40.97%	34.03%	
Return on assets	**15.60%**	**16.02%**	

* Income Taxes Expense ÷ Income before Taxes

$$\text{Return on Equity} = \frac{\text{Net Income}}{\text{Average Equity*}}$$

$$\text{*Average Balance} = \frac{(\text{Beginning Balance} + \text{Ending Balance})}{2}$$

	2012	2011	2010
Net income	$ 52,558	$ 38,979	
Stockholders' equity	280,485	214,388	$150,830
Return on equity	**21.24%**	**21.35%**	

5. Stockholder ratios:

$$\text{Earnings per Share Ratio} = \frac{\text{Net Income} - \text{Preferred Dividends}}{\text{Average Number of Common Shares Outstanding}}$$

(Continued)

	2012	2011
Net income	$52,558	$38,979
Preferred dividends	0	0
Average common shares*	48,021	46,983
EPS	**1.09**	**0.83**

*Provided in the Information section.

$$\text{Return on Common Equity} = \frac{\text{Net Income}}{\text{Average Common Equity*}}$$

*Common Equity = Total Equity − Preferred Stock − Additional Paid-In Capital—Preferred Stock

	2012	2011	2010
Net income	$ 52,558	$ 38,979	
Stockholders' equity	280,485	214,388	$150,830
Preferred stock	0	0	0
Additional paid-in capital—preferred stock	0	0	0
Return on common equity	**21.24%**	**21.35%**	

$$\text{Dividend Yield Ratio} = \frac{\text{Dividends per Common Share}}{\text{Closing Market Price per Share for the Year}}$$

	2012	2011
Dividends per share*	$ 0	$ 0
Closing market price for year*	43.67	50.45
Dividend yield ratio	**0.0%**	**0.0%**

*Provided in the Information section.

$$\text{Dividend Payout Ratio} = \frac{\text{Common Dividends}}{\text{Net Income}}$$

	2012	2011
Common dividends*	$ 0	$ 0
Net income	52,558	38,979
Dividend yield ratio	**0.0%**	**0.0%**

*Provided in the Information section.

$$\text{Total Payout Ratio} = \frac{\text{Common Dividends} + \text{Common Stock Repurchases}}{\text{Net Income}}$$

	2012	2011
Common dividends*	$ 0	$ 0
Common stock repurchases*	0	0
Net income	52,558	38,979
Total payout ratio	**0%**	**0%**

*Provided in the Information section.

6. Dupont analysis:

$$\text{ROE} = \frac{\text{Net Income}}{\text{Sales}} \times \frac{\text{Sales}}{\text{Average Total Assets}} \times \frac{\text{Average Total Assets}}{\text{Average Equity}}$$
$$= \text{Net Profit Margin} \times \text{Asset Turnover} \times \text{Total Leverage}$$

2012:

$$= \frac{\$52,558}{\$606,561} \times \frac{\$606,561}{(\$390,613 + \$289,368) \div 2} \times \frac{(\$390,613 + \$289,368) \div 2}{(\$280,485 + \$214,388) \div 2}$$
$$= 8.67\% \times 1.78 \times 1.37$$
$$= \underline{\underline{21.14\%^*}}$$

*Does not equal ROE of 21.24% shown in Parts 4 and 5 because of rounding in the individual components.

2011:

$$= \frac{\$38,979}{\$430,689} \times \frac{\$430,689}{(\$289,368 + \$203,687) \div 2} \times \frac{(\$289,368 + \$203,687) \div 2}{(\$214,388 + \$150,830) \div 2}$$

$$= 9.05\% \times 1.75 \times 1.35$$

$$= \underline{\underline{21.38\%}}^{*}$$

*Does not equal ROE of 21.35% shown in Parts 4 and 5 because of rounding in the individual components.

DISCUSSION QUESTIONS

1. Describe how some of the primary groups of users use financial statements.
2. What is a 10-K?
3. How does the 10-K differ from the 10-Q?
4. Describe the information provided in Item 1 of the 10-K.
5. Describe the information provided in Item 7 of the 10-K.
6. Describe the information provided in Item 8 of the 10-K.
7. What is the difference between time series and cross sectional analysis?
8. What is the difference between horizontal and vertical analysis?
9. How do the current and quick ratios differ? Which is a more conservative measure of short-term liquidity? Support your answer.
10. How does the operating cash flow ratio differ from the current, quick, and cash ratios?
11. What are you trying to learn by calculating debt management ratios?
12. Why are higher asset turnover ratios considered to be better than lower turnover ratios?
13. What two aspects of a company's profitability are measured by profitability ratios?
14. What are the two major categories of stockholder ratios?
15. A Dupont analysis breaks down return on equity into what three components?
16. Why must you analyze the accounting policies of a company when performing financial statement analysis? Provide an example of how knowledge of accounting policies would affect your analysis of inventory.

MULTIPLE-CHOICE QUESTIONS

12-1 Which of the following use financial statement data to make decisions?

a. customers
b. investors
c. suppliers
d. all of these

12-2 Which statement would best provide information about a company's current liquidity?

a. income statement
b. balance sheet
c. statement of cash flows
d. none of these

12-3 A banker is analyzing a company that operates in the petroleum industry. Which of the following might be a major consideration in determining whether the company should receive a loan?

a. The petroleum industry suffers from political pressures concerning the selling price of its products.
b. All companies in the petroleum industry use the same accounting principles.
c. The company has a large amount of interest payments related to many outstanding loans.
d. Inflation has been high for several years in a row.

12-4 Which of the following filings includes unaudited financial statements, provides a continuing view of the corporation's financial position during the year, and must be filed for each of the first three fiscal quarters of the corporation's fiscal year?

a. 10-Q
b. 10-K
c. 8-K
d. Form 13F

12-5 Which of the following filings is known as the "current report" that companies must file with the SEC to announce major events that are important to investors and creditors?

a. 10-Q
b. 10-K
c. 8-K
d. Form 13F

12-6 Which section of the Form 10-K includes an analysis of the company's financial condition and performance of the company?

a. Item 4—Submission of Matters to Vote
b. Item 5—Market for Common Stock
c. Item 6—Selected Financial Data
d. Item 7—Management Discussion and Analysis

12-7 Which of the following are required to be included in the Form 10-K?

a. the name of every person or group who owns more than 5% of a class of stock
b. a list of all financial statements and exhibits required to be filed
c. information on the salary and other forms of compensation paid to executive officers and directors
d. all of the above

12-8 Which type of analysis compares a single corporation across time?

a. timetable analysis
b. time series analysis
c. company analysis
d. cross sectional analysis

12-9 Which of the following types of analysis compares one corporation to another corporation and to industry averages?

a. timetable analysis
b. time series analysis
c. company analysis
d. cross sectional analysis

12-10 Which of the following types of analysis is particularly useful for trend analysis?

a. vertical analysis
b. horizontal analysis
c. trend-setting analysis
d. timetable analysis

12-11 Vertical analysis expresses each financial statement line item as a percent of the:

a. smallest statement amount.
b. largest statement amount.
c. average statement amount.
d. mean statement amount.

12-12 Horizontal analysis expresses each financial statement line item as a percent of:

a. base year.
b. total assets.
c. net income.
d. stockholders' equity.

12-13 How is the current ratio calculated?

a. Cash Flows from Operating Activities ÷ Current Liabilities
b. (Cash + Marketable Securities + Accounts Receivable) ÷ Current Liabilities
c. Current Assets ÷ Current Liabilities
d. (Cash + Marketable Securities) ÷ Current Liabilities

12-14 Partial information from Fabray Company's balance sheet is:

Current Assets:		**Current Liabilities:**	
Cash	$ 1,200,000	Notes payable	$ 750,000
Marketable securities	3,750,000	Accounts payable	9,750,000
Accounts receivable	28,800,000	Accrued expenses	6,250,000
Inventories	33,150,000	Income taxes payable	250,000
Prepaid expenses	600,000	Total current liabilities	$17,000,000
Total current assets	$67,500,000		

What is Fabray's current ratio?

a. 0.25
b. 1.8
c. 3.0
d. 3.97

12-15 Hummel Inc. has $30,000 in current assets and $15,000 in current liabilities. What is Hummel's current ratio?

a. 3
b. 2
c. 1
d. 0.5

12-16 How is the cash ratio calculated?

a. (Cash + Marketable Securities) ÷ Current Liabilities
b. (Cash + Marketable Securities + Accounts Receivable) ÷ Current Liabilities
c. Current Assets ÷ Current Liabilities
d. Cash Flows from Operating Activities ÷ Current Liabilities

12-17 A firm's quick ratio is typically computed as:

a. (Cash + Marketable Securities + Accounts Receivable) ÷ Current Liabilities.
b. Total Liabilities ÷ Total Assets.
c. Current Liabilities ÷ Current Assets.
d. Current Assets ÷ Current Liabilities.

12-18 Schuester Company has $40,000 in current liabilities, $20,000 in cash, and $25,000 in marketable securities. What Schuester's cash ratio?

a. 0.625
b. 0.889
c. 1.125
d. 1.6

12-19 What ratio is used to measure a firm's liquidity?

a. current ratio
b. debt ratio
c. asset turnover
d. return on equity

12-20 Which of the following transactions could increase a firm's current ratio?

a. purchase of inventory for cash
b. purchase of temporary investments for cash
c. collection of accounts receivable
d. payment of accounts payable

12-21 Total Liabilities ÷ Total Equity equals:

a. Receivables Turnover Ratio
b. Accounts Payable Turnover Ratio
c. Debt to Equity Ratio
d. Times Interest Earned Ratio

12-22 Which of the following ratios is *not* a debt management ratio?

a. return on equity ratio
b. debt to equity ratio
c. long-term debt to equity ratio
d. times interest earned

12-23 The balance sheet for Sylvester Inc. at the end of the first year of operations indicates the following:

	2011		2011
Total current assets	$600,000	Total long-term liabilities	$350,000
Total investments	85,000	Common stock, $10 par	600,000
Total property, plant, and equipment	900,000	Additional paid-in capital—common stock	60,000
Current portion of long-term debt	250,000	Retained earnings	325,000

What is the long-term debt to total assets ratio for 2011 (rounded to one decimal place)?

a. 22.1%
b. 37.9%
c. 40.0%
d. 41.7%

12-24 When analyzing a company's debt to equity ratio, if the ratio has a value that is greater than one, then the company has:

a. equal amounts of debt and equity.
b. more debt than equity.
c. less debt than equity.
d. none of these.

12-25 Cost of goods sold divided by average inventory is the formula to compute:

a. gross profit percentage.
b. return on sales percentage.
c. inventory turnover.
d. accounts receivable turnover.

12-26 A firm's asset turnover ratio is typically computed as:

a. Operating Income ÷ Net Sales.
b. Gross Profit ÷ Net Sales.
c. Net Sales ÷ Average Total Assets.
d. Net Income + [Interest Expense × (1 − Tax Rate)] ÷ Average Total Assets.

12-27 Which of the following ratios is used to measure a firm's efficiency at using its assets?

a. asset turnover ratio
b. current ratio
c. return on sales ratio
d. return on equity

12-28 Which of the following ratios is used to measure a firm's efficiency?

a. Net Income ÷ Equity
b. Assets ÷ Equity
c. Net Income ÷ Sales
d. Net Sales ÷ Average Total Assets

12-29 Pillsbury Corporation has \$65,000 of cost of goods sold and average inventory of \$30,000. What is Pillsbury's inventory turnover ratio?

a. 2.17
b. 1.46
c. 1.17
d. 0.46

12-30 If Abrams Company has an inventory turnover of 7.3 and a receivables turnover of 9.6, approximately how long is its operating cycle?

a. 95 days
b. 88 days
c. 72 days
d. There is not enough information to calculate the operating cycle.

12-31 Which of the following ratios is used to measure the profit earned on each dollar invested in a firm?

a. return on sales ratio
b. return on equity
c. current ratio
d. asset turnover ratio

12-32 Which of the following is the formula to compute the net profit margin percentage?

a. Operating Income ÷ Net Sales
b. Net Income ÷ Net Sales
c. Net Income ÷ Average Equity
d. Net Income + [Interest Expense × (1 − Tax Rate)] ÷ Average Total Assets

12-33 Selected information for Berry Company is as follows:

Average common stock	\$600,000
Average additional paid-in capital	250,000
Average retained earnings	370,000
Sales revenue for year	915,000
Net income for year	240,000

Berry's return on equity, rounded to the nearest percentage point, is:

a. 20%.
b. 21%.
c. 28%.
d. 40%.

12-34 Which of the following ratios is used to measure a firm's profitability?

a. Liabilities ÷ Equity
b. Assets ÷ Equity
c. Sales ÷ Assets
d. Net Income ÷ Net Sales

12-35 Why might an industry group have higher 5-year average returns on equity than do other industries?

a. It is a lower-risk industry.
b. It is a higher-risk industry.
c. It is a high-growth industry.
d. None of these.

12-36 The dividend yield ratio measures the:

a. income available for common stockholders on a per-share basis.
b. profit earned by a firm through the use of capital supplied by stockholders.
c. proportion of a corporation's profits that are returned to the stockholders immediately as dividends.
d. rate at which dividends provide a return to stockholders.

12-37 Corporations are required to disclose earnings per share on which of the following statements?

a. statement of cash flows
b. balance sheet
c. income statement
d. all of these

12-38 Hudson Company has preferred dividends of $15,000, a net income of $40,000, and average common shares outstanding of 8,000. What is Hudson's earnings per share?

a. $2.13
b. $2.67
c. $3.13
d. $5.00

12-39 Which of the following are *not* part of common equity?

a. preferred stock
b. common stock
c. retained earnings
d. treasury stock

12-40 A Dupont analysis recognizes that return on equity can be broken down into three important aspects of return, which are:

a. net profit margin, asset turnover, and leverage
b. net profit margin, asset turnover, and average assets
c. sales, income, and leverage
d. sales, income, and equity

12-41 If a company has a higher net profit margin than most of its competitors, this means that the company:

a. has a lower proportion of debt financing.
b. has more loyal customers.
c. is more efficient with its assets.
d. has a higher proportion of each sales dollar that is profit.

12-42 Which of the following ratios is decomposed using the Dupont framework?

a. assets-to-equity ratio
b. asset turnover
c. return on equity
d. return on sales

12-43 Which of the following is *not* included in the Dupont framework?

a. a measure of profitability
b. a measure of efficiency
c. a measure of leverage
d. a measure of market share

12-44 When a Dupont analysis reveals that a company has much higher than average asset turnover and much lower than average profit margin, what can be concluded about the company's strategy?

a. It is a product differentiator.
b. It needs to concentrate on improving its profit margins.
c. It has no strategy.
d. It is a low-cost provider

12-45 Which of the following questions would be appropriate for an analyst to investigate regarding a company's liabilities?

a. Are the liabilities properly classified?
b. Are estimated liabilities large enough?
c. Are the liabilities reported?
d. All of these would be appropriate.

CORNERSTONE EXERCISES

OBJECTIVE 3
CORNERSTONE 12.1

Cornerstone Exercise 12-46 Cross Sectional Analysis

Cross sectional analysis entails comparing a company to its competitors.

Required:

Indicate one of the biggest weaknesses of using cross sectional analysis when analyzing a company.

OBJECTIVE 3
CORNERSTONE 12.1

Cornerstone Exercise 12-47 Time Series Analysis

Time series analysis involves comparing a company's income statement and balance sheet for the current year to its previous years' income statements and balance sheets.

Required:

Explain whether it is always bad if a company's cost of goods sold is increasing from year to year.

OBJECTIVE 4
CORNERSTONE 12.2
CORNERSTONE 12.3

Cornerstone Exercise 12-48 Horizontal and Vertical Analysis

Selected data from the financial statements of Jones Hardware Company follows.

	2013	2012
Accounts receivable	$ 60,000	$ 38,000
Merchandise inventory	12,000	16,000
Total assets	450,000	380,000
Net sales	380,000	270,000
Cost of goods sold	160,000	210,000

Required:

1. Calculate by how much accounts receivable, merchandise inventory, total assets, net sales, and cost of goods sold increased or decreased in dollar terms from 2012 to 2013.
2. Indicate what happened from 2012 to 2013 to accounts receivable and merchandise inventory as a percentage of total assets (rounded to the nearest whole percent). Indicate what happened from 2012 to 2013 to cost of goods sold as a percentage of net sales (rounded to the nearest whole percent).

OBJECTIVE 3
CORNERSTONE 12.4

Cornerstone Exercise 12-49 Short-Term Liquidity Ratios

Three ratios calculated for Puckerman, Cohen, and Chang companies for 2012 and 2013 follow.

(in millions)		Puckerman	Cohen	Chang
Current ratio	12/31/13	2.8 to 1	2.3 to 1	1.8 to 1
	12/31/12	2.0 to 1	1.5 to 1	2.2 to 1
Inventory turnover ratio	12/31/13	6.9 times	5.8 times	8.0 times
	12/31/12	7.6 times	5.8 times	9.6 times
Quick ratio	12/31/13	2.5 to 1	2.1 to 1	0.5 to 1
	12/31/12	1.0 to 1	1.4 to 1	1.2 to 1

Required:

Explain which company appears to be the most liquid.

OBJECTIVE 5
CORNERSTONE 12.5

Cornerstone Exercise 12-50 Debt Management Ratios

Selected data from the financial statements of Lopez Company follow.

	2013	2012
Total liabilities	$1,205,000	$952,000
Common stock ($30 par)	250,000	225,000
Additional paid-in capital—common stock	150,000	135,000
Retained earnings	155,000	145,000

Required:

Determine whether the debt to equity ratio is increasing or decreasing and whether Lopez should be concerned.

Cornerstone Exercise 12-51 Debt Management and Short-Term Liquidity Ratios

OBJECTIVE 5
CORNERSTONE 12.4
CORNERSTONE 12.5

The following items appear on the balance sheet of Figgins Company at the end of 2012 and 2013:

	2013	2012
Current assets	$6,000	$3,000
Long-term assets	7,000	4,000
Current liabilities	2,000	3,000
Long-term liabilities	7,000	0
Stockholders' equity	4,000	4,000

Required:

Between 2012 and 2013, indicate whether Figgins' debt to equity ratio increased or decreased. Also, indicate whether Figgins' current ratio increased or decreased. Interpret these ratios.

Cornerstone Exercise 12-52 Asset Efficiency Ratios

OBJECTIVE 5
CORNERSTONE 12.6

Selected financial statement numbers for Rutherford Company follow.

Net sales	$277,480	Average inventory	$ 4,145
Cost of goods sold	179,000	Average property, plant, and equipment	75,705
Average accounts receivable	20,730	Average total assets	126,127

Required:

1. Using this information, calculate Rutherford's receivable turnover ratio (rounded to two decimal places.)
2. Using this information, calculate Rutherford's asset turnover ratio (rounded to two decimal places) and also convert the ratio into days (rounded to the nearest whole day).

Cornerstone Exercise 12-53 Profitability Ratios

OBJECTIVE 5
CORNERSTONE 12.7

The following data came from the financial statements of Israel Company:

Revenue	$900,000	Assets	$600,000
Expenses	600,000	Liabilities	100,000
Net income	300,000	Average equity	500,000

Required:

Compute Israel's return on equity (in percentage terms, rounded to two decimal places).

Cornerstone Exercise 12-54 Profitability Ratios

OBJECTIVE 5
CORNERSTONE 12.7

Tanaka Corporation's balance sheet indicates the following balances as of December 31, 2013.

Cash	$ 70,000	Bonds payable (due in 2017)	$100,000
Accounts receivable	80,000	Common stock (12/31/2012)	275,000
Inventory	55,000	Common stock (12/31/2013)	325,000
Property, plant, and equipment	500,000	Retained earnings (12/31/2012)	200,000
Accounts payable	75,000	Retained earnings (12/31/2013)	260,000

Required:

If Tanaka's 2013 net income is $80,000, determine its return on equity (in percentage terms, rounded to two decimal places).

OBJECTIVE 5
CORNERSTONE 12.7

Cornerstone Exercise 12-55 Profitability Ratios

The following data came from the financial statements of St. James Corp. for 2013 and 2012.

	2013	2012
Net income	$150,000	$120,000
Cash dividends paid on preferred stock	$15,000	$15,000
Cash dividends paid on common stock	$42,000	$38,000
Weighted average number of preferred shares outstanding	20,000	20,000
Weighted average number of common shares outstanding	105,000	95,000

Required:

Calculate St. James' earnings per share as it would be reported on the 2013 income statement.

OBJECTIVE 5
CORNERSTONE 12.8

Cornerstone Exercise 12-56 Stockholder Ratios

The following data came from the financial statements of Ryerson Corp. for 2013 and 2012.

	2013	2012
Net income	$110,000	$123,000
Cash dividends paid on common stock	$42,000	$38,000
Market price per share of common stock at the end of the year	$16.00	$13.00
Shares of common stock outstanding	140,000	140,000

Required:

Calculate Ryerson's dividend payout ratio for 2013 (in percentage terms, rounded to two decimal places).

BRIEF EXERCISES

OBJECTIVE 3

Brief Exercise 12-57 Cross Sectional Analysis

Cross sectional analysis entails comparing a company to its competitors.

Required:

Indicate one of the biggest weaknesses of using cross sectional analysis when analyzing a company.

OBJECTIVE 3

Brief Exercise 12-58 Time Series Analysis

Time series analysis involves comparing a company's income statement and balance sheet for the current year to its previous years' income statements and balance sheets.

Required:

CONCEPTUAL CONNECTION Explain whether it is always bad if a company's cost of goods sold is increasing from year to year.

OBJECTIVE 4

Brief Exercise 12-59 Horizontal and Vertical Analysis

Venus Clothing Company specializes in selling apparel for special occasions. In 2012 and 2013, Venus' account balances were as follows:

	2013	2012
Accounts receivable	$ 45,000	$ 32,000
Merchandise inventory	9,000	11,000
Total assets	375,000	340,000
Net sales	330,000	260,000
Cost of goods sold	145,000	185,000

Required:

1. Calculate the change in each of the Venus' accounts from 2012 to 2013.
2. Indicate what happened from 2012 to 2013 to accounts receivable and merchandise inventory as a percentage of total assets. Indicate what happened from 2012 to 2013 to cost of goods sold as a percentage of net sales.

Brief Exercise 12-60 Short-Term Liquidity Ratios

OBJECTIVE 3

Larry, Curly, and Moe companies operate in the same industry. Each company provided financial information to the public containing three ratios for 2012 and 2013.

(in millions)		Larry	Curly	Moe
Current ratio	12/31/13	2.3 to 1	1.9 to 1	1.8 to 1
	12/31/12	2.0 to 1	1.5 to 1	2.2 to 1
Inventory turnover ratio	12/31/13	5.6 times	4.6 times	6.0 times
	12/31/12	7.6 times	5.8 times	9.6 times
Quick ratio	12/31/13	2.2 to 1	1.9 to 1	0.7 to 1
	12/31/12	1.0 to 1	1.4 to 1	1.2 to 1

Required:

Explain which company appears to be the most liquid at December 31, 2013.

Brief Exercise 12-61 Debt Management Ratios

OBJECTIVE 5

Glow Corporation provides annual and quarterly financial data to the public. For the years of 2012 and 2013, Glow's financial data included the following account balances:

	2013	2012
Total liabilities	$1,390,000	$988,000
Common stock ($25 par)	270,000	235,000
Paid-in capital in excess of par—common stock	155,000	140,000
Retained earnings	167,000	152,000

Required:

Determine whether the debt to equity ratio is increasing or decreasing and whether Glow should be concerned.

Brief Exercise 12-62 Debt Management and Short-Term Liquidity Ratios

OBJECTIVE 5

Magellan Company is an international travel agency providing travel planning services to customers in over 20 countries. Recently, the travel industry has been experiencing volatility as a result of increases in oil prices. Magellan's investors have been following its financial information closely to determine its ability to continue as a going concern. Its investors have used the following information to determine financial ratios:

	2013	2012
Current assets	$5,000	$3,600
Long-term assets	6,000	3,900
Current liabilities	1,500	2,200
Long-term liabilities	5,000	0
Stockholders' equity	3,900	3,900

Required:

Between 2012 and 2013, indicate whether Magellan's debt to equity ratio increased or decreased. Also, indicate whether Magellan's current ratio increased or decreased. Interpret these ratios.

OBJECTIVE 5

Brief Exercise 12-63 Asset Efficiency Ratios

Rumsford Inc.'s financial statements for 2013 indicate the following account balances:

Net sales	$256,340
Cost of goods sold	162,000
Average accounts receivable	18,710
Average inventory	3,845
Average property, plant, and equipment	72,345
Average total assets	119,124

Required:

1. Using this information, calculate Rumsford's receivable turnover ratio. (*Note:* Round to two decimal places.)
2. Using this information, calculate Rumsford's asset turnover ratio and also convert the ratio into days.

OBJECTIVE 5

Brief Exercise 12-64 Profitability Ratios

Meade Publications is a magazine publisher established in Southern California. Financial analysts are concerned about Meade's ability to generate positive returns as printed material becomes less popular than digital material. Financial analysts observe the following account balances from Meade to determine financial ratios:

Revenue	$1,100,000
Expenses	700,000
Net income	350,000
Assets	625,000
Liabilities	175,000
Average equity	600,000

Required:

Compute Meade's return on equity.

OBJECTIVE 5

Brief Exercise 12-65 Profitability Ratios

Tinker Corporation operates in the highly competitive consulting industry. Tinker's balance sheet indicates the following balances as of December 31, 2013.

Cash	$ 80,000
Accounts receivable	87,000
Inventory	52,000
Property, plant, and equipment	485,000
Accounts payable	73,000
Bonds payable (due in 2015)	110,000
Common stock (12/31/2012)	250,000
Common stock (12/31/2013)	275,000
Retained earnings (12/31/2012)	180,000
Retained earnings (12/31/2013)	220,000

Required:

Calculate Tinker's return on equity if Tinker's 2013 net income is $90,000.

OBJECTIVE 5

Brief Exercise 12-66 Profitability Ratios

Katrina Corp. is a publicly traded company on a large stock exchange. Katrina's financial statement for 2013 and 2012 included the following data:

	2013	2012
Net income	$140,000	$115,000
Cash dividends paid on preferred stock	11,000	11,000
Cash dividends paid on common stock	38,000	34,000

	2013	2012
Weighted average number of preferred shares outstanding	18,000	18,000
Weighted average number of common shares outstanding	97,000	94,000

Required:

Calculate Katrina's earnings per share as it would be reported on the 2013 income statement.

Brief Exercise 12-67 Stockholder Ratios OBJECTIVE 5

Orion Corp.'s financial data for 2013 and 2012 included the following:

	2013	2012
Net income	$120,000	$135,000
Cash dividends paid on common stock	49,000	42,000
Market price per share of common stock at the end of the year	19.00	17.00
Shares of common stock outstanding	150,000	150,000

Required:

Calculate Orion's dividend payout ratio for 2013.

EXERCISES

Exercise 12-68 Sec Filings OBJECTIVE 2

The SEC requires publicly traded companies to file many different forms.

Required:

Describe the Form 10-Q.

Exercise 12-69 Form 10-K OBJECTIVE 2

Form 10-K has many different items.

Required:

1. Indicate what is included in the Management's Discussion and Analysis section of the 10-K.
2. List five important things that are included in the Form 10-K.

Exercise 12-70 Getting Familiar with the Format of the 10-K OBJECTIVE 2

Look up VF's 10-K for 2011 (filed February 29, 2012). It can be found online (which allows you to search and reference the entire 10-K) by searching for "VF investor relations." Once at that site click on "SEC Filings," move the "Groupings Filter (View SEC Groupings descriptions)" pull down menu to "Annual Filings," and click the "Search" button.

Required:

Answer the following questions and include in which item number of the 10-K the information was found:

1. How is VF's strategy transforming its mix of business?
2. VF divides its brands into 5 "coalitions." Name these coalitions.
3. Describe the seasonality of VF's business. Specifically, in which quarter did VF experience the highest proportion of its 2011 revenues and operating income? Why is this quarter higher than the other quarters?
4. Is VF involved in any litigation that may materially affect its financial position?
5. In analyzing the results of operations, what 4 factors are presented as the sources of growth in revenues from 2010 to 2011? Which factor is the primary source of the growth?
6. What method of depreciation does VF use? What is the range of useful lives for machinery and equipment?
7. Who audits VF?

OBJECTIVE 3

Exercise 12-71 Financial Statement Users

Many groups analyze financial statements to make decisions.

Required:

1. **CONCEPTUAL CONNECTION** Explain why a person who is selecting an employer should be sure to view and analyze the company's financial statements.
2. **CONCEPTUAL CONNECTION** Explain why a business that is considering selling goods or providing services to another business should review the company's financial statements.

OBJECTIVE 3 4

Exercise 12-72 Horizontal Analysis of Income Statements

Consolidated income statements for Winged Manufacturing follow.

Winged Manufacturing
Consolidated Income Statements
(in thousands except per share amounts)

	Three fiscal years ended December 31		
	2013	**2012**	**2011**
Sales	$9,188,748	$7,976,954	$7,086,542
Costs and expenses:			
Cost of goods sold	$6,844,915	$5,248,834	$3,991,337
Research and development	564,303	664,564	602,135
Selling, general, and administrative	1,384,111	1,632,362	1,637,262
Restructuring costs and other	(126,855)	320,856	50,000
	$8,666,474	$7,866,616	$6,280,734
Operating income	$ 522,274	$ 110,338	$ 805,808
Interest and other income, net	(21,988)	29,321	49,634
Income before income taxes	$ 500,286	$ 139,659	$ 855,442
Provision for income taxes	190,108	53,070	325,069
Net income	$ 310,178	$ 86,589	$ 530,373
Earnings per common and common equivalent share	$ 2.61	$ 0.73	$ 4.33
Common and common equivalent shares used in the calculations of earnings per share	118,735	119,125	122,490

Required:

1. Prepare common size income statements for horizontal analysis (in percentage terms, rounded to two decimal places). You do not need to include the actual dollar amounts shown above.
2. **CONCEPTUAL CONNECTION** Explain why net income decreased in 2012 and increased in 2013.

OBJECTIVE 3

Exercise 12-73 Vertical Analysis of Balance Sheets

Consolidated balance sheets for Winged Manufacturing follow.

Winged Manufacturing
Consolidated Balance Sheets
(dollars in thousands)

	December 31	
	2013	**2012**
ASSETS		
Current assets:		
Cash and cash equivalents	$1,203,488	$ 676,413
Short-term investments	54,368	215,890
Accounts receivable, net of allowance for doubtful accounts of $90,992 ($83,776 in 2012)	1,581,347	1,381,946
Inventories	1,088,434	1,506,638
Deferred tax assets	293,048	268,085
Other current assets	255,767	289,383
Total current assets	$4,476,452	$4,338,355

Property, plant, and equipment:		
Land and buildings	$ 484,592	$ 404,688
Machinery and equipment	572,728	578,272
Office furniture and equipment	158,160	167,905
Leasehold improvements	236,708	261,792
	$1,452,188	$1,412,657
Accumulated depreciation and amortization	(785,088)	(753,111)
Net property, plant, and equipment	$ 667,100	$ 659,546
Other assets	159,194	173,511
Total assets	$5,302,746	$5,171,412
LIABILITIES AND STOCKHOLDERS' EQUITY		
Current liabilities:		
Short-term borrowings	$ 292,200	$ 823,182
Accounts payable	881,717	742,622
Accrued compensation and employee benefits	136,895	144,779
Accrued marketing and distribution	178,294	174,547
Accrued restructuring costs	58,238	307,932
Other current liabilities	396,961	315,023
Total current liabilities	$1,944,305	$2,508,085
Long-term debt	304,472	7,117
Deferred tax liabilities	670,668	629,832
Total liabilities	$2,919,445	$3,145,034
Stockholders' equity:		
Common stock, no par value: 320,000,000 shares authorized; 119,542,527 shares issued and outstanding in 2013 (116,147,035 shares in 2012)	$ 297,929	$ 203,613
Retained earnings	2,096,206	1,842,600
Accumulated translation adjustment	(10,834)	(19,835)
Total stockholders' equity	$2,383,301	$2,026,378
Total liabilities and stockholders' equity	$5,302,746	$5,171,412

Required:

1. Prepare common size balance sheets for vertical analysis (in percentage terms, rounded to two decimal places). You do not need to include the actual dollar amounts shown above.
2. Indicate from what sources Winged appears to have secured the resources for its asset increase.

Exercise 12-74 Horizontal Analysis Using Income Statements

OBJECTIVE 3 4

The consolidated 2013, 2012, and 2011 income statements for Butler Corporation follow.

Butler Corporation
Consolidated Income Statements
(in millions except per share amounts)

	December 31,		
	2013	**2012**	**2011**
Net sales	$ 25,020.7	$ 21,970.0	$19,292.2
Costs and expenses:			
Cost of goods sold	(11,946.1)	(10,611.7)	(9,366.2)
Selling, general, and administrative	(9,864.4)	(8,721.2)	(7,605.9)
Amortization of intangible assets	(303.7)	(265.9)	(208.3)
Operating income	$ 2,906.5	$ 2,371.2	$ 2,111.8

(Continued)

	December 31,		
	2013	2012	2011
Interest expense	(572.7)	(586.1)	(613.7)
Interest income	88.7	113.7	161.6
Income before income taxes	$ 2,422.5	$ 1,898.8	$ 1,659.7
Provision for income taxes	834.6	597.1	597.5
Net income	$ 1,587.9	$ 1,301.7	$ 1,062.2

Required:

1. Prepare common size income statements for horizontal analysis (in percentage terms, rounded to two decimal places). You do not need to include the actual dollar amounts shown above.
2. Indicate what Butler's 2013, 2012, and 2011 tax rates were on its income before taxes (in percentage terms, rounded to two decimal places).
3. **CONCEPTUAL CONNECTION** Explain why net income increased by a larger percentage than sales in 2013 and 2012.

OBJECTIVE 3 4

Exercise 12-75 Horizontal Analysis Using Balance Sheets

The consolidated 2013 and 2012 balance sheets for Butler Corporation follow.

Butler Corporation
Consolidated Balance Sheets
(in millions except per share amounts)

	December 31,	
	2013	2012
ASSETS		
Current assets:		
Cash and cash equivalents	$ 226.9	$ 169.9
Short-term investments at cost which approximates market	1,629.3	1,888.5
Accounts and notes receivable, less allowance: $128.3 in 2013 and $112.0 in 2012	1,883.4	1,588.5
Inventories	924.7	768.8
Prepaid expenses, taxes, and other current assets	499.8	426.6
Total current assets	$ 5,164.1	$ 4,842.3
Investments in affiliates and other assets	1,756.6	1,707.9
Property, plant, and equipment, net	8,855.6	7,442.0
Intangible assets, net	7,929.5	6,959.0
Total assets	$23,705.8	$20,951.2
LIABILITIES AND STOCKHOLDERS' EQUITY		
Current liabilities:		
Short-term borrowings	$ 2,191.2	$ 706.8
Accounts payable	1,390.0	1,164.8
Income taxes payable	823.7	621.1
Accrued compensation and benefits	726.0	638.9
Accrued marketing	400.9	327.0
Other current liabilities	1,043.1	1,099.0
Total current liabilities	$ 6,574.9	$ 4,557.6
Long-term debt	7,442.6	7,964.8
Other liabilities	1,342.0	1,390.8
Deferred income taxes	2,007.6	1,682.3
Total liabilities	$17,367.1	$15,595.5

Stockholders' equity:		
Capital stock, par value $1 per share: authorized 1,800.0 million shares, 14.4 million and 7.4 million shares issued at December 31, 2013 and 2012, respectively	$ 14.4	$ 7.4
Capital in excess of par value	879.5	674.6
Retained earnings	6,541.9	5,439.7
Other comprehensive income (loss)	(183.9)	(99.0)
Less: Treasury stock, at cost: 64.3 shares in 2013 and 2012	(913.2)	(667.0)
Total stockholders' equity	$ 6,338.7	$ 5,355.7
Total liabilities and stockholders' equity	$23,705.8	$20,951.2

Required:

1. Calculate the percentage that Butler's total assets increased by during 2013 (in percentage terms, rounded to one decimal place). You do not need to include the actual dollar amounts shown above.
2. Determine whether any of the asset categories experienced larger increases than others.
3. Indicate where Butler acquired the capital to finance its asset growth.
4. Indicate whether any of the individual liability or equity items increased at a rate different from the rate at which total liabilities and equity increased.

Exercise 12-76 Preparation of Common Size Statements for Vertical Analysis

OBJECTIVE 3 4

Financial statements for Steele Inc. follow.

Steele Inc.
Consolidated Income Statements
(in thousands except per share amounts)

	2013	2012	2011
Net sales	$ 7,245,088	$ 6,944,296	$ 6,149,218
Cost of goods sold	(5,286,253)	(4,953,556)	(4,355,675)
Gross margin	$ 1,958,835	$ 1,990,740	$ 1,793,543
General and administrative expenses	(1,259,896)	(1,202,042)	(1,080,843)
Special and nonrecurring items	2,617	0	0
Operating income	$ 701,556	$ 788,698	$ 712,700
Interest expense	(63,685)	(62,398)	(63,927)
Other income	7,308	10,080	11,529
Gain on sale of investments	0	9,117	0
Income before income taxes	$ 645,179	$ 745,497	$ 660,302
Provision for income taxes	(254,000)	(290,000)	(257,000)
Net income	$ 391,179	$ 455,497	$ 403,302

Steele Inc.
Consolidated Balance Sheets
(in thousands)

ASSETS	Dec. 31, 2013	Dec. 31, 2012
Current assets:		
Cash and equivalents	$ 320,558	$ 41,235
Accounts receivable	1,056,911	837,377
Inventories	733,700	803,707
Other	109,456	101,811
Total current assets	$2,220,625	$1,784,130
Property and equipment, net	1,666,588	1,813,948
Other assets	247,892	248,372
Total assets	$4,135,105	$3,846,450

(Continued)

LIABILITIES AND STOCKHOLDERS' EQUITY		
Current liabilities:		
Accounts payable	$ 250,363	$ 309,092
Accrued expenses	347,892	274,220
Other current liabilities	15,700	0
Income taxes	93,489	137,466
Total current liabilities	$ 707,444	$ 720,778
Long-term debt	650,000	541,639
Deferred income taxes	275,101	274,844
Other long-term liabilities	61,267	41,572
Total liabilities	$1,693,812	$1,578,833
Stockholders' equity:		
Preferred stock	$ 100,000	$ 100,000
Common stock	89,727	89,727
Additional paid-in capital—common stock	128,906	127,776
Retained earnings	2,397,112	2,136,794
	$2,715,745	$2,454,297
Less: Treasury stock, at cost	(274,452)	(186,680)
Total stockholders' equity	$2,441,293	$2,267,617
Total liabilities and stockholders' equity	$4,135,105	$3,846,450

Required:

1. Prepare common size income statements and balance sheets for Steele to be used in vertical analysis (in percentage terms, rounded to two decimal places). You do not need to include the actual dollar amounts shown above.
2. **CONCEPTUAL CONNECTION** Indicate whether gross margin grew as much as sales between 2011 and 2012 and between 2012 and 2013, and, if so, why it grew.
3. **CONCEPTUAL CONNECTION** Indicate whether the relative proportion of Steele's assets changed between 2012 and 2013, and, if so, explain the change.
4. **CONCEPTUAL CONNECTION** Indicate whether the relative proportion of Steele's liabilities and equity changed between 2012 and 2013, and, if so, explain the change.
5. **CONCEPTUAL CONNECTION** Explain how Steele appears to have financed the 7.5% increase in assets that occurred between 2012 and 2013.

OBJECTIVE 3 4

Exercise 12-77 Common Size Statements for Vertical Analysis

The following consolidated income statements and balance sheets are available for Azure Inc.:

Azure Inc.
Consolidated Income Statements

	Year ended December 31,					
	2013		2012		2011	
	Amount	%	Amount	%	Amount	%
Revenues	$901,170	100.0	$728,035	100.0	$661,850	100.0
Costs and expenses:						
Cost of goods sold	$539,801	59.9	$439,005	60.3	$401,743	60.7
Selling and administrative	318,113	35.3	206,034	28.3	176,052	26.6
Interest	17,122	1.9	18,201	2.5	17,208	2.6
Other expenses (income)	9,913	1.1	2,912	0.4	(1,324)	(0.2)
Total costs and expenses	$884,949	98.2	$666,152	91.5	$593,679	89.7
Income before provision for income taxes	$ 16,221	1.8	$ 61,883	8.5	$ 68,171	10.3
Provision for income taxes	4,506	0.5	22,569	3.1	23,827	3.6
Net income	$ 11,715	1.3	$ 39,314	5.4	$ 44,344	6.7

Azure Inc.
Consolidated Balance Sheets

	December 31,					
	2013		2012		2011	
	Amount	%	Amount	%	Amount	%
ASSETS						
Current assets	$147,129	31.4	$ 62,417	14.3	$ 66,927	16.1
Investment	30,925	6.6	95,589	21.9	91,453	22.0
Property, plant, and equipment (net)	270,831	57.8	261,015	59.8	241,519	58.1
Other assets	19,680	4.2	17,459	4.0	15,796	3.8
Total assets	$468,565	100.0	$436,480	100.0	$415,695	100.0
LIABILITIES AND STOCKHOLDERS' EQUITY						
Current liabilities	$ 68,410	14.6	$ 29,244	6.7	$ 28,683	6.9
Long-term debt	152,284	32.5	162,807	37.3	152,976	36.8
Total liabilities	$220,694	47.1	$192,051	44.0	$181,659	43.7
Common stock	$183,209	39.1	$182,332	41.8	$171,266	41.2
Retained earnings	64,662	13.8	62,097	14.2	62,770	15.1
Total stockholders' equity	$247,871	52.9	$244,429	56.0	$234,036	56.3
Total liabilities and stockholders' equity	$468,565	100.0	$436,480	100.0	$415,695	100.0

Required:

1. **CONCEPTUAL CONNECTION** Explain why income from operations decreased in 2012 and 2013 while sales increased.
2. Determine whether the proportion of resources invested in the various asset categories changed from 2011 to 2013.
3. Determine whether the proportion of capital supplied by creditors changed.
4. Indicate from what sources Azure secured the capital to finance its increase in current assets in 2013.

Exercise 12-78 Short-Term Liquidity Ratios

OBJECTIVE 5

The financial statements for Seek Enterprises, a retailer, follow.

Seek Enterprises
Consolidated Income Statements
(millions of dollars except per share data)

	December 31		
	2013	2012	2011
Revenues	$19,233	$17,927	$16,115
Costs and expenses:			
Cost of retail sales, buying, and occupancy	$14,164	$13,129	$11,751
Selling, publicity, and administration	3,175	2,978	2,801
Depreciation	498	459	410
Interest expense, net	446	437	398
Taxes other than income taxes	343	313	283
Total costs and expenses	$18,626	$17,316	$15,643
Earnings before income taxes	$ 607	$ 611	$ 472
Provision for income taxes	232	228	171
Net earnings	$ 375	$ 383	$ 301

(Continued)

Seek Enterprises
Consolidated Balance Sheets
(millions of dollars)

	December 31, 2013	December 31, 2012
ASSETS		
Current assets:		
Cash and cash equivalents	$ 321	$ 117
Accounts receivable	1,536	1,514
Merchandise inventories	2,497	2,618
Other	157	165
Total current assets	$ 4,511	$ 4,414
Property and equipment:		
Land	$ 1,120	$ 998
Buildings and improvements	4,753	4,342
Fixtures and equipment	2,162	2,197
Construction-in-progress	248	223
Accumulated depreciation	(2,336)	(2,197)
Net property and equipment	$ 5,947	$ 5,563
Other	320	360
Total assets	$10,778	$10,337
LIABILITIES AND STOCKHOLDERS' EQUITY		
Current liabilities:		
Notes payable	$ 200	$ 23
Accounts payable	1,654	1,596
Accrued liabilities	903	849
Income taxes payable	145	125
Current portion of long-term debt	173	371
Total current liabilities	$ 3,075	$ 2,964
Long-term debt	4,279	4,330
Deferred income taxes and other	536	450
Loan to ESOP	(217)	(267)
Total liabilities	$ 7,673	$ 7,477
Stockholders' equity:		
Preferred stock	368	374
Common stock	72	71
Additional paid-in capital—common	73	58
Retained earnings	2,592	2,357
Total stockholders' equity	$ 3,105	$ 2,860
Total liabilities and stockholders' equity	$10,778	$10,337

Required:

1. Compute the four short-term liquidity ratios (rounded to two decimal places) for 2012 and 2013, assuming operating cash flows are $281 million and $483 million, respectively.
2. **CONCEPTUAL CONNECTION** Indicate which ratios appear to be most appropriate for a retail organization. Indicate what other information you would like to know to comment on Seek's short-term liquidity.

OBJECTIVE 5

Exercise 12-79 Debt Management Ratios

Refer to Steele's financial statements in **Exercise 12-76**.

Required:

1. Compute the five debt management ratios for 2012 and 2013 (rounded to two decimal places).
2. **CONCEPTUAL CONNECTION** Indicate whether the ratios have changed and whether the ratios suggest that Steele is more or less risky for long-term creditors at December 31, 2013, than at December 31, 2012.

Exercise 12-80 Asset Efficiency Ratios

OBJECTIVE 5

Refer to Steele's financial statements in **Exercise 12-76** and the information below.

Statement Item	January 1, 2012 (in thousands)
Accounts receivable	$ 752,945
Inventories	698,604
Total assets	3,485,233

Required:

1. Compute the three asset efficiency ratios (rounded to two decimal places) for 2012 and 2013.
2. Indicate the length of Steele's operating cycle in days (rounded to two decimal places) for the years ended December 31, 2013, and December 31, 2012.

Exercise 12-81 Profitability Ratios

OBJECTIVE 5

Refer to Steele's financial statements in **Exercise 12-76** and the information below.

Statement Item	January 1, 2012 (in thousands)
Total assets	$3,485,233
Total stockholders' equity	2,083,122

Required:

1. Compute the five profitability ratios (in percentage terms, rounded to two decimal places) for 2012 and 2013.
2. **CONCEPTUAL CONNECTION** Explain what these ratios suggest about Steele's profitability. Indicate what other information you would like to know to further assess Steele's profitability.

Exercise 12-82 Stockholder Ratios

OBJECTIVE 5

Refer to Steele's financial statements in **Exercise 12-76** and the information below.

	Year ended December 31,	
Item	2013	2012
Average number of common shares outstanding (thousands)	362,202	364,398
Preferred dividends (thousands)	$ 24,000	$ 24,000
Dividends per common share	0.36	1.54
Common dividends (thousands)	130,861.00	561,172.30
Common stock repurchases	0	0
Market price per share:		
High	83.25	79.10
Low	63.25	59.00
Close	78.42	66.36

At January 1, 2012, total stockholders' equity was $2,083,122 and there was no preferred stock.

Required:

1. Compute the earnings per share, return on common equity, dividend yield ratio, and dividend payout ratio (in percentage terms, rounded to two decimal places except for EPS, which should be rounded to nearest cent) for 2012 and 2013.
2. **CONCEPTUAL CONNECTION** Indicate whether there were significant changes in these ratios between the years ended December 31, 2013, and December 31, 2012. Determine whether the stockholder ratios suggest that Steele was a better investment at December 31, 2013, or December 31, 2012.

Exercise 12-83 Dupont Analysis

OBJECTIVE 5

Refer to Steele's financial statements in **Exercise 12-76** and the information below.

Statement Item	January 1, 2012 (in millions)
Total assets	$3,485,233
Total stockholders' equity	2,083,122

(Continued)

	Year ended December 31,	
Industry Averages	**2013**	**2012**
Return on equity	5.31%	12.54%
Profit margin	4.00	6.21
Asset turnover	0.83	1.96
Leverage	1.60	1.03

Required:

1. Perform a Dupont analysis (in percentage terms, rounded to two decimal places) for 2012 and 2013.
2. **CONCEPTUAL CONNECTION** Explain what you learn about Steele's trends from 2012 to 2013 by comparing its performance to the industry averages.

PROBLEM SET A

OBJECTIVE 3 4

Problem 12-84A Using Common Size Data for Credit Analysis

You are the credit manager for London Supplies. One of your sales staff has made a $50,000 credit sale to Bing Company, an electronics manufacturer. Your responsibility is to decide whether to approve the sale. You have the following data for the electronics industry and Bing:

For the Years 2009–2013	Industry	Bing Company
Average annual sales growth	13.4%	17.6%
Average annual operating income growth	10.8%	9.7%
Average annual net income growth	14.4%	9.9%
Average annual asset growth	10.3%	14.2%
Average debt to equity ratio	0.32	0.26
Average current ratio	4.04	3.71
Average inventory turnover ratio	2.53	2.06
Average accounts receivable turnover ratio	3.95	4.18

For Bing, you have the following data for the year ended December 31, 2013:

Sales revenue	$3,908,000
Net income	$359,000
Total assets	$3,626,000
Current ratio	1.82
Debt to equity ratio	0.37
Inventory turnover ratio	1.79
Accounts receivable turnover ratio	3.62

The salesperson believes that Bing would order about $200,000 per year of materials that would provide a gross margin of $35,000 to London if reasonable credit terms could be arranged.

Required:

CONCEPTUAL CONNECTION State whether you would grant authorization for Bing to purchase on credit and support your decision.

OBJECTIVE 3 4

Problem 12-85A Using Common Size Data for Investment Analysis

Assume that you are a trust officer for the Joss Bank. You are attempting to select a pharmaceutical manufacturer's stock for a client's portfolio. You have secured the following data:

	5-Year Averages				
	Industry Average	**Opal**	**Main**	**Darcy**	**Hunt**
Sales growth	8.3%	9.8%	7.9%	7.2%	10.1%
Net income growth	13.0	12.0	10.7	4.2	16.1
Asset growth	5.0	6.1	4.6	4.4	6.2

	Current Year				
	Industry Average	Opal	Main	Darcy	Hunt
Return on equity	16.2%	17.5%	17.5%	19.4%	21.6%
Return on assets	8.5	7.8	12.7	8.4	11.4
Dividend payout	43.0	40.0	23.0	31.0	31.0

Required:

CONCEPTUAL CONNECTION Comment on the relative performance of these firms.

Problem 12-86A Using Common Size Income Statement Data

OBJECTIVE 3 4

The 2013, 2012, and 2011 income statements for Jolly Fun Inc. follow.

Jolly Fun Inc.
Consolidated Income Statements

	Year ended December 31,		
	2013	2012	2011
Revenues:			
Theme parks and resorts	$3,440.7	$3,306.9	$2,794.3
Filmed entertainment	3,673.4	3,115.2	2,593.7
Consumer products	1,415.1	1,081.9	724.0
	$8,529.2	$7,504.0	$6,112.0
Costs and expenses:			
Theme parks and resorts	$2,693.8	$2,662.9	$2,247.7
Filmed entertainment	3,051.2	2,606.9	2,275.6
Consumer products	1,059.7	798.9	494.2
	$6,804.7	$6,068.7	$5,017.5
Operating income:			
Theme parks and resorts	$ 746.9	$ 644.0	$ 546.6
Filmed entertainment	622.2	508.3	318.1
Consumer products	355.4	283.0	229.8
	$1,724.5	$1,435.3	$1,094.5
Corporate activities:			
General and administrative expenses	$ 164.2	$ 148.2	$ 160.8
Interest expense	157.7	126.8	105.0
Investment and interest income	(186.1)	(130.3)	(119.4)
	$ 135.8	$ 144.7	$ 146.4
Income (loss) on investment in Asian theme park	$ (514.7)	$ 11.2	$ 63.8
Income before income taxes	$1,074.0	$1,301.8	$1,011.9
Income taxes	402.7	485.1	375.3
Net income	$ 671.3	$ 816.7	$ 636.6

Required:

1. Calculate how much each of the revenues and expenses changed from 2011 through 2013 (in percentage terms, rounded to two decimal places). Utilize 2011 as the base year for both 2012 and 2013. You do not need to include the actual dollar amounts shown above.
2. **CONCEPTUAL CONNECTION** Explain the primary causes of Jolly's increase in net income in 2012 and the decrease in 2013.

OBJECTIVE 3 4

Problem 12-87A Using Common Size Statements

The following income statement and vertical analysis data are available for Riley Manufacturing:

Riley Manufacturing
Consolidated Income Statements

	Year ended June 30,					
	2013		2012		2011	
(in thousands)	Amount	%	Amount	%	Amount	%
Sales	$2,970.0	100.0	$3,465.0	100.0	$3,960.0	100.0
Other income, net	23.7	0.8	34.6	1.0	39.6	1.0
Total revenues	$2,993.7	100.8	$3,499.6	101.0	$3,999.6	101.0
Costs and expenses:						
Cost of goods sold	$1,303.8	43.9	$1,566.2	45.2	$1,920.6	48.5
Selling and administrative	1,571.1	52.9	1,593.9	46.0	1,564.2	39.5
Interest	62.4	2.1	65.8	1.9	59.4	1.5
Total costs and expenses	$2,937.3	98.9	$3,225.9	93.1	$3,544.2	89.5
Income before income taxes	$ 56.4	1.9	$ 273.7	7.9	$ 455.4	11.5
Income taxes expense	14.8	0.5	107.4	3.1	182.2	4.6
Net income	$ 41.6	1.4	$ 166.3	4.8	$ 273.2	6.9

Required:

1. **CONCEPTUAL CONNECTION** Suggest why net income declined from $273,200 to $41,600 while the cost of goods sold percentage decreased each year and selling and administrative expenses remained nearly constant.
2. **CONCEPTUAL CONNECTION** Determine what could cause sales to decline while the gross margin percentage increases.

OBJECTIVE 3 4

ILLUSTRATING RELATIONSHIPS

Problem 12-88A Using Common Size Statements

Twisted Company owns and operates a small chain of pretzel stands located near colleges and universities. Twisted has experienced significant growth in recent years. The following data are available for Twisted:

Twisted Company
Consolidated Income Statements
(in thousands)

	Year ended December 31,		
	2013	2012	2011
Sales	$51,638	$41,310	$34,425
Cost of goods sold	31,050	24,840	20,700
Gross margin	$20,588	$16,470	$13,725
Other income, net	383	426	405
	$20,971	$16,896	$14,130
Costs and expenses:			
Selling and administrative	$16,570	$13,465	$11,350
Interest	1,237	765	554
Total costs and expenses	$17,807	$14,230	$11,904
Income before income taxes	$ 3,164	$ 2,666	$ 2,226
Provision for income taxes	885	746	623
Net income	$ 2,279	$ 1,920	$ 1,603

Twisted Company
Consolidated Balance Sheets
(in thousands)

	December 31, 2013	2012	2011
ASSETS			
Current assets:			
Cash	$ 360	$ 293	$ 236
Accounts receivable	4,658	3,690	3,285
Inventories	6,064	4,478	3,442
Total current assets	$11,082	$ 8,461	$ 6,963
Property, plant, and equipment (net)	4,860	3,600	2,756
Other assets	574	585	562
Total assets	$16,516	$12,646	$10,281
LIABILITIES AND STOCKHOLDERS' EQUITY			
Current liabilities:			
Short-term notes payable	$ 4,230	$ 1,620	$ 450
Accounts payable	1,147	1,013	720
Total current liabilities	$ 5,377	$ 2,633	$ 1,170
Long-term debt	3,150	3,150	3,150
Total liabilities	$ 8,527	$ 5,783	$ 4,320
Common stock & additional paid-in capital	$ 4,725	$ 4,725	$ 4,725
Retained earnings	3,264	2,138	1,236
Total stockholders' equity	$ 7,989	$ 6,863	$ 5,961
Total liabilities and stockholders' equity	$16,516	$12,646	$10,281

Required:

1. Determine how much Twisted's sales, net income, and assets have grown during these 3 years.
2. Explain how Twisted has financed the increase in assets.
3. Determine whether Twisted's liquidity is adequate.
4. **CONCEPTUAL CONNECTION** Explain why interest expense is growing.
5. If Twisted's sales grow by 25% in 2014, what would you expect net income to be?
6. If Twisted's assets must grow by 25% to support the 25% sales increase and if 50% of net income is paid in dividends, how much capital must Twisted raise in 2014?

Problem 12-89A Preparing Common Size Statements

OBJECTIVE 3 4

The financial statements for Burch Industries follow:

Burch Industries
Consolidated Income Statements
(in thousands, except per share data)

	Year ended December 31, 2013	2012	2011
Revenues	$3,930,984	$3,405,211	$3,003,610
Costs and expenses:			
Cost of goods sold	$2,386,993	$2,089,089	$1,850,530
Selling and administrative	922,261	761,498	664,061
Interest	25,739	30,665	27,316
Other expenses (income)	1,475	2,141	(43)
Total costs and expenses	$3,336,468	$2,883,393	$2,541,864
Income before income taxes	$ 594,516	$ 521,818	$ 461,746
Income taxes	229,500	192,600	174,700
Net income	$ 365,016	$ 329,218	$ 287,046

(Continued)

Burch Industries
Consolidated Balance Sheets (in thousands)

	December 31,	
	2013	**2012**
ASSETS		
Current assets:		
Cash and equivalents	$ 291,284	$ 260,050
Accounts receivable, less allowance for doubtful accounts of $19,447 and $20,046	667,547	596,018
Inventories	592,986	471,202
Deferred income taxes	26,378	27,511
Prepaid expenses	42,452	32,977
Total current assets	$1,620,647	$1,387,758
Property, plant, and equipment	$ 571,032	$ 497,795
Less accumulated depreciation	(193,037)	(151,758)
Net property, plant, and equipment	$ 377,995	$ 346,037
Goodwill	157,894	110,363
Other assets	30,927	28,703
Total assets	$2,187,463	$1,872,861
LIABILITIES AND STOCKHOLDERS' EQUITY		
Current liabilities:		
Current portion of long-term debt	$ 52,985	$ 3,652
Notes payable	108,165	105,696
Accounts payable	135,701	134,729
Accrued liabilities	138,563	134,089
Income taxes payable	17,150	42,422
Total current liabilities	$ 452,564	$ 420,588
Long-term debt	15,033	77,022
Noncurrent deferred income taxes	29,965	27,074
Other noncurrent liabilities	43,575	23,728
Commitments and contingencies	0	0
Redeemable preferred stock	300	300
Total liabilities	$ 541,437	$ 548,712
Stockholders' equity:		
Common stock at stated value:		
Class A convertible—26,691 and 26,919 shares outstanding	$ 159	$ 161
Class B—49,161 and 48,591 shares outstanding	2,720	2,716
Capital in excess of stated value	108,451	93,799
Treasury stock (common at cost)	(7,790)	(6,860)
Retained earnings	1,542,486	1,234,333
Total stockholders' equity	$1,646,026	$1,324,149
Total liabilities and stockholders' equity	$2,187,463	$1,872,861

Required:

1. Prepare common size income statements to be used for horizontal analysis for Burch for 2011 to 2013 (in percentage terms, rounded to two decimal places). Utilize 2011 as the base year for both 2012 and 2013. You do not need to include the actual dollar amounts shown above.
2. **CONCEPTUAL CONNECTION** Indicate why Burch's net income increased between 2011 and 2013.
3. Prepare common size balance sheets to be used for vertical analysis for 2013 and 2012 (in percentage terms, rounded to two decimal places). You do not need to include the actual dollar amounts shown above.
4. Indicate whether the proportion of dollars invested in the various categories of assets has changed significantly between 2012 and 2013.

5. Indicate whether the proportion of capital raised from the various liability categories and common stockholders' equity has changed significantly between 2012 and 2013.
6. **CONCEPTUAL CONNECTION** Describe Burch's performance and financial position.

Problem 12-90A Preparation of Ratios

OBJECTIVE 5

Refer to the financial statements for Twisted Company in **Problem 12-88A**.

Required:

1. **CONCEPTUAL CONNECTION** Compute the asset efficiency ratios (rounded to two decimal places) for Twisted for 2013 and 2012 (in percentage terms, rounded to two decimal places). Indicate whether efficiency has changed.
2. **CONCEPTUAL CONNECTION** Compute the profitability ratios (rounded to two decimal places) for Twisted for 2013 and 2012. Determine by how much Twisted's profitability ratios have changed (in percentage terms, rounded to two decimal places) for the 2-year period.
3. **CONCEPTUAL CONNECTION** Compute the debt management ratios (in percentage terms, rounded to two decimal places) for Twisted for 2012 and 2013. Discuss whether creditors are as secure in 2013 as they were in 2012.

Problem 12-91A Comparing Financial Ratios

OBJECTIVE 5

Presented below are selected ratios for four firms. Badgley is a heavy equipment manufacturer, Reagan is a newspaper publisher, Klein is a food manufacturer, and Taylor is a grocery chain.

	Badgley	Reagan	Klein	Taylor
Short-term liquidity ratio				
Current ratio	1.3	1.7	1.0	1.6
Debt management ratio				
Long-term debt to equity	1.81	0.45	0.30	0.09
Asset efficiency ratios				
Accounts receivable turnover	4.66	8.28	11.92	116.15
Inventory turnover	6.26	40.26	7.29	8.43
Profitability ratios				
Operating income	12.6%	25.4%	21.2%	3.8%
Net income	5.9	10.9	10.8	1.9
Return on assets	4.7	10.6	16.8	10.3
Return on equity	36.0	22.6	38.0	21.2

Required:

1. Which firm has the weakest current ratio?
2. **CONCEPTUAL CONNECTION** Explain why the turnover ratios vary so much among the four firms.
3. **CONCEPTUAL CONNECTION** Explain why the return on equity ratio is larger than the return on asset ratio for all four firms.
4. **CONCEPTUAL CONNECTION** Discuss whether the large differences in the return on equity ratios can exist over long periods of time.

Problem 12-92A Preparation of Ratios

OBJECTIVE 5

Refer to the financial statements for Burch Industries in **Problem 12-89A** and the following data.

	2013	2012	2011
Average number of common shares outstanding	77,063	76,602	76,067
Accounts receivable, net	$ 667,547	$ 596,018	$ 521,588
Inventories	592,986	471,202	586,594
Total assets	2,187,463	1,872,861	1,708,430
Stockholders' equity	1,646,026	1,324,149	1,032,789
Stock repurchases	930,111	581,134	288,320
Cash flows from operating activities	190,000	150,000	137,000

(Continued)

	2013	2012	2011
Common dividends paid	$ 57,797	$ 45,195	$ 39,555
Dividends per common share	0.75	0.59	0.52
Market price per share:			
High	90.25	77.45	54.50
Low	55.00	35.12	26.00
Close	86.33	71.65	43.22

	Year ended December 31,	
Industry Averages	**2013**	**2012**
Return on equity	25.98%	23.04%
Profit margin	0.05	0.04
Asset turnover	2.24	2.56
Leverage	2.32	2.25

Required:

1. Prepare all the financial ratios for Burch for 2013 and 2012 (using percentage terms where appropriate and rounding all answers to two decimal places).
2. **CONCEPTUAL CONNECTION** Explain whether Burch's short-term liquidity is adequate.
3. **CONCEPTUAL CONNECTION** Discuss whether Burch uses its assets efficiently.
4. **CONCEPTUAL CONNECTION** Determine whether Burch is profitable.
5. **CONCEPTUAL CONNECTION** Discuss whether long-term creditors should regard Burch as a high-risk or a low-risk firm.
6. Perform a Dupont analysis (rounding to two decimal places) for 2012 and 2013.

OBJECTIVE 6

Problem 12-93A Accounting Alternatives and Financial Analysis

Lemon Automobiles has asked your bank for a $100,000 loan to expand its sales facility. Lemon provides you with the following data:

	2013	2012	2011
Sales revenue	$6,100,000	$5,800,000	$5,400,000
Net income	119,000	112,000	106,000
Ending inventory (FIFO)*	665,000	600,000	500,000
Purchases	5,370,000	5,105,000	4,860,000
Depreciable assets	1,240,000	1,150,000	1,090,000

* The 2010 ending inventory was $470,000 (FIFO).

Your inspection of the financial statements of other automobiles sales firms indicates that most of these firms adopted the LIFO method in the late 1970s. You further note that Lemon has used 5% of depreciable asset cost when computing depreciation expense and that other automobile dealers use 10%. Assume that Lemon's effective tax rate is 25% of income before tax. Also assume the following:

	2013	2012	2011
Ending inventory (LIFO)*	$508,000	$495,000	$480,000

* The 2010 ending inventory was $470,000 (LIFO).

Required:

1. Compute cost of goods sold for 2011–2013, using both the FIFO and the LIFO methods.
2. Compute depreciation expense for Lemon for 2011–2013, using both 5% and 10% of the cost of depreciable assets.
3. Recompute Lemon's net income for 2011–2013, using LIFO and 10% depreciation. (Don't forget the tax impact of the increases in cost of goods sold and depreciation expense.)
4. **CONCEPTUAL CONNECTION** Explain whether Lemon appears to have materially changed its financial statements by the selection of FIFO (rather than LIFO) and 5% (rather than 10%) depreciation.

PROBLEM SET B

Problem 12-84B Using Common Size Data for Credit Analysis

OBJECTIVE 3 4

You are the credit manager for Meyer Company. One of your sales staff has made a $60,000 credit sale to Rudy Technology, a manufacturer of small computers. Your responsibility is to decide whether to approve the sale. You have the following data for the computer industry and Rudy:

For the Years 2009–2013	Industry	Rudy
Average annual sales growth	12.6%	16.8%
Average annual operating income growth	11.2%	10.2%
Average annual net income growth	15.3%	10.6%
Average annual asset growth	9.9%	13.9%
Average debt to equity ratio	0.36	0.29
Average current ratio	4.12	3.88
Average inventory turnover ratio	2.61	2.19
Average accounts receivable turnover ratio	3.89	4.11

For Rudy, you have the following data for the year ended December 31, 2013:

Sales revenue	$4,120,000
Net income	$367,000
Total assets	$3,752,000
Current ratio	1.79
Debt to equity ratio	0.42
Inventory turnover ratio	1.83
Accounts receivable turnover ratio	3.71

The salesperson believes that Rudy would order about $240,000 per year of materials that would provide a gross margin of $40,000 to Meyer if reasonable credit terms could be arranged.

Required:

CONCEPTUAL CONNECTION State whether you would grant authorization for Rudy to purchase on credit and support your decision.

Problem 12-85B Using Common Size Data for Investment Analysis

OBJECTIVE 3 4

Assume that you are a trust officer for Second Fourth Bank. You are attempting to select a pharmaceutical manufacturer's stock for a client's portfolio. You have secured the following data:

	5-Year Averages				
	Industry Average	Van	Mitchell	Dawson	Bronze
Sales growth	9.3%	8.8%	10.2%	10.0%	7.9%
Net income growth	6.0	1.5	1.9	1.4	1.6
Asset growth	7.0	6.6	8.3	8.9	6.3
	Current Year				
Return on equity	19.5%	18.4%	22.7%	20.8%	17.3%
Return on assets	11.7	10.4	13.7	12.8	11.1
Dividend payout	31.0	30.0	39.0	37.0	29.0

Required:

CONCEPTUAL CONNECTION Comment on the relative performance of these firms.

OBJECTIVE 3 4

Problem 12-86B Using Common Size Income Statement Data

The 2013, 2012, and 2011 income statements for Spinner Entertainment Inc. follow.

Spinner Entertainment Inc. Consolidated Income Statements			
	Year ended December 31,		
	2013	2012	2011
Revenues:			
Theme parks and resorts	$2,723.8	$3,299.9	$3,502.7
Filmed entertainment	2,601.4	3,127.3	3,682.4
Consumer products	752.3	1,121.6	1,493.5
	$6,077.5	$7,548.8	$8,678.6
Costs and expenses:			
Theme parks and resorts	$2,263.9	$2,723.4	$2,703.7
Filmed entertainment	2,300.2	2,566.3	3,104.9
Consumer products	503.7	804.5	1,120.6
	$5,067.8	$6,094.2	$6,929.2
Operating income:			
Theme parks and resorts	$ 459.9	$ 576.5	$ 799.0
Filmed entertainment	301.2	561.0	577.5
Consumer products	248.6	317.1	372.9
	$1,009.7	$1,454.6	$1,749.4
Corporate activities:			
General and administrative expenses	$ 161.2	$ 150.2	$ 165.3
Interest expense	103.7	130.8	158.9
Investment and interest income	(121.1)	(127.4)	(193.6)
	$ 143.8	$ 153.6	$ 130.6
Income (loss) on investment in Asian theme park	$ 62.1	$ 13.6	$ (520.8)
Income before income taxes	$ 928.0	$1,314.6	$1,098.0
Income taxes	376.2	492.3	410.4
Net income	$ 551.8	$ 822.3	$ 687.6

Required:

1. Calculate how much each of the revenues and expenses changed from 2011 through 2013 using horizontal analysis (in percentage terms, rounded to two decimal places). Utilize 2011 as the base year for both 2012 and 2013. You do not need to include the actual dollar amounts shown above.
2. **CONCEPTUAL CONNECTION** Discuss the primary causes of Spinner's increase in net income in 2012 and the decrease in 2013.

OBJECTIVE 3 4

Problem 12-87B Using Common Size Statements

The following income statement and vertical analysis data are available for Westman Company:

Westman Company Consolidated Income Statements (in thousands)						
	Year ended June 30,					
	2013		2012		2011	
	Amount	%	Amount	%	Amount	%
Sales	$4,122.0	100.0	$3,566.0	100.0	$2,965.0	100.0
Other income, net	39.7	1.0	36.7	1.0	21.3	0.7
Total revenues	$4,161.7	101.0	$3,602.7	101.0	$2,986.3	100.7
Costs and expenses:						
Cost of goods sold	$1,893.6	45.9	$1,610.3	45.2	$1,310.8	44.2

(Continued)

	Year ended June 30,					
	2013		2012		2011	
	Amount	%	Amount	%	Amount	%
Selling and administrative	1,610.3	39.1	1,603.6	45.0	1,505.3	50.8
Interest	61.4	1.5	69.7	2.0	63.2	2.1
Total costs and expenses	$3,565.3	86.5	$3,283.6	92.2	$2,879.3	97.1
Income before income taxes	$ 596.4	14.5	$ 319.1	8.9*	$ 107.0	3.6
Income taxes expense	181.5	4.4	109.6	3.1	14.5	0.5
Net income	$ 414.9	10.1	$ 209.5	5.9*	$ 92.5	3.1

* Differences due to rounding.

Required:

1. **CONCEPTUAL CONNECTION** Suggest why net income increased from $92,500 to $414,900 while the cost of goods sold percentage increased each year and selling and administrative expenses have decreased.
2. **CONCEPTUAL CONNECTION** Explain what could cause sales to increase while the gross margin percentage decreases.

Problem 12-88B Using Common Size Statements

OBJECTIVE 3 4

ILLUSTRATING RELATIONSHIPS

Austin Logo Inc. owns and operates a small chain of sportswear stores located near colleges and universities. Austin has experienced significant growth in recent years. The following data are available for Austin:

Austin Logo Inc.
Consolidated Income Statements
(in thousands)

	Year ended December 31,		
	2013	2012	2011
Sales	$54,922	$42,893	$35,526
Cost of goods sold	32,936	25,682	21,721
Gross margin	$21,986	$17,211	$13,805
Other income, net	397	439	421
	$22,383	$17,650	$14,226
Costs and expenses:			
Selling and administrative	$17,857	$14,665	$12,754
Interest	1,356	863	622
	$19,213	$15,528	$13,376
Income before income taxes	$ 3,170	$ 2,122	$ 850
Provision for income taxes	885	746	623
Net income	$ 2,285	$ 1,376	$ 227

Austin Logo Inc.
Consolidated Balance Sheets
(in thousands)

	December 31,		
ASSETS	2013	2012	2011
Current assets:			
Cash	$ 372	$ 301	$ 245
Accounts receivable	4,798	3,546	3,369
Inventories	5,673	4,521	3,389
Total current assets	$10,843	$ 8,368	$ 7,003
Property, plant, and equipment (net)	4,912	3,541	2,937
Other assets	592	592	552
Total assets	$16,347	$12,501	$10,492

(Continued)

	December 31,		
LIABILITIES AND STOCKHOLDERS' EQUITY	**2013**	**2012**	**2011**
Current liabilities:			
Short-term notes payable	$ 4,314	$ 1,731	$ 463
Accounts payable	1,256	987	783
Total current liabilities	$ 5,570	$ 2,718	$ 1,246
Long-term debt	3,241	3,234	3,266
Total liabilities	$ 8,811	$ 5,952	$ 4,512
Common stock & additional paid-in capital	$ 4,367	$ 4,598	$ 4,725
Retained earnings	3,169	1,951	1,255
Total stockholders' equity	$ 7,536	$ 6,549	$ 5,980
Total liabilities and stockholders' equity	$16,347	$12,501	$10,492

Required:

1. Calculate how much Austin's sales, net income, and assets have grown during these 3 years.
2. Explain how Austin has financed the increase in assets.
3. **CONCEPTUAL CONNECTION** Discuss whether Austin's liquidity is adequate.
4. **CONCEPTUAL CONNECTION** Explain why interest expense is growing.
5. If Austin's sales grow by 25% in 2014, what would you expect net income to be?
6. If Austin's assets must grow by 25% to support the 25% sales increase and if 50% of net income is paid in dividends, how much capital must Austin raise in 2014?

OBJECTIVE 3 4

Problem 12-89B Preparing Common Size Statements

The financial statements for Richardson Socks Company follow.

Richardson Socks Company
Consolidated Income Statements
(in thousands except per share data)

	Year ended December 31,		
	2013	**2012**	**2011**
Revenues	$4,102,721	$3,652,412	$3,178,569
Costs and expenses:			
Cost of goods sold	$2,256,236	$2,234,985	$1,952,123
Selling and administrative	927,412	653,986	598,236
Interest	23,974	32,596	31,853
Other expenses (income)	1,925	2,254	(102)
Total costs and expenses	$3,209,547	$2,923,821	$2,582,110
Income before income taxes	$ 893,174	$ 728,591	$ 596,459
Income taxes	247,692	183,456	163,524
Net income	$ 645,482	$ 545,135	$ 432,935

Richardson Socks Company
Consolidated Balance Sheets
(in thousands)

	December 31,	
ASSETS	**2013**	**2012**
Current assets:		
Cash and equivalents	$ 301,695	$ 269,648
Accounts receivable, less allowance for doubtful accounts of $20,568 and $18,322	670,469	604,236
Inventories	601,396	469,582

(Continued)

	December 31,	
	2013	2012
Deferred income taxes	23,415	24,397
Prepaid expenses	43,624	36,478
Total current assets	$1,640,599	$1,404,341
Property, plant, and equipment	$ 583,152	$ 501,239
Less accumulated depreciation	(206,452)	(148,231)
Net property, plant, and equipment	$ 376,700	$ 353,008
Goodwill	162,325	127,695
Other assets	29,158	23,598
Total assets	$2,208,782	$1,908,642
LIABILITIES AND STOCKHOLDERS' EQUITY		
Current liabilities:		
Current portion of long-term debt	$ 63,169	$ 5,665
Notes payable	112,596	110,423
Accounts payable	128,696	139,364
Accrued liabilities	143,874	133,569
Income taxes payable	23,541	38,972
Total current liabilities	$ 471,876	$ 427,993
Long-term debt	16,254	83,456
Noncurrent deferred income taxes	33,489	31,238
Other noncurrent liabilities	46,685	27,434
Commitments and contingencies	0	0
Redeemable preferred stock	200	200
Total liabilities	$ 568,504	$ 570,321
Stockholders' equity:		
Common stock at stated value:		
Class A convertible—27,723 and 25,832 shares outstanding	$ 164	$ 175
Class B—49,756 and 47,652 shares outstanding	3,152	3,120
Capital in excess of stated value	110,596	96,546
Treasury stock (common at cost)	(8,741)	(7,859)
Retained earnings	1,535,107	1,246,339
Total stockholders' equity	$1,640,278	$1,338,321
Total liabilities and stockholders' equity	$2,208,782	$1,908,642

Required:

1. Prepare common size income statements to be used for horizontal analysis for Richardson for 2011 and 2013 (in percentage terms, rounded to two decimal places). Utilize 2011 as the base year for both 2012 and 2013. You do not need to include the actual dollar amounts shown above.
2. Indicate why Richardson's net income increased between 2011 and 2013.
3. Prepare common size balance sheets to be used for vertical analysis for 2013 and 2012 (in percentage terms, rounded to two decimal places). You do not need to include the actual dollar amounts shown above.
4. Determine whether the proportion of dollars invested in the various categories of assets has changed significantly between 2012 and 2013.
5. Determine whether the proportion of capital raised from the various liability categories and common stockholders' equity has changed significantly between 2012 and 2013.
6. **CONCEPTUAL CONNECTION** How would you describe Richardson's performance and financial position?

OBJECTIVE 5

Problem 12-90B Preparation of Ratios

Refer to the financial statements for Austin Logo Inc. in **Problem 12-88B**.

Required:

1. **CONCEPTUAL CONNECTION** Compute the asset efficiency ratios for Austin for 2013 and 2012 (in percentage terms, rounded to two decimal places) and determine whether its asset efficiency has changed.
2. **CONCEPTUAL CONNECTION** Compute the profitability ratios (rounded to two decimal places) for Austin for 2013 and 2012. Determine by how much Austin's profitability ratios have changed (in percentage terms, rounded to two decimal places) during the 2-year period.
3. **CONCEPTUAL CONNECTION** Compute the debt management ratios for 2012 and 2013. Discuss whether creditors are as secure in 2013 as they were in 2012.

OBJECTIVE 5

Problem 12-91B Comparing Financial Ratios

Presented below are selected ratios for four firms. Tweeter is a distiller, Clinton is a jewelry retailer, Smith is an airline, and Orlando is a hotel chain.

	Tweeter	Clinton	Smith	Orlando
Short-term liquidity ratio				
Current ratio	1.5	3.5	0.9	1.4
Debt management ratio				
Long-term debt to equity	0.24	0.20	562.11	209.48
Asset efficiency ratios				
Accounts receivable turnover	7.66	17.07	19.72	11.09
Inventory turnover	2.30	0.95	31.43	7.24
Profitability ratios				
Operating income	17.7%	15.5%	4.2%	9.2%
Net income	13.1	9.6	2.2	5.4
Return on assets	11.9	8.6	1.8	7.9
Return on equity	23.7	14.9	49.2	34.5

Required:

1. **CONCEPTUAL CONNECTION** Explain why the long-term debt to equity ratio is so much higher for the airline and hotel chain than it is for the distiller and jewelry retailer.
2. **CONCEPTUAL CONNECTION** Explain why the turnover ratios vary so much among the four firms.
3. **CONCEPTUAL CONNECTION** Explain why the return on equity for the airline and hotel chain is higher than for the distiller and jewelry retailer when their operating income and net income percentages are considerably smaller.

OBJECTIVE 5

Problem 12-92B Preparation of Ratios

Refer to the financial statements for Richardson Socks Company in **Problem 12-89B** and the data below.

	2013	2012	2011
Average number of common shares outstanding	78,273	77,325	77,021
Accounts receivable, net	$ 670,469	$ 604,236	$ 545,556
Inventories	601,396	469,582	592,524
Total assets	2,208,782	1,908,642	1,699,432
Stockholders' equity	1,640,278	1,338,321	1,075,952
Stock repurchases	990,521	623,259	310,132
Cash flows from operating activities	495,000	380,000	265,000
Common dividends paid	61,836	49,488	37,740
Dividends per common share	0.79	0.64	0.49
Market price per share:			
High	92.17	79.13	56.22
Low	56.59	37.23	27.10
Close	88.47	73.83	44.26

Industry Averages	Year ended December 31, 2013	2012
Return on equity	32.71%	27.86%
Profit margin	0.06	0.05
Asset turnover	2.31	2.51
Leverage	2.36	2.22

Required:

1. Prepare all the financial ratios for Richardson for 2013 and 2012 (using percentage terms where appropriate and rounding all answers to two decimal places).
2. **CONCEPTUAL CONNECTION** Indicate whether Richardson's short-term liquidity is adequate.
3. **CONCEPTUAL CONNECTION** Discuss whether Richardson uses its assets efficiently.
4. **CONCEPTUAL CONNECTION** Determine whether Richardson is profitable.
5. **CONCEPTUAL CONNECTION** Discuss whether long-term creditors should regard Richardson as a high-risk or a low-risk firm.
6. Perform a Dupont analysis (rounding to two decimal places) for 2013 and 2012.

Problem 12-93B Accounting Alternatives and Financial Analysis

OBJECTIVE 6

Affordable Autos Inc. has asked your bank for a $100,000 loan to expand its sales facility. Affordable Autos provides you with the following data:

	2013	2012	2011
Sales revenue	$6,900,000	$6,400,000	$6,100,000
Net income	120,000	113,000	109,000
Ending inventory (FIFO)*	675,000	620,000	510,000
Purchases	5,410,000	5,200,000	4,990,000
Depreciable assets	1,320,000	1,230,000	1,120,000

* The 2010 ending inventory was $420,000 (FIFO).

Your inspection of the financial statements of other automobiles sales firms indicates that most of these firms adopted the LIFO method in the late 1970s. You further note that Affordable Autos has used 10% of depreciable asset cost when computing depreciation expense and that other automobile dealers use 20%. Assume that Affordable Autos's effective tax rate is 30% of income before tax. Also assume the following:

	2013	2012	2011
Ending inventory (LIFO)*	$518,000	$512,000	$500,000

* The 2010 ending inventory was $420,000 (LIFO).

Required:

1. Compute cost of goods sold for 2011–2013, using both the FIFO and the LIFO methods.
2. Compute depreciation expense for Affordable Autos for 2011–2013, using both 10% and 20% of the cost of depreciable assets.
3. Recompute Affordable Autos's net income for 2011–2013, using LIFO and 20% depreciation. (Don't forget the tax impact of the increases in cost of goods sold and depreciation expense.)
4. **CONCEPTUAL CONNECTION** Does Affordable Autos appear to have materially changed its financial statements by the selection of FIFO (rather than LIFO) and 10% (rather than 20%) depreciation?

CASES

Case 12-94 Ethics and Equity

Kelsey Calhoun is employed as a financial analyst at a large brokerage house. Her job is to follow companies in the computer hardware sector and issue reports that will be used by her firm's brokers in making recommendations to the brokerage house's clients. Her reports are summarized by her ratings of the company—strong buy, buy, hold, sell, or strong sell. She is in frequent contact with the top management of the companies she follows.

After a thorough investigation, she believes she should downgrade Protech from a "strong buy" to a "hold." However, when she informs Protech's CFO, the CFO threatens to call her boss. Later that week, her boss calls her to request that she reconsider her downgrade and states that her cooperation will be "greatly appreciated."

Required:

How should Kelsey respond to her boss? Are there any other steps she should consider taking?

Case 12-95 Assessing the Effects of the "Clean Air" Legislation

Congress is considering legislation that would require significant reductions over a several-year period in the quantity of emissions that electric utilities will be allowed to discharge into the air. Electric utilities that generate their electricity by burning inexpensive, but relatively high-sulfur, coal will be most affected by this legislation. Some utilities plan to comply with this legislation by burning coal with a lower sulfur content. Other utilities plan to comply with this legislation by installing devices on power plant smokestacks that would filter emissions before it is discharged into the air.

Required:

1. In what places on the financial statements of coal-dependent electric utilities do you expect to observe the effects of this legislation?
2. In what places on the financial statements of companies that mine coal do you expect to observe the effects of this legislation?

Case 12-96 Changes in the Price of Fuel for Aircraft

The cost of fuel is reported to be about 20% of the total operating cost for a major airline. Events in the Middle East caused jet fuel costs to nearly double from 2008 to 2011.

Required:

1. If you were the CEO of a major airline, how would you suggest that the airline respond to the fuel price increase?
2. How would you expect the financial statements of major airlines to be affected by the fuel price increase and the actions that the airlines would take in response?

Case 12-97 Analyzing Growth

Consolidated financial statements for Initech Corporation follow.

Initech Corporation
Consolidated Income Statements
(in millions except per share amounts)

	Three years ended December 31,		
	2013	2012	2011
Net revenues	$8,782	$5,844	$4,779
Cost of goods sold	$3,252	$2,557	$2,316
Research and development	970	780	618
Marketing, general, and administrative expenses	1,168	1,017	765
Operating costs and expenses	$5,390	$4,354	$3,699

	Three years ended December 31,		
	2013	2012	2011
Operating income	$3,392	$1,490	$1,080
Interest expense	(50)	(54)	(82)
Interest income and other, net	188	133	197
Income before taxes	$3,530	$1,569	$1,195
Provision for taxes	1,235	502	376
Net income	$2,295	$1,067	$ 819

Initech Corporation
Consolidated Balance Sheets
(in millions except per share amounts)

	December 31,	
ASSETS	**2013**	**2012**
Current assets:		
Cash and cash equivalents	$ 1,659	$ 1,843
Short-term investments	1,477	993
Accounts and notes receivable, net of allowance for doubtful accounts of $22 ($26 in 2012)	1,448	1,069
Inventories	838	535
Deferred tax assets	310	205
Other current assets	70	46
Total current assets	$ 5,802	$ 4,691
Property, plant, and equipment:		
Land and buildings	$ 1,848	$ 1,463
Machinery and equipment	4,148	2,874
Construction in progress	317	311
	$ 6,313	$ 4,648
Less accumulated depreciation	(2,317)	(1,832)
Property, plant, and equipment, net	$ 3,996	$ 2,816
Long-term investments	1,416	496
Other assets	130	86
Total assets	$11,344	$ 8,089
LIABILITIES AND STOCKHOLDERS' EQUITY		
Current liabilities:		
Short-term debt	$ 399	$ 202
Long-term debt redeemable within 1 year	98	110
Accounts payable	427	281
Deferred income on shipments to distributors	200	149
Accrued compensation and benefits	544	435
Other accrued liabilities	374	306
Income taxes payable	391	359
Total current liabilities	$ 2,433	$ 1,842
Long-term debt	426	249
Deferred tax liabilities	297	180
Other long-term liabilities	688	373
Total liabilities	$ 3,844	$ 2,644
Stockholders' equity:		
Preferred stock, $0.001 par value, 50 shares authorized; none issued	$ 0	$ 0
Common stock, $0.001 par value, 1,400 shares authorized, issued, and outstanding in 2013 and 2012	1	1
Additional paid-in capital—common stock	2,193	1,775
Retained earnings	5,306	3,669
Total stockholders' equity	$ 7,500	$ 5,445
Total liabilities and stockholders' equity	$11,344	$ 8,089

(Continued)

Required:

1. Prepare common size income statements to be used for both vertical and horizontal analysis for 2011–2013 (in percentage terms, rounded to two decimal places). You do not need to include the actual dollar amounts shown above.
2. Using the common size income statements for both vertical and horizontal analysis prepared in Requirement 1, indicate why Initech's profits increased more rapidly than sales for 2012 and 2013.
3. Prepare common size balance sheets for vertical analysis for 2012 and 2013 (in percentage terms, rounded to two decimal places). You do not need to include the actual dollar amounts shown above.
4. Did the proportion of assets invested in the various classes of assets change significantly from 2012 to 2013?
5. How has Initech financed its growth in assets?
6. Did the income statement change as much between 2012 and 2013 as the balance sheet?

Case 12-98 Identifying the Causes of Profitability Changes

The consolidated financial statements for Dowsett Shipping Corporation and Subsidiaries follow.

Dowsett Shipping Corporation and Subsidiaries
Consolidated Income Statements
(in thousands, except per share amounts)

	Fiscal year ended May 31,		
	2013	2012	2011
Revenues	$7,808,043	$7,550,060	$7,688,296
Operating expenses:			
Salaries and employee benefits	$3,807,493	$3,637,080	$3,438,391
Rentals and landing fees	658,138	672,341	650,001
Depreciation and amortization	579,896	577,157	562,207
Fuel	495,384	508,386	663,327
Maintenance and repairs	404,639	404,311	449,394
Restructuring charges	(12,500)	254,000	121,000
Other	1,497,820	1,473,818	1,551,850
	$7,430,870	$7,527,093	$7,436,170
Operating income	$ 377,173	$ 22,967	$ 252,126
Other income (expenses):			
Interest, net	$(160,923)	$(164,315)	$(181,880)
Gain on disposition of aircraft and related equipment	4,633	2,832	11,375
Other, net	(17,307)	(8,312)	(8,679)
Payroll tax loss	0	0	(32,000)
Other income (expenses), net	$(173,597)	$(169,795)	$(211,184)
Income (loss) before income taxes and extraordinary loss	$ 203,576	$(146,828)	$ 40,942
Provision (credit) for income taxes	93,767	(33,046)	35,044
Income (loss) before extraordinary loss	$ 109,809	$(113,782)	$ 5,898
Extraordinary loss, net of tax benefit of $34,287	(55,943)	0	0
Net income (loss)	$ 53,866	$(113,782)	$ 5,898

Dowsett Shipping Corporation and Subsidiaries
Consolidated Balance Sheets
(in thousands)

	May 31, 2013	May 31, 2012
ASSETS		
Current assets:		
Cash and cash equivalents	$ 155,456	$ 78,177
Receivable, less allowance for doubtful accounts of $31,308 and $32,074	922,727	899,773
Spare parts, supplies and fuel	164,087	158,062
Prepaid expenses and other	63,573	69,994
Deferred income taxes	133,875	0
Total current assets	$ 1,439,718	$ 1,206,006
Property and equipment, at cost		
Flight equipment	$ 2,843,253	$ 2,540,350
Package handling and ground support equipment	1,413,793	1,352,659
Computer and electronic equipment	947,913	851,686
Other	1,501,250	1,433,212
	$ 6,706,209	$ 6,177,907
Less accumulated depreciation and amortization	(3,229,941)	(2,766,610)
Net property and equipment	$ 3,476,268	$ 3,411,297
Other assets:		
Goodwill	$ 432,215	$ 487,780
Equipment deposits and other assets	444,863	358,103
Total other assets	$ 877,078	$ 845,883
Total assets	$ 5,793,064	$ 5,463,186
LIABILITIES AND STOCKHOLDERS' EQUITY		
Current liabilities:		
Current portion of long-term debt	$ 133,797	$ 155,257
Accounts payable	554,111	430,130
Accrued expenses	761,357	799,468
Total current liabilities	$ 1,449,265	$ 1,384,855
Long-term debt, less current portion	1,882,279	1,797,844
Deferred income taxes	72,479	123,715
Other liabilities	717,660	577,050
Total liabilities	$ 4,121,683	$ 3,883,464
Common stockholders' equity:		
Common stock, $0.10 par value, 100,000 shares authorized, 54,743 and 54,100 shares issued	$ 5,474	$ 5,410
Additional paid-in capital—common stock	699,385	672,727
Retained earnings	969,515	906,555
	$ 1,674,374	$ 1,584,692
Less treasury stock and deferred compensation related to stock plans	(2,993)	(4,970)
Total common stockholders' equity	$ 1,671,381	$ 1,579,722
Total liabilities and stockholders' equity	$ 5,793,064	$ 5,463,186

Required:

1. Evaluate Dowsett's performance in 2013.
2. What were the primary factors responsible for Dowsett's loss in 2012 and return to profitability in 2013?
3. How did Dowsett finance the $329,878,000 increase in assets in 2013?

Case 12-99 CONTINUING PROBLEM: FRONT ROW ENTERTAINMENT

The income statement and consolidated balance sheets for Front Row Entertainment follow.

Front Row Entertainment Inc.
Consolidated Balance Sheets

	December 31	
ASSETS	**2014**	**2013**
Current assets:		
Cash	$ 30,322	$ 9,005
Accounts receivable, net	98,250	17,000
Prepaid expenses	133,400	57,200
Supplies	2,200	3,700
Inventory	61,380	2,850
Total current assets	$ 325,552	$89,755
Property, plant, and equipment:		
Building	1,857,250	0
Equipment	27,350	7,000
Accumulated depreciation	(53,835)	(2,160)
Trademark	25,000	0
Total assets	$2,181,317	$94,595
LIABILITIES AND EQUITY		
Current liabilities:		
Accounts payable	$ 2,450	$12,240
Salaries payable	2,500	3,690
Interest payable	40,917	2,250
Unearned sales revenue	1,780	28,650
Income taxes payable	550	2,180
Notes payable (short-term)	8,000	0
Total current liabilities	$ 56,197	$49,010
Long-term liabilities:		
Notes payable	$ 405,000	$25,000
Bonds payable, net	1,500,000	0
Less: Discount on bond payable	(109,530)	
Total long-term liabilities	$1,795,470	$25,000
Equity:		
Preferred stock	$ 150,000	$ 0
Common stock	18,000	16,000
Additional paid-in capital:		
Preferred stock	75,000	0
Common stock	38,000	0
Treasury stock	1,800	0
Retained earnings	53,250	4,585
Less: Treasury stock	(6,400)	0
Total stockholders' equity	$ 329,650	$20,585
Total liabilities and equity	$2,181,317	$94,595

Front Row Entertainment Inc. Income Statement For the year ended December 31, 2014	
Revenues:	
Sales revenue	$3,142,800
Service revenue	636,000
Total revenues	$3,778,800
Expenses:	
Artist Fee Expense	$2,134,260
Rent expense	952,663
Cost of goods sold	74,800
Salaries and wages expense	345,100
Depreciation expense	51,675
Interest expense	98,087
Income taxes expense	22,000
Other expenses	26,550
Total expenses	$3,705,135
Net income	$ 73,665

Additional information:

- The market price of the common shares at the end of the year is $17.55 per share.
- The average number of common shares outstanding for 2014 is 16,400.
- The dividends per common share for 2014 were $25,000, which is approximately $1.45 per share ($25,000/17,300 common shares). The 17,300 shares can be calculated from information in Chapter 10 (16,000 shares at Jan. 1, 2014 + 2,000 shares issued on June 15, 2014 – 700 shares repurchased on July 10, 2014).
- Common stock repurchases for 2014 were $11,200. This is taken from Chapter 10 as 700 common shares were repurchased as treasury stock at a cost of $16 per share.
- Cash flows used in operating activities for 2014 were $(77,783).
- Preferred dividends for 2014 were $0.

Note: Round all answers to two decimal places.

Required:

1. Calculate the short-term liquidity ratios for Front Row for 2014.
2. Calculate the debt management ratios for Front Row for 2014.
3. Calculate the asset efficiency ratios for Front Row for 2014.
4. Calculate the profitability ratios for Front Row for 2014.*
5. Calculate the stockholder ratios for Front Row for 2014.

*In computing gross margin, include only the expenses of Cost of Goods Sold and Artist Fee Expense.

1 Appendix

International Financial Reporting Standards

© Pixelfabrik/Alamy

After studying Appendix 1, you should be able to:

1. Understand and describe some of the important aspects of international financial reporting standards.
2. Understand key differences between IFRS and U.S. GAAP.

CAN BALCIOGLU/Shutterstock.com

INTERNATIONAL FINANCIAL REPORTING

OBJECTIVE 1

Understand and describe some of the important aspects of international financial reporting standards.

Business is becoming an increasingly global activity as companies conduct operations across national boundaries. Not only are more and more companies engaging in international transactions, they are also seeking capital from foreign stock exchanges. Due to a variety of factors (such as differences in culture, legal systems, and business environments), the historical development of accounting standards on a country-by-country basis has led to considerable diversity in financial accounting practices. To facilitate the conduct of business in an international environment, there has been heightened interest in the development of international accounting standards. This appendix will address some of the more frequently asked questions with regard to **international financial reporting standards (IFRS)**.

What Are IFRS?

IFRS have both a narrow and a broad meaning. Narrowly, IFRS refer to the accounting standards issued by the International Accounting Standards Board after 2001. More broadly, IFRS describe the entire international set of generally accepted accounting standards. IFRS encompass:

- international accounting standards (IAS) issued prior to 2001
- international financial reporting standards (IFRS) issued after 2001
- interpretations of these standards

IFRS are generally considered less detailed and more concept-based than U.S. GAAP. Over the last several years, IFRS have assumed the role as the common language of financial reporting in much of the world.

Who Develops IFRS?

The following bodies play an instrumental role in the development of IFRS.

International Accounting Standards Board (IASB) IFRS are developed by the **International Accounting Standards Board (IASB)**, which is headquartered in London. The IASB is an independent, privately funded accounting standard-setting body that consists of 16 members from nine countries (at the time of this writing, the IASB has only 15 members). To ensure geographical diversity, members of the IASB normally include four members from the Asia/Oceania region, four members from Europe, four members from North America, one each from Africa and South America, and two members from any area. The goal of the IASB is to develop a single set of high-quality accounting standards that result in transparent and comparable information reported in general purpose financial statements. The general structure of the IASB is shown in Exhibit A1.1.

Monitoring Board The Monitoring Board's purpose is to enhance public accountability of the IFRS Foundation through oversight of the IFRS Foundation Trustees. Its main responsibilities are to participate in the trustee nomination process, approve appointments to the trustees, and ensure that the trustees continue to discharge their duties according to their mandate.

International Financial Reporting Standards (IFRS) Foundation The IASB is overseen by the International Financial Reporting Standards Foundation. The IFRS Foundation funds, appoints the members of, and oversees the IASB. The IFRS Foundation is composed of 22 trustees who possess a wide degree of professional experience—including auditors, preparers, users, academics, and others.

IFRS Interpretations Committee The IFRS Interpretations Committee interprets the application of and provides guidance on financial reporting issues not specifically addressed in IFRS. Any interpretations must be reported to the IASB for approval.

IFRS Advisory Council The IFRS Advisory Council advises the IASB and the IFRS Foundation on a number of issues, such as items that should be on the IASB agenda, input on the timetable of the various IASB projects, and advice on various aspects of these projects.

EXHIBIT A1.1

Structure of the IASB

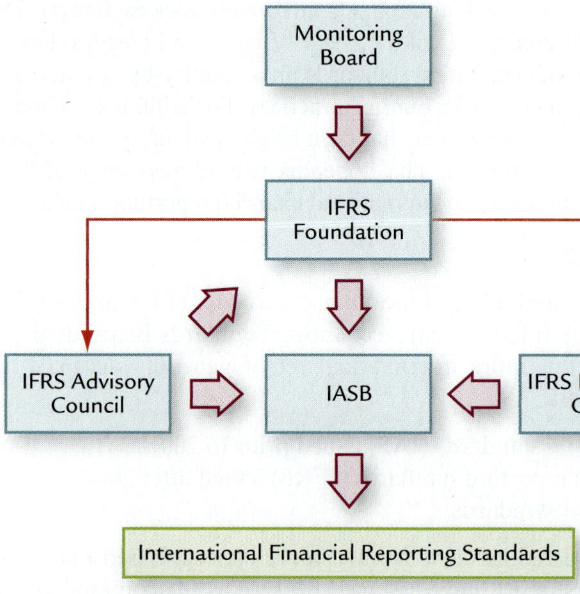

Source: Based on information found at www.iasplus.com.

How Long Has the IASB Been Issuing Standards?

International standard setting began in 1973 with the formation of the International Accounting Standards Committee (IASC). Between 1973 and 1988, the IASC completed a set of core standards, which began to gain global acceptance. In all, the IASC issued 41 International Accounting Standards (IAS).

In 2001, the IASB was established as the successor organization of the IASC and assumed the standard-setting responsibilities from the IASC. The IASB endorsed the standards of the IASC and began issuing its own standards, which are called International Financial Reporting Standards (IFRS). At this point, with support from the Securities and Exchange Commission (SEC), the Financial Accounting Standards Board (FASB), the European Union (EU), and others, the movement to a single set of high-quality international accounting standards began to pick up considerable momentum. Therefore, IFRS represent a relatively young body of accounting literature. Exhibit A1.2 outlines key dates in the development of IFRS.

EXHIBIT A1.2

Key Dates in the Development of IFRS

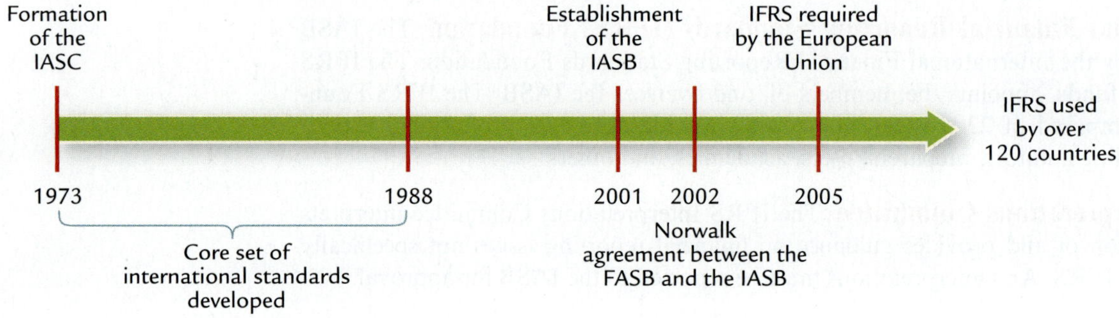

Source: Based on information found at www.iasplus.com.

What Organizations Have Played a Role in the Development of IFRS?

In 2002, the FASB and the IASB reached an agreement, known as the Norwalk Agreement, in which both standard setters formalized their commitment to develop "as quickly as practicable" a common set of accounting standards. This process, commonly referred to as **convergence** or **harmonization** of U.S. GAAP and IFRS, involves removing existing differences between the two sets of accounting standards and working together on future accounting standards. The FASB and the IASB are currently involved in several joint standard setting projects aimed at reducing the differences between U.S. GAAP and IFRS.

The Securities and Exchange Commission (SEC) has long supported (as early as 1988) the development of an internationally acceptable set of accounting standards, and it publicly supported the Norwalk Agreement. Current statements by the SEC have reiterated its support for a single set of high-quality globally accepted accounting standards and encouraged continued convergence of U.S. GAAP and IFRS. The SEC plans to make a determination in 2012 regarding the use of IFRS for publicly traded U.S. companies.

The EU has been instrumental to the global acceptance of IFRS. In a pivotal event for the use of IFRS, the EU, in 2002, required its member countries to use IFRS by 2005. With the EU adoption of IFRS, the number of countries using IFRS more than doubled between 2003 and 2006.

Who Uses IFRS?

IFRS are quickly gaining global acceptance and are currently used by over 120 countries, including over 30 member-states of the European Union, Australia, and Israel. Exhibit A1.3 highlights the use of IFRS around the world. Countries such as Canada, India, Mexico, Japan, and Taiwan are expected to transition to IFRS in the near future.

EXHIBIT A1.3

IFRS Around the World

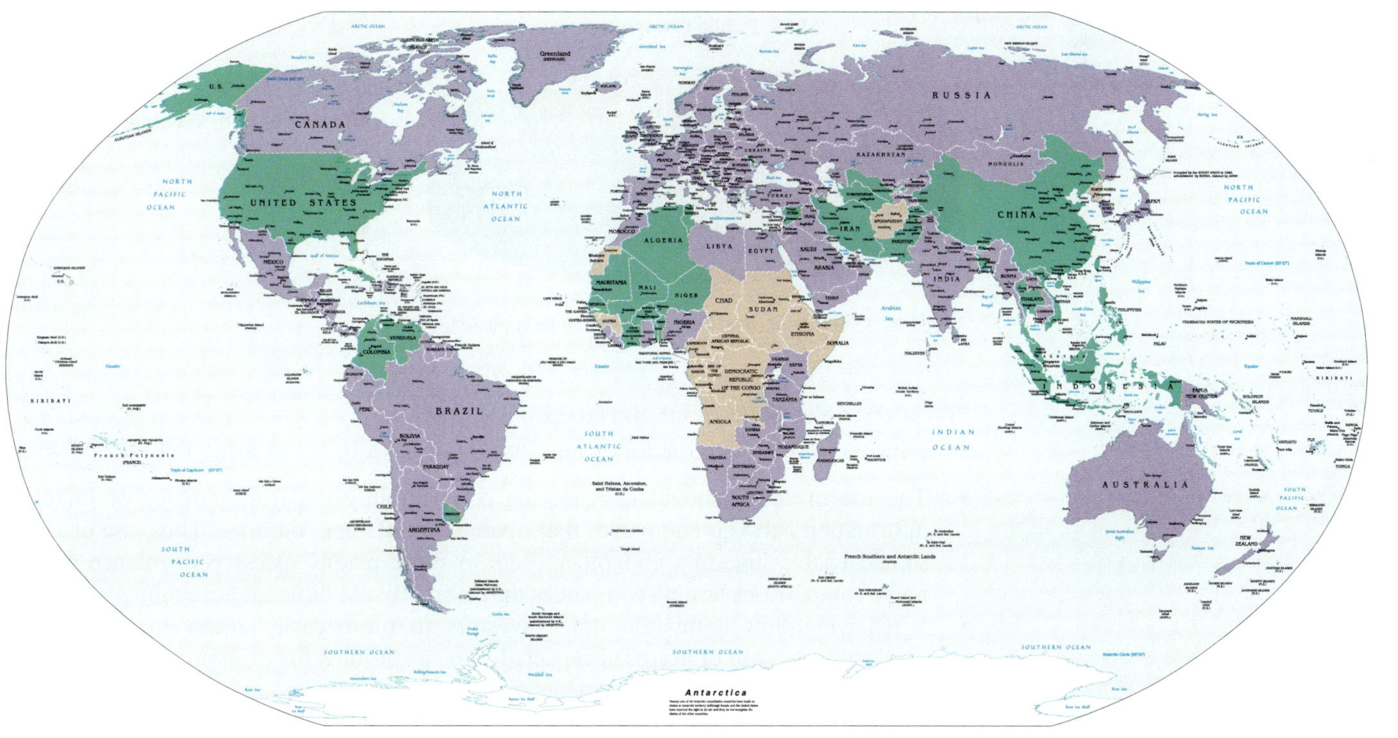

IFRS Required or Permitted IFRS Not Permitted Information Not Yet Available

Source: Based on information found at http://www.iasplus.com/country/useias.htm.

When Are IFRS Expected to Be Used in the United States?

With the majority of companies throughout the world following IFRS, there is considerable pressure for the United States to adopt IFRS. The United States currently allows foreign companies who trade on U.S. stock exchanges to use IFRS without reconciliation to U.S. GAAP. While the SEC had originally envisioned 2015 as the earliest possible date for the mandatory adoption of IFRS by U.S. companies, a 2012 SEC staff paper on incorporating IFRS into U.S. financial reporting is widely viewed as advocating a "go-slow" approach. In considering the adoption of IFRS, the SEC has identified several key issues that will be considered in transitioning to IFRS, including:

- determining whether IFRS are sufficiently developed and applied consistently enough to be used in the United States
- understanding the impact of IFRS adoption on companies
- evaluating whether the financial statement preparers and auditors are sufficiently prepared to convert to IFRS
- determining if investors have adequate preparation and understanding of IFRS and how they differ from U.S. GAAP

Exhibit A1.4 reveals the results of a recent survey conducted by the American Institute of CPAs (AICPA) regarding the public attitude to IFRS adoption. The majority of respondents (52%) thought that IFRS should be required. However, the vast majority of these companies (34%) desire further convergence of IFRS and U.S. GAAP prior to this requirement. Further, another 26% of companies feel that, while IFRS should not be required, companies should be given the option to use IFRS. While the exact timing of IFRS adoption in the United States is unknown, all indicators point to the fact that the use of IFRS in the United States is not a matter of "if" it will occur but "when" it will occur.

EXHIBIT A1.4

Should the SEC Require IFRS Adoption?

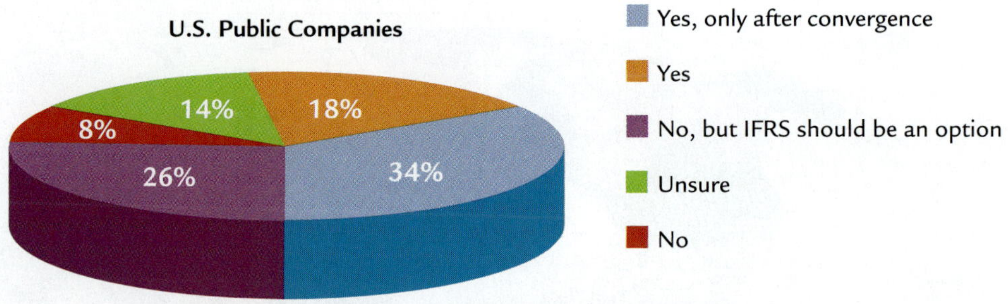

Source: Based on AICPA's IFRS Readiness Tracking Survey (Fall 2011).

What Are the Advantages of IFRS?

Proponents of IFRS cite the following four major advantages of using IFRS:

- The use of IFRS should increase the comparability and transparency of financial information between companies that operate in different countries. Thus, use of IFRS should enable investors and other users to more readily assess performance and to make comparisons among companies that currently use different accounting standards.
- IFRS will allow companies and investors to more easily access foreign capital markets. This ease of access is expected to be a stimulus for economic growth.
- IFRS should allow for a more efficient use of company resources as companies streamline their financial reporting processes. Thus, there is an opportunity for companies to lower costs by standardizing and centralizing the financial reporting function.

- IFRS generally require more judgments than the strict application of rules. The use of judgment is seen as a means of preventing the financial abuses that have occurred under U.S. GAAP.

Overall, the reduction in complexities from the use of a single set of high-quality standards is expected to have major benefits for investors, companies, and the capital markets in general.

Are There Potential Problems with Adopting IFRS?

The movement toward IFRS presents many challenges as well as opportunities, including:

- IFRS, which are relatively young, may be viewed by some as a lower quality set of standards compared to U.S. GAAP, which has stood the test of time.
- There are inherent difficulties involved with integrating worldwide cultural differences to ensure that IFRS are applied and interpreted consistently.
- IFRS generally require more judgment and less reliance on rules than U.S. GAAP. While this exercise of judgment can be a positive aspect of IFRS, many see the potential abuses of judgment as a key problem with IFRS.
- Not all countries will use the same version of IFRS. Many countries that currently use IFRS have selectively modified (or carved out) certain standards with which they do not agree. Such modification will reduce comparability and increase complexity in financial reporting.
- Companies will incur significant transition costs in creating new accounting policies, modifying their accounting systems, and training their employees with regard to IFRS.

Exhibit A1.5 lists the major challenges that companies foresee in implementing IFRS.

What Do Financial Statements Look Like Under IFRS?

While the details of preparing financial statements under IFRS is a topic more appropriately covered in intermediate accounting courses, it is helpful to identify a few of the major differences between financial statements prepared under U.S. GAAP and those prepared under IFRS. As an example of financial statements prepared according to IFRS, Exhibit A1.6 (pp. 734–735) shows the income statement and balance sheet of

EXHIBIT A1.5

IFRS Implementation Challenges

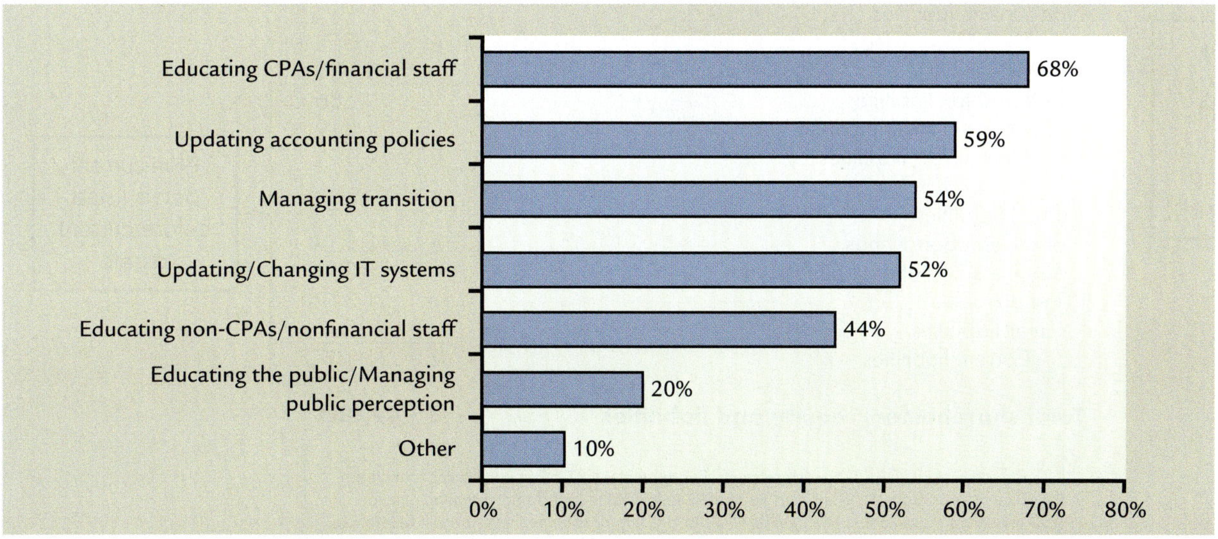

Source: Based on AICPA's IFRS Readiness Tracking Survey (Fall 2011).

EXHIBIT A1.6

Financial Statements Prepared Under IFRS

Carrefour S.A.
Consolidated Statement of Financial Position
December 31, 2011

Assets		
Non-current assets		
Goodwill	€	8,740
Other intangible assets		966
Tangible fixed assets		13,771
Investment property		507
Investments—equity method		280
Other non-current financial assets		1,432
Consumer credit from financial services companies		2,236
Deferred tax on assets		745
Non-current assets	€	28,677
Current assets		
Inventories	€	6,848
Commerical receivables		2,782
Consumer credit from financial companies—short-term		3,384
Other current financial assets		911
Tax receivables		468
Other assets		1,012
Cash and cash equivalents		3,849
Current assets	€	19,254
Total assets	**€**	**47,931**
Shareholders' Equity		
Share capital	€	1,698
Consolidated reserves (including income)		4,919
Minority interests		1,009
Shareholders' equity	€	7,626
Liabilities		
Non-current liabilities		
Long-term borrowings	€	9,513
Provisions		3,680
Deferred tax liabilities		586
Other non-current liabilities		419
Non-current liabilities	€	14,198
Current liabilities		
Short-term borrowings	€	2,159
Suppliers and other creditors		15,362
Tax payables		1,319
Other liabilities		7,267
Current liabilities	€	26,107
Total shareholders' equity and liabilities	**€**	**47,931**

*IFRS differ from U.S. GAAP in many respects. For example, IFRS allow companies to increase the value of their property, plant, and equipment to fair value and do not permit the use of LIFO for valuing inventories. See Exhibit A1.7 for a listing of some of these specific differences.

Source: Carrefour, S.A. 2011 10K

Preferred title for the balance sheet

Classifications are often listed in reverse liquidity order

Specific measurement differences exist for certain accounts*

Note terminology differences for common stock and retained earnings

Equities are listed before liabilities

Provisions refers to contingent and other liabilities (e.g., retirement costs)

Non-current assets listed before current assets

(Continued)

Carrefour S.A.
Consolidated Income Statement
For the Year Ended December 31, 2011

S.A. is a common way to refer to a corporation in many countries

The currency used will differ between countries

(in millions of euros)		
Net sales (net of loyalty program costs)	€	80,455
Other revenue		2,309
Total revenue	€	82,764
Cost of sales		(64,912)
Gross margin from recurring operations	€	17,852
Sales, general, and administrative expenses		(13,969)
Depreciation, amortization, and provisions		(1,701)
Recurring operating income	€	2,182
Non-recurring income and expenses, net		(2,663)
Operating (loss)/income	€	(481)
Financial income (expense)		(757)
(Loss)/income before taxes	€	(1,238)
Income tax expense		(1,002)
Net income from companies accounted for by the equity method		64
Net (loss)/income from continuing operations	€	(2,176)
Net income from discontinued operations		2,580
Net income for the year	€	404

Expenses may be classified by their nature or function**

Diversity is allowed with regard to definitions and captions of subtotals

The term "Financial income (expense)" refers to "Interest income (expense)"

**Classification by nature results in classifications reflecting the economic benefit received for an expense—e.g., salaries expense, depreciation expense. Classification by function identifies the purpose of the expense—e.g., cost of goods sold, selling expense, administrative expense. If a functional classification is used, IFRS require disclosure by nature in the notes to the financial statements.

Source: Carrefour, S.A. 2011 10K

Carrefour S.A., a French retailer that operates in Europe, South America, North Africa, and parts of Asia.[1] Carrefour is the second largest retailer in the world in terms of revenue, trailing only **Wal-Mart**.

[1] The differences between the retained earnings statement and the statement of cash flows under U.S. GAAP and IFRS are relatively minor, so we will focus on the balance sheet and income statement here.

OBJECTIVE 2

Understand key differences between IFRS and U.S. GAAP.

KEY DIFFERENCES BETWEEN IFRS AND U.S. GAAP

While IFRS are expected to have far-reaching impacts on financial accounting, there are more similarities than differences between IFRS and U.S. GAAP.

How Will IFRS Impact My Study of Accounting?

To aid in understanding the impact of IFRS on the cornerstones of financial accounting, review Exhibit A1.7. As you can see, the Cornerstones of accounting covered in this text will still provide you with a solid foundation for your study of accounting.

EXHIBIT A1.7

Effect of IFRS on Cornerstones of Financial Accounting (as of July 2012)

Chapter	Cornerstones Affected	Comments
1	Cornerstone 1.1: Using the Fundamental Accounting Equation	• The fundamental accounting equation is the same under IFRS as under U.S. GAAP.
	Cornerstone 1.2: Preparing a Classified Balance Sheet	• The elements of the balance sheet are the same as under U.S. GAAP; however, IFRS do not specify a particular format. Therefore, the balance sheet classifications are often listed in the reverse order as compared to U.S. GAAP. For example, IFRS classify assets as either noncurrent or current. Noncurrent assets are typically presented first, followed by current assets. Additionally, stockholders' equity is often presented, followed by noncurrent liabilities, and then current liabilities.
	Cornerstone 1.3: Preparing an Income Statement	• IFRS do not prescribe a specific format for the income statement (e.g., single-step or multiple-step). In addition, IFRS allow income statement items to be classified either by their nature or their function. U.S. GAAP classifies income statement items by their function (e.g., cost of goods sold).
	Cornerstone 1.4: Preparing a Retained Earnings Statement	• IFRS do not specify the retained earnings statement as a required financial statement. Instead, IFRS require the change in retained earnings be shown on the statement of changes in equity. • IFRS require the presentation of a statement of cash flows whose format is similar to the one prescribed by U.S. GAAP. However, some items (as described on page 40 for Chapter 11) may be classified differently. • Terminology differences exist. For example, on the balance sheet, stockholders' equity may be called "capital and reserves," and retained earnings may be called "accumulated profits and losses." On the income statement, sales may be referred to as "turnover" or interest expense may be referred to as "finance costs."
2	No Cornerstones Affected	• The IASB and the FASB are currently working on a joint conceptual framework. The first phase of this framework that describes the objective of financial accounting and the qualitative characteristics of accounting information has been completed and is discussed in Chapter 2. • In general, IFRS are considered more "principles-based" than U.S. GAAP. • IFRS and U.S. GAAP use the identical double-entry accounting system. • Under IFRS, transactions are analyzed, journalized, and posted in the same manner as under U.S. GAAP.
3	No Cornerstones Affected	• The adjustment process under IFRS is the same as the adjustment process under U.S. GAAP. • While revenue recognition concepts under IFRS are similar to U.S. GAAP, IFRS contain less detailed guidance.

(Continued)

Chapter	Cornerstones Affected	Comments
4	No Cornerstones Affected	• Internal control issues are company and financial accounting system-specific, and the issues would be similar in an international environment. However, the documentation and assessment requirements of Section 404 of the Sarbanes-Oxley Act (SOX) impose a much greater burden on U.S. companies compared to international companies. • The management, control, and accounting for cash are the same under IFRS as under U.S. GAAP.
5	No Cornerstones Affected	• The recognition of sales revenue under IFRS is generally similar to U.S. GAAP. However, the amount of guidance provided by IFRS as to when revenue should be recognized is considerably less and more principles-based than the amount of guidance provided by U.S. GAAP. • The recognition and valuation of receivables under IFRS is generally the same as U.S. GAAP.
6	Cornerstone 6.6: Applying the LIFO Inventory Costing Method Cornerstone 6.8: Valuing Inventory at Lower of Cost or Market	• The purchase and sale of inventory is generally the same under IFRS as under U.S. GAAP. • IFRS do not allow the use of LIFO for determining the cost of inventory. • IFRS require the use of the lower of cost or market method, but it defines market value as net realizable value (the estimated selling price minus costs of completion and disposal) instead of replacement cost. IFRS also permit reversal of inventory write-downs.
7	Cornerstone 7.1: Measuring and Recording the Cost of a Fixed Asset Cornerstones 7.2, 7.3, and 7.4: Depreciation Cornerstone 7.8: Accounting for Intangible Assets Cornerstone 7.10: Recording an Impairment of Property, Plant, and Equipment	• While the accounting for an asset's initial cost is similar under IFRS and U.S. GAAP, IFRS allow for companies to increase the value of their property, plant, equipment, and intangible assets up to fair value. This is not permitted under U.S. GAAP. • While similar depreciation methods are used, IFRS require depreciating each component of an asset separately (component depreciation); this is permitted, but not required, by U.S. GAAP. • Generally the accounting for intangible assets under IFRS is similar to U.S. GAAP. However, under IFRS, research costs are expensed while development costs are capitalized as an intangible asset if it is probable that future benefits will be generated. • The impairment model under IFRS is a single-step process rather than the two-step process used in U.S. GAAP. In addition, IFRS allow recovery of impairment losses, which is not allowed under U.S. GAAP.
8	No Cornerstones Affected	• While the accounting for current liabilities is generally the same under IFRS and U.S. GAAP, IFRS commonly report liabilities in reverse order relative to U.S. GAAP—from least liquid to most liquid. • IFRS refer to loss contingencies that are recognized in the financial statements as "provisions." Loss contingencies that are not recognized in the financial statements are referred to as "contingencies." • Similar to U.S. GAAP, IFRS recognize provisions when the contingent event is probable. However, IFRS define probable as "more likely than not" while U.S. GAAP defines probable as "likely." Therefore, more events will be recognized as provisions under IFRS.
9	No Cornerstones Affected	• The accounting for bonds and notes payable is generally the same under IFRS as under U.S. GAAP. • A capital lease under U.S. GAAP is referred to as a finance lease under IFRS.
10	No Cornerstones Affected	• The accounting for equity is generally the same under IFRS as under U.S. GAAP. However, some terminology differences exist. For example, under IFRS, stockholders' equity is typically called "capital and reserves." The use of the term "reserves" has generally been discouraged under U.S. GAAP.

(Continued)

Chapter	Cornerstones Affected	Comments
11	Cornerstone 11.1: Classifying Business Activities	• The classification of certain business activities differs under IFRS relative to U.S. GAAP. For example, IFRS allow companies to report the payment of dividends and interest as either an operating cash outflow or a financing cash outflow. In addition, the payment of income taxes can be reported as an investing or financing transaction if it can be identified with an investing or financing activity. Finally, interest or dividends received may be reported as either operating or investing cash inflows.
12	No Cornerstones Affected	• The analysis of financial statements is the same under IFRS as it is under U.S. GAAP.

Where Can I Go to Find Out More About IFRS?

IFRS Foundation website:
www.ifrs.org

American Institute of Certified Public Accountants (AICPA) website for IFRS Resources:
www.IFRS.com

Ernst & Young IFRS page:
www.ey.com/GL/en/Issues/IFRS

Deloitte IFRS page:
www.iasplus.com

International Association for Accounting Education & Research:
www.iaaer.org/resources

PricewaterhouseCoopers IFRS page:
www.pwc.com/gx/en/ifrs-reporting/index.jhtml

KPMG IFRS page:
www.kpmginstitutes.com/ifrs-institute/

SUMMARY OF LEARNING OBJECTIVES

LO 1. Understand and describe some of the important aspects of international financial reporting standards.

- International financial reporting standards (IFRS) are an international set of generally accepted accounting standards.
- IFRS are developed by the International Accounting Standards Board (IASB), an independent, privately funded standard-setting body consisting of 16 members from nine countries.
- International standard setting began in 1973; however, the development of a single-set of high quality international accounting standards accelerated in 2001 with the establishment of the IASB and the European Union's requirement of the use of IFRS.
- IFRS are currently used in more than 120 countries and are currently being considered in the United States.
- The reduction in complexities from the use of a single set of high-quality standards is expected to have major benefits for investors, companies and capital markets in general. However, the movement toward IFRS presents many challenges as well.
- A familiarity with financial statements prepared under IFRS is useful for financial statement users.

LO 2. Understand key differences between IFRS and U.S. GAAP.

- IFRS are expected to have far-reaching impacts on financial accounting; however, the cornerstones of accounting will provide a strong foundation for the study of accounting.
- Within each topical area of accounting, financial statement users need to be able to identify key differences between U.S. GAAP and IFRS.

KEY TERMS

Convergence (harmonization), 731
International Accounting Standards Board (IASB), 729
International financial reporting standards (IFRS), 729

MULTIPLE-CHOICE QUESTIONS

A1-1 Which of the following best describes international financial reporting standards?

a. IFRS describe the generally accepted accounting principles that are currently used by all companies in the United States.
b. IFRS consist only of standards that have been issued since the IASB was formed in 2001.
c. IFRS are considered to be more concept-based than U.S. GAAP.
d. IFRS will be required to be used in the United States beginning in 2015.

A1-2 Which of the following statements is true?

a. The FASB has consistently resisted the adoption of IFRS in the United States for fear that it will lose its standard-setting authority.
b. The requirement to use IFRS by the European Union led to a significant increase in the global acceptance of IFRS.
c. IFRS have existed for nearly as long as U.S. GAAP; however, it only recently began to gain acceptance as a body of high-quality accounting standards.
d. The SEC is considering allowing foreign companies who trade stock on the U.S. stock exchanges to use IFRS.

A1-3 Convergence of U.S. GAAP and IFRS is best described as:

a. the replacement of U.S. GAAP by IFRS.
b. the replacement of IFRS by U.S. GAAP.
c. changing existing U.S. GAAP so that any differences in IFRS will be insignificant.
d. changing both existing U.S. GAAP and IFRS to reduce differences and developing new GAAP through a joint standard-setting process.

A1-4 Which of the following organizations has the responsibility to create IFRS?

a. Financial Accounting Standards Board
b. International Financial Reporting Standards Foundation
c. International Accounting Standards Board
d. Securities and Exchange Commission

A1-5 Which of the following is *not* an advantage of IFRS?

a. The use of IFRS should increase the comparability and transparency of financial information.
b. The use of IFRS will make it easier to access foreign capital markets.
c. IFRS require more judgments than U.S. GAAP.
d. IFRS are less conservative than U.S. GAAP, so net income under IFRS will generally be higher than net income under U.S. GAAP.

A1-6 Which of the following is *not* a disadvantage of IFRS?

a. The use of IFRS will lead to an outflow of capital from the U.S. to foreign countries.
b. The use of IFRS could be viewed as adopting a lower quality standard.
c. Due to cultural differences among countries, it will be difficult to ensure consistent application and interpretation of IFRS.
d. Different versions of IFRS exist that may cause confusion for users of financial statements.

A1-7 With regard to the presentation of financial information under IFRS, which of the following is true?

a. The terminology on the balance sheet and the income statement is the same under IFRS and U.S. GAAP.
b. Under IFRS, the elements of the balance sheet are often presented in reverse order relative to U.S. GAAP, with noncurrent assets presented before current assets and stockholders' equity presented before liabilities.
c. Under IFRS, the elements of the income statement are often presented in reverse order, with expenses presented first followed by revenues.
d. IFRS do not require the presentation of a statement of cash flows.

A1-8 Which of the following inventory costing methods is *not* allowed under IFRS?

a. FIFO
b. specific identification
c. average cost
d. LIFO

A1-9 Which of the following is true?

a. IFRS allow property, plant, and equipment to be revalued upward if fair value is higher than historical cost.
b. IFRS contain more extensive guidance on revenue recognition than U.S. GAAP.
c. IFRS have a much more broad definition of cash than U.S. GAAP.
d. The accounting for research and development costs is identical under IFRS and U.S. GAAP.

A1-10 Which of the following is true with regard to contingent liabilities?

a. IFRS and U.S. GAAP use the same terminology to refer to contingent liabilities.
b. A contingent liability is recognized under IFRS when it is more likely than not that the contingent event will occur.
c. Fewer events will be recognized as contingent liabilities under IFRS than under U.S. GAAP.
d. Provisions are contingent liabilities that are not recognized in the financial statements.

2 Appendix

© Pixelfabrik/Alamy

After studying Appendix 2, you should be able to:

1. Choose between and use the amortized cost, fair value, and equity methods for reporting investments.
2. Describe the consolidated balance sheet and income statement.
3. Describe accounting for business combinations.

Investments

iStockphoto.com/Amanda Rohde

Although companies can invest in virtually any asset (such as land), here we will concentrate on the most common investments—buying equity or debt securities.

- *Equity Securities*: An **equity security** represents an ownership interest in a corporation. Although most equity securities are common stock, preferred stock is also an equity security.
- *Debt Securities*: A **debt security** exists when another entity owes the security holder some combination of interest and principal. Debt securities include corporate bonds, U.S. treasury securities, and municipal bonds.

A company buys debt or equity securities with either short- or long-term investment horizons. As discussed in Chapter 4, short-term investment horizons are typically attempts to earn greater returns with cash that is not immediately needed for operations. Such "excess cash" results when cash inflows are not evenly distributed throughout the year. For example, many retail businesses, such as **Abercrombie & Fitch**, **Aeropostale**, and **Toys"R"Us**, collect significantly more cash around Christmas than in the summer. Consequently, they may need to save some of the cash collected at Christmas to meet operational needs during the summer. Other companies, such as banks, mutual funds, and insurance companies, buy and sell securities to profit from day-to-day changes in security prices.

Companies also attempt to maximize returns over long-term investment horizons. For insurance companies, such as **State Farm**, and mutual funds, such as **Fidelity**, for example, long-term investment income generated from debt and equity securities is a core part of operations. Or, companies may accumulate capital for future expansion to avoid having to borrow or sell additional stock. Companies may also invest in equity securities to establish long-term relationships, obtain significant influence, or control the other company. For example, to assure itself of access to high quality raw materials, a company may purchase the common stock of a supplier—the more common stock purchased, the more influence that can be exerted.

OVERVIEW OF ACCOUNTING FOR INVESTMENTS IN DEBT AND EQUITY

OBJECTIVE 1

Choose between and use the amortized cost, fair value, and equity methods for reporting investments.

Accounting for investments in equity securities differs depending upon the amount of common stock owned. The difference exists because of the nature of the ownership interest.

- *Passive:* If an investor owns less than 20% of the common stock, the investment is generally considered to be passive; that is, the investor is not attempting to exert influence over the operating and financial policies of the investee. In this case, the *fair value method* is used.
- *Significant Influence*: Because owning stock entitles the investor to vote for members of the board of directors, if the investor owns 20% to 50% of the outstanding common stock, then the investor is assumed to possess significant influence over the operating and financial policies of the investee. In this case, the *equity method* is used to account for the investment.
- *Control*: If the investor owns over 50% of the outstanding common stock, the investor is deemed to have control over the operating and financial policies of the investee. The investor is then called the **parent** and the investee is called a **subsidiary**. In these cases, the subsidiary's financial statements are combined with the parent's into a single set of **consolidated financial statements**.

Each of the methods for accounting for investments in debt and equity will be discussed in the sections that follow.

Classifying and Accounting for Equity Securities

When an investor owns less than 20% of the outstanding common stock of a corporation, the equity securities are classified as either *trading securities* or *available-for-sale securities*. Debt securities are also classified as trading or available-for-sale, but debt securities may also be classified in a third category—*held-to-maturity*. The distinction between these classifications is as follows:

- **Held-to-maturity securities** are debt investments (not equity, because stock does not mature) that management intends to hold until the debt contract requires the borrower to repay the debt in its entirety. On the balance sheet, held-to-maturity securities are classified as noncurrent assets unless the date of maturity is within 1 year or one operating cycle, whichever is longer.
- **Trading securities** are equity or debt investments that management intends to sell in the near term. Trading securities are bought and sold frequently and typically are owned for under 1 month. Trading securities are always classified as current assets on the balance sheet.
- **Available-for-sale securities** are equity or debt investments that management intends to sell in the future, but not necessarily in the near term. Therefore, investments that don't warrant inclusion as trading securities or held-to-maturity securities are considered available-for-sale. On the balance sheet, available-for-sale securities are classified as current or noncurrent assets depending on whether they will be sold within 1 year or one operating cycle, whichever is longer.

Debt securities that are classified as "held-to-maturity" are valued at an amortized cost basis. Securities (both debt and equity) that are classified as trading or available-for-sale are valued at fair market value. An overview of the accounting for investments in debt and equity securities is shown in Exhibit A2.1. We will illustrate these different methods of accounting for investments using Redbird Corporation.

EXHIBIT A2.1

Accounting for Investments in Debt and Equity Securities

Investments in Equity Securities	Method	Reporting of Dividends	Reporting of Unrealized Gains and Losses
1. Passive investment (own <20% of the stock)			
a. Trading	Fair value	Net Income	Net income
b. Available-for-sale	Fair value	Net Income	Other comprehensive income
2. Significant influence (own 20% to 50% of the stock)	Equity	Reduces investment account	Not recognized
3. Control (own >50% of the stock)	Equity plus consolidation	Eliminated	Not recognized
Investments in Debt Securities		**Reporting of Interest Income**	
1. Held-to-maturity	Amortized cost	Net Income	Not recognized
2. Trading	Fair value	Net Income	Net income
3. Available-for-sale	Fair value	Net Income	Other comprehensive income

Amortized Cost Method

All investments in debt securities that are classified as held-to-maturity are accounted for by the **amortized cost method** (also called *the cost method*). Investments are recorded at cost when acquired, and interest income is recognized with appropriate amortization of premiums and discounts. In other words, the amortized cost method closely parallels accounting for long-term liabilities, which is described in Chapter 9.

Purchase of Bonds On December 31, 2013, Redbird Corporation purchases 10-year, 5% bonds with a face value of $100,000 for $96,000 cash. Redbird would record the purchase with the following journal entry:

Dec. 31, 2013	Investments—Held to Maturity	96,000	
	Cash		96,000
	(Record issuance of bonds at discount)		

Assets	= Liabilities +	Stockholders' Equity
+96,000		
−96,000		

Receipt of Interest Payment These bonds pay interest of $2,500 ($100,000 × 5% × 6/12) every 6 months. Additionally, you will recall from Chapter 9 that any premium or discount must be amortized over the life of the bond. For simplicity, we will amortize the discount on a straight-line basis. This results in discount amortization of $200 {[($100,000 – $96,000)/10 years] × 6/12} every 6 months. The following entries would be made to record receipt of the interest payments during 2014:

June 30, 2014	Cash	2,500	
	Investments—Held-to-Maturity	200	
	Interest Income		2,700
	(Record receipt of interest payment)		

Assets	= Liabilities +	Stockholders' Equity
+2,500		+2,700
+200		

Dec. 31, 2014	Cash	2,500	
	Investments—Held-to-Maturity	200	
	Interest Income		2,700
	(Record receipt of interest payment)		

Assets	= Liabilities +	Stockholders' Equity
+2,500		
+200		+2,700

The same entries would be made each year to record receipt of the interest payments.

Reporting in the Financial Statements As shown in the preceding entries, at December 31, 2014, $400 of the discount has been amortized to the investment account. This means the book value of the held-to-maturity investments is $96,400 ($96,000 + $400). Assume that the fair market value of these bonds is $98,000 at December 31, 2014. The 2014 financial statements would report this investment as:

Redbird Corporation
Partial Balance Sheet
At December 31, 2014

Noncurrent assets:	
Investments (held-to-maturity), net of unamortized discount	$96,400

Redbird Corporation
Partial Income Statement
For the year ended December 31, 2014

Interest income	$5,400

Because the market value of Redbird's investment is $1,600 ($98,000 − $96,400) more than its book value, there is an unrealized gain of $1,600. The rationale for not recognizing unrealized gains or losses on held-to-maturity investments is that changes in market value do not affect the amount that is realized from such investments. If securities are held to maturity, the amount that is realized is the face value—as determined by the debt agreement.

Receipt of Principal Payment When the bonds mature on December 31, 2023, the following journal entry is made:

Assets	= Liabilities +	Stockholders' Equity
+100,000		
−100,000		

Dec. 31, 2023	Cash	100,000	
	Investments—Held-to-Maturity		100,000
	(Record receipt of principal payment)		

Note that this entry zeros out the investment account because, at maturity, the discount has been fully amortized, which makes the balance in the investment account equal to the face value of the bonds.

Fair Value Method

Recall that when an investment is considered passive (less than 20% common stock ownership), the investor usually cannot significantly influence the investee. These investments are classified as trading or available-for-sale securities. In such cases, the investor must use the **fair value method** to account for the investment. This means the investment is valued at the price for which the investor could sell the asset in an orderly transaction between market participants. For most securities, this price is a quoted price in an active market, but if no active market exists, other techniques are used to estimate the fair market value.

Purchase of Securities Like other assets, trading and available-for-sale securities are recorded at cost, which is also fair value on the date of purchase. To illustrate, on August 1, 2014, Redbird Corporation made the following purchases of securities:

Security	Type	Classification	Amount
Illinois Enterprises	Equity	Trading	$10,000
Metzler Design	Debt	Trading	6,000
IMG	Equity	Trading	4,100
Total Trading Securities			**$20,100**
Alabama Co.	Debt	AFS	$ 8,100
Mutare Inc.	Debt	AFS	6,300
ABC	Equity	AFS	12,000
Total Available-for-Sale Securities			**$26,400**

These acquisitions are recorded by the following journal entry:

Assets	= Liabilities +	Stockholders' Equity
+20,100		
+26,400		
−46,500		

Date	Account and Explanation	Debit	Credit
Aug. 1, 2014	Investments—Trading Securities	20,100	
	Investments—Available-for-Sale Securities	26,400	
	Cash		46,500
	(Record purchase of investments)		

Receipt of Dividend Payment On September 30, 2014, Redbird received cash dividends of $300 from IMG and $200 from ABC, which are recorded by the following journal entry:[1]

[1] Dividend income should be recognized by investors at the dividend declaration date rather than the dividend payment date. When a cash dividend is declared in 1 year and paid in the following year, the investor should record the dividend declaration at year end by a debit to dividends receivable and a credit to dividend income. In the following year, when the related cash is received, the investor should debit cash and credit dividends receivable.

Date	Account and Explanation	Debit	Credit
Sept. 30, 2014	Cash	500	
	Dividend Income		500
	(Record receipt of dividends)		

Assets	= Liabilities +	Stockholders' Equity
+500		+500

Selling Securities On December 20, 2014, the market price of IMG stock had climbed to $4,900, and Redbird decided to sell its entire holding. The following journal entry records the sale:

Date	Account and Explanation	Debit	Credit
Dec. 20, 2014	Cash	4,900	
	Investments—Trading Securities		4,100
	Gain on Sale of Investments		800
	(Record sale of security)		

Assets	= Liabilities +	Stockholders' Equity
+4,900 −4,100		+800

The $800 gain will be included in Redbird's year end net income, as will the $500 of dividends received on September 30.

In summary, this investment yielded two forms of income—dividends ($500) and a gain on sale ($800)—giving Redbird additional net income of $1,300.

Receipt of Interest Payments In addition, Mutare, Metzler Design, and Alabama (the three debt securities) pay interest totaling $1,500 on December 31, 2014, which is recorded with the following journal entry:

Date	Account and Explanation	Debit	Credit
Dec. 31, 2014	Cash	1,500	
	Interest Income		1,500
	(Record receipt of interest payment)		

Assets	= Liabilities +	Stockholders' Equity
+1,500		+1,500

Reporting on the Financial Statements On the balance sheet, both trading and available-for-sale securities are recorded at fair value. Use of the fair value method results in **unrealized gains** and/or **unrealized losses** because the value of the securities must be written up or down to fair market value at the balance sheet date (often called "marking to market"). For example, consider the securities shown in Exhibit A2.2.

EXHIBIT A2.2

Investment Portfolio Data

Redbird Corporation
Investment Portfolio
December 31, 2014

Security	Classification	Acquisition Cost	Market Value at 12/31
Illinois Enterprises	Trading	$ 10,000	$ 8,800
Metzler Design	Trading	6,000	6,400
Total Trading Securities		**$16,000**	**$15,200**
Alabama Co.	AFS	$ 8,100	$ 8,600
Mutare Inc.	AFS	6,300	6,500
ABC	AFS	12,000	13,500
Total Available-for-Sale Securities		**$26,400**	**$28,600**

On December 31, Redbird Corporation would make the following entries to "mark the investments to market:"

Assets	= Liabilities +	Stockholders' Equity
+2,200		+2,200

Date	Account and Explanation	Debit	Credit
Dec. 31, 2014	Allowance to Adjust Available-for-Sale Securities to Market	2,200	
	Unrealized Gain (Loss) on Available-for-Sale Securities*		2,200
	(Record available-for-sale securities at fair value)		

* Recognize that for available-for-sale securities, any unrealized gain or loss goes to the "accumulated other comprehensive income" portion of stockholders' equity—not to the income statement.

Assets	= Liabilities +	Stockholders' Equity
−800		−800

Date	Account and Explanation	Debit	Credit
Dec. 31, 2014	Unrealized Gain (Loss) on Trading Securities**	800	
	Allowance to Adjust Trading Securities to Market		800
	(Record trading securities at fair value)		

** Recognize that for trading securities, any unrealized gain or loss goes to the income statement.

The allowance accounts (both Available-for-Sale and Trading) are valuation accounts containing the unrealized gains and losses for the Available-for-Sale and Trading investment portfolios, respectively. Valuation accounts are used to record changes in the fair values of the investments so that the investment accounts (both Available-for-Sale and Trading) reflect the original cost. At the balance sheet date, the allowance accounts are adjusted to reflect the current amount of unrealized gain or loss in the investment portfolio. On the balance sheet, the allowance accounts are netted with the respective investment accounts (added if the allowance has a debit balance and subtracted if it has a credit balance) to report the investments at fair value as:

Redbird Corporation
Partial Balance Sheet
December 31, 2014

Current assets:		
Trading securities, at cost	$16,000	
Less: Allowance to adjust trading securities to market	(800)	
Trading securities, at market*		$15,200
Noncurrent assets:		
Available-for-sale securities, at cost	$26,400	
Add: Allowance to adjust available-for-sale securities to market	2,200	
Available-for-sale securities, at market*		$28,600
Stockholders' equity:		
Accumulated other comprehensive income		$ 2,200

* While trading securities will always be classified as current assets, available-for-sale securities are classified as current or noncurrent assets depending on whether they will be sold within 1 year or one operating cycle, whichever is longer.

Redbird Corporation
Partial Income Statement
For the year ended December 31, 2014

Other income:	
Interest income	$1,500
Dividend income	500
Other loss:	
Unrealized loss on trading securities	$ 800

To summarize, the debits and credits for trading securities and available-for-sale securities are identical. The only difference is that unrealized gains and losses affect the financial statements differently:

- Unrealized gains and losses for trading securities are included on the income statement and, thus, flow into retained earnings.
- Unrealized gains and losses for available-for-sale securities, on the other hand, are *not* included on the income statement. Instead, they are included as part of "accumulated other comprehensive income," a separate account in stockholders' equity.

Equity Method

The fair value method should be used when investments are considered passive. But when the investor possesses significant influence over the operating and financial policies of the investee (20 to 50% common stock ownership), the investor must use the *equity method* to account for the investment. The **equity method** requires an investor to recognize income when it is reported as earned by the investee, rather than when dividends accrue. The earlier recognition of investment income and loss under the equity method is consistent with the close relationship between the investor and investee.

Purchase of Stock On January 1, 2014, Redbird purchases 25% of the common stock of one of its major suppliers—Korsgard Mining, a newly formed corporation—for $4,000,000 cash. Redbird would record the purchase with the following journal entry:

Date	Account and Explanation	Debit	Credit
Jan. 1, 2014	Investments—Equity Method	4,000,000	
	Cash		4,000,000
	(Record purchase of Korsgard stock)		

Assets	= Liabilities +	Stockholders' Equity
+4,000,000		
−4,000,000		

Note that the investment is recorded at cost, just as it is in the amortized cost and fair value methods. In addition, the investment is recorded in a separate account, not with the trading or available-for-sale securities.

Investee Income and Dividends On November 1, 2014, Korsgard declared and paid a cash dividend of $60,000. Further, for the year ended December 31, 2014, Korsgard reported net income of $440,000. Under the equity method, these events would have the following effect on Redbird's accounts:

Date	Account and Explanation	Debit	Credit
Nov. 1, 2014	Cash*	15,000	
	Investments—Equity Method		15,000
	(Record receipt of dividends)		

* 25% × $60,000 = $15,000

Assets	= Liabilities +	Stockholders' Equity
+15,000		
−15,000		

Date	Account and Explanation	Debit	Credit
Dec. 31, 2014	Investments—Equity Method**	110,000	
	Investment Income—Equity Method		110,000
	(Record Redbird's share of Korsgard net income)		

** 25% × $440,000 = $110,000

Assets	= Liabilities +	Stockholders' Equity
+110,000		+110,000

Unlike the fair value method, the equity method recognizes income when income is earned by the investee, not when a dividend is declared and paid. Instead, the dividend paid by Korsgard is a distribution to owners and therefore reduces the amount of Redbird's investment.

Reporting on the Financial Statements Equity method investments are carried on the balance sheet as:

Acquisition Cost + Investor's Share of the Investee's Income (Loss)
− Investor's Share of the Investee's Dividends

This means the investment account is not adjusted for changes in the fair market value of the common stock. Redbird would account for its investment in Korsgard as follows:

Investments—Equity Method (Korsgard Mining)

Purchase of Korsgard stock, 1/1/14	4,000,000	15,000	Receipt of Korsgard dividends, 11/1/14
Redbird's share of Korsgard net income, 12/31/14	110,000		
	4,095,000		

Redbird Corporation
Partial Balance Sheet
At December 31, 2014

Noncurrent assets:	
Investments—equity method (Korsgard Mining)	$4,095,000

Redbird Corporation
Partial Income Statement
For the year ended December 31, 2014

Investment income—equity method (Korsgard)	$110,000

One advantage of the equity method over the fair value method is that it prevents an investor from manipulating its own income by exerting influence over the amount and timing of investee dividends.

OBJECTIVE 2

Describe the consolidated balance sheet and income statement.

CONSOLIDATED FINANCIAL STATEMENTS

If the investor holds enough common stock to control the investee (50% or more common stock ownership), then the two corporations are no longer separate reporting entities. In such cases, the investor must prepare consolidated financial statements, which combine the financial statements of the two corporations as if they were a single company. In this case the investor is referred to as the parent and the investee is called the subsidiary. Of course, the parent and subsidiary continue to maintain separate accounting records. As such, the parent must continue to account for its investment in the subsidiary. This is done with equity method accounting entries; however, the *reporting* requires consolidation.

Preparing Consolidated Statements

Consolidated financial statements are prepared from information contained in the separate financial statements of the parent and subsidiary:

- The consolidated balance sheet is essentially the same as the parent's balance sheet, except the parent's "investment in subsidiary" account is replaced by the subsidiary's assets and liabilities.
- The consolidated income statement is essentially the parent's income statement, except the parent's "income from subsidiary" is replaced by the subsidiary's revenues and expenses.

Consolidated Balance Sheet To illustrate the preparation of consolidated balance sheets, consider the following situation in which a parent owns all the outstanding stock of its subsidiary.[2]

On January 1, 2014, Parent Inc. purchases all the outstanding common stock of Sub Corporation for $2,750,000. In this case, since Parent has control over Sub, a consolidated balance sheet needs to be prepared from the individual balance sheets of both companies. To do so, a **consolidation worksheet** must be prepared. Exhibit A2.3 presents the worksheet that is used to prepare the consolidated income statement for Parent and Sub at acquisition. The corporate balance sheets for Parent and Sub are listed in the two left columns of the worksheet. Consolidation adjustments are entered into the third column. The amounts in the fourth column can be computed by adding the first two columns and the adjustments.

EXHIBIT A2.3

Worksheet for Preparing the Consolidated Balance Sheet on January 1, 2014

			Adjustments		
	Parent	Sub	Debit	Credit	Consolidated
Assets:					
Current assets	$ 9,250,000	$ 700,000			$ 9,950,000
Investment—equity method	2,750,000			2,750,000	—
Property, plant, and equipment	68,000,000	2,300,000			70,300,000
Total assets	$80,000,000	$3,000,000			$80,250,000
Liabilities	$10,000,000	$ 250,000			$10,250,000
Stockholders' equity:					
Common stock	40,000,000	1,000,000	1,000,000		40,000,000
Retained earnings	30,000,000	1,750,000	1,750,000		30,000,000
Total liabilities and stockholders' equity	$80,000,000	$3,000,000			$80,250,000

As you can see in Exhibit A2.3, the consolidation of these two balance sheets requires a credit adjustment that eliminates the Parent's Investment—Equity Method account. This is offset by debits to Common Stock and Retained Earnings, which eliminates the related stockholders' equity of Sub. These worksheet adjustments are not entered on the accounting records of either Parent or Sub.

Consolidated Income Statement Just as a consolidation worksheet was used to prepare the consolidated balance sheet for Parent and Sub, a similar worksheet is prepared for the consolidated income statement. Exhibit A2.4 presents the worksheet used to prepare the consolidated income statement for Parent and Sub 1 year after acquisition.

Notice that the consolidated net income is exactly the same as Parent's net income. From Parent's viewpoint, the consolidation procedure does not change net income, only the revenues and expenses on which net income is based. The credit needed to offset the $600,000 debit adjustment (and keep everything in balance) occurs on the balance sheet—against the Investment—Equity Method account. Preparation of the consolidated balance sheet on December 31, 2014, 1 year after the acquisition, follows the same principles. However, it is complicated by Parent's equity method journal entries. Further, adjustments are required to eliminate any transactions between Parent and Sub (such as the sale or other

[2] Many large corporations have a complex network of many subsidiaries. However, for the sake of simplicity, the examples here discuss a two-corporation structure involving one parent and one subsidiary.

EXHIBIT A2.4

Worksheet for Preparing the Consolidated Income Statement on December 31, 2014

	Parent	Sub	Adjustments Debit	Adjustments Credit	Consolidated
Revenue	$9,000,000	$2,000,000			$11,000,000
Cost of goods sold	3,200,000	950,000			4,150,000
Depreciation expense	2,100,000	220,000			2,320,000
Other expenses	1,600,000	230,000			1,830,000
Investment income—equity method	600,000		600,000		
Net income	$2,700,000	$ 600,000			$ 2,700,000

transfer of assets). Because you cannot make a sale to yourself, such transactions between the two corporations must be eliminated to present the two corporations as a single accounting entity.

Reporting a Noncontrolling Interest

Consolidation is required when a parent acquires between 50% and 100% of the subsidiary's stock. Any voting stock not held by the parent is called the **noncontrolling interest**, and the holders of such shares are called noncontrolling stockholders (or minority stockholders). However, even when the parent owns less than 100% of the subsidiary's stock, 100% of the subsidiary's assets and liabilities are included in the consolidated balance sheet. In other words, if the parent controls the subsidiary, it controls *all* of the subsidiary's assets and liabilities.

For example, assume Parent had acquired only 80% of Sub. The consolidated total assets still would have been $80,250,000 because Parent controls all of the assets of Sub. However, the noncontrolling interest would have been $550,000 [20% × ($1,000,000 + $1,750,000)], and this amount must be shown as a component of stockholders' equity on the consolidated balance sheet. Further, the consolidated income statement would show 100% of Sub's revenues and expenses, but 20% of net income would be deducted as belonging to the noncontrolling interest.

OBJECTIVE 3

Describe accounting for business combinations.

BUSINESS COMBINATIONS

Any transaction or set of transactions that brings together two or more previously separate entities to form a single accounting entity is called a **business combination**. Business combinations take many forms. Some, like Parent–Sub described in the previous section, involve the acquisition of another corporation's stock in exchange for cash. Others involve the acquisition of another corporation's stock with the parent's own common stock. In either case, these are called **stock acquisitions** because the stock of the other corporation is being acquired. The parent could also purchase some or all of the assets of the other corporation. This is referred to as an **asset acquisition**. In this case, the two entities actually become a single legal entity.

Business combinations usually, but not always, transfer ownership of the acquired business entity from one stockholder group to another. In general, purchased assets are recorded at current cost, which is measured as the fair value of the cash and other consideration given up to acquire the asset. Thus, a purchased asset is recorded at its current value to the purchaser, without regard to its recorded value to the seller. Applying this logic to a business combination, a purchased company must be recorded at the value of the cash and other consideration given by the acquiring company.

To illustrate, consider the acquisition of all the assets and liabilities (i.e., an asset acquisition) of Landron Bottling Works by CactusCo for $12,000,000. With the approval of Landron's stockholders and creditors, Landron transfers all of its assets and liabilities to CactusCo and distributes the cash to Landron's stockholders. On the acquisition date, Landron's stockholders' equity was $6,500,000. CactusCo determines that Landron's liabilities of $1,000,000 are correctly valued, but its identifiable assets have a fair value of $3,800,000 more than their book value of $7,500,000. Thus, the acquisition cost exceeds the fair value of the net assets (assets minus liabilities) acquired by $1,700,000:

Acquisition cost			$12,000,000
Current value of identifiable net assets acquired:			
Book value of assets acquired	$7,500,000		
Adjustment to current value	3,800,000	$11,300,000	
Less:			
Book value of liabilities acquired	$1,000,000		
Adjustment to current value	0	1,000,000	10,300,000
Excess of acquisition cost over current value (goodwill)			$ 1,700,000

The excess of acquisition cost over the fair value of Landron's identifiable net assets is recorded as goodwill. **Goodwill** is an intangible asset arising from attributes that are not separable from the business—such as customer satisfaction, product quality, skilled employees, and business location. CactusCo's recording of the acquisition would be recorded with following journal entry:

Account and Explanation	Debit	Credit
Assets (various accounts)	11,300,000	
Goodwill	1,700,000	
Liabilities (various accounts)		1,000,000
Cash		12,000,000
(Record the acquisition of Landron's net assets)		

Assets	=	Liabilities	+	Stockholders' Equity
+11,300,000		+1,000,000		
+1,700,000				
−12,000,000				

This entry assumes that Landron goes out of existence as a corporation. If, instead of selling its net assets to CactusCo, Landron stockholders sell all their stock (as in a stock acquisition) to CactusCo, Landron will continue as a legal entity and the journal entry would be as follows:

Account and Explanation	Debit	Credit
Investments—Equity Method	12,000,000	
Cash		12,000,000
(Record the acquisition of Landron's stock)		

Assets	=	Liabilities	+	Stockholders' Equity
+12,000,000				
−12,000,000				

In this case, CactusCo must also consolidate Landron's financial statements, substituting the detailed assets (including goodwill) and liabilities for the investment account. The financial statements for a 100% asset acquisition will be identical to the consolidated financial statements for a 100% stock acquisition.

SUMMARY OF LEARNING OBJECTIVES

LO 1. Choose between and use the amortized cost, fair value, and equity methods for reporting investments.

- There are three methods of accounting for investments.
  - The amortized cost method is used only for debt securities that the business plans to hold until maturity.
  - The fair value method is used for both debt and equity securities that are classified as either trading securities or available-for-sale securities (less than 20% common stock ownership).
  - The equity method is used for equity securities in which 20% or more of the outstanding common stock is owned.
- Investments in equity securities in which more than 50% of the outstanding common stock is owned are also required to issue consolidated financial statements.

LO 2. Describe the consolidated balance sheet and income statement.

- When a company owns more than 50% of the outstanding common stock of another corporation, the investor (parent) is deemed to control the other corporation (subsidiary).
- In this case, the parent is required to issue consolidated financial statements in which the parent's and subsidiary's financial statements are combined.
- Noncontrolling interest is disclosed when the parent owns more than 50%, but less than 100% of the outstanding common stock.

LO 3. Describe accounting for business combinations.

- Business combinations can occur through either an asset or stock acquisition.
- The business combination is recorded at the cost of acquisition, without regard to the seller's book value.
- The excess of acquisition cost over the current value of identifiable net assets is recorded as goodwill.

KEY TERMS

Amortized cost method, 745
Asset acquisition, 752
Available-for-sale securities, 744
Business combination, 752
Consolidated financial statements, 743
Consolidation worksheet, 751
Debt security, 743
Equity method, 749
Equity security, 743
Fair value method, 746
Goodwill, 753
Held-to-maturity securities, 744
Noncontrolling interest, 752
Parent, 743
Stock acquisitions, 752
Subsidiary, 743
Trading securities, 744
Unrealized gains, 747
Unrealized losses, 747

DISCUSSION QUESTIONS

1. How do long-term investments differ from short-term investments?
2. Describe the three classifications that are possible for investments in debt securities.
3. Describe the amortized cost method of accounting for investments. Under which circumstances should it be used?
4. Describe the fair value method of accounting for investments. Under which circumstances should it be used?

5. Describe the equity method of accounting for investments. Under which circumstances should it be used?
6. How do available-for-sale securities differ from trading securities?
7. What event triggers the recognition of investment income under the amortized cost method? Under the fair value method? Under the equity method?
8. How does the equity method discourage the manipulation of net income by investors?
9. Define the terms *parent* and *subsidiary*.
10. What is noncontrolling interest and where is it reported on the consolidated balance sheet?
11. How does the consolidated balance sheet differ from the balance sheet of the parent?
12. What is the allowance to adjust short-term investments to market, and why is it used?
13. Why is it necessary to eliminate transactions between the parent and subsidiary in consolidation?
14. What is the difference between an asset acquisition and a stock acquisition?
15. What is goodwill, and how is it calculated?

MULTIPLE-CHOICE QUESTIONS

A2-1 Investments in equity securities are deemed to be "passive" if:

a. less than 20% of the firm's stock is owned.
b. between 20% and 50% of the firm's stock is owned.
c. between 50% and 100% of the firm's stock is owned.
d. 100% of the firm's stock is owned.

A2-2 Equity and debt investments that management intends to sell in the future, but not necessarily in the near term, are called:

a. available-for-sale securities.
b. trading securities.
c. debt securities.
d. stock securities.

A2-3 Which of the following is a reason businesses purchase securities?

a. To save (and earn returns on) money from uneven cash flows
b. To diversify risk
c. To profit from changes in day-to-day security prices
d. All of the above

A2-4 Which of the following terms is not used for debt securities?

a. Trading securities
b. Held-to-maturity securities
c. Available-for-sale securities
d. Fair value securities

A2-5 How are held-to-maturity securities valued?

a. Historical cost
b. Amortized cost
c. Fair market value
d. Amortized fair value

A2-6 The Boss Inc. reported an unrealized gain *on its income statement* due to appreciation in the stock price of AMW Corp. How much of AMW does The Boss own, and how has The Boss classified this investment?

a. Owns 35%, trading security
b. Owns 18%, available-for-sale security
c. Owns 9%, trading security
d. Owns over half of AMW and has consolidated the companies' income statement information

A2-7 EMK Corp. is holding two bonds to maturity, both of which have a book value of $132,000. At the end of the fiscal year, the fair market value of Bond A is $118,000, and the fair market value of Bond B is $136,000. What is the unrealized gain or loss for EMK on these two bonds?

a. Unrealized gain of $4,000
b. Unrealized loss of $10,000
c. Unrealized loss of $14,000
d. No unrealized gain or loss

Refer to the following information for Multiple-Choice Questions A2-8 and A2-9:
Shackley Inc. owns three available-for-sale equity securities which have yielded the following fiscal year end results:

A. Dividend income: $350
B. Gain on sale: $2,000
C. Unrealized loss: $600

A2-8 Refer to the information for Shackley above. Which of these are reported on Shackley's income statement?

a. B only
b. A and B
c. A and C
d. B and C

A2-9 Refer to the information for Shackley above. Assume that one of the securities was solely responsible for the $600 unrealized loss and was responsible for $150 of the dividend income. If Shackley bought that security for $3,500, what is the value of the security on the year end balance sheet?

a. $2,900
b. $3,050
c. $3,500
d. $3,650

A2-10 JFK Inc. buys 30% of the shares outstanding for KLN Company. What account will JFK debit?

a. Investments—Equity Method
b. Investments
c. Trading Securities
d. Available-for-Sale Securities

A2-11 Whopper Corporation owns a 40% interest in BigMac Corporation, which it purchased for $2.5 million. During fiscal year 2014, BigMac paid cash dividends of $50,000 and reported net income of $700,000. What is the value of Whopper's investment in BigMac reported on its 2014 balance sheet?

a. $3,150,000
b. $2,760,000
c. $2,500,000
d. $2,450,000

A2-12 When the market value of a company's available-for-sale securities is lower than its cost, the difference should be:

a. shown as a liability.
b. shown as a valuation allowance added to the historical cost of the investments.
c. shown as a valuation allowance subtracted from the historical cost of the investments.
d. No entry is made, the securities are shown at historical cost.

A2-13 What account title will *not* appear on consolidated financial statements?

a. Investment in MJK Corporation (35% ownership)
b. Inventory
c. Investment in EBL Corporation (80% ownership)
d. Common Stock

A2-14 Consolidated financial statements are required:

a. only when 100% of the common stock of another corporation is owned.
b. when over 50% of the common stock of another corporation is owned.
c. only when significant influence or control can be exerted over another company.
d. whenever the commons stock of another corporation is owned.

A2-15 Assume a parent has total assets of \$6,000,000 and a subsidiary has total assets of \$4,000,000. If the parent owns 70% of the subsidiary's common stock, what amount of total assets will be reported on the consolidated balance sheet?

a. \$10,000,000
b. \$7,000,000
c. \$6,000,000
d. \$0, consolidation is not necessary

A2-16 Goodwill is calculated as the excess of the cost of an acquired company over the:

a. book value of net assets acquired.
b. fair value of assets acquired.
c. book value of identifiable net assets acquired.
d. fair value of identifiable net assets acquired.

EXERCISES

Exercise A2-17 Matching Accounting Methods and Investments

OBJECTIVE 1

Consider the following accounting methods for long-term investments:

a. Amortized cost method
b. Fair value method
c. Equity method
d. Consolidation of parent and sub

Required:

Match one or more of these methods with each of the investments described below:

1. Mueller Inc. owns 75% of Johnston Corporation's outstanding common stock.
2. Anderson Inc. owns 25% of Peterson Corporation's outstanding common stock.
3. Wixon Corporation owns 12% of the outstanding common stock of Gilman Inc., which is classified as available-for-sale.
4. Kohler Corporation holds a \$40,000 long-term note receivable from Bennett Inc., a major customer. Kohler expects to sell the note within the next 2 or 3 years.
5. Janis Products Inc. holds \$200,000 in Gibson Manufacturing bonds. Janis plans to hold these until they mature.

Exercise A2-18 Trading Securities

OBJECTIVE 1

Pear Investments began operations in 2014 and invests in securities classified as trading securities. During 2014, it entered into the following trading security transactions:

Purchased 20,000 shares of ABC common stock at \$38 per share
Purchased 32,000 shares of XYZ common stock at \$17 per share

At December 31, 2014, ABC common stock was trading at \$39.50 per share and XYZ common stock was trading at \$16.50 per share.

Required:

1. Prepare the necessary adjusting entry to value the trading securities at fair market value.
2. **CONCEPTUAL CONNECTION** What is the income statement effect of this adjusting entry?

OBJECTIVE 1

Exercise A2-19 Available-for-Sale Securities

Tolland Financial began operators in 2014 and invests in securities classified as available-for-sale. During 2014, it entered into the following available-for-sale security transactions:

Purchased 10,000 shares of DTR common stock at $50 per share
Purchased 44,000 shares of MJO common stock at $22 per share

At December 31, 2014, DTR common stock was trading at $62 per share and MJO common stock was trading at $21 per share.

Required:

1. Prepare the necessary adjusting entry to value the available-for-sale securities at fair market value.
2. **CONCEPTUAL CONNECTION** What is the income statement effect of this adjusting entry?

OBJECTIVE 1

Exercise A2-20 Allowance for Available-for-Sale Securities

McCarthy Corporation's allowance to reduce available-for-sale securities to market has a $7,200 credit balance on December 31, 2014, before the lower-of-cost-or-market adjustment. The cost and market value of the available-for-sale portfolio at December 31, 2014, are $120,000 and $117,000, respectively.

Required:

Prepare the adjusting entry, if any, to adjust the allowance at year end.

OBJECTIVE 1

Exercise A2-21 Adjusting the Allowance to Adjust Trading Securities to Market

Caesar Corporation has the following information for its portfolio of trading securities at the end of the past 4 years:

Date	Portfolio Cost	Portfolio Market Value
12/31/11	$162,300	$153,800
12/31/12	109,600	106,200
12/31/13	148,900	151,300
12/31/14	139,000	138,700

Required:

1. Prepare the journal entries, if necessary, to adjust the allowance account at the end of 2012, 2013, and 2014.
2. **CONCEPTUAL CONNECTION** What is the income statement effect of the 2014 entry?
3. **CONCEPTUAL CONNECTION** How would your answer to Requirement 2 change if this was an available-for-sale portfolio?

OBJECTIVE 1

Exercise A2-22 Investments in Available-for-Sale Securities

Williams Corporation acquired the following equity securities during 2014:

200 shares of Southwestern Company capital stock	$14,600
500 shares of Montgomery Products capital stock	14,500

Williams's investment in both of these companies is passive, and Williams classifies these securities as available-for-sale. During 2014, Southwestern paid a dividend of $1.20 per share, and Montgomery paid a dividend of $1.80 per share. At December 31, 2014, the Southwestern stock has a market value of $75 per share, and the Montgomery stock has a market value of $25 per share.

Required:

1. Prepare entries for Williams's journal to record these two investments and the receipt of the dividends.

2. Calculate the market value of Williams's short-term investment portfolio at December 31, 2014.
3. Prepare the necessary adjusting entry at December 31, 2014.
4. How would these securities be disclosed on the December 31, 2014 balance sheet?

Exercise A2-23 Fair Value and Equity Methods

OBJECTIVE 1

Nadal Corporation purchased 10,000 shares of Cutler Inc.'s common stock, on January 1, 2013, for $100,000. During 2013, Cutler declared and paid cash dividends to Nadal in the amount of $8,000. Nadal's share of Cutler's net income for 2013 was $12,400. At December 31, 2013, the fair value of 10,000 shares of Cutler's common stock was $120,000. This is Nadal's only investment.

Required:

1. Assume that Cutler has 75,000 shares of common stock outstanding. What journal entries will Nadal make during 2013 relative to this investment?
2. Assume that Cutler has 40,000 shares of common stock outstanding. What journal entries will Nadal make during 2013 relative to this investment?

Exercise A2-24 Fair Value Method

OBJECTIVE 1

On January 1, 2013, Miller Inc. acquired 1,500 shares of the outstanding common stock of Graceland Industries for $16 per share, or $24,000. On that date, Graceland had 10,000 shares of common stock outstanding. On October 1, 2013, Graceland declared and paid a cash dividend of $2 per share. On November 13, 2013, Miller sold 300 shares of Graceland for $5,000. Graceland reported 2013 net income of $36,000. Graceland's stock sold for $15 per share at December 31, 2013. This is Miller's only investment, and Miller plans on remaining invested in Graceland for a number of years.

Required:

1. Prepare Miller's journal entries to record the transactions related to its investment in Graceland.
2. Give the title and amount of each item (except Cash) related to this investment on the December 31, 2013 balance sheet. Name the balance sheet section in which each item appears.

Exercise A2-25 Equity Method

OBJECTIVE 1

On January 1, 2013, Hill Corporation acquired 40% of the outstanding common stock (400 of 1,000 outstanding shares) of Valley Manufacturing Inc. for $60,000, which equals the book value of Valley. On December 31, 2013, Valley reported net income of $30,000 and declared and paid a cash dividend of $11,500.

Required:

1. Prepare the journal entries made by Hill to record the transactions related to its investment in Valley.
2. Give the title and amount of each item (except Cash) related to the investment on the December 31, 2013 balance sheet. Name the balance sheet section in which each item appears.

Exercise A2-26 Accounting for Investments in Equity Securities

OBJECTIVE 1

On January 1, 2013, Stern Corporation purchased 100 shares of common stock issued by Milstein Inc. (representing 12% of the total shares outstanding) for $6,000 and 500 shares of Heifetz Inc. (representing 25% of the total shares outstanding) for $20,000. Assume that the acquisition cost of each investment equals the book value of the related stockholders' equity on the records of the investee. During 2013, Milstein declared and paid cash dividends to Stern of $500, and Heifetz declared and paid cash dividends to Stern of $1,700. Milstein reported 2013 net income of $12,000, and Heifetz reported 2013 net income of $15,000. On December 31, 2013, the market value of 100 shares of Milstein was $6,450, and the market value of 500 shares of Heifetz was $19,720.

Required:

Answer the following questions for both investments:

	Milstein	Heifetz
1. Which accounting method is applicable?		
2. What amount is recorded in the investment account on the date of acquisition?		
3. What amount is recorded in Stern's net income from the investment?		
4. What amount is reported for the investment on the balance sheet at December 31, 2013?		

OBJECTIVE 1

Exercise A2-27 Investments in Trading Securities

Maxwell Company engaged in the following transactions involving short-term investments:

a. Purchased 200 shares of Bartco stock for $12,800.
b. Received a $1.60-per-share dividend on the Bartco stock.
c. Sold 40 shares of the Bartco stock for $61 per share.
d. Purchased 380 shares of Newton stock for $20,900.
e. Received a dividend of $1.00 per share on the Newton stock.

At December 31, the Bartco stock has a market value of $60 per share, and the Newton stock has a market value of $59 per share.

Required:

1. Prepare entries for Maxwell's journal to record these transactions assuming they are trading securities.
2. Calculate the market value of Maxwell's short-term investment portfolio at December 31.
3. Prepare the necessary adjusting entry at December 31.
4. CONCEPTUAL CONNECTION What is the income statement effect of the adjusting entry?
5. How would these investments be reported on the December 31 balance sheet?

OBJECTIVE 2 3

Exercise A2-28 Consolidated Balance Sheet

Augusta Inc. acquired 100% of the outstanding common stock of Dear Corporation in a business combination. Immediately before the business combination, the two businesses had the following balance sheets:

Augusta		Dear	
Cash	$ 3,100	Cash	$ 180
Equipment (net)	9,500	Equipment (net)	930
Total assets	$12,600	Total assets	$1,110
Common stock	$ 9,100	Common stock	$ 700
Retained earnings	3,500	Retained earnings	410
Total liabilities & equity	$12,600	Total liabilities & equity	$1,110

Augusta agreed to give Dear's stockholders $1,500 cash in exchange for all their Dear common stock. Dear's equipment has a fair value of $1,100.

Required:

1. Prepare the entries for Augusta and Dear to record the business combination.
2. Prepare the balance sheet of Augusta immediately after the business combination.
3. Prepare the balance sheet of Dear immediately after the business combination.
4. Calculate the amount of the adjustment to the book value of Dear's equity and the amount of goodwill.
5. Prepare a consolidated balance sheet immediately after the combination.

Exercise A2-29 Consolidated Income Statement

OBJECTIVE 2 3

Johnson Inc. is the wholly owned subsidiary of Stuart Corporation. The 2014 income statements for the two corporations are as follows:

Stuart			Johnson		
Sales revenue		$3,200	Sales revenue		$500
Income from investment in Johnson		?			
Total revenue		$?	Total revenue		$500
Cost of goods sold	$920		Cost of goods sold	$160	
Depreciation expense	410		Depreciation expense	95	
Other expenses	680	2,010	Other expenses	135	390
Net income		$?	Net income		$110

The acquisition cost of Stuart's 100% ownership interest in Johnson equaled its book value on Johnson's records. During 2014, Johnson pays a cash dividend of $25 to Stuart.

Required:

1. Calculate the income from investment in Johnson as reported on Stuart's income statement.
2. Calculate the 2014 net income reported by the parent company (Stuart) on its income statement.
3. Prepare the 2014 consolidated income statement for Stuart and Johnson.

Exercise A2-30 Goodwill

OBJECTIVE 3

Pindar Corporation acquired all the outstanding stock of Strauss Company for $23,000,000 on January 1, 2014. On the date of acquisition, Strauss had the following balance sheet:

Strauss Company
Balance Sheet
January 1, 2014

Assets		Liabilities	
Accounts receivable	$ 6,800,000	Accounts payable	$ 2,000,000
Inventory	4,700,000	Notes payable	8,000,000
Property, plant & equipment (net)	16,300,000	Total liabilities	$10,000,000
		Stockholders' Equity	
		Common stock	$ 2,000,000
		Additional paid-in capital—common stock	8,000,000
		Retained earnings	7,800,000
		Total stockholders' equity	$17,800,000
Total assets	$27,800,000	Total liabilities & stockholders' equity	$27,800,000

All Strauss' assets and liabilities have book values equal to their fair values except for equipment, which has a fair value of $20,700,000.

Required:

1. Calculate the amount of goodwill.
2. Prepare the journal entry by Pindar to record the acquisition.
3. Assume that instead of acquiring all the outstanding common stock of Strauss, Pindar acquired 100% of Strauss' net assets. What would Pindar's journal entry be in this case?

3 Appendix

© Pixelfabrik/Alamy

After studying Appendix 3, you should be able to:

1. Explain how compound interest works.
2. Use future value and present value tables to apply compound interest to accounting transactions.

Time Value of Money

iStockphoto.com/BrooksElliott

Time value of money is widely used in business to measure today's value of future cash outflows or inflows and the amount to which liabilities (or assets) will grow when compound interest accumulates.

In transactions involving the borrowing and lending of money, the borrower usually pays *interest*. In effect, interest is the **time value of money**. The amount of interest paid is determined by the length of the loan and the interest rate.

However, interest is not restricted to loans made to borrowers by banks. Investments (particularly, investments in debt securities and savings accounts), installment sales, and a variety of other contractual arrangements all include interest. In all cases, the arrangement between the two parties—the note, security, or purchase agreement—creates an asset in the accounting records of one party and a corresponding liability in the accounting records of the other. All such assets and liabilities increase as interest is earned by the asset holder and decrease as payments are made by the liability holder.

COMPOUND INTEREST CALCULATIONS

OBJECTIVE 1

Explain how compound interest works.

Compound interest is a method of calculating the time value of money in which interest is earned on the previous periods' interest. That is, interest for the period is added to the account balance and interest is earned on this new balance in the next period. In computing compound interest, it's important to understand the difference between the *interest period* and the *interest rate*:

- The **interest period** is the time interval between interest calculations.
- The **interest rate** is the percentage that is multiplied by the beginning-of-period balance to yield the amount of interest for that period.

The interest rate must agree with the interest period. For example, if the interest period is 1 month, then the interest rate used to calculate interest must be stated as a percentage "per month."

When an interest rate is stated in terms of a time period that differs from the interest period, the rate must be adjusted before interest can be calculated. For example, suppose that a bank advertises interest at a rate of 12% per year compounded monthly. Here, the interest period would be 1 month. Since there are 12 interest periods in 1 year, the interest rate for 1 month is one-twelfth the annual rate, or 1%. In other words, if the *rate statement period* differs from the *interest period*, the stated rate must be divided by the number of interest periods included in the rate statement period. A few examples of adjusted rates follow:

Stated Rate	Adjusted Rate for Computations
12% per year compounded semiannually	6% per 6-month period (12% ÷ 2)
12% per year compounded quarterly	3% per quarter (12% ÷ 4)
12% per year compounded monthly	1% per month (12% ÷ 12)

If an interest rate is stated without reference to a rate statement period or an interest period, assume that the period is 1 year. For example, both "12%" and "12% per year" should be interpreted as 12% per year compounded annually.

Compound interest means that interest is computed on the original amount plus undistributed interest earned in previous periods. The simplest compound interest calculation involves putting a single amount into an account and adding interest to it at the end of each period. Cornerstone A3.1 shows how to compute future values using compound interest.

CORNERSTONE

A3.1

Computing Future Values Using Compound Interest

Why:

When deposits earn compound interest, interest is earned on the interest.

Information:

An investor deposits $20,000 in a savings account on January 1, 2014. The bank pays interest of 6% per year compounded monthly.

Required:

Assuming that the only activity to the account is the deposit of interest at the end of each month, how much money will be in the account after the interest payment on March 31, 2014?

Solution:

Monthly interest will be ½% (6% per year ÷ 12 months).

Account balance, 1/1/14	$20,000.00
January interest ($20,000.00 × ½%)	100.00
Account balance, 1/31/14	$20,100.00
February interest ($20,100.00 × ½%)	100.50
Account balance, 2/28/14	$20,200.50
March interest ($20,200.50 × ½%)	101.00
Account balance, 3/31/14	$20,301.50

Note: Here, interest was the only factor that altered the account balance after the initial deposit. In more complex situations, the account balance is changed by subsequent deposits and withdrawals as well as by interest. Withdrawals reduce the balance and therefore, the amount of interest in subsequent periods. Additional deposits have the opposite effect, increasing the balance and the amount of interest earned.

As you can see in Cornerstone A3.1, the balance in the account continues to grow each month by an increasing amount of interest. The amount of monthly interest increases because interest is *compounded.* In other words, interest is computed on accumulated interest as well as on principal. For example, February interest of $100.50 consists of $100 interest on the $20,000 principal and 50¢ interest on the $100 January interest ($100 × 0.005 = 50¢).

In Cornerstone A3.1, the compound interest only amounts to 25¢. That might seem relatively insignificant, but if the investment period is sufficiently long, the amount of compound interest grows large even at relatively small interest rates. For example, suppose your parents invested $1,000 at ½% per month when you were born with the objective of giving you a college graduation present at age 21. How much would that investment be worth after 21 years? The answer is $3,514. In 21 years, the compound interest is $2,514—more than 2½ times the original principal. Without compounding, interest over the same period would have been only $1,260.

The amount to which an account will grow when interest is compounded is the **future value** of the account. Compound interest calculations can assume two fundamentally different forms:

- calculations of future values
- calculations of present values

As shown, calculations of future values are projections of future balances based on *past and future* cash flows and interest payments. In contrast, calculations of present values are determinations of present amounts based on *expected* future cash flows.

PRESENT VALUE OF FUTURE CASH FLOWS

Whenever a contract establishes a relationship between an initial amount borrowed or loaned and one or more future cash flows, the initial amount borrowed or loaned is the **present value** of those future cash flows. The present value can be interpreted in two ways:

- From the borrower's viewpoint, it is the liability that will be exactly paid by the future payments.
- From the lender's viewpoint, it is the receivable balance that will be exactly satisfied by the future receipts.

In understanding cash flows, cash flow diagrams that display both the amounts and the times of the cash flows specified by a contract can be quite help helpful. In these diagrams, a time line runs from left to right. Inflows are represented as arrows pointing upward and outflows as arrows pointing downward. For example, suppose that the Hilliard Corporation borrows $100,000 from Citizens Bank of New Hope on January 1, 2015. The note requires three $38,803.35 payments, one each at the end of 2015, 2016, and 2017, and includes interest at 8% per year. The cash flows for Hilliard are shown in Exhibit A3.1.

EXHIBIT A3.1

Cash Flow Diagram

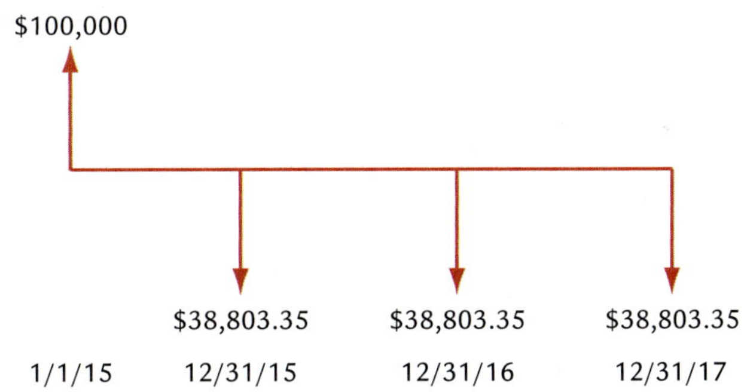

The calculation that follows shows, from the borrower's perspective, the relationship between the amount borrowed (*the present value*) and the future payments (*future cash flows*) required by Hilliard's note.

Amount borrowed, 1/1/15	$100,000.00
Add: 2015 interest ($100,000.00 × 0.08)	8,000.00
Subtract payment on 12/31/15	(38,803.35)
Liability at 12/31/15	$ 69,196.65
Add: 2016 interest ($69,196.65 × 0.08)	5,535.73
Subtract payment on 12/31/16	(38,803.35)
Liability at 12/31/16	$ 35,929.03
Add: 2017 interest ($35,929.03 × 0.08)	2,874.32
Subtract payment on 12/31/17	(38,803.35)
Liability at 12/31/17	$ 0.00

Present value calculations like this one are future value calculations in reverse. Here, the three payments of $38,803.35 exactly pay off the liability created by the note.

Because the reversal of future value calculations can present a burdensome and sometimes difficult algebraic problem, shortcut methods using tables have been developed (see Exhibits A3.7, A3.8, A3.9, and A3.10, discussed later in this appendix).

Interest and the Frequency of Compounding

The number of interest periods into which a compound interest problem is divided can make a significant difference in the amount of compound interest. For example, assume that you are evaluating four 1-year investments, each of which requires an initial $10,000 deposit. All four investments earn interest at a rate of 12% per year, but they have different compounding periods. The data in Exhibit A3.2 show the impact of compounding frequency on future value. Investment D, which offers monthly compounding, accumulates $68 more interest by the end of the year than Investment A, which offers only annual compounding.

EXHIBIT A3.2

Effect of Interest Periods on Compound Interest

Investment	Interest Period	*I*	*N*	Calculation of Future Amount in One Year*
A	1 year	12%	1	($10,000 × 1.12000) = $11,200
B	6 months	6%	2	($10,000 × 1.12360) = 11,236
C	1 quarter	3%	4	($10,000 × 1.12551) = 11,255
D	1 month	1%	12	($10,000 × 1.12683) = 11,268

*The multipliers (1.12000 for Investment A, 1.12360 for Investment B, etc.) are taken from the future value table in Exhibit A3.7 (p. 783).

OBJECTIVE 2

Use future value and present value tables to apply compound interest to accounting transactions.

FOUR BASIC COMPOUND INTEREST PROBLEMS

Any present value or future value problems can be broken down into one or more of the following four basic problems:

- computing the future value of a single amount
- computing the present value of a single amount
- computing the value of an annuity
- computing the present value of an annuity

Computing the Future Value of a Single Amount

In computing the future value of a single amount, the following elements are used:

- f: the cash flow
- FV: the future value
- n: the number of periods between the cash flow and the future value
- i: the interest rate per period

To find the future value of a single amount, establish an account for f dollars and add compound interest at i% to that account for n periods:

$$FV = (f)(1 + i)^n$$

The balance of the account after n periods is the future value.

Because people frequently need to compute the future value of a single amount, tables have been developed to make it easier. Therefore, instead of using the formula above, you could use the future value table in Exhibit A3.7 (p. 783), where M_1 is the multiple that corresponds to the appropriate values of n and i:

$$FV = (f)(M_1)$$

For example, suppose Allied Financial loans $200,000 at a rate of 6% per year compounded annually to an auto dealership for 4 years. Exhibit A3.3 shows how to compute the future value (FV) at the end of the 4 years—the amount that will be repaid.

EXHIBIT A3.3

Future Value of a Single Amount: An Example

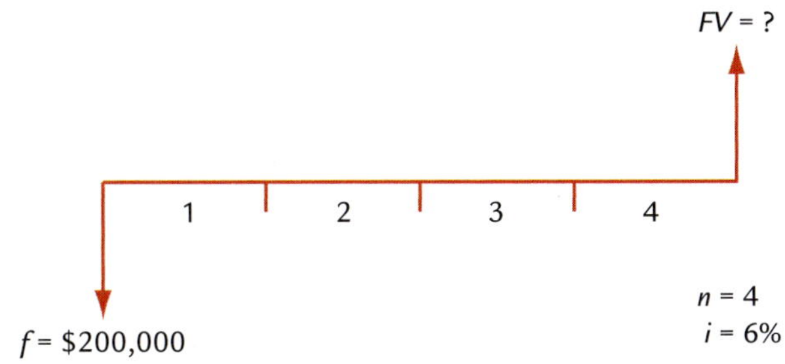

Assuming Allied's viewpoint (the lender's), using a compound interest calculation, the unknown future value (FV) would be found as follows:

Amount loaned	$200,000.00
First year's interest ($200,000.00 × 0.06)	12,000.00
Loan receivable at end of first year	$212,000.00
Second year's interest ($212,000.00 × 0.06)	12,720.00
Loan receivable at end of second year	$224,720.00
Third year's interest ($224,720.00 × 0.06)	13,483.20
Loan receivable at end of third year	$238,203.20
Fourth year's interest ($238,203.20 × 0.06)	14,292.19
Loan receivable at end of the fourth year	$252,495.39

As you can see, the amount of interest increases each year. This growth is the effect of computing interest for each year based on an amount that includes the interest earned in prior years.

The shortcut calculation, using the future value table (Exhibit A3.7, p. 783), would be:

$$\begin{aligned} FV &= (f)(M_1) \\ &= (\$200{,}000)(1.26248) \\ &= \underline{\underline{\$252{,}496}} \end{aligned}$$

You can find M_1 at the intersection of the 6% column ($i = 6\%$) and the fourth row ($n = 4$) or by calculating 1.06^4. This multiple is the future value of the single amount after having been borrowed (or invested) for 4 years at 6% interest. The future value of $200,000 is 200,000 times the multiple.

Note that there is a difference between the answer ($252,495.39) developed in the compound interest calculation and the answer ($252,496) determined using the future value table. This is because the numbers in the table have been rounded to five decimal places. If they were taken to eight digits ($1.06^4 = 1.26247696$), the two answers would be equal. Cornerstone A3.2 shows how to compute the future value of a single amount.

CORNERSTONE

A3.2

Computing Future Value of a Single Amount

Why:

The future value of a single amount is the original cash flow plus compound interest as of a specific future date.

Information:

The Kitchner Company sells an unneeded factory site for $200,000 on July 1, 2014. Kitchner expects to purchase a different site in 18 months so that it can expand into a new market. Meanwhile, Kitchner decides to invest the $200,000 in a money market fund that is guaranteed to earn 6% per year compounded semiannually (3% per 6-month period).

Required:

1. Draw a cash flow diagram for this investment from Kitchner's perspective.
2. Calculate the amount of money in the money market fund on December 31, 2014, and prepare the journal entry necessary to recognize interest income.
3. Calculate the amount of money in the money market fund on December 31, 2015, and prepare the journal entry necessary to recognize interest *i*.

Solution:

1.

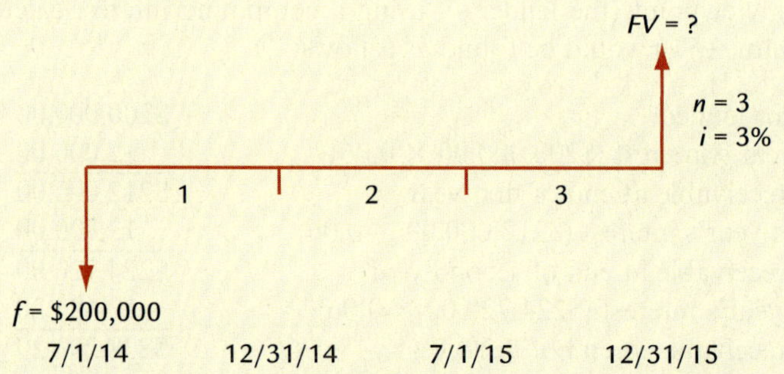

2. Because we are calculating the value at 12/31/14, there is only one period:

$$\begin{aligned} FV &= (f)(FV\ of\ a\ Single\ Amount,\ 1\ period,\ 3\%) \\ &= (\$200{,}000)(1.03) \\ &= \underline{\underline{\$206{,}000}} \end{aligned}$$

The excess of the amount of money over the original deposit is the interest earned from July 1 through December 31, 2014.

Assets	=	Liabilities	+	Stockholders' Equity
+6,000				+6,000

Dec. 31, 2014	Cash	6,000	
	Interest Income		6,000
	(Record interest income)		

3.

$$\begin{aligned} FV &= (f)(FV\ of\ a\ Single\ Amount,\ 3\ periods,\ 3\%) \\ &= (\$200{,}000)(1.09273) \\ &= \underline{\underline{\$218{,}546}} \end{aligned}$$

(Continued)

CORNERSTONE **A3.2** *(Continued)*

The interest income for the year is the increase in the amount of money during 2015, which is $12,546 ($218,546 – $206,000). The journal entry to record interest income would be:

Dec. 31, 2015	Cash	12,546	
	Interest Income		12,546
	(Record interest income)		

Assets	= Liabilities +	Stockholders' Equity
+12,546		+12,546

Computing the Present Value of a Single Amount

In computing the present value of a single amount, the following elements are used:

- f: the future cash flow
- PV: the present value
- n: the number of periods between the present time and the future cash flow
- i: the interest rate per period

In present value problems, the interest rate is sometimes called the *discount rate*.

To find the present value of a single amount, use the following equation:

$$PV = \frac{f}{(1+i)^n}$$

You could use the present value table in Exhibit A3.8 (p. 784), where M_2 is the multiple from Exhibit A3.8 that corresponds to the appropriate values of n and i:

$$PV = (f)(M_2)$$

Suppose **Marathon Oil** has purchased property on which it plans to develop oil wells. The seller has agreed to accept a single $150,000,000 payment 3 years from now, when Marathon expects to be selling oil from the field. Assuming an interest rate of 7% per year, the (PV) at the end of the 3 years from the borrower's perspective can be calculated as shown in Exhibit A3.4.

EXHIBIT A3.4

Present Value of a Single Amount: An Example

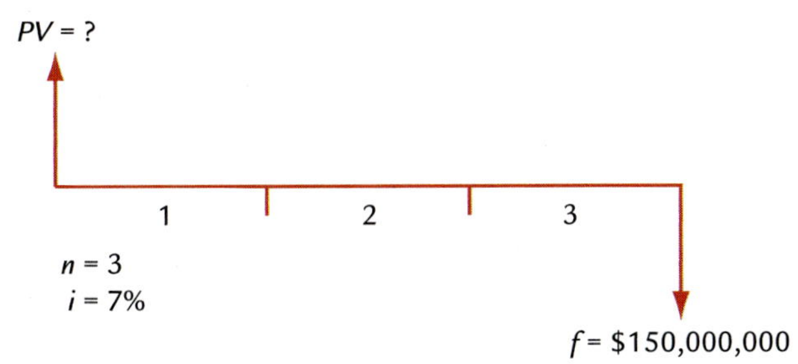

The shortcut calculation, using the present value table (Exhibit A3.8, p. 784), would be:

$$\begin{aligned} PV &= (f)(M_2) \\ &= (\$150{,}000{,}000)(0.81630) \\ &= \underline{\underline{\$122{,}445{,}000}} \end{aligned}$$

You can find M_2 at the intersection of the 7% column ($i = 7\%$) and the third row ($n = 3$) in Exhibit A3.8 or by calculating $[1/(1.07)^3]$. This multiple is the present value of a $1 cash inflow or outflow in 3 years at 7%. Thus, the present value of $150,000,000 is 150,000,000 times as much as the multiple.

Although the future value calculation cannot be used to determine the present value, it can be used to verify that the present value calculated by using the table is correct. The following calculation is proof for the present value problem:

Calculated present value *(PV)*	$122,445,000
First year's interest ($122,445,000 × 0.07)	8,571,150
Loan payable at end of first year	$131,016,150
Second year's interest ($131,016,150 × 0.07)	9,171,131
Loan payable at end of second year	$140,187,281
Third year's interest ($140,187,281 × 0.07)	9,813,110
Loan payable at end of the third year (*f*)	$150,000,391

Again, the $391 difference between the amount here and the assumed $150,000,000 cash flow is due to rounding.

When interest is compounded on the calculated present value of $122,445,000, then the present value calculation is reversed, and we return to the future cash flow of $150,000,000. This reversal proves that $122,445,000 is the correct present value. Cornerstone A3.3 shows how to compute the present value of a single amount.

CORNERSTONE

A3.3

Computing Present Value of a Single Amount

Why:

The present value of a single cash flow is the original cash flow that must be invested to produce a known value at a specific future date.

Information:

On October 1, 2014, Adelsman Manufacturing Company sold a new machine to Randell Inc. The machine represented a new design that Randell was eager to place in service. Since Randell was unable to pay for the machine on the date of purchase, Adelsman agreed to defer the $60,000 payment for 15 months. The appropriate rate of interest in such transactions is 8% per year compounded quarterly (2% per 3-month period).

Required:

1. Draw the cash flow diagram for this deferred-payment purchase from Randell's (the borrower's) perspective.
2. Calculate the present value of this deferred-payment purchase.
3. Prepare the journal entry necessary to record the acquisition of the machine.

(Continued)

CORNERSTONE

A3.3

(Continued)

Solution:

1.

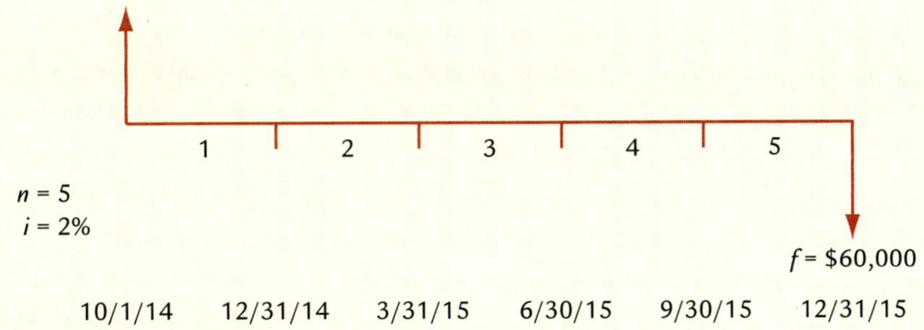

2. The present value of the $60,000 payment.

$PV = (f)(PV\ of\ a\ Single\ Amount,\ 5\ periods,\ 2\%)$
$= (\$60{,}000)(0.90573)$
$= \underline{\underline{\$54{,}344}}$

3.

Oct. 1, 2014	Equipment	54,344	
	Notes Payable		54,344
	(Record purchase of equipment)		

Assets	=	Liabilities	+	Stockholders' Equity
+54,344		+54,344		

Computing the Future Value of an Annuity

So far, we have been discussing problems that involve a single cash flow. However, there are also instances of multiple cash flows one period apart. An **annuity** is a number of equal cash flows; one to each interest period. For example, an investment in a security that pays $1,000 to an investor every December 31 for 10 consecutive years is an annuity. A loan repayment schedule that calls for a payment of $367.29 on the first day of each month can also be considered an annuity. (Although the number of days in a month varies from 28 to 31, the interest period is defined as 1 month without regard to the number of days in each month.)

In computing the future value of an annuity, the following elements are used:

- f: the amount of each repeating cash flow
- FV: the future value after the last (n^{th}) cash flow
- n: the number of cash flows
- i: the interest rate per period

To find the future value of an annuity, use the following equation:

$$FV = (f)\left[\frac{(1+i)^n - 1}{i}\right]$$

Alternatively, you could use the future value table in Exhibit A3.9 (p. 785), where M_3 is the multiple from Exhibit A3.9 that corresponds to the appropriate values of n and i compound interest calculations:

$$FV = (f)(M_3)$$

Assume that **Chase** wants to advertise a new savings program to its customers. The savings program requires the customers to make four annual payments of $5,000 each, with the first payment due 3 years before the program ends. Chase advertises a 6% interest rate compounded annually. The future value of this annuity immediately after the fourth cash payment from the investor's perspective is shown in Exhibit A3.5.

EXHIBIT A3.5

Future Value of an Annuity: An Example

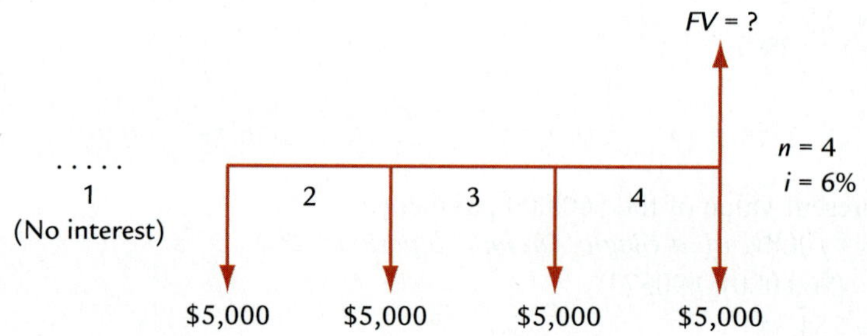

Note that the first period in Exhibit A3.5 is drawn with a dotted line. When using annuities, the time-value-of-money model assumes that all cash flows occur at the end of a period. Therefore, the first cash flow in the future value of an annuity occurs at the end of the first period. However, since interest cannot be earned until the first deposit has been made, the first period is identified as a no-interest period.

The future value (*FV*) can be computed as:

Interest for first period ($0 × 6%)	$ 0.00
First deposit	5,000.00
Investment balance at end of first year	$ 5,000.00
Second year's interest ($5,000.00 × 0.06)	300.00
Second deposit	5,000.00
Investment balance at end of second year	$10,300.00
Third year's interest ($10,300.00 × 0.06)	618.00
Third deposit	5,000.00
Investment balance at end of third year	$15,918.00
Fourth year's interest ($15,918.00 × 0.06)	955.08
Fourth deposit	5,000.00
Investment at end of the fourth year	$21,873.08

This calculation shows that the lender has accumulated a future value (*FV*) of $21,873.08 by the end of the fourth period, immediately after the fourth cash investment.

The shortcut calculation, using the future value table (Exhibit A3.9, p. 785), would be:

$$
\begin{aligned}
FV &= (f)(M_3) \\
&= (\$5{,}000)(4.37462) \\
&= \underline{\underline{\$21{,}873}}
\end{aligned}
$$

You can find M_3 at the intersection of the 6% column ($i = 6\%$) and the fourth row ($n = 4$) in the Exhibit A3.9 (p. 785) or by calculating $(1.06^4 - 1) \div 0.06$. This multiple is the future value of an annuity of four cash flows of $1 each at 6%. The future value of an annuity of $5,000 cash flows is 5,000 times the multiple. Thus, the table allows us to calculate the future value of an annuity by a single multiplication, no matter how many cash flows are involved. Cornerstone A3.4 shows how to compute the future value of an annuity.

Computing Future Value of an Annuity

CORNERSTONE A3.4

Why:

The future value of an annuity is the value of a series of equal cash flows made at regular intervals with compound interest at some specific future date.

Information:

Greg Smith is a lawyer and CPA specializing in retirement and estate planning. One of Greg's clients, the owner of a large farm, wants to retire in 5 years. To provide funds to purchase a retirement annuity from New York Life at the date of retirement, Greg asks the client to give him annual payments of \$170,000, which Greg will deposit in a special fund that will earn 7% per year.

Required:

1. Draw the cash flow diagram for the fund from Greg's client's perspective.
2. Calculate the future value of the fund immediately after the fifth deposit.
3. If Greg's client needs \$1,000,000 to purchase the annuity, how much must be deposited every year?

Solution:

1.

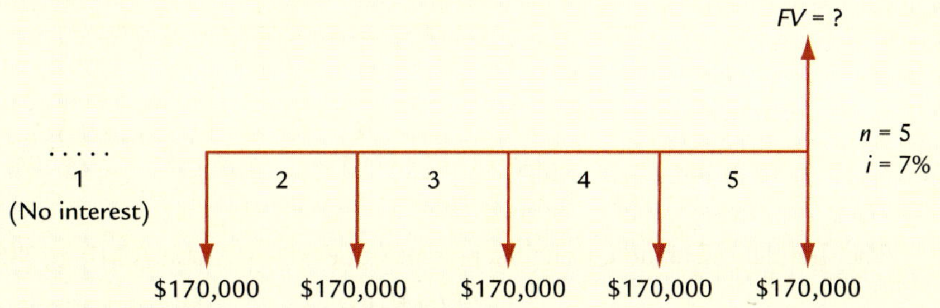

2. $FV = (f)(FV\ of\ an\ Annuity,\ 5\ periods,\ 7\%)$
$= (\$170{,}000)(5.75074)$
$= \underline{\underline{\$977{,}626}}$

3. In this case, the future value is known, but the annuity amount (f) is not:

$\$1{,}000{,}000 = (f)(FV\ of\ an\ Annuity,\ 5\ periods,\ 7\%)$
$\$1{,}000{,}000 = (f)(5.75074)$
$f = \$1{,}000{,}000/5.75074$
$f = \underline{\underline{\$173{,}890.66}}$

Present Value of an Annuity

In computing the present value of an annuity, the following elements are used:

- f: the amount of each repeating cash flow
- PV: the present value of the n future cash flows
- n: the number of cash flows and periods
- i: the interest (or discount) rate per period

To find the present value of an annuity, use the following equation:

$$PV = (f)\frac{1 - \dfrac{1}{(1+i)^n}}{i}$$

You could also use the present value table in Exhibit A3.10 (p. 786), where M_4 is the multiple from Exhibit A3.10 that corresponds to the appropriate values of n and i:

$$PV = (f)(M_4)$$

For example, assume that **Xerox Corporation** purchased a new machine for its manufacturing operations. The purchase agreement requires Xerox to make four annual payments of \$24,154 each. The interest rate is 8% compounded annually and the first cash flow occurs 1 year after the purchase. Exhibit A3.6 shows how to determine the present value of this annuity from Xerox's (the borrower's) perspective. Note that the same concept applies to both the lender's and borrower's perspectives.

EXHIBIT A3.6

Present Value of An Annuity: An Example

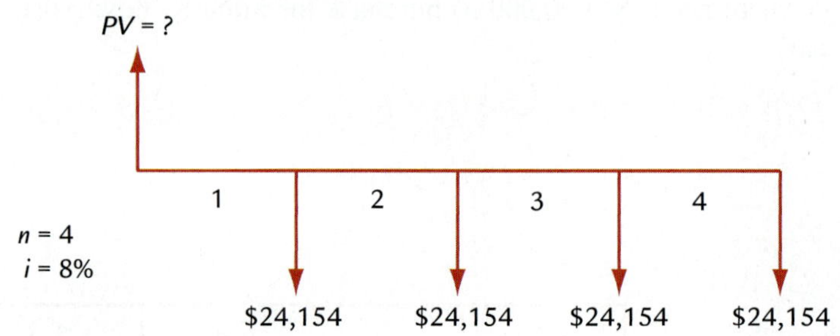

The shortcut calculation, using the present value table (Exhibit A3.10, p. 786), would be:

$$\begin{aligned} PV &= (f)(M_4) \\ &= (\$24{,}154)(3.31213) \\ &= \$80{,}001.19 \end{aligned}$$

You can find M_4 at the intersection of the 8% column ($i = 8\%$) and the fourth row ($n = 4$) in Exhibit A3.10 or by solving for $[1 - (1 \div 1.08^4)] \div 0.08$. This multiple is the present value of an annuity of four cash flows of \$1 each at 8%. The present value of an annuity of four \$24,154 cash flows is 24,154 times the multiple.

Again, although the compound interest calculation is not used to determine the present value, it can be used to prove that the present value found using the table is correct. The following calculation verifies the present value in the problem:

Calculated present value *(PV)*	\$ 80,001.19
Interest for first year (\$80,001.19 × 0.08)	6,400.10
Less: First cash flow	(24,154.00)
Balance at end of first year	\$ 62,247.29
Interest for second year (\$62,247.29 × 0.08)	4,979.78
Less: Second cash flow	(24,154.00)
Balance at end of second year	\$ 43,073.07
Interest for third year (\$43,073.07 × 0.08)	3,445.85
Less: Third cash flow	(24,154.00)
Balance at end of third year	\$ 22,364.92
Interest for fourth year (\$22,364.92 × 0.08)	1,789.19
Less: Fourth cash flow	(24,154.00)
Balance at end of fourth year	\$ 0.11

This proof uses a compound interest calculation that is the reverse of the present value formula. If the present value (*PV*) calculated with the formula is correct, then the proof should end with a balance of zero immediately after the last cash flow. This proof ends with a balance of $0.11 because of rounding in the proof itself and in the table in Exhibit A3.10 (p. 786).

Cornerstone A3.5 shows how to compute the present value of an annuity.

Computing Present Value of an Annuity

CORNERSTONE

A3.5

Why:

The present value of an annuity is the value of a series of equal future cash flows made at regular intervals with compound interest discounted back to today.

Information:

Bates Builders purchased a subdivision site from the Second National Bank and Trust Co. on January 1, 2014. Bates gave the bank an installment note. The note requires Bates to make four annual payments of $600,000 each on December 31 of each year, beginning in 2014. Interest is computed at 9%.

Required:

1. Draw the cash flow diagram for this purchase from Bates' perspective.
2. Calculate the cost of the land as recorded by Bates on January 1, 2014.
3. Prepare the journal entry that Bates will make to record the purchase of the land.

Solution:

1.

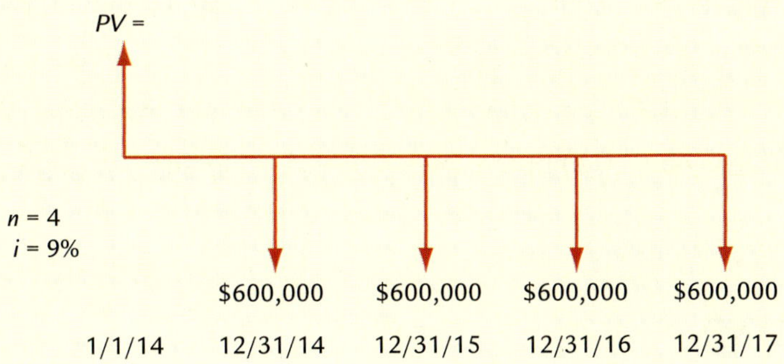

2. $PV = (f)(PV\ of\ an\ Annuity,\ 4\ periods,\ 9\%)$
   $= (\$600{,}000)(3.23972)$
   $= \$1{,}943{,}832$

3.

Jan. 1, 2014	Land	1,943,832	
	Notes Payable		1,943,832
	(Record purchase of land)		

Assets	=	Liabilities	+	Stockholders' Equity
+1,943,832		+1,943,832		

SUMMARY OF LEARNING OBJECTIVES

LO 1. Explain how compound interest works.

- In transactions involving the borrowing and lending of money, it is customary for the borrower to pay interest.
- With compound interest, interest for the period is added to the account and interest is earned on the total balance in the next period.
- Compound interest calculations require careful specification of the interest period and the interest rate.

LO 2. Use future value and present value tables to apply compound interest to accounting transactions.

- Cash flows are described as either:
  - single cash flows
  - annuities
- An annuity is a number of equal cash flows made at regular intervals.
- All other cash flows are a series of one or more single cash flows.
- Accounting for such cash flows may require:
  - calculation of the amount to which a series of cash flows will grow when interest is compounded (i.e., the future value)
  - the amount a series of future cash flows is worth today after taking into account compound interest (i.e., the present value)

CORNERSTONE A3.1 Computing future values using compound interest, page 764
CORNERSTONE A3.2 Computing future value of a single amount, page 768
CORNERSTONE A3.3 Computing present value of a single amount, page 770
CORNERSTONE A3.4 Computing future value of an annuity, page 773
CORNERSTONE A3.5 Computing present value of an annuity, page 775

KEY TERMS

Annuity, 771
Compound interest, 763
Future value, 764
Interest period, 763
Interest rate, 763
Present value, 765
Time value of money, 763

DISCUSSION QUESTIONS

1. Why does money have a time value?
2. Describe the four basic time-value-of-money problems.
3. How is compound interest computed? What is a future value? What is a present value?
4. Define an annuity in general terms. Describe the cash flows related to an annuity from the viewpoint of the lender in terms of receipts and payments.
5. Explain how to use time-value-of-money calculations to measure an installment note liability.

CORNERSTONE EXERCISES

Cornerstone Exercise A3-1 Explain How Compound Interest Works

OBJECTIVE 1
CORNERSTONE A3.1

Jim Emig has $6,000.

Required:

Calculate the future value of the $6,000 at 12% compounded quarterly for 5 years. (*Note:* Round answers to two decimal places.)

Cornerstone Exercise A3-2 Use Future Value and Present Value Tables to Apply Compound Interest to Accounting Transactions

OBJECTIVE 2
CORNERSTONE A3.2

Cathy Lumbattis inherited $140,000 from an aunt.

Required:

If Cathy decides not to spend her inheritance but to leave the money in her savings account until she retires in 15 years, how much money will she have, assuming an annual interest rate of 8%, compounded semiannually? (*Note:* Round answers to two decimal places.)

Cornerstone Exercise A3-3 Use Future Value and Present Value Tables to Apply Compound Interest to Accounting Transactions

OBJECTIVE 2
CORNERSTONE A3.3

LuAnn Bean will receive $7,000 in 7 years.

Required:

What is the present value at 7% compounded annually? (*Note:* Round answers to two decimal places.)

Cornerstone Exercise A3-4 Use Future Value and Present Value Tables to Apply Compound Interest to Accounting Transactions

OBJECTIVE 2
CORNERSTONE A3.3

A bank is willing to lend money at 6% interest, compounded annually.

Required:

How much would the bank be willing to loan you in exchange for a payment of $600 4 years from now? (*Note:* Round answers to two decimal places.)

Cornerstone Exercise A3-5 Use Future Value and Present Value Tables to Apply Compound Interest to Accounting Transactions

OBJECTIVE 2
CORNERSTONE A3.4

Ed Walker wants to save some money so that he can make a down payment of $3,000 on a car when he graduates from college in 4 years.

Required:

If Ed opens a savings account and earns 3% on his money, compounded annually, how much will he have to invest now? (*Note:* Round answers to two decimal places.)

Cornerstone Exercise A3-6 Use Future Value and Present Value Tables to Apply Compound Interest to Accounting Transactions

OBJECTIVE 2
CORNERSTONE A3.4

Kristen Quinn makes equal deposits of $500 semiannually for 4 years.

Required:

What is the future value at 8%? (*Note:* Round answers to two decimal places.)

Cornerstone Exercise A3-7 Use Future Value and Present Value Tables to Apply Compound Interest to Accounting Transactions

OBJECTIVE 2
CORNERSTONE A3.4

Chuck Russo, a high school math teacher, wants to set up an IRA account into which he will deposit $2,000 per year. He plans to teach for 20 more years and then retire.

(Continued)

Required:

If the interest on his account is 7% compounded annually, how much will be in his account when he retires? (*Note:* Round answers to two decimal places.)

OBJECTIVE 2
CORNERSTONE A3.4

Cornerstone Exercise A3-8 Use Future Value Tables to Apply Compound Interest to Accounting Transactions

Larson Lumber makes annual deposits of $500 at 6% compounded annually for 3 years.

Required:

What is the future value of these deposits? (*Note:* Round answers to two decimal places.)

OBJECTIVE 2
CORNERSTONE A3.5

Cornerstone Exercise A3-9 Use Future Value and Present Value Tables to Apply Compound Interest to Accounting Transactions

Michelle McFeaters can earn 6%.

Required:

How much would have to be deposited in a savings account in order for Michelle to be able to make equal annual withdrawals of $200 at the end of each of 10 years? (*Note:* Round answers to two decimal places.) The balance at the end of the last year would be zero.

OBJECTIVE 2
CORNERSTONE A3.5

Cornerstone Exercise A3-10 Use Future Value and Present Value Tables to Apply Compound Interest to Accounting Transactions

Barb Muller wins the lottery. She wins $20,000 per year to be paid for 10 years. The state offers her the choice of a cash settlement now instead of the annual payments for 10 years.

Required:

If the interest rate is 6%, what is the amount the state will offer for a settlement today? (*Note:* Round answers to two decimal places.)

EXERCISES

OBJECTIVE 2

Exercise A3-11 Practice with Tables

Refer to the appropriate tables on pages 783–786.

Required:

Note: Round answers to two decimal places. Determine the:

a. future value of a single cash flow of $5,000 that earns 7% interest compounded annually for 10 years.
b. future value of an annual annuity of 10 cash flows of $500 each that earns 7% compounded annually.
c. present value of $5,000 to be received 10 years from now, assuming that the interest (discount) rate is 7% per year.
d. present value of an annuity of $500 per year for 10 years for which the interest (discount) rate is 7% per year and the first cash flow occurs 1 year from now.

OBJECTIVE 2

Exercise A3-12 Practice with Tables

Refer to the appropriate tables on pages 783–786.

Required:

Note: Round answers to two decimal places. Determine the:

a. present value of $1,200 to be received in 7 years, assuming that the interest (discount) rate is 8% per year.

b. present value of an annuity of seven cash flows of $1,200 each (one at the end of each of the next 7 years) for which the interest (discount) rate is 8% per year.
c. future value of a single cash flow of $1,200 that earns 8% per year for 7 years.
d. future value of an annuity of seven cash flows of $1,200 each (one at the end of each of the next 7 years), assuming that the interest rate is 8% per year.

Exercise A3-13 Future Values

OBJECTIVE 2

Refer to the appropriate tables on pages 783–786.

Required:

Note: Round answers to two decimal places. Determine the:

a. future value of a single deposit of $15,000 that earns compound interest for 4 years at an interest rate of 10% per year.
b. annual interest rate that will produce a future value of $13,416.80 in 6 years from a single deposit of $8,000.
c. size of annual cash flows for an annuity of nine cash flows that will produce a future value of $79,428.10 at an interest rate of 9% per year.
d. number of periods required to produce a future value of $17,755.50 from an initial deposit of $7,500 if the annual interest rate is 9%.

Exercise A3-14 Future Values and Long-Term Investments

OBJECTIVE 2

Portman Corporation engaged in the following transactions during 2014:

a. On January 1, 2014, Portman deposited $12,000 in a certificate of deposit paying 6% interest compounded semiannually (3% per 6-month period). The certificate will mature on December 31, 2017.
b. On January 1, 2014, Portman established an account with Lee County Bank. Portman will make quarterly payments of $2,500 to Lee beginning on March 31, 2014, and ending on December 31, 2015. Lee guarantees an interest rate of 8% compounded quarterly (2% per 3-month period).

Required:

1. Prepare the cash flow diagram for each of these two investments.
2. Calculate the amount to which each of these investments will accumulate at maturity. (*Note:* Round answers to two decimal places.)

Exercise A3-15 Future Values

OBJECTIVE 2

On January 1, Beth Woods made a single deposit of $8,000 in an investment account that earns 8% interest.

Required:

Note: Round answers to two decimal places.

1. Calculate the balance in the account in 5 years assuming the interest is compounded annually.
2. Determine how much interest will be earned on the account in 7 years if interest is compounded annually.
3. Calculate the balance in the account in 5 years assuming the 8% interest is compounded quarterly.

Exercise A3-16 Future Values

OBJECTIVE 2

Palmer Transit Company invested $70,000 in a tax-anticipation note on June 30, 2014. The note earns 12% interest compounded monthly (1% per month) and matures on March 31, 2015.

Required:

Note: Round answers to two decimal places.

1. Prepare the cash flow diagram for this investment.
2. Determine the amount Palmer will receive when the note matures.

(Continued)

3. Determine how much interest Palmer will earn on this investment from June 30, 2014, through December 31, 2014.

OBJECTIVE 2

Exercise A3-17 Present Values

Refer to the appropriate tables on pages 783–786.

Required:

Note: Round answers to two decimal places. Determine the:

a. present value of a single $14,000 cash flow in 7 years if the interest (discount) rate is 8% per year.
b. number of periods for which $5,820 must be invested at an annual interest (discount) rate of 7% to produce an investment balance of $10,000.
c. size of the annual cash flow for a 25-year annuity with a present value of $49,113 and an annual interest rate of 9%. One payment is made at the end of each year.
d. annual interest rate at which an investment of $2,542 will provide for a single $4,000 cash flow in 4 years.
e. annual interest rate earned by an annuity that costs $17,119 and provides 15 payments of $2,000 each, one at the end of each of the next 15 years.

OBJECTIVE 2

Exercise A3-18 Present Values

Phillips Enterprises signed notes to make the following two purchases on January 1, 2014:

a. new piece of equipment for $60,000, with payment deferred until December 31, 2015. The appropriate interest rate is 9% compounded annually.
b. small building from Richter Construction. The terms of the purchase require a $75,000 payment at the end of each quarter, beginning March 31, 2014, and ending June 30, 2016. The appropriate interest rate is 2% per quarter.

Required:

Note: Round answers to two decimal places.

1. Prepare the cash flow diagrams for these two purchases.
2. Prepare the entries to record these purchases in Phillips' journal.
3. Prepare the cash payment and interest expense entries for Purchase b at March 31, 2014, and June 30, 2014.
4. Prepare the adjusting entry for Purchase a at December 31, 2014.

OBJECTIVE 2

Exercise A3-19 Present Values

Krista Kellman has an opportunity to purchase a government security that will pay $200,000 in 5 years.

Required:

Note: Round answers to two decimal places.

1. Calculate what Krista would pay for the security if the appropriate interest (discount) rate is 6% compounded annually.
2. Calculate what Krista would pay for the security if the appropriate interest (discount) rate is 10% compounded annually.
3. Calculate what Krista would pay for the security if the appropriate interest (discount) rate is 6% compounded semiannually.

OBJECTIVE 2

Exercise A3-20 Future Values of an Annuity

On December 31, 2014, Natalie Livingston signs a contract to make annual deposits of $4,200 in an investment account that earns 10%. The first deposit is made on December 31, 2014.

Required:

Note: Round answers to two decimal places.

1. Calculate what the balance in this investment account will be just after the seventh deposit has been made if interest is compounded annually.
2. Determine how much interest will have been earned on this investment account just after the seventh deposit has been made if interest is compounded annually.

Exercise A3-21 Future Values of an Annuity

OBJECTIVE 2

Devon National Bank pays 8% interest compounded weekly (0.154% per week) on savings accounts. The bank has asked your help in preparing a table to show potential customers the number of dollars that will be available at the end of 10-, 20-, 30-, and 40-week periods during which there are weekly deposits of $1, $5, $10, or $50. The following data are available:

Length of Annuity	Future Value of Annuity at an Interest Rate of 0.154% per Week
10 weeks	10.0696
20 weeks	20.2953
30 weeks	30.6796
40 weeks	41.2250

Required:

Complete a table similar to the one below. (*Note:* Round answers to two decimal places.)

	Amount of Each Deposit			
Number of Deposits	$1	$5	$10	$50
10				
20				
30				
40				

Exercise A3-22 Future Value of a Single Cash Flow

OBJECTIVE 2

Jenkins Products has just been paid $25,000 by Shirley Enterprises, which has owed Jenkins this amount for 30 months but been unable to pay because of financial difficulties. Had it been able to invest this cash, Jenkins assumes that it would have earned an interest rate of 12% compounded monthly (1% per month).

Required:

Note: Round answers to two decimal places.

1. Prepare a cash flow diagram for the investment that could have been made if Shirley had paid 30 months ago.
2. Determine how much Jenkins has lost by not receiving the $25,000 when it was due 30 months ago.
3. **CONCEPTUAL CONNECTION** Indicate whether Jenkins would make an entry to account for this loss. Why or why not?

Exercise A3-23 Installment Sale

OBJECTIVE 2
CORNERSTONE A3.5

Wilke Properties owns land on which natural gas wells are located. Cincinnati Gas Company signs a note to buy this land from Wilke on January 1, 2014. The note requires Cincinnati to pay Wilke $775,000 per year for 25 years. The first payment is to be made on December 31, 2014. The appropriate interest rate is 9% compounded annually.

(Continued)

Required:

Note: Round answers to two decimal places.

1. Prepare a diagram of the appropriate cash flows from Cincinnati Gas's perspective.
2. Determine the present value of the payments.
3. Indicate what entry Cincinnati Gas should make at January 1, 2014.

OBJECTIVE 2
CORNERSTONE A3.5

Exercise A3-24 Installment Sale

Bailey's Billiards sold a pool table to Sheri Sipka on October 31, 2014. The terms of the sale are no money down and payments of $50 per month for 30 months, with the first payment due on November 30, 2014. The table they sold to Sipka cost Bailey's $800, and Bailey uses a perpetual inventory system. Bailey's uses an interest rate of 12% compounded monthly (1% per month).

Required:

Note: Round answers to two decimal places.

1. Prepare the cash flow diagram for this sale.
2. Calculate the amount of revenue Bailey's should record on October 31, 2014.
3. Prepare the journal entry to record the sale on October 31. Assume that Bailey's records cost of goods sold at the time of the sale (perpetual inventory accounting).
4. Determine how much interest income Bailey's will record from October 31, 2014, through December 31, 2014.
5. Determine how much Bailey's 2014 income before taxes increased by this sale.

EXHIBIT A3.7

Future Value of a Single Amount

$FV = 1(1 + i)^n$

n/i	1%	2%	3%	4%	5%	6%	7%	8%	9%	10%	12%	14%	16%	18%	20%	25%	30%
1	1.01000	1.02000	1.03000	1.04000	1.05000	1.06000	1.07000	1.08000	1.09000	1.10000	1.12000	1.14000	1.16000	1.18000	1.20000	1.25000	1.30000
2	1.02010	1.04040	1.06090	1.08160	1.10250	1.12360	1.14490	1.16640	1.18810	1.21000	1.25440	1.29960	1.34560	1.39240	1.44000	1.56250	1.69000
3	1.03030	1.06121	1.09273	1.12486	1.15763	1.19102	1.22504	1.25971	1.29503	1.33100	1.40493	1.48154	1.56090	1.64303	1.72800	1.95313	2.19700
4	1.04060	1.08243	1.12551	1.16986	1.21551	1.26248	1.31080	1.36049	1.41158	1.46410	1.57352	1.68896	1.81064	1.93878	2.07360	2.44141	2.85610
5	1.05101	1.10408	1.15927	1.21665	1.27628	1.33823	1.40255	1.46933	1.53862	1.61051	1.76234	1.92541	2.10034	2.28776	2.48832	3.05176	3.71293
6	1.06152	1.12616	1.19405	1.26532	1.34010	1.41852	1.50073	1.58687	1.67710	1.77156	1.97382	2.19497	2.43640	2.69955	2.98598	3.81470	4.82681
7	1.07214	1.14869	1.22987	1.31593	1.40710	1.50363	1.60578	1.71382	1.82804	1.94872	2.21068	2.50227	2.82622	3.18547	3.58318	4.76837	6.27485
8	1.08286	1.17166	1.26677	1.36857	1.47746	1.59385	1.71819	1.85093	1.99256	2.14359	2.47596	2.85259	3.27841	3.75886	4.29982	5.96046	8.15731
9	1.09369	1.19509	1.30477	1.42331	1.55133	1.68948	1.83846	1.99900	2.17189	2.35795	2.77308	3.25195	3.80296	4.43545	5.15978	7.45058	10.60450
10	1.10462	1.21899	1.34392	1.48024	1.62889	1.79085	1.96715	2.15892	2.36736	2.59374	3.10585	3.70722	4.41144	5.23384	6.19174	9.31323	13.78585
11	1.11567	1.24337	1.38423	1.53945	1.71034	1.89830	2.10485	2.33164	2.58043	2.85312	3.47855	4.22623	5.11726	6.17593	7.43008	11.64153	17.92160
12	1.12683	1.26824	1.42576	1.60103	1.79586	2.01220	2.25219	2.51817	2.81266	3.13843	3.89598	4.81790	5.93603	7.28759	8.91610	14.55192	23.29809
13	1.13809	1.29361	1.46853	1.66507	1.88565	2.13293	2.40985	2.71962	3.06580	3.45227	4.36349	5.49241	6.88579	8.59936	10.69932	18.18989	30.28751
14	1.14947	1.31948	1.51259	1.73168	1.97993	2.26090	2.57853	2.93719	3.34173	3.79750	4.88711	6.26135	7.98752	10.14724	12.83918	22.73737	39.37376
15	1.16097	1.34587	1.55797	1.80094	2.07893	2.39656	2.75903	3.17217	3.64248	4.17725	5.47357	7.13794	9.26552	11.97375	15.40702	28.42171	51.18589
16	1.17258	1.37279	1.60471	1.87298	2.18287	2.54035	2.95216	3.42594	3.97031	4.59497	6.13039	8.13725	10.74800	14.12902	18.48843	35.52714	66.54166
17	1.18430	1.40024	1.65285	1.94790	2.29202	2.69277	3.15882	3.70002	4.32763	5.05447	6.86604	9.27646	12.46768	16.67225	22.18611	44.40892	86.50416
18	1.19615	1.42825	1.70243	2.02582	2.40662	2.85434	3.37993	3.99602	4.71712	5.55992	7.68997	10.57517	14.46251	19.67325	26.62333	55.51115	112.45541
19	1.20811	1.45681	1.75351	2.10685	2.52695	3.02560	3.61653	4.31570	5.14166	6.11591	8.61276	12.05569	16.77652	23.21444	31.94800	69.38894	146.19203
20	1.22019	1.48595	1.80611	2.19112	2.65330	3.20714	3.86968	4.66096	5.60441	6.72750	9.64629	13.74349	19.46076	27.39303	38.33760	86.73617	190.04946
21	1.23239	1.51567	1.86029	2.27877	2.78596	3.39956	4.14056	5.03383	6.10881	7.40025	10.80385	15.66758	22.57448	32.32378	46.00512	108.42022	247.06453
22	1.24472	1.54598	1.91610	2.36992	2.92526	3.60354	4.43040	5.43654	6.65860	8.14027	12.10031	17.86104	26.18640	38.14206	55.20614	135.52527	321.18389
23	1.25716	1.57690	1.97359	2.46472	3.07152	3.81975	4.74053	5.87146	7.25787	8.95430	13.55235	20.36158	30.37622	45.00763	66.24737	169.40659	417.53905
24	1.26973	1.60844	2.03279	2.56330	3.22510	4.04893	5.07237	6.34118	7.91108	9.84973	15.17863	23.21221	35.23642	53.10901	79.49685	211.75824	542.80077
25	1.28243	1.64061	2.09378	2.66584	3.38635	4.29187	5.42743	6.84848	8.62308	10.83471	17.00006	26.46192	40.87424	62.66863	95.39622	264.69780	705.64100
26	1.29526	1.67342	2.15659	2.77247	3.55567	4.54938	5.80735	7.39635	9.39916	11.91818	19.04007	30.16658	47.41412	73.94898	114.47546	330.87225	917.33330
27	1.30821	1.70689	2.22129	2.88337	3.73346	4.82235	6.21387	7.98806	10.24508	13.10999	21.32488	34.38991	55.00038	87.25980	137.37055	413.59031	1192.53329
28	1.32129	1.74102	2.28793	2.99870	3.92013	5.11169	6.64884	8.62711	11.16714	14.42099	23.88387	39.20449	63.80044	102.96656	164.84466	516.98788	1550.29328
29	1.33450	1.77584	2.35657	3.11865	4.11614	5.41839	7.11426	9.31727	12.17218	15.86309	26.74993	44.69312	74.00851	121.50054	197.81359	646.23485	2015.38126
30	1.34785	1.81136	2.42726	3.24340	4.32194	5.74349	7.61226	10.06266	13.26768	17.44940	29.95992	50.95016	85.84988	143.37064	237.37631	807.79357	2619.99564

EXHIBIT A3.8

Present Value of a Single Amount

$$PV = \frac{1}{(1+i)^n}$$

n/i	1%	2%	3%	4%	5%	6%	7%	8%	9%	10%	12%	14%	16%	18%	20%	25%	30%
1	0.99010	0.98039	0.97087	0.96154	0.95238	0.94340	0.93458	0.92593	0.91743	0.90909	0.89286	0.87719	0.86207	0.84746	0.83333	0.80000	0.76923
2	0.98030	0.96117	0.94260	0.92456	0.90703	0.89000	0.87344	0.85734	0.84168	0.82645	0.79719	0.76947	0.74316	0.71818	0.69444	0.64000	0.59172
3	0.97059	0.94232	0.91514	0.88900	0.86384	0.83962	0.81630	0.79383	0.77218	0.75131	0.71178	0.67497	0.64066	0.60863	0.57870	0.51200	0.45517
4	0.96098	0.92385	0.88849	0.85480	0.82270	0.79209	0.76290	0.73503	0.70843	0.68301	0.63552	0.59208	0.55229	0.51579	0.48225	0.40960	0.35013
5	0.95147	0.90573	0.86261	0.82193	0.78353	0.74726	0.71299	0.68058	0.64993	0.62092	0.56743	0.51937	0.47611	0.43711	0.40188	0.32768	0.26933
6	0.94205	0.88797	0.83748	0.79031	0.74622	0.70496	0.66634	0.63017	0.59627	0.56447	0.50663	0.45559	0.41044	0.37043	0.33490	0.26214	0.20718
7	0.93272	0.87056	0.81309	0.75992	0.71068	0.66506	0.62275	0.58349	0.54703	0.51316	0.45235	0.39964	0.35383	0.31393	0.27908	0.20972	0.15937
8	0.92348	0.85349	0.78941	0.73069	0.67684	0.62741	0.58201	0.54027	0.50187	0.46651	0.40388	0.35056	0.30503	0.26604	0.23257	0.16777	0.12259
9	0.91434	0.83676	0.76642	0.70259	0.64461	0.59190	0.54393	0.50025	0.46043	0.42410	0.36061	0.30751	0.26295	0.22546	0.19381	0.13422	0.09430
10	0.90529	0.82035	0.74409	0.67556	0.61391	0.55839	0.50835	0.46319	0.42241	0.38554	0.32197	0.26974	0.22668	0.19106	0.16151	0.10737	0.07254
11	0.89632	0.80426	0.72242	0.64958	0.58468	0.52679	0.47509	0.42888	0.38753	0.35049	0.28748	0.23662	0.19542	0.16192	0.13459	0.08590	0.05580
12	0.88745	0.78849	0.70138	0.62460	0.55684	0.49697	0.44401	0.39711	0.35553	0.31863	0.25668	0.20756	0.16846	0.13722	0.11216	0.06872	0.04292
13	0.87866	0.77303	0.68095	0.60057	0.53032	0.46884	0.41496	0.36770	0.32618	0.28966	0.22917	0.18207	0.14523	0.11629	0.09346	0.05498	0.03302
14	0.86996	0.75788	0.66112	0.57748	0.50507	0.44230	0.38782	0.34046	0.29925	0.26333	0.20462	0.15971	0.12520	0.09855	0.07789	0.04398	0.02540
15	0.86135	0.74301	0.64186	0.55526	0.48102	0.41727	0.36245	0.31524	0.27454	0.23939	0.18270	0.14010	0.10793	0.08352	0.06491	0.03518	0.01954
16	0.85282	0.72845	0.62317	0.53391	0.45811	0.39365	0.33873	0.29189	0.25187	0.21763	0.16312	0.12289	0.09304	0.07078	0.05409	0.02815	0.01503
17	0.84438	0.71416	0.60502	0.51337	0.43630	0.37136	0.31657	0.27027	0.23107	0.19784	0.14564	0.10780	0.08021	0.05998	0.04507	0.02252	0.01156
18	0.83602	0.70016	0.58739	0.49363	0.41552	0.35034	0.29586	0.25025	0.21199	0.17986	0.13004	0.09456	0.06914	0.05083	0.03756	0.01801	0.00889
19	0.82774	0.68643	0.57029	0.47464	0.39573	0.33051	0.27651	0.23171	0.19449	0.16351	0.11611	0.08295	0.05961	0.04308	0.03130	0.01441	0.00684
20	0.81954	0.67297	0.55368	0.45639	0.37689	0.31180	0.25842	0.21455	0.17843	0.14864	0.10367	0.07276	0.05139	0.03651	0.02608	0.01153	0.00526
21	0.81143	0.65978	0.53755	0.43883	0.35894	0.29416	0.24151	0.19866	0.16370	0.13513	0.09256	0.06383	0.04430.	0.03094	0.02174	0.00922	0.00405
22	0.80340	0.64684	0.52189	0.42196	0.34185	0.27751	0.22571	0.18394	0.15018	0.12285	0.08264	0.05599	0.03819	0.02622	0.01811	0.00738	0.00311
23	0.79544	0.63416	0.50669	0.40573	0.32557	0.26180	0.21095	0.17032	0.13778	0.11168	0.07379	0.04911	0.03292	0.02222	0.01509	0.00590	0.00239
24	0.78757	0.62172	0.49193	0.39012	0.31007	0.24698	0.19715	0.15770	0.12640	0.10153	0.06588	0.04308	0.02838	0.01883	0.01258	0.00472	0.00184
25	0.77977	0.60953	0.47761	0.37512	0.29530	0.23300	0.18425	0.14602	0.11597	0.09230	0.05882	0.03779	0.02447	0.01596	0.01048	0.00378	0.00142
26	0.77205	0.59758	0.46369	0.36069	0.28124	0.21981	0.17220	0.13520	0.10639	0.08391	0.05252	0.03315	0.02109	0.01352	0.00874	0.00302	0.00109
27	0.76440	0.58586	0.45019	0.34682	0.26785	0.20737	0.16093	0.12519	0.09761	0.07628	0.04689	0.02908	0.01818	0.01146	0.00728	0.00242	0.00084
28	0.75684	0.57437	0.43708	0.33348	0.25509	0.19563	0.15040	0.11591	0.08955	0.06934	0.04187	0.02551	0.01567	0.00971	0.00607	0.00193	0.00065
29	0.74934	0.56311	0.42435	0.32065	0.24295	0.18456	0.14056	0.10733	0.08215	0.06304	0.03738	0.02237	0.01351	0.00823	0.00506	0.00155	0.00050
30	0.74192	0.55207	0.41199	0.30832	0.23138	0.17411	0.13137	0.09938	0.07537	0.05731	0.03338	0.01963	0.01165	0.00697	0.00421	0.00124	0.00038

EXHIBIT A3.9

Future Value of an Annuity

$$FVA = \frac{(1+i)^n - 1}{i}$$

n/i	1%	2%	3%	4%	5%	6%	7%	8%	9%	10%	12%	14%	16%	18%	20%	25%	30%
1	1.00000	1.00000	1.00000	1.00000	1.00000	1.00000	1.00000	1.00000	1.00000	1.00000	1.00000	1.00000	1.00000	1.00000	1.00000	1.00000	1.00000
2	2.01000	2.02000	2.03000	2.04000	2.05000	2.06000	2.07000	2.08000	2.09000	2.10000	2.12000	2.14000	2.16000	2.18000	2.20000	2.25000	2.30000
3	3.03010	3.06040	3.09090	3.12160	3.15250	3.18360	3.21490	3.24640	3.27810	3.31000	3.37440	3.43960	3.50560	3.57240	3.64000	3.81250	3.99000
4	4.06040	4.12161	4.18363	4.24646	4.31013	4.37462	4.43994	4.50611	4.57313	4.64100	4.77933	4.92114	5.06650	5.21543	5.36800	5.76563	6.18700
5	5.10101	5.20404	5.30914	5.41632	5.52563	5.63709	5.75074	5.86660	5.98471	6.10510	6.35285	6.61010	6.87714	7.15421	7.44160	8.20703	9.04310
6	6.15202	6.30812	6.46841	6.63298	6.80191	6.97532	7.15329	7.33593	7.52333	7.71561	8.11519	8.53552	8.97748	9.44197	9.92992	11.25879	12.75603
7	7.21354	7.43428	7.66246	7.89829	8.14201	8.39384	8.65402	8.92280	9.20043	9.48717	10.08901	10.73049	11.41387	12.14152	12.91590	15.07349	17.58284
8	8.28567	8.58297	8.89234	9.21423	9.54911	9.89747	10.25980	10.63663	11.02847	11.43589	12.29969	13.23276	14.24009	15.32700	16.49908	19.84186	23.85769
9	9.36853	9.75463	10.15911	10.58280	11.02656	11.49132	11.97799	12.48756	13.02104	13.57948	14.77566	16.08535	17.51851	19.08585	20.79890	25.80232	32.01500
10	10.46221	10.94972	11.46388	12.00611	12.57789	13.18079	13.81645	14.48656	15.19293	15.93742	17.54874	19.33730	21.32147	23.52131	25.95868	33.25290	42.61950
11	11.56683	12.16872	12.80780	13.48635	14.20679	14.97164	15.78360	16.64549	17.56029	18.53117	20.65458	23.04452	25.73290	28.75514	32.15042	42.56613	56.40535
12	12.68250	13.41209	14.19203	15.02581	15.91713	16.86994	17.88845	18.97713	20.14072	21.38428	24.13313	27.27075	30.85017	34.93107	39.58050	54.20766	74.32695
13	13.80933	14.68033	15.61779	16.62684	17.71298	18.88214	20.14064	21.49530	22.95338	24.52271	28.02911	32.08865	36.78620	42.21866	48.49660	68.75958	97.62504
14	14.94742	15.97394	17.08632	18.29191	19.59863	21.01507	22.55049	24.21492	26.01919	27.97498	32.39260	37.58107	43.67199	50.81802	59.19592	86.94947	127.91255
15	16.09690	17.29342	18.59891	20.02359	21.57856	23.27597	25.12902	27.15211	29.36092	31.77248	37.27971	43.84241	51.65951	60.96527	72.03511	109.68684	167.28631
16	17.25786	18.63929	20.15688	21.82453	23.65749	25.67253	27.88805	30.32428	33.00340	35.94973	42.75328	50.98035	60.92503	72.93901	87.44213	138.10855	218.47220
17	18.43044	20.01207	21.76159	23.69751	25.84037	28.21288	30.84022	33.75023	36.97370	40.54470	48.88367	59.11760	71.67303	87.06804	105.93056	173.63568	285.01386
18	19.61475	21.41231	23.41444	25.64541	28.13238	30.90565	33.99903	37.45024	41.30134	45.59917	55.74971	68.39407	84.14072	103.74028	128.11667	218.04460	371.51802
19	20.81090	22.84056	25.11687	27.67123	30.53900	33.75999	37.37896	41.44626	46.01846	51.15909	63.43968	78.96923	98.60323	123.41353	154.74000	273.55576	483.97343
20	22.01900	24.29737	26.87037	29.77808	33.06595	36.78559	40.99549	45.76196	51.16012	57.27500	72.05244	91.02493	115.37975	146.62797	186.68800	342.94470	630.16546
21	23.23919	25.78332	28.67649	31.96920	35.71925	39.99273	44.86518	50.42292	56.76453	64.00250	81.69874	104.76842	134.84051	174.02100	225.02560	429.68087	820.21510
22	24.47159	27.29898	30.53678	34.24797	38.50521	43.39229	49.00574	55.45676	62.87334	71.40275	92.50258	120.43600	157.41499	206.34479	271.03072	538.10109	1067.27963
23	25.71630	28.84496	32.45288	36.61789	41.43048	46.99583	53.43614	60.89330	69.53194	79.54302	104.60289	138.29704	183.60138	244.48685	326.23686	673.62636	1388.46351
24	26.97346	30.42186	34.42647	39.08260	44.50200	50.81558	58.17667	66.76476	76.78981	88.49733	118.15524	158.65862	213.97761	289.49448	392.48424	843.03295	1806.00257
25	28.24320	32.03030	36.45926	41.64591	47.72710	54.86451	63.24904	73.10594	84.70090	98.34706	133.33387	181.87083	249.21402	342.60349	471.98108	1054.79118	2348.80334
26	29.52563	33.67091	38.55304	44.31174	51.11345	59.15638	68.67647	79.95442	93.32398	109.18177	150.33393	208.33274	290.08827	405.27211	567.37730	1319.48898	3054.44434
27	30.82089	35.34432	40.70963	47.08421	54.66913	63.70577	74.48382	87.35077	102.72313	121.09994	169.37401	238.49933	337.50239	479.22109	681.85276	1650.36123	3971.77764
28	32.12910	37.05121	42.93092	49.96758	58.40258	68.52811	80.69769	95.33883	112.96822	134.20994	190.69889	272.88923	392.50277	566.48089	819.22331	2063.95153	5164.31093
29	33.45039	38.79223	45.21885	52.96629	62.32271	73.63980	87.34653	103.96594	124.13536	148.63093	214.58275	312.09373	456.30322	669.44745	984.06797	2580.93941	6714.60421
30	34.78489	40.56808	47.57542	56.08494	66.43885	79.05819	94.46079	113.28321	136.30754	164.49402	241.33268	356.78685	530.31173	790.94799	1181.88157	3227.17427	8729.98548

EXHIBIT A3.10

Present Value of an Annuity

$$PVA = \frac{1 - \frac{1}{(1+i)^n}}{i}$$

n/i	1%	2%	3%	4%	5%	6%	7%	8%	9%	10%	12%	14%	16%	18%	20%	25%	30%
1	0.99010	0.98039	0.97087	0.96154	0.95238	0.94340	0.93458	0.92593	0.91743	0.90909	0.89286	0.87719	0.86207	0.84746	0.83333	0.80000	0.76923
2	1.97040	1.94156	1.91347	1.88609	1.85941	1.83339	1.80802	1.78326	1.75911	1.73554	1.69005	1.64666	1.60523	1.56564	1.52778	1.44000	1.36095
3	2.94099	2.88388	2.82861	2.77509	2.72325	2.67301	2.62432	2.57710	2.53129	2.48685	2.40183	2.32163	2.24589	2.17427	2.10648	1.95200	1.81611
4	3.90197	3.80773	3.71710	3.62990	3.54595	3.46511	3.38721	3.31213	3.23972	3.16987	3.03735	2.91371	2.79818	2.69006	2.58873	2.36160	2.16624
5	4.85343	4.71346	4.57971	4.45182	4.32948	4.21236	4.10020	3.99271	3.88965	3.79079	3.60478	3.43308	3.27429	3.12717	2.99061	2.68928	2.43557
6	5.79548	5.60143	5.41719	5.24214	5.07569	4.91732	4.76654	4.62288	4.48592	4.35526	4.11141	3.88867	3.68474	3.49760	3.32551	2.95142	2.64275
7	6.72819	6.47199	6.23028	6.00205	5.78637	5.58238	5.38929	5.20637	5.03295	4.86842	4.56376	4.28830	4.03857	3.81153	3.60459	3.16114	2.80211
8	7.65168	7.32548	7.01969	6.73274	6.46321	6.20979	5.97130	5.74664	5.53482	5.33493	4.96764	4.63886	4.34359	4.07757	3.83716	3.32891	2.92470
9	8.56602	8.16224	7.78611	7.43533	7.10782	6.80169	6.51523	6.24689	5.99525	5.75902	5.32825	4.94637	4.60654	4.30302	4.03097	3.46313	3.01900
10	9.47130	8.98259	8.53020	8.11090	7.72173	7.36009	7.02358	6.71008	6.41766	6.14457	5.65022	5.21612	4.83323	4.49409	4.19247	3.57050	3.09154
11	10.36763	9.78685	9.25262	8.76048	8.30641	7.88687	7.49867	7.13896	6.80519	6.49506	5.93770	5.45273	5.02864	4.65601	4.32706	3.65640	3.14734
12	11.25508	10.57534	9.95400	9.38507	8.86325	8.38384	7.94269	7.53608	7.16073	6.81369	6.19437	5.66029	5.19711	4.79322	4.43922	3.72512	3.19026
13	12.13374	11.34837	10.63496	9.98565	9.39357	8.85268	8.35765	7.90378	7.48690	7.10336	6.42355	5.84236	5.34233	4.90951	4.53268	3.78010	3.22328
14	13.00370	12.10625	11.29607	10.56312	9.89864	9.29498	8.74547	8.24424	7.78615	7.36669	6.62817	6.00207	5.46753	5.00806	4.61057	3.82408	3.24867
15	13.86505	12.84926	11.93794	11.11839	10.37966	9.71225	9.10791	8.55948	8.06069	7.60608	6.81086	6.14217	5.57546	5.09158	4.67547	3.85926	3.26821
16	14.71787	13.57771	12.56110	11.65230	10.83777	10.10590	9.44665	8.85137	8.31256	7.82371	6.97399	6.26506	5.66850	5.16235	4.72956	3.88741	3.28324
17	15.56225	14.29187	13.16612	12.16567	11.27407	10.47726	9.76322	9.12164	8.54363	8.02155	7.11963	6.37286	5.74870	5.22233	4.77463	3.90993	3.29480
18	16.39827	14.99203	13.75351	12.65930	11.68959	10.82760	10.05909	9.37189	8.75563	8.20141	7.24967	6.46742	5.81785	5.27316	4.81219	3.92794	3.30369
19	17.22601	15.67846	14.32380	13.13394	12.08532	11.15812	10.33560	9.60360	8.95011	8.36492	7.36578	6.55037	5.87746	5.31624	4.84350	3.94235	3.31053
20	18.04555	16.35143	14.87747	13.59033	12.46221	11.46992	10.59401	9.81815	9.12855	8.51356	7.46944	6.62313	5.92884	5.35275	4.86958	3.95388	3.31579
21	18.85698	17.01121	15.41502	14.02916	12.82115	11.76408	10.83553	10.01680	9.29224	8.64869	7.56200	6.68696	5.97314	5.38368	4.89132	3.96311	3.31984
22	19.66038	17.65805	15.93692	14.45112	13.16300	12.04158	11.06124	10.20074	9.44243	8.77154	7.64465	6.74294	6.01133	5.40990	4.90943	3.97049	3.32296
23	20.45582	18.29220	16.44361	14.85684	13.48857	12.30338	11.27219	10.37106	9.58021	8.88322	7.71843	6.79206	6.04425	5.43212	4.92453	3.97639	3.32535
24	21.24339	18.91393	16.93554	15.24696	13.79864	12.55036	11.46933	10.52876	9.70661	8.98474	7.78432	6.83514	6.07263	5.45095	4.93710	3.98111	3.32719
25	22.02316	19.52346	17.41315	15.62208	14.09394	12.78336	11.65358	10.67478	9.82258	9.07704	7.84314	6.87293	6.09709	5.46691	4.94759	3.98489	3.32861
26	22.79520	20.12104	17.87684	15.98277	14.37519	13.00317	11.82578	10.80998	9.92897	9.16095	7.89566	6.90608	6.11818	5.48043	4.95632	3.98791	3.32970
27	23.55961	20.70690	18.32703	16.32959	14.64303	13.21053	11.98671	10.93516	10.02658	9.23722	7.94255	6.93515	6.13636	5.49189	4.96360	3.99033	3.33054
28	24.31644	21.28127	18.76411	16.66306	14.89813	13.40616	12.13711	11.05108	10.11613	9.30657	7.98442	6.96066	6.15204	5.50160	4.96967	3.99226	3.33118
29	25.06579	21.84438	19.18845	16.98371	15.14107	13.59072	12.27767	11.15841	10.19828	9.36961	8.02181	6.98304	6.16555	5.50983	4.97472	3.99381	3.33168
30	25.80771	22.39646	19.60044	17.29203	15.37245	13.76483	12.40904	11.25778	10.27365	9.42691	8.05518	7.00266	6.17720	5.51681	4.97894	3.99505	3.33206

GLOSSARY

A

account a record of increases and decreases in each of the basic elements of the financial statements (each of the company's asset, liability, stockholders' equity, revenue, expense, gain, and loss items).

account payable an obligation that arises when a business purchases goods or services on credit.

account receivable money due from another business or individual as payment for services performed or goods delivered. Payment is typically due in 30 to 60 days and does not involve a formal note between the parties nor does it include interest.

accounting the process of identifying, measuring, recording, and communicating financial information about a company's activities so decision makers can make informed decisions.

accounting cycle the procedures that a company uses to transform the results of its business activities into financial statements.

accounting system the methods and records used to identify, measure, record, and communicate financial information about a business.

accounts receivable turnover ratio net credit sales or net sales divided by average accounts receivable.

accrual accounting see *accrual-basis accounting*

accrual-basis accounting a method of accounting in which revenues are generally recorded when earned (rather than when cash is received) and expenses are matched to the periods in which they help produce revenues (rather than when cash is paid).

accrued expenses previously unrecorded expenses that have been incurred, but not yet paid in cash.

accrued liabilities liabilities that usually represent the completed portion of activities that are in process at the end of the period.

accrued revenues previously unrecorded revenues that have been earned but for which no cash has yet been received.

accumulated depreciation the total amount of depreciation expense that has been recorded for an asset since the asset was acquired. It is reported on the balance sheet as a contra-asset.

accumulated other comprehensive income the total of comprehensive income for all periods and conveys the changes in assets and liabilities resulting from all transactions with nonowners.

additional paid-in capital the amount received in excess of the par value.

adjusted trial balance an updated trial balance that reflects the changes to account balances as the result of adjusting entries.

adjusting entries journal entries that are made at the end of an accounting period to record the completed portion of partially completed transactions.

aging method a method in which bad debt expense is estimated indirectly by determining the ending balance desired in the allowance for doubtful accounts and then computing the necessary adjusting entry to achieve this balance; the amount of this adjusting entry is also the amount of bad debt expense.

allowance for doubtful accounts a contra-asset account that is established to "store" the estimate of uncollectible accounts until specific accounts are identified as uncollectible.

amortization the process whereby companies systematically allocate the cost of their intangible operating assets as an expense among the accounting periods in which the asset is used and the benefits are received.

annuity a series of equal cash flows at regular intervals.

articles of incorporation a document that authorizes the creation of the corporation, setting forth its name, purpose, and the names of the incorporators.

asset efficiency ratios (operating ratios) ratios that measure how efficiently a company uses its assets.

asset turnover ratio a ratio that measures the efficiency with which a corporation's assets (usually accounts receivable or inventory) are used to produce sales revenues.

assets economic resources representing expected future economic benefits controlled by the business (e.g., cash, accounts receivable, inventory, land, buildings, equipment, and intangible assets).

audit report the auditor's opinion as to whether the company's financial statements are fairly stated in accordance with generally accepted accounting principles (GAAP).

authorized shares the maximum number of shares a company may issue in each class of stock.

average age of fixed assets a rough estimate of the age of fixed assets that can be computed by dividing accumulated depreciation by depreciation expense.

average cost method an inventory costing method that allocates the cost of goods available for sale between ending inventory and cost of goods sold based on a weighted average cost per unit.

average days to sell inventory an estimate of the number of days it takes a company to sell its inventory. It is found by dividing 365 days by the inventory turnover ratio.

B

bad debt expense the expense that results from receivables that are not paid.

balance sheet a financial statement that reports the resources (assets) owned by a company and the claims against those resources (liabilities and stockholders' equity) at a specific point in time.

bank reconciliation the process of reconciling any differences between a company's accounting records and the bank's accounting records.

bond a type of note that requires the issuing entity to pay the face value of the bond to the holder when it matures and, usually, periodic interest at a specified rate.

book value (carrying value) the value of an asset or a liability as it appears on the balance sheet. Book value is calculated as the cost of the asset or liability minus the balance in its related contra-account (e.g., cost of equipment less accumulated depreciation; notes payable less discount on notes payable).

business process risks threats to the internal processes of a company.

C

callable bonds bonds that give the borrower the right to pay off (or call) the bonds prior to their due date. The borrower typically "calls" debt when the interest rate being paid is much higher than the current market conditions.

capital a company's assets less its liabilities. Capital is also known as stockholders' equity.

capital expenditures expenditures to acquire long-term assets or extend the life, expand the productive capacity, increase the efficiency, or improve the quality of existing long-term assets.

capital lease a noncancelable agreement that is in substance a purchase of the leased asset.

capital stock the portion of a corporation's stockholders' equity contributed by investors (owners) in exchange for shares of stock.

cash-basis accounting a method of accounting in which revenue is recorded when cash is received, regardless of when it is actually earned. Similarly, an expense is recorded when cash is paid, regardless of when it is actually incurred. Cash-basis accounting does not tie recognition of revenues and expenses to the actual business activity but rather to the exchange of cash.

cash equivalents short-term, highly liquid investments that are readily convertible to cash and have original maturities of three months or less.

cash flow adequacy ratio the cash flow adequacy ratio provides a measure of the company's ability to meet its debt obligations and is calculated as: Cash Flow Adequacy = Free Cash Flow ÷ Average Amount of Debt Maturing over the Next Five Years.

cash flows from financing activities any cash flow related to obtaining resources from creditors or owners, which includes the issuance and repayment of debt, common and preferred stock transactions, and the payment of dividends.

cash flows from investing activities the cash inflows and outflows that relate to acquiring and disposing of operating assets, acquiring and selling investments (current and long-term), and lending money and collecting loans.

cash flows from operating activities any cash flows directly related to earning income, including cash sales and collections of accounts receivable as well as cash payments for goods, services, salaries, and interest.

cash over and short an account that records the discrepancies between deposited amounts of actual cash received and the total of the cash register tape.

cash ratio a short-term liquidity ratio that is calculated as: (Cash + Short-Term Investments) ÷ Current Liabilities.

chart of accounts the list of accounts used by a company.

common-size statements financial statements that express each financial statement line item in percentage terms.

common stock the basic ownership interest in a corporation. Owners of common stock have the right to vote in the election of the board of directors, share in the profits and dividends of the company, keep the same percentage of ownership if new stock is issued (preemptive right), and share in the assets in liquidation in proportion to their holdings.

comparability one of the four qualitative characteristics that useful information should possess. Information has comparability if it allows comparisons to be made between companies.

compound interest a method of calculating the time value of money in which interest is earned on the previous periods' interest.

conservatism principle a principle which states that when more than one equally acceptable accounting method exists, the method that results in the lower assets and revenues or higher liabilities and expenses should be selected.

consignment an arrangement where goods owned by one party are held and offered for sale by another.

consistency one of the four qualitative characteristics that useful information should possess. Consistency refers to the application of the same accounting principles by a single company over time.

contingent liability an obligation whose amount or timing is uncertain and depends on future events. For example, a firm may be contingently liable for damages under a lawsuit that has yet to be decided by the courts.

continuity (or going concern) assumption one of the four basic assumptions that underlie accounting that assumes a company will continue to operate long enough to carry out its existing commitments.

contra accounts accounts that have a balance that is opposite of the balance in the related account.

contract rate see *interest rate*

control activities the policies and procedures that top management establishes to help insure that its objectives are met.

control environment the collection of environmental factors that influence the effectiveness of control procedures such as the philosophy and operating style of management, the personnel policies and practices of the business, and the overall integrity, attitude, awareness, and actions of everyone in the business concerning the importance of control.

convertible bonds bonds that allow the bondholder to convert the bond into another security—typically common stock.

copyright an intangible asset that grants the holder the right to publish, sell, or control a literary or artistic work. The legal life is the life of the author plus 70 years.

corporate charter see *articles of incorporation*

corporation a company chartered by the state to conduct business as an "artificial person" and owned by one or more stockholders.

cost any expenditure necessary to acquire the asset and to prepare the asset for use.

cost constraint qualitative characteristic of useful information that states that the benefit received from accounting information should be greater than the cost of providing that information.

cost of goods available for sale the sum of the cost of beginning inventory and the cost of purchases.

cost of goods sold an expense that represents the outflow of resources caused by the sale of inventory. This is often computed as the cost of goods available for sale less the cost of ending inventory.

coupon rate see *interest rate*

credit the right side of a T-account; alternatively, credit may refer to the act of entering an amount on the right side of an account.

credit cards a card that authorizes the holder to make purchases up to some limit from specified retailers. Credits cards are a special form of factoring in which the issuer of the credit card pays the seller the amount of each sale less a service charge and then collects the full amount of the sale from the buyer at some later date.

creditor the person to whom money is owed.

cross sectional analysis a type of analysis that compares one corporation to another corporation and to industry averages.

cumulative dividend preference a provision that requires the eventual payment of all preferred dividends—both dividends in arrears and current dividends—to preferred stockholders before any dividends are paid to common stockholders.

current assets cash and other assets that are reasonably expected to be converted into cash within one year or one operating cycle, whichever is longer.

current dividend preference a provision that requires that current dividends must be paid to preferred stockholders before any dividends are paid to common stockholders.

current liabilities obligations that require a firm to pay cash or another current asset, create a new current liability, or provide goods or services within one year or one operating cycle, whichever is longer.

current ratio a measure of liquidity that is computed as: Current Assets ÷ Current Liabilities.

D

date of record the date on which a stockholder must own one or more shares of stock in order to receive the dividend.

debenture bonds another name for unsecured bonds.

debit the left side of a T-account; alternatively, debit may refer to the act of entering an amount on the left side of an account.

debit card a card that authorizes a bank to make an immediate electronic withdrawal (debit) from the holder's bank account and a corresponding deposit to another party's account.

debt management ratios a type of ratio that provides information on two aspects of debt: (1) the relative mix of debt and equity financing (often referred to as its capital structure) and (2) the corporation's ability to meet its debt obligations through operations because interest and principal payments must be made as scheduled, or a company can be declared bankrupt.

debt to equity ratio a measure of the proportion of capital provided by creditors relative to that provided by stockholders. This ratio is calculated as: Total Liabilities ÷ Total Equity.

debt to total assets ratio a measure of the proportion of capital provided by creditors. This ratio is calculated as: Total Liabilities ÷ Total Assets.

declaration date the date on which a corporation announces its intention to pay a dividend on common stock.

declining balance depreciation method an accelerated depreciation method that produces a declining amount of depreciation expense each period by multiplying the declining book value of an asset by a constant depreciation rate. Declining balance depreciation expense for each period of an asset's useful life equals the declining balance rate times the asset's book value (cost less accumulated depreciation) at the beginning of the period.

deferred (or prepaid) expenses asset arising from the payment of cash which has not been used or consumed by the end of the period.

deferred (or unearned) revenues liability arising from the receipt of cash for which revenue has not yet been earned.

deficit the accumulated losses over the entire life of a corporation that have not been paid out in dividends.

depletion the process of allocating the cost of a natural resource to each period in which the resource is removed from the earth.

deposit in transit an amount received and recorded by a company, but which has not been recorded by the bank in time to appear on the current bank statement.

depreciable cost depreciable cost is calculated as the cost of the asset less its residual (or salvage) value. This amount will be depreciated (expensed) over the asset's useful life.

depreciation the process whereby companies systematically allocate the cost of their tangible operating assets (other than land) as an expense in each period in which the asset is used.

depreciation expense the amount of depreciation recorded on the income statement.

direct method a method of computing net cash flow from operating activities by adjusting each item on the income statement by the changes in the related current asset or liability accounts. Typical cash flow categories reported are cash collected from customers, cash paid to suppliers, cash paid to employees, cash paid for interest, and cash paid for taxes.

discount when a bond sells at a price below face value, due to the yield being greater than the stated rate of interest.

discount period the reduced payment period associated with purchase discounts.

dividend amounts paid periodically by a corporation to its stockholders as a return of their invested capital. Dividends represent a distribution of retained earnings, not an expense.

dividend payout ratio a ratio that measures the proportion of a corporation's profits that are returned to the stockholders immediately as dividends. It is calculated as: Common Dividends ÷ Net Income.

dividend yield ratio a ratio that measures the rate at which dividends provide a return to stockholders, by comparing dividends with the market price of a share of stock. It is calculated as: Dividends per Common Share ÷ Closing Market Price per Share for the Year.

dividends in arrears cumulative preferred stock dividends remaining unpaid for one or more years are considered to be in arrears.

double-entry accounting a type of accounting in which the two-sided effect that every transaction has on the accounting equation is recorded in the accounting system.

Dupont analysis a type of analysis that recognizes that ROE can be broken down into three important components—net profit margin, asset turnover, and leverage.

E

earned one of two requirements for the recognition of revenue. Revenues are considered "earned" when the earnings process is substantially complete. This typically happens when the goods are delivered or the service is provided.

earnings per share (EPS) a ratio that measures the income available for common stockholders on a per-share basis. EPS is calculated as net income less preferred dividends divided by the average number of common shares outstanding.

economic entity assumption one of the four basic assumptions that underlie accounting that assumes each company is accounted for separately from its owners.

effective interest rate method a method of interest amortization that is based on compound interest calculations.

equity see *stockholders' equity*

events events make up the multitude of activities in which companies engage. External events result from exchange between the company and another outside entity, and internal events result from a company's own actions that do not involve other companies.

exercise (or strike) price the price at which employees can buy stock when their employer grants stock options.

expenses the cost of assets used, or the liabilities created, in the operation of the business.

F

face value the amount of money that a borrower must repay at maturity; also called par value or principal.

factor a method of handling receivables in which the seller receives an immediate cash payment reduced by the factor's fees. The factor, the buyer of the receivables, acquires the right to collect the receivables and the risk of uncollectibility. In a typical factoring arrangement, the sellers of the receivables have no continuing responsibility for their collection.

faithful representation qualitative characteristic of information stipulating it should be complete, neutral, and free from error.

financial accounting accounting and reporting to satisfy the outside demand (primarily investors and creditors) for accounting information.

Financial Accounting Standards Board (FASB) the primary accounting standard-setter in the United States which has been granted this power to set standards by the Securities and Exchange Commission.

financial statements a set of standardized reports in which the detailed transactions of a company's activities are reported and summarized so they can be communicated to decision-makers.

finished goods inventory the account in manufacturing firms that represents the cost of the final product that is available for sale.

first-in, first-out (FIFO) method an inventory costing system in which the earliest (oldest) purchases (the first in) are assumed to be the first sold (the first out) and the more recent purchases are in ending inventory.

fiscal year an accounting period that runs for one year.

fixed asset turnover ratio a ratio that indicates how efficiently a company uses its fixed assets. This ratio is calculated by dividing net sales by average fixed assets.

F.O.B. destination a shipping arrangement in which ownership of inventory passes when the goods are delivered to the buyer.

F.O.B. shipping point a shipping arrangement in which ownership of inventory passes from the seller to the buyer at the shipping point.

footnotes notes to the financial statements that help clarify and expand upon the information presented in those statements.

Form 8-K the "current report" companies must file with the SEC to announce major events that are important to investors and creditors.

Form 10-K the annual report on Form 10-K provides a comprehensive overview of the corporation's business and financial condition and includes *audited* financial statements. Although similarly named, the annual report on Form 10-K is distinct from the "annual report to shareholders," which a corporation must send to its shareholders when it holds an annual meeting to elect directors. For larger filers, the 10-K must be filed within 60 days of their fiscal year end.

Form 10-Q the Form 10-Q includes *unaudited* financial statements and provides a continuing view of the corporation's financial position during the year. The report must be filed for each of the first three fiscal quarters of the corporation's fiscal year. For larger filers, this must be done within 40 days of the end of the quarter.

franchise an exclusive right to conduct a certain type of business in some particular geographic area.

free cash flow the cash flow that a company is able to generate after considering the maintenance or expansion of its assets (capital expenditures) and the payment of dividends. Free cash flow is calculated as Net Cash Flow from Operating Activities – Capital Expenditures – Cash Dividends.

freight-in the transportation costs that are normally paid by the buyer under F.O.B. shipping point terms.

freight-out the transportation costs that the seller is usually responsible for paying under F.O.B. destination shipping terms.

full disclosure a policy that requires any information that would make a difference to financial statement users to be revealed.

fundamental accounting equation Assets = Liabilities + Stockholders' Equity. The left side of the accounting equation shows the assets, or economic resources, of a company. The right side of the accounting equation indicates who has a claim on the company's assets.

G

general ledger a collection of all the individual financial statement accounts that a company uses in its financial statements.

goodwill an unidentifiable intangible asset that arises from factors such as customer satisfaction, quality products, skilled employees, and business location.

gross margin (gross profit) a key performance measure that is computed as sales revenue less cost of goods sold.

gross profit percentage a measurement of the proportion of each sales dollar that is available to pay other expenses and provide profit for owners.

gross profit ratio a measurement of the proportion of each sales dollar that is available to pay other expenses and provide profit for owners; it is computed by dividing gross margin by net sales.

H

historical cost principle a principle that requires the activities of a company to be initially measured at their cost—the exchange price at the time the activity occurs.

horizontal analysis a type of analysis in which each financial statement line item is expressed as a percent of the base year (typically the first year shown).

I

impairment a permanent decline in the future benefits or service potential of an asset.

income from operations gross margin less operating expenses. This represents the results of the core operations of the business.

income statement a financial statement that reports the profitability of a business over a specific period of time.

indirect method a method that computes operating cash flows by adjusting net income for items that do not affect cash flows.

intangible operating assets assets that provide a benefit to a company over a number of years but lack physical substance. Examples of intangible assets include patents, copyrights, trademarks, and goodwill.

interest the excess of the total amount of money paid to a lender over the amount borrowed.

interest amortization the process used to determine the amount of interest to be recorded in each of the periods a liability is outstanding.

interest period the time interval between interest calculations.

interest rate a percentage of the principal that must be paid in order to have use of the principal. It is multiplied by the beginning-of-period balance to yield the amount of interest for the period.

internal control system the policies and procedures established by top management and the board of directors to provide reasonable assurance that the company's objectives are being met in three areas: (1) effectiveness and efficiency of operations, (2) reliability of financial reporting, and (3) compliance with applicable laws and regulations.

International Accounting Standards Board (IASB) an independent, privately funded accounting standard-setting body with the goal of developing a single set of high-quality accounting standards that result in transparent and comparable information reported in general purpose financial statements.

international financial reporting standards (IFRS) a general term that describes an international set of generally accepted accounting standards.

inventory products held for resale that are classified as current assets on the balance sheet.

inventory turnover ratio a ratio that describes how quickly inventory is purchased (or produced) and sold. It is calculated as cost of goods sold divided by average inventory.

involuntary disposal a type of disposal that occurs when assets are lost or destroyed through theft, acts of nature, or by accident.

issued shares the number of shares actually sold to stockholders.

J

journal a chronological record showing the debit and credit effects of transactions on a company.

journal entry a record of a transaction that is made in a journal so that the entire effect of the transaction is contained in one place.

junk bonds unsecured bonds where the risk of the borrower failing to make the payments is relatively high.

L

last-in, first-out (LIFO) method an inventory costing system that allocates the cost of goods available for sale between ending inventory and cost of goods sold based on the assumption that the most recent purchases (the last in) are the first to be sold (the first out).

lease an agreement that enables a company to use property without legally owning it.

lessee one who uses an asset during the term of the lease.

lessor the legal owner of an asset that retains substantially all of the risks and obligations of ownership.

leverage the use of borrowed capital to produce more income than needed to pay the interest on a debt.

liabilities probable future sacrifices of economic benefits; liabilities usually require the payment of cash, the transfer of assets other than cash, or the performance of services.

LIFO reserve the amount that inventory would increase (or decrease) if the company had used FIFO.

liquidating dividends dividends that return paid-in capital to stockholders; liquidating dividends occur when retained earnings has been reduced to zero.

liquidity a company's ability to pay obligations as they become due.

long-term debt obligations that extend beyond one year.

long-term debt to equity ratio a ratio that provides information on the proportion of capital provided by this type of debt and by stockholders. It is calculated as: Long-Term Debt (including current portion) ÷ Total Equity.

long-term debt to total assets ratio a measure of the proportion of capital provided by long-term creditors which is calculated as: Long-Term Debt (including current portion) ÷ Total Assets.

long-term investments investments that the company expects to hold for longer than one year. This includes land or buildings that a company is not currently using in operations, as well as debt and equity securities.

long-term liabilities the obligations of the company that will require payment beyond one year or the operating cycle, whichever is longer.

lower of cost or market (LCM) rule a rule that requires a company to reduce the carrying value of its inventory to its market value if the market value is lower than its cost.

M

management's discussion and analysis (MD&A) a section of the annual report that provides a discussion and explanation of various items reported in the financial statements. Management uses this section to highlight favorable and unfavorable trends and significant risks facing the company.

manufacturers companies that buy and transform raw materials into a finished product which is then sold.

market rate the market rate of interest demanded by creditors.

matching principle a principle that requires an expense to be recorded and reported in the same period as the revenue that it helped generate.

maturity the date on which a borrower agrees to pay the creditor the face (or par) value.

merchandise inventory the inventory held by merchandisers.

merchandisers companies, either retailers or wholesalers, that purchase inventory in a finished condition and hold it for resale without further processing.

monetary unit assumption one of the four basic assumptions that underlie accounting that requires that a company account for and report its financial results in monetary terms (e.g., U.S. dollar, euro, Japanese yen).

mortgage bonds bonds that are secured by real estate.

N

natural resources resources, such as coal deposits, oil reserves, and mineral deposits, that are physically consumed as they are used by a company and that can generally be replaced or restored only by an act of nature.

net income the excess of a company's revenue over its expenses during a period of time.

net loss the excess of a company's expenses over its revenues during a period of time.

net profit margin percentage a measure of the proportion of each sales dollar that is profit, determined by dividing net income by net sales.

net sales revenue computed as gross sales revenue minus sales returns and allowances, as well as sales discounts.

no-par stock stock without a par value.

non-sufficient funds (NSF) check a check that has been returned to the depositor because funds in the issuer's account are not sufficient to pay the check (also called a "bounced" check).

noncash investing and financing activities investing and financing activities that take place without affecting cash. For example, a company may choose to acquire an operating asset (e.g., building) by issuing long-term debt.

nontrade receivables receivables that arise from transactions not involving inventory (e.g., interest receivable or cash advances to employees).

normal balance the type of balance expected of an account based on its effect on the fundamental accounting equation. Assets, expenses, and dividends have normal debit balances while liabilities, stockholders' equity, and revenues have normal credit balances.

note(s) payable a payable that arises when a business borrows money or purchases goods or services from a company that requires a formal agreement or contract.

notes receivable receivables that generally specify an interest rate and a maturity date at which any interest and principal must be repaid.

notes to the financial statements (or footnotes) notes that clarify and expand upon the information presented in the financial statements.

O

operating assets the long-lived assets that are used by the company in the normal course of operations.

operating cash flow ratio a ratio that looks at the ability of operations to generate cash, which recognizes the more general concept that current obligations will be paid through operations (after all, selling inventory and collecting receivables is a big part of operations). This ratio is calculated as Cash Flows from Operating Activities ÷ Current Liabilities.

operating cycle the average time that it takes a company to purchase goods, resell the goods, and collect the cash from customers.

operating lease the most common form of lease in which the lessor (the legal owner of the asset) retains the risks and obligations of ownership, while the lessee uses the asset during the term of the lease.

operating margin percentage a measure of the profitability of a company's operations in relation to its sales that is calculated as Income from Operations ÷ Net Sales.

organizational costs significant costs such as legal fees, stock issue costs, accounting fees, and promotional fees that a company may incur when it is formed.

outstanding check a check that has been issued and recorded by the business but that has not been "cashed" by the recipient of the check.

outstanding shares the number of issued shares actually in the hands of stockholders.

P

par value for stock, it is an arbitrary monetary amount printed on each share of stock that establishes a minimum price for the stock when issued, but does not determine its market value. For debt, par value is the amount of money the borrower agrees to repay at maturity.

participating dividend preference a provision that stockholders of participating preferred shares receive, in addition to the stated dividend, a share of amounts available for distribution as dividends to other classes of stock.

partnership a business owned jointly by two or more individuals.

patent a type of intangible asset that grants the holder the right to manufacture, sell, or use a product. The legal life is 20 years from the date of the grant.

payment date the date on which the dividend will actually be paid.

payroll taxes taxes that businesses must pay based on employee payrolls; these amounts are not withheld from employee pay, rather they are additional amounts that must be paid over and above gross pay.

percentage of credit sales method a method of determining bad debt expense whereby past experience and management's view of how the future may differ from the past are used to estimate the percentage of the current period's credit sales that will eventually become uncollectible.

periodic inventory system an inventory system that records the cost of purchases as they occur (in an account separate from the Inventory account), takes a physical count of inventory at the end of the period, and applies the cost of goods sold model to determine the balances of ending inventory and cost of goods sold. The Inventory account reflects the correct inventory balance only at the end of each accounting period.

permanent accounts accounts of asset, liability, and stockholders' equity items whose balances are carried forward from the current accounting period to future accounting periods.

perpetual inventory system an inventory system in which balances for inventory and cost of goods sold are continually (perpetually) updated with each sale or purchase of inventory. The accounts reflect the correct inventory and cost of goods sold balances throughout the period.

petty cash a fund used to pay for small dollar amounts.

posting the process of transferring information from journalized transactions to the general ledger.

preferred stock a class of stock that generally does not give voting rights, but grants specific guarantees and dividend preferences.

premium when a bond's selling price is above face value.

present value determinations of present amounts based on expected future cash flows.

principal the amount of money borrowed and promised to be repaid (usually with interest).

prior period adjustment the correction of an error made in the financial statements of a prior period. The adjustment is entered as a direct adjustment to retained earnings.

profitability ratios ratios that measure two aspects of a corporation's profits: (1) those elements of operations that contribute to profit and (2) the relationship of profit to total investment and investment by stockholders.

property, plant, and equipment the tangible, long-lived, productive assets used by a company in its operations to produce revenue. This includes land, buildings, machinery, manufacturing equipment, office equipment, and furniture.

purchase allowance a situation in which the purchaser chooses to keep the merchandise if the seller is willing to grant a deduction (allowance) from the purchase price.

purchase discounts price reductions (usually expressed as a percentage of the purchase price) that companies offer their customers to encourage prompt payment.

purchase returns the cost of merchandise returned to suppliers.

purchases the cost of merchandise acquired for resale during the accounting period.

Q

quick ratio a measure of a company's short-term liquidity that is calculated as follows: (Cash + Short-Term Investments + Receivables) ÷ Current Liabilities.

R

ratio analysis an examination of financial statements conducted by preparing and evaluating a series of ratios.

ratios (financial ratios) data that provide meaningful information only when compared with ratios from previous periods for the same firm or similar firms; they help by removing most of the effects of size differences.

raw materials inventory the account in manufacturing firms that includes the basic ingredients to make a product.

realized/realizable one of two requirements for revenue to be recognized. An item is realized, or realizable, if noncash resources (i.e., inventory) have been exchanged for cash or near cash (e.g., accounts receivable).

relevance one of the four qualitative characteristics that useful information should possess. Accounting information is said to be relevant if it is capable of making a difference in a business decision by helping users predict future events or by providing feedback about prior expectations. Relevant information must also be provided in a timely manner.

research and development (R&D) expense the cost of internal development of intangible assets that is expensed as incurred.

residual value (salvage value) the amount of cash or trade-in consideration that the company expects to receive when an asset is retired from service.

retailers merchandisers that sell directly to consumers.

retained earnings (or deficit) the accumulated earnings (or losses) over the entire life of the corporation that have not been paid out in dividends.

return on assets a ratio that measures the profit earned by a corporation through use of all its capital, or the total of the investment by both creditors and owners. Return on assets is calculated as: [Net Income + Interest (1 – Tax Rate)]/Average Total Assets.

return on common equity ratio a ratio that is basically the same as the return on equity ratio. It is calculated as: Net Income/(Total Equity + Preferred Stock + Paid-In Capital – Preferred Stock).

return on equity a ratio that measures the profit earned by a firm through the use of capital supplied by stockholders. Return on equity is computed as net income divided by average equity.

revenue the increase in assets that results from the sale of products or services.

revenue expenditures expenditures that do not increase the future economic benefits of the asset. These expenditures are expensed as they are incurred.

revenue recognition principle a principle that requires revenue to be recognized or recorded in the period in which it is earned and the collection of cash is reasonably assured.

S

safeguarding the physical protection of assets through, for example, fireproof vaults, locked storage facilities, keycard access, and anti-theft tags on merchandise.

sales allowance a price reduction offered by the seller to induce the buyer to keep the goods when the goods are only slightly defective, are shipped late, or in some other way are rendered less valuable.

sales discount a price reduction (usually expressed as a percentage of the selling price) that companies may offer to encourage prompt payment.

sales returns merchandise or goods returned by the customer to the seller.

sales taxes money collected from the customer for the governmental unit levying the tax.

secured a term used for a bond that has some collateral pledged against the corporation's ability to pay.

Securities and Exchange Commission (SEC) the federal agency established by Congress to regulate securities markets and ensure effective public disclosure of accounting information. The SEC has the power to set accounting rules for publicly traded companies.

securitization a process in which large businesses and financial institutions frequently package factored receivables as financial instruments or securities and sell them to investors.

segregation of duties the idea that accounting and administrative duties should be performed by different individuals, so that no one person has access to the asset and prepares all the documents and records for an activity.

service charges fees charged by the bank for checking account services.

shareholders see *stockholders*

short-term liquidity ratios a type of ratio that compares some combination of current assets or operations to current liabilities.

sole proprietorship a business owned by one person.

specific identification method an inventory costing method that determines the cost of ending inventory and the cost of goods sold based on the identification of the actual units sold and in inventory. This method does not require an assumption about the flow of costs but actually assigns cost based on the specific flow of inventory.

stated capital (legal capital) the amount of capital that, under law, cannot be returned to the corporation's owners unless the corporation is liquidated.

stated rate see *interest rate*

statement of cash flows a financial statement that provides relevant information about a company's cash receipts (inflows of cash) and cash payments (outflows of cash) during an accounting period.

statement of retained earnings a financial statement that reports how much of the company's income was retained in the business and how much was distributed to owners for a period of time.

stock dividend a dividend paid to stockholders in the form of additional shares of stock (instead of cash).

stock repurchase payout ratio a ratio that addresses the distribution of company value and can be calculated directly as Common Stock Repurchase ÷ Net Income, or indirectly as Stock Repurchase Payout Ratio = Total Payout Ratio – Dividend Payout Ratio.

stock split a stock issue that increases the number of outstanding shares of a corporation without changing the balances of its equity accounts.

stock warrant the right granted by a corporation to purchase a specified number of shares of its capital stock at a stated price and within a stated time period.

stockholder ratios ratios such as earnings per share and return on common equity that provide information about the creation of value for shareholders.

stockholders the owners of a corporation who own its shares in varying numbers.

stockholders' equity the owners' claims against the assets of a corporation after all liabilities have been deducted.

straight-line depreciation a depreciation method that allocates an equal amount of an asset's cost to depreciation expense for each year of the asset's useful life. Straight-line depreciation expense for each period is calculated by dividing the depreciable cost of an asset by the asset's useful life.

strategic risks possible threats to the organization's success in accomplishing its objectives that are external to the organization.

T

T-account a graphical representation of an account that gets its name because it resembles the capital letter T. A T-account is a two-column record that consists of an account title and two sides divided by a vertical line—the left side is called the debit side and the right side is called the credit side.

temporary accounts the accounts of revenue, expense, and dividend items that are used to collect the activities of only one period.

time period assumption one of the four basic assumptions that underlie accounting that allows the life of a company to be divided into artificial time periods so net income can be measured for a specific period of time (e.g., monthly, quarterly, annually).

time series (or trend) analysis a type of analysis that compares a single corporation across time.

time value of money the idea that a cash flow in the future is less valuable than a cash flow at present.

timeliness quality of information where it is available to users before it loses its ability to influence decisions.

times interest earned ratio a ratio that measures the excess of net income over interest to gauge a firm's ability to repay its debt. It is calculated as: Income from Operations ÷ Interest Expense.

total payout ratio a ratio that adds stock repurchases to common dividends and compares this to net income. It is calculated as: Total Payout Ratio = (Common Dividends + Common Stock Repurchases)/Net Income.

trade receivable an account receivable that is due from a customer purchasing inventory in the ordinary course of business.

trademark an intangible asset that grants the holder the right to the exclusive use of a distinctive name, phrase, or symbol. The legal life is 20 years but it can be renewed indefinitely.

transaction any event, external or internal, that is recognized in the financial statements.

transaction analysis the process of determining the economic effects of a transaction on the elements of the accounting equation.

transportation-in see *freight-in*

treasury stock previously issued stock that is repurchased by the issuing corporation.

trial balance a list of all active accounts and each account's debit or credit balance.

turnover the average length of time required for assets to be consumed or replaced.

U

understandability quality of information whereby users with a reasonable knowledge of accounting and business can comprehend the meaning of that information.

unearned revenue a liability that occurs when a company receives payment for goods that will be delivered or services that will be performed in the future.

units-of-production method a depreciation method that allocates the cost of an asset over its expected life in direct proportion to the actual use of the asset; depreciation expense is computed by multiplying an asset's depreciable cost by a usage ratio.

unsecured a term used for bonds in which the lender is relying on the general credit of the borrowing corporation rather than on collateral.

useful life the period of time over which the company anticipates deriving benefit from the use of the asset.

V

verifiability quality of information indicating the information is verifiable when independent parties can reach a consensus on the measurement of the activity.

vertical analysis a type of analysis that expresses each financial statement line item as a percent of the largest amount on the statement.

voluntary disposal a type of disposal that occurs when a company determines that the asset is no longer useful; the disposal may occur at the end of the asset's useful life or at some other time.

W

warranty a guarantee to repair or replace defective goods during a period (ranging from a few days to several years) following the sale.

wholesalers merchandisers that sell to other retailers.

withholding businesses are required to withhold taxes from employees' earnings; standard withholdings include federal, state, and possibly city or county income taxes, as well as Social Security and Medicare. Employees may also have amounts withheld for such things as retirement accounts and health insurance.

work-in-process inventory the account in manufacturing firms that consists of the raw materials that are used in production as well as other production costs such as labor and utilities.

working capital a measure of liquidity computed as: Current Assets – Current Liabilities.

worksheet an informal schedule that accountants use to assist them in organizing and preparing the information necessary to perform the end-of-period steps in the accounting cycle—namely the preparation of adjusting entries, financial statements, and closing entries.

Y

yield the market rate of interest demanded by creditors; yield may differ from stated rate because the underwriter disagrees with the borrower as to the correct yield or because of changes in the economy or creditworthiness of the borrower between the setting of the stated rate and the date of issue.

CHECK FIGURES

Check figures are given for selected problems here. For the complete Check Figures for all applicable Cornerstone Exercises, Exercises, Problems, and Cases, please visit the companion website at www.cengagebrain.com.

Chapter 1

P 1-56A		12/31/13 Liabilities = $90,550
P 1-57A	(b)	Equity at the beginning of the year = $52,600
	(d)	Expenses = $477,300
P 1-58A		Net income = $102,450
P 1-59A	(d)	Total liabilities = $1,165
	(e)	Total revenue = $72
P 1-60A		Net income = $30,100
		Retained earnings = $135,710
P 1-61A		2013 ending retained earnings = $36,050
P 1-62A	(d)	2013 dividends = $3,700
P 1-63A	1.	Net income = $36,000
		Ending retained earnings = $90,000
		Total current liabilities = $35,990
P 1-64A	(f)	Manning Company 2013 ending retained earnings = $7,500
	(m)	Corey Company 2013 net income = $7,100
P 1-65A	2.	Net loss = $(9,050)
	4.	Net income = $15,950
P 1-56B		12/31/13 Liabilities = $264,700
P 1-57B	(b)	Total liabilities at the end of the year = $426,630
	(d)	Net income for the year = $94,120
P 1-58B		Net income = $143,425
P 1-59B	(d)	Total liabilities = $860
	(e)	Total revenue = $503
P 1-60B		Net income = $12,250
		Retained earnings = $48,200
P 1-61B		2013 ending retained earnings = $74,700
P 1-62B	(c)	Net income = $12,400
P 1-63B		Net income = $76,500
		Ending retained earnings = $179,800
		Total current liabilities = $68,400
P 1-64B	(f)	Compton Company total equity = $60,600
	(m)	Merlotte Company total equity = $34,400
P 1-65B	2.	Net income = $57,450
	4.	Net income = $64,450

Chapter 2

P 2-56A	1.	Cash column total = $31,410
		Retained Earnings column total = $8,940
	2.	Trial balance total = $58,790
P 2-57A	2.	Trial balance total = $8,200
P 2-60A	2.	Ending Cash balance = $25,890
P 2-61A	3.	Ending Cash balance = $9,820
	4.	Trial balance total = $168,850
P 2-62A	3.	Ending Cash balance = $520,400
		Ending Accounts Receivable balance = $11,000
	4.	Trial balance total = $1,372,100
P 2-56B	1.	Cash column total = $14,910
		Retained Earnings column total = $5,740
	2.	Trial balance total = $33,495
P 2-57B	2.	Trial balance total = $6,335
P 2-60B	2.	Ending Cash balance = $20,835
P 2-61B	3.	Ending Cash balance = $57,220
	4.	Trial balance total = $178,800
P 2-62B	3.	Ending Cash balance = $226,700
		Ending Accounts Receivable balance = $121,000
	4.	Trial balance total = $914,000

Chapter 3

P 3-70A	1. b.	Credit to Accounts Receivable = $2,332,028
	e.	Debit to Accounts Payable = $39,200
	h.	Debit to Interest Expense = $30,000
	2.	Ending Cash balance = $2,012,324
		Ending Interest Payable balance = $30,000
	3.	Net income = $1,125,948
	4.	Ending retained earnings = $1,563,323
	5.	Total current liabilities = $578,707
P 3-71A	1.	Adjusted Trial Balance columns totals = $5,581,688
		Net income = $32,512
		Ending retained earnings = $71,712
	2.	Total current liabilities = $159,438
P 3-62B	1.	Cash-basis March income = $2,910
	2.	Accrual-basis March income = $2,395
P 3-63B	1.	2013 total expenses = $71,720
P 3-64B	2. b.	Credit to Service Revenue = $3,300
	d.	Credit to Prepaid Insurance = $500
	g.	Debit to Supplies Expense = $265
P 3-65B	1. b.	Debit to Accounts Receivable = $17,640
	e.	Debit to Supplies Expense = $661
	2.	Net understatement of income would be $32,734
P 3-67B	2.	Total operating expenses = $923,890
		Ending retained earnings = $67,730
		Total current liabilities = $69,130

P 3-68B 1. (a) Adjusted Prepaid Insurance = $4,144
(d) Adjusted Service Revenue = $132,130
(e) Adjusted Depreciation Expense = $10,500
2. (b) Credit to Interest Payable = $4,175
(c) Credit to Wages Payable = $17,600

P 3-69B 1. Credit to Retained Earnings = $49,250
2. Net income = $49,250

P 3-70B 1. b. Credit to Accounts Receivable = $199,100
g. Debit to Accounts Payable = $73,000
h. Debit to Interest Expense = $2,700
2. Ending Cash balance = $12,300
Ending Interest Payable balance = $2,700
3. Net income = $38,500
4. Ending retained earnings = $86,500
5. Total current liabilities = $36,800

P 3-71B 1. Adjusted Trial Balance columns totals = $2,204,300
Net income = $148,900
Ending retained earnings = $135,600
2. Total current liabilities = $88,600

Chapter 4

P 4-58A 1. Adjusted cash balance = $5,805
P 4-59A 1. Adjusted cash balance = $7,806.81
P 4-60A 1. Adjusted cash balance = $7,550
P 4-61A f. Credit to Cash = $340
P 4-58B 1. Adjusted cash balance = $5,725
P 4-59B 1. Adjusted cash balance = $8,100
P 4-60B 1. Adjusted cash balance = $9,500
P 4-61B f. Credit to Cash = $675

Chapter 5

P 5-80A 1. Expected gross margin with discount policy = $147,675

P 5-81A 2. Cash collected = $2,810,700

P 5-82A 2. Debit to Cash = $84,150
4. Implied interest rate = 24% (approximate)

P 5-84A 1. 2013 loss rate = 0.082
6. Increase in income from operations = $49,034

P 5-85A 3. Credit to Allowance for Doubtful Accounts = $9,785

P 5-86A 4. Credit to Allowance for Doubtful Accounts = $17,438

P 5-87A Mar. 1, 2014 credit to Interest Income = $116.67
Sept. 1, 2014 credit to Interest Receivable = $45

P 5-88A 1. b. 2012 operating margin = 37.04%
d. 2012 accounts receivable turnover = 10.34

P 5-80B 1. Expected gross margin with discount policy = $277,500

P 5-81B 2. Cash collected = $2,677,763

P 5-82B 2. Debit to Cash = $242,500
4. Implied interest rate = 36% (approximate)

P 5-84B 1. 2013 loss rate = 0.082
6. Increase in income from operations = $4,911

P 5-85B 3. Credit to Allowance for Doubtful Accounts = $16,993

P 5-86B 4. Credit to Allowance for Doubtful Accounts = $29,954

P 5-87B May 1, 2014 credit to Interest Income = $267
Sept. 1, 2014 credit to Interest Receivable = $120

P 5-88B 1. b. 2012 operating margin = 17.95%
d. 2012 accounts receivable turnover = 5.38

Chapter 6

P 6-65A (c) 2012 cost of goods sold = $243,170
(f) 2013 ending inventory = $54,680

P 6-66A 2. Gross margin = $12,444

P 6-67A 1. FIFO cost of goods sold = $567.70
2. LIFO ending inventory = $48
3. Average cost method cost of goods sold = $571.01

P 6-68A 1. FIFO 2012 cost of goods sold = $9,540
2. LIFO 2013 ending inventory = $1,420
3. Average cost 2013 cost of goods sold = $4,491
6. Weighted average 2013 inventory turnover = 1.73

P 6-69A 2. Credit to inventory = $1,225

P 6-70A 1. FIFO cost of goods sold = $36,700,000
LIFO cost of goods sold = $37,200,000
Average cost method cost of goods sold = $36,753,500
2. FIFO final inventory valuation = $4,060,000

P 6-71A 2. 2012 gross margin = $2,035,400

P 6-72A 1. FIFO ending inventory = $58.80
2. LIFO ending inventory = $48.00
3. Weighted average cost per unit = $8.95

P 6-73A 1. FIFO 2012 gross margin = $12,210
2. LIFO 2012 gross margin = $11,380
3. Weighted average 2012 cost per unit = $11.3478

P 6-65B (c) 2012 goods available for sale = $111,670
(f) 2013 ending inventory = $11,670

P 6-66B 2. Gross margin = $6,524

P 6-67B 1. FIFO cost of goods sold = $2,848
2. LIFO ending inventory = $174
3. Average cost method cost of goods sold = $2,875.81

P 6-68B 1. FIFO 2012 cost of goods sold = $63,300
2. LIFO 2013 ending inventory = $47,900
3. Average cost 2013 cost of goods sold = $35,235
6. Weighted average 2013 inventory turnover = 0.92

P 6-69B 2. Credit to Inventory = $1,200

P 6-70B 1. FIFO cost of goods sold = $32,180
LIFO cost of goods sold = $32,490
Average cost method cost of goods sold = $32,224
2. LIFO final inventory valuation = $740

P 6-71B 2. 2012 gross margin = $372,750
P 6-72B 1. FIFO ending inventory = $288
2. LIFO ending inventory = $174
3. Weighted average cost per unit = $78.40
P 6-73B 1. FIFO 2012 gross margin = $44,700
2. LIFO 2012 gross margin = $41,200
3. Weighted average 2012 cost per unit = $54.1765

Chapter 7

P 7-68A Total property, plant, and equipment = $226,700
P 7-69A 1. Acquisition cost = $46,180
2. Two items were expensed.
P 7-70A 3. Straight-line year 2 book value = $145,500
Double-declining year 2 book value = $106,875
Units-of-production year 2 book value = $148,348
P 7-71A 2. Year 3 ending book value = $11,750
P 7-72A 2. Book value after renovation = $17,800
3. Revised yearly depreciation = $1,630
P 7-74A 1. Gain on building = $30,000
Loss on furniture and fixtures = $32,500
P 7-75A 1. Debit to Goodwill = $85,000
3. Credit to Accumulated Depletion = $225,000
P 7-76A 1. Credit to Patent = $178,000
2. Debit to Patent = $50,000
4. Debit to Loss from Impairment = $534,000
P 7-68B Total property, plant, and equipment = $303,155
P 7-69B 1. Acquisition cost = $65,380
2. One item is expensed.
P 7-70B 3. Straight-line year 2 book value = $53,800
Double-declining year 2 book value = $41,728
Units-of-production year 2 book value = $55,510
P 7-71B 2. Year 3 ending book value = $29,160
P 7-72B 2. Book value after renovation = $39,535
3. Revised yearly depreciation = $3,211
P 7-74B 1. Gain on truck = $1,350
Loss on furniture = $350
P 7-75B 1. Debit to Goodwill = $1,250,000
3. Credit to Accumulated Depletion = $3,696,429
P 7-76B 2. Credit to Copyright = $165,000

Chapter 8

P 8-73A 1. h. Credit to Cash = $547,266
i. Debit to Unearned Sales Revenue = $22,000
2. Debit to Interest Expense = $25,000
P 8-74A 1. Credit to Cash = $355,597.50
2. Total cost = 132.65% of gross pay
P 8-75A 2. Credit to Interest Payable = $12,000
4. Debit to Interest Expense = $16,000
P 8-76A 2. No journal entry necessary.
4. Credit to Cash = $81,600
P 8-77A 1. Total bill = $3,596,640
P 8-78A 1. Reported as current liability = $50,000
2. Debit to Cash = $150,000
Reported as noncurrent liability = $62,500
3. Debit to Unearned Sales Revenue = $75,000
P 8-79A 1. 2013 warranty expense = $21,780
3. Balance 12/31/13 = $23,580
P 8-80A 2. 2014 quick ratio = 0.81
3. 2013 cash ratio = 0.29
4. 2014 operating cash flow ratio = 0.33
P 8-73B 1. h. Credit to Cash = $1,075,484
i. Debit to Unearned Sales Revenue = $40,000
2. Debit to Interest Expense = $12,250
P 8-74B 1. Credit to Cash = $973,775
2. Total cost = 135.65% of gross pay
P 8-75B 2. Credit to Interest Payable = $8,500
4. Debit to Interest Expense = $8,500
P 8-76B 2. No journal entry necessary.
4. Credit to Cash = $823,900
P 8-77B 1. Total billing = $413,449.50
P 8-78B 1. Reported as current liability = $26,250
2. Debit to Cash = $140,000
Reported as noncurrent liability = $45,000
3. Debit to Unearned Sales Revenue = $48,750
P 8-79B 1. 2013 warranty expense = $101,250
3. Balance 12/31/13 = $16,250
P 8-80B 2. 2013 quick ratio = 0.81
3. 2012 cash ratio = 0.29
4. 2013 operating cash flow ratio = 0.33

Chapter 9

P 9-96A Current liabilities = $158,100
P 9-97A 2. Credit to Interest Payable = $5,600
3. Debit to Interest Expense = $4,000
P 9-98A Carrying value 12/31/15 = $101,800
P 9-99A 2. Credit to Discount on Notes Payable = $360
4. Carrying value = $796,400
P 9-100A 1. Carrying value 12/31/16 = $710,400
2. Debit to Interest Expense = $30,650
P 9-101A 1. Carrying value, 06/30/17 = $738,435
2. 06/30/14 credit to Discount on Bonds Payable = $3,855
P 9-102A 1. Carrying value, 12/31/15 = $5,100,000
P 9-103A 2. Debit to Interest Expense = $22,500
P 9-104A Carrying value, 12/31/15 = $2,590,000
P 9-105A 3. Debit to Lease Liability = $48,187
P 9-96B Current liabilities = $144,500
P 9-97B 2. Credit to Interest Payable = $15,767
3. Debit to Interest Expense = $1,433
P 9-98B Carrying value 12/31/15 = $415,666
P 9-99B 2. Credit to Discount on Notes Payable = $725
4. Carrying value = $992,750
P 9-100B 1. Carrying value 12/31/16 = $920,000
2. Debit to Interest Expense = $28,750

P 9-101B 1. Carrying value, 06/30/18 = $694,000
2. 06/30/15 credit to Discount on Bonds Payable = $2,000

P 9-102B 1. Carrying value, 12/31/15 = $6,860,000

P 9-103B 2. Debit to Interest Expense = $10,150

P 9-104B Carrying value, 12/31/15 = $2,620,000

P 9-105B 3. Debit to Lease Liability = $20,980

Chapter 10

P 10-81A Total stockholders' equity = $3,403,000

P 10-82A b. Credit to Additional Paid-In Capital—Common Stock = $56,000
c. Credit to Additional Paid-In Capital—Preferred Stock = $60,000

P 10-83A 1. b. Debit to Retained Earnings = $16,000
d. Credit to Treasury Stock = $173,200
2. Cumulative effect on equity = $(138,700)

P 10-84A 1. e. Credit to Treasury Stock = $7,200
2. Total stockholders' equity = $1,549,500

P 10-85A 1. e. Credit to Dividends Payable = $165,825
g. Debit to Retained Earnings = $460,625
h. Credit to Dividends Payable = $193,463
2. Total dividends for the year = $932,413
3. Cumulative effect on assets = $(471,788)

P 10-86A 2. Retained earnings reported = $73,000
Credit to Additional Paid-In Capital—Common Stock = $120,000

P 10-87A 1. Total annual dividends = $93,300
2. Total dividends in arrears = $27,900

P 10-88A Stock repurchase payout = 61.44%
Return on common equity = 43.13%

P 10-81B Total stockholders' equity = $9,883,000

P 10-82B b. Credit to Additional Paid-In Capital—Common Stock = $55,000
c. Credit to Additional Paid-In Capital—Preferred Stock = $40,000

P 10-83B 1. b. Debit to Retained Earnings = $13,000
d. Credit to Treasury Stock = $83,800
2. Cumulative effect on equity = $(61,400)

P 10-84B 1. e. Credit to Treasury Stock = $15,200
2. Total stockholders' equity = $6,275,300

P 10-85B 1. e. Credit to Dividends Payable = $323,800
g. Debit to Retained Earnings = $1,214,250
h. Credit to Dividends Payable = $400,703
2. Total dividends for the year = $2,102,753
3. Cumulative effect on assets = $(888,503)

P 10-86B 2. Retained earnings reported = $383,400
Credit to Additional Paid-In Capital—Common Stock = $21,600

P 10-87B 1. Total annual dividends = $275,500
2. Total dividends in arrears = $157,500

P 10-88B 1. Stock repurchase payout = 53.66%
Return on common equity = 48.89%

Chapter 11

P 11-52A 1. Financing = 4 items
2. No cash effect = 2 items

P 11-53A 1. Total adjustments = $179,525

P 11-54A 1. Total adjustments = $35,560
Net cash used for investing activities = $(72,300)

P 11-55A Gain on disposal of equipment = $(2,500)
Gain on sale of investments = $(4,100)
Net cash provided by operating activities = $27,100
Net cash used for investing activities = $(5,250)

P 11-56A 1. Total adjustments = $12,400
Net cash used for investing activities = $(84,200)

P 11-57A 1. Net cash provided by operating activities = $8,765
Net cash provided by financing activities = $92,000

P 11-58A Cash paid for operating expenses = $(887,700)
Net cash provided by operating activities = $287,645

P 11-59A 1. Total of Adjustments columns = $1,276,000
Total adjustments to net income = $257,000
Net cash used for investing activities = $(419,000)

P 11-52B 1. Financing = 3 items
2. No cash effect = 3 items

P 11-53B 1. Total adjustments = $313,945

P 11-54B 1. Total adjustments = $157,910
Net cash used for investing activities = $(78,475)

P 11-55B Loss on disposal of PP&E = $4,200
Loss on sale of investments = $1,500
Net cash provided by operating activities = $58,125
Net cash used for investing activities = $(45,725)

P 11-56B 1. Total adjustments = $301,000
Net cash used for investing activities = $(295,000)

P 11-57B 1. Net cash provided by operating activities = $170,700
Net cash provided by financing activities = $(28,000)

P 11-58B Cash paid for operating expenses = $(824,400)
Net cash provided by operating activities = $359,245

P 11-59B 1. Purchase of investments = $15,000
Total of Adjustments columns = $965,600
Total adjustments to net income = $63,800
Net cash used for investing activities = $(434,400)

Chapter 12

P 12-86A 2013 total revenues = 139.55%
2012 total costs and expenses = 120.95%
2013 total operating income = 157.56%
2012 net income = 128.29%

P 12-88A
1. Net income growth = 42%
3. Quick ratio = 0.93
5. 2014 expected net income = $2,849
6. Capital to be raised = $2,704.50

P 12-89A
1. 2013 revenues = 130.88%
2013 total costs and expenses = 131.26%
2013 net income = 127.16%
2012 revenues = 113.37%
2012 total costs and expenses = 113.44%
2012 net income = 114.69%
3. 2013 current assets = 74.09%
2013 total liabilities = 24.75%
2013 shareholders' equity = 75.25%
2012 current assets = 74.10%
2012 total liabilities = 29.30%
2012 shareholders' equity = 70.70%

P 12-90A
1. 2013 average accounts receivable = $4,174
2012 accounts receivable turnover ratio = 11.85
2013 average inventories = $5,271
2012 inventory turnover ratio = 6.27
2013 average total assets = $14,581
2012 asset turnover ratio = 3.60
2. 2012 gross profit percentage = 39.87%
2012 operating margin percentage = 8.31%
2012 net profit margin percentage = 4.65%
2013 interest expense net of tax = $890.64
2013 average total assets = $14,581
2012 return on assets = 21.55%
2013 average equity = $7,426
2012 return on equity = 29.94%
3. 2013 operating income = $4,401
2012 operating income = $3,431
2012 long-term debt to equity ratio = 0.46
2012 long-term debt to total assets ratio = 0.25

P 12-92A
1. 2013 quick assets = $958,831
2012 quick assets = $856,068
2012 cash ratio = 0.62
2012 operating cash flow ratio = 0.36
2013 EBIT = $620,255
2012 times interest earned ratio = 18.02
2012 long-term debt to equity ratio = 0.06
2012 long-term debt to total assets ratio = 0.04
2013 average accounts receivable = $631,782.50
2012 accounts receivable turnover ratio = 6.09
2013 average inventory = $532,094
2012 inventory turnover ratio = 3.95
2013 average total assets = $2,030,162
2012 asset turnover ratio = 1.90
2013 income from operations = $620,255
2012 income from operations = $552,483
2013 net income + interest net of tax = $380,819.02
2012 average total assets = $1,790,646
2013 average common equity = $1,485,087.50
2012 return on common equity ratio = 27.94%
2012 total payout ratio = 190.25%
2013 stock repurchase payout = 254.82%

P 12-93A
1. 2012 LIFO cost of goods sold = $5,090,000
2012 FIFO cost of goods sold = $5,005,000
2. 2012 depreciation at 10% = $115,000

P 12-86B
2013 total revenues =70.03%
2012 total costs and expenses = 87.95%
2013 total operating income = 57.72%
2012 net income = 119.59%

P 12-88B
1. Net income growth = 907%
3. Quick ratio = 0.93
5. 2014 expected net income = $2,856
6. Capital to be raised = $2,658.75

P 12-89B
1. 2013 revenues = 129.07%
2013 total costs and expenses = 124.30%
2013 net income = 149.09%
2012 revenues = 114.91%
2012 total costs and expenses = 113.23%
2012 net income = 125.92%
3. 2013 current assets = 74.28%
2013 total liabilities = 25.74%
2013 shareholders' equity = 74.26%
2012 current assets = 73.58%
2012 total liabilities = 29.88%
2012 shareholders' equity = 70.12%

P 12-90B
1. 2013 average accounts receivable = $4,172
2012 accounts receivable turnover ratio = 12.41
2013 average inventories = $5,097
2012 inventory turnover ratio = 6.49
2013 average total assets = $14,424
2012 asset turnover ratio = 3.73
2. 2012 gross profit percentage = 40.13%
2012 operating margin percentage = 6.96%
2012 net profit margin percentage = 3.21%
2013 interest expense net of tax = $976.3
2013 average total assets = $14,424
2012 return on assets = 16.85%
2013 average equity = $7,043
2012 return on equity = 21.96%
3. 2013 operating income = $4,526
2012 operating income = $2,985
2012 long-term debt to equity ratio = 0.49
2012 long-term debt to total assets ratio= 0.26

P 12-92B
1. 2013 quick assets = $972,164
2012 quick assets = $873,884
2012 cash ratio = 0.63
2012 operating cash flow ratio = 0.89
2013 operating income = $917,148
2012 times interest earned ratio = 23.35
2012 long-term debt to equity ratio = 0.07
2012 long-term debt to total assets ratio = 0.05

2013 average accounts receivable = $637,352.50
2012 accounts receivable turnover ratio = 6.35
2013 average inventory = $535,489
2012 inventory turnover ratio = 4.21
2013 average total assets = $2,058,712
2012 asset turnover ratio = 2.02
2013 income from operations = $917,148
2012 income from operations = $761,187
2013 net income + interest net of tax = $662,815.20
2012 average total assets = $1,804,037
2013 average equity = $1,489,299.5
2012 return on equity ratio = 45.16%
2012 total payout ratio = 123.41%
2013 stock repurchase payout = 153.45%

P 12-93B
1. 2012 LIFO cost of goods sold = $5,188,000
   2012 FIFO cost of goods sold = $5,090,000
2. 2012 depreciation at 20% = $246,000

INDEX

A

J

K

L

M

N

O

S

T